Publications of the

National Bureau of Economic Research, Inc.

Number 38

**Residential Real Estate, its Economic Position
as shown by Values, Rents, Family Incomes, Financing
and Construction, together with Estimates for All
Real Estate**

Residential Real Estate

its Economic Position as shown by

Values, Rents, Family Incomes, Financing, and Construction,

together with Estimates for All Real Estate

David L. Wickens

NATIONAL BUREAU OF ECONOMIC RESEARCH

NEW YORK · 1941

Printed in the United States of America

RELATION OF THE DIRECTORS
TO THE WORK OF THE NATIONAL BUREAU

1. The object of the National Bureau of Economic Research is to ascertain and to present to the public important economic facts and their interpretation in a scientific and impartial manner. The Board of Directors is charged with the responsibility of ensuring that the work of the Bureau is carried on in strict conformity with this object.

2. To this end the Board of Directors shall appoint one or more Directors of Research.

3. The Director or Directors of Research shall submit to the members of the Board, or to its Executive Committee, for their formal adoption, all specific proposals concerning researches to be instituted.

4. No study shall be published until the Director or Directors of Research shall have submitted to the Board a summary report drawing attention to the character of the data and their utilization in the study, the nature and treatment of the problems involved, the main conclusions and such other information as in their opinion will serve to determine the suitability of the study for publication in accordance with the principles of the Bureau.

5. A copy of any manuscript proposed for publication shall also be submitted to each member of the Board. If publication is approved each member is entitled to have published also a memorandum of any dissent or reservation he may express, together with a brief statement of his reasons. The publication of a volume does not, however, imply that each member of the Board of Directors has read the manuscript and passed upon its validity in every detail.

6. The results of an inquiry shall not be published except with the approval of at least a majority of the entire Board and a two-thirds majority of all those members of the Board who shall have voted on the proposal within the time fixed for the receipt of votes on the publication proposed. The limit shall be forty-five days from the date of the submission of the synopsis and manuscript of the proposed publication unless the Board extends the limit; upon the request of any member the limit may be extended for not more than thirty days.

7. A copy of this resolution shall, unless otherwise determined by the Board, be printed in each copy of every Bureau publication.

(Resolution of October 25, 1926, revised February 6, 1933)

Foreword

The Division of Industry and Trade of the Committee on Credit and Banking of the Social Science Research Council outlined in December 1932 a program of studies in banking policy and credit control in relation to economic stability. Three stages of inquiry were proposed: (1) a statistical study of the formation of capital during the 1920's in terms of commodities and services rather than values; (2) measurement and analysis of the manner in which capital expansion in that period was financed, with attention to the sources and flow of savings and credit; (3) analysis of the implications of the studies at the first two stages with reference to the potentialities of credit control and banking policy and their bearing upon the stabilization of industry. The inquiries at the final stage were planned to include institutional studies of banking structure and policy and to emphasize the potentialities and limitations of credit control as a device for stabilization.

The initial project, a study of durable goods and capital formation in the United States, 1919–1933, was started in January 1933 by the National Bureau of Economic Research under the direction of Simon Kuznets. The National Bureau has so far published: *National Income and Capital Formation, 1919–1935* (1937); *Commodity Flow and Capital Formation,* Vol. I (1938); National Bureau *Bulletin 52,* "Gross Capital Formation, 1919–1933" (1934), and *Bulletin 74,* "Commodity Flow and Capital Formation in the Recent Recovery and Decline" (1939). In addition to these reports Dr. Kuznets is now preparing the second volume of *Commodity Flow and Capital Formation,* and William H. Shaw, a report on capital formation, 1879–1919.

The second stage of the program was concerned with the volume of capital funds and their flow through various channels, with the techniques and policies of the institutions that handle the funds, and with the effects of the flow and its volume upon the expansion and shrinkage of production of durable goods. The only project undertaken under this part of the program is the investigation by David L. Wickens of real estate financing and economic stability. Some of the results were released in National Bureau *Bulletin 65,* "Non-Farm Residential Construction, 1920–1936" (1937), and *Bulletin 75,* "Differentials in Housing Costs" (1939). The basic tables are published in this book and the methods described in detail. Both projects

were financed in part by the Social Science Research Council and in part by the National Bureau.

The Committee recommended the study of real estate financing because of the importance of real estate in national wealth. It is one of the greatest outlets for long term investment by banks, insurance companies, and private investors, and economic stability generally is influenced in large degree by what happens in real estate. The Committee was of the opinion also that real estate financing had been commonly understressed in the discussions of banking and credit phases of stabilization problems and that a major effort was necessary to organize the field by a comprehensive study on a national scale. With the results of such an effort the Committee believed that the ground would be laid for more fruitful work in the future, as had been the case with early studies of national income, and for a deeper understanding of the importance of real estate in the national economy.

Since effective measurements of real estate phenomena incident to financing are fundamental to an understanding of the problems of financing and stability, Mr. Wickens found it necessary to concentrate upon developing them. His task was more difficult because of the lack of any comprehensive information of a census character such as that available in the censuses of agriculture, population, and manufactures. As he points out, he used widely scattered sources and attempted by various methods to arrive at basic estimates.

As a result of his efforts, the fullest and most reliable data on values of urban residential properties, the relation of these values to mortgage debts, current rentals, construction, incomes of occupants, rates of obsolescence of properties, terms of financing, and sources of funds are now available in one book. In it one finds that urban real estate had a total value in 1930 of $266,300,000,000, of which $122,600,000,000 represented urban residential properties; that about 49 per cent of residential properties were held free of mortgages and 51 per cent were mortgaged; that in 1934 indebtedness on owner-occupied residential properties amounted to 55.6 per cent of their value; and that the total mortgage debt against urban residential properties amounted to $26,078,000,000.

The facts made available in the tables, which constitute the greater part of this volume, remove real estate and mortgage financing from the list of economic and financial factors about which we know least. They provide a basis for a better understanding of real estate financing and mortgage operations whose relations to the economy as a whole can now be seen. They are a ready source to which makers of public policy and directors of private enterprises as well as students generally can turn.

The Committee is deeply indebted to the National Bureau for assuming responsibility for and active technical direction of the investigation and for handling the details of publication.

David Friday, Chairman

Committee on Credit and Banking
of the
Social Science Research Council

Alvin H. Hansen	Jesse H. Riddle
Charles O. Hardy	Winfield W. Riefler
Frederick C. Mills	Woodlief Thomas

Contents

Part Three

Tables

Section C

Section E

Charts

Preface

This volume presents the results of several years of intensive study of the statistics of real property, especially nonfarm residential real estate. Farm real estate has been depressed since 1920. In the late '20's and early '30's, the impact of depression on nonfarm real estate and the urban construction industries reawakened public interest in construction and real estate. It became evident that the stagnation of urban real estate, construction, and trade, coming in the wake of the agricultural depression, implied grave dangers for the stability of the entire economic structure. But knowledge did not exist upon which to base sound public policy and sound private judgments with respect to real property and its many long-range commitments. Especially was there a dearth of reliable, integrated data concerning nonfarm residential real estate whose study had been much neglected compared with agricultural realty. Even the aggregate value of nonfarm residential real estate in the United States was unknown. No estimate was available for any more recent year than 1922, and fluctuations in this value during booms and depressions had not been studied. Comprehensive data on the amount of new dwelling construction and year to year changes were lacking. Little was known of the relation between the value of houses occupied by their owners and the value of tenant-occupied dwellings, or of the relation between the value of dwellings and the incomes of owners and tenants, or of how much it cost to buy or to rent a house in various parts of the country or among population groups of different sizes. For nearly two decades no inquiry had been made concerning the number of urban houses mortgaged, nor was there information on the holders of mortgages, the rates of interest charged, the number of residential loans delinquent, and the risk of loss assumed by investors in real estate mortgages.

As early as 1933 the Committee on Banking and Industry of the Social Science Research Council outlined a comprehensive program of research into the problems of real estate and economic stability. This was postponed until the completion of the principal phases of the Financial Survey of Urban Housing, conducted in 1934 as a CWA project and directed by the author under the sponsorship of the Bureau of Foreign and Domestic Commerce. The study planned by the Council was finally inaugurated early in 1935, financed generously by the Social Science Research Council, and carried on under the auspices of the National Bureau of Economic Research. This volume is a product of that study. Based on a wide range of data, the preparation of its estimates and the compilation of its tables have required extensive work with primary data and a variety of methods and intricate computations. The text is restricted to relatively brief descriptions of some of the main features of the new data and the methods of estimating. The major portion of the volume consists of tables in Part Three whose structure is described in Part Two, Chapter I. The ten tables in Part One have Roman numerals; the tables in Part Two have the same classification letters as the tables in Part Three, but they carry in addition the letter M to signify that they are used in the exposition of method.

These statistics, prepared for publication in 1937 and relating to the period prior to that date, are made available prior to the completion of related analytical studies that are based partly on these data because of the current widespread interest in real property, especially housing, and because of the assistance they may render other students.

Many individuals and agencies have contributed generously of their time and resources in the interest of this study. Especial recognition is due the Committee on Banking and Industry of the Social Science Research Council and particularly its Chairman, David Friday, for the impetus his stimulating suggestions and never failing encouragement have given, and Winfield W. Riefler, whose counsel has been invaluable during the entire course of the study.

Grateful acknowledgment is made to the Bureau of the Census for permitting the use of its records and for the tabulations and transcriptions essential to the estimates of rents and values of urban properties, and in particular to Leon E. Truesdell, Chief Statistician for Population; to the Bureau of Foreign and Domestic Commerce for permission to use unpublished materials from the Financial Survey of Urban Housing; to Herman Byer, Chief of the Division of Construction and Public Employment, Bureau of Labor Statistics, for permission to use data on building permits collected by the Bureau as well as for numerous special tabulations; to Arthur Holden of the New York Building Congress for permission to use primary data gathered by that organization; and to the Mayor's Planning Committee of New York for making available personnel needed for the tabulation of real property values and debt in New York City.

Among my associates at the National Bureau of Economic Research, I am deeply indebted to Wesley C. Mitchell, Joseph H. Willits, formerly Executive Director, and William J. Carson, the present Executive Director, for their helpful cooperation in arranging for the conduct of the inquiry, and to the project committee, Simon Kuznets, Leo Wolman, and Solomon Fabricant, for its counsel concerning use of the material; also to Frederick C. Mills for stimulating suggestions in the interest of accuracy and for encouraging a comprehensive attack on this field of research, as well as to all other individual members of the staff who have contributed their comments and advice in the editing of this volume. Particular acknowledgment is due Raymond T. Bowman, a research associate at the National Bureau, 1938–39, who rendered extremely valuable assistance during the concluding months of the study by his critical reading of the manuscript and by his improvement of the order and clarity of statements concerning the statistical processes.

To William Hoad, formerly of the Central Statistical Board staff, who gave the manuscript critical review, I am also indebted for many ideas and helpful suggestions.

Great credit is due the members of the Washington staff who were actively engaged on the entire project and whose loyal work made its completion possible. Ray R. Foster performed the principal part of the work on Construction and shared responsibility for carrying through many of the other statistical processes involved in the numerous estimates presented. Other staff members who gave valuable service in the statistical and research work are Melvin F. Miller, Katherine Kates, Gladys Wilson, Marie Evans, and Mabel Demond.

D. L. W.

RESIDENTIAL REAL ESTATE

PART ONE

The Economic Significance of Nonfarm Residential Real Estate

The value [1] of real property exceeds that of any other form of wealth in the United States. During 1900–22 more than half of the national wealth was in land and buildings, and today they probably make up fully as large a share. Residential real estate in particular is important not only because of its wide geographical distribution, but also because of its great aggregate value. In 1930 nonfarm residential [2] property constituted 46 per cent of the total value of all nonfarm real estate, and farm residences constituted 19 per cent of the value of all farm real estate.

Although this volume is concerned chiefly with nonfarm residential property, the most important single type, certain aspects of farm real estate are considered and estimates are given of the value of all real estate as well as of the principal types. Partly owing to the sparsity of data these estimates were not made in as much detail or as precisely as those of nonfarm residential real estate, but they are useful not only to indicate the importance of all these forms of wealth combined but also for furnishing a ground of comparison for the nonfarm residential data. A brief discussion of the economic significance of total real estate as well as of the major classes precedes the more comprehensive analysis of nonfarm residential.

In the analysis of nonfarm residential real estate, five aspects are considered: value, rent, incomes of owner-occupants and of tenants, financing, and new construction. For each, numerous statistical tables are presented in Part Three covering various aspects of the situation in various areas of the United States. Estimates for the country as a whole, for the respective states, or for population groups appear first in each section and are followed by estimates for the chief regions, by type of dwelling or other category.

Value of Real Estate: Aggregate and Major Components

In 1900 all real property, residential and nonresidential, was valued at about $52.5 billion; by 1912 its

[1] *Value as used here refers to the amount of money the property would command in the market.*
[2] *City and village real estate is used interchangeably with nonfarm in this discussion. The term residential is used in this volume as synonymous with housekeeping units; that is, it includes houses and apartments, but not hotels or other nonhousekeeping dwellings. The term dwelling or dwelling unit refers to the quarters designed for the use of one family and includes both land and building.*

value had doubled. By 1930 it had trebled the 1912 total and, according to the estimates in Table I, amounted to more than $314 billion. This rise in total value reflects not only more costly structures, enhanced ground rents and speculative values in urban centers, but also a larger number of structures as population expanded, particularly in towns and cities.[3] The farm population changed little during this period. From 5.7 million in 1900 farm families increased to only 6.7 million in 1930. Nonfarm families, on the other hand, increased from 10.3 million in 1900 to 17.6 million in 1920 and 23.2 million in 1930 (Table II).

TABLE I

National Wealth and the Value of Real Estate (billions of dollars)

	1900	1904	1912	1922	1930	1934
Estimated total wealth [1]	88.5	107.1	186.3	320.8	..	..
Total value, real property and improvements [2]	52.5	62.3	109.2	176.4	314.2 [3]	203.6 [3]
Percentage real property is of total wealth	59.4	58.2	58.6	55.0	..	..

[1] *Department of Commerce Bulletin*, Estimated National Wealth—Wealth, Public Debt and Taxation, 1922, *p. 18*.
[2] Ibid. (*sum of real property and improvements, taxed and exempt*).
[3] *NBER estimate; see Note to Part One.*

During times of extreme economic changes, the market value of real estate may fluctuate markedly within a short period. From 1930 to 1934, for example, the value of both farm and nonfarm residential property fell about one-third. Although smaller than in some other important forms of investment and less than in many commodity prices, this decline had far-reaching repercussions because of the great aggregate value involved. All classes of real property in all sections of the country were affected. The important role real estate values play in the economy is most clearly evident at such times. Not only the owners of real estate and the holders of real estate mortgages but also bank depositors and other persons whose savings are

[3] For the method used to obtain Tables I–V see the Note to Part One, Estimates of the Aggregate Value of Real Estate.

committed to financial institutions having substantial real estate investments may feel directly or indirectly the effects of radical fluctuations in real property prices. The disturbing effect of interrupted financing, of fluctuations in income from real property and hence in its value and salability, inevitably makes less secure the status of financial institutions and of their owners and depositors.

TABLE II

Number of Families, 1900–1930 (millions)

	1900	1910	1920	1930
Total [1]	16.0	20.3	24.4	29.9
Farm [2]	5.7	6.1	6.8	6.7
Nonfarm [2]	10.3	14.2	17.6	23.2

[1] Census of Population, 1930, *VI, Families, Table 14, p. 11.*
[2] Population Bulletin, *Families, U. S. Summary, Table 16, p. 11.*

Within the total, there were interesting differences in the rate of growth of farm and nonfarm realty values. These were caused not only by the shift of population to cities, but also by the difference in general economic conditions prevailing in agriculture on the one hand and in urban industries on the other. Agricultural depression began in 1920 while urban values did not decline until after the 1929 crash.

Partly because of rising commodity prices for farm products, farm values doubled from 1900 to 1910 and again by 1920. With the severe post-war decline in agricultural prices, farm real estate values, according to decennial Census reports, fell from $66 billion in 1920 to $48 billion in 1930 and $32 billion in 1934.

TABLE III

Farm and Nonfarm Real Estate Value and Percentage Distribution

	1900	1904	1912	1922	1930	1934
VALUE (BILLIONS OF DOLLARS)						
Farm	16.6	23.9	37.8	54.2	47.9	31.6
Nonfarm	35.9	38.5	71.4	122.2	266.3	172.0
Total	52.5	62.3	109.2	176.4	314.2	203.6
PERCENTAGE DISTRIBUTION OF VALUE						
Farm	31.6	38.3	34.6	30.7	15.2	15.5
Nonfarm	68.4	61.7	65.4	69.3	84.8	84.5
Total	100.0	100.0	100.0	100.0	100.0	100.0

Total value figures for 1900, 1904, 1912, and 1922 are from Department of Commerce Bulletin, Estimated National Wealth —Wealth, Public Debt and Taxation, 1922, p. 18 (sum of real property and improvements, taxed and exempt). Total values for 1930 and 1934 are NBER estimates (sum of farm and nonfarm values). Farm value figures for 1900 and 1930 are from Census of Agriculture, 1930, IV, Table 4, p. 39. Farm values for 1904, 1912, 1922, and 1934, and nonfarm for 1934 are NBER estimates (see Note to Part One). Nonfarm values for 1900, 1904, 1912, and 1922 are obtained by subtracting farm value from value of total real estate, but the value for 1930 includes real estate used by utilities (Table IV, NBER estimate).

Total nonfarm real estate values increased from $36 billion in 1900 to $71 billion in 1912, $122 billion in 1922, $266 billion in 1930. Four years of depression following 1930 brought nonfarm realty values down to approximately $172 billion, a shrinkage of more than one-third from the peak. From 1900 to 1922, therefore, the value of nonfarm real estate constituted between 60 and 70 per cent of the total value of real estate in the country as a whole. By 1930 it had risen to nearly 85 per cent (Table III).

CHART 1

Total Value of Nonfarm Real Estate by Classes, 1930

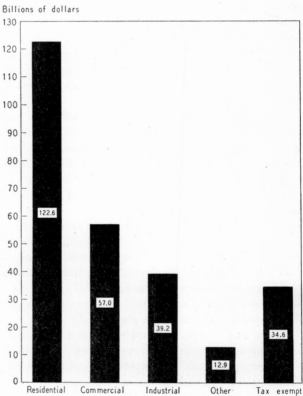

On the basis of value, residential property by itself dominates nonfarm real estate (Chart 1). Nearly half of the aggregate value of city and village realty in 1930 consisted of residential property, estimated at $123 billion, and of this, $76 billion was concentrated in the Middle Atlantic and East North Central states, the most thickly populated sections of the country (Table IV). Commercial property was less than half this amount, with values aggregating about $57 billion or 21 per cent of total property. Industrial property made up 15 per cent of the total, with a value of $39 billion. Property exempt from taxation, such as public buildings and churches, was valued at about $35 billion or 13 per cent. A minor share of all property, about $13 billion or 5 per cent, was devoted to various other private uses. These estimates cover all major

TABLE IV

Nonfarm Real Estate Taxed by Type and Real Estate Exempt, Value and
Percentage Distribution by Geographic Division, 1930

	Nonfarm residential	Commercial	Industrial	Other	Total	REAL ESTATE EXEMPT	TOTAL REAL ESTATE
			A VALUE (BILLIONS OF DOLLARS)				
United States	122.6	57.0	39.2	12.9	231.7	34.6	266.3
New England	9.6	2.1	2.5	1.3	15.5	4.1	19.6
Mid. Atlantic	45.7	17.4	14.9	4.4	82.4	15.7	98.1
E. N. Central	30.0	12.1	7.9	1.6	51.6	4.8	56.4
W. N. Central	8.1	4.7	2.0	0.7	15.5	1.7	17.2
South [1]	16.9	14.1	9.5	4.5	45.0	7.4	52.4
Mountain	2.0	0.6	0.6	0.3	3.5	0.2	3.7
Pacific	10.3	6.0	1.8	0.1	18.2	0.7	18.9
			B PERCENTAGE DISTRIBUTION OF VALUE				
United States	46.1	21.4	14.7	4.8	87.0	13.0	100.0
New England	48.6	10.8	12.9	6.6	78.9	21.1	100.0
Mid. Atlantic	46.6	17.7	15.2	4.5	84.0	16.0	100.0
E. N. Central	53.1	21.5	14.0	2.9	91.5	8.5	100.0
W. N. Central	46.8	27.3	11.7	4.1	89.9	10.1	100.0
South [1]	32.3	26.9	18.1	8.6	85.9	14.1	100.0
Mountain	53.5	15.5	16.0	9.1	94.1	5.9	100.0
Pacific	54.6	31.9	9.3	0.4	96.2	3.8	100.0

[1] Includes South Atlantic, East South Central, and West South Central geographic divisions.

types of nonfarm property except railroad rights of way, utility lines, and other industrial property outside cities. The total of such items, however, constitutes merely a small fraction, probably less than 3 per cent,[4] of the total value of urban and village real estate.

Value of Nonfarm Residential Real Estate
Slightly less than half of the nonfarm families in the United States own the houses in which they live; but dwellings occupied by their owners are in general worth about one-third more per unit than those which are rented. As a result, owner-occupied properties total somewhat more in value for the country as a whole than rented. In 1930 the former were valued at $65 billion, the latter at $58 billion (Table V). The smallness of the difference in aggregate value for the country as a whole is explained chiefly by the fact that owner-occupied dwellings in large cities are relatively fewer than in small towns and cities of moderate size. This fact explains also the substantially greater value of rented properties as a group in the Middle Atlantic states where realty values are highest. Over 42 per cent of the value of all the nonfarm rented units in the United States is in the three states of that area, and of this a great part is concentrated in New York City.

The majority of urban dwellings have values of less than $5,000. In 1930 [5] when values were high, 51 per cent of American families owned and lived in dwell-

[4] This estimate is based on data gathered by the Federal Trade Commission.
[5] Census, 1930, VI, Table 23, p. 17.

ings of this class, while the average value of all owner-occupied dwellings the country over was about $5,800 and that of dwellings occupied by tenants about $4,300, or three-fourths as large. Four years later, in the depression year 1934, when values of all dwellings averaged nearly one-third lower than in 1930, a survey of 61 cities showed that the proportion of owner-occupied houses with values under $5,000 had increased from 46 per cent in 1930 to 70 per cent.

TABLE V

Value of Nonfarm Residential Real Estate by Geographic Division and Tenure, 1930 (billions of dollars)

	TOTAL*	OWNER-OCCUPIED	RENTED
United States	122.6	64.7	57.9
New England	9.5	5.7	3.8
Middle Atlantic	45.7	20.8	24.9
East North Central	29.9	16.8	13.1
West North Central	8.1	5.1	3.0
South Atlantic	8.3	4.8	3.5
East South Central	3.4	1.9	1.5
West South Central	5.3	2.8	2.5
Mountain	2.0	1.1	0.9
Pacific	10.4	5.7	4.7

* The slight differences between this column and the first column of Table IV are due to rounding.

Within the totals represented by these average values, marked differences arise in different parts of the country from many climatic, economic, and social causes as well as from differences in the houses themselves. Housing costs most in the North and East, where population and wealth are concentrated to a greater degree in high-cost metropolitan areas, where a more rigorous climate requires better construction, and where most dwellings are larger and more elaborate. The greatest contrast is with the South where the average value of dwellings in 1930 was three-fifths of that for the country as a whole, and where a large proportion of the houses, particularly those occupied by negroes, are below the average value for the United States, and few rise much above it.[6]

Even more important than regional differentials in housing values is the general rule that the smaller the population group, the lower the cost of housing. As shown in detail in Table A 3, the prospective owner in 1930 would have found that an average house in the group of cities over 100,000 in population was valued at about $6,500; in towns and villages less than 2,500 in population at about $2,700. Farm dwellings averaged only about $1,240. The principal exception to lower residential values in smaller centers is in the exclusive suburban developments near large cities (Chart 2).

The land or site on which the dwelling stands is an important element in property values, especially in explaining differences between farm and nonfarm property values, although the difference in the value of the structures themselves is even greater. For nonfarm dwellings, the site accounts on the average for about one-fifth of the value of the property; for new dwellings the percentage is somewhat smaller.[7] For farms, even when an entire acre is allowed for the site, the value of the land averages less than 0.3 per cent of the total and ranges from less than 1 per cent to 4 per cent in various parts of the country.

These variations in average property values among regions and in population groups of different size and between farm and nonfarm emphasize the danger of generalizations concerning housing costs for the country as a whole, especially on the basis of information solely for the largest cities and their immediate surroundings. Value levels in large cities are not typical of housing in the United States.

Rent of Nonfarm Residential Real Estate

Over 12 million nonfarm families paid an aggregate rent in 1929, of $4.6 billion. The secular trend in the amount paid in rent has been upward owing to the increase in the number of rented dwellings and the rent paid per dwelling. During short periods the controlling factor in the fluctuating amount of gross annual rent is the latter. From late 1929 to the beginning of 1934, the estimated total annual rent bill for nonfarm dwellings declined to $3.2 billion, although the number of families or houses did not change materially.

[6] See National Bureau Bulletin 75.
[7] For new single-family homes securing mortgages accepted for insurance by the Federal Housing Administration in 1937, the average land valuation was 15.3 per cent of the average property valuation (4th Annual Report, year ending Dec. 31, 1937, Federal Housing Administration), p. 72.

Of the 12 million families who lived in rented houses in April 1930, more than half (55 per cent) were paying less than $30 per month, and 80 per cent, less than $50. A monthly rent as high as $75 was paid by only 2 per cent. The 31 per cent decline in rents during the succeeding four years naturally placed a larger proportion in the lower rent paying groups.

Annual rents are commonly so set as to approximate 10 per cent of the value of dwelling property, except for apartments and other structures that include various services and facilities in the rent charged and therefore have higher rent-value ratios. Rent is related roughly to the reproduction cost of the structure, with allowances for age, obsolescence, depreciation, risk, upkeep and management costs. The value of the site and the character of the facilities or furnishings provided are other important factors in determining differences in residential costs and rents in the same city.

CHART 2

Average Value per Dwelling Unit
by Population Groups and on Farms, 1930

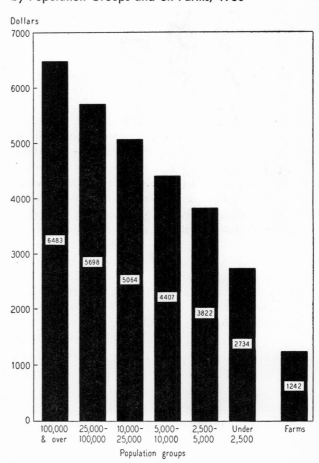

Rent levels in the larger cities, which are those most commonly discussed in housing programs, are no more representative of the country as a whole than are value levels. Much lower rents prevail in towns and villages. In 1929 monthly rents in population groups under 2,500 averaged $14 as compared with $40 in cities of more than 100,000. Part of this difference is probably due to the more frequent inclusion of such facilities as heat, light, furnishings, and refrigeration in the rent bill in the larger cities (Chart 3).

CHART 3

Average Monthly Rent of Nonfarm Dwelling Units by Population Groups, 1930

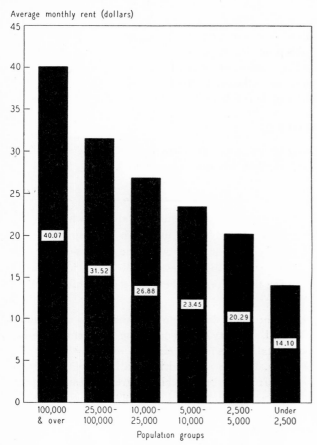

Average monthly rent (dollars)

Population groups

Rents are commonly much affected by the character of the neighborhood and section of the city. In larger population centers families who can afford only small rents frequently live in old and poorly equipped dwellings in once prosperous sections, in the outlying suburbs, or in nearby small towns where the cost of land and construction is lower than near the center of the city or in the exclusive suburbs. The lower rents charged for the same space in new and often better constructed dwellings in these outlying areas and smaller towns suggest an important possible method of providing low cost dwellings that can be rented, as transportation becomes available and industries choose more economical sites.

Rents are highest in the North and East, lowest in the South and Mountain states. These wide regional variations in rent are due to much the same factors as those which influence value, and include differences in the cost and type of construction because of climate, the cost of sites and of labor and materials of construction, as well as in the quality of the structures. Aside from these peculiarities of renting costs due to geographic location, the nation's urban rent bill is distributed roughly in proportion to population.

It may be assumed that, so long as population is concentrated in highly congested urban areas, where property values are high, many American families will continue to rent. Some families prefer not to have the responsibilities of ownership; many are unable to save enough money to make the down payment and the long series of subsequent payments necessary for purchase. Moreover, the traditionally high mobility of the American people and the infrequency of zoning laws that tend to protect property values have often made ownership somewhat hazardous, particularly in view of the lack of any organization of the residential market that would assure the ready sale of property. Consequently, at least half the task of supplying better housing for the nonfarm population will doubtless continue for some time to be the provision of suitable houses or apartments for rent. In such a housing program the lag between declines in rents and in family incomes is of paramount importance, for the size of the income determines the amount of money that can be expended for living quarters, which in turn limits the amount of capital that can be invested with economy and safety by landlords who construct or purchase dwellings for rent.

For the greater part of the population that lives in rented dwellings, rent ordinarily consumes from one-fifth to one-third of the family income. Food and clothing are the only larger items in the family budget. The proportion of income spent for rent tends to hold within a limited range from one year to another, although during depressions it usually increases because the rent structure is more rigid than are incomes. That is, incomes fluctuate with employment and wage rates while rents are fixed for the period of the lease. In the lower income groups a much higher percentage of income is spent for rent than in the higher. In 33 typical cities surveyed in 1934, average monthly rent took 21 per cent of the average family income in 1929, and 25 per cent in 1933.[8] In 1933, 47 per cent of the income of families receiving $250 to $500 would have been spent for rent had the bills been paid; of incomes between $1,500 and $2,000, 19.7 per cent was absorbed by rent, while in families with incomes above $7,500 only 9.2 per cent was spent for rent.

When the rent bill exacts more than about one-fourth or one-fifth of the family income, increasing

[8] *Reports from the Financial Survey of Urban Housing.*

CHART 4

Families by Income Groups
Percentage Distribution, 33 Cities, 1929 and 1933

Percentage of total families

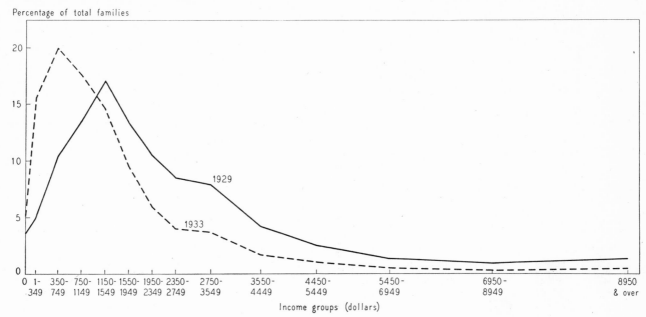

Income groups (dollars)

difficulty is encountered in its payment and delinquencies become much more common. Thus there are practical limits to the proportion of the income that can be expended for rent. For these reasons the predominance of moderate rents is a significant indication of the cost level at which new rental dwellings may be expected to find a market.

Relation of Value and Rent of Rented Properties
Comparison of the value of rented properties as declared by their owners with the rent reported by tenants, on a per room basis for 1933–34 in 42 cities, showed that on the average value was 8 times rent for 1-family dwellings, 9.4 for 2-family dwellings, and 10.8 for apartments. In some cities the range was from 4.3 to 18 times the annual rent and the ratio was generally lower in the South than in the North and West. For 1-family dwellings in most cities, however, the average value-rent ratio ranged from 8.9 in the West North Central to 12.6 in the East North Central. These ratios indicate the relation between the declared market value of the property and gross rents received. The furnishings or facilities included in the rent bill differ with the type and class of property and with local rental practice. On a net basis, with allowance for these charges, rent would constitute a lower proportion of value than here indicated, since the market value of the property would be unchanged and net rent, after operation costs had been deducted, would of course be less than gross. The large amount of service value added by the common practice of including furnish-

ings and facilities in rents for apartments and, less commonly, for 2-family dwellings, is responsible for the marked difference between the ratios for 1-family dwellings and other types, and to a considerable degree for the differences between geographic divisions.

Family Income in Relation to Rent and Value of Dwellings
The real property situation during the last decade has been vitally affected by changes in individual family incomes. Income received from all sources, including returns from business, declined greatly from the prosperity period that ended in 1929 to the depression years 1932 and 1933 (Chart 4). This decline was closely related to the serious reduction in employment, since both owner and tenant families derive most of their income from wages and salaries. Of the owner-occupant families reporting income in 1934,[9] 79 per cent of the family income was from this source, and of the tenant families, 91 per cent. Moreover, the average percentage of full time worked by the chief wage earner of the family ranged from very low figures for the lower income groups to high figures for the upper income groups. The incomes of both owner-occupant and tenant families who reported incomes for 1929 and 1933 in 33 cities were concentrated in 1929 between $1,150 and $1,549. Four years later the incomes of approximately the same group of families were concentrated between $350 and $749. For the prosperous

[9] *Percentages computed from Tables 20 and 21,* Financial Survey of Urban Housing.

year 1929, families who owned their houses in 52 representative American cities reported annual incomes averaging $2,300. By 1933, the low point of the depression, average income had declined 36.4 per cent, to $1,465, an amount equal to 33 per cent of the value of their dwellings. The decline was more severe than in the incomes of tenants, which fell 31.9 per cent. A greater dependence by the owner-occupant families on business profits accounts in part for this difference.

Families that live in rented dwellings have average incomes substantially less than owners, partly because they are smaller, have fewer mature members and fewer income earners. In 52 cities incomes of tenant families averaged $1,590 in 1929 and $1,080 in 1933, or about one-third less than incomes of owners. Rent paid by these families averaged $30 a month in 1929 and $20 in 1933.

The change in incomes for individual families was highly irregular, and for a large proportion the decline was much more severe than is indicated by the averages. In Cleveland, for example, 38 per cent of the incomes of 1,725 families receiving between $950 and $1,149 in 1929 fell below $500 in 1933. For another 25 per cent, income fell into the $500–749 class. Only 18 per cent retained their 1929 incomes or received larger incomes (Table VI). Such drastic changes deprived many families of the means of paying the usual amount of rent or of maintaining installments on mortgages. This situation was a prime cause of the widespread delinquency in rents and defaults on real estate loans, and of the decline in realty values.

TABLE VI

Percentage Distribution of 1933 Incomes of 1,725 Families receiving Incomes of $950–1,149 in 1929, Cleveland, Ohio [1]

INCOME GROUP 1933	PERCENTAGE DISTRIBUTION
No income	5.0
$ 1– 249	11.8
250– 499	21.7
500– 749	25.4
750– 999	18.4
1,000–1,499	14.5
1,500–1,999	2.0
2,000–2,999	1.0
3,000–4,499	0.1
4,500–7,499	0.1
7,500 and over	0.0

[1] *Special tabulation by the National Bureau of Economic Research of data obtained by the Financial Survey of Urban Housing. The 1929 income group is the modal or typical income group for the 1929 distribution of family incomes in Cleveland.*

The value of houses in 1934, as reported in the Financial Survey of Urban Housing by nearly 125,000 owner-occupant families, averaged about 3.2 times the 1933 family income. This ratio varied from about 2 to 4. In the northeastern cities, where residential values are considerably higher than in the West and South and incomes are somewhat larger, the value of the family residence in relation to income was commonly above the national average.

The ratios of the values of dwellings to the annual incomes of owner-occupant families with low incomes were very much higher than the average for all owner-occupant families. Owner-occupant families with annual incomes ranging between $500 and $750 had houses valued, on the average, at 6 times their income, while those with incomes between $3,000 and $4,500 had houses with values averaging twice their incomes. In other years, when property values and particularly family incomes may have been different, other ratios may have prevailed.

For owner-occupant families whose houses are mortgaged the ratio between the value of the property and annual income is smaller than in the case of properties owned free from debt. The schedule of payments covering interest and principal must be met periodically as a recurrent cash expense similar to rent. If the loan is to be kept in good standing, income must be sufficient to provide for the regular payments as well as the family's other expenses. When incomes decline severely, many loans become delinquent, particularly on houses of families with small incomes and little or no margin of saving. This danger of loan delinquency among owners is similar to that of tenant families whose rent delinquency increases sharply as the rent-income ratio rises to 20 per cent or above.

Financing Nonfarm Residential Real Estate

The price for which real estate can be bought or sold provides the security for its financing, thereby determining the size of the credit structure that can be erected on mortgages. It is greatly influenced by the peculiarly local nature and inherent immobility of real property. In the market, which is essentially local with limits defined by local conditions, real estate may sell much more readily at some times than at others, unlike a commodity that sells on an organized exchange where all offerings may be sold at any time for some price. Land values may rise or decline as the neighborhood improves or goes downhill. The value of buildings declines as they age, become obsolete, and deteriorate. The major hazard for real property owners and investors, however, may be the wide fluctuations in value that accompany national or local economic changes.

Over long periods measures of value for American real estate are modified when, as in the case of such other durable goods as automobiles, new materials or equipment are introduced or styles are radically altered. For example, residential units now have facilities built in as standard equipment that a few years ago were considered luxuries. A house built in 1940

CHART 5

**Mortgaged Properties, Owner-Occupied, 52 Cities, Rented, 44 Cities
Percentage Distribution by Ratio of Debt to Value, 1934**

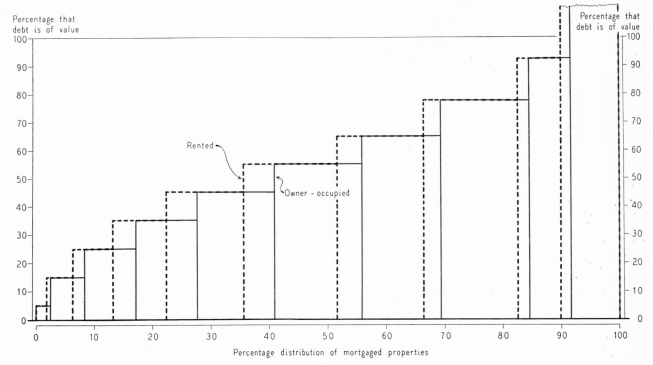

may differ only slightly in exterior design and construction from its predecessor of 1930, or even 1910, but its fixtures are much more complete. Electricity, improved plumbing and heating, refrigeration, garages and, more recently, air-conditioning, are illustrations of improvements in housing that have come as a result of industrial progress and that reflect the rising standard of living. Similar improvements have been made in nonresidential construction. Hence a part of the increase in the value of properties during the last 20 or 30 years is attributable to qualitative improvements in construction.

When a property is covered by a loan or a purchase-money mortgage, the problems associated with the fulfillment of the credit part of the transaction are to that extent postponed to the time payment falls due. By then or before, there may be a different relation between debt service and income, and even a major change in values as compared with the time the credit arrangement was made. This uncertainty as to the future relation of these factors and the effect on the economic system as compared with that originally contemplated is a central problem in real estate financing.

Real estate loans constitute the largest single form of credit, a predominance that reflects the leading position of real estate in the nation's wealth. Nonfarm residential property constitutes the security for most realty financing. In 1934 this class of indebtedness outstanding was estimated as approximately $26 billion, an amount probably considerably less than the outstanding debt in 1930, prior to the severe liquidation of mortgages during the depression.

Like the property that constitutes their security, real estate loans are widely distributed geographically, representing the obligations of many individuals and firms, secured in most instances by relatively small properties. The widespread and increasing use of realty credit is indicated by a comparison of owner-occupied residential properties mortgaged in 50 representative cities covered by the Census in 1920 and by the Financial Survey in 1934: the percentage rose from 49 to 55 per cent.

This growing use of credit was due in large part to rising values, the construction of new buildings at higher costs, and the more liberal provisions of mortgage credit by financial agencies. Existing structures also were used as the basis for larger mortgages as property values rose. Those properties which were free from debt, if transferred to others, were commonly used as collateral for the unpaid balance. This was true in most American cities of medium or large size where a majority of the properties are encumbered by one or more mortgages. The Financial Survey, covering 52 cities, showed an average of 56 per cent of owner-occupied dwellings and 40 per cent of rented dwellings mortgaged in 1934. Cities that are new or that have recently experienced a period of active building are likely to have relatively more of their properties encumbered because they have more recently incurred capital loans. A substantial part of total encumbrance comes into existence at the time the property is acquired; though many other mortgages in the form of new financing, renewals, or refinancing are placed upon the property subsequent to its purchase.

The percentage of the value that the mortgage constitutes is a gauge of the financial soundness of the loan. The Financial Survey showed that in 1934 encumbered owner-occupied dwellings in most of the 52 cities covered were mortgaged on the average up to 50 or 60 per cent of their value; 59 per cent had mortgages amounting to more than one-half, and 31 per cent to more than 70 per cent of their value (Table VII and Chart 5). The unpaid balances vary from small percentages to the full value of the property and on some properties exceed it. New properties, or those recently bought, are likely to have larger proportions of the value remaining unpaid. A high debt ratio is produced also by a decline in the value of the property after a mortgage has been placed on it.

TABLE VII

68,385 Mortgaged Owner-Occupied Properties, Percentage Distribution by Debt-Value Ratios, 52 Cities, 1934

DEBT-VALUE RATIO (per cent)	PERCENTAGE DISTRIBUTION	CUMULATIVE PERCENTAGE
1– 9	2.5	2.5
10–19	5.8	8.3
20–29	8.8	17.1
30–39	10.6	27.7
40–49	13.2	40.9
50–59	14.9	55.8
60–69	13.6	69.4
70–84	14.7	84.1
85–99	7.6	91.7
100 and over	8.3	100.0

Compiled from Financial Survey of Urban Housing data

The institutions or agencies that provide mortgage credit differ widely in their practices, deriving and expending their loan funds through different channels and on different terms and conditions. Life insurance companies, commercial and savings banks, building and loan associations, mortgage companies, and individuals, are the principal sources. Their relative importance as mortgage holders in representative cities prior to the refunding operations that began in 1934 is shown in Chart 6. Since that time, the relative position has changed owing to the more rapid liquidation of loans by some agencies through the elimination of many of their active sources of credit and to the greatly expanded operations of federally sponsored agencies.

The changes in credit sources have been reflected also in the terms of loans. Formerly most loans were made for relatively few years. The prevailing practice of the chief classes of lenders is illustrated by the terms of outstanding loans reported in 1934 in the 52 Financial Survey cities. Three-year loans were held largely by commercial banks, 5-year loans by life insurance companies, 10- to 12-year loans by building and loan associations; loans for 15 years or more were usually held by individual investors, the Home Owners Loan Corporation, and a few life insurance companies. Since the advent of the Federal Housing Administration commercial banks have taken a leading part in originating long term loans incident to qualifying mortgages for insurance.

CHART 6

Residential Mortgage Debt on Owner-Occupied and Rented Properties, Percentage Distribution by Holding Agency 52 Cities, 1934

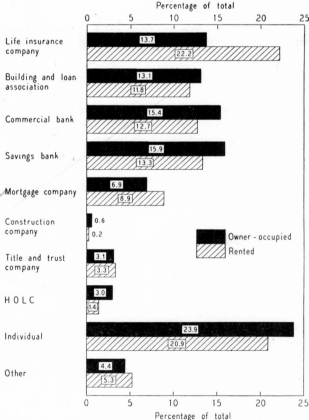

Distinctive features of changing loan practices in recent years have been the lengthening of terms and the inclusion of provisions for amortization and more frequent payments (Chart 7). This tendency has been strongly influenced by the use of long term amortized loans of the Home Owners Loan Corporation and by the requirement of the Federal Housing Administration that all loans on which insurance is granted shall

CHART 7

First Mortgages, Owner-Occupied, 52 Cities, Rented, 47 Cities
Percentage Distribution by Term, 1934

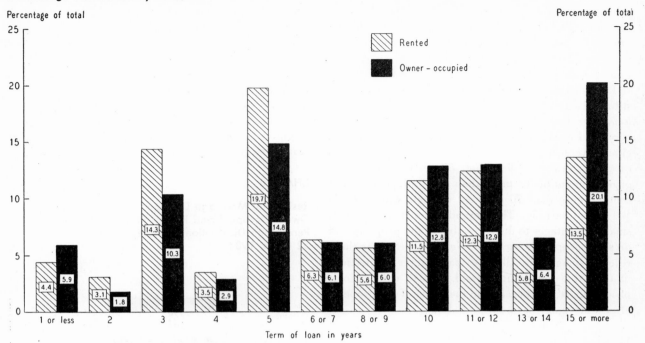

Percentage of total

Rented

Owner – occupied

Term of loan in years

have long terms and carry amortization provisions. These changes have brought many more mortgages within the reach of more families.

Perhaps no development of recent years has been more significant for the future real estate situation than the marked reduction in interest rates on all types of loans. In 1934 contract interest rates in 52 cities averaged approximately 6.3 per cent on first mortgage loans on owner-occupied properties and 6.4 per cent on rented properties. Higher rates prevailed on second mortgages. Effective rates, which included incidental financing costs, were nearly one-half per cent higher than contract rates. Especially since federally sponsored agencies entered the field of housing, many loans have been made at 5 and 4½ per cent, and large loans at even lower rates. At the end of 1938 two federal agencies had made or insured a total of $5 billion loans with contract interest rates of 5 per cent; in 1939 their prevailing rate was lowered to 4½ per cent. Vast quantities of private funds became available for mortgage loans at 4½ per cent or even lower rates. Low interest rates, especially if they continue to be generally available, will greatly affect real estate values and the credit structure through new loans and refinancing, at values based on low capitalization rates. On the whole, recent changes in credit regulations and in the institutions financing residential property in the United States have tended toward greater availability of funds and more liberal arrangements for credit. Since longer terms and lower rates have enabled bor-

rowers to carry loans more easily, the size of loans has increased.

Nonfarm Residential Construction

The rate of construction of new dwellings has far reaching economic consequences, not only for the industries that supply construction materials and the workmen who are directly employed in building, but also upon overcrowding or vacancy, the character of housing, the levels of rents, and the value of existing properties. Never has this subject been more widely considered in the United States. After nearly a decade of relative inactivity, general interest has again revived in construction and in the purchase and sale of existing properties, partly as a consequence of improved conditions of financing. Supplementing these economic forces a general movement for better housing began in 1935–36, and continued at a somewhat diminished rate in 1937–38. This revival in nonfarm residential building and related activity started a full two years after the beginning of the general business recovery in 1933–34 (Chart 8).[10] Improvement in employment and trade and an increase in family incomes and in business earnings were apparently a necessary prelude.

The seventeen years following 1920 were noteworthy

[10] *This chart and some other parts of the material on construction that appear in this volume were first published on September 15, 1937 in National Bureau Bulletin 65, by D. L. Wickens and R. R. Foster.*

both for the great activity in new residential building and for its violent fluctuations. During the decade 1920–29 construction was started on 7,035,000 new nonfarm dwelling units; during the next seven years, 1930–36, on only 1,106,000.[11] The 1920's thus produced 86 per cent of total nonfarm residential construction accomplished during these seventeen years.

The timing of the crest of building activity is of vital economic importance. Beginning at a moderate rate with 247,000 units in 1920, building activity rose to boom proportions within a few years. An all-time record of nearly one million dwelling units, including apartments and houses (Tables E 1 and 2), was reached in 1925 rather than in 1928, as has been generally assumed. By 1930–31 construction had declined to the level of a decade earlier. The decline began four years before the industrial decline of 1929. A rapid further descent to a nominal building rate during the depression 1932–34 was followed by a revival, and in 1936 the 1920 and 1930 volume was again equaled (Chart 8).

CHART 8

**Nonfarm Dwelling Units Built
Number and Value, 1920–1936**

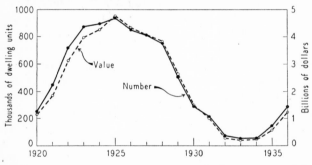

Construction in various parts of the country followed widely divergent courses, and even within re-

gions trends for individual cities have differed widely from the trend for the region as a whole. In nonmetropolitan urban centers, that is, those places not in metropolitan districts but with populations of 2,500 or more, construction fluctuated less violently than in metropolitan areas, and in recent years has been a larger proportion of the total than formerly. Many of these urban places not in metropolitan districts are in predominantly agricultural regions.

The tables in Part Three, section E, measure the fluctuations in residential construction since 1920, showing regional differences, the types of structure erected, and the total value of new nonfarm construction from year to year. Also, aggregate building from 1920 to 1936 is compared with that during the three decades 1890–1919. For many years building in the United States has been concentrated chiefly in a small area, over half of all new nonfarm residential units having been built in the industrial Northeast; during 1920–36 nearly three-fourths were built in the 96 metropolitan districts as defined by the Bureau of the Census. Residential construction in the 120 central cities of these metropolitan districts far exceeded that in any other group of urban centers. The concentration of nonfarm construction in metropolitan districts is even more pronounced on a value basis.

Reflecting the generally upward trend of average cost per dwelling unit throughout much of this period,[12] the total value of new housekeeping units built in nonfarm areas rose more rapidly than the number of units from 1922 to 1925, and declined less rapidly from 1925 to 1928. A part of this increase in cost per unit was due to the construction of more elaborate and expensive houses. Average costs of dwelling construction in small population centers, aside from environs of metropolitan centers, were substantially less than in large cities.

Note: Estimates of the Aggregate Value of Real Estate

The data on national wealth and on total value of real estate, 1900–22 (Tables I and III), are taken from the Department of Commerce Bulletin, *Estimated National Wealth—Wealth, Public Debt and Taxation, 1922.* Total real property and improvements for 1930 and 1934 represent the total value of urban real estate estimated by this study as described in Part Two and of farm real estate estimated as follows: For 1910,

1920, 1925, and 1930 values were taken from the Census of Agriculture; for 1912 and 1922 estimates were made by a straight line interpolation between Census years. Table III gives the NBER estimates and their percentage distributions. In estimating the total value of all real estate in 1934 it was assumed that the decline from 1930 had been in the same proportion as for 1-family residential property, the index number being 65.6 (1930=100).

Method of Estimating Total Value of Nonfarm Real Estate, 1930 and 1934

The method was determined by the lack of materials comparable to those available for nonfarm residential

---

[11] *These totals compare with approximately 3,900,000 units built during each of the decades 1910–19 and 1900–09, and 2,400,000 during 1890–99. Despite the drastic curtailment in building during the 1930's the 8,142,000 units built during the 17 years 1920–36 exceeds the 7,840,000 units in the two decades prior to 1920, owing partly to the construction during the early 1920's of buildings that had been postponed during the War.*

[12] *Cost here means the average cost of dwellings actually built, as distinct from the trend of labor-materials price indexes.*

real estate. Although less detailed and less exact than the nonfarm residential estimates, tests indicate that the estimates of the value of all nonfarm real estate are reasonably dependable. The data were obtained by sending inquiries to city assessors, banks, and tax authorities in many cities. A total of 533 returns (Table VIII) reported the actual or estimated assessed value of each of the following principal types of real estate (see Table IV for estimates of market values): (a) residential, (b) commercial real estate, (c) industrial real estate, (d) other real estate taxed, (e) real estate exempt.

The kinds of real estate included in these general groups and as shown on the schedule used were:

"A Real estate taxed
    1 Residential property. (Include site and structure) houses, apartments, hotels, other dwelling units
    2 Commercial property. (Include site and structure) office buildings, stores, garages, service stations, theaters, loft buildings, warehouses, storage plants, and real estate occupied by banks and financial institutions
    3 Industrial property. Include: land and buildings of manufacturing establishments, processing plants; real estate owned by utilities, including street car lines, gas and electric power plants (omit franchises), and railroad real estate in city, including bridges, right of way, barns, and shops.
    4 All other real estate taxed
    Total assessed value of real estate taxed
B Real estate exempt from taxation
Total real estate."

The city assessor was requested to report assessed values as of June 30, 1936, or on the most recent assessment date, and to indicate whether the figures were actual amounts or estimates. Only those schedules which included a report on residential real estate were used in summarizing the results, since that was the only classification for which aggregate estimates could be obtained. The replies were tabulated by geographic divisions. Table VIII shows the distribution by geographic divisions and population groups, and the percentage of each group represented by the sample.

In those cases in which the data for other items were missing from the schedule, the omitted data were estimated by applying a relative derived in a percentage distribution from paired items, expressing the total for the individual item as a percentage of total real estate reported. In this process, "total real estate" includes real estate exempt from taxation. Aggregates of these assessed values, actual or estimated, for all schedules were then totaled for each of the five types of real estate by geographic divisions. A percentage distribution was then made of the aggregate assessed values of these five classes of property by geographic divisions with "total real estate" as 100 per cent.

To convert assessed values into market values, data on the relative size of market and assessed values were obtained for cities throughout the country. Commercial and savings banks and tax experts returned 796 schedules reporting their estimates of the relation between assessed and market value of real property in their respective cities, giving assessed value as an estimated percentage of market value for each of the four classes of taxed real estate described above. Table IX shows

TABLE VIII

Cities and Villages for which Tax Assessors reported Total Value of Real Estate, June 30, 1936, Number and Percentage of Total, Summary by Geographic Division and Population Group

	ALL POPULATION GROUPS	100,000 OR MORE	25,000–100,000	10,000–25,000	5,000–10,000	2,500–5,000	1,000–2,500	UNDER 1,000
				A NUMBER				
United States	533	20	51	110	65	63	99	125
New England	36	1	4	17	8	1	4	1
Mid. Atlantic	106	7	10	34	11	14	15	15
E. N. Central	144	6	24	24	19	14	29	28
W. N. Central	95	2	1	14	5	11	12	50
S. Atlantic	45	1	4	7	3	4	10	16
E. S. Central	24	..	..	4	1	7	6	6
W. S. Central	45	..	2	5	10	7	16	5
Mountain	18	..	1	3	3	3	5	3
Pacific	20	3	5	2	5	2	2	1
	B PERCENTAGE OF TOTAL NUMBER OF CITIES AND VILLAGES (CENSUS 1930)							
United States	3.2	21.5	18.0	18.2	7.6	4.7	3.2	1.2
New England	11.0	7.7	9.5	21.8	11.8	3.2	11.4	1.7
Mid. Atlantic	5.5	38.9	17.2	21.0	5.7	4.9	3.4	2.0
E. N. Central	4.1	31.6	30.8	19.8	10.2	5.5	4.4	1.3
W. N. Central	2.3	22.2	5.6	22.6	6.1	6.1	2.1	1.5
S. Atlantic	2.0	11.1	12.5	13.7	3.4	2.5	2.3	1.1
E. S. Central	2.0	..	..	12.5	2.2	7.0	2.5	0.8
W. S. Central	2.7	..	11.1	11.9	11.2	4.2	4.0	0.5
Mountain	2.1	..	12.5	26.3	17.6	7.7	4.7	3.0	0.5
Pacific	2.8	33.3	26.3	4.8	8.2	2.2	1.4	0.3

TABLE IX

Cities and Villages for which Banks reported Estimated Percentage Market Value is of Assessed Value, 1936, Number and Percentage of Total, Summary by Geographic Division and Population Group

	ALL POPU-LATION GROUPS	100,000 OR MORE	25,000–100,000	10,000–25,000	5,000–10,000	2,500–5,000	1,000–2,500	UNDER 1,000
	A NUMBER							
United States	786	30	22	80	108	121	145	280
New England	31	4	3	12	5	1	5	1
Mid. Atlantic	117	3	4	18	24	30	18	20
E. N. Central	172	6	9	18	30	25	28	56
W. N. Central	177	5	1	9	13	20	30	99
S. Atlantic	61	4	1	3	7	7	13	26
E. S. Central	60	3	2	3	5	12	13	22
W. S. Central	75	3	1	6	8	11	21	25
Mountain	45	..	..	3	7	5	11	19
Pacific	48	2	1	8	9	10	6	12
	B PERCENTAGE OF TOTAL NUMBER OF CITIES (CENSUS 1930)							
United States	4.7	32.3	7.8	13.2	12.7	9.1	4.7	2.7
New England	9.5	30.8	7.1	15.4	7.4	3.2	14.3	1.7
Mid. Atlantic	6.1	16.7	6.9	11.1	12.4	10.5	4.0	2.6
E. N. Central	4.9	31.6	11.5	14.9	16.1	9.9	4.2	2.6
W. N. Central	4.3	55.6	5.6	14.5	15.9	11.1	5.4	3.1
S. Atlantic	2.7	44.4	3.1	5.9	8.0	4.3	3.0	1.7
E. S. Central	5.0	50.0	20.0	9.4	11.1	12.0	5.4	2.8
W. S. Central	4.4	37.5	5.6	14.3	9.0	6.6	5.3	2.6
Mountain	5.4	..	..	17.6	17.9	7.8	6.7	3.5
Pacific	6.8	22.2	5.3	19.0	14.8	11.1	4.1	3.6

the distribution of reports by geographic divisions and population groups and the percentage in each group represented by the sample. All reports that included data for residential and commercial real estate were tabulated by geographic divisions. Items for "industrial property" and "other real estate taxed" that were not reported on individual schedules were estimated by assuming that the ratio of assessed to market value was the same as that shown by the aggregates of the corresponding types for all those cities that reported these items. A total and an average was computed for each city reporting and averages of the city percentages were computed for: (1) residential real estate, (2) commercial real estate, (3) industrial real estate, (4) other real estate taxed, (5) total for each geographic division. These average percentages representing ratios of assessed to market value were used in connection with the actual data obtained from the schedules sent to the city assessors, as follows: The percentage that assessed value is of market value for each of the four types of taxed real estate by geographic divisions was divided into the corresponding assessed value, as described in the first paragraph above, to get an estimated market value. An average of the four percentages for residential, commercial, industrial, and other taxed real estate was used to convert the value reported for exempt real estate to full market value.

These percentages thus used as correction factors varied relatively little among the different types of real estate in most geographic divisions (Table X). Consequently the resulting aggregates of value varied little in relative importance from that indicated by their assessed values. The percentage assessed is of

market value for industrial real estate in New England, 99.9, is the outstanding exception, since the percentages for the three other classes in that region ranged from 81.9 to 88.6. In this case the high figure was due to the inclusion of reports for several cities indicating that assessed value was much above market value for industrial property. The aggregates by type were totaled for all real estate and upon the basis of this total a percentage distribution was computed showing the value of the sample for each type—residential, commercial, industrial, other real estate taxed, and real estate exempt. By substituting this study's estimated aggregate residential value for each geographic division for the residential property's percentage in the percentage distribution by type of real estate for the same geographic division, the value of each of the other types of real estate was computed. The estimated values of the respective types were totaled to obtain the estimated value of all real estate.

The fact that the city assessors' reports covered only the property within city limits probably results, as noted above, in a slight underestimate for certain types of property such as railroad rights of way, utility lines, and industrial property outside cities.

With a fair representation of population groups of different size, though the percentage in towns and villages was a smaller part of the total than the percentage in cities, the returns covered all parts of the country. The coverage of the reports on the ratio of assessed to market value varied somewhat among geographic divisions and population groups (see Tables VIII and IX).

The method used here differs in three respects from

that used by the Bureau of the Census in its estimate of wealth for 1900, 1904, 1912, 1922 as published in *Estimated National Wealth—Wealth, Public Debt and Taxation, 1922.* (1) In the Census study the assessed values for all real estate were combined without differentiation as to type. (2) The Census study undertook to adjust assessed to market values by means of a

TABLE X

Assessed Value as Percentage of Estimated Market Value of City and Village Real Estate Taxed; Bank Schedules, 1936, Average Percentages, by Type of Property, by Geographic Division

	No. of Schedules	ASSESSED VALUE AS PERCENTAGE OF ESTIMATED MARKET VALUE, BY TYPE OF PROPERTY			
		Residential	Commercial	Industrial	Other real estate taxed
United States	796	65.3	67.0	64.0	65.1
New England	34	83.8	88.6	99.9	81.9
Mid. Atlantic	120	66.6	64.5	62.1	67.2
E. N. Central	173	70.9	73.7	69.7	70.9
W. N. Central	178	67.6	69.3	66.0	68.8
S. Atlantic	61	59.9	60.4	57.9	57.6
E. S. Central	61	61.5	65.1	59.5	58.2
W. S. Central	75	59.1	58.6	54.5	55.3
Mountain	45	64.0	70.2	63.1	69.8
Pacific	49	44.2	45.7	44.4	43.7

SOURCE: *Special reports to the National Bureau from commercial and savings banks and taxation authorities*

correction factor derived from replies to an inquiry to state and county tax officials on the relation between assessed and sales values. To avoid the difficulties that confront tax officials in carrying out legal instructions which often require that real estate be assessed at full value, whereas actual practice usually indicates a level of assessed values that is considerably below market value, though in some cities it is above, the estimates, by this project, of the relation between assessed and market value were obtained from private sources, including banks and real estate firms specializing in tax work. (3) The Census study combined the real estate with the other property of corporations. Real property and improvements for steam railways, electrical railways, telegraph and telephone systems, and privately owned steam railways, central light and power enterprises and water works were combined in making an estimate of wealth by the ownership classification. The Census procedure probably resulted in an understatement of the real estate reported for Census years. This study sought to include the real estate of corporate enterprises as well as individually and publicly owned property and to classify it according to its general uses, under the general types of residential, commercial, industrial, other real estate taxed, and real estate exempt from taxation.

PART TWO

CHAPTER I

Sources, Method of Presentation, and Important Characteristics of the Statistical Data

Part Three presents the statistical information in five sections: A, the value of nonfarm residential real estate (Tables A 3 and 17 contain some farm data); B, rents; C, the relation between values, rents, and the incomes of owner-occupant and tenant families; D, the financial aspects of residential real estate; E, estimates of new nonfarm residential construction. Within these classifications the tables are numbered consecutively. Brief topical paragraphs giving the main qualifications of the data precede each section as half-title pages.

In the five chapters in Part Two the methods used to obtain the estimates presented in Part Three are described in some detail. But first we discuss: (1) the principal sources from which the statistical data were derived; (2) certain general principles that have guided their presentation; (3) the reliability and significance of owners' estimates of the value of residential real estate.

1 Principal Sources

The statistical data rest heavily upon four main sources: (1) *Census of Population, 1930*, VI, Families; (2) Federal Real Property Inventory of 1934; (3) Financial Survey of Urban Housing; (4) Bureau of Labor Statistics reports on building permits.

The *Census of Population, 1930*, VI, provides the basic material for estimating the aggregate value of nonfarm residential real estate in 1930. This material was supplemented by a special tabulation of unpublished data prepared by this project from primary schedules of the Census Bureau covering 139 cities and by related information in the Federal Real Property Inventory and the Financial Survey of Urban Housing, the latter an intensive sample survey of the properties covered by the former. In estimating nonfarm residential construction the Census data on families were also used extensively in connection with the Bureau of Labor Statistics building permits data.

The Federal Real Property Inventory and the Financial Survey of Urban Housing provide the detailed housing data, chiefly for 1934, for selected cities throughout the United States. Of the 64 cities covered by the Federal Real Property Inventory, 61 were included in the more intensive Financial Survey of Urban Housing, but 9 were covered incompletely so that the more detailed tabulations are available only for 52 cities. Until the publication of this volume, complete data had been published [1] for only 22 of the 52 cities though press releases had appeared for each city.

The Financial Survey of Urban Housing, undertaken in 1934, obtained reports from owner-occupants, tenants, and landlords on the physical characteristics of dwellings and their value, rent, and debt status, and the income of the occupant family. Value and debt reports were for January 1, 1930, 1933, and 1934; rent and income for 1929, 1932, and 1933. The Financial Survey reports constitute a sample varying from 5 to 30 per cent of the families in individual cities and averaging close to 12 per cent for tenant families and 15 per cent for owner-occupant families for all 61 cities.

2 Presentation

The statistical evidence is presented in tabular form that is readily usable by those who may wish to know "the facts" concerning residential real estate. Where estimates have been made, details of methods are set forth so that each user may judge their validity and the proper fields for their application. Where sample data are used, the number of reports or a cross reference to other tables where they can be found has also been given to provide the analyst with a basis for judging their adequacy. The representativeness of the Financial Survey samples for each city is fairly accurate, as is evident from a comparison of similar items reported by the Real Property Inventory.[2] They have not been raised to represent full coverage in each city, and the geographic division totals of the number

[1] *Financial Survey of Urban Housing (Department of Commerce, Washington, 1937).*
[2] *These comparisons are given at the beginning of the data for each of the 22 cities for which results were published in November 1937 and for the 30 cities not yet published, all covered by the Financial Survey of Urban Housing.*

reporting for the cities in each division are totals of the sample data.

The material is so voluminous that it has not been practicable to appraise it other than by these comparisons of the basic data. It must be used at the reader's discretion. As an additional aid in determining appropriate uses each section of tables is introduced by a brief summary of technical considerations or other pertinent items of information concerning the data or their derivation. Footnotes to individual tables serve a similar purpose.

The Financial Survey of Urban Housing data gave information on specific items for all 61 cities covered. Some tables from it are reprinted in this volume chiefly in summary form with certain related items for each city in which reports were adequate. Most data cover 52 cities, some, 61, and, for certain data from the Real Property Inventory, even 64 cities. Some data from owner-landlord reports relating to tenants or tenant-occupied property cover 44 or fewer cities.

For values, rents, and reports on financial items, the tables give, in addition to information for individual cities, weighted figures for the group of cities within each geographic division and for all reporting cities combined. The weighting on which such geographic division figures are based is explained in the footnotes to each table where they appear. The arithmetic averages for the cities included in the several geographic divisions were derived by weighting the sample data for each city on the basis of its relative importance in the group of cities reporting. The averages thus derived from the combination of data for cities covered may not be identical with, or even approximate to, the averages that would be derived from data for all cities or from a different selection of cities in each geographic division. In the absence of data for complete coverage it is impossible to determine the actual representation given by the weighted means for the selected cities. The weighted figures for the cities in each geographic division had often to be used as the true figures for the area as a whole, since it seemed the preferable alternative to use all the data available weighted on the basis of their relative importance, but it is believed that no considerable error has resulted from this procedure. These points are emphasized for the assistance of the reader who desires to use the weighted figures for the cities in each geographic division. The cities included, their importance in their regions, and other factors connected with the particular item of information must be appraised in conjunction with the purpose to be served and the requisite accuracy. Certainly in the absence of additional information the weighted figures may be assumed to be more representative of the geographic division than the figures for any one city.

The method of weighting the sample data for geographic division totals does not correct for any bias in the data for individual cities. These division totals merely weight the sample results on the basis of the relative importance of the several cities in terms of the items covered. Certain tables, e.g., A 11 and B 8, do attempt to present data for each city and for the combination of cities in each geographic division that represents complete coverage. The introductory comments to each section of tables call readers' attention to these.

3 Owners' Estimates

Owners' estimates, of which extensive use is made in this study, are the chief source of information concerning the value of real estate. They are provided by the 1930 Population Census, the Financial Survey of Urban Housing, and the Federal Real Property Inventory, as well as by numerous subsequent real property inventories in other cities. The Census of Agriculture has obtained reports on the value of individual farms, with occasional separate reports for buildings and land, as estimated by the farm operator in each Census of Agriculture since 1850 (Table A 17).

Market value of property rather than some other concept, such as the cost of the property plus additions and less depreciation, reproduction cost new less depreciation, the amount the owner would be willing to accept for the property, or the value at which the property is assessed for taxation purposes, has been established as the preferred concept in practice. It is assumed that the market value reported approximates the probable sale price under the usual terms and conditions of sale prevailing in the community. Market value does not mean, necessarily, that if all properties in the community were offered for sale at the time in question the stated value could be obtained. Rather, market value as usually defined means that under prevailing conditions of sales activity property similar to that for which the value was estimated is or could be sold at the stated price. Unusual conditions of sale, either in the terms of credit or cash required or in the forced character of the sale, are not ordinarily considered in quoting market value.

For a staple commodity such as wheat the value of the stock on hand is usually based upon the prices prevailing in the market for the different grades of wheat actually being sold currently. Such a valuation is possible since the commodity can be divided into a reasonably small number of fairly homogeneous grades which are sold on a continuous, organized, and broad market. Residential properties are sold under quite different conditions. Virtually every parcel is different from every other and is sold with particular reference to these differences on narrow, discontinuous, and only slightly organized markets. Consequently, the market value of a particular parcel cannot be determined precisely unless it is actually sold.

Market values of properties may be estimated regardless of tenure, though those of owner-occupied are most commonly used because of the presumed familiarity of the owner with such values. Furthermore, the value of properties, rented or otherwise used for income, may be estimated by capitalizing income to approximate investment and market values; or, as done in this study, the value may be estimated by applying to rent an empirical ratio between rent and value. Since properties inhabited by their owners do not yield rents their value cannot be estimated by this procedure unless the rent is first estimated.

Partial evidence for the assumption that owners' estimates do approximate market values as defined above is at hand. It is sometimes held that owners consider the value of their residences as continuously identical with the original cost to them. This contention is definitely not supported by experience with owners' estimates. The Department of Agriculture index of the value of farm land and buildings per acre, based largely on owners' reports, increased from 100 for 1912–14 to 170 in 1920, and declined to 73 in 1933, with changes in every intervening year. Moreover, the index for each of the 48 states behaved differently. The same variability in the average of owners' reports has been evident in the Census returns at 5- and 10-year intervals.

Original costs by year of acquisition and the values estimated by the owners on January 1, 1934 for identical properties, reported to the Financial Survey, indicate clearly that owners do not estimate value in terms of cost. The movement of the series indicates also that the deviations of estimated value in 1934 from original cost in the year of acquisition are more closely related to economic shifts in values than to depreciation resulting from the passage of time. The mere fact that owners do vary their estimates of market value and do not maintain them at cost of acquisition does not establish the correctness of the level of their estimates or of the trend. The values estimated for individual properties may deviate considerably from approximate market values or from the trends of such values. The values of groups of properties are much more reliable as measures of price movements.

So far as absolute levels are concerned, it is virtually impossible to secure information on a comprehensive scale that would indicate how much owners' average estimates deviate from actual market values. The extensive use of owners' estimates is occasioned partly by the absence of other data. However, the owner is familiar with the property evaluated. Usually he has purchased it; often he has built it. If his name is not made public and if no offer to purchase is given, he has little or no motive for misrepresenting the value. Although not an expert appraiser, he usually has gained a good idea of its value from the expert opinion

of appraisers who valued the property when he bought it or by his knowledge of prices paid for other similar properties that have been bought or sold in the same community. A tendency to understate value in order to avoid a high tax appraisal may be offset by overstatement for sale purposes.

So far as farm values reported by farm operators are concerned, experience indicates that they follow the general direction of sales price indexes. They reach high and low points at about the same time, but tend to lag behind sales price indexes during the early part of either an upward or downward movement. Table M 1 presents such index numbers for three states. In

TABLE M 1

Estimated Farm Values and Sales Prices per Acre
Ohio, Minnesota, and Vermont, 1912–1937

Index Numbers (1929 = 100.0) [1]

| | OHIO | | MINNESOTA [2] | | VERMONT | |
	B. A. E. [3] estimated value	Sales price [4]	B. A. E. [3] estimated value	Sales price [5]	B. A. E. [3] estimated value	Sales price [6]
1912			70.1	69	82	88.3
1913					82	94.9
1914			76.2	81	80	89.9
1915					85	77.3
1916			93.5	96	93	99.2
1917					103	110.1
1918			115.8	115	108	111.7
1919					111	115.9
1920			152.8		122	127.8
1921				146	122	125.2
1922			130.9	119	118	109.2
1923	129.7	119.1			109	119.3
1924	125.5	113.1	118.3		106	95.8
1925	116.9	112.0		110	102	92.4
1926	111.7	112.0	107.9		102	110.9
1927	105.3	108.4		107	102	100.0
1928	102.0	101.3	100.0		100	100.8
1929	100.0	100.0		100	100	100.0
1930	95.7	95.3	89.6		100	84.9
1931	87.1	90.5		84	98	83.2
1932	74.4	73.2	63.7		91	86.5
1933	62.7	71.5		63	82	80.6
1934	67.0	81.0	59.7	55		
1935	70.2	84.5				
1936	75.5	90.0	61.9	54		
1937	79.7	90.5				

[1] *Index numbers shifted from other base years for better comparability.*
[2] *Since data for Minnesota are for crop years, 1912 is really 1912–13 and the base year is 1928–29.*
[3] *Bureau of Agricultural Economics.*
[4] *Semi-annual index of farm real estate values in Ohio, March 1938 (mimeographed release).*
[5] *Minnesota Farm Business Notes, June 20, 1938.*
[6] *Vermont Agricultural Experiment Station, Bulletin 391.*

terms of dollar values per acre, estimated values tend on the whole to be somewhat higher than sales values. In Kansas estimated values per acre as reported to the Census in 1920, 1925, and 1930 were 3, 6, and 6 per cent higher, respectively, than average sales prices. In Ohio estimated values were 5 and 11 per cent higher in 1925 and 1930 respectively but 12 per cent lower in

1935. In Minnesota sales prices could not be directly compared with census estimates since the former were given for crop years. However, the estimates seem to be from 4 to 10 per cent higher than the sales prices in the four Census years 1920, 1925, 1930, and 1935. These differences may be accounted for by the fact that the properties sold were probably the less valuable ones, especially in depression years, since "distress" properties are likely to be less productive.

Estimates of farm values by farm operators may not be strictly comparable with estimates by urban families of the values of the houses they own and occupy since farmers operate their farms for profit and are more likely to have a business outlook, whereas the owner-occupant of an urban dwelling derives only a use value from the property. However, landlords who lease their properties for a cash rent also have the business man's outlook, and the relative changes in their estimates of the value of nonfarm residential real estate and in the estimates of owner-occupant families

during the same period are very similar. Evidence from the Financial Survey of Urban Housing indicates that in 37 cities from 1930 to 1934 the percentage decline in values as estimated by landlords did not differ more than 5 per cent from owner-occupants' estimates. In 2 cities the percentage changes were identical; in 32 cities landlords' estimates of values showed percentage declines greater than the estimates of owner-occupants, but the declines in 4 cities of the 32 differed less than 1 per cent, in 11 cities less than 2 per cent, in 19 cities less than 3 per cent, in 25 cities less than 5 per cent, and in only 1 city more than 10 per cent (10.5). Of the 10 cities in which owner-occupant estimated values indicated greater percentage declines than landlord estimated values, only 1 city showed a difference of more than 3 per cent (3.9) and for 7 of the 10 cities the difference was less than 2 per cent. It is quite possible that rented properties may have declined somewhat more in value than owner-occupied.

CHAPTER II

Value and Rent of Nonfarm Residential Real Estate, 1930 and 1934

The estimated total value of nonfarm residential real estate in the United States in 1930 is presented in Part Three, section A, Tables A 1–5. Table A 1 shows the number of dwelling units, Table A 2 their value by geographic division, state, tenure, and population group, and Table A 3 the average values per dwelling unit. Tables A 4 and 5 give the number of dwelling units and their values for each geographic division by type of dwelling. The value estimates for 1934 are presented by geographic division and tenure in Table A 8.

1 General Problems and Information Utilized in the 1930 Estimates

The total value of nonfarm residential real estate in the United States had to be estimated because the Census of Population returns for 1930 show only the number of nonfarm families occupying dwelling units distributed by value or rent classes. Median values and rents but no totals or arithmetic average values or rents are given.

In the 1930 Census families are distributed by value of dwelling unit classes whenever a related member of the family owned the structure or dwelling unit occupied by the family. The dwelling units occupied by these families constitute the tenure class "owner-occupied dwellings." [1] When a residential structure

contained more than one dwelling unit and one of the dwelling units was inhabited by the family owning the structure, the Census enumerator obtained the value of the unit, not the value of the entire structure. [2] Families are distributed by rent classes when the dwelling unit

_____

of home" the following explanation is given: "Since a home is defined as the living quarters occupied by a family, the number of homes is always the same as the number of families. In the classification by tenure a home is counted as owned if it is owned wholly or in part by any related member of the family."

[2] Ibid., p. 6. Under the heading "Value or rental of home," the following statement appears: "The enumerator was instructed to report on the population schedule for each nonfarm family returned as owning its home, the approximate current market value of the home, and for each nonfarm family returned as occupying rented quarters the monthly rental, or if rental was not paid by the month, then the equivalent monthly rental or the approximate rental value per month." Information obtained from the special tabulations of census data undertaken by this project and by inquiry from the Bureau of the Census indicates that "home" as used here refers to dwelling unit and not structure. Leon E. Truesdell of the Census Bureau in a letter reply to an inquiry from this project states: "The owners were expected to return, in cases where they occupied only a part of the structure, the value of that part occupied by the owner's family. Specific instructions to this effect were given wherever the question was raised, though this point was unfortunately not covered in the printed instruction pamphlet. Because of this there are doubtless some cases in which the owner returned the entire value of the structure rather than only that part which he occupied as a residence."

[1] Census of Population, 1930, _VI, 6. Under the heading "Tenure_

is rented, i.e., not owned by a related member of the occupant family. For multiple dwelling units the Census enumerator was instructed to secure the estimated rent for the dwelling unit actually occupied by the primary lessee and the actual rents paid by the secondary lessee families for the dwelling units they occupy.[3] Dwelling units occupied by families that do not own them constitute the tenure class "rented dwelling units" or "tenant-occupied dwelling units." [3]

The preceding explanation indicates that values and rents are for dwelling units, not structures (dwellings), unless the structure contains only one dwelling unit. When residential real estate is classified by "class of dwelling" (Census terminology) or by "type of dwelling" (terminology in this volume) reference is made to the number of dwelling units contained in the structure, e.g., 1-family, 2-family dwelling, etc.[4]

The Census enumeration of families by value and rent classes does not include vacant units. Furthermore, it was impossible to secure values or rents from every occupant family reporting tenure, and some families were enumerated as "not reporting value" or "not reporting rent." Similarly, since reports on tenure were incomplete some families are listed as "not reporting tenure." Attention has already been called to the fact that the data are presented in the form of frequency distributions; it should be noted also that the frequency distributions have open ends, that is, no definite limits are assigned to the end classes.

[3] Ibid., p. 6. "A home is counted as rented if it is not owned by any member of the family even though no cash rental is paid."
[4] Ibid., p. 10. "Dwellings. A dwelling, for Census purposes, is a place in which one or more persons regularly sleep. It need not be a house in the usual sense of the word. A boat, a tent, or a room in a factory or office building, although occupied by only one person, is also counted as a dwelling; while, on the other hand, an entire apartment house, although containing many families, constitutes but one dwelling. Dwellings have been classified for 1930 into three groups, namely, (a) those occupied by one family only, (b) those occupied by two families, and (c) those occupied by three or more families. It has been found difficult in some cases, particularly in cities where the houses are built in solid blocks, to make this classification. The enumerators were instructed to return as 1 dwelling a 2-family house with one apartment above the other, even though there was a separate front door for each apartment. On the other hand, where two families occupied parts of a building separated by a solid wall running up through the building, each part was counted as a 1-family dwelling, and likewise each 'house' in a section of 'row' houses." The number of dwellings of the three classes or types noted does not correspond to the number of standing structures, since only occupied units are enumerated. Furthermore, the statement as quoted, and further information received by correspondence with the Bureau of Census, indicates that when a multiple dwelling structure is occupied by only one family it is enumerated as a 1-family dwelling. This tends to give an excess number of occupied 1-family dwellings from the standpoint of class of structure (dwelling), an understated number of multiple family dwellings, and an understated number of 2-family dwellings. It also explains why the 2-family dwellings are shown as housing exactly two families per dwelling.

To estimate the total value of all nonfarm residential real estate in the United States in 1930 three major steps are necessary. First, total values or rents must be obtained from the frequency distributions as published in the *Census of Population, 1930,* VI, for those families reporting value or rent. Second, to the total value or rent derived for those families reporting must be added the value or rent of (1) dwelling units occupied by families that reported tenure but not value or rent; (2) dwelling units occupied by families not reporting tenure; (3) vacant units. Third, the total rent thus derived for the rented dwelling units must be converted to values by the use of value-rent ratios.

The estimation of total values and rents was facilitated by the 139 city special tabulation, which provided average values or rents for each Census value and rent group for each city.[5] This tabulation made possible the computation of average values or rents for the open end classes in the published Census distributions, that is, the two value groups reported as "under $1000" and "$20,000 and over," and the rent groups "under $10" and "$200 and over." Furthermore, it made unnecessary the use of mid-point values or rents as representative averages for those classes with specified boundaries. Moreover, it showed clearly that actual values and rents as reported cluster near the lower limits of the Census value or rent boundaries, so that if mid-points had been used as averages they would have given the estimates an upward bias.

To allow for the value or rent of those dwelling units for which tenure was designated but no values or rents given some representative value or rent had to be assigned to the known number of such units. Since few units are involved they were assigned the average value or rent derived from the frequency distributions for those units reporting values or rents.

Those dwelling units for which tenure, value, or rent was not reported had first to be allocated to the two tenure classes. This was done by assuming that the proportions of the two tenures for those dwelling units for which tenure was reported applied to those units for which tenure was not reported. This seemed reasonable since the number of units for which tenure was not designated was small and any error arising from this apportionment would not be significant. To the units thus allocated were assigned the average values and rents determined for those units reporting values and rents.

Vacant units and the values or rents assigned to them were estimated from sources described in further detail in sections 2 c and 3 a and c of this chapter.

[5] For cities with populations under 100,000 the average values or rents were obtained for 10 value or rent classes rather than the 6 classes in the Census volume; see explanation in sec. 2 a of this chapter.

2 Nonfarm Dwelling Units, 1930, Details of the Estimates

The *Census of Population, 1930,* VI, shows for each state, in frequency distribution form, the number of nonfarm families reporting values and rents in each population group of 2,500 or more. It shows also, without reference to tenure, values or rents, the number of occupied residential structures in each city and town by type of structure, i.e., 1-, 2-, and 3-or-more family dwellings (footnote 4 above).

Since the Census does not cover vacant units it was necessary to estimate the number of units before estimating value. It was possible to group the units and estimate their values for population groups of different sizes from Census data, but it was not possible to make the further important breakdown by metropolitan and nonmetropolitan areas. The significance of this shortcoming of the estimates is discussed on the half-title page to section A, Part Three. The estimates were prepared so as to show (Tables A 1–3) the number of dwelling units and their value by geographic division, state, tenure, and population group, and also by type of dwelling (Tables A 4–5).

Nonfarm dwelling units were estimated first by geographic division, state, tenure, and population group, without respect to type of dwelling. In some instances information by type of dwelling was used but in general the procedure followed the pattern outlined.

a Transcription of Number of Families reporting Value or Rent by Value or Rent Group for each Geographic Division by Population Group

For each state, and for each population group of 2,500 or more within the state, the number of nonfarm owner-occupant and tenant families was transcribed in separate tabulations for each tenure by the Census value and rent group classifications. Within each state five population classifications were arranged in descending order: 100,000 or more; 25,000–100,000; 10,000–25,000; 5,000–10,000; and 2,500–5,000. State subtotals by value or rent groups were obtained for each population group. The distribution for places under 2,500 in population was derived by obtaining totals in each value or rent group for places with populations above 2,500 and subtracting them from those for the state as a whole as given in the Census. A tabulation for Connecticut is given in Table ABM 1. Although statistically possible to provide for an additional classification showing metropolitan and nonmetropolitan areas, this was not practicable.

When the tabulations were complete for each state the states were grouped into the nine Census geographic divisions and subtotals prepared for each division having the same classification as the states. Table ABM 2 presents a complete recapitulation for the New England division.

TABLE ABM 1

Occupied Dwelling Units, Number reporting Value or Rent by Value or Rent Group, State, Tenure, and Population Group, April 1, 1930

Connecticut (similar tabulation for each state)

VALUE OR RENT GROUP	STATE TOTAL	POP. GROUP 100,000 AND OVER	VALUE OR RENT GROUP	25,000– 100,000	10,000– 25,000	5,000– 10,000	2,500– 5,000	Under 2,500
A OWNER-OCCUPIED								
All groups	154,880	31,611	All groups	38,930	23,671	3,610	1,579	55,479
Under $1,000	1,254	64	Under $1,500	278	322	29	31	2,370
1,000– 1,499	1,990	150	1,500–2,999	1,310	1,635	285	123	6,162
1,500– 1,999	2,392	201	3,000–4,999	5,852	4,996	984	474	12,267
2,000– 2,999	8,095	771	5,000–7,499	11,745	6,963	1,028	585	14,845
3,000– 4,999	28,210	3,637	7,500–9,999	7,096	3,386	352	174	7,025
5,000– 7,499	42,541	7,375	10,000 and over	11,925	5,977	903	185	11,974
7,500– 9,999	23,201	5,168	Not reported	724	392	29	7	836
10,000–14,999	24,653	7,018						
15,000–19,999	10,190	3,850						
20,000 and over	9,879	2,890						
Not reported	2,475	487						
B RENTED								
All groups	210,605	83,167	All groups	54,281	24,667	4,757	2,285	41,448
Under $10	7,528	561	Under $15	2,715	2,712	1,106	513	11,923
10– 14	16,125	4,123	15–29	24,569	12,226	2,409	1,336	17,064
15– 19	26,695	8,556	30–49	20,234	7,191	646	406	8,244
20– 29	64,047	24,582	50–99	5,747	2,032	375	21	2,983
30– 49	68,478	31,757	100 and over	462	277	181	4	609
50– 74	19,822	10,423	Not reported	554	229	40	5	625
75– 99	3,208	1,449						
100–149	1,773	748						
150–199	383	144						
200 and over	378	109						
Not reported	2,168	715						

Source: Census, 1930, *VI*

TABLE ABM 2

Dwelling Units, Number reporting Value or Rent by Value or Rent Group,
Geographic Division, Tenure, and Population Group, April 1, 1930

New England (similar tabulation for each geographic division)

VALUE OR RENT GROUP	GEOGRAPHIC DIVISION	POP. GROUP 100,000 OR MORE	VALUE OR RENT GROUP	25,000– 100,000	10,000– 25,000	5,000– 10,000	2,500– 5,000	Under 2,500
			A OWNER-OCCUPIED					
All groups	802,593	175,601	All groups	193,293	151,456	61,245	14,971	206,027
Under $1,000	21,612	451	Under $1,500	2,782	4,058	3,512	1,435	33,118
1,000– 1,499	25,422	1,678	1,500–2,999	12,659	16,073	9,552	3,023	45,279
1,500– 1,999	26,304	2,344	3,000–4,999	37,588	38,288	18,489	4,018	51,498
2,000– 2,999	70,795	8,169	5,000–7,499	58,409	46,485	16,817	3,497	38,810
3,000– 4,999	179,693	29,812	7,500–9,999	30,659	18,218	5,104	979	12,637
5,000– 7,499	212,943	48,925	10,000 and over	49,016	26,385	6,932	1,786	19,902
7,500– 9,999	97,294	29,697	Not reported	2,180	1,949	839	233	4,783
10,000–14,999	96,496	32,084						
15,000–19,999	31,003	10,684						
20,000 and over	28,194	8,904						
Not reported	12,837	2,853						
			B RENTED					
All groups	1,025,519	414,343	All groups	267,515	139,228	53,141	14,129	137,163
Under $10	46,608	4,877	Under $15	21,645	20,395	13,606	4,578	58,221
10– 14	102,656	25,942	15–29	118,111	70,248	27,893	7,111	54,732
15– 19	139,308	43,696	30–49	92,505	36,222	8,875	1,916	15,584
20– 29	299,291	116,808	50–99	28,713	10,188	1,841	292	4,315
30– 49	309,949	154,847	100 and over	4,358	782	339	39	821
50– 74	87,816	49,770	Not reported	2,183	1,393	587	193	3,490
75– 99	16,396	9,093						
100–149	7,996	3,469						
150–199	1,872	809						
200 and over	1,481	732						
Not reported	12,146	4,300						

In order that the value or rent classes might be the same for all population groups (for differences see Tables ABM 1 and 2) cumulative frequency curves were prepared for each population group under 100,-000 in each geographic division covering the value classes up to $3,000 and the rental classes up to $100. Intermediate values or rentals in line with the group limits for cities with populations of 100,000 or more were read from the graphs and first differences taken so as to determine the frequencies in the finer breakdown of value and rent classes for the largest city group. In order to distribute the frequencies above the level of $10,000 for values and $100 for rents so as to obtain value and rent classes comparable to those for the largest cities it was necessary to use a slightly different expedient than the one outlined above, since the small numbers made interpolation from graphs very difficult. The frequencies in these classes for all places under 100,000 in population were obtained by subtraction and the percentage in each derived. These percentages were then used to distribute the number above the specified value ($10,000) and rent ($100) levels among the proper value or rent class for each population group under 100,000.

When this process had been completed the tabulations contained, for each geographic division by the six nonfarm population groups, (1) owner-occupied dwelling units for which values were reported, distributed by ten value classes, and the number not reporting value; (2) rented dwelling units for which rents

were reported, distributed by ten rent classes and the number not reporting rent (see Table ABM 7). To obtain total nonfarm dwelling units in each geographic division by population groups the dwelling units not classified by tenure and the vacant dwelling units were added to the totals described above for each geographic division by population groups.

b Addition of Dwelling Units for which Tenure was not reported

The Census enumeration of the number of dwellings by type and the number of families occupying them (Table ABM 10) makes it possible, as will be shown later, to obtain by population groups total occupied nonfarm dwelling units for each geographic division (see Table ABM 3). From tabulations for each geographic division, e.g., Table ABM 2 for New England, were obtained the number of dwelling units for which tenure was reported. The totals for the two tenure classes are shown in Table ABM 3, column 2. A simple subtraction indicates the number of dwelling units in each population group for which tenure was not reported, and the ratio of total occupied units (col. 1) to those reporting tenure (col. 2) is shown in column 4.

On the assumption that the dwelling units for which tenure was not reported are distributed between the two tenure classes in the same proportion as those reporting tenure the number of dwelling units reporting tenure in each tenure group (Table ABM 2) was multiplied by the factors in Table ABM 3, column 4. This

TABLE ABM 3

Dwelling Units, Total Occupied, Number reporting and not reporting Tenure; Ratio of Total to those reporting Tenure: by Geographic Division and Population Group

New England (similar tabulation for each geographic division)

POPULATION GROUP	TOTAL [1] (1)	REPORT- ING TENURE[2] (2)	NOT REPORT- ING TENURE (3) = (1)−(2)	RATIO OF TOTAL TO THOSE RE- PORTING TENURE (4) =(1)÷(2)
All groups	1,848,887	1,828,112	20,775	1.0113642
100,000 and over	597,405	589,944	7,461	1.0126470
25,000–100,000	465,812	460,808	5,004	1.0108592
10,000– 25,000	293,422	290,684	2,738	1.0094192
5,000– 10,000	115,622	114,386	1,236	1.0108055
2,500– 5,000	29,496	29,100	396	1.0136082
Under 2,500	347,130	343,190	3,940	1.0114805

[1] *From Table ABM 10, col. 3.*   [2] *Table ABM 2.*

procedure adds to the number reporting tenure in each tenure group the number not reporting tenure assignable to the tenure group on the basis of the above assumption.

c Addition of Vacant Dwelling Units

The data for 1930 on vacant dwelling units by geographic division and population group are few. The differences in vacancies among 1-, 2-, and 3-or-more family dwellings, however, are sufficiently marked to

furnish a basis for estimating vacancies by type of dwelling that indicate roughly the vacancies by geographic division and population group on the assumption that vacancies are by and large related to the type of dwelling. The information used consisted of: (1) vacancy data for 1930 for all types of dwellings in 42 cities, and for 1-family dwellings in 37 cities (Residential Vacancy Surveys in the United States, 1930–34, Federal Housing Administration, March 1935); (2) vacancies in apartments in New York City (New York Tenement House Department), Washington, D. C. (Federal Housing Administration), and Los Angeles (Eberle Economic Service, unpublished data); (3) detailed data on relative vacancies by type of dwelling in 64 cities in 1934 (Federal Real Property Inventory).

The vacancy data from the Real Property Inventory are presented in Table ABM 4 with a reclassification according to the three Census types of dwelling. The residential vacancy surveys in 37 cities showed modal groups for 1-family dwellings ranging from 2 to 4 per cent in 1930; the median vacancy was 3.4, the arithmetic mean, 4.1. The median vacancy for 1-family dwellings, as shown by the 64 Real Property Inventory cities in 1934, was 5.1 and the arithmetic mean, 5.2, or nearly the same as the median. A vacancy figure of 3.5 per cent was therefore taken for 1-family dwellings for the country as a whole for 1930. Since the vacancy

TABLE ABM 4

Vacant Dwelling Units, Number as Percentage of Total, by Type, 64 Real Property Inventory Cities by Geographic Division, January 1, 1934

A REAL PROPERTY INVENTORY CLASSIFICATION
PERCENTAGE VACANCY

	NO. OF CITIES	1- family	2- family	3- family	4- family	5-or-more family	Row house	Other	All types
New England	6	3.8	8.1	7.5	15.3	15.0	15.8	13.3	8.4
Middle Atlantic	5	3.8	7.3	9.7	13.5	13.9	7.9	14.2	7.2
East North Central	8	4.2	10.3	11.8	16.9	15.8	21.4	14.6	8.7
West North Central	10	4.1	8.5	10.4	12.3	10.7	17.7	10.6	6.3
South Atlantic	11	6.3	8.1	9.1	12.2	11.1	5.6	9.2	7.5
East South Central	4	5.8	11.2	8.1	12.1	11.3	18.2	8.4	7.5
West South Central	7	5.6	7.2	6.3	11.4	9.6	16.5	8.7	6.4
Mountain	9	6.3	11.5	18.6	16.2	12.3	25.3	12.7	8.8
Pacific	4	6.8	17.8	18.2	21.7	12.9	16.9	15.4	9.3
Total	64	5.2	9.3	8.1	14.7	12.9	10.7	12.7	7.8

B CENSUS CLASSIFICATION
PERCENTAGE VACANCY

	1-FAMILY [1]	2-FAMILY	3-OR-MORE FAMILY [2]	ALL TYPES
New England	4.0	8.1	10.6	8.4
Middle Atlantic	4.3	7.3	13.5	7.2
East North Central	4.4	10.3	15.4	8.7
West North Central	4.1	8.5	11.0	6.3
South Atlantic	6.2	8.1	10.6	7.5
East South Central	5.9	11.2	10.8	7.5
West South Central	5.6	7.2	9.9	6.4
Mountain	7.1	11.5	13.2	8.8
Pacific	6.9	17.8	14.2	9.3
Total, 64 Cities	5.4	9.3	12.5	7.8

[1] *1-family and row houses combined.*   [2] *3-, 4-, 5-or-more families, and other combined.*

TABLE ABM 5

Dwelling Units, Number Occupied, Vacancy Factor, and Total by Geographic
Division, Population Group, and Type of Dwelling, April 1, 1930

New England (similar tabulation for each geographic division)

TYPE OF DWELLING	ALL POPULATION GROUPS	100,000 OR OVER	25,000– 100,000	10,000– 25,000	5,000– 10,000	2,500– 5,000	UNDER 2,500
1 1-family							
a Occupied dwelling units [1]	991,754	182,451	225,764	192,146	84,026	22,486	284,881
b Vacancy factor	1.037	1.037	1.037	1.037	1.037	1.037	1.037
c Total dwelling units (a × b)	1,028,449	189,202	234,117	199,255	87,135	23,318	295,422
2 2-family							
a Occupied dwelling units [2]	448,510	170,432	133,294	69,008	21,980	5,002	48,794
b Vacancy factor	1.065	1.065	1.065	1.065	1.065	1.065	1.065
c Total dwelling units (a × b)	477,663	181,510	141,958	73,493	23,409	5,327	51,966
3 3-or-more family							
a Occupied dwelling units [3]	408,623	244,522	106,754	32,268	9,616	2,008	13,455
b Vacancy factor	1.088	1.088	1.088	1.088	1.088	1.088	1.088
c Total dwelling units (a × b)	444,582	266,040	116,148	35,108	10,462	2,185	14,639
4 All types							
a Occupied dwelling units [4]	1,848,887	597,405	465,812	293,422	115,622	29,496	347,130
b Vacant dwelling units	101,807	39,347	26,411	14,434	5,384	1,334	14,897
c Total dwelling units	1,950,694	636,752	492,223	307,856	121,006	30,830	362,027

[1] *Table ABM 10, col. 4.*
[2] *Table ABM 10, col. 6.*
[3] *Table ABM 10, col. 8.*
[4] *Table ABM 10, col. 2.*

TABLE ABM 6

Total Dwelling Units, including Vacant, by Geographic Division, Population Group,
Type of Dwelling, and Tenure, April 1, 1930

New England (similar tabulation for each geographic division)

TYPE OF DWELLING	ALL POPULATION GROUPS (1)	100,000 OR MORE (2)	25,000– 100,000 (3)	10,000– 25,000 (4)	5,000– 10,000 (5)	2,500– 5,000 (6)	UNDER 2,500 (7)
1 1-family							
a Total [1]	1,028,449	189,202	234,117	199,255	87,135	23,318	295,422
b Percentage of owner-occupied [2]	......	61.9	65.9	67.9	66.0	58.5	68.4
c No. owner-occupied or for sale (a × b)	679,930 [9]	117,127	154,344	135,239	57,473	13,639	202,108
d No. rented or for rent (a − c)	348,519	72,075	79,773	64,016	29,662	9,679	93,314
2 2-family							
a Total [3]	477,663	181,510	141,958	73,493	23,409	5,327	51,966
b Percentage of owner-occupied [4]	......	23.8	26.7	27.2	26.0	33.2	23.4
c No. owner-occupied or for sale (a × b)	121,089 [9]	43,200	37,917	19,956	6,076	1,769	12,171
d No. rented or for rent (a − c)	356,574	138,310	104,041	53,537	17,333	3,558	39,795
3 3-or-more family							
a Total [5]	444,582	266,040	116,148	35,108	10,462	2,185	14,639
b No. owner-occupied [6]	42,363	24,311	10,956	3,735	782	362	2,217
c No. rented or for rent (a − b)	402,219	241,729	105,192	31,373	9,680	1,823	12,422
4 All types							
a Total [7]	1,950,694	636,752	492,223	307,856	121,006	30,830	362,027
b No. owner-occupied or for sale [8]	843,382	184,638	203,217	158,930	64,331	15,770	216,496
c No. rented or for rent [8]	1,107,312	452,114	289,006	148,926	56,675	15,060	145,531

[1] *Table ABM 5, line 1 c.*
[2] *Owner-occupied dwelling units, as shown for 1-family dwellings in Table ABM 11, col. 1, as percentage of total occupied dwelling units (sum of col. 1 and 4 of Table ABM 11, or line 1 a, Table ABM 5).*
[3] *Table ABM 5, line 2 c.*
[4] *Owner-occupied dwelling units, as shown for 2-family dwellings in Table ABM 11, col. 1, as percentage of total occupied dwelling units (sum of col. 1 and 4 of Table ABM 11, or line 2 a, Table ABM 5).*
[5] *Table ABM 5, line 3 c.*
[6] *Table ABM 11, col. 1, 3-or-more family dwellings (see explanation, Ch. II, sec. 2 f).*
[7] *Table ABM 5, line 4 c.*
[8] *Grand totals, Table ABM 7.*
[9] *Obtained by addition of figures for population groups.*

data for 1930, that is, in 37 cities, showed vacancies only for 1-family dwellings and for all types combined, the estimates of vacancy for the 2-family and for the 3-or-more family dwellings were based on the relations of these types to the vacancy of 1-family dwellings as shown in the 64 Real Property Inventory cities.

These estimated percentages are in terms of total

TABLE ABM 7

Dwelling Units, Number reporting Value or Rent by Value or Rent Group; and Number
not reporting Value or Rent, Number not reporting Tenure, and Number Vacant:
by Geographic Division and Population Group, April 1, 1930

New England (similar tabulation for each geographic division)

VALUE OR RENT GROUP	ALL POPULATION GROUPS (1)	100,000 OR MORE (2)	25,000– 100,000 (3)	10,000– 25,000 (4)	5,000– 10,000 (5)	2,500– 5,000 (6)	UNDER 2,500 (7)
A OWNER-OCCUPIED							
Under $1,000	21,612	451	1,000	1,800	1,500	500	16,361
1,000– 1,499	25,422	1,678	1,782	2,258	2,012	935	16,757
1,500– 1,999	26,304	2,344	2,718	3,942	2,188	865	14,247
2,000– 2,999	70,795	8,169	9,941	12,131	7,364	2,158	31,032
3,000– 4,999	179,693	29,812	37,588	38,288	18,489	4,018	51,498
5,000– 7,499	212,943	48,925	58,409	46,485	16,817	3,497	38,810
7,500– 9,999	97,294	29,697	30,659	18,218	5,104	979	12,637
10,000–14,999	96,496	32,084	30,352	16,338	4,292	1,106	12,324
15,000–19,999	31,003	10,684	9,575	5,154	1,354	349	3,887
20,000 and over	28,194	8,904	9,089	4,893	1,286	331	3,691
Not reporting value	12,837	2,853	2,180	1,949	839	233	4,783
Total reporting tenure [1]	802,593	175,601	193,293	151,456	61,245	14,971	206,027
Not reporting tenure [2]	9,121	2,221	2,090	1,427	662	204	2,517
Total occupied [3]	811,714	177,822	195,383	152,883	61,907	15,175	208,544
Vacancies [4]	31,668	6,816	7,834	6,047	2,424	595	7,952
Grand total [5]	843,382	184,638	203,217	158,930	64,331	15,770	216,496
B RENTED							
Under $10	46,608	4,877	5,831	6,400	3,200	1,400	24,900
10– 14	102,656	25,942	15,814	13,995	10,406	3,178	33,321
15– 19	139,308	43,696	34,155	23,605	14,994	3,379	19,479
20– 29	299,291	116,808	83,956	46,643	12,899	3,732	35,253
30– 49	309,949	154,847	92,505	36,222	8,875	1,916	15,584
50– 74	87,816	49,770	24,152	8,135	1,526	170	4,063
75– 99	16,396	9,093	4,561	2,053	315	122	252
100–149	7,996	3,469	3,112	558	242	27	586
150–199	1,872	809	732	132	57	7	138
200 and over	1,481	732	514	92	40	5	97
Not reporting rent	12,146	4,300	2,183	1,393	587	193	3,490
Total reporting tenure [1]	1,025,519	414,343	267,515	139,228	53,141	14,129	137,163
Not reporting tenure [2]	11,654	5,240	2,914	1,311	574	192	1,423
Total occupied [3]	1,037,173	419,583	270,429	140,539	53,715	14,321	138,586
Vacancies [4]	70,139	32,531	18,577	8,387	2,960	739	6,945
Grand total [5]	1,107,312	452,114	289,006	148,926	56,675	15,060	145,531

[1] See Tables ABM 1 and 2 and explanation in Ch. II, sec. 2 a.

[2] Total occupied less total reporting tenure.

[3] Total reporting tenure in each size group multiplied by the factors in Table ABM 3, col. 4. See explanation in Ch. II, sec. 2 b.

[4] Grand total less total occupied.

[5] Table ABM 6, lines 13 and 14 (see explanation, Ch. II, sec. 2 f).

units rather than of those occupied and are for the type of dwelling without reference to location and population group (except in the instance noted above). It was necessary to convert these percentages into factors applicable to the number of occupied units and to determine the number of occupied units by type of dwelling, geographic division, and population group. The estimate of the number of dwelling units by geographic division, type of dwelling, tenure, and population group is explained below in section 2 f; it was multiplied by the following factors (Table ABM 5):

$$\text{1-family dwellings, } 1.037[6] = \frac{1}{1-0.035}; \text{ 2-family}$$

[6] The ratio 1.037 is slightly in error; the correct figure is 1.036. The numerical error was not discovered until all the operations had been completed, and its effect on the estimates was so small that it was not considered sufficiently important to attempt to correct them.

$$\text{dwellings, } 1.065 = \frac{1}{1-0.06}; \text{ and 3-or-more family}$$

$$\text{dwellings, } 1.088 = \frac{1}{1-0.08}, \text{ except in New York City}$$

and cities over 100,000 in population in the Pacific division, for which the factor was $1.111 = \frac{1}{1-0.10}$.

Table ABM 5 for the New England division gives the information desired except that it is for both tenures combined rather than for each tenure separately. In some vacancy surveys [7] all vacant units are classified as rental units. Some vacancies are, however, not in rental units: they are in structures that are for sale or are units that have been vacated only temporarily by their owners; they are not for rent and should be considered as belonging to the owner-occupant tenure.

[7] See Federal Real Property Inventory, 64 cities.

In order to allocate the vacant units by tenure, it was assumed that vacancies were distributed between the two tenure classes in the same proportion as occupied units for 1- and 2-family dwellings, but that all vacancies in 3-or-more-family dwellings were for rent. However, since the distribution of occupied units by tenure in the Census was not given by type of dwelling, an estimate had to be prepared. As explained in section 2 f of this chapter, information derived from the special tabulation for the 139 cities was used.

From the distribution by tenure and type for occupied units (Table ABM 11, col. 1 and 4) the percentages that were owner-occupied in the 1- and 2-family dwelling types were computed. These percentages are used in Table ABM 6 to allocate total dwelling units (including vacant) by type of dwelling to the two tenure groups. The footnotes to Table ABM 6 explain the process in detail.

d Estimates by Tenure, Value or Rent Group, Population Group, and Geographic Division, Recapitulation

The several steps described in the preceding sections made it possible to estimate for each geographic division, tenure, and population group the number of nonfarm dwelling units for which values or rents were reported by 10 value or rent groups. In addition, the number of nonfarm dwelling units occupied but not reporting value or rent and the number of vacant units were estimated for each geographic division by tenure and population group. This information is presented for New England in Table ABM 7 with footnote references to the specific sections where the methods are explained in detail.

e Distribution by States in each Geographic Division, by Tenure and Population Group

The preliminary transcription of Census data gave for each state the dwelling units reporting tenure (i.e., those reporting value plus those not reporting value) by population group and tenure. The geographic division totals were obtained by adding these state figures. To the geographic division totals, in turn, were added, as explained above, those units not reporting tenure and vacant units. The state figures for those reporting tenure were then increased to include the nonfarm dwelling units not reporting tenure or vacant. The increase for each state (Table ABM 1) was assumed to be proportional to the increase for the geographic division as a whole. For the addition of dwelling units not reporting tenure all that was required on this assumption was to raise the state figures on units reporting tenure in each tenure class by using the ratios in Table ABM 3, column 4, as factors. A similar assumption with reference to vacant units makes it possible to increase the totals (including tenure not reported) to include them. Table ABM 7 shows the grand total for New England. The ratio of the grand totals for each tenure class by population groups to total occupied units gives the ratios of increase for the individual states.

This method of determining the number of nonfarm dwelling units by states involves a slight error. To obtain for each state the exact addition of units not reporting tenure would have required the calculation of factors like those in Table ABM 3, column 4. This would have involved an extensive preliminary tabulation for each state similar to that for the geographic division in Tables ABM 9 and 10. The differences in the results obtained by the two methods tried out in

TABLE ABM 8

Total Nonfarm Dwelling Units by State, Population Group, and Tenure, April 1, 1930

Connecticut (similar tabulation for each state)

	ALL POPULATION GROUPS (1)	100,000 AND OVER (2)	25,000–100,000 (3)	10,000–25,000 (4)	5,000–10,000 (5)	2,500–5,000 (6)	UNDER 2,500 (7)
Owner-occupied (number)							
1 Reporting tenure [1]	154,880	31,611	38,930	23,671	3,610	1,579	55,479
2 Not reporting tenure [2]	1,783	400	421	223	39	22	678
3 Occupied [3]	156,663	32,011	39,351	23,894	3,649	1,601	56,157
4 Vacant [4]	6,097	1,227	1,578	945	143	63	2,141
5 Total [5]	162,760	33,238	40,929	24,839	3,792	1,664	58,298
Rented (number)							
1 Reporting tenure [1]	210,605	83,167	54,281	24,667	4,757	2,285	41,448
2 Not reporting tenure [2]	2,388	1,052	591	232	52	31	430
3 Occupied [3]	212,993	84,219	54,872	24,899	4,809	2,316	41,878
4 Vacant [4]	14,269	6,530	3,769	1,486	265	120	2,099
5 Total [5]	227,262	90,749	58,641	26,385	5,074	2,436	43,977

[1] See Table ABM 1.

[2] Line 3 minus line 1.

[3] Obtained by multiplying factors in Table ABM 3, col. 4, by line 1. Some slight adjustments were necessary to tie into figures with geographic division totals.

[4] Line 5 minus line 3.

[5] Obtained by multiplying ratio of grand total of units to occupied units for the tenure classes (Table ABM 7) by the figures in line 3 for the respective tenure class.

TABLE ABM 9

Occupied Dwellings and Families (Dwelling Units), Number by Type of Dwelling, State, and Population Group, 1930

Connecticut (similar tabulation for each state)

TYPE OF DWELLING	ALL POPULATION GROUPS (1)	100,000 OR MORE (2)	25,000– 100,000 (3)	10,000– 25,000 (4)	5,000– 10,000 (5)	2,500– 5,000 (6)	UNDER 2,500 (7)
1 All types							
a Dwellings	280,552	63,735	64,114	37,995	6,463	3,455	104,790
b Dwelling units	388,645	116,007	94,747	49,497	8,510	3,910	115,974
2 1-family							
a Dwellings (and dwelling units)	214,588	36,371	44,855	29,522	5,046	3,111	95,683
3 2-family							
a Dwellings	46,302	17,295	13,228	6,670	1,061	270	7,778
b Dwelling units [1]	92,604	34,590	26,456	13,340	2,122	540	15,556
4 3-or-more family							
a Dwellings	19,662	10,069	6,031	1,803	356	74	1,329
b Dwelling units [2]	81,453	45,046	23,436	6,635	1,342	259	4,735

[1] *Number of dwellings multiplied by 2.*
[2] *Total families (line 1 b) minus sum of families in 1- and 2-family dwellings (lines 2 a and 3 b).*

several states did not seem to warrant this additional labor.

Similarly the distribution of vacant units by states is not entirely accurate because it was based upon type of dwelling. Since the distribution of dwelling types in the several states is not identical with the distribution for the geographic division, the vacancy factors for each state would be slightly different from those for the geographic divisions. The error is so small, however, as compared with the possibility of error in the general data for vacancy, that the simple method seemed more appropriate. These decisions also simplified the estimates of values by states and involved no substantial error.[8]

Table ABM 8 shows for Connecticut how total dwelling units were estimated. The footnotes explain in detail the factors used and their sources. When this process had been completed for each state the sum of the dwelling units for the states in each geographic division was identical with the figures for the geographic divisions.

f Distribution of Estimates by Geographic Division, Type of Dwelling, Tenure, and Population Group

Since in Census state totals the number of both nonfarm dwellings, by type, and of farm families are given, it is possible to estimate for each state the number of nonfarm dwellings by type on the assumption that farm families occupy only 1-family dwellings. The Census number of dwellings by type for each population group of 2,500 or more, some of which include a few farm dwellings, must be corrected, as

explained later, in order to obtain the number of nonfarm dwellings by type and population group in each geographic division. For population groups under 2,500 the same information can be obtained by subtracting the totals for all larger places from the state totals.

The number of dwelling *units* by type of dwelling can be obtained as follows: the number of 2-family dwellings is multiplied by two; the sum of this product and the number of 1-family dwellings subtracted from the total number of families gives the number of dwelling units in 3-or-more family dwellings.[9]

This information is given for Connecticut in Table ABM 9. When the states are grouped the same type of information can be obtained for the nine geographic divisions, as shown, with certain additional information, for New England in Table ABM 10. The number of dwellings and of dwelling units, by type, opposite the "total" for each population group are the summations of state figures similar to those for Connecticut in Table ABM 9.

The nonfarm dwellings and dwelling units by type were obtained as follows: for all cities the known [10] number of farm dwellings and families was allocated to the 1-family type of dwelling and subtracted from total dwellings and families; for the several population groups (except that under 2,500) the ratio of nonfarm families reporting tenure to total families reporting tenure (Table ABM 10, col. 9) was used as indicative of the relative number of nonfarm dwellings; finally the number of nonfarm families in the population group under 2,500 was obtained by subtraction.

[8] *Checking for both tenures combined for the New England states indicated a possible difference in state figures of three-tenths of 1 per cent.*

[9] *See footnote 4 above for a criticism of Census type of dwelling data.*
[10] Census, 1930, *VI, Table 60, p. 53.*

TABLE ABM 10

Occupied Dwellings and Families (Dwelling Units), Number by Type of Dwelling, Geographic Division and Population Group, 1930

New England (similar tabulation for each geographic division)

		ALL TYPES		1-Family Dwellings (and dwelling units)	2-Family		3-or-more Family		FAMILIES REPORTING TENURE [3]	RATIO OF NONFARM FAMILIES REPORTING TENURE TO ALL FAMILIES REPORTING TENURE [4]
		Dwellings	Dwelling units		Dwellings	Dwelling units [1]	Dwellings	Dwelling units [2]		
		(1)	(2)	(3)	(4)	(5)	(6)	(7)	(8)	(9)
All groups	Total [5]	1,453,222	1,981,499	1,124,366	224,255	448,510	104,601	408,623	1,957,962	....
	Farm [6]	132,612	132,612	132,612	......	......	....	......	......	
	Nonfarm [7]	1,320,610	1,848,887	991,754	224,255	448,510	104,601	408,623	1,828,112	.934
100,000 and over	Total	329,656	598,003	183,049	85,216	170,432	61,391	244,522	590,343	
	Nonfarm	329,058	597,405 [9]	182,451 [10]	85,216	170,432	61,391	244,522	589,944	.999
25,000–100,000	Total	322,478	468,318	228,270	66,647	133,294	27,561	106,754	463,473	
	Nonfarm	319,972	465,812 [9]	225,764 [10]	66,647	133,294	27,561	106,754	460,808	.994
10,000–25,000	Total	241,753	299,716	198,440	34,504	69,008	8,809	32,268	296,797	
	Nonfarm	235,459	293,422 [9]	192,146 [10]	34,504	69,008	8,809	32,268	290,684	.979
5,000–10,000	Total	103,225	121,324	89,728	10,990	21,980	2,507	9,616	119,983	
	Nonfarm	97,523	115,622 [9]	84,026 [10]	10,990	21,980	2,507	9,616	114,386	.953
2,500–5,000	Total	26,809	30,757	23,747	2,501	5,002	561	2,008	30,335	
	Nonfarm	25,548	29,496 [9]	22,486 [10]	2,501	5,002	561	2,008	29,100	.959
Under 2,500	Total [8]	429,301	463,381	401,132	24,397	48,794	3,772	13,455	457,031	
	Nonfarm [8]	313,050	347,130	284,881	24,397	48,794	3,772	13,455	343,190	.751

[1] *Dwellings in col. 4 multiplied by 2.*
[2] *Sum of col. 3 and 5 subtracted from col. 2.*
[3] *Totals include urban farm families.*
[4] *Nonfarm in col. 8 divided by "total" in col. 8.*
[5] *Census of Population, 1930, VI, Table 62, p. 55.*
[6] *Ibid., Table 60, p. 53. Farm dwellings assumed to be all 1-family.*

[7] *Total less farm.*
[8] *All cities, total and nonfarm, less sum of similar items for cities with populations over 2,500.*
[9] *Total multiplied by ratio for given size group (col. 9).*
[10] *Total less difference between total and nonfarm (col. 2).*

In using the ratios in column 8 of Table ABM 10 it was again assumed that all farm families live in 1-family dwellings so that the ratio, when applied to all types of dwelling units, gave the necessary correction for the 1-family type and left the numbers in the other types unchanged.

For a breakdown by tenure the procedure outlined above and illustrated in Tables ABM 9 and 10 provided the number of occupied nonfarm dwelling units by type but without any division by tenure. Information derived from the special tabulation for 139 cities was used. For each city the percentages of the total number of 2- and 3-or-more family dwellings (structures) that contained an owner-occupant family were estimated. These individual city percentages were then grouped by population groups and geographic divisions and weighted by the total population of the several cities in each population group. Because of the thinness of the sample in certain regions and population groups the geographic divisions were combined as shown in Table ABM 20 where the final results of this process are recorded.

Multiplying the divisional percentages in Table ABM 20 (New England combined with Middle Atlantic) by the number of nonfarm dwellings (structures) in the same geographic division, illustrated for New England in columns 4 and 6 of Table ABM 10, yielded the number (excluding vacant units) of owner-occupied 2- and 3-or-more family dwellings (structures); that is, owner-occupied dwelling units (Table ABM 7), excluding vacant, since the owner-occupant family would not occupy more than one dwelling unit. The number of 1-family owner-occupied dwelling units was secured by subtracting the sum of owner-occupied 2- and 3-or-more family dwelling units from the number of owner-occupied dwelling units of all types.

The number of rented dwelling units by type, excluding vacant (Table ABM 11, col. 4), was estimated by subtracting the owner-occupied dwelling units of each type from total nonfarm dwelling units (Table ABM 10, col. 3, 5, and 7). Columns 3 and 6 of Table ABM 11 were taken from Table ABM 6 and the number of vacant units (col. 2 and 5) obtained by subtraction.

The number of dwelling units as classified in Table ABM 7 was distributed by states as explained in sec-

TABLE ABM 11

Occupied Dwelling Units, Vacant, and Total including Vacant, by Type of Dwelling,
Geographic Division, Population Group, and Tenure, April 1, 1930

New England (similar tabulation for each geographic division)

TYPE OF DWELLING AND POPULATION GROUP	OWNER-OCCUPIED			RENTED		
	Occupied (1)	Vacant (2)	Total (3)	Occupied (4)	Vacant (5)	Total (6)
All types						
All population groups	811,714	31,668	843,382	1,037,173	70,139	1,107,312
100,000 and over	177,822	6,816	184,638	419,583	32,531	452,114
25,000–100,000	195,383	7,834	203,217	270,429	18,577	289,006
10,000– 25,000	152,883	6,047	158,930	140,539	8,387	148,926
5,000– 10,000	61,907	2,424	64,331	53,715	2,960	50,675
2,500– 5,000	15,175	595	15,770	14,321	739	15,060
Under 2,500	208,544	7,952	216,496	138,586	6,945	145,531
1-family						
All population groups	655,654	24,276	679,930	336,100	12,419	348,519
100,000 and over	112,948	4,179	117,127	69,503	2,572	72,075
25,000–100,000	148,823	5,521	154,344	76,941	2,832	79,773
10,000– 25,000	130,412	4,827	135,239	61,734	2,282	64,016
5,000– 10,000	55,421	2,052	57,473	28,605	1,057	29,662
2,500– 5,000	13,152	487	13,639	9,334	345	9,679
Under 2,500	194,898	7,210	202,108	89,983	3,331	93,314
2-family						
All population groups	113,697	7,392	121,089	334,813	21,761	356,574
100,000 and over	40,563	2,637	43,200	129,869	8,441	138,310
25,000–100,000	35,604	2,313	37,917	97,690	6,351	104,041
10,000– 25,000	18,736	1,220	19,956	50,272	3,265	53,537
5,000– 10,000	5,704	372	6,076	16,276	1,057	17,333
2,500– 5,000	1,661	108	1,769	3,341	217	3,558
Under 2,500	11,429	742	12,171	37,365	2,430	39,795
3-or-more family						
All population groups	42,363	....	42,363	366,260	35,959	402,219
100,000 and over	24,311	....	24,311	220,211	21,518	241,729
25,000–100,000	10,956	....	10,956	95,798	9,394	105,192
10,000– 25,000	3,735	....	3,735	28,533	2,840	31,373
5,000– 10,000	782	....	782	8,834	846	9,680
2,500– 5,000	362	....	362	1,646	177	1,823
Under 2,500	2,217	....	2,217	11,238	1,184	12,422

tion 2 e of this chapter and illustrated in Table ABM 8. The information on tenure by type of dwelling does not warrant a distribution by states of the dwelling units in Table ABM 11.

The proportion of each of the three dwelling types in the two tenure classes was based upon data derived from the 139 city special tabulation. Application of the tenure proportions to the several states is not warranted, but they should be fairly reliable for the geographic division as a whole.

The procedure explained above and illustrated by the tables for New England was applied to each geographic division in exactly the same way with one exception, the Middle Atlantic. Each borough in New York City was treated separately because of the wide variation in the percentages of owner-occupancy of apartments and 2-family dwellings. The percentages actually used for New York City were based on special tabulations made for this project by the Bureau of the Census for selected areas in each borough. In Manhattan, Bronx, and Brooklyn the percentages derived for 1- and 2-family dwellings were applied to the number of dwellings of these types to obtain the number of owner-occupied units, and their sum was sub-

tracted from total owner-occupied units to obtain the number of owner-occupied units in 3-or-more family dwellings. For Queens and Richmond boroughs percentages for the 2- and 3-or-more family types were used and the 1-family units obtained by subtraction.

3 Value of Nonfarm Residential Real Estate, 1930

The estimates of value by population group, tenure, state, and geographic division consist of three main parts: (1) values are estimated for the owner-occupant tenure group; (2) rents are estimated for the occupied rental dwelling units; (3) value-rent ratios are applied to the rent estimates to obtain the value of occupied rental dwelling units and also of vacant rental units.

a Value of Owner-Occupied Dwelling Units

Table ABM 7 presents the number of nonfarm dwelling units. Section A provides the essential data for value estimates. The number of units in each value group is multiplied by an average value for each group derived from the 139 city special tabulation. The calculated average value per dwelling unit for all dwelling units reporting value is then assigned to the dwelling units not reporting value or not reporting tenure. The same procedure is followed for vacant units except that the average value derived for the units

TABLE ABM 12

Derivation of Total Value of All Owner-occupied Dwelling Units by Geographic Division and Population Group

Population group 100,000 and over, New England (similar tabulation for each population group in each geographic division)

VALUE CLASS	NO. OF DWELLING UNITS [1]	PRELIMINARY TOTAL VALUE [2] (DOLLARS)	CORRECTION FACTOR [3]	FINAL TOTAL VALUE (DOLLARS)
	(1)	(2)	(3)	(4) = (2) × (3)
Under $1,000	451	245,344	1.000	245,344
1,000– 1,499	1,678	2,120,000	.912	1,933,440
1,500– 1,999	2,344	4,127,250	.917	3,784,688
2,000– 2,999	8,169	20,801,250	.912	18,970,740
3,000– 4,999	29,812	121,496,000	.924	112,262,304
5,000– 7,499	48,925	305,301,875	.951	290,342,083
7,500– 9,999	29,697	259,848,750	.945	245,557,069
10,000–14,999	32,084	401,050,000	.892	357,736,600
15,000–19,999	10,684	186,970,000	.913	170,703,610
20,000 and over	8,904	294,633,360	1.000	294,633,360
All classes	172,748	1,596,593,829	.937 [4]	1,496,169,238
Not reporting value	2,853	26,367,426 [5]		
Not reporting tenure	2,221	20,526,482 [5]		
Total occupied units	177,822	1,643,487,737	.937	1,539,948,010
Vacant units	6,816			
Total units	184,638			1,596,926,086 [6]

[1] See Table ABM 7.

[2] The total values in this column were obtained as follows:

1) The number of units in the class "Under $1,000" was multiplied by the average value of $544 derived from the special tabulation for 139 cities; see Table ABM 17.

2) The 5 classes from $1,000 to $7,499 were divided into 10 classes with frequencies of 749, 929, 1,071, 1,273, 3,327, 4,842, 12,658, 17,154, 24,846, and 24,079, as explained in Ch. II, sec. 3 a, and each frequency multiplied by the new value class mid-points of $1,125, $1,375, etc. The frequencies in the 3 value classes from $7,500 to $19,999 were multiplied by the mid-points of these classes.

3) The number of units having values of $20,000 and over was multiplied by the average value of $33,090 determined from the special tabulation for 139 cities; see Table ABM 17.

[3] For adjustment from mid-point of group basis to empirical average basis; see Table ABM 18.

[4] Obtained by dividing the total value for all classes (col. 4) by the total for all value classes (col. 2).

[5] Obtained by multiplying the number of units not reporting value and not reporting tenure by the average value of $9,242, derived by dividing the total value for all value groups (col. 2) by the total units reporting value (col. 1).

[6] Obtained by raising the total value for occupied dwelling units (col. 4) by the ratio 1.037, based on the ratio of 1.038, which is the ratio of total units (184,638) to occupied units (177,822), corrected for the relationship of the value of vacant units to occupied units, which is .974. The computation to obtain the ratio 1.037 is [1.000 + (1.038 − 1.000) × .974].

reporting value is adjusted to take into account the estimated differences (based on rent differentials) between the values of vacant and occupied units.

The value estimates involved more steps than explained above, but the end results are virtually the same as if the above procedure had been followed. The value estimates were undertaken before the 139 city special tabulation had been completed. The first procedure used average values for the value groups "under $1,000" and "$20,000 and over" from the 139 city special tabulation, the aggregate values for the other value groups being obtained by using the midpoint values of the groups, after obtaining a finer breakdown of value groups, as the assumed average values. For instance, each of the 5 value groups from $1,000 to $7,499 was divided into 2 groups and the frequencies in each group subdivision determined by taking first differences from interpolated figures on a cumulative frequency curve.

A preliminary estimate was made following the procedure outlined above before the more extensive special tabulation and the determination of the empirical averages for each value and rent class for the 139 cities was carried out. Table ABM 12 shows in column 2 the total values actually obtained for the original 10 value classes for New England cities with populations of 100,000 or more. The details of the method are explained in the footnotes.

When the more extensive tabulation for the 139 cities was made available it was obvious that the midpoint values were not representative average values. Table A 6 gives the average values by the 10 value classes for each of the 139 cities; Table ABM 17, the average values finally accepted as representative of the value classes in each geographic division by population groups; and Table ABM 18 the ratio of the average values for each class that resulted from the use of value class mid-points.

These ratios were then used to adjust the total values previously obtained; the procedure is outlined in the detailed footnotes to Table ABM 12. This procedure essentially is equivalent to multiplying the average values obtained from the 139 city special tabulation by the several value class frequencies. The differences in the mechanics of procedure make for slight differences in the numerical results so that a perfect numerical correspondence would be impossible unless the steps actually taken were carried out in extreme detail.

b Value of Owner-Occupied Dwelling Units, Distribution by States

Within each geographic division it is possible to obtain, by states, the percentage distribution of dwelling units reporting value for the 6 Census value classes.[11]

[11] Six value groups were used since the Census data on dwelling units reporting value are restricted to 6 value classes rather than

These percentages were used to distribute, by states, the total value for each value class as determined for the geographic division. The sum of the values thus distributed to each state gives for the individual states the value of owner-occupied dwelling units reporting value. This procedure had been carried out before the correction for the displacement of the mid-points had been undertaken and the results are shown, for Connecticut, in Table ABM 13, columns 2 and 3.

TABLE ABM 13

Geographic Division Total Value of All Owner-occupied Dwelling Units, Distribution by States

Population group 100,000 and over, Connecticut (similar tabulations by each population group for the states in each geographic division)

VALUE CLASS	NEW ENGLAND Uncorrected values [1] (dollars)	CONNECTICUT Percentage of dwelling units in state [2]	CONNECTICUT Value allocated to state (dollars)
	(1)	(2)	(3) = (1) × (2)
Under $1,500	2,365,344	10.052	237,764
1,500–2,999	24,928,500	9.246	2,304,889
3,000–4,999	121,496,000	12.200	14,822,512
5,000–7,499	305,301,875	15.074	46,021,205
7,500–9,999	259,848,750	17.402	45,218,880
10,000 and over	882,653,360	26.626	235,015,284
All value classes	1,596,593,829		343,620,534
Correction factor [3]			1.000208
Total adjusted value (all dwellings) [4]			343,692,007

[1] Table ABM 12, col 2, with certain value classes combined.
[2] These percentages were obtained from Tables ABM 1 and 2 where dwelling units reporting value by value classes for the states and geographic divisions are shown by population groups.
[3] For adjustment from mid-point of group basis to empirical average basis, including, in total value, dwelling units not reporting value, not reporting tenure, and vacant, see explanation Ch. II, sec. 3 b.
[4] 343,620,534 × 1.000208.

To correct for mid-point displacement and also include the values of dwelling units not reporting value, not reporting tenure, and vacant, a ratio was derived from Table ABM 12. In Table ABM 12 the uncorrected total value for all dwelling units reporting value in population groups of 100,000 or more in New England is $1,596,593,829 (col. 2). The total *corrected* value for all dwelling units, including those not reporting value, not reporting tenure, and vacant is $1,596,926,086. The ratio between the total corrected value, all dwelling units, and the uncorrected value for dwelling units reporting value is 1.000208 $\left(\dfrac{1,596,926,086}{1,596,593,829}\right)$. By multiplying this ratio by the value derived for each state for those dwellings re-

10, except for cities with populations of 100,000 or more. For the method used to obtain 10 value classes for each population group, see sec. 2 a of this chapter.

porting value, as illustrated for Connecticut in Table ABM 13, column 3, we obtain the total value in each state for all units corrected for adjustment from mid-point of group basis to empirical average basis.

TABLE ABM 14

Derivation of Total Monthly Rent of Occupied Rented Dwelling Units by Geographic Division and Population Group

Population group 100,000 and over, New England (similar tabulations by each population group for each geographic division)

RENT GROUP	NO. OF DWELLING UNITS [1]	PRELIMINARY TOTAL RENT [2] (DOLLARS)	CORRECTION FACTOR [3]	FINAL TOTAL RENT (DOLLARS)
	(1)	(2)	(3)	(4) = (2) × (3)
Under $10	4,877	34,139	1.000	34,139
10– 14	25,942	336,395	.919	309,147
15– 19	43,696	770,347	.933	718,734
20– 29	116,808	2,913,296	.944	2,750,151
30– 49	154,847	5,980,345	.919	5,495,937
50– 74	49,770	2,975,063	.933	2,775,734
75– 99	9,093	781,719	.937	732,471
100–149	3,469	412,813	.902	372,357
150–199	809	141,575	.913	129,258
200 and over	732	197,398	1.000	197,398
All groups	410,043	14,543,090	.929 [4]	13,515,326
Not reporting rent	4,300			
Not reporting tenure	5,240			
Total occupied	419,583			13,825,260 [5]
Vacant	32,531			
Total, all units	452,114			

[1] See Table ABM 7.
[2] The total rents in this column were obtained as follows:
1) The number of units in the class "Under $10" was multiplied by the average rent of $7 derived from the special tabulation for 139 cities; see Table ABM 17.
2) The 7 rent classes from $10 to $149.99 were divided into 14 classes with frequencies of 8,123, 17,819, 19,581, 24,115, 59,785, 57,023, 98,777, 56,070, 35,730, 14,040, 5,660, 3,433, 2,567, and 902 as explained in Ch. II, sec. 3 c, and each frequency multiplied by the new rent class mid-points of $11.25, $13.75, etc. The frequencies in the rent class from $150 to $199 were multiplied by its mid-points.
3) The number of dwelling units having rents of $200.00 or more was multiplied by an average rent of $269.67 determined from the special tabulation for 139 cities; see Table ABM 17.
[3] For adjustment from mid-point of group basis to empirical average basis, see Table ABM 18.
[4] Derived by dividing for "All groups" the final total rent (col. 4) by the preliminary total rent (col. 2).
[5] Obtained by multiplying total occupied units (419,583) by the average rent of rented units reporting, as determined by dividing $14,543,090 (col. 2) by 410,043 units (col. 1), and correcting the average rent obtained ($35.47) by the correction factor .929 to give $32.95.

c Rent of Rented Dwelling Units

The total monthly rent of occupied rental dwelling units was estimated in exactly the same manner as the values of owner-occupied dwelling units (described in sec. 3 a). Table ABM 14 illustrates the method used for rents, the footnotes giving in detail the processes followed. The essential steps, including the processes for deriving and applying the mid-point correction factors, are presented in Tables ABM 17 and 18 in connection with the description of the 139 city special tabulation.

The annual rent (Table B 1) was obtained by multiplying the monthly rents as determined above from the Census reports for April 1, 1930 by 12. This assumes, of course, that the rents for that one month are the true arithmetic means for the year.

The distribution of monthly rents by states (Table ABM 15) involves exactly the same procedure as the distribution of the values of owner-occupied dwelling units except that vacant units are not considered. The annual rent is obtained by multiplying by 12.

TABLE ABM 15

Geographic Division Total Monthly Rent of All Occupied Rented Dwelling Units, Distribution by States

Population group 100,000 and over, Connecticut (similar tabulation by each population group for the states in each geographic division)

	NEW ENGLAND	CONNECTICUT	
	Uncorrected rents [1] (dollars)	Percentage of dwelling units in state [2]	Rent allocated to state (dollars)
RENT CLASS	(1)	(2)	(3) = (1) × (2)
Under $15	370,534	15.199	56,317
15–29	3,683,643	20.646	760,525
30–49	5,980,345	20.509	1,226,509
50–99	3,756,782	20.169	757,705
100 and over	751,786	19.980	150,207
All rent classes	14,543,090		2,951,263
Correction factor [3]			.950641
Total adjusted rent [4]			2,805,592

[1] *Table ABM 14, col. 2, with certain rent groups combined.*

[2] *These percentages were obtained from Tables ABM 1 and 2, where the number of dwelling units reporting rent by rent classes for states and geographic divisions are shown by population groups as illustrated by Connecticut and New England.*

[3] *For adjustment for mid-point of group basis to empirical group basis, including, in total rent, the rent of dwelling units not reporting value or tenure. Derived by dividing corrected monthly rent for all occupied dwellings (Table ABM 14, col. 4) by the uncorrected monthly rent for dwellings reporting rent (col 2):*

$$\frac{13,825,260}{14,543,090} = .950641.$$

[4] *2,951,263 × .950641.*

d Value of Rented Dwelling Units

The values of occupied rental dwelling units were obtained by means of value-rent ratios. The derivation of these ratios is explained below in section 5; Table B 20 presents the ratios actually derived for 1930. Since they reveal significant differences by type of dwelling, it was necessary to determine aggregate rents

by type of dwelling for each geographic division and population group. This step was possible with data derived from the 139 city special tabulation. As explained in section 4 d the special tabulation of rented dwelling units in the 139 cities was so prepared as to secure average monthly rents per dwelling unit for each type of dwelling. The average monthly rents per dwelling unit for the 2- and 3-or-more family dwellings were then expressed as percentages of the average monthly rents for 1-family dwellings (Table ABM 19).

Table ABM 16 illustrates how these relative rents, weighted by the number of occupied rental units of each type, were used to obtain the distribution of monthly rents by type of dwelling for cities in the population group 100,000 and over in New England. These monthly rents by type were then converted into annual rents (line 1 f 2) and multiplied by the value-rent ratios (line g) to obtain the aggregate values (line h). As a final step the value of vacant units was included by multiplying the total value of occupied units for each type of dwelling by the ratios of total units to occupied units after adjusting the ratio by the differential in rents between occupied and vacant units.

e Value of Rented Dwelling Units, Distribution by States

The derived value-rent ratio as determined for all types of occupied rental dwellings (see Table ABM 16, line g) was assumed to hold for each state for the respective population groups. These value-rent ratios were then multiplied by the aggregate rents for each state, determined as in the illustration for the 100,000 or more population group for Connecticut in the New England division (Table ABM 15). The value of vacant units was then allowed for by increasing the values for each state in the same proportion as the values had been increased for the geographic division as a whole (Table ABM 16).

This method of distributing the value of rented dwelling units by states involves some error, as the distribution of rented dwellings by type may differ from state to state. Since it was impossible to estimate the number of dwelling units for each state by type and tenure (see Ch. II, 2 f), without pressing certain assumptions too far, the values of rented dwelling units were distributed by states without reference to type of dwelling.

f Value of Dwelling Units, Distribution by Type

In deriving the number of nonfarm dwelling units a distribution of the number of units for each geographic division was obtained by tenure, population group, and type of dwelling (see Tables ABM 11 and A 4). From the tabulations completed thus far, a similar distribution could be made for rented dwelling units (see Table A 5), but not for values for each tenure.

TABLE ABM 16

Derivation of Value of Rented Dwelling Units, including Vacant, by Geographic
Division and Population Group

Population group 100,000 and over in New England (similar tabulation
by each population group for each geographic division)

1 OCCUPIED UNITS	1-FAMILY	2-FAMILY	3-OR-MORE FAMILY	ALL TYPES
	(1)	(2)	(3)	(4)
a Relative rents (base, 1-family) [1]	100.0	85.0	94.0	92.2 [7]
b Estimated no. of rented units [2]	69,503	129,869	220,211	419,583
c Equivalent units in 1-family rental rates (used to obtain relative, all types) a × b	69,503	110,389	206,998	386,890 [8]
d Relative rents (base, all types) [3]	108,5	92.2	102.0	100.0
e Estimated avg. monthly rent per unit [4] (dollars)	35.75	30.38	33.58	32.95 [9]
f Aggregate rent, 1930 (dollars) per				
1) month e × b	2,484,732	3,945,420	7,395,108 [10]	13,825,260
2) year 12 × f(1)	29,816,784	47,345,040	88,741,296	165,903,120
g Value-rent ratio [5]	13.1	9.1	8.2	9.3 [11]
h Aggregate value of occupied units, 1930 (thousands of dollars) g × f(2)	390,600	430,840	727,679	1,549,119 [12]
2 Vacancy value correction factor [6]	1.036	1.063	1.095	1.071 [13]
3 Aggregate value, all units, 1930 (thousands of dollars) h × (2)	404,662	457,983	796,809	1,659,454

[1] See Table ABM 19.   [2] See Table ABM 11.

[3] Based on line 1 a, all types = 100.0.

[4] Relative, line 1 d, applied to average, all types (32.95).

[5] See explanation, Ch. II, sec. 5, and Table B 20.

[6] Ratios of total rented dwelling units by type (including vacant) to total occupied units, adjusted to take account of the difference in rent between vacant and occupied units. The rent of vacant units was 97.4 per cent of that of occupied units. The unadjusted vacancy ratios were 1.037, 1.065, and 1.098. These ratios can be obtained from Table ABM 14. The adjustment was made as follows: [1.000 + (unadjusted ratio − 1.000) × .974].

[7] Derived: line 1 b ÷ line 1 c.   [8] Added total.

[9] Equals $35.47 (uncorrected average rent for dwellings reporting value) corrected for mid-point of group basis by use of ratio .929; see footnote 5, Table ABM 14.

[10] Aggregate "All types" less aggregates for 1- and 2-family dwellings so as to give arithmetic check.

[11] Derived: line 1 h ÷ line 1 f (2).

[12] Added total.

[13] Derived: line 3 ÷ line 1 h.

The method of deriving the values of rented dwellings made it necessary to distribute rents of occupied units by type of dwelling, since value-rent ratios showed marked differences by type of dwelling. Consequently, the differentials in rent for the several types of dwellings were derived from the 139 city special tabulation.

Since in order to estimate the total value of owner-occupied dwelling units it was not necessary to differentiate by type, no attempt was made to derive the representative differential average values of the several types of dwellings from the 139 city special tabulation for owner-occupants. Although statistically possible to estimate such values by type, it was not practicable.

4 Special Tabulation of Census Data for 139 Selected Cities

The special tabulation of Census data covering 139 selected cities was used in deriving the number and value of nonfarm dwelling units. Its earlier description would have interfered with the logical presentation of the basic methods.

a Character and Content of the Special Tabulation

Tables A 6 and B 5 list the 139 cities in the tabulation, classified by geographic division, and indicate the population of each city and the average values or rents, by value or rent groups, of the dwelling units for which values or rents were reported. The tabulation is based upon complete coverage for 90 cities and sample coverage for 49 cities.[12] Among the 139 cities are the 61 cities [13] included in both the Real Property Inventory and the Financial Survey of Urban Housing. The sample in the 49 cities varied with the size of the city. In cities of 100,000 or more, every 9th family was covered; in cities of 50,000–100,000, every 7th family; in cities of 25,000–50,000, every 6th family; in cities under 25,000, every 4th family.

To make the area covered by this tabulation for Atlanta, Georgia; Birmingham, Alabama; Cleveland, Ohio; Providence, Rhode Island; San Diego, California; Seattle, Washington; and Wheeling, West Virginia (which were among the 49 sample coverage cities) comparable to the area used by the Financial Survey, their environs were included in the respective metropolitan areas.

[12] The sample coverage cities are indicated by footnote references in Tables A 6 and B 5.

[13] For a list of these cities see Table A 9. The 9 cities of the 61 cities not included among the 52 cities of Table A 15 received only simplified tabulation by the Financial Survey of Urban Housing because of incomplete sample coverage.

b Type of Tabulation and Methods

For each city the value or rent of each dwelling unit (or a sample of such values or rents in the 49 cities) was entered under the value or rent group to which it belonged. The types differentiated in the two parts of the tabulation are shown herewith. The number of value entries in each value class gave the number of owner-occupied dwelling units and also of structures, since the owner-occupied dwelling units in a multiple

90 CITY COMPLETE TABULATION		49 CITY SAMPLE TABULATION
Owner-occupied	Rented	Owner-occupied and rented
Total (structures)	Total (dwelling units)	Total (structures or dwelling units)
1-family	1-family	1-family
2-family	2-family	2-family
	3-or-more family	3-family
		4-family
		5-or-more family

family dwelling would not be duplicated among the owner-occupant tenure group. The rent entries gave the number of rented dwelling units but not of structures, since multiple dwelling structures may be represented by two or more entries in the rented tenure group or by one entry in the owner-occupant tenure group and one or more entries in the rented tenure group.

The sum of all the value entries in each value class divided by the total entries gave the average value per dwelling unit by value groups. Similarly, the rent entries served as the basis for determining the average rent per dwelling unit by rent groups.

For rented dwelling units the rents of each type of dwelling also were cumulated to determine the average rents for dwelling units in 2- and 3-or-more family dwellings. This was not done for owner-occupied dwelling units since, as explained in section 3 f, the information by type was not required for estimate purposes. The average values of all types and of 1-family types alone were obtained for the owner-occupant tenure.

c Average Values or Rents by Value or Rent Group by Geographic Division and Population Group

From the individual city data on average values or rents by value or rent groups (Tables A 6 and B 5) were derived representative average values for geographic divisions by population groups. The size of the sample made it necessary to combine certain geographic divisions to provide a sufficient number of cities of each size to yield fairly representative average values.

Table ABM 17 presents for the group of cities with populations of 100,000 or more the geographic division average values or rents. On these average values were calculated the correction factors used to adjust the class mid-points from a preliminary to an actual

TABLE ABM 17

Average Values or Rents by Value or Rent Group as Derived from the 139 City Special Tabulation by Geographic Regions

Population group 100,000 and over by geographic region (similar tabulation for each population group)

A AVERAGE VALUE (DOLLARS)[1]

	Under 1,000[3]	1,000– 1,499	1,500– 1,999	2,000– 2,999	3,000– 4,999	5,000– 7,499	7,500– 9,999	10,000– 14,999	15,000– 19,999	20,000 and over[4]
North East[2] (5 cities)	544	1,157	1,619	2,320	3,768	5,938	8,273	11,146	15,982	33,090
North Central (7 cities)	597	1,121	1,622	2,321	3,742	5,807	8,175	10,999	15,758	33,090
South (7 cities)	587	1,077	1,592	2,271	3,645	5,813	8.179	10,956	15,696	33,090
West (4 cities)	551	1,101	1,604	2,305	3,738	5,703	8,160	10,906	15,708	33,090

B AVERAGE MONTHLY RENT (DOLLARS)[1]

	Under 10.00[3]	10.00– 14.99	15.00– 19.99	20.00– 29.99	30.00– 49.99	50.00– 74.99	75.00– 99.99	100.00– 149.99	150.00– 199.99	200.00 and over[4]
North East[2] (5 cities)	7.00	11.85	16.53	23.65	35.95	56.34	80.25	108.02	159.76	242.58
North Central (7 cities)	6.80	11.55	16.28	23.28	36.71	56.25	80.01	110.32	157.28	206.55
South (7 cities)	6.60	11.47	16.04	22.95	36.18	56.19	79.52	109.06	157.73	240,18
West (4 cities)	6.30	11.23	16.16	23.18	36.22	55.82	80.72	112.26	160.86	318.23

[1] *Average values and rents for all except open end groups are merely simple arithmetic averages of the individual city averages for those cities in the specified areas having populations within the population groups noted; see Tables A 6 and B 5.*

[2] *North East combines New England and Middle Atlantic; North Central combines East and West North Central; South combines South Atlantic, East South Central, and West South Central; West combines Mountain and Pacific.*

[3] *Simple arithmetic average of weighted averages for population groups of different size in each geographic division. Size groups were restricted to "Over 25,000"; "5,000–25,000" and "Under 5,000."*

[4] *Assigned after studying calculations similar to those noted in footnote 3.*

basis (Table ABM 18). The methods by which these correction ratios were calculated are explained in the footnotes to Table ABM 18.

TABLE ABM 18

Correction Factors [1] for Adjustment of Total Values and Rents as Derived from the Use of Class Mid-Points

Population group 100,000 and over by geographic region (similar tabulation for each population group)

A   OWNER-OCCUPIED

	NORTH EAST [2]	NORTH CENTRAL	SOUTH	WEST
Value Group				
Under $1,000	1.000	1.000	1.000	1.000
1,000– 1,499	.912	.874	.851	.872
1,500– 1,999	.917	.918	.904	.910
2,000– 2,999	.912	.916	.902	.914
3,000– 4,999	.924	.921	.915	.933
5,000– 7,499	.951	.940	.944	.930
7,500– 9,999	.945	.934	.935	.933
10,000–14,999	.892	.880	.876	.872
15,000–19,999	.913	.900	.897	.898
20,000 and over	1.000	1.000	1.000	1.000

B   RENTED

	NORTH EAST [2]	NORTH CENTRAL	SOUTH	WEST
Rent Group				
Under $10.00	1.000	1.000	1.000	1.000
10.00– 14.99	.919	.904	.908	.883
15.00– 19.99	.933	.921	.917	.914
20.00– 29.99	.944	.930	.928	.926
30.00– 49.99	.919	.932	.936	.933
50.00– 74.99	.933	.928	.935	.926
75.00– 99.99	.937	.933	.926	.956
100.00–149.99	.902	.938	.913	.908
150.00–199.99	.913	.899	.901	.919
200.00 and over	1.000	1.000	1.000	1.000

[1] *The correction factors or ratios in this table were derived as follows: the aggregate values or rents by value or rent groups were first obtained as explained in Table ABM 12, footnote 4, for each of the 9 geographic divisions. Simple averages were then computed for the geographic divisions that were combined. These were divided into the averages of Table ABM 17. For the use of these factors see Tables ABM 12 and 14.*

[2] *North East combines New England and Middle Atlantic; North Central combines East and West North Central; South combines South Atlantic, East South Central, and West South Central; West combines Mountain and Pacific.*

d Relative Rents by Type of Dwelling for each Geographic Division

In order to obtain total monthly rents for each type of dwelling as illustrated in Table ABM 16 it was necessary to have a set of percentages for each geographic division that would indicate the differentials in rents for the different types of dwellings. Weighted average rents by type of dwelling were computed for population groups of a given size in each geographic division. The rents thus computed for the 2- and 3-or-more family dwelling units were expressed as percentages of the 1-family dwelling rents. Curves were then drawn with population groups as abscissa and percentages as ordinates for each geographic division. From the general trend of these percentages by population groups for all geographic divisions, a set of percentages was selected as representative for a combination of geographic areas (Table ABM 19).

e Percentage of Nonfarm Residential Structures Inhabited by Their Owners

In deriving the distribution of types of dwellings by tenure (Table ABM 20) information gained from the 139 city special tabulation was used. The method of obtaining this information is described above in section 4 b. The percentages were used in deriving Table ABM 11.

f Data for Population Groups under 2,500

Among the 139 cities of the special Census tabulation 25 had populations under 2,500. Since the *Census of Population, 1930* does not show distributions of dwelling units by value or rent groups for towns and villages with fewer than 2,500 inhabitants, distributions of number of dwelling units, all types, by value or rent groups were made for this group (Tables A 7 and B 6). Table A 7 gives also total 1-family dwelling units and Table B 6 total dwelling units in each of the

TABLE ABM 19

Average Monthly Rents for 2- and 3-or-more Family Dwellings as Percentages of Monthly Rents for 1-Family Dwellings by Geographic Division and Population Group [1]

	2-FAMILY DWELLINGS						3-OR-MORE FAMILY DWELLINGS ALL POPULATION GROUPS
	100,000 and over	25,000– 100,000	10,000– 25,000	5,000– 10,000	2,500– 5,000	Under 2,500	
				(percentages)			
New England	85.0	87.0	88.0	89.0	91.0	92.0	94.0
Middle Atlantic	85.0	87.0	88.0	89.0	91.0	92.0	112.0
East North Central	94.0	95.0	96.0	98.0	99.0	100.0	121.0
West North Central	94.0	95.0	96.0	98.0	99.0	100.0	136.0
South Atlantic	97.0	98.0	99.0	100.0	101.0	102.0	150.0
East South Central	97.0	98.0	99.0	100.0	101.0	102.0	150.0
West South Central	97.0	98.0	99.0	100.0	101.0	102.0	150.0
Mountain	88.0	89.0	90.0	92.0	93.0	94.0	133.0
Pacific	88.0	89.0	90.0	92.0	93.0	94.0	133.0

[1] *For method of derivation and source see explanation in text. These percentages were used as illustrated in Table ABM 16.*

TABLE ABM 20

Percentage of Residential Structures Inhabited by Their Owners, by Geographic Division, Type of Dwelling, and Population Group, April 1, 1930

GEOGRAPHIC DIVISION AND TYPE OF DWELLING	ALL POPULATION GROUPS	100,000 AND OVER	25,000– 100,000	10,000– 25,000	5,000– 10,000	2,500– 5,000
New England and Middle Atlantic						
2-family dwelling	50.7	47.6	53.4	54.3	51.9	66.4
3-or-more family dwelling	40.5	39.6	39.8	42.4	31.2	64.6
East and West North Central						
2-family dwelling	51.5	46.7	53.2	57.3	60.0	63.8
3-or-more family dwelling	37.8	30.2	48.9	36.3	53.7	53.7
South Atlantic						
2-family dwelling	36.5	32.3	34.7	39.3	40.0	51.2
3-or-more family dwelling	34.5	24.8	25.0	55.3	36.4	69.3
East and West South Central						
2-family dwelling	45.2	41.3	40.9	53.6	53.7	45.1
3-or-more family dwelling	45.3	34.7	32.3	56.7	60.1	68.7
Mountain and Pacific						
2-family dwelling	45.3	44.7	45.9	47.6	49.2	37.9
3-or-more family dwelling	33.4	28.5	41.4	36.8	48.6	28.7

Derived from special tabulation of 139 cities for NBER

three types of dwelling classifications, information not available elsewhere.

5 Value-Rent Ratios, Method of Deriving

To estimate the value of rented properties, value-rent ratios (Table ABM 16) were derived from information in the Financial Survey of Urban Housing with the aid of weights from the Real Property Inventory. Since the best information in these surveys relates to 1934, the method of deriving the value-rent ratios for that year is explained first.

a 1934

The value-rent ratios derived for 1934 by type of dwelling are shown in Table B 19 for 42 cities, with weighted averages for the cities in each geographic division. Since the number of tenant and landlord reports in the Financial Survey of Urban Housing was not the same, average rents derived from tenant reports and average values derived from landlord reports were used.

Financial Survey of Urban Housing reports were classified into 1-family, 2-family, apartments, and "other dwellings" and average rents and values derived for each type. Ratios of value per room to rent per room were computed for each type. Financial Survey sample data are available for 1-family dwellings for 1, 2, 3, 4, 5, 6, and "7-or-more" rooms. For each city, value-rent ratios were computed for each room size and reweighted by total rented 1-family dwelling units classified by number of rooms, as reported by the Real Property Inventory. This reweighting served to overcome the tendency of the Financial Survey sample of rented dwellings as reported by landlords to be biased toward the larger room sizes.

In order to match the Census "1-family dwelling unit" classification, which includes row houses, the value-rent ratios for 1-family dwellings for the cities within each geographic division were combined with similar value-rent ratios for row houses by using weights of the number in each city derived from the Real Property Inventory. To give geographic division ratios the ratios thus obtained for each city were combined by weighting total 1-family and row houses in each city as reported by the Real Property Inventory.

A breakdown by number of rooms similar to that for 1-family dwellings was not feasible for 2-family dwellings, and the value-rent ratios for the cities as derived from the Financial Survey sample data were accepted and reweighted by the Real Property Inventory number of rented 2-family dwelling units in the several cities to obtain average ratios for the geographic divisions.

In order to match the Census "3-or-more family dwellings" classification it was necessary to combine the sample data for several types of dwellings as given in the Financial Survey and reweight them accordingly. Rents per room were obtainable from the sample as reported by tenants for 3- and 4-family dwellings and "larger apartments" (5-or-more family). However, the values of multi-family rented dwellings as reported by landlords covered only "apartments" that contained 4-or-more family dwelling units and "other dwellings," which included, without possibility of segregation, 3-family dwellings, row houses, flats over stores, and miscellaneous units not otherwise classified. Consequently, in each city, value-rent ratios were computed for "apartments" (4-or-more family dwellings) and "other dwellings." A composite 3-or-more family dwelling value-rent ratio was then obtained by weighting this "apartment" ratio by the rented apartment units and weighting the "other dwelling" ratio by total rented dwelling units in "3-family dwellings," "flats over stores," and "other," both as reported in the Financial Survey tenant sample. The Financial Survey sample data were used for weighting because the corresponding Real Property Inventory data on "other dwellings" include, in addition to flats over stores, several essentially 1-family dwellings, such as single dwellings with business offices or stores. In some cities, Cleveland in particular, the Real Property Inventory full coverage data would have seriously over-weighted the "other dwelling" value-rent ratio.

b 1930

Ratios of 1930 value and 1929 rent, by type of dwelling, similar to those described above for 1933–34, cannot be derived directly from the Financial Survey data. A composite ratio for all types is obtainable for 1930, but it is not possible to make the detailed adjustments outlined for 1934. Furthermore, the 1930 values and 1929 rents reported to the Financial Survey in 1934, when compared with the 1930 Census data, seem to be understated in varying degree. Consequently, the 1933–34 ratios by type, described above, seemed to offer a more reliable basis for deriving a 1929–30 ratio. They were accordingly used to estimate value, adjustment being made for changes in the value-rent relationship between 1930 and 1934. In making this adjustment, which is based on the differential changes in values and rents between 1930 and 1934, two difficulties had to be overcome: first, as noted above, the objection to using the retrospective values and rents reported by the Financial Survey for 1930; second, the trend in values required was that for rented properties, which was available from the Financial Survey alone. The trend in rents, 1930–34, was based upon the full coverage rent data for 1930 derived from the Census taken in that year (Table B 8) while the 1934 rents are Financial Survey average rents by rent classes obtained in that year and weighted by the Real Property Inventory number of rented dwellings by rent classes.

To obtain the value trend for 1930–34 certain additional steps were necessary. Table A 10 presents the average values of 1-family owner-occupied dwellings on a full coverage basis in 1930 and on a sample basis in 1934 and the percentage change. To obtain the change in the value of all rented dwellings between 1930 and 1934 it was assumed that the relative difference between the value of 1-family dwellings as reported to the Financial Survey for these two years and the full coverage averages in Table A 10 would be fairly representative measures of the difference between full coverage values of rented properties and the values reported by landlords to the Financial Survey for rented properties in 1930 and 1934.

The 1930 and 1934 values for rented properties were corrected by the method described above, and the percentage change between the two years was thus obtained for individual cities (similar to Table A 10). With comparable percentage changes in values and rents between the two years for individual cities it is possible to obtain for each city the relative percentage changes in values and rents. This was done first for each city; then the ratios in each city were weighted by the number of rented dwellings as reported by the Real Property Inventory in 1934 to give geographic division weighted figures (Table ABM 21). Where the ratio exceeds unity it indicates that values were higher relative to rents in 1930 than in 1934 and hence the value-rent ratio in 1930 should be higher than the value-rent ratio in 1934 by the amount indicated.

TABLE ABM 21

Ratio of Percentage Change in Value (1930–1934) to Percentage Change in Rent (1930–1934) and Correction Factors for Incomplete Coverage of Financial Survey Value-Rent Ratios for 1934, by Geographic Division

	RATIO OF CHANGE IN VALUE TO CHANGE IN RENT 1930–34	FACTOR TO CORRECT FOR INCOMPLETE COVERAGE [2]
New England	1.114	0.967
Mid. Atlantic	1.202	0.958
E. N. Central	0.960	1.044
W. N. Central	1.053	1.058
S. Atlantic	1.100	1.007
E. S. Central [1]	1.138	0.998
W. S. Central	1.191	0.984
Mountain	1.034	1.059
Pacific	1.167	1.010

[1] *The East South Central is a weighted average of the South Atlantic and the West South Central geographic divisions.*
[2] *Percentage of full coverage average value for 1-family dwellings to sample coverage divided by percentage of full coverage average annual rent to sample coverage average annual rent.*

These adjustment factors were not applied to the value-rent ratios for 1934 in Table B 19 since the latter were based upon sample data and the measurement of trends was on a full coverage basis. The 1934 value-rent ratios by type for the geographic divisions were instead adjusted by a ratio based on the percentage relationship between (a) full coverage owner-occupied 1-family dwelling values and sample coverage values in 1934, and (b) full coverage average annual rents and sample coverage rents in 1934.

The correction factors in Table ABM 21 were multiplied by the value-rent ratios for 1934 by type (Table B 19) to obtain the 1934 value-rent ratios for the separate types, excluding "all types" (Table B 20). The 1934 value-rent ratios for the separate types, excluding "all types," in Table B 20 were then multiplied by the correction factors in Table ABM 21 to give the 1930 value-rent ratios in Table B 20 for the separate types, excluding "all types." It was these 1930 value-rent ratios by type that were used to estimate aggregate values for 1930 (Table ABM 16). The value-rent ratio for "all types" (Table B 20) for 1930 was obtained as a result of the aggregate estimate (all cities), illustrated in Table ABM 16 for the population group 100,000 and over in New England. The "all types" ratio for 1934 (Table B 20) was then obtained by dividing by the correction factors in Table ABM 21. The weighted "all types" value-rent ratio for 1934 is used in estimating aggregate value of rented properties for 1934 (Table A 8).

6 Value of Nonfarm Residential Real Estate, including Vacant, Estimates, 1934

The total value of nonfarm residential real estate in 1934 (Table A 8) was estimated separately for owner-occupied and rented properties in each geographic division, but not by population groups.

a Value of Owner-Occupied Dwelling Units

To estimate the average value of owner-occupied dwelling units in 1934, the average 1930 value of owner-occupied dwellings, including vacant, in each geographic division was multiplied by a correction factor representing the relative change in the value of 1-family dwellings between 1930 and 1934, as shown in Table A 10 by geographic division. The resulting average value per unit in 1934 was multiplied by the dwelling units standing in 1934 to obtain the estimated aggregate value of owner-occupied residential property for the geographic division. The units standing in 1934 were estimated on the basis of additions through new construction and decreases through demolitions, estimates for which were made in connection with the estimates of construction (see Ch. V). The United States total was then obtained by addition of the products for the geographic divisions. This procedure assumes, in the absence of more conclusive

data, that average values of 2- and 3-or-more family dwellings declined by the same percentage as those of 1-family dwellings. While values of these other types of structure may have declined at different rates, the error in the total is probably small, since 1-family dwellings comprised 89 per cent of all owner-occupied dwelling units in 1930.

b Value of Rented Dwelling Units

Aggregate value of rented dwelling units in 1934 was estimated after the average value per unit and the number of rented dwelling units standing in 1934 had been determined. The average value of rented dwellings was obtained by using the product of the percentage change in the value-rent ratios and in rents. In order to adjust to 1934 values the following steps were taken: The value-rent ratios for all types in 1929–30 by geographic division were divided into the corresponding ratios for 1933–34 (Table B 20) to obtain a correction factor reflecting the change in these ratios. This correction factor was multiplied by the ratio of average rent for all types in 1933, expressed as a percentage of the average rent for 1929, to give an estimated ratio of the value of rented units of all types in 1934 expressed as a percentage of the value of rented units in 1930. The percentage so obtained was multiplied by the average value per unit in 1930 (Table A 3) to obtain an estimated average value per unit in 1934. This average value per unit in 1934 was multiplied by the estimated number of units on January 1, 1934 to obtain an estimated aggregate value of rented units in 1934. Addition of values of owner-occupied and rented gave an aggregate value for the two tenures for 1934. Total dwelling units standing on January 1, 1934 were derived on the basis of estimated net additions through new construction and demolitions between April 1, 1930 and January 1, 1934. These net additions were added to total dwelling units standing on April 1, 1930 (Table A 4).

CHAPTER III

Source of Income Data and Method of Tabulating

The income data in Part Three, section C, Tables C 1–15, were derived from information collected by the Financial Survey of Urban Housing. Tables C 1–3 are the results of special tabulations made in connection with this study and these data have not been published previously.

1 Tables Derived from Special Tabulations

The income tables in Part Three, section C, may be conveniently divided into two parts. The first three, C 1–3, present income information for 33 cities for 1929 and 1933. Since the data result from special tabulations for cities providing the largest number of returns, they warranted greater subdivision. These more elaborate tabulations were made after digit sorting of punch cards covering income data for both 1929 and 1933, by 39 income groups. The tabulation by the Financial Survey covered 1933 alone and gave only 11 income groups.

In Table C 1 the number and percentage of owner-occupant and tenant families reporting income in 1933 for the years 1929 and 1933 are shown by 39 income groups for the 33 cities combined. The combination of the reports for each city to obtain the totals for the 33 cities is based upon the sample data, no attempt being made to increase the reports in each city to full coverage or to equal percentage coverage.

Table C 2 is identical with Table C 1 except that it shows the income (to the nearest $100) reported by families in each income group and the percentage distribution of the amounts by the 39 income groups.

Table C 3 presents for tenant families for the 33 cities combined and for each city individually: (1) the number of families reporting income and rent by the 39 income groups, (2) the average income and rent reported by families in each income group, (3) the percentage rent is of income by income groups. The information for the tenant families that had reported through mail returns and for those that had been personally enumerated is presented separately. A similar table showing the relation between income and value of residence cannot be presented for owner-occupant families without considerable additional machine tabulation since the income and value data are on different punch cards.

In tabulating the income data for 1929 in conjunction with 1933 those schedules were eliminated from the 1929 distribution which indicated that the families reporting income in 1933 were non-existent as families in 1929.

2 Tables Derived Directly from Financial Survey Tabulations

Tables C 4–13 present real estate information for 1933 for 52 cities by 11 income groups. These materials were originally prepared by the Financial Survey, but the results have as yet been published for only 22 cities. The totals for the cities in each geographic division and for all 52 cities combined (Tables C 4–13) were weighted as explained in the footnotes to the tables (see also Part Two, Ch. I, sec. 2). Therefore, the weight of each city in the combinations of cities is

based upon estimated full coverage rather than actual sample coverage.

3 Character of the Income Data

The unit of enumeration for all data collected by the Financial Survey was the dwelling. Income was that received by the family living in the dwelling unit. The family was not necessarily coextensive with the number of persons living in the dwelling unit since enumerators were specifically instructed to ascertain the number of persons living in the dwelling unit and also the number of persons making up the family. Lodgers, roomers, other paying guests, and servants on January 1 of each year for which the reports were received were excluded from the family proper. There was no formal definition of family per se, but the substance of the instructions and the arrangement of the schedules defined it as the persons living in the dwelling unit less those mentioned above. Presumably a person might be excluded as a family member, even though he was related to other persons within the family by blood or marriage, if he paid board or room rent and was thought of as a lodger or roomer. Persons temporarily absent but normally members of the family were included as members. In requesting the amount of the family income the enumerators were instructed to state that there was no desire to pry into personal affairs or to acquire information for taxation purposes, but that it was "necessary to get reliable statistics showing the relation between family income and the type and value or rent of the house owned or used"; only an approximation of family income was desired.

The family income data applied to the 12 months of each calendar year reported on: the amount received in the form of wages and salaries and from roomers or lodgers was reported separately. To the total income from these two sources was to be added any net income from investments, from rental of a garage or other properties or part thereof, or from relatives, relief agencies, or other sources. The income from wages or salaries and all other income was the total for all members of the family. The schedule and instructions made no specific differentiation or reference to the form of income, whether cash or income received in the form of goods, services, or commodity orders.

Many of the Financial Survey schedules, especially

Used, Rejected, and Total Schedules Received, Percentage Distribution by 11 Income Groups, 33 Cities, 1933

	All Income Groups	No Income	$1– 249	$250– 499	$500– 749	$750– 999	$1,000– 1,499	$1,500– 1,999	$2,000– 2,999	$3,000– 4,499	$4,500– 7,499	$7,500 and over
Used	100.0	5.2	10.3	11.9	13.5	10.3	18.5	13.3	10.4	4.3	1.7	0.6
Rejected	100.0	9.1	14.8	12.8	12.6	10.2	16.1	10.7	8.0	3.5	1.4	0.8
Total	100.0	5.6	10.7	11.9	13.4	10.3	18.2	13.1	10.2	4.3	1.7	0.6

Special tabulation of Financial Survey of Urban Housing schedules

among those returned by mail, were rejected in editing because of incomplete data. Subsequent analysis indicates a downward bias in favor of the smaller income groups. When the rejected schedules containing income information are added to the used schedules, however, the total varies only slightly from the distri-

bution of the used returns, as shown by the accompanying table.

A more detailed presentation of the income data here shown in part and of the method of collection and tabulation is being prepared.

CHAPTER IV

Financing Nonfarm Residential Real Estate

With the exception of Tables D 1, 2, 4, and 48 all tables in Part Three, section D, are derived from Financial Survey data. The principal estimate of this section is for debt in 1934 (Table D 4). The percentages of owner-occupied nonfarm properties mortgaged and the debt-value ratios expressed in percentage form for 1920 are presented in Table D 1 by population group, state, and geographic division. Table D 2 presents for 1920 and 1934 for 50 cities the percentage of properties mortgaged and for 45 cities the debt-value ratios of mortgaged properties. The 1934 data are from the Financial Survey. Table D 48 presents data on financing of real estate in two New York City areas as derived from a special study.

Before the methods used to derive the mortgage estimates for 1934 are explained, the sources and methods used to obtain the data for 1920 and the information available for 1930 and 1934 from the Financial Survey are described.

1 Percentage of Owner-Occupied Houses Mortgaged and Percentage that Debt is of Value, 1920

Census Monograph II, *Mortgages on Homes in the United States, 1920,* provides the information from which Table D 1 and the 1920 section of Table D 2 were derived. These census data were based on a mailed survey of 66.3 per cent of owner-occupied residences. The percentages of owner-occupied residences mortgaged and the debt-value ratios for all population groups combined (Table D 1) are transcribed directly from Tables 26 and 30 of the Census Monograph II. The percentages of residences mortgaged for each population group (Table D 1) are derived from Tables 26, 27, 28, 30, 31, and 33 of the Monograph.

The percentages of houses mortgaged in cities with populations of 100,000 and over (Table 27) and between 25,000 and 100,000 (Table 28) were used in conjunction with the number of mortgaged houses (Tables 31 and 33) to obtain total owner-occupied houses in each city in the respective population groups. The cities in both size groups were then arranged by

states in each geographic division and totals obtained by states and geographic divisions of the number of owner-occupied and mortgaged houses. From these totals were computed the percentages mortgaged in each state and geographic division for both population groups.

To obtain similar percentages for population groups under 25,000 the combined total of mortgaged dwellings for the larger cities, computed as described above, was subtracted from total mortgaged dwellings for states and geographic divisions in Census Monograph Table 30. Since the percentage mortgaged by states and geographic divisions for all cities was given in Table 26 it was possible to obtain total owner-occupied residences and derive by subtraction the number in population groups under 25,000. From total owner-occupied and mortgaged houses in population groups under 5,000 it was then possible to compute the percentage mortgaged.

The debt-value ratio by population groups (Table D 1) was transcribed directly from Census Monograph Table 34.

2 Percentage of Owner-Occupied and Rented Houses Mortgaged and Debt-Value Ratios in Individual Cities

The city percentages for 1920 in Table D 2 were transcribed directly from Census Monograph Tables 27, 28, 31, and 33; the 1934 percentages and ratios are from the Financial Survey of Urban Housing. The debt-value ratios in Table D 3 for owner-occupied and rented properties for 1930, 1933, and 1934 are based on sample data derived from the Financial Survey. The number of reports on which they are based is shown in Tables D 5 and 6 by value groups together with the percentage mortgaged by value groups. Tables D 7 and 8 present Financial Survey data on the value of and the debt outstanding (principal only) on mortgaged properties by value groups and thus provide the basic sample data from which the debt-value ratios of mortgaged properties in 1934 are derived. Table D 9 presents, by type of dwelling, for each tenure separately the percentage of properties mortgaged in 1934 as reported to the Financial Survey.

Tables D 11 and 12 present the number and percentage distribution of mortgaged properties by debt-value ratio groups; Table D 13, the debt-value ratios of mortgaged properties by value groups (derived from Tables D 7 and 8); Table D 14, the ratios of debt on mortgaged properties to the values of all properties, including properties not mortgaged (derived from Tables A 12 and 13, D 5 and 6).

3 Estimated Total Mortgage Debt on Nonfarm Residential Properties, 1934

The preliminary estimate of total mortgage debt on residential properties, Table D 4, was obtained by means of separate operations for owner-occupied and rented properties in each geographic division.

a Estimated Debt on Rented Properties

Debt on rented properties was estimated by multiplying the estimated 1934 value of rented residential properties [1] (Table A 8) in each geographic division by a weighted average debt-value ratio derived from Financial Survey data in 44 cities (Table D 14, col. 2). This ratio is the relation of debt on mortgaged rented properties to the total value of all rented properties, including those not mortgaged. This direct method of estimating debt on rented properties was used primarily because of the absence of other mortgage data on rented properties which would allow more detailed methods similar to those employed in estimating debt on owner-occupied properties described below. The 1920 Census and the various Real Property Inventory studies obtained no mortgage data on rented properties. The only specific data on debt of mortgaged rented properties are those in the Financial Survey.

b Estimated Debt on Owner-Occupied Properties

In estimating debt on owner-occupied residential properties the percentage of properties mortgaged and the debt-value ratio of mortgaged properties were determined separately. Forty-six of the Financial Survey cities were classified into groups of cities 100,000 or more and 25,000–100,000 in population by geographic division. The debt-value ratio in each city was recorded as shown by the 1920 Census and by the Financial Survey for 1934. Data for a third population group, under 25,000, were derived by subtracting the totals for the cities over 25,000 in population from the geographic division total. A weighted debt-value ratio of mortgaged owner-occupied dwellings was computed for the 46 cities by three population groups, in each geographic division for 1920 and 1934. The 1934 ratio

[1] *Includes value of land and improvements; does not include nonhousekeeping dwellings (hotels, clubs, lodging houses).*

was then expressed as a percentage of the 1920 ratio for each city. From these results was derived a weighted percentage for the size group. This was used as a correction factor to compute a debt-value ratio for 1934 by multiplying the percentage by the 1920 debt-value ratio of all mortgaged properties. This process was performed for each of the three population groups within each geographic division. These ratios were later used in connection with the aggregate value of mortgaged properties, described below, in estimating debt in 1934.

The aggregate value of mortgaged owner-occupied properties in 1934 was obtained by first estimating their average value in 1934 for three population groups, by geographic divisions. This was done by multiplying the average value of all such units as shown by the special Census tabulation of 46 Financial Survey cities for 1930 by a percentage expressing the average value of all owner-occupied 1-family dwelling units in 1934, for the same 46 Financial Survey cities, in relation to the average value of 1-family units in 1930 as estimated by this project. A weighted percentage was derived from the individual city percentages and applied to the size group average within each division to obtain an estimated average value for all properties. This process assumed that the changes in value for 1-family units during these four years applied to other types of dwellings also. The total value of all owner-occupied units was estimated by multiplying these average values by the number of all owner-occupied units in 1934. The average value of all mortgaged properties was computed by multiplying the average just found by a ratio expressing the average value of mortgaged properties as a percentage of the average value of all properties, as shown by the Financial Survey cities in 1934.

The 1920 Census reported the number of mortgages for 68 cities 100,000 or more in population and for 219 cities 25,000–100,000 in population and also for each geographic division as a whole. By subtracting the number of mortgaged properties in these 287 cities from the geographic division total of mortgaged properties, the number mortgaged in population groups under 25,000 was obtained. This total number mortgaged was divided by the total number of properties to obtain the percentage mortgaged. A similar process gave the percentages of properties mortgaged in 1934 for the same population and geographic division classifications. A ratio between the percentage mortgaged in 1934 and the percentage for 1920 was computed and applied as a correction factor to the percentage of all owner-occupied properties as reported by the 1920 Census to obtain an estimated percentage of all owner-occupied properties mortgaged in 1934. The number of owner-occupied houses mortgaged was estimated by multiplying this percentage by the total number of owner-occupied houses standing, including vacant, in 1934. This number, in turn, was multiplied by the average value of mortgaged owner-occupied houses for each population group by geographic divisions, found as previously described, to obtain an estimated total value of all owner-occupied mortgaged properties in 1934. Finally, this aggregate value of owner-occupied mortgaged properties was multiplied by the debt-value ratio of mortgaged properties derived as described in the first part of this section, to estimate total mortgage debt on owner-occupied residential properties as of January 1, 1934.

In this preliminary estimate of debt, the different types of residential structures are not treated separately. The validity of using composite figures on debt frequency and debt-value ratios for all types combined, as is done here, rests upon the representativeness of the data. The representativeness of apartment dwellings is probably most doubtful. Such properties are usually encumbered more frequently than others and it is more difficult to obtain credit data on them. Consequently the sample data probably do not adequately represent that type and mortgages are probably underestimated, at least on rented properties.

4 Mortgage Loans, Two New York City Areas

The data for the Lower East Side and Harlem in New York City, Table D 48, were collected in 1934 by a CWA project on residential property conditions of these areas, sponsored by the New York Building Congress under the direction of Arthur Holden. The value and finance data on the schedules were analyzed as part of this study by the National Bureau with the cooperation and assistance of the Mayor's Planning Committee.

The primary data on assessed value, mortgage debt, priority of liens, source and terms of loans, were obtained from public records. The mortgage data were checked with the holder of the loan.

CHAPTER V

Method of Estimating Nonfarm Residential Construction

The estimates of residential construction summarized in Part Three, Tables E 1–5, were published in National Bureau *Bulletin 65*, together with a condensed statement of method. The estimates were made in five stages: (1) organization and adjustment of data; (2) estimate, in detail, by geographic division, population group, and type of dwelling, of aggregate nonfarm dwelling units built during 1920–29, corrected for bias in the basic building permit series; (3) estimate, based on the relationships found in (2), of aggregate nonfarm dwelling units built each year since 1920, and separate estimates for 1935 and 1936; (4) estimate, by applying average costs per dwelling unit to estimated units built, of the dollar value of new residential building each year since 1920; (5) estimate of aggregate nonfarm dwelling units built by decades, 1890–1929.

1 Description of Data: Organization and Adjustment
a Primary Data Used

The estimates are based primarily on reported building permits for principal cities of the United States as published by the Bureau of Labor Statistics for the years since 1920,[1] and on changes in the number of families as derived from Census data. The permit data were adjusted for undervaluation and for under- and over-representation of actual construction, as described below. The data on number of families were adjusted to allow for changes in the boundaries of cities and for the varying area coverage of building permit reports.[2]

Among the items in the permit data are type of structure (i.e., 1- or 2-family dwellings, apartments, hotels, clubs, and lodging houses); number of family dwelling units; and estimated cost of the proposed structure, all as declared by the applicant for the permit. The permit data are available on an annual basis from 1920 to 1930, and monthly since September 1929. For 1920–32 reports are available only for cities having populations of 25,000 or more, the number of cities varying from 189 in 1920 to 360 in 1932.[3] In 1933 the number of cities covered by the permit reports of the Bureau of Labor Statistics was increased to 811 by the addition of population groups 10,000–25,000. During 1936 the number was again increased to nearly 2,000 by the addition of population groups

[1] *Bulding Permits in the Principal Cities of the United States, Bulletins 295, 318, 347, 368, 397, 424, 449, 469, 500, 524, and 545;* Monthly Labor Review, *March and April 1932, March and April 1933, and April 1934; Building Construction, Serial No. R-219, R-351, and R-538.*
[2] *Estimates based on contracts awarded are discussed in Note A.*
[3] *The total number of cities in the United States with populations over 25,000 was 287 in 1920 and 376 in 1930.*

2,500–10,000. Data for 1,689 of the 2,000 cities were available for the entire year 1936.

As the number of reporting cities has varied considerably during the period, principal reliance was placed on data for 257 cities with populations over 25,000 and reporting continuously since 1921. Data for 1920 were estimated on the basis of the 189 cities reporting. For estimating construction in 1935 and 1936 the enlarged samples of 811 and 1,689 cities then available were used in combination with the data for the 257 cities. The data for recent years give some representation in all 48 states, but the coverage is not uniform for states or regions.[4] Neither suburban developments nor farms outside city limits are represented by permits, and throughout most of the period for which estimates were made small cities and towns of less than 25,000 population were not covered.

The 257 reporting cities accounted for about one-half of total nonfarm population, or approximately two-thirds of the population in centers with 2,500 or more, usually designated as urban. Thus, to estimate total nonfarm building, the amount in areas having in the aggregate approximately half the total nonfarm population had to be determined.

In order to establish rates of change in population and building for different classes of cities, the 257 cities were classified into three groups, based on their location within or outside metropolitan districts: (1) 113 central cities included in the 96 metropolitan districts as defined by the Bureau of the Census and containing 120 central cities, ranging in population from 25,000 to over 6,000,000; (2) 64 satellite cities of from 25,000 to 116,000 population in the environs of 14 of the 96 metropolitan districts, with 33 of the 64 cities in the environs of New York City and Boston, and none in the environs of central cities in the South, West Central, or Mountain regions; (3) 80 nonmetropolitan cities with populations of from 25,000 to 100,000.

These three groups of cities, which provide the sample data used in the estimates, constitute differing proportions of the total urban population in the three classes of cities. The 113 central cities cover all but 1.5 per cent of the population in the 120 central cities; however, the population in the 7 central cities not included among the 257 cities grew more than twice as fast as that in the 113 cities (Table EM 1). The population in the urban environs represented by the 64 reporting satellite cities was only about one-fourth of that in all environs, and the rate of growth in the reporting cities was only half that in the unreported areas. Population of the 80 reporting cities comprised

[4] There is no reporting city among the 257 cities in Vermont, North Dakota, Mississippi, Idaho, Wyoming, New Mexico, or Nevada, but the aggregate nonfarm population of these states is only 2 per cent of the United States total.

one-fifth of that in the urban areas outside metropolitan districts here classified as "nonmetropolitan urban." While the two groups of 64 and 80 cities constitute relatively small parts of the population of their re-

TABLE EM 1

Population of 257 Cities reporting Building Permits, and Unreported Urban and Nonfarm Areas, by Class of City, 1920 and 1930 [1]

	POPULATION			
	1920 Jan. 1 [2]	1930 April 1	Increase 1920–30	Distribution 1930
	(thousands)		(percentage)	
Metropolitan districts	42,680	54,753	28.3	59.3
113 reporting central cities [3]	30,913	37,253	20.5	40.3
7 unreported central cities [4]	394	562	42.6	0.6
Total, 120 central cities	31,307	37,815	20.8	40.9
64 reporting satellite cities [5]	3,024	3,810	26.0	4.1
Unreported urban environs	4,667	7,517	61.1	8.1
Total urban environs (pop. 2,500 and over) [6]	7,691	11,327	47.3	12.2
Rural environs (pop. under 2,500)	3,682	5,612	52.4	6.1
Total, environs	11,373 [7]	16,939	48.9	18.3
177 reporting metropolitan district cities	33,937	41,063	21.0	44.5
Unreported Metropolitan district areas	8,743	13,690	56.6	14.8
Nonmetropolitan cities	16,142	19,813	22.7	21.5
80 reporting	3,351	3,846	14.8	4.2
Unreported	12,791	15,967	24.8	17.3
All urban areas [8]	58,822	74,567	26.8	80.8
257 reporting cities	37,288	44,909	20.6	48.6
Unreported urban areas	21,534	29,658	37.7	32.2
Rural nonfarm [9]	15,274	17,763	16.6	19.2
Total nonfarm	74,096	92,330	24.6	100.0

[1] "Reporting cities" are those in the U. S. Bureau of Labor Statistics series of 257 cities; "unreported areas" are cities or unincorporated areas not among the 257 cities.

[2] Population of reporting cities includes estimated 1920 population of areas annexed during 1920–30 to obtain comparable areas on the 1930 basis.

[3] In 91 of 96 metropolitan districts.

[4] In 5 metropolitan districts: Evansville, Ind; Johnstown and Reading, Pa; Miami, Tampa, and St. Petersburg, Fla; and Ashland, Ky.

[5] In 14 of 96 metropolitan districts.

[6] Obtained by combination of special tabulations of the population of satellite cities with 2,500–25,000 (furnished by Division of Construction and Public Employment, Bureau of Labor Statistics); and satellite cities with 25,000 and over (by National Bureau of Economic Research).

[7] Partly estimated. Census data available for environs of only 85 metropolitan districts in 1920.

[8] National Bureau classification: includes places under 2,500 in environs usually classified as "rural" but considered as urban for estimating building. Census total, 1930: 68,954,823; 1920 total for identical areas on 1930 classification: 55,140,358, special tabulation by Bureau of the Census, unpublished.

[9] National Bureau classification: excludes places under 2,500 in environs of metropolitan districts.

spective groups of cities, their representation is greatly strengthened when they are used in conjunction with the enlarged samples of 811 cities with populations over 10,000 and available since 1933, and the 1,689 cities with populations over 2,500 reporting in 1936.

Rural nonfarm areas were not represented in the permit data. As defined by the Census their aggregate population increased 23 per cent between 1920 and 1930 (Table EM 1), but that portion included in metropolitan districts and designated in this study as "rural environs" increased 52.4 per cent while the other, more typically rural areas, increased only 16.3 per cent.

b Statistical Advantages in Using Data on Number of Families rather than Population

In the early stages of this study total dwelling units built during 1920–29 in metropolitan, nonmetropolitan, and rural nonfarm areas were estimated by computing per capita building rates in reporting cities and applying similar rates to the population of unreported areas. The building rate to be applied to the population of an unreported area was selected from the regression line derived in a computation for the corresponding group of reporting cities, determining the correlation of (1) families provided for per 10,000 population during 1920–29 and (2) the percentage increase in population between Census dates 1920 and 1930.[5] The correlation of building rates and population increase was high and almost entirely independent of size of population group or geographic location. However, the method proved too unwieldy to apply on a regional basis and was not carried further.[6]

The method finally adopted to estimate aggregate building during 1920–29 was based directly on Census data on families, utilizing ratios of dwelling units built to the increase in the number of families in cities reporting building permits, and applying these ratios or modifications of them to the increase in the number of families in areas not covered by building permits.[7]

The elements included in these ratios may be illustrated by the final estimate. Approximately 7,035,000 nonfarm dwelling units were built between 1920 and 1929, while the Census indicates a 5,541,000 net increase in the number of nonfarm families. The indicated ratio of units built to the increase in the number of families is 1.27, i.e., for an increase of 100 families, approximately 127 units were built. The additional 27 units per 100 families, or 1,494,000 dwellings in all, are accounted for as follows. By definition, the Census enumeration of families is also a count of the occupied dwelling units; when vacant units in 1920 and 1930 are added to the Census count of families (occupied dwellings) in 1920 and 1930, the net increase for the decade in all units standing is approximately 6,580,-

000. Vacant units in 1920 were estimated at 177,000 and in 1930 at 1,216,000, indicating an increase of 1,039,000, which may be apportioned roughly into three parts: (1) building to make up the housing shortage that had accumulated at the beginning of the decade; (2) building to provide a nominal vacancy accompanying the 5,541,000 increase in occupied units; (3) excess building which resulted in greater than "normal" vacancy by 1930.

In addition to providing for the estimated increase of nearly 6,580,000 units in the total of all units standing, some building was necessary to replace dwellings demolished either to make way for other buildings or by fire, flood, and other causes. This was estimated to be nearly 580,000 units which, added to the 6,580,000 net increase in units standing, would indicate a gross volume of building of 7,160,000 units. However, when allowance is made for the net increase of 125,000 units, resulting from remodeling and conversion of many existing buildings, the net new construction is indicated as only 7,035,000 dwelling units. The excess in

[5] *This is the same general principle used recently by F. J. Hallauer for estimating construction during 1920–29 (*Population and Building Construction*, Journal of Land and Public Utility Economics, February 1934; and *Population and Building Construction, a Revision*, Journal of Land and Public Utility Economics, February 1936) and anticipated by King and Leven in 1924 (*Population Growth and Building*, Journal of American Statistical Association, Vol. XIX, 1924) and the Federal Trade Commission in its report, *The National Wealth and Income* (1926), p. 368.*

[6] *Other factors that led to the abandonment of the use of per capita rates (except for 1935 and 1936 when there is practically no alternative) were: (1) any per capita building rate computed on the basis of total population in a city or other area at a given time is essentially an average of new building related to "old" population. It assumes, and imposes on the figures, a relationship that does not exist except indirectly, since over a period of years dwelling units equal to 85 to 90 per cent of all residential building have been required to house the increase in population, with only 10 to 15 per cent to replace losses of dwellings occupied by the "old" population and maintained a supply of vacant units. Consequently per capita building rates applied to the population in unreported areas produce erroneous results unless adjusted for differences in the rates of growth of the reporting cities and unreported areas. (2) The use of per capita rates usually involves averaging rates for a group of cities having an extremely wide dispersion about the mean, overweighting the rates for the most rapidly growing cities since they account for most of the construction within the group. (3) Population growth is only an indirect and not always accurate measure of the increase in the number of families, which is the more direct measure of housing requirements over a period of years. A given increase in population may mean an 8 to 10 per cent greater increase in the number of families in large cities than in rural areas, owing to the difference in the rate of decline in the average size of family. In certain regions, as the Pacific Coast, the number of families increased 14 per cent more than population while in some southern states it increased only 2 to 5 per cent more than population, 1920–30.*

[7] *This is application in more detail of the method developed by George Terborgh, to whom acknowledgment is due for many helpful suggestions during the progress of this study.*

construction of 1,494,000 dwelling units over the increase in the number of families is accounted for, therefore, by the 1,039,000 increase in vacancy, plus 580,000 dwellings constructed to replace those demolished or destroyed, less 125,000 units added by conversions.[8]

Certain important differences among population groups are to be considered in measuring their rates of new construction. The ratio of units built to the increase in the number of families, which was 1.27 for the entire nonfarm area, is higher for large cities than for small towns for several reasons: (a) The additional building required to maintain a "normal" vacancy tends to be relatively greater in large cities, mainly because of the many apartments, in which vacancies ordinarily average much higher than in 1-family dwellings which predominate in small communities. During 1920–30 the percentage increase in vacancy was greater in apartments than in other types. (b) Building to replace dwellings demolished because of the encroachment of business on residential sections, physical deterioration, or other causes is proportionately greater in large cities. In a new residential area outside city limits building to replace demolitions would be virtually nil, and new construction would usually be in the proportion of one unit to each family moving into the area, since in most instances the family's moving would depend upon the completion of a dwelling unit to accommodate it. (c) The majority of the largest cities, except Los Angeles, Detroit, and Queens and Bronx Boroughs in New York City, have been growing more slowly than smaller cities; consequently building on account of demolitions and vacancy change in large cities would be greater relative to the absolute increase in the number of families.[9]

The differences in the ratios of units built to the increase in the number of families as found in the 1920–29 data for the various classes of the 257 cities are: 113 central cities in metropolitan districts, 1.415; 64 satellite cities in metropolitan districts, 1.279; 80 nonmetropolitan cities, 1.182.

c Special Problems in Adjusting the Primary Data

As an aid in describing in detail the method of using these ratios (Table EM 2) to estimate building in unreported areas, the steps involved in assembling the basic data on families in all areas and on building in the reporting cities are presented below.[10]

[8] *See Tables EM 12 and 13 for the details mentioned above.*

[9] *This would be true of any city, regardless of size, having a low rate of growth. At some future date, if the number of families reaches a maximum and the net increase becomes zero, the present method will no longer be applicable. Building will then be primarily to replace losses and to accommodate intraregional migration.*

1) Basic population and family data

Estimates by population groups were of particular significance in considering the construction work of the period covered, since, as stated in Part One, the latest building boom was predominantly in metropolitan districts. However, this detailed treatment of population groups and geographic divisions introduces several difficulties. Since Census data on families in metropolitan districts are provided for neither 1920 or 1930, the distribution of urban families between metropolitan districts and the areas outside was estimated from Census data on population. The overlapping of some metropolitan districts across regional boundaries made it necessary to adjust the number of families in each geographic division to correspond to the population. Also, the metropolitan districts as defined by the Census include many towns and villages under 2,500 and unincorporated areas usually classified by the Census as rural. From the standpoint of building, these small places in environs of metropolitan districts are essentially urban in character, since their activities are strongly influenced by the larger centers of which they are a part. To obtain the population of these "rural" environs the population in both 1920 and 1930 of all satellite cities over 2,500 in each region [11] was subtracted from the total population in environs. Since the population in "rural" environs was considered urban in this study, total urban population is correspondingly increased and the other rural nonfarm population is less than that shown by the Census (see Table EM 1). The number of families was distributed, as between urban and rural environs, on the basis of population in each region.

Part of the increase in urban population and in the number of urban families, 1920–30, was due to the classification of some towns as urban in 1930 that in 1920 had a population less than 2,500 and were then classified as rural nonfarm. Furthermore, the 1930 Census modified the definition of urban areas as applied to some towns in the New England and Middle Atlantic states and in California.[12] In all these instances comparability was established by the use of the 139 city special tabulation which gave the estimated urban population in identical areas in 1920, by states

[10] *Throughout this discussion reference is made to the "number of families" and "ratios of building to the increase in the number of families." This is largely a matter of convenience, since the family data are actually used as measures of the number of occupied dwelling units rather than the number of married couples or families as social units.*

[11] *This was made possible by a special tabulation of population in 1920 and 1930 of the 2,798 cities with populations from 2,500 to 25,000, segregated by satellite and nonsatellite cities, and by regions, prepared by the Division of Construction and Public Employment, Bureau of Labor Statistics. Corresponding data for cities 25,000 and over were tabulated by the National Bureau of Economic Research.*

[12] Census of Population, 1930, I, 7.

and regions, based on the 1930 classification. It was assumed that any shift in the total nonfarm population from farm to nonfarm classification, or vice versa, would be negligible.

The 1930 Census data on families were first adjusted to include quasi-families living in hotels, clubs, and institutions to make them comparable with population figures, as well as with the 1920 family data; then the 1920–30 increase was corrected to a "private family" basis, since the estimates of building are for number of housekeeping units alone.

Corresponding data on the increase in the number of families in the 257 Bureau of Labor Statistics cities were assembled in a table which is summarized in Table EM 2, column 1, for reporting cities. In 121 of these cities a part of the increase was due to the annexation of territory between 1920 and 1930, which increased the area and population reported by the Census as within the city limits, and consequently changed the coverage of the Bureau of Labor Statistics permit data. The total population involved in annexations during the decade amounted to 3 per cent of the 1930 population of the 257 cities, though in some cities annexations caused as much as a 20 or 30 per cent increase.

Since the area and population involved in annexations to cities between 1930 and 1936 were negligible except in a few cities, 1930 was taken as a base; the adjustment for annexations was made by estimating the 1920 population in territory annexed during 1920–30 from data on population in counties outside the cities in question, and adding this estimated annexed population to the population enumerated in 1920 for the 1920 areas. As published by the Bureau of the Census, annexation data cover only a few of the annexations occurring between Census dates and are in terms of population rather than families. Special tabulations, prepared by the Bureau of the Census from unpublished data on population in annexed areas,[13] made possible their conversion to a family basis on the assumption that the same proportionate changes occurred in the number of families.

Building in reporting cities was estimated from a tabulation[14] of Bureau of Labor Statistics data on the number of families provided for in each of the 257 cities annually during 1920–36. "Families provided for" include total family dwelling units in 1- and 2-family dwellings and apartments, also dwellings and apartments with stores, for which building permits are granted. Since in 1920 family dwelling unit data were incomplete in 22 cities and were not available in 66 of the smaller cities, part of the number of units built had to be estimated. The units thus estimated amounted to

12.8 per cent of the combined total of reported and estimated units for 1920, but only 0.4 per cent of the total for 1920–29, hence any error introduced by these estimates would be negligible relatively to the ten-year total, except possibly in a few cities. Ten-year subtotals of the "families provided for" were obtained for the cities grouped within each geographic division as: (a) central, (b) satellite, (c) nonmetropolitan.

Seven of the 120 central cities were not included by the Bureau of Labor Statistics in the 257 city series because reports for them were lacking in one year or more. For these cities estimates were made for the few missing years, thus giving complete data for all 120 central cities for the entire period.

Estimates of "families provided for" in the 7 cities were made as follows: Johnstown, Pennsylvania (1925), Reading, Pennsylvania (1921), Evansville, Indiana (1920), based on data for adjacent years; Miami and Tampa, Florida (1920–21), based on Bradstreet's total building permit data; St. Petersburg, Florida (1920–25), based on the trend for Tampa, the other central city in the same metropolitan district; and Ashland, Kentucky (1920–31), based on data for Huntington, West Virginia. The units thus estimated amounted to 17.6 per cent of the 17-year total for the 7 cities but only 0.3 per cent of the total for all 120 cities. The chief advantage of adding data for these 7 cities to the basic 257 city series is the representation given the cities prominent in the Florida boom. Jacksonville, the only Florida city among the 257 cities, was not representative.

In the cities in which annexations increased the coverage of the building permit series as discussed above, the number of families provided for reported by building permits was increased in each year affected in proportion to the population, which had been raised to include the current population of areas annexed after 1920.[15] The greatest percentage correction was in 1920 when absolute volume was low, the correction gradually declining to zero by 1930. The net effect for the 264 cities, including the additional 7 central cities, was an increase of 2.7 per cent in the number of families provided for in 1920 and 1.4 per cent in 1920–29. Though a correction for this amount would have been of minor importance in the estimate for the country as a whole, it was a significant factor in individual regions, particularly in the South. The figures for the three northeastern regions and the Pacific coast required virtually no correction.

2) *Correction for lapsed permits and underreporting*
The other principal adjustment to the building data in reporting cities was for lapsed permits. An inquiry ad-

---

[13] *Portions of these data had been made available previously through the courtesy of F. J. Hallauer.*

[14] *Too voluminous to be included.*

[15] *This correction is probably conservative since higher building rates could be expected in the annexed territory because of their more rapid rate of growth generally.*

dressed to building officials in 30 large cities brought replies from 22 [16] which disclosed that, both before and after 1929, except in two cities, very few residential permits were allowed to lapse, averaging less than 2 or 3 per cent in most cities.[17] Philadelphia and New York City were the exceptions, and for these cities the records are such that correction can be made. In certain years proposed changes in building codes and tax laws affecting apartment buildings in both cities caused a large number of permits to be taken out that were not acted upon, notably in 1929 in Philadelphia, and in 1923 and 1929 in New York City. The figures on number and cost of buildings for New York City in the building permit series are for "plans filed" which indicate a larger volume of building than in permits granted or buildings actually completed, not only in 1923 and 1929 but also in nearly all years. On the basis of data on apartments completed, obtainable over a period of years from the annual reports of the New York City Tenement House Department,[18] the New York City figures were corrected to eliminate the apartment units for which plans were filed but that were not actually built. In order to keep the figures comparable, a 6-month time lag was allowed between the series for plans filed and buildings completed, based on the above-mentioned Bureau of Labor Statistics study and on a comparison of the timing of the curves for plans filed and apartments completed in New York City, 1918–36. The correction to the New York City data for 1920–29 amounted to over 97,000 apartment units, or nearly 18 per cent of all apartments and 10 per cent of all dwelling units built in New York City, as reported by the Bureau of Labor Statistics. The correction for the 257 cities amounted to 6 per cent of total apartments built and nearly 3 per cent of all dwelling units built. In some years the correction was sufficient to modify the trend for the 257 cities; for example, published data on dwelling units built in the 257 cities show a decline from 1923 to 1924, while the corrected figures show a continued uptrend.[19]

Lapsed permits in Philadelphia were not similarly corrected because the data were not received until after the basic tabulations on dwelling units had been made, and a correction was not warranted, most lapses occurring in 1929. The units involved constituted less than 2 per cent of the total for all reporting cities in the Middle Atlantic division, and less than 0.7 per cent of the total for the 120 central cities in 1929, the totals that would be affected in the present estimates.

Offsetting the tendency of building permits in some cities to overstate actual building, because of the inclusion of some permits that are allowed to lapse, there appears to be a tendency in some cities to underreport actual construction. For example, a study of construction during the 15-year period 1919–33 in 46 of the 64 Real Property Inventory cities showed that the units reported by the Bureau of Labor Statistics permit data [20] were 10 per cent fewer than those estimated by this project from Real Property Inventory data.

The apparent underreporting may arise in some instances from local building regulations which require permits only in fire zones rather than in the entire area within city limits, or because permit regulations are not fully enforced. The 46 cities provide only a small sample on which to draw conclusions concerning possible underreporting in all cities. On the other hand, the data on lapsed permits are not a satisfactory basis for correcting for lapsed permits annually over a period of years. Consequently, Bureau of Labor Statistics figures on dwelling units, other than those for apartments in New York City, were not corrected. There is, accordingly, still some uncertainty in the figures, with respect to both lapsed permits and underreporting. Any corrections for these two items for the country as a whole would tend to offset one another.

2 Dwelling Units Built, 10-Year Aggregate, 1920–1929
The basic data on families and construction assembled, ratios were computed showing the relation of aggregate dwelling units built during 1920–29 to the increase in the number of families (occupied units) in reporting cities. These ratios, with certain modifications, were then applied to the increase in the number of families in unreported areas. The complete table of these computations in detail for all nine geographic divisions is not presented, because of its size, but the United States totals are summarized by classes of cities in Table EM 2. Table EM 3 gives the ratios as derived for the reporting cities, by geographic division, and as applied in estimating building in the unreported areas. These two summary tables illustrate the method and range of estimate.

a Use of Ratios of Dwelling Units Built to Increase in Number of Families
The highest ratio in Table EM 3 is 1.955, for the group of 13 reporting central cities in New England, which

---

[16] *Having an aggregate population of 22 million in 1930 and accounting for one-half of the total building reported in the 257 cities.*

[17] *This is in accord with the study of lapsed permits in 10 large cities in 1929 and 1931 made by the Bureau of Labor Statistics (Monthly Labor Review, Jan. 1933).*

[18] *Acknowledgment is due James Taylor of the Federal Housing Administration for suggestions concerning use of these data.*

[19] *Data on the completion of other types of dwellings, including 1- and 2-family dwellings, hotels, and lodging houses, are also obtainable for the five boroughs of New York City separately in the Bureau of Building records of each borough, but they are not uniform in items covered in the different boroughs, and as the completeness of coverage is in doubt they were not used.*

[20] *Units in 1919 estimated on the basis of U. S. Geological Survey building permit data.*

TABLE EM 2

Dwelling Units Built, Estimated Aggregate, 1920–1929, Summary by Class of City

	INCREASE IN NUMBER OF FAMILIES (THOUSANDS)			RATIO OF UNITS BUILT TO INCREASE IN NUMBER OF FAMILIES			DWELLING UNITS BUILT (THOUSANDS)		
	Reporting cities (1)	Unreported areas (2)	Total (3)	Reporting cities (4) = (7)÷(1)	Unreported areas (5)	Total (6) = (9)÷(3)	Reporting cities (7)	Unreported areas (8) = (2)×(5)	Total (9) = (7)+(8)
96 Metropolitan districts	2,440	1,356	3,744	1.401	1.185	1.326	3,419	1,546	4,965
120 Central cities	2,192	..	2,192	1.415	..	1.415	3,102	..	3,102
Urban environs	248	768	1,016	1.279	1.211	1.227	317	930	1,247
Rural environs	..	536	536	..	1.148	1.148	..	616	616
Total environs	248	1,304	1,552	1.279	1.185	1.200	317	1,546	1,863
Nonmetropolitan cities	160	927	1,087	1.182	1.163	1.166	190	1,077	1,267
Total urban	2,600	2,231	4,831	1.388	1.176	1.290	3,609	2,623	6,232
Rural nonfarm	..	710	710	..	1.132	1.132	..	803	803
Total nonfarm	2,600	2,941	5,541	1.388	1.165	1.270	3,609	3,426	7,035

had the lowest percentage increase in the number of families between 1920 and 1930, and which had building on account of vacancy changes and to replace losses nearly equal to that needed to house the increment in the number of families. The lowest ratio was 1.007, the average for the 9 reporting central cities in the West South Central area. Building to replace losses would be a relatively small portion of total construction in these new, rapidly growing cities, since the aggregate number of families in the 9 cities increased 57 per cent between 1920 and 1930, and the change in vacancy was probably small, possibly decreasing in some cities affected by the oil boom in the late 1920's.

TABLE EM 3

Ratio of Dwelling Units Built to Increase in Number of Families, by Geographic Division, 1920–1929

	REPORTING CITIES			UNREPORTED AREAS			
	113 central (1)	64 satellite (2)	80 Non-met. dist. (3)	Urban environs (4)	Rural environs (5)	Non-met. urban (6)	Rural nonfarm (7)
Total	1.415	1.279	1.182	1.211	1.148	1.163	1.132
New England	1.955	1.252	1.304	1.252	1.149	1.222	1.144
Mid. Atlantic	1.687	1.544	1.023	1.283	1.168	1.017	1.138
E. N. Central	1.266	1.059	1.093	1.059	1.035	1.068	1.042
W. N. Central	1.468	..	1.073	1.279	1.165	1.053	1.078
S. Atlantic	1.559	..	1.395	1.477	1.283	1.289	1.196
E. S. Central	1.173	..	1.350	1.173	1.103	1.256	1.146
W. S. Central	1.007	..	1.257	1.007	1.004	1.188	1.106
Mountain	1.379	..	1.231	1.305	1.181	1.169	1.116
Pacific	1.260	1.257	1.778	1.257	1.152	1.133	1.125

Because of the completeness of reporting in the larger cities it was not necessary to use the high ratios in Table EM 3, columns 1, 2, and 3. The highest ratio actually applied was 1.477 in the environs of South Atlantic central cities, but the building to be estimated there was relatively small. The major portion of building in unreported areas was estimated on the basis of ratios under 1.200 and approaching 1.000, the equivalent of one dwelling unit for each additional family.

In determining the increase in the number of fami-

lies in the unreported areas, the ratios for the most appropriate population groups were used as follows:

1) Urban environs

For the New England, East North Central, and Pacific divisions the same ratios were used as for reporting satellite cities; for the Middle Atlantic, average ratios for reporting satellite and nonmetropolitan urban cities; for the West North Central, South Atlantic, and Mountain, average ratios of reporting central and nonmetropolitan urban cities, there being no reporting satellite cities in these areas; for the East and West South Central, the same ratios as for central cities, since little building had to be estimated.

2) Rural environs and rural nonfarm areas

An estimate of the distribution, by population group, for the country as a whole indicates average ratios of dwelling units built to the increase in the number of families as follows: rural environs, 1.125; all nonmetropolitan cities, 1.166; rural nonfarm, 1.110. Owing to the limitations of the data on vacancies, demolitions, and conversions, it was not feasible to estimate the ratios directly by geographic divisions, but using each of the above United States figures as a base, the ratios for unreported areas were assigned in the several divisions in the same proportions as previously found for areas most nearly corresponding to the unreported areas. For example, ratios for the rural environs were assumed to have the same divisional patterns in relation to the United States average of 1.125 indicated above as had been derived for the unreported urban environs. When the ratios were applied to the increase in the number of families in the rural environs in each division the resulting ratio for all rural environs was 1.148 rather than 1.125, because the divisional distribution of families in the rural environs was different from that in the urban environs, from which the ratios had originally been derived. Similarly, ratios for rural nonfarm areas were assigned the divisional pattern that had been derived for unreported urban areas, and the resulting weighted average in Table EM 2 was 1.132 instead of 1.110.

3) Nonmetropolitan urban

For nonmetropolitan urban areas the same divisional pattern of ratios was used as for reporting nonmetropolitan cities, except in the Pacific region, where the sample consisted of only one city, Stockton, California, which was not considered representative. The unweighted United States average for unreported nonmetropolitan cities was therefore applied to the Pacific division. The weighted average, derived after application of these ratios in all divisions, was 1.163, which, combined with 1.182 for reporting cities, results in the estimated ratio of 1.166 for all nonmetropolitan cities.

3 Dwelling Units Built Annually, 1920–1936

After the dwelling units built during 1920–29 had been established (Table EM 2) those built each year were estimated (Table EM 10). Preliminary annual totals were first projected from the data for reporting cities,[21] by applying relationships shown in Table EM 2 to 1930–36 as well as to 1920–29 (discussed under a below). Then the entire series for 1920–36 was corrected for the downward bias in the 257 city series (discussed under b below).

a Preliminary Totals, Uncorrected for Bias

Units built in the 120 central cities, comprising those reported for 113 central cities and those (partly estimated) for the 7 central cities are given in Table EM 10, lines 1 and 2. Total building in the environs was derived by averaging two estimates made as follows: The first was an expansion to full coverage based on the trend of the 64 satellite cities (line 5, Table EM 10) by multiplying the dwelling units reported to have been built in the 64 cities each year by 5.875.[22] The second estimate followed the trend of building in all 184 of the reporting cities, which was applied to both central and satellite cities in metropolitan districts and established the multiplier, 0.545.[23] This procedure was evolved as the most satisfactory compromise of several methods tested, including attempts to estimate for separate metropolitan districts and groups of metropolitan districts within geographic divisions. If the trend of building in the environs were assumed to follow the trend in the 64 reporting cities, a trend that is dominated by reporting cities in the environs of Boston and

New York would be imposed on environs in some of the southern and western metropolitan districts. Furthermore, building in the 64 cities constituted less than one-sixth of building in all the environs; therefore, the year-to-year changes cannot be assumed to be satisfactorily representative. In the South and West the central cities constitute the only representation in the metropolitan districts.

Building in urban and rural environs was estimated as 0.669 and 0.331 respectively of the total for all environs (Table EM 2).

Building in nonmetropolitan urban areas was estimated on the basis of the 80 reporting cities (Table EM 10, lines 11–12). Estimated total urban building is shown in line 16. The trend of building in rural nonfarm areas was derived by averaging two estimates based on: (a) the 80 nonmetropolitan cities; (b) total urban building. The sum of the urban and rural nonfarm estimates obtained above gives tentative nonfarm totals in line 20.

The use of the above method involves the assumption that building outside reporting cities follows the trend of building within the cities, year by year. The assumption is not valid if the trend of all the reporting cities combined is applied directly to the entire unreported nonfarm area as a unit, because of the downward bias of the 257 city series, as will be shown later. Likewise the year-to-year trend of building outside some individual cities may differ considerably from that within. However, for groups of cities within reasonably large areas such as metropolitan districts, building in the environs follows that in the central city quite closely. For example, the year-to-year building trends in the 14 reporting satellite cities in the Boston metropolitan district taken individually had apparently little relation to one another or to the trend in Boston from 1920 to 1936, but the combined annual totals of the 14 cities, representing a sizeable sample of the environs, followed the trend for Boston. Similarly, in the environs of Providence, New York City, and Philadelphia, the trend for each group of reporting satellite cities conformed in general to that of its central city. Because the sample of reporting cities was small, comparisons in other metropolitan districts are less conclusive.

Similar relationships are evident in new residential construction in 31 metropolitan districts as shown in the 1934 Real Property Inventory of 64 cities; also, cities that have much the same general economic conditions and rates of growth have similar building trends even though they are in different states. Thus the tentative assumption that building in unreported areas followed the trend of reporting cities seems to be applicable to areas that are homogeneous with respect to the factors influencing building. For these reasons, the estimates of year-to-year trends, made by metro-

---

[21] Corrected for change in coverage due to annexations, for lapsed permits on apartments in New York City, and including data (partly estimated) for 7 central cities not among the 257 cities.

[22] Relation of units built in all environs to units built in 64 reporting cities, 1920–29, as shown in Table EM 2 (1,862,941 ÷ 317,117 = 5.875).

[23] Relation of units built in all environs to units built in 184 reporting cities (1,862,941 ÷ 3,418,921 = 0.545).

politan and nonmetropolitan areas, probably give more accurate results than if made by regions.

b Correction for Bias

The preliminary totals of dwelling units built (Table EM 10, lines 1–20) were corrected in lines 22–34 for the downward bias in the 257 city series. Evidence of this bias is given by estimates of total nonfarm building based on the larger sample of cities in 1935 and 1936 (Tables EM 14 and 15), which show that all non-farm building increased to about 2.5 times that for the 257 cities during the depression, in contrast to an average of about twice during 1920–29. This bias continued throughout the 17 years, though it was much less prior to 1928–29, as indicated by data for 31 metropolitan districts included in the Real Property Inventory of 64 cities. The percentage corrections are smallest in the years of greatest activity in the middle 1920's, and most pronounced during the depression when absolute volume was low.

The preliminary totals of nonfarm units built (Table EM 10, line 20) were multiplied by the factors in line 22, derived from the sources mentioned in the preceding paragraph, to obtain the corrected nonfarm totals in line 23, except in 1935 and 1936 when the estimates based on 811 and 1,689 cities were used (Tables EM 14 and 15). Since the central cities were covered almost completely by the permit reports, their estimated building would not be affected, but the estimates for building in the areas outside them required adjustment so that the total would equal line 23. These steps are indicated in lines 27–34. In the absence of conclusive evidence to the contrary, it was assumed that the adjustment for each year applied equally to all the areas outside the central cities for 1920–30, but additional adjustments were made for 1931–36. Comparison of the estimate for 1936 (Table EM 15) with that based on 257 cities indicated that the process used in the latter produced virtually the same number of units in the total environs as the former, but tended to overestimate for the urban environs by 8½ per cent, and consequently to underestimate for the rural environs; therefore a correction was applied to the estimates for urban environs based on the 257 cities, graduated from zero in 1930 to 7 per cent in 1935. Similarly, the estimates based on 257 cities would have overestimated building in the nonmetropolitan cities 15½ per cent in 1936; hence a graduated correction was applied, ranging from zero in 1930 to 12½ per cent in 1935. Thus lines 26–34, Table EM 10, present estimates of building annually in five segments of the nonfarm areas that reflect the separate trends of subgroups of the 257 cities, yet correct for the tendency of building to shift outward from the large cities.[24]

[24] See Note B for comparisons with other estimates.

c Comparison of Estimated Trend with Shipments of Materials

To check the trend of nonfarm residential units built, as estimated above, comparisons were made with other available indexes of the physical volume of residential building, including shipments of bathtubs, lavatories, and kitchen sinks (Table EM 4). Although comparison of relative volumes is not clear-cut because of the considerable number of bathtubs, sinks, and lavatories going into replacements and the modernization of old buildings in cities, as well as into farm dwellings, shipments seem to confirm the trend of nonfarm units built.

TABLE EM 4

Dwelling Units Built, and Factory Shipments of Baths, Lavatories, Kitchen Sinks, and Radiators, 1920–1936

	DWELLING UNITS BUILT [1] (thousands)	FACTORY SHIPMENTS [2]			
		BATHS	LAVA-TORIES	KITCHEN SINKS	RADIATORS (millions of sq. ft. of heating surface)
		(thousands of pieces)			
1920	247	617	617	723	..
1921	449	498	698	797	..
1922	716	898	1,098	1,144	..
1923	871	1,085	1,326	1,370	143
1924	893	1,148	1,323	1,445	148
1925	937	1,326	1,528	1,551	165
1926	849	1,195	1,365	1,364	172
1927	810	1,133	1,253	1,315	162
1928	753	1,117	1,266	1,318	161
1929	509	938	1,118	1,159	127
1930	286	592	743	760	86
1931	212	461	550	565	79
1932	74	(series discontinued)			45
1933	54				39
1934	55				50
1935	144				58
1936	282				78

[1] From Table EM 10, line 34.
[2] Survey of Current Business.

Shipments of radiators (Table EM 4) differ in trend from all nonfarm units built because of the relatively larger number of radiators used in apartments and hotels as well as in office buildings, schools, and other non-residential structures, than in small dwellings. Radiator shipments reached a peak in 1926 and remained at high levels in 1927 and 1928, showing a trend not unlike that in apartment building, which reached a maximum later than 1- and 2-family dwellings.

Shipments of other materials used largely, but not exclusively, in residential building, such as lumber, common brick, lime, plaster, lath, and shingles, confirm the general pattern of estimated dwelling units built. Though less conclusive for year-to-year comparisons, the general trend is the same in biennial figures on production of window glass, putty, fillers, and sewer pipe.

d Method of Estimating Dwelling Units Built, by Geographic Division

Estimates for different geographic divisions were obtained by different methods. In the New England, North Central, and South Central divisions preliminary totals of nonfarm units built each year were estimated in one process by raising the number of units built in the reporting cities of the 257 city series in each geographic division in the same proportions as indicated for 1920–29 in the detailed tables from which the United States summary (Table EM 2) was derived. In the Middle Atlantic division separate estimates were made for environs, nonmetropolitan cities, and rural nonfarm areas, based on the corresponding groups of reporting cities, but excluding New York City. In the South Atlantic and Mountain regions separate estimates were also made by population group in order to give the sample of nonmetropolitan cities proper weighting. In the Pacific division estimates for unreported areas were based on the 14 reporting cities, excluding Los Angeles; inclusion of Los Angeles would have given a disproportionate weighting. The entire series of estimates was then corrected for the downward bias of the 257 cities,[25] so that the resulting United States totals matched those previously derived in Table EM 10. This procedure assumes that the correction for bias is approximately the same for all regions, since data on which to base corrections for each region, with any degree of certainty, are insufficient.

e Dwelling Units Built, by Type of Dwelling

The units of each type of dwelling (apartments, 1- and 2-family dwellings) built each year were calculated in the same general manner as the total of all units as described above. First, aggregate units of each type built during 1920–29 in each population group were estimated on the basis of the 257 reporting cities and Census data on dwellings in 1930. The 2-family dwelling and apartment units built each year were then distributed according to the trends of these types in the 257 reporting cities, which included a large portion of the total building of these types. The difference between the total of 2-family and apartment units thus obtained and the nonfarm total of all units built each year as previously estimated in Table EM 10 gave 1-family dwellings. The 1-family dwelling classification includes not only detached 1-family houses but also dwelling units in row houses, the two types not being reported separately in the basic building permit data.

Estimates of dwelling units of various types built since 1920, by years, are summarized in Table E 1, section A. They are confined to nonfarm totals for each type: 1-, 2-, and 3-or-more-family (apartment) dwellings. Separate estimates on an annual basis for geo-

[25] Table showing these computations omitted; see Part Three, Table E 1, sec. C.

graphic divisions or for metropolitan and nonmetropolitan areas within divisions were not attempted, owing to the extensive tabulations necessary.

Aggregate units of each type built during 1921–30[26] were obtained as follows: The 10-year totals of 2-family and apartment units built in (a) 113 central cities, (b) 64 satellite cities, (c) 80 nonmetropolitan cities were estimated by means of the basic tabulations for all units built and a special study of 1-family dwellings built in the 257 cities. Subtracting 1-family units from total units built gave a combined total for 2- and 3-family dwellings. The proportion of units in each type was estimated in accordance with the totals for the two types as reported in the 257 cities.[27] Then the 2- and 3-or-more family units built were estimated for each unreported area: (a) 7 central cities, (b) environs, (c) nonmetropolitan urban, (d) rural nonfarm, by means of the percentage distribution of units by type, derived from the 1930 Census data on dwellings in different population groups and described in Chapter I. The percentage distribution thus obtained of all nonfarm units built, by type, 1921–30, was applied to the 1920–29 aggregate of 7,035,473 units built as derived in Table EM 10, resulting in the accompanying estimates.

	DISTRIBUTION (Per Cent)	DWELLING UNITS (Number)
All types	100.0	7,035,473
1-family dwellings	60.7	4,270,532
2-family dwellings	15.5	1,090,498
Apartments	23.8	1,674,443

The 257 cities reported 38, 55, and 77 per cent respectively of the estimated nonfarm totals of 1-, 2-, and 3-or-more family dwelling units for 1920–29. Because of the dominance of the 257 cities it was assumed that the annual trend of the nonfarm totals of the 2-family and apartment units would follow the respective trends for the 257 cities, and that this would apply during 1930–36 as well as 1920–29. Consequently an index of the 2-family units built in the 257 cities was computed with the 1920–29 average as 100 and applied to the ten-year average of all nonfarm 2-family dwelling units. A similar procedure was followed for apartments. An additional adjustment was made in the indexes for 2-family dwellings and for apartments, 1931–36, based on: (a) Bureau of Labor Statistics estimates of dwelling units provided in urban areas during 1936 by type of dwelling and de-

[26] The period 1921–30 was used instead of 1920–29 because detailed data by type of dwelling for 1920 are few; aggregate units and proportions by type are virtually the same for both periods.

[27] Since the 113 central cities accounted for 89 per cent of all 2-family and apartment units built in the 257 cities, the proportions would be virtually the same for both groups of cities.

rived from building permit reports from 1,689 places over 2,500 in population (press release, February 19, 1938); (b) the relation of total 2-family and apartment dwelling units standing in 1930 in nonfarm and urban areas, developed in connection with the estimates on aggregate values and rents in 1930 (Ch. II); (c) the shifts between 1930 and 1936 in the proportions that 2-family and apartment dwelling units were of the total units provided in the 257 cities. Estimates of the nonfarm totals of 2-family and apartment dwelling units provided in 1936 were then revised on the basis of these adjusted indexes. They resulted in estimates somewhat higher for 2-family dwellings and lower for apartments than the estimates based on the 257 city series alone. The indexes for these two types of dwellings were then adjusted to the revised 1936 level, with corrections each year graduated from the full correction in 1936 to zero in 1930. Subtracting the sum of the 2-family and apartment units built each year from total nonfarm units of all three types built, previously estimated in Table EM 10, gave the number of 1-family units built. The results of these estimates are summarized in Table E 1, section A.

4 New Dwelling Units Built, Estimated Value

The value of new nonfarm dwelling units built annually since 1920 was estimated (Table EM 11) by applying average costs per dwelling unit to the corresponding number of dwelling units built (Table EM 10). The derivation of the average costs per unit is described below.

a Unit Costs

A special study on unit costs of 1-family dwellings built in the 257 cities showed marked differences in satellite and nonmetropolitan cities (Part Three Table E 7). The regional differences were even wider, costs in the northeastern states averaging nearly double those in the South. Because the sample was small, however, it was not feasible to estimate cost of residential building by regions without considerable further study of the distribution of the number of units by type of dwelling in each region.

b Basic Data on Unit Costs, Building Permits

Table EM 11, lines 35–39 show basic data on unit costs as derived from the Bureau of Labor Statistics data for 257 cities, while lines 40–42, 45, and 47 show these data after correction for undervaluation of permits and as used in estimating cost of dwellings in urban areas.[28]

The unit costs for the reporting 113 central and 64 satellite cities (lines 36 and 37) are composite averages for all housekeeping units, including 1-, 2-, and

[28] *Table EM 11, and the line numbering, is a continuation of Table EM 10.*

3-or-more family dwellings, derived by substracting the value of nonhousekeeping dwellings from the value of all new residential building as published by the Bureau of Labor Statistics and dividing by the number of families provided for. In the central cities this average is usually lower than the average for 1-family dwellings in Table E 7, because of the large number of apartments and 2-family dwellings which average lower in cost per unit than 1-family dwellings. Line 39 shows the unit costs for 1-family dwellings alone in the 80 nonmetropolitan cities as derived in the special study of average costs of 1-family dwellings. Since most of the nonmetropolitan cities for which building must be estimated are in the 2,500–25,000 population group, in which 1-family dwellings predominate, the 1-family average unit cost is more representative than a composite average including apartments.

c Adjustment for Undervaluation

Each series (Table EM 11, lines 35, 37, and 39) was increased 18 per cent as a tentative correction for undervaluation of permits. This adjustment is based on several sets of data, all of which indicate that average values of permits were understated. Such comparisons as can be made with the F. W. Dodge Corporation data on contracts awarded support the reasonableness of the 18 per cent correction.

Among the evidence used to correct permit valuations is that given in a release entitled "Construction Statistics Analyzed: Permit Records and Contract Records Compared," dated July 20, 1936, in which the F. W. Dodge Corporation discuss undervaluation in building permits, stating in part:

"Permit valuations are generally recorded considerably below actual cost, for the following reasons:
1. Applicants expect tax assessments to be based upon permit valuations given.
2. In many cases, permit fees are charged in proportion to valuation given in the application.
3. In some places, costs of heating, plumbing, and wiring are not included.

In one of the largest cities of the country, projects are very generally undervalued one-third for purposes of the permit record. The degree of undervaluation varies from place to place. Here are some actual instances, reported by Dodge field men who interviewed building department heads:

3 cities	30 per cent undervalued
1 city	30 per cent to 40 per cent undervalued
2 cities	30 per cent undervalued
2 cities	25 per cent undervalued
2 cities	15 per cent to 20 per cent undervalued."

In many large cities permit valuations are rather carefully checked against architects' estimates of current

costs for finished structures of similar type on a square or cubic foot basis. Significant undervaluations in such cities would be the exception rather than the rule.

A comparison of permit valuations and loan appraisal values of 255 residential structures built in Minneapolis, 1922–32, indicated an undervaluation in permits of approximately one-third.[29] However, the appraised loan values, reflecting the selling price of the dwelling to the purchaser, may include items other than the actual cost of construction, which would reduce the permit undervaluation.

In contrast to these indications of undervaluation of permits, it is possible that in boom times some speculative builders overstate valuation in permit applications in order to cite these "official" records as sales arguments.

If these instances are typical for the country as a whole, unit costs reported in permit data evidently cannot be taken as accurate measures of value, since they tend toward understatement. However, despite their limitations, the building permit cost data proved to be a more homogeneous and usable series than contracts awarded, as discussed in more detail in Note A.

Any correction for undervaluation of permits should possibly be less in recent years because of the increasing strictness of permit regulations and checking of permit values. In the absence of specific data on which to base such graduated correction, the 18 per cent was applied throughout the period.

Another difficulty in using average unit costs derived from building permits is that they are at times distorted by the inclusion of a few very expensive dwellings, as became apparent in the course of the special study on 1-family dwelling unit costs.[30] However, in the absence of data on the actual dispersion of unit costs about the average in the unreported areas, it is difficult to state what correction, if any, is necessary. To the extent that the derived average costs are too high to apply to dwellings built in the unreported areas, they tend to offset any undervaluation in permits. This was one factor in limiting the correction for undervaluation to 18 per cent rather than using the 25–40 per cent indicated as necessary by other data cited above.

An additional correction must be made for the 64 satellite and 80 nonmetropolitan cities, because the unit costs derived for these groups of cities—all of which have populations of more than 25,000—are not representative of the corresponding unreported areas,

which include many smaller places. The average for the 64 cities was increased 5 per cent to approximate the average for all urban environs, while the 80 city average was decreased 18 per cent because of the large number of low priced units built in the nonmetropolitan areas with populations between 2,500 and 25,000. The need for such adjustment was demonstrated by comparison of averages for the 64 satellite and 80 nonmetropolitan areas with data for the 1,689 cities reporting permits in 1936, from which the average cost per dwelling unit, all types, by population group, was derived.[31]

	NO. OF REPORTING CITIES	AVG. COST PER DWELLING UNIT
All reporting cities	1,689	$4,048
Central	120	3,992
Satellite	613	5,467
Nonmetropolitan	956	2,965

The average for all 1,689 cities obscures the very marked differences between average costs in the environs of metropolitan centers and in nonmetropolitan areas. Furthermore, the average of $5,467 per unit for the 613 satellite cities reporting in 1936 is 5 per cent higher than the corresponding 1936 average for the 64 satellite cities among the 257 cities. This was to be expected because of the greater number of relatively expensive 1-family dwellings in the small cities in the environs of metropolitan centers. The composite correction for both undervaluation and nonrepresentativeness of the sample becomes 1.18 x 1.05 = 1.24, applied to line 37, Table EM 11, to obtain line 41.

The average of $2,965 (for all types) in the 956 nonmetropolitan cities reporting in 1936 is lower than the average of $3,410 for 1-family dwellings in the 80 nonmetropolitan cities, the series upon which estimates are based for the earlier years. This relationship is consistent with the findings of a study of Census data for 1930: the average value of houses in small towns outside metropolitan districts was found to be much lower than in larger cities or cities of the same size within metropolitan districts. When estimates based on the averages for reporting cities in each size group are extended to all nonmetropolitan cities, the average becomes $2,818 (compared with $2,965 in the 956 reporting cities), only 82 per cent of the 1-family average, $3,410, for the 80 cities. The composite correction is then 1.18 x 0.82 = 0.97, which, applied to line 39, gives line 45 (Table EM 11).

d Unit Costs in Rural Areas

Virtually no information is available on the year-to-year cost of construction of dwellings in either the

[29] The Construction Industry in Minnesota (*University of Minnesota, Employment Stabilization Research Institute, II, No. 9, June 1934*), p. 20.

[30] *Confirmed by data recently published by the Bureau of Labor Statistics showing cost arrays for different types of dwellings and materials of construction for 815 cities with populations over 10,000 in which detailed studies were made of building permits for 1929–35.*

[31] *Based on Bureau of Labor Statistics data on "number of families provided for" and "estimated valuation of new residential buildings," the latter corrected to exclude nonhousekeeping dwellings (Building Construction, February 1937, p. 62).*

rural environs of metropolitan districts or the strictly rural areas. The Bureau of Labor Statistics receives no reports from these areas and the F. W. Dodge data on contracts awarded do not lend themselves to a segregation of urban and rural nonfarm construction. Consequently, the trend of the average cost of dwelling units built in rural environs, predominantly 1-family dwellings, is estimated on the basis of the trend for 1-family dwellings in the reporting satellite cities, but at a level 24 per cent lower. This relatively lower level was determined by a detailed study of the estimated average value of all dwellings in places over and under 2,500, in environs of metropolitan districts, based on the 1930 Census data on values and rents. Since the Census data are for 1930 alone, and include value of land and both new and old dwellings, they may not represent the relative costs of new dwellings built either during 1930 or over a period of years. However, analysis of the unit costs for new dwellings during 1936 in the 1,689 reporting cities, by size groups, shows much the same relations in average costs between cities of different size as were found in the 1930 value data (after allowances for differences in land values), when the cities are segregated by metropolitan and nonmetropolitan areas, indicating that the Census data give a reasonable basis for estimating relative average costs.

Similarly, unit costs of new dwellings in rural nonfarm areas were estimated as 66 per cent of those in nonmetropolitan urban centers (line 45), on the basis of the relation of estimated values of structures in rural nonfarm areas and of values in nonmetropolitan urban cities as shown in the 1930 Census.

Partial confirmation of the correctness of these estimated average costs is contained in Part VII of the Report of the President's Conference on Housing (1931), *Farm and Village Housing*. The results of a mailed inquiry on the cost of houses built in rural areas in 18 states during 1926–30 are summarized. The sample was rather small, comprising 1,546 returns, 970 of which were for houses on farms, 312 in villages, and 264 in other rural areas; location within or outside metropolitan districts was not designated. New York and Georgia had the highest and lowest averages. The average values of $3,912 for new village houses

	FARM	VILLAGE	OTHER RURAL	TOTAL RURAL
18 states, average	$2,789	$3,912	$3,556	$3,146
New York (highest)	3,235	6,113	5,545	4,894
Georgia (lowest)	1,607	2,088	1,739	1,706

and $3,556 for other rural houses for the 18 states are lower than the average of $4,788 per unit for "rural" environs (Table EM 11, line 42), but higher than the average of $2,508 for rural nonfarm dwellings (line 47) for the corresponding period, 1926–30. However, if rural environs and rural nonfarm areas are combined, a composite average of $3,525 per unit is de-

rived, only slightly lower than the averages of $3,912 and $3,556 for "village" and "other rural" dwellings in the sample study above. Extension, by the Bureau of Labor Statistics, of the reporting of building permits to places with populations under 2,500 will in time provide a basis for revising, if necessary, the average unit costs tentatively assumed in Table EM 11.

The unit costs as derived above (Table EM 11, lines 40, 41, 42, 45, and 47), when multiplied by the number of units built each year for the respective population group (Table EM 10, lines 26, 27, 28, 31, and 33), result in the estimated value of new housekeeping dwellings (Table EM 11, lines 49–57).

In order to have estimates of the cost of all residential construction, including nonhousekeeping units (hotels, clubs, and lodging houses), comparable to other estimates previously available, the cost of nonhousekeeping units was estimated tentatively (Table EM 11, line 58). These estimates are subject to revision when the basic data for the 257 cities in earlier years are corrected by the Bureau of Labor Statistics. To allocate the estimates for nonhousekeeping units by geographic division or population group was not attempted.

The estimates described above are for new construction alone; they do not include expenditures for repairs and alterations of residential buildings.

5 Aggregate Nonfarm Dwelling Units Built by Decades, 1890–1929

Estimates of aggregate new nonfarm dwelling units built by decades since 1890 are summarized in Tables E 6 and EM 5. Estimates for the three decades prior to 1920 were derived by the method described for 1920–29. That is, it was assumed that net new dwelling units built each decade were equal to the total increase in dwelling units standing, obtained by adding the increase in the number of families (number of occupied units) and in vacant units, plus building to replace losses, less units added by conversions. The estimates for earlier years are subject to a wider range of uncertainty than those for the period since 1920. They are tentative, subject to revision if more reliable data become available. Even if the estimates for the earlier decades are slightly inaccurate, they, together with the 1920–36 estimates, provide basic data for gauging current developments against a background of nearly half a century. They provide also a means of checking estimates of total units built annually prior to 1920. The methods used in deriving the component parts of the estimates are summarized below in the order in which they appear in Table EM 5.

a Increase in Number of Families, 1890–1930
1) Necessary adjustments of Census data
Basic data on total nonfarm families as published by

the Bureau of the Census for the five Census dates between 1890 and 1930 (Table EM 6) require several adjustments before they can safely be used in estimating construction in the manner described above.

TABLE EM 5

Dwelling Units Built by Decades, 1890–1929 (thousands)

	1890–99	1900–09	1910–19	1920–29
Increase in no. of				
1 Occupied units	2,262	3,445	4,109	5,541
2 Vacant units	9	291	−530	1,039
3 Demolitions, fire, flood, and other losses	208	297	414	580
4 Total units built (1+2+3)	2,479	4,033	3,993	7,160
5 Conversions	62	81	103	125
6 Net new units built (4−5)	2,417	3,952	3,890	7,035

The reasons for the adjustments are:

a) The Census data for 1900 and 1930 are for private families only, while the 1890, 1910, and 1920 figures include quasi-family groups, e.g., groups living in hotels, lodging houses, schools, institutions, labor camps, or army posts.

b) The number of persons included in the quasi-family classification in 1900 was not comparable with that in 1930 for several reasons: relatively more persons were counted as living in lodging houses in 1900 than would have been counted on the basis of the 1930 classification; the average number per lodging house in 1900 was under 10; in 1930 the minimum was 11 and the average over 20. Because of greater care in reporting transient residents in hotels in 1930 according to their permanent residence, probably fewer persons were counted as quasi-families in hotels in 1930 than in 1900. Also, the Census of 1900, taken June 1, apparently included relatively more farm labor groups than the later censuses taken in January or April.

c) The intercensal periods vary in length because the Census enumerations were made on June 1 in 1890 and 1900, April 15, 1910, January 1, 1920, and April 1, 1930.

d) The distribution of total families between farm and nonfarm as published for 1900 and 1910 appears to be inconsistent with that for other years because of some possible change in classification or other cause as yet undetermined by the Bureau of the Census. Farm families exceeded farms by 4.4, 4.7, and 6.0 per cent in 1890, 1920, and 1930, respectively; [32] in 1900 and 1910 farm families were reported as 0.8 and 3.7 per cent *less* than the number of farms (see Table EM 6). These variations are small in terms of the totals, but, as will be shown later, they affect considerably

[32] *If the number of occupied farm dwellings in 1935 is considered as a minimum count of farm families, there were at least 8 per cent more farm families than farms in 1935 (see Farm Dwellings, Census of Agriculture, 1935, release, June 12, 1936).*

the *increases* in the number of both farm and nonfarm families between Census dates.

2) *Methods used in making adjustments*

The adjustments made to the Census data on families are summarized below.

a) The family data for all five Census dates were reduced to a "private-family" basis by applying the ratio of private families to all families in the 1930 Census. Since the Census Bureau did not tabulate separately private and quasi-family groups for farm and nonfarm families in 1930, the same ratio was applied to both farm and nonfarm totals. The correction to the totals is of course small (one-fourth of 1 per cent),

TABLE EM 6

Families and Farms, United States, Census Data, 1890–1930 (thousands)

No. of families [1]	1890 June 1	1900 June 1	1910 April 15	1920 Jan. 1	1930 April 1
1) Total	12,690	15,964	20,256	24,351	29,905
2) Farm	4,767	5,690	6,124	6,751	6,669
3) Nonfarm	7,923	10,274	14,132	17,600	23,236
4) No. of farms [2]	4,565	5,738	6,362	6,448	6,289
5) Ratio of farm families to farms	1.044	0.992	0.963	1.047	1.060

Increase in no. of families	1890–00	1900–10	1910–20	1920–30
6) Total	3,274	4,292	4,096	5,553
7) Farm	923	434	628	−83
8) Nonfarm	2,351	3,858	3,468	5,636

[1] Census, 1930, *VI, Table 16, p. 11. The headnote to this table reads in part: "Figures for 1930 and 1900 represent private family homes alone; those for 1920, 1910 and 1890 include the premises occupied by the small number of institutions and other quasi-family groups which were counted as families in the respective censuses. . . ."*
[2] Census, 1930, *VI, 50.*

but its effect is more pronounced on the increases between Census dates, and was made for the sake of consistency in the figures rather than for the fine degree of accuracy implied (see Table EM 7).

b) Farm families in 1900 and 1910 were estimated to be respectively 1.045 and 1.046 times the number of farms. These ratios were interpolations between the 1890 and 1920 ratios, 1.044 and 1.047, of farm families to farms (Table EM 6). This adjustment was made after consultation with Bureau of the Census officials and study of state-by-state comparisons of the number of farm families and of farms at each of the five Census dates, made possible by a special Bureau of the Census tabulation. Nonfarm families were obtained by subtracting farm families from the United States totals.

c) The increases in the number of families between Census dates were adjusted to a uniform ten-year interval, equivalent to a January 1 basis throughout (Table EM 7, lines 6–8). The 1900–10, 1910–20, and the 1920–30 increases based on Table EM 7, lines 2,

4, and 5, were divided by 0.9875, 0.9708, and 1.025 respectively, to correct for the uneven intercensal periods of 9.875, 9.708, and 10.25 years instead of 10 years. Comparison with the corresponding data published by the Census (Table EM 6) shows an increase in the number of farm families from 1890 to 1900, and 1900 to 1910, a third to a half greater, and an increase from 1910 to 1920, only one-sixth as much. Furthermore, the adjusted increases in farm families show a steady decline from 1890 to 1930, whereas the published Census data indicate a greater increase from 1910 to 1920 than in the preceding decade. Likewise, the adjusted data (Table EM 7) show successively larger increases in nonfarm families each decade from 1890 to 1930 instead of the interruption to the rate of increase indicated in 1910–20 (Table EM 6, line 8).

TABLE EM 7

Number of Families, 1890–1930, and Adjusted Increase in Number of Private Families by 10-Year Intervals (thousands)

Number of families, Census dates

	1890 June 1	1900 June 1	1910 April 15	1920 Jan. 1	1930[1] April 1
1 Total, all families [1]	12,690	16,188	20,256	24,351	29,980
2 Total, private families only [2]	12,658 [3]	16,147	20,204	24,290	29,905
3 Farm, all families [1]	4,767	5,997 [4]	6,654 [5]	6,751	..
4 Farm, private families only [2]	4,755	5,982	6,637	6,734	6,669
5 Nonfarm, private families only (2) − (4)	7,903	10,165	13,567	17,556	23,236

Increase in no. of private families, adj. to 10-year intervals, January 1–January 1

	1890–00	1900–10	1910–20	1920–30
6 Total	3,488	4,109	4,209	5,477
7 Farm	1,226	664	100	−64
8 Nonfarm	2,262	3,445	4,109	5,541

[1] *Source:* Census, 1930, *VI, Table 14, p. 10.*

[2] *Estimated as same proportion of "all families" as in 1930 = 0.9975.*

[3] *Census count of private families in 1900 was not used, as it is not strictly comparable with private families as enumerated in 1930.*

[4] *Estimated at 1.045 times the number of farms (see Table EM 6).*

[5] *Estimated at 1.046 times the number of farms (see Table EM 6).*

[6] *Not tabulated separately by the Census Bureau.*

b Change in Percentage of Vacant Units

Total units standing January 1 of each Census year were estimated and the ten-year increases obtained by the method described in Note C for 1920–29. The difference between the increase in the dwelling units standing and in occupied dwelling units (increase in number of families) in each decade is the net change in vacant units (Table EM 5). Vacant units, as percentages of the total standing at the beginning of each decade, were estimated to be: 1890, 5; 1900, 4; 1910,

5; 1920, 1; 1930, 5. The basis of selection of the 1920 and 1930 vacancy percentages is described in Note C. For earlier years data are exceedingly scanty, but from the available evidence on vacancies and building activity it was concluded that vacancies were probably fairly numerous at the beginning of 1890 and 1910 following active periods of building.[33] The situation was probably similar to that which followed the active building of the middle 1920's. On the other hand, less building during the 1890's, together with continued increase in the number of families and immigration, probably resulted in somewhat fewer vacancies in 1900.

1) Supporting evidence on variations in the percentage of vacancies

This general pattern of vacancies is confirmed by the following information:

a) Vacancies in St. Louis were reported by Wenzlick to be approximately 6.7 per cent in 1900; 8.9 in 1910; 3.6 in 1920, and 9.5 per cent in 1930. They average higher than for the country as a whole, as might be expected because of the larger than average proportion of 2- and 3-or-more family dwellings there,[34] in which types vacancies on the average are higher than in 1-family dwellings.

b) Vacancy surveys in apartment buildings made by the New York Tenement House Department [35] reported apartment vacancies at 8.08 per cent in early 1909 and 5.60 per cent in early 1916. At the beginning of 1920, however, apartment vacancies in New York City were probably less than 1 per cent, since they were 2.18 per cent in March 1919 and 0.36 per cent in March 1920.

c) Vacancies in dwellings (only those fit for occupancy) in Philadelphia averaged 5 per cent in 1912, the date of the first vacancy survey made by the Philadelphia Housing Association. At the next surveys in 1917 and 1921 they were 1.65 and 0.67 per cent respectively, indicating a vacancy of not more than about 1 per cent at the beginning of 1920.

The above data furnish a very inadequate basis on which to estimate total vacancies in nonfarm areas. Furthermore, a change of only 1 per cent in total vacancy at the beginning or end of a decade can affect appreciably the estimate of change during it. However, variations in the assumed percentages of vacancy would have a relatively small effect on the estimate of total building, and would not materially change the

[33] *See J. R. Riggleman, Building Cycles in the United States, 1875–1932, Journal of the American Statistical Association, June 1933. The data are for total building but presumably residential building fluctuated in essentially the same manner.*

[34] *Of all occupied dwelling units in St. Louis, 58 per cent were in 2- and 3-or-more family dwellings combined compared with 30 per cent in all nonfarm areas, 1930 (Census, 1930, VI).*

[35] *Tenth Annual Report, Table 28, pp. 162–3.*

longer term proportions of construction done during the several decades.

c Demolitions and Other Losses

The basis of estimating the reduction in dwelling units during 1920–29 due to demolitions, fire, flood, and other losses is described in Note C. For the earlier decades there are virtually no empirical data. Aggregate property loss by fire in the United States as reported by the National Board of Fire Underwriters in the four decades following 1890 totaled $1,373, $2,168, $2,457, and $5,053 million respectively, only a portion of which was in residential property (see Note C). Even if the proportion of the total that was residential property were known, it would be difficult even to approximate the number of dwelling units destroyed by fire, owing to the lack of a satisfactory measure of urban property values over a long period. The larger loss that might be expected in later years because of the larger number of dwellings in existence, might be partly or wholly offset by improved fire protection methods and equipment.

During the 1920's demolitions of dwellings (many in good condition) to make way for other buildings constituted a large proportion of all losses. This accompanied the rapid urbanization, most pronounced in large metropolitan areas, and was probably a much less important factor in earlier years. Consequently, it was estimated that average annual losses, including those from demolitions, fire, flood, and other causes were 5, 5½, and 6 units per 10,000 population respectively in the three decades 1890–99, 1900–09, and 1910–19, comparable with 6.97 units during 1920–29 derived from empirical data and separate estimates for demolitions and other losses as described in Note C.

d Conversions

In the absence of empirical data for earlier years, annual conversions were estimated on the same basis as for 1920–29, namely, at 1½ units per 10,000 population. Since, as thus estimated, they averaged less than 3 per cent of total building, a considerable margin of error in the conversions estimate would not materially affect estimated total new building.

6 Limitations of the Estimates

The chief limitations of the estimates are due to the nature and scope of the data available. The estimates

for 1920–36 are based on a sample of building permits for cities, which, in terms of both population and dwelling units built over a period, has varied from about 40 to 60 per cent of total nonfarm dwellings. While this is a fairly large sample for the country as a whole, the representation varies widely by regions and size of population groups.

Any estimate of the value of construction based on either building permits or contracts awarded presents difficulties in interpretation with respect to the time at which construction actually occurs. Both permits and contracts report a lump sum as of a given date, but the actual expenditure for materials and labor is usually spread over several months. The estimates presented herewith are annual totals; monthly trends are not attempted. Owing to the marked concentration of residential building in the summer, particularly in 1-family dwellings which comprise the bulk of residential building, there is no serious distortion to the annual figures due to carry-overs from one year to the next, and any error that may arise from this cause is much smaller than for certain types of nonresidential and heavy engineering construction. Furthermore, the extreme range of fluctuation in the national totals over a period of years and the marked differences in regional trends tend to reduce the significance of short term fluctuations in the national totals.

The tables in this chapter should not be taken as implying as fine a degree of accuracy as might be inferred from computations to the last digit or to thousands of dollars. The figures were carried out for the purpose of checking with reported data and other computations. Furthermore, important parts of the basic material refer to items that cannot be defined exactly. For example, a family dwelling unit may be any one of several types—an apartment, a flat over a store, a row house, in a 2-family dwelling, or a 1-family detached dwelling. Dwelling units may vary in size from 1 to 10 or more rooms. A single family dwelling may be anything from a 1-room shack with a minimum of improvements to a 10- or 20-room mansion on an estate. While these represent extremes they are included in the figures currently reported by the Bureau of Labor Statistics without segregation by number of rooms or material of structure. Despite these variations, the series of dwelling units and average values for the last 17 years are quite consistent.

Notes: Supplementary Information concerning Construction

A Value of Residential Construction, Present Estimates Compared with F. W. Dodge Corporation and Other Estimates

Unlike previous estimates of the total value of new residential construction, the present estimates are based primarily on building permits in relation to

changes in the number of families, rather than on contracts awarded. This method was chosen only after detailed analysis of both series. The advantages and disadvantages of the permits series are discussed in Chapter V. Contracts awarded, as published by the F. W. Dodge Corporation, are gathered for a commer-

TABLE EM 8

Value of Residential Building (millions of dollars), Comparison of Estimates and Reported Data [1]

	NBER ESTIMATE 48 states [2]	CONTRACTS AWARDED 48 STATES		37 states [5]	BUILDING PERMITS 257 cities [6]	EXPENDITURES, 48 STATES	
		FESB estimate [3]	F. W. Dodge estimate [4]			WPA estimates [7]	Dept. of Commerce estimates [8]
	(1)	(2)	(3)	(4)	(5)	(6)	(7)
1920	1,122	..	743	673	..	..	1,545
1921	1,841	..	1,146	1,027	937	..	1,661
1922	3,115	..	1,735	1,555	1,612	..	2,734
1923	3,980	..	2,073	1,807	2,001	..	3,640
1924	4,244	..	2,399	2,112	2,070	..	4,195
1925	4,754	3,050	3,076	2,748	2,462	4,253	4,505
1926	4,314	2,965	2,958	2,671	2,256	4,056	4,496
1927	4,064	2,856	2,879	2,573	1,906	4,204	4,175
1928	3,813	3,095	3,069	2,788	1,859	4,338	3,869
1929	2,623	2,127	2,139	1,916	1,433	3,098	3,324
1930	1,456	1,222	1,240	1,101	601	1,654	2,118
1931	1,005	900	901	811	426	1,222	1,343
1932	282	311	..	280	103	432	615
1933	204	..	..	249	91	398	287
1934	214	..	..	249	76	416	235
1935	585	..	..	479	212	764	467
1936	1,202	..	..	802	473	1,245	964

[1] *Other than on farms; includes nonhousekeeping dwellings (hotels, clubs, etc.)*

[2] *New building only.*

[3] *Federal Employment Stabilization Board, published in National Bureau Bulletin 52, November 15, 1934, p. 17*

[4] *F. W. Dodge Corporation; excludes new construction and remodeling projects under $5,000*

[5] *F. W. Dodge Corporation; totals for 1920–22 estimated (by F. W. Dodge Corporation) on basis of actual contract totals in 27 states; 1923 and 1924, on basis of 36 states. Includes repair contracts over $5,000 prior to 1930, over $2,000 in 1930 and 1931, and over $1,000 since 1932.*

[6] *Bureau of Labor Statistics*, Building Construction, *February 1937, p. 65*

[7] *Construction Expenditures and Employment, 1925–36, Table 1, p. 39, June 1, 1937*

[8] *Construction Activity in the United States, 1915–37 (Department of Commerce, Domestic Commerce Series, No. 99, Jan. 1938), Table 12, p. 43. (Figures in col. 7 are for new construction alone. For totals including additions, alterations, repairs, and maintenance see* ibid., *Table 5, col. 1, p. 22, and Table 12, col. 4, p. 43.)*

cial news service, and adaptation of the data for statistical purposes is of secondary importance. The chief difficulties in attempting to use them as the basis for estimating in the earlier years were, first, the distortion in total residential construction and 1-family unit costs caused by the exclusion of contracts under $5,000 prior to 1930. Nor could this omitted construction be measured accurately from the reported data themselves. Second, the data on the number of family units constructed are incomplete. Finally, 11 western states are not represented. Since 1935 the F. W. Dodge Corporation has undertaken to provide virtually complete coverage of new nonfarm residential building within the 37 eastern states, except for that covered by contracts under $2,000, an undetermined amount. The exclusion of contracts under $5,000 [1] prior to 1930 caused a greater understatement of residential construction than is gen-

[1] *The minimum was lowered to $2,000 in 1930; in 1932 it was lowered to $1,000 for both new and alteration work. Beginning in 1935 the minimum for new work was restored to $2,000, the minimum for repairs remaining at $1,000. The $5,000 minimum was apparently not always strictly adhered to, as the average value of 1-family dwellings reported in some southern and western states in earlier years was as low as $4,700–4,800, or below the nominal minimum of $5,000.*

erally recognized, and the resulting trend of the contracts reported is not representative for either the 37 states or the country as a whole, as may be demonstrated by the following rough tests for 1920–29. In Table EM 8, column 3, are F. W. Dodge Corporation estimates of contracts awarded for residential structures in all 48 states, involving contracts over $5,000 each, amounting to an aggregate of $22 billion. This total includes cost of hotels. Even if this indicated volume of construction were all in housekeeping dwellings and the average cost per family unit were as low as $5,000, it would represent only 4,400,000 units for the decade. This falls considerably short of the ten-year increase of 5,541,000 in occupied nonfarm dwelling units shown by the 1930 Census. It is 2,600,-000 units less than the probable total of about 7,000,-000 units built during the decade, when allowance is made for the 1,500,000 additional units built to offset demolitions, fire, and other losses, and for the increase in vacancy. For the total of $22 billion to have accounted for 7,000,000 dwelling units built, the average cost per unit would have had to be as low as $3,143, which is much less than actual unit costs indicate.

This understatement is confirmed by contract data on residential floor space for 1920–29, which in 37 eastern states amounted to 4,143,859,000 square feet.[2] Table E 5 indicates that the dwelling units built in the 11 western states (Mountain and Pacific divisions) were approximately 19 per cent of the number in the 37 eastern states. Thus, if the floor space for 37 states is raised 19 per cent to include the 11 western states, a total of approximately 4,931,000,000 square feet is indicated for all 48 states. With an average as low as 1,000 square feet per dwelling unit this would mean only 4,931,000 units. However, it is unlikely that the floor space per unit for all types could have averaged as low as 1,000 square feet, since many 1-family dwellings averaged 1,500 to 2,500 or more square feet, and this type predominates. Apartments usually range from 700 to 1,000 square feet, but their number would be insufficient to reduce the average to 1,000. Thus a composite average of 1,200–1,500 square feet per unit seems more likely, and if applied to the 4,931,-000,000 square feet would represent between 4,100,-000 and 3,287,000 units in contrast to the net increase of 5,541,000 occupied dwelling units and the total of 7,035,000 units built.

Further evidence of the omission of a considerable number of 1-family and possibly 2-family dwellings is disclosed by a comparison of permits and contracts. In 1925 the aggregate value of 1- and 2-family dwellings for which permits were issued in 257 cities was approximately $1,425 million; contracts awarded in 37 eastern states for 1- and 2-family dwellings totaled $1,295 million,[3] an amount actually less than shown by building permits in the 257 cities, although the non-farm area presumably covered by the contracts data was more than 80 per cent greater than that of the 257 cities in terms of population, and 66 per cent greater in terms of the 1920–29 increase in families as shown by the 1930 Census. In 1928 contracts for 1- and 2-family dwellings in 37 states totaled $1,409 million. If this high level had been maintained every year throughout 1920–29 the total would have been nearly $14.1 billion; a liberal allowance of 20 per cent for the 11 western states would raise this hypothetical total to $16.9 billion for all 48 states. At $5,000 per unit, the Dodge minimum for single contracts, this would have represented 3,390,000 units, or approximately 2 million fewer than the 5,360,000 units that the estimates in this study indicate as the ten-year total of 1- and 2-family dwelling units (Table E 3). Or, for the Dodge data to have accounted for the 5,360,000 1- and 2-family dwelling units, with the aggregate value of $16.9 billion, would imply an average cost per unit of only $3,150, an average clearly too low in view of the large number of contracts actually reported averag-

ing $6,000–9,000 and higher for 1-family dwellings. The actual level of contracts awarded during the decade of course averaged less than the reported 1928 peak level of $1,409 million, probably one-third to one-half. Thus, contracts data, if available for all 48 states throughout 1920–29, would probably have included considerably fewer than 3,000,000 1- and 2-family dwelling units, owing chiefly to the exclusion of contracts under $5,000.

Exclusion, because of the $5,000 minimum, of as many 1-family dwellings from the contracts data as are indicated above would go far toward explaining the difference in trend in the contracts awarded and building permit series. For example, the estimates in this study based on the latter indicate that in terms of family units, building of 1-family dwellings reached a peak in 1925, while apartment building reached highest levels during 1926–28. Also, exclusion of many 1-family dwellings because of the $5,000 limit, and possible underreporting in small centers where the 1-family type prevails, would tend to overweight the contracts series with apartments. Inclusion of contracts for all 1-family dwellings, with a peak in 1925, would probably have brought the combined total of contracts awarded to a maximum in 1925 instead of 1928, with the totals in earlier years much higher than reported. Thus the contracts series as reported for 37 states were not representative of the trend of total residential building throughout much of the period under consideration.

In an effort to determine average unit costs from contracts the following difficulties were encountered: since during most of the period covered by the estimates, contracts for repairs were not segregated, the cost of new buildings alone cannot be derived with certainty. Nor can accurate unit costs be obtained directly from contracts for all types of dwellings in earlier years, as the number of family units in apartment buildings, and hence average unit costs, can be merely approximated from the data on square feet of floor space—an uncertain method.

While family units in detached 1- and 2-family dwellings can be derived from the number of buildings reported in contracts, 1-family unit costs cannot be taken as representing actual averages throughout much of the period because the exclusion of contracts under $5,000 prior to 1930 probably excluded one-half or more of all 1-family dwellings built.[4]

Also, average unit costs in different regions would

---

[2] *Reported in contracts for 37 states, 1925–29, and estimated by F. W. Dodge Corporation for 1920–24 on the basis of contracts in 27–36 states (Table EM 9).*

[3] Architectural Record, *July 1936, Vol. 80, No. 1, p. 24.*

[4] *A study of over 25,000 residential building permits in Minneapolis, 1920–32, classified according to size of project, showed that on the average over three-fourths of all the permits were for projects under $5,000 (The Construction Industry in Minnesota, p. 63). Even if liberal allowance is made for the probable undervaluation of these permits, more than half would remain in the less than $5,000 classification.*

be affected in varying degree by the $5,000 minimum, as it would tend to exclude a much larger proportion of dwellings in the southern and western than in the northeastern states.

Another complication is introduced by the fact that the F. W. Dodge 1-family classification did not include all 1-family dwellings. Row houses or groups of 2-or-more detached dwellings (both 1- and 2-family) that were built by one contractor were classed as "housing developments." Two-family dwellings have been segregated only since 1928; i.e., prior to 1928, many 1- and 2-family dwellings were included in the "housing developments" classification.

Despite the difficulties in applying contracts cost data, they might still seem preferable on the ground that they would constitute a larger sample. Within the 37 eastern states, at least, they presumably had nearly double the coverage of the permit series for 257 cities, on a population basis, since contracts were reported for villages and suburban areas outside city limits. Though the permit series covers only areas within city limits, it furnishes virtually as large an absolute sample as contracts which cover the entire nonfarm area within the 37 states. In 1922 and 1923 the value of residential building permits in 257 cities (Table EM 8) actually exceeded contracts awarded in 37 states (col. 4) and averaged only slightly less than the estimated total of contracts in all 48 states (col. 3). Since building permits are not distorted by the exclusion of any one type of dwelling or range of values, they constitute a more representative and dependable sample for the cities reported. Adjustments must be made for undervaluation in permits and for the differences in unit costs between unreported areas and reporting cities, but they can be made with less uncertainty than is involved in attempting to adjust contracts for those excluded, for lack of data on family units, and for non-representation in the 11 western states.

Acknowledgment is due the F. W. Dodge Corporation for making available to the National Bureau of Economic Research many detailed data on contracts awarded, ordinarily available only to subscribers to the Dodge Statistical Service. While these data were not used in the National Bureau's estimates, they serve as valuable collateral material on building trends.

Estimates of the value of residential construction in the United States annually, 1925–32 (Table EM 8, col. 2), prepared by the Federal Employment Stabilization Board from contracts awarded, and published in National Bureau *Bulletin 52*, are almost identical with F. W. Dodge Corporation estimates (col. 3), and, for 1925–29, considerably lower than National Bureau estimates (col. 1).

Two additional series of estimates on the value of nonfarm residential construction have been published

recently in connection with estimates of total expenditures for all types of construction (Table EM 8). The estimates prepared for the Works Progress Administration by Peter A. Stone for 1925–36 [5] (col. 6) were based on residential contracts awarded and have a different trend from the estimates presented in this volume. Instead of a peak in residential construction in 1925 and a continuous decline to 1928, the WPA estimates decrease from 1925 to 1926, but increase in 1927 to a peak in 1928. Although projects under $5,000, excluded from contracts awarded, were allowed for, year-to-year changes in the contracts as reported were assumed to be representative of the course of all residential construction, resulting in the 1928 peak. As explained above, this assumption is not valid. The estimates (col. 7) prepared under the direction of L. J. Chawner and published by the Department of Commerce are based mainly on building permits. For rural nonfarm areas and population groups under 25,000 the estimates of value were obtained by multiplying estimated nonfarm dwelling units by average costs per dwelling unit for population groups classified by size and relation to metropolitan districts. For the larger cities the method is described as follows:

"The cost of residential buildings for which permits are estimated to have been issued in all cities having a population of more than 25,000 during the years 1921 to 1932 (and more than 10,000 during the years 1933 to 1935) was calculated for each group in the proportion which the total population of all cities in each group was to the population of the reporting cities in each group. This adjustment was not large, because of the fact that the population of the reporting cities over this period was more than 90 per cent of all cities exceeding 25,000 in population." [6]

The adjustment would have been larger had building in non-reporting cities been estimated on the basis of their population growth rather than on total population. Since Department of Commerce estimates for residential construction were to be combined with data for other types of construction, for which the time of completion differed widely, the residential estimates were converted to a calendar year expenditures basis ". . . by adding one-third of the cost of the buildings for which permits were issued in the preceding year to two-thirds of the cost in a given year." [7] This apparently overcorrects for the difference between the value of residential construction started in a given calendar year and of expenditures on work in progress during the year, especially during periods of rapid change in construction such as the early 1920's and 1930's. In those years, a correction based on actual monthly data

[5] Construction Expenditures and Employment, 1925–36 (*WPA, June 1937*).
[6] Construction Activity in the United States, 1915–37 (*Domestic Commerce Series, No. 99, January 1938*), p. 38.
[7] Ibid., *footnote to col. 2, Table 12, p. 43.*

TABLE EM 9

Dwelling Units Built, Square Feet of Floor Space in Residential Contracts Awarded in 37 States, and Number
of Families Provided for in 257 Cities, 1920–1936

	NEW NONFARM DWELLING UNITS BUILT			SQ. FT. OF FLOOR SPACE, RESIDENTIAL CONTRACTS AWARDED [3] 37 STATES	FAMILIES PROVIDED FOR, 257 CITIES [4]
	NBER estimates	Brookings [1]	Dept. of Commerce [2]		
	(thousands of units)			(millions of square feet)	(thousands)
	(1)	(2)	(3)	(4)	(5)
1920	247	213	300	174	...
1921	449	446	432	237	225
1922	716	705	676	358	377
1923	871	846	814	407	454
1924	893	872	827	436	443
1925	937	951	894	560	491
1926	849	845	841	521	462
1927	810	781	757	495	406
1928	753	736	713	568	389
1929	509	472	510	388	244
1930	286	260	303	230	125
1931	212	200	219	190	98
1932	74	80	94	74	27
1933	54	70	64	73	26
1934	55	60	59	64	22
1935	144	150	138	136	56
1936	282	300	275	223	115

[1] The Recovery Problem in the United States (*Brookings Institution, 1937*), p. 639. The estimates carry this footnote: "Data which became available after this table went to press indicate that the estimates for 1925, 1926 and 1936 should be reduced by 30,000–50,000 while those for 1920 and 1929 should be increased by a similar amount."

[2] Construction Activity in the United States, 1915–37 (*Department of Commerce, Domestic Commerce Series, No. 99, Jan. 1938*), Table 10, p. 41
[3] *F. W. Dodge Corporation; includes nonhousekeeping dwellings*
[4] *Bureau of Labor Statistics*, Building Construction, Feb. 1937, p. 65

for the closing months of each year results in a much smaller adjustment than a one-third—two-thirds allocation of annual totals.

The discussion of Department of Commerce methods of estimating residential construction concludes with the statement:

". . . it is believed that estimates have been secured for the years 1921 to 1936 which do not have a margin of error in excess of plus or minus 15 per cent." [8]

[8] Ibid., *p. 45.*

B Comparison with Other Estimates of Physical Volume

Although the aggregate value of residential construction had been estimated at various times, no series was generally available prior to 1936 of total family units built annually in nonfarm areas over a period of years. Reflecting the widespread interest in the problem and research by several interested agencies, results of four sets of estimates [1] were presented between December 1936 and March 1937. These estimates are compared in Table EM 9 together with related data on residential floor space reported in contracts awarded and number of families provided for as reported in building permits. Certain features of the Brookings estimates (col. 2) are described in *The Recovery Problem in the United States* (p. 650):

"For the nonfarm area outside of the 257 cities, an estimate for the decade 1920–29 was first obtained by assuming that the number of new units erected bore the same relation to the increase in the number of families that prevailed in a group of smaller cities included in the 257 (82 cities with a population of 25,000–50,000). This estimated total for the decade

[1] *Preliminary results of National Bureau estimates of both value and number of nonfarm dwellings built annually since 1920, together with discussion of some problems encountered in their preparation, were presented at the meeting of the American Statistical Association, December 28, 1936 (see Journal of the American Statistical Association, March 1937, p. 97). In January 1937 the Brookings Institution published estimates of new nonfarm dwelling units built annually, 1920–36, as part of a chapter on accumulated needs in durable goods, in The Recovery Problem in the United States, pp. 183–8. In March 1937 L. J. Chawner of the Bureau of Foreign and Domestic Commerce presented estimates on nonfarm dwelling units built annually, 1915–36, in The Annals, American Academy of Political and Social Science, Vol. 190, p. 25. These estimates have since been published in revised form in Construction Activity in the United States, 1915–37. Notice of the completion of a report ". . . embodying a series of estimates on housing construction during the years 1920–36, with a forecast for 1937 . . ." by the Federal Housing Administration was made in the Journal of the American Statistical Association, March 1937, but the complete series was not cited. Estimates for selected years were referred to in a press release, December 27, 1936, and in the third annual report of the Federal Housing Administration, January 28, 1937.*

as a whole was then distributed among the ten years in accordance with the distribution of the decade's construction, shown by these 82 cities. For years since 1929, construction in the nonfarm area outside the 257 cities has been estimated by other methods, too varied to detail here."

Although the estimates for unreported nonfarm areas are based on a rather small sample, 82 cities, they do not differ materially from the NBER estimates (col. 1) which are based on more cities and more detailed processes. The Brookings estimates, prepared by George Terborgh, pioneered in basing the estimates of construction upon the relation of building to the increase in the number of families.

The methods by which the Department of Commerce estimates (col. 3) were obtained are described in *Construction Activity in the United States, 1915–37* (pp. 40–41):

"The estimation of the number of new family units involved two steps. First, by using the number of family units for which permits were issued in each size group of cities, classified according to their satellite and nonsatellite character, rates showing the number of units per 10,000 persons annually were computed. These rates formed the basis for estimating the number of family units in smaller cities, for which actual reports were not available. The actual rates used were determined after a careful study of the relationships between building rates in cities of different size and relationship to metropolitan areas. In calculating the rates for satellite cities, an adjustment based upon the Real Property Inventory was used. In the case of nonsatellite communities the building rates used as the basis of estimation were substantially less than those obtained directly from the larger reporting cities. The second step involved the extension of these rates to the cities in rural nonfarm areas from which actual reports were not received. This extension was based upon the population of the smaller cities and rural nonfarm areas."

Considerable uncertainty is introduced into the estimates of building in small cities and rural nonfarm areas, when their population is taken as a basis and building rates from larger cities are projected, without adjustment for differences in population growth as between reporting and unreported areas. Analyses made in connection with the present study indicate

that per capita building rates of a town or city are closely related to population growth (see Ch. V, sec. 1 b).

Although not strictly comparable with the data on family units, the F. W. Dodge data on square feet of floor space in residential construction (col. 4) constituted the other chief series previously available that directly measured the trend of physical volume of residential building over a period of years. As mentioned in Note A it is difficult to translate the data on square feet of floor space into number of dwelling units.

Our estimates were based upon the number of families provided for, as reported in building permits in 257 cities and published by the Bureau of Labor Statistics, (col. 5).

C Fire, Flood, and Other Losses

Demolition permits are not usually issued for dwellings completely destroyed by fire, flood, windstorm, or earthquake. Fire losses in residential buildings alone are not available on a national basis, but reports from 7 states (Illinois, Indiana, Iowa, Kansas, Louisiana, Massachusetts, Oregon; *President's Conference on Housing*, 1931, Part VIII, p. 5) for 1930 indicate that 58 per cent of the total number and 32 per cent of the aggregate fire losses were in dwellings. On the basis of a ten-year average of approximately $500 million aggregate property loss reported by the National Board of Fire Underwriters, a loss of $160 million is indicated for dwellings. If this represented the complete destruction of dwellings averaging, say, $5,000, it would mean a loss of some 32,000 dwellings a year. However, only a small portion of the aggregate dollar loss represents complete destruction of dwellings. (Average loss per fire in dwellings in the 7 reporting states in 1930 was only $770.) Most of the loss is repaired and the property continued in use. Consequently 15,000 dwellings per year would probably be a generous estimate of the units completely destroyed by fire, even allowing for losses not covered by insurance and for relatively higher losses in rural than in urban areas. In the absence of specific data, it was assumed that losses due to floods, earthquakes, windstorms, and other causes would raise the total losses (other than by demolition) to 25,000 units per year, with a range of 20,000–30,000.

Note to Part Two: Supplementary material developed by the NBER, but not included in detail in this volume. The following bodies of data not reproduced in Part Three are in the form of tabulations unless otherwise designated.

I Supplementary Value and Rent Data
1) Values and rents for 139 cities from *1930 Census of Population* (for complete list see Tables A 6

and B 5). The description of this tabulation in Part Two, Ch. II, sec. 2 indicates the character of the material.

Folder 32: Miscellaneous tables on average rent and value, 139 cities, 1930

Work-table	Sheets	Work-table	Sheets
C 3	1–5	C 36	
C 9		C 37	1–4
C 11	1–4	C 40	
C 26	1–4		18 miscellaneous

Folder 33: Owner-occupied and rented dwelling units by value and rent groups. Special Census tabulation of 1930 data (full coverage).

Section A: 6 New England cities, 77 sheets

1–10 Summaries of rent data	17–19 Orange, Mass.
11 Pittsfield, Me.	20–33 Central Falls, R. I.
12–16 Greenwich, Conn.	34–56 Nashua, N. H.
	57–77 Burlington, Vt.

Section B: 10 Middle Atlantic cities, 198 sheets

1– 68 Trenton, N. J.	168–180 Peekskill, N. Y.
69–127 Binghamton, N. Y.	181–184 Latrobe, Pa.
128–153 Williamsport, Pa.	185–188 Corry, Pa.
	189–191 Dansville, N. Y.
154–167 Carbondale City, Pa.	192–196 Hoosick Falls, N. Y.
	197–198 Canton, N. Y.

Section C: 12 East North Central cities, 111 sheets

1– 26 Portsmouth, Ohio	87– 90 West Bend, Wis.
27– 54 La Crosse, Wis.	91– 95 Barnesville, Ohio
55– 68 Findlay, Ohio	96–100 Vandalia, Ill.
69– 73 Macomb, Ill.	101–104 Mitchell, Ind.
74– 81 Valparaiso, Ind.	105–107 Crystal Falls, Mich.
82– 86 Ionia, Mich.	108–111 Franklin Park, Ill.

Section D: 13 West North Central cities, 87 sheets

1–36 Springfield, Mo.	70–73 Richmond, Mo.
37–55 Sioux Falls, S. D.	74–78 Alexandria, Minn.
56–60 So. St. Paul, Minn.	79–81 Gering, Neb.
61–65 Abilene, Kans.	82 Forest City, Iowa
	83 St. Paul, Neb.
66–69 Chariton, Iowa	84–85 Wilton, N. D.
	86 Belle Plaine, Kans.
	87 Avon, S. D.

Section E: 13 South Atlantic cities, 87 sheets

1–22 Wilmington, N. C.	74–77 Milledgeville, Ga.
	78–81 Franklin, Va.
23–50 Hagerstown, Md.	82 Calhoun, Ga.
	83 Jesup, Ga.

51–58 Martinsburg, W. Va.	84 Chesterfield, S. C.
	85 Boca Raton, Fla.
59–68 Tallahassee, Fla.	86 Odessa, Del.
	87 Wilson Mills, N. C.
69–73 Richwood, W. Va.	

Section F: 7 East South Central cities, 30 sheets

1–13 Johnson City, Tenn.	24–27 Andalusia, Ala.
	28 Carbon Hill, Ala.
14–17 Paris, Tenn.	29 Durant, Miss.
18–23 Somerset, Ky.	30 Woodbury, Tenn.

Section G: 8 West South Central cities, 65 sheets

1–30 Austin, Texas	53–56 Hope, Ark.
31–46 Baton Rouge, La.	57–60 Conway, Ark.
	61–63 Chandler, Okla.
47–52 Greenville, Texas	64 Vivian, La.
	65 Lockney, Tex.

Section H: 10 Mountain cities, 39 sheets

1–14 Casper, Wyo.	33–34 Gooding, Idaho
15–22 Bozeman, Mont.	35 Salina, Utah
	36–37 Florence, Ariz.
23–29 Salida, Colo.	38 Lovelock, Nev.
30 Roundup, Mont.	39 Los Lunas, N. M.
31–32 Bountiful, Utah	

Section I: 10 Pacific cities, 83 sheets

1–25 Santa Barbara, Calif.	63–67 Porterville, Calif.
	68–75 Ashland, Ore.
26–37 Vancouver, Wash.	76–79 Burns, Ore.
	80–81 North Sacramento, Calif.
38–50 Modesto, Calif.	
	82 Marcus, Wash.
51–62 Oregon City, Ore.	83 Grandview, Wash.

Section J: Peoria, Ill., 139 sheets

Section K: Rent summaries of full coverage data for 90 cities, 96 sheets

1– 7 Miscellaneous	64–71 South Atlantic
8–15 New England	72–75 East South Central
16–35 Middle Atlantic	76–83 West South Central
36–51 East North Central	84–88 Mountain
52–63 West North Central	89–96 Pacific

Section L: Value summaries of full coverage data for 90 cities, 104 sheets

1– 3 Owner-occupied 1-family dwellings, average value by value groups for 139 cities

4– 7 Summary of owner-occupied dwelling units; number, aggregate, and average value by value groups for 49 cities, sample coverage.

8– 13 Summary of owner-occupied dwelling units; number, aggregate, and average value by value groups for 90 cities, full **coverage.**

14– 15 Owner-occupied dwelling units, number and average value by value groups of 25 cities having populations less than 2,500 in 1930, full coverage.

16 Summary of 1-family owner-occupied dwellings; number, aggregate, and average value for 86 cities.

17–104 Summaries by geographic divisions

17– 23 New England

24– 43 Middle Atlantic

44– 59 East North Central

60– 69 West North Central

70– 77 South Atlantic

78– 81 East South Central

82– 89 West South Central

90– 95 Mountain

96–104 Pacific

Folder 34: Owner-occupied and rented dwellings by value and rent groups. Special Census tabulation of 1930 data (sample coverage)

Section A: 3 New England cities, 176 sheets

1–144 Providence, R. I.   163–176 Portland, Me.

145–162 Waterbury, Conn.

Section B: 1 Middle Atlantic city, 20 sheets

1–20 Erie, Pa.

Section C: 6 East North Central cities, 286 sheets

1–179 Cleveland, Ohio

180–242 Indianapolis, Ind.

243–255 Lansing, Mich.

256–267 Racine, Wis.

268–277 Decatur, Ill.

278–286 Kenosha, Wis.

Section D: 5 West North Central cities, 124 sheets

1– 70 Minneapolis, Minn.

71– 86 Wichita, Kans.

87–100 St. Joseph, Mo.

101–113 Lincoln, Neb.

114–124 Topeka, Kans.

Section E: 8 South Atlantic cities, 163 sheets

1– 49 Atlanta, Ga.

50– 81 Richmond, Va.

82– 98 Jacksonville, Fla.

99–111 Charleston, S. C.

112–136 Wheeling, W. Va.

137–145 Greensboro, N. C.

146–154 Columbia, S. C.

155–163 Asheville, N. C.

Section F: 2 East South Central cities, 62 sheets

1–47 Birmingham, Ala.

48–62 Knoxville, Tenn.

Section G: 4 West South Central cities, 90 sheets

1–33 Dallas, Texas

34–63 Oklahoma City, Okla.

64–76 Little Rock, Ark.

77–90 Shreveport, La.

Section H: 7 Mountain cities, 59 sheets

1–25 Salt Lake City, Utah

26–35 Pueblo, Colo.

36–42 Phoenix, Ariz.

43–48 Butte, Mont.

49–51 Albuquerque, N. M.

52–56 Boise, Idaho

57–59 Reno, Nev.

Section I: 4 Pacific cities, 192 sheets

1– 69 Seattle, Wash.

70–137 Portland, Ore.

138–174 San Diego, Calif.

175–192 Sacramento, Calif.

Section J: 8 Miscellaneous cities, 133 sheets

1– 33 Worcester, Mass., N. E.

34– 68 Syracuse, N. Y., M. A.

69–112 St. Paul, Minn., W. N. C.

113–116 Fargo, N. D., W. N. C.

117–118 Frederick, Md., M. A.

119–123 Jackson, Miss., E. S. C.

124–127 Paducah, Ky., E. S. C.

128–133 Wichita Falls, Texas, W. S. C.

Folder 35: Des Moines, Iowa alone, Special Census tabulation of 1930 data (part sample and part full coverage) 87 sheets

2) Dwellings and dwelling units: detailed work tables, derived from *1930 Census of Population,* showing the mechanics by which the number of units were obtained by states and geographic divisions, give the number of dwelling units by value and rent classes for the 3,165 cities with populations over 2,500 classified by states and geographic divisions and further subdivided into five population groups.

Folder 21: Work-table C 38, sheets 1–58

Folder 22: Work-table C 4, sheets 1–58

3) Dwellings and dwelling units by type, population group, state, and geographic division (Folder 25): Work-table C 1; C 2, sheets 1–61; C 15, sheets 1–9.

4) Dwelling units in New York City: a special tabulation to show distribution by type of structure, made by the Census Bureau for use in estimating the value of residential properties of various classes in New York City (Files on "Construction Correspondence," letters of March 9 and 24, 1937)

II Family Income Data

1) Owner-occupant and tenant families: rent, income, and rent delinquency by personal enumeration and mail returns in 33 cities in 1929 and 1933

by 39 income groups, 8 tables for each of 33 cities. This material is designed for a monograph.

Folder 39: Income data for 33 cities—special tabulation from Financial Survey of Urban Housing by 39 income groups for personal enumeration and mail returns by tenure

Table 3: Tenant families: mail returns by 39 income groups for 1929
Annual rent bill, 1929
Number reporting, total rent, average rent per unit
Total family income, 1929, 1932, and 1933
Number reporting, total and average family income
Total family income, 1933, by 11 income groups
A cross tabulation of number reporting 1929 income by 39 groups and 1933 income by 11 groups

Table 4: Tenant families: personal enumeration by 39 income groups for 1929 for same items as in Table 3

Table 5: Owner-occupant families: mail returns by 39 income groups for 1929
Total family income, 1929, 1932, and 1933
Number reporting, total and average family income
Total family income, 1933, by 11 income groups
A cross tabulation of number reporting 1929 income by 39 income groups and 1933 income by 11 groups

Table 6: Owner-occupant families: personal enumeration by 39 income groups for 1929 for same items as in Table 5

Table 7: Tenant families: mail returns by 39 income groups for 1933
Annual rent bill, 1933
A cross tabulation of number reporting 1933 income for 39 income groups and number reporting 1933 rent for 11 rent groups, total and average rent per unit
Total family income, 1929, 1932, and 1933
Number reporting, total and average family income
Rent delinquency, 1933
Number reporting on rent status, number reporting rent not fully paid, percentage with rent not fully paid, number reporting months unpaid, total months unpaid, average months unpaid, number reporting amount unpaid, total and average amount unpaid

Table 8: Tenant families: personal enumeration by 39 income groups for 1933 for same items as in Table 7

Table 9: Owner-occupant families: mail returns by 39 income groups for 1933
Total family income, 1929, 1932, and 1933
Number reporting, total and average family income
Number reporting value of all properties, January 1, 1934
A cross tabulation of number reporting 1933 income for 39 income groups and number reporting value Jan. 1, 1934 by 11 value groups

Table 10: Owner-occupant families: personal enumeration by 39 income groups for 1933 for same items as in Table 9

III Real Estate Financial Data

A Apartment Buildings: Value, Income, Operating Expenses, and Financing, by Years (Folder 28):

1) Sixteen apartment buildings in Indianapolis: gross income, vacancy and concessions, actual rentals; operating expenses, including taxes before interest, net operating income before interest, income expressed as number of times mortgage interest was earned before refunding capital invested, and interest. Annual data and trends of items, 1937–33 (5 sheets). Data obtained for this project through the cooperation of D. T. Rowlands, University of Pennsylvania.

2) Twenty-one apartment buildings in St. Paul: gross income, net income before interest; operating expenses, payrolls, commissions, fuel, gas and electricity, water, telephone, miscellaneous; repairs, plumbing and heating, painting, fixed charges, taxes, insurance. Data complete for 21 properties in 1935 and 1936; for 16 properties in 1934, 1935, and 1936; and for 10 properties in 1933, 1934, 1935, and 1936. Data obtained for this project through the cooperation of D. T. Rowlands (10 sheets)

3) Sixty-eight apartment buildings in Philadelphia: year built, number of rooms; gross income, total expense, operating expenses, net income, rental income, maintenance and repairs, management expenses, taxes, interest, net income before interest, assessment, senior, junior, and total financing, interest rate, interest charged, services included in rent, by years, 1925–35. Tabulations by gross income groups. Series not complete for all properties. Data collected by and used in project by permission of D. T. Rowlands (81 sheets)

B Apartment and other buildings: Value and Financing (Folder 29):

1) 1,869 properties on Lower East Side, New York City: assessed value of land and of improvements; original debt, amount of first, second, and third mortgage; total payments of interest and principal; total payments of interest first year; total payments on principal, first year; outstanding debt, 1934, interest and principal, payments on outstanding loans in 1934, ratio of outstanding debt to assessed value of property, by Census tract and block number (1 sheet)

2) 1,301 indebted properties among the 1,869 properties: items under (1) (2 sheets)

3) 568 properties free from debt among the 1,869: items under (1) except financing (1 sheet)

4) Commercial and industrial buildings in Harlem: items under (1) (3 sheets)

5) 1,303 mortgaged properties among the 1,869 properties in (1) classified by 11 sources of credit and by first, second, and third mortgage: number of loans held, original amount, interest rate, total annual payments, total interest payments, and average term (1 sheet)

6) Same properties as in (5): distribution by debt-value ratios, by 11 classifications for each by Census tract and block number (2 sheets)

7) Same properties as in (5) classified by area: number, original mortgage, interest rates, payments, term, outstanding amount of first, second, third, and fourth mortgage by agency holding the mortgage (24 sheets)

8) 1,564 properties, Harlem, New York, for all properties, indebted properties, and properties free from debt, by Census tract and block number. Number, total and average value, original debt; outstanding debt, 1934, and as percentage of original debt; interest and principal payments, and payments as percentage of total debt, 1934; number and percentage of properties mortgaged, and properties free from debt (5 sheets)

9) Lower East Side area: number and percentage distribution of properties by type, age, condition, and Census tract (1 sheet)

10) Harlem: number and percentage distribution of properties by type, age, condition, and Census tract (1 sheet)

11) Harlem: number and percentage distribution of mortgaged properties by debt-value ratios, by Census tract and block number; by source of credit and priority, covering 1,198

first mortgages, 426 second mortgages, 75 third mortgages, and 5 fourth mortgages: number of mortgages held, average original mortgage, average mortgage outstanding; interest rate, amortization required in first year of mortgage, aggregate annual payments, annual interest payments for first year; average term, total outstanding debt, 1934 (3 sheets)

12) Harlem: distribution of mortgages by Census tract and block number, items in (11) by lending agency and priority of loan (31 sheets)

C Assessed values of urban real estate and their relation to sales or market values (Folder 19):

1) Schedules received from the tax assessors of 522 cities: assessed value of residential, commercial, industrial, and other taxable real estate, and real estate exempt from taxation, tabulated by states and geographic divisions. Work-table R 166, sheets 1–17

2) Original schedules used in C 1

3) 789 schedules received from commercial banks, savings banks, and real estate tax specialists, with their estimates of the percentage relation between assessed and market values in their respective cities, for residential, commercial, industrial, and other real estate taxed, June 30, 1936. Tabulated by states and geographic divisions. Work-table UR 167, sheets 1–21

4) Original schedules used in C 3 (Folder 29)

5) Several thousand properties in New York City, Borough of Manhattan, assessed and market values, 1935. Real estate foreclosure sales: assessed value of land and of improvements; selling price and ratio to assessed value; debt, taxes, total amount due, ratio of debt to assessed value, and ratio of market land value to assessed value (8 sheets)

6) Summary of the data referred to in C 5 by class of property: dwellings, apartments, commercial, and vacant (1 sheet)

7) Lower East Side and Harlem, voluntary sales, 1935: total value, value of land and of improvements, mortgage, value above mortgage, selling price, ratio of assessed value to selling price for residential and nonresidential properties (2 sheets)

8) Lower East Side and Harlem areas by Census tract and block number: number of properties, value and financing by type of property: residential, commercial, and industrial; value of land and of improvements, original and outstanding debt, payments by priority; properties held by institutions; and for vacant properties in Harlem, free and indebted: number, total

value, value of land and of improvements, original mortgage, payments, outstanding debt by priority, ratio of outstanding debt to assessed value (3 sheets)

9) New York areas and the Bronx in 1935, distribution of number of foreclosure sales by class of property and of ownership (2 sheets)

D Real estate in relation to commercial banking and other financing agencies (Folder 31):

1) Principal provisions of state and federal laws governing lending regulations with respect to real estate loans by each main class of financial agency, digest and tabulation: insurance requirements for mortgaged property, issuance or mortgage participation certificates, construction loans, power to make and insure Federal Housing Administration loans, limitations on lending, on aggregate funds lent on real estate security (by states), location of real estate, type of lien, basis of valuation, and repayment provisions (29 sheets)

2) Real estate loans by national and state banks: amount of farm loans, loans on other real estate, total real estate loans, loans and investments, and total resources, with ratios for the United States and by states, by years, 1911–36 (50 sheets)

3) Estimate of total maximum real estate loans that are legal for banks (51 sheets)

IV Nonfarm Residential Construction: (A) Building permits, (B) Contracts awarded (Folder 3)

A Building permits

1) "Families provided for" (dwelling units, all types) as reported by the Bureau of Labor Statistics, with annual totals for each of 311 cities each year for which data were reported, 1920–36, by states and geographic divisions. Subtotals for each year by population group and geographic division, 257 cities.

Note: Until recent years, the Bureau of Labor Statistics published data for cities arranged alphabetically with subtotals for regions or population groups, and it has not yet published many data by population groups (Work-table UR 106, sheets 1–9)

2) "Cost of new residential building," including non-housekeeping dwellings: hotels, clubs, etc. Similar to material described in IV A 1, giving total cost of new residential construction as reported in building permits, by states and geographic divisions, subtotals for each year, by population group and geographic division, 257 cities (Work-table UR 51, sheets 1–13)

3) Cost of non-housekeeping dwellings only,

similar to IV A 2 for 257 cities, by population group, state, and geographic division (Work-table UR 151, sheets 1–3)

4) Number, total and average cost of one-family dwellings as reported in building permits for each of 257 cities by years, 1921–36, by population group, state, and geographic division. Tabulation from bulletins published by the Bureau of Labor Statistics during 1921–30 and from its office records for 1931–36. Average cost per dwelling computed for reporting cities in each population group and each region annually; averages compiled, computed for approximately half of the 257 cities (Work-table UR 119, sheets 1–12); see Table E 7 for summary of averages

5) Summary tabulation of number of buildings and estimated total cost of new construction, all types, as reported in Bureau of Labor Statistics building permit data, 1920–36, by type of building; annual totals for varying number of reporting cities (189 in 1920 to 1,689 in 1936) (Work-table UR 135, sheets 1–2)

Residential	*Nonresidential*
1-family	Amusement and recreation
2-family	Churches
1- and 2-family dwellings with stores	Factories, shops, etc.
	Garages, public
Multi-family	Garages, private
Multi-family dwellings with stores	Gasoline and service stations
Hotels	Institutions
Lodging houses	Office buildings
Other	Public buildings
Total new residential	Public works and utilities
	Schools, libraries, etc.
	Sheds
	Stables and barns
	Stores, warehouses, etc.
	All other
Total, new building	*Total new nonresidential*

Additions, alterations, and repairs

Residential
Nonresidential

Grand Total

6) Demolitions: number of units for which demolition permits were issued in 7 large cities during various periods from 1918 to 1936, summary of Bureau of Labor Statistics building permit survey data for 159 cities, 1929–35

(Work-table UR 155, UR 156, sheets 1–3, and UR 118, sheets 1–5)

7) Residential repairs: building permit data on repairs to housekeeping and non-housekeeping dwellings each year, 1921–36, in 257 cities by population group, state, and geographic division. Tabulation from bulletins published by Bureau of Labor Statistics for 1921–30 and from its office records (Work-table UR 195, sheets 1–10)

8) Building permits, 1908–20: tabulation of U. S. Geological Survey building permit data on number of buildings (in some cities number of permits) and total cost (including repairs) in varying number of cities (43 in 1908 to 134 in 1920) by states and geographic divisions. Subtotals by regions for each year for identical groups of cities reporting in current and preceding year (Work-table UR 46, sheets 1–3)

9) Building permits, 1910–20, by type of construction: tabulation of U. S. Geological Survey building permit data on number and cost of new wooden buildings (96–120 cities), and new brick or hollow tile buildings (87–110 cities), by states and geographic divisions (tabulation for 1910–13 not completed) (Work-table UR 183, sheets 1–7)

B Contracts awarded (F. W. Dodge data)

1) Residential: tabulation of value of residential contracts awarded (thousands of dollars): states and geographic divisions, 37 states, 1925–36, and 27–36 states, 1919–24 (Work-table UR 149)

2) Apartments: tabulation similar to (1) of value of apartment contracts awarded (Work-table UR 183)

3) 1-family dwellings: summary of average value by states and geographic divisions, average values for each state annually, 1919–33, computed on basic tabulation sheets furnished by F. W. Dodge Corporation. Data for 11 cities: Boston, Providence, New York, Philadelphia, Pittsburgh, Cleveland, Detroit, Chicago, Miami, Atlanta, and Houston (Work-table UR 150)

4) New York City Tenement House data: tabulation of plans filed, buildings completed, demolitions, conversions, 1918–36, by boroughs, number of buildings, apartments, and rooms completed each year, average costs per building, apartment, and room, and average number of rooms per apartment, by boroughs, 1902–36; a tabulation of 11 vacancy surveys, various dates, 1919–33, by type of tenement (old or new law), by boroughs. Data from New York City Tenement House Department annual reports and special tabulations obtained by correspondence. (Work-table UR 52, sheets 1–5, UR 53, sheets 1–2, and UR 105)

TABLE EM 10

Dwelling Units Built by Class of City, 1920-1936

	Source	1920	1921	1922	1923	1924	1925	1926
Dwelling Units Built, Preliminary, Not Corrected for Bias in 257 City Series[1]								
1 113 central cities	2/	93,619	188,319	314,728	387,023	389,624	412,712	384,932
2 120 central cities	2/	95,427	192,414	318,504	393,212	403,868	431,002	395,536
3 64 satellite cities	2/	10,382	19,510	32,713	39,953	39,637	40,912	37,928
4 184 met. dist. cities	lines 2 + 3	105,809	211,924	351,217	433,165	443,505	471,914	433,464
5 Total environs based on 64 cities[3]	5.875 x line 3	60,994	114,621	192,189	234,724	232,867	240,358	222,827
6 Total environs based on 184 cities[3]	0.545 x line 4	57,666	115,499	191,413	236,075	241,710	257,193	236,238
7 Total environs, average	(lines 5+6)/2	59,330	115,060	191,801	235,400	237,289	248,776	229,533
8 Urban environs (2,500 and over)[3]	0.669 x line 7	39,692	76,975	128,315	157,483	158,746	166,431	153,558
9 Rural environs (under 2,500)[3]	0.331 x line 7	19,638	38,085	63,486	77,917	78,543	82,345	75,975
10 96 metropolitan districts	lines 2 + 7	154,757	307,474	510,305	628,612	641,157	679,778	625,069
11 80 BLS nonmet. dist. cities	2/	10,472	15,526	21,486	23,762	23,809	23,168	19,019
12 Unreported nonmet. dist. urban	lines 13 - 11	59,502	88,219	122,083	135,016	135,283	131,641	108,066
13 Total nonmet. dist. urban[3]	6.682 x line 11	69,974	103,745	143,569	158,778	159,092	154,809	127,085
14 257 cities	2/	114,473	223,355	368,927	450,738	453,070	476,792	441,879
15 Unreported urban	lines 16 - 14	110,258	187,864	284,947	336,652	347,179	357,795	310,275
16 Total urban	lines 10 + 13	224,731	411,219	653,874	787,390	800,249	834,587	752,154
17 Rural nonfarm based on total urban[3]	0.129 x line 16	28,990	53,047	84,350	101,573	103,232	107,662	97,028
18 Rural nonfarm based on 80 nonmet. dist. cities[3]	4.236 x line 11	44,359	65,768	91,015	100,656	100,855	98,140	80,564
19 Rural nonfarm, average	(lines 17+18)/2	36,674	59,408	87,682	101,114	102,044	102,901	88,796
20 Total nonfarm	lines 16 + 19	261,405	470,627	741,556	888,504	902,293	937,488	840,950
21 Total nonfarm outside 120 central cities	lines 20 - 2	165,978	278,213	423,052	495,292	498,425	506,486	445,414
Dwelling Units Built, Corrected for Bias								
22 Factor "A"	4/	0.945	0.955	0.965	0.980	0.990	1.000	1.010
23 Total nonfarm, corrected for bias	lines 20 x 22	247,028	449,449	715,602	870,734	893,270	937,488	849,360
24 Total nonfarm outside 120 central cities	lines 23 - 2	151,601	257,035	397,098	477,522	489,402	506,486	453,824
25 Correction for areas outside 120 central cities	lines 24/21	0.913,380	0.923,878	0.938,651	0.964,122	0.981,897	1.000,000	1.018,881
Redistribution of Corrected Nonfarm								
26 120 central cities	line 2	95,427	192,414	318,504	393,212	403,868	431,002	395,536
27 Urban environs (2,500 and over)	lines 8 x 25[6]	36,254	71,116	120,443	151,833	155,872	166,431	156,457
28 Rural environs (under 2,500)	lines 29 - 27	17,937	35,185	59,591	75,121	77,121	82,345	77,410
29 Total environs	lines 7 x 25	54,191	106,301	180,034	226,954	232,993	248,776	233,867
30 96 metropolitan districts	lines 26 + 29	149,618	298,715	498,538	620,166	636,861	679,778	629,403
31 Nonmet. dist. urban	lines 13 x 25[6]	63,913	95,848	134,761	153,082	156,212	154,809	129,484
32 Total urban	lines 30 + 31	213,531	394,563	633,299	773,248	793,073	834,587	758,887
33 Rural nonfarm	lines 19 x 25[7]	33,497	54,886	82,303	97,486	100,197	102,901	90,473
34 Total nonfarm	lines 32 + 33	247,028	449,449	715,602	870,734	893,270	937,488	849,360

[1] Unreported refers to all cities or nonfarm areas not included in the Bureau of Labor Statistics list of 257 cities reporting continuously since 1921, even though reports may be available for some years for portions of the areas designated as unreported.

[2] Source of basic data: Bureau of Labor Statistics, Building Permits. Corrected for 'plans filed' on apartments in New York City but not executed; also for effect of increased coverage due to annexations.

[3] Factors based on Table C 9. See text.

[4] Based on estimates for 1935 and 1936 (Tables C 17 and C 18) and data for 31 metropolitan districts included in federal Real Property Inventory of 64 cities, 1934. See text.

[5] Bureau of Labor Statistics.

[6] Modified correction for bias applied 1931-35. See text for method.

[7] Except 1931-35 = lines 34 - 32. Line 34 same as line 23.

TABLE EM 10 (Cont'd)

Dwelling Units Built by Class of City, 1920-1936

	1927	1928	1929	Subtotal 1920-29	1930	1931	1932	Source
Dwelling Units Built, Preliminary, Not Corrected for Bias in 257 City Series[1]								
1 113 central cities	352,358	311,732	201,991	3,037,038	112,538	82,057	23,908	2/
2 120 central cities	355,217	313,481	203,143	3,101,804	113,159	82,535	24,150	2/
3 64 satellite cities	39,792	35,686	20,604	317,117	9,865	6,968	2,231	2/
4 184 met. dist. cities	395,009	349,167	223,747	3,418,921	123,024	89,503	26,381	lines 2 + 3
5 Total environs based on 64 cities[3]	233,778	209,655	121,049	1,863,062	57,957	40,937	13,107	5.875 x line 3
6 Total environs based on 184 cities[3]	215,280	190,296	121,942	1,863,312	67,048	48,779	14,378	0.545 x line 4
7 Total environs, average	224,529	199,976	121,496	1,863,190	62,503	44,858	13,743	(lines 5+6)/2
8 Urban environs (2,500 and over)[3]	150,210	133,784	81,281	1,246,475	41,815	30,010	9,194	0.669 x line 7
9 Rural environs (under 2,500)[3]	74,319	66,192	40,215	616,715	20,688	14,848	4,549	0.331 x line 7
10 96 metropolitan districts	579,746	513,457	324,639	4,964,994	175,662	127,393	37,893	lines 2 + 7
11 80 BLS nonmet. dist. cities	18,784	19,238	14,350	189,614	7,116	5,089	2,342	2/
12 Unreported nonmet. dist. urban	106,731	109,310	81,537	1,077,388	40,433	28,916	13,307	lines 13 - 11
13 Total nonmet. dist. urban[3]	125,515	128,548	95,887	1,267,002	47,549	34,005	15,649	6.682 x line 11
14 257 cities	410,934	366,656	236,945	3,543,769	129,519	94,114	28,481	2/
15 Unreported urban	294,327	275,349	183,581	2,688,227	93,692	67,284	25,061	lines 16 - 14
16 Total urban	705,261	642,005	420,526	6,231,996	223,211	161,398	53,542	lines 10 + 15
17 Rural nonfarm based on total urban[3]	90,979	82,819	54,248	803,928	28,794	20,820	6,907	0.129 x line 16
18 Rural nonfarm based on 80 nonmet. dist. cities[3]	79,569	81,492	60,787	803,205	30,143	21,557	9,921	4.236 x line 11
19 Rural nonfarm, average	85,274	82,156	57,518	803,567	29,469	21,188	8,414	(lines 17+18)/2
20 Total nonfarm	790,535	724,161	478,044	7,035,563	252,680	182,586	61,956	lines 16 + 19
21 Total nonfarm outside 120 central cities	435,318	410,680	274,901	3,933,759	139,521	100,051	37,806	lines 20 - 2
Dwelling Units Built, Corrected for Bias								
22 Factor "A"	1.025	1.040	1.065		1.130	1.160	1.190	4/
23 Total nonfarm, corrected for bias	810,298	753,127	509,117	7,035,473	285,528	211,800	73,728	lines 20 x 22
24 Total nonfarm outside 120 central cities	455,081	439,646	305,974	3,933,669	172,369	129,265	49,578	lines 23 - 2
25 Correction for areas outside 120 central cities	1.045,399	1.070,532	1.113,033		1.235,434	1.291,991	1.311,379	lines 24/21
Redistribution of Corrected Nonfarm								
26 120 central cities	355,217	313,481	203,143	3,101,804	113,159	82,535	24,150	line 2
27 Urban environs (2,500 and over)	157,029	143,220	90,468	1,249,123	51,660	38,235	11,782	lines 8 x 25[6]
28 Rural environs (under 2,500)	77,694	70,861	44,761	618,026	25,558	19,721	6,240	lines 29 - 27
29 Total environs	234,723	214,081	135,229	1,869,149	77,218	57,956	18,022	lines 7 x 25
30 96 metropolitan districts	589,940	527,562	338,372	4,968,953	190,377	140,491	42,172	lines 26 + 29
31 Nonmet. dist. urban	131,213	137,615	106,725	1,263,662	58,744	43,017	19,641	lines 13 x 25[6]
32 Total urban	721,153	665,177	445,097	6,232,615	249,121	183,508	61,813	lines 30 + 31
33 Rural nonfarm	89,145	87,950	64,020	802,858	36,407	28,292	11,915	lines 19 x 25[7]
34 Total nonfarm	810,298	753,127	509,117	7,035,473	285,528	211,800	73,728	lines 32 + 33

[1] Unreported refers to all cities or nonfarm areas not included in the Bureau of Labor Statistics list of 257 cities reporting continuously since 1921, even though reports may be available for some years for portions of the areas designated as unreported.

[2] Source of basic data: Bureau of Labor Statistics, Building Permits. Corrected for 'plans filed' on apartments in New York City but not executed; also for effect of increased coverage due to annexations.

[3] Factors based on Table C 9. See text.

[4] Based on estimates for 1935 and 1936 (Tables C 17 and C 18) and data for 31 metropolitan districts included in federal Real Property Inventory of 64 cities, 1934. See text.

[5] Bureau of Labor Statistics.

[6] Modified correction for bias applied 1931-35. See text for method.

[7] Except 1931-35 = lines 34 - 32. Line 34 same as line 23.

TABLE EM 10

Dwelling Units Built by Class of City, 1920-1936

Source	1933	1934	1935	1936	Subtotal 1930-36	Grand total 1920-36		
							Dwelling Units Built, Preliminary, Not Corrected for Bias in 257 City Series[1]	
2/	16,964	19,014	49,472	101,057	405,010	3,442,048	113 central cities	1
2/	17,140	19,391	50,765	103,887	411,027	3,512,831	120 central cities	2
2/	1,615	1,182	2,439	6,693	30,993	348,110	64 satellite cities	3
lines 2 + 3	18,755	20,573	53,204	110,580	442,020	3,860,941	184 met. dist. cities	4
5.875 x line 3	9,488	6,944	14,329	39,321	182,083	2,045,145	Total environs based on 64 cities[3]	5
0.545 x line 4	10,221	11,212	28,996	60,266	240,900	2,104,212	Total environs based on 184 cities[3]	6
(lines 5+6)/2	9,855	9,078	21,663	49,794	211,494	2,074,684	Total environs, average	7
0.669 x line 7	6,593	6,073	14,493	33,312	141,490	1,387,965	Urban environs (2,500 and over)[3]	8
0.331 x line 7	3,262	3,005	7,170	16,482	70,004	686,719	Rural environs (under 2,500)[3]	9
lines 2 + 7	26,995	28,469	72,428	153,681	622,521	5,587,515	96 metropolitan districts	10
2/	1,631	1,500	3,907	7,615	29,200	218,814	80 BLS nonmet. dist. cities	11
lines 13 - 11	9,267	8,523	22,200	43,268	165,914	1,243,302	Unreported nonmet. dist. urban	12
6.682 x line 11	10,898	10,023	26,107	50,883	195,114	1,462,116	Total nonmet. dist. urban[3]	13
2/	20,210	21,696	55,818	115,365	465,203	4,008,972	257 cities	14
lines 16 - 14	17,683	16,796	42,717	89,199	352,432	3,040,659	Unreported urban	15
lines 10 + 15	37,893	38,492	98,535	204,564	817,635	7,049,631	Total urban	16
0.129 x line 16	4,888	4,965	12,711	26,389	105,474		Rural nonfarm based on total urban[3]	17
4.236 x line 11	6,909	6,354	16,550	32,257	123,691		Rural nonfarm based on 80 nonmet. dist. cities[3]	18
(lines 17+18)/2	5,899	5,660	14,630	29,323	114,583		Rural nonfarm, average	19
lines 16 + 19	43,792	44,152	113,165	233,887	932,218		Total nonfarm	20
lines 20 - 2	26,652	24,761	62,400	130,000	521,191		Total nonfarm outside 120 central cities	21
							Dwelling Units Built, Corrected for Bias	
4/	1.225	1.255	....	....			Factor "A"	22
lines 20 x 22	53,645	55,411	144,015[5]	....			Total nonfarm, corrected for bias	23
lines 23 - 2	36,505	36,020	93,250	....			Total nonfarm outside 120 central cities	24
lines 24/21	1.369,691	1.454,707	1.494,391	....			Correction for areas outside 120 central cities	25
							Redistribution of Corrected Nonfarm	
line 2	17,140	19,391	50,765	103,887[5]	411,027	3,512,831	120 central cities	26
lines 8 x 25[6]	8,671	8,368	20,258	40,305	179,279	1,428,402	Urban environs (2,500 and over)	27
lines 29 - 27	4,827	4,838	12,115	27,361	100,660	718,686	Rural environs (under 2,500)	28
lines 7 x 25	13,498	13,206	32,373	67,666	279,939	2,147,088	Total environs	29
lines 26 + 29	30,638	32,597	83,138	171,553	690,966	5,659,919	96 metropolitan districts	30
lines 13 x 25[6]	13,959	13,315	34,813	60,587	244,076	1,507,738	Nonmet. dist. urban	31
lines 30 + 31	44,597	45,912	117,951	232,140	935,042	7,167,657	Total urban	32
lines 19 x 25[7]	9,048	9,499	26,064	50,087	171,312	974,170	Rural nonfarm	33
lines 32 + 33	53,645	55,411	144,015	282,227	1,106,354	8,141,827	Total nonfarm	34

TABLE EM II

Dwelling Units Built, Aggregate Value, 1920-1936

	Source	1920	1921	1922	1923	1924	1925	1926
Unit Costs, Basic Data								
35 Average, all types, 257 cities	1/		$ 3,947	$ 4,005	$ 4,127	$ 4,352	$ 4,464	$ 4,422
36 Average, all types, 113 central cities	2/	$ 4,216	4,008	4,055	4,147	4,378	4,450	4,376
37 Average, all types, 64 satellite cities	2/	4,729	4,038	3,945	4,363	4,715	5,019	5,097
38 Average, 1-fam. dwellings, 64 satellite cities	3/	6,773	4,771	5,183	5,273	5,399	5,695	5,972
39 Average, 1-fam. dwellings, 80 non-metropolitan district cities	3/	3,456	2,946	3,323	3,454	3,484	3,794	3,973
Unit Costs, as Applied[4]								
40 Central cities, assigned	1.18 x line 36	4,975	4,729	4,785	4,893	5,166	5,251	5,164
41 Urban environs, assigned	1.24 x line 37	5,864	5,007	4,892	5,410	5,847	6,224	6,320
42 Rural environs, assigned	0.76 x line 38	5,147	3,626	3,939	4,007	4,103	4,328	4,539
43 Total environs, derived	lines 52/29	5,627	4,550	4,577	4,946	5,270	5,596	5,730
44 96 metropolitan districts, derived	lines 53/30	5,211	4,665	4,710	4,912	5,204	5,377	5,374
45 Nonmetropolitan districts urban, assigned	0.97 x line 39	3,352	2,858	3,223	3,350	3,379	3,680	3,854
46 Total urban, derived	lines 55/32	4,655	4,226	4,393	4,603	4,844	5,063	5,115
47 Rural nonfarm, assigned	0.66 x line 45	2,212	1,886	2,127	2,211	2,230	2,429	2,544
48 Total nonfarm, derived	lines 57/34	4,323	3,940	4,133	4,335	4,551	4,773	4,841
Estimated Value, Housekeeping Units, (thousands of dollars)								
49 120 central cities	lines 26* x 40	474,749	909,926	1,524,042	1,923,986	2,086,382	2,263,192	2,042,548
50 Urban environs (2,500 and over)	lines 27* x 41	212,593	356,078	589,207	821,417	911,384	1,035,867	988,808
51 Rural environs (under 2,500)	lines 28* x 42	92,322	127,581	234,729	301,010	316,427	356,389	351,364
52 Total environs	lines 50 + 51	304,915	483,659	823,936	1,122,427	1,227,811	1,392,256	1,340,172
53 96 metropolitan districts	lines 49 + 52	779,664	1,393,585	2,347,978	3,046,413	3,314,193	3,655,448	3,382,720
54 Nonmetropolitan districts urban	lines 31* x 45	214,236	273,934	434,335	512,825	527,840	569,697	499,031
55 Total urban	lines 53 + 54	993,900	1,667,519	2,782,313	3,559,238	3,842,033	4,225,145	3,881,751
56 Rural nonfarm	lines 33* x 47	74,095	103,515	175,058	215,542	223,439	249,947	230,163
57 Total nonfarm	lines 55 + 56	1,067,995	1,771,034	2,957,371	3,774,780	4,065,472	4,475,092	4,111,914
Estimated Value, Total New Residential Building (thousands of dollars)								
58 Nonhousekeeping dwellings	5/	54,166	69,801	157,214	205,689	178,580	278,603	202,326
59 Total new residential building	lines 57 + 58	1,122,161	1,840,835	3,114,585	3,980,469	4,244,052	4,753,695	4,314,240

*Line numbering refers to Table EM 10, as Table EM 11 is a continuation of EM 10.

[1] Bureau of Labor Statistics, _Building Construction_ (Feb. 1937), p. 68.

[2] Source of basic data: Bureau of Labor Statistics, Building Permits.

[3] Bureau of Labor Statistics.

[4] See text for method of deriving factors used in lines 40, 41, 42, 45, and 47.

[5] Hotels, clubs, lodging houses. Preliminary, subject to revision of basic data for 257 cities by Bureau of Labor Statistics.

TABLE EM 11

Dwelling Units Built, Aggregate Value, 1920-1936

1927	1928	1929	1920-29	1930	1931	1932	Source		
			Arithmetic average					**Unit Costs, Basic Data**	
$ 4,449	$ 4,407	$ 4,566	$ 4,304	$ 4,385	$ 4,225	$ 3,705	1/	Average, all types, 257 cities	35
4,416	4,357	4,597	4,300	4,385	4,225	3,705	2/	Average, all types, 113 central cities	36
5,023	5,063	5,068	4,706	5,392	5,366	4,670	2/	Average, all types, 64 satellite cities	37
6,239	6,471	6,429	5,820	6,779	6,784	5,312	3/	Average, 1-fam. dwellings, 64 satellite cities	38
3,864	3,969	3,901	3,616	3,820	3,669	3,004	3/	Average, 1-fam. dwellings, 80 non-metropolitan district cities	39
			Weighted average					**Unit Costs, as Applied** [4]	
5,211	5,141	5,424	5,074	5,174	4,986	4,372	1.18 x line 36	Central cities, assigned	40
6,229	6,278	6,284	5,835	6,686	6,654	5,791	1.24 x line 37	Urban environs, assigned	41
4,742	4,918	4,886	4,423	5,152	5,156	4,037	0.76 x line 38	Rural environs, assigned	42
5,737	5,828	5,821	5,391	6,178	6,144	5,184	lines 52/29	Total environs, derived	43
5,420	5,420	5,583	5,205	5,581	5,464	4,719	lines 53/30	96 metropolitan districts, derived	44
3,748	3,850	3,784	3,508	3,705	3,559	2,914	0.97 x line 39	Nonmetropolitan districts urban, assigned	45
5,116	5,095	5,151	4,865	5,139	5,017	4,145	lines 55/32	Total urban, derived	46
2,474	2,541	2,497	2,315	2,445	2,349	1,923	0.66 x line 45	Rural nonfarm, assigned	47
4,825	4,797	4,818	4,577	4,795	4,661	3,786	lines 57/34	Total nonfarm, derived	48
			Subtotal 1920-29					**Estimated Value, Housekeeping Units, (thousands of dollars)**	
1,851,036	1,611,606	1,101,848	15,789,315	585,485	411,520	105,584	lines 26* x 40	120 central cities	49
978,134	899,135	568,501	7,361,124	345,399	254,416	68,230	lines 27* x 41	Urban environs (2,500 and over)	50
368,425	348,494	218,702	2,715,443	131,675	101,681	25,191	lines 28* x 42	Rural environs (under 2,500)	51
1,346,559	1,247,629	787,203	10,076,567	477,074	356,097	93,421	lines 50 + 51	Total environs	52
3,197,595	2,859,235	1,889,051	25,865,882	1,062,559	767,617	199,005	lines 49 + 52	96 metropolitan districts	53
491,786	529,818	403,847	4,457,349	217,647	153,098	57,234	lines 31* x 45	Nonmetropolitan districts urban	54
3,689,381	3,389,053	2,292,898	30,323,231	1,280,206	920,715	256,239	lines 53 + 54	Total urban	55
220,545	223,481	159,858	1,875,643	89,015	66,458	22,913	lines 33* x 47	Rural nonfarm	56
3,909,926	3,612,534	2,452,756	32,198,874	1,369,221	987,173	279,152	lines 55 + 56	Total nonfarm	57
								Estimated Value, Total New Residential Building (thousands of dollars)	
154,381	200,234	170,619	1,671,613	86,407	17,402	2,990	5/	Nonhousekeeping dwellings	58
4,064,307	3,812,768	2,623,375	33,870,487	1,455,628	1,004,575	282,142	lines 57 + 58	Total new residential building	59

TABLE EM 11 (Cont'd)

Dwelling Units Built, Aggregate Value, 1920-1936

	Source	1933	1934	1935	1936	1930-36	1920-36
						Arithmetic average	
Unit Costs, Basic Data							
35 Average, all types, 257 cities	1/	$ 3,494	$ 3,381	$ 3,759	$ 4,073	$ 3,860	$ 4,082
36 Average, all types, 113 central cities	2/	3,494	3,381	3,759	4,073	3,860	4,080
37 Average, all types, 64 satellite cities	2/	5,325	5,597	5,521	5,226	5,342	5,024
38 Average, 1-fam. dwellings, 64 satellite cities	3/	5,625	5,840	5,754	5,785	5,983	5,902
39 Average, 1-fam. dwellings, 80 non-metropolitan district cities	3/	2,804	2,816	3,224	3,410	3,250	3,433
Unit Costs, as Applied[4]						Weighted average	
40 Central cities, assigned	1.18 x line 36	4,123	3,990	4,436	4,806	4,555	4,814
41 Urban environs, assigned	1.24 x line 37	6,603	6,940	6,846	6,480	6,624	6,230
42 Rural environs, assigned	0.76 x line 38	4,275	4,438	4,373	4,397	4,547	4,486
43 Total environs, derived	lines 52/29	5,770	6,023	5,921	5,638	5,919	5,465
44 96 metropolitan districts, derived	lines 53/30	4,849	4,814	5,014	5,134	5,256	5,212
45 Nonmetropolitan districts urban, assigned	0.97 x line 39	2,720	2,732	3,127	3,308	3,153	3,330
46 Total urban, derived	lines 55/32	4,182	4,210	4,457	4,657	4,752	4,851
47 Rural nonfarm, assigned	0.66 x line 45	1,795	1,803	2,064	2,183	2,081	2,198
48 Total nonfarm, derived	lines 57/34	3,780	3,797	4,024	4,218	4,355	4,547
Estimated Value, Housekeeping Units, (thousands of dollars)						Subtotal 1930-36	Grand total 1920-36
49 120 central cities	lines 26* x 40	70,668	77,370	225,194	499,281	1,975,102	17,764,417
50 Urban environs (2,500 and over)	lines 27* x 41	57,255	58,074	138,686	261,176	1,183,236	8,544,360
51 Rural environs (under 2,500)	lines 28* x 42	20,635	21,471	52,979	120,306	473,938	3,189,381
52 Total environs	lines 50 + 51	77,890	79,545	191,665	381,482	1,657,174	11,733,741
53 96 metropolitan districts	lines 49 + 52	148,558	156,915	416,859	880,763	3,632,276	29,498,158
54 Nonmetropolitan districts urban	lines 31* x 45	37,968	36,377	108,860	200,422	811,606	5,268,955
55 Total urban	lines 53 + 54	186,526	193,292	525,719	1,081,185	4,443,882	34,767,113
56 Rural nonfarm	lines 33* x 47	16,241	17,127	53,796	109,340	374,890	2,250,533
57 Total nonfarm	lines 55 + 56	202,767	210,419	579,515	1,190,525	4,818,772	37,017,646
Estimated Value, Total New Residential Building (thousands of dollars)							
58 Nonhousekeeping dwellings	5/	1,507	3,262	5,052	11,025	127,645	1,799,258
59 Total new residential building	lines 57 + 58	204,274	213,681	584,567	1,201,550	4,946,417	38,816,905

*Line numbering refers to Table EM 10, as Table EM 11 is a continuation of EM 10.

[1] Bureau of Labor Statistics, *Building Construction* (Feb. 1937), p. 68.

[2] Source of basic data: Bureau of Labor Statistics, *Building Permits*.

[3] Bureau of Labor Statistics.

[4] See text for method of deriving factors used in lines 40, 41, 42, 45, and 47.

[5] Hotels, clubs, lodging houses. Preliminary, subject to revision of basic data for 257 cities by Bureau of Labor Statistics.

TABLE EM 12

Dwelling Units Built, Estimated Aggregate for 1920-1929

		Mean	Minimum	Maximum
		(thousands of dwelling units)		
Occupied dwelling units,				
January 1 [1]	1930	23,097	...	...
	1920	17,556	...	...
10-year increase		5,541	...	...
Dwelling units standing,				
January 1 [2]	1930	24,313	24,313	24,571
	1920	17,733	17,914	17,733
10-year increase		6,580	6,399	6,838
10-year change in vacancy		1,039	858	1,297
Losses, total [3]		580	450	715
Demolitions [3]		330	250	415
Fire, flood, wind, and other losses [4]		250	200	300
Total units built		7,160	6,849	7,553
Units added by conversions, net [5]		125	166	83
Total new units built		7,035	6,683	7,470

[1] Based on *Census of Population, 1930*, VI, 11. The Census figure 23,235,982 for nonfarm families (private) April 1, 1930 was adjusted to a January 1 basis by straight line interpolation. Nonfarm families (including quasi-families) January 1, 1920 numbered 17,600,472. In estimating the number of private families in 1920, the relationship between private and quasi-families in 1930 was assumed to apply.

[2] Estimated vacancy, percentage:
Mean change   - from 1 per cent in 1920 to 5 per cent in 1930
Minimum change - from 2 per cent in 1920 to 5 per cent in 1930
Maximum change - from 1 per cent in 1920 to 6 per cent in 1930

These data are based on the following sources: weighted average of vacancies, early 1930, all types of dwellings in 16 large cities, was 6.0 per cent (Residential Vacancy Surveys in the United States, 1930-34, Federal Housing Administration, March 9, 1935). Apartment vacancies, New York City, probably 10 per cent (7.8 per cent, Nov. 1928, and 12.0 per cent, June 1932), New York City Tenement House Department reports. Vacancies in dwellings, only those fit for occupancy, in Philadelphia, 4.0 per cent (Philadelphia Housing Association). Beginning of 1920, apartment vacancies 0.4 per cent in New York City; dwelling vacancies in Philadelphia probably less than 1.0 per cent (1.65 in 1917 and 0.67 in 1921). On the other hand, some cities were temporarily overbuilt following cessation of war-time activity in principal industries, e.g., Chester, Pa., and Camden, N.J. (shipbuilding), Charleston, W.Va. (armor plate, chemicals), Gary, Hammond, and East Chicago, Ind. (steel), Peoria, Ill. (tractors), but since dwellings are predominantly of the 1-family type and vacancies in this type are generally lower than for other types, vacancies probably are relatively low in any event.

[3] Estimated units demolished annually per 10,000 population: mean 4, minimum 3, maximum 5 (see Table EM 8).

[4] See text accompanying Table EM 8.

[5] Estimated units added by conversions annually per 10,000 population: mean 1½, minimum 1, maximum 2. (The maximum number of conversions was subtracted from the minimum number of total units built to estimate the minimum number of new units built. Likewise, the minimum number of conversions was subtracted from the maximum number of units built to estimate the maximum number of new units built). Based on: (a) 1921-27 data for 25-68 cities over 25,000 in population reported in building permits (BLS) indicating an annual increase of 3.5 to 6.0 units per 10,000 population; (b) 1923-35 data for Philadelphia averaging 3.7 units increase per 10,000 population (Philadelphia Housing Association); (c) conversions in apartment buildings, New York City, indicating a small net decrease (N.Y. City Tenement House Department); (d) allowance for conversion of residential buildings to non-residential use in areas not covered by permits, and for a probably lower rate of conversions, and an increasing number of units in small cities and rural areas.

TABLE EM 13

Demolitions, Selected Cities, 1918-1935

		Dwelling Units Demolished Annually per 10,000 Pop.		
		Entire period	Prior to & inc. 1929	Since 1929
Dwellings, all types				
Philadelphia [1]	1923-35	6.4	4.1	6.9
Minneapolis [2]	1923-32	4.7	...	...
Cleveland [3]	1932-35	8.3	...	8.3
Denver [4]	1931-35	4.7	...	4.7
Manhattan, New York City [5]	1918-32	19.3	15.8	29.0
78 central cities [6]	1929-35	3.2	...	3.2 [7]
44 satellite cities [6]	1929-35	2.2	...	2.2 [7]
37 nonmetropolitan cities [6]	1929-35	1.3	...	1.3 [7]
Apartments only [5]				
Manhattan	1918-35	16.0	13.0	23.1
Bronx	1918-35	0.8	0.4	1.5
Brooklyn	1918-35	2.3	1.8	3.1
Queens	1918-35	0.7	0.3	1.2
Richmond	1918-35	0.4	0.3	0.4
Total New York City	1918-35	6.2	5.3	7.9

[1] Philadelphia Housing Association, *Housing in Philadelphia, 1932-35*

[2] University of Minnesota, Employment Stabilization Research Institute, *The Construction Industry in Minnesota*, June 1934, p.30

[3] H. W. Green, Real Property Inventory, Cleveland, 1935.

[4] University of Denver, *Business Review*, Nov. 1931, 1933, 1934, 1935.

[5] Apartment demolitions from New York City Tenement House Department, annual reports; 1- and 2-family dwelling units demolished in Manhattan, estimated from number of buildings demolished (2-family not segregated) in annual report, Borough President, 1932-33, Borough of Manhattan.

[6] Special tabulation furnished by Bureau of Labor Statistics, Division of Construction and Public Employment. Partial list from 810 cities with populations over 10,000; does not include large cities listed separately above.

[7] Includes 1929.

TABLE EM 14

Dwelling Units Built, 1935, Based on 811 Bureau of Labor Statistics reporting Cities 10,000 and over in Population

	POP. 1930 (000's)	DWELLING UNITS BUILT, 1935	
		Number	Per 10,000 population (3)=(2)÷(1)10
	(1)	(2)	(3)
257 cities, pop. 25,000 and over	44,909	55,810[1]	12.44
554 cities, pop. 10,000-25,000	10,515	20,705[1]	19.68
811 cities, pop. 10,000 and under	55,424	76,515[1]	13.82
Nonfarm outside 811 cities	38,906	67,500[3]	18.30[2]
Total nonfarm	92,330	144,015	15.62

[1]*Source: Bureau of Labor Statistics, 'Families Provided For', 811 cities.*

[2]*Based on average of 19.68 units per 10,000 population for 554 reporting cities with populations of from 10,000 to 25,000, but modified to conform to relationships found in 1936 estimate based on 1,689 cities having populations over 2,500. Ratio of building rates for first two groups of cities for 1935: $\frac{554\ cities\ 19.68}{257\ cities\ 12.44} = 1.582$; but for 1936, ratio is: $\frac{32.21}{25.60} = 1.258$, indicating that the 1935 rate for cities with populations of from 10,000 to 25,000 is too high to use unchanged for estimating unreported nonfarm, since population and building in unreported areas were over three times as large as for sample cities with populations from 10,000 to 25,000. On the other hand, the 1936 estimate indicates that the building rate in unreported nonfarm areas under 10,000 was 1.17 times as great as the reporting group of cities with populations from 10,000 to 25,000 ($\frac{37.60}{32.21} = 1.17$). Thus $19.68 \times 1.17 \times \frac{1.258}{1.582} = 18.30$ units per 10,000 population. This building rate may be an underestimate to a minor degree since the nonfarm population outside 811 cities was probably a slightly larger percentage of the total population in 1935 than in 1930.*

[3][*Col.(1)÷10*]×*col.(2)*.

TABLE EM 15

Dwelling Units Built, 1936[1].

←——————— DWELLING UNITS BUILT, 1936 ———————→

	NUMBER OF CITIES			POPULATION, 1930 (thousands)			PER 10,000 POPULATION					
	B.L.S.[2]	Unre-ported	Total	B.L.S.[2]	Unre-ported	Total	B.L.S.[2]	Unre-ported	Total	B.L.S.[2]	UNRE-PORTED	TOTAL
	(1)	(2)	(3)	(4)	(5)	(6)	(7) $\frac{(10)\times10}{(4)}$	(8)[6]	(9) $\frac{(12)\times10}{(6)}$	(10)	(11) $\frac{(5)\times(8)}{10}$	(12)
Metropolitan districts												
Central cities[3]	120	...	120	37,815	...	37,815	27.47	...	27.47	103,887	...	103,887
Urban environs, 2,500 and over[3]	613	252	865	9,580	1,747	11,327	35.39	(36.62)	35.58	33,906	6,399	40,305
Rural environs, under 2,500	...	...	...	...	5,645	5,645	...	(48.47)[4]	48.47[4]	...	27,361	27,361
Total environs	613	252	865	9,580	7,392	16,972	35.39	(45.67)	39.86	33,906	33,760	67,666
Total metropolitan districts	733	252	985	47,395	7,392	54,787	29.07	(45.67)	31.31	137,793	33,760	171,553
Nonmetropolitan urban[3]	956	1,224	2,180	13,185	6,628	19,813	29.61	(32.50)	30.58	39,045	21,542	60,587
Total urban	1,689	1,476	3,165	60,580	14,020	74,600	29.19	(39.45)	31.12	176,838	55,302	232,140
Rural nonfarm	...	...	...	...	17,730	17,730	...	(28.25)[5]	28.25[5]	...	50,087	50,087
Total nonfarm	1,689	...	...	60,580	31,750	92,330	29.19	(33.19)	30.57	176,838	105,389	282,227

[1]*Preliminary. Subject to revision when basic data for reporting cities are available in sufficient detail to make possible estimating totals by region and population group, and for rural environs and other rural areas on the basis of current empirical data.*

[2]*Cities reporting building permits to the Bureau of Labor Statistics.*

[3]*Derived from totals for cities by size of population groups, thus: 500,000 and over, 100,000-500,000, 50,000-100,000, 25,000-50,000, 10,000-25,000, 5,000-10,000, 2,500-5,000. Dwelling units per 10,000 population for unreported cities in each size group [col. (8)] were assigned on the basis of data for reporting cities of the same size [col. (7)], but corrected for differences in rates of growth of population in reporting and unreported cities.*

[4]*Estimated on basis of average for all urban environs [col. (9)], corrected for differences in rates of growth of population in urban and rural environs.*

[5]*Estimated on basis of average for reporting nonmetropolitan cities [col. (7)], corrected for differences in rates of growth of population.*

[6]*Parentheses indicate derived data.*

PART THREE

SECTION A

Value of Residential Real Estate

Section A has 17 tables. The number and value of non-farm dwelling units in 1930 are covered in the first 7. Tables A 1–5 are based upon estimates prepared by the National Bureau as described in detail in Chapter II. The value estimates are based upon owners' statements of value and tenants' statements of rent. The probable accuracy of owners' appraisals is discussed in Chapter I, section 2, and the technical methods used in estimating aggregate values are presented in the Note to Part One.

The information on values in Tables A 1–5 is given for six population groups. As explained in Chapter II, section 2 a, it was not possible to make the further important breakdown by metropolitan and nonmetropolitan areas. For this reason, it should be borne in mind that average values and rents by population groups obscure variations within the groups, depending on the proportion of satellite and non-satellite cities included. Other evidence indicates that in certain areas the location of cities within or outside metropolitan districts reflects the degree of urbanization better than the grouping by size. Preliminary estimates of values and rents for several metropolitan districts and adjacent nonmetropolitan areas on a county basis showed generally much higher average values and rents within metropolitan districts. These relationships were utilized in connection with the estimates of residential construction (see Ch. V, sec. 1 a). Furthermore, values and rents in satellite cities within metropolitan districts within a given population group averaged higher than in cities of the same size group outside metropolitan districts, particularly in the case of small population groups.

Tables A 6 and 7 are based upon the special tabulation of 1930 Census data for 139 cities. The essential details concerning this tabulation are presented in Chapter II, section 4. Table A 6 gives, for owner-occupied dwellings, average value per dwelling unit, all types, by value classes for each of the 139 cities and the average values of 1-family dwellings for all value classes combined. In Table B 5 similar data are presented for monthly rents of rented dwelling units and, in addition, monthly rents of 2- and 3-or-more

family dwellings. The reasons for giving rents for the two types of multiple dwelling units but not value data by similar classifications for the owner-occupied properties are stated in Chapter II, section 3 f.

The number of dwelling units for which average values (Table A 6) and rents (Table B 5) are derived for population groups of 2,500 or more can be determined from the *Census of Population, 1930,* Volume VI, Families. Since the Census does not publish data for smaller population groups separately, Tables A 7 and B 6 were prepared to show the distribution of the number of units by value and rent groups for a sample of these small population centers.

The estimate of the value of nonfarm residential real estate for 1934 (Table A 8) was based upon the value derived for 1930 from Census data and the change in values from 1930 to 1934 as determined from other sources, as explained in Chapter II, sections 5 and 6.

Tables A 9–16, derived almost entirely from either the Federal Real Property Inventory or the Financial Survey of Urban Housing, present data for 1934 and in some instances corresponding data for 1930. Table A 17 is derived from Census reports and provides information on farm residences in 1930.

The number of dwelling units by value classes (Table A 9) for 1930 and 1934 is derived from various sources, as indicated in the source note. To make the data comparable it is necessary to restrict the coverage to 1-family dwellings, since Census values are for dwelling units and the Federal Real Property Inventory obtained values of structures. Furthermore, the Census definition of 1-family dwellings differs from that used by the Federal Real Property Inventory (see Ch. II, sec. 1). Only part of the discrepancy arising from the difference in definition can be eliminated. The Federal Real Property Inventory count of 1-family dwellings excludes row houses and 2-family side-by-side houses having a common wall (see Ch. II, sec. 1, footnote 4). Row houses are shown separately; hence it was possible to add them to the number of 1-family dwellings. But since 2-family side-by-side houses were not similarly segregated it was not possible to add them to the number of 1-family dwellings. They were, however, included in the Census count. Owing to the lack of strict comparability the decrease (101,556) in the number of 1-family owner-occupied dwellings between the two years cannot be interpreted as an actual reduction in comparable units. Table A 9 is useful chiefly in studying the relative shift in the number of dwelling units among the value classes. Table B 7, which presents similar information for rented dwellings, indicates an increase of 72,635 rented dwelling units of all types for the 61 cities covered. It is probable that the decrease in 1-family owner-occupied dwellings for the 61 cities (101,556) is partly the result of the failure to include 2-family side-by-side houses for 1934 and the shift in dwelling units from the owner-occupied to the rented class. The increase in rented dwellings is due largely to a shift in tenure, which was accentuated by the depression during those years. Tables A 9 and B 7 are included primarily to show the shifts in the relative number of dwellings in the several value or rent classes. The absolute number of units indicates merely the magnitude of the quantities distributed.

The average values per dwelling unit for 50 cities in 1934 (Table A 10) are reasonably comparable with the Census average values for 1930 since the weighting of the Financial Survey average values for each value class by the number of dwelling units in that value class as reported by the Real Property Inventory should approximate average values on a full coverage basis. Only average values of 1-family dwellings are compared, for the reason cited in the comments on Table A 9. The difference between the average values so computed for 1934 and the average values derived directly from the Financial Survey sample is revealed when Tables A 10 and 14 are compared.

Table A 17 shows the difference in the values of nonfarm and farm dwellings. The value of an acre of farm land is included with the farm dwelling to make the physical specifications of the two classes of property more alike though the land site for the farm dwelling is usually much lower in value than the land on which city dwellings are built. The construction of the dwellings must also be considered, though it is doubtful whether this difference in materials of construction and workmanship is any greater than that between many towns and cities, especially when they are in different parts of the country. For further discussion concerning the accuracy of the data see Part One, Chapter II.

TABLE A I

Dwelling Units[1] by Tenure, Population Group, State, and Geographic Division, April 1, 1930

	All population groups	100,000 or more	25,000-100,000	10,000-25,000	5,000-10,000	2,500-5,000	Under 2,500	All population groups	100,000 or more	25,000-100,000
	TOTAL							OWNER-OCCUPIED		
United States	24,409,239	9,699,008	3,382,608	2,368,309	1,541,259	1,249,423	6,168,632	11,089,450	3,471,464	1,559,062
New England	1,950,694	636,752	492,223	307,856	121,006	30,830	362,027	843,382	184,638	203,217
Maine	164,524		33,432	22,533	16,631	7,139	84,789	89,279		12,572
New Hampshire	108,573		33,991	24,153	6,235	4,686	39,508	53,531		12,942
Vermont	66,919			13,852	13,449	3,882	35,736	33,307		
Massachusetts	1,049,389	447,258	261,912	172,966	68,941	10,106	88,206	436,741	130,647	110,988
Rhode Island	171,267	65,507	63,318	23,128	6,884	917	11,513	67,764	20,753	25,786
Connecticut	390,022	123,987	99,570	51,224	8,866	4,100	102,275	162,760	33,238	40,929
Mid. Atlantic	6,343,035	3,319,460	730,702	627,064	339,439	268,556	1,057,814	2,656,209	995,373	327,132
New York	3,194,659	2,267,523	209,335	191,742	71,827	84,219	370,013	1,071,754	535,964	94,555
New Jersey	1,004,641	316,130	241,018	156,325	89,645	49,394	152,129	472,103	101,246	89,573
Pennsylvania	2,143,735	735,807	280,349	278,997	177,967	134,943	535,672	1,112,352	358,163	143,004
E. N. Central	5,571,481	2,474,379	907,896	473,421	351,602	253,350	1,110,833	2,840,959	965,604	488,434
Ohio	1,529,047	711,866	201,587	140,045	100,593	64,697	310,259	787,417	301,363	101,873
Indiana	672,259	212,652	126,317	66,788	50,258	36,304	179,940	365,822	99,094	63,243
Illinois	1,781,033	923,208	272,356	125,915	106,505	75,533	277,516	805,400	289,256	146,301
Michigan	1,043,906	475,412	182,541	82,525	57,083	41,027	205,318	570,443	212,027	103,987
Wisconsin	545,236	151,241	125,095	58,148	37,163	35,789	137,800	311,877	63,864	73,030
W. N. Central	2,269,737	721,248	227,227	237,723	149,050	170,691	763,798	1,195,512	305,751	117,381
Minnesota	436,264	219,951		38,826	29,859	33,641	114,187	240,135	107,383	
Iowa	430,238	39,786	111,024	46,222	26,594	47,525	159,087	246,438	20,232	58,841
Missouri	700,806	339,238	54,374	44,133	41,874	34,285	187,102	316,951	115,657	26,171
N. Dakota	69,525		6,865	10,411	8,190	1,346	42,713	37,915		2,986
S. Dakota	80,301		8,532	15,263	3,046	7,084	46,376	42,249		3,943
Nebraska	219,370	57,273	20,921	20,682	16,453	15,575	88,466	124,272	29,339	11,163
Kansas	333,233	65,000	25,511	62,186	23,434	31,235	125,867	187,552	33,140	14,277
S. Atlantic	2,454,335	605,465	381,598	178,291	147,522	138,059	1,003,400	981,703	244,107	132,787
Delaware	50,719	26,885				4,595	19,239	25,510	12,215	
Maryland	350,345	202,271	17,407	9,511	5,543	11,545	104,068	187,281	103,209	6,995
D. C.	131,058	131,058						49,970	49,970	
Virginia	356,411	81,239	54,992	25,829	18,409	16,285	159,657	158,192	26,763	21,645
W. Virginia	298,487		64,952	21,577	19,898	15,205	176,855	110,000		27,052
N. Carolina	358,884		98,323	40,617	25,605	23,313	171,026	143,457		34,139
S. Carolina	199,786		43,735	15,568	18,166	14,855	107,462	59,026		12,017
Georgia	380,901	71,915	64,729	39,861	29,055	28,223	147,118	121,652	20,809	15,378
Florida	327,744	92,097	37,460	25,328	30,846	24,038	117,975	126,615	31,141	15,561
E. S. Central	1,235,048	319,478	116,320	125,715	79,020	91,680	502,835	492,188	120,660	46,192
Kentucky	374,323	84,776	55,585	23,422	30,189	23,520	156,831	163,712	34,910	23,901
Tennessee	355,463	166,977	5,413	11,829	25,283	24,072	121,889	147,335	62,850	2,324
Alabama	331,743	67,725	35,304	47,079	17,122	23,537	140,976	112,070	22,900	12,302
Mississippi	173,519		20,018	43,385	6,426	20,551	83,139	69,071		7,665
W. S. Central	1,794,442	482,519	195,141	173,732	159,184	152,387	631,479	765,988	176,452	80,059
Arkansas	198,608		29,470	29,802	15,489	28,218	95,629	87,310		12,821
Louisiana	324,461	118,055	35,862	17,183	18,156	24,944	110,261	118,696	32,485	13,667
Oklahoma	362,644	87,802	16,229	45,846	43,517	28,094	141,156	159,739	33,600	7,865
Texas	908,729	276,662	113,580	80,901	82,022	71,131	284,433	400,243	110,367	45,706
Mountain	686,877	118,842	80,776	66,137	71,247	54,906	294,969	326,877	55,201	36,957
Montana	90,601		18,383	15,554	10,234	4,741	41,689	42,023		7,185
Idaho	68,636			10,472	11,792	11,880	34,492	34,236		
Wyoming	41,370			9,625	7,120	2,769	21,856	16,291		
Colorado	211,297	82,827	23,354	16,453	16,261	8,455	63,947	102,641	37,387	12,630
New Mexico	66,429		7,198	5,540	6,548	7,946	39,197	32,825		3,527
Arizona	88,020		21,480		11,579	6,265	48,696	35,302		7,988
Utah	97,888	36,015	10,361	3,218	5,931	9,782	32,581	53,965	17,814	5,627
Nevada	22,636			5,275	1,782	3,068	12,511	9,594		
Pacific	2,103,590	1,020,865	250,725	178,370	123,189	88,964	441,477	986,632	423,878	126,903
Washington	360,858	170,943	17,538	39,978	7,885	18,281	106,233	199,511	91,887	10,483
Oregon	218,566	91,328	7,068	16,078	18,124	13,181	72,787	118,432	49,509	4,156
California	1,524,166	758,594	226,119	122,314	97,180	57,502	262,457	668,689	282,282	112,264

[1] Includes vacant.

TABLE A I

Dwelling Units[1] by Tenure, Population Group, State, and Geographic Division, April 1, 1930

OWNER-OCCUPIED				RENTED							
10,000-25,000	5,000-10,000	2,500-5,000	Under 2,500	All population groups	100,000 or more	25,000-100,000	10,000-25,000	5,000-10,000	2,500-5,000	Under 2,500	
1,233,793	832,701	690,130	3,302,300	13,319,789	6,227,544	1,823,546	1,134,516	708,558	559,293	2,866,332	**United States**
158,930	64,331	15,770	216,496	1,107,312	452,114	289,006	148,926	56,675	15,060	145,531	**New England**
10,756	8,802	4,196	52,953	75,245		20,860	11,777	7,829	2,943	31,836	Maine
11,388	2,956	2,378	23,867	55,042		21,049	12,765	3,279	2,308	15,641	New Hampshire
6,204	5,858	1,633	19,612	33,612			7,648	7,591	2,249	16,124	Vermont
94,468	39,492	5,484	55,662	612,648	316,611	150,924	78,498	29,449	4,622	32,544	Massachusetts
11,275	3,431	415	6,104	103,503	44,754	37,532	11,853	3,453	502	5,409	Rhode Island
24,839	3,792	1,664	58,298	227,262	90,749	58,641	26,385	5,074	2,436	43,977	Connecticut
343,592	192,921	161,909	635,282	3,686,826	2,324,087	403,570	283,472	146,518	106,647	422,532	**Mid. Atlantic**
107,720	41,151	51,428	240,936	2,122,905	1,731,559	114,780	84,022	30,676	32,791	129,077	New York
93,408	55,271	31,509	101,096	532,538	214,884	151,445	62,917	34,374	17,885	51,033	New Jersey
142,464	96,499	78,972	293,250	1,031,383	377,644	137,345	136,533	81,468	55,971	242,422	Pennsylvania
284,222	219,973	162,419	720,307	2,730,522	1,508,775	419,462	189,199	131,629	90,931	390,526	**E. N. Central**
83,453	61,696	40,841	198,191	741,630	410,503	99,714	56,592	38,897	23,856	112,068	Ohio
37,341	28,957	22,312	114,875	306,437	113,558	63,074	29,447	21,301	13,992	65,065	Indiana
76,099	67,463	48,711	177,570	975,633	633,952	126,055	49,816	39,042	26,822	99,946	Illinois
50,759	36,848	27,212	139,610	473,463	263,385	78,554	31,766	20,235	13,815	65,708	Michigan
36,570	25,009	23,343	90,061	233,359	87,377	52,065	21,578	12,154	12,446	47,739	Wisconsin
127,374	83,743	99,933	461,330	1,074,225	415,497	109,846	110,349	65,307	70,758	302,468	**W. N. Central**
21,594	17,868	21,112	72,178	196,129	112,568		17,232	11,791	12,529	42,009	Minnesota
25,083	14,973	28,467	98,842	183,800	19,554	52,183	21,139	11,621	19,058	60,245	Iowa
24,246	22,811	18,714	109,352	383,855	223,581	28,203	19,887	18,863	15,571	77,750	Missouri
4,748	4,086	794	25,301	31,610		3,879	5,663	4,104	552	17,412	N. Dakota
7,242	1,537	3,626	25,901	38,052		4,589	8,021	1,509	3,458	20,475	S. Dakota
11,203	9,253	9,231	54,083	95,098	27,934	9,758	9,479	7,200	6,344	34,383	Nebraska
33,258	13,215	17,989	75,673	145,681	31,860	11,234	28,928	10,219	13,246	50,194	Kansas
71,091	63,105	59,681	410,932	1,472,632	361,358	248,811	107,200	84,417	78,378	592,468	**S. Atlantic**
		2,441	10,854	25,209	14,670				2,154	8,385	Delaware
4,318	2,884	6,071	63,804	163,064	99,062	10,412	5,193	2,659	5,474	40,264	Maryland
				81,088	81,088						D. C.
11,516	9,032	7,978	81,258	198,219	54,476	33,347	14,313	9,377	8,307	78,399	Virginia
10,469	9,224	7,413	55,842	188,487		37,900	11,108	10,674	7,792	121,013	W. Virginia
15,493	11,299	10,157	72,369	215,427		64,184	25,124	14,306	13,156	98,657	N. Carolina
5,304	6,508	5,731	29,466	140,760		31,718	10,284	11,658	9,124	77,996	S. Carolina
13,321	11,040	9,268	51,836	259,249	51,106	49,351	26,540	18,015	18,955	95,282	Georgia
10,670	13,118	10,622	45,503	201,129	60,956	21,899	14,658	17,728	13,416	72,472	Florida
48,825	34,254	41,372	200,885	742,860	198,818	70,128	76,890	44,766	50,308	301,950	**E. S. Central**
11,032	14,748	11,276	67,845	210,611	49,866	31,684	12,390	15,441	12,244	88,986	Kentucky
5,026	10,737	11,369	55,029	208,128	104,127	3,089	6,803	14,546	12,703	66,860	Tennessee
16,430	6,063	9,491	44,884	219,673	44,825	23,002	30,649	11,059	14,046	96,092	Alabama
16,337	2,706	9,236	33,127	104,448		12,353	27,048	3,720	11,315	50,012	Mississippi
76,433	75,105	73,650	284,289	1,028,454	306,067	115,082	97,299	84,079	78,737	347,190	**W. S. Central**
12,398	7,127	12,784	42,180	111,298		16,649	17,404	8,362	15,434	53,449	Arkansas
7,246	8,024	11,291	45,983	205,765	85,570	22,195	9,937	10,132	13,653	64,278	Louisiana
19,933	20,248	13,975	64,118	202,905	54,202	8,364	25,913	23,269	14,119	77,038	Oklahoma
36,856	39,706	35,600	132,008	508,486	166,295	67,874	44,045	42,316	35,531	152,425	Texas
31,795	34,982	27,565	140,377	360,000	63,641	43,819	34,342	36,265	27,341	154,592	**Mountain**
7,088	4,903	2,540	20,307	48,578		11,198	8,466	5,331	2,201	21,382	Montana
4,940	6,383	6,138	16,775	34,400			5,532	5,409	5,742	17,717	Idaho
4,108	3,205	1,164	7,814	25,079			5,517	3,915	1,605	14,042	Wyoming
8,493	8,579	4,591	30,961	108,656	45,440	10,724	7,960	7,682	3,864	32,986	Colorado
2,746	3,113	4,024	19,416	33,604		3,671	2,794	3,436	3,922	19,781	New Mexico
	4,469	2,186	20,659	52,718		13,492		7,110	4,079	28,037	Arizona
2,027	3,739	5,543	19,215	43,923	18,201	4,734	1,191	2,192	4,239	13,366	Utah
2,393	592	1,379	5,230	13,042			2,882	1,190	1,689	7,281	Nevada
91,531	64,287	47,831	232,402	1,116,958	597,187	123,822	86,839	58,902	41,133	209,075	**Pacific**
20,922	4,316	10,092	61,811	161,347	79,056	7,055	19,056	3,569	8,189	44,422	Washington
7,717	9,700	7,257	40,093	100,134	41,819	2,912	8,361	8,424	5,924	32,694	Oregon
62,892	50,271	30,482	130,498	855,477	476,312	113,855	59,422	46,909	27,020	131,959	California

TABLE A 2

Dwelling Units,[1] Total Value (thousands of dollars) by Tenure, Population Group, State, and Geographic Division, April 1, 1930

	TOTAL							OWNER-OCCUPIED		
	All population groups	100,000 or more	25,000-100,000	10,000-25,000	5,000-10,000	2,500-5,000	Under 2,500	All population groups	100,000 or more	25,000-100,000
United States	122,578,481	62,877,941	19,274,857	11,992,130	6,792,361	4,775,663	16,865,529	64,681,033	27,060,650	11,222,093
New England	9,529,852	3,256,380	2,717,849	1,567,805	511,063	122,170	1,354,585	5,691,304	1,596,926	1,634,162
Maine	549,592		158,377	93,860	53,915	21,824	221,596	349,564		86,797
New Hampshire	355,444		130,392	89,428	18,187	15,939	101,498	216,329		74,441
Vermont	241,288			71,629	58,022	15,756	95,881	153,512		
Massachusetts	5,427,070	2,247,189	1,539,949	929,127	309,633	47,818	353,354	3,160,507	1,072,180	919,895
Rhode Island	800,925	328,743	309,786	94,923	25,496	3,755	38,222	483,202	181,054	191,712
Connecticut	2,155,533	680,448	579,345	288,818	45,810	17,078	544,034	1,328,190	343,692	361,317
Mid. Atlantic	45,701,866	27,590,281	5,553,554	4,240,089	2,200,347	1,582,838	4,534,757	20,782,511	9,470,295	2,961,038
New York	25,971,965	20,227,599	1,577,714	1,245,259	536,869	506,456	1,878,068	9,688,474	5,984,632	861,742
New Jersey	7,688,795	2,330,057	2,118,453	1,337,584	718,983	346,306	837,412	4,215,989	916,477	1,020,705
Pennsylvania	12,041,106	5,032,625	1,857,387	1,657,246	944,495	730,076	1,819,277	6,878,048	2,569,186	1,078,591
E. N. Central	29,954,726	15,978,156	5,606,308	2,556,845	1,584,321	1,033,360	3,195,736	16,838,971	7,392,402	3,510,795
Ohio	7,856,262	4,063,506	1,345,202	721,092	471,286	290,012	965,164	4,703,521	2,138,879	829,393
Indiana	2,609,943	1,081,488	587,687	258,371	161,870	108,117	412,410	1,556,264	591,878	341,315
Illinois	10,980,130	6,609,189	1,871,300	808,725	568,485	318,572	803,859	5,524,270	2,532,008	1,184,068
Michigan	5,830,956	3,317,248	1,089,873	430,453	225,169	176,598	591,615	3,373,448	1,688,846	680,824
Wisconsin	2,677,435	906,725	712,246	338,204	157,511	140,061	422,688	1,681,468	440,991	475,195
W. N. Central	8,054,868	3,246,863	957,450	925,847	537,833	539,227	1,847,648	5,085,010	1,861,317	598,885
Minnesota	1,713,710	1,032,888		158,701	102,236	119,017	300,868	1,127,952	649,429	
Iowa	1,469,416	163,232	462,287	185,814	94,781	159,598	403,904	985,378	101,880	293,873
Missouri	2,704,755	1,595,303	228,536	190,193	164,674	97,224	428,825	1,576,786	829,828	139,139
N. Dakota	208,869		35,674	45,697	31,327	4,000	92,171	122,611		19,404
S. Dakota	249,489		38,948	62,541	9,119	24,980	113,901	151,131		21,837
Nebraska	761,144	236,791	97,672	82,421	60,562	48,812	234,886	507,228	147,068	62,808
Kansas	947,485	218,649	94,333	200,680	75,134	85,596	273,093	613,924	133,112	61,824
S. Atlantic	8,337,445	3,126,148	1,561,919	639,822	508,217	408,687	2,092,652	4,793,861	1,709,521	862,532
Delaware	230,405	149,140				17,591	63,674	145,560	88,774	
Maryland	1,594,753	1,026,257	83,477	42,794	25,558	45,310	371,357	1,057,315	648,269	47,784
D. C.	920,719	920,719						477,487	477,487	
Virginia	1,188,445	363,539	202,696	111,764	69,890	56,313	384,243	716,425	178,712	116,423
W. Virginia	900,325		335,032	102,411	82,484	56,425	323,973	500,395		193,564
N. Carolina	1,009,431		422,816	129,309	81,784	68,694	306,828	590,518		235,498
S. Carolina	453,652		156,960	49,528	48,787	37,667	160,710	237,071		82,358
Georgia	1,005,443	300,703	196,337	113,718	73,473	60,011	261,201	501,047	136,703	87,227
Florida	1,034,272	365,790	164,601	90,298	126,241	66,676	220,666	568,043	179,576	99,678
E. S. Central	3,348,891	1,254,312	439,382	364,212	227,055	222,291	841,639	1,892,735	680,528	246,580
Kentucky	1,132,250	361,956	235,057	83,439	98,719	64,623	288,456	672,456	199,975	136,406
Tennessee	1,030,525	633,048	20,693	37,853	66,324	57,873	214,734	582,542	340,457	12,125
Alabama	799,337	259,308	114,198	126,964	44,265	50,327	204,275	425,804	140,096	59,888
Mississippi	386,779		69,434	115,956	17,747	49,468	134,174	211,933		38,161
W. S. Central	5,323,606	2,124,571	738,982	549,654	462,820	384,052	1,063,527	2,843,314	1,072,868	406,153
Arkansas	447,881		112,040	91,798	41,793	64,699	137,551	250,732		65,174
Louisiana	967,308	509,634	144,797	49,492	43,817	55,469	164,099	491,049	243,264	78,334
Oklahoma	1,099,378	456,739	58,667	156,029	129,049	68,475	230,419	549,567	221,232	33,776
Texas	2,809,039	1,158,198	423,478	252,335	248,161	195,409	531,458	1,551,966	608,372	228,869
Mountain	1,982,162	495,557	316,612	249,435	222,426	149,708	548,424	1,065,214	284,630	166,529
Montana	252,147		70,889	55,124	35,696	13,049	77,389	123,376		30,682
Idaho	171,736			39,831	36,859	33,149	61,897	93,388		
Wyoming	121,235			36,860	26,781	9,431	48,163	58,115		
Colorado	681,499	352,030	78,266	57,397	48,196	20,902	124,708	389,125	198,777	46,651
New Mexico	139,468		29,752	19,088	19,427	19,850	51,351	71,263		17,191
Arizona	248,438		100,528		31,320	18,881	97,709	112,348		48,605
Utah	296,166	143,527	37,177	11,320	17,385	23,675	63,082	183,380	85,853	23,400
Nevada	71,473			29,815	6,762	10,771	24,125	34,219		
Pacific	10,345,065	5,805,673	1,382,801	898,421	538,279	333,330	1,386,561	5,688,113	2,992,163	835,419
Washington	1,312,813	758,856	62,408	153,288	24,151	54,775	259,335	769,915	435,762	39,233
Oregon	798,427	422,744	29,951	68,396	64,603	40,194	172,539	481,815	261,055	19,850
California	8,233,825	4,624,073	1,290,442	676,737	449,525	238,361	954,687	4,436,383	2,295,346	776,336

[1] Includes value of vacant units.

TABLE A 2

Dwelling Units,[1] Total Value (thousands of dollars) by Tenure, Population Group, State, and Geographic Division, April 1, 1930

OWNER-OCCUPIED				RENTED							
10,000-25,000	5,000-10,000	2,500-5,000	Under 2,500	All population groups	100,000 or more	25,000-100,000	10,000-25,000	5,000-10,000	2,500-5,000	Under 2,500	
7,644,403	4,421,057	3,163,597	11,169,233	57,897,448	35,817,291	8,052,764	4,347,727	2,371,304	1,612,066	5,696,296	United States
1,060,864	349,950	81,216	968,186	3,838,548	1,659,454	1,083,687	506,941	161,113	40,954	386,399	New England
59,514	34,368	14,719	154,166	200,028		71,580	34,366	19,547	7,105	67,430	Maine
53,249	10,563	9,897	68,179	139,115		55,951	36,179	7,624	6,042	33,319	New Hampshire
45,504	35,558	9,174	63,276	87,776			26,125	22,464	6,582	32,605	Vermont
645,169	224,449	35,200	263,614	2,266,563	1,175,009	620,054	283,958	85,184	12,618	89,740	Massachusetts
64,815	17,132	2,163	26,326	317,723	147,689	118,074	30,108	8,364	1,592	11,896	Rhode Island
192,613	27,880	10,063	392,625	827,343	336,756	218,028	96,205	17,930	7,015	151,409	Connecticut
2,668,295	1,427,838	1,080,412	3,174,633	24,919,355	18,119,986	2,592,516	1,571,794	772,509	502,426	1,360,124	Mid. Atlantic
799,212	339,286	342,778	1,360,824	16,283,491	14,242,967	715,972	446,047	197,583	163,678	517,244	New York
901,635	505,996	248,630	622,546	3,472,806	1,413,580	1,097,748	435,949	212,987	97,676	214,866	New Jersey
967,448	582,556	489,004	1,191,263	5,163,058	2,463,439	778,796	689,798	361,939	241,072	628,014	Pennsylvania
1,768,141	1,128,470	740,103	2,299,060	13,115,755	8,585,754	2,095,513	788,704	455,851	293,257	896,676	E. N. Central
499,924	335,639	207,497	692,189	3,152,741	1,924,627	515,809	221,168	135,647	82,515	272,975	Ohio
161,968	103,807	72,800	284,696	1,053,679	489,810	246,372	96,403	58,063	35,317	127,714	Indiana
579,754	417,100	232,148	579,192	5,455,860	4,077,181	687,232	228,971	151,385	86,424	224,667	Illinois
289,257	156,382	127,575	430,564	2,457,508	1,628,402	409,049	141,196	68,787	49,023	161,051	Michigan
237,238	115,542	100,083	312,419	995,967	465,734	237,051	100,966	41,969	39,978	110,269	Wisconsin
592,493	356,222	367,234	1,308,859	2,969,858	1,385,546	358,565	333,354	181,611	171,993	538,789	W. N. Central
103,801	70,480	85,332	218,910	585,758	383,459		54,900	31,756	33,685	81,958	Minnesota
119,076	64,088	111,866	294,595	484,038	61,352	168,414	66,538	30,693	47,732	109,309	Iowa
132,855	109,256	64,727	300,981	1,127,969	765,475	89,397	57,338	55,418	32,497	127,844	Missouri
23,507	17,640	2,339	59,721	86,258		16,270	22,190	13,687	1,661	32,450	N. Dakota
35,233	5,266	14,600	74,195	98,358		17,111	27,308	3,853	10,380	39,706	S. Dakota
53,583	40,589	33,147	170,033	253,916	89,723	34,864	28,838	19,973	15,665	64,853	Nebraska
124,438	48,903	55,223	190,424	333,561	85,537	32,509	76,242	26,231	30,373	82,669	Kansas
378,756	308,051	255,616	1,279,385	3,543,584	1,416,627	699,387	261,066	200,166	153,071	813,267	S. Atlantic
		12,055	44,731	84,845	60,366				5,536	18,943	Delaware
26,120	18,133	31,322	285,687	537,438	377,988	35,693	16,674	7,425	13,988	85,670	Maryland
				443,232	443,232						D. C.
69,469	45,836	38,435	267,550	472,020	184,827	86,273	42,295	24,054	17,878	116,693	Virginia
63,923	49,081	33,268	160,559	399,930		141,468	38,488	33,403	23,157	163,414	W. Virginia
76,999	51,893	44,096	182,032	418,913		187,318	52,310	29,891	24,598	124,796	N. Carolina
28,781	28,780	23,443	73,709	216,581		74,602	20,747	20,007	14,224	87,001	S. Carolina
60,196	41,436	32,015	143,470	504,396	164,000	109,110	53,522	32,037	27,996	117,731	Georgia
53,268	72,892	40,982	121,647	466,229	186,214	64,923	37,030	53,349	25,694	99,019	Florida
209,034	140,598	135,561	480,434	1,456,156	573,784	192,802	155,178	86,457	86,730	361,205	E. S. Central
55,095	64,583	40,622	175,775	459,794	161,981	98,651	28,344	34,136	24,001	112,681	Kentucky
22,672	39,013	36,262	132,013	447,983	292,591	8,568	15,181	27,311	21,611	82,721	Tennessee
68,935	26,406	29,074	101,405	373,533	119,212	54,310	58,029	17,859	21,253	102,870	Alabama
62,332	10,596	29,603	71,241	174,846		31,273	53,624	7,151	19,865	62,933	Mississippi
298,940	272,755	226,979	565,619	2,480,292	1,051,703	332,829	250,714	190,065	157,073	497,908	W. S. Central
49,111	24,900	38,298	73,249	197,149		46,866	42,687	16,893	26,401	64,302	Arkansas
28,877	25,168	33,080	82,326	476,259	266,370	66,463	20,615	18,649	22,389	81,773	Louisiana
75,521	69,733	38,660	110,645	549,811	235,507	24,891	80,508	59,316	29,815	119,774	Oklahoma
145,431	152,954	116,941	299,399	1,257,073	549,826	194,609	106,904	95,207	78,468	232,059	Texas
139,083	121,613	79,273	274,086	916,948	210,927	150,083	110,352	100,813	70,435	274,338	Mountain
28,338	18,857	7,204	38,295	128,771		40,207	26,786	16,839	5,845	39,094	Montana
21,868	21,389	18,505	31,626	78,348			17,963	15,470	14,644	30,271	Idaho
18,872	14,437	4,514	20,292	63,120			17,988	12,344	4,917	27,871	Wyoming
34,665	28,273	12,274	68,485	292,374	153,253	31,615	22,732	19,923	8,628	56,223	Colorado
10,928	10,485	10,362	22,297	68,205		12,561	8,160	8,942	9,488	29,054	New Mexico
	12,884	7,536	43,323	136,090		51,923		18,436	11,345	54,386	Arizona
8,164	12,392	13,455	40,116	112,786	57,674	13,777	3,156	4,993	10,220	22,966	Utah
16,248	2,896	5,423	9,652	37,254			13,567	3,866	5,348	14,473	Nevada
528,797	315,560	197,203	818,971	4,656,952	2,813,510	547,382	369,624	222,719	136,127	567,590	Pacific
83,624	14,033	30,277	166,986	542,898	323,094	23,175	69,664	10,118	24,498	92,349	Washington
35,376	35,974	23,194	106,366	316,612	161,689	10,101	33,020	28,629	17,000	66,173	Oregon
409,797	265,553	143,732	545,619	3,797,442	2,328,727	514,106	266,940	183,972	94,629	409,068	California

TABLE A 3

Dwelling Units, Average Value (dollars) by Tenure, Population Group, State, Geographic Division, and on Farms, 1930

	←————— TOTAL POPULATION GROUP* —————→								←——— OWNER-OCCUPIED ———→			
	All non-farm groups	100,000 or more	25,000-100,000	10,000-25,000	5,000-10,000	2,500-5,000	Under 2,500	Farm[1][2]	All non-farm groups	100,000 or more	25,000-100,000	10,000-25,000
United States	5,022	6,483	5,698	5,064	4,407	3,822	2,734	1,242	5,833	7,795	7,198	6,196
New England	4,885	5,114	5,522	5,093	4,223	3,963	3,742	2,356	6,748	8,649	8,041	6,675
Maine	3,340		4,737	4,166	3,242	3,057	2,613	1,542	3,915		6,904	5,533
New Hampshire	3,274		3,836	3,703	2,917	3,401	2,569	1,844	4,041		5,752	4,676
Vermont	3,606			5,171	4,314	4,059	2,683	1,789	4,609			7,335
Massachusetts	5,172	5,024	5,880	5,372	4,491	4,732	4,006	3,310	7,237	8,207	8,288	6,829
Rhode Island	4,676	5,018	4,893	4,104	3,704	4,095	3,320	3,208	7,131	8,724	7,435	5,749
Connecticut	5,527	5,488	5,818	5,638	5,167	4,165	5,319	3,947	8,160	10,340	8,828	7,754
Mid. Atlantic	7,205	8,312	7,600	6,762	6,482	5,894	4,287	2,375	7,824	9,514	9,052	7,766
New York	8,130	8,921	7,537	6,494	7,474	6,014	5,076	2,429	9,040	11,166	9,114	7,419
New Jersey	7,653	7,371	8,790	8,556	8,020	7,011	5,505	3,496	8,930	9,052	11,395	9,653
Pennsylvania	5,617	6,840	6,625	5,940	5,307	5,410	3,396	2,164	6,183	7,173	7,542	6,791
E. N. Central	5,376	6,457	6,175	5,401	4,506	4,079	2,877	1,750	5,927	7,656	7,188	6,221
Ohio	5,138	5,708	6,673	5,149	4,685	4,483	3,111	1,740	5,973	7,097	8,141	5,990
Indiana	3,882	5,086	4,652	3,869	3,221	2,978	2,292	1,477	4,254	5,971	5,397	4,338
Illinois	6,165	7,159	6,871	6,423	5,338	4,218	2,897	1,956	6,859	8,754	8,093	7,618
Michigan	5,586	6,978	5,971	5,216	3,945	4,304	2,881	1,694	5,914	7,965	6,547	5,699
Wisconsin	4,911	5,995	5,694	5,816	4,238	3,914	3,067	1,984	5,391	6,905	6,507	6,487
W. N. Central	3,549	4,502	4,214	3,895	3,608	3,159	2,419	1,677	4,253	6,088	5,102	4,652
Minnesota	3,928	4,696		4,087	3,447	3,538	2,635	1,804	4,697	6,048		4,807
Iowa	3,415	4,103	4,164	4,016	3,564	3,358	2,539	2,387	3,998	5,036	4,994	4,747
Missouri	3,859	4,703	4,203	4,310	3,951	2,836	2,292	1,188	4,975	7,175	5,317	5,479
N. Dakota	3,004		5,197	4,389	3,825	2,972	2,158	1,520	3,234		6,498	4,951
S. Dakota	3,107		4,565	4,098	2,994	3,526	2,456	1,548	3,577		5,538	4,865
Nebraska	3,470	4,134	4,669	3,985	3,681	3,134	2,655	1,852	4,082	5,013	5,626	4,783
Kansas	2,843	3,364	3,698	3,227	3,206	2,740	2,170	1,394	3,273	4,017	4,331	3,742
S. Atlantic	3,397	5,163	4,093	3,589	3,445	2,960	2,086	876	4,883	7,003	6,496	5,328
Delaware	4,543	5,547				3,828	3,310	1,929	5,706	7,268		
Maryland	4,552	5,074	4,796	4,499	4,611	3,925	3,568	2,183	5,646	6,281	6,831	6,049
D. C.	7,025	7,025						6,500	9,555	9,555		
Virginia	3,334	4,475	3,686	4,327	3,797	3,458	2,407	1,326	4,529	6,678	5,379	6,032
W. Virginia	3,016		5,158	4,746	4,145	3,711	1,832	1,009	4,549		7,155	6,106
N. Carolina	2,813		4,300	3,184	3,194	2,947	1,794	733	4,116		6,898	4,970
S. Carolina	2,271		3,589	3,181	2,686	2,536	1,496	585	4,016		6,853	5,426
Georgia	2,640	4,181	3,033	2,853	2,529	2,126	1,775	546	4,119	6,569	5,672	4,519
Florida	3,156	3,972	4,394	3,565	4,093	2,774	1,870	1,072	4,486	5,767	6,406	4,992
E. S. Central	2,712	3,926	3,777	2,897	2,873	2,425	1,674	575	3,846	5,640	5,338	4,281
Kentucky	3,025	4,270	4,229	3,562	3,270	2,748	1,839	760	4,108	5,728	5,707	4,994
Tennessee	2,899	3,791	3,823	3,200	2,623	2,404	1,762	683	3,954	5,417	5,217	4,511
Alabama	2,410	3,829	3,235	2,697	2,585	2,138	1,449	458	3,799	6,118	4,868	4,196
Mississippi	2,229		3,469	2,673	2,762	2,407	1,614	441	3,068		4,979	3,815
W. S. Central	2,967	4,403	3,787	3,164	2,907	2,520	1,684	670	3,712	6,080	5,073	3,911
Arkansas	2,255		3,802	3,080	2,698	2,293	1,438	457	2,872		5,083	3,961
Louisiana	2,981	4,317	4,038	2,880	2,413	2,224	1,488	517	4,137	7,489	5,732	3,985
Oklahoma	3,032	5,202	3,615	3,403	2,965	2,437	1,632	704	3,440	6,584	4,294	3,789
Texas	3,091	4,186	3,728	3,119	3,026	2,747	1,868	816	3,878	5,512	5,007	3,946
Mountain	2,886	4,170	3,920	3,771	3,122	2,727	1,859	1,102	3,259	5,156	4,506	4,374
Montana	2,783		3,856	3,544	3,488	2,752	1,856	969	2,936		4,270	3,998
Idaho	2,502		3,804	3,126	2,790		1,795	1,238	2,728			4,427
Wyoming	2,931			3,830	3,761	3,406	2,204	1,052	3,567			4,594
Colorado	3,225	4,250	3,351	3,489	2,964	2,472	1,950	1,185	3,791	5,317	3,694	4,082
New Mexico	2,100		4,133	3,445	2,967	2,498	1,310	601	2,171		4,874	3,980
Arizona	2,823		4,680	.	2,705	3,014	2,007	1,229	3,182		6,085	
Utah	3,026	3,985	3,588	3,518	2,931	2,420	1,936	1,472	3,398		4,159	4,028
Nevada	3,157			5,652	3,795	3,511	1,928	1,748	3,567			6,790
Pacific	4,918	5,687	5,515	5,037	4,370	3,747	3,141	1,820	5,765	7,062	6,583	5,777
Washington	3,638	4,439	3,558	3,834	3,063	2,996	2,441	1,429	3,859	4,742	3,743	3,997
Oregon	3,653	4,629	4,238	4,254	3,565	3,049	2,370	1,410	4,068	5,273	4,776	4,584
California	5,402	6,096	5,707	5,533	4,626	4,145	3,637	2,215	6,634	8,131	6,915	6,516

Source: Based on number and aggregate value from Tables A 1 and 2
*Based on number and aggregate value of all units, including vacant.
[1] Average value of farm dwelling plus average value of one acre of land.
[2] Average value of all farm dwellings includes value of farm managers' dwellings.

TABLE A 3

Dwelling Units, Average Value (dollars) by Tenure, Population Group, State, Geographic Division, and on Farms, 1930

← OWNER-OCCUPIED →				← RENTED →								
5,000-10,000	2,500-5,000	Under 2,500	Farm [1]	All non-farm groups	100,000 or more	25,000-100,000	10,000-25,000	5,000-10,000	2,500-5,000	Under 2,500	Farm [1]	
5,309	4,584	3,382	1,511	4,347	5,751	4,416	3,832	3,347	2,882	1,987	826	**United States**
5,440	5,150	4,472	2,304	3,467	3,670	3,750	3,404	2,843	2,719	2,655	2,064	**New England**
3,905	3,508	2,911	1,539	2,658		3,431	2,918	2,497	2,414	2,118	1,261	Maine
3,573	4,162	2,857	1,815	2,527		2,658	2,834	2,325	2,618	2,130	1,476	New Hampshire
6,070	5,618	3,226	1,760	2,611			3,416	2,959	2,927	2,022	1,754	Vermont
5,683	6,419	4,736	3,221	3,700	3,711	4,108	3,617	2,893	2,730	2,757	2,798	Massachusetts
4,993	5,212	4,313	3,205	3,070	3,300	3,146	2,540	2,422	3,171	2,199	2,523	Rhode Island
7,352	6,047	6,735	3,820	3,640	3,711	3,718	3,646	3,534	2,880	3,443	3,540	Connecticut
7,401	6,673	4,997	2,341	6,759	7,797	6,424	5,545	5,272	4,711	3,219	2,278	**Mid. Atlantic**
8,245	6,665	5,648	2,401	7,670	8,226	6,238	5,309	6,441	4,992	4,007	2,242	New York
9,155	7,891	6,158	3,509	6,521	6,578	7,248	6,929	6,196	5,461	4,210	3,038	New Jersey
6,037	6,192	4,062	2,116	5,006	6,523	5,670	5,052	4,443	4,307	2,591	2,202	Pennsylvania
5,130	4,557	3,192	1,784	4,803	5,691	4,996	4,169	3,463	3,225	2,296	1,716	**E. N. Central**
5,440	5,081	3,493	1,749	4,251	4,688	5,173	3,908	3,487	3,459	2,436	1,655	Ohio
3,585	3,263	2,478	1,488	3,438	4,313	3,906	3,274	2,726	2,524	1,963	1,428	Indiana
6,183	4,766	3,262	2,024	5,592	6,431	5,452	4,596	3,877	3,222	2,248	1,831	Illinois
4,244	4,688	3,084	1,669	5,190	6,183	5,207	4,445	3,399	3,549	2,451	1,699	Michigan
4,620	4,287	3,469	1,977	4,268	5,330	4,553	4,679	3,453	3,212	2,310	1,959	Wisconsin
4,254	3,675	2,837	1,827	2,765	3,335	3,264	3,021	2,781	2,431	1,781	1,432	**W. N. Central**
3,944	4,042	3,033	1,855	2,987	3,406		3,186	2,693	2,689	1,951	1,668	Minnesota
4,280	3,930	2,980	2,716	2,634	3,138	3,227	3,148	2,641	2,505	1,814	2,013	Iowa
4,790	3,459	2,752	1,303	2,939	3,424	3,170	2,883	2,938	2,087	1,644	940	Missouri
4,317	2,946	2,350	1,649	2,729		4,194	3,918	3,335	3,009	1,864	1,259	N. Dakota
3,426	4,026	2,865	1,702	2,585		3,729	3,405	2,553	3,002	1,939	1,346	S. Dakota
4,387	3,591	3,144	2,189	2,670	3,212	3,573	3,042	2,774	2,469	1,886	1,465	Nebraska
3,701	3,070	2,516	1,595	2,290	2,685	2,894	2,636	2,567	2,293	1,647	1,099	Kansas
4,882	4,283	3,113	1,149	2,406	3,920	2,811	2,435	2,371	1,953	1,373	524	**S. Atlantic**
	4,939	4,121	1,969	3,366	4,115				2,570	2,259	1,724	Delaware
6,287	5,159	4,478	2,231	3,296	3,816	3,428	3,211	2,792	2,555	2,128	1,818	Maryland
			6,202	5,466	5,466						3,529	D. C.
5,075	4,818	3,293	1,452	2,381	3,393	2,587	2,955	2,565	2,152	1,488	843	Virginia
5,321	4,488	2,875	1,063	2,122		3,733	3,465	3,129	2,972	1,350	713	W. Virginia
4,593	4,341	2,515	900	1,945		2,918	2,082	2,089	1,870	1,265	538	N. Carolina
4,422	4,091	2,501	920	1,539		2,352	2,021	1,716	1,559	1,115	386	S. Carolina
3,753	3,454	2,768	835	1,946	3,209	2,211	2,017	1,778	1,477	1,236	389	Georgia
5,557	3,858	2,673	1,235	2,318	3,055	2,965	2,526	3,009	1,915	1,366	450	Florida
4,105	3,277	2,392	790	1,960	2,886	2,749	2,018	1,931	1,724	1,196	382	**E. S. Central**
4,379	3,603	2,591	853	2,183	3,248	3,114	2,288	2,211	1,960	1,266	548	Kentucky
3,634	3,190	2,399	848	2,152	2,810	2,774	2,232	1,878	1,701	1,237	459	Tennessee
4,355	3,063	2,259	691	1,700	2,659	2,361	1,893	1,615	1,513	1,071	319	Alabama
3,916	3,205	2,151	694	1,674		2,532	1,983	1,922	1,756	1,258	330	Mississippi
3,632	3,082	1,990	965	2,412	3,436	2,892	2,577	2,261	1,995	1,434	474	**W. S. Central**
3,494	2,996	1,737	622	1,771		2,815	2,453	2,020	1,711	1,203	348	Arkansas
3,137	2,930	1,791	819	2,315	3,113	2,995	2,075	1,841	1,640	1,272	346	Louisiana
3,444	2,766	1,726	1,001	2,710	4,345	2,976	3,107	2,549	2,112	1,555	503	Oklahoma
3,852	3,285	2,268	1,155	2,472	3,306	2,867	2,427	2,250	2,208	1,522	575	Texas
3,476	2,876	1,952	1,152	2,547	3,314	3,425	3,213	2,780	2,576	1,775	891	**Mountain**
3,846	2,836	1,886	1,018	2,651		3,591	3,164	3,159	2,656	1,828	777	Montana
3,351	3,015	1,885	1,306	2,278			3,247	2,860	2,550	1,709	1,015	Idaho
4,505	3,878	2,597	1,063	2,517			3,260	3,153	3,064	1,985	871	Wyoming
3,296	2,673	2,212	1,287	2,691	3,373	2,948	2,856	2,593	2,233	1,704	992	Colorado
3,369	2,575	1,148	608	2,030		3,422	2,921	2,602	2,419	1,469	513	New Mexico
2,883	3,447	2,097	1,254	2,581		3,848		2,593	2,781	1,940	925	Arizona
3,314	2,427	2,088	1,527	2,568	3,169	2,910	2,650	2,278	2,411	1,718	1,044	Utah
4,892	3,933	1,846	1,766	2,856			4,707	3,249	3,166	1,988	1,350	Nevada
4,909	4,123	3,524	1,919	4,169	4,711	4,421	4,256	3,781	3,309	2,715	1,265	**Pacific**
3,251	3,000	2,702	1,476	3,365	4,087	3,285	3,656	2,835	2,992	2,079	1,159	Washington
3,709	3,196	2,653	1,462	3,162	3,866	3,469	3,949	3,399	2,870	2,024	1,135	Oregon
5,282	4,715	4,181	2,396	4,439	4,889	4,515	4,492	3,922	3,500	3,100	1,381	California

TABLE A 4

Dwelling Units[1] by Tenure, Population Group, Geographic Division, and Type, April 1, 1930

	TOTAL							OWNER-OCCUPIED		
	All population groups	100,000 and over	25,000-100,000	10,000-25,000	5,000-10,000	2,500-5,000	Under 2,500	All population groups	100,000 and over	25,000-100,000
United States										
All types	24,409,239	9,699,008	3,382,608	2,368,309	1,541,259	1,249,423	6,168,632	11,089,450	3,471,464	1,559,062
1-family	16,762,514	4,786,154	2,328,884	1,857,060	1,288,852	1,081,791	5,419,773	9,940,707	2,893,808	1,371,054
2-family	3,680,826	1,811,791	599,602	338,024	174,157	123,540	633,712	903,488	418,093	150,508
3-or-more family	3,965,899	3,101,063	454,122	173,225	78,250	44,092	115,147	245,255	159,563	37,500
New England										
All types	1,950,694	636,752	492,223	307,856	121,006	30,830	362,027	843,382	184,638	203,217
1-family	1,028,449	189,202	234,117	199,255	87,135	23,318	295,422	679,930	117,127	154,344
2-family	477,663	181,510	141,958	73,493	23,409	5,327	51,966	121,089	43,200	37,917
3-or-more family	444,582	266,040	116,148	35,108	10,462	2,185	14,639	42,363	24,311	10,956
Mid. Atlantic										
All types	6,343,035	3,319,460	730,702	627,064	339,439	268,556	1,057,814	2,656,209	995,373	327,132
1-family	3,463,993	1,135,522	423,212	468,137	270,339	225,529	941,254	2,289,932	773,781	272,578
2-family	1,066,203	620,103	165,669	104,951	47,160	31,724	96,596	272,278	149,573	44,157
3-or-more family	1,812,839	1,563,835	141,821	53,976	21,940	11,303	19,964	93,999	72,019	10,397
E. N. Central										
All types	5,571,481	2,474,379	907,896	473,421	351,602	253,350	1,110,833	2,840,959	965,604	488,434
1-family	3,816,456	1,183,676	680,677	394,891	311,024	225,319	1,020,869	2,555,555	792,523	442,861
2-family	904,304	575,914	139,877	56,085	30,725	22,218	79,485	232,873	134,493	37,206
3-or-more family	850,721	714,789	87,342	22,445	9,853	5,813	10,479	52,531	38,588	8,367
W. N. Central										
All types	2,269,737	721,248	227,227	237,723	149,050	170,691	763,798	1,195,512	305,751	117,381
1-family	1,778,877	433,260	187,167	196,875	124,738	152,394	684,443	1,104,982	262,066	110,070
2-family	297,879	157,096	20,201	23,662	15,511	12,729	68,680	76,704	36,687	5,448
3-or-more family	192,981	130,892	19,859	17,186	8,801	5,568	10,675	13,826	6,998	1,863
S. Atlantic										
All types	2,454,335	605,465	381,598	178,291	147,522	138,059	1,003,400	981,703	244,107	132,787
1-family	1,973,962	412,622	290,538	147,118	122,582	119,314	881,788	910,933	224,942	120,613
2-family	316,961	96,327	59,738	23,134	17,645	14,463	105,654	60,827	15,559	10,385
3-or-more family	163,412	96,516	31,322	8,039	7,295	4,282	15,958	9,943	3,606	1,789
E. S. Central										
All types	1,235,048	319,478	116,320	125,715	79,020	91,680	502,835	492,188	120,660	46,192
1-family	957,229	234,043	83,957	99,518	63,975	75,987	399,749	437,927	108,119	40,720
2-family	208,300	48,434	23,083	20,139	11,856	12,418	92,370	47,074	10,000	4,725
3-or-more family	69,519	37,001	9,280	6,058	3,189	3,275	10,716	7,187	2,541	747
W. S. Central										
All types	1,794,442	482,519	195,141	173,732	159,184	152,387	631,479	765,988	176,452	80,059
1-family	1,458,240	366,783	154,542	143,115	136,708	131,527	525,565	703,333	160,178	73,736
2-family	228,730	59,548	25,639	20,772	16,047	15,762	90,962	51,693	12,295	5,219
3-or-more family	107,472	56,188	14,960	9,845	6,429	5,098	14,952	10,962	3,979	1,104
Mountain										
All types	686,877	118,842	80,776	66,137	71,247	54,906	294,969	326,877	55,201	36,957
1-family	574,165	88,919	64,785	53,417	61,094	47,444	258,506	310,367	52,415	34,710
2-family	58,788	8,644	6,944	5,930	5,625	4,588	27,057	13,316	1,932	1,596
3-or-more family	53,924	21,279	9,047	6,790	4,528	2,874	9,406	3,194	854	651
Pacific										
All types	2,103,590	1,020,865	250,725	178,370	123,189	88,964	441,477	986,632	423,678	126,903
1-family	1,711,143	742,127	209,889	154,734	111,257	80,959	412,177	947,748	402,657	121,422
2-family	121,998	64,215	16,493	9,858	6,179	4,311	20,942	27,634	14,354	3,855
3-or-more family	270,449	214,523	24,343	13,778	5,753	3,694	8,358	11,250	6,667	1,626

[1] Includes vacant.

TABLE A 4

Dwelling Units[1] by Tenure, Population Group, Geographic Division, and Type, April 1, 1930

——— OWNER-OCCUPIED ——→				← ——————— RENTED ——————— →							
10,000-25,000	5,000-10,000	2,500-5,000	Under 2,500	All population groups	100,000 and over	25,000-100,000	10,000-25,000	5,000-10,000	2,500-5,000	Under 2,500	
1,233,793	832,701	690,130	3,302,300	13,319,789	6,227,544	1,823,546	1,134,516	708,558	559,293	2,866,332	**United States** — All types
1,126,675	778,981	649,649	3,120,540	6,821,807	1,892,346	957,830	730,385	509,871	432,142	2,299,233	1-family
90,564	46,109	34,528	163,686	2,777,338	1,393,698	449,094	247,460	128,048	89,012	470,026	2-family
16,554	7,611	5,953	18,074	3,720,644	2,941,500	416,622	156,671	70,639	38,139	97,073	3-or-more family
158,930	64,331	15,770	216,496	1,107,312	452,114	289,006	148,926	56,675	15,060	145,531	**New England** — All types
135,239	57,473	13,639	202,108	348,519	72,075	79,773	64,016	29,662	9,679	93,314	1-family
19,956	6,076	1,769	12,171	356,574	138,310	104,041	53,537	17,333	3,558	39,795	2-family
3,735	782	362	2,217	402,219	241,729	105,192	31,373	9,680	1,823	12,422	3-or-more family
343,592	192,921	161,909	635,282	3,686,826	2,324,087	403,570	283,472	146,518	106,647	422,532	**Mid. Atlantic** — All types
310,048	179,231	149,685	604,609	1,174,061	361,741	150,634	158,089	91,108	75,844	336,645	1-family
28,497	12,239	10,533	27,279	793,925	470,530	121,512	76,454	34,921	21,191	69,317	2-family
5,047	1,451	1,691	3,394	1,718,840	1,491,816	131,424	48,929	20,489	9,612	16,570	3-or-more family
284,222	219,973	162,419	720,307	2,730,522	1,508,775	419,462	189,199	131,629	90,931	390,526	**E. N. Central** — All types
266,312	209,496	154,538	689,825	1,260,901	391,153	237,816	128,579	101,528	70,781	331,044	1-family
16,067	9,218	7,088	28,801	671,431	441,421	102,671	40,018	21,507	15,130	50,684	2-family
1,843	1,259	793	1,681	798,190	676,201	78,975	20,602	8,594	5,020	8,798	3-or-more family
127,374	83,743	99,933	461,330	1,074,225	415,497	109,846	110,349	65,307	70,758	302,468	**W. N. Central** — All types
119,322	78,014	95,178	440,332	673,895	171,194	77,097	77,553	46,724	57,216	244,111	1-family
6,778	4,653	4,061	19,077	221,175	120,409	14,753	16,884	10,858	8,668	49,603	2-family
1,274	1,076	694	1,921	179,155	123,894	17,996	15,912	7,725	4,874	8,754	3-or-more family
71,091	63,105	59,681	410,932	1,472,632	361,358	248,811	107,200	84,417	78,378	592,468	**S. Atlantic** — All types
65,453	58,950	56,134	384,841	1,063,029	187,680	169,925	81,665	63,632	63,180	496,947	1-family
4,545	3,529	3,037	23,772	256,134	80,768	49,353	18,589	14,116	11,426	81,882	2-family
1,093	626	510	2,319	153,469	92,910	29,533	6,946	6,669	3,772	13,639	3-or-more family
48,825	34,254	41,372	200,885	742,860	198,818	70,128	76,890	44,766	50,308	301,950	**E. S. Central** — All types
42,554	30,592	37,974	177,968	519,302	125,924	43,237	56,964	33,383	38,013	221,781	1-family
5,397	3,183	2,800	20,969	161,226	38,434	18,358	14,742	8,673	9,618	71,401	2-family
874	479	598	1,948	62,332	34,460	8,533	5,184	2,710	2,677	8,768	3-or-more family
76,433	75,105	73,650	284,289	1,028,454	306,067	115,082	97,299	84,079	78,737	347,190	**W. S. Central** — All types
69,522	69,847	69,189	260,861	754,907	206,605	80,806	73,593	66,861	62,338	264,704	1-family
5,567	4,308	3,554	20,750	177,037	47,253	20,420	15,205	11,739	12,208	70,212	2-family
1,344	950	907	2,678	96,510	52,209	13,856	8,501	5,479	4,191	12,274	3-or-more family
31,795	34,982	27,565	140,377	360,000	63,641	43,819	34,342	36,265	27,341	154,592	**Mountain** — All types
29,934	33,153	26,513	133,642	263,798	36,504	30,075	23,483	27,941	20,931	124,864	1-family
1,411	1,383	869	6,125	45,472	6,712	5,348	4,519	4,242	3,719	20,932	2-family
450	446	183	610	50,730	20,425	8,396	6,340	4,082	2,691	8,796	3-or-more family
91,531	64,287	47,831	232,402	1,116,958	597,187	123,822	86,839	58,902	41,133	209,075	**Pacific** — All types
88,291	62,225	46,799	226,354	763,395	339,470	88,467	66,443	49,032	34,160	185,823	1-family
2,346	1,520	817	4,742	94,364	49,861	12,638	7,512	4,659	3,494	16,200	2-family
894	542	215	1,306	259,199	207,856	22,717	12,884	5,211	3,479	7,052	3-or-more family

TABLE A 5

Rented Dwelling Units,[1] Total and Average Value by Population Group, Geographic Division, and Type, April 1, 1930

	All population groups	100,000 and over	25,000-100,000	10,000-25,000	5,000-10,000	2,500-5,000	Under 2,500
United States							
All types	57,897,448	35,817,291	8,052,764	4,347,727	2,371,304	1,612,066	5,696,296
1-family	24,528,711	9,653,445	4,286,386	2,877,700	1,737,994	1,263,788	4,709,398
2-family	10,255,541	6,326,069	1,728,641	820,476	372,946	225,863	781,546
3-or-more family	23,113,196	19,837,777	2,037,737	649,551	260,364	122,415	205,352
New England							
All types	3,838,548	1,659,454	1,083,687	506,941	161,113	40,954	386,399
1-family	1,529,594	404,662	422,907	281,712	103,747	30,509	286,057
2-family	1,057,137	457,983	332,823	143,905	37,446	7,082	77,898
3-or-more family	1,251,817	796,809	327,957	81,324	19,920	3,363	22,444
Mid. Atlantic							
All types	24,919,355	18,119,986	2,592,516	1,571,794	772,509	502,426	1,360,124
1-family	6,377,553	2,533,283	985,066	900,683	491,668	364,048	1,102,805
2-family	4,158,894	2,710,025	648,684	359,995	157,402	86,812	195,976
3-or-more family	14,382,908	12,876,678	958,766	311,116	123,439	51,566	61,343
E. N. Central							
All types	13,115,755	8,585,754	2,095,513	788,704	455,851	293,257	896,676
1-family	5,562,973	2,381,776	1,250,429	558,738	361,846	234,709	775,475
2-family	2,927,990	2,144,172	435,335	141,773	63,759	42,177	100,774
3-or-more family	4,624,792	4,059,806	409,749	88,193	30,246	16,371	20,427
W. N. Central							
All types	2,969,858	1,385,546	358,565	333,354	181,611	171,993	538,789
1-family	1,954,404	678,126	272,487	254,368	140,755	146,858	461,810
2-family	470,463	301,785	33,340	35,787	21,578	14,827	63,146
3-or-more family	544,991	405,635	52,738	43,199	19,278	10,308	13,833
S. Atlantic							
All types	3,543,584	1,416,627	699,387	261,066	200,166	153,071	813,267
1-family	2,366,787	725,606	479,267	200,321	151,161	124,029	686,403
2-family	598,257	276,410	124,325	41,135	30,567	20,627	105,193
3-or-more family	578,540	414,611	95,795	19,610	18,438	8,415	21,671
E. S. Central							
All types	1,456,156	573,784	192,802	155,178	86,457	86,730	361,205
1-family	986,732	356,308	118,472	114,986	64,475	65,566	266,925
2-family	283,307	97,861	45,728	27,317	15,537	15,515	81,349
3-or-more family	186,117	119,615	28,602	12,875	6,445	5,649	12,931
W. S. Central							
All types	2,480,292	1,051,703	332,829	250,714	190,065	157,073	497,908
1-family	1,750,377	682,193	228,404	186,844	149,511	123,515	379,910
2-family	365,636	138,468	51,761	34,958	24,020	22,347	94,082
3-or-more family	364,279	231,042	52,664	28,912	16,534	11,211	23,916
Mountain							
All types	916,948	210,927	150,083	110,352	100,813	70,435	274,338
1-family	700,645	134,942	111,821	81,887	82,382	57,188	232,425
2-family	88,532	17,369	14,076	11,274	9,151	7,519	29,143
3-or-more family	127,771	58,616	24,186	17,191	9,280	5,728	12,770
Pacific							
All types	4,656,952	2,813,510	547,382	369,624	222,719	136,127	567,590
1-family	3,299,646	1,756,549	417,533	298,161	192,449	117,366	517,588
2-family	305,325	181,996	42,569	24,332	13,486	8,957	33,985
3-or-more family	1,051,981	874,965	87,280	47,131	16,784	9,804	16,017

[1] Includes value of vacant units.
[2] Based on number and aggregate value, including vacant units, as shown in Tables A 4 and 5.

Rented Dwelling Units,[1] Total and Average Value by Population Group, Geographic Division, and Type, April 1, 1930

| ← A V E R A G E V A L U E[2] P E R D W E L L I N G U N I T (dollars) → | | | | | | | |
All population groups	100,000 and over	25,000-100,000	10,000-25,000	5,000-10,000	2,500-5,000	Under 2,500	
							United States
4,347	5,751	4,416	3,832	3,347	2,882	1,987	All types
3,596	5,101	4,475	3,940	3,409	2,924	2,048	1-family
3,693	4,539	3,849	3,316	2,913	2,537	1,663	2-family
6,212	6,744	4,891	4,146	3,686	3,210	2,115	3-or-more family
							New England
3,467	3,670	3,750	3,404	2,843	2,719	2,655	All types
4,389	5,614	5,301	4,401	3,498	3,152	3,066	1-family
2,965	3,311	3,199	2,688	2,160	1,990	1,957	2-family
3,112	3,296	3,118	2,592	2,058	1,845	1,807	3-or-more family
							Mid. Atlantic
6,759	7,797	6,424	5,545	5,272	4,711	3,219	All types
5,432	7,003	6,539	5,697	5,397	4,800	3,276	1-family
5,238	5,760	5,338	4,709	4,507	4,097	2,827	2-family
8,368	8,632	7,295	6,359	6,025	5,365	3,702	3-or-more family
							E. N. Central
4,803	5,691	4,996	4,169	3,463	3,225	2,296	All types
4,412	6,089	5,258	4,345	3,564	3,316	2,343	1-family
4,361	4,857	4,240	3,543	2,965	2,788	1,988	2-family
5,794	6,004	5,188	4,281	3,519	3,261	2,322	3-or-more family
							W. N. Central
2,765	3,335	3,264	3,021	2,781	2,431	1,781	All types
2,900	3,961	3,534	3,280	3,012	2,567	1,892	1-family
2,127	2,506	2,260	2,120	1,987	1,711	1,273	2-family
3,042	3,274	2,931	2,715	2,496	2,115	1,580	3-or-more family
							S. Atlantic
2,406	3,920	2,811	2,435	2,371	1,953	1,373	All types
2,226	3,866	2,820	2,453	2,376	1,963	1,381	1-family
2,336	3,422	2,519	2,213	2,165	1,805	1,285	2-family
3,770	4,463	3,244	2,823	2,765	2,231	1,589	3-or-more family
							E. S. Central
1,960	2,886	2,749	2,018	1,931	1,724	1,196	All types
1,900	2,830	2,740	2,019	1,931	1,725	1,204	1-family
1,757	2,546	2,491	1,853	1,791	1,613	1,139	2-family
2,986	3,471	3,352	2,484	2,378	2,110	1,475	3-or-more family
							W. S. Central
2,412	3,436	2,892	2,577	2,261	1,995	1,434	All types
2,319	3,302	2,827	2,539	2,236	1,981	1,435	1-family
2,065	2,930	2,535	2,299	2,046	1,831	1,340	2-family
3,775	4,425	3,801	3,401	3,018	2,675	1,949	3-or-more family
							Mountain
2,547	3,314	3,425	3,213	2,780	2,576	1,775	All types
2,656	3,697	3,718	3,487	2,948	2,732	1,861	1-family
1,947	2,588	2,632	2,495	2,157	2,022	1,392	2-family
2,519	2,870	2,881	2,712	2,273	2,129	1,452	3-or-more family
							Pacific
4,169	4,711	4,421	4,256	3,781	3,309	2,715	All types
4,322	5,174	4,720	4,487	3,925	3,436	2,785	1-family
3,236	3,650	3,368	3,239	2,895	2,564	2,098	2-family
4,059	4,209	3,842	3,658	3,221	2,818	2,271	3-or-more family

TABLE A 6

Owner-occupied Dwelling Units, Average Value, All Types combined, by Value Groups: 1-Family, All Value Groups combined, 139 Cities Towns, and Villages in Descending Order of Population, by Geographic Division, April 1, 1930

	POPULATION	ALL TYPES — All value groups	Under $1,000	$1,000-1,499	$1,500-1,999	$2,000-2,999	$3,000-4,999	$5,000-7,499	$7,500-9,999	$10,000-14,999	$15,000-19,999	$20,000 and over	1-FAMILY All value groups
10 New England cities													
Providence, R.I.[1]	252,981	$8,525	$675	$1,112	$1,586	$2,331	$3,733	$5,913	$8,287	$11,146	$16,079	$29,541	$9,106
Worcester, Mass.[1]	195,311	8,957	520	1,097.	1,587	2,273	3,826	6,014	8,348	11,286	16,241	27,135	8,144
Waterbury, Conn.[1]	99,902	9,155	540	1,083	1,593	2,381	3,878	5,992	8,272	11,289	16,157	30,964	8,995
Portland, Me.[1]	70,810	7,044	458	1,091	1,602	2,248	3,728	5,847	8,318	10,955	15,986	29,296	6,875
Nashua, N.H.	31,463	5,843	560	1,081	1,582	2,288	3,742	5,765	7,926	10,828	15,716	24,935	5,796
Central Falls, R.I.	25,898	7,921	700	1,093	1,517	2,295	3,714	6,003	8,369	11,008	15,535	24,483	7,739
Burlington, Vt.	24,789	7,830	600	1,071	1,598	2,284	3,722	5,876	8,196	11,050	15,902	26,874	7,920
Greenwich, Conn.	5,981	23,469	740		1,500	2,500	3,754	6,123	8,386	11,376	15,867	40,545	23,727
Orange, Mass.	5,365	3,691	594	1,125	1,661	2,424	3,542	5,703	8,194	10,333	15,500	25,000	3,603
Pittsfield, Me.	2,075	3,773	563	1,050	1,625	2,326	3,599	5,567	8,214	10,000		27,000	3,743
12 Mid. Atlantic cities													
Syracuse, N.Y.[1]	209,326	10,435		1,167	1,645	2,322	3,799	6,070	8,318	11,362	16,002	31,252	10,340
Trenton, N.J.	123,356	6,502	675	1,342	1,666	2,340	3,681	5,854	8,193	10,820	15,684	31,153	6,360
Erie, Pa.[1]	115,967	7,772	525	1,067	1,613	2,334	3,803	5,841	8,219	11,115	15,906	30,293	7,905
Binghamton, N.Y.	76,662	8,449	560	1,089	1,596	2,314	3,936	5,979	8,234	11,125	15,874	30,170	8,232
Williamsport, Pa.	45,729	6,529	554	1,125	1,621	2,290	3,679	5,854	8,167	10,785	15,543	29,950	6,393
Carbondale, Pa.	20,061	5,631	598	1,137	1,620	2,185	3,522	5,631	8,193	10,701	15,455	28,974	5,587
Peekskill, N.Y.	17,125	9,652	700	1,115	1,692	2,295	3,675	5,886	8,249	10,921	15,674	28,180	9,541
Latrobe, Pa.	10,644	6,016	750	1,100	1,577	2,272	3,627	5,785	8,201	10,859	15,757	30,536	5,846
Corry, Pa.	7,152	4,191	581	1,076	1,583	2,293	3,649	5,665	8,125	10,561	15,429	35,000	4,181
Dansville, N.Y.	4,928	4,932	612	1,089	1,656	2,407	3,663	5,834	8,228	10,900	15,000	30,400	4,943
Hoosick Falls, N.Y.	4,755	4,181	681	1,102	1,565	2,282	3,471	5,496	8,155	10,429	15,833	30,200	4,239
Canton, N.Y.	2,822	5,189	698	1,069	1,593	2,336	3,668	5,978	8,191	10,351	15,583	37,000	5,159
19 E. N. Central cities													
Cleveland, Ohio[1]	900,429	7,843	671	1,176	1,654	2,326	3,825	6,026	8,260	11,099	15,947	33,556	7,533
Indianapolis, Ind.[1]	364,161	6,043	669	1,163	1,649	2,344	3,744	5,802	8,242	11,126	15,976	30,777	5,985
Peoria, Ill.	104,969	6,326	416	1,118	1,613	2,312	3,717	5,833	8,210	11,082	15,768	29,949	6,168
Lansing, Mich.[1]	78,397	6,312	690	1,124	1,641	2,412	3,868	5,921	8,175	11,040	16,157	27,333	6,192
Racine, Wis.[1]	67,542	7,265	800	1,071	1,670	2,302	3,894	6,072	8,228	11,120	15,917	28,075	7,224
Decatur, Ill.[1]	57,510	5,603	639	1,118	1,587	2,343	3,800	5,713	8,209	10,932	16,238	30,929	5,575
Kenosha, Wis.[1]	50,262	8,037		1,250	1,600	2,196	3,971	6,114	8,180	11,137	15,811	33,719	8,140
Portsmouth, Ohio	42,560	6,149	631	1,147	1,678	2,387	3,875	5,898	8,154	10,898	15,621	29,973	6,009
La Crosse, Wis.	39,614	4,583	563	1,139	1,642	2,341	3,541	5,769	8,148	11,032	15,729	29,664	4,541
Findlay, Ohio	19,363	4,613	639	1,115	1,595	2,282	3,607	5,763	8,147	11,019	16,264	26,981	4,407
Macomb, Ill.	8,509	5,112	595	1,163	1,607	2,330	3,639	5,807	8,143	10,736	15,391	25,667	5,079
Valparaiso, Ind.	8,079	6,380	635	1,045	1,583	2,361	3,788	5,829	8,151	10,569	15,379	25,560	6,230
Ionia, Mich.	6,562	3,674	646	1,146	1,645	2,294	3,627	5,521	8,000	10,471	15,600	31,667	3,654
West Bend, Wis.	4,760	6,017	750	1,100	1,690	2,377	3,912	5,928	8,140	10,669	16,167	32,500	6,053
Barnesville, Ohio	4,602	3,386	634	1,128	1,674	2,276	3,545	5,745	8,000	10,308	15,667		3,402
Vandalia, Ill.	4,342	3,342	505	1,056	1,587	2,274	3,558	5,522	8,115	10,308			3,360
Mitchell, Ind.	3,226	2,304	635	1,138	1,595	2,285	3,553	5,579	7,950	10,400			2,343
Crystal Falls, Mich.	2,995	2,573	513	1,060	1,547	2,200	3,395	5,476	7,833	11,333	16,500		2,551
Franklin Park, Ill.	2,425	7,204	500	1,160	1,675	2,286	3,555	6,179	8,148	10,777	15,833	24,857	7,114
21 W. N. Central cities													
Minneapolis, Minn.[1]	464,356	6,381	539	1,106	1,616	2,324	3,816	5,797	8,188	11,137	15,756	32,720	6,346
St. Paul, Minn.[1]	271,606	5,594	547	1,078	1,603	2,296	3,743	5,776	8,166	10,921	15,554	28,800	5,604
Des Moines, Iowa[1]	142,559	5,091	602	1,101	1,595	2,313	3,656	5,747	8,070	10,835	15,525	32,043	5,026
Wichita, Kan.[1]	111,110	4,685	563	1,103	1,623	2,332	3,696	5,670	8,086	10,796	15,780	23,019	4,649
St. Joseph, Mo.[1]	80,935	4,452	663	1,109	1,607	2,245	3,579	5,717	8,140	10,981	15,636	27,625	4,419
Lincoln, Neb.[1]	75,933	5,710	627	1,127	1,612	2,344	3,662	5,792	8,134	11,193	15,905	30,990	5,583
Topeka, Kan.	64,120	4,342	631	1,113	1,636	2,301	3,729	5,769	8,229	10,830	15,447	31,583	4,176
Springfield, Mo.	57,527	4,285	636	1,098	1,606	2,283	3,589	5,745	8,133	10,839	15,653	27,347	4,172
Sioux Falls, S.D.	33,362	5,304	598	1,082	1,585	2,281	3,712	5,782	8,135	10,572	15,761	24,000	5,218
Fargo, N.D.[1]	28,619	6,677	490	1,200	1,640	2,347	3,868	5,748	8,158	10,808	15,917	30,750	6,561
So. St. Paul, Minn.	10,009	4,276	591	1,083	1,585	2,269	3,696	5,663	8,047	10,640	15,571	30,000	4,176
Abilene, Kan.	5,658	4,258	707	1,082	1,610	2,315	3,683	5,771	8,069	10,986	15,615	21,667	4,252
Chariton, Iowa	5,365	3,465	633	1,122	1,599	2,257	3,618	5,506	8,000	10,320	15,250	20,000	3,397
Richmond, Mo.	4,129	2,953	641	1,078	1,573	2,243	3,640	5,662	7,895	10,000	15,000		2,933
Alexandria, Minn.	3,876	3,836	700	1,133	1,604	2,279	3,604	5,671	8,026	10,714	18,000	20,000	3,774
Gering, Neb.	2,531	3,420	575	1,088	1,605	2,319	3,578	5,502	8,188	10,960	16,333	20,000	3,432
Forest City, Iowa	2,016	3,850	605	1,150	1,581	2,331	3,642	5,593	7,778	10,417	15,000		3,852
St. Paul, Neb.	1,621	2,978	668	1,098	1,563	2,238	3,681	5,511	8,125	10,000			2,944
Wilton, N.D.	1,001	2,241	517	1,022	1,578	2,105	3,719	5,857		10,000	15,000		2,101
Belle Plaine, Kan.	825	2,249	623	1,169	1,573	2,307	3,455	5,600	8,000				2,249
Avon, S.D.	670	3,103	642	1,133	1,594	2,215	3,585	5,417	8,667	11,000	15,000		3,141
22 S. Atlantic cities													
Atlanta, Ga.[1]	270,366	6,615	650	1,095	1,613	2,294	3,695	5,864	8,252	11,113	15,784	34,461	6,556
Richmond, Va.[1]	182,929	7,155	663	1,094	1,606	2,261	3,620	5,972	8,278	11,122	16,000	29,474	7,197
Jacksonville, Fla.[1]	129,549	6,279	565	1,065	1,581	2,216	3,555	5,738	8,221	10,735	15,586	31,379	6,128
Charleston, S.C.[1]	62,265	6,669	599	1,061	1,569	2,197	3,596	5,686	8,140	10,984	15,897	40,095	6,446
Wheeling, W.Va.[1]	61,659	7,170	635	1,138	1,620	2,275	3,676	5,855	8,165	10,785	15,837	29,304	7,111
Greensboro, N.C.[1]	53,569	7,530	571	1,077	1,590	2,297	3,673	5,855	8,249	10,962	15,618	28,451	7,432
Columbia, S.C.[1]	51,581	6,598	531	1,052	1,543	2,144	3,802	5,884	8,041	10,770	15,550	26,920	6,617
Asheville, N.C.[1]	50,193	8,295	636	1,080	1,581	2,147	3,628	5,834	8,191	10,795	15,769	31,143	8,342
Wilmington, N.C.	32,270	4,543	727	1,089	1,586	2,245	3,624	5,647	8,126	10,701	15,508	29,259	4,493
Hagerstown, Md.	30,861	7,034	593	1,134	1,601	2,287	3,661	5,854	8,295	11,323	15,612	29,457	6,709
Martinsburg, W.Va.	14,857	5,060	663	1,099	1,596	2,261	3,500	5,708	8,035	10,808	15,446	34,855	4,856
Frederick, Md.[1]	14,434	6,324	750	1,085	1,613	2,327	3,702	5,699	8,116	11,038	15,886	26,737	6,219
Tallahassee, Fla.	10,700	4,823	547	1,072	1,537	2,241	3,666	5,627	7,946	10,560	15,524	29,102	4,685
Richwood, W.Va.	5,720	2,435	572	1,095	1,575	2,221	3,380	5,279	8,083	10,667	15,375	50,000	2,427
Milledgeville, Ga.	5,534	3,359	481	1,078	1,550	2,158	3,638	5,613	8,175	10,405	15,571	33,750	3,249
Franklin, Va.	2,930	3,799	557	1,075	1,600	2,214	3,606	5,774	8,125	10,500	15,600	20,000	3,761
Calhoun, Ga.	2,371	3,624	540	1,080	1,538	2,303	3,487	5,698	8,025	10,222	15,000	20,000	3,600
Jesup, Ga.	2,303	2,362	604	1,000	1,538	2,176	3,392	5,650	8,000	10,000			2,299
Chesterfield, S.C.	1,030	3,115	405	1,050	1,500	2,200	3,500	5,500	8,000	10,000			3,193
Boca Raton, Fla.	447	4,537	642	1,000	1,500	2,167	3,500	5,000	8,000	10,500	15,250	25,000	4,616
Odessa, Del.	385	2,174	645	1,022	1,593	2,291	3,650	5,600	7,750	10,000			2,192
Wilson Mills, N.C.	359	1,539	650	1,050	1,500	2,125	3,300						1,539

TABLE A 6 (Cont'd)

Owner-occupied Dwelling Units, Average Value, All Types combined, by Value Groups: 1-Family, All Value Groups combined, 139 Cities, Towns, and Villages in Descending Order of Population, by Geographic Division, April 1, 1930

	POPU-LATION	All value groups	Under $1,000	$1,000-1,499	$1,500-1,999	$2,000-2,999	$3,000-4,999	$5,000-7,499	$7,500-9,999	$10,000-14,999	$15,000-19,999	$20,000 and over	1-FAMILY All value groups
11 E. S. Central cities													
Birmingham, Ala. [1]	259,678	$6,358	$638	$1,080	$1,577	$2,300	$3,691	$5,805	$8,159	$10,798	$15,604	$31,889	$6,280
Knoxville, Tenn. [1]	105,802	5,109	636	1,073	1,563	2,252	3,533	5,769	8,040	10,966	15,556	32,535	4,976
Jackson, Miss. [1]	48,282	5,566	706	1,100	1,592	2,232	3,694	5,744	8,255	10,743	15,457	26,895	5,535
Paducah, Ky. [1]	33,541	3,875	520	1,062	1,585	2,238	3,586	5,805	8,073	11,048	16,300	27,750	3,780
Johnson City, Tenn.	25,080	5,388	589	1,085	1,603	2,276	3,650	5,819	8,153	10,917	15,613	31,738	5,193
Paris, Tenn.	8,164	3,229	520	1,077	1,603	2,233	3,497	5,792	8,007	10,273	15,000	26,429	3,175
Somerset, Ky.	5,506	2,412	552	1,085	1,582	2,206	3,462	5,667	8,194	10,286	15,000		2,388
Andalusia, Ala.	5,154	4,705	561	1,098	1,588	2,211	3,526	5,513	7,833	10,265	15,231	28,333	4,741
Carbon Hill, Ala.	2,519	1,727	503	1,062	1,524	2,181	3,454	5,292	7,875				1,740
Durant, Miss.	2,480	2,163	623	1,106	1,695	2,363	3,594	5,382	8,000	10,000			2,114
Woodbury, Tenn.	502	1,953	491	1,090	1,558	2,083	3,545	5,000			15,000		1,954
13 W. S. Central cities													
Dallas, Tex. [1]	260,475	6,128	598	1,081	1,584	2,296	3,735	5,719	8,138	11,051	15,604	33,675	5,973
Oklahoma City, Okla. [1]	185,389	5,980	560	1,053	1,601	2,277	3,689	5,821	8,166	10,910	15,756	31,451	5,871
Little Rock, Ark. [1]	81,679	5,532	587	1,076	1,558	2,291	3,630	5,782	8,119	10,758	15,610	29,394	5,533
Shreveport, La. [1]	76,655	6,238	525	1,056	1,567	2,200	3,601	5,879	8,166	11,122	15,477	35,039	6,193
Austin, Tex.	53,120	5,049	586	1,103	1,591	2,288	3,648	5,720	8,118	10,938	15,840	29,298	4,918
Wichita Falls, Tex. [1]	43,690	5,321	541	1,074	1,578	2,283	3,654	5,652	8,187	10,657	15,429	35,862	5,364
Baton Rouge, La.	30,729	5,497	695	1,102	1,572	2,210	3,646	5,782	8,156	10,613	15,635	28,374	5,449
Greenville, Tex.	12,407	3,819	546	1,080	1,561	2,275	3,514	5,646	7,955	10,450	15,231	27,105	3,700
Hope, Ark.	6,008	3,149	496	1,074	1,592	2,278	3,418	5,581	8,000	10,300	15,600	31,000	3,051
Conway, Ark.	5,534	3,674	516	1,102	1,567	2,288	3,483	5,484	8,042	10,681	15,000	26,429	3,626
Chandler, Okla.	2,717	2,768	512	1,081	1,580	2,281	3,512	5,505	8,250	10,750	16,000		2,743
Vivian, La.	1,646	2,146	589	1,074	1,568	2,229	3,554	5,353				20,000	2,170
Lockney, Tex.	1,466	2,748	494	1,024	1,527	2,214	3,328	5,429	8,000	10,000			2,736
17 Mountain cities													
Salt Lake City, Utah [1]	140,267	4,756	607	1,106	1,619	2,289	3,761	5,669	8,362	10,909	15,605	30,536	4,566
Pueblo, Colo. [1]	50,096	2,992	612	1,123	1,614	2,292	3,558	5,553	8,100	10,643	15,500	37,500	2,884
Phoenix, Ariz. [1]	48,118	7,132	500	1,100	1,587	2,270	3,717	5,664	8,125	10,987	15,424	36,563	7,080
Butte, Mont. [1]	39,532	3,292	585	1,093	1,604	2,238	3,554	5,755	8,000	10,782	16,000	32,500	3,254
Albuquerque, N.M. [1]	26,570	4,832	576	1,069	1,621	2,289	3,696	5,698	8,145	10,517	15,100	29,167	4,731
Boise, Idaho [1]	21,544	4,579	584	1,059	1,591	2,271	3,605	5,636	8,199	10,804	15,600	27,190	4,463
Reno, Nev. [1]	18,529	7,362	571	1,123	1,574	2,238	3,674	5,796	8,114	10,772	15,425	35,621	6,673
Casper, Wyo.	16,619	4,050	503	1,069	1,567	2,242	3,601	5,608	8,183	10,653	15,636	43,565	3,684
Bozeman, Mont.	6,855	3,836	570	1,129	1,590	2,285	3,630	5,772	7,988	10,370	15,167	20,000	3,712
Salida, Colo.	5,065	2,600	615	1,083	1,615	2,274	3,456	5,353	8,071	10,778	15,000	28,750	2,506
Roundup, Mont.	2,577	2,708	442	1,131	1,669	2,184	3,621	5,548	7,750	10,000	15,000		2,678
Bountiful, Utah	2,571	2,964	683	1,083	1,549	2,191	3,487	5,561	7,917	10,000			2,968
Gooding, Idaho	1,592	2,733	580	1,091	1,556	2,293	3,569	5,478	7,667	10,000			2,670
Salina, Utah	1,333	2,286	618	1,083	1,551	2,078	3,405	5,308	8,000		15,000		2,275
Florence, Ariz.	1,318	2,974	646	1,078	1,592	2,332	3,775	5,643	7,500	10,333			2,899
Lovelock, Nev.	1,263	2,732	461	1,048	1,500	2,155	3,434	5,615	8,000	11,000	15,000		2,736
Los Lunas, N.M.	513	1,157	347	1,000	1,500	2,000	3,000	5,000		12,000			1,210
14 Pacific cities													
Seattle, Wash. [1]	365,583	5,646	403	1,109	1,611	2,333	3,739	5,684	8,125	10,813	15,615	39,194	5,335
Portland, Ore. [1]	301,815	5,145	641	1,121	1,604	2,328	3,748	5,719	8,071	10,899	15,875	32,796	5,004
San Diego, Calif. [1]	147,995	7,052	572	1,066	1,582	2,289	3,702	5,740	8,082	11,001	15,735	36,621	6,640
Sacramento, Calif. [1]	93,750	5,987	800	1,112	1,603	2,368	3,806	5,705	8,170	10,977	15,667	30,167	5,803
Santa Barbara, Calif.	33,613	8,956	520	1,079	1,591	2,309	3,757	5,794	8,214	10,943	15,758	35,106	8,679
Vancouver, Wash.	15,766	3,413	576	1,123	1,604	2,313	3,604	5,554	8,064	10,750	15,667	53,667	3,270
Modesto, Calif.	13,842	4,902	638	1,066	1,631	2,356	3,619	5,590	8,127	10,943	15,548	40,957	4,695
Oregon City, Ore.	5,761	3,071	518	1,110	1,593	2,262	3,527	5,726	8,000	10,580	15,000	20,000	3,082
Porterville, Calif.	5,303	4,134	523	1,080	1,574	2,345	3,617	5,641	8,284	10,650	15,333	24,000	4,098
Ashland, Ore.	4,544	3,456	659	1,091	1,580	2,258	3,547	5,562	8,052	10,773	15,500	26,250	3,420
Burns, Ore.	2,599	3,062	432	1,074	1,527	2,246	3,550	5,539	8,200	10,000			3,040
N. Sacramento, Calif.	2,097	3,920	480	1,079	1,566	2,325	3,606	5,659	8,200	10,286	15,000	25,000	3,890
Grandview, Wash.	1,085	2,355	631	1,122	1,633	2,275	3,516	5,900	8,000	12,000			2,342
Marcus, Wash.	583	1,407	580	1,065	1,508	2,227	3,050	5,500					1,407

Source: Special Census tabulation of 139 cities for NBER

[1] *Average values derived from sampling of complete Census data, by population group:*
  100,000 or more population, and Wheeling, W.Va., every 9th family.
  50,000-100,000   "   , every 7th family.
  25,000-50,000   "   ,   " 6th family.
  Under 25,000   "   ,   " 4th family.

The other 90 cities, towns, and villages listed in this table and not carrying this footnote had full coverage.

TABLE A 7

Owner-occupied Dwelling Units, All Types combined, by Value Groups: 1-Family, All Value Groups combined, 25 Urban Places with Populations under 2,500, by Geographic Division, April 1, 1930

	All value groups	Under $1,000	$1,000-1,499	$1,500-1,999	$2,000-2,999	$3,000-4,999	$5,000-7,499	$7,500-9,999	$10,000-14,999	$15,000-19,999	$20,000 and over	1-FAMILY All value groups
1 New England city												
Pittsfield, Me.	346	4	8	12	76	167	67	7	4		1	284
1 E. N. Central city												
Franklin Park, Ill.	344	1	5	4	7	61	136	64	47	12	7	318
5 W. N. Central cities												
Forest City, Iowa	285	10	16	21	55	92	74	9	6	2		242
Wilton, N.D.	114	25	18	18	21	23	7		1	1		105
Avon, S.D.	112	12	6	16	26	34	12	3	2	1		102
St. Paul, Neb.	307	25	43	31	64	90	44	8	2			304
Belle Plaine, Kan.	154	15	29	24	41	39	5	1				154
6 S. Atlantic cities												
Odessa, Del.	74	22	9	14	11	10	5	2	1			72
Wilson Mills, N.C.	28	8	8	3	4	5						28
Chesterfield, S.C.	97	19	12	6	12	25	14	4	5			84
Calhoun, Ga.	235	31	5	16	45	76	43	8	9	1	1	216
Jesup, Ga.	218	51	21	26	37	60	20	2	1			204
Boca Raton, Fla.	46	12	3	2	9	7	3	1	4	4	1	45
2 E. S. Central cities												
Woodbury, Tenn.	65	17	10	12	12	11	2			1		62
Durant, Miss.	304	106	18	22	59	80	17	2				259
2 W. S. Central cities												
Vivian, La.	211	46	33	36	41	37	17				1	191
Lockney, Tex.	208	9	19	31	62	61	21	2	3			201
5 Mountain cities												
Gooding, Idaho	205	27	29	24	41	54	23	3	4			197
Los Lunas, N.M.	53	34	5	5	3	3	2		1			50
Florence, Ariz.	130	20	18	12	25	34	14	1	6			117
Salina, Utah	196	25	27	35	51	42	13	2		1		189
Lovelock, Nev.	168	36	27	8	22	43	26	3	2	1		167
3 Pacific cities												
Marcus, Wash.	68	25	13	13	11	4	2					68
N. Sacramento, Calif.	342	6	14	22	61	154	66	8	7	2	2	340
Grandview, Wash.	157	23	23	15	56	28	10	1	1			151

Source: Special Census tabulation of 139 cities for NBER, full coverage

TABLE A 8

Dwelling Units,[1] Total Value (thousands of dollars) by Tenure and Geographic Division, April 1, 1930 and January 1, 1934

	TOTAL 1930	TOTAL 1934	OWNER-OCCUPIED 1930	OWNER-OCCUPIED 1934	RENTED 1930	RENTED 1934
United States	122,578,481	79,170,161	64,681,033	42,416,386	57,897,448	36,753,775
New England	9,529,852	7,242,013	5,691,304	4,380,497	3,838,548	2,861,516
Middle Atlantic	45,701,866	27,584,422	20,782,511	12,461,525	24,919,355	15,122,897
East North Central	29,954,726	20,222,148	16,838,971	11,480,545	13,115,755	8,741,603
West North Central	8,054,868	5,728,483	5,085,010	3,665,563	2,969,858	2,062,920
South Atlantic	8,337,445	5,649,639	4,793,861	3,255,062	3,543,584	2,394,577
East South Central	3,348,891	1,765,663	1,892,735	1,023,988	1,456,156	741,675
West South Central	5,323,606	3,276,979	2,843,314	1,806,342	2,480,292	1,470,637
Mountain	1,982,162	1,374,670	1,065,214	755,221	916,948	619,449
Pacific	10,345,065	6,326,144	5,688,113	3,587,643	4,656,952	2,738,501

[1] *Includes value of vacant units.*

TABLE A 9

Owner-occupied 1-Family Dwellings, Number and Percentage Distribution by Value Groups, 61 Cities by Geographic Division, April 1, 1930 and January 1, 1934

	All value groups		Under $1,500		$1,500- 2,999		$3,000- 4,999		$5,000- 7,499		$7,500- 9,999	
	1930	1934	1930	1934	1930	1934	1930	1934	1930	1934	1930	1934
61 cities	846,813	745,257	47,653	102,323	116,930	192,397	222,971	223,515	236,518	134,089	91,258	42,552
6 New England cities	72,738	59,454	1,603	2,783	6,208	9,222	16,838	19,485	23,290	16,120	9,399	5,242
Portland, Me.[1]	4,767	3,863	238	299	497	589	1,078	1,056	1,414	1,044	602	388
Nashua, N.H.	2,456	1,852	56	97	273	367	495	661	505	503	327	229
Burlington, Vt.[1]	2,089	1,896	28	69	165	210	495	506	505	503	327	229
Worcester, Mass.[1]	9,747	8,552	153	213	396	742	1,791	2,864	3,501	2,784	1,422	889
Providence, R.I.[1]*	47,799	38,934	1,044	2,008	4,590	6,815	11,673	13,090	15,300	10,062	5,913	3,143
Waterbury, Conn.[1]	5,880	4,357	84	97	287	499	1,008	1,308	1,799	1,262	882	451
5 Mid. Atlantic cities	56,289	40,354	530	1,049	3,409	6,327	11,080	12,810	17,987	11,032	9,155	4,347
Binghamton, N.Y.	6,028	5,372	40	168	196	611	1,068	2,314	2,269	1,482	1,003	395
Syracuse, N.Y.[1]	19,350	15,411	81	128	324	1,192	1,593	3,696	5,175	5,053	4,707	2,658
Trenton, N.J.	13,626	6,463	117	241	1,972	1,999	4,357	2,158	3,942	984	1,384	357
Erie, Pa.[1]	12,123	9,275	99	277	351	1,552	2,619	3,431	5,004	2,554	1,476	722
Williamsport, Pa.	5,162	3,833	193	235	566	973	1,443	1,211	1,597	959	585	215
7 E. N. Central cities	185,517	163,772	2,524	7,844	13,565	30,183	38,035	52,339	59,123	40,994	31,029	14,693
Cleveland, Ohio[1]*	100,305	93,799	756	1,913	3,159	10,679	13,518	28,132	31,743	28,184	20,826	10,922
Indianapolis, Ind.[1]	40,302	32,730	900	3,615	6,102	10,289	13,113	9,986	11,349	4,930	3,852	1,775
Decatur, Ill.[1]	8,211	6,520	175	826	1,225	2,131	3,045	2,420	2,394	749	630	199
Peoria, Ill.	11,968	11,282	378	684	1,588	2,355	3,410	4,004	3,571	2,806	1,381	753
Lansing, Mich.[1]	11,011	8,577	238	568	1,022	3,332	3,059	3,328	4,060	908	1,351	247
Kenosha, Wis.[1]	5,593	4,420	21	93	91	438	651	1,645	2,653	1,630	1,099	349
Racine, Wis.[1]	8,127	6,444	56	145	378	959	1,239	2,824	3,353	1,787	1,890	448
10 W. N. Central cities	151,614	138,809	8,924	17,510	23,476	37,617	45,198	48,458	47,034	23,467	12,755	5,971
Minneapolis, Minn.[1]	48,402	42,654	882	1,699	3,879	8,665	13,959	18,526	19,035	9,082	5,166	2,369
St. Paul, Minn.[1]	30,258	28,451	1,017	1,963	4,158	7,091	8,973	11,079	10,719	5,792	2,709	1,328
Des Moines, Iowa.[1]	18,197	17,444	1,837	3,414	3,560	5,411	5,386	4,964	4,414	2,326	1,435	652
St. Joseph, Mo.[1]	8,288	7,153	987	1,585	2,263	2,718	2,555	1,754	1,491	696	350	171
Springfield, Mo.	7,538	7,091	974	2,316	2,186	2,235	2,105	1,487	1,374	680	405	162
Fargo, N.D.[1]	2,442	2,284	72	98	138	288	552	929	1,056	681	300	180
Sioux Falls, S.D.	3,487	3,624	202	546	587	939	955	1,238	1,065	602	347	172
Lincoln, Neb.[1]	10,094	9,992	518	1,377	1,806	2,941	3,101	3,166	2,758	1,622	742	486
Topeka, Kan.[1]	9,345	8,578	1,211	1,793	2,338	2,784	2,779	2,531	1,981	1,067	518	193
Wichita, Kan.[1]	13,563	11,538	1,224	2,719	2,556	4,545	4,833	2,784	3,141	919	783	258
10 S. Atlantic cities	85,147	74,493	9,040	14,090	14,804	19,818	19,137	17,819	18,513	12,329	8,371	4,568
Frederick, Md.[1]	1,752	978	80	78	296	200	532	321	424	191	124	62
Hagerstown, Md.	2,522	1,734	85	144	409	441	657	479	625	325	260	139
Richmond, Va.[1]	13,446	11,888	1,035	1,467	1,881	2,538	2,610	2,952	2,835	2,620	2,016	1,253
Wheeling, W.Va.[1]*	17,820	16,229	2,052	3,834	4,005	5,018	4,815	3,957	3,915	2,110	1,224	604
Asheville, N.C.[1]	3,808	3,287	252	882	525	1,103	840	694	889	326	364	91
Greensboro, N.C.[1]	3,752	3,398	273	576	644	863	777	819	735	602	357	220
Charleston, S.C.[1]	2,954	2,166	427	414	483	382	616	463	511	346	245	174
Columbia, S.C.[1]	3,255	2,699	525	482	378	471	469	675	812	582	406	173
Atlanta, Ga.[1]*	26,037	23,846	2,700	4,427	4,356	6,608	5,931	5,598	5,670	3,899	2,727	1,444
Jacksonville, Fla.[1]	9,801	8,268	1,611	1,786	1,827	2,194	1,890	1,863	2,097	1,328	648	408
4 E. S. Central cities	45,675	40,074	6,795	14,114	10,302	11,323	10,863	7,871	8,640	3,764	3,411	1,146
Paducah, Ky.[1]	2,892	2,642	930	1,376	648	661	534	303	360	221	144	42
Knoxville, Tenn.[1]	9,603	8,380	1,269	2,095	2,610	2,856	2,646	1,815	1,539	895	558	303
Birmingham, Ala.[1]*	29,448	25,978	4,122	9,760	6,264	7,188	6,849	4,967	6,021	2,168	2,385	682
Jackson, Miss.[1]	3,732	3,074	474	883	780	638	834	786	720	480	324	119
7 W. S. Central cities	67,672	58,760	6,809	13,137	11,865	17,851	18,385	15,578	15,689	7,174	5,875	2,121
Little Rock, Ark.[1]	7,959	6,677	826	1,524	1,596	2,203	2,240	1,667	1,463	700	700	274
Baton Rouge, La.	2,583	2,093	329	421	534	479	670	582	489	357	205	111
Shreveport, La.[1]	7,532	6,615	1,036	1,781	1,533	1,554	1,498	1,710	1,477	1,014	847	212
Oklahoma City, Okla.[1]	16,038	14,441	1,377	2,812	2,538	4,132	4,581	3,895	4,077	2,161	1,152	720
Austin, Tex.[1]	5,342	5,693	1,234	1,416	1,008	1,567	1,209	1,379	902	666	322	219
Dallas, Tex.[1]	23,922	20,000	1,215	3,762	3,780	6,955	7,209	5,853	6,399	2,104	2,331	518
Wichita Falls, Tex.[1]	4,296	3,241	792	1,421	876	961	978	492	882	172	318	67
8 Mountain cities	39,641	37,093	5,067	9,018	8,883	11,968	12,528	10,064	8,069	4,033	2,004	937
Butte, Mont.[1]	3,678	3,388	1,014	1,271	1,080	1,141	966	604	366	262	84	51
Boise, Idaho[1]	2,736	2,690	304	469	708	1,010	876	762	552	305	92	63
Casper, Wyo.[1]	1,632	1,790	478	676	344	470	358	447	267	154	89	23
Pueblo, Colo.[1]	6,272	5,292	1,701	2,542	1,988	1,673	1,659	807	658	219	140	33
Albuquerque, N.M.[1]	3,108	2,827	486	743	522	709	930	786	702	383	180	106
Phoenix, Ariz.[1]	3,996	3,543	108	428	474	951	1,182	1,149	1,020	619	462	175
Salt Lake City, Utah[1]	16,047	15,416	900	2,594	3,483	5,526	6,057	4,819	3,816	1,640	765	369
Reno, Nev.[1]	2,172	2,147	76	295	284	488	500	690	688	451	192	117
4 Pacific cities	142,520	132,448	6,361	22,778	24,418	48,088	50,907	39,091	38,173	15,176	9,259	3,527
Seattle, Wash.[1]*	60,516	57,748	3,492	12,985	11,988	21,443	21,087	15,216	15,381	5,463	3,654	1,267
Portland, Ore.[1]	45,531	41,955	1,593	5,506	7,920	15,415	18,279	13,546	12,078	5,160	2,412	1,108
Sacramento, Calif.[1]	11,039	9,369	133	739	1,036	2,954	4,116	3,462	3,640	1,610	952	371
San Diego, Calif.[1]*	25,434	23,376	1,143	3,548	3,474	8,276	7,425	6,867	7,074	2,943	2,241	781

Source: 1930, special Census tabulation; 1934, *Real Property Inventory*, Table II. Classification of dwelling units by type not strictly comparable in the two enumerations, as explained on the half-title page to sec. A. Furthermore, there is some question as to the completeness of coverage in the *Real Property Inventory*. The absolute differences in number of dwelling units cannot, therefore, be stressed. The emphasis should be on the major shifts of dwelling units among the value classes, as shown by the percentage distributions.

*Metropolitan district.

[1] 1930 Census sample data raised to full coverage by using sampling factor (see Table A 6, footnote 1).

TABLE A 9

Owner-occupied 1-Family Dwellings, Number and Percentage Distribution by Value Groups, 61 Cities by Geographic Division, April 1, 1930 and January 1, 1934

NUMBER $10,000 and over 1930	1934	All value groups 1930	1934	Under $1,500 1930	1934	$1,500-2,999 1930	1934	$3,000-4,999 1930	1934	$5,000-7,499 1930	1934	$7,500-9,999 1930	1934	$10,000 and over 1930	1934	
131,483	50,381	100.0	100.0	5.6	13.7	13.8	25.8	26.3	30.0	28.0	18.0	10.8	5.7	15.5	6.8	61 cities
15,400	6,602	100.0	100.0	2.2	4.7	8.5	15.5	23.2	32.8	32.0	27.1	12.9	8.8	21.2	11.1	6 New England cities
938	487	100.0	100.0	5.0	7.7	10.4	15.3	22.6	27.3	29.7	27.0	12.6	10.1	19.7	12.6	Portland, Me.[1]
310	120	100.0	100.0	2.3	5.2	11.1	19.8	32.3	35.7	31.4	25.1	10.3	7.7	12.6	6.5	Nashua, N.H.
569	379	100.0	100.0	1.3	3.6	7.9	11.1	23.7	26.7	24.2	26.5	15.7	12.1	27.2	20.0	Burlington, Vt.
2,484	1,060	100.0	100.0	1.6	2.5	4.0	8.7	18.4	33.5	35.9	32.5	14.6	10.4	25.5	12.4	Worcester, Mass.[1]
9,279	3,816	100.0	100.0	2.2	5.2	9.6	17.5	24.4	33.6	32.0	25.8	12.4	8.1	19.4	9.8	Providence, R.I.[1]*
1,820	740	100.0	100.0	1.4	2.2	4.9	11.5	17.1	30.0	30.6	29.0	15.0	10.3	31.0	17.0	Waterbury, Conn.[1]
14,128	4,789	100.0	100.0	0.9	2.6	6.1	15.7	19.7	31.7	31.9	27.3	16.3	10.8	25.1	11.9	5 Mid. Atlantic cities
1,452	402	100.0	100.0	0.7	3.1	3.3	11.4	17.7	43.1	37.6	27.6	16.6	7.3	24.1	7.5	Binghamton, N.Y.[1]
7,470	2,684	100.0	100.0	0.4	0.8	1.7	7.7	8.2	24.0	26.8	32.8	24.3	17.3	38.6	17.4	Syracuse, N.Y.[1]
1,854	724	100.0	100.0	0.9	3.8	14.5	30.9	32.0	33.4	28.9	15.2	10.1	5.5	13.6	11.2	Trenton, N.J.
2,574	739	100.0	100.0	0.8	3.0	2.9	16.7	21.6	37.0	41.3	27.5	12.2	7.8	21.2	8.0	Erie, Pa.[1]
778	240	100.0	100.0	3.7	6.1	11.0	25.4	28.0	31.6	30.9	25.0	11.3	5.6	15.1	6.3	Williamsport, Pa.
41,241	17,719	100.0	100.0	1.4	4.8	7.3	18.4	20.5	32.0	31.9	25.0	16.7	9.0	22.2	10.8	7 E. N. Central cities
30,303	13,969	100.0	100.0	0.8	2.0	3.1	11.4	13.5	30.0	31.6	30.1	20.8	11.6	30.2	14.9	Cleveland, Ohio[1]*
4,986	2,135	100.0	100.0	2.2	11.1	15.1	31.4	32.5	30.5	28.2	15.1	9.6	5.4	12.4	6.5	Indianapolis, Ind.[1]
742	195	100.0	100.0	2.1	12.7	14.9	32.7	37.1	37.1	29.2	11.5	7.7	3.0	9.0	3.0	Decatur, Ill.[1]
1,640	680	100.0	100.0	3.2	6.0	13.3	20.9	28.5	35.5	29.8	24.9	11.5	6.7	13.7	6.0	Peoria, Ill.
1,281	194	100.0	100.0	2.1	6.6	9.3	38.8	27.8	38.8	36.9	10.6	12.3	2.9	11.6	2.3	Lansing, Mich.[1]
1,078	265	100.0	100.0	0.4	2.1	1.6	9.9	11.6	37.2	47.4	36.9	19.7	7.9	19.3	6.0	Kenosha, Wis.[1]
1,211	281	100.0	100.0	0.7	2.2	4.6	14.9	15.2	43.8	41.3	27.7	23.3	7.0	14.9	4.4	Racine, Wis.[1]
14,227	5,786	100.0	100.0	5.9	12.6	15.5	27.1	29.8	34.9	31.0	16.9	8.4	4.3	9.4	4.2	10 W. N. Central cities
5,481	2,313	100.0	100.0	1.8	4.0	8.0	20.3	28.9	43.4	39.3	21.3	10.7	5.6	11.3	5.4	Minneapolis, Minn.[1]
2,682	1,198	100.0	100.0	3.4	6.9	13.7	24.9	29.7	38.9	35.4	20.4	8.9	4.7	8.9	4.2	St. Paul, Minn.[1]
1,565	677	100.0	100.0	10.1	19.6	19.6	31.0	29.6	28.5	24.2	13.3	7.9	3.7	8.6	3.9	Des Moines, Iowa[1]
637	229	100.0	100.0	11.9	22.2	27.4	38.0	30.8	24.5	18.0	9.7	4.2	2.4	7.7	3.2	St. Joseph, Mo.[1]
494	211	100.0	100.0	12.9	32.6	29.0	31.5	27.9	21.0	18.2	9.6	5.4	2.3	6.6	3.0	Springfield, Mo.
324	108	100.0	100.0	2.9	4.3	5.7	12.6	22.6	40.7	43.2	29.8	12.3	7.9	13.3	4.7	Fargo, N.D.
331	127	100.0	100.0	5.8	15.1	16.8	25.9	27.4	34.2	30.5	16.6	10.0	4.7	9.5	3.5	Sioux Falls, S.D.
1,169	400	100.0	100.0	5.1	13.8	17.9	29.4	30.7	31.7	27.3	16.2	7.4	4.9	11.6	4.0	Lincoln, Neb.[1]
518	210	100.0	100.0	12.9	20.9	25.0	32.5	29.7	29.5	21.2	12.4	5.6	2.3	5.6	2.4	Topeka, Kan.[1]
1,026	313	100.0	100.0	9.0	23.6	18.8	39.4	35.6	24.1	23.2	8.0	5.8	2.2	7.6	2.7	Wichita, Kan.[1]
15,282	5,869	100.0	100.0	10.6	18.9	17.4	26.6	22.5	23.9	21.7	16.6	9.8	6.1	18.0	7.9	10 S. Atlantic cities
296	126	100.0	100.0	4.6	8.0	16.9	20.5	30.3	32.8	24.2	19.5	7.1	6.3	16.9	12.9	Frederick, Md.[1]
486	206	100.0	100.0	3.4	8.3	16.2	25.4	26.0	27.6	24.8	18.8	10.3	8.0	19.3	11.9	Hagerstown, Md.
3,069	1,058	100.0	100.0	7.7	12.4	14.0	21.4	19.4	24.8	21.1	22.0	15.0	10.5	22.8	8.9	Richmond, Va.[1]
1,809	706	100.0	100.0	11.5	23.6	22.5	30.9	27.0	24.4	22.0	13.0	6.9	3.7	10.1	4.4	Wheeling, W.Va.[1]*
938	191	100.0	100.0	6.6	26.8	13.8	33.6	22.1	21.1	23.3	9.9	9.6	2.8	24.6	5.8	Asheville, N.C.[1]
966	318	100.0	100.0	7.3	16.9	17.2	25.4	20.7	24.1	19.6	17.7	9.5	6.5	25.7	9.4	Greensboro, N.C.[1]
672	387	100.0	100.0	14.5	19.1	16.3	17.6	20.9	21.4	17.3	16.0	8.3	8.0	22.7	17.9	Charleston, S.C.[1]
665	316	100.0	100.0	16.1	17.9	11.6	17.4	14.4	25.0	25.0	21.6	12.5	6.4	20.4	11.7	Columbia, S.C.[1]
4,653	1,872	100.0	100.0	10.3	18.6	16.7	27.7	22.8	23.5	21.8	16.3	10.5	6.1	17.9	7.8	Atlanta, Ga.[1]*
1,728	689	100.0	100.0	16.4	21.6	18.7	26.6	19.3	22.5	21.4	16.1	6.6	4.9	17.6	8.3	Jacksonville, Fla.[1]
5,664	1,856	100.0	100.0	14.9	35.2	22.5	28.3	23.8	19.6	18.9	9.4	7.5	2.9	12.4	4.6	4 E. S. Central cities
276	39	100.0	100.0	32.2	52.1	22.4	25.0	18.5	11.5	12.4	8.3	5.0	1.6	9.5	1.5	Paducah, Ky.[1]
981	416	100.0	100.0	13.2	25.0	27.2	34.1	27.6	21.6	16.0	10.7	5.8	3.6	10.2	5.0	Knoxville, Tenn.[1]
3,807	1,233	100.0	100.0	14.0	37.6	21.3	27.6	23.3	19.1	20.4	8.4	8.1	2.6	12.9	4.7	Birmingham, Ala.[1]*
600	168	100.0	100.0	12.7	28.7	20.9	20.7	22.3	25.6	19.3	15.6	8.7	3.9	16.1	5.5	Jackson, Miss.[1]
9,049	2,899	100.0	100.0	10.0	22.4	17.5	30.4	27.2	26.5	23.2	12.2	8.7	3.6	13.4	4.9	7 W. S. Central cities
1,134	309	100.0	100.0	10.4	22.8	20.1	33.0	28.1	25.0	18.4	10.5	8.8	3.6	13.4	4.9	Little Rock, Ark.[1]
356	143	100.0	100.0	12.7	20.1	20.7	22.9	25.9	27.8	18.9	17.1	8.0	4.1	14.2	4.6	Baton Rouge, La.[1]
1,141	344	100.0	100.0	13.8	26.9	20.4	23.5	19.9	25.9	19.6	15.3	8.0	5.3	13.8	6.8	Shreveport, La.[1]
2,313	721	100.0	100.0	8.6	19.5	15.8	28.6	28.6	27.0	25.4	14.9	11.2	3.2	15.1	5.2	Oklahoma City, Okla.[1]
667	446	100.0	100.0	23.1	24.9	18.9	27.5	22.6	24.2	16.9	11.7	7.2	5.0	14.4	5.0	Austin, Tex.[1]
2,988	808	100.0	100.0	5.1	18.8	15.8	34.8	30.1	29.3	26.8	10.5	6.0	3.9	12.5	7.8	Dallas, Tex.[1]
450	128	100.0	100.0	18.4	43.8	20.4	29.7	22.8	15.2	20.5	5.3	9.7	2.6	12.5	4.0	Wichita Falls, Tex.[1]
3,090	1,073	100.0	100.0	12.8	24.3	22.4	32.3	31.6	27.1	20.4	10.9	5.0	2.5	7.8	2.9	8 Mountain cities
168	59	100.0	100.0	27.6	37.5	29.3	33.7	26.3	17.8	9.9	7.7	2.3	1.5	4.6	1.8	Butte, Mont.[1]
204	81	100.0	100.0	11.1	17.4	25.9	37.6	32.0	28.3	20.2	11.3	3.4	2.4	7.4	3.0	Boise, Idaho[1]
96	20	100.0	100.0	29.3	37.8	21.1	26.2	21.9	25.0	16.4	8.6	5.4	1.3	5.9	1.1	Casper, Wyo.[1]
126	18	100.0	100.0	27.1	48.0	31.7	31.6	26.5	15.3	10.5	4.1	2.2	0.6	2.0	0.4	Pueblo, Colo.[1]
288	100	100.0	100.0	15.6	26.3	16.8	25.1	29.9	27.8	22.6	13.6	5.8	3.7	9.3	3.5	Albuquerque, N.M.[1]
750	221	100.0	100.0	2.7	12.1	11.9	26.8	29.6	32.4	25.5	17.5	11.5	5.0	18.8	6.2	Phoenix, Ariz.[1]
1,026	468	100.0	100.0	5.6	16.8	21.7	35.9	37.7	31.3	23.8	10.6	4.8	2.4	6.4	3.0	Salt Lake City, Utah[1]
432	106	100.0	100.0	3.5	13.8	13.1	22.7	23.0	32.1	31.7	21.0	8.8	5.5	19.9	4.9	Reno, Nev.[1]
13,402	3,788	100.0	100.0	4.5	17.2	17.1	36.3	35.7	29.5	26.8	11.4	6.5	2.7	9.4	2.9	4 Pacific cities
4,914	1,374	100.0	100.0	5.8	22.5	19.8	37.1	34.9	26.3	25.4	9.5	6.0	2.2	8.1	2.4	Seattle, Wash.[1]*
3,249	1,220	100.0	100.0	3.5	13.1	17.4	36.8	40.2	32.3	26.5	12.3	5.3	2.6	7.1	2.9	Portland, Ore.[1]
1,162	233	100.0	100.0	1.2	7.9	9.4	31.5	37.3	36.9	33.0	17.2	8.6	4.0	10.5	2.5	Sacramento, Calif.[1]
4,077	961	100.0	100.0	4.5	15.2	13.7	35.4	29.2	29.4	27.8	12.6	8.8	3.3	16.0	4.1	San Diego, Calif.[1]*

TABLE A 10

Owner-occupied 1-Family Dwellings, Average Value, 50 Cities by Geographic Division, April 1, 1930 and January 1, 1934, and Percentage 1934 is of 1930

	1930	1934	1934 as percentage of 1930		1930	1934	1934 as percentage of 1930
	(dollars)				(dollars)		
50 cities[1]	6,619	4,439	67.1	**7 S. Atlantic cities**	6,342	4,216	66.5
				Hagerstown, Md.	6,709	4,973	74.1
4 New England cities	7,344	5,614	76.4	Richmond, Va.	7,197	4,967	69.0
Portland, Me.	6,875	5,453	79.3	Wheeling, W.Va.*	5,026	3,411	67.9
Worcester, Mass.	8,144	6,038	74.1	Greensboro, N.C.	7,432	4,663	62.7
Providence, R.I.*	6,981	5,370	76.9	Columbia, S.C.	6,617	4,730	71.5
Waterbury, Conn.	8,995	6,822	75.8	Atlanta, Ga.*	6,701	4,286	64.0
				Jacksonville, Fla.	6,128	3,980	64.9
4 Mid. Atlantic cities	8,541	5,056	59.2				
Binghamton, N.Y.	8,232	5,240	63.7	**3 E. S. Central cities**	5,482	2,943	53.7
Syracuse, N.Y.	10,340	5,580	54.0	Paducah, Ky.	3,780	2,124	56.2
Trenton, N.J.	6,360	4,029	63.3	Birmingham, Ala.*	5,662	2,939	51.9
Erie, Pa.	7,905	5,127	64.9	Jackson, Miss.	5,535	3,652	66.0
6 E. N. Central cities	8,440	5,761	68.3	**6 W. S. Central cities**	5,723	3,517	61.5
Cleveland, Ohio*	9,684	6,596	68.1	Little Rock, Ark.	5,533	3,280	59.3
Indianapolis, Ind.	5,985	4,238	70.8	Baton Rouge, La.	5,449	4,124	75.7
Peoria, Ill.	6,168	4,590	74.4	Oklahoma City, Okla.	5,871	3,773	64.3
Lansing, Mich.	6,192	3,545	57.3	Austin, Tex.	4,918	3,779	76.8
Kenosha, Wis.	8,140	5,249	64.5	Dallas, Tex.	5,973	3,422	57.3
Racine, Wis.	7,224	4,863	67.3	Wichita Falls, Tex.	5,364	2,574	47.9
10 W. N. Central cities	5,504	3,948	71.7	**6 Mountain cities**	4,370	3,066	70.2
Minneapolis, Minn.	6,346	4,643	73.2	Butte, Mont.	3,254	2,412	74.1
St. Paul, Minn.	5,604	4,142	73.9	Boise, Idaho	4,463	3,323	74.5
Des Moines, Iowa	5,026	3,458	68.8	Casper, Wyo.	3,684	2,455	66.6
St. Joseph, Mo.	4,419	3,153	71.4	Pueblo, Colo.	2,884	1,889	65.5
Springfield, Mo.	4,172	2,863	68.6	Phoenix, Ariz.	7,080	4,175	59.0
Fargo, N.D.	6,561	4,850	73.9	Salt Lake City, Utah	4,566	3,398	74.4
Sioux Falls, S.D.	5,218	3,744	71.8				
Lincoln, Neb.	5,583	3,775	67.6	**4 Pacific cities**	5,446	3,341	61.3
Topeka, Kan.	4,176	3,203	76.7	Seattle, Wash.*	5,166	3,086	59.7
Wichita, Kan.	4,649	2,938	63.2	Portland, Ore.	5,004	3,434	68.6
				Sacramento, Calif.	5,803	3,837	66.1
				San Diego, Calif.*	6,747	3,583	53.1

Source: 1930, special Census tabulation; 1934, _Financial Survey of Urban Housing_. Average value by value groups weighted by number of 1-family dwelling units by value groups (RPI). Note differences between 1934 average values in this table and those in Table A 14 which are unweighted.

* Metropolitan district.

[1] Geographic division and 50-city averages weighted by number of 1-family dwelling units in each city (RPI).

TABLE A II

Dwelling Units, Number and Percentage Distribution by Age Groups, 64 Cities by Geographic Division, January 1, 1934

	All age groups	Under 5 years	5-9	10-14	15-19	20-24	25-29	30-34	35-39	40-49	50-74	75 years and over	Not reporting
64 cities	1,491,223	76,912	263,210	197,128	181,915	168,223	123,627	158,694	68,113	135,769	97,637	16,418	3,577
6 New England cities	88,247	4,343	10,949	6,580	6,865	6,079	4,978	8,880	5,811	12,731	15,191	5,511	329
Portland, Me.	10,475	455	938	729	779	708	573	1,005	655	1,276	2,234	1,082	41
Nashua, N.H.	4,646	375	460	299	196	180	121	286	362	837	945	530	55
Burlington, Vt.	4,252	275	368	205	167	183	200	476	337	675	922	422	22
Worcester, Mass.	23,546	1,112	3,650	2,236	2,209	2,004	1,222	2,047	1,398	3,184	3,514	864	106
Providence, R.I.	33,525	1,493	3,662	1,965	1,956	2,173	2,026	3,907	2,290	5,343	6,471	2,154	85
Waterbury, Conn.	11,803	633	1,871	1,146	1,558	831	836	1,159	769	1,416	1,105	459	20
5 Mid. Atlantic cities	92,961	3,429	13,253	8,385	9,477	8,190	5,953	9,024	5,490	13,831	13,396	2,286	247
Binghamton, N.Y.	12,279	416	1,441	1,207	1,430	1,096	777	1,298	850	2,058	1,471	190	45
Syracuse, N.Y.	35,764	1,574	6,520	3,292	3,003	3,110	2,342	3,396	2,023	5,077	4,557	743	127
Trenton, N.J.	14,841	208	1,661	1,246	1,348	1,394	835	1,677	884	2,252	2,856	454	26
Erie, Pa.	21,618	979	2,672	2,054	3,269	2,148	1,551	1,855	1,167	2,613	2,683	585	42
Williamsport, Pa.	8,459	252	959	586	427	442	448	798	566	1,831	1,829	314	7
8 E. N. Central cities	302,782	10,500	43,523	34,773	37,469	30,723	24,803	33,967	18,254	36,845	29,019	2,571	335
Cleveland, Ohio	136,628	3,477	17,214	15,765	18,460	13,503	11,275	16,466	8,929	17,419	13,122	927	71
Zanesville, Ohio	9,042	284	1,188	670	545	658	871	773	486	1,296	1,756	511	4
Indianapolis, Ind.	79,623	2,865	11,324	9,013	8,886	8,970	6,781	9,484	4,971	10,191	6,738	297	103
Decatur, Ill.	14,662	470	3,181	1,776	1,399	1,619	1,084	1,534	639	1,535	1,279	36	110
Peoria, Ill.	21,828	1,345	2,567	1,646	2,039	1,913	1,582	2,751	1,273	3,174	3,252	267	19
Lansing, Mich.	18,144	845	3,500	3,190	3,196	1,954	1,543	1,223	715	1,148	762	59	9
Kenosha, Wis.	9,508	437	2,182	1,376	1,511	899	784	721	393	662	378	156	9
Racine, Wis.	13,347	777	2,367	1,337	1,433	1,207	883	1,015	848	1,420	1,732	318	10
10 W. N. Central cities	274,037	13,974	42,279	37,008	34,467	31,131	24,324	28,218	14,620	30,793	16,164	514	545
Minneapolis, Minn.	83,604	4,735	14,508	11,994	11,028	9,125	7,163	7,084	4,176	9,001	4,450	151	189
St. Paul, Minn.	51,578	1,851	7,350	6,930	6,772	6,094	4,192	4,270	3,074	7,027	3,854	103	61
Des Moines, Iowa	34,183	1,520	4,403	5,632	5,740	3,654	2,907	3,357	1,632	3,109	2,109	78	42
St. Joseph, Mo.	16,686	418	1,132	935	938	1,908	2,057	3,192	1,359	2,475	2,152	111	9
Springfield, Mo.	14,801	773	2,615	1,656	1,465	1,760	1,392	1,820	904	1,662	688	29	37
Fargo, N.D.	5,209	403	747	700	764	584	514	608	347	414	84		44
Sioux Falls, S.D.	7,561	813	1,107	1,167	1,181	808	570	624	352	708	202		29
Lincoln, Neb.	18,780	804	2,908	2,441	2,173	2,339	1,855	2,799	924	1,902	573		62
Topeka, Kan.	16,390	610	2,208	1,251	1,190	1,657	1,446	2,179	1,088	2,933	1,775	34	19
Wichita, Kan.	25,245	2,047	5,301	4,302	3,216	3,202	2,228	2,285	764	1,562	277	8	53
11 S. Atlantic cities	184,305	7,135	28,990	21,597	19,276	22,205	15,264	24,880	7,590	17,420	14,348	4,889	711
Wilmington, Del.	10,990	508	774	386	907	1,003	676	847	635	2,171	2,376	661	46
Frederick, Md.	2,635	71	248	143	165	195	127	250	139	262	504	501	30
Hagerstown, Md.	5,035	205	457	411	528	634	453	689	305	580	451	241	81
Richmond, Va.	32,191	932	4,140	3,284	2,611	3,605	2,388	3,540	1,821	4,899	4,395	554	22
Wheeling, W.Va.	11,780	255	1,179	1,062	933	965	1,006	1,220	644	1,556	2,191	688	81
Asheville, N.C.	10,833	220	3,511	1,583	1,262	1,107	716	961	366	708	345	15	39
Greensboro, N.C.	11,000	429	2,303	1,816	1,599	1,449	1,110	1,561	307	293	98	21	14
Charleston, S.C.	10,759	236	198	599	860	871	611	1,247	427	1,367	2,130	2,023	190
Columbia, S.C.	10,009	646	1,234	1,322	972	1,240	726	2,091	321	810	449	106	92
Atlanta, Ga.	48,976	2,317	7,961	6,798	5,596	6,118	4,221	8,467	2,165	3,999	1,218	41	75
Jacksonville, Fla.	30,097	1,316	6,985	4,193	3,843	5,018	3,330	4,007	460	775	191	38	41
4 E. S. Central cities	94,183	3,512	22,322	12,608	10,418	11,538	9,035	12,994	3,608	5,385	2,389	181	193
Paducah, Ky.	7,765	412	1,111	574	467	612	760	1,426	537	1,173	492	69	132
Knoxville, Tenn.	22,828	930	3,894	2,976	2,411	2,741	2,647	3,280	1,106	1,853	923	52	15
Birmingham, Ala.	54,027	1,495	14,497	7,822	6,369	7,163	5,001	7,064	1,769	2,104	708	20	15
Jackson, Miss.	9,563	675	2,820	1,236	1,171	1,022	627	1,224	196	255	266	40	31
7 W. S. Central cities	156,949	14,256	38,524	32,363	22,668	17,418	10,285	12,569	2,697	3,980	1,649	139	401
Little Rock, Ark.	17,771	894	3,483	2,735	2,150	1,969	1,206	2,788	678	1,174	608	38	48
Baton Rouge, La.	6,951	373	1,158	1,478	1,240	942	499	856	86	167	98	17	37
Shreveport, La.	19,722	1,134	4,384	5,148	3,048	2,402	1,216	1,725	206	298	124	4	33
Oklahoma City, Okla.	34,755	5,677	9,340	6,858	4,243	3,884	2,619	1,617	209	184			124
Austin, Tex.	12,849	2,277	2,283	1,540	1,391	1,234	881	1,416	449	818	500	48	12
Dallas, Tex.	55,234	3,681	14,606	11,973	8,679	6,126	3,498	3,848	1,033	1,303	318	32	137
Wichita Falls, Tex.	9,667	220	3,270	2,631	1,917	861	366	319	36	36	1		10
9 Mountain cities	78,735	5,367	12,026	10,653	10,217	8,932	7,108	9,904	4,161	6,766	2,906	221	474
Butte, Mont.	7,358	66	116	309	1,264	836	822	1,490	902	1,239	255	15	44
Boise, Idaho	5,167	274	284	450	594	1,043	807	1,018	358	278	34		27
Casper, Wyo.	4,227	48	526	1,759	1,432	237	105	55	40	17			8
Pueblo, Colo.	10,882	482	1,622	1,073	740	952	960	1,910	813	1,530	633		167
Albuquerque, N.M.	6,458	804	1,490	1,114	746	673	552	445	206	246	142	40	40
Santa Fe, N.M.	2,145	466	436	174	146	165	65	100	67	191	211	119	5
Phoenix, Ariz.	10,519	1,209	3,018	1,960	1,469	1,227	455	760	128	184	38		71
Salt Lake City, Utah	27,327	1,170	3,674	3,307	3,407	3,366	2,847	3,512	1,571	2,847	1,497	87	42
Reno, Nev.	4,652	848	860	507	419	433	495	614	76	234	96		70
4 Pacific cities	219,024	14,396	51,344	33,161	31,058	32,007	21,877	18,258	5,882	8,018	2,575	106	342
Seattle, Wash.	81,334	5,840	16,080	11,409	13,244	12,274	9,514	8,282	2,148	2,150	292	22	79
Portland, Ore.	74,818	3,428	15,989	11,531	10,205	11,939	8,641	6,392	2,232	3,356	1,004	19	84
Sacramento, Calif.	19,919	1,465	5,175	2,767	2,143	2,216	1,419	1,454	793	1,392	966	40	89
San Diego, Calif.	42,953	3,665	14,100	7,454	5,466	5,578	2,303	2,130	709	1,120	313	25	90

Source: *Real Property Inventory.* *Percentage not shown if less than one-tenth of one per cent.*

TABLE A II

Dwelling Units, Number and Percentage Distribution by Age Groups, 64 Cities by Geographic Division, January 1, 1934

All age groups	Under 5 years	5-9	10-14	15-19	20-24	25-29	30-34	35-39	40-49	50-74	75 years and over	Not reporting	
100.0	5.2	17.7	13.2	12.2	11.3	8.3	10.6	4.6	9.1	6.5	1.1	0.2	64 cities
100.0	4.9	12.4	7.5	7.8	6.9	5.6	10.1	6.6	14.4	17.2	6.2	0.4	6 New England cities
100.0	4.3	9.0	7.0	7.4	6.8	5.5	9.6	6.2	12.2	21.3	10.3	0.4	Portland, Me.
100.0	8.1	9.9	6.4	4.2	3.9	2.6	6.2	7.8	18.0	20.3	11.4	1.2	Nashua, N.H.
100.0	6.5	8.7	4.8	3.9	4.3	4.7	11.2	7.9	15.9	21.7	9.9	0.5	Burlington, Vt.
100.0	4.7	15.5	9.5	9.4	8.5	5.2	8.7	5.9	13.5	14.9	3.7	0.5	Worcester, Mass.
100.0	4.5	10.9	5.9	5.8	6.5	6.0	11.7	6.8	15.9	19.3	6.4	0.3	Providence, R.I.
100.0	5.4	15.8	9.7	13.2	7.0	7.1	9.8	6.5	12.0	9.4	3.9	0.2	Waterbury, Conn.
100.0	3.7	14.2	9.0	10.2	8.8	6.4	9.7	5.9	14.9	14.4	2.5	0.3	5 Mid. Atlantic cities
100.0	3.4	11.7	9.8	11.7	8.9	6.3	10.6	6.9	16.8	12.0	1.5	0.4	Binghamton, N.Y.
100.0	4.4	18.2	9.2	8.4	8.7	6.5	9.5	5.7	14.2	12.7	2.1	0.4	Syracuse, N.Y.
100.0	1.4	11.2	8.4	9.1	9.4	5.6	11.3	5.9	15.2	19.2	3.1	0.2	Trenton, N.J.
100.0	4.5	12.4	9.5	15.1	9.9	7.2	8.6	5.4	12.1	12.4	2.7	0.2	Erie, Pa.
100.0	3.0	11.3	6.9	5.1	5.2	5.3	9.4	6.7	21.7	21.6	3.7	0.1	Williamsport, Pa.
100.0	3.5	14.4	11.5	12.4	10.1	8.2	11.2	6.0	12.2	9.6	0.8	0.1	8 E. N. Central cities
100.0	2.5	12.6	11.5	13.5	9.9	8.3	12.1	6.5	12.7	9.6	0.7	0.1	Cleveland, Ohio
100.0	3.2	13.1	7.4	6.0	7.3	9.6	8.5	5.4	14.3	19.4	5.7	0.1	Zanesville, Ohio
100.0	3.6	14.2	11.3	11.2	11.3	8.5	11.9	6.2	12.8	8.5	0.4	0.1	Indianapolis, Ind.
100.0	3.2	21.7	12.1	9.5	11.0	7.4	10.5	4.4	10.5	8.7	0.2	0.8	Decatur, Ill.
100.0	6.2	11.8	7.6	9.3	8.8	7.2	12.6	5.8	14.5	14.9	1.2	0.1	Peoria, Ill.
100.0	4.7	19.3	17.6	17.6	10.8	8.5	6.7	3.9	6.3	4.2	0.3	0.1	Lansing, Mich.
100.0	4.6	22.9	14.5	15.9	9.5	8.2	7.6	4.1	7.0	4.0	1.6	0.1	Kenosha, Wis.
100.0	5.8	17.7	10.0	10.7	9.1	6.6	7.6	6.4	10.6	13.0	2.4	0.1	Racine, Wis.
100.0	5.1	15.4	13.5	12.6	11.4	8.9	10.3	5.3	11.2	5.9	0.2	0.2	10 W. N. Central cities
100.0	5.7	17.3	14.3	13.2	10.9	8.6	8.5	5.0	10.8	5.3	0.2	0.2	Minneapolis, Minn.
100.0	3.6	14.3	13.4	13.1	11.8	8.1	8.3	6.0	13.6	7.5	0.2	0.1	St. Paul, Minn.
100.0	4.4	12.9	16.5	16.8	10.7	8.5	9.8	4.8	9.1	6.2	0.2	0.1	Des Moines, Iowa
100.0	2.5	6.8	5.6	5.6	11.4	12.3	19.1	8.2	14.8	12.9	0.7	0.1	St. Joseph, Mo.
100.0	5.2	17.7	11.2	9.9	11.9	9.4	12.3	6.1	11.2	4.6	0.2	0.3	Springfield, Mo.
100.0	7.7	14.3	13.4	14.7	11.2	9.9	11.7	6.7	7.9	1.6		0.9	Fargo, N.D.
100.0	10.7	14.6	15.4	15.6	10.7	7.5	8.3	4.7	9.4	2.7		0.4	Sioux Falls, S.D.
100.0	4.3	15.5	13.0	11.6	12.5	9.9	14.9	4.9	10.1	3.0		0.3	Lincoln, Neb.
100.0	3.7	13.5	7.6	7.3	10.1	8.8	13.3	6.7	17.9	10.8	0.2	0.1	Topeka, Kan.
100.0	8.1	21.0	17.0	12.7	12.7	8.8	9.1	3.0	6.2	1.1	0.1	0.2	Wichita, Kan.
100.0	3.8	15.7	11.7	10.5	12.0	8.3	13.5	4.1	9.5	7.8	2.7	0.4	11 S. Atlantic cities
100.0	4.6	7.0	3.5	8.3	9.1	6.2	7.7	5.8	19.8	21.6	6.0	0.4	Wilmington, Del.
100.0	2.7	9.4	5.4	6.3	7.4	4.8	9.5	5.3	10.0	19.1	19.0	1.1	Frederick, Md.
100.0	4.1	9.1	8.2	10.5	12.6	9.0	13.7	6.0	11.5	8.9	4.8	1.6	Hagerstown, Md.
100.0	2.9	12.9	10.2	8.1	11.2	7.4	11.0	5.7	15.2	13.6	1.7	0.1	Richmond, Va.
100.0	2.2	10.0	9.0	7.9	8.2	8.5	10.4	5.5	13.2	18.6	5.8	0.7	Wheeling, W. Va.
100.0	2.0	32.4	14.6	11.7	10.2	6.6	8.9	3.4	6.5	3.2	0.1	0.4	Asheville, N. C.
100.0	3.9	20.9	16.5	14.5	13.2	10.1	14.2	2.8	2.7	0.9	0.2	0.1	Greensboro, N. C.
100.0	2.2	1.8	5.6	8.0	8.1	5.7	11.6	4.0	12.7	19.8	18.8	1.7	Charleston, S. C.
100.0	6.5	12.3	13.2	9.7	12.4	7.2	20.9	3.2	8.1	4.5	1.1	0.9	Columbia, S. C.
100.0	4.7	16.2	13.9	11.4	12.5	8.6	17.3	4.4	8.2	2.5	0.1	0.2	Atlanta, Ga.
100.0	4.4	23.2	14.0	12.8	16.7	10.7	13.3	1.5	2.6	0.6	0.1	0.1	Jacksonville, Fla.
100.0	3.7	23.7	13.4	11.1	12.3	9.6	13.8	3.8	5.7	2.5	0.2	0.2	4 E. S. Central cities
100.0	5.3	14.3	7.4	6.0	7.9	9.8	18.4	6.9	15.1	6.3	0.9	1.7	Paducah, Ky.
100.0	4.1	17.1	13.0	10.6	12.0	11.6	14.4	4.8	8.1	4.0	0.2	0.1	Knoxville, Tenn.
100.0	2.8	28.8	14.5	11.8	13.3	9.2	13.1	3.3	3.9	1.3			Birmingham, Ala.
100.0	7.1	29.5	12.9	12.2	10.7	6.6	12.8	2.0	2.7	2.8	0.4	0.3	Jackson, Miss.
100.0	9.1	24.5	20.6	14.4	11.1	6.6	8.0	1.7	2.5	1.1	0.1	0.3	7 W. S. Central cities
100.0	5.0	19.6	15.4	12.1	11.1	6.8	15.7	3.8	6.6	3.4	0.2	0.3	Little Rock, Ark.
100.0	5.4	16.7	21.3	17.8	13.6	7.2	12.3	1.2	2.4	1.4	0.2	0.5	Baton Rouge, La.
100.0	5.7	22.2	26.1	15.5	12.2	6.2	8.7	1.0	1.5	0.6	0.1	0.2	Shreveport, La.
100.0	16.3	26.9	19.7	12.2	11.2	7.5	4.7	0.6	0.5			0.4	Oklahoma City, Okla.
100.0	17.7	17.8	12.0	10.8	9.6	6.8	11.0	3.5	6.4	3.9	0.4	0.1	Austin, Tex.
100.0	6.7	26.4	21.7	15.7	11.1	6.3	7.0	1.9	2.3	0.6	0.1	0.2	Dallas, Tex.
100.0	2.3	33.8	27.2	19.8	8.9	3.8	3.3	0.4	0.4			0.1	Wichita Falls, Tex.
100.0	6.8	15.3	13.5	13.0	11.3	9.0	12.6	5.3	8.6	3.7	0.3	0.6	9 Mountain cities
100.0	0.9	1.6	4.2	17.2	11.4	11.2	20.2	12.2	16.8	3.5	0.2	0.6	Butte, Mont.
100.0	5.3	5.5	8.7	11.5	20.2	15.6	19.7	6.9	5.4	0.7		0.5	Boise, Idaho
100.0	1.1	12.5	41.6	33.9	5.6	2.5	1.3	0.9	0.4			0.2	Casper, Wyo.
100.0	4.4	14.9	9.9	6.8	8.7	8.8	17.6	7.5	14.1	5.8		1.5	Pueblo, Colo.
100.0	12.5	23.1	17.2	11.6	10.4	8.5	6.9	3.2	3.8	2.2		0.6	Albuquerque, N.M.
100.0	21.7	20.3	8.1	6.8	7.7	3.0	4.7	3.1	8.9	9.9	5.6	0.2	Santa Fe, N.M.
100.0	11.5	28.7	18.6	14.0	11.7	4.3	7.2	1.2	1.7	0.4		0.7	Phoenix, Ariz.
100.0	4.3	13.4	12.1	12.5	12.3	10.4	12.9	5.7	10.4	5.5	0.3	0.2	Salt Lake City, Utah
100.0	18.2	18.5	10.9	9.0	9.3	10.7	13.2	1.6	5.0	2.1		1.5	Reno, Nev.
100.0	6.6	23.4	15.1	14.2	14.6	10.0	8.3	2.7	3.7	1.2		0.2	4 Pacific cities
100.0	7.2	19.8	14.0	16.3	15.1	11.7	10.2	2.6	2.6	0.4		0.1	Seattle, Wash.
100.0	4.6	21.4	15.4	13.7	16.0	11.5	8.5	3.0	4.5	1.3		0.1	Portland, Ore.
100.0	7.4	26.0	13.9	10.8	11.1	7.1	7.3	4.0	7.0	4.8	0.2	0.4	Sacramento, Calif.
100.0	8.5	32.8	17.4	12.7	13.0	5.4	5.0	1.6	2.6	0.7	0.1	0.2	San Diego, Calif.

291375

TABLE A 12

Owner-occupied Dwellings, Number reporting Value and Percentage Distribution by Value Groups, 61 Cities by Geographic Division, January 1, 1934

	NUMBER										
All value groups	$1-499	$500-999	$1,000-1,499	$1,500-1,999	$2,000-2,999	$3,000-3,999	$4,000-4,999	$5,000-7,499	$7,500-9,999	$10,000-14,999	$15,000 and over
61 cities[1] 133,251	1,246	4,903	7,475	9,994	23,571	24,189	18,255	25,971	8,762	5,493	3,392
6 New England cities 7,469	12	23	76	118	524	959	1,079	2,417	1,121	793	347
Portland, Me. 1,448	5	9	23	38	99	201	208	449	213	150	53
Nashua, N.H. 377			4	12	44	82	59	113	37	19	7
Burlington, Vt. 336		1	4	5	24	53	54	90	48	40	17
Worcester, Mass. 1,423	1		7	5	53	124	216	513	249	182	73
Providence, R.I.* 3,290	5	13	34	58	277	462	465	1,070	458	311	137
Waterbury, Conn. 595	1		4		27	37	77	182	116	91	60
5 Mid. Atlantic cities 8,196	4	34	165	371	1,286	1,660	1,399	2,106	650	359	162
Binghamton, N.Y. 590		1		1	37	81	85	218	97	47	23
Syracuse, N.Y. 1,314		3	10	10	68	176	184	509	213	110	31
Trenton, N.J. 2,364		11	85	194	553	479	387	483	96	50	26
Erie, Pa. 3,125	2	8	28	109	461	766	628	727	210	124	62
Williamsport, Pa. 803	2	11	42	57	167	158	115	169	34	28	20
7 E. N. Central cities 33,257	45	262	602	1,139	3,678	5,297	5,432	9,664	3,634	2,095	1,409
Cleveland, Ohio* 22,036	17	114	295	522	1,910	3,066	3,475	6,956	2,815	1,686	1,180
Indianapolis, Ind. 2,780	6	57	95	189	458	513	418	569	240	144	91
Decatur, Ill. 851	8	23	66	117	300	195	74	53	11	4	
Peoria, Ill. 2,740	6	38	92	180	486	556	437	584	187	109	65
Lansing, Mich. 1,149	8	20	29	68	227	315	215	197	54	11	5
Kenosha, Wis. 1,145		1	4	17	81	232	256	398	88	47	21
Racine, Wis. 2,556		9	21	46	216	420	557	907	239	94	47
10 W. N. Central cities 24,577	293	1,068	1,718	2,286	4,941	5,066	3,585	3,846	920	540	314
Minneapolis, Minn. 7,519	9	79	216	416	1,281	1,784	1,455	1,534	412	209	124
St. Paul, Minn. 1,899	3	22	61	127	386	503	359	350	44	30	14
Des Moines, Iowa 3,422	109	257	302	353	746	670	360	463	83	45	34
St. Joseph, Mo. 1,262	15	83	128	144	296	240	128	127	46	24	15
Springfield, Mo. 1,594	43	154	251	253	357	195	124	243	50	38	14
Fargo, N.D. 845		1	10	15	75	206	193	243	50	38	21
Sioux Falls, S.D. 1,224	13	32	46	91	220	250	197	231	72	51	21
Lincoln, Neb. 1,715	17	78	109	188	413	331	215	233	63	35	33
Topeka, Kan. 2,518	27	146	251	293	517	479	347	342	63	38	15
Wichita, Kan. 2,579	57	216	344	406	650	408	207	183	49	32	27
10 S. Atlantic cities 13,456	133	698	888	1,163	2,288	2,187	1,588	2,543	887	639	442
Frederick, Md. 515	1	7	25	47	110	131	65	72	22	20	15
Hagerstown, Md. 740	5	10	34	61	124	120	99	159	55	41	32
Richmond, Va. 2,238	24	109	146	168	253	247	240	591	233	152	75
Wheeling, W.Va.* 2,351	30	132	170	214	424	440	323	387	110	74	47
Asheville, N.C. 898	12	78	92	86	171	142	103	112	37	34	28
Greensboro, N.C. 569	1	29	39	43	69	73	67	128	58	34	28
Charleston, S.C. 647	9	53	37	48	78	90	71	148	45	41	27
Columbia, S.C. 598	9	37	39	37	76	79	71	133	53	47	17
Atlanta, Ga.* 4,274	31	200	251	392	863	770	489	705	240	182	151
Jacksonville, Fla. 626	11	43	55	67	120	95	60	108	34	18	15
4 E. S. Central cities 6,020	158	644	684	671	1,249	934	595	690	188	134	73
Paducah, Ky. 782	62	158	124	95	141	81	40	51	18	5	7
Knoxville, Tenn. 802	17	89	100	103	170	127	80	79	21	12	4
Birmingham, Ala.* 3,989	74	374	439	448	863	653	390	476	126	96	50
Jackson, Miss. 447	5	23	21	25	75	73	85	84	23	21	12
7 W. S. Central cities 10,992	236	683	867	1,035	2,370	2,093	1,130	1,508	496	344	230
Little Rock, Ark. 1,995	56	195	203	184	441	361	156	239	90	42	28
Baton Rouge, La. 381	12	38	31	37	62	63	35	52	19	26	6
Shreveport, La. 476	4	45	56	44	85	70	38	77	23	20	14
Oklahoma City, Okla. 2,944	47	128	178	273	626	561	330	448	159	115	79
Austin, Tex. 1,082	25	81	120	102	199	167	105	154	50	52	27
Dallas, Tex. 3,220	17	73	167	273	780	759	415	473	138	75	50
Wichita Falls, Tex. 894	75	123	112	122	177	112	51	65	17	14	26
8 Mountain cities 10,436	232	829	1,078	1,216	2,343	1,847	1,115	1,112	308	213	143
Butte, Mont. 1,989	59	233	341	300	391	255	157	163	36	33	21
Boise, Idaho 1,318	12	80	93	138	328	273	164	149	36	26	19
Casper, Wyo. 708	65	89	73	72	144	98	62	58	25	13	9
Pueblo, Colo. 1,039	70	216	183	145	240	105	31	37	6	4	2
Albuquerque, N.M. 291	2	10	10	26	71	63	46	43	8	6	6
Phoenix, Ariz. 998	2	30	65	84	210	205	138	155	51	32	26
Salt Lake City, Utah 3,587	19	164	297	430	901	764	425	384	107	63	33
Reno, Nev. 506	3	7	16	21	58	84	92	123	39	36	27
4 Pacific cities 18,848	133	662	1,397	1,995	4,892	4,146	2,332	2,085	558	376	272
Seattle, Wash.* 6,705	73	328	618	795	1,860	1,367	700	618	155	100	91
Portland, Ore. 5,065	32	189	453	640	1,414	1,073	596	440	116	65	47
Sacramento, Calif. 2,343	5	35	72	144	457	567	436	410	104	80	33
San Diego, Calif.* 4,735	23	110	254	416	1,161	1,139	600	617	183	131	101

Source: *Financial Survey of Urban Housing*   *Percentage not shown if less than one-tenth of one per cent.*

* Metropolitan district.

[1] Geographic division and 61-city percentage distributions weighted by number of owner-occupied dwelling units in each city (RPI).

Owner-occupied Dwellings, Number reporting Value and Percentage Distribution by Value Groups, 61 Cities by Geographic Division, January 1, 1934

<────────────────── P E R C E N T A G E   D I S T R I B U T I O N ──────────────────>

All value groups	$1-499	$500-999	$1,000-1,499	$1,500-1,999	$2,000-2,999	$3,000-3,999	$4,000-4,999	$5,000-7,499	$7,500-9,999	$10,000-14,999	$15,000 and over	
100.0	0.8	3.3	5.2	7.1	17.3	18.1	13.8	20.3	7.0	4.5	2.6	61 cities[1]
100.0	0.2	0.3	0.9	1.5	7.3	12.8	14.3	32.6	14.9	10.5	4.7	6 New England cities
100.0	0.3	0.6	1.6	2.6	6.8	13.9	14.4	31.0	14.7	10.4	3.7	Portland, Me.
100.0			1.0	3.2	11.7	21.8	15.6	30.0	9.8	5.0	1.9	Nashua, N.H.
100.0		0.3	1.2	1.5	7.1	15.8	16.1	26.8	14.3	11.9	5.0	Burlington, Vt.
100.0	0.1		0.5	0.3	3.7	8.7	15.2	36.1	17.5	12.8	5.1	Worcester, Mass.
100.0	0.2	0.4	1.0	1.8	8.4	14.0	14.1	32.5	13.9	9.5	4.2	Providence, R.I.*
100.0	0.2		0.7		4.5	6.2	12.9	30.6	19.5	15.3	10.1	Waterbury, Conn.
100.0	0.1	0.3	1.7	3.4	12.6	17.8	15.9	29.8	10.6	5.6	2.2	5 Mid. Atlantic cities
100.0		0.2		0.2	6.3	13.7	14.4	36.9	16.4	8.0	3.9	Binghamton, N.Y.
100.0		0.2	0.8	0.8	5.2	13.4	14.0	38.7	16.2	8.4	2.3	Syracuse, N.Y.
100.0		0.4	3.6	8.2	23.4	20.3	16.4	20.4	4.1	2.1	1.1	Trenton, N.J.
100.0	0.1	0.2	0.9	3.5	14.7	24.5	20.1	23.3	6.7	4.0	2.0	Erie, Pa.
100.0	0.3	1.4	5.2	7.1	20.8	19.7	14.3	21.0	4.2	3.5	2.5	Williamsport, Pa.
100.0	0.1	0.9	2.0	3.9	12.1	16.4	16.0	27.6	10.6	6.2	4.2	7 E. N. Central cities
100.0		0.5	1.3	2.3	8.7	13.9	15.8	31.6	12.8	7.7	5.4	Cleveland, Ohio*
100.0	0.2	2.0	3.4	6.8	16.5	18.5	15.0	20.5	8.6	5.2	3.3	Indianapolis, Ind.
100.0	0.9	2.7	7.8	13.7	35.3	22.9	8.7	6.2	1.3	0.5		Decatur, Ill.
100.0	0.2	1.4	3.4	6.6	17.7	20.3	15.9	21.3	6.8	4.0	2.4	Peoria, Ill.
100.0	0.7	1.8	2.5	5.9	19.8	27.4	18.7	17.1	4.7	1.0	.4	Lansing, Mich.
100.0			0.3	1.5	7.1	20.3	22.4	34.8	7.7	4.1	1.8	Kenosha, Wis.
100.0		0.3	0.8	1.8	8.5	16.4	21.8	35.5	9.4	3.7	1.8	Racine, Wis.
100.0	1.0	3.6	6.1	8.6	20.0	21.8	15.6	16.3	3.7	2.1	1.2	10 W. N. Central cities
100.0	0.1	1.1	2.9	5.5	17.0	23.7	19.4	20.4	5.5	2.8	1.6	Minneapolis, Minn.
100.0	0.2	1.2	3.2	6.7	20.3	26.5	18.9	18.4	2.3	1.6	0.7	St. Paul, Minn.
100.0	3.2	7.5	8.8	10.3	21.8	19.6	10.5	13.6	2.4	1.3	1.0	Des Moines, Iowa
100.0	1.2	6.6	10.2	11.4	23.5	19.0	10.1	10.1	3.6	3.0	1.3	St. Joseph, Mo.
100.0	2.7	9.7	15.7	15.9	22.4	12.2	7.8	8.8	2.4	1.5	0.9	Springfield, Mo.
100.0		0.1	1.2	1.8	8.9	24.4	22.8	28.7	5.9	4.5	1.7	Fargo, N.D.
100.0	1.0	2.6	3.8	7.4	18.0	20.4	16.1	18.9	5.9	4.2	1.7	Sioux Falls, S D.
100.0	1.0	4.5	6.4	11.0	24.1	19.3	12.5	13.6	3.7	2.0	1.9	Lincoln, Neb.
100.0	1.1	5.8	10.0	11.6	20.5	19.0	13.8	13.6	2.5	1.5	0.6	Topeka, Kan.
100.0	2.2	8.4	13.3	15.8	25.2	15.8	8.0	7.1	1.9	1.3	1.0	Wichita, Kan.
100.0	1.1	5.3	6.8	8.8	17.1	16.2	11.7	18.8	6.5	4.6	3.1	10 S. Atlantic cities
100.0	0.2	1.3	4.9	9.1	21.4	25.4	12.6	14.0	4.3	3.9	2.9	Frederick, Md.
100.0	0.7	1.4	4.6	8.2	16.8	16.2	13.4	21.5	7.4	5.5	4.3	Hagerstown, Md.
100.0	1.1	4.9	6.5	7.5	11.3	11.0	10.7	26.4	10.4	6.8	3.4	Richmond, Va.
100.0	1.3	5.6	7.2	9.1	18.0	18.7	13.7	16.5	4.7	3.2	2.0	Wheeling, W.Va.*
100.0	1.3	8.7	10.3	9.6	19.0	15.8	11.5	12.5	4.1	3.3	3.9	Asheville, N.C.
100.0	0.2	5.1	6.8	7.6	12.1	12.8	11.8	22.5	10.2	6.0	4.9	Greensboro, N.C.
100.0	1.4	8.2	5.7	7.4	12.0	13.9	11.0	22.9	7.0	6.3	4.2	Charleston, S.C.
100.0	1.5	6.2	6.5	6.2	12.7	13.2	11.9	22.2	8.9	7.9	2.8	Columbia, S.C.
100.0	0.7	4.7	5.9	9.2	20.2	18.0	11.4	16.5	5.6	4.3	3.5	Atlanta, Ga.*
100.0	1.7	6.8	8.8	10.7	19.2	15.2	9.6	17.3	5.4	2.9	2.4	Jacksonville, Fla.
100.0	2.2	10.2	11.1	11.1	20.9	15.8	10.3	11.7	3.2	2.3	1.2	4 E. S. Central cities
100.0	7.9	20.2	15.9	12.2	18.0	10.4	5.1	6.5	2.3	0.6	0.9	Paducah, Ky.
100.0	2.1	11.1	12.5	12.8	21.2	15.8	10.0	9.9	2.6	1.5	0.5	Knoxville, Tenn.
100.0	1.8	9.4	11.0	11.2	21.6	16.4	9.8	11.9	3.2	2.4	1.3	Birmingham, Ala.*
100.0	1.1	5.2	4.7	5.6	16.8	16.3	19.0	18.8	5.1	4.7	2.7	Jackson, Miss.
100.0	1.7	5.7	7.7	9.3	21.5	19.3	10.6	14.2	4.6	3.3	2.1	7 W. S. Central cities
100.0	2.8	9.8	10.2	9.2	22.1	18.1	7.8	12.0	4.5	2.1	1.4	Little Rock, Ark.
100.0	3.2	10.0	8.1	9.7	16.3	16.5	9.2	13.6	5.0	6.8	1.6	Baton Rouge, La.
100.0	0.8	9.5	11.8	9.2	17.9	14.7	8.0	16.2	4.8	4.2	2.9	Shreveport, La.
100.0	1.6	4.3	6.0	9.3	21.3	19.1	11.2	15.2	5.4	3.9	2.7	Oklahoma City, Okla.
100.0	2.3	7.5	11.1	9.4	18.4	15.4	9.7	14.3	4.6	4.8	2.5	Austin, Tex.
100.0	0.5	2.2	5.2	8.5	24.2	23.6	12.9	14.7	4.3	2.3	1.6	Dallas, Tex.
100.0	8.4	13.8	12.5	13.6	19.8	12.5	5.7	7.3	1.9	1.6	2.9	Wichita Falls, Tex.
100.0	2.1	7.7	9.6	11.3	22.8	18.1	10.9	11.0	3.0	2.1	1.4	8 Mountain cities
100.0	2.9	11.7	17.1	15.1	19.7	12.8	7.9	8.2	1.8	1.7	1.1	Butte, Mont.
100.0	0.9	6.1	7.1	10.5	24.9	20.7	12.4	11.3	2.7	2.0	1.4	Boise, Idaho
100.0	9.2	12.6	10.3	10.2	20.3	13.8	8.8	8.2	3.5	1.8	1.3	Casper, Wyo.
100.0	6.7	20.8	17.6	13.9	23.1	10.1	3.0	3.6	0.6	0.4	0.2	Pueblo, Colo.
100.0	0.7	3.4	3.4	8.9	24.4	21.7	15.8	14.8	2.7	2.1	2.1	Albuquerque, N.M.
100.0	0.2	3.0	6.5	8.4	21.1	20.6	13.8	15.5	5.1	3.2	2.6	Phoenix, Ariz.
100.0	0.5	4.6	8.3	12.0	25.1	21.3	11.8	10.7	3.0	1.8	0.9	Salt Lake City, Utah
100.0	0.6	1.4	3.1	4.2	11.5	16.6	18.2	24.3	7.7	7.1	5.3	Reno, Nev.
100.0	0.8	3.8	8.0	11.1	26.5	21.6	11.9	10.4	2.7	1.8	1.4	4 Pacific cities
100.0	1.1	4.9	9.2	11.9	27.7	20.4	10.4	9.2	2.3	1.5	1.4	Seattle, Wash.*
100.0	0.6	3.7	9.0	12.6	27.9	21.2	11.8	8.7	2.3	1.3	0.9	Portland, Ore.
100.0	0.2	1.5	3.1	6.2	19.5	24.2	18.6	17.5	4.4	3.4	1.4	Sacramento, Calif.
100.0	0.5	2.3	5.3	8.8	24.5	24.1	12.7	13.0	3.9	2.8	2.1	San Diego, Calif.*

TABLE A 13

Rented Dwellings, Number reporting Value and Percentage Distribution by Value Groups, 58 Cities by Geographic Division, January 1, 1934

	All value groups	$1–499	$500–999	$1,000–1,499	$1,500–1,999	$2,000–2,999	$3,000–3,999	$4,000–4,999	$5,000–7,499	$7,500–9,999	$10,000–14,999	$15,000 and over
58 cities [1]	36,688	1,011	2,666	3,213	3,648	6,949	5,769	3,823	5,248	1,957	1,330	1,074
4 New England cities	1,667		19	44	61	180	227	214	485	246	124	67
Portland, Me.	470		10	20	21	56	51	62	121	75	36	18
Burlington, Vt.	91		1	3	7	16	12	8	20	11	11	2
Worcester, Mass.	300			4	2	10	36	40	102	58	28	20
Providence, R.I.*	806		8	17	31	98	128	104	242	102	49	27
5 Mid. Atlantic cities	2,088	9	45	87	146	372	340	284	472	174	105	54
Binghamton, N.Y.	179		1	2	3	13	20	23	61	25	22	9
Syracuse, N.Y.	334			2	1	13	31	45	132	60	35	15
Trenton, N.J.	623	2	24	48	71	181	97	63	95	25	8	8
Erie, Pa.	778	2	5	13	43	128	170	142	162	57	37	19
Williamsport, Pa.	174	5	15	22	28	37	22	11	22	7	2	3
7 E. N. Central cities	8,032	27	206	349	458	1,135	1,211	1,144	1,869	746	496	391
Cleveland, Ohio*	4,481	8	58	125	134	430	549	657	1,281	557	375	307
Indianapolis, Ind.	1,000	5	42	62	110	226	168	117	160	51	37	22
Decatur, Ill.	267	5	26	40	45	74	40	15	21		1	20
Peoria, Ill.	922	4	55	80	102	190	168	125	123	29	26	20
Lansing, Mich.	455	2	18	23	56	112	136	51	42	9	4	2
Kenosha, Wis.	284	2		4	4	20	55	58	82	26	19	14
Racine, Wis.	623	1	7	15	7	83	95	121	160	74	34	26
10 W. N. Central cities	8,187	182	685	946	1,028	1,727	1,456	808	827	221	147	160
Minneapolis, Minn.	2,158	15	64	143	179	445	465	287	314	93	67	86
St. Paul, Minn.	548		15	26	47	115	129	88	85	22	13	8
Des Moines, Iowa	1,168	52	119	128	179	266	207	84	81	21	14	17
St. Joseph, Mo.	457	10	53	95	46	96	74	35	32	5	2	3
Springfield, Mo.	732	35	133	152	134	139	58	24	41	7	7	2
Fargo, N.D.	173	1		4	6	19	38	35	49	12	7	2
Sioux Falls, S.D.	461	4	14	33	41	80	91	82	75	19	10	12
Lincoln, Neb.	551	10	50	52	84	133	106	49	38	13	6	10
Topeka, Kan.	993	23	110	142	159	223	162	77	68	13	9	7
Wichita, Kan.	946	32	127	171	153	211	126	47	44	16	11	8
9 S. Atlantic cities	3,894	153	382	366	362	741	585	371	495	189	155	95
Hagerstown, Md.	270	7	19	33	24	61	38	32	28	14	10	4
Richmond, Va.	392	6	32	31	35	55	65	51	69	19	15	14
Wheeling, W. Va.*	549	6	28	40	34	109	111	54	89	26	36	16
Asheville, N.C.	316	15	22	28	31	71	49	38	38	15	8	1
Greensboro, N.C.	259	15	36	27	19	33	37	21	34	19	11	7
Charleston, S.C.	318	11	48	43	33	55	32	22	43	15	13	3
Columbia, S.C.	258	26	31	22	15	32	37	26	37	20	8	4
Atlanta, Ga.*	1,335	52	151	132	159	289	189	104	137	45	41	36
Jacksonville, Fla.	197	15	15	10	12	36	27	23	20	16	13	10
4 E. S. Central cities	1,752	198	348	204	189	278	200	119	115	48	31	22
Paducah, Ky.	354	85	109	42	41	26	20	8	14	3	3	3
Knoxville, Tenn.	246	17	76	48	32	36	16	9	5	5	1	1
Birmingham, Ala.*	963	67	144	106	102	193	134	82	69	32	21	13
Jackson, Miss.	189	29	19	8	14	23	30	20	27	8	6	5
7 W. S. Central cities	3,828	294	458	418	472	741	518	262	353	122	95	95
Little Rock, Ark.	770	137	123	127	94	129	67	24	38	9	12	10
Baton Rouge, La.	140		12	4	14	32	20	13	26	8	5	6
Shreveport, La.	205	23	32	10	24	33	26	19	21	6	6	5
Oklahoma City, Okla.	932	40	84	84	118	172	122	69	118	35	39	51
Austin, Tex.	360	16	84	44	31	51	46	22	31	20	8	7
Dallas, Tex.	1,035	61	57	78	122	247	189	95	106	41	25	14
Wichita Falls, Tex.	386	17	66	71	69	77	48	20	13	3		2
8 Mountain cities	2,302	101	218	305	271	483	343	206	216	64	36	59
Butte, Mont.	390	33	56	64	55	68	33	19	34	7	7	14
Boise, Idaho	100	6	5	18	14	26	16	7	3	2	1	2
Casper, Wyo.	198	11	26	29	12	36	32	19	16	8	4	5
Pueblo, Colo.	244	28	59	41	32	47	13	8	8	4	2	
Albuquerque, N.M.	102	1	2	4	16	21	23	10	15	6	2	2
Phoenix, Ariz.	381	5	14	29	38	87	75	44	57	17	9	6
Salt Lake City, Utah	716	9	45	110	89	156	124	76	58	15	9	25
Reno, Nev.	171	8	11	10	15	42	27	23	25	5		5
4 Pacific cities	4,938	47	305	494	661	1,292	889	415	416	147	141	131
Seattle, Wash.*	1,403	8	83	172	216	381	235	98	96	29	30	55
Portland, Ore.	1,316	18	106	163	177	330	249	103	91	31	24	24
Sacramento, Calif.	527	2	15	31	51	140	98	65	68	28	22	7
San Diego, Calif.*	1,692	19	101	128	217	441	307	149	161	59	65	45

Source: *Financial Survey of Urban Housing*

* Metropolitan district.

[1] *Geographic division and 58-city percentage distributions weighted by number of rented dwelling units in each city (RPI).*

TABLE A 13

Rented Dwellings, Number reporting Value and Percentage Distribution by Value Groups, 58 Cities by Geographic Division, January 1, 1934

←————————————————————— P E R C E N T A G E   D I S T R I B U T I O N ————————————————————→

All value groups	$1 - 499	$500- 999	$1,000- 1,499	$1,500- 1,999	$2,000- 2,999	$3,000- 3,999	$4,000- 4,999	$5,000- 7,499	$7,500- 9,999	$10,000- 14,999	$15,000 and over	
100.0	2.4	6.4	7.5	8.9	17.9	15.5	10.8	16.5	6.5	4.3	3.3	58 cities[1]
100.0		0.9	2.1	3.3	10.4	14.6	12.9	30.3	14.4	7.1	4.0	4 New England cities
100.0		2.1	4.2	4.5	11.9	10.9	13.2	25.7	16.0	7.7	3.8	Portland, Me.
100.0		1.1	3.3	7.7	17.5	13.2	8.8	22.0	12.1	12.1	2.2	Burlington, Vt.
100.0			1.3	0.7	3.3	12.0	13.3	34.0	19.4	9.3	6.7	Worcester, Mass.
100.0		1.0	2.1	3.8	12.2	15.9	12.9	30.0	12.7	6.1	3.3	Providence, R.I.*
100.0	0.3	1.6	3.1	4.8	12.7	13.4	13.1	28.6	11.7	7.3	3.4	5 Mid. Atlantic cities
100.0		0.5	1.1	1.7	7.3	11.2	12.8	34.1	14.0	12.3	5.0	Binghamton, N.Y.
100.0			0.6	0.3	3.9	9.3	13.5	39.5	17.9	10.5	4.5	Syracuse, N.Y.
100.0	0.3	3.9	7.7	11.4	29.1	15.6	10.1	15.2	4.0	1.4	1.3	Trenton, N.J.
100.0	0.3	0.6	1.7	5.5	16.5	21.8	18.3	20.8	7.3	4.8	2.4	Erie, Pa.
100.0	2.9	8.6	12.7	16.1	21.3	12.7	6.3	12.6	4.0	1.1	1.7	Williamsport, Pa.
100.0	0.3	2.5	4.2	5.8	14.2	14.4	13.8	23.7	9.5	6.5	5.1	7 E. N. Central cities
100.0	0.2	1.3	2.8	3.0	9.6	12.2	14.6	28.6	12.4	8.4	6.9	Cleveland, Ohio*
100.0	0.5	4.2	6.2	11.0	22.6	16.8	11.7	16.0	5.1	3.7	2.2	Indianapolis, Ind.
100.0	1.9	9.7	15.0	16.8	27.7	15.0	5.6	7.9		0.4		Decatur, Ill.
100.0	0.4	6.0	8.7	11.1	20.6	18.2	13.6	13.3	3.1	2.8	2.2	Peoria, Ill.
100.0	0.4	4.0	5.1	12.3	24.6	29.9	11.2	9.2	2.0	0.9	0.4	Lansing, Mich.
100.0	0.7		1.4	1.4	7.0	19.4	20.4	28.9	9.2	6.7	4.9	Kenosha, Wis.
100.0	0.2	1.1	2.4	1.1	13.3	15.2	19.4	25.7	11.9	5.5	4.2	Racine, Wis.
100.0	1.6	6.5	9.6	11.1	21.0	19.4	11.4	11.7	3.2	2.2	2.3	10 W. N. Central cities
100.0	0.7	3.0	6.6	8.3	20.6	21.5	13.3	14.6	4.3	3.1	4.0	Minneapolis, Minn.
100.0		2.7	4.7	8.6	21.0	23.5	16.1	15.5	4.0	2.4	1.5	St. Paul, Minn.
100.0	4.4	10.2	11.0	15.3	22.8	17.7	7.2	6.9	1.8	1.2	1.5	Des Moines, Iowa
100.0	2.2	11.6	20.7	10.0	21.0	16.2	7.7	7.0	1.1	1.8	0.7	St. Joseph, Mo.
100.0	4.8	18.1	20.7	18.3	19.0	7.9	3.3	5.6	1.0	0.3	1.0	Springfield, Mo.
100.0	0.6		2.3	3.5	11.0	22.0	20.2	28.3	6.9	4.0	1.2	Fargo, N.D.
100.0	0.8	3.0	7.2	8.9	17.4	19.7	17.8	16.3	4.1	2.2	2.6	Sioux Falls, S.D.
100.0	1.8	9.1	9.4	15.3	24.1	19.2	8.9	6.9	2.4	1.1	1.8	Lincoln, Neb.
100.0	2.3	11.1	14.3	16.0	22.5	16.3	7.8	6.8	1.3	0.9	0.7	Topeka, Kan.
100.0	3.4	13.4	18.1	16.2	22.3	13.3	4.9	4.7	1.7	1.2	0.8	Wichita, Kan.
100.0	4.0	9.6	8.8	9.2	18.7	15.0	9.8	12.8	5.0	4.2	2.9	9 S. Atlantic cities
100.0	2.6	7.0	12.2	8.9	22.6	14.1	11.8	10.4	5.2	3.7	1.5	Hagerstown, Md.
100.0	1.5	8.2	7.9	8.9	14.0	16.6	13.0	17.6	4.9	3.8	3.6	Richmond, Va.
100.0	1.1	5.1	7.3	6.2	19.9	20.2	9.8	16.2	4.7	6.6	2.9	Wheeling, W.Va.*
100.0	4.8	7.0	8.9	9.8	22.5	15.5	12.0	12.0	4.7	2.5	0.3	Asheville, N.C.
100.0	5.8	13.9	10.4	7.4	12.8	14.3	8.1	13.1	7.3	4.2	2.7	Greensboro, N.C.
100.0	3.5	15.1	13.5	10.4	17.3	10.1	6.9	13.5	4.7	4.1	0.9	Charleston, S.C.
100.0	10.1	12.0	8.5	5.8	12.4	14.3	10.1	14.3	7.8	3.1	1.6	Columbia, S.C.
100.0	3.9	11.3	9.9	11.9	21.6	14.1	7.8	10.3	3.4	3.1	2.7	Atlanta, Ga.*
100.0	7.6	7.6	5.1	6.1	18.2	13.7	11.7	10.2	8.1	6.6	5.1	Jacksonville, Fla.
100.0	8.6	18.1	11.9	10.8	17.9	12.4	7.5	6.7	3.0	1.9	1.2	4 E. S. Central cities
100.0	24.0	30.8	11.9	11.6	7.4	5.6	2.3	4.0	0.8	0.8	0.8	Paducah, Ky.
100.0	6.9	30.9	19.5	13.0	14.7	6.5	3.7	2.0	2.0	0.4	0.4	Knoxville, Tenn.
100.0	7.0	15.0	11.0	10.6	20.0	13.9	8.5	7.2	3.3	2.2	1.3	Birmingham, Ala.*
100.0	15.3	10.1	4.2	7.4	12.2	15.9	10.6	14.3	4.2	3.2	2.6	Jackson, Miss.
100.0	7.0	10.6	9.2	12.1	20.0	14.6	7.7	10.1	3.5	2.7	2.5	7 W. S. Central cities
100.0	17.8	16.0	16.5	12.2	16.7	8.7	3.1	4.9	1.2	1.6	1.3	Little Rock, Ark.
100.0		8.6	2.8	10.0	22.8	14.3	9.3	18.6	5.7	3.6	4.3	Baton Rouge, La.
100.0	11.2	15.6	4.9	11.7	16.1	12.7	9.3	10.3	2.9	2.9	2.4	Shreveport, La.
100.0	4.3	9.0	9.0	12.6	18.4	13.1	7.4	12.7	3.8	4.2	5.5	Oklahoma City, Okla.
100.0	4.5	23.3	12.2	8.6	14.2	12.8	6.1	8.6	5.6	2.2	1.9	Austin, Tex.
100.0	5.9	5.5	7.5	11.8	23.8	18.3	9.2	10.2	4.0	2.4	1.4	Dallas, Tex.
100.0	4.4	17.1	18.4	17.9	19.9	12.4	5.2	3.4	0.8		0.5	Wichita Falls, Tex.
100.0	3.9	8.8	13.0	12.0	21.3	15.5	9.1	9.4	2.9	1.6	2.5	8 Mountain cities
100.0	8.4	14.4	16.4	14.1	17.4	8.5	4.9	8.7	1.8	1.8	3.6	Butte, Mont.
100.0	6.0	5.0	18.0	14.0	26.0	16.0	7.0	3.0	2.0	1.0	2.0	Boise, Idaho
100.0	5.6	13.1	14.6	6.1	18.2	16.2	9.6	8.1	4.0	2.0	2.5	Casper, Wyo.
100.0	11.5	24.2	16.8	13.1	19.3	5.3	3.3	3.3	1.6	1.6		Pueblo, Colo.
100.0	1.0	2.0	3.9	15.7	20.6	22.5	9.8	14.7	5.8	2.0	2.0	Albuquerque, N.M.
100.0	1.3	3.8	7.6	10.0	22.8	19.7	11.5	15.0	4.5	2.4	1.6	Phoenix, Ariz.
100.0	1.2	6.3	15.4	12.4	21.8	17.3	10.6	8.1	2.1	1.3	3.5	Salt Lake City, Utah
100.0	4.7	6.4	5.8	8.8	24.6	15.8	13.5	14.6	2.9		2.9	Reno, Nev.
100.0	0.9	6.3	10.7	13.7	26.3	17.8	8.1	8.0	2.8	2.6	2.8	4 Pacific cities
100.0	0.6	5.9	12.3	15.4	27.2	16.7	7.0	6.8	2.1	2.1	3.9	Seattle, Wash.*
100.0	1.4	8.1	12.4	13.4	25.1	18.9	7.8	6.9	2.4	1.8	1.8	Portland, Ore.
100.0	0.4	2.8	5.9	9.7	26.6	18.6	12.3	12.9	5.3	4.2	1.3	Sacramento, Calif.
100.0	1.1	6.0	7.6	12.8	26.1	18.1	8.8	9.5	3.5	3.8	2.7	San Diego, Calif.*

TABLE A 14

Dwellings, Average Value (dollars) by Value Groups: Owner-occupied, 52 Cities; Rented, 44 Cities, by Geographic Division, January 1, 1934

	All value groups	$1-499	$500-999	$1,000-1,499	$1,500-1,999	$2,000-2,999	$3,000-3,999	$4,000-4,999	$5,000-7,499	$7,500-9,999	$10,000-14,999	$15,000 and over
52 cities[1]	4,997	401	824	1,209	1,694	2,415	3,305	4,260	5,757	8,167	11,035	21,143
4 New England cities	6,607	477	759	1,172	1,624	2,575	3,345	4,244	5,883	8,330	10,990	19,546
Portland, Me.	6,088	360	722	1,117	1,642	2,348	3,264	4,222	5,886	8,169	10,807	17,913
Worcester, Mass.	6,975			1,143	1,560	2,591	3,509	4,287	5,924	8,315	10,998	17,796
Providence, R.I.*	6,244	480	762	1,185	1,640	2,618	3,309	4,238	5,870	8,339	10,977	19,456
Waterbury, Conn.	8,415			1,175		2,426	3,338		5,893	8,393	11,157	23,767
4 Mid. Atlantic cities	5,672		763	1,300	1,666	2,436	3,306	4,255	5,812	8,165	10,887	20,626
Binghamton, N.Y.	6,356					2,527	3,383	4,333	5,928	8,055	10,719	18,891
Syracuse, N.Y.	6,251		767	1,230	1,620	2,437	3,290	4,250	5,864	8,277	11,075	22,239
Trenton, N.J.	4,029		791	1,358	1,649	2,395	3,289	4,248	5,630	8,164	10,354	19,808
Erie, Pa.	4,751		738	1,428	1,785	2,384	3,290	4,205	5,703	7,995	10,917	18,806
6 E. N. Central cities	5,914	443	911	1,269	1,790	2,466	3,355	4,330	5,814	8,205	11,076	21,691
Cleveland, Ohio*	6,388	494	960	1,281	1,842	2,494	3,348	4,361	5,811	8,234	11,170	22,625
Indianapolis, Ind.	4,969	300	818	1,275	1,678	2,374	3,388	4,256	5,900	8,149	10,838	20,310
Peoria, Ill.	4,549	267	763	1,173	1,680	2,347	3,309	4,229	5,713	8,030	10,848	18,086
Lansing, Mich.	3,876	350	710	1,155	1,628	2,418	3,304	4,287	5,660	8,178	11,318	19,980
Kenosha, Wis.	5,252			1,125	1,724	2,457	3,338	4,258	5,764	8,214	10,513	19,257
Racine, Wis.	5,326		778	1,352	1,665	2,547	3,454	4,294	5,793	8,171	10,885	18,672
10 W. N. Central cities	3,899	359	808	1,159	1,659	2,337	3,255	4,210	5,631	8,026	10,745	21,383
Minneapolis, Minn.	4,440	489	929	1,196	1,700	2,401	3,296	4,231	5,679	8,099	10,895	23,425
St. Paul, Minn.	3,831	133	723	1,148	1,647	2,345	3,278	4,230	5,591	8,170	10,697	19,286
Des Moines, Iowa	3,224	337	714	1,169	1,615	2,319	3,279	4,218	5,635	8,035	10,144	20,868
St. Joseph, Mo.	3,468	494	831	1,234	1,639	2,377	3,201	4,452	5,991	7,930	11,021	18,847
Springfield, Mo.	2,840	330	698	1,116	1,652	2,271	3,221	4,236	5,704	8,053	10,500	25,820
Fargo, N.D.	4,982			1,150	1,660	2,411	3,304	4,251	5,742	8,144	10,853	19,714
Sioux Falls, S.D.	4,266	246	741	1,148	1,636	2,490	3,256	4,239	5,707	8,068	10,971	16,071
Lincoln, Neb.	3,692	300	751	1,131	1,672	2,314	3,249	4,214	5,755	8,046	11,289	19,727
Topeka, Kan.	3,303	333	897	1,159	1,652	2,311	3,311	4,211	5,623	8,073	11,124	20,353
Wichita, Kan.	2,828	365	785	1,142	1,631	2,289	3,229	4,218	5,626	8,076	11,194	21,733
9 S. Atlantic cities	4,499	402	747	1,187	1,690	2,331	3,272	4,209	5,773	8,115	10,890	19,948
Hagerstown, Md.	4,940	300	700	1,124	1,844	2,327	3,296	4,256	5,736	7,955	11,093	18,338
Richmond, Va.	5,209	367	717	1,199	1,807	2,287	3,271	4,244	5,868	8,157	11,318	21,301
Wheeling, W.Va.*	3,927	403	711	1,139	1,621	2,321	3,240	4,228	5,736	8,169	10,742	19,117
Asheville, N.C.	3,929	358	762	1,229	1,623	2,343	3,407	4,179	5,645	7,984	10,290	18,880
Greensboro, N.C.	5,337		697	1,144	1,642	2,306	3,285	4,272	5,797	8,078	10,432	23,239
Charleston, S.C.	4,967	444	694	1,341	1,602	2,295	3,223	4,106	5,749	7,987	10,907	23,259
Columbia, S.C.	4,773	450	768	1,121	1,597	2,557	3,280	4,196	5,723	8,006	10,225	17,188
Atlanta, Ga.*	4,418	448	780	1,235	1,710	2,357	3,292	4,196	5,810	8,125	11,020	20,262
Jacksonville, Fla.	3,768	327	828	1,084	1,601	2,287	3,228	4,152	5,612	8,118	10,556	16,700
3 E. S. Central cities	3,357	465	779	1,155	1,598	2,295	3,230	4,301	5,590	8,099	10,476	18,942
Paducah, Ky.	2,311	352	782	1,100	1,565	2,222	3,237	4,228	5,806	8,044	11,700	19,000
Birmingham, Ala.*	3,238	490	797	1,165	1,601	2,296	3,223	4,319	5,568	8,037	10,358	18,530
Jackson, Miss.	4,465	380	678	1,124	1,596	2,323	3,262	4,234	5,614	8,465	10,581	21,167
6 W. S. Central cities	3,855	367	840	1,228	1,702	2,330	3,251	4,206	5,790	8,005	10,775	19,990
Little Rock, Ark.	3,291	336	739	1,168	1,754	2,333	3,205	4,162	5,681	7,940	10,264	17,993
Baton Rouge, La.	3,992	267	726	1,171	1,649	2,339	3,256	4,226	5,894	8,179	11,112	24,000
Oklahoma City, Okla.	4,139	309	797	1,117	1,678	2,332	3,244	4,208	5,762	8,153	10,718	20,694
Austin, Tex.	3,880	260	821	1,302	1,786	2,303	3,284	4,226	5,742	7,908	10,669	18,581
Dallas, Tex.	3,878	465	932	1,322	1,698	2,335	3,261	4,219	5,866	7,922	10,976	19,772
Wichita Falls, Tex.	2,933	297	691	1,131	1,634	2,319	3,232	4,114	5,566	8,000	10,536	21,577
6 Mountain cities	3,318	339	782	1,153	1,643	2,329	3,272	4,244	5,680	8,467	11,611	24,550
Butte, Mont.	2,707	369	831	1,109	1,595	2,270	3,234	4,099	5,557	8,175	10,300	19,843
Boise, Idaho	3,512	492	723	1,278	1,667	2,362	3,266	4,211	5,899	8,053	10,923	21,410
Casper, Wyo.	2,880	320	755	1,122	1,632	2,322	3,256	4,219	5,616	8,184	10,462	18,889
Pueblo, Colo.	1,910	351	751	1,129	1,606	2,341	3,236	4,248	5,500	7,917	11,000	
Phoenix, Ariz.	4,148		753	1,089	1,640	2,301	3,236	4,212	5,638	8,225	11,059	20,485
Salt Lake City, Utah	3,481	305	800	1,165	1,658	2,342	3,299	4,288	5,720	8,806	12,386	27,791
4 Pacific cities	3,511	310	803	1,167	1,641	2,335	3,275	4,239	5,625	8,113	11,670	23,585
Seattle, Wash.*	3,347	289	787	1,201	1,646	2,340	3,256	4,268	5,621	8,039	12,576	25,730
Portland, Ore.	3,207	331	821	1,136	1,627	2,307	3,293	4,228	5,595	7,992	10,818	23,664
Sacramento, Calif.	4,290	300	794	1,172	1,660	2,384	3,326	4,237	5,760	8,955	12,316	18,130
San Diego, Calif.*	3,916	326	816	1,139	1,644	2,341	3,265	4,194	5,612	8,039	10,694	21,613

Source: Financial Survey of Urban Housing. Average not shown for fewer than 3 reports.
* *Metropolitan district.*
[1] *Geographic division, 52-city, and 44-city averages weighted by number of dwelling units, by tenure, in each city (RPI).*

TABLE A 14

Dwellings, Average Value (dollars) by Value Groups: Owner-occupied, 52 Cities; Rented, 44 Cities, by Geographic Division, January 1, 1934

←─────────────────────────────────────── R E N T E D ───────────────────────────────────────→

All value groups	$1-499	$500-999	$1,000-1,499	$1,500-1,999	$2,000-2,999	$3,000-3,999	$4,000-4,999	$5,000-7,499	$7,500-9,999	$10,000-14,999	$15,000 and over	
4,878	371	767	1,213	1,715	2,369	3,317	4,264	5,782	8,246	11,269	32,016	44 cities
6,103		763	1,263	1,609	2,370	3,315	4,254	5,909	8,280	11,022	25,880	3 New England cities
5,963		760	1,075	1,662	2,329	3,253	4,224	5,940	8,083	10,803	25,922	Portland, Me.
7,083			1,125		2,470	3,397	4,238	6,029	8,291	11,318	19,390	Worcester, Mass.
5,860		763	1,323	1,603	2,349	3,301	4,262	5,874	8,301	10,971	27,596	Providence, R.I.*
6,272		710	1,160	1,650	2,327	3,335	4,215	5,748	8,195	10,928	23,817	3 Mid. Atlantic cities
7,444					2,300	3,368	4,209	5,802	8,215	10,789	25,233	Syracuse, N.Y.
3,496		688	1,175	1,627	2,319	3,256	4,183	5,538	8,192	11,344	19,613	Trenton, N.J.
4,868		720	1,154	1,660	2,393	3,297	4,244	5,719	8,151	11,057	22,500	Erie, Pa.
6,193	447	870	1,326	1,904	2,498	3,353	4,306	5,866	8,617	11,333	27,842	6 E. N. Central cities
7,141	475	929	1,413	1,984	2,575	3,384	4,330	5,929	8,420	11,437	29,687	Cleveland, Ohio*
4,181	380	767	1,158	1,828	2,290	3,283	4,280	5,716	9,576	11,108	22,291	Indianapolis, Ind.
4,037	350	711	1,160	1,600	2,427	3,280	4,149	5,787	8,007	10,996	33,230	Peoria, Ill.
3,186		656	1,204	1,657	2,344	3,276	4,190	5,767	8,000	11,500		Lansing, Mich.
5,873			1,125	1,650	2,655	3,418	4,322	5,795	8,358	11,068	18,686	Kenosha, Wis.
5,823		743	1,127	1,600	2,384	3,281	4,293	5,804	8,199	11,147	25,046	Racine, Wis.
3,799	405	721	1,188	1,695	2,313	3,325	4,280	5,726	8,197	11,102	27,973	9 W. N. Central cities
4,729	493	712	1,270	1,627	2,335	3,302	4,357	5,743	8,458	11,029	29,347	Minneapolis, Minn.
4,132		700	1,123	1,985	2,303	3,374	4,299	5,813	8,332	11,354	28,500	St. Paul, Minn.
2,984	298	767	1,158	1,625	2,298	3,242	4,221	5,711	8,133	11,643	29,753	Des Moines, Iowa
2,653	490	677	1,108	1,613	2,271	3,682	4,223	5,738	7,700	10,150	16,800	St. Joseph, Mo.
2,117	357	711	1,141	1,642	2,240	3,221	4,300	5,551	8,271		20,314	Springfield, Mo.
4,355	250	743	1,164	1,654	2,371	3,287	4,177	5,692	7,963	11,350	30,600	Sioux Falls, S.D.
3,115	270	722	1,169	1,626	2,305	3,285	4,200	5,750	8,192	10,000	23,450	Lincoln, Neb.
2,755	343	783	1,134	1,653	2,309	3,319	4,168	5,624	7,885	10,722	37,571	Topeka, Kan.
2,479	338	726	1,144	1,622	2,303	3,287	4,185	5,607	7,406	11,727	25,925	Wichita, Kan.
4,123	319	699	1,139	1,629	2,287	3,289	4,211	5,645	8,009	11,949	33,988	8 S. Atlantic cities
3,766	271	721	1,179	1,683	2,275	3,200	4,284	5,636	8,014	10,750	36,750	Hagerstown, Md.
4,339	367	675	1,126	1,643	2,284	3,208	4,276	5,801	7,768	10,820	23,014	Richmond, Va.
4,362	317	754	1,100	1,632	2,256	3,183	4,133	5,627	8,177	10,744	21,863	Wheeling, W.Va.*
3,244	307	732	1,086	1,616	2,393	3,269	4,274	5,653	7,580	10,625		Asheville, N.C.
3,767	380	647	1,119	1,611	2,321	3,173	4,267	5,838	7,879	10,991	19,014	Greensboro, N.C.
3,200	300	785	1,081	1,591	2,233	3,250	4,209	5,744	7,807	11,462	15,000	Charleston, S.C.
3,607	200	639	1,564	1,633	2,263	3,285	4,262	5,603	8,225	11,188	20,375	Columbia, S.C.
4,308	312	687	1,119	1,629	2,292	3,401	4,188	5,547	8,118	13,468	50,117	Atlanta, Ga.*
3,197	366	708	1,127	1,608	2,343	3,325	4,278	5,539	7,743	10,533	47,468	2 E. S. Central cities
1,579	222	651	1,093	1,578	2,292	3,170	4,150	5,571	8,667	11,700	21,000	Paducah, Ky.
3,262	372	710	1,128	1,609	2,345	3,331	4,283	5,538	7,706	10,486	48,538	Birmingham, Ala.*
3,681	310	707	1,131	1,624	2,312	3,311	4,218	5,749	8,059	11,175	28,176	5 W. S. Central cities
2,194	304	792	1,112	1,610	2,247	3,654	4,113	5,882	7,811	12,958	17,560	Little Rock, Ark.
4,733	338	686	1,131	1,611	2,306	3,308	4,262	5,701	8,011	10,782	31,120	Oklahoma City, Okla.
3,100	338	762	1,236	1,677	2,361	3,300	4,127	5,784	7,995	10,937	21,500	Austin, Tex.
3,446	292	696	1,122	1,625	2,318	3,256	4,222	5,732	8,227	11,160	29,293	Dallas, Tex.
2,034	235	714	1,080	1,638	2,332	3,192	4,225	5,938	7,500			Wichita Falls, Tex.
4,062	353	744	1,261	1,712	2,314	3,250	4,239	5,663	8,292	11,526	43,889	4 Mountain cities
4,205	391	784	1,350	1,607	2,268	3,152	4,200	5,721	8,329	11,571	52,607	Butte, Mont.
1,873	332	707	1,110	1,634	2,300	3,238	4,150	5,375	7,850	12,625		Pueblo, Colo.
3,862	380	771	1,479	1,961	2,320	3,311	4,236	5,718	8,359	10,889	23,116	Phoenix, Ariz.
4,546	333	727	1,156	1,630	2,327	3,248	4,268	5,674	8,333	11,622	51,924	Salt Lake City, Utah
4,298	298	757	1,140	1,624	2,324	3,276	4,271	5,877	8,119	11,219	41,852	4 Pacific cities
5,080	275	713	1,131	1,618	2,284	3,218	4,207	6,190	8,041	11,090	60,449	Seattle, Wash.*
3,307	344	758	1,183	1,620	2,375	3,277	4,223	5,551	8,100	11,629	29,813	Portland, Ore.
4,051		753	1,155	1,641	2,400	3,569	4,255	5,771	8,389	11,282	23,643	Sacramento, Cal.
3,792	300	847	1,112	1,636	2,328	3,287	4,451	5,607	8,200	11,049	22,764	San Diego, Cal.*

TABLE A 15

1-Family Dwellings by Material of Construction: Owner-occupied, Average Value per Dwelling Unit, per Room, and per Person,
52 Cities; Rented, Average Value per Dwelling Unit and per Room, 44 Cities, by Geographic Division, January 1, 1934

OWNER - OCCUPIED

	PER DWELLING UNIT				PER ROOM				PER PERSON	
	All materials	Wood	Brick	Other	All materials	Wood	Brick	Other	All materials	Wood
52 cities[1]	$4,283	$3,693	$9,298	$6,360	$ 689	$ 606	$1,234	$931	$1,076	$928
4 New England cities	6,186	5,777	18,023	7,552	832	789	1,874	974	1,447	1,356
Portland, Me.	6,051	5,459	11,283	8,031	766	724	998	988	1,510	1,364
Worcester, Mass.*	6,642	6,205	12,872	10,506	906	857	1,542	1,280	1,552	1,450
Providence, R.I.	5,903	5,560	19,308	6,459	791	753	2,018	863	1,376	1,302
Waterbury, Conn.	8,001	7,224	23,280	11,182	1,109	1,033	2,024	1,348	1,821	1,642
4 Mid. Atlantic cities	5,409	5,074	10,254	6,557	761	722	1,262	880	1,297	1,220
Binghamton, N.Y.	6,163	5,988	8,500	7,222	817	803	882	966	1,433	1,430
Syracuse, N.Y.	5,901	5,695	13,958	7,750	839	814	1,700	1,013	1,477	1,424
Trenton, N.J.	4,200	3,820	4,500	4,220	622	597	638	647	935	868
Erie, Pa.	4,576	3,942	7,276	5,027	654	572	996	700	1,062	896
6 E. N. Central cities	5,592	4,784	12,418	9,502	868	763	1,646	1,226	1,363	1,169
Cleveland, Ohio*	6,249	5,390	14,327	11,553	943	841	1,812	1,377	1,442	1,252
Indianapolis, Ind.	4,890	3,815	11,092	7,723	801	640	1,618	1,143	1,363	1,063
Peoria, Ill.	4,405	3,888	9,965	5,338	758	683	1,456	893	1,185	1,050
Lansing, Mich.	3,813	3,578	7,482	5,409	588	557	988	829	975	917
Kenosha, Wis.	5,069	4,639	8,258	5,758	820	757	1,248	920	1,204	1,101
Racine, Wis.	4,961	4,734	6,536	5,651	782	749	1,000	896	1,212	1,155
10 W. N. Central cities	3,663	3,129	7,690	4,674	606	523	1,033	777	922	782
Minneapolis, Minn.	4,204	3,506	8,919	4,879	671	549	1,106	807	1,013	814
St. Paul, Minn.	3,766	3,319	7,066	4,741	631	556	929	815	943	810
Des Moines, Iowa	3,157	2,717	6,543	4,178	547	478	999	711	829	715
St. Joseph, Mo.	3,296	2,669	6,841	5,172	585	498	901	865	917	745
Springfield, Mo.	2,651	2,279	6,556	3,829	489	432	1,020	619	732	634
Fargo, N.D.	4,811	4,434	12,450	5,892	752	695	1,445	928	1,071	986
Sioux Falls, S.D.	4,101	3,859	9,875	5,190	691	655	1,266	860	1,053	989
Lincoln, Neb.	3,548	2,963	8,310	5,136	572	489	1,118	774	889	741
Topeka, Kan.	3,186	3,053	5,416	4,702	543	524	813	773	892	857
Wichita, Kan.	2,722	2,392	7,227	3,904	493	439	1,093	670	777	682
9 S. Atlantic cities	4,310	3,321	7,310	6,936	683	548	1,021	1,003	1,005	773
Hagerstown, Md.	4,601	2,752	5,614	6,059	665	438	767	845	1,184	675
Richmond, Va. *	5,218	3,237	7,679	6,312	766	525	1,009	872	1,187	750
Wheeling, W. Va.*	3,768	3,491	5,704	5,757	641	605	827	908	877	810
Asheville, N.C.	3,807	3,131	7,932	4,281	580	491	1,053	637	913	752
Greensboro, N.C.	5,226	4,397	7,752	8,565	750	637	1,104	1,110	1,146	981
Charleston, S.C.	5,023	4,123	10,200	6,453	722	613	1,208	906	1,148	939
Columbia, S.C.	4,779	3,988	6,452	7,931	733	609	972	1,173	1,061	846
Atlanta, Ga.*	4,339	3,097	7,535	8,773	701	524	1,093	1,211	1,007	718
Jacksonville, Fla.	3,499	3,042	8,659	5,185	584	512	1,187	884	880	763
3 E. S. Central cities	3,240	2,760	7,257	6,959	555	478	1,021	962	765	649
Paducah, Ky.	2,106	1,633	4,962	3,489	413	336	783	600	549	418
Birmingham, Ala.*	3,198	2,732	7,646	7,490	547	472	1,046	1,005	759	649
Jackson, Miss.	4,462	3,866	6,215	5,803	745	650	1,025	925	1,006	850
6 W. S. Central cities	3,632	2,946	6,974	5,458	645	538	1,072	904	911	738
Little Rock, Ark.	3,230	2,622	5,668	5,049	562	469	877	815	849	687
Baton Rouge, La.	3,806	3,696	6,133	6,131	672	656	920	972	821	795
Oklahoma City, Okla.	3,838	3,074	6,571	5,357	688	565	1,084	919	955	765
Austin, Tex.	3,732	2,985	9,951	6,545	701	586	1,434	1,037	935	748
Dallas, Tex.	3,695	3,026	6,596	5,549	637	537	1,005	906	924	757
Wichita Falls, Tex.	2,933	2,089	9,219	4,036	550	406	1,301	725	777	546
6 Mountain cities	2,946	2,056	3,619	3,484	553	425	621	638	742	536
Butte, Mont.	2,355	2,091	3,091	2,930	459	434	509	583	620	565
Boise, Idaho	3,147	2,953	4,649	3,900	570	541	706	728	895	844
Casper, Wyo.	2,594	2,378	5,847	2,863	562	531	964	552	708	649
Pueblo, Colo.	1,830	1,435	2,334	2,237	364	297	426	458	481	377
Phoenix, Ariz.	4,143	2,082	4,412	5,431	744	453	760	902	1,125	598
Salt Lake City, Utah	3,224	2,062	3,534	3,629	593	430	629	647	751	505
4 Pacific cities	3,220	2,953	7,465	4,601	582	540	1,080	784	961	878
Seattle, Wash.*	3,043	2,863	6,321	4,310	559	528	986	734	899	841
Portland, Ore.	3,104	2,920	9,144	4,720	533	504	1,219	791	914	859
Sacramento, Calif.	3,995	3,278	6,087	5,135	718	599	1,042	891	1,169	952
San Diego, Calif.*	3,568	3,107	7,800	4,895	673	610	1,080	853	1,114	973

Source: _Financial Survey of Urban Housing._ _Average not shown for fewer than 3 reports._
*Metropolitan district.
[1]Geographic division, 52-city, and 44-city averages weighted by number of 1-family dwelling units, by tenure, in each city (RPI).

TABLE A 15

1-Family Dwellings by Material of Construction: Owner-occupied, Average Value per Dwelling Unit, per Room, and per Person, 52 Cities; Rented, Average Value per Dwelling Unit and per Room, 44 Cities, by Geographic Division, January 1, 1934

RENTED

←— PER PERSON —→		←—— PER DWELLING UNIT ——→				←—— PER ROOM ——→				
Brick	Other	All materials	Wood	Brick	Other	All materials	Wood	Brick	Other	
$2,291	$1,503	$3,142	$2,798	$5,880	$3,508	$552	$499	$904	$608	44 cities[1]
4,245	1,732	4,832	4,770	6,835	4,281	657	659	752	567	4 New England cities
2,414	1,868	4,445	3,919	5,438	6,846	608	578	551	814	Portland, Me.
2,841	2,985	6,133	6,186	6,433	5,571	826	852	919	629	Worcester, Mass.
4,633	1,386	4,706	4,692	7,083	3,750	636	639	750	528	Providence, R.I.*
5,173	2,236									Waterbury, Conn.
2,378	1,495	4,459	4,204	5,506	4,681	662	639	641	720	4 Mid. Atlantic cities
1,793	1,537									Binghamton, N.Y.
3,246	1,802	5,436	5,279	5,900	6,086	791	782	567	918	Syracuse, N.Y.
981	959	3,135	3,051	3,339	2,250	483	483	494	386	Trenton, N.J.
1,817	1,169	3,786	3,353	5,829	3,904	581	531	791	621	Erie, Pa.
3,024	1,965	4,305	3,946	8,982	4,362	700	649	1,275	705	6 E. N. Central cities
3,323	2,188	5,464	5,017	11,061	5,172	843	779	1,463	807	Cleveland, Ohio*
3,005	1,924	3,126	2,761	8,408	3,364	550	498	1,277	579	Indianapolis, Ind.
2,685	1,417	3,087	2,937	6,578	3,329	582	554	1,108	638	Peoria, Ill.
2,113	1,258	2,970	2,834	4,050	3,459	506	488	642	561	Lansing, Mich.
1,965	1,440	4,969	4,724	6,144	5,895	806	797	1,007	778	Kenosha, Wis.
1,578	1,385	4,342	4,101	5,404	5,439	719	693	795	864	Racine, Wis.
1,832	1,212	2,713	2,461	4,930	3,144	494	451	830	570	10 W. N. Central cities
1,878	1,218	3,375	2,966	7,180	3,844	577	508	1,122	659	Minneapolis, Minn.
1,627	1,190	3,285	2,840	5,238	3,992	578	495	799	738	St. Paul, Minn.
1,759	1,127	2,486	2,288	3,637	2,905	460	426	673	524	Des Moines, Iowa
1,724	1,481	2,483	2,206	2,826	3,500	486	458	481	595	St. Joseph, Mo.
1,883	987	1,940	1,743	5,184	2,322	398	361	918	493	Springfield, Mo.
2,762	1,378									Fargo, N.D.
2,469	1,311	3,291	3,160	5,163	3,790	587	562	879	682	Sioux Falls, S.D.
1,998	1,398	2,524	2,418	3,930	2,670	445	426	690	477	Lincoln, Neb.
1,504	1,283	2,258	2,200	2,404	2,563	437	429	401	493	Topeka, Kan.
2,017	1,063	2,066	1,970	5,450	2,050	400	385	1,025	396	Wichita, Kan.
1,754	1,601	3,128	2,497	5,498	3,701	542	455	829	614	9 S. Atlantic cities
1,523	1,478	2,535	1,762	3,247	3,131	413	297	516	490	Hagerstown, Md.
1,748	1,373	3,640	2,577	4,539	4,944	593	468	675	730	Richmond, Va.
1,432	1,339	3,519	2,810	6,035	4,513	607	510	882	747	Wheeling, W. Va.*
1,983	1,037	3,234	3,008	5,341	3,261	541	518	861	502	Asheville, N.C.
1,685	1,749	3,382	2,753	7,468	4,360	561	478	1,035	736	Greensboro, N.C.
2,318	1,666	2,723	2,380	7,000	2,750	485	450	750	391	Charleston, S.C.
1,576	1,983	2,907	2,348	5,457	3,193	562	480	899	556	Columbia, S.C.
1,794	1,943	2,793	2,232	5,154	3,055	500	410	821	553	Atlanta, Ga.*
2,165	1,498									Jacksonville, Fla.
1,698	1,567	2,567	2,284	6,282	3,298	485	435	1,022	617	3 E. S. Central cities
1,369	969	1,188	995	3,271	1,905	289	249	574	426	Paducah, Ky.
1,769	1,624	2,703	2,411	6,579	3,436	503	452	1,064	635	Birmingham, Ala.*
1,390	1,617									Jackson, Miss.
1,789	1,328	2,488	2,167	5,102	2,818	491	441	867	501	6 W. S. Central cities
1,498	1,296	1,794	1,506	4,380	2,161	386	332	735	466	Little Rock, Ark.
1,305	1,202									Baton Rouge, La.
1,767	1,347	2,580	2,153	4,466	3,542	509	453	823	571	Oklahoma City, Okla.
2,492	1,615	2,529	2,236	7,477	2,627	571	513	1,130	606	Austin, Tex.
1,642	1,307	2,796	2,475	5,428	2,914	523	475	907	492	Dallas, Tex.
2,492	1,022	1,970	1,836	3,914	1,770	383	360	742	300	Wichita Falls, Tex.
884	871	2,466	1,731	2,842	2,560	483	339	523	540	6 Mountain cities
776	771	1,719	1,521	2,552	1,470	348	329	384	351	Butte, Mont.
1,178	1,114									Boise, Idaho
1,624	730									Casper, Wyo.
611	589	1,503	1,273	1,679	1,997	320	279	332	435	Pueblo, Colo.
1,165	1,482	3,368	1,707	3,905	3,319	649	340	715	678	Phoenix, Ariz.
804	826	2,677	2,068	2,923	2,743	509	372	549	568	Salt Lake City, Utah
2,073	1,341	2,726	2,513	4,475	3,273	521	484	745	612	4 Pacific cities
1,720	1,212	2,587	2,500	4,911	2,540	495	479	814	500	Seattle, Wash.*
2,471	1,402	2,655	2,479		3,684	469	440		626	Portland, Ore.
1,743	1,427	3,255	2,628	5,047	4,246	645	524	861	843	Sacramento, Calif.
2,364	1,519	2,872	2,538	3,667	3,648	584	529	611	700	San Diego, Calif.*

TABLE A 16

I-Family Dwellings, Wood Construction, Average Value (dollars) by Tenure and Period of Construction: Owner-occupied, 52 Cities; Rented, 44 Cities, by Geographic Division, January 1, 1934

	All periods of construction	1839 or before	1840-49	1850-59	1860-69	1870-79	1880-89	1890-99	1900-09	1910-19	1920-29	1930-33
52 cities[1]	3,712	5,650	4,617	4,070	5,154	3,221	3,167	3,194	3,525	3,845	4,062	3,850
4 New England cities	5,796	5,647	3,711	6,090	4,859	4,605	5,331	5,755	6,160	5,791	6,349	5,765
Portland, Me.	5,529	3,618	5,000	4,983	4,650	3,963	4,722	6,217	6,428	5,078	6,016	5,869
Worcester, Mass.	6,193			5,176	4,887	4,940	6,194	7,637	7,775	6,087	5,597	6,168
Providence, R.I.	5,575	5,913	3,570	5,032	4,788	4,668	4,940	5,067	5,336	5,778	6,500	5,636
Waterbury, Conn.	7,300	5,233		18,725	5,667	4,000	7,793	7,829	10,219	6,032	6,803	6,036
4 Mid. Atlantic cities	5,114	5,320	4,745	4,427	3,798	4,113	4,349	4,627	5,065	5,422	5,720	5,707
Binghamton, N.Y.	6,078				3,500	5,250	6,838	6,042	5,397	6,232	6,415	5,000
Syracuse, N.Y.	5,725		5,750	4,809	3,986	4,188	4,418	4,968	5,667	6,191	6,296	7,259
Trenton, N.J.	3,912	5,633		6,283	4,283	2,650	2,735	3,628	3,818	4,288	5,060	5,333
Erie, Pa.	3,950	5,200	3,043	3,066	3,475	3,848	3,322	3,564	4,320	4,057	4,572	3,661
6 E. N. Central cities	4,808	6,530	5,511	3,919	5,138	3,673	3,516	3,352	4,368	4,990	5,362	5,168
Cleveland, Ohio	5,417	6,735	5,511	4,603	4,790	4,119	3,963	3,308	4,866	5,508	6,044	6,149
Indianapolis, Ind.	3,843			2,833	7,775	2,591	2,369	3,178	3,399	4,253	4,190	3,061
Peoria, Ill.	3,905			2,186	2,700	2,915	2,832	3,184	3,527	4,446	4,811	4,738
Lansing, Mich.	3,582	2,667			3,250	3,500	3,250	3,382	3,925	3,597	3,766	4,187
Kenosha, Wis.	4,632				3,689	5,510	4,889	4,506	4,454	4,499	4,908	4,420
Racine, Wis.	4,753	8,833		3,143	4,007	3,477	3,951	4,365	4,532	4,803	5,416	5,113
10 W. N. Central cities	3,146			3,204	3,145	2,254	2,482	2,701	3,021	3,327	3,531	3,762
Minneapolis, Minn.	3,514			3,083	3,744	2,450	2,674	3,028	3,679	3,652	3,683	4,515
St. Paul, Minn.	3,327					2,286	2,369	2,953	3,095	3,806	3,962	4,371
Des Moines, Iowa	2,735			4,317	1,954	1,956	2,062	2,349	2,523	2,874	3,171	2,417
St. Joseph, Mo.	2,694					2,144	2,346	2,361	2,406	2,983	3,487	3,758
Springfield, Mo.	2,300					1,912	1,972	2,275	2,195	2,555	2,269	2,026
Fargo, N.D.	4,430						4,033	3,893	4,156	4,355	5,033	4,338
Sioux Falls, S.D.	3,868					6,417	3,863	3,603	3,917	4,151	3,583	3,868
Lincoln, Neb.	2,996					1,488	2,467	2,162	2,671	3,159	3,596	2,950
Topeka, Kan.	3,126			1,500	2,583	1,870	2,406	2,497	2,888	3,494	3,907	4,346
Wichita, Kan.	2,413					1,828	2,452	1,951	1,910	2,352	2,593	2,655
9 S. Atlantic cities	3,352	2,992	2,274	2,876	4,127	3,020	2,687	3,071	3,020	3,628	3,674	2,746
Hagerstown, Md.	2,805					1,500	3,244	2,192	2,097	2,956	1,444	2,000
Richmond, Va.	3,298	1,000		1,600	1,856	1,371	1,761	2,170	2,879	3,431	4,815	3,683
Wheeling, W. Va.	3,515	3,425	2,038	2,916	5,564	3,544	3,325	3,180	3,365	3,850	3,754	3,176
Asheville, N.C.	3,132					967	2,838	4,331	2,837	3,202	3,046	1,600
Greensboro, N.C.	4,351					7,000	3,167	4,875	4,160	3,890	4,717	
Charleston, S.C.	4,169	6,424	4,086	3,700	4,278	3,167	4,084	3,154	2,733	4,624	5,784	2,800
Columbia, S.C.	4,029	5,900		7,162	5,057	4,220	1,870	4,480	4,530	4,157	3,434	1,600
Atlanta, Ga.	3,144				4,100	3,093	2,634	2,990	2,756	3,608	3,090	2,357
Jacksonville, Fla.	3,039						2,412	2,675	2,619	3,273	3,402	
3 E. S. Central cities	2,763			1,967	3,731	1,433	2,514	2,258	2,681	2,849	2,863	1,872
Paducah, Ky.	1,624			1,967	1,244	1,433	1,696	1,565	1,541	1,728	1,699	1,320
Birmingham, Ala.	2,737				4,000		2,602	2,278	2,476	2,804	2,908	1,874
Jackson, Miss.	3,864						2,667	5,106	4,079	3,458		2,300
6 W. S. Central cities	2,959			4,429	3,202	4,982	3,347	2,887	2,991	3,070	2,816	2,352
Little Rock, Ark.	2,624				3,657	3,506	2,610	2,396	2,622	2,587	2,573	2,843
Baton Rouge, La.	3,721			7,350		12,000	4,940	4,368	3,471	3,595	3,191	3,133
Oklahoma City, Okla.	3,084							3,862	3,387	3,154	2,801	2,303
Austin, Tex.	3,013			3,333	2,633	4,194	4,250	3,196	2,855	2,850	3,172	2,437
Dallas, Tex.	3,039						3,188	2,397	3,058	3,311	2,908	2,113
Wichita Falls, Tex.	2,100							1,233	1,610	2,321	2,030	
6 Mountain cities	2,047					1,277	1,817	1,969	1,947	2,155	2,390	2,217
Butte, Mont.	2,091						1,346	1,537	1,795	2,568	2,434	2,000
Boise, Idaho	2,945					2,500	3,631	2,218	2,684	3,042	3,678	2,629
Casper, Wyo.	2,374							2,550	4,715	2,532	2,115	2,429
Pueblo, Colo.	1,445					1,275	792	1,145	1,009	1,676	1,906	
Phoenix, Ariz.	2,023						2,000	3,770	1,494	2,110	1,916	2,000
Salt Lake City, Utah	2,054					1,056	1,926	1,834	1,914	2,032	2,468	2,211
4 Pacific cities	2,967				12,900	3,176	2,948	2,813	2,686	2,955	3,175	3,055
Seattle, Wash.	2,870					4,000	2,255	2,577	2,657	2,861	3,138	2,285
Portland, Ore.	2,941				12,900	1,977	3,037	2,411	2,354	2,823	3,330	4,223
Sacramento, Calif.	3,296					3,507	4,746	3,528	3,354	3,153	3,254	3,319
San Diego, Calif.	3,125						3,800	3,850	3,098	3,350	2,954	2,740

O W N E R - O C C U P I E D

Source: Financial Survey of Urban Housing. Average not shown for fewer than 3 reports.
[1] *Geographic division, 52-city, and 44-city averages weighted by number of 1-family dwelling units, by tenure, in each city (RPI).*

1-Family Dwellings, Wood Construction, Average Value (dollars) by Tenure and Period of Construction: Owner-occupied, 52 Cities; Rented, 44 Cities, by Geographic Division, January 1, 1934

◄——————————————————— R E N T E D ———————————————————►

All periods of construction	1839 or before	1840-49	1850-59	1860-69	1870-79	1880-89	1890-99	1900-09	1910-19	1920-29	1930-33	
2,812	5,567	3,790	2,817	2,625	2,777	2,594	2,398	2,765	2,747	3,217	2,886	**44 cities**[1]
4,530			2,740	5,765	3,729	3,775	4,235	4,433	4,257	5,682	4,683	**3 New England cities**
3,984				3,414	1,953	3,680	5,757	5,009	5,200	4,059	4,767	Portland, Me.
6,220				3,366	4,375	4,800		7,362	7,912	5,829	5,020	Worcester, Mass.
4,372			2,740	6,420	3,885	3,647	4,025	3,949	3,623	5,886	4,625	Providence, R.I.
4,254			3,554	3,405	2,517	3,287	3,677	4,072	4,209	4,961	5,525	**3 Mid. Atlantic cities**
5,333			3,500	.....		4,529	4,800	5,143	5,007	5,773	7,000	Syracuse, N.Y.
3,095				2,940	2,100	1,985	2,152	2,404	3,140	4,665		Trenton, N.J.
3,401			3,617	3,575	2,669	2,292	2,904	3,413	3,654	4,110	3,783	Erie, Pa.
3,969		3,750	3,068	1,800	3,106	4,373	3,124	3,974	3,969	4,497	4,379	**6 E. N. Central cities**
5,012		4,200	3,386	1,784	2,882	6,240	3,798	5,177	4,750	5,726	5,985	Cleveland, Ohio
2,808				3,767	2,445	2,135	2,574	3,060	3,152	2,475		Indianapolis, Ind.
2,986		1,200	1,067	1,080	1,981	2,905	2,534	2,986	3,491	3,871	2,630	Peoria, Ill.
2,872					2,571	2,667	2,963	2,988	2,707			Lansing, Mich.
4,779							5,190	4,613	4,265	5,091	3,250	Kenosha, Wis.
4,163			3,571	3,833	3,130	3,441	3,382	3,992	4,488	4,729	4,075	Racine, Wis.
2,499			1,260	2,189	1,878	2,002	1,999	2,344	2,650	2,882	2,832	**9 W. N. Central cities**
2,994				2,333	2,271	2,506	2,718	2,965	3,090	3,257	4,643	Minneapolis, Minn.
2,922						1,840	2,160	2,756	3,184	3,534	3,667	St. Paul, Minn.
2,347					1,092	2,067	1,874	2,167	2,340	2,855	2,157	Des Moines, Iowa
2,309			1,575	1,800	1,917	1,800	1,597	2,510	2,539	2,835		St. Joseph, Mo.
1,678			920			1,323	1,764	1,279	1,912	1,791	1,278	Springfield, Mo.
3,209					3,167	3,231	2,590	3,114	3,539	3,207	3,045	Sioux Falls, S.D.
2,429						2,138	1,871	2,066	2,610	2,971	2,538	Lincoln, Neb.
2,233					1,708	1,834	1,628	2,054	2,639	2,809	2,800	Topeka, Kan.
1,992						1,418	1,258	1,703	2,007	2,158	2,529	Wichita, Kan.
2,566	5,567	4,367		2,048	2,368	1,626	2,095	2,276	2,707	3,060	2,411	**8 S. Atlantic cities**
1,925						1,700	1,356	1,814	2,683	2,783		Hagerstown, Md.
2,733					850	1,323	2,527	1,881	3,855	3,832	4,180	Richmond, Va.
2,844				2,000	3,886	2,600	2,515	2,779	3,313		2,967	Wheeling, W. Va.
3,051						2,333	2,210	2,700	3,368			Asheville, N.C.
2,815						2,188	2,948	2,314	3,146			Greensboro, N.C.
2,454	5,567	4,367		2,213	3,283	1,682	3,248	1,569	1,851	3,179	1,000	Charleston, S.C.
2,317				1,650		929	1,228	3,150	2,436	2,763	960	Columbia, S.C.
2,303						1,409	1,692	2,134	2,467	2,613	1,925	Atlanta, Ga.
2,273					1,100	2,221	1,466	2,029	2,123	2,641	1,103	**2 E. S. Central cities**
993					1,100	681	580	1,106	1,070	1,570	800	Paducah, Ky.
2,399						2,373	1,553	2,120	2,227	2,747	1,133	Birmingham, Ala.
2,182					6,925	1,628	2,324	2,820	1,833	2,347	1,315	**5 W. S. Central cities**
1,516						1,267	984	1,451	1,502	1,961	633	Little Rock, Ark.
2,145							3,000	5,278	1,043	1,887	1,125	Oklahoma City, Okla.
2,294					6,925	1,421	2,767	2,853	2,002	2,575	1,716	Austin, Tex.
2,490						1,811	2,307	2,149	2,419	2,790	1,580	Dallas, Tex.
1,872								1,536	1,657	1,967		Wichita Falls, Tex.
1,682					2,380	2,088	1,625	1,794	1,407	1,878	1,933	**4 Mountain cities**
1,532						2,385	1,282	1,467	1,378	2,400		Butte, Mont.
1,303						767	514	966	1,379	1,964		Pueblo, Colo.
1,744							1,850	2,643	1,164	1,773		Phoenix, Ariz.
1,902					2,380	2,738	2,216	1,831	1,584	1,732	1,933	Salt Lake City, Utah
2,527						2,444	2,440	2,375	2,337	2,778	3,075	**4 Pacific cities**
2,497						2,520	2,931	2,347	2,212	2,826	2,421	Seattle, Wash.
2,510						2,615	2,045	2,109	2,415	2,863	3,250	Portland, Ore.
2,700						3,686	1,760	2,269	2,409	2,917	4,500	Sacramento, Calif.
2,544						1,800	2,331	2,746	2,417	2,571	3,473	San Diego, Calif.

TABLE A 17

Number of Farm Operators reporting Value of Farm Dwelling and Average Value of Farm Dwelling plus Average Value of one Acre of Land, by State, Geographic Division, and Tenure, April 1, 1930

	←————FARM OPERATORS REPORTING VALUE OF————→ FARM DWELLING, 1930				←—AVERAGE VALUE OF FARM DWELLING PLUS AVERAGE—→ VALUE OF ONE ACRE OF LAND				
	Total[1]	Owners[2]	Managers[2]	Tenants[2]	Subtotal: M'g'rs + Ten.	Total[3]	Owners[4]	Managers[4]	Tenants[4]	Subtotal:[4] M'g'rs + Ten.
United States	5,866,446	3,430,944	48,185	2,387,317	2,435,502	1,242	1,511	2,990	826	867
New England	119,207	109,754	2,566	6,887	9,453	2,356	2,304	5,329	2,064	2,956
Maine	37,175	35,241	456	1,478	1,934	1,542	1,539	2,645	1,261	1,589
New Hampshire	14,168	13,154	312	702	1,014	1,844	1,815	3,935	1,476	2,235
Vermont	24,247	21,503	441	2,303	2,744	1,789	1,760	3,432	1,754	2,025
Massachusetts	24,018	22,080	795	1,143	1,938	3,310	3,221	6,411	2,798	4,291
Rhode Island	3,128	2,693	85	350	435	3,208	3,205	6,043	2,523	3,217
Connecticut	16,471	15,083	477	911	1,388	3,947	3,820	8,663	3,540	5,305
Mid. Atlantic	343,145	289,023	5,479	47,643	53,122	2,375	2,341	4,936	2,278	2,555
New York	153,133	131,396	2,400	19,337	21,737	2,429	2,401	5,402	2,242	2,594
New Jersey	23,958	19,933	577	3,448	4,025	3,496	3,509	5,731	3,038	3,430
Pennsylvania	165,054	137,694	2,502	24,858	27,360	2,164	2,116	4,308	2,202	2,397
E. N. Central	929,022	673,378	7,825	247,819	255,644	1,750	1,784	3,279	1,716	1,765
Ohio	209,767	154,533	1,618	53,616	55,234	1,740	1,749	3,625	1,655	1,715
Indiana	172,708	120,989	1,318	50,401	51,719	1,477	1,488	2,154	1,428	1,448
Illinois	206,475	116,417	1,950	88,108	90,058	1,956	2,024	3,431	1,831	1,866
Michigan	163,135	137,378	1,399	24,358	25,757	1,694	1,669	3,909	1,699	1,821
Wisconsin	176,937	144,061	1,540	31,336	32,876	1,984	1,977	3,117	1,959	2,014
W. N. Central	1,062,535	642,220	6,870	413,445	420,315	1,677	1,827	2,374	1,432	1,447
Minnesota	179,731	123,883	970	54,878	55,848	1,804	1,855	3,001	1,668	1,692
Iowa	207,319	108,713	1,829	96,777	98,606	2,387	2,716	2,618	2,013	2,024
Missouri	244,848	161,010	1,429	82,409	83,838	1,188	1,303	2,440	940	977
North Dakota	73,159	48,008	432	24,719	25,151	1,520	1,649	2,032	1,259	1,272
South Dakota	78,336	43,971	415	33,950	34,365	1,548	1,702	1,896	1,346	1,352
Nebraska	123,205	65,426	942	56,837	57,779	1,852	2,189	1,971	1,465	1,472
Kansas	155,937	91,209	853	63,875	64,728	1,394	1,595	2,047	1,099	1,112
S. Atlantic	979,797	517,751	7,017	455,029	462,046	876	1,149	3,291	524	569
Delaware	9,189	6,131	139	2,919	3,058	1,929	1,969	4,514	1,724	1,852
Maryland	41,447	30,054	846	10,547	11,393	2,183	2,231	4,985	1,818	2,056
D.C.	97	58	15	24	39	6,500	6,202	9,864	3,529	6,462
Virginia	161,605	117,836	1,436	42,333	43,769	1,326	1,452	5,103	843	986
West Virginia	79,070	64,342	657	14,071	14,728	1,009	1,063	2,006	713	772
North Carolina	260,504	136,885	560	123,059	123,619	733	900	2,807	538	548
South Carolina	146,478	52,669	601	93,208	93,809	585	920	2,107	386	397
Georgia	233,928	76,441	1,261	156,226	157,487	546	835	2,408	389	406
Florida	47,479	33,335	1,502	12,642	14,144	1,072	1,235	2,407	450	690
E. S. Central	972,905	449,541	2,462	520,902	523,364	575	790	2,575	382	393
Kentucky	224,232	151,189	578	72,465	73,043	760	853	2,941	548	569
Tennessee	226,060	127,338	540	98,182	98,722	683	848	2,618	459	471
Alabama	239,637	87,981	471	151,185	151,656	458	691	1,921	319	325
Mississippi	282,976	83,033	873	199,070	199,943	441	694	2,674	330	341
W. S. Central	999,921	392,688	4,804	602,429	607,233	670	965	1,935	474	481
Arkansas	219,381	85,958	568	132,855	133,423	457	622	1,908	348	355
Louisiana	149,166	51,418	673	97,075	97,748	517	819	2,665	346	360
Oklahoma	187,766	74,287	738	112,741	113,479	704	1,001	1,565	503	509
Texas	443,608	181,025	2,825	259,758	262,583	816	1,155	1,874	575	582
Mountain	219,338	164,013	3,075	52,250	55,325	1,102	1,152	2,050	891	951
Montana	45,073	33,978	462	10,633	11,095	969	1,018	1,848	777	820
Idaho	38,723	28,721	494	9,508	10,002	1,238	1,306	1,713	1,015	1,047
Wyoming	15,186	11,683	257	3,246	3,503	1,052	1,063	2,908	871	1,018
Colorado	55,151	36,002	729	18,420	19,149	1,185	1,287	2,142	992	1,032
New Mexico	27,771	21,949	287	5,535	5,822	601	608	1,846	513	575
Arizona	11,807	9,389	446	1,972	2,418	1,229	1,254	2,122	925	1,132
Utah	22,405	19,665	193	2,547	2,740	1,472	1,527	1,840	1,044	1,084
Nevada	3,222	2,626	207	389	596	1,748	1,766	2,297	1,350	1,680
Pacific	241,576	192,576	8,087	40,913	49,000	1,820	1,919	2,199	1,265	1,421
Washington	67,552	55,355	1,064	11,133	12,197	1,429	1,476	1,828	1,159	1,218
Oregon	52,620	42,822	737	9,061	9,798	1,410	1,462	1,825	1,135	1,186
California	121,404	94,399	6,286	20,719	27,005	2,215	2,396	2,305	1,381	1,594

[1] _Census, 1930_, IV, 61.

[2] _Bureau of the Census, special tabulation._

[3] _Average value of farm dwelling (Census, 1930, IV, 61) plus average value of one acre of land (Census, 1930, IV, 259-65)._

[4] _Average value of farm operator's dwelling (total value of farm operators' dwellings, Census, IV, 225-39, divided by respective number of farm operators reporting value of dwelling, cols. 2-5 above) plus average value of one acre of land (Census, 1930, IV, 259-65)._

SECTION B

Rent of Nonfarm Residential Real Estate

Of the 20 tables in section B the first 4 give estimates of aggregate annual or average monthly rent per occupied dwelling unit in 1930. The method used in deriving these estimates is described in Chapter II, section 3 c. Aggregate annual rent for all units is based on monthly rents as reported April 1, 1930, multiplied by 12, and is, therefore, the rent bill at April rates and not the actual rent bill for 1930 unless April rents were identical with the true mean rents for the year. That the April rents were at least approximately representative of the year is indicated by rent indexes for that period.

The index of rents as published by the Bureau of Labor Statistics (1913 = 100) for all reporting cities is 151.9 for December 1929, 149.6 for June 1930, and 146.5 for December 1930. Converted to a June 1930 base these index numbers become 101.5 for December 1929 and 97.9 for December 1930. A straight line interpolation between December 1929 and June 1930 would indicate that the rents for April were approximately .3 per cent higher than those for June. The rents for June were probably very close to the mean rent for the year although the sharper decline during the last six months of the year would imply that June rents were higher than the year's average. It is also possible that the number of occupied dwelling units in April may have been larger than the mean number for the year. The total 12 month rent bill at April rents and for April occupancy is probably close to the actual rent bill for 1930.

Table B 5 presents average monthly rents April 1, 1930 by rent groups for each of the 139 cities in the special tabulation of Census data (Ch. II, sec. 4). It gives also average monthly rents per dwelling unit for each city by the three principal types, 1-, 2-, and 3-or-more family dwellings, but not by rent groups. Though it was possible to present rents for each of these types of dwellings and all types combined, it was not practicable to present values (Table A 6) except for 1-family dwellings and for "all types," as explained in Chapter II, section 3 f. Table B 7 is similar to Table A 9, which shows distributions of owner-occupied 1-family dwellings by value groups (see half-title page to sec. A), except that the number of rented dwelling units could be presented for both

1930 and 1934 for all types of dwellings combined since both the census enumeration and the Real Property Inventory count were in terms of dwelling units. Comparisons of the absolute figures in Tables A 9 and B 7 must take into consideration the factors discussed in connection with Table A 9 on the half-title page to section A.

Table B 8 shows the percentage change in average annual rent per dwelling unit between 1930 and 1933 for 50 cities and is similar to Table A 10 for average values. Average annual rents for 1933 were derived from the average annual rents reported to the Financial Survey of Urban Housing classified by rent groups and weighted by the number of rented dwelling units in each rent group as reported by the Federal Real Property Inventory for the same cities. The effect of so weighting the Financial Survey reports appears from a comparison of Tables B 8 and 10. Tables B 14–18 present information concerning the frequency with which facilities are provided and their cost, which was included in the rent bill. Table B 14 presents the number of dwelling units reporting such facilities and the number and percentage having the respective types of facility as derived from a summary of data on the primary schedules from tenant families reporting in the Financial Survey.

Table B 15 gives the number of replies to a special sample mail inquiry on facility cost and the average cost thus reported for each of seven facilities after correction for bias in the sample. The method of correction assumes that the cost of facilities included in the rent for those reporting such costs varies directly with the rent bill. For example, if all dwellings reporting the cost of facilities have rents averaging 10 per cent higher than the average rent reported for the city, then the facility costs reported would also be considered 10 per cent higher than average and hence reduced in proportion.

Table B 16 presents the average cost of each facility included in rent, expressed as a dollar charge and as a percentage of the average rent per dwelling unit for the dwellings of the entire city, including those for which no such facilities are included in the rent. It is derived from Table B 15; the method is specified in the footnotes to Table B 16. Table B 17 is similar to

Table B 16, but presents the cost of all facilities by rent groups.

Table B 18 shows for 11 cities the result of applying the data on cost of facilities as obtained in the special survey by comparing the gross and net rent excluding the cost of facilities. The figures for these 11 cities are based upon the number of reports shown in the table.

The special survey referred to was made by sending questionnaires to the tenants and their landlords who had reported to the Financial Survey requesting them to report the actual or estimated cost of each facility mentioned in the Financial Survey. The replies of tenants and landlords were combined in summarizing the returns. The rents for the properties reported by landlords in the special inquiry were higher than in the Financial Survey. Hence in applying the cost data to the city average, the facility cost was adjusted in proportion to this rent differential, the facility cost having been found to vary with the rent level. The method by which the value-rent ratios in Tables B 19 and 20 are derived is explained in Chapter II, section 5 a.

TABLE B 1

Total Annual Rent (thousands of dollars) by Population Group, State, and Geographic Division, 1930

	All population groups	100,000 or more	25,000– 100,000	10,000– 25,000	5,000– 10,000	2,500– 5,000	Under 2,500
United States	4,573,098	2,787,025	652,637	348,139	190,265	130,207	464,825
New England	361,371	165,903	102,092	44,675	13,736	3,351	31,614
Maine	17,537		6,743	3,029	1,666	582	5,517
New Hampshire	12,330		5,271	3,189	650	494	2,726
Vermont	7,424			2,302	1,915	539	2,668
Massachusetts	216,546	117,471	58,414	25,024	7,263	1,032	7,342
Rhode Island	30,358	14,765	11,124	2,653	713	130	973
Connecticut	77,176	33,667	20,540	8,478	1,529	574	12,388
Mid. Atlantic	1,630,762	1,177,329	171,888	104,992	51,676	33,634	91,243
New York	1,057,109	920,971	47,470	29,795	13,217	10,957	34,699
New Jersey	230,573	93,469	72,783	29,120	14,248	6,539	14,414
Pennsylvania	343,080	162,889	51,635	46,077	24,211	16,138	42,130
E. N. Central	1,087,587	727,442	169,200	62,653	35,746	22,972	69,574
Ohio	260,566	163,067	41,648	17,569	10,637	6,464	21,181
Indiana	86,279	41,500	19,893	7,658	4,553	2,766	9,909
Illinois	455,198	345,446	55,490	18,189	11,871	6,770	17,432
Michigan	203,943	137,969	33,028	11,216	5,394	3,840	12,496
Wisconsin	81,601	39,460	19,141	8,021	3,291	3,132	8,556
W. N. Central	313,723	157,367	36,254	33,618	18,171	16,591	51,722
Minnesota	63,383	43,552		5,537	3,177	3,249	7,868
Iowa	48,875	6,968	17,028	6,710	3,071	4,605	10,493
Missouri	122,715	86,941	9,039	5,782	5,545	3,135	12,273
N. Dakota	8,528		1,645	2,238	1,370	160	3,115
S. Dakota	9,682		1,730	2,754	386	1,001	3,811
Nebraska	26,359	10,191	3,525	2,908	1,998	1,511	6,226
Kansas	34,181	9,715	3,287	7,689	2,624	2,930	7,936
S. Atlantic	322,577	132,982	63,317	23,260	17,905	13,559	71,554
Delaware	7,823	5,667				490	1,666
Maryland	49,641	35,483	3,231	1,486	664	1,239	7,538
D. C.	41,607	41,607					
Virginia	42,932	17,350	7,811	3,768	2,152	1,584	10,267
W. Virginia	35,653		12,807	3,429	2,988	2,051	14,378
N. Carolina	37,452		16,958	4,661	2,674	2,179	10,980
S. Carolina	19,306		6,754	1,848	1,789	1,260	7,655
Georgia	45,746	15,395	9,878	4,769	2,866	2,480	10,358
Florida	42,417	17,480	5,878	3,299	4,772	2,276	8,712
E. S. Central	133,468	53,203	17,765	14,106	7,850	7,862	32,682
Kentucky	42,156	15,019	9,090	2,577	3,099	2,176	10,195
Tennessee	41,223	27,130	789	1,380	2,480	1,959	7,485
Alabama	34,189	11,054	5,004	5,275	1,622	1,926	9,308
Mississippi	15,900		2,882	4,874	649	1,801	5,694
W. S. Central	231,501	98,496	31,108	23,334	17,649	14,586	46,328
Arkansas	18,354		4,380	3,972	1,568	2,451	5,983
Louisiana	44,498	24,947	6,212	1,919	1,732	2,079	7,609
Oklahoma	51,297	22,056	2,327	7,493	5,508	2,769	11,144
Texas	117,352	51,493	18,189	9,950	8,841	7,287	21,592
Mountain	90,429	22,375	14,995	10,992	9,657	6,730	25,680
Montana	12,515		4,017	2,668	1,613	558	3,659
Idaho	7,504			1,789	1,482	1,399	2,834
Wyoming	6,053			1,792	1,182	470	2,609
Colorado	29,676	16,257	3,159	2,264	1,909	824	5,263
New Mexico	6,551		1,255	813	857	907	2,719
Arizona	13,129		5,188		1,766	1,084	5,091
Utah	11,414	6,118	1,376	315	478	977	2,150
Nevada	3,587			1,351	370	511	1,355
Pacific	401,680	251,928	46,018	30,509	17,875	10,922	44,428
Washington	46,635	28,931	1,948	5,750	812	1,966	7,228
Oregon	26,895	14,478	850	2,725	2,298	1,364	5,180
California	328,150	208,519	43,220	22,034	14,765	7,592	32,020

Based on average monthly rent, April 1, 1930, occupied units only; see Part Two, Ch. II, sec. 1 c.

TABLE B 2

Occupied Rented Dwelling Units, Average Monthly Rent (dollars) by Population Group, State, and Geographic Division, 1930

	All Population Groups	100,000 or more	25,000–100,000	10,000–25,000	5,000–10,000	2,500–5,000	Under 2,500
United States	30.34	40.07	31.52	26.88	23.45	20.29	14.10
New England	29.03	32.95	31.46	26.49	21.31	19.50	19.01
Maine	20.53		28.79	22.71	18.72	17.31	15.16
New Hampshire	19.78		22.30	22.06	17.43	18.77	15.25
Vermont	19.39			26.58	22.19	20.98	14.48
Massachusetts	31.52	33.32	34.47	28.15	21.68	19.58	19.74
Rhode Island	26.15	29.62	26.40	19.77	18.16	22.75	15.75
Connecticut	30.20	33.31	31.19	28.38	26.49	20.65	24.65
Mid. Atlantic	39.66	46.00	37.76	32.55	30.90	27.55	18.79
New York	45.26	48.73	36.67	31.16	37.75	29.19	23.39
New Jersey	38.20	38.49	42.61	40.68	36.31	31.94	24.58
Pennsylvania	29.26	38.17	33.33	29.66	26.04	25.19	15.12
E. N. Central	35.19	42.99	35.46	28.95	23.66	22.00	15.47
Ohio	31.03	35.42	36.72	27.14	23.83	23.60	16.41
Indiana	24.78	32.59	27.73	22.74	18.62	17.22	13.22
Illinois	41.30	48.59	38.70	31.92	26.49	21.98	15.15
Michigan	38.06	46.71	36.96	30.87	23.22	24.21	16.51
Wisconsin	30.78	40.27	32.32	32.49	23.59	21.91	15.56
W. N. Central	25.60	33.50	28.88	26.64	24.32	20.41	14.87
Minnesota	28.40	34.22		28.09	23.55	22.57	16.29
Iowa	23.23	31.52	28.55	27.76	23.10	21.03	15.15
Missouri	28.10	34.39	28.04	25.43	25.69	17.52	13.73
North Dakota	23.52		37.11	34.55	29.16	25.29	15.56
South Dakota	22.18		32.99	30.02	22.33	25.20	16.19
Nebraska	24.26	32.27	31.61	26.83	24.26	20.74	15.75
Kansas	20.52	26.97	25.60	23.24	22.45	19.25	13.75
S. Atlantic	19.12	32.41	22.24	18.91	18.49	15.05	10.49
Delaware	27.18	34.02				19.81	17.26
Maryland	26.68	31.55	27.12	24.93	21.77	19.69	16.26
Dist. of Columbia	45.19	45.19					
Virginia	18.91	28.05	20.47	22.94	20.00	16.59	11.37
West Virginia	16.46		29.53	26.91	24.40	22.90	10.32
North Carolina	15.14		23.09	16.17	16.29	14.41	9.67
South Carolina	11.94		18.61	15.70	13.38	12.01	8.52
Georgia	15.40	26.53	17.49	15.66	13.87	11.38	9.44
Florida	18.42	25.26	23.46	19.62	23.47	14.76	10.44
E. S. Central	15.69	23.46	22.19	16.00	15.29	13.62	9.43
Kentucky	17.48	26.41	25.13	18.14	17.50	15.49	9.98
Tennessee	17.31	22.84	22.39	17.69	14.86	13.44	9.75
Alabama	13.59	21.62	19.06	15.01	12.79	11.95	8.44
Mississippi	13.28		20.43	15.72	15.22	13.87	9.92
W. S. Central	19.64	28.18	23.62	20.92	18.28	16.13	11.62
Arkansas	14.37		22.99	19.91	16.34	13.83	9.75
Louisiana	18.88	25.53	24.46	16.84	14.88	13.26	10.31
Oklahoma	22.06	35.63	24.31	25.22	20.61	17.07	12.60
Texas	20.15	27.11	23.42	19.71	18.19	17.86	12.34
Mountain	21.94	30.97	29.91	28.03	23.23	21.46	14.45
Montana	22.47		31.36	27.60	26.39	22.12	14.89
Idaho	19.01			28.33	23.90	21.24	13.91
Wyoming	21.04			28.44	26.35	25.52	16.16
Colorado	23.91	31.52	25.75	24.91	21.67	18.60	13.88
New Mexico	16.99		29.88	25.47	21.75	20.15	11.96
Arizona	21.70		33.61		21.67	23.17	15.80
Utah	22.74	29.61	25.41	23.12	19.03	20.08	13.99
Nevada	23.98			41.07	27.14	26.39	16.19
Pacific	31.64	37.46	32.52	30.67	26.41	23.10	18.44
Washington	25.40	32.50	24.16	26.34	19.80	20.88	14.12
Oregon	23.56	30.74	25.52	28.46	23.74	20.03	13.75
California	33.77	38.87	33.22	32.37	27.39	24.45	21.06

Source: Based on aggregate rents as shown in Table B 1 and number of occupied units. The number of rented dwelling units in table A 1 includes vacant units and was not used in deriving this table. The number of occupied rented units is not shown, but their relative importance is indicated in Part Two, Ch. II, sec. 2c.

TABLE B 3

Total Annual Rent (thousands of dollars) by Population Group, Geographic Division, and Type, 1930

	All population groups	100,000 and over	25,000– 100,000	10,000– 25,000	5,000– 10,000	2,500– 5,000	Under 2,500
United States							
All types	4,573,098	2,787,025	652,636	348,138	190,265	130,207	464,827
1-family	1,906,321	745,046	331,555	221,159	135,283	99,628	373,650
2-family	871,847	530,472	148,083	70,159	32,046	19,562	71,525
3-or-more family	1,794,930	1,511,507	172,998	56,820	22,936	11,017	19,652
New England							
All types	361,371	165,903	102,092	44,675	13,736	3,351	31,614
1-family	112,705	29,817	31,161	20,757	7,644	2,248	21,078
2-family	109,284	47,345	34,406	14,878	3,871	732	8,052
3-or-more family	139,382	88,741	36,525	9,040	2,221	371	2,484
Mid. Atlantic							
All types	1,630,762	1,177,329	171,888	104,992	51,676	33,634	91,243
1-family	427,174	169,983	65,903	60,258	32,894	24,356	73,780
2-family	290,284	189,699	45,033	24,992	10,928	6,027	13,605
3-or-more family	913,304	817,647	60,952	19,742	7,854	3,251	3,858
E. N. Central							
All types	1,087,587	727,442	169,200	62,652	35,746	22,972	69,575
1-family	423,217	181,200	95,129	42,508	27,528	17,856	58,996
2-family	255,523	187,120	37,991	12,372	5,564	3,681	8,795
3-or-more family	408,847	359,122	36,080	7,772	2,654	1,435	1,784
W. N. Central							
All types	313,723	157,367	36,253	33,618	18,171	16,591	51,723
1-family	175,968	61,056	24,534	22,902	12,673	13,223	41,580
2-family	61,297	39,320	4,344	4,663	2,811	1,932	8,227
3-or-more family	76,458	56,991	7,375	6,053	2,687	1,436	1,916
S. Atlantic							
All types	322,577	132,982	63,317	23,260	17,905	13,559	71,554
1-family	205,221	62,916	41,557	17,370	13,107	10,754	59,517
2-family	55,410	25,601	11,514	3,810	2,831	1,911	9,743
3-or-more family	61,946	44,465	10,246	2,080	1,967	894	2,294
E. S. Central							
All types	133,468	53,203	17,765	14,106	7,850	7,862	32,682
1-family	87,850	31,723	10,548	10,237	5,740	5,837	23,765
2-family	26,477	9,146	4,273	2,553	1,452	1,450	7,603
3-or-more family	19,141	12,334	2,944	1,316	658	575	1,314
W. S. Central							
All types	231,501	98,496	31,108	23,334	17,649	14,586	46,328
1-family	160,600	62,592	20,957	17,143	13,718	11,333	34,857
2-family	35,696	13,518	5,053	3,413	2,345	2,182	9,185
3-or-more family	35,205	22,386	5,098	2,778	1,586	1,071	2,286
Mountain							
All types	90,429	22,375	14,995	10,992	9,657	6,730	25,680
1-family	62,315	11,996	9,970	7,279	7,324	5,084	20,662
2-family	9,637	1,891	1,532	1,227	996	819	3,172
3-or-more family	18,477	8,488	3,493	2,486	1,337	827	1,846
Pacific							
All types	401,680	251,928	46,018	30,509	17,875	10,922	44,428
1-family	251,271	133,763	31,796	22,705	14,655	8,937	39,415
2-family	28,239	16,832	3,937	2,251	1,248	828	3,143
3-or-more family	122,170	101,333	10,285	5,553	1,972	1,157	1,870

Based on average monthly rent, April 1, 1930, occupied units only; see Part Two, Ch. II, sec. 1 c.

TABLE B 4

Rented Dwelling Units, Average Monthly Rent (dollars) by Population Group, Geographic Division, and Type, April 1, 1930

	All population groups	100,000 and over	25,000– 100,000	10,000– 25,000	5,000– 10,000	2,500– 5,000	Under 2,500
United States							
All types	30.34	40.07	31.52	26.88	23.45	20.29	14.10
1-family	24.15	34.01	29.91	26.17	22.93	19.92	14.04
2-family	27.84	33.73	29.26	25.16	22.21	19.50	13.51
3-or-more family	44.38	47.34	37.95	33.19	29.72	26.56	18.66
New England							
All types	29.03	32.95	31.46	26.49	21.31	19.50	19.01
1-family	27.94	35.75	33.75	28.02	22.27	20.07	19.52
2-family	27.20	30.38	29.35	24.66	19.82	18.26	17.96
3-or-more family	31.71	33.58	31.77	26.40	20.95	18.78	18.42
Mid. Atlantic							
All types	39.66	46.00	37.76	32.55	30.90	27.55	18.79
1-family	31.43	40.55	37.80	32.94	31.20	27.75	18.94
2-family	32.37	35.63	32.89	29.01	27.77	25.24	17.42
3-or-more family	49.21	50.85	42.34	36.92	34.98	31.15	21.50
E. N. Central							
All types	35.19	42.99	35.46	28.95	23.66	22.00	15.47
1-family	29.01	40.03	34.57	28.57	23.43	21.80	15.40
2-family	33.77	37.62	32.84	27.44	22.96	21.59	15.40
3-or-more family	46.71	48.40	41.81	34.48	28.36	26.28	18.70
W. N. Central							
All types	25.60	33.50	28.88	26.64	24.32	20.41	14.87
1-family	22.56	30.82	27.49	25.52	23.44	19.97	14.72
2-family	24.60	28.98	26.14	24.51	22.98	19.78	14.72
3-or-more family	38.96	41.92	37.50	34.73	31.92	27.06	20.23
S. Atlantic							
All types	19.12	32.41	22.24	18.91	18.49	15.05	10.49
1-family	16.68	28.97	21.13	18.38	17.80	14.71	10.35
2-family	19.20	28.13	20.70	18.19	17.80	14.84	10.56
3-or-more family	36.81	43.54	31.62	27.54	26.96	21.75	15.49
E. S. Central							
All types	15.69	23.46	22.19	16.00	15.29	13.62	9.43
1-family	14.62	21.77	21.08	15.53	14.86	13.27	9.26
2-family	14.58	21.12	20.66	15.37	14.86	13.38	9.45
3-or-more family	28.13	32.67	31.53	23.36	22.36	19.84	13.86
W. S. Central							
All types	19.64	28.18	23.62	20.92	18.28	16.13	11.62
1-family	18.38	26.18	22.41	20.13	17.73	15.71	11.38
2-family	17.89	25.39	21.96	19.92	17.73	15.86	11.61
3-or-more family	33.41	39.14	33.59	30.05	26.65	23.63	17.22
Mountain							
All types	21.94	30.97	29.91	28.03	23.23	21.46	14.45
1-family	20.41	28.40	28.56	26.79	22.65	20.99	14.30
2-family	18.81	25.00	25.42	24.10	20.84	19.53	13.45
3-or-more family	33.21	37.82	37.98	35.76	30.00	28.06	19.14
Pacific							
All types	31.64	37.46	32.52	30.67	26.41	23.10	18.44
1-family	28.44	34.05	31.06	29.53	25.88	22.61	18.33
2-family	26.56	29.96	27.65	26.59	23.76	21.04	17.22
3-or-more family	43.68	45.34	41.31	39.32	34.63	30.30	24.44

Based on aggregate rents as shown in Table B 3 and number of occupied rented units. The number of rented dwelling units in Table A 5 includes vacant units and was not used in deriving this table.

TABLE B 5

Rented Dwelling Units, Average Monthly Rent, All Types combined, by Rent Groups; All Rent Groups combined, by Type, 139 Cities, Towns, and Villages in Descending Order of Population by Geographic Division, April 1, 1930

	POPU-LATION 1930	All rent groups	Under $10	$10.-14.99	$15.-19.99	$20.-29.99	$30.-49.99	$50.-74.99	$75.-99.99	$100.-149.99	$150.-199.99	$200 and over	1-family	2-family	3-or-more family
New England															
Providence, R.I.[1]	252,981	$29.60	$7.48	$12.07	$16.52	$23.31	$35.62	$57.22	$80.06	$114.33	$161.82	$269.67	$36.43	$25.43	$27.15
Worcester, Mass.[1]	195,311	30.61	6.83	11.78	16.63	24.05	35.25	56.66	79.49	108.64	168.33		32.56	30.20	30.35
Waterbury, Conn.[1]	99,902	30.64	7.83	12.03	16.58	23.98	35.43	56.39	79.69	106.86	160.00		34.32	29.20	29.02
Portland, Me.[1]	70,810	31.73	7.21	11.99	16.21	23.46	36.92	54.64	79.28	113.70		250.00	31.64	29.00	34.39
Nashua, N.H.	31,463	23.01	7.20	11.89	16.81	23.36	34.87	52.94	78.50	100.00			23.01	20.22	24.55
Central Falls, R.I.	25,898	22.82	7.56	12.51	16.65	23.31	33.57	54.32	80.00	100.00			24.42	22.93	22.05
Burlington, Vt.	24,789	26.59	6.99	11.98	16.42	22.88	35.46	55.06	77.30	101.00	150.00		27.66	25.46	25.39
Greenwich, Conn.	5,981	79.86		12.00	15.00	24.60	37.69	56.30	78.94	115.24	165.08	274.04	103.87	60.81	67.40
Orange, Mass.	5,365	17.80	6.82	12.10	16.39	22.36	33.17	50.00	75.00	100.00	150.00		18.58	16.58	17.35
Pittsfield, Me.	2,075	15.37	6.53	11.36	15.99	22.22	33.13						15.32	14.72	20.69
Mid. Atlantic															
Syracuse, N.Y.[1]	209,326	38.60	6.33	11.52	16.40	23.67	37.36	56.51	79.91	109.83	155.00	221.00	40.66	34.31	40.97
Trenton, N.J.[1]	123,356	32.39	7.46	11.75	16.54	23.40	35.80	55.83	79.41	106.65	163.67	222.73	31.23	31.23	44.64
Erie, Pa.[1]	115,967	31.16	7.00	12.13	16.58	23.80	35.71	55.47	82.37	100.63	150.00	200.00	33.21	26.18	34.11
Binghamton, N.Y.	76,662	33.40	6.67	11.78	16.41	23.71	36.36	55.35	79.53	111.84	169.88	235.00	35.49	30.85	34.94
Williamsport, Pa.	45,729	30.02	7.00	12.01	16.45	23.47	35.67	54.69	77.93	105.00	160.83	200.00	29.18	30.68	34.76
Carbondale, Pa.	20,061	28.29	6.92	11.32	16.01	23.16	34.86	53.77	81.25	100.00	175.00	200.00	29.73	26.23	26.98
Peekskill, N.Y.	17,125	35.30	7.18	11.99	16.18	23.27	36.18	56.07	81.39	106.67	150.00	230.67	38.72	32.03	34.84
Latrobe, Pa.	10,644	27.40	6.69	11.53	15.96	22.84	35.34	55.59	83.00	120.00			27.18	24.34	32.30
Corry, Pa.	7,152	20.88	6.10	11.28	16.25	22.67	34.34	53.75				200.00	21.17	19.95	20.08
Dansville, N.Y.	4,928	25.29	6.00	11.39	16.18	23.40	33.26	58.90	80.00				26.49	23.12	20.00
Hoosick Falls, N.Y.	4,755	15.66	7.70	11.72	15.98	22.69	35.26	50.00					16.80	14.62	15.27
Canton, N.Y.	2,822	25.39	5.71	11.00	16.04	22.83	35.19	53.67	80.00	120.00			26.75	21.41	23.17
E. N. Central															
Cleveland, Ohio[1]	900,429	36.44	7.20	11.66	16.38	23.70	37.01	55.19	80.78	113.07	155.38	285.22	38.14	31.73	39.15
Indianapolis, Ind.[1]	364,161	31.02	7.28	11.70	16.43	23.12	36.44	56.79	81.26	111.19	164.27	263.33	27.54	27.48	46.93
Peoria, Ill.	104,969	33.80	5.36	11.80	16.43	23.15	36.83	56.59	79.52	111.31	154.69	335.42	31.19	33.92	41.92
Lansing, Mich.[1]	78,397	37.82	7.00	11.17	16.31	23.51	36.84	55.09	78.16	112.70	150.00		37.46	33.95	45.13
Racine, Wis.[1]	67,542	35.23		11.59	16.19	23.41	36.70	56.42	78.93	111.67		250.00	35.31	31.78	43.90
Decatur, Ill.[1]	57,510	28.53	6.93	11.32	15.91	22.82	34.88	55.21	75.77	100.00			27.86	27.08	35.11
Kenosha, Wis.[1]	50,262	33.55	8.00	11.45	16.06	23.77	36.21	55.57	81.83	110.00	150.00		36.31	29.19	40.15
Portsmouth, Ohio	42,560	25.94	6.77	11.38	16.06	22.95	35.24	55.22	77.45	112.14	150.00		27.54	22.38	23.49
La Crosse, Wis.	39,614	26.49	6.86	11.67	16.39	23.07	35.85	54.88	77.32	105.00	150.00		27.37	24.08	25.91
Findlay, Ohio	19,363	23.13	6.71	11.22	16.00	22.76	35.29	53.22	80.00	100.00			24.06	22.77	17.78
Macomb, Ill.	8,509	24.02	6.08	11.40	15.96	22.63	36.03	52.33	78.33				24.09	22.22	26.01
Valparaiso, Ind.	8,079	32.89	6.57	10.90	16.24	23.26	36.62	54.58	75.00	100.00	163.75		29.54	30.63	47.34
Ionia, Mich.	6,562	22.21	6.69	11.28	16.01	23.10	33.25	52.83					23.04	21.33	16.81
West Bend, Wis.	4,760	28.59	6.50	11.25	15.88	23.29	36.01	56.18	80.00	130.00			30.70	24.51	29.20
Barnesville, Ohio	4,602	16.57	6.24	11.19	15.82	22.21	32.31	50.00				250.00	17.47	13.39	13.50
Vandalia, Ill.	4,342	19.42	6.13	11.09	15.71	22.62	33.70	55.00	75.00				20.00	17.06	18.48
Mitchell, Ind.	3,226	12.03	6.38	11.01	15.64	21.92	32.27	50.00					12.31	8.78	
Crystal Falls, Mich.	2,995	17.53	5.48	10.65	15.45	22.98	34.08	57.00		125.00		400.00	18.92	9.89	18.25
Franklin Park, Ill.	2,425	36.46	9.00	11.33	15.43	23.98	37.26	53.11	75.00				36.24	36.58	37.70
W. N. Central															
Minneapolis, Minn.[1]	464,356	36.40	6.59	11.75	16.30	23.40	37.40	56.75	80.06	112.14	157.75	251.71	35.26	30.21	43.06
St. Paul, Minn.[1]	271,606	32.59	6.45	11.43	16.26	23.20	37.06	55.51	79.97	109.25	154.17	241.67	32.34	26.46	39.11
Des Moines, Iowa[1]	142,559	31.40	6.50	11.04	15.94	23.18	36.21	56.88	79.49	115.27	164.67	200.00	28.12	28.86	42.74
Wichita, Kan.[1]	111,110	30.94	6.09	11.48	16.24	23.19	36.04	56.23	78.97	100.00	150.00		29.80	28.45	36.46
St. Joseph, Mo.[1]	80,935	24.22	6.78	11.48	16.15	22.54	35.27	54.94	77.14	103.33			22.62	24.89	36.76
Lincoln, Neb.[1]	75,933	31.97	6.59	11.30	16.00	23.25	36.56	55.70	78.35	102.75	155.00		30.48	30.51	37.29
Topeka, Kan.[1]	64,120	27.75	6.49	11.12	15.97	23.06	36.46	54.99	82.95	100.00			25.36	28.26	40.23
Springfield, Mo.	57,527	20.45	6.65	11.24	16.09	22.38	36.34	54.73	77.83	101.00			19.82	18.21	27.20
Sioux Falls, S.D.	33,362	33.01	6.59	11.15	15.89	23.03	36.85	54.89	77.37	101.33		200.00	32.60	31.24	36.12
Fargo, N.D.[1]	28,619	39.10	6.50	11.06	15.80	23.46	38.69	55.85	81.00	110.00			40.25	33.21	40.13
S. St. Paul, Minn.	10,009	25.93	6.95	11.52	16.10	22.85	37.30	56.54	78.50	125.00	150.00		26.83	21.74	31.15
Abilene, Kan.	5,658	26.15	7.25	11.00	15.94	22.63	35.80	51.32					25.92	28.06	25.51
Chariton, Iowa	5,365	19.20	6.38	11.29	16.01	22.65	35.53	50.40	75.00				19.17	18.81	19.88
Richmond, Mo.	4,129	12.34	6.34	10.82	15.75	22.29	33.13						12.43	11.97	9.30
Alexandria, Minn.	3,876	21.95	6.89	11.55	16.13	22.80	35.27	51.15		100.00			21.02	19.13	32.37
Gering, Neb.	2,531	24.55	6.22	10.53	15.46	23.13	34.53	55.00					21.71	20.73	17.89
Forest City, Iowa	2,016	23.63	6.92	11.48	15.68	22.88	34.48	50.00		110.00	150.00		23.67	24.62	22.03
St. Paul, Neb.	1,621	17.37	6.20	11.48	16.07	23.11	32.57	50.00					16.77	26.11	
Wilton, N.D.	1,001	15.87	6.71	10.77	15.33	22.69	30.83	50.00					15.99	13.86	17.50
Belle Plaine, Kan.	825	15.01	5.62	10.76	15.73	24.10	32.08						15.01		
Avon, S.D.	670	18.17	5.67	11.13	15.60	21.50	36.25	50.00		100.00			19.74	9.43	15.00
S. Atlantic															
Atlanta, Ga.[1]	270,366	25.63	6.64	11.55	16.11	23.04	36.55	57.24	78.92	111.31	153.75	272.50	23.80	20.60	34.59
Richmond, Va.[1]	182,929	27.55	7.10	11.33	15.90	22.98	36.35	57.53	79.90	110.70	164.10	287.50	24.31	23.26	42.65
Jacksonville, Fla.[1]	129,549	25.66	6.98	11.62	16.27	22.81	36.14	55.28	78.84	103.67	158.33	225.00	24.28	26.70	35.48
Charleston, S.C.[1]	62,265	16.43	5.64	11.01	15.93	23.26	35.57	54.59	77.14	108.33	150.00		21.24	17.09	9.65
Wheeling, W.Va.[1]	61,659	31.12	7.10	11.51	16.18	22.92	35.28	55.33	78.88	108.32	150.00	250.00	32.88	26.12	35.93
Greensboro, N.C.[1]	53,569	24.84	4.85	11.68	16.02	22.57	35.68	56.37	79.60	107.50	175.00		22.95	26.13	41.41
Columbia, S.C.[1]	51,581	20.06	6.54	11.11	15.72	22.84	35.79	56.38	76.55	112.50	150.00		20.05	19.96	20.37
Asheville, N.C.[1]	50,193	25.52	6.60	11.23	15.80	22.48	35.52	54.27	78.52	108.00	150.00	200.00	26.00	20.76	29.75
Wilmington, N.C.	32,270	17.19	6.54	10.97	15.56	22.58	35.61	53.99	79.22	101.67	156.25		16.16	19.24	24.51
Hagerstown, Md.	30,861	25.89	7.09	12.05	16.47	23.15	35.22	54.91	77.33	110.00	151.00		23.81	28.21	35.04
Martinsburg, W.Va.	14,857	21.56	6.35	11.24	16.23	22.96	33.94	51.70	75.00				21.05	21.20	27.52
Frederick, Md.[1]	14,434	20.93	6.75	11.37	16.45	22.97	35.81	55.88					19.74	24.43	26.40
Tallahassee, Fla.	10,700	22.54	6.00	10.98	15.81	23.01	36.45	55.66	76.72	105.00	163.00	212.50	22.71	18.24	32.94
Richwood, W.Va.	5,720	14.94	6.85	11.37	15.76	21.69	33.22	51.79	75.00				14.77	15.92	15.30
Milledgeville, Ga.	5,534	12.87	4.34	10.98	15.88	23.02	34.70	54.43	75.00				13.01	10.95	17.81
Franklin, Va.	2,930	15.29	5.62	10.54	15.51	23.50	33.10	55.00					14.11	16.21	28.63
Calhoun, Ga.	2,371	12.21	6.61	10.88	15.58	22.23	30.92			100.00			12.91	9.33	9.46
Jesup, Ga.	2,303	13.64	5.54	10.73	15.72	22.79	31.89						13.49	14.39	13.60
Chesterfield, S.C.	1,030	11.09	4.01	10.71	15.40	22.89	33.00		90.00				11.29	10.13	
Boca Raton, Fla.	447	12.81	7.65	10.00	15.00	23.80	35.00	50.00					12.80	17.50	10.00
Odessa, Del.	385	13.95	5.72	10.82	15.75	22.00					150.00		14.18	11.00	
Wilson Mills, N.C.	359	5.26	4.11	10.67		20.00							5.26		

TABLE B 5 (Cont'd)

Rented Dwelling Units, Average Monthly Rent, All Types combined, by Rent Groups; All Rent Groups combined, by Type, 139 Cities, Towns, and Villages in Descending Order of Population by Geographic Division, April 1, 1930

	Population 1930	All rent groups	Under $10	$10.-14.99	$15.-19.99	$20.-29.99	$30.-49.99	$50.-74.99	$75.-99.99	$100.-149.99	$150.-199.99	$200 and over	1-family	2-family	3-or-more family
E. S. Central															
Birmingham, Ala.[1]	259,678	21.53	7.26	11.27	15.79	22.82	35.82	56.19	80.18	110.69	159.17	200.00	19.69	18.40	39.16
Knoxville, Tenn.[1]	105,802	23.42	6.81	11.68	16.12	22.49	36.12	55.61	78.89	109.25	150.00		22.46	19.67	35.53
Jackson, Miss.[1]	48,282	24.70	6.86	11.80	16.13	22.71	36.32	54.24	78.28	104.58			23.41	26.27	32.98
Paducah, Ky.[1]	33,541	18.19	6.91	11.43	16.06	22.79	35.26	54.93	78.00	100.00			16.63	18.78	35.08
Johnson City, Tenn.	25,080	22.13	6.04	11.18	15.63	22.56	35.22	55.72	76.40	104.38		250.00	20.29	21.22	32.33
Paris, Tenn.	8,164	16.91	6.06	10.75	15.60	22.62	34.70	51.38	82.50	112.50			16.22	16.66	27.12
Somerset, Ky.	5,506	14.92	5.83	11.00	15.66	22.50	34.60	50.00	80.00				14.79	12.51	25.72
Andalusia, Ala.	5,154	13.17	5.73	10.87	15.60	22.47	34.63	56.71					13.34	12.60	11.52
Carbon Hill, Ala.	2,519	10.85	5.78	10.37	15.67	22.53	30.00	50.00	75.00	100.00	150.00		11.44	7.32	6.00
Durant, Miss.	2,480	13.89	6.95	10.18	15.00	22.49	33.67	50.00					11.76	16.92	26.18
Woodbury, Tenn.	502	8.14	5.14	11.09	15.00	20.67							8.35	6.88	
W. S. Central															
Dallas, Texas[1]	260,475	29.80	6.78	11.46	16.16	23.26	35.75	55.72	79.30	112.71	161.63	247.00	28.70	25.21	41.72
Oklahoma City, Okla.[1]	185,389	34.22	5.86	11.37	15.93	23.26	36.50	55.76	80.62	105.11	157.14	295.00	34.18	32.18	36.10
Little Rock, Ark.[1]	81,679	26.00	6.56	11.17	15.96	23.02	35.82	55.09	82.96	108.33	180.00		24.03	27.26	35.81
Shreveport, La.[1]	76,655	25.02	6.53	11.88	16.20	23.02	35.84	55.39	77.60	101.11			24.02	26.65	32.67
Austin, Tex.	53,120	23.33	6.53	11.21	16.04	23.09	36.01	55.41	78.25	105.43	155.00	262.50	23.28	21.08	27.26
Wichita Falls, Tex.[1]	43,690	23.65	5.86	11.21	15.58	22.64	35.18	55.87	77.73	100.50			22.82	24.19	33.10
Baton Rouge, La.	30,729	25.52	7.49	11.23	15.77	23.23	36.08	54.66	78.54	100.00	161.00	275.00	25.00	26.02	34.55
Greenville, Tex.	12,407	14.46	6.44	10.81	15.66	22.15	34.88	54.29	76.25	100.00			14.32	13.48	20.65
Hope, Ark.	6,008	16.05	6.83	11.15	15.82	22.41	33.12	56.63	83.33	100.00	150.00		15.37	17.94	18.77
Conway, Ark.	5,534	16.52	5.90	10.98	15.67	22.68	33.40	52.50	90.00				16.71	15.63	15.43
Chandler, Okla.	2,717	19.22	6.40	11.14	15.43	22.78	32.97	57.50	80.00				19.11	21.11	23.00
Vivian, La.	1,646	14.36	5.72	11.12	15.32	22.77	32.91	50.00					14.07	14.93	21.20
Lockney, Tex.	1,466	18.56	7.44	11.00	15.64	23.09	31.50	50.00	75.00				19.46	17.35	18.00
Mountain															
Salt Lake City, Utah[1]	140,267	28.67	6.28	11.41	16.15	22.86	36.58	55.75	82.00	111.25	151.40		24.87	22.58	38.32
Pueblo, Colo.[1]	50,096	25.23	6.26	11.46	16.05	23.03	35.73	56.48	80.00	115.00	158.33		26.07	21.62	24.54
Phoenix, Ariz.[1]	48,118	34.25	6.71	11.36	15.92	23.27	36.52	55.71	79.54	106.14	175.00	311.00	36.34	26.37	31.99
Butte, Mont.[1]	39,532	28.30	6.73	11.65	16.48	23.17	34.99	56.50	80.65	100.00	151.25	253.33	27.04	29.71	32.01
Albuquerque, N.M.[1]	26,570	29.52	5.36	11.35	16.12	23.75	37.05	54.78	77.08	100.00	175.00		30.92	19.23	28.31
Boise, Idaho[1]	21,544	27.46	5.61	11.27	15.97	23.31	36.14	54.08	80.71	100.00	150.00		27.69	25.01	28.04
Reno, Nev.[1]	18,529	43.13	6.64	10.79	15.91	23.67	37.11	57.20	77.42	107.26	150.00	307.14	39.09	36.13	58.03
Casper, Wyo.	16,619	25.48	6.39	11.06	16.02	22.94	35.51	55.01	77.50	103.57			25.23	24.08	27.54
Bozeman, Mont.	6,855	29.09	5.60	11.45	15.61	23.04	37.09	54.34	75.00	110.00		250.00	27.74	28.59	32.76
Salida, Colo.	5,065	20.60	5.81	11.14	16.33	23.21	33.36	55.00	75.00				20.92	16.95	22.78
Roundup, Mont.	2,577	21.40	7.05	11.02	15.63	22.50	33.54	60.00	75.00				20.64	25.63	29.53
Bountiful, Utah	2,571	14.92	6.22	10.82	15.59	22.16	34.17	65.00					14.67	14.17	24.50
Gooding, Idaho	1,592	17.55	6.21	10.86	15.77	23.56	32.89	60.00					17.65	13.25	19.08
Salina, Utah	1,383	14.44	5.56	10.74	15.05	21.87	35.25		75.00				14.23	15.29	16.67
Florence, Ariz.	1,318	15.48	5.91	10.46	16.06	22.42	33.78	50.00					15.56	15.15	14.67
Lovelock, Nev.	1,263	17.36	4.95	10.28	15.49	23.23	32.08		75.00	100.00			17.43	5.00	
Los Lunas, N.M.	513	10.93	4.83	10.83	15.67	22.50	40.00			100.00			11.15	7.00	
Pacific															
Seattle, Wash.[1]	365,583	35.08	5.99	11.31	16.23	23.29	36.96	56.51	81.27	110.67	163.75	337.13	30.26	27.10	43.22
Portland, Ore.[1]	301,815	29.77	6.71	11.32	16.09	23.16	35.95	55.32	79.85	110.69	163.89	360.00	27.19	25.11	36.20
San Diego, Calif.[1]	147,995	31.33	6.28	10.87	16.15	23.39	35.38	55.71	79.78	116.43	164.38	325.00	30.92	24.96	36.73
Sacramento, Calif.[1]	93,750	33.20	6.89	11.23	16.19	23.62	35.89	55.44	79.11	105.71	154.50	324.00	33.15	29.03	35.88
Santa Barbara, Calif.	33,613	36.60	6.63	11.28	16.06	23.65	36.28	55.44	78.77	108.43	159.33	347.73	36.81	30.64	38.82
Vancouver, Wash.	15,766	21.30	6.02	11.14	16.06	22.84	35.04	54.22	77.50	110.00			20.36	20.73	25.31
Modesto, Calif.	13,842	28.65	6.74	10.86	16.33	23.72	35.22	55.03	79.55	100.00	150.00	243.75	28.25	27.03	32.28
Oregon City, Ore.	5,761	17.91	6.28	11.31	15.86	22.47	35.67	55.00	75.00				16.96	15.74	25.00
Porterville, Calif.	5,303	21.29	6.11	11.31	15.86	22.81	34.94	52.00	77.50	102.50	150.00		21.23	22.30	21.10
Ashland, Ore.	4,544	18.98	6.03	11.19	15.72	22.61	33.18	56.00					18.96	19.69	18.64
Burns, Ore.	2,599	22.71	5.29	10.87	16.23	22.53	35.47	53.18	78.40				23.01	22.43	18.43
N. Sacramento, Calif.	2,097	25.20	5.00	11.41	15.94	23.23	34.61	54.00				250.00	25.33	24.80	22.44
Grandview, Wash.	1,085	18.77	6.06	11.07	15.70	22.77	33.24			125.00			18.77	18.67	
Marcus, Wash.	583	10.56	5.97	10.72	15.00	20.00	32.50	50.00					10.56		

Source: Special Census tabulation

[1] Average rents derived from sampling of complete Census data by population group:
  Cities 100,000 or more population and Wheeling, W.Va., every 9th dwelling unit.
  Cities 50,000-100,000 population, every 7th dwelling unit.
  Cities 25,000-50,000   "   ,   " 6th dwelling unit.
  Cities under 25,000   "   ,   " 4th dwelling unit.
The other 90 cities, towns, and villages listed in this table and not carrying this footnote had full coverage.

TABLE B 6

Rented Dwelling Units, All Types combined, by Rent Groups; All Rent Groups combined, by Type, 25 Urban places with populations under 2,500, by Geographic Division, April 1, 1930

| | | | | ALL | TYPES | | | | | | ALL RENT GROUPS BY TYPE | | |
	All rent groups	Under $10	$10-14.99	$15-19.99	$20-29.99	$30-49.99	$50-74.99	$75-99.99	$100-149.99	$150-199.99	$200 and over	1-family	2-family	3-or-more family
New England														
Pittsfield, Me.	278	32	94	75	69	8						173	92	13
E. N. Central														
Franklin Park, Ill.	205	1	3	7	41	114	38	1				135	50	20
W. N. Central														
Forest City, Iowa	193	12	27	31	66	54	1		1	1		122	42	29
Wilton, N.D.	100	17	26	24	26	6	1					91	7	2
Avon, S.D.	52	6	15	15	10	4	1		1			43	7	2
St. Paul, Neb.	139	30	29	28	28	23	1					130	9	
Belle Plaine, Kan.	79	21	25	11	10	12						79		
S. Atlantic														
Odessa, Del.	42	18	11	8	4					1		39	3	
Wilson Mills, N.C.	31	27	3		1							31		
Chesterfield, S.C.	129	68	17	20	18	5		1				106	23	
Calhoun, Ga.	343	161	73	43	52	13			1			275	55	13
Jesup, Ga.	298	119	55	36	61	27						242	51	5
Boca Raton, Fla.	95	26	36	20	10	2	1					90	2	3
E. S. Central														
Woodbury, Tenn.	57	37	11	6	3							49	8	
Durant, Miss.	353	150	71	26	75	30	1					238	98	17
W. S. Central														
Vivian, La.	212	74	33	37	56	11	1					177	30	5
Lockney, Tex.	150	9	22	50	56	10	2	1				127	17	6
Mountain														
Gooding, Idaho	177	19	50	39	50	18	1					157	8	12
Los Lunas, N.M.	55	30	12	9	2	1			1			52	3	
Florence, Ariz.	197	67	37	17	52	23	1					164	27	6
Salina, Utah.	105	25	35	21	15	8		1				88	14	3
Lovelock, Nev.	201	42	36	37	60	24		1	1			200	1	
Pacific														
Marcus, Wash.	96	39	36	16	2	2	1					96		
N. Sacramento, Calif.	231	5	17	34	115	54	5				1	217	5	9
Grandview, Wash.	137	18	27	30	44	17			1			131	6	

Source: *Special Census tabulation of 139 cities for NBER, full coverage.*

TABLE B 7

Rented Dwelling Units, Number and Percentage Distribution by Monthly Rent Groups, 61 Cities by Geographic Division, 1930 and 1934

← ———————————————————————————————— N U M B E R ————————————————————————————————

	All rent groups		Under $15		$15-29		$30-49		$50-99		$100 and over	
	1930	1934	1930	1934	1930	1934	1930	1934	1930	1934	1930	1934
61 cities	1,200,525	1,273,160	195,381	420,416	452,315	571,335	375,785	231,302	163,441	47,182	13,603	2,925
6 New England cities	154,402	157,950	18,156	31,099	79,323	93,378	44,481	27,655	11,374	5,474	1,068	344
Portland, Me.	10,805	11,340	825	1,508	4,474	5,859	4,098	3,365	1,335	599	73	9
Nashua, N.H.	4,502	4,579	861	1,306	2,623	2,622	895	592	122	56	1	3
Burlington, Vt.	3,453	3,596	503	738	1,784	1,944	796	721	361	188	9	5
Worcester, Mass.	29,222	29,279	1,624	3,579	13,822	18,427	10,769	5,824	2,845	1,400	162	49
Providence, R.I.*	92,268	94,423	13,797	21,395	49,932	55,309	22,257	14,596	5,517	2,870	765	253
Waterbury, Conn.	14,152	14,733	546	2,573	6,688	9,217	5,666	2,557	1,194	361	58	25
5 Mid. Atlantic cities	70,631	73,674	2,615	11,399	26,207	40,550	29,952	18,321	11,113	3,249	744	155
Binghamton, N.Y.	10,234	10,946	365	698	3,954	6,005	4,463	3,567	1,373	656	79	20
Syracuse, N.Y.	28,356	29,981	729	3,956	7,782	15,439	12,876	9,018	6,614	1,503	355	65
Trenton, N.J.	12,079	13,198	491	2,349	5,625	7,290	4,349	2,810	1,445	704	169	45
Erie, Pa.	14,053	13,609	678	2,690	6,187	8,500	5,849	2,127	1,228	269	111	23
Williamsport, Pa.	5,909	5,940	352	1,706	2,659	3,316	2,415	799	453	117	30	2
7 E. N. Central cities	267,490	273,396	16,108	65,802	84,496	136,261	106,002	56,594	55,833	13,512	5,051	1,227
Cleveland, Ohio*	173,115	168,179	7,101	26,801	47,322	88,857	72,153	41,478	42,444	10,048	4,095	995
Indianapolis, Ind.	55,362	60,091	6,789	24,204	23,446	24,288	17,091	9,141	7,382	2,291	654	187
Decatur, Ill.	6,592	8,067	630	3,542	3,057	3,733	2,281	688	606	100	18	4
Peoria, Ill.	12,499	12,602	1,065	2,932	4,688	6,228	4,387	2,802	2,245	620	114	20
Lansing, Mich.	7,873	10,576	197	3,913	1,858	5,332	4,199	1,119	1,553	200	66	12
Kenosha, Wis.	5,086	5,858	140	1,565	1,818	3,674	2,477	525	607	93	44	1
Racine, Wis.	6,963	8,023	186	2,845	2,307	4,169	3,414	841	996	160	60	8
10 W. N. Central cities	168,777	184,268	17,540	44,606	63,351	83,751	59,927	46,850	26,444	8,731	1,515	330
Minneapolis, Minn.	60,006	65,917	2,994	8,940	20,340	31,843	24,023	20,845	11,819	4,114	830	175
St. Paul, Minn.	32,504	34,102	2,713	5,385	12,442	16,292	12,229	10,545	4,860	1,798	260	82
Des Moines, Iowa	17,832	20,847	2,533	5,658	6,811	9,531	5,726	4,443	2,791	1,180	171	35
St. Joseph, Mo.	11,702	10,552	2,589	4,742	5,667	4,246	2,636	1,330	760	227	50	7
Springfield, Mo.	7,176	7,727	2,526	4,656	3,179	2,313	1,118	672	345	79	8	2
Fargo, N.D.	3,501	4,194	126	665	857	1,789	1,531	1,506	973	234	14	
Sioux Falls, S.D.	4,265	4,919	269	910	1,493	2,616	1,824	1,256	668	133	11	4
Lincoln, Neb.	9,052	10,414	869	2,708	3,488	4,983	3,374	2,403	1,255	310	66	10
Topeka, Kan.	7,164	8,949	1,395	3,475	2,918	3,601	1,981	1,623	848	248	22	2
Wichita, Kan.	15,575	16,647	1,526	7,467	6,356	6,532	5,485	2,227	2,125	408	83	13
10 S. Atlantic cities	172,838	178,904	59,635	92,947	61,818	56,722	32,086	22,805	17,543	6,113	1,756	317
Frederick, Md.	1,897	2,074	609	822	824	964	364	260	95	27	5	1
Hagerstown, Md.	4,746	4,968	553	1,630	2,665	2,608	1,223	640	291	86	14	4
Richmond, Va.	29,527	27,568	8,250	10,139	10,847	9,876	6,021	5,636	4,029	1,825	380	92
Wheeling, W.Va.*	22,896	22,456	5,787	11,329	10,854	8,786	4,554	1,910	1,476	401	225	30
Asheville, N.C.	7,083	7,541	1,974	4,420	2,815	2,258	1,529	686	663	170	102	7
Greensboro, N.C.	6,960	7,902	2,478	4,538	2,321	1,980	1,170	1,136	939	242	52	6
Charleston, S.C.	12,747	13,157	7,348	8,736	3,056	3,060	1,819	1,146	485	206	39	9
Columbia, S.C.	7,312	8,169	3,888	5,152	1,684	1,853	1,060	946	646	215	34	3
Atlanta, Ga.*	58,977	60,946	23,283	33,319	18,189	17,003	9,594	8,005	7,164	2,478	747	141
Jacksonville, Fla.	20,693	24,123	5,465	12,862	8,563	8,334	4,752	2,440	1,755	463	158	24
4 E. S. Central cities	85,304	92,394	41,720	68,768	25,869	17,166	11,542	5,457	5,667	960	506	43
Paducah, Ky.	5,204	5,306	2,524	3,899	1,820	990	564	365	286	50	10	2
Knoxville, Tenn.	13,551	15,350	4,031	9,263	6,009	4,292	2,251	1,506	1,196	280	64	9
Birmingham, Ala.*	59,895	64,142	32,589	51,073	15,993	9,938	7,542	2,601	3,402	502	369	28
Jackson, Miss.	6,654	7,596	2,576	4,533	2,047	1,946	1,185	985	783	128	63	4
7 W. S. Central cities	104,819	110,893	21,274	44,529	37,754	44,914	31,498	18,416	13,524	2,857	769	177
Little Rock, Ark.	10,405	11,114	2,973	5,918	3,682	3,969	2,718	1,094	974	131	58	2
Baton Rouge, La.	4,499	4,742	1,441	2,174	1,388	1,609	1,203	820	450	135	17	4
Shreveport, La.	11,416	13,067	3,745	7,586	3,842	3,680	2,486	1,621	1,266	174	77	6
Oklahoma City, Okla.	26,953	25,983	2,769	8,496	8,373	11,790	10,556	5,012	5,020	665	235	20
Austin, Tex.	6,414	7,742	2,415	3,235	2,090	2,681	1,277	1,474	588	344	44	8
Dallas, Tex.	38,494	42,194	6,092	13,036	15,529	19,522	11,797	8,103	4,761	1,396	315	137
Wichita Falls, Tex.	6,638	6,051	1,839	4,084	2,850	1,663	1,461	292	465	12	23	
8 Mountain cities	47,194	49,784	7,261	18,009	19,225	21,344	14,485	8,761	5,681	1,601	542	69
Butte, Mont.	5,978	4,717	684	1,928	3,209	2,006	1,546	646	486	137	53	
Boise, Idaho	2,779	3,131	494	884	1,146	1,454	826	690	296	98	17	5
Casper, Wyo.	2,623	2,671	444	1,030	1,256	1,131	754	468	163	42	6	
Pueblo, Colo.	5,260	5,460	1,093	3,069	2,400	1,930	1,382	432	359	28	26	1
Albuquerque, N.M.	3,421	3,971	773	1,250	1,051	1,761	1,119	862	443	96	35	2
Phoenix, Ariz.	7,726	9,119	1,199	3,908	2,220	3,518	2,732	1,281	1,386	391	189	21
Salt Lake City, Utah	16,744	17,832	2,365	5,414	7,347	8,298	5,100	3,450	1,820	635	112	35
Reno, Nev.	2,663	2,883	209	526	596	1,246	1,026	932	728	174	104	5
4 Pacific cities	129,070	151,897	11,072	43,257	54,272	77,249	45,812	26,443	16,262	4,685	1,652	263
Seattle, Wash.*	51,885	60,963	3,978	17,820	19,998	29,509	18,666	11,528	8,559	1,978	684	128
Portland, Ore.	37,904	44,236	3,974	16,977	17,775	20,937	12,276	5,517	3,517	772	362	33
Sacramento, Calif.	12,263	13,878	663	2,156	4,853	7,398	5,060	3,774	1,540	536	147	14
San Diego, Calif.*	27,018	32,820	2,457	6,304	11,646	19,405	9,810	5,624	2,646	1,399	459	88

Source: 1930, *Census,* VI; 1934, *Real Property Inventory,* Table I
The number of dwelling units obtained in the two enumerations are not strictly comparable, as explained in the half-title page to sec. A, and there is some doubt concerning the completeness of coverage by the Real Property Inventory. The absolute differences in number of dwelling units cannot, therefore, be stressed. The emphasis should be on the shift of dwelling units among the rent classes, as shown by the percentage distributions.
*Metropolitan district.

[1]*Percentage not shown if less than one-tenth of one per cent.*

Rented Dwelling Units, Number and Percentage Distribution by Monthly Rent Groups, 61 Cities by Geographic Division, 1930 and 1934

← ——————————————— P E R C E N T A G E   D I S T R I B U T I O N [1] ——————————————— →

All rent groups		Under $15		$15-29		$30-49		$50-99		$100 and over		
1930	1934	1930	1934	1930	1934	1930	1934	1930	1934	1930	1934	
100.0	100.0	16.3	33.0	37.7	44.9	31.3	18.2	13.6	3.7	1.1	0.2	61 cities
100.0	100.0	11.7	19.7	51.4	59.1	28.8	17.5	7.4	3.5	0.7	0.2	6 New England cities
100.0	100.0	7.6	13.3	41.4	51.6	37.9	29.7	12.4	5.3	0.7	0.1	Portland, Me.
100.0	100.0	19.1	28.5	58.3	57.3	19.9	12.9	2.7	1.2		0.1	Nashua, N.H.
100.0	100.0	14.6	20.5	51.7	54.1	23.0	20.1	10.4	5.2	0.3	0.1	Burlington, Vt.
100.0	100.0	5.6	12.2	47.3	62.9	36.8	19.9	9.7	4.8	0.6	0.2	Worcester, Mass.
100.0	100.0	15.0	22.6	54.1	58.6	24.1	15.5	6.0	3.0	0.8	0.3	Providence, R.I.*
100.0	100.0	3.9	17.5	47.3	62.6	40.0	17.3	8.4	2.4	0.4	0.2	Waterbury, Conn.
100.0	100.0	3.7	15.5	37.1	55.0	42.4	24.9	15.7	4.4	1.1	0.2	5 Mid. Atlantic cities
100.0	100.0	3.6	6.4	38.6	54.8	43.6	32.6	13.4	6.0	0.8	0.2	Binghamton, N.Y.
100.0	100.0	2.6	13.2	27.4	51.5	45.4	30.1	23.3	5.0	1.3	0.2	Syracuse, N.Y.
100.0	100.0	4.1	17.8	46.5	55.2	36.0	21.3	12.0	5.3	1.4	0.4	Trenton, N.J.
100.0	100.0	4.8	19.8	44.0	62.4	41.6	15.6	8.8	2.0	0.8	0.2	Erie, Pa.
100.0	100.0	5.9	28.7	45.0	55.8	40.9	13.5	7.7	2.0	0.5		Williamsport, Pa.
100.0	100.0	6.0	24.1	31.6	49.9	39.6	20.7	20.9	4.9	1.9	0.4	7 E. N. Central cities
100.0	100.0	4.1	15.9	27.3	52.8	41.7	24.7	24.5	6.0	2.4	0.6	Cleveland, Ohio*
100.0	100.0	12.3	40.3	42.3	40.4	30.9	15.2	13.3	3.8	1.2	0.3	Indianapolis, Ind.
100.0	100.0	9.5	43.9	46.4	46.3	34.6	8.5	9.2	1.2	0.3	0.1	Decatur, Ill.
100.0	100.0	8.5	23.3	37.5	49.4	35.1	22.2	18.0	4.9	0.9	0.2	Peoria, Ill.
100.0	100.0	2.5	37.0	23.6	50.4	53.4	10.6	19.7	1.9	0.8	0.1	Lansing, Mich.
100.0	100.0	2.8	26.7	35.7	62.7	48.7	9.0	11.9	1.6	0.9		Kenosha, Wis.
100.0	100.0	2.7	35.5	33.1	51.9	49.0	10.5	14.3	2.0	0.9	0.1	Racine, Wis.
100.0	100.0	10.4	24.2	37.5	45.5	35.5	25.4	15.7	4.7	0.9	0.2	10 W. N. Central cities
100.0	100.0	5.0	13.6	33.9	48.3	40.0	31.6	19.7	6.2	1.4	0.3	Minneapolis, Minn.
100.0	100.0	8.3	15.8	38.3	47.8	37.6	30.9	15.0	5.3	0.8	0.2	St. Paul, Minn.
100.0	100.0	14.2	27.1	37.1	45.7	32.1	21.3	15.7	5.7	0.9	0.2	Des Moines, Iowa
100.0	100.0	22.1	44.9	48.5	40.2	22.5	12.6	6.5	2.1	0.4	0.2	St. Joseph, Mo.
100.0	100.0	35.2	60.3	44.3	30.0	15.6	8.7	4.8	1.0	0.1		Springfield, Mo.
100.0	100.0	3.6	15.8	24.5	42.7	43.7	35.9	27.8	5.6	0.4		Fargo, N.D.
100.0	100.0	6.3	18.5	35.0	53.2	42.8	25.5	15.7	2.7	0.2	0.1	Sioux Falls, S.D.
100.0	100.0	9.6	26.0	38.5	47.8	37.3	23.1	13.9	3.0	0.7	0.1	Lincoln, Neb.
100.0	100.0	19.5	38.8	40.7	40.3	27.7	18.1	11.8	2.8	0.3		Topeka, Kan.
100.0	100.0	9.8	44.9	40.8	39.2	35.2	13.4	13.7	2.4	0.5	0.1	Wichita, Kan.
100.0	100.0	34.5	52.0	35.8	31.7	18.6	12.7	10.1	3.4	1.0	0.2	10 S. Atlantic cities
100.0	100.0	32.1	39.6	43.4	46.5	19.2	12.5	5.0	1.3	0.3	0.1	Frederick, Md.
100.0	100.0	11.7	32.8	56.1	52.5	25.8	12.9	6.1	1.7	0.3	0.1	Hagerstown, Md.
100.0	100.0	28.0	36.8	36.7	35.8	20.4	20.5	13.6	6.6	1.3	0.3	Richmond, Va.
100.0	100.0	25.3	50.5	47.4	39.1	19.9	8.5	6.4	1.8	1.0	0.1	Wheeling, W.Va.*
100.0	100.0	27.9	58.6	39.7	29.9	21.6	9.1	9.4	2.3	1.4	0.1	Asheville, N.C.
100.0	100.0	35.6	57.4	33.4	25.0	16.8	14.4	13.5	3.1	0.7	0.1	Greensboro, N.C.
100.0	100.0	57.6	66.4	24.0	23.2	14.3	8.7	3.8	1.6	0.3	0.1	Charleston, S.C.
100.0	100.0	53.2	63.1	23.0	22.7	14.5	11.6	8.8	2.6	0.5		Columbia, S.C.
100.0	100.0	39.5	54.7	30.8	27.9	16.3	13.1	12.1	4.1	1.3	0.2	Atlanta, Ga.*
100.0	100.0	26.4	53.3	41.4	34.6	22.9	10.1	8.5	1.9	0.8	0.1	Jacksonville, Fla.
100.0	100.0	48.9	74.4	30.3	18.6	13.5	5.9	6.7	1.0	0.6	0.1	4 E. S. Central cities
100.0	100.0	48.5	73.5	35.0	18.7	10.8	6.9	5.5	0.9	0.2		Paducah, Ky.
100.0	100.0	29.8	60.3	44.3	28.0	16.6	9.8	8.8	1.8	0.5	0.1	Knoxville, Tenn.
100.0	100.0	54.4	79.6	26.7	15.5	12.6	4.1	5.7	0.8	0.6		Birmingham, Ala.*
100.0	100.0	38.7	59.7	30.8	25.6	17.8	13.0	11.8	1.7	0.9		Jackson, Miss.
100.0	100.0	20.3	40.2	36.0	40.5	30.1	16.6	12.9	2.6	0.7	0.1	7 W. S. Central cities
100.0	100.0	28.6	53.3	35.4	35.7	26.1	9.8	9.4	1.2	0.5		Little Rock, Ark.
100.0	100.0	32.0	45.9	30.9	33.9	26.7	17.3	10.0	2.8	0.4	0.1	Baton Rouge, La.
100.0	100.0	32.8	58.0	33.6	28.2	21.8	12.4	11.1	1.3	0.7	0.1	Shreveport, La.
100.0	100.0	10.3	32.7	31.0	45.4	39.2	19.3	18.6	2.5	0.9	0.1	Oklahoma City, Okla.
100.0	100.0	37.6	41.8	32.6	34.6	19.9	19.0	9.2	4.5	0.7	0.1	Austin, Tex.
100.0	100.0	15.8	30.9	40.4	46.3	30.6	19.2	12.4	3.3	0.8	0.3	Dallas, Tex.
100.0	100.0	27.7	67.5	42.9	27.5	22.0	4.8	7.0	0.2	0.4		Wichita Falls, Tex.
100.0	100.0	15.4	36.2	40.7	42.9	30.7	17.6	12.0	3.2	1.2	0.1	8 Mountain cities
100.0	100.0	11.4	40.9	53.7	42.5	25.9	13.7	8.1	2.9	0.9		Butte, Mont.
100.0	100.0	17.8	28.2	41.2	46.5	29.7	22.0	10.7	3.1	0.6	0.2	Boise, Idaho
100.0	100.0	16.9	38.6	47.9	42.3	28.8	17.5	6.2	1.6	0.2		Casper, Wyo.
100.0	100.0	20.8	56.2	45.6	35.4	26.3	7.9	6.8	0.5	0.5		Pueblo, Colo.
100.0	100.0	22.6	31.5	30.7	44.3	32.7	21.7	13.0	2.4	1.0	0.1	Albuquerque, N.M.
100.0	100.0	15.5	42.9	28.7	38.6	35.4	14.0	17.9	4.3	2.5	0.2	Phoenix, Ariz.
100.0	100.0	14.1	30.4	43.9	46.5	30.4	19.3	10.9	3.6	0.7	0.2	Salt Lake City, Utah
100.0	100.0	7.9	18.3	22.4	43.2	38.5	32.3	27.3	6.0	3.9	0.2	Reno, Nev.
100.0	100.0	8.6	28.5	42.0	50.8	35.5	17.4	12.6	3.1	1.3	0.2	4 Pacific cities
100.0	100.0	7.7	29.2	38.5	48.4	36.0	18.9	16.5	3.3	1.3	0.2	Seattle, Wash.*
100.0	100.0	10.5	38.4	46.9	47.3	32.4	12.5	9.3	1.7	0.9	0.1	Portland, Ore.
100.0	100.0	5.4	15.5	39.6	53.3	41.3	27.2	12.5	3.9	1.2	0.1	Sacramento, Calif.
100.0	100.0	9.1	19.2	43.1	59.1	36.3	17.1	9.8	4.3	1.7	0.3	San Diego, Calif.*

TABLE B 8

Rented Dwelling Units, Average Annual Rent, 50 Cities by Geographic Division, 1930 and 1933, and Percentage 1933 is of 1930

	1930	1933	1933 as percentage of 1930		1930	1933	1933 as percentage of 1930
	(dollars)				(dollars)		
50 cities[1]	372	258	69.4	7 S. Atlantic cities	302	219	72.5
				Hagerstown, Md.	311	233	74.9
4 New England cities	337	276	81.9	Richmond, Va.	331	273	82.5
Portland, Me.	381	315	82.7	Wheeling, W. Va.*	287	201	70.0
Worcester, Mass.	367	298	81.2	Greensboro, N.C.	298	198	66.4
Providence, R.I.*	317	266	83.9	Columbia, S.C.	241	186	77.2
Waterbury, Conn.	368	269	73.1	Atlanta, Ga.*	299	215	71.9
				Jacksonville, Fla.	308	198	64.3
4 Mid. Atlantic cities	420	300	71.4				
Binghamton, N.Y.	401	332	82.8	3 E. S. Central cities	230	133	57.8
Syracuse, N.Y.	463	312	67.4	Paducah, Ky.	218	148	67.9
Trenton, N.J.	389	291	74.8	Birmingham, Ala.*	224	125	55.8
Erie, Pa.	374	259	69.3	Jackson, Miss.	296	193	65.2
				6 W. S. Central cities	353	241	68.3
6 E. N. Central cities	448	286	63.8	Little Rock, Ark.	312	194	62.2
Cleveland, Ohio*	481	309	64.2	Baton Rouge, La.	306	231	75.5
Indianapolis, Ind.	372	247	66.4	Oklahoma City, Okla.	411	248	60.3
Peoria, Ill.	406	282	69.5	Austin, Tex.	280	246	87.9
Lansing, Mich.	454	218	48.0	Dallas, Tex.	358	263	73.5
Kenosha, Wis.	403	226	56.1	Wichita Falls, Tex.	284	149	52.5
Racine, Wis.	423	226	53.4	6 Mountain cities	348	239	68.7
				Butte, Mont.	340	228	67.1
10 W. N. Central cities	391	286	73.1	Boise, Idaho	330	265	80.3
Minneapolis, Minn.	437	324	74.1	Casper, Wyo.	306	229	74.8
St. Paul, Minn.	391	309	79.0	Pueblo, Colo.	303	179	59.1
Des Moines, Iowa	377	280	74.3	Phoenix, Ariz.	411	235	57.2
St. Joseph, Mo.	291	217	74.6	Salt Lake City, Utah	344	261	75.9
Springfield, Mo.	245	179	73.1				
Fargo, N.D.	469	320	68.2	4 Pacific cities	387	255	65.9
Sioux Falls, S.D.	396	283	71.5	Seattle, Wash.*	411	258	62.8
Lincoln, Neb.	384	269	70.1	Portland, Ore.	357	220	61.6
Topeka, Kan.	333	240	72.1	Sacramento, Calif.	398	300	75.4
Wichita, Kan.	371	216	58.2	San Diego, Calif.*	375	276	73.6

Source: 1930, special Census tabulation, average yearly rent based on monthly rent reported, April 1, 1930; 1933, average rent by rent groups (Financial Survey of Urban Housing) weighted by number of rental units by rent groups (RPI). Note differences between 1933 average rents in this table and those in Table B 10 which are unweighted.
*Metropolitan district.
[1]Geographic division and 50-city averages weighted by number of rental units in each city (RPI).

TABLE B 9

Rented Dwelling Units reporting Annual Rent and Percentage Distribution by Annual Rent Groups, 52 Cities by Geographic Division, 1933

	All rent groups	$1-59	$60-119	$120-179	$180-239	$240-299	$300-359	$360-479	$480-599	$600-899	$900-1,199	$1,200 and over
52 cities[1]	156,165	3,722	16,781	27,043	27,986	23,648	20,743	21,642	8,446	5,246	661	247
4 New England cities	12,520	30	255	1,415	2,617	2,571	2,152	2,027	804	548	69	32
Portland, Me.	2,728	7	43	211	416	489	472	668	260	156	6	
Worcester, Mass.	2,805	9	65	222	560	631	592	415	154	134	18	5
Providence, R.I.*	5,857	12	132	857	1,385	1,200	899	768	324	217	38	25
Waterbury, Conn.	1,130	2	15	125	256	251	189	176	66	41	7	2
4 Mid. Atlantic cities	7,260	14	156	1,043	1,610	1,420	1,256	1,126	401	193	32	9
Binghamton, N.Y.	773	4	7	43	132	168	133	150	83	45	7	1
Syracuse, N.Y.	1,515	1	26	218	262	218	299	339	110	40	1	1
Trenton, N.J.	2,063	2	48	320	493	435	331	270	93	53	15	3
Erie, Pa.	2,909	7	75	462	723	599	493	367	115	55	9	4
6 E. N. Central cities	36,466	171	1,609	4,952	6,993	6,265	5,904	6,065	2,348	1,739	286	134
Cleveland, Ohio*	27,191	93	849	3,145	4,986	4,830	4,670	4,960	1,899	1,405	233	121
Indianapolis, Ind.	3,132	30	282	535	474	407	452	455	249	200	40	8
Peoria, Ill.	2,305	8	86	377	512	373	333	375	132	97	8	4
Lansing, Mich.	968	12	156	237	217	156	97	72	12	7	2	
Kenosha, Wis.	995	8	42	187	325	195	144	72	13	8	1	
Racine, Wis.	1,875	20	194	471	479	304	208	131	43	22	2	1
10 W. N. Central cities	24,663	194	1,755	3,990	4,432	3,823	3,534	4,165	1,711	948	92	19
Minneapolis, Minn.	9,224	32	245	967	1,673	1,560	1,484	1,845	854	485	64	15
St. Paul, Minn.	1,814	3	43	260	366	272	302	370	135	62	1	
Des Moines, Iowa	3,069	17	212	475	506	527	479	517	189	132	14	1
St. Joseph, Mo.	1,270	10	130	330	252	180	139	153	46	25	4	1
Springfield, Mo.	1,184	30	268	394	199	98	85	74	21	15		
Fargo, N.D.	906		12	91	106	116	155	251	125	50		
Sioux Falls, S.D.	1,514	7	41	165	262	275	268	320	124	51	1	
Lincoln, Neb.	1,275	5	82	219	268	211	176	191	80	38	5	
Topeka, Kan.	2,053	42	273	472	314	266	250	288	96	50	2	
Wichita, Kan.	2,354	48	449	617	486	318	196	156	41	40	1	2
9 S. Atlantic cities	26,503	1,547	6,050	5,881	3,627	2,509	2,140	2,556	1,229	851	88	25
Hagerstown, Md.	1,261	5	81	314	350	185	144	123	44	14	1	
Richmond, Va.	4,146	34	628	836	547	370	381	588	422	308	25	7
Wheeling, W.Va.*	2,184	35	243	554	483	322	251	199	58	26	11	2
Asheville, N.C.	1,632	136	428	421	251	154	105	95	25	13	3	1
Greensboro, N.C.	1,208	213	315	156	132	91	70	125	68	34	2	2
Charleston, S.C.	2,507	459	745	330	231	202	221	219	55	34	7	4
Columbia, S.C.	1,564	173	540	295	129	99	97	137	49	42	2	1
Atlanta, Ga.*	9,481	356	2,360	2,195	1,175	860	730	949	458	357	33	8
Jacksonville, Fla.	2,520	136	710	780	329	226	141	121	50	23	4	
3 E. S. Central cities	9,115	1,259	2,957	1,984	1,032	561	509	542	171	82	15	3
Paducah, Ky.	1,289	98	547	321	122	51	46	73	21	10		
Birmingham, Ala.*	7,121	1,136	2,286	1,485	826	437	387	374	116	57	14	3
Jackson, Miss.	705	25	124	178	84	73	76	95	34	15	1	
6 W. S. Central cities	12,960	285	1,862	2,600	2,242	1,944	1,531	1,624	591	259	17	5
Little Rock, Ark.	2,594	113	667	632	433	280	198	203	44	22		2
Baton Rouge, La.	860	12	174	231	92	84	92	105	48	22		
Oklahoma City, Okla.	3,659	58	298	684	704	656	493	537	160	65	3	1
Austin, Tex.	1,010	16	220	168	118	111	111	137	73	48	6	2
Dallas, Tex.	3,793	18	173	598	718	738	591	596	252	101	8	
Wichita Falls, Tex.	1,044	68	330	287	177	75	46	46	14	1		
6 Mountain cities	9,881	105	966	2,115	2,036	1,491	1,154	1,223	478	284	25	4
Butte, Mont.	1,939	6	118	481	438	323	219	191	82	77	4	
Boise, Idaho	1,093	6	52	173	197	161	156	220	90	36	2	
Casper, Wyo.	673	21	120	129	113	105	79	71	27	8		
Pueblo, Colo.	901	28	213	227	168	95	83	74	11	2		
Phoenix, Ariz.	1,642	14	191	341	368	247	197	166	58	50	9	1
Salt Lake City, Utah	3,633	30	272	764	752	560	420	501	210	111	10	3
4 Pacific cities	16,797	117	1,171	3,063	3,397	3,064	2,563	2,314	713	342	37	16
Seattle, Wash.*	5,935	60	409	1,124	1,223	1,074	858	813	214	146	6	8
Portland, Ore.	3,965	34	533	1,202	840	565	370	321	62	30	8	
Sacramento, Calif.	2,145	4	52	188	344	375	385	479	226	77	11	4
San Diego, Calif.*	4,752	19	177	549	990	1,050	950	701	211	89	12	4

Source: Financial Survey of Urban Housing

*Metropolitan district.

[1]Geographic division and 52-city percentage distributions weighted by number of rental units in each city (RPI).

[2]Percentage not shown if less than one-tenth of one per cent.

Rented Dwelling Units reporting Annual Rent and Percentage Distribution by Annual Rent Groups, 52 Cities by Geographic Division, 1933

← P E R C E N T A G E   D I S T R I B U T I O N [2] →

All rent groups	$1-59	$60-119	$120-179	$180-239	$240-299	$300-359	$360-479	$480-599	$600-899	$900-1.199	$1,200 and over	
100.0	2.2	10.0	17.2	18.2	15.4	13.6	13.9	5.4	3.4	0.5	0.2	**52 cities**[1]
100.0	0.2	2.1	12.4	22.2	20.8	16.8	14.6	5.9	4.1	0.6	0.3	**4 New England cities**
100.0	0.3	1.6	7.7	15.2	17.9	17.3	24.5	9.6	5.7	0.2		Portland, Me.
100.0	0.3	2.3	7.9	20.0	22.5	21.1	14.8	5.5	4.8	0.6	0.2	Worcester, Mass.
100.0	0.2	2.3	14.6	23.6	20.5	15.4	13.1	5.5	3.7	0.7	0.4	Providence, R.I. *
100.0	0.2	1.3	11.1	22.7	22.2	16.7	15.6	5.8	3.6	0.6	0.2	Waterbury, Conn.
100.0	0.2	1.9	13.6	20.2	18.1	18.0	18.0	6.5	3.0	0.4	0.1	**4 Mid. Atlantic cities**
100.0	0.5	0.9	5.6	17.1	21.7	17.2	19.4	10.7	5.9	0.9	0.1	Binghamton, N.Y.
100.0	0.1	1.7	14.4	17.3	14.4	19.7	22.4	7.2	2.6	0.1	0.1	Syracuse, N.Y.
100.0	0.1	2.3	15.5	23.9	21.1	16.0	13.1	4.5	2.6	0.7	0.2	Trenton, N.J.
100.0	0.2	2.6	15.9	24.9	20.6	16.9	12.6	4.0	1.9	0.3	0.1	Erie, Pa.
100.0	0.5	5.2	14.1	18.4	16.5	15.9	16.3	6.7	5.2	0.9	0.3	**6 E. N. Central cities**
100.0	0.3	3.1	11.6	18.3	17.8	17.2	18.2	7.0	5.2	0.9	0.4	Cleveland, Ohio*
100.0	1.0	9.0	17.1	15.1	13.0	14.4	14.5	7.9	6.4	1.3	0.3	Indianapolis, Ind.
100.0	0.3	3.7	16.4	22.2	16.2	14.4	16.3	5.7	4.2	0.4	0.2	Peoria, Ill.
100.0	1.2	16.1	24.5	22.4	16.1	10.0	7.5	1.2	0.8	0.2		Lansing, Mich.
100.0	0.8	4.2	18.8	32.7	19.6	14.5	7.2	1.3	0.8	0.1		Kenosha, Wis.
100.0	1.1	10.3	25.1	25.5	16.2	11.1	7.0	2.3	1.2	0.1	0.1	Racine, Wis.
100.0	0.7	6.6	15.9	18.5	15.5	14.5	17.1	6.9	3.8	0.4	0.1	**10 W. N. Central cities**
100.0	0.3	2.7	10.5	18.1	16.9	16.1	20.0	9.3	5.2	0.7	0.2	Minneapolis, Minn.
100.0	0.2	2.4	14.3	20.2	15.0	16.6	20.4	7.4	3.4	0.1		St. Paul, Minn.
100.0	0.5	6.9	15.5	16.5	17.2	15.6	16.8	6.2	4.3	0.5	0.0	Des Moines, Iowa
100.0	0.8	10.2	26.0	19.8	14.2	10.9	12.1	3.6	2.0	0.3	0.1	St. Joseph, Mo.
100.0	2.5	22.6	33.3	16.8	8.3	7.2	6.2	1.8	1.3			Springfield, Mo.
100.0		1.3	10.1	11.7	12.8	17.1	27.7	13.8	5.5			Fargo, N.D.
100.0	0.4	2.7	10.9	17.3	18.2	17.7	21.1	8.2	3.4	0.1		Sioux Falls, S.D.
100.0	0.4	6.4	17.2	21.0	16.5	13.8	15.0	6.3	3.0	0.4		Lincoln, Neb.
100.0	2.0	13.3	23.0	15.3	13.0	12.2	14.0	4.7	2.4	0.1		Topeka, Kan.
100.0	2.0	19.1	26.2	20.7	13.5	8.3	6.6	1.8	1.7	0.0	0.1	Wichita, Kan.
100.0	5.4	22.4	22.8	13.9	9.7	8.1	9.5	4.6	3.2	0.3	0.1	**9 S. Atlantic cities**
100.0	0.4	6.4	24.9	27.7	14.7	11.4	9.8	3.5	1.1	0.1		Hagerstown, Md.
100.0	0.8	15.1	20.2	13.2	8.9	9.2	14.2	10.2	7.4	0.6	0.2	Richmond, Va.
100.0	1.6	11.1	25.4	22.1	14.7	11.5	9.1	2.7	1.2	0.5	0.1	Wheeling, W.Va.*
100.0	8.3	26.2	25.8	15.4	9.5	6.4	5.8	1.5	0.8	0.2	0.1	Asheville, N.C.
100.0	17.6	26.1	12.9	10.9	7.5	5.8	10.4	5.6	2.8	0.2	0.2	Greensboro, N.C.
100.0	18.3	29.7	13.2	9.2	8.1	8.8	8.7	2.2	1.3	0.3	0.2	Charleston, S.C.
100.0	11.1	34.5	18.9	8.2	6.3	6.2	8.8	3.1	2.7	0.1	0.1	Columbia, S.C.
100.0	3.8	24.9	23.1	12.4	9.1	7.7	10.0	4.8	3.8	0.3	0.1	Atlanta, Ga. *
100.0	5.4	28.2	30.9	13.0	9.0	5.6	4.8	2.0	0.9	0.2		Jacksonville, Fla.
100.0	14.3	31.5	21.6	11.5	6.3	5.8	6.0	1.9	0.9	0.2		**3 E. S. Central cities**
100.0	7.6	42.4	24.9	9.5	3.9	3.6	5.7	1.6	0.8			Paducah, Ky.
100.0	16.0	32.1	20.9	11.6	6.1	5.4	5.3	1.6	0.8	0.2	0.0	Birmingham, Ala. *
100.0	3.6	17.6	25.2	11.9	10.4	10.8	13.5	4.8	2.1	0.1		Jackson, Miss.
100.0	1.8	11.8	18.9	17.7	16.1	12.8	13.4	5.1	2.2	0.2		**6 W. S. Central cities**
100.0	4.4	25.7	24.4	16.7	10.8	7.6	7.8	1.7	0.8		0.1	Little Rock, Ark.
100.0	1.4	20.2	26.9	10.7	9.8	10.7	12.2	5.6	2.5			Baton Rouge, La.
100.0	1.6	8.1	18.7	19.2	17.9	13.5	14.7	4.4	1.8	0.1	0.0	Oklahoma City, Okla.
100.0	1.6	21.8	16.6	11.7	11.0	11.0	13.6	7.2	4.7	0.6	0.2	Austin, Tex.
100.0	0.5	4.6	15.8	18.9	19.4	15.6	15.7	6.6	2.7	0.2		Dallas, Tex.
100.0	6.5	31.6	27.5	17.0	7.2	4.4	4.4	1.3	0.1			Wichita Falls, Tex.
100.0	1.2	10.8	21.5	20.6	14.8	11.5	12.0	4.6	2.6	0.3	0.1	**6 Mountain cities**
100.0	0.3	6.1	24.8	22.6	16.7	11.3	9.8	4.2	4.0	0.2		Butte, Mont.
100.0	0.6	4.8	15.8	18.0	14.7	14.3	20.1	8.2	3.3	0.2		Boise, Idaho
100.0	3.1	17.8	19.2	16.8	15.6	11.7	10.6	4.0	1.2			Casper, Wyo.
100.0	3.1	23.6	25.2	18.7	10.6	9.2	8.2	1.2	0.2			Pueblo, Colo.
100.0	0.9	11.6	20.8	22.4	15.0	12.0	10.1	3.5	3.0	0.6	0.1	Phoenix, Ariz.
100.0	0.8	7.5	21.0	20.7	15.4	11.6	13.8	5.8	3.0	0.3	0.1	Salt Lake City, Utah
100.0	0.8	7.7	19.7	20.4	17.8	14.4	13.1	3.8	2.0	0.2	0.1	**4 Pacific cities**
100.0	1.0	6.9	18.9	20.6	18.1	14.5	13.7	3.6	2.5	0.1	0.1	Seattle, Wash. *
100.0	0.9	13.4	30.3	21.2	14.2	9.3	8.1	1.6	0.8	0.2		Portland, Ore.
100.0	0.2	2.4	8.8	16.0	17.5	17.9	22.3	10.6	3.6	0.5	0.2	Sacramento, Calif.
100.0	0.4	3.7	11.6	20.8	22.1	20.0	14.7	4.4	1.9	0.3	0.1	San Diego, Calif. *

TABLE B 10

Rented Dwelling Units, Average Annual Rent (dollars) by Annual Rent Groups, 52 Cities by Geographic Division, 1933

	All[2] rent groups	$1-59	$60-119	$120-179	$180-239	$240-299	$300-359	$360-479	$480-599	$600-899	$900-1,199	$1,200 and over
52 cities[1]	262	45	99	142	196	252	309	391	504	656	956	1,438
4 New England cities	294	42	109	148	200	253	311	390	506	665	960	1,467
Portland, Me.	328	43	105	155	200	255	311	394	508	655	920	
Worcester, Mass.	304	47	94	155	202	254	314	391	506	665	998	1,332
Providence, R.I.*	287	40	115	146	200	253	310	389	505	665	956	1,508
Waterbury, Conn.	293	45	100	142	199	252	309	387	508	676	947	
4 Mid. Atlantic cities	289	38	93	144	200	249	308	388	499	657	940	1,563
Binghamton, N.Y.	329	43	81	144	202	254	309	393	504	642	967	
Syracuse, N.Y.	295		94	145	201	247	307	388	500	654		
Trenton, N.J.	273		97	143	198	249	311	385	499	666	940	1,500
Erie, Pa.	264	34	98	142	197	250	308	389	492	668	921	1,620
6 E. N. Central cities	298	43	104	144	198	252	309	390	509	665	952	1,449
Cleveland, Ohio*	310	44	110	147	198	252	309	390	509	664	953	1,403
Indianapolis, Ind.	298	40	94	140	202	253	309	393	511	679	947	1,536
Peoria, Ill.	282	43	96	142	196	253	308	388	508	663	964	1,650
Lansing, Mich.	203	43	90	135	189	247	307	390	490	647		
Kenosha, Wis.	226	50	106	142	188	247	305	376	505	660		
Racine, Wis.	220	47	98	141	199	249	308	388	528	605		
10 W. N. Central cities	281	46	99	141	196	252	310	393	507	658	944	1,309
Minneapolis, Minn.	317	57	106	146	197	254	311	396	510	664	937	1,309
St. Paul, Minn.	291	40	90	139	194	249	312	391	510	652		
Des Moines, Iowa	284	31	106	141	197	254	307	394	505	651	971	
St. Joseph, Mo.	234	44	92	136	193	250	308	385	505	658	945	
Springfield, Mo.	182	45	88	136	192	248	310	386	497	618		
Fargo, N.D.	336		97	138	196	250	308	393	506	638		
Sioux Falls, S.D.	299	41	105	142	194	252	308	392	504	642		
Lincoln, Neb.	268	38	102	135	196	251	314	389	490	652	938	
Topeka, Kan.	242	46	96	137	196	251	312	393	504	688		
Wichita, Kan.	200	45	84	135	195	253	306	390	510	667		
9 S. Atlantic cities	217	48	92	138	196	253	309	395	502	647	937	1,358
Hagerstown, Md.	232	42	101	143	194	251	311	392	496	659		
Richmond, Va.	285	46	93	138	195	251	306	402	515	662	984	1,330
Wheeling, W. Va.*	226	42	100	136	196	256	310	394	502	651	940	
Asheville, N.C.	170	52	87	134	187	245	304	378	486	632	920	
Greensboro, N.C.	198	48	80	136	200	274	309	396	492	649		
Charleston, S.C.	176	51	86	135	195	251	307	387	491	610	931	1,300
Columbia, S.C.	185	51	91	138	192	252	309	418	500	639		
Atlanta, Ga.*	222	49	91	141	198	251	310	395	510	658	920	1,383
Jacksonville, Fla.	172	49	90	138	196	253	308	389	485	625	930	
3 E. S. Central cities	158	46	85	133	189	247	305	387	498	668	1,007	1,680
Paducah, Ky.	146	51	84	131	191	245	306	385	487	650		
Birmingham, Ala.*	151	45	83	132	188	247	305	387	498	674	1,007	1,680
Jackson, Miss.	228	49	102	140	192	246	306	391	511	629		
6 W. S. Central cities	248	43	96	144	195	253	307	393	500	632	968	
Little Rock, Ark.	191	50	95	137	190	275	305	407	488	637		
Baton Rouge, La.	227	43	95	137	196	252	308	384	497	679		
Oklahoma City, Okla.	251	48	98	143	192	253	306	389	506	627	960	
Austin, Tex.	257	41	98	138	196	248	308	396	508	628	930	
Dallas, Tex.	276	38	96	151	197	249	309	395	500	629	980	
Wichita Falls, Tex.	154	45	84	133	193	250	303	380	497			
6 Mountain cities	244	44	95	138	193	249	309	396	506	661	928	1,450
Butte, Mont.	247	33	97	136	194	252	307	389	510	644	990	
Boise, Idaho	287	40	108	141	195	251	307	392	505	639		
Casper, Wyo.	220	41	85	134	190	249	313	395	514	661		
Pueblo, Colo.	186	55	92	130	191	246	308	393	504			
Phoenix, Ariz.	243	44	93	148	193	247	308	391	503	667	929	
Salt Lake City, Utah	259	46	97	137	193	250	309	403	505	667	908	1,450
4 Pacific cities	251	46	98	138	194	250	311	389	498	642	966	1,355
Seattle, Wash.*	255	44	109	139	192	250	313	391	502	658	943	1,301
Portland, Ore.	204	43	91	136	191	249	306	385	486	609	1,008	
Sacramento, Calif.	319	43	87	138	198	251	308	397	504	646	991	1,948
San Diego, Calif.*	275	53	91	139	199	252	313	388	502	655	943	1,200

Source: *Financial Survey of Urban Housing.* Based on number of dwelling units reporting rent as shown in Table B 9. Average not shown for fewer than 3 reports.
*Metropolitan district.
[1]Geographic division and 52-city averages weighted by number of rental units in each city (RPI).
[2]Note differences between average rent 'All rent groups' in this table and those in Table B 8 which are weighted.

TABLE B 11

Rented Dwelling Units reporting Annual Rent and Average Annual Rent per Dwelling Unit, by Type, 52 Cities by Geographic Division, 1933

	← NUMBER →					← AVERAGE ANNUAL RENT →				
	All types	1-family	2-family	Apart-ments	Other	All[2] types	1-family	2-family	Apart-ments	Other
52 cities[1]	149,754	67,855	39,446	25,794	16,659	$263	$248	$246	$317	$241
4 New England cities	11,927	1,068	3,964	2,060	4,835	294	352	300	260	273
Portland, Me.	2,621	277	1,000	630	714	328	363	311	374	298
Worcester, Mass.	2,593	143	488	469	1,493	305	428	341	313	280
Providence, R.I.*	5,632	586	2,268	731	2,047	287	329	293	292	267
Waterbury, Conn.	1,081	62	208	230	581	293	457	301	280	278
4 Mid. Atlantic cities	6,962	2,091	3,103	607	1,161	290	329	275	320	251
Binghamton, N.Y.	735	102	365	153	115	330	445	317	353	235
Syracuse, N.Y.	1,449	386	722	166	175	296	354	276	300	246
Trenton, N.J.	1,989	568	699	79	643	273	265	282	390	257
Erie, Pa.	2,789	1,035	1,317	209	228	264	289	243	271	264
6 E. N. Central cities	34,935	11,438	12,619	6,263	4,615	297	307	274	361	234
Cleveland, Ohio*	26,101	6,976	9,892	5,137	4,096	311	363	290	344	231
Indianapolis, Ind.	2,912	1,146	1,085	582	99	300	277	256	435	246
Peoria, Ill.	2,242	1,455	315	295	177	283	258	307	384	274
Lansing, Mich.	922	762	82	41	37	204	200	196	255	237
Kenosha, Wis.	962	438	399	74	51	226	251	196	236	232
Racine, Wis.	1,796	661	846	134	155	219	230	202	285	209
10 W. N. Central cities	23,757	12,582	4,866	4,912	1,397	282	266	267	342	247
Minneapolis, Minn.	8,988	2,527	2,888	2,966	607	318	338	277	348	272
St. Paul, Minn.	1,768	706	560	300	202	290	316	264	333	205
Des Moines, Iowa	2,914	2,202	155	455	102	285	262	327	388	262
St. Joseph, Mo.	1,209	752	294	107	56	235	223	223	357	233
Springfield, Mo.	1,141	982	69	64	26	183	173	179	366	146
Fargo, N.D.	891	622	95	141	33	337	340	299	341	358
Sioux Falls, S.D.	1,469	911	239	206	113	299	288	288	377	264
Lincoln, Neb.	1,221	887	113	172	49	268	257	270	339	224
Topeka, Kan.	1,908	1,340	185	253	130	243	224	268	335	227
Wichita, Kan.	2,248	1,653	268	248	79	200	188	215	257	216
9 S. Atlantic cities	25,293	12,133	7,425	3,762	1,973	218	213	185	317	177
Hagerstown, Md.	1,207	204	663	115	225	232	242	218	329	214
Richmond, Va.	3,976	1,568	1,104	995	309	283	274	230	377	219
Wheeling, W.Va.*	2,093	954	704	200	235	227	234	204	250	243
Asheville, N.C.	1,589	1,251	162	95	81	169	173	129	171	189
Greensboro, N.C.	1,160	954	81	90	35	200	184	212	372	180
Charleston, S.C.	2,402	961	927	102	412	177	198	171	160	142
Columbia, S.C.	1,412	978	288	70	76	187	187	180	258	159
Atlanta, Ga.*	9,012	3,644	2,950	1,912	506	223	233	156	326	149
Jacksonville, Fla.	2,442	1,619	546	183	94	172	157	185	241	211
3 E. S. Central cities	8,787	5,446	2,248	879	214	159	153	98	337	144
Paducah, Ky.	1,222	852	257	75	38	145	130	130	322	221
Birmingham, Ala.*	6,894	4,142	1,877	735	140	151	148	87	336	110
Jackson, Miss.	671	452	114	69	36	232	213	224	356	257
6 W. S. Central cities	12,401	8,353	2,190	1,309	549	248	234	259	318	238
Little Rock, Ark.	2,476	1,999	231	133	113	192	183	222	287	184
Baton Rouge, La.	820	687	75	13	45	227	217	256	384	281
Oklahoma City, Okla.	3,487	1,995	752	584	156	251	235	257	303	242
Austin, Tex.	974	787	94	36	57	260	244	321	379	306
Dallas, Tex.	3,621	2,070	875	514	162	277	270	267	332	241
Wichita Falls, Tex.	1,023	815	163	29	16	153	149	155	263	159
6 Mountain cities	9,584	4,969	1,639	2,092	864	249	223	216	337	229
Butte, Mont.	1,918	714	368	588	248	248	220	228	281	275
Boise, Idaho	1,074	643	105	246	80	286	248	318	373	291
Casper, Wyo.	650	376	70	136	68	222	218	205	252	196
Pueblo, Colo.	876	627	114	96	39	187	171	214	255	190
Phoenix, Ariz.	1,575	922	351	105	197	243	245	221	347	220
Salt Lake City, Utah	3,471	1,687	631	921	232	260	232	199	362	221
4 Pacific cities	16,128	9,775	1,392	3,910	1,051	251	240	235	276	257
Seattle, Wash.*	5,704	2,870	320	2,118	396	255	233	204	295	244
Portland, Ore.	3,859	2,518	334	786	221	204	198	195	231	188
Sacramento, Calif.	2,081	1,108	365	438	170	319	326	281	313	365
San Diego, Calif.*	4,484	3,279	373	568	264	276	275	276	290	256

Source: Financial Survey of Urban Housing

*Metropolitan district.

[1] *Geographic division and 52-city averages weighted by number of rental units, by type, in each city (RPI).*

[2] *Slight differences between average rents in this table and in Tables B 10 and 13 are due to differences in the number reporting rent by type of dwelling as compared with the number reporting rents irrespective of type.*

TABLE B 12

Rented 1-Family Dwellings, Number and Average Annual Rent for Units reporting Annual Rent per Dwelling Unit, per Room, and per Person, by Material of Construction, 52 Cities by Geographic Division, 1933

| | ← NUMBER → | | | | ← AVERAGE ANNUAL RENT → | | | |
| | | | | | PER UNIT | | | |
	All materials	Wood	Brick	Other	All materials	Wood	Brick	Other
52 cities[1]	67,855	57,095	5,611	5,149	$248	$229	$424	$333
4 New England cities	1,068	992	25	51	352	347	600	396
Portland, Me.	277	254	16	7	363	349	575	380
Worcester, Mass.	143	131	3	9	428	416	810	478
Providence, R.I.*	586	552	4	30	329	325	570	381
Waterbury, Conn.	62	55	2	5	457	458		440
4 Mid. Atlantic cities	2,091	1,590	408	93	329	315	457	354
Binghamton, N.Y.	102	91	5	6	445	425	692	553
Syracuse, N.Y.	386	373	4	9	354	353	495	362
Trenton, N.J.	568	281	244	43	265	235	298	283
Erie, Pa.	1,035	845	155	35	289	267	402	309
6 E. N. Central cities	11,438	10,603	483	352	307	291	565	447
Cleveland, Ohio*	6,976	6,555	281	140	363	348	629	530
Indianapolis, Ind.	1,146	1,050	69	27	277	251	610	460
Peoria, Ill.	1,455	1,327	46	82	258	249	460	299
Lansing, Mich.	762	716	14	32	200	196	336	221
Kenosha, Wis.	438	377	28	33	251	245	338	242
Racine, Wis.	661	578	45	38	230	225	268	261
10 W. N. Central cities	12,582	10,385	344	1,853	266	244	378	334
Minneapolis, Minn.	2,527	1,505	37	985	338	287	412	413
St. Paul, Minn.	706	513	24	169	316	283	385	408
Des Moines, Iowa.	2,202	1,914	73	215	262	249	389	333
St. Joseph, Mo.	752	637	48	67	223	209	288	304
Springfield, Mo.	982	889	42	51	173	163	319	219
Fargo, N.D.	622	519	13	90	340	326	462	408
Sioux Falls, S.D.	911	831	15	65	288	279	367	386
Lincoln, Neb.	887	781	25	81	257	245	396	327
Topeka, Kan.	1,340	1,239	25	76	224	219	219	306
Wichita, Kan.	1,653	1,557	42	54	188	180	455	203
9 S. Atlantic cities	12,133	10,177	1,408	548	213	185	387	298
Hagerstown, Md.	204	117	77	10	242	188	326	213
Richmond, Va.	1,568	1,009	426	133	274	201	392	448
Wheeling, W.Va.*	954	803	111	40	234	220	326	267
Asheville, N.C.	1,251	1,025	89	137	173	159	298	197
Greensboro, N.C.	954	822	82	50	184	161	346	297
Charleston, S.C.	961	873	56	32	198	186	345	289
Columbia, S.C.	978	869	89	20	187	166	363	311
Atlanta, Ga.*	3,644	3,141	458	45	233	199	456	321
Jacksonville, Fla.	1,619	1,518	20	81	157	151	378	217
3 E. S. Central cities	5,446	5,042	280	124	153	143	296	272
Paducah, Ky.	852	768	41	43	130	122	242	163
Birmingham, Ala.*	4,142	3,886	199	57	148	139	294	279
Jackson, Miss.	452	388	40	24	213	193	360	305
6 W. S. Central cities	8,353	7,378	684	291	234	214	409	290
Little Rock, Ark.	1,999	1,751	167	81	183	163	367	218
Baton Rouge, La.	687	665	1	21	217	216		266
Oklahoma City, Okla.	1,995	1,730	203	62	235	216	383	285
Austin, Tex.	787	710	22	55	244	228	514	352
Dallas, Tex.	2,070	1,771	248	51	270	244	437	331
Wichita Falls, Tex.	815	751	43	21	149	139	308	190
6 Mountain cities	4,969	2,502	1,830	637	223	175	262	261
Butte, Mont.	714	508	195	11	220	203	259	329
Boise, Idaho	643	560	38	45	248	236	311	333
Casper, Wyo.	376	313	18	45	218	205	338	257
Pueblo, Colo.	627	388	142	97	171	155	189	211
Phoenix, Ariz.	922	344	277	301	245	147	295	311
Salt Lake City, Utah	1,687	389	1,160	138	232	172	254	222
4 Pacific cities	9,775	8,426	149	1,200	240	228	441	316
Seattle, Wash.*	2,870	2,717	85	68	233	226	393	318
Portland, Ore.	2,518	2,352	6	160	198	194	507	253
Sacramento, Calif.	1,108	805	54	249	326	288	466	417
San Diego, Calif.*	3,279	2,552	4	723	275	252	430	357

Source: *Financial Survey of Urban Housing*   *Average not shown for fewer than 3 reports.*
* Metropolitan district.
[1] Geographic division and 52-city averages weighted by number of 1-family rental units in each city (RPI).

TABLE B 12

Rented 1-Family Dwellings, Number and Average Annual Rent for Units reporting Annual Rent per Dwelling Unit, per Room, and per Person, by Material of Construction, 52 Cities by Geographic Division, 1933

←———————— AVERAGE ANNUAL RENT ————————→								
PER ROOM				**PER PERSON**				
All materials	Wood	Brick	Other	All materials	Wood	Brick	Other	52 cities[1]
$48	$45	$70	$60	$58	$53	$101	$79	
54	53	78	59	74	74	150	65	**4 New England cities**
54	53	67	58	75	72	114	81	Portland, Me.
67	65	110	74	93	90	162	113	Worcester, Mass.
50	49	74	57	69	69	152	53	Providence, R.I.*
72	75		52	101	105		92	Waterbury, Conn.
51	49	61	57	70	67	95	84	**4 Mid. Atlantic cities**
62	60	91	71	94	89	157	128	Binghamton, N.Y.
55	55	58	62	77	76	90	96	Syracuse, N.Y.
44	42	46	49	55	50	59	57	Trenton, N.J.
45	42	62	50	61	56	95	66	Erie, Pa.
53	51	86	71	70	65	132	99	**6 E. N. Central cities**
60	58	89	79	79	75	141	117	Cleveland, Ohio*
51	47	99	79	67	60	151	102	Indianapolis, Ind.
51	50	81	57	61	58	106	72	Peoria, Ill.
34	33	51	36	47	46	96	46	Lansing, Mich.
45	44	57	42	55	54	61	56	Kenosha, Wis.
40	40	42	43	50	50	53	55	Racine, Wis.
51	47	64	62	62	56	86	83	**10 W. N. Central cities**
61	52	60	74	75	60	81	100	Minneapolis, Minn.
59	53	66	74	73	64	92	100	St. Paul, Minn.
51	49	79	63	64	60	103	86	Des Moines, Iowa
47	45	52	60	54	51	63	78	St. Joseph, Mo.
37	35	58	44	41	39	81	54	Springfield, Mo.
67	66	76	72	72	69	94	87	Fargo, N.D.
56	55	57	67	66	64	71	95	Sioux Falls, S.D.
47	45	64	56	59	56	95	77	Lincoln, Neb.
44	43	42	62	55	53	54	85	Topeka, Kan.
38	37	75	41	47	45	102	53	Wichita, Kan.
45	41	65	56	46	40	86	64	**9 S. Atlantic cities**
41	34	49	38	54	43	72	44	Hagerstown, Md.
53	43	63	76	58	44	76	96	Richmond, Va.
47	45	56	54	51	48	69	60	Wheeling, W.Va.*
31	29	46	32	38	35	68	40	Asheville, N.C.
36	32	60	52	36	32	74	53	Greensboro, N.C.
52	50	67	58	45	42	81	66	Charleston, S.C.
46	43	65	59	40	35	85	63	Columbia, S.C.
49	44	74	62	49	41	105	69	Atlanta, Ga.*
36	35	65	45	37	35	88	52	Jacksonville, Fla.
32	31	49	47	34	32	66	61	**3 E. S. Central cities**
34	32	46	45	34	31	55	51	Paducah, Ky.
30	29	48	46	33	31	64	61	Birmingham, Ala.*
49	47	61	61	47	42	88	68	Jackson, Miss.
50	47	71	60	52	48	100	68	**6 W. S. Central cities**
40	37	65	44	43	38	93	55	Little Rock, Ark.
52	52		59	52	51		63	Baton Rouge, La.
50	47	71	60	52	47	94	64	Oklahoma City, Okla.
55	53	82	71	53	50	108	76	Austin, Tex.
56	52	75	67	60	54	107	78	Dallas, Tex.
31	29	54	38	34	32	86	48	Wichita Falls, Tex.
48	41	51	54	53	42	63	64	**6 Mountain cities**
50	50	50	57	57	56	59	71	Butte, Mont.
49	47	51	68	58	55	66	86	Boise, Idaho
51	48	79	53	61	57	122	65	Casper, Wyo.
37	35	38	47	43	38	46	61	Pueblo, Colo.
53	39	58	62	61	37	73	78	Phoenix, Ariz.
48	40	50	48	49	36	53	50	Salt Lake City, Utah
49	47	82	62	64	61	122	91	**4 Pacific cities**
46	45	73	63	60	58	100	92	Seattle, Wash.*
39	37	74	48	53	52	117	71	Portland, Ore.
65	59	89	79	85	74	134	113	Sacramento, Calif.
59	56	101	72	78	71	156	106	San Diego, Calif.*

TABLE B 13

Rented Dwelling Units, Average Annual Rent (dollars), 1929, 1932, and 1933, reported by Tenants, January 1, 1934,
52 Cities by Geographic Division

	1929	1932	1933		1929	1932	1933
52 cities[1]	341	297	262	9 S. Atlantic cities	261	237	217
				Hagerstown, Md.	282	261	232
				Richmond, Va.	311	302	285
4 New England cities	340	317	294	Wheeling, W.Va.*	296	256	226
Portland, Me.	364	349	328	Asheville, N.C.	233	194	170
Worcester, Mass.	359	332	304	Greensboro, N.C.	229	208	198
Providence, R.I.*	327	306	287	Charleston, S.C.	180	177	176
Waterbury, Conn.	367	329	293	Columbia, S.C.	207	197	185
				Atlanta, Ga.*	273	246	222
				Jacksonville, Fla.	217	187	172
4 Mid. Atlantic cities	366	329	289				
Binghamton, N.Y.	374	350	329	3 E. S. Central cities	243	190	158
Syracuse, N.Y.	390	339	295	Paducah, Ky.	200	169	146
Trenton, N.J.	322	298	273	Birmingham, Ala.*	241	185	151
Erie, Pa.	354	313	264	Jackson, Miss.	279	252	228
				6 W. S. Central cities	336	286	248
6 E. N. Central cities	416	348	298	Little Rock, Ark.	267	226	191
Cleveland, Ohio*	435	364	310	Baton Rouge, La.	269	252	227
Indianapolis, Ind.	393	336	298	Oklahoma City, Okla.	383	299	251
Peoria, Ill.	371	326	282	Austin, Tex.	289	276	257
Lansing, Mich.	364	256	203	Dallas, Tex.	350	313	276
Kenosha, Wis.	355	269	226	Wichita Falls, Tex.	280	195	154
Racine, Wis.	374	274	220				
				6 Mountain cities	316	278	244
				Butte, Mont.	319	280	247
10 W. N. Central cities	351	314	281	Boise, Idaho	331	302	287
Minneapolis, Minn.	386	348	317	Casper, Wyo.	282	254	220
St. Paul, Minn.	340	314	291	Pueblo, Colo.	266	224	186
Des Moines, Iowa	352	316	284	Phoenix, Ariz.	358	293	243
St. Joseph, Mo.	303	272	234	Salt Lake City, Utah	320	285	259
Springfield, Mo.	237	208	182				
Fargo, N.D.	422	390	336	4 Pacific cities	339	289	251
Sioux Falls, S.D.	387	341	299	Seattle, Wash.*	358	300	255
Lincoln, Neb.	345	306	268	Portland, Ore.	283	235	204
Topeka, Kan.	313	276	242	Sacramento, Calif.	380	354	319
Wichita, Kan.	323	251	200	San Diego, Calif.*	358	313	275

Source: *Financial Survey of Urban Housing*
*Metropolitan district.
[1] *Geographic division and 52-city averages weighted by number of rental units in each city (RPI).*

TABLE B 14

Rented Dwelling Units reporting Facilities included in Rent,[2] Number and Percentage of Dwelling Units with each Type of Facility, 51 Cities by Geographic Division, 1933

	NUMBER REPORTING	Furnishings	Elec-tricity	Gas	Water	Heat	Mechanical refrigeration	Garage
51 cities[1]	155,052	16,681	11,650	9,137	90,024	23,633	10,973	51,231
4 New England cities	12,592	350	545	358	9,958	1,355	354	1,445
Portland, Me.	2,752	203	171	89	2,338	619	156	323
Worcester, Mass.	2,815	52	162	106	1,918	293	48	280
Providence, R.I.*	5,892	77	174	136	4,787	335	135	740
Waterbury, Conn.	1,133	18	38	27	915	108	15	102
4 Mid. Atlantic cities	7,311	227	306	274	4,959	730	108	1,627
Binghamton, N.Y.	774	26	49	40	638	144	18	208
Syracuse, N.Y.	1,526	84	90	76	1,256	218	29	414
Trenton, N.J.	2,083	26	77	53	1,299	208	34	121
Erie, Pa.	2,928	91	90	105	1,766	160	27	884
6 E. N. Central cities	36,847	1,687	2,536	2,550	27,553	6,121	2,771	14,374
Cleveland, Ohio*	27,471	1,029	1,489	1,532	22,695	4,259	1,988	10,728
Indianapolis, Ind.	3,176	146	529	535	1,634	761	440	1,288
Peoria, Ill.	2,329	250	249	230	1,435	565	184	887
Lansing, Mich.	977	76	62	59	134	87	24	558
Kenosha, Wis.	1,001	68	86	66	771	132	16	331
Racine, Wis.	1,893	118	121	128	884	317	119	582
10 W. N. Central cities	24,873	3,018	2,748	2,547	12,437	5,770	2,488	9,768
Minneapolis, Minn.	9,280	1,411	1,029	1,053	7,545	2,926	1,507	2,944
St. Paul, Minn.	1,828	121	132	124	706	445	126	639
Des Moines, Iowa	3,112	363	416	345	766	708	244	1,290
St. Joseph, Mo.	1,282	83	81	88	335	118	51	507
Springfield, Mo.	1,196	71	74	52	598	75	39	619
Fargo, N.D.	908	85	99	18	254	177	58	337
Sioux Falls, S.D.	1,523	172	191	126	463	378	108	696
Lincoln, Neb.	1,293	117	93	65	707	223	87	629
Topeka, Kan.	2,077	223	280	304	529	381	145	752
Wichita, Kan.	2,374	372	353	372	534	339	123	1,355
8 S. Atlantic cities	24,164	657	1,302	414	11,799	2,770	1,322	4,525
Hagerstown, Md.	1,275	22	46	14	1,060	236	21	200
Richmond, Va.	4,172	92	130	87	807	739	443	343
Wheeling, W.Va.*	2,213	60	161	102	251	121	25	310
Asheville, N.C.	1,642	36	27	9	229	60	24	613
Greensboro, N.C.	1,223	30	322	7	671	94	53	386
Columbia, S.C.	1,579	37	66	12	1,042	42	18	351
Atlanta, Ga.*	9,534	260	497	158	5,812	1,431	701	1,927
Jacksonville, Fla.	2,526	120	53	25	1,927	47	37	395
3 E. S. Central cities	9,188	313	247	121	2,668	815	535	2,088
Paducah, Ky.	1,309	31	45	12	248	84	15	214
Birmingham, Ala.*	7,172	219	167	77	2,156	689	504	1,675
Jackson, Miss.	707	63	35	32	264	42	16	199
6 W. S. Central cities	13,066	1,769	1,195	1,186	3,014	764	501	6,162
Little Rock, Ark.	2,614	190	82	83	465	60	63	922
Baton Rouge, La.	865	28	15	10	138	11	2	271
Oklahoma City, Okla.	3,693	723	518	560	1,391	351	262	1,829
Austin, Tex.	1,016	73	25	15	172	10	15	463
Dallas, Tex.	3,821	617	492	456	737	302	152	1,984
Wichita Falls, Tex.	1,057	138	63	62	111	30	7	693
6 Mountain cities	10,041	2,928	762	582	7,239	2,017	938	3,637
Butte, Mont.	1,998	806	209	114	1,638	385	60	340
Boise, Idaho	1,112	282	72	5	502	299	71	415
Casper, Wyo.	697	298	106	129	499	137	33	270
Pueblo, Colo.	915	171	102	37	774	141	37	464
Phoenix, Ariz.	1,665	805	83	28	932	84	101	846
Salt Lake City, Utah	3,654	566	190	269	2,894	971	636	1,302
4 Pacific cities	16,970	5,732	2,009	1,105	10,397	3,291	1,956	7,605
Seattle, Wash.*	5,985	1,833	1,041	628	4,189	2,256	1,282	1,987
Portland, Ore.	4,017	968	469	87	1,232	732	283	1,473
Sacramento, Calif.	2,165	521	99	52	1,864	87	91	1,188
San Diego, Calif.*	4,803	2,410	400	338	3,112	216	300	2,957

Source: _Financial Survey of Urban Housing_
*Metropolitan district.
[1] _Geographic division and 51-city percentages weighted by number of rental units in each city (RPI)._
[2] _Sum of number with each type of facility does not equal total number of reports since some dwelling units have more than one type of facility. Similarly, percentages do not add to 100.0_

Rented Dwelling Units reporting Facilities included in Rent,[2] Number and Percentage of Dwelling Units with each Type of Facility, 51 Cities by Geographic Division, 1933

Furnishings	Electricity	Gas	Water	Heat	Mechanical refrigeration	Garage	PERCENTAGE WITH EACH TYPE
10.3	7.9	6.2	57.9	15.4	7.2	32.3	51 cities[1]
1.9	3.8	2.7	78.9	8.3	2.4	11.7	4 New England cities
7.4	6.2	3.2	85.0	22.5	5.7	11.7	Portland, Me.
1.8	5.8	3.8	68.1	10.4	1.7	9.9	Worcester, Mass.
1.3	3.0	2.3	81.2	5.7	2.3	12.6	Providence, R.I.*
1.6	3.4	2.4	80.8	9.5	1.3	9.0	Waterbury, Conn.
3.8	4.9	4.3	73.8	12.3	1.7	23.7	4 Mid. Atlantic cities
3.4	6.3	5.2	82.4	18.6	2.3	26.9	Binghamton, N.Y.
5.5	5.9	5.0	82.3	14.3	1.9	27.1	Syracuse, N.Y.
1.2	3.7	2.5	62.4	10.0	1.6	5.8	Trenton, N.J.
3.1	3.1	3.6	60.3	5.5	0.9	30.2	Erie, Pa.
4.5	8.4	8.5	70.6	17.6	8.5	39.7	6 E. N. Central cities
3.7	5.4	5.6	82.6	15.5	7.2	39.1	Cleveland, Ohio*
10.7	10.7	9.9	61.6	24.3	7.9	38.1	Peoria, Ill.
7.8	6.3	6.0	13.7	8.9	2.5	57.1	Lansing, Mich.
6.8	8.6	6.6	77.0	13.2	1.6	33.1	Kenosha, Wis.
6.2	6.4	6.8	46.7	16.7	6.3	30.7	Racine, Wis.
11.6	10.4	9.8	50.6	23.4	9.9	38.7	10 W. N. Central cities
15.2	11.1	11.3	81.3	31.5	16.2	31.7	Minneapolis, Minn.
6.6	7.2	6.8	38.6	24.3	6.9	35.0	St. Paul, Minn.
11.7	13.4	11.1	24.6	22.8	7.8	41.5	Des Moines, Iowa
6.5	6.3	6.9	26.1	9.2	4.0	39.5	St. Joseph, Mo.
5.9	6.2	4.3	50.0	6.3	3.3	51.8	Springfield, Mo.
9.4	10.9	2.0	28.0	19.5	6.4	37.1	Fargo, N.D.
11.3	12.5	8.3	30.4	24.8	7.1	45.7	Sioux Falls, S.D.
9.0	7.2	5.0	54.7	17.2	6.7	48.6	Lincoln, Neb.
10.7	13.5	14.6	25.5	18.3	7.0	36.2	Topeka, Kan.
15.7	14.9	15.7	22.5	14.3	5.2	57.1	Wichita, Kan.
2.8	5.4	1.9	47.7	10.8	5.3	17.9	8 S. Atlantic cities
1.7	3.6	1.1	83.1	18.5	1.6	15.7	Hagerstown, Md.
2.2	3.1	2.1	19.3	17.7	10.6	8.2	Richmond, Va.
2.7	7.3	4.6	11.3	5.5	1.1	14.0	Wheeling, W.Va.*
2.2	1.6	0.5	13.9	3.7	1.5	37.3	Asheville, N.C.
2.5	26.3	0.6	54.9	7.7	4.3	31.6	Greensboro, N.C.
2.3	4.2	0.8	66.0	2.7	1.1	22.2	Columbia, S.C.
2.7	5.2	1.7	61.0	15.0	7.4	20.2	Atlanta, Ga.*
4.8	2.1	1.0	76.3	1.9	1.5	15.6	Jacksonville, Fla.
3.6	2.6	1.4	30.0	9.1	6.2	23.3	3 E. S. Central cities
2.4	3.4	0.9	18.9	6.4	1.1	16.3	Paducah, Ky.
3.1	2.3	1.1	30.1	9.6	7.0	23.4	Birmingham, Ala.*
8.9	5.0	4.5	37.3	5.9	2.3	28.1	Jackson, Miss.
14.5	10.2	10.0	22.9	6.5	4.0	48.8	6 M. S. Central cities
7.3	3.1	3.2	17.8	2.3	2.4	35.3	Little Rock, Ark.
3.2	1.7	1.2	16.0	1.3	0.2	31.3	Baton Rouge, La.
19.6	14.0	15.2	37.7	9.5	7.1	49.5	Oklahoma City, Okla.
7.2	2.5	1.5	16.9	1.0	1.5	45.6	Austin, Tex.
16.1	12.9	11.9	19.3	7.9	4.0	51.9	Dallas, Tex.
13.1	6.0	5.9	10.5	2.8	0.7	65.6	Wichita Falls, Tex.
28.2	7.4	5.9	72.8	19.4	9.9	38.6	6 Mountain cities
40.3	10.5	5.7	82.0	19.3	3.0	17.0	Butte, Mont.
25.4	6.5	0.4	45.1	26.9	6.4	37.3	Boise, Idaho
42.8	15.2	18.5	71.6	19.7	4.7	38.7	Casper, Wyo.
18.7	11.1	4.0	84.6	15.4	4.0	50.7	Pueblo, Colo.
48.3	5.0	1.7	56.0	5.0	6.1	50.8	Phoenix, Ariz.
15.5	5.2	7.4	79.2	26.6	17.4	35.6	Salt Lake City, Utah
32.3	12.7	6.6	59.1	22.0	12.5	42.2	4 Pacific cities
30.6	17.4	10.5	70.0	37.7	21.4	33.2	Seattle, Wash.*
24.1	11.7	2.2	30.7	18.2	7.0	36.7	Portland, Ore.
24.1	4.6	2.4	86.1	4.0	4.2	54.9	Sacramento, Calif.
50.2	8.3	7.0	64.8	4.5	6.2	61.6	San Diego, Calif.*

TABLE B 15

Rented Dwelling Units reporting Cost of Facilities included in Rent, Number and Average Cost of each Type of Facility for Dwelling Units using Facility, 51 Cities by Geographic Division, 1933

| | NUMBER REPORTING | NUMBER REPORTING EACH TYPE | | | | | | |
		Furnishings	Electricity	Gas	Water	Heat	Mechanical refrigeration	Garage
51 cities[1]	3,421	1,087	2,624	2,299	2,851	2,679	283	970
4 New England cities	217	33	152	139	152	150	9	70
Portland, Me.	39	6	26	25	27	27		15
Worcester, Mass.	76	11	60	55	54	58	3	26
Providence, R.I.*	32	6	20	18	22	19	1	11
Waterbury, Conn.	70	10	46	41	49	46	5	18
4 Mid. Atlantic cities	220	42	163	156	170	172	21	72
Binghamton, N.Y.	41	9	34	33	23	33		18
Syracuse, N.Y.	36	11	29	25	26	28	6	15
Trenton, N.J.	61	7	37	34	48	48	13	23
Erie, Pa.	82	15	63	64	73	63	2	16
6 E. N. Central cities	689	161	517	484	543	536	54	240
Cleveland, Ohio*	274	54	194	190	198	187	23	92
Indianapolis, Ind.	89	18	73	63	74	77	7	27
Peoria, Ill.	127	30	98	90	108	103	6	38
Lansing, Mich.	88	27	68	60	70	74	7	40
Kenosha, Wis.	61	16	47	44	48	50		22
Racine, Wis.	50	16	37	37	45	45	11	21
10 W. N. Central cities	736	221	585	554	612	612	57	204
Minneapolis, Minn.	153	38	114	119	118	119	8	48
St. Paul, Minn.	92	27	74	71	80	81	5	22
Des Moines, Iowa	69	22	65	62	65	64	5	18
St. Joseph, Mo.	22	7	16	18	20	19	1	5
Springfield, Mo.	58	21	41	28	51	48	9	14
Fargo, N.D.	65	18	50	55	58	59	5	16
Sioux Falls, S.D.	66	10	59	55	60	59	2	14
Lincoln, Neb.	78	29	63	55	71	65	12	26
Topeka, Kan.	70	20	51	46	35	47	8	31
Wichita, Kan.	63	29	52	45	54	51	2	10
8 S. Atlantic cities	405	110	292	262	352	311	38	81
Hagerstown, Md.	49	8	36	31	42	42	3	13
Richmond, Va.	72	22	54	51	61	55	13	13
Wheeling, W.Va.*	42	7	27	28	32	27	1	16
Asheville, N.C.	42	18	39	23	40	33	4	9
Greensboro, N.C.	49	8	32	22	45	30	2	3
Columbia, S.C.	31	10	21	23	25	27	1	2
Atlanta, Ga.*	84	25	61	62	80	70	11	19
Jacksonville, Fla.	36	12	22	22	27	27	3	6
3 E. S. Central cities	140	38	94	72	123	106	13	23
Paducah, Ky.	32	9	18	7	28	27	1	6
Birmingham, Ala.*	79	16	57	48	71	61	11	12
Jackson, Miss.	29	13	19	17	24	18	1	5
6 W. S. Central cities	304	129	246	212	284	217	38	54
Little Rock, Ark.	56	16	39	30	53	43	4	8
Baton Rouge, La.	20	9	15	15	20	13	2	3
Oklahoma City, Okla.	45	21	30	23	38	27	8	13
Austin, Tex.	48	18	44	38	45	41	6	7
Dallas, Tex.	105	47	87	80	98	69	12	18
Wichita Falls, Tex.	30	18	31	26	30	24	6	5
6 Mountain cities	401	204	311	197	339	307	34	123
Butte, Mont.	58	33	40	13	58	40	2	16
Boise, Idaho	76	33	68	33	71	69	4	21
Casper, Wyo.	76	40	64	48	59	56	4	19
Pueblo, Colo.	62	35	41	30	49	45	2	16
Phoenix, Ariz.	49	31	43	42	41	40	2	14
Salt Lake City, Utah	80	32	55	31	61	57	20	37
4 Pacific cities	309	149	264	223	276	268	19	103
Seattle, Wash.*	109	52	94	66	103	102	14	42
Portland, Ore.	112	53	98	84	107	100	5	31
Sacramento, Calif.	56	25	44	43	42	42		19
San Diego, Calif.*	32	19	28	30	24	24		11

Source: _Financial Survey of Urban Housing_

*Metropolitan district.

[1] _Geographic division and 51-city averages weighted by estimated number of facilities by type in each city._

[2] _Adjusted on basis of percentage city average rent is of rent of all dwelling units reporting cost of facilities; see half-title page to sec. B._

Rented Dwelling Units reporting Cost of Facilities included in Rent, Number and Average Cost of each Type of Facility for Dwelling Units using Facility, 51 Cities by Geographic Division, 1933

Furnishings	Electricity	Gas	Water	Heat	Mechanical refrigeration	Garage	
←			AVERAGE COST OF EACH TYPE	(DOLLARS)		→	
76.08	30.24	28.62	11.25	54.96	23.66	28.48	51 cities[1]
94.93	29.39	30.12	9.62	73.39	17.31	37.72	4 New England cities
64.87	28.98	34.63	10.53	94.17		29.11	Portland, Me.
130.58	27.75	33.55	10.73	82.48	23.85	44.75	Worcester, Mass.
99.88	29.88	26.10	9.02	58.14	14.18	36.97	Providence, R.I.*
102.87	32.75	39.24	10.93	72.37	35.99	38.50	Waterbury, Conn.
89.49	29.27	28.98	9.59	61.43	20.65	33.29	4 Mid. Atlantic cities
109.33	36.27	35.43	7.71	77.48		41.55	Binghamton, N.Y.
85.87	25.84	25.96	6.72	56.56	16.49	31.34	Syracuse, N.Y.
72.80	31.11	28.93	9.14	53.82	30.99	35.44	Trenton, N.J.
92.70	30.42	30.86	19.89	60.60	22.82	31.16	Erie, Pa.
95.62	30.07	29.46	13.13	55.51	27.37	30.39	6 E. N. Central cities
103.68	26.45	30.01	12.25	54.78	27.19	32.15	Cleveland, Ohio*
95.19	34.30	29.42	17.67	62.90	27.94	29.17	Indianapolis, Ind.
90.99	28.51	28.54	15.08	24.97	24.82	26.23	Peoria, Ill.
62.86	19.28	22.15	11.23	47.65	43.78	22.34	Lansing, Mich.
95.96	27.26	30.71	7.67	55.94		26.67	Kenosha, Wis.
59.24	27.37	29.48	9.88	57.00	18.66	24.46	Racine, Wis.
81.58	30.64	30.07	10.09	67.95	30.28	27.89	10 W. N. Central cities
82.06	34.27	32.33	9.41	74.92	33.08	34.13	Minneapolis, Minn.
76.47	26.75	29.14	8.46	69.95	15.12	27.59	St. Paul, Minn.
95.83	29.29	31.71	10.50	56.66	39.04	26.62	Des Moines, Iowa
141.80	40.07	29.56	18.42	64.68	36.36	31.03	St. Joseph, Mo.
50.86	17.50	15.39	10.37	34.99	19.30	16.89	Springfield, Mo.
112.12	34.38	33.28	9.18	83.98	24.75	35.34	Fargo, N.D.
103.67	37.13	35.61	28.04	75.22	14.94	26.15	Sioux Falls, S.D.
70.29	30.24	26.82	9.31	58.91	23.00	26.17	Lincoln, Neb.
62.01	22.88	24.19	14.52	50.41	20.55	23.24	Topeka, Kan.
62.92	26.72	27.60	10.54	40.17	40.49	20.64	Wichita, Kan.
63.12	30.59	28.88	9.39	41.08	22.83	25.07	8 S. Atlantic cities
67.01	28.65	25.30	11.35	49.57	16.76	23.52	Hagerstown, Md.
98.21	35.03	33.20	6.58	49.87	19.95	38.18	Richmond, Va.
40.57	25.88	26.93	10.46	28.50	27.57	35.42	Wheeling, W.Va.*
73.65	30.35	20.82	13.13	48.60	22.19	27.10	Asheville, N.C.
61.19	27.18	30.88	10.40	41.98	9.62	23.10	Greensboro, N.C.
60.73	25.53	29.28	8.18	25.96	17.53	17.53	Columbia, S.C.
57.80	34.61	29.55	10.10	38.28	25.78	23.10	Atlanta, Ga.*
62.55	30.68	25.34	8.13	20.77	21.53	18.45	Jacksonville, Fla.
52.87	21.33	20.05	10.74	19.20	15.44	20.20	3 E. S. Central cities
49.72	20.50	26.92	8.99	30.42	19.25	23.12	Paducah, Ky.
49.30	20.34	21.73	10.50	18.41	15.01	20.00	Birmingham, Ala.*
65.23	26.06	15.12	13.17	22.08	26.44	20.49	Jackson, Miss.
83.06	29.97	26.36	13.86	31.11	26.66	23.22	6 W. S. Central cities
72.17	29.87	28.27	13.92	36.74	20.37	20.37	Little Rock, Ark.
80.35	35.80	36.57	18.51	31.26	22.90	43.24	Baton Rouge, La.
85.17	30.25	18.06	13.11	31.72	20.73	14.19	Oklahoma City, Okla.
102.83	29.24	20.73	14.14	17.95	13.88	22.26	Austin, Tex.
83.33	29.75	32.64	14.33	30.69	34.38	27.73	Dallas, Tex.
67.52	29.77	24.25	12.70	28.04	38.12	22.72	Wichita Falls, Tex.
71.25	31.13	27.41	15.83	54.32	18.89	23.88	6 Mountain cities
57.88	31.24	45.11	24.84	98.69	15.57	38.15	Butte, Mont.
83.12	43.29	22.55	17.01	73.06	22.32	23.62	Boise, Idaho
60.77	33.40	27.07	18.80	43.09	35.53	33.75	Casper, Wyo.
80.12	31.53	27.43	17.91	39.41	13.35	27.61	Pueblo, Colo.
74.22	33.49	41.84	23.10	24.79	47.52	19.35	Phoenix, Ariz.
75.92	25.92	21.63	9.05	47.94	13.60	21.26	Salt Lake City, Utah
69.22	31.16	26.83	10.96	48.76	16.28	31.02	4 Pacific cities
62.52	33.05	24.97	8.14	50.75	15.50	28.54	Seattle, Wash.*
59.56	27.02	26.24	9.59	49.37	19.65	23.86	Portland, Ore.
93.92	39.33	33.07	13.85	32.73		37.72	Sacramento, Calif.
78.19	29.41	31.53	16.04	19.30		36.76	San Diego, Calif.*

TABLE B 16

Rented Dwelling Units, Computed Average Cost of Facility for All Units by Type of Facility and Average Cost as Percentage of Average Rent, 51 Cities by Geographic Division, 1933

	All types of facility	Furnishings	Electricity	Gas	Water	Heat	Mechanical refrigeration	Garage
	◄──────── A V E R A G E C O S T [1] (DOLLARS) ─────────►							
51 cities	37.87	7.84	2.39	1.77	6.51	8.46	1.70	9.20
4 New England cities	22.24	1.80	1.12	0.81	7.59	6.09	0.42	4.41
Portland, Me.	41.25[3]	4.80	1.79	1.11	8.95	21.19		3.41
Worcester, Mass.*	25.95	2.35	1.61	1.27	7.31	8.57	0.41	4.43
Providence, R.I.*	18.43	1.30	0.90	0.60	7.33	3.31	0.33	4.66
Waterbury, Conn.	23.34	1.65	1.11	0.94	8.83	6.87	0.47	3.47
4 Mid. Atlantic cities	28.96	3.40	1.43	1.25	7.08	7.56	0.35	7.89
Binghamton, N.Y.	39.79[3]	3.72	2.29	1.84	6.35	14.41		11.18
Syracuse, N.Y.	29.97	4.72	1.53	1.30	5.53	8.09	0.31	8.49
Trenton, N.J.	16.38	0.87	1.15	0.72	5.70	5.38	0.50	2.06
Erie, Pa.	29.87	2.88	0.94	1.11	11.99	3.33	0.21	9.41
6 E. N. Central cities	42.76	4.30	2.53	2.50	9.27	9.77	2.33	12.06
Cleveland, Ohio*	40.09	3.84	1.43	1.68	10.12	8.49	1.96	12.57
Indianapolis, Ind.	54.96	4.38	5.73	4.95	9.08	15.10	3.88	11.84
Peoria, Ill.	42.93	9.74	3.05	2.83	9.29	6.07	1.96	9.99
Lansing, Mich.	27.08	4.90	1.21	1.33	1.54	4.24	1.10	12.76
Kenosha, Wis.	33.01[3]	6.53	2.35	2.02	5.90	7.38		8.83
Racine, Wis.	30.25	3.67	1.75	2.00	4.61	9.52	1.18	7.52
10 W. N. Central cities	50.40	9.46	3.19	2.95	5.11	15.90	3.00	10.79
Minneapolis, Minn.	67.36	12.47	3.81	3.66	7.65	23.59	5.36	10.82
St. Paul, Minn.	39.92	5.05	1.93	1.98	3.26	16.99	1.05	9.66
Des Moines, Iowa	48.24	11.22	3.92	3.52	2.59	12.91	3.04	11.04
St. Joseph, Mo.	38.24	9.21	2.52	2.04	4.81	5.95	1.45	12.26
Springfield, Mo.	21.51	3.00	1.08	0.66	5.18	2.20	0.64	8.75
Fargo, N.D.	48.60	10.54	3.75	0.67	2.57	16.38	1.58	13.11
Sioux Falls, S.D.	59.51	11.71	4.64	2.95	8.53	18.66	1.06	11.96
Lincoln, Neb.	39.33	6.33	2.18	1.34	5.09	10.13	1.54	12.72
Topeka, Kan.	36.57	6.63	3.09	3.53	3.70	9.22	1.99	8.41
Wichita, Kan.	40.20	9.88	3.98	4.34	2.37	5.74	2.10	11.79
8 S. Atlantic cities	18.59	1.77	1.65	0.55	4.48	4.44	1.21	4.49
Hagerstown, Md.	25.00	1.14	1.03	0.28	9.42	9.17	0.27	3.69
Richmond, Va.	19.29	2.16	1.08	0.70	1.27	8.83	2.12	3.13
Wheeling, W.Va.*	11.22	1.09	1.89	1.24	1.18	1.56	0.39	3.87
Asheville, N.C.	16.26	1.62	0.48	0.10	1.83	1.80	0.31	10.12
Greensboro, N.C.	25.51	1.53	7.14	0.19	5.71	3.23	0.41	7.30
Columbia, S.C.	12.89	1.40	1.07	0.24	5.40	0.70	0.19	3.89
Atlanta, Ga.*	22.34	1.56	1.80	0.50	6.17	5.74	1.90	4.67
Jacksonville, Fla.	13.70	3.00	0.65	0.25	6.20	0.40	0.32	2.88
3 E. S. Central cities	13.37	1.90	0.55	0.28	3.22	1.75	0.96	4.71
Paducah, Ky.	9.75	1.19	0.70	0.24	1.70	1.95	0.21	3.76
Birmingham, Ala.*	12.89	1.53	0.47	0.24	3.16	1.77	1.05	4.67
Jackson, Miss.	20.37	5.81	1.30	0.68	4.91	1.30	0.61	5.76
6 W. S. Central cities	35.33	12.04	3.06	2.64	3.17	2.02	1.07	11.33
Little Rock, Ark.	18.10	5.27	0.92	0.91	2.48	0.85	0.49	7.18
Baton Rouge, La.	20.58	2.58	0.61	0.44	2.96	0.41	0.05	13.53
Oklahoma City, Okla.	40.11	16.69	4.23	2.74	4.95	3.01	1.47	7.02
Austin, Tex.	21.37	7.40	0.73	0.31	2.39	0.18	0.21	10.15
Dallas, Tex.	42.09	13.42	3.84	3.88	2.77	2.42	1.37	14.39
Wichita Falls, Tex.	29.36	8.85	1.79	1.43	1.33	0.78	0.26	14.92
6 Mountain cities	57.16	20.09	2.30	1.62	11.52	10.54	1.87	9.22
Butte, Mont.	75.56	23.33	3.28	2.57	20.37	19.05	0.47	6.49
Boise, Idaho	61.60	21.13	2.81	0.09	7.68	19.65	1.43	8.81
Casper, Wyo.	72.76	26.01	5.07	5.00	13.46	8.49	1.67	13.06
Pueblo, Colo.	55.34	14.99	3.50	1.10	15.15	6.07	0.53	14.00
Phoenix, Ariz.	65.14	35.85	1.67	0.71	12.94	1.24	2.90	9.83
Salt Lake City, Utah	44.59	11.78	1.35	1.60	7.17	12.76	2.36	7.57
4 Pacific cities	60.43	22.36	3.96	1.77	6.48	10.73	2.04	13.09
Seattle, Wash.*	65.12	19.13	5.75	2.62	5.70	19.13	3.32	9.47
Portland, Ore.	40.15[3]	14.36	3.16	0.57	2.95	8.98	1.37	8.76
Sacramento, Calif.	59.18[3]	22.64	1.81	0.79	11.93	1.30		20.71
San Diego, Calif.*	77.80[3]	39.25	2.44	2.20	10.40	0.87		22.64

Source: Financial Survey of Urban Housing
*Metropolitan district.
[1]Based on the percentage of dwelling units having each type of facility and the average cost of each type of facility for dwelling units using such facility as shown in Tables B 14 and 15.
[2]Based on average cost of facilities and average rents as shown in this table and Table B 13.
[3]Excludes mechanical refrigeration.

Rented Dwelling Units, Computed Average Cost of Facility for All Units by Type of Facility and Average Cost as Percentage of Average Rent, 51 Cities by Geographic Division, 1933

All types of facility	Furnishings	Electricity	Gas	Water	Heat	Mechanical refrigeration	Garage	— AVERAGE COST AS PERCENTAGE OF ANNUAL RENT [2] —
14.5	3.0	0.9	0.7	2.5	3.2	0.6	3.5	51 cities
7.6	0.6	0.4	0.3	2.6	2.1	0.1	1.5	4 New England cities
12.5[3]	1.5	0.5	0.3	2.7	6.5		1.0	Portland, Me.
8.5	0.8	0.5	0.4	2.4	2.8	0.1	1.5	Worcester, Mass.
6.4	0.4	0.3	0.2	2.6	1.2	0.1	1.6	Providence, R.I.*
8.0	0.6	0.4	0.3	3.0	2.3	0.2	1.2	Waterbury, Conn.
10.0	1.2	0.5	0.4	2.5	2.6		2.7	4 Mid. Atlantic cities
12.1[3]	1.1	0.7	0.6	1.9	4.4	0.1	3.4	Binghamton, N.Y.
10.2	1.6	0.5	0.4	1.9	2.7		3.0	Syracuse, N.Y.
6.0	0.3	0.4	0.3	2.0	2.0	0.2	0.8	Trenton, N.J.
11.3	1.1	0.4	0.4	4.4	1.3	0.1	3.6	Erie, Pa.
14.3	1.4	0.9	0.8	3.1	3.3	0.8	4.0	6 E. N. Central cities
12.9	1.2	0.5	0.5	3.3	2.7	0.6	4.1	Cleveland, Ohio*
18.4	1.5	1.9	1.7	3.0	5.0	1.3	4.0	Indianapolis, Ind.
15.2	3.5	1.1	1.0	3.3	2.1	0.7	3.5	Peoria, Ill.
18.3	2.4	0.6	0.7	0.8	2.1	0.5	6.2	Lansing, Mich.
14.6[3]	2.9	1.0	0.9	2.6	3.3		3.9	Kenosha, Wis.
13.8	1.7	0.8	0.9	2.1	4.4	0.5	3.4	Racine, Wis.
17.9	3.4	1.1	1.0	1.8	5.7	1.1	3.8	10 W. N. Central cities
21.2	3.9	1.2	1.1	2.4	7.4	1.7	8.4	Minneapolis, Minn.
13.7	1.7	0.7	0.7	1.1	5.8	0.4	3.3	St. Paul, Minn.
17.0	3.9	1.4	1.2	0.9	4.6	1.1	3.9	Des Moines, Iowa
16.3	3.9	1.1	0.9	2.1	2.5	0.6	5.2	St. Joseph, Mo.
11.8	1.6	0.6	0.4	2.8	1.2	0.4	4.8	Springfield, Mo.
14.5	3.1	1.1	0.2	0.8	4.9	0.5	3.9	Fargo, N.D.
19.9	3.9	1.6	1.0	2.8	6.2	0.4	4.0	Sioux Falls, S.D.
14.7	2.4	0.8	0.5	1.9	3.8	0.6	4.7	Lincoln, Neb.
15.1	2.7	1.3	1.5	1.5	3.8	0.8	3.5	Topeka, Kan.
20.1	4.9	2.0	2.2	1.2	2.9	1.0	5.9	Wichita, Kan.
8.6	0.8	0.8	0.2	2.1	2.0	0.6	2.1	8 S. Atlantic cities
10.8	0.5	0.4	0.1	4.1	4.0	0.1	1.6	Hagerstown, Md.
6.8	0.8	0.4	0.2	0.4	3.2	0.7	1.1	Richmond, Va.
5.0	0.5	0.9	0.5	0.5	0.7	0.2	1.7	Wheeling, W.Va.*
9.6	1.0	0.3	0.1	1.1	1.1	0.2	5.8	Asheville, N.C.
12.9	0.8	3.6	0.1	2.9	1.6	0.2	3.7	Greensboro, N.C.
7.0	0.8	0.6	0.1	2.9	0.4	0.1	2.1	Columbia, S.C.
10.1	0.7	0.8	0.2	2.8	2.6	0.9	2.1	Atlanta, Ga.*
8.0	1.7	0.4	0.1	3.7	0.2	0.2	1.7	Jacksonville, Fla.
8.5	1.2	0.4	0.2	2.0	1.1	0.6	3.0	3 E. S. Central cities
6.7	0.8	0.5	0.2	1.2	1.3	0.1	2.6	Paducah, Ky.
8.5	1.0	0.2	0.2	2.1	1.2	0.7	3.1	Birmingham, Ala.*
8.9	2.5	0.6	0.3	2.2	0.6	0.3	2.4	Jackson, Miss.
14.3	4.9	1.2	1.1	1.3	0.8	0.4	4.6	6 W. S. Central cities
9.5	2.8	0.5	0.5	1.3	0.4	0.3	3.7	Little Rock, Ark.
9.1	1.1	0.3	0.2	1.3	0.2	0.1	5.9	Baton Rouge, La.
16.0	6.6	1.7	1.1	2.0	1.2	0.6	2.8	Oklahoma City, Okla.
8.3	2.9	0.3	0.1	0.9	0.1	0.1	3.9	Austin, Tex.
15.3	4.9	1.4	1.4	1.0	0.9	0.5	5.2	Dallas, Tex.
19.1	5.7	1.2	0.9	0.9	0.5	0.2	9.7	Wichita Falls, Tex.
23.4	8.2	0.9	0.7	4.7	4.3	0.8	3.8	6 Mountain cities
30.6	9.5	1.3	1.0	8.3	7.7	0.2	2.6	Butte, Mont.
21.5	7.3	1.0	0.1	2.7	6.8	0.5	3.1	Boise, Idaho
33.1	11.7	2.3	2.3	6.1	3.9	0.8	6.0	Casper, Wyo.
29.8	8.1	1.8	0.6	8.2	3.3	0.3	7.5	Pueblo, Colo.
26.8	14.8	0.7	0.3	5.3	0.5	1.2	4.0	Phoenix, Ariz.
17.2	4.6	0.5	0.6	2.8	4.9	0.9	2.9	Salt Lake City, Utah
24.1	8.9	1.6	0.7	2.6	4.3	0.8	5.2	4 Pacific cities
25.5	7.5	2.2	1.0	2.2	7.6	1.3	3.7	Seattle, Wash.*
19.7	7.0	1.6	0.3	1.4	4.4	0.7	4.3	Portland, Ore.
18.5[3]	7.1	0.6	0.2	3.7	0.4		6.5	Sacramento, Calif.
28.3[3]	14.3	0.9	0.8	3.8	0.3		8.2	San Diego, Calif.*

TABLE B 17

Rented Dwelling Units, Average Cost (dollars) of Facilities included in Annual Rent by Rent Groups, 50 Cities by Geographic Division, 1933

	All rent groups	$1–59	$60–119	$120–179	$180–239	$240–299	$300–359	$360–479	$480–599	$600–899	$900–1,199	$1,200 and over
50 cities[1]	37.85	18.26	18.56	24.05	28.87	41.04	53.09	70.70	91.29	110.39	149.40	264.19
4 New England cities	22.19			21.06	14.02	20.78	33.30	38.82	78.83	90.70	153.36	209.33
Portland, Me.	41.25					38.00	32.90	58.53	63.64			
Worcester, Mass.	25.95			24.90	17.87	15.39	23.31	43.97	89.11	98.68		
Providence, R.I.*	18.43				12.59	20.87	38.39	34.95	78.12			209.33
Waterbury, Conn.	23.34			13.44	15.60	16.67	20.53	37.42	75.59	74.87	153.36	
4 Mid. Atlantic cities	28.87		22.35	14.62	19.64	25.99	35.96	50.67	66.50	81.27		
Binghamton, N.Y.	39.79				17.04	20.64	36.26	60.49	93.07			
Syracuse, N.Y.	29.97				21.08	27.25	44.44	58.17		99.13		
Trenton, N.J.	16.38			11.82	17.77	22.94	16.68	33.19	37.84	69.26		
Erie, Pa.	29.87		22.35	17.12	20.24	30.00	35.58	43.82	72.83	55.50		
6 E. N. Central cities	42.80		15.39	20.10	25.14	39.97	53.79	72.18	90.21	107.76	149.06	294.41
Cleveland, Ohio*	40.09			19.37	22.02	35.87	50.84	63.56	86.09	92.49	149.06	294.41
Indianapolis, Ind.	54.96		16.17	18.31	29.64	48.38	60.26	88.69	91.35	147.22		
Peoria, Ill.	42.93		13.54	23.12	37.12	54.08	58.60	86.26	122.65	122.99		
Lansing, Mich.	27.08		12.65	20.59	24.69	47.31	55.46	80.70	125.18			
Kenosha, Wis.	33.01			49.16	38.23	34.17	49.58	56.46		92.20		
Racine, Wis.	30.25			24.84	29.41	34.48	58.84	103.23	77.48			
10 W. N. Central cities	50.40		32.23	28.72	35.53	47.00	60.87	83.29	104.29	149.04		
Minneapolis, Minn.	67.36		44.89	31.63	39.30	53.81	65.88	109.63	120.00	198.44		
St. Paul, Minn.	39.92			40.87	32.76	38.27	46.57	56.72	79.36	112.29		
Des Moines, Iowa	48.24		26.10	15.61	31.81	39.02	60.40	76.56	119.86	134.92		
St. Joseph, Mo.	38.24			12.89	19.92	32.96						
Springfield, Mo.	21.51		10.42	19.16	38.54	29.51	53.85	76.43		94.90		
Fargo, N.D.	48.60					53.83	50.24	41.27	54.90	54.22		
Sioux Falls, S.D.	59.51			34.30	42.30	55.88	63.16	54.53	84.82	140.52		
Lincoln, Neb.	39.34		28.07	19.54	27.33	40.60	49.96	59.94	85.27	78.75		
Topeka, Kan.	36.57		12.82	18.01	34.53	42.03	53.26	76.67	101.74	163.52		
Wichita, Kan.	40.20		12.61	33.43	43.04	66.59	86.23	80.59		133.39		
8 S. Atlantic cities	18.48	18.26	7.71	11.01	16.30	26.57	33.02	58.19	87.11	107.21		
Hagerstown, Md.	25.00			15.14	23.97	37.53	36.82	68.72	77.33			
Richmond, Va.	19.29		1.49	4.78	5.26	15.10	15.56	53.38	72.07	105.32		
Wheeling, W.Va.*	11.22			4.34	10.30	15.72	23.24	41.84		58.07		
Asheville, N.C.	16.26		8.94	19.47	41.40	57.13	44.75	48.54				
Greensboro, N.C.	25.51	18.26	20.01	11.64	20.36	38.19	40.57	54.33	87.96	79.18		
Columbia, S.C.	12.86		13.61			42.62	14.90	41.49	67.10	117.09		
Atlanta, Ga.*	22.34		8.87	13.74	18.04	26.40	40.22	72.02	97.36	128.48		
Jacksonville, Fla.	13.70		5.84	13.75	19.21	29.22	43.15	52.08				
2 E. S. Central cities	13.60		8.69	13.43	18.39	36.59	50.16	65.57		72.85		
Birmingham, Ala.*	12.89		8.69	13.43	18.32	35.16	52.16	67.66		71.80		
Jackson, Miss.	20.37				19.09	50.16	31.19	45.82		82.74		
6 W. S. Central cities	35.30		9.45	18.04	27.03	42.92	58.59	72.40	87.87	107.35		
Little Rock, Ark.	18.10		7.26	13.13	21.29	36.97	42.37	52.93	41.79			
Baton Rouge, La.	20.58			12.21		27.55		32.57				
Oklahoma City, Okla.	40.11			30.79	26.39	65.02	65.22	68.03	92.20	101.16		
Austin, Tex.	21.37			9.47	17.67		34.25	40.71	49.65	87.82		
Dallas, Tex.	42.09		10.05	14.97	27.90	33.25	54.74	90.16	104.45	114.36		
Wichita Falls, Tex.	29.36			11.76	44.68		114.86					
6 Mountain cities	57.20		41.77	51.36	50.86	66.56	87.37	101.69	107.07	119.68		
Butte, Mont.	75.56		46.57	53.20	58.45	71.25	71.62	137.23		158.58		
Boise, Idaho	61.60			29.93	31.99	52.72	98.39	87.76	157.54			
Casper, Wyo.	72.76		33.85	64.90	109.75	81.16	106.28	105.26		145.17		
Pueblo, Colo.	55.34		42.48	46.42	67.04	63.88	107.50	130.22	136.47			
Phoenix, Ariz.	65.14			91.87	50.08	88.68	92.75	133.62	135.06	189.29		
Salt Lake City, Utah	44.59		41.40	33.68	36.32	54.81	77.86	66.94	75.00	68.51		
4 Pacific cities	60.07		24.05	40.63	56.01	69.77	77.99	98.08	103.06	104.26		
Seattle, Wash.*	65.12			41.82	56.53	83.71	103.10	94.67	104.50	106.89		
Portland, Ore.	40.15		24.05	31.84	39.84	49.04	53.27	86.04				
Sacramento, Calif.	59.18			28.58	44.83	48.74	54.27	75.82	149.93	92.68		
San Diego, Calif.*	77.80			55.58	81.93	80.25	73.47	130.87	79.63			

Source: Financial Survey of Urban Housing. Based on number of dwelling units reporting facilities and those reporting cost of facilities as shown in Tables B 14 and 15. Averages shown here similar to those shown for all dwelling units in Table B 16. Average not shown for fewer than 3 reports.

*Metropolitan district.

[1]Geographic division and 50-city averages weighted by number of rental units (RPI).

TABLE B 18

Rented Dwelling Units reporting Gross and Net Rent, Average Annual Gross Rent including Facilities, Net Rent for Space per Dwelling Unit, and Average Cost of Facilities included in Rent as Percentage of Gross and Net Rent, by Type, 11 Cities, 1933

	NUMBER REPORTING	AVERAGE ANNUAL RENT PER UNIT, 1933		COST OF FACILITIES INCLUDED IN RENT AS PERCENTAGE OF	
		Gross rent	Net rent for space	Gross rent	Net rent for space
		(dollars)		(per cent)	

1 - F A M I L Y   D W E L L I N G S

	NUMBER REPORTING	Gross rent	Net rent for space	Gross rent	Net rent for space
11 cities[1]		257	234	8.9	9.9
Atlanta, Ga.	45	233	218	6.6	7.0
Birmingham, Ala.	65	148	140	5.5	5.9
Cleveland, Ohio	110	363	323	11.1	12.5
Dallas, Tex.	67	270	247	8.6	9.4
Indianapolis, Ind.	50	277	255	7.8	8.4
Lincoln, Neb.	65	257	234	9.1	10.0
Minneapolis, Minn.	98	338	306	9.4	10.3
Peoria, Ill.	106	258	234	9.4	10.4
Portland, Ore.	87	198	179	9.6	10.7
St. Paul, Minn.	56	316	296	6.5	6.9
Seattle, Wash.	96	233	203	13.0	14.9

2 - F A M I L Y   D W E L L I N G S

	NUMBER REPORTING	Gross rent	Net rent for space	Gross rent	Net rent for space
11 cities[1]		238	210	11.4	12.9
Atlanta, Ga.	36	156	145	7.2	7.8
Birmingham, Ala.	9	87	77	11.5	13.0
Cleveland, Ohio	123	290	258	10.9	12.3
Dallas, Tex.	18	267	228	14.6	17.0
Indianapolis, Ind.	53	256	223	12.8	14.6
Lincoln, Neb.	7	270	231	14.5	17.0
Minneapolis, Minn.	51	277	245	11.7	13.2
Peoria, Ill.	14	307	246	19.8	24.7
Portland, Ore.	11	195	161	17.6	21.3
St. Paul, Minn.	33	264	242	8.2	8.9
Seattle, Wash.	9	204	164	19.7	24.6

A P A R T M E N T S

	NUMBER REPORTING	Gross rent	Net rent for space	Gross rent	Net rent for space
11 cities[1]		330	249	24.7	33.9
Atlanta, Ga.	18	326	266	18.5	22.6
Birmingham, Ala.	16	336	279	16.9	20.3
Cleveland, Ohio	58	344	280	18.5	22.7
Dallas, Tex.	17	332	212	36.2	56.8
Indianapolis, Ind.	14	435	314	27.8	38.6
Lincoln, Neb.	12	339	249	26.5	36.1
Minneapolis, Minn.	17	348	250	28.0	38.9
Peoria, Ill.	16	384	240	37.5	60.0
Portland, Ore.	11	231	147	36.2	56.7
St. Paul, Minn.	12	333	270	18.8	23.1
Seattle, Wash.	27	295	219	25.8	34.7

Source: *Financial Survey of Urban Housing*
[1]*11-city averages weighted by number of rental units in each city (RPI).*

TABLE B 19

Rented Dwelling Units, Ratio of Value to Annual Rent by Type, 42 Cities by Geographic Division, 1934

	1–family	2–family	3–or more family		1–family	2–family	3–or more family
42 cities[1]	10.8	9.4	8.0	8 S. Atlantic cities	10.0	9.1	7.6
				Hagerstown, Md.	9.4	10.5	8.7
				Richmond, Va.	9.2	9.0	7.2
3 New England cities	12.2	8.5	7.7	Wheeling, W. Va.*	11.9	9.1	9.2
Portland, Me.	10.2	8.1	6.9	Asheville, N.C.	15.2	10.4	7.9
Worcester, Mass.	11.5	8.7	7.8	Greensboro, N.C.	11.6	9.5	7.4
Providence, R.I.*	12.5	8.5	7.7	Charleston, S.C.	7.9	7.9	6.4
				Columbia, S.C.	7.7	13.8	8.8
3 Mid. Atlantic cities	12.5	11.7	12.4	Atlanta, Ga.*	8.7	8.7	7.6
Syracuse, N.Y.	14.5	11.9	13.3				
Trenton, N.J.	10.3	11.7	10.7	E. S. Central[2]	9.5	8.8	7.7
Erie, Pa.	12.8	11.1	10.0				
				5 W. S. Central cities	8.9	8.2	8.0
6 E. N. Central cities	12.6	10.7	10.3	Little Rock, Ark.	9.9	7.8	8.7
Cleveland, Ohio*	13.3	10.6	11.0	Oklahoma City, Okla.	9.3	8.4	9.8
Indianapolis, Ind.	10.1	9.9	6.6	Austin, Tex.	9.4	9.4	9.3
Peoria, Ill.	11.0	8.4	9.0	Dallas, Tex.	7.9	7.9	6.5
Lansing, Mich.	14.6	12.2	8.6	Wichita Falls, Tex.	9.7	8.7	7.8
Kenosha, Wis.	18.0	15.5	13.3				
Racine, Wis.	18.0	14.9	17.2	4 Mountain cities	9.9	7.9	5.9
				Butte, Mont.	6.2	5.7	5.6
9 W. N. Central cities	9.6	6.4	5.9	Pueblo, Colo.	8.2	8.8	4.3
Minneapolis, Minn.	9.5	4.9	5.5	Phoenix, Ariz.	11.9	8.2	8.6
St. Paul, Minn.	10.0	7.8	6.1	Salt Lake City, Utah	10.4	8.1	5.5
Des Moines, Iowa	8.9	7.1	5.9				
St. Joseph, Mo.	9.6	7.9	5.6	4 Pacific cities	10.8	8.6	6.6
Springfield, Mo.	10.5	8.9	6.2	Seattle, Wash.*	10.5	8.4	6.8
Sioux Falls, S.D.	10.5	8.3	7.8	Portland, Ore.	12.4	9.2	6.3
Lincoln, Neb.	9.2	7.6	6.5	Sacramento, Calif.	9.9	8.4	6.2
Topeka, Kan.	9.5	8.0	7.1	San Diego, Calif.*	9.5	8.5	7.1
Wichita, Kan.	10.1	9.2	6.4				

Source: Financial Survey of Urban Housing
*Metropolitan district.
[1]Geographic division and 42-city ratios weighted by number of rental units, by type, in each city (RPI).
[2]Weighted average of S. Atlantic and W. S. Central.

TABLE B 20

Rented Dwelling Units, Ratio of Value to Annual Rent by Type and Geographic Division, 1930 and 1934

	1930	1934		1930	1934
New England			**E. S. Central**		
All types	10.0	9.0	All types	10.4	9.1
1-family	13.1	11.8	1-family	10.8	9.5
2-family	9.1	8.2	2-family	10.0	8.8
3-or-more family	8.2	7.4	3-or-more family	8.8	7.7
Mid. Atlantic			**W. S. Central**		
All types	14.2	11.8	All types	10.2	8.6
1-family	14.4	12.0	1-family	10.5	8.8
2-family	13.5	11.2	2-family	9.6	8.1
3-or-more family	14.3	11.9	3-or-more family	9.4	7.9
E. N. Central			**Mountain**		
All types	11.4	11.9	All types	9.7	9.4
1-family	12.7	13.2	1-family	10.9	10.5
2-family	10.8	11.2	2-family	8.7	8.4
3-or-more family	10.4	10.8	3-or-more family	6.4	6.2
W. N. Central			**Pacific**		
All types	9.0	8.5	All types	11.0	9.4
1-family	10.7	10.2	1-family	12.7	10.9
2-family	7.2	6.8	2-family	10.2	8.7
3-or-more family	6.5	6.2	3-or-more family	7.8	6.7
S. Atlantic					
All types	10.4	9.5			
1-family	11.1	10.1			
2-family	10.1	9.2			
3-or-more family	8.5	7.7			

[1]See Part Two, Ch. II, sec. 5.

SECTION C

Family Income

The 13 tables in section C are discussed in general in Part Two, Chapter III. Table C 1 is a simple summary of total owner-occupant and tenant families by 39 income groups for 1929 and 1933 for the 33 cities covered in the detailed tabulations in Table C 3. Table C 2 presents a similar summary for the income reported in Table C 3 for each city separately. Table C 3 gives average annual rent and income for 1929 and 1933 and the percentage relationship between them.

In all the tables, because of rounding in editing the schedules, average family income appears in even hundreds of dollars for the first 17 of the 39 income groups above "no income." This rounding is also responsible for the unevenness of the successive income class intervals (see footnote to Table C 1).

Tables C 4–13 show results of combining the two methods of enumeration. Table C 4 presents average annual income for 1929, 1932, and 1933 as reported in 1934 by families of the respective tenures. The figures for 1929 and 1932 are therefore retrospective reporting. Covering only those families reporting as such in 1934 the reports exclude the incomes of those families which may have existed in 1929–32 but not at the date of the survey in 1934. To obtain geographic division and all city totals in Tables C 4–13, the number of dwelling units or families of the appropriate tenure as shown by the Federal Real Property Inventory were uniformly used as weights. The figures in Table C 13 are simple averages of the percentages reported as the proportion of full time that the head of the family was employed.

Many of the schedules were rejected in the course of editing the field returns, especially schedules returned by mail. An examination of these rejected schedules shows that they had two biases as compared with the used schedules: the first was a concentration in the lowest income groups; the second, a smaller concentration in the higher income groups. When all rejected schedules are combined with the used schedules, however, the pattern of the distribution by income groups changes little in any of the 52 cities by each tenure and both canvasses. For owner-occupant families the concentration in the upper groups was more pronounced than for tenants.

TABLE C I

Owner-occupant and Tenant Families, Number and Percentage Distribution by 39 Income Groups, 33 Cities combined, 1929 and 1933

Annual income group[1]	TOTAL 1929 Number	TOTAL 1929 Percentage distribution	TOTAL 1933 Number	TOTAL 1933 Percentage distribution	OWNER-OCCUPANT 1929 Number	OWNER-OCCUPANT 1929 Percentage distribution	OWNER-OCCUPANT 1933 Number	OWNER-OCCUPANT 1933 Percentage distribution	TENANT 1929 Number	TENANT 1929 Percentage distribution	TENANT 1933 Number	TENANT 1933 Percentage distribution
All groups	213,522	100.0	241,207	100.0	102,824	100.0	108,229	100.0	110,698	100.0	132,978	100.0
No income	7,782	3.6	12,304	5.1	3,944	3.8	6,014	5.6	3,838	3.5	6,290	4.7
$1- 149	2,489	1.2	11,621	4.8	1,232	1.2	4,400	4.1	1,257	1.1	7,221	5.4
150- 250	4,265	2.0	14,655	6.1	1,950	1.9	5,635	5.2	2,315	2.1	9,020	6.8
251- 349	3,865	1.8	11,165	4.6	1,594	1.5	4,343	4.0	2,271	2.1	6,822	5.1
350- 450	5,127	2.4	12,961	5.4	2,096	2.1	5,154	4.8	3,031	2.7	7,807	5.9
451- 549	5,941	2.8	12,704	5.3	2,374	2.3	5,172	4.8	3,567	3.2	7,532	5.7
550- 650	6,328	2.9	13,128	5.4	2,475	2.4	5,451	5.0	3,853	3.5	7,677	5.8
651- 749	4,890	2.3	9,447	3.9	1,862	1.8	3,760	3.5	3,028	2.7	5,687	4.2
750- 850	7,258	3.4	12,609	5.2	2,728	2.6	5,092	4.7	4,530	4.1	7,517	5.7
851- 949	5,773	2.7	9,029	3.8	2,161	2.1	3,715	3.4	3,612	3.3	5,314	4.0
950-1,050	11,852	5.6	14,751	6.1	4,792	4.7	6,365	5.9	7,060	6.4	8,386	6.3
1,051-1,149	3,898	1.8	6,096	2.5	1,574	1.5	2,586	2.4	2,324	2.1	3,510	2.6
1,150-1,250	14,193	6.6	13,746	5.7	5,787	5.6	5,948	5.5	8,406	7.6	7,798	5.9
1,251-1,349	4,906	2.3	5,650	2.3	1,983	1.9	2,391	2.2	2,973	2.7	3,259	2.5
1,350-1,450	6,247	2.9	6,717	2.8	2,666	2.6	2,979	2.8	3,581	3.2	3,738	2.8
1,451-1,549	11,230	5.3	9,215	3.8	5,207	5.1	4,374	4.0	6,023	5.4	4,841	3.6
1,550-1,650	6,923	3.2	6,285	2.6	2,950	2.8	2,878	2.6	3,973	3.6	3,407	2.6
1,651-1,749	4,374	2.0	4,297	1.8	1,936	1.9	2,028	1.9	2,438	2.2	2,269	1.7
1,750-1,949	17,184	8.1	12,375	5.1	7,888	7.7	5,929	5.5	9,296	8.4	6,446	4.8
1,950-2,149	15,443	7.3	9,530	3.9	8,065	7.9	4,967	4.6	7,378	6.7	4,563	3.4
2,150-2,349	6,856	3.2	4,755	2.0	3,734	3.6	2,542	2.4	3,122	2.8	2,213	1.7
2,350-2,549	13,198	6.2	6,692	2.8	7,070	6.9	3,595	3.3	6,123	5.5	3,097	2.4
2,550-2,749	4,936	2.3	2,899	1.2	2,746	2.7	1,539	1.4	2,190	2.0	1,360	1.0
2,750-3,149	11,584	5.4	5,875	2.5	6,608	6.4	3,284	3.0	4,976	4.5	2,591	2.0
3,150-3,549	5,295	2.5	2,966	1.2	3,269	3.2	1,727	1.6	2,026	1.8	1,239	0.9
3,550-3,949	4,660	2.2	2,000	0.8	2,640	2.6	1,115	1.0	2,010	1.8	885	0.7
3,950-4,450	4,205	2.0	2,044	0.9	2,628	2.5	1,306	1.2	1,577	1.4	738	0.5
4,451-4,949	2,367	1.1	1,113	0.5	1,509	1.5	693	0.6	858	0.8	420	0.3
4,950-5,450	2,910	1.4	1,373	0.6	1,882	1.8	916	0.9	1,028	0.9	457	0.4
5,451-5,949	701	0.3	350	0.1	484	0.5	232	0.2	217	0.2	118	0.1
5,950-6,949	2,181	1.0	944	0.4	1,505	1.4	652	0.6	676	0.6	292	0.2
6,950-7,949	1,227	0.6	511	0.2	869	0.9	357	0.3	358	0.3	154	0.1
7,950-8,949	740	0.3	350	0.1	542	0.5	254	0.2	198	0.2	96	0.1
8,850-9,949	398	0.2	186	0.1	291	0.3	135	0.1	107	0.1	51	0.1
9,950-11,949	812	0.4	331	0.1	615	0.6	265	0.3	197	0.2	66	0.1
11,950-13,949	425	0.2	174	0.1	346	0.3	146	0.1	79	0.1	28	
13,950-15,949	317	0.1	119	0.1	255	0.3	87	0.1	62	0.1	32	
15,950-19,949	216	0.1	75	0.1	162	0.2	63	0.1	54	0.1	12	
19,950 and over	536	0.3	165	0.1	455	0.4	140	0.1	81	0.1	25	

Source: Financial Survey of Urban Housing (special tabulation). Based on empirical data obtained by personal enumeration and mail return. Distributions uncorrected for non-representativeness of size of population groups or for differences in size of samples. Total is simple addition of two tenures. Percentage not shown if less than one-tenth of one per cent.

TABLE C 2

Owner-occupant and Tenant Families, Annual Family Income, Amount and Percentage Distribution by 39[2] Income Groups, 33 Cities combined, 1929 and 1933

All groups	420,856.6	100.0	299,677.0	100.0	234,773.7	100.0	154,255.3	100.0	186,082.9	100.0	145,421.7	100.0
$1– 149	248.9	0.1	1,162.1	0.4	123.2	0.1	440.0	0.3	125.7	0.1	722.1	0.5
150– 250	853.0	0.2	2,931.0	1.0	390.0	0.2	1,127.0	0.7	463.0	0.2	1,804.0	1.2
251– 349	1,159.5	0.3	3,349.5	1.1	478.2	0.2	1,302.9	0.8	681.3	0.4	2,046.6	1.4
350– 450	2,050.8	0.5	5,184.4	1.7	838.4	0.3	2,061.6	1.3	1,212.4	0.7	3,122.8	2.1
451– 549	2,970.5	0.7	6,352.0	2.1	1,187.0	0.5	2,586.0	1.7	1,783.5	1.0	3,766.0	2.6
550– 650	3,796.8	0.9	7,876.8	2.6	1,485.0	0.6	3,270.6	2.1	2,311.8	1.2	4,606.2	3.2
651– 749	3,423.0	0.8	6,612.9	2.2	1,303.4	0.6	2,632.0	1.7	2,119.6	1.1	3,980.9	2.7
750– 850	5,806.4	1.4	10,087.2	3.4	2,182.4	0.9	4,073.6	2.6	3,624.0	1.9	6,013.6	4.1
851– 949	5,195.7	1.2	8,126.1	2.7	1,944.9	0.8	3,343.5	2.2	3,250.8	1.7	4,782.6	3.3
950– 1,050	11,852.0	2.8	14,750.9	4.9	4,792.0	2.0	6,365.0	4.1	7,060.0	3.8	8,385.9	5.8
1,051– 1,149	4,287.8	1.0	6,705.6	2.2	1,731.4	0.7	2,844.6	1.8	2,556.4	1.4	3,861.0	2.7
1,150– 1,250	17,031.6	4.0	16,495.2	5.5	6,944.4	3.0	7,187.6	4.6	10,087.2	5.4	9,357.6	6.4
1,251– 1,349	6,377.8	1.5	7,345.0	2.5	2,512.9	1.1	3,108.3	2.0	3,864.9	2.1	4,236.7	2.9
1,350– 1,450	8,745.8	2.1	9,403.8	3.1	3,732.4	1.6	4,170.6	2.7	5,013.4	2.7	5,238.2	3.6
1,451– 1,549	16,845.0	4.0	13,822.5	4.6	7,810.5	3.3	6,561.0	4.3	9,034.5	4.9	7,261.5	5.0
1,550– 1,650	11,076.8	2.6	10,056.0	3.4	4,720.0	2.0	4,604.8	3.0	6,356.8	3.4	5,451.2	3.8
1,651– 1,749	7,435.8	1.8	7,304.9	2.4	3,291.2	1.4	3,447.6	2.2	4,144.6	2.2	3,857.3	2.6
1,750– 1,949	31,381.9	7.5	22,611.7	7.5	14,394.6	6.1	10,832.3	7.0	16,987.3	9.1	11,779.4	8.1
1,950– 2,149	31,490.6	7.5	19,350.5	6.5	16,418.9	7.0	10,076.3	6.5	15,071.7	8.1	9,274.2	6.4
2,150– 2,349	15,341.3	3.6	10,639.0	3.6	8,357.7	3.6	5,687.6	3.7	6,983.6	3.8	4,951.4	3.4
2,350– 2,549	32,320.0	7.7	16,363.0	5.5	17,325.4	7.4	8,803.3	5.7	14,994.6	8.1	7,559.7	5.2
2,550– 2,749	13,045.1	3.1	7,667.4	2.6	7,258.7	3.1	4,069.3	2.6	5,786.4	3.1	3,598.1	2.5
2,750– 3,149	34,425.5	8.2	17,318.3	5.8	19,658.2	8.4	9,671.8	6.3	14,767.3	7.9	7,646.5	5.3
3,150– 3,549	17,863.3	4.2	9,931.2	3.3	11,033.0	4.7	5,783.8	3.8	6,830.3	3.7	4,147.4	2.9
3,550– 3,949	17,134.2	4.1	7,404.4	2.5	9,726.6	4.1	4,136.0	2.7	7,407.6	4.0	3,268.4	2.3
3,950– 4,450	17,348.5	4.1	8,400.6	2.8	10,864.8	4.6	5,364.6	3.5	6,483.7	3.5	3,036.0	2.1
4,451– 4,949	11,003.3	2.6	5,171.1	1.7	7,008.4	3.0	3,219.7	2.1	3,994.9	2.1	1,951.4	1.3
4,950– 5,450	14,808.5	3.5	6,966.8	2.3	9,596.4	4.1	4,646.2	3.0	5,212.1	2.8	2,320.6	1.6
5,451– 5,949	3,944.0	0.9	1,971.4	0.7	2,725.3	1.2	1,304.5	0.9	1,218.7	0.7	666.9	0.5
5,950– 6,949	13,486.2	3.2	5,843.6	1.9	9,314.1	4.0	4,033.2	2.6	4,172.1	2.2	1,810.4	1.2
6,950– 7,949	8,980.0	2.1	3,711.6	1.2	6,369.0	2.7	2,593.5	1.7	2,611.0	1.4	1,118.1	0.8
7,950– 8,949	6,100.9	1.5	2,871.3	1.0	4,480.7	1.9	2,077.7	1.4	1,620.2	0.9	793.6	0.5
8,950– 9,949	3,659.6	0.9	1,699.5	0.6	2,675.4	1.1	1,233.3	0.8	984.2	0.5	466.2	0.3
9,950–11,949	8,289.6	2.0	3,393.3	1.1	6,292.9	2.7	2,715.8	1.8	1,996.7	1.1	677.5	0.5
11,950–13,949	5,221.9	1.2	2,160.7	0.7	4,250.5	1.8	1,815.2	1.2	971.4	0.5	345.5	0.2
13,950–15,949	4,680.3	1.1	1,758.9	0.6	3,770.7	1.6	1,287.3	0.8	909.6	0.5	471.6	0.3
15,950–19,949	3,739.6	0.9	1,303.2	0.4	2,812.6	1.2	1,094.4	0.7	927.0	0.5	208.8	0.1
19,950 and over	17,435.1	4.2	5,573.6	1.9	14,972.5	6.4	4,732.8	3.1	2,462.6	1.3	840.8	0.6

Source: Financial Survey of Urban Housing (special tabulation). Based on empirical data obtained by personal enumeration and mail return. Distributions uncorrected for non-representativeness of population group or for differences in size of samples. Total is simple addition of two tenures.
1See Table C 1, footnote 1.
2Only 38 income groups shown since an amount of income cannot be shown for the 'no income' group.

TABLE C 3

Tenant Families, Number reporting Rent and Income, Average Annual Rent and Income, and Ratio of Rent to Income by 39 Income Groups; Personal Enumeration and Mail Returns, 33 Cities, combined and Each Individual City, 1929 and 1933

33 CITIES COMBINED

Column groups (each with: Rent — No. of Reports, Average (dollars); Income — No. of Reports, Average (dollars); Rent-Income Ratio):

Annual Income group[1]	1929 PERSONAL ENUMERATION					1929 MAIL RETURNS					1933 PERSONAL ENUMERATION					1933 MAIL RETURNS				
	Rent No. Rep.	Rent Avg. (\$)	Inc. No. Rep.	Inc. Avg. (\$)	Ratio	Rent No. Rep.	Rent Avg. (\$)	Inc. No. Rep.	Inc. Avg. (\$)	Ratio	Rent No. Rep.	Rent Avg. (\$)	Inc. No. Rep.	Inc. Avg. (\$)	Ratio	Rent No. Rep.	Rent Avg. (\$)	Inc. No. Rep.	Inc. Avg. (\$)	Ratio
All groups	53,293	338	61,894	1,809	0.210	37,438	371	46,804	1,772	0.209	67,693	258	68,283	1,025	0.252	64,088	278	64,695	1,166	0.238
No Income	1,292	271	1,458	0		1,580	258	2,380	0		2,684	197	2,725	0		3,567	199	3,565	0	
\$1- 149	510	162	623	100	1.620	481	196	634	100	1.960	3,444	135	3,491	100	1.350	3,682	160	3,730	100	1.600
150- 250	1,129	169	1,351	200	0.845	722	200	964	200	1.000	5,156	151	5,221	200	0.755	3,754	170	3,799	200	0.850
251- 349	1,186	177	1,397	300	0.590	659	208	874	300	0.693	4,053	167	4,109	300	0.557	2,686	178	2,713	300	0.593
350- 450	1,635	183	1,891	400	0.458	877	204	1,140	400	0.510	4,464	179	4,508	400	0.448	3,251	189	3,299	400	0.473
451- 549	1,918	206	2,232	500	0.412	1,016	231	1,335	500	0.462	4,302	197	4,351	500	0.394	3,142	204	3,181	500	0.408
550- 650	2,074	214	2,400	600	0.357	1,094	231	1,453	600	0.385	4,272	210	4,305	600	0.350	3,325	213	3,372	600	0.355
651- 749	1,675	222	1,879	700	0.317	877	240	1,149	700	0.343	2,970	216	2,997	700	0.309	2,660	219	2,690	700	0.313
750- 850	2,517	231	2,885	800	0.289	1,236	257	1,645	800	0.321	3,977	231	4,007	800	0.289	3,472	233	3,510	800	0.291
851- 949	2,005	247	2,285	900	0.274	1,022	253	1,327	900	0.281	2,729	244	2,750	900	0.271	2,535	242	2,564	900	0.269
950- 1,050	3,783	269	4,375	1,000	0.269	1,998	274	2,685	1,000	0.274	4,429	282	4,456	1,000	0.262	3,895	259	3,930	1,000	0.259
1,051- 1,149	1,186	270	1,353	1,100	0.245	748	282	971	1,100	0.256	1,661	283	1,687	1,100	0.239	1,835	264	1,843	1,100	0.240
1,150- 1,250	4,558	299	5,320	1,200	0.249	2,310	304	3,086	1,200	0.253	4,222	290	4,261	1,200	0.242	3,506	285	3,537	1,200	0.238
1,251- 1,349	1,501	296	1,667	1,300	0.228	1,041	299	1,306	1,300	0.230	1,510	288	1,517	1,300	0.222	1,730	284	1,742	1,300	0.218
1,350- 1,450	1,674	315	1,915	1,400	0.225	1,314	321	1,666	1,400	0.229	1,674	300	1,679	1,400	0.214	2,043	298	2,059	1,400	0.213
1,451- 1,549	2,991	335	3,535	1,500	0.223	1,910	338	2,488	1,500	0.225	2,450	328	2,469	1,500	0.219	2,349	322	2,372	1,500	0.215
1,550- 1,650	1,861	336	2,104	1,600	0.210	1,491	337	1,869	1,600	0.211	1,506	323	1,514	1,600	0.202	1,887	318	1,893	1,600	0.199
1,651- 1,749	1,029	350	1,206	1,700	0.206	993	355	1,232	1,700	0.209	950	323	953	1,700	0.190	1,305	329	1,316	1,700	0.194
1,760- 1,949	4,344	376	5,058	1,821	0.206	3,316	368	4,240	1,835	0.201	3,084	355	3,095	1,824	0.195	3,333	351	3,351	1,850	0.192
1,950- 2,149	3,247	409	3,780	2,048	0.200	2,816	410	3,598	2,037	0.201	2,149	391	2,161	2,033	0.192	2,378	386	2,402	2,032	0.190
2,150- 2,349	1,333	421	1,519	2,236	0.188	1,288	433	1,603	2,238	0.193	896	396	900	2,235	0.177	1,302	408	1,313	2,239	0.182
2,350- 2,549	2,908	461	3,420	2,446	0.188	2,109	473	2,708	2,448	0.193	1,498	435	1,506	2,439	0.178	1,572	436	1,591	2,443	0.178
2,550- 2,749	908	457	1,060	2,641	0.173	908	498	1,130	2,643	0.188	566	444	570	2,646	0.168	780	447	790	2,645	0.169
2,750- 3,149	2,164	519	2,545	2,963	0.175	1,891	523	2,431	2,973	0.176	1,196	489	1,203	2,961	0.165	1,378	477	1,388	2,943	0.162
3,150- 3,549	827	552	968	3,381	0.163	835	555	1,058	3,363	0.165	476	518	479	3,354	0.154	754	517	760	3,343	0.155
3,550- 3,949	882	575	1,050	3,675	0.156	719	593	960	3,697	0.160	376	531	379	3,682	0.144	502	567	506	3,702	0.153
3,950- 4,450	624	631	749	4,125	0.153	656	638	828	4,101	0.156	305	595	310	4,105	0.145	424	593	428	4,120	0.144
4,451- 4,949	365	642	434	4,652	0.138	323	688	424	4,660	0.148	179	596	180	4,647	0.128	236	618	240	4,645	0.135
4,950- 5,450	413	708	509	5,063	0.140	387	743	519	5,077	0.146	213	703	214	5,067	0.139	240	708	243	5,087	0.139
5,451- 5,949	80	677	93	5,612	0.121	101	768	124	5,619	0.137	33	674	34	5,659	0.119	84	702	84	5,649	0.124
5,950- 6,949	265	773	338	6,138	0.126	247	812	338	6,205	0.131	115	691	115	6,164	0.112	175	767	177	6,223	0.123
6,950- 7,949	150	857	177	7,296	0.117	130	841	181	7,291	0.115	56	819	57	7,258	0.113	96	827	97	7,262	0.114
7,950- 8,949	63	949	81	8,157	0.116	88	888	117	8,201	0.108	27	699	27	8,204	0.085	69	764	69	8,291	0.092
8,950- 9,949	28	908	34	9,197	0.099	53	1,089	73	9,199	0.118	14	874	14	9,079	0.096	37	932	37	9,165	0.102
9,950-11,949	64	912	84	10,061	0.091	87	1,100	113	10,191	0.108	23	806	24	10,046	0.080	42	1,210	42	10,390	0.116
11,950-13,949	30	932	35	12,280	0.076	32	1,173	44	12,325	0.095	8	968	9	12,444	0.078	19	1,008	19	12,289	0.082
13,950-15,949	20	1,484	24	14,833	0.100	29	1,191	38	14,568	0.082	15	1,541	15	14,927	0.090	17	888	17	14,571	0.061
15,950-19,949	17	1,209	20	17,410	0.069	26	1,353	34	17,024	0.079	2	1,080	2	18,000	0.060	10	1,385	10	17,280	0.080
19,950 and over	37	1,629	42	31,631	0.052	28	1,803	39	29,079	0.062	9	1,031	9	35,122	0.029	16	1,337	16	32,794	0.041

TABLE C 3 (Cont'd)

I PORTLAND, MAINE

Annual Income group[1]	1929 PERSONAL ENUMERATION Rent No. of Reports	Rent Average (dollars)	Income No. of Reports	Income Average (dollars)	Rent-Income Ratio	1929 MAIL RETURNS Rent No. of Reports	Rent Average (dollars)	Income No. of Reports	Income Average (dollars)	Rent-Income Ratio	1933 PERSONAL ENUMERATION Rent No. of Reports	Rent Average (dollars)	Income No. of Reports	Income Average (dollars)	Rent-Income Ratio	1933 MAIL RETURNS Rent No. of Reports	Rent Average (dollars)	Income No. of Reports	Income Average (dollars)	Rent-Income Ratio
All groups	853	354	1,002	1,670	0.212	1,081	374	1,284	1,880	0.199	1,098	323	1,112	1,208	0.267	1,622	332	1,637	1,351	0.246
No income	15	331	19	0		27	329	27	0		43	251	44	0		49	281	49	0	
$1- 149	2	415	3	100	4.150	7	324	10	100	3.240	22	234	22	100	2.340	40	231	40	100	2.310
150- 250	7	221	9	200	1.105	11	283	12	200	1.415	44	228	45	200	1.140	58	215	59	200	1.075
251- 349	7	180	10	300	0.600	12	242	15	300	0.807	53	216	53	300	0.720	46	239	47	300	0.797
350- 450	9	222	13	400	0.555	18	219	19	400	0.548	38	221	38	400	0.552	58	242	58	400	0.605
451- 549	34	242	36	500	0.484	21	282	28	500	0.524	56	250	56	500	0.500	82	253	85	500	0.506
550- 650	20	239	22	600	0.398	26	261	33	600	0.435	51	286	51	600	0.443	84	258	84	600	0.430
651- 749	11	280	11	700	0.371	21	255	24	700	0.364	42	274	42	700	0.391	50	254	51	700	0.363
750- 850	37	276	47	800	0.345	23	285	29	800	0.356	64	287	65	800	0.359	80	303	80	800	0.379
851- 949	27	292	29	900	0.324	29	248	33	900	0.276	44	281	46	900	0.312	81	283	82	900	0.314
950- 1,050	74	307	89	1,000	0.307	64	296	84	1,000	0.296	99	300	102	1,000	0.300	117	293	117	1,000	0.293
1,051- 1,149	19	307	24	1,100	0.279	38	292	44	1,100	0.265	35	313	35	1,100	0.285	57	308	57	1,100	0.280
1,150- 1,250	54	295	67	1,200	0.246	57	296	74	1,200	0.247	78	364	78	1,200	0.303	90	315	92	1,200	0.263
1,251- 1,349	48	284	53	1,300	0.218	47	302	56	1,300	0.232	56	313	56	1,300	0.241	62	332	63	1,300	0.255
1,350- 1,450	25	325	29	1,400	0.232	45	322	60	1,400	0.230	25	376	25	1,400	0.269	61	319	61	1,400	0.228
1,451- 1,549	55	357	66	1,500	0.238	59	333	70	1,500	0.222	49	376	50	1,500	0.251	73	356	73	1,500	0.237
1,550- 1,650	56	331	65	1,600	0.207	68	338	77	1,600	0.211	46	365	46	1,600	0.228	88	367	88	1,600	0.229
1,651- 1,749	16	350	22	1,700	0.206	34	352	39	1,700	0.207	25	369	25	1,700	0.217	39	346	39	1,700	0.204
1,750- 1,949	81	381	93	1,820	0.209	91	376	108	1,819	0.207	60	401	62	1,832	0.219	110	400	110	1,828	0.219
1,950- 2,149	68	407	78	2,040	0.200	86	393	103	2,048	0.192	45	426	46	2,039	0.209	65	401	65	2,035	0.197
2,150- 2,349	28	380	33	2,248	0.169	40	458	46	2,248	0.204	29	436	29	2,248	0.194	43	459	44	2,232	0.206
2,350- 2,549	47	456	51	2,469	0.185	46	435	52	2,460	0.177	27	461	27	2,481	0.186	41	423	42	2,452	0.173
2,550- 2,749	21	401	24	2,621	0.153	33	489	36	2,628	0.186	17	431	17	2,635	0.164	23	486	24	2,650	0.183
2,750- 3,149	38	513	42	2,962	0.173	63	499	73	2,921	0.171	23	457	23	2,991	0.153	43	478	43	2,984	0.160
3,150- 3,549	22	517	28	3,364	0.154	32	499	36	3,353	0.149	9	419	9	3,378	0.124	22	550	22	3,341	0.165
3,550- 3,949	7	464	8	3,738	0.124	17	535	19	3,658	0.146	2	510	2	3,800	0.134	20	513	20	3,710	0.138
3,950- 4,450	8	461	8	4,113	0.112	22	584	25	4,092	0.143	9	460	9	4,133	0.111	11	555	12	4,125	0.135
4,451- 4,949	4	430	5	4,620	0.093	8	533	9	4,700	0.113	2	525	2	4,750	0.111	5	572	5	4,660	0.122
4,950- 5,450	6	680	8	5,088	0.134	7	617	8	5,038	0.122	2	340	2	5,000	0.088	10	546	10	5,090	0.107
5,451- 5,949	2	650	2	5,650	0.115	3	720	5	5,600	0.129	1	360	1	5,800	0.062	4	575	4	5,725	0.100
5,950- 6,949	1	480	2	6,400	0.075	10	662	13	6,354	0.104	1	300	1	6,000	0.050	3	720	4	6,375	0.113
6,950- 7,949	2	960	2	7,300	0.132	3	900	3	7,287	0.124	1	660	1	7,500	0.088	2	520	2	7,400	0.070
7,950- 8,949						2	780	2	8,250							1	720	1	8,000	0.090
8,950- 9,949	1	300	1	9,000	0.033	2	745	3	9,233	0.081										
9,950- 11,949	3	430	3	10,000	0.043	2	480	2	11,400	0.042	1	650	1	9,000	0.072	2	900	2	10,000	0.090
11,950- 13,949						4	630	4	12,750	0.049	1	780	1	10,000	0.078	1	600	1	13,500	0.044
13,950- 15,949						1	840	1	15,000	0.056						1	400	1	15,000	0.027
15,950- 19,949						2	950	2	17,500	0.054										
19,950 and over																				

TABLE C 3 (Cont'd)

2 WORCESTER, MASSACHUSETTS

Annual Income group[1]	1929 PERSONAL ENUMERATION — RENT No. of Reports	RENT Average (dollars)	INCOME No. of Reports	INCOME Average (dollars)	Rent-Income Ratio	1929 MAIL RETURNS — RENT No. of Reports	RENT Average (dollars)	INCOME No. of Reports	INCOME Average (dollars)	Rent-Income Ratio	1933 PERSONAL ENUMERATION — RENT No. of Reports	RENT Average (dollars)	INCOME No. of Reports	INCOME Average (dollars)	Rent-Income Ratio	1933 MAIL RETURNS — RENT No. of Reports	RENT Average (dollars)	INCOME No. of Reports	INCOME Average (dollars)	Rent-Income Ratio
All groups	281	407	321	2,138	0.190	1,660	353	1,920	1,644	0.215	360	362	361	1,512	0.239	2,440	295	2,450	1,181	0.250
No Income	8	384	8	0		79	223	95	0		15	325	15	0		145	215	145	0	
$1- 149	1	360	1	100	3.600	13	238	15	100	2.380	7	236	7	100	2.360	103	193	104	100	1.930
150- 250	1	300	1	200	1.500	25	316	32	200	1.580	3	233	3	200	1.165	85	221	86	200	1.105
251- 349	2	300	2	300	1.000	17	271	20	300	0.903	7	226	7	300	0.753	86	210	86	300	0.700
350- 450	5	248	6	400	0.620	36	226	40	400	0.565	13	242	13	400	0.605	109	232	110	400	0.580
451- 549	10	313	10	500	0.626	46	269	50	500	0.538	20	262	20	500	0.524	129	248	129	500	0.496
550- 650	2	210	2	600	0.350	53	274	62	600	0.457	12	298	12	600	0.497	105	240	106	600	0.400
651- 749	9	330	9	700	0.471	29	280	36	700	0.400	16	285	16	700	0.379	105	240	106	700	0.343
750- 850	9	248	10	800	0.308	51	275	64	800	0.344	23	316	23	800	0.395	150	257	150	800	0.321
851- 949	3	350	5	900	0.389	41	289	47	900	0.299	18	241	16	900	0.288	105	271	106	900	0.301
950- 1,050	22	320	24	1,000	0.320	102	284	123	1,000	0.284	24	327	25	1,000	0.327	186	270	187	1,000	0.270
1,051- 1,149	7	339	9	1,100	0.308	35	294	43	1,100	0.267	6	292	6	1,100	0.285	102	281	102	1,100	0.255
1,150- 1,250	17	315	19	1,200	0.262	93	298	114	1,200	0.248	22	318	22	1,200	0.285	129	313	130	1,200	0.261
1,251- 1,349	8	284	8	1,300	0.218	66	316	77	1,300	0.243	12	353	12	1,300	0.272	93	282	93	1,300	0.217
1,350- 1,450	3	213	6	1,400	0.152	69	332	79	1,400	0.237	12	355	12	1,400	0.254	84	305	84	1,400	0.218
1,451- 1,549	21	322	24	1,500	0.215	91	322	113	1,500	0.215	23	362	23	1,500	0.241	106	309	107	1,500	0.206
1,550- 1,650	18	335	22	1,600	0.209	95	345	108	1,600	0.216	20	382	20	1,600	0.239	93	315	93	1,600	0.197
1,651- 1,749	8	389	10	1,700	0.229	55	324	60	1,700	0.191	7	346	7	1,700	0.204	60	351	61	1,700	0.206
1,750- 1,949	17	412	17	1,824	0.226	146	366	157	1,832	0.200	17	422	17	1,835	0.230	127	346	127	1,835	0.189
1,950- 2,149	26	404	29	2,031	0.199	163	384	184	2,034	0.189	21	399	21	2,029	0.197	97	373	97	2,030	0.184
2,150- 2,349	10	455	12	2,233	0.195	81	423	89	2,229	0.190	6	412	6	2,250	0.183	48	413	48	2,244	0.184
2,350- 2,549	13	495	15	2,480	0.200	70	440	76	2,454	0.179	14	461	14	2,457	0.188	41	463	41	2,446	0.189
2,550- 2,749	5	480	5	2,620	0.183	41	463	44	2,636	0.176	4	583	4	2,600	0.228	27	439	27	2,648	0.166
2,750- 3,149	18	494	18	2,978	0.166	68	476	82	2,946	0.162	11	565	11	2,955	0.191	37	428	38	2,971	0.144
3,150- 3,549	11	531	12	3,333	0.159	28	507	30	3,380	0.150	7	537	7	3,329	0.161	17	538	17	3,335	0.161
3,550- 3,949	3	600	4	3,600	0.167	14	441	17	3,706	0.119	4	423	4	3,725	0.114	18	504	18	3,739	0.135
3,950- 4,450	6	687	7	4,057	0.164	16	542	17	4,118	0.132	6	675	6	4,167	0.162	13	572	13	4,138	0.138
4,451- 4,949	5	564	5	4,520	0.125	5	820	6	4,700	0.174	3	577	3	4,533	0.127	9	676	9	4,611	0.147
4,950- 5,450	3	840	7	5,029	0.167	9	753	10	5,090	0.148	2	720	2	5,050	0.143	8	709	8	5,075	0.140
5,451- 5,949	1	600	2	5,500	0.109	6	808	7	5,671	0.142	1	600	1	5,500	0.109	2	780	2	5,650	0.138
5,950- 6,949	4	750	4	6,500	0.115	4	560	5	6,420	0.087	3	850	3	6,333	0.131	7	680	7	6,243	0.109
6,950- 7,949	3	850	4	7,250	0.117	3	887	4	7,200	0.120	1	960	1	7,500	0.128	3	960	3	7,287	0.132
7,950- 8,949						3	1,273	3	8,167	0.156	1	840	1	8,800	0.095	4	860	4	8,275	0.104
8,950- 9,949						1	1,080	2	9,100	0.119						4	790	1	9,000	0.088
9,950-11,949						1	1,050	1	10,167	0.101						4	1,215	4	10,325	0.118
11,950-13,949	1	660	1	12,000	0.055	2	1,440	1	12,000	0.120						1	1,060	1	12,000	0.090
13,950-15,949						1	1,110	2	15,000	0.074	1	110	1	15,000	0.007					
15,950-19,949	2	960	2	17,600	0.055	3	900	3	16,833	0.053						1	300	1	18,000	0.017
19,950 and over	1	1,200	1	20,000	0.060															

TABLE C 3 (Cont'd)

3 PROVIDENCE, RHODE ISLAND

	1929 PERSONAL ENUMERATION					1929 MAIL RETURNS					1933 PERSONAL ENUMERATION					1933 MAIL RETURNS				
Annual Income group	Rent No. of Reports	Rent Average (dollars)	Income No. of Reports	Income Average (dollars)	Rent-Income Ratio	Rent No. of Reports	Rent Average (dollars)	Income No. of Reports	Income Average (dollars)	Rent-Income Ratio	Rent No. of Reports	Rent Average (dollars)	Income No. of Reports	Income Average (dollars)	Rent-Income Ratio	Rent No. of Reports	Rent Average (dollars)	Income No. of Reports	Income Average (dollars)	Rent-Income Ratio
All groups	3,063	312	3,257	1,579	0.198	1,522	356	1,791	1,807	0.197	3,530	278	3,552	1,065	0.264	2,323	299	2,332	1,254	0.258
No Income	96	250	97	0		60	256	82	0		238	215	240	0		125	243	125	0	
$1- 149	13	164	15	100	1.640	11	185	12	100	1.850	73	173	78	100	1.730	80	220	82	100	2.200
150- 250	31	249	32	200	1.250	21	231	24	200	1.165	145	192	146	200	0.980	90	199	91	200	0.995
251- 349	34	227	37	300	0.757	16	206	21	300	0.887	137	193	137	300	0.643	77	207	77	300	0.690
350- 450	59	225	66	400	0.563	20	229	25	400	0.573	212	203	213	400	0.508	110	216	110	400	0.540
451- 549	78	213	95	500	0.426	39	498	48	500	0.996	237	216	239	500	0.432	128	229	128	500	0.458
550- 650	86	235	93	600	0.392	38	260	44	600	0.433	244	223	246	600	0.372	141	224	141	600	0.373
651- 749	68	229	72	700	0.327	25	213	32	700	0.304	149	225	150	700	0.321	106	245	107	700	0.350
750- 850	159	214	173	800	0.288	54	256	67	800	0.320	272	236	274	800	0.295	152	242	152	800	0.303
851- 949	110	242	114	900	0.269	50	249	62	900	0.277	149	248	151	900	0.276	116	254	116	900	0.282
950- 1,050	309	218	321	1,000	0.218	96	264	110	1,000	0.284	310	266	311	1,000	0.286	174	257	175	1,000	0.257
1,051- 1,149	97	263	100	1,100	0.239	41	285	52	1,100	0.259	90	263	90	1,100	0.239	63	262	63	1,100	0.238
1,150- 1,250	285	275	303	1,200	0.229	87	293	102	1,200	0.244	241	298	242	1,200	0.248	138	297	138	1,200	0.248
1,251- 1,349	154	272	161	1,300	0.209	72	283	86	1,300	0.218	112	294	114	1,300	0.226	83	298	83	1,300	0.229
1,350- 1,450	112	290	114	1,400	0.207	67	284	75	1,400	0.203	84	292	85	1,400	0.209	68	281	68	1,400	0.201
1,451- 1,549	203	298	218	1,500	0.199	95	322	107	1,500	0.215	136	315	137	1,500	0.210	72	315	72	1,500	0.210
1,550- 1,650	159	304	166	1,600	0.190	63	301	73	1,600	0.188	107	340	107	1,600	0.213	62	341	62	1,600	0.213
1,651- 1,749	54	329	58	1,700	0.194	39	335	45	1,700	0.197	50	320	50	1,700	0.188	45	357	45	1,700	0.210
1,750- 1,949	223	324	233	1,818	0.178	141	339	156	1,824	0.186	143	353	143	1,814	0.195	110	348	111	1,832	0.190
1,950- 2,149	225	379	240	2,040	0.186	141	368	165	2,034	0.181	112	420	112	2,033	0.207	74	368	75	2,027	0.182
2,150- 2,349	68	395	74	2,236	0.177	48	401	54	2,253	0.180	48	412	48	2,242	0.184	38	433	39	2,241	0.193
2,350- 2,549	118	412	124	2,464	0.167	59	422	68	2,457	0.172	66	418	66	2,467	0.169	50	419	50	2,446	0.171
2,550- 2,749	48	408	54	2,628	0.155	31	438	35	2,837	0.166	30	484	30	2,620	0.185	27	447	27	2,637	0.170
2,750- 3,149	95	456	101	2,968	0.154	63	480	73	2,951	0.163	56	511	56	2,957	0.173	70	485	70	2,949	0.164
3,150- 3,549	35	514	38	3,421	0.150	35	515	37	3,351	0.154	23	551	23	3,404	0.162	27	454	27	3,533	0.136
3,550- 3,949	28	511	26	3,731	0.137	16	574	24	3,725	0.154	15	564	15	3,753	0.150	21	568	21	3,738	0.152
3,950- 4,450	35	730	37	4,068	0.179	23	571	28	4,089	0.140	18	737	18	4,011	0.184	17	614	17	4,076	0.151
4,451- 4,949	16	623	17	4,653	0.134	11	635	13	4,685	0.136	7	563	7	4,586	0.123	11	690	11	4,882	0.147
4,950- 5,450	29	676	36	5,056	0.134	23	759	28	5,065	0.150	11	1,075	11	5,000	0.215	12	598	12	5,075	0.118
5,451- 5,949	2	840	2	5,650	0.149	4	540	5	5,600	0.096	2	780	2	5,800	0.158	9	733	9	5,611	0.131
5,950- 6,949	9	780	11	6,218	0.125	6	880	9	6,333	0.139	5	648	5	6,040	0.107	11	911	12	6,308	0.144
6,950- 7,949	11	929	11	7,264	0.128	7	741	8	7,338	0.101	4	848	4	7,400	0.115	8	998	8	7,350	0.136
7,950- 8,949	4	1,225	6	8,050	0.152	7	849	7	8,271	0.103	1	1,200	1	8,000	0.150	1	160	1	8,000	0.020
8,950- 9,949	1	1,020	1	9,000	0.113	2	960	3	9,187	0.105						2	1,590	2	9,000	0.177
9,950-11,949	4	790	4	10,000	0.079	3	880	4	10,425	0.084						3	887	3	10,687	0.083
11,950-13,949	2	500	2	12,500	0.040			1	12,200		1	420	1	13,000	0.032					
13,950-15,949	1	2,220	1	14,000	0.159	3	480	3	14,133	0.033	1	600	1	14,000	0.043	1	720	1	14,000	0.051
15,950-19,949	3	1,037	3	17,500	0.059	2	2,550	2	17,950	0.142										
19,950 and over	1	500	1	35,000	0.014	3	1,510	3	24,853	0.061	1	470	1	27,000	0.017	1	450	1	35,000	0.013

TABLE C 3 (Cont'd)

4 SYRACUSE, NEW YORK

Annual Income group [1]	1929 PERSONAL ENUMERATION					1929 MAIL RETURNS					1933 PERSONAL ENUMERATION					1933 MAIL RETURNS				
	RENT No. of Reports	RENT Average (dollars)	INCOME No. of Reports	INCOME Average (dollars)	Rent-Income Ratio	RENT No. of Reports	RENT Average (dollars)	INCOME No. of Reports	INCOME Average (dollars)	Rent-Income Ratio	RENT No. of Reports	RENT Average (dollars)	INCOME No. of Reports	INCOME Average (dollars)	Rent-Income Ratio	RENT No. of Reports	RENT Average (dollars)	INCOME No. of Reports	INCOME Average (dollars)	Rent-Income Ratio
All groups	662	360	709	1,490	0.242	453	436	588	1,879	0.232	759	276	764	949	0.291	756	314	761	1,217	0.258
No income	28	315	28	0		8	274	15	0		44	226	45	0		38	264	38	0	
$1- 149	5	208	5	100	2.080	1	420	2	100	4.200	16	167	16	100	1.670	21	202	21	100	2.020
150- 250	7	301	8	200	1.505	3	280	5	200	1.400	31	223	32	200	1.115	21	216	21	200	1.080
261- 349	10	232	12	300	0.773	3	240	6	300	0.800	34	221	35	300	0.737	31	219	31	300	0.730
350- 450	9	286	11	400	0.715	7	276	8	400	0.690	39	205	40	400	0.513	38	208	38	400	0.520
451- 549	17	287	17	500	0.534	12	267	13	500	0.534	86	213	86	500	0.426	52	238	54	500	0.476
550- 650	15	205	15	600	0.342	7	296	13	600	0.493	69	200	69	600	0.333	34	229	34	600	0.382
651- 749	10	255	10	700	0.364	10	339	12	700	0.484	50	225	50	700	0.321	28	282	28	700	0.403
750- 850	31	260	34	800	0.325	15	283	16	800	0.354	50	275	50	800	0.344	52	281	53	800	0.351
851- 949	22	298	22	900	0.331	10	384	15	900	0.427	28	276	23	900	0.307	37	264	37	900	0.293
950- 1,050	72	281	77	1,000	0.281	26	318	34	1,000	0.318	49	282	49	1,000	0.282	46	283	46	1,000	0.283
1,051- 1,149	12	313	14	1,100	0.285	8	358	9	1,100	0.307	20	323	20	1,100	0.294	19	303	19	1,100	0.275
1,150- 1,250	69	286	74	1,200	0.238	24	327	33	1,200	0.273	44	311	44	1,200	0.259	44	309	44	1,200	0.258
1,261- 1,349	37	336	37	1,300	0.258	6	323	13	1,300	0.248	27	306	27	1,300	0.235	19	359	19	1,300	0.281
1,350- 1,450	15	300	16	1,400	0.214	18	406	25	1,400	0.290	20	318	20	1,400	0.227	23	318	23	1,400	0.227
1,451- 1,549	33	339	34	1,500	0.226	28	409	34	1,500	0.273	25	342	25	1,500	0.228	28	339	27	1,500	0.226
1,550- 1,650	47	332	48	1,600	0.208	18	399	24	1,600	0.249	16	374	16	1,600	0.234	21	321	21	1,600	0.201
1,651- 1,749	11	448	15	1,700	0.264	9	414	14	1,700	0.244	10	372	11	1,700	0.219	19	382	19	1,700	0.225
1,750- 1,949	47	435	55	1,818	0.239	40	420	46	1,828	0.230	41	390	41	1,817	0.215	54	390	55	1,836	0.212
1,950- 2,149	62	453	66	2,030	0.223	50	463	61	2,028	0.228	23	423	23	2,030	0.208	31	378	31	2,026	0.187
2,150- 2,349	12	471	13	2,246	0.210	17	466	24	2,250	0.207	3	440	3	2,200	0.200	22	447	22	2,245	0.199
2,350- 2,549	27	481	29	2,452	0.196	35	523	46	2,457	0.213	10	420	10	2,450	0.171	17	444	17	2,453	0.181
2,550- 2,749	17	485	18	2,628	0.185	10	516	12	2,617	0.197	6	477	6	2,650	0.180	12	423	12	2,625	0.161
2,750- 3,149	22	621	22	2,941	0.211	47	550	53	2,947	0.180	6	493	6	2,917	0.169	25	464	25	2,920	0.159
3,150- 3,549	9	620	10	3,400	0.182	13	611	15	3,387	0.180	4	470	4	3,300	0.142	7	594	7	3,371	0.178
3,550- 3,949	5	658	5	3,660	0.180	10	580	13	3,746	0.155	2	430	2	3,700	0.116	8	563	8	3,688	0.153
3,950- 4,450	2	810	3	4,033	0.201	10	600	11	4,109	0.146	3	517	3	4,533	0.114	10	569	10	4,180	0.138
4,451- 4,949	3	660	4	4,625	0.143	1	540	2	4,600	0.117	1	420	1	5,000	0.084	1	480	1	4,500	0.107
4,950- 5,450	2	420	2	5,150	0.082	5	780	7	5,029	0.155										
5,451- 5,949	2	510	2	5,500	0.093	1	600	1	5,800	0.103										
5,950- 6,949	2	575	2	6,000	0.096	1	900	4	6,125	0.147	2	580	2	6,300	0.092	2	690	2	6,000	0.115
6,950- 7,949			1	7,000																
7,950- 8,949																				
8,950- 9,949						1	1,200	1	9,100	0.132										
9,950-11,949						1	1,800	1	10,000	0.180										
11,950-13,949																				
13,950-15,949																				
15,950-19,949																				
19,950 and over																				

TABLE C 3 (Cont'd)

5 TRENTON, NEW JERSEY

Annual Income group[1]	1929 PERSONAL ENUMERATION					1929 MAIL RETURNS					1933 PERSONAL ENUMERATION					1933 MAIL RETURNS				
	RENT No. of Reports	RENT Average (dollars)	INCOME No. of Reports	INCOME Average (dollars)	Rent-Income Ratio	RENT No. of Reports	RENT Average (dollars)	INCOME No. of Reports	INCOME Average (dollars)	Rent-Income Ratio	RENT No. of Reports	RENT Average (dollars)	INCOME No. of Reports	INCOME Average (dollars)	Rent-Income Ratio	RENT No. of Reports	RENT Average (dollars)	INCOME No. of Reports	INCOME Average (dollars)	Rent-Income Ratio
All groups	1,038	318	1,152	1,318	0.241	475	336	617	1,402	0.240	1,231	272	1,242	859	0.317	830	277	839	965	0.287
No Income	39	250	39	0		32	208	54	0		117	204	117	0		88	214	91	0	
$1- 149	18	229	19	100	2.290	7	214	10	100	2.140	49	186	50	100	1.860	49	223	50	100	2.230
150- 250	17	225	19	200	1.125	11	186	13	200	0.930	80	213	80	200	1.065	58	226	58	200	1.130
251- 349	20	290	22	300	0.967	13	261	17	300	0.870	61	207	62	300	0.690	43	203	43	300	0.677
350- 450	20	249	26	400	0.623	14	257	18	400	0.643	86	218	86	400	0.545	39	210	39	400	0.525
451- 549	51	255	58	500	0.510	21	277	23	500	0.554	121	229	121	500	0.458	45	237	45	500	0.474
550- 650	39	220	39	600	0.377	6	235	9	600	0.392	77	238	78	600	0.397	53	234	53	600	0.390
651- 749	34	288	36	700	0.383	8	274	12	700	0.391	49	223	50	700	0.319	28	253	29	700	0.361
750- 850	55	288	62	800	0.335	23	288	26	800	0.360	81	256	83	800	0.320	43	261	44	800	0.326
851- 949	48	278	52	900	0.309	15	269	22	900	0.299	56	290	57	900	0.322	40	240	40	900	0.287
950- 1,050	141	293	162	1,000	0.293	32	284	46	1,000	0.284	90	288	90	1,000	0.288	51	287	52	1,000	0.287
1,051- 1,149	22	253	22	1,100	0.230	8	311	13	1,100	0.283	28	318	28	1,100	0.289	18	259	18	1,100	0.235
1,150- 1,250	112	294	121	1,200	0.245	34	327	45	1,200	0.273	66	305	67	1,200	0.254	46	294	46	1,200	0.245
1,251- 1,349	33	298	36	1,300	0.229	20	294	24	1,300	0.226	35	304	36	1,300	0.234	22	336	22	1,300	0.258
1,350- 1,450	59	291	65	1,400	0.208	12	285	15	1,400	0.204	32	319	32	1,400	0.228	24	303	24	1,400	0.216
1,451- 1,549	52	321	61	1,500	0.214	28	333	32	1,500	0.222	30	328	30	1,500	0.219	15	367	15	1,500	0.245
1,550- 1,650	36	364	38	1,600	0.228	17	313	21	1,600	0.196	21	303	21	1,600	0.189	12	337	12	1,600	0.211
1,651- 1,749	18	390	19	1,700	0.229	13	344	16	1,700	0.202	12	356	12	1,700	0.209	11	316	11	1,700	0.186
1,750- 1,949	46	376	53	1,826	0.206	31	340	42	1,814	0.187	42	375	42	1,833	0.205	49	346	49	1,839	0.188
1,950- 2,149	49	371	53	2,028	0.183	41	423	45	2,033	0.208	37	397	37	2,032	0.195	26	355	26	2,031	0.175
2,150- 2,349	26	422	26	2,235	0.189	20	389	25	2,244	0.173	14	359	14	2,243	0.160	13	344	13	2,246	0.153
2,350- 2,549	44	414	49	2,457	0.168	19	452	22	2,436	0.186	17	505	17	2,459	0.205	11	487	11	2,445	0.199
2,550- 2,749	8	593	10	2,620	0.226	10	397	11	2,600	0.153	4	493	4	2,600	0.190	6	367	7	2,643	0.139
2,750- 3,149	23	439	26	2,954	0.149	20	451	25	2,948	0.153	9	417	10	2,970	0.140	15	389	16	2,888	0.135
3,150- 3,549	6	527	9	3,422	0.154	8	495	12	3,325	0.149	3	647	4	3,375	0.192	9	572	9	3,387	0.170
3,550- 3,949	7	704	9	3,756	0.187	5	704	6	3,750	0.187	3	940	3	3,667	0.256	5	396	5	3,660	0.108
3,950- 4,450	5	576	7	4,000	0.144	2	1,210	3	4,000	0.303	5	636	5	4,120	0.154	2	540	2	4,000	0.135
4,451- 4,949	1	420	3	4,567	0.092			1	4,800		1	1,200	1	4,500	0.237	1	420	1	4,600	0.091
4,950- 5,450	5	1,104	6	5,067	0.218	5	660	6	5,000	0.132	4	1,005	4	5,050	0.199	5	718	5	5,100	0.141
5,451- 5,949						1	220	1	5,600	0.039						1	720	1	5,700	0.128
5,950- 6,949	3	700	3	6,000	0.117	1	1,500	1	6,500	0.231	1	480	1	6,000	0.080	1	540	1	6,300	0.086
6,950- 7,949	1	280	1	7,000	0.040			1	7,000							1	740	1	7,100	0.104
7,950- 8,949																				
8,950- 9,949																				
9,950-11,949																				
11,950-13,949																				
13,950-15,949																				
15,950-19,949																				
19,950 and over			1	20,000																

TABLE C 3 (Cont'd)

6 ERIE, PENNSYLVANIA

Annual Income group[1]	1929 PE Rent No. of Reports	1929 PE Rent Average (dollars)	1929 PE Income No. of Reports	1929 PE Income Average (dollars)	1929 PE Rent-Income Ratio	1929 MR Rent No. of Reports	1929 MR Rent Average (dollars)	1929 MR Income No. of Reports	1929 MR Income Average (dollars)	1929 MR Rent-Income Ratio	1933 PE Rent No. of Reports	1933 PE Rent Average (dollars)	1933 PE Income No. of Reports	1933 PE Income Average (dollars)	1933 PE Rent-Income Ratio	1933 MR Rent No. of Reports	1933 MR Rent Average (dollars)	1933 MR Income No. of Reports	1933 MR Income Average (dollars)	1933 MR Rent-Income Ratio
All groups	843	337	963	1,518	0.222	1,099	368	1,426	1,674	0.220	1,082	252	1,086	848	0.297	1,822	272	1,836	958	0.284
No Income	20	282	20	0		74	306	112	0		95	179	95	0		206	225	211	0	
$1- 149	6	192	7	100	1.920	10	247	14	100	2.470	70	187	70	100	1.870	104	192	104	100	1.920
150- 250	10	229	11	200	1.145	17	305	21	200	1.525	82	190	82	200	0.950	126	213	126	200	1.085
251- 349	14	259	16	300	0.863	10	305	18	300	1.017	71	197	71	300	0.657	81	212	82	300	0.707
350- 450	16	229	17	400	0.573	15	287	25	400	0.668	77	205	77	400	0.513	106	210	107	400	0.525
451- 549	26	287	34	500	0.514	33	270	40	500	0.540	86	225	86	500	0.450	93	225	93	500	0.450
550- 650	37	228	44	600	0.380	33	285	41	600	0.475	68	240	68	600	0.400	83	235	83	600	0.392
651- 749	31	273	34	700	0.390	20	300	26	700	0.429	42	208	42	700	0.297	85	224	85	700	0.320
750- 850	49	240	56	800	0.300	41	277	51	800	0.346	84	243	84	800	0.304	115	245	115	800	0.306
851- 949	27	294	33	900	0.327	28	253	37	900	0.281	36	253	36	900	0.281	74	241	74	900	0.268
950- 1,050	65	283	76	1,000	0.283	56	291	84	1,000	0.291	72	249	72	1,000	0.249	107	265	109	1,000	0.265
1,051- 1,149	18	332	21	1,100	0.302	14	314	18	1,100	0.285	27	280	27	1,100	0.255	51	287	51	1,100	0.243
1,150- 1,250	78	299	83	1,200	0.249	61	288	82	1,200	0.240	42	314	42	1,200	0.262	88	294	88	1,200	0.245
1,251- 1,349	22	308	28	1,300	0.237	40	292	49	1,300	0.225	31	280	31	1,300	0.215	49	289	50	1,300	0.207
1,350- 1,450	34	314	40	1,400	0.224	39	304	46	1,400	0.217	18	314	19	1,400	0.224	50	312	51	1,400	0.223
1,451- 1,549	53	291	60	1,500	0.194	54	314	77	1,500	0.209	25	328	26	1,500	0.219	56	340	56	1,500	0.227
1,550- 1,650	41	338	49	1,600	0.211	51	351	65	1,600	0.219	21	295	21	1,600	0.184	35	327	35	1,600	0.204
1,651- 1,749	22	366	24	1,700	0.215	38	362	39	1,700	0.213	13	314	13	1,700	0.185	30	300	31	1,700	0.176
1,750- 1,949	73	363	83	1,825	0.199	104	356	133	1,832	0.194	43	341	43	1,826	0.187	77	366	77	1,832	0.200
1,950- 2,149	65	384	76	2,030	0.189	73	430	90	2,026	0.212	27	368	28	2,021	0.182	54	387	55	2,029	0.191
2,150- 2,349	15	475	15	2,253	0.213	54	414	60	2,238	0.185	9	363	9	2,256	0.161	25	423	25	2,256	0.188
2,350- 2,549	34	432	38	2,458	0.176	57	452	76	2,451	0.184	12	416	12	2,450	0.170	42	445	42	2,440	0.182
2,550- 2,749	16	424	16	2,625	0.162	31	453	39	2,636	0.172	3	493	3	2,633	0.187	17	435	17	2,624	0.166
2,750- 3,149	32	481	38	2,971	0.162	51	497	62	2,939	0.169	12	403	12	2,942	0.137	21	454	22	2,941	0.154
3,150- 3,549	13	494	13	3,338	0.148	19	498	27	3,356	0.148	5	612	5	3,340	0.183	12	444	12	3,417	0.130
3,550- 3,949	8	691	11	3,655	0.189	18	557	23	3,709	0.150	3	753	4	3,625	0.208	6	548	6	3,700	0.148
3,950- 4,450	6	597	6	4,100	0.146	17	487	19	4,063	0.120						8	474	8	4,063	0.117
4,451- 4,949	1	1,000	3	4,533	0.221	10	780	11	4,664	0.167	1	650	1	4,500	0.144	7	479	7	4,643	0.103
4,950- 5,450	3	660	3	5,000	0.132	11	594	15	5,093	0.117	1	540	1	5,000	0.108	5	662	5	5,000	0.132
5,451- 5,949	1	720	1	5,500	0.131	1	480	2	5,600	0.086	2	660	2	5,700	0.116	2	420	2	5,500	0.076
5,950- 6,949						9	674	12	6,225	0.108						4	535	4	6,175	0.087
6,950- 7,949	3	707	3	7,153	0.099	5	720	6	7,333	0.098	2	1,140	2	7,100	0.161	1	260	1	7,000	0.037
7,950- 8,949	1	840	1	8,600	0.098	1	580	2	8,100	0.072						1	900	1	8,000	0.113
8,950- 9,949						2	1,050	2	9,150	0.115										
9,950-11,949	1	900	1	10,000	0.090						1	1,320	1	10,000	0.132					
11,950-13,949																				
13,950-15,949	1	1,500	1	15,000	0.100	1	600	1	15,000	0.040	1	900	1	15,000	0.060	1	2,400	1	16,000	0.150
15,950-19,949																				
19,950 and over	1	1,800	1	20,000	0.090	1	2,580	1	22,000	0.117										

TABLE C 3 (Cont'd)

7 CLEVELAND, OHIO

Annual Income group [1]	1929 PERSONAL ENUMERATION RENT No. of Reports	RENT Average (dollars)	INCOME No. of Reports	INCOME Average (dollars)	Rent-Income Ratio	1929 MAIL RETURNS RENT No. of Reports	RENT Average (dollars)	INCOME No. of Reports	INCOME Average (dollars)	Rent-Income Ratio	1933 PERSONAL ENUMERATION RENT No. of Reports	RENT Average (dollars)	INCOME No. of Reports	INCOME Average (dollars)	Rent-Income Ratio	1933 MAIL RETURNS RENT No. of Reports	RENT Average (dollars)	INCOME No. of Reports	INCOME Average (dollars)	Rent-Income Ratio
All groups	10,557	418	11,707	1,756	.241	8,128	464	10,628	1,969	.236	12,877	297	12,990	1,022	.291	14,205	323	14,360	1,252	.258
No Income	383	316	383	0		545	290	838	0		667	233	668	0		1,064	234	1,064	0	
$1- 149	81	285	95	100	2.850	67	283	93	100	2.830	466	204	471	100	2.040	732	211	743	100	2.110
150- 250	186	249	213	200	1.245	101	294	142	200	1.470	1,028	204	1,046	200	1.020	675	213	687	200	1.065
251- 349	187	252	217	300	0.840	103	310	142	300	1.033	859	206	871	300	.687	526	226	531	300	.753
350- 450	200	274	221	400	0.685	121	287	167	400	.718	915	217	925	400	.543	651	229	662	400	.573
451- 549	312	292	351	500	0.584	161	288	215	500	.576	864	234	876	500	.468	641	238	656	500	.476
550- 650	321	291	355	600	0.485	163	319	229	600	.532	813	249	818	600	.415	633	246	649	600	.410
651- 749	266	294	288	700	0.420	182	285	243	700	.407	588	254	592	700	.363	614	245	624	700	.350
750- 850	439	315	474	800	0.394	231	297	308	800	.371	769	257	778	800	.321	782	267	792	800	.334
851- 949	335	310	367	900	0.344	179	313	233	900	.358	482	275	485	900	.306	498	266	509	900	.296
950- 1,050	764	340	839	1,000	0.340	369	323	494	1,000	.323	917	293	927	1,000	.293	831	284	839	1,000	.284
1,051- 1,149	224	315	244	1,100	0.286	126	344	163	1,100	.313	255	296	255	1,100	.269	363	295	366	1,100	.268
1,150- 1,250	900	365	1,010	1,200	0.304	441	383	592	1,200	.319	781	324	787	1,200	.270	769	315	774	1,200	.263
1,251- 1,349	323	333	342	1,300	0.256	179	325	230	1,300	.250	234	314	234	1,300	.242	366	306	368	1,300	.235
1,350- 1,450	358	365	383	1,400	0.261	273	384	351	1,400	.274	317	330	318	1,400	.237	453	325	458	1,400	.232
1,451- 1,549	652	399	727	1,500	0.266	384	404	501	1,500	.269	457	359	463	1,500	.239	559	352	564	1,500	.235
1,550- 1,650	349	383	386	1,600	0.239	272	394	341	1,600	.246	256	345	257	1,600	.216	381	341	384	1,600	.213
1,651- 1,749	219	390	235	1,700	0.229	216	421	272	1,700	.248	160	351	160	1,700	.206	293	357	295	1,700	.210
1,750- 1,949	890	438	983	1,819	0.241	709	440	905	1,858	.237	509	386	510	1,823	.212	765	374	769	1,827	.205
1,950- 2,149	748	471	845	2,064	0.228	609	473	793	2,033	.233	407	416	408	2,024	.206	590	429	593	2,032	.211
2,150- 2,349	281	492	305	2,236	0.220	275	508	349	2,238	.227	155	441	156	2,231	.198	340	431	340	2,236	.193
2,350- 2,549	650	531	707	2,479	0.214	575	533	725	2,469	.216	259	480	261	2,436	.197	393	472	401	2,447	.193
2,550- 2,749	186	515	209	2,637	0.195	228	586	277	2,643	.222	86	501	86	2,651	.189	171	513	172	2,646	.194
2,750- 3,149	457	596	534	2,953	0.202	492	590	612	3,022	.195	236	556	236	2,964	.188	348	513	350	2,947	.174
3,150- 3,549	172	603	191	3,451	0.175	238	622	298	3,356	.185	78	600	78	3,385	.178	197	560	198	3,348	.187
3,550- 3,949	169	632	192	3,665	0.172	192	683	235	3,683	.185	77	644	78	3,696	.174	144	616	145	3,702	.166
3,950- 4,450	137	678	164	4,205	0.161	199	707	243	4,098	.173	67	680	67	4,088	.166	114	645	115	4,104	.157
4,451- 4,949	87	704	96	4,649	0.151	97	764	123	4,667	.164	45	618	45	4,636	.133	59	648	59	4,646	.139
4,950- 5,450	102	792	118	5,024	0.158	119	810	151	5,077	.160	55	761	55	5,038	.151	71	819	71	5,086	.161
5,451- 5,949	15	708	17	5,582	0.127	30	886	38	5,605	.158	6	1,035	7	5,643	.183	25	813	25	5,612	.145
5,950- 6,949	64	947	79	6,172	0.153	81	961	104	6,197	.155	27	749	27	6,263	.120	48	880	48	6,192	.142
6,950- 7,949	43	928	46	7,270	0.127	44	1,019	59	7,348	.139	11	990	11	7,273	.136	31	947	31	7,300	.130
7,950- 8,949	18	1,088	22	8,091	0.134	26	1,006	35	8,263	.122	9	576	9	8,289	.069	21	999	21	8,319	.120
8,950- 9,949	8	1,018	10	9,220	0.110	19	1,217	22	9,227	.132	4	1,420	4	9,250	.154	16	989	16	9,175	.108
9,950-11,949	17	1,013	18	10,167	0.100	34	1,304	43	10,240	.127	7	960	8	10,138	.095	15	1,479	15	10,253	.144
11,950-13,949	12	848	15	12,287	0.069	16	1,375	22	12,245	.112	3	1,280	3	12,500	.102	8	1,228	8	12,125	.101
13,950-15,949	5	1,604	6	15,000	0.107	14	1,454	14	14,521	.100	6	1,525	6	15,150	.101	6	1,007	6	14,867	.068
15,950-19,949	5	1,878	5	17,800	0.094	6	1,818	8	17,200	.106						3	1,900	3	16,933	.112
19,950 and over	12	2,188	15	32,473	0.067	10	2,178	16	30,600	.071	4	1,973	4	31,500	.063	9	1,541	9	36,300	.042

TABLE C 3 (Cont'd)

8 INDIANAPOLIS, INDIANA

Annual Income group[1]	1929 PERSONAL ENUMERATION RENT No. of Reports	RENT Average (dollars)	INCOME No. of Reports	INCOME Average (dollars)	Rent-Income Ratio	1929 MAIL RETURNS RENT No. of Reports	RENT Average (dollars)	INCOME No. of Reports	INCOME Average (dollars)	Rent-Income Ratio	1933 PERSONAL ENUMERATION RENT No. of Reports	RENT Average (dollars)	INCOME No. of Reports	INCOME Average (dollars)	Rent-Income Ratio	1933 MAIL RETURNS RENT No. of Reports	RENT Average (dollars)	INCOME No. of Reports	INCOME Average (dollars)	Rent-Income Ratio
All groups	900	367	1,076	1,841	0.199	1,090	418	1,390	2,083	0.201	1,198	290	1,225	1,178	0.246	1,930	304	1,945	1,366	0.223
No income	43	189	51	0		45	232	60	0		109	143	114	0		95	172	95	0	
$1- 149	5	144	6	100	1.440	10	228	13	100	2.280	56	161	60	100	1.610	89	151	93	100	1.510
150- 250	13	176	18	200	0.880	10	206	13	200	1.030	64	161	67	200	0.805	90	181	91	200	0.905
251- 349	9	241	11	300	0.803	12	277	14	300	0.923	51	166	53	300	0.553	52	154	53	300	0.513
350- 450	23	183	28	400	0.458	19	256	25	400	0.640	54	195	54	400	0.488	75	197	75	400	0.493
451- 549	26	215	35	500	0.430	28	288	31	500	0.576	84	185	90	500	0.370	66	230	68	500	0.460
550- 650	29	243	35	600	0.405	35	222	40	600	0.370	48	224	49	600	0.373	113	213	114	600	0.355
651- 749	28	240	33	700	0.343	13	246	17	700	0.351	54	225	57	700	0.321	69	226	71	700	0.323
750- 850	43	234	51	800	0.293	30	298	47	800	0.373	68	232	68	800	0.290	94	244	94	800	0.305
851- 949	34	247	39	900	0.274	28	281	32	900	0.290	46	247	47	900	0.274	95	245	95	900	0.272
950- 1,050	70	284	84	1,000	0.284	56	289	75	1,000	0.289	82	268	82	1,000	0.268	122	279	122	1,000	0.279
1,051- 1,149	23	314	24	1,100	0.285	24	330	27	1,100	0.300	32	259	32	1,100	0.235	47	246	47	1,100	0.224
1,150- 1,250	78	280	85	1,200	0.233	69	300	89	1,200	0.250	50	306	51	1,200	0.255	110	284	112	1,200	0.237
1,251- 1,349	22	280	22	1,300	0.215	30	378	38	1,300	0.291	20	290	20	1,300	0.223	52	283	52	1,300	0.218
1,350- 1,450	23	291	25	1,400	0.208	28	359	43	1,400	0.256	30	321	30	1,400	0.229	53	308	53	1,400	0.220
1,451- 1,549	45	327	56	1,500	0.218	41	329	49	1,500	0.219	47	359	47	1,500	0.239	63	315	63	1,500	0.210
1,550- 1,650	33	354	41	1,600	0.221	31	347	44	1,600	0.217	21	339	21	1,600	0.212	54	329	54	1,600	0.206
1,651- 1,749	16	359	19	1,700	0.211	24	357	27	1,700	0.210	12	313	12	1,700	0.184	47	303	47	1,700	0.178
1,750- 1,949	59	381	64	1,820	0.209	66	385	88	1,820	0.212	49	395	49	1,827	0.216	101	360	101	1,832	0.197
1,950- 2,149	47	423	52	2,029	0.208	86	390	114	2,007	0.194	41	442	41	2,020	0.219	95	412	96	2,027	0.203
2,150- 2,349	22	457	25	2,244	0.204	59	447	65	2,248	0.199	20	425	20	2,245	0.189	53	398	53	2,236	0.178
2,350- 2,549	50	503	58	2,448	0.205	75	489	90	2,441	0.200	32	434	32	2,444	0.178	71	430	71	2,445	0.176
2,550- 2,749	16	502	19	2,637	0.190	28	535	33	2,636	0.203	12	471	13	2,646	0.178	38	472	38	2,634	0.179
2,750- 3,149	36	528	46	2,954	0.179	88	525	116	2,950	0.178	37	496	37	2,965	0.167	63	519	63	2,943	0.176
3,150- 3,549	17	530	21	3,429	0.155	29	581	34	3,368	0.173	21	597	21	3,390	0.176	36	520	36	3,361	0.155
3,550- 3,949	22	737	29	3,690	0.200	32	662	41	3,729	0.178	8	664	8	3,700	0.179	18	573	18	3,722	0.154
3,950- 4,450	18	650	27	4,078	0.159	31	681	39	4,141	0.164	11	615	11	4,145	0.148	23	633	23	4,109	0.154
4,451- 4,949	13	734	14	4,571	0.161	6	608	11	4,582	0.133	10	661	10	4,680	0.141	8	629	9	4,600	0.137
4,950- 5,450	10	666	22	5,068	0.131	20	778	25	5,080	0.153	20	737	20	5,060	0.146	8	551	8	5,050	0.109
5,451- 5,949	1	450	2	5,500	0.082	6	787	6	5,667	0.139	2	720	2	5,850	0.123	4	653	4	5,875	0.115
5,950- 6,949	14	750	21	6,157	0.122	9	713	11	6,236	0.114	2	660	2	6,000	0.110	13	784	13	6,331	0.124
6,950- 7,949	4	983	5	7,460	0.132	7	731	9	7,378	0.099	3	920	3	7,333	0.125	4	983	4	7,250	0.136
7,950- 8,949	2	690	3	8,200	0.084	5	872	7	8,257	0.106						2	420	2	8,400	0.050
8,950- 9,949	1	1,110	1	9,000	0.123	1	1,200	1	9,600	0.125										
9,950- 11,949	1	600	2	10,000	0.060	7	901	7	10,086	0.089	1	840	1	10,000	0.084	3	1,167	3	10,533	0.111
11,950- 13,949	1	1,680	1	12,000	0.140	1	1,020	1	12,000	0.085						2	1,320	2	12,250	0.108
13,950- 15,949	2	1,750	2	15,000	0.117	1	1,320	2	14,250	0.093	1	3,000	1	15,000	0.200	1	900	1	14,500	0.062
15,950- 19,949						5	1,404	5	17,320	0.081						1	1,370	1	18,000	0.076
19,950 and over	1	1,360	1	23,500	0.059	1	1,380	1	23,500	0.059										

TABLE C 3 (Cont'd)

9 PEORIA, ILLINOIS

PE = Personal Enumeration, MR = Mail Returns

Annual Income group	1929 PE RENT Reports	1929 PE RENT Avg ($)	1929 PE INCOME Reports	1929 PE INCOME Avg ($)	1929 PE Rent-Income Ratio	1929 MR RENT Reports	1929 MR RENT Avg ($)	1929 MR INCOME Reports	1929 MR INCOME Avg ($)	1929 MR Rent-Income Ratio	1933 PE RENT Reports	1933 PE RENT Avg ($)	1933 PE INCOME Reports	1933 PE INCOME Avg ($)	1933 PE Rent-Income Ratio	1933 MR RENT Reports	1933 MR RENT Avg ($)	1933 MR INCOME Reports	1933 MR INCOME Avg ($)	1933 MR Rent-Income Ratio
All groups	799	366	907	1,662	0.220	707	381	960	1,721	0.221	1,008	282	1,022	1,108	0.255	1,294	282	1,304	1,153	0.245
No income	23	321	25	0		22	275	33	0		29	248	32	0		36	214	36	0	
$1- 149	2	100	3	100	1.000	3	167	5	100	1.670	40	191	40	100	1.910	45	163	46	100	1.630
150- 250	9	261	13	200	1.305	12	288	21	200	1.440	44	186	47	200	0.930	64	190	64	200	0.950
251- 349	8	194	12	300	0.647	10	226	18	300	0.753	62	208	62	300	0.693	55	205	56	300	0.683
350- 450	28	224	30	400	0.560	7	204	13	400	0.510	54	187	54	400	0.468	72	190	73	400	0.475
451- 549	21	235	25	500	0.470	13	288	18	500	0.536	48	206	51	500	0.412	76	236	77	500	0.472
550- 650	28	245	31	600	0.408	15	237	24	600	0.395	64	221	65	600	0.368	67	223	68	600	0.372
651- 749	20	276	22	700	0.394	15	306	24	700	0.437	60	239	61	700	0.341	66	229	67	700	0.327
750- 850	35	243	41	800	0.304	27	226	36	800	0.283	69	233	69	800	0.291	78	229	79	800	0.286
851- 949	23	283	23	900	0.326	14	280	22	900	0.311	50	241	50	900	0.268	62	239	63	900	0.266
950- 1,050	54	312	62	1,000	0.312	39	270	60	1,000	0.270	84	277	85	1,000	0.277	112	236	112	1,000	0.236
1,051- 1,149	25	239	28	1,100	0.217	12	271	21	1,100	0.246	28	225	26	1,100	0.205	41	287	41	1,100	0.243
1,150- 1,250	36	310	68	1,200	0.258	42	270	62	1,200	0.225	52	304	52	1,200	0.253	70	289	71	1,200	0.224
1,251- 1,349	42	297	42	1,300	0.228	27	315	34	1,300	0.242	30	297	30	1,300	0.228	47	296	47	1,300	0.228
1,350- 1,450	30	323	32	1,400	0.231	34	332	47	1,400	0.237	42	293	42	1,400	0.209	43	313	43	1,400	0.224
1,451- 1,549	54	333	62	1,500	0.222	45	307	64	1,500	0.205	33	324	33	1,500	0.216	59	342	59	1,500	0.228
1,550- 1,650	40	342	44	1,600	0.214	40	342	51	1,600	0.214	34	285	34	1,600	0.178	38	299	38	1,600	0.187
1,651- 1,749	25	356	28	1,700	0.209	25	317	32	1,700	0.186	14	336	14	1,700	0.198	29	321	29	1,700	0.189
1,750- 1,949	62	376	70	1,819	0.207	65	379	85	1,828	0.207	46	349	46	1,826	0.191	61	367	61	1,852	0.198
1,950- 2,149	52	422	57	2,030	0.208	57	459	68	2,032	0.228	30	402	30	2,040	0.197	37	390	37	2,051	0.190
2,150- 2,349	25	415	29	2,231	0.186	20	425	24	2,246	0.189	13	420	13	2,238	0.188	19	439	19	2,221	0.198
2,350- 2,549	29	529	34	2,432	0.218	38	470	46	2,443	0.192	30	442	31	2,442	0.181	33	478	33	2,448	0.195
2,550- 2,749	14	493	18	2,650	0.186	19	507	21	2,652	0.191	7	403	8	2,663	0.151	12	421	13	2,646	0.159
2,750- 3,149	30	530	38	2,961	0.179	36	524	46	2,961	0.177	14	566	14	2,993	0.189	22	474	22	2,941	0.161
3,150- 3,549	14	551	16	3,344	0.165	19	638	21	3,314	0.193	9	580	9	3,311	0.175	13	552	13	3,369	0.164
3,550- 3,949	10	688	11	3,682	0.187	13	667	19	3,658	0.182	5	598	5	3,680	0.163	15	579	15	3,680	0.157
3,950- 4,450	10	720	11	4,055	0.178	12	734	15	4,113	0.178	4	525	4	4,150	0.127	4	505	4	4,200	0.120
4,451- 4,949	10	608	10	4,700	0.129	7	600	7	4,686	0.128	4	815	4	4,575	0.178	8	611	8	4,675	0.131
4,950- 5,450	9	580	9	5,056	0.115	6	630	7	5,086	0.124	5	720	5	5,000	0.144	3	687	3	5,000	0.137
5,451- 5,949	1	360	1	5,900	0.061	3	757	3	5,500	0.138	1	600	1	5,500	0.109					
5,950- 6,949	5	895	5	6,160	0.145	4	695	5	6,300	0.110	2	690	2	6,000	0.115	4	958	4	6,450	0.149
6,950- 7,949	3	733	3	7,233	0.101			1	7,000		1	840	1	7,200	0.117	1	540	1	7,000	0.077
7,950- 8,949			1	8,900		3	867	3	8,167	0.106										
8,950- 9,949	1	1,020	1	9,000	0.113											1	1,080	1	9,000	0.120
9,950-11,949	1	900	1	10,000	0.090	2	780	2	10,000	0.078	1	780	1	9,000	0.087	1	1,200	1	10,800	0.010
11,950-13,949	2	900	2	12,450	0.072			1	13,000											
13,950-15,949	1	3,000	1	15,000	0.200	1	1,200	1	15,000	0.080	1	2,700	1	15,000	0.180					
15,960-19,949																				
19,950 and over																				

TABLE C 3 (Cont'd)

10 LANSING, MICHIGAN

Annual Income group[1]	1929 — PERSONAL ENUMERATION					1929 — MAIL RETURNS					1933 — PERSONAL ENUMERATION					1933 — MAIL RETURNS				
	RENT No. of Reports	RENT Average (dollars)	INCOME No. of Reports	INCOME Average (dollars)	Rent-Income Ratio	RENT No. of Reports	RENT Average (dollars)	INCOME No. of Reports	INCOME Average (dollars)	Rent-Income Ratio	RENT No. of Reports	RENT Average (dollars)	INCOME No. of Reports	INCOME Average (dollars)	Rent-Income Ratio	RENT No. of Reports	RENT Average (dollars)	INCOME No. of Reports	INCOME Average (dollars)	Rent-Income Ratio
All groups	409	362	465	1,707	0.212	298	367	378	1,712	0.214	500	205	505	963	0.213	465	201	469	976	0.206
No income	2	240	7	0		4	250	12	0		4	125	5	0		22	125	22	0	
$1- 149	2	155	3	100	1.550	2	230	4	100	2.300	12	128	13	100	1.280	18	154	18	100	1.540
150- 250	3	180	6	200	0.900	4	218	6	200	1.090	39	132	39	200	0.660	20	122	20	200	0.610
251- 349	5	200	6	300	0.667	4	190	5	300	0.633	25	146	25	300	0.487	18	114	18	300	0.380
350- 450	13	154	17	400	0.385	3	453	3	400	1.133	48	132	48	400	0.330	37	155	37	400	0.388
451- 549	13	224	13	500	0.448	7	243	10	500	0.486	38	158	38	500	0.316	38	165	38	500	0.330
550- 650	6	290	6	600	0.483	2	330	4	600	0.550	35	161	35	600	0.268	28	173	28	600	0.288
651- 749	7	249	8	700	0.356	4	223	4	700	0.319	25	162	25	700	0.231	24	158	24	700	0.226
750- 850	20	292	24	800	0.365	9	301	11	800	0.376	50	193	51	800	0.241	42	181	42	800	0.226
851- 949	13	272	14	900	0.302	12	263	13	900	0.292	21	180	21	900	0.200	24	185	24	900	0.206
950- 1,050	21	271	26	1,000	0.271	19	294	24	1,000	0.294	35	218	36	1,000	0.218	28	200	29	1,000	0.200
1,051- 1,149	10	271	11	1,100	0.246	9	328	9	1,100	0.298	25	237	26	1,100	0.215	17	205	17	1,100	0.186
1,150- 1,250	41	332	44	1,200	0.277	18	328	22	1,200	0.273	29	255	29	1,200	0.213	32	223	34	1,200	0.186
1,251- 1,349	16	276	19	1,300	0.212	6	320	9	1,300	0.246	10	229	8	1,300	0.176	12	218	12	1,300	0.168
1,350- 1,450	14	344	15	1,400	0.246	13	294	19	1,400	0.210	8	260	8	1,400	0.186	12	253	12	1,400	0.181
1,451- 1,549	36	337	40	1,500	0.225	24	368	28	1,500	0.245	14	259	14	1,500	0.173	14	250	14	1,500	0.167
1,550- 1,650	12	368	15	1,600	0.230	16	324	17	1,600	0.203	12	228	12	1,600	0.143	13	228	13	1,600	0.143
1,651- 1,749	8	291	8	1,700	0.171	9	314	10	1,700	0.185	6	280	6	1,700	0.165	6	207	6	1,700	0.122
1,750- 1,949	32	392	36	1,814	0.216	28	354	36	1,822	0.194	18	316	18	1,844	0.171	15	261	15	1,820	0.143
1,950- 2,149	31	398	33	2,021	0.197	31	410	38	2,039	0.201	16	331	16	2,025	0.163	11	287	11	2,036	0.141
2,150- 2,349	24	425	24	2,229	0.191	16	344	19	2,221	0.155	3	260	3	2,200	0.118	7	327	7	2,243	0.146
2,350- 2,549	31	419	31	2,442	0.172	19	447	25	2,448	0.183	6	293	6	2,467	0.119	9	342	9	2,467	0.139
2,550- 2,749	3	287	4	2,600	0.110	9	538	11	2,655	0.203	2	350	2	2,650	0.132	2	300	2	2,600	0.115
2,750- 3,149	14	490	17	2,959	0.166	15	508	20	2,940	0.173	4	345	4	2,950	0.117	10	387	10	2,920	0.133
3,150- 3,549	6	690	6	3,383	0.204	1	780	1	3,200	0.244	8	468	8	3,375	0.139	1	600	1	3,300	0.182
3,550- 3,949	10	484	10	3,690	0.131	5	588	5	3,600	0.163	3	420	3	3,687	0.115	2	810	2	3,600	0.225
3,950- 4,450	9	506	8	4,075	0.124	2	840	2	4,000	0.210	3	507	3	4,100	0.124	2	510	2	4,100	0.124
4,451- 4,949	7	705	5	4,560	0.155	3	670	4	4,675	0.143	1	540	1	4,800	0.113					
4,950- 5,450	5	900	1	5,000	0.180	2	490	2	5,000	0.098						2	645	2	5,200	0.124
5,451- 5,949	1	480	2	5,800	0.083	1	420	2	5,700	0.074										
5,950- 6,949	2	750	2	6,000	0.125															
6,950- 7,949	1	2,400	1	7,800	0.308			1	7,200											
7,950- 8,949	2	1,100	2	8,050	0.137	1	840	2	8,250	0.102										
8,950- 9,949																				
9,950-11,949																				
11,950-13,949																				
13,950-15,949																				
15,950-19,949																				
19,950 and over	1		1	15,000																

TABLE C 3 (Cont'd)

II RACINE, WISCONSIN

Annual Income group[1]	PERSONAL ENUMERATION — 1929					MAIL RETURNS — 1929					PERSONAL ENUMERATION — 1933					MAIL RETURNS — 1933				
	RENT No. of Reports	RENT Average (dollars)	INCOME No. of Reports	INCOME Average (dollars)	Rent-Income Ratio	RENT No. of Reports	RENT Average (dollars)	INCOME No. of Reports	INCOME Average (dollars)	Rent-Income Ratio	RENT No. of Reports	RENT Average (dollars)	INCOME No. of Reports	INCOME Average (dollars)	Rent-Income Ratio	RENT No. of Reports	RENT Average (dollars)	INCOME No. of Reports	INCOME Average (dollars)	Rent-Income Ratio
All groups	536	371	687	1,526	0.243	581	384	805	1,756	0.219	789	211	795	787	0.275	1,081	225	1,091	883	0.255
No Income	37	286	48	0		33	248	50	0		102	160	103	0		112	156	112	0	
$1- 149	4	303	7	100	3.030	2	290	5	100	2.900	62	139	62	100	1.390	107	159	109	100	1.590
150- 250	9	256	16	200	1.280	6	190	12	200	0.950	64	156	66	200	0.780	88	181	89	200	0.905
251- 349	6	283	10	300	0.943	6	297	10	300	0.990	55	190	55	300	0.633	49	179	50	300	0.597
350- 450	11	259	16	400	0.648	7	301	9	400	0.753	49	186	49	400	0.465	64	176	65	400	0.440
451- 549	12	283	18	500	0.566	8	263	14	500	0.526	56	185	56	500	0.370	48	186	49	500	0.372
550- 650	15	256	23	600	0.427	11	285	14	600	0.475	44	200	44	600	0.333	44	198	51	600	0.330
651- 749	12	297	14	700	0.424	12	329	17	700	0.470	30	192	30	700	0.274	44	202	44	700	0.289
750- 850	23	278	29	800	0.348	10	300	19	800	0.375	40	241	40	800	0.301	65	193	65	800	0.241
851- 949	8	361	15	900	0.401	10	371	13	900	0.412	28	202	28	900	0.224	41	213	42	900	0.237
950- 1,050	41	376	47	1,000	0.376	23	323	34	1,000	0.323	47	213	47	1,000	0.213	56	257	58	1,000	0.257
1,051- 1,149	13	349	16	1,100	0.317	17	308	23	1,100	0.280	23	219	23	1,100	0.199	34	241	34	1,100	0.219
1,150- 1,250	34	327	48	1,200	0.273	33	311	46	1,200	0.259	31	256	31	1,200	0.213	43	239	43	1,200	0.199
1,251- 1,349	12	329	15	1,300	0.253	12	338	15	1,300	0.280	19	248	20	1,300	0.191	32	281	32	1,300	0.201
1,350- 1,450	17	310	18	1,400	0.221	25	331	29	1,400	0.256	20	263	20	1,400	0.188	36	269	37	1,400	0.192
1,451- 1,549	31	350	36	1,500	0.253	38	341	50	1,500	0.227	21	272	22	1,500	0.181	31	267	31	1,500	0.178
1,550- 1,650	27	335	34	1,600	0.209	37	314	56	1,600	0.196	15	303	15	1,600	0.189	31	271	31	1,600	0.189
1,651- 1,749	12	426	18	1,700	0.251	22	340	33	1,700	0.200	13	285	13	1,700	0.168	16	276	16	1,700	0.162
1,750- 1,949	63	374	74	1,824	0.205	66	361	94	1,800	0.201	18	302	19	1,826	0.165	36	280	37	1,800	0.156
1,950- 2,149	45	437	54	2,035	0.215	55	457	70	2,009	0.227	13	347	13	2,015	0.172	31	360	31	2,000	0.180
2,150- 2,349	16	405	22	2,232	0.181	30	474	34	2,200	0.215	7	361	7	2,257	0.160	10	327	10	2,200	0.149
2,350- 2,549	34	468	43	2,440	0.192	33	480	41	2,400	0.200	10	346	10	2,420	0.143	12	378	12	2,400	0.158
2,550- 2,749	8	520	11	2,673	0.195	11	389	17	2,635	0.148	8	281	8	2,633	0.107	7	380	7	2,643	0.144
2,750- 3,149	18	504	21	2,990	0.169	27	458	37	2,962	0.155	5	402	5	2,840	0.142	15	369	15	2,800	0.132
3,150- 3,549	6	580	7	3,271	0.177	11	508	18	3,344	0.152	1	480	1	3,400	0.141	6	470	6	3,333	0.141
3,550- 3,949	8	615	10	3,710	0.166	6	488	8	3,700	0.132	3	497	3	3,633[1]	0.137	4	435	4	3,600	0.121
3,950- 4,450	4	498	5	4,040	0.123	8	563	8	4,038	0.139	1	780	1	4,000	0.195	3	480	3	4,067	0.113
4,451- 4,949	2	455	2	4,700	0.097	4	760	5	4,800	0.158	1	600	1	4,800	0.125	3	870	3	4,667	0.186
4,950- 5,450	2	630	3	5,133	0.123	10	752	14	5,379	0.140	1	660	1	5,400	0.122	1	600	1	5,400	0.111
5,451- 5,949	2	450	2	5,550	0.081															
5,950- 6,949	2	890	3	6,300	0.141	1	520	1	6,500	0.080	1	480	1	6,000	0.080	2	900	2	6,350	0.142
6,950- 7,949	2	810	2	7,550	0.107	4	565	5	7,220	0.076						2	600	2	7,250	0.083
7,950- 8,949						1	1,200	1	8,000	0.150	1	580	1	8,000	0.073	1	840	1	8,600	0.098
8,950- 9,949																				
9,950-11,949			2	10,000		2	1,380	2	10,000	0.138										
11,950-13,949																				
13,950-15,949																1	1,020	1	15,000	0.068
15,950-19,949																				
19,950 and over								1	25,000											

TABLE C 3 (Cont'd)

12 MINNEAPOLIS, MINNESOTA

Annual Income group[1]	1929 PERSONAL ENUMERATION					1929 MAIL RETURNS					1933 PERSONAL ENUMERATION					1933 MAIL RETURNS				
	RENT No. of Reports	RENT Average (dollars)	INCOME No. of Reports	INCOME Average (dollars)	Rent-Income Ratio	RENT No. of Reports	RENT Average (dollars)	INCOME No. of Reports	INCOME Average (dollars)	Rent-Income Ratio	RENT No. of Reports	RENT Average (dollars)	INCOME No. of Reports	INCOME Average (dollars)	Rent-Income Ratio	RENT No. of Reports	RENT Average (dollars)	INCOME No. of Reports	INCOME Average (dollars)	Rent-Income Ratio
All groups	4,258	378	4,893	1,711	0.221	2,258	403	2,933	1,890	0.213	5,290	313	5,313	1,168	0.288	3,923	323	3,957	1,294	0.250
No Income	33	263	33	0		67	261	105	0		66	255	66	0		216	218	216	0	
$1- 149	18	255	20	100	2.550	22	300	27	100	3.000	88	200	89	100	2.000	178	194	180	100	1.940
150- 250	34	219	40	200	1.095	23	248	30	200	1.240	169	202	169	200	2.010	158	225	159	200	1.125
251- 349	51	184	67	300	0.613	19	284	33	300	0.880	256	200	259	300	0.667	114	209	117	300	0.697
350- 450	74	187	98	400	0.468	30	230	38	400	0.575	380	209	383	400	0.523	156	218	158	400	0.545
451- 549	96	225	113	500	0.450	33	248	48	500	0.496	348	215	353	500	0.450	150	231	151	500	0.462
550- 650	134	252	156	600	0.420	50	269	63	600	0.448	409	242	409	600	0.403	172	243	172	600	0.405
651- 749	105	280	113	700	0.400	49	277	61	700	0.396	237	260	238	700	0.471	152	250	153	700	0.357
750- 850	192	264	218	800	0.330	61	285	85	800	0.331	335	266	336	800	0.333	215	247	218	800	0.309
851- 949	168	288	191	900	0.320	57	288	75	900	0.320	260	284	261	900	0.316	158	264	161	900	0.293
950- 1,050	329	289	375	1,000	0.289	116	297	155	1,000	0.297	379	313	379	1,000	0.313	242	284	243	1,000	0.284
1,051- 1,149	127	398	137	1,100	0.271	45	304	63	1,100	0.276	169	299	169	1,100	0.272	135	284	135	1,100	0.258
1,150- 1,250	410	308	471	1,200	0.257	156	311	208	1,200	0.259	407	336	408	1,200	0.280	241	320	242	1,200	0.267
1,251- 1,349	129	326	148	1,300	0.251	57	297	79	1,300	0.228	151	337	151	1,300	0.259	121	311	121	1,300	0.239
1,350- 1,450	163	353	190	1,400	0.252	112	340	139	1,400	0.243	152	347	152	1,400	0.248	157	321	157	1,400	0.229
1,451- 1,549	281	351	328	1,500	0.234	121	369	167	1,500	0.246	245	366	245	1,500	0.244	169	356	172	1,500	0.237
1,550- 1,650	205	368	233	1,600	0.230	114	356	133	1,600	0.223	146	370	148	1,600	0.231	146	359	148	1,600	0.224
1,651- 1,749	99	396	115	1,700	0.233	81	369	103	1,700	0.217	79	351	79	1,700	0.206	89	367	92	1,700	0.216
1,750- 1,949	405	409	456	1,820	0.225	230	388	287	1,825	0.213	289	403	289	1,824	0.221	224	397	225	1,828	0.217
1,950- 2,149	289	430	306	2,040	0.211	193	449	246	2,038	0.220	197	446	199	2,048	0.218	175	415	176	2,032	0.204
2,150- 2,349	122	453	137	2,244	0.202	78	465	97	2,237	0.208	79	445	79	2,229	0.200	94	428	95	2,236	0.191
2,350- 2,549	210	507	249	2,427	0.209	137	485	182	2,438	0.199	134	484	134	2,428	0.199	127	471	127	2,444	0.193
2,550- 2,749	70	477	83	2,642	0.181	63	519	74	2,654	0.196	55	432	56	2,648	0.163	56	483	57	2,647	0.182
2,750- 3,149	214	554	236	2,956	0.187	92	533	128	2,946	0.181	107	499	108	2,946	0.169	92	547	94	2,946	0.186
3,150- 3,549	67	579	79	3,361	0.172	54	561	68	3,369	0.187	42	507	42	3,319	0.153	53	544	53	3,351	0.162
3,550- 3,949	93	582	106	3,661	0.159	38	586	53	3,694	0.159	32	593	32	3,669	0.162	31	642	31	3,708	0.173
3,950- 4,450	47	666	55	4,089	0.163	45	667	56	4,093	0.163	28	686	28	4,114	0.167	35	619	36	4,133	0.150
4,451- 4,949	27	654	31	4,632	0.141	24	700	31	4,671	0.150	17	614	18	4,711	0.130	10	670	10	4,620	0.145
4,950- 5,450	38	759	50	5,098	0.149	27	841	38	5,034	0.187	15	757	15	5,113	0.148	17	741	18	5,111	0.145
5,451- 5,949	2	540	3	5,667	0.095	2	690	2	5,850	0.118	3	430	3	5,667	0.076	3	500	3	5,700	0.088
5,950- 6,949	23	720	28	6,107	0.118	13	861	17	6,171	0.140	6	800	6	6,133	0.130	10	735	10	6,230	0.118
6,950- 7,949	11	1,222	11	7,345	0.166	6	662	5	7,138	0.093	4	650	4	7,375	0.088	7	974	7	7,414	0.131
7,950- 8,949	4	795	7	8,214	0.097	4	540	8	8,300	0.065	3	713	3	8,000	0.089	6	710	6	8,333	0.085
8,950- 9,949	1	3,100	1	9,600	0.323	4	1,578	9	9,211	0.171	1	880	1	9,000	0.098	4	980	4	9,225	0.106
9,950-11,949	3	1,120	5	10,000	0.112	5	1,008	8	10,150	0.099						3	1,280	3	10,000	0.128
11,950-13,949						3	1,080	5	12,240	0.088						1	840	1	12,500	0.067
13,950-15,949						2	1,500	4	14,850	0.101						3	960	3	14,333	0.067
15,950-19,949						1	1,200	1	16,000	0.075						2	1,350	2	17,000	0.079
19,950 and over	4	755	4	42,500	0.018	4	1,545	4	24,750	0.062	2	390	2	42,220	0.009	1	1,500	1	22,000	0.068

TABLE C 3 (Cont'd)

13 ST. PAUL, MINNESOTA

Annual Income group	1929 PERSONAL ENUMERATION					1929 MAIL RETURNS					1933 PERSONAL ENUMERATION					1933 MAIL RETURNS				
	Rent No. of Reports	Rent Average (dollars)	Income No. of Reports	Income Average (dollars)	Rent-Income Ratio	Rent No. of Reports	Rent Average (dollars)	Income No. of Reports	Income Average (dollars)	Rent-Income Ratio	Rent No. of Reports	Rent Average (dollars)	Income No. of Reports	Income Average (dollars)	Rent-Income Ratio	Rent No. of Reports	Rent Average (dollars)	Income No. of Reports	Income Average (dollars)	Rent-Income Ratio
All groups	1,045	323	1,198	1,390	0.232	325	392	432	1,800	0.218	1,246	276	1,255	962	0.287	567	325	572	1,288	0.256
No income	40	242	53	0		12	268	22	0		91	179	91	0		26	228	26	0	
$1- 149	4	178	6	100	1.780	1	190	1	100	1.900	66	183	88	100	1.830	23	203	24	100	2.030
150- 250	12	166	12	200	.840	4	238	5	200	1.190	65	188	65	200	.940	16	186	16	200	.930
251- 349	15	228	19	300	.760	...	:	...	.....	.....	58	204	59	300	.680	14	252	14	300	.840
350- 450	21	226	25	400	.565	3	187	4	400	.468	63	205	64	400	.513	18	204	20	400	.510
451- 549	30	210	35	500	.420	3	190	3	500	.380	51	235	52	500	.470	16	249	16	500	.498
550- 650	42	252	47	600	.420	3	260	7	600	.433	87	224	87	600	.373	41	289	41	600	.448
651- 749	23	260	25	700	.371	4	245	7	700	.350	60	248	61	700	.354	15	221	15	700	.316
750- 850	50	247	54	800	.309	9	271	13	800	.339	84	250	84	800	.313	31	289	31	800	.338
851- 949	64	244	72	900	.271	8	300	12	900	.333	75	264	76	900	.293	20	285	20	900	.317
950- 1,050	78	287	92	1,000	.287	10	393	17	1,000	.393	90	266	90	1,000	.266	40	278	41	1,000	.278
1,051- 1,149	38	287	46	1,100	.243	10	289	12	1,100	.245	36	277	36	1,100	.252	27	271	27	1,100	.246
1,150- 1,250	133	291	150	1,200	.243	27	337	34	1,200	.281	92	300	93	1,200	.250	35	324	35	1,200	.270
1,251- 1,349	35	324	35	1,300	.249	16	331	19	1,300	.255	24	312	24	1,300	.240	18	343	18	1,300	.264
1,350- 1,450	46	315	56	1,400	.225	11	295	18	1,400	.211	38	305	38	1,400	.218	28	325	28	1,400	.232
1,451- 1,549	69	334	75	1,500	.223	23	324	35	1,500	.216	55	356	55	1,500	.237	25	368	25	1,500	.245
1,550- 1,650	42	330	44	1,600	.206	18	367	20	1,600	.229	31	382	31	1,600	.239	19	382	19	1,600	.239
1,651- 1,749	23	369	28	1,700	.217	15	385	19	1,700	.226	20	385	20	1,700	.215	14	389	14	1,700	.229
1,750- 1,949	86	376	106	1,824	.206	38	375	46	1,837	.204	41	378	41	1,820	.208	40	384	40	1,835	.209
1,950- 2,149	47	396	51	2,053	.195	29	382	36	2,036	.188	36	391	36	2,036	.192	29	402	29	2,024	.199
2,150- 2,349	19	433	24	2,229	.194	12	509	14	2,287	.226	8	431	8	2,283	.190	10	413	11	2,238	.185
2,350- 2,549	54	460	59	2,439	.189	23	490	27	2,433	.201	25	483	26	2,442	.198	21	465	21	2,438	.191
2,550- 2,749	10	508	11	2,673	.190	5	494	6	2,683	.184	10	488	10	2,640	.185	6	487	6	2,683	.182
2,750- 3,149	27	459	31	2,971	.154	16	561	19	2,974	.189	22	543	22	2,968	.183	11	544	11	2,955	.184
3,150- 3,549	9	577	10	3,370	.171	5	728	7	3,386	.215	7	480	7	3,386	.142	11	518	11	3,282	.158
3,550- 3,949	12	520	13	3,669	.142	2	510	4	3,625	.141	3	610	3	3,700	.165	3	553	3	3,733	.148
3,950- 4,450	3	680	6	4,033	.169	9	561	13	4,131	.141	3	533	3	4,200	.127	8	608	8	4,113	.148
4,451- 4,949	4	720	5	4,540	.159	2	735	4	4,525	.162	1	720	1	4,500	.160	3	700	3	4,500	.156
4,950- 5,450	3	760	4	5,050	.150	3	820	4	5,025	.163	2	560	2	5,100	.108					
5,451- 5,949	1	1,080	1	5,500	.196															
5,950- 6,949	5	784	5	6,320	.124															
6,950- 7,949						1	700	1	6,600	.106	1	300	1	6,200	.046	1	600	1	7,000	.086
7,950- 8,949						2	840	2	7,000	.120	1	700	1	7,100	.099					
8,950- 9,949								1	8,400											
9,950-11,949						1	850	1	9,600	.089										
11,950-13,949								1	12,000											
13,950-15,949																				
15,850-19,949																				
19,950 and over																				

TABLE C 3 (Cont'd)

14 DES MOINES, IOWA

Annual Income group[1]	1929 — PERSONAL ENUMERATION — RENT No. of Reports	RENT Average (dollars)	INCOME No. of Reports	INCOME Average (dollars)	Rent-Income Ratio	1929 — MAIL RETURNS — RENT No. of Reports	RENT Average (dollars)	INCOME No. of Reports	INCOME Average (dollars)	Rent-Income Ratio	1933 — PERSONAL ENUMERATION — RENT No. of Reports	RENT Average (dollars)	INCOME No. of Reports	INCOME Average (dollars)	Rent-Income Ratio	1933 — MAIL RETURNS — RENT No. of Reports	RENT Average (dollars)	INCOME No. of Reports	INCOME Average (dollars)	Rent-Income Ratio
All groups	973	362	1,178	1,716	0.211	930	352	1,259	1,690	0.208	1,330	291	1,353	1,155	0.252	1,727	279	1,751	1,197	0.253
No income	8	168	9	0		30	240	50	0		33	195	36	0		59	180	59	0	
$1- 149	1	300	1	100	3.000	7	199	10	100	1.990	57	161	57	100	1.610	85	168	88	100	1.680
150- 250	9	168	11	200	.840	12	273	22	200	1.365	70	189	72	200	.945	84	190	86	200	.950
251- 349	16	236	18	300	.787	12	147	17	300	.490	39	186	45	300	.620	65	178	65	300	.593
350- 450	20	151	25	400	.378	15	255	23	400	.638	48	167	49	400	.418	82	182	83	400	.455
451- 549	21	174	24	500	.348	17	195	27	500	.390	73	190	74	500	.380	78	190	77	500	.380
550- 650	24	233	28	600	.388	28	220	36	600	.367	61	240	63	600	.400	111	200	113	600	.333
651- 749	23	238	27	700	.340	28	208	36	700	.297	67	228	70	700	.326	60	209	60	700	.299
750- 850	51	223	60	800	.279	33	499	49	800	.624	97	235	98	800	.294	81	231	84	800	.289
851- 949	38	240	44	900	.287	16	281	28	900	.312	71	251	71	900	.279	87	240	87	900	.287
950- 1,050	81	280	109	1,000	.280	50	289	75	1,000	.289	98	253	98	1,000	.253	119	253	120	1,000	.253
1,051- 1,149	22	279	25	1,100	.254	28	247	36	1,100	.225	34	306	35	1,100	.278	61	286	61	1,100	.242
1,150- 1,250	76	291	98	1,200	.243	77	276	98	1,200	.230	100	305	100	1,200	.254	105	283	106	1,200	.219
1,251- 1,349	41	347	45	1,300	.287	40	287	46	1,300	.221	34	313	34	1,300	.241	66	288	66	1,300	.206
1,350- 1,450	23	285	29	1,400	.204	41	295	48	1,400	.211	30	315	30	1,400	.225	69	309	71	1,400	.221
1,451- 1,549	71	339	85	1,500	.228	57	313	78	1,500	.209	80	333	81	1,500	.222	53	301	53	1,500	.201
1,550- 1,650	34	354	37	1,600	.221	52	315	64	1,600	.197	35	378	35	1,600	.236	43	335	43	1,600	.209
1,651- 1,749	14	355	18	1,700	.209	16	321	21	1,700	.189	21	351	22	1,700	.206	42	311	42	1,700	.183
1,750- 1,949	100	385	114	1,813	.212	85	238	104	1,833	.130	89	389	89	1,818	.214	98	344	98	1,828	.188
1,950- 2,149	71	415	88	2,032	.204	67	387	98	2,038	.190	51	452	52	2,025	.223	66	391	68	2,034	.192
2,150- 2,349	30	462	38	2,250	.205	30	436	39	2,251	.194	22	383	22	2,223	.172	41	377	41	2,244	.168
2,350- 2,549	48	450	58	2,422	.186	56	473	70	2,443	.194	40	472	40	2,420	.195	49	468	49	2,429	.193
2,560- 2,749	19	523	26	2,673	.196	17	469	23	2,635	.178	13	523	13	2,654	.197	21	425	23	2,628	.162
2,750- 3,149	40	638	53	2,985	.214	50	543	68	2,938	.185	25	518	25	2,976	.174	39	496	39	2,933	.169
3,150- 3,549	20	577	25	3,388	.170	10	548	13	3,392	.162	17	472	17	3,329	.142	13	531	14	3,279	.162
3,550- 3,949	27	571	30	3,650	.158	14	594	22	3,705	.160	8	519	8	3,650	.142	15	595	16	3,650	.163
3,950- 4,450	22	686	28	4,092	.168	10	632	15	4,093	.154	8	541	8	4,063	.133	16	657	16	4,125	.159
4,451- 4,949	7	844	9	4,700	.180	9	767	13	4,638	.165	6	505	6	4,650	.109	7	664	7	4,657	.143
4,950- 5,450	9	450	11	5,100	.088	10	824	13	5,131	.161	2	510	2	5,100	.100	10	660	10	5,130	.129
5,451- 5,949						4	805	5	5,600	.144						1	1,080	1	5,700	.189
5,950- 6,949	2	900	4	6,000	.150	8	828	9	6,178	.134						1	880	1	6,000	.147
6,950- 7,949	3	713	3	7,467	.095	2	570	2	7,100	.080	1	600	1	7,200	.083	2	840	2	7,250	.116
7,950- 8,949						1	960	2	8,250	.116						1	960	1	8,000	.120
8,950- 9,949	2	450	2	9,000	.050	1	600	1	9,000	.067										
9,950-11,949						1	960	2	14,500	.066						1	900	1	12,500	.072
11,950-13,949																				
13,950-15,949																				
15,950-19,949																				
19,950 and over																				

TABLE C 3 (Cont'd)

15 ST. JOSEPH, MISSOURI

Annual Income group [1]	1929 PERSONAL ENUMERATION					1929 MAIL RETURNS					1933 PERSONAL ENUMERATION					1933 MAIL RETURNS				
	Rent No. of Reports	Rent Average (dollars)	Income No. of Reports	Income Average (dollars)	Rent-Income Ratio	Rent No. of Reports	Rent Average (dollars)	Income No. of Reports	Income Average (dollars)	Rent-Income Ratio	Rent No. of Reports	Rent Average (dollars)	Income No. of Reports	Income Average (dollars)	Rent-Income Ratio	Rent No. of Reports	Rent Average (dollars)	Income No. of Reports	Income Average (dollars)	Rent-Income Ratio
All groups	350	303	450	1,528	0.198	439	304	583	1,622	0.187	511	234	517	1,116	0.210	758	235	784	1,201	0.196
No income	8	130	15	0		10	243	15	0		13	130	13	0		18	140	18	0	
$1- 149	3	120	5	100	1.200	8	113	8	100	1.130	17	155	17	100	1.550	38	124	39	100	1.240
150- 250	6	142	11	200	0.710	7	169	10	200	0.845	46	147	49	200	0.735	47	129	49	200	0.645
251- 349	12	145	14	300	0.483	6	113	7	300	0.377	19	130	20	300	0.433	34	129	35	300	0.430
350- 450	10	181	16	400	0.478	15	161	18	400	0.403	35	164	36	400	0.410	28	138	28	400	0.345
451- 549	13	223	18	500	0.456	11	200	21	500	0.400	17	171	17	500	0.342	27	166	27	500	0.332
550- 650	13	205	19	600	0.342	5	152	12	600	0.253	28	185	29	600	0.308	43	178	43	600	0.297
651- 749	9	210	10	700	0.300	9	273	12	700	0.390	26	167	26	700	0.239	29	186	29	700	0.266
750- 850	28	215	32	800	0.269	13	188	22	800	0.235	37	206	37	800	0.258	46	185	46	800	0.206
851- 949	16	254	20	900	0.282	19	239	23	900	0.266	33	210	33	900	0.233	47	210	47	900	0.233
950- 1,050	28	271	34	1,000	0.271	31	244	46	1,000	0.244	24	228	24	1,000	0.228	54	237	54	1,000	0.237
1,051- 1,149	8	219	9	1,100	0.199	14	280	17	1,100	0.236	10	242	10	1,100	0.220	20	190	20	1,100	0.173
1,150- 1,250	25	260	34	1,200	0.217	43	273	50	1,200	0.228	29	217	29	1,200	0.181	42	265	42	1,200	0.221
1,251- 1,349	9	260	10	1,300	0.200	18	245	21	1,300	0.188	12	273	12	1,300	0.210	28	234	28	1,300	0.180
1,350- 1,450	13	292	20	1,400	0.209	17	232	20	1,400	0.166	24	251	24	1,400	0.179	33	239	33	1,400	0.171
1,451- 1,549	16	316	22	1,500	0.211	28	371	34	1,500	0.247	15	307	15	1,500	0.205	30	258	30	1,500	0.172
1,550- 1,650	8	276	11	1,600	0.173	30	287	37	1,600	0.179	19	286	19	1,600	0.179	27	287	27	1,600	0.179
1,651- 1,749	7	340	11	1,700	0.200	10	314	15	1,700	0.185	11	267	11	1,700	0.157	18	290	19	1,700	0.171
1,750- 1,949	28	351	33	1,830	0.192	33	345	41	1,822	0.189	31	314	31	1,861	0.169	47	313	47	1,840	0.170
1,950- 2,149	14	348	16	2,013	0.173	20	348	30	2,027	0.172	18	349	18	2,028	0.172	33	338	34	2,041	0.166
2,150- 2,349	11	400	12	2,242	0.178	16	363	17	2,241	0.162	7	317	7	2,243	0.141	11	412	11	2,227	0.185
2,350- 2,549	22	385	28	2,427	0.159	21	399	27	2,433	0.164	14	379	14	2,493	0.152	13	388	13	2,431	0.160
2,550- 2,749	6	385	7	2,629	0.146	11	408	11	2,645	0.154	5	420	5	2,640	0.159	8	365	8	2,650	0.138
2,750- 3,149	19	468	21	3,000	0.156	18	403	29	2,941	0.137	7	454	7	2,971	0.153	10	367	10	2,860	0.128
3,150- 3,549	1	480	2	3,500	0.145	10	409	13	3,392	0.121	4	368	4	3,450	0.107	7	414	7	3,543	0.124
3,550- 3,949	4	630	5	3,600	0.175	5	528	5	3,720	0.142	1	190	1	3,600	0.053	5	518	5	3,740	0.139
3,950- 4,450	3	660	4	4,075	0.162	3	433	6	4,200	0.103	3	640	3	4,287	0.150	5	414	5	4,140	0.100
4,451- 4,949	1	300	1	4,800	0.063	3	630	4	4,725	0.133	2	540	2	4,800	0.113	2	690	2	4,650	0.148
4,950- 5,450	3	620	3	5,167	0.120	1	1,220	1	5,000	0.244	1	900	1	5,000	0.180	1	520	1	5,100	0.102
5,451- 5,949																				
5,950- 6,949	2	720	2	6,000	0.120	3	620	5	6,140	0.101						2	600	2	6,250	0.096
6,950- 7,949	2	750	4	7,300	0.103			2	7,000		2	780	2	7,100	0.110	2	750	2	7,250	0.103
7,950- 8,949	1	1,140	1	8,500	0.134	2	1,200	2	8,100	0.148						2	750	2	8,000	0.094
8,950- 9,949																1	540	1	9,000	0.060
9,950-11,949						1	1,200	1	10,800	0.111						1	900	1	10,800	0.083
11,950-13,949	1		1	12,000							1	840	1	13,500	0.062					
13,950-15,949																1	1,400	1	15,000	0.093
15,950-19,949						1		1	16,000											
19,950 and over	1	1,080	1	21,400	0.050															

TABLE C 3 (Cont'd)

16 SPRINGFIELD, MISSOURI

Annual Income group	1929 PERSONAL ENUMERATION — Rent No. of Reports	Rent Average (dollars)	Income No. of Reports	Income Average (dollars)	Rent-Income Ratio	1929 MAIL RETURNS — Rent No. of Reports	Rent Average (dollars)	Income No. of Reports	Income Average (dollars)	Rent-Income Ratio	1933 PERSONAL ENUMERATION — Rent No. of Reports	Rent Average (dollars)	Income No. of Reports	Income Average (dollars)	Rent-Income Ratio	1933 MAIL RETURNS — Rent No. of Reports	Rent Average (dollars)	Income No. of Reports	Income Average (dollars)	Rent-Income Ratio
All groups	394	226	480	1,308	.173	355	249	491	1,418	.176	518	187	521	890	.210	666	179	676	905	.198
No income	9	141	16	0		11	115	18	0		19	131	19	0		36	115	39	0	
$1- 149	7	114	7	100	1.140	9	113	14	100	1.130	35	101	38	100	1.010	68	90	69	100	.900
150- 250	15	169	18	200	.845	10	124	15	200	.620	53	116	53	200	.580	57	111	57	200	.555
251- 349	11	175	11	300	.583	9	124	12	300	.413	31	128	31	300	.427	45	128	45	300	.420
350- 450	14	131	20	400	.328	13	127	20	400	.318	32	132	32	400	.330	42	125	42	400	.313
451- 549	17	141	22	500	.282	14	148	20	500	.298	29	156	29	500	.312	29	130	29	500	.260
550- 650	13	160	17	600	.267	10	155	22	600	.258	40	150	40	600	.250	40	135	40	600	.225
651- 749	18	148	24	700	.211	12	181	14	700	.259	19	157	19	700	.224	34	152	35	700	.217
750- 850	11	165	13	800	.206	12	201	28	800	.251	27	193	27	800	.241	36	158	36	800	.198
851- 949	17	158	22	900	.178	13	175	19	900	.194	38	180	36	900	.200	23	180	23	900	.200
950- 1,050	32	169	37	1,000	.169	22	179	26	1,000	.179	25	230	25	1,000	.230	42	191	42	1,000	.191
1,051- 1,149	14	201	18	1,100	.183	5	272	8	1,100	.247	18	188	18	1,100	.171	17	191	17	1,100	.174
1,150- 1,250	50	227	58	1,200	.189	37	227	45	1,200	.189	40	214	40	1,200	.178	34	214	34	1,200	.178
1,251- 1,349	13	210	13	1,300	.162	9	256	15	1,300	.197	14	211	14	1,300	.162	15	240	15	1,300	.185
1,350- 1,450	11	262	11	1,400	.187	20	272	25	1,400	.194	12	213	12	1,400	.152	17	228	17	1,400	.163
1,451- 1,549	15	301	20	1,500	.201	18	258	24	1,500	.172	15	331	15	1,500	.221	20	232	20	1,500	.155
1,550- 1,650	15	227	18	1,600	.142	15	222	19	1,600	.139	11	259	11	1,600	.162	11	240	11	1,600	.150
1,651- 1,749	11	200	13	1,700	.118	5	214	5	1,700	.128	4	205	4	1,700	.121	10	240	11	1,700	.141
1,750- 1,949	30	279	33	1,815	.154	23	289	33	1,830	.147	21	288	21	1,805	.148	27	283	28	1,832	.154
1,950- 2,149	24	275	30	2,020	.136	16	317	22	2,023	.157	13	288	13	2,038	.141	12	357	13	2,015	.177
2,150- 2,349	7	380	9	2,233	.161	10	451	18	2,244	.201	5	320	5	2,220	.144	8	325	8	2,238	.145
2,350- 2,549	18	417	25	2,468	.169	17	385	21	2,448	.157	10	398	10	2,470	.161	10	373	11	2,418	.154
2,550- 2,749	4	358	5	2,660	.135	8	385	8	2,650	.145	1	240	1	2,700	.089	5	430	5	2,640	.163
2,750- 3,149	9	348	12	2,983	.117	11	405	15	2,973	.136	4	363	4	3,000	.121	13	325	13	2,954	.110
3,150- 3,549	4	485	5	3,380	.144	5	550	7	3,329	.165	2	270	2	3,300	.082	6	467	6	3,367	.139
3,550- 3,949	1	380	1	3,800	.095	5	434	6	3,667	.118	2	435	2	3,750	.118	3	490	4	3,825	.135
3,950- 4,450						2	630	3	4,100	.154	1	390	1	4,000	.098	1	540	1	4,100	.132
4,451- 4,949	1		1	4,500	0	1	630	3	4,633	.136						1	480	1	4,500	.107
4,950- 5,450	2	390	2	5,050	.077	2	470	4	5,075	.093	2	480	2	5,150	.093	1	600	1	5,000	.120
5,451- 5,949						1	420	1	5,800	.072						1	300	1	5,800	.052
5,950- 6,949						2	690	3	6,000	.115	1	600	1	6,000	.100	2	525	2	6,000	.088
6,950- 7,949	1	420	2	7,000	.060	1	600	1	7,200	.083										
7,950- 8,949																				
8,950- 9,949	1	480	1	9,000	.053	1	100	1	9,600	.010										
9,950-11,949																				
11,950-13,949																				
13,950-15,949																				
15,950-19,949																				
19,950 and over																				

TABLE C 3 (Cont'd)

17 LINCOLN, NEBRASKA

Annual Income group [1]	1929 PERSONAL ENUMERATION					1929 MAIL RETURNS					1933 PERSONAL ENUMERATION					1933 MAIL RETURNS				
	RENT No. of Reports	RENT Average (dollars)	INCOME No. of Reports	INCOME Average (dollars)	Rent-Income Ratio	RENT No. of Reports	RENT Average (dollars)	INCOME No. of Reports	INCOME Average (dollars)	Rent-Income Ratio	RENT No. of Reports	RENT Average (dollars)	INCOME No. of Reports	INCOME Average (dollars)	Rent-Income Ratio	RENT No. of Reports	RENT Average (dollars)	INCOME No. of Reports	INCOME Average (dollars)	Rent-Income Ratio
All groups	289	334	453	1,589	0.210	446	351	580	1,749	0.201	535	254	545	1,069	0.238	736	278	745	1,222	0.227
No income	6	302	8	0		19	204	29	0		7	170	7	0		31	168	31	0	
$1- 149	2	185	3	100	1.850	5	158	6	100	1.580	29	144	30	100	1.440	30	162	30	100	1.620
150- 250	11	177	12	200	0.885	3	280	4	200	1.400	38	163	38	200	0.815	47	161	47	200	0.805
251- 349	6	163	12	300	.543	...	...	2	300		32	158	32	300	.527	20	177	21	300	.590
350- 450	2	205	5	400	.513	7	237	10	400	0.718	30	187	31	400	.393	34	194	35	400	.485
451- 549	5	178	10	500	.356	8	189	12	500	.378	24	188	25	500	.376	34	187	35	500	.374
550- 650	11	253	20	600	.422	8	255	10	600	.425	34	214	36	600	.357	34	220	34	600	.367
651- 749	8	171	17	700	.244	14	256	18	700	.366	29	189	29	700	.270	36	226	36	700	.323
750- 850	6	172	16	800	.215	17	258	22	800	.323	28	195	28	800	.244	43	235	43	800	.294
851- 949	9	224	15	900	.249	21	234	24	900	.260	27	261	27	900	.290	35	259	35	900	.288
950- 1,050	17	254	25	1,000	.254	32	255	42	1,000	.255	37	281	37	1,000	.281	52	235	52	1,000	.235
1,051- 1,149	7	311	14	1,100	.283	13	260	17	1,100	.236	24	235	24	1,100	.259	24	246	24	1,100	.225
1,150- 1,250	31	286	46	1,200	.222	29	284	43	1,200	.237	34	276	35	1,200	.230	54	280	56	1,200	.233
1,251- 1,349	10	286	18	1,300	.205	14	273	19	1,300	.210	12	313	12	1,300	.241	21	273	21	1,300	.210
1,350- 1,450	13	271	19	1,400	.194	19	302	24	1,400	.216	16	301	16	1,400	.215	21	280	21	1,400	.200
1,451- 1,549	15	379	33	1,500	.253	31	328	34	1,500	.219	25	294	25	1,500	.196	27	340	27	1,500	.227
1,550- 1,650	6	312	13	1,600	.195	15	341	19	1,600	.213	11	279	13	1,600	.174	18	297	18	1,600	.186
1,651- 1,749	5	342	7	1,700	.201	15	351	19	1,700	.206	8	306	8	1,700	.180	10	354	10	1,700	.208
1,750- 1,949	22	365	32	1,819	.201	28	378	37	1,827	.207	16	354	16	1,819	.195	41	337	41	1,834	.184
1,950- 2,149	17	428	24	2,029	.211	38	363	45	2,044	.178	27	381	27	2,019	.189	32	413	33	2,042	.202
2,150- 2,349	10	397	15	2,233	.178	15	409	17	2,235	.183	6	352	6	2,200	.160	16	410	16	2,256	.182
2,350- 2,549	16	420	23	2,439	.172	21	457	27	2,437	.188	16	456	16	2,438	.187	18	404	19	2,442	.165
2,550- 2,749	12	390	14	2,636	.148	11	424	13	2,638	.161	3	590	3	2,633	.224	7	430	7	2,671	.161
2,750- 3,149	20	471	23	2,970	.159	23	509	28	2,979	.171	12	395	12	2,983	.132	10	452	10	2,930	.154
3,150- 3,549	8	549	9	3,333	.165	13	569	15	3,333	.171	3	640	3	3,367	.190	14	519	14	3,350	.155
3,550- 3,949	3	473	4	3,725	.127	5	562	8	3,600	.156	3	487	3	3,833	.127	8	536	8	3,763	.142
3,960- 4,450	4	630	5	4,120	.153	7	609	10	4,120	.148	1	520	1	4,200	.124	8	543	8	4,213	.129
4,451- 4,949	2	585	5	4,700	.124	7	587	10	4,610	.121	2	340	2	4,650	.073	3	720	3	4,787	.151
4,950- 5,450	3	620	5	5,080	.122	4	660	5	5,040	.131	2	540	2	5,000	.108	6	592	6	5,033	.118
5,461- 5,949			1	5,500		1	600	1	5,600	.107										
5,950- 6,949	1	600	2	6,000	.100	1	900	3	6,333	.142						1	720	1	6,500	.111
6,950- 7,949						1	1,320	1	7,200	.183						1	600	1	7,300	.082
7,950- 8,949						2	990	4	8,125	.122						1	840	1	8,500	.099
8,950- 9,949	1	690	1	9,000	.077	1	900	1		.090	1	540	1	9,000	.060	1	960	1	9,500	.101
9,950-11,949								1	10,000											
11,950-13,949								1	13,500											
13,950-15,949																				
15,950-19,949																				
19,950 and over																				

TABLE C 3 (Cont'd)

18 TOPEKA, KANSAS

Annual Income group	1929 PERSONAL ENUMERATION					1929 MAIL RETURNS					1933 PERSONAL ENUMERATION					1933 MAIL RETURNS				
	RENT No. of Reports	RENT Average (dollars)	INCOME No. of Reports	INCOME Average (dollars)	Rent-Income Ratio	RENT No. of Reports	RENT Average (dollars)	INCOME No. of Reports	INCOME Average (dollars)	Rent-Income Ratio	RENT No. of Reports	RENT Average (dollars)	INCOME No. of Reports	INCOME Average (dollars)	Rent-Income Ratio	RENT No. of Reports	RENT Average (dollars)	INCOME No. of Reports	INCOME Average (dollars)	Rent-Income Ratio
All groups	667	319	806	1,631	0.196	672	313	888	1,503	0.208	872	245	881	1,110	0.221	1,178	240	1,193	1,043	0.230
No Income	15	303	25	0		16	203	33	0		15	235	15	0		27	157	27	0	
$1- 149	11	102	19	100	1.020	7	259	16	100	2.590	54	122	56	100	1.220	57	147	60	100	1.470
150- 250	14	139	20	200	0.695	17	124	25	200	0.620	85	115	85	200	0.575	76	126	76	200	0.630
251- 349	19	129	20	300	0.430	11	216	13	300	0.720	51	131	51	300	0.437	52	130	52	300	0.433
350- 450	20	178	23	400	0.445	13	135	24	400	0.333	50	173	51	400	0.433	70	151	72	400	0.378
451- 549	27	162	31	500	0.324	21	218	28	500	0.456	40	160	41	500	0.320	63	168	65	500	0.336
550- 650	30	190	36	600	0.317	18	192	41	600	0.320	45	179	47	600	0.298	80	172	80	600	0.287
651- 749	19	189	25	700	0.270	10	177	17	700	0.253	47	183	49	700	0.261	66	216	67	700	0.309
750- 850	25	173	29	800	0.216	19	253	33	800	0.316	40	206	40	800	0.258	86	199	87	800	0.249
851- 949	16	247	24	900	0.274	27	239	33	900	0.266	38	211	39	900	0.234	52	227	52	900	0.252
950- 1,050	40	222	46	1,000	0.222	52	207	60	1,000	0.207	43	202	43	1,000	0.202	79	227	80	1,000	0.227
1,051- 1,149	18	235	20	1,100	0.214	20	232	23	1,100	0.211	24	279	24	1,100	0.254	38	261	39	1,100	0.237
1,150- 1,250	67	286	77	1,200	0.222	54	289	66	1,200	0.224	53	270	53	1,200	0.225	67	277	68	1,200	0.231
1,251- 1,349	17	223	23	1,300	0.172	27	263	31	1,300	0.202	10	299	10	1,300	0.230	24	270	24	1,300	0.208
1,350- 1,450	27	281	30	1,400	0.201	31	294	34	1,400	0.210	23	298	23	1,400	0.213	48	308	48	1,400	0.220
1,451- 1,549	25	327	28	1,500	0.218	35	293	47	1,500	0.195	25	337	25	1,500	0.225	49	312	50	1,500	0.208
1,550- 1,650	19	280	22	1,600	0.163	16	348	20	1,600	0.218	19	332	19	1,600	0.208	25	309	25	1,600	0.193
1,651- 1,749	17	303	21	1,700	0.178	23	288	29	1,700	0.169	18	289	18	1,700	0.170	24	362	24	1,700	0.213
1,750- 1,949	52	378	64	1,823	0.208	71	349	89	1,827	0.191	55	339	55	1,825	0.186	66	344	67	1,821	0.189
1,950- 2,149	37	387	46	2,050	0.179	47	369	59	2,032	0.182	37	381	37	2,043	0.186	34	354	35	2,031	0.174
2,150- 2,349	18	446	19	2,237	0.199	22	398	28	2,252	0.178	17	385	17	2,253	0.171	23	359	23	2,239	0.160
2,350- 2,549	36	508	41	2,424	0.210	34	464	43	2,430	0.191	24	407	24	2,425	0.168	22	419	22	2,450	0.171
2,550- 2,749	11	441	11	2,664	0.166	19	423	22	2,632	0.161	15	504	15	2,660	0.189	8	408	8	2,650	0.154
2,750- 3,149	25	552	29	2,979	0.185	29	494	30	2,943	0.168	18	478	18	2,978	0.161	18	454	18	2,928	0.155
3,150- 3,549	17	561	17	3,290	0.171	9	448	11	3,345	0.134	4	398	4	3,325	0.120	8	504	8	3,413	0.148
3,550- 3,949	15	527	17	3,676	0.143	6	548	10	3,730	0.147	6	453	6	3,617	0.125	7	439	7	3,700	0.119
3,950- 4,450	10	678	12	4,083	0.166	4	668	5	4,140	0.161	6	660	6	4,233	0.156	3	640	3	4,200	0.152
4,451- 4,949	7	669	9	4,744	0.141	3	900	4	4,750	0.189	2	540	2	4,850	0.111	3	603	3	4,567	0.132
4,950- 5,450	4	680	5	5,060	0.134	3	643	4	5,000	0.129	1	880	1	5,000	0.176					
5,451- 5,949	2	570	2	5,600	0.102	1	900	1	5,600	0.161	1	500	1	5,700	0.088					
5,950- 6,949	4	1,010	7	6,157	0.164	3	777	4	6,400	0.121	2	660	2	6,350	0.104	2	645	2	6,300	0.102
6,950- 7,949						2	540	2	7,250	0.074	3	650	3	7,200	0.090					
7,950- 8,949	1	470	1	8,000	0.059	1	640	1	8,400	0.076										
8,950- 9,949	1	480	1	9,000	0.053															
9,950- 11,949							780	2	10,000	0.078										
11,950- 13,949	1	600	1	12,000	0.050						1	840	1	12,000	0.070	1	720	1	12,000	0.060
13,950- 15,949																				
15,950- 19,949	1		1	17,000																
19,950 and over	1		1	35,000																

TABLE C 3 (Cont'd)

19 WICHITA, KANSAS

Annual Income group¹	1929 — Personal Enumeration					1929 — Mail Returns					1933 — Personal Enumeration					1933 — Mail Returns				
	Rent No. of Reports	Rent Average (dollars)	Income No. of Reports	Income Average (dollars)	Rent-Income Ratio	Rent No. of Reports	Rent Average (dollars)	Income No. of Reports	Income Average (dollars)	Rent-Income Ratio	Rent No. of Reports	Rent Average (dollars)	Income No. of Reports	Income Average (dollars)	Rent-Income Ratio	Rent No. of Reports	Rent Average (dollars)	Income No. of Reports	Income Average (dollars)	Rent-Income Ratio
All groups	755	329	947	1,688	0.195	695	323	920	1,701	0.190	1,071	202	1,080	1,023	0.197	1,282	197	1,292	1,041	0.189
No income																				
$1- 149	6	343	21	0		11	235	21	0		23	206	24	0		23	158	23	0	
150- 250	4	140	7	100	1.400	5	178	10	100	1.780	23	139	23	100	1.390	61	121	61	100	1.210
251- 349	5	258	9	200	1.290	14	229	20	200	1.145	90	119	91	200	0.595	100	122	100	200	0.610
350- 450	8	123	12	300	0.410	11	145	18	300	0.483	76	115	76	300	0.383	72	117	72	300	0.390
451- 549	20	177	24	400	0.443	11	238	13	400	0.595	69	136	70	400	0.340	77	140	78	400	0.350
550- 650	16	227	23	500	0.454	20	198	31	500	0.396	84	138	84	500	0.276	76	136	76	500	0.272
651- 749	33	190	43	600	0.317	15	190	23	600	0.317	68	167	69	600	0.278	58	168	59	600	0.280
750- 850	21	200	22	700	0.286	15	211	17	700	0.301	67	166	69	700	0.237	67	165	67	700	0.236
851- 949	31	217	39	800	0.271	12	223	17	800	0.279	67	177	67	800	0.221	87	170	89	800	0.213
950- 1,050	23	198	28	900	0.220	27	224	32	900	0.249	47	172	48	900	0.191	71	189	71	900	0.210
1,051- 1,149	60	224	80	1,000	0.224	46	208	60	1,000	0.208	70	194	70	1,000	0.194	100	196	101	1,000	0.196
1,150- 1,250	25	203	28	1,100	0.185	22	225	28	1,100	0.205	28	211	28	1,100	0.192	40	186	40	1,100	0.169
1,251- 1,349	61	261	76	1,200	0.218	50	271	68	1,200	0.226	53	209	53	1,200	0.174	88	209	89	1,200	0.174
1,350- 1,450	28	274	32	1,300	0.211	21	304	24	1,300	0.234	32	221	32	1,300	0.170	29	226	29	1,300	0.174
1,451- 1,549	34	340	45	1,400	0.243	30	274	39	1,400	0.196	33	240	33	1,400	0.171	40	231	41	1,400	0.165
1,550- 1,650	37	319	45	1,500	0.213	41	288	53	1,500	0.192	29	239	29	1,500	0.159	44	240	45	1,500	0.160
1,651- 1,749	27	279	34	1,600	0.174	26	360	35	1,600	0.225	31	272	31	1,600	0.170	37	241	37	1,600	0.151
1,750- 1,949	18	369	20	1,700	0.217	13	309	23	1,700	0.182	14	286	14	1,700	0.168	23	261	23	1,700	0.154
1,950- 2,149	76	329	90	1,819	0.181	69	316	79	1,820	0.174	45	292	45	1,849	0.158	59	266	59	1,829	0.145
2,150- 2,349	35	364	44	2,045	0.178	61	372	76	2,028	0.183	36	308	37	2,049	0.150	28	284	28	2,050	0.139
2,350- 2,549	19	347	23	2,226	0.156	22	409	28	2,246	0.182	11	309	11	2,255	0.137	18	356	18	2,233	0.159
2,550- 2,749	52	487	64	2,431	0.200	34	420	53	2,442	0.172	23	363	23	2,435	0.149	23	322	23	2,430	0.133
2,750- 3,149	19	441	23	2,639	0.167	21	451	25	2,680	0.168	7	411	7	2,657	0.155	13	363	13	2,662	0.136
3,150- 3,549	30	491	35	2,914	0.168	42	452	51	2,965	0.152	14	437	14	2,957	0.148	16	366	16	2,900	0.128
3,550- 3,949	10	499	14	3,357	0.149	12	489	15	3,407	0.144	7	447	7	3,286	0.136	14	414	14	3,321	0.125
3,950- 4,450	14	555	16	3,700	0.150	16	469	22	3,691	0.127	8	461	8	3,725	0.124	2	540	2	3,650	0.148
4,451- 4,949	19	628	20	4,125	0.152	11	558	15	4,067	0.137	8	560	8	4,050	0.138	4	458	4	4,150	0.110
4,950- 5,450	6	747	8	4,688	0.159	8	660	8	4,700	0.140	4	655	4	4,675	0.140	4	603	4	4,700	0.128
5,451- 5,949	6	590	8	5,175	0.114	5	768	7	5,029	0.153	6	438	6	5,133	0.085	3	760	3	5,033	0.151
5,950- 6,949	1	1,320	1	5,600	0.236	1	720	2	5,650	0.127						1	480	1	5,800	0.083
6,950- 7,949	7	744	8	6,275	0.119	3	660	4	6,100	0.108	3	740	3	6,000	0.123	2	560	2	6,350	0.088
7,950- 8,949	1	600	2	7,250	0.083	1	600	2	7,550	0.795						2	780	2	7,000	0.111
8,950- 9,949						1	140	1	8,000	0.018										
9,950-11,949	3	880	4	10,000	0.088											1	720	1	9,000	0.080
11,950-13,949			1	12,000												1	180	1	10,000	0.018
13,950-15,949																				
15,950-19,949																				
19,950 and over																				

TABLE C 3 (Cont'd)

20 RICHMOND, VIRGINIA

	1929 — PERSONAL ENUMERATION					1929 — MAIL RETURNS					1933 — PERSONAL ENUMERATION					1933 — MAIL RETURNS				
Annual Income group[1]	Rent No. of Reports	Rent Average (dollars)	Income No. of Reports	Income Average (dollars)	Rent-Income Ratio	Rent No. of Reports	Rent Average (dollars)	Income No. of Reports	Income Average (dollars)	Rent-Income Ratio	Rent No. of Reports	Rent Average (dollars)	Income No. of Reports	Income Average (dollars)	Rent-Income Ratio	Rent No. of Reports	Rent Average (dollars)	Income No. of Reports	Income Average (dollars)	Rent-Income Ratio
All groups	2,039	270	2,348	1,333	0.203	879	406	1,130	1,995	0.204	2,820	254	2,838	1,095	0.232	1,517	340	1,529	1,498	0.227
No Income	32	215	32	0		29	261	51	0		54	182	54	0		60	190	60	0	
$1- 149	17	121	18	100	1.210	16	168	22	100	1.680	94	127	94	100	1.270	53	135	57	100	1.350
150- 250	62	111	68	200	0.555	16	221	20	200	1.105	235	122	237	200	0.610	60	183	60	200	0.815
251- 349	107	132	117	300	0.440	20	212	28	300	0.707	200	130	201	300	0.433	44	177	45	300	0.590
350- 450	139	142	147	400	0.355	18	202	19	400	0.505	204	145	204	400	0.363	59	190	59	400	0.475
451- 549	188	150	183	500	0.300	14	241	17	500	0.482	193	149	195	500	0.298	53	180	53	500	0.360
550- 650	189	162	182	600	0.270	38	223	45	600	0.372	175	154	178	600	0.257	63	224	63	600	0.373
651- 749	78	193	84	700	0.276	17	207	22	700	0.296	76	189	96	700	0.270	50	199	50	700	0.284
750- 850	183	163	183	800	0.204	27	233	32	800	0.291	150	200	150	800	0.250	72	246	73	800	0.308
851- 949	110	187	124	900	0.208	34	210	41	900	0.233	92	216	92	900	0.240	55	253	55	900	0.281
950- 1,050	124	229	144	1,000	0.229	39	277	50	1,000	0.277	181	261	182	1,000	0.281	77	285	79	1,000	0.285
1,051- 1,149	34	231	38	1,100	0.210	17	281	24	1,100	0.255	41	257	42	1,100	0.234	34	312	34	1,100	0.284
1,150- 1,250	124	287	148	1,200	0.223	43	283	58	1,200	0.236	159	303	183	1,200	0.253	78	363	78	1,200	0.303
1,251- 1,349	33	283	42	1,300	0.202	18	362	24	1,300	0.278	46	301	46	1,300	0.232	41	334	42	1,300	0.257
1,350- 1,450	42	303	48	1,400	0.216	18	327	27	1,400	0.234	40	308	40	1,400	0.220	55	321	55	1,400	0.229
1,451- 1,549	78	291	87	1,500	0.194	27	460	37	1,500	0.307	81	334	83	1,500	0.223	71	356	72	1,500	0.237
1,550- 1,650	57	330	65	1,600	0.206	34	321	43	1,600	0.201	64	334	64	1,600	0.209	59	330	59	1,600	0.206
1,651- 1,749	23	320	25	1,700	0.188	24	385	27	1,700	0.226	35	343	35	1,700	0.202	33	389	34	1,700	0.229
1,750- 1,949	116	380	144	1,810	0.210	73	343	92	1,827	0.188	135	406	137	1,810	0.224	98	387	98	1,827	0.212
1,950- 2,149	85	432	105	2,071	0.209	65	420	83	2,035	0.206	87	442	87	2,021	0.219	84	442	84	2,032	0.218
2,150- 2,349	30	447	40	2,245	0.199	40	437	48	2,256	0.194	38	461	38	2,234	0.206	62	453	63	2,240	0.202
2,350- 2,549	65	533	82	2,435	0.219	46	501	55	2,438	0.205	53	500	53	2,449	0.204	43	493	43	2,440	0.202
2,550- 2,749	22	497	25	2,640	0.188	25	563	33	2,655	0.212	28	532	28	2,665	0.200	33	522	33	2,648	0.197
2,750- 3,149	55	559	65	2,978	0.187	48	569	62	2,981	0.191	67	550	67	2,990	0.184	63	526	63	2,938	0.179
3,150- 3,549	24	671	34	3,350	0.200	32	606	36	3,350	0.181	17	529	17	3,371	0.157	36	595	38	3,328	0.179
3,550- 3,949	28	854	39	3,867	0.178	21	620	32	3,681	0.168	21	539	22	3,641	0.148	13	610	13	3,677	0.166
3,950- 4,450	16	684	22	4,064	0.168	21	645	27	4,059	0.159	16	641	17	4,108	0.156	15	689	15	4,133	0.167
4,451- 4,949	9	727	11	4,582	0.159	10	625	11	4,718	0.132	15	679	15	4,553	0.149	12	718	12	4,687	0.154
4,950- 5,450	14	730	18	5,022	0.145	8	858	11	5,091	0.169	5	628	5	5,040	0.125	13	815	13	5,138	0.159
5,451- 5,949	3	700	4	5,850	0.124	4	758	6	5,517	0.137	1	540	1	5,800	0.098	8	805	8	5,675	0.142
5,950- 6,949	5	1,074	8	6,225	0.173	19	847	21	6,238	0.136	6	790	6	6,217	0.127	10	681	10	6,130	0.111
6,950- 7,949	3	1,000	7	7,200	0.139	8	1,031	10	7,290	0.141	3	1,007	3	7,233	0.139	2	765	2	7,550	0.101
7,950- 8,949	1	540	1	8,000	0.068	3	943	4	8,025	0.118	2	600	2	8,000	0.075	4	690	4	8,300	0.083
8,950- 9,949			2	9,000		3	1,160	4	9,000	0.129	3	730	3	9,000	0.081	3	593	3	9,287	0.064
9,950-11,949	3	987	3	10,000	0.097	3	1,120	6	10,100	0.111	3	1,060	3	10,000	0.106					
11,950-13,949	1	960	1	12,000	0.080	2	670	2	13,000	0.052										
13,950-15,949			1	15,000				1	14,000		1	960	1	15,000	0.064					
15,950-19,949																				
19,950 and over	1	140	1	20,000	0.007	1	2,400	1	20,000	0.120	1	70	1	48,500	0.001	1	1,280	1	23,000	0.056

TABLE C 3 (Cont'd)

21 WHEELING, WEST VIRGINIA

Annual Income group[1]	1929 PERSONAL ENUMERATION					1929 MAIL RETURNS					1933 PERSONAL ENUMERATION					1933 MAIL RETURNS				
	RENT No. of Reports	RENT Average (dollars)	INCOME No. of Reports	INCOME Average (dollars)	Rent-Income Ratio	RENT No. of Reports	RENT Average (dollars)	INCOME No. of Reports	INCOME Average (dollars)	Rent-Income Ratio	RENT No. of Reports	RENT Average (dollars)	INCOME No. of Reports	INCOME Average (dollars)	Rent-Income Ratio	RENT No. of Reports	RENT Average (dollars)	INCOME No. of Reports	INCOME Average (dollars)	Rent-Income Ratio
All groups	876	287	1,012	1,397	0.205	665	312	820	1,444	0.216	1,101	218	1,116	892	0.244	1,083	234	1,101	959	0.244
No Income	32	212	36	0		36	221	46	0		37	191	38	0		50	147	50	0	
$1- 149	17	172	23	100	1.720	12	175	14	100	1.750	85	150	89	100	1.500	58	157	62	100	1.570
150- 250	24	143	28	200	0.715	19	202	25	200	1.010	94	134	95	200	0.670	83	151	84	200	0.755
251- 349	24	180	26	300	0.600	13	194	20	300	0.647	56	145	57	300	0.483	59	161	60	300	0.537
350- 450	24	198	32	400	0.495	21	184	24	400	0.460	86	162	86	400	0.405	81	174	82	400	0.435
451- 549	33	224	37	500	0.448	23	169	28	500	0.338	81	173	81	500	0.346	74	203	74	500	0.406
550- 650	28	202	37	600	0.337	27	223	36	600	0.372	71	201	71	600	0.335	72	193	73	600	0.322
651- 749	31	206	35	700	0.294	16	218	22	700	0.311	43	190	44	700	0.271	38	172	41	700	0.246
750- 850	49	208	55	800	0.260	24	240	29	800	0.300	70	202	70	800	0.253	47	206	49	800	0.258
851- 949	31	247	40	900	0.274	25	251	33	900	0.279	38	234	38	900	0.260	33	205	33	900	0.228
950- 1,050	57	225	67	1,000	0.225	39	217	51	1,000	0.217	78	224	80	1,000	0.224	74	265	75	1,000	0.265
1,051- 1,149	22	250	26	1,100	0.227	16	235	22	1,100	0.214	39	240	40	1,100	0.218	41	241	41	1,100	0.219
1,150- 1,250	67	251	76	1,200	0.209	42	283	47	1,200	0.236	65	230	65	1,200	0.192	65	258	66	1,200	0.215
1,251- 1,349	43	285	44	1,300	0.219	18	278	24	1,300	0.214	34	303	34	1,300	0.233	29	242	30	1,300	0.186
1,350- 1,450	28	271	33	1,400	0.194	23	271	26	1,400	0.194	29	259	29	1,400	0.185	36	249	37	1,400	0.178
1,451- 1,549	40	306	45	1,500	0.204	36	284	43	1,500	0.189	38	290	39	1,500	0.193	32	291	32	1,500	0.194
1,550- 1,650	28	290	32	1,600	0.181	28	311	38	1,600	0.194	21	307	21	1,600	0.192	39	283	39	1,600	0.164
1,651- 1,749	28	309	29	1,700	0.182	14	324	17	1,700	0.191	13	312	13	1,700	0.184	36	310	36	1,700	0.182
1,750- 1,949	71	323	83	1,817	0.178	73	323	89	1,826	0.177	34	279	35	1,817	0.154	45	356	45	1,831	0.194
1,950- 2,149	51	319	60	2,032	0.157	48	353	55	2,038	0.173	24	327	24	2,033	0.161	22	350	22	2,036	0.172
2,150- 2,349	21	354	25	2,244	0.158	17	444	22	2,255	0.197	18	388	18	2,228	0.174	11	385	11	2,245	0.171
2,350- 2,549	42	446	45	2,438	0.183	25	515	29	2,448	0.210	16	403	16	2,425	0.166	18	387	19	2,437	0.159
2,550- 2,749	25	390	28	2,621	0.149	13	447	15	2,660	0.168	6	337	7	2,614	0.129	13	412	13	2,631	0.157
2,750- 3,149	24	414	29	2,948	0.140	23	523	25	2,976	0.176	11	523	12	2,917	0.179	10	495	10	2,950	0.168
3,150- 3,549	7	456	9	3,289	0.139	8	450	10	3,390	0.133	6	373	6	3,367	0.111	3	443	3	3,367	0.132
3,550- 3,949	9	783	9	3,711	0.211	4	528	6	3,633	0.145	1	340	1	3,800	0.089	4	490	4	3,675	0.133
3,950- 4,450	7	474	8	4,138	0.115	6	653	7	4,057	0.161	1	480	1	4,200	0.114	1	540	1	4,000	0.135
4,451- 4,949	5	520	5	4,600	0.113	2	940	2	4,550	0.207						3	760	3	4,600	0.165
4,950- 5,450	3	560	5	5,000	0.112	7	744	8	5,013	0.148	2	550	2	5,000	0.106	2	930	2	5,000	0.186
5,451- 5,949	2	900	2	5,600	0.161	1	1,200	1	5,500	0.218	1	480	1	5,600	0.086	1	900	1	5,800	0.155
5,950- 6,949	3	487	3	6,167	0.079	3	1,047	3	6,400	0.164	1	420	1	6,000	0.070					
6,950- 7,949											1	900	1	7,200	0.125	3	720	3	7,200	0.100
7,950- 8,949	1	1,080	1	8,300	0.130															
8,950- 9,949											1	560	1	9,000	0.062					
9,950-11,949	1	900	1	12,000	0.075	2	910	2	10,150	0.090										
11,950-13,949																				
13,950-15,949																				
15,950-19,949						1	1,200	1	17,100	0.070										
19,950 and over																				

TABLE C 3 (Cont'd)

22 ATLANTA, GEORGIA

Annual Income group	1929 PERSONAL ENUMERATION RENT No. of Reports	RENT Average (dollars)	INCOME No. of Reports	INCOME Average (dollars)	Rent-Income Ratio	1929 MAIL RETURNS RENT No. of Reports	RENT Average (dollars)	INCOME No. of Reports	INCOME Average (dollars)	Rent-Income Ratio	1933 PERSONAL ENUMERATION RENT No. of Reports	RENT Average (dollars)	INCOME No. of Reports	INCOME Average (dollars)	Rent-Income Ratio	1933 MAIL RETURNS RENT No. of Reports	RENT Average (dollars)	INCOME No. of Reports	INCOME Average (dollars)	Rent-Income Ratio
All groups	4,141	231	4,554	1,456	.193	3,000	284	3,773	1,356	.195	4,802	222	4,825	972	.228	4,655	221	4,689	987	.224
No income	34	252	42	0		118	205	162	0		84	184	84	0		273	128	273	0	
$1- 149	30	92	35	100	.920	107	134	119	100	1.340	258	92	260	100	.920	509	114	509	100	1.140
150- 250	122	114	144	200	.570	165	134	190	200	.670	582	108	584	200	.540	521	116	525	200	.580
251- 349	188	114	203	300	.380	180	136	206	300	.453	437	123	440	300	.410	343	134	345	300	.447
350- 450	257	142	280	400	.355	261	148	292	400	.370	390	133	394	400	.333	345	144	350	400	.360
451- 549	252	153	278	500	.306	238	160	271	500	.320	366	153	368	500	.306	307	157	308	500	.314
550- 650	273	154	293	600	.257	224	159	263	600	.285	330	172	331	600	.287	270	174	272	600	.290
651- 749	232	172	242	700	.246	160	173	181	700	.247	189	166	189	700	.237	191	192	191	700	.274
750- 850	283	188	302	800	.210	186	174	221	800	.218	252	199	253	800	.249	160	182	182	800	.228
851- 949	155	196	163	900	.218	91	178	111	900	.198	149	200	149	900	.222	111	195	113	900	.217
950- 1,050	238	205	257	1,000	.205	131	227	170	1,000	.227	228	231	226	1,000	.231	159	247	161	1,000	.247
1,051- 1,149	74	194	79	1,100	.176	52	205	59	1,100	.186	86	248	86	1,100	.225	72	256	72	1,100	.233
1,150- 1,250	259	245	275	1,200	.204	112	265	161	1,200	.221	195	282	196	1,200	.235	166	245	166	1,200	.204
1,251- 1,349	95	284	106	1,300	.203	57	283	67	1,300	.218	82	283	83	1,300	.218	62	277	62	1,300	.213
1,350- 1,450	80	289	88	1,400	.206	52	268	64	1,400	.191	76	288	78	1,400	.206	104	294	105	1,400	.210
1,451- 1,549	163	303	180	1,500	.202	68	312	91	1,500	.208	157	342	157	1,500	.228	83	322	84	1,500	.215
1,550- 1,650	82	289	90	1,600	.181	52	314	69	1,600	.196	78	300	77	1,600	.188	93	332	93	1,600	.208
1,651- 1,749	49	330	59	1,700	.194	38	337	45	1,700	.198	64	317	84	1,700	.186	55	317	55	1,700	.186
1,750- 1,949	284	366	294	1,816	.202	122	354	184	1,827	.194	200	359	201	1,821	.197	162	338	164	1,830	.185
1,950- 2,149	180	389	204	2,086	.186	104	369	151	2,022	.182	164	402	164	2,030	.198	124	360	126	2,033	.177
2,150- 2,349	68	430	75	2,245	.192	43	393	60	2,236	.176	55	433	55	2,238	.193	93	409	94	2,244	.182
2,350- 2,549	219	477	247	2,455	.196	91	476	125	2,430	.196	136	460	137	2,446	.188	96	435	98	2,439	.178
2,550- 2,749	62	438	67	2,640	.166	39	481	61	2,644	.182	51	431	51	2,641	.163	64	445	64	2,650	.168
2,750- 3,149	174	517	199	2,947	.175	103	567	147	2,957	.192	101	507	101	2,948	.172	90	473	92	2,949	.160
3,150- 3,549	68	563	82	3,368	.167	35	550	48	3,377	.163	35	561	35	3,377	.166	50	512	51	3,310	.155
3,550- 3,949	81	596	84	3,689	.162	47	643	76	3,709	.173	30	516	30	3,717	.139	34	561	34	3,732	.150
3,950- 4,450	54	655	62	4,081	.160	29	643	42	4,088	.160	16	532	16	4,113	.129	29	577	30	4,100	.141
4,451- 4,949	25	608	25	4,652	.131	21	756	32	4,666	.162	6	553	6	4,635	.119	23	576	24	4,604	.125
4,950- 5,450	35	721	41	5,076	.142	19	749	30	5,073	.148	15	605	15	5,040	.120	18	674	18	5,156	.131
5,451- 5,949	8	546	9	5,622	.097	9	867	11	5,645	.154	2	420	2	5,550	.076	5	724	5	5,620	.129
5,950- 6,949	12	831	14	6,121	.136	14	671	21	6,187	.109	11	745	11	6,100	.122	14	705	14	6,371	.111
6,950- 7,949	13	714	14	7,336	.097	7	944	11	7,200	.131	3	607	4	7,425	.082	11	760	11	7,136	.107
7,950- 8,949	5	1,100	5	8,000	.138	12	931	14	8,093	.115	1	780	1	8,200	.095	4	750	4	8,100	.093
8,950- 9,949			1	9,700		2	1,110	4	9,250	.120						2	890	2	9,000	.099
9,950-11,949	6	970	13	10,000	.097	3	750	3	10,000	.075	7	543	7	10,000	.054	4	1,365	4	10,900	.125
11,950-13,949						2	1,800	2	12,000	.150						3	710	3	12,500	.057
13,950-15,949	1	2,100	2	14,500	.145			2	15,000							2	810	2	14,000	.058
15,950-19,949						2	1,155	2	17,000	.068										
19,950 and over						4	1,395	5	26,500	.053						3	1,377	3	29,333	.047

TABLE C 3 (Cont'd)

23 BIRMINGHAM, ALABAMA

Annual Income group[1]	1929 PERSONAL ENUMERATION Rent No.	Rent Avg	Inc No.	Inc Avg	R/I Ratio	1929 MAIL RETURNS Rent No.	Rent Avg	Inc No.	Inc Avg	R/I Ratio	1933 PERSONAL ENUMERATION Rent No.	Rent Avg	Inc No.	Inc Avg	R/I Ratio	1933 MAIL RETURNS Rent No.	Rent Avg	Inc No.	Inc Avg	R/I Ratio
All groups	4,771	234	5,075	1,399	0.167	1,189	287	1,562	1,533	0.174	5,253	145	5,279	732	0.198	1,864	167	1,890	854	0.196
No Income	101	189	101	0		39	173	71	0		258	106	263	0		105	119	105	0	
$1- 149	152	97	164	100	0.970	50	129	59	100	1.290	885	73	888	100	0.730	246	79	250	100	0.790
150- 250	266	121	280	200	0.605	54	123	63	200	0.615	758	87	785	200	0.435	214	101	218	200	0.505
251- 349	194	125	202	300	0.417	42	144	53	300	0.480	446	93	451	300	0.310	112	106	113	300	0.353
350- 450	283	127	293	400	0.318	44	155	52	400	0.388	395	108	397	400	0.270	100	114	103	400	0.285
451- 549	243	134	252	500	0.268	46	152	56	500	0.304	301	119	301	500	0.238	107	128	108	500	0.256
550- 650	257	144	273	600	0.240	50	143	64	600	0.238	271	131	272	600	0.218	103	145	103	600	0.242
651- 749	277	137	288	700	0.196	41	178	53	700	0.254	194	137	194	700	0.196	77	147	77	700	0.210
750- 850	252	148	261	800	0.185	48	170	62	800	0.213	193	156	193	800	0.195	97	150	98	800	0.188
851- 949	220	158	230	900	0.176	41	171	52	900	0.190	116	154	117	900	0.171	56	199	57	900	0.221
950- 1,050	287	171	305	1,000	0.171	81	170	103	1,000	0.170	183	168	184	1,000	0.168	71	158	71	1,000	0.158
1,051- 1,149	99	176	101	1,100	0.160	18	158	25	1,100	0.144	80	172	80	1,100	0.156	41	207	41	1,100	0.188
1,150- 1,250	306	215	338	1,200	0.179	69	232	87	1,200	0.193	223	206	223	1,200	0.172	78	214	80	1,200	0.178
1,251- 1,349	78	203	79	1,300	0.156	21	241	25	1,300	0.185	84	210	84	1,300	0.162	40	201	41	1,300	0.155
1,350- 1,450	102	251	107	1,400	0.179	40	253	50	1,400	0.181	83	213	83	1,400	0.152	48	222	49	1,400	0.159
1,451- 1,549	125	274	144	1,500	0.183	51	266	68	1,500	0.177	95	262	95	1,500	0.175	54	248	55	1,500	0.165
1,550- 1,650	110	276	118	1,600	0.173	36	288	44	1,600	0.180	76	251	76	1,600	0.157	40	246	40	1,600	0.154
1,651- 1,749	76	265	81	1,700	0.156	26	290	32	1,700	0.171	54	240	54	1,700	0.141	26	220	26	1,700	0.129
1,750- 1,949	314	295	339	1,807	0.163	83	314	110	1,866	0.168	155	287	155	1,852	0.144	75	276	78	1,825	0.151
1,950- 2,149	204	338	218	2,045	0.165	78	366	98	2,089	0.175	93	291	93	2,039	0.143	44	305	44	2,041	0.149
2,150- 2,349	97	332	102	2,239	0.148	32	328	44	2,234	0.147	41	323	41	2,234	0.145	22	347	23	2,235	0.155
2,350- 2,549	197	362	220	2,418	0.150	54	394	72	2,435	0.162	74	329	74	2,434	0.135	35	361	36	2,447	0.148
2,550- 2,749	62	372	68	2,638	0.141	23	458	29	2,628	0.174	28	337	28	2,646	0.127	13	319	15	2,620	0.122
2,750- 3,149	151	465	168	2,965	0.157	39	490	62	2,979	0.164	73	385	73	2,958	0.130	19	384	19	2,937	0.131
3,150- 3,549	64	464	68	3,371	0.138	21	489	30	3,350	0.146	25	450	25	3,372	0.133	16	431	17	3,376	0.128
3,550- 3,949	83	485	94	3,655	0.133	18	557	29	3,731	0.149	24	454	24	3,683	0.123	5	402	5	3,600	0.112
3,950- 4,450	50	538	52	4,160	0.129	12	628	21	4,129	0.152	8	473	8	4,138	0.114	9	427	9	4,211	0.101
4,451- 4,949	22	636	24	4,704	0.135	6	642	8	4,713	0.136	9	496	9	4,622	0.107	4	565	4	4,650	0.122
4,950- 5,450	20	688	21	5,100	0.135	9	677	12	5,083	0.133	9	646	10	5,070	0.127	2	650	2	5,000	0.126
5,451- 5,949	9	813	9	5,644	0.144	2	900	3	5,633	0.160	2	890	2	5,600	0.159					
5,950- 6,949	26	662	28	6,136	0.108	10	659	13	6,100	0.108	12	699	12	6,058	0.115	1	420	1	6,000	0.070
6,950- 7,949	10	796	11	7,355	0.108	1	900	2	7,350	0.122	2	570	2	7,150	0.080	1	620	1	7,100	0.087
7,950- 8,949	8	746	9	8,133	0.092	1	840	1	8,000	0.105	2	1,070	2	8,500	0.126	1	780	1	8,500	0.092
8,950- 9,949	5	555	4	9,150	0.061															
9,950- 11,949	4	1,350	5	10,060	0.134	3	980	5	10,280	0.095	1	480	1	10,000	0.048	1	900	1	9,000	0.100
11,950- 13,949	4	1,283	4	12,500	0.101	1	1,200	1	12,000	0.100	1	600	1	12,000	0.050	1	420	1	11,000	0.038
13,950- 15,949	4	1,518	4	15,000	0.101	1	1,210	2	14,500	0.083										
15,950- 19,949	3	823	4	17,250	0.048															
19,950 and over	6	1,612	6	29,183	0.055			1	25,000		1	70	1	30,200	0.002					

TABLE C 3 (Cont'd)

24 LITTLE ROCK, ARKANSAS

Annual Income group	1929 PERSONAL ENUMERATION					1929 MAIL RETURNS					1933 PERSONAL ENUMERATION					1933 MAIL RETURNS				
	RENT No. of Reports	RENT Average (dollars)	INCOME No. of Reports	INCOME Average (dollars)	Rent-Income Ratio	RENT No. of Reports	RENT Average (dollars)	INCOME No. of Reports	INCOME Average (dollars)	Rent-Income Ratio	RENT No. of Reports	RENT Average (dollars)	INCOME No. of Reports	INCOME Average (dollars)	Rent-Income Ratio	RENT No. of Reports	RENT Average (dollars)	INCOME No. of Reports	INCOME Average (dollars)	Rent-Income Ratio
All groups	925	264	1,160	1,483	0.178	730	276	1,025	1,489	0.185	1,230	187	1,243	932	0.201	1,355	189	1,363	917	0.206
No Income	15	151	16	0		45	153	65	0		33	75	36	0		111	102	111	0	
$1- 149	21	91	28	100	0.910	19	154	29	100	1.540	118	94	119	100	0.940	147	101	147	100	1.010
150- 250	49	101	57	200	0.505	29	123	47	200	0.615	131	119	132	200	0.595	127	126	128	200	0.630
251- 349	40	130	48	300	0.433	27	142	38	300	0.473	88	126	89	300	0.420	96	119	96	300	0.397
350- 450	47	126	54	400	0.315	33	144	53	400	0.360	70	142	71	400	0.355	98	130	98	400	0.325
451- 549	34	116	44	500	0.232	20	145	28	500	0.290	76	153	77	500	0.306	63	187	63	500	0.374
550- 650	47	167	55	600	0.278	27	159	35	600	0.265	73	162	73	600	0.270	79	159	80	600	0.265
651- 749	30	180	31	700	0.257	27	173	35	700	0.247	45	172	45	700	0.246	44	152	44	700	0.217
750- 850	45	203	56	800	0.254	28	191	41	800	0.239	61	195	61	800	0.244	49	166	49	800	0.208
851- 949	42	219	53	900	0.243	29	199	39	900	0.221	50	200	51	900	0.222	52	180	52	900	0.200
950- 1,050	52	263	71	1,000	0.263	39	240	55	1,000	0.240	77	198	78	1,000	0.198	58	213	60	1,000	0.213
1,051- 1,149	19	231	22	1,100	0.210	16	253	20	1,100	0.230	29	230	29	1,100	0.209	38	207	38	1,100	0.188
1,150- 1,250	70	257	90	1,200	0.214	43	246	60	1,200	0.205	61	237	61	1,200	0.198	36	231	36	1,200	0.193
1,251- 1,349	12	278	14	1,300	0.214	13	284	15	1,300	0.218	20	218	21	1,300	0.168	29	222	29	1,300	0.171
1,350- 1,450	25	291	29	1,400	0.208	11	239	19	1,400	0.171	33	210	33	1,400	0.150	30	237	30	1,400	0.169
1,451- 1,549	42	301	54	1,500	0.201	35	291	43	1,500	0.194	43	235	43	1,500	0.157	41	232	41	1,500	0.155
1,550- 1,650	25	284	30	1,600	0.178	15	270	28	1,600	0.169	12	265	12	1,600	0.166	26	262	26	1,600	0.164
1,651- 1,749	17	354	22	1,700	0.208	15	307	21	1,700	0.181	16	287	16	1,700	0.169	18	251	18	1,700	0.148
1,750- 1,949	61	328	83	1,812	0.181	56	339	75	1,817	0.187	57	257	57	1,819	0.141	43	358	43	1,886	0.190
1,950- 2,149	33	355	46	2,028	0.175	37	354	50	2,088	0.170	37	283	37	2,038	0.139	47	290	47	2,028	0.143
2,150- 2,349	15	363	24	2,233	0.163	17	395	25	2,228	0.177	20	307	20	2,220	0.138	17	311	17	2,241	0.139
2,350- 2,549	64	366	78	2,426	0.151	37	387	53	2,475	0.156	29	357	29	2,431	0.147	33	346	34	2,431	0.142
2,550- 2,749	12	355	15	2,640	0.134	11	461	15	2,660	0.173	9	273	9	2,633	0.104	10	351	10	2,660	0.132
2,750- 3,149	39	413	52	2,973	0.139	39	453	44	3,000	0.151	14	362	14	2,936	0.123	16	407	16	2,963	0.137
3,150- 3,549	21	463	22	3,400	0.136	12	480	19	3,374	0.142	8	395	8	3,363	0.117	14	485	14	3,343	0.145
3,550- 3,949	22	500	27	3,622	0.138	21	486	23	3,665	0.133	10	387	10	3,650	0.106	13	435	13	3,715	0.117
3,950- 4,450	8	625	12	4,087	0.154	7	517	13	4,100	0.126	6	410	6	4,133	0.099	8	510	8	4,125	0.124
4,451- 4,949	3	420	6	4,683	0.090	5	588	6	4,633	0.127	2	360	2	4,700	0.077	4	555	4	4,725	0.117
4,950- 5,450	6	520	10	5,050	0.103	10	468	17	5,053	0.093	2	530	2	5,050	0.105	5	392	6	5,033	0.078
5,451- 5,949	1	300	1	5,500	0.055	4	515	6	6,083	0.085						1	480	1	6,900	0.070
5,950- 6,949	4	345	5	6,180	0.056	1	900	4	7,450	0.121	1	300	1	7,000	0.043	1	660	2	7,250	0.091
6,950- 7,949	3	740	5	7,080	0.105	2	705	4	8,225	0.086						2	540	2	8,150	0.066
7,950- 8,949																				
8,950- 9,949																				
9,950-11,949	1	780	2	10,000	0.078						1	1,200	1	15,000	0.080					
11,950-13,949																				
13,950-15,949																				
15,950-19,949																				
19,950 and over																				

TABLE C 3 (Cont'd)

25 OKLAHOMA CITY, OKLAHOMA

Annual Income group	1929 PERSONAL ENUMERATION Rent No. of Reports	Rent Average (dollars)	Income No. of Reports	Income Average (dollars)	Rent-Income Ratio	1929 MAIL RETURNS Rent No. of Reports	Rent Average (dollars)	Income No. of Reports	Income Average (dollars)	Rent-Income Ratio	1933 PERSONAL ENUMERATION Rent No. of Reports	Rent Average (dollars)	Income No. of Reports	Income Average (dollars)	Rent-Income Ratio	1933 MAIL RETURNS Rent No. of Reports	Rent Average (dollars)	Income No. of Reports	Income Average (dollars)	Rent-Income Ratio
All groups	1,599	382	2,140	1,727	0.221	610	388	915	1,838	0.211	2,302	253	2,328	1,056	0.240	1,341	245	1,351	1,157	0.212
No income	35	368	39	0		27	255	42	0		74	250	74	0		49	147	49	0	
$1– 149	2	140	13	100	1.400	7	220	14	100	2.200	110	133	113	100	1.330	88	142	89	100	1.420
150– 250	37	148	51	200	0.740	10	223	14	200	1.115	146	141	149	200	0.705	84	170	84	200	0.850
251– 349	34	187	51	300	0.623	7	228	12	300	0.753	134	183	137	300	0.610	45	166	45	300	0.553
350– 450	48	223	59	400	0.558	7	307	16	400	0.768	142	187	143	400	0.468	59	187	59	400	0.418
451– 549	54	289	74	500	0.538	9	181	24	500	0.322	96	219	97	500	0.438	79	181	81	500	0.362
550– 650	39	250	61	600	0.417	13	388	19	600	0.547	137	207	139	600	0.345	68	218	69	600	0.363
651– 749	43	307	54	700	0.439	12	280	18	700	0.400	97	224	100	700	0.320	42	194	42	700	0.277
750– 850	53	288	71	800	0.335	16	228	24	800	0.285	110	249	110	800	0.311	61	204	61	800	0.255
851– 949	58	286	65	900	0.298	16	284	24	900	0.316	106	231	108	900	0.257	53	232	53	900	0.258
950–1,050	82	323	106	1,000	0.323	43	287	57	1,000	0.287	172	246	174	1,000	0.246	97	227	97	1,000	0.227
1,051–1,149	23	314	28	1,100	0.285	13	312	18	1,100	0.284	60	251	60	1,100	0.228	46	258	46	1,100	0.235
1,150–1,250	153	342	200	1,200	0.285	41	318	60	1,200	0.263	229	283	233	1,200	0.219	101	262	102	1,200	0.218
1,251–1,349	34	317	45	1,300	0.244	16	330	20	1,300	0.254	47	291	48	1,300	0.224	41	232	41	1,300	0.178
1,350–1,450	59	325	69	1,400	0.232	18	335	28	1,400	0.239	65	272	65	1,400	0.194	59	258	59	1,400	0.184
1,451–1,549	110	363	149	1,500	0.242	34	372	47	1,500	0.248	95	297	95	1,500	0.198	56	284	58	1,500	0.189
1,550–1,650	41	399	52	1,600	0.249	30	328	43	1,600	0.204	45	305	45	1,600	0.191	56	284	58	1,600	0.185
1,651–1,749	21	337	32	1,700	0.198	19	413	24	1,700	0.243	31	325	31	1,700	0.191	28	280	28	1,700	0.185
1,750–1,949	188	395	231	1,811	0.218	64	369	100	1,829	0.202	120	332	120	1,824	0.182	57	318	57	1,833	0.173
1,950–2,149	89	539	119	2,037	0.265	38	427	60	2,032	0.210	82	348	82	2,045	0.170	41	330	42	2,029	0.163
2,150–2,349	43	437	54	2,226	0.196	17	410	27	2,244	0.183	36	355	37	2,224	0.160	28	325	28	2,231	0.146
2,350–2,549	128	465	170	2,421	0.192	37	453	53	2,428	0.187	69	407	69	2,423	0.168	35	353	35	2,440	0.145
2,550–2,749	32	493	40	2,650	0.186	10	429	19	2,853	0.182	19	453	19	2,632	0.172	21	415	21	2,657	0.156
2,750–3,149	91	529	119	2,961	0.179	31	579	51	2,975	0.195	25	419	25	2,924	0.143	29	424	29	2,941	0.144
3,150–3,549	23	629	30	3,343	0.188	20	496	23	3,370	0.147	18	493	19	3,300	0.149	9	382	10	3,310	0.115
3,550–3,949	33	569	53	3,615	0.155	12	640	16	3,656	0.175	16	422	16	3,619	0.117	8	530	8	3,713	0.143
3,950–4,449	22	575	35	4,149	0.139	18	646	24	4,100	0.158	6	457	7	4,071	0.112	6	483	6	4,083	0.118
4,450–4,949	14	488	18	4,839	0.105	11	619	14	4,879	0.132	4	525	4	4,550	0.115	3	440	4	4,575	0.096
4,950–5,449	16	601	19	5,079	0.118	7	627	10	5,060	0.124	5	542	5	5,000	0.108	6	583	6	5,117	0.114
5,450–5,949	2	760	2	5,800	0.136	1	540	1	5,800	0.098	2	780	2	5,800	0.134	2	420	2	5,500	0.076
5,950–6,949	5	492	16	6,000	0.082	1	600	4	6,125	0.098						3	800	3	6,000	0.133
6,950–7,949	8	677	7	7,286	0.093	1	900	1	7,200	0.125						1	660	1	7,000	0.094
7,950–8,949	1	720	1	8,000	0.090	2	750	4	8,025	0.093						1	1,200	1	8,000	0.150
8,950–9,949	1	1,270	1	9,000	0.141			1	9,000											
9,950–11,949	2	480	3	10,000	0.048	1	720	1	10,000	0.072						1	1,020	1	10,500	0.097
11,950–13,949	1	200	1	12,000	0.017															
13,950–15,949	1	150	1	15,000	0.010															
15,950–19,949											3	347	3	7,187	0.048					
19,950 and over	1	540	1	25,000	0.022	1	3,600	2	31,000	0.116	1	600	1	8,000	0.075					

TABLE C 3 (Cont'd)

26 DALLAS, TEXAS

Annual Income group	PERSONAL ENUMERATION 1929 Rent — No. of Reports	Rent — Average (dollars)	Income — No. of Reports	Income — Average (dollars)	Rent-Income Ratio	MAIL RETURNS 1929 Rent — No. of Reports	Rent — Average (dollars)	Income — No. of Reports	Income — Average (dollars)	Rent-Income Ratio	PERSONAL ENUMERATION 1933 Rent — No. of Reports	Rent — Average (dollars)	Income — No. of Reports	Income — Average (dollars)	Rent-Income Ratio	MAIL RETURNS 1933 Rent — No. of Reports	Rent — Average (dollars)	Income — No. of Reports	Income — Average (dollars)	Rent-Income Ratio
All groups	1,452	339	1,710	1,756	0.193	914	376	1,348	1,947	0.193	1,859	269	1,874	1,181	0.228	1,930	283	1,950	1,288	0.220
No Income	7	376	7	0		12	183	21	0		34	204	36	0		55	185	55	0	
$1- 149	1	140	2	100	1.400	12	245	20	100	1.830	33	157	34	100	1.570	80	172	81	100	1.720
150- 250	8	191	17	200	0.955	23	342	28	200	1.225	88	157	89	200	0.785	82	242	82	200	1.210
251- 349	11	395	17	300	1.317	22	279	35	300	1.140	92	173	92	300	0.577	74	201	74	300	0.670
350- 450	35	200	43	400	0.500	19	195	31	400	0.698	100	179	100	400	0.448	92	181	93	400	0.453
451- 549	43	206	55	500	0.412	17	224	34	500	0.390	100	205	101	500	0.410	78	203	78	500	0.408
550- 650	43	223	49	600	0.372	19	294	25	600	0.373	125	194	125	600	0.323	101	208	103	600	0.347
651- 749	43	240	51	700	0.343	17	287	43	700	0.420	94	222	95	700	0.317	72	224	73	700	0.320
750- 850	57	234	72	800	0.293	25	260	34	800	0.359	114	234	116	800	0.293	109	214	110	800	0.288
851- 949	54	227	58	900	0.252	26	280	68	900	0.289	82	271	82	900	0.301	81	244	82	900	0.271
950- 1,050	100	240	117	1,000	0.240	41	250	28	1,000	0.280	143	254	143	1,000	0.254	120	242	122	1,000	0.242
1,051- 1,149	31	282	36	1,100	0.238	15	287	84	1,100	0.227	53	247	53	1,100	0.225	53	255	54	1,100	0.232
1,150- 1,250	145	290	171	1,200	0.242	55	281	46	1,200	0.239	173	281	178	1,200	0.234	126	269	128	1,200	0.224
1,251- 1,349	23	256	27	1,300	0.197	33	282	36	1,300	0.216	39	271	39	1,300	0.208	47	282	48	1,300	0.217
1,350- 1,450	50	290	59	1,400	0.207	25	318	83	1,400	0.201	41	300	41	1,400	0.214	57	303	57	1,400	0.216
1,451- 1,549	102	325	115	1,500	0.217	58	314	50	1,500	0.212	85	321	85	1,500	0.214	91	296	93	1,500	0.197
1,550- 1,650	58	313	64	1,600	0.196	38	334	30	1,600	0.196	42	300	42	1,600	0.188	71	316	71	1,600	0.198
1,651- 1,749	26	315	31	1,700	0.185	21	379	140	1,700	0.196	30	323	30	1,700	0.190	40	337	41	1,700	0.198
1,750- 1,949	134	358	166	1,811	0.198	105	372	107	1,823	0.208	108	342	108	1,821	0.188	122	356	122	1,848	0.182
1,950- 2,149	98	374	110	2,029	0.184	69	414	32	2,059	0.181	84	391	85	2,032	0.192	93	380	94	2,028	0.187
2,150- 2,349	34	358	37	2,227	0.161	19	456	84	2,259	0.183	22	375	22	2,227	0.168	48	376	48	2,246	0.167
2,350- 2,549	122	416	146	2,432	0.171	55	507	31	2,430	0.188	51	401	51	2,425	0.165	72	417	73	2,441	0.171
2,550- 2,749	21	440	26	2,654	0.166	21	455	87	2,652	0.191	18	426	18	2,644	0.161	33	408	34	2,650	0.154
2,750- 3,149	74	469	83	2,969	0.158	58	525	38	2,955	0.154	45	395	45	2,951	0.134	45	456	45	2,953	0.154
3,150- 3,549	29	498	30	3,370	0.148	30	524	40	3,389	0.155	19	454	19	3,363	0.135	27	490	27	3,322	0.148
3,550- 3,949	32	588	37	3,889	0.159	27	522	22	3,660	0.143	14	439	14	3,700	0.119	11	465	11	3,700	0.126
3,950- 4,450	17	579	19	4,084	0.142	17	687	15	4,164	0.125	12	486	13	4,138	0.117	21	542	21	4,110	0.132
4,451- 4,949	19	545	26	4,688	0.116	12	687	19	4,613	0.149	5	414	5	4,720	0.088	9	529	10	4,640	0.114
4,950- 5,450	15	737	16	5,044	0.146	12	675	5	5,095	0.135	7	794	7	5,100	0.156	5	672	5	5,100	0.132
5,451- 5,949	5	514	6	5,650	0.091	4	770	16	5,660	0.119	...	...	...	...	...	2	665	7	5,600	0.119
5,950- 6,949	8	600	9	6,111	0.098	12	493	5	6,063	0.127	4	540	4	6,200	0.087	7	661	6	6,086	0.109
6,950- 7,949	3	530	4	7,125	0.074	4	810	2	7,200	0.068	1	390	1	7,000	0.056	3	510	3	7,233	0.071
7,950- 8,949	...	...	...	...	...	2	1,500	2	8,000	0.101	...	...	...	...	...	3	600	3	8,167	0.073
8,950- 9,949	...	...	...	...	...	3	940	4	9,400	0.160	...	...	...	...	...	...	...	...	...	...
9,950-11,949	1	110	1	10,000	0.011	...	...	...	10,000	0.094	1	900	1	14,000	0.064	...	...	...	...	...
11,950-13,949	...	...	...	...	...	...	...	...	...	...	...	...	...	...	...	...	...	...	...	...
13,950-15,949	1	1,080	1	14,000	0.077	1	1,000	2	16,000	0.063	...	...	...	...	...	...	...	...	...	...
15,950-19,949	2	1,140	2	16,000	0.071	1	900	1	20,000	0.045	...	...	...	...	...	...	...	...	...	...
19,950 and over	...	...	...	...	...	...	...	...	...	...	...	...	...	...	...	...	...	...	...	...

TABLE C 3 (Cont'd)

27 BUTTE, MONTANA

Annual Income group	1929 PERSONAL ENUMERATION					1929 MAIL RETURNS					1933 PERSONAL ENUMERATION					1933 MAIL RETURNS				
	RENT No. of Reports	RENT Average (dollars)	INCOME No. of Reports	INCOME Average (dollars)	Rent-Income Ratio	RENT No. of Reports	RENT Average (dollars)	INCOME No. of Reports	INCOME Average (dollars)	Rent-Income Ratio	RENT No. of Reports	RENT Average (dollars)	INCOME No. of Reports	INCOME Average (dollars)	Rent-Income Ratio	RENT No. of Reports	RENT Average (dollars)	INCOME No. of Reports	INCOME Average (dollars)	Rent-Income Ratio
All groups	483	338	541	1,969	0.172	1,144	312	1,280	1,842	0.169	553	253	587	1,024	0.247	1,382	246	1,412	977	0.252
No Income	9	199	9	0	.....	62	245	62	0	0	56	184	62	0	0	140	206	140	0	0
$1- 149	2	250	3	100	2.500	8	228	7	100	2.280	44	188	47	100	1.880	112	171	117	100	1.710
150- 250	3	187	4	200	0.835	10	184	11	200	0.920	31	174	33	200	0.870	83	166	88	200	0.830
251- 349	2	150	2	300	0.500	9	212	13	300	0.707	21	220	22	300	0.733	74	180	74	300	0.600
350- 450	10	296	11	400	0.740	13	224	14	400	0.560	36	212	40	400	0.530	70	177	75	400	0.443
451- 549	10	277	11	500	0.554	25	225	28	500	0.450	29	204	31	500	0.408	70	174	70	500	0.348
550- 650	9	213	9	600	0.355	27	220	36	600	0.387	49	184	53	600	0.307	118	186	125	600	0.310
651- 749	7	284	11	700	0.377	12	288	14	700	0.383	20	195	21	700	0.279	69	209	70	700	0.299
750- 850	8	234	9	800	0.293	29	332	30	800	0.415	25	242	25	800	0.303	82	213	63	800	0.266
851- 949	11	257	12	900	0.286	30	255	32	900	0.283	19	214	25	900	0.238	46	247	46	900	0.274
950- 1,050	18	263	22	1,000	0.283	62	288	64	1,000	0.288	24	237	26	1,000	0.237	80	275	80	1,000	0.275
1,051- 1,149	7	287	9	1,100	0.261	15	224	18	1,100	0.204	6	252	6	1,100	0.229	24	280	24	1,100	0.255
1,150- 1,250	29	338	34	1,200	0.280	69	267	75	1,200	0.223	18	232	20	1,200	0.193	55	254	56	1,200	0.212
1,251- 1,349	9	409	9	1,300	0.315	17	249	18	1,300	0.192	5	320	5	1,300	0.246	23	250	24	1,300	0.192
1,350- 1,450	13	270	17	1,400	0.193	38	239	42	1,400	0.171	18	269	18	1,400	0.192	34	271	34	1,400	0.194
1,451- 1,549	57	243	62	1,500	0.162	93	282	103	1,500	0.175	23	279	23	1,500	0.186	41	314	41	1,500	0.209
1,550- 1,650	29	296	30	1,600	0.185	88	253	76	1,600	0.158	12	369	12	1,600	0.231	28	300	28	1,600	0.188
1,651- 1,749	20	305	20	1,700	0.179	27	287	30	1,700	0.169	11	292	11	1,700	0.172	19	291	19	1,700	0.171
1,750- 1,949	71	328	80	1,820	0.180	154	295	178	1,819	0.182	24	328	24	1,833	0.179	48	333	50	1,822	0.183
1,950- 2,149	31	345	33	2,039	0.189	90	319	95	2,032	0.157	15	372	15	2,033	0.183	50	334	51	2,075	0.181
2,150- 2,349	18	346	21	2,229	0.155	44	355	47	2,228	0.159	15	357	16	2,244	0.159	20	361	20	2,240	0.161
2,350- 2,549	25	340	31	2,419	0.141	67	373	71	2,434	0.153	14	456	17	2,424	0.188	24	401	24	2,433	0.165
2,550- 2,749	10	394	10	2,640	0.149	27	397	32	2,650	0.150	6	415	6	2,650	0.157	12	331	12	2,650	0.125
2,750- 3,149	30	482	30	2,973	0.162	38	417	42	2,987	0.141	11	479	12	2,992	0.160	32	413	32	2,958	0.140
3,150- 3,549	5	624	13	3,300	0.189	24	518	28	3,357	0.154	3	453	3	3,333	0.136	20	486	20	3,320	0.146
3,550- 3,949	12	524	5	3,854	0.143	29	480	31	3,671	0.131	6	455	6	3,717	0.122	8	717	8	3,683	0.198
3,950- 4,450	4	393	8	4,180	0.094	20	524	21	4,148	0.126	5	535	5	4,120	0.130	5	660	5	4,180	0.159
4,451- 4,949	5	396	5	4,617	0.086	12	494	12	4,825	0.107	2	645	2	4,750	0.136	5	438	5	4,700	0.093
4,950- 5,450	5	804	5	5,120	0.157	8	514	10	5,050	0.122	2	600	2	5,100	0.118	3	550	3	5,187	0.108
5,451- 5,949																2	570	2	5,800	0.098
5,950- 6,949	4	535	5	6,000	0.089	6	645	7	6,243	0.103	3	613	3	6,267	0.098	3	757	3	6,000	0.128
6,950- 7,949	4	705	5	7,500	0.094	6	655	6	7,250	0.090										
7,950- 8,949	1	780	1	8,000	0.098											1	600	1	8,000	0.075
8,950- 9,949	2	790	2	9,600	0.082	2	735	4	9,000	0.082										
9,950-11,949						2	435	2	10,000	0.044										
11,950-13,949	1	720	1	13,200	0.055								1	12,000						
13,950-15,949						1	480	2	14,000	0.034										
15,950-19,949								1	16,300							2	690	2	18,000	0.038
19,950 and over	2	780	2	20,700	0.038	2	780	2	20,500	0.038										

TABLE C 3 (Cont'd)

28 BOISE, IDAHO

Column groups: **1929 — PERSONAL ENUMERATION** and **1929 — MAIL RETURNS**; **1933 — PERSONAL ENUMERATION** and **1933 — MAIL RETURNS**. For each group: RENT (No. of Reports, Average dollars), INCOME (No. of Reports, Average dollars), Rent-Income Ratio.

Annual Income group[1]	1929 PE Rent No.	1929 PE Rent Avg	1929 PE Inc. No.	1929 PE Inc. Avg	1929 PE Ratio	1929 Mail Rent No.	1929 Mail Rent Avg	1929 Mail Inc. No.	1929 Mail Inc. Avg	1929 Mail Ratio	1933 PE Rent No.	1933 PE Rent Avg	1933 PE Inc. No.	1933 PE Inc. Avg	1933 PE Ratio	1933 Mail Rent No.	1933 Mail Rent Avg	1933 Mail Inc. No.	1933 Mail Inc. Avg	1933 Mail Ratio
All groups	353	337	470	1,542	0.219	358	322	500	1,615	0.199	543	290	550	1,138	0.255	550	283	563	1,240	0.228
No income	14	317	25	0		13	258	27	0		19	285	20	0		13	229	13	0	
$1- 149	3	130	3	100	1.300			1	100		13	148	13	100	1.480	14	145	15	100	1.450
150- 250	4	208	10	200	1.040	2	120	4	200	0.600	42	159	43	200	0.795	23	169	24	200	0.845
251- 349	5	284	10	300	0.947	2	130	5	300	0.433	18	209	19	300	0.697	22	155	22	300	0.517
350- 450	7	200	9	400	0.500	3	97	7	400	0.243	32	178	32	400	0.445	27	200	28	400	0.500
451- 549	9	219	13	500	0.438	7	174	13	500	0.348	30	250	30	500	0.500	27	187	31	500	0.374
550- 650	10	196	15	600	0.327	4	165	7	600	0.275	37	222	37	600	0.370	29	230	31	600	0.383
651- 749	10	274	10	700	0.391	7	240	10	700	0.343	24	205	24	700	0.293	21	227	21	700	0.324
750- 850	17	295	23	800	0.369	19	216	28	800	0.270	18	289	19	800	0.361	32	234	34	800	0.293
851- 949	10	312	10	900	0.347	12	218	20	900	0.242	18	254	19	900	0.282	23	231	23	900	0.257
950- 1,050	30	287	38	1,000	0.287	24	200	35	1,000	0.200	41	270	41	1,000	0.270	28	257	27	1,000	0.257
1,051- 1,149	9	312	10	1,100	0.284	9	257	12	1,100	0.234	15	342	15	1,100	0.311	20	277	20	1,100	0.252
1,150- 1,250	35	284	43	1,200	0.237	35	289	45	1,200	0.241	39	306	39	1,200	0.255	47	274	47	1,200	0.228
1,251- 1,349	9	276	10	1,300	0.212	9	278	13	1,300	0.212	18	297	18	1,300	0.228	10	320	11	1,300	0.246
1,350- 1,450	14	353	17	1,400	0.252	9	277	15	1,400	0.198	19	336	19	1,400	0.240	19	295	19	1,400	0.211
1,451- 1,549	25	305	33	1,500	0.203	23	337	25	1,500	0.225	19	318	19	1,500	0.212	27	314	27	1,500	0.209
1,550- 1,650	8	316	13	1,600	0.198	11	328	14	1,600	0.205	11	378	11	1,600	0.236	19	312	19	1,600	0.195
1,651- 1,749	3	280	3	1,700	0.153	4	318	4	1,700	0.187	6	363	6	1,700	0.214	12	287	12	1,700	0.169
1,750- 1,949	35	388	47	1,815	0.203	37	357	54	1,826	0.198	42	374	43	1,809	0.207	32	354	32	1,813	0.195
1,950- 2,149	30	399	37	2,032	0.198	28	334	31	2,029	0.165	21	373	22	2,023	0.184	35	405	35	2,009	0.202
2,150- 2,349	5	506	8	2,213	0.229	14	340	17	2,200	0.155	17	393	17	2,241	0.175	15	465	15	2,240	0.208
2,350- 2,549	18	418	25	2,424	0.172	38	424	46	2,428	0.175	11	414	11	2,436	0.170	15	437	15	2,433	0.180
2,550- 2,749	11	448	13	2,846	0.169	9	429	11	2,645	0.162	3	423	3	2,687	0.159	9	360	9	2,656	0.136
2,750- 3,149	13	475	19	2,974	0.160	21	433	32	2,959	0.146	15	513	15	2,940	0.174	14	409	14	2,979	0.137
3,150- 3,549	7	527	7	3,386	0.156	4	403	4	3,425	0.118	6	457	6	3,333	0.137	7	397	7	3,300	0.120
3,550- 3,949	4	500	8	3,638	0.137	7	447	10	3,700	0.121	1	600	1	3,600	0.167	7	416	7	3,714	0.112
3,950- 4,450	2	750	3	4,033	0.186	7	570	8	4,083	0.140	4	548	4	4,000	0.137	1	720	1	4,000	0.180
4,451- 4,949	2	750	3	4,700	0.160	1	670	1	4,800	0.140										
4,950- 5,450	2	510	2	5,000	0.102	1	880	2	5,000	0.178	3	520	3	5,200	0.100	1	900	1	5,000	0.180
5,451- 5,949			1	5,500												1	540	1	5,700	0.095
5,950- 6,949	2	450	2	6,250	0.072			1	6,800		1	660	1	6,000	0.110	2	630	2	6,000	0.105
6,950- 7,949																				
7,950- 8,949			1	8,400																
8,950- 9,949																				
9,950-11,949			1	10,000																
11,950-13,949																				
13,950-15,949																				
15,950-19,949																				
19,950 and over																				

TABLE C 3 (Cont'd)

29 SALT LAKE CITY, UTAH

Each year block shows **← PERSONAL ENUMERATION →** and **← MAIL RETURNS →**. Under each: RENT (No. of Reports, Average (dollars)); INCOME (No. of Reports, Average (dollars)); Rent-Income Ratio.

Annual Income group[1]	1929 PE Rent No.	1929 PE Rent Avg	1929 PE Inc No.	1929 PE Inc Avg	1929 PE Ratio	1929 Mail Rent No.	1929 Mail Rent Avg	1929 Mail Inc No.	1929 Mail Inc Avg	1929 Mail Ratio	1933 PE Rent No.	1933 PE Rent Avg	1933 PE Inc No.	1933 PE Inc Avg	1933 PE Ratio	1933 Mail Rent No.	1933 Mail Rent Avg	1933 Mail Inc No.	1933 Mail Inc Avg	1933 Mail Ratio
All groups	1,368	313	1,672	1,592	.197	991	334	1,303	1,834	.182	1,884	256	1,886	1,012	.253	1,741	263	1,758	1,172	.224
No Income	38	238	38	0		19	253	44	0		56	204	56	0		54	159	54	0	
$1- 149	26	174	32	100	1.740	11	180	16	100	1.800	152	162	152	100	1.620	133	143	140	100	1.430
150- 250	30	209	46	200	1.045	22	179	31	200	.895	147	163	147	200	.815	118	186	119	200	.930
251- 349	20	221	27	300	.737	10	206	15	300	.687	90	191	92	300	.637	60	161	61	300	.537
350- 450	26	250	32	400	.625	19	208	16	400	.520	121	186	121	400	.465	80	192	80	400	.480
451- 549	57	207	68	500	.414	28	209	30	500	.418	109	200	109	500	.400	84	173	84	500	.346
550- 650	67	241	79	600	.402	17	209	35	600	.348	105	211	105	600	.352	90	204	90	600	.340
651- 749	40	222	48	700	.317	22	192	21	700	.274	94	210	94	700	.300	70	213	71	700	.304
750- 850	54	262	66	800	.328	18	201	28	800	.251	113	225	113	800	.281	94	208	97	800	.260
851- 949	55	208	67	900	.231		219	25	900	.243	79	238	79	900	.264	52	229	52	900	.254
950- 1,050	71	251	89	1,000	.251	60	232	74	1,000	.232	119	242	119	1,000	.242	105	240	105	1,000	.240
1,051- 1,149	32	267	37	1,100	.243	15	199	19	1,100	.181	57	253	57	1,100	.230	73	230	74	1,100	.209
1,150- 1,250	139	283	165	1,200	.236	74	248	103	1,200	.207	113	273	113	1,200	.228	101	266	102	1,200	.222
1,251- 1,349	38	284	43	1,300	.218	44	263	52	1,300	.202	47	312	47	1,300	.240	57	263	58	1,300	.202
1,350- 1,450	37	247	54	1,400	.176	47	275	54	1,400	.196	56	285	56	1,400	.204	49	297	49	1,400	.212
1,451- 1,549	79	276	97	1,500	.184	52	288	75	1,500	.192	50	331	50	1,500	.221	58	309	58	1,500	.206
1,550- 1,650	50	323	57	1,600	.202	48	316	59	1,600	.198	38	299	38	1,600	.187	53	316	53	1,600	.198
1,651- 1,749	29	313	37	1,700	.184	32	304	36	1,700	.179	35	310	35	1,700	.182	49	306	49	1,700	.180
1,750- 1,949	127	330	149	1,815	.182	88	311	116	1,824	.171	81	356	81	1,822	.195	89	344	89	1,829	.188
1,950- 2,149	82	352	105	2,031	.173	71	378	94	2,028	.186	49	361	49	2,039	.177	56	372	56	2,039	.182
2,150- 2,349	37	356	43	2,240	.159	43	350	47	2,221	.158	28	365	28	2,235	.163	29	437	29	2,248	.194
2,350- 2,549	62	421	82	2,429	.173	57	426	71	2,439	.175	40	452	40	2,438	.185	35	438	35	2,434	.180
2,550- 2,749	24	435	31	2,635	.165	28	447	33	2,642	.169	19	452	19	2,653	.170	26	412	26	2,662	.155
2,750- 3,149	51	438	62	2,971	.147	58	506	75	2,955	.171	37	560	37	2,943	.190	46	493	46	2,946	.167
3,150- 3,549	24	476	25	3,328	.143	26	475	30	3,393	.140	14	538	14	3,321	.162	31	471	31	3,388	.140
3,550- 3,949	21	550	26	3,669	.150	21	529	29	3,662	.144	10	524	10	3,730	.140	12	564	12	3,700	.152
3,950- 4,450	18	549	21	4,076	.135	10	579	19	4,105	.141	11	517	11	4,109	.126	9	506	9	4,078	.124
4,451- 4,949	13	708	14	4,636	.153	7	579	8	4,538	.128	4	485	4	4,700	.103	8	558	8	4,675	.119
4,950- 5,450	8	585	12	5,067	.115	14	646	22	5,069	.128	3	630	3	5,133	.123	7	736	8	5,058	.146
5,451- 5,949	2	420	2	5,650	.074	3	610	3	5,633	.108	1	600	1	5,500	.109	2	750	2	5,500	.136
5,950- 6,949	7	677	9	6,056	.112	6	738	8	6,113	.121	3	730	3	6,100	.120	4	610	4	6,175	.099
6,950- 7,949	3	473	3	7,333	.065	2	570	2	7,250	.079	2	645	2	7,000	.092	1	480	1	7,000	.069
7,950- 8,949	2	675	3	8,133	.083	1	720	2	8,300	.087	1	1,020	1	8,400	.121	3	680	3	8,233	.083
8,950- 9,949						2	1,365	3	9,300	.147	1	670	1	9,100	.074					
9,950-11,949			2	10,000		3	1,410	4	10,000	.141	1	450	1	10,000	.045	3	923	3	10,333	.089
11,950-13,949						2	585	2	12,000	.049										
13,950-15,949																				
15,950-19,949																				
19,950 and over	1	5,600	1	75,000	.075	1	720	2	17,500	.041										

TABLE C 3 (Cont'd)

30 SEATTLE, WASHINGTON

Annual Income group[1]	1929 PERSONAL ENUMERATION					1929 MAIL RETURNS					1933 PERSONAL ENUMERATION					1933 MAIL RETURNS				
	RENT No. of Reports	RENT Average (dollars)	INCOME No. of Reports	INCOME Average (dollars)	Rent-Income Ratio	RENT No. of Reports	RENT Average (dollars)	INCOME No. of Reports	INCOME Average (dollars)	Rent-Income Ratio	RENT No. of Reports	RENT Average (dollars)	INCOME No. of Reports	INCOME Average (dollars)	Rent-Income Ratio	RENT No. of Reports	RENT Average (dollars)	INCOME No. of Reports	INCOME Average (dollars)	Rent-Income Ratio
All groups	2,615	359	2,892	1,782	.201	1,647	362	2,159	1,827	.198	3,206	253	3,221	1,102	.230	2,717	258	2,757	1,120	.230
No Income	14	309	44	0		38	377	60	0		7	266	7	0		96	213	96	0	
$1- 149	14	139	16	100	1.390	22	270	27	100	2.700	99	153	100	100	1.530	159	163	162	100	1.630
150- 250	55	185	67	200	.925	39	163	53	200	.815	237	150	237	200	.750	191	165	195	200	.825
251- 349	52	201	63	300	.671	29	203	37	300	.677	202	179	202	300	.597	120	173	124	300	.577
350- 450	70	200	77	400	.500	35	225	55	400	.563	222	192	228	400	.455	159	178	166	400	.445
451- 549	82	227	89	500	.454	38	216	54	500	.432	216	207	216	500	.414	141	203	142	500	.406
550- 650	101	266	115	600	.443	45	263	57	600	.438	205	216	206	600	.360	138	214	141	600	.357
651- 749	69	242	77	700	.346	35	268	49	700	.383	144	221	144	700	.316	122	202	125	700	.289
750- 850	87	245	103	800	.306	44	275	61	800	.344	194	228	195	800	.285	158	234	159	800	.293
851- 949	92	288	96	900	.298	43	260	53	900	.289	148	244	148	900	.271	111	229	113	900	.254
950- 1,050	162	285	175	1,000	.285	90	295	120	1,000	.295	189	254	189	1,000	.254	163	258	165	1,000	.258
1,051- 1,149	27	315	30	1,100	.286	30	305	40	1,100	.277	87	236	88	1,100	.215	67	244	69	1,100	.222
1,150- 1,250	240	322	262	1,200	.268	139	295	179	1,200	.246	214	260	215	1,200	.217	159	274	161	1,200	.228
1,251- 1,349	55	281	59	1,300	.216	43	289	54	1,300	.222	73	255	73	1,300	.181	70	285	71	1,300	.204
1,350- 1,450	66	313	70	1,400	.224	57	367	67	1,400	.262	109	289	109	1,400	.206	85	291	85	1,400	.208
1,451- 1,549	158	341	175	1,500	.227	87	308	115	1,500	.205	139	325	140	1,500	.217	110	316	112	1,500	.211
1,550- 1,650	74	327	75	1,600	.204	60	322	78	1,600	.201	82	292	83	1,600	.183	90	298	90	1,600	.186
1,651- 1,749	52	344	57	1,700	.202	52	338	64	1,700	.199	51	291	51	1,700	.171	54	318	54	1,700	.187
1,750- 1,949	244	371	265	1,858	.200	148	355	190	1,876	.189	191	317	191	1,825	.174	149	319	149	1,828	.175
1,950- 2,149	184	384	200	2,089	.184	141	396	173	2,087	.190	100	350	100	2,032	.172	94	344	95	2,033	.169
2,150- 2,349	100	391	104	2,229	.175	57	402	74	2,234	.180	47	336	48	2,238	.150	46	391	47	2,240	.175
2,350- 2,549	193	426	204	2,482	.172	99	478	133	2,442	.196	72	390	72	2,436	.160	60	420	60	2,440	.172
2,550- 2,749	65	474	70	2,647	.179	38	468	51	2,635	.178	27	418	27	2,644	.158	33	376	33	2,642	.142
2,750- 3,149	119	490	134	3,022	.162	77	498	101	2,964	.168	60	403	61	2,956	.136	50	407	51	2,933	.139
3,150- 3,549	46	502	50	3,364	.149	30	524	40	3,375	.155	23	456	23	3,352	.136	27	500	27	3,341	.150
3,550- 3,949	55	528	61	3,805	.139	45	556	58	3,850	.144	19	449	19	3,621	.124	14	565	14	3,679	.154
3,950- 4,450	35	624	36	4,142	.151	38	617	43	4,086	.151	13	533	13	4,108	.130	15	555	15	4,100	.135
4,451- 4,949	25	642	31	4,694	.137	11	609	20	4,670	.130	9	599	9	4,700	.127	8	564	8	4,613	.122
4,950- 5,450	24	711	28	5,082	.140	10	630	14	5,086	.124	12	516	12	5,083	.102	5	564	5	5,000	.113
5,451- 5,949	5	932	6	5,617	.166	2	720	2	5,550	.130	2	465	2	5,750	.081	5	516	5	5,660	.091
5,950- 6,949	24	801	27	6,115	.131	7	649	14	6,243	.104	8	661	8	6,138	.108	7	666	7	6,100	.109
6,950- 7,949	6	720	6	7,417	.097	6	555	7	7,300	.076	3	820	3	7,233	.113	2	360	2	7,200	.050
7,950- 8,949	8	950	9	8,200	.116	4	655	4	8,350	.078	1	610	1	8,000	.076	5	518	5	8,360	.062
8,950- 9,949			1	9,800		4	870	4	9,200	.095						2	855	2	9,050	.094
9,950-11,949	5	672	5	10,100	.067	2	810	3	10,467	.077										
11,950-13,949	2	1,500	2	12,000	.125						1	1,200	1	12,000	0.100	1	120	1	14,000	.009
13,950-15,949	2	570	2	14,500	.039	2	555	4	16,700	.033										
15,950-19,949	1	1,200	1	17,500	.069											1	160	1	30,000	.005
19,950 and over	2	900	2	27,500	.033	1	555	1	100,000	0										

TABLE C 3 (Cont'd)

31 PORTLAND, OREGON

Each year (1929, 1933) is split into PERSONAL ENUMERATION and MAIL RETURNS. Within each: RENT (No. of Reports, Average dollars), INCOME (No. of Reports, Average dollars), and Rent-Income Ratio.

Annual Income group	1929 PE Rent No. Reports	1929 PE Rent Avg ($)	1929 PE Income No. Reports	1929 PE Income Avg ($)	1929 PE Rent-Income Ratio	1929 MR Rent No. Reports	1929 MR Rent Avg ($)	1929 MR Income No. Reports	1929 MR Income Avg ($)	1929 MR Rent-Income Ratio	1933 PE Rent No. Reports	1933 PE Rent Avg ($)	1933 PE Income No. Reports	1933 PE Income Avg ($)	1933 PE Rent-Income Ratio	1933 MR Rent No. Reports	1933 MR Rent Avg ($)	1933 MR Income No. Reports	1933 MR Income Avg ($)	1933 MR Rent-Income Ratio
All groups	1,724	276	2,393	1,417	0.195	672	304	954	1,652	0.184	2,677	200	2,720	853	0.234	1,283	212	1,293	1,028	0.206
No Income	74	251	108	0		14	233	30	0		145	171	145	0		52	151	52	0	
$1- 149	22	170	35	100	1.700	7	163	10	100	1.630	219	132	223	100	1.320	63	129	64	100	1.290
150- 250	32	179	42	200	0.895	10	148	20	200	0.740	284	139	269	200	0.695	99	143	99	200	0.715
251- 349	39	176	60	300	0.587	11	207	16	300	0.690	154	149	160	300	0.497	68	144	68	300	0.480
350- 450	55	183	81	400	0.483	17	236	25	400	0.590	185	149	188	400	0.373	91	162	92	400	0.405
451- 549	59	199	81	500	0.398	10	279	21	500	0.558	164	169	165	500	0.338	73	161	73	500	0.322
550- 650	70	183	96	600	0.305	31	197	36	600	0.328	181	176	183	600	0.293	70	172	72	600	0.287
651- 749	39	208	66	700	0.297	12	217	20	700	0.310	114	177	115	700	0.253	61	183	62	700	0.261
750- 850	84	201	113	800	0.251	28	219	41	800	0.274	173	181	177	800	0.226	77	185	77	800	0.231
851- 949	88	231	128	900	0.257	21	161	29	900	0.179	107	194	109	900	0.216	55	187	55	900	0.208
950- 1,050	119	231	167	1,000	0.231	41	241	66	1,000	0.241	166	223	168	1,000	0.223	57	215	58	1,000	0.215
1,051- 1,149	34	246	46	1,100	0.224	15	259	16	1,100	0.235	69	222	69	1,100	0.202	43	224	43	1,100	0.204
1,150- 1,250	189	253	251	1,200	0.211	47	267	68	1,200	0.223	157	232	162	1,200	0.193	69	244	70	1,200	0.203
1,251- 1,349	33	262	44	1,300	0.202	12	213	16	1,300	0.164	51	240	51	1,300	0.185	31	225	31	1,300	0.173
1,350- 1,450	60	267	81	1,400	0.191	28	261	32	1,400	0.186	67	265	67	1,400	0.189	37	229	37	1,400	0.164
1,451- 1,549	125	256	169	1,500	0.171	41	286	55	1,500	0.191	93	263	96	1,500	0.175	51	261	53	1,500	0.174
1,550- 1,650	52	319	63	1,600	0.199	18	308	23	1,600	0.193	45	257	46	1,600	0.161	36	243	36	1,600	0.152
1,651- 1,749	28	331	46	1,700	0.195	19	289	27	1,700	0.170	28	282	27	1,700	0.166	25	263	25	1,700	0.155
1,750- 1,949	137	297	187	1,856	0.180	72	298	103	1,823	0.163	105	286	105	1,818	0.157	73	284	73	1,826	0.156
1,950- 2,149	101	317	136	2,032	0.156	49	364	66	2,030	0.179	55	285	55	2,025	0.141	40	307	40	2,050	0.151
2,150- 2,349	36	308	48	2,221	0.139	27	355	38	2,237	0.159	25	326	25	2,228	0.146	17	291	18	2,239	0.130
2,350- 2,549	98	364	133	2,429	0.150	41	412	54	2,441	0.169	33	356	33	2,455	0.145	36	349	36	2,442	0.143
2,550- 2,749	21	376	32	2,647	0.142	18	434	26	2,646	0.164	13	396	13	2,654	0.149	11	382	11	2,645	0.144
2,750- 3,149	59	428	75	2,951	0.145	32	416	41	2,956	0.141	30	399	31	3,094	0.129	19	374	19	2,932	0.128
3,150- 3,549	11	443	18	3,372	0.131	12	489	17	3,312	0.148	9	421	10	3,330	0.126	11	402	11	3,336	0.121
3,550- 3,949	16	546	25	3,688	0.149	15	520	19	3,653	0.142	6	398	6	3,600	0.111	9	466	9	3,689	0.126
3,950- 4,450	14	478	22	4,105	0.116	12	451	15	4,053	0.111	8	345	9	4,111	0.084	3	440	3	4,067	0.108
4,451- 4,949	7	513	9	4,667	0.110	4	510	7	4,586	0.111	8	690	2	4,550	0.152	1	480	1	4,500	0.107
4,950- 5,450	10	504	12	5,017	0.100	4	430	4	5,000	0.086	6	615	6	5,353	0.115	2	330	2	5,050	0.065
5,451- 5,949	1	240	2	5,650	0.042	4	480	4	5,550	0.086										
5,950- 6,949	4	525	7	6,071	0.086			4	6,000		2	570	2	6,000	0.095					
6,950- 7,949	3	1,040	6	7,367	0.141			3	7,233							1	900	1	7,000	0.129
7,950- 8,949	1	1,500	1	8,600	0.174						2	780	2	8,000	0.098					
8,950- 9,949																2	655	2	9,500	0.069
9,950-11,949	1	3,010	1	10,000	0.301	2	660	2	10,000	0.066										
11,950-13,949																				
13,950-15,949	1	900	1	15,000	0.060						1	600	1	15,000	0.040					
15,950-19,949																				
19,950 and over	1	1,280	1	20,000	0.064															

TABLE C 3 (Cont'd)

32 SACRAMENTO, CALIFORNIA

Annual Income group [1]	1929 PERSONAL ENUMERATION RENT No. of Reports	RENT Average (dollars)	INCOME No. of Reports	INCOME Average (dollars)	Rent-Income Ratio	1929 MAIL RETURNS RENT No. of Reports	RENT Average (dollars)	INCOME No. of Reports	INCOME Average (dollars)	Rent-Income Ratio	1933 PERSONAL ENUMERATION RENT No. of Reports	RENT Average (dollars)	INCOME No. of Reports	INCOME Average (dollars)	Rent-Income Ratio	1933 MAIL RETURNS RENT No. of Reports	RENT Average (dollars)	INCOME No. of Reports	INCOME Average (dollars)	Rent-Income Ratio
All groups	928	375	1,381	1,816	0.206	314	396	428	2,031	0.195	1,580	317	1,599	1,299	0.244	559	325	563	1,485	0.219
No Income	21	251	21	0		2	300	3	0		54	234	54	0		5	188	5	0	
$1- 149	10	214	14	100	2.140	1	360	3	100	3.600	46	206	48	100	2.060	13	221	14	100	2.210
150- 250	19	213	27	200	1.065	7	246	9	200	1.230	69	191	69	200	0.955	24	214	24	200	1.070
251- 349	9	252	13	300	0.840	3	470	3	300	1.567	56	224	60	300	0.747	15	229	15	300	0.763
350- 450	24	211	28	400	0.528	3	167	3	400	0.418	59	218	61	400	0.545	14	199	14	400	0.498
451- 549	17	240	27	500	0.480	3	210	5	500	0.420	83	241	86	500	0.482	20	233	20	500	0.466
550- 650	22	280	37	600	0.467	7	256	8	600	0.427	79	251	80	600	0.418	22	209	22	600	0.348
651- 749	23	263	32	700	0.376	5	288	6	700	0.411	54	258	54	700	0.369	25	246	25	700	0.351
750- 850	20	287	29	800	0.359	8	299	13	800	0.374	72	251	72	800	0.314	28	255	28	800	0.319
851- 949	28	306	43	900	0.340	9	299	12	900	0.332	57	308	57	900	0.342	15	258	15	900	0.287
950- 1,050	49	277	67	1,000	0.277	7	344	11	1,000	0.344	90	300	90	1,000	0.300	42	301	42	1,000	0.301
1,051- 1,149	18	332	29	1,100	0.302	3	380	5	1,100	0.345	35	303	36	1,100	0.275	19	274	19	1,100	0.249
1,150- 1,250	95	327	145	1,200	0.273	19	307	26	1,200	0.256	162	302	163	1,200	0.252	32	300	32	1,200	0.250
1,251- 1,349	16	363	24	1,300	0.279	9	348	11	1,300	0.268	34	287	34	1,300	0.221	22	310	22	1,300	0.238
1,350- 1,450	31	322	38	1,400	0.230	14	331	18	1,400	0.236	35	337	35	1,400	0.241	20	282	20	1,400	0.201
1,451- 1,549	55	360	96	1,500	0.240	19	327	26	1,500	0.218	84	337	85	1,500	0.225	21	321	21	1,500	0.214
1,550- 1,650	26	387	37	1,600	0.242	9	358	14	1,600	0.224	35	337	35	1,600	0.211	15	339	15	1,600	0.212
1,651- 1,749	23	376	35	1,700	0.221	7	320	8	1,700	0.188	35	370	35	1,700	0.218	19	345	19	1,700	0.203
1,750- 1,949	72	382	122	1,818	0.210	40	387	50	1,822	0.212	115	373	117	1,824	0.204	46	357	47	1,821	0.196
1,950- 2,149	70	383	112	2,033	0.188	34	411	41	2,044	0.201	81	386	83	2,046	0.189	36	399	38	2,034	0.196
2,150- 2,349	36	410	44	2,254	0.184	9	391	16	2,225	0.176	36	406	36	2,228	0.182	16	371	16	2,244	0.165
2,350- 2,549	77	461	119	2,427	0.190	28	458	42	2,456	0.188	74	442	74	2,428	0.182	19	416	19	2,463	0.169
2,550- 2,749	22	436	32	2,665	0.164	8	570	9	2,667	0.214	25	412	25	2,644	0.156	12	438	12	2,633	0.166
2,750- 3,149	62	496	88	2,950	0.168	19	493	25	2,960	0.167	54	486	54	2,948	0.165	22	469	22	2,964	0.158
3,150- 3,549	23	536	33	3,342	0.160	16	481	24	3,400	0.141	21	489	21	3,343	0.146	8	523	8	3,313	0.158
3,550- 3,949	17	483	29	3,666	0.132	8	540	13	3,669	0.147	10	401	10	3,700	0.108	11	566	11	3,645	0.155
3,950- 4,450	9	536	14	4,150	0.129	5	630	8	4,175	0.151	10	561	10	4,070	0.138	7	626	7	4,129	0.152
4,451- 4,949	9	630	13	4,623	0.136	4	513	4	4,625	0.111	4	613	4	4,675	0.131	5	648	5	4,740	0.137
4,950- 5,450	7	681	9	5,078	0.134	2	.570	3	5,300	0.108	2	570	2	5,100	0.112	3	730	3	5,133	0.142
5,451- 5,949	2	560	2	5,650	0.099	1	600	1	5,700	0.105	2	505	2	5,550	0.091					
5,950- 6,949	9	652	10	6,080	0.107	2	660	3	6,187	0.107	3	660	3	6,367	0.104	2	675	2	6,000	0.113
6,950- 7,949	2	840	4	7,375	0.114	2	900	3	7,167	0.126	2	1,890	2	7,500	0.252					
7,950- 8,949	1	600	3	8,333	0.072	1	100	2	8,250	0.012	1	630	1	8,400	0.075	1	600	1	8,500	0.071
8,950- 9,949	2	1,020	2	9,300	0.110															
9,950-11,949	2	750	2	10,650	0.070															
11,950-13,949																				
13,950-15,949																				
15,950-19,949	1		1	18,000							1	960	1	18,000	0.053					
19,950 and over																				

33 SAN DIEGO, CALIFORNIA

Annual Income group[1]	1929 PERSONAL ENUMERATION RENT No. of Reports	RENT Average (dollars)	INCOME No. of Reports	INCOME Average (dollars)	Rent-Income Ratio	1929 MAIL RETURNS RENT No. of Reports	RENT Average (dollars)	INCOME No. of Reports	INCOME Average (dollars)	Rent-Income Ratio	1933 PERSONAL ENUMERATION RENT No. of Reports	RENT Average (dollars)	INCOME No. of Reports	INCOME Average (dollars)	Rent-Income Ratio	1933 MAIL RETURNS RENT No. of Reports	RENT Average (dollars)	INCOME No. of Reports	INCOME Average (dollars)	Rent-Income Ratio
All groups	1,335	356	1,895	1,693	0.210	1,133	365	1,756	1,786	0.207	2,278	270	2,298	1,172	0.230	2,472	278	2,502	1,214	0.229
No Income	35	309	35	0		33	256	46	0		43	215	47	0		74	216	75	0	
$1- 149	4	115	7	100	1.150	14	207	17	100	2.070	48	176	48	100	1.760	80	180	82	100	1.800
150- 250	19	201	33	200	1.005	16	256	25	200	1.280	115	163	117	200	0.815	85	192	87	200	0.960
251- 349	21	243	30	300	0.810	9	218	14	300	0.727	82	179	83	300	0.597	74	196	76	300	0.653
350- 450	40	230	58	400	0.575	18	218	27	400	0.545	130	200	130	400	0.500	110	212	110	400	0.530
451- 549	32	224	54	500	0.448	31	286	49	500	0.572	96	205	100	500	0.410	97	224	98	500	0.448
550- 650	41	276	66	600	0.460	30	270	51	600	0.450	148	212	149	600	0.353	132	223	136	600	0.372
651- 749	31	255	52	700	0.364	21	286	44	700	0.360	105	218	106	700	0.311	102	229	102	700	0.327
750- 850	51	260	78	800	0.325	34	302	53	800	0.378	149	234	151	800	0.293	148	249	150	800	0.311
851- 949	52	298	69	900	0.331	25	281	47	900	0.312	125	244	126	900	0.271	129	254	131	900	0.282
950- 1,050	96	288	147	1,000	0.288	60	318	112	1,000	0.318	184	247	185	1,000	0.247	208	252	211	1,000	0.252
1,051- 1,149	28	318	54	1,100	0.289	25	305	41	1,100	0.277	96	245	96	1,100	0.223	90	287	90	1,100	0.234
1,150- 1,250	130	318	190	1,200	0.265	90	305	160	1,200	0.254	172	285	174	1,200	0.238	168	275	169	1,200	0.229
1,251- 1,349	28	312	34	1,300	0.240	24	295	36	1,300	0.227	55	261	55	1,300	0.201	71	288	71	1,300	0.222
1,350- 1,450	49	300	62	1,400	0.214	34	325	54	1,400	0.232	67	319	67	1,400	0.228	92	292	95	1,400	0.209
1,451- 1,549	68	324	109	1,500	0.216	51	343	82	1,500	0.229	99	295	99	1,500	0.197	122	313	122	1,500	0.209
1,550- 1,650	47	337	60	1,600	0.211	52	355	66	1,600	0.222	75	310	75	1,600	0.194	108	299	109	1,600	0.187
1,651- 1,749	32	382	44	1,700	0.189	33	342	46	1,700	0.201	46	311	46	1,700	0.183	66	317	66	1,700	0.186
1,750- 1,849	138	390	179	1,828	0.213	137	368	195	1,821	0.202	144	355	144	1,824	0.195	189	324	189	1,830	0.177
1,850- 1,949	77	371	107	2,029	0.183	105	393	153	2,029	0.194	70	374	71	2,031	0.184	92	347	95	2,028	0.171
1,950- 2,149	32	370	41	2,234	0.166	44	409	61	2,239	0.183	38	345	38	2,245	0.154	42	371	43	2,253	0.165
2,150- 2,349	87	434	114	2,434	0.178	65	389	103	2,443	0.159	57	354	57	2,446	0.145	48	383	50	2,444	0.157
2,350- 2,549	26	433	35	2,643	0.164	35	435	47	2,636	0.165	30	400	30	2,663	0.150	24	412	24	2,650	0.155
2,550- 2,749	57	450	79	2,962	0.152	53	455	72	2,957	0.154	32	445	32	2,934	0.152	45	455	45	2,920	0.156
2,750- 3,149	28	607	40	3,363	0.180	16	533	33	3,345	0.159	18	574	18	3,356	0.171	23	458	23	3,370	0.136
3,150- 3,549	28	468	38	3,642	0.129	25	517	38	3,655	0.141	20	495	20	3,660	0.135	19	554	19	3,728	0.149
3,550- 3,949	22	595	27	4,104	0.145	21	609	25	4,144	0.147	12	555	12	4,108	0.135	8	534	8	4,338	0.123
3,950- 4,450	7	574	13	4,685	0.123	10	590	15	4,640	0.127	5	562	5	4,740	0.119	6	517	6	4,750	0.109
4,451- 4,949	8	740	10	5,140	0.144	4	783	10	5,070	0.154	7	871	7	5,071	0.172	5	668	5	5,000	0.134
4,950- 5,450	6	762	6	5,600	0.136	4	745	5	5,640	0.132	1	630	1	5,500	0.115	3	577	3	5,867	0.098
5,451- 5,949	3	660	7	6,000	0.110	3	713	6	6,317	0.113	4	550	4	6,275	0.088	6	835	6	6,267	0.133
5,950- 6,949	3	617	4	7,175	0.086	4	735	10	7,380	0.100	1	540	1	7,000	0.077	2	530	2	7,500	0.071
6,950- 7,949	1	480	2	8,250	0.058			2	8,000		1	380	1	8,100	0.047	3	447	3	8,833	0.051
7,950- 8,949																				
8,950- 9,949	4	1,080	1	9,000	0.120	4	715	5	9,100	0.079	1	280	1	9,000	0.031					
9,950-11,949	5	624	6	10,000	0.062	2	1,710	5	10,000	0.171	1	960	1	10,000	0.096					
11,950-13,949	1	1,200	1	12,000	0.100											1	420	1	12,000	0.035
13,950-15,949																				
15,950-19,949	1	1,200	1	18,000	0.067	1	900	1	15,000	0.060	1	1,200	1	10,000	0.067					
19,950 and over	2	2,225	2	42,500	0.052															

Source: Special tabulation of Financial Survey of Urban Housing data
[1] See Table C 1, footnote 1.

TABLE C 4

Owner-occupant and Tenant Families, Average Annual Family Income (dollars), 1929, 1932, and 1933, reported by Families in 1934, 52 Cities by Geographic Division

| | ←O W N E R — O C C U P A N T→ | | | ←————T E N A N T————→ | | |
	1929	1932	1933	1929	1932	1933
52 cities[1]	2,304	1,654	1,465	1,589	1,183	1,082
4 New England cities	2,505	1,869	1,710	1,659	1,260	1,171
Portland, Me.	2,773	2,188	1,842	1,744	1,415	1,290
Worcester, Mass.	2,784	2,089	1,907	1,686	1,306	1,221
Providence, R.I.	2,339	1,733	1,606	1,630	1,239	1,124
Waterbury, Conn.	3,086	2,233	2,073	1,742	1,286	1,223
4 Mid. Atlantic cities	2,212	1,576	1,394	1,571	1,196	1,071
Binghamton, N.Y.	2,421	2,051	2,019	1,694	1,439	1,408
Syracuse, N.Y.	2,450	1,714	1,507	1,665	1,231	1,082
Trenton, N.J.	1,917	1,377	1,174	1,317	1,010	902
Erie, Pa.	1,943	1,281	1,080	1,549	1,050	924
6 E. N. Central cities	2,478	1,683	1,430	1,774	1,253	1,149
Cleveland, Ohio	2,463	1,669	1,391	1,757	1,240	1,138
Indianapolis, Ind.	2,899	2,078	1,821	1,896	1,422	1,289
Peoria, Ill.	2,203	1,614	1,454	1,691	1,220	1,131
Lansing, Mich.	2,146	1,337	1,204	1,632	1,016	966
Kenosha, Wis.	1,855	1,067	959	1,378	831	803
Racine, Wis.	1,939	1,052	918	1,589	913	837
10 W. N. Central cities	2,173	1,659	1,449	1,611	1,248	1,141
Minneapolis, Minn.	2,304	1,742	1,530	1,730	1,349	1,220
St. Paul, Minn.	2,060	1,633	1,469	1,454	1,139	1,056
Des Moines, Iowa	2,138	1,653	1,455	1,660	1,307	1,174
St. Joseph, Mo.	2,196	1,727	1,473	1,555	1,261	1,176
Springfield, Mo.	1,753	1,288	1,162	1,365	1,003	899
Fargo, N.D.	2,399	1,932	1,682	1,679	1,420	1,304
Sioux Falls, S.D.	2,283	1,748	1,545	1,635	1,309	1,229
Lincoln, Neb.	2,294	1,630	1,404	1,591	1,251	1,153
Topeka, Kan.	1,981	1,512	1,373	1,492	1,172	1,070
Wichita, Kan.	2,112	1,471	1,271	1,652	1,149	1,035
9 S. Atlantic cities	2,270	1,730	1,620	1,268	1,028	958
Hagerstown, Md.	2,064	1,435	1,315	1,312	1,029	920
Richmond, Va.	2,715	2,154	1,999	1,508	1,352	1,285
Wheeling, W.Va.	1,594	1,121	1,073	1,379	982	925
Asheville, N.C.	2,126	1,544	1,393	1,155	900	821
Greensboro, N.C.	2,915	2,208	2,000	1,462	1,226	1,217
Charleston, S.C.	2,454	2,060	1,927	880	745	734
Columbia, S.C.	2,315	1,829	1,737	1,015	879	812
Atlanta, Ga.	2,701	2,088	1,906	1,377	1,124	979
Jacksonville, Fla.	1,593	1,291	1,224	873	680	626
3 E. S. Central cities	2,275	1,425	1,275	1,349	889	778
Paducah, Ky.	1,667	1,231	1,134	1,019	731	680
Birmingham, Ala.	2,267	1,390	1,211	1,385	880	769
Jackson, Miss.	2,703	1,891	1,707	1,250	965	899
6 W. S. Central cities	2,500	1,809	1,647	1,641	1,244	1,128
Little Rock, Ark.	2,591	1,763	1,502	1,445	1,063	940
Baton Rouge, La.	2,153	1,707	1,532	1,371	1,118	1,009
Oklahoma City, Okla.	2,580	1,791	1,617	1,627	1,172	1,096
Austin, Tex.	2,070	1,710	1,534	1,450	1,282	1,168
Dallas, Tex.	2,564	1,883	1,712	1,751	1,350	1,233
Wichita Falls, Tex.	2,706	1,832	1,650	1,612	1,114	1,048
6 Mountain cities	2,146	1,463	1,341	1,595	1,135	1,027
Butte, Mont.	2,257	1,261	1,155	1,732	1,038	986
Boise, Idaho	1,812	1,395	1,266	1,493	1,259	1,194
Casper, Wyo.	2,064	1,602	1,441	1,569	1,213	1,099
Pueblo, Colo.	1,570	1,043	933	1,290	843	783
Phoenix, Ariz.	2,880	1,919	1,590	1,681	1,204	1,114
Salt Lake City, Utah	2,270	1,600	1,417	1,603	1,193	1,094
4 Pacific cities	2,098	1,491	1,307	1,626	1,198	1,092
Seattle, Wash.	2,122	1,453	1,278	1,693	1,206	1,125
Portland, Ore.	1,994	1,381	1,218	1,423	1,017	905
Sacramento, Calif.	2,465	1,914	1,712	1,805	1,456	1,344
San Diego, Calif.	2,047	1,583	1,371	1,670	1,336	1,192

Source: *Financial Survey of Urban Housing*. Based upon the combined schedules of personal enumeration and mail return.
[1]Geographic division and 52-city averages weighted by number of dwelling units, by tenure, in each city (RPI).

TABLE C 5

Owner-occupant Families reporting Annual Income, Number and Percentage Distribution by 11 Income Groups, 61 Cities by Geographic Division, 1933

	NUMBER										
	All income groups	No income	$1-249	$250-499	$500-749	$750-999	$1,000-1,499	$1,500-1,999	$2,000-2,999	$3,000-4,499	$4,500-7,499	$7,500 and over
61 cities [1]	127,074	6,984	11,385	13,379	15,478	11,810	22,485	17,883	15,656	7,342	3,218	1,454
6 New England cities	7,030	249	440	634	735	611	1,365	1,030	1,055	488	266	157
Portland, Me.	1,366	46	69	118	132	96	259	192	255	109	56	34
Nashua, N.H.	359	12	22	33	38	35	82	61	44	22	7	3
Burlington, Vt.	309	10	13	26	23	93	247	188	207	109	62	37
Worcester, Mass.	1,307	45	83	108	128	93	247	188	207	109	62	37
Providence. R.I.	3,125	119	233	295	355	306	608	475	417	160	101	56
Waterbury, Conn.	564	17	20	54	59	46	108	60	92	62	26	20
5 Mid. Atlantic cities	7,686	589	723	855	1,072	794	1,424	909	769	336	144	71
Binghamton, N.Y.	560	11	14	38	46	41	126	87	105	50	24	18
Syracuse, N.Y.	1,262	53	84	113	178	116	258	172	168	74	29	17
Trenton, N.J.	2,223	152	171	230	348	267	414	270	227	97	40	7
Erie, Pa.	2,933	307	367	378	403	292	512	291	226	97	37	23
Williamsport, Pa.	708	66	87	96	97	78	114	89	43	18	14	6
7 E. N. Central cities	31,630	2,370	3,002	3,703	4,153	3,018	5,328	3,917	3,403	1,581	765	390
Cleveland, Ohio	20,999	1,561	1,972	2,469	2,768	1,994	3,497	2,580	2,289	1,064	517	288
Indianapolis, Ind.	2,552	185	161	190	278	190	415	354	369	216	134	60
Decatur, Ill.	822	119	100	114	114	68	120	96	60	25	4	2
Peoria, Ill.	2,618	139	182	243	319	261	508	393	316	160	69	28
Lansing, Mich.	1,111	59	108	121	146	133	231	138	116	38	15	6
Kenosha, Wis.	1,100	76	127	186	155	139	183	119	77	32	6	
Racine, Wis.	2,428	231	352	380	373	233	374	237	176	46	20	6
10 W. N. Central cities	23,489	1,006	1,687	2,246	2,797	2,475	4,572	3,639	3,005	1,285	551	226
Minneapolis, Minn.	7,226	219	434	629	808	782	1,470	1,158	1,028	419	205	74
St. Paul, Minn.	1,850	83	102	155	206	190	397	310	268	90	32	17
Des Moines, Iowa	3,236	189	249	298	363	297	651	514	380	180	75	40
St. Joseph, Mo.	1,211	70	69	118	136	115	250	193	159	53	32	16
Springfield, Mo.	1,523	94	168	164	216	153	289	205	144	63	22	5
Fargo, N.D.	817	37	31	76	63	68	131	153	156	68	27	7
Sioux Falls, S.D.	1,165	44	85	86	115	142	236	190	143	77	31	16
Lincoln, Neb.	1,623	85	144	173	213	165	274	215	198	98	43	15
Topeka, Kan.	2,385	79	184	225	347	297	419	358	294	124	40	18
Wichita, Kan.	2,453	106	221	322	330	266	455	343	235	113	44	18
10 S. Atlantic cities	12,773	490	1,079	1,272	1,424	1,052	2,134	1,728	1,846	1,066	478	204
Frederick, Md.	454	9	40	40	48	51	111	63	48	27	11	6
Hagerstown, Md.	702	32	66	92	87	63	141	89	63	48	17	4
Richmond, Va.	2,133	70	104	147	176	147	349	322	398	261	114	45
Wheeling, W. Va.	2,233	158	299	311	331	217	369	249	190	65	31	13
Asheville, N.C.	882	29	73	110	123	89	135	128	114	53	21	7
Greensboro, N.C.	535	8	32	64	63	46	73	67	84	46	33	19
Charleston, S.C.	601	15	52	48	59	47	93	75	110	58	33	11
Columbia, S.C.	569	18	64	51	68	39	73	66	94	64	23	9
Atlanta, Ga.	4,068	117	256	326	403	311	703	598	672	413	183	86
Jacksonville, Fla.	596	34	93	83	66	42	87	71	73	31	12	4
4 E. S. Central cities	5,846	329	839	698	653	497	930	799	660	288	124	29
Paducah, Ky.	757	56	145	84	90	68	109	96	69	25	9	6
Knoxville, Tenn.	781	26	89	89	95	83	145	111	86	41	13	3
Birmingham, Ala.	3,879	229	564	484	434	318	613	528	429	179	89	12
Jackson, Miss.	429	18	41	41	34	28	63	64	76	43	13	8
7 W. S. Central cities	10,387	475	882	955	1,133	869	1,698	1,555	1,506	791	364	159
Little Rock, Ark.	1,855	118	209	158	182	148	298	240	273	156	48	25
Baton Rouge, La.	346	27	47	37	41	27	51	33	42	17	16	8
Shreveport, La.	455	7	49	49	47	45	65	65	57	39	23	9
Oklahoma City, Okla.	2,813	119	229	273	335	233	476	424	376	196	106	46
Austin, Tex.	1,036	43	95	120	119	99	155	146	128	71	48	12
Dallas, Tex.	3,058	120	175	244	311	256	527	523	522	247	89	44
Wichita Falls, Tex.	824	41	78	74	98	61	126	124	108	65	34	15
8 Mountain cities	10,191	630	1,070	1,070	1,283	901	1,746	1,458	1,183	550	199	101
Butte, Mont.	1,969	206	228	196	344	202	284	222	161	76	30	20
Boise, Idaho	1,278	71	97	132	180	105	256	190	169	49	26	3
Casper, Wyo.	686	21	41	72	82	64	158	125	74	27	14	8
Pueblo, Colo.	1,019	68	203	168	116	70	150	122	82	33	5	2
Albuquerque, N.M.	282	9	6	17	40	21	57	39	57	26	6	4
Phoenix, Ariz.	988	68	95	112	99	69	161	130	126	78	26	24
Salt Lake City, Utah	3,494	163	370	331	381	331	608	545	445	213	75	32
Reno, Nev.	475	24	30	42	41	39	72	85	69	48	17	8
4 Pacific cities	18,042	846	1,663	1,946	2,228	1,593	3,288	2,848	2,229	957	327	117
Seattle, Wash.	6,474	183	739	824	884	542	1,124	986	732	314	104	42
Portland, Ore.	4,830	341	487	531	593	466	844	744	506	227	65	26
Sacramento, Calif.	2,260	115	125	133	226	209	365	388	405	198	74	22
San Diego, Calif.	4,478	207	312	458	525	376	955	730	586	218	84	27

Source: Financial Survey of Urban Housing
[1] *Geographic division and 61-city percentage distributions weighted by number of owner-occupied units in each city (RPI).*

TABLE C 5

Owner-occupant Families reporting Annual Income, Number and Percentage Distribution by 11 Income Groups, 61 Cities by Geographic Division, 1933

← ————————————————— P E R C E N T A G E   D I S T R I B U T I O N ————————————————— →

All income groups	No income	$1-249	$250-499	$500-749	$750-999	$1,000-1,499	$1,500-1,999	$2,000-2,999	$3,000-4,499	$4,500-7,499	$7,500 and over	
100.0	5.2	8.7	10.4	12.0	9.2	17.9	14.3	12.6	5.9	2.6	1.2	61 cities[1]
100.0	3.6	6.7	9.2	10.8	9.1	19.4	14.8	14.3	6.4	3.6	2.1	6 New England cities
100.0	3.4	5.0	8.6	9.7	7.0	19.0	14.0	18.7	8.0	4.1	2.5	Portland, Me.
100.0	3.3	6.1	9.2	10.6	9.8	22.8	17.0	12.3	6.1	2.0	.8	Nashua, N.H.
100.0	3.2	4.2	8.4	7.5	11.3	19.7	17.5	13.0	8.4	4.5	2.3	Burlington, Vt.
100.0	3.4	6.4	8.3	9.8	7.1	18.9	14.4	15.8	8.3	4.8	2.8	Worcester, Mass.
100.0	3.8	7.5	9.4	11.4	9.8	19.5	15.2	13.3	5.1	3.2	1.8	Providence, R.I.
100.0	3.0	3.5	9.6	10.5	8.2	19.2	10.6	16.3	11.0	4.6	3.5	Waterbury, Conn.
100.0	6.2	8.0	10.1	13.6	9.9	19.3	12.7	11.6	5.2	2.2	1.2	5 Mid. Atlantic cities
100.0	2.0	2.5	6.8	8.2	7.3	22.5	15.5	18.8	8.9	4.3	3.2	Binghamton, N.Y.
100.0	4.2	6.7	9.0	14.1	9.2	20.4	13.6	13.3	5.9	2.3	1.3	Syracuse, N.Y.
100.0	6.8	7.7	10.4	15.7	12.0	18.6	12.1	10.2	4.4	1.8	.3	Trenton, N.J.
100.0	10.5	12.5	12.9	13.7	9.9	17.5	9.9	7.7	3.3	1.3	.8	Erie, Pa.
100.0	9.3	12.3	13.6	13.7	11.0	16.1	12.6	6.1	2.5	2.0	.8	Williamsport, Pa.
100.0	7.4	9.1	11.2	12.8	9.4	16.8	12.6	11.2	5.4	2.7	1.4	7 E. N. Central cities
100.0	7.4	9.4	11.7	13.2	9.5	16.6	12.3	10.9	5.1	2.5	1.4	Cleveland, Ohio
100.0	7.2	6.3	7.4	10.9	7.4	16.3	13.9	14.5	8.5	5.2	2.4	Indianapolis, Ind.
100.0	14.5	12.1	13.9	13.9	8.3	14.6	11.7	7.3	3.0	.5	.2	Decatur, Ill.
100.0	5.3	6.9	9.3	12.2	10.0	19.4	15.0	12.1	6.1	2.6	1.1	Peoria, Ill.
100.0	5.3	9.7	10.9	13.2	12.0	20.8	12.4	10.4	3.4	1.4	.5	Lansing, Mich.
100.0	6.9	11.6	16.9	14.1	12.6	16.6	10.8	7.0	2.9	0.6	.0	Kenosha, Wis.
100.0	9.5	14.5	15.7	15.4	9.6	15.4	9.8	7.2	1.9	0.8	.2	Racine, Wis.
100.0	4.2	6.8	9.4	11.7	10.4	19.9	15.7	13.2	5.4	2.3	1.0	10 W. N. Central cities
100.0	3.0	6.0	8.7	11.2	10.8	20.4	16.0	14.2	5.8	2.9	1.0	Minneapolis, Minn.
100.0	4.5	5.5	8.4	11.1	10.3	21.5	16.7	14.5	4.9	1.7	.9	St. Paul, Minn.
100.0	5.8	7.7	9.2	11.2	9.2	20.1	15.9	11.8	5.5	2.4	1.2	Des Moines, Iowa
100.0	5.8	5.7	9.8	11.2	9.5	20.7	15.9	13.1	4.4	2.6	1.3	St. Joseph, Mo.
100.0	6.2	11.0	10.8	14.2	10.0	19.0	13.5	9.5	4.1	1.4	.3	Springfield, Mo.
100.0	4.5	3.8	9.3	7.7	8.3	16.1	18.7	19.1	8.3	3.3	.9	Fargo, N.D.
100.0	3.8	7.3	7.4	9.9	12.2	20.2	16.3	12.3	6.6	2.6	1.4	Sioux Falls, S.D.
100.0	5.2	8.9	10.7	13.1	10.2	16.9	13.2	12.2	6.0	2.7	.9	Lincoln, Neb.
100.0	3.3	7.7	9.4	14.5	12.5	17.6	15.0	12.4	5.2	1.6	.8	Topeka, Kan.
100.0	4.3	9.0	13.1	13.5	10.8	18.6	14.0	9.6	4.6	1.8	.7	Wichita, Kan.
100.0	4.2	9.1	10.3	11.3	8.1	16.5	13.3	14.2	8.0	3.5	1.5	10 S. Atlantic cities
100.0	2.0	8.8	8.8	10.6	11.2	24.5	13.9	10.6	5.9	2.4	1.3	Frederick, Md.
100.0	4.5	9.4	13.1	12.4	9.0	20.1	12.7	9.0	6.8	2.4	.6	Hagerstown, Md.
100.0	3.3	4.9	6.9	8.2	6.9	16.4	15.1	18.7	12.2	5.3	2.1	Richmond, Va.
100.0	7.1	13.4	13.9	14.8	9.7	16.5	11.2	8.5	2.9	1.4	.6	Wheeling, W. Va.
100.0	3.3	8.3	12.5	13.9	10.1	15.3	14.5	12.9	6.0	2.4	.8	Asheville, N.C.
100.0	1.5	6.0	12.0	11.8	8.6	13.6	12.5	15.7	8.6	6.2	3.5	Greensboro, N.C.
100.0	2.5	8.7	8.0	9.8	7.8	15.5	12.5	18.3	9.6	5.5	1.8	Charleston, S.C.
100.0	3.2	11.2	9.0	12.0	6.9	12.8	11.6	16.5	11.2	4.0	1.6	Columbia, S.C.
100.0	2.9	6.3	8.0	9.9	7.6	17.3	14.7	16.5	10.2	4.5	2.1	Atlanta, Ga.
100.0	5.7	15.6	13.9	11.1	7.0	14.6	11.9	12.3	5.2	2.0	.7	Jacksonville, Fla.
100.0	5.3	13.8	11.9	11.2	8.6	16.2	13.8	11.5	5.1	2.1	0.5	4 E. S. Central cities
100.0	7.4	19.1	11.1	11.9	9.0	14.4	12.7	9.1	3.3	1.2	.8	Paducah, Ky.
100.0	3.3	11.4	11.4	12.2	10.6	18.6	14.2	11.0	5.2	1.7	.4	Knoxville, Tenn.
100.0	5.9	14.5	12.5	11.2	8.2	15.8	13.6	11.1	4.6	2.3	.3	Birmingham, Ala.
100.0	4.2	9.6	9.6	7.9	6.5	14.7	14.9	17.7	10.0	3.0	1.9	Jackson, Miss.
100.0	4.2	8.3	9.3	10.9	8.5	18.3	15.2	14.6	7.6	3.6	1.5	7 W. S. Central cities
100.0	6.4	11.3	8.5	9.8	8.0	16.1	12.9	14.7	8.4	2.6	1.3	Little Rock, Ark.
100.0	7.8	13.6	10.7	11.9	7.8	14.8	9.5	12.1	4.9	4.6	2.3	Baton Rouge, La.
100.0	1.5	10.8	10.8	10.3	9.9	14.3	14.3	12.5	8.6	5.0	2.0	Shreveport, La.
100.0	4.2	8.1	9.7	11.9	8.3	16.9	15.1	13.4	7.0	3.8	1.6	Oklahoma City, Okla.
100.0	4.1	9.2	11.6	11.5	9.6	15.0	14.1	12.3	6.8	4.6	1.2	Austin, Tex.
100.0	3.9	5.7	8.0	10.2	8.4	17.2	17.1	17.1	8.1	2.9	1.4	Dallas, Tex.
100.0	5.0	9.5	9.0	11.9	7.4	15.3	15.0	13.1	7.9	4.1	1.8	Wichita Falls, Tex.
100.0	5.7	10.5	10.5	11.9	8.6	17.2	14.5	12.2	5.9	2.0	1.0	8 Mountain cities
100.0	10.5	11.6	10.0	17.5	10.2	14.4	11.3	8.2	3.8	1.5	1.0	Butte, Mont.
100.0	5.6	7.6	10.3	14.1	8.2	20.0	14.9	13.2	3.8	2.1	.2	Boise, Idaho
100.0	3.1	6.0	10.5	12.0	9.3	23.0	18.2	10.8	3.9	2.0	1.2	Casper, Wyo.
100.0	6.7	19.9	16.5	11.4	6.9	14.7	12.0	8.0	3.2	.5	.2	Pueblo, Colo.
100.0	3.2	2.1	6.0	14.2	7.5	20.2	13.9	20.2	9.2	2.1	1.4	Albuquerque, N.M.
100.0	6.9	9.6	11.3	10.0	7.0	16.3	13.2	12.8	7.9	2.6	2.4	Phoenix, Ariz.
100.0	4.7	10.6	9.5	10.9	9.5	17.4	15.6	12.7	6.1	2.1	.9	Salt Lake City, Utah
100.0	5.1	6.3	8.8	8.6	8.2	15.2	17.9	14.5	10.1	3.6	1.7	Reno, Nev.
100.0	4.6	9.7	11.2	12.6	8.9	18.0	15.6	11.9	5.2	1.8	0.6	4 Pacific cities
100.0	2.8	11.4	12.7	13.7	8.4	17.4	15.2	11.3	4.9	1.6	.6	Seattle, Wash.
100.0	7.1	10.1	11.0	12.3	9.6	17.5	15.4	10.5	4.7	1.3	.5	Portland, Ore.
100.0	5.1	5.5	5.9	10.0	9.2	16.1	17.2	17.9	8.8	3.3	1.0	Sacramento, Calif.
100.0	4.6	7.0	10.2	11.7	8.4	21.3	16.3	13.1	4.9	1.9	.6	San Diego, Calif.

TABLE C 6

Tenant Families reporting Annual Income, Number and Percentage Distribution by 11 Income Groups, 61 Cities by Geographic Division, 1933

	All income groups	No income	$1-249	$250-499	$500-749	$750-999	$1,000-1,499	$1,500-1,999	$2,000-2,999	$3,000-4,499	$4,500-7,499	$7,500 and over
61 cities[1]	162,982	7,656	20,380	22,098	23,613	17,826	29,988	20,200	14,086	5,171	1,601	363
6 New England cities	13,460	696	812	1,336	1,983	1,690	3,088	1,912	1,252	473	175	43
Portland, Me.	2,755	97	150	227	355	302	676	487	301	120	31	9
Nashua, N.H.	400	21	19	30	48	46	110	64	40	17	5	
Burlington, Vt.	465	17	29	62	70	60	110	50	45	18	4	
Worcester, Mass.	2,816	163	196	252	361	339	652	446	261	94	38	14
Providence, R.I.	5,891	374	368	633	940	798	1,311	703	480	192	73	19
Waterbury, Conn.	1,133	24	50	132	209	145	229	162	125	32	24	1
5 Mid. Atlantic cities	7,994	705	795	1,024	1,235	971	1,486	908	603	190	72	5
Binghamton, N.Y.	774	25	26	52	76	97	203	137	105	33	20	
Syracuse, N.Y.	1,526	84	83	176	295	192	294	217	131	45	9	
Trenton, N.J.	2,081	207	222	281	338	254	390	194	140	39	16	
Erie, Pa.	2,928	311	365	384	425	349	512	300	198	54	26	4
Williamsport, Pa.	685	78	99	131	101	79	87	60	29	19	1	1
7 E. N. Central cities	37,634	2,521	3,829	4,878	5,410	4,130	6,982	4,542	3,358	1,373	478	133
Cleveland, Ohio	27,473	1,844	2,694	3,569	3,907	2,928	5,049	3,412	2,540	1,057	360	113
Indianapolis, Ind.	3,183	219	299	275	428	330	583	399	391	176	71	14
Decatur, Ill.	775	72	123	149	145	77	114	61	27	6	1	
Peoria, Ill.	2,330	70	181	278	370	307	519	304	196	72	29	4
Lansing, Mich.	977	30	77	163	169	151	201	96	61	26	3	
Kenosha, Wis.	1,002	64	146	172	153	133	190	87	45	9	3	
Racine, Wis.	1,894	222	309	272	240	204	326	183	98	27	11	2
10 W. N. Central cities	24,891	811	2,135	2,886	3,549	3,219	5,275	3,517	2,405	823	223	48
Minneapolis, Minn.	9,282	295	560	1,081	1,336	1,138	2,058	1,390	972	334	88	30
St. Paul, Minn.	1,830	120	169	183	254	258	381	246	151	58	10	
Des Moines, Iowa	3,117	105	297	268	442	383	690	461	317	122	30	2
St. Joseph, Mo.	1,282	32	141	147	156	188	259	195	116	30	11	7
Springfield, Mo.	1,196	57	193	181	183	140	215	125	69	25	8	
Fargo, N.D.	909	21	44	84	122	93	221	162	112	38	12	
Sioux Falls, S.D.	1,525	45	95	141	186	252	327	230	181	55	10	3
Lincoln, Neb.	1,295	43	133	150	175	161	280	152	131	51	16	3
Topeka, Kan.	2,078	46	256	269	325	262	381	278	187	58	14	2
Wichita, Kan.	2,377	47	247	382	370	344	463	278	169	52	24	1
10 S. Atlantic cities	27,268	852	5,180	4,891	4,243	2,434	3,789	2,667	2,125	783	246	58
Frederick, Md.	573	13	54	78	96	99	127	56	40	8	2	
Hagerstown, Md.	1,275	63	141	199	229	159	233	136	90	18	7	
Richmond, Va.	4,172	118	401	628	561	435	705	573	455	205	71	20
Wheeling, W.Va.	2,218	88	313	333	349	230	472	254	136	29	13	1
Asheville, N.C.	1,644	32	307	316	316	154	237	141	112	24	5	
Greensboro, N.C.	1,221	10	91	151	211	200	224	130	136	48	15	5
Charleston, S.C.	2,535	82	824	482	345	149	280	192	116	50	12	3
Columbia, S.C.	1,583	50	505	260	214	112	141	128	105	56	11	1
Atlanta, Ga.	9,520	327	1,806	1,746	1,517	745	1,192	901	843	313	102	28
Jacksonville, Fla.	2,527	69	738	698	405	151	178	156	92	32	8	
4 E. S. Central cities	10,178	475	2,823	1,759	1,345	811	1,283	874	546	202	55	5
Paducah, Ky.	1,313	70	430	215	152	110	138	116	65	17		
Knoxville, Tenn.	982	18	139	170	196	117	163	93	61	18	7	
Birmingham, Ala.	7,175	370	2,068	1,249	917	535	893	584	364	147	43	5
Jackson, Miss.	708	17	186	125	80	49	89	81	56	20	5	
7 W. S. Central cities	13,890	478	1,742	1,861	1,952	1,386	2,706	1,815	1,340	470	120	20
Little Rock, Ark.	2,613	146	518	377	374	224	408	262	209	77	14	4
Baton Rouge, La.	865	42	184	139	101	62	107	98	86	38	6	2
Shreveport, La.	815	24	127	191	113	53	115	103	68	17	2	2
Oklahoma City, Okla.	3,691	128	386	437	508	383	880	489	351	96	29	4
Austin, Tex.	1,018	18	147	144	153	92	175	113	100	57	16	3
Dallas, Tex.	3,831	98	261	422	537	446	822	594	443	163	40	5
Wichita Falls, Tex.	1,057	22	119	151	166	126	199	156	83	22	13	
8 Mountain cities	10,682	612	1,373	1,279	1,525	1,090	1,933	1,419	954	372	101	24
Butte, Mont.	2,009	206	278	253	345	181	270	209	170	72	21	4
Boise, Idaho	1,114	34	79	132	151	125	236	168	135	46	8	
Casper, Wyo.	698	58	75	81	96	44	120	117	75	26	5	1
Pueblo, Colo.	917	68	192	135	140	78	135	110	50	8	1	
Albuquerque, N.M.	268	3	10	24	48	23	57	51	33	15	3	1
Phoenix, Ariz.	1,666	112	183	193	199	186	327	260	122	55	22	7
Salt Lake City, Utah	3,654	119	534	432	502	424	722	439	310	129	35	8
Reno, Nev.	356	12	22	29	44	29	66	65	59	21	6	3
4 Pacific cities	16,985	506	1,691	2,184	2,371	2,095	3,446	2,546	1,503	485	131	27
Seattle, Wash.	5,990	110	638	891	859	725	1,153	861	521	163	58	11
Portland, Ore.	4,023	205	604	611	618	485	706	466	236	75	14	3
Sacramento, Calif.	2,167	64	142	192	258	211	461	374	328	112	20	5
San Diego, Calif.	4,805	127	307	490	636	674	1,126	845	418	135	39	8

Source: Financial Survey of Urban Housing
[1]*Geographic division and 61-city percentage distributions weighted by number of tenant occupied units in each city (RPI).*

TABLE C 6

Tenant Families reporting Annual Income, Number and Percentage Distribution by 11 Income Groups, 61 Cities by Geographic Division, 1933

⟵——————————————————— P E R C E N T A G E   D I S T R I B U T I O N [1] ———————————————————⟶

All income groups	No income	$1-249	$250-499	$500-749	$750-999	$1,000-1,499	$1,500-1,999	$2,000-2,999	$3,000-4,499	$4,500-7,499	$7,500 and over	
100.0	4.6	12.0	13.4	14.6	11.1	18.7	12.5	8.7	3.2	1.0	0.2	61 cities[1]
100.0	5.6	6.1	10.3	15.2	12.9	22.6	13.4	8.9	3.3	1.4	0.3	6 New England cities
100.0	3.5	5.5	8.2	12.9	11.0	24.5	17.7	10.9	4.4	1.1	.3	Portland, Me.
100.0	5.2	4.8	7.5	12.0	11.5	27.5	16.0	10.0	4.3	1.2	.0	Nashua, N.H.
100.0	3.7	6.2	13.3	15.1	12.9	23.6	10.8	9.7	3.9	.8	.0	Burlington, Vt.
100.0	5.8	7.0	9.0	12.8	12.0	23.2	15.8	9.3	3.3	1.3	.5	Worcester, Mass.
100.0	6.4	6.2	10.7	16.0	13.5	22.3	11.9	8.2	3.3	1.2	.3	Providence, R.I.
100.0	2.1	4.4	11.7	18.4	12.8	20.2	14.3	11.1	2.8	2.1	.1	Waterbury, Conn.
100.0	7.4	8.2	12.1	16.1	12.3	19.3	12.4	8.5	2.7	0.9	0.1	5 Mid. Atlantic cities
100.0	3.2	3.4	6.7	9.8	12.5	26.2	17.7	13.6	4.3	2.6	.0	Binghamton, N.Y.
100.0	5.5	5.4	11.5	19.3	12.6	19.3	14.2	8.6	3.0	.6	.0	Syracuse, N.Y.
100.0	10.0	10.7	13.5	16.2	12.2	18.7	9.3	6.7	1.9	.8	.0	Trenton, N.J.
100.0	10.6	12.5	13.1	14.5	11.9	17.5	10.2	6.8	1.9	.9	.1	Erie, Pa.
100.0	11.4	14.5	19.1	14.8	11.5	12.7	8.8	4.2	2.8	.1	.1	Williamsport, Pa.
100.0	6.7	10.0	12.4	14.3	10.9	18.5	12.1	9.4	4.0	1.4	0.3	7 E. N. Central cities
100.0	6.7	9.8	13.0	14.2	10.7	18.4	12.4	9.2	3.9	1.3	.4	Cleveland, Ohio
100.0	6.9	9.4	8.7	13.4	10.4	18.3	12.5	12.3	5.5	2.2	.4	Indianapolis, Ind.
100.0	9.3	15.9	19.2	18.7	9.9	14.7	7.9	3.5	.8	.1	.0	Decatur, Ill.
100.0	3.0	7.8	11.9	15.9	13.2	22.3	13.0	8.4	3.1	1.2	.2	Peoria, Ill.
100.0	3.1	7.9	16.7	17.3	15.4	20.6	9.8	6.2	2.7	.3	.0	Lansing, Mich.
100.0	6.4	14.6	17.1	15.3	13.3	18.9	8.7	4.5	.9	.3	.0	Kenosha, Wis.
100.0	11.7	16.3	14.4	12.7	10.8	17.2	9.7	5.1	1.4	.6	.1	Racine, Wis.
100.0	3.7	8.6	11.5	14.2	13.0	21.2	14.0	9.4	3.3	0.9	0.2	10 W. N. Central cities
100.0	3.2	6.0	11.6	14.4	12.3	22.2	15.0	10.4	3.6	1.0	.3	Minneapolis, Minn.
100.0	6.6	9.2	10.0	13.9	14.1	20.8	13.4	8.3	3.1	.6	.0	St. Paul, Minn.
100.0	3.3	9.5	8.6	14.2	12.3	22.1	14.8	10.2	3.9	1.0	.1	Des Moines, Iowa
100.0	2.5	11.0	11.5	12.2	14.7	20.2	15.2	9.0	2.3	.9	.5	St. Joseph, Mo.
100.0	4.8	16.1	15.1	15.3	11.7	18.0	10.4	5.8	2.1	.7	.0	Springfield, Mo.
100.0	2.3	4.9	9.3	13.4	10.2	24.3	17.8	12.3	4.2	1.3	.0	Fargo, N.D.
100.0	3.0	6.2	9.2	12.2	16.5	21.4	15.1	11.9	3.6	.7	.2	Sioux Falls, S.D.
100.0	3.3	10.3	11.6	13.5	12.4	21.6	11.8	10.1	4.0	1.2	.2	Lincoln, Neb.
100.0	2.2	12.3	13.0	15.6	12.6	18.3	13.4	9.0	2.8	.7	.1	Topeka, Kan.
100.0	2.0	10.4	16.1	15.5	14.4	19.5	11.7	7.1	2.2	1.0	.1	Wichita, Kan.
100.0	3.1	19.0	18.3	15.5	8.8	13.9	9.8	7.7	2.8	0.9	0.2	10 S. Atlantic cities
100.0	2.3	9.4	13.6	16.8	17.3	22.1	9.8	6.9	1.4	.4	.0	Frederick, Md.
100.0	4.9	11.1	15.6	18.0	12.4	18.3	10.7	7.0	1.4	.6	.0	Hagerstown, Md.
100.0	2.8	9.6	15.1	13.5	10.4	16.9	13.7	10.9	4.9	1.7	.5	Richmond, Va.
100.0	4.0	14.1	15.0	15.7	10.3	21.3	11.5	6.1	1.3	.6	.1	Wheeling, W.Va.
100.0	1.9	18.7	19.2	19.2	9.4	14.4	8.6	6.8	1.5	.3	.0	Asheville, N.C.
100.0	.8	7.5	12.4	17.3	16.4	18.3	10.6	11.1	4.0	1.2	.4	Greensboro, N.C.
100.0	3.2	32.5	19.0	13.6	5.9	11.0	7.6	4.6	2.0	.5	.1	Charleston, S.C.
100.0	3.2	31.9	16.4	13.5	7.1	8.9	8.1	6.6	3.5	.7	.1	Columbia, S.C.
100.0	3.4	19.0	18.4	15.9	7.8	12.5	9.5	8.8	3.3	1.1	.3	Atlanta, Ga.
100.0	2.7	29.2	27.6	16.0	6.0	7.1	6.2	3.6	1.3	.3	.0	Jacksonville, Fla.
100.0	4.4	26.5	17.3	13.8	8.2	13.0	8.6	5.5	2.0	0.6	0.1	4 E. S. Central cities
100.0	5.3	32.8	16.4	11.6	8.4	10.5	8.8	4.9	1.3	.0	.0	Paducah, Ky.
100.0	1.8	14.2	17.3	20.0	11.9	16.6	9.5	6.2	1.8	.7	.0	Knoxville, Tenn.
100.0	5.2	28.3	17.4	12.8	7.5	12.4	8.1	5.1	2.0	.6	.1	Birmingham, Ala.
100.0	2.4	26.3	17.7	11.3	6.9	12.6	11.4	7.9	2.8	.7	.0	Jackson, Miss.
100.0	3.2	11.4	13.7	14.0	10.1	19.6	13.6	10.0	3.4	0.9	0.1	7 W. S. Central cities
100.0	5.6	19.8	14.4	14.3	8.6	15.6	10.0	8.0	3.0	.5	.2	Little Rock, Ark.
100.0	4.8	21.3	16.1	11.7	7.2	12.4	11.3	9.9	4.4	.7	.2	Baton Rouge, La.
100.0	2.9	15.6	23.4	13.9	6.5	14.1	12.6	8.3	2.1	.3	.3	Shreveport, La.
100.0	3.5	10.5	11.8	13.8	10.4	23.8	13.2	9.5	2.6	.8	.1	Oklahoma City, Okla.
100.0	1.8	14.4	14.2	15.0	9.0	17.2	11.1	9.8	5.6	1.6	.3	Austin, Tex.
100.0	2.6	6.8	11.0	14.0	11.6	21.5	15.5	11.6	4.3	1.0	.1	Dallas, Tex.
100.0	2.1	11.3	14.3	15.7	11.9	18.8	14.7	7.9	2.1	1.2	.0	Wichita Falls, Tex.
100.0	5.3	12.6	11.7	14.2	10.1	18.4	13.9	9.1	3.5	1.0	0.2	8 Mountain cities
100.0	10.3	13.8	12.6	17.2	9.0	13.4	10.4	8.5	3.6	1.0	.2	Butte, Mont.
100.0	3.1	7.1	11.8	13.6	11.2	21.2	15.1	12.1	4.1	.7	.0	Boise, Idaho
100.0	8.3	10.7	11.6	13.8	6.3	17.2	16.8	10.7	3.7	.7	.2	Casper, Wyo.
100.0	7.4	20.9	14.7	15.3	8.5	14.7	12.0	5.5	.9	.1	.0	Pueblo, Colo.
100.0	1.1	3.7	9.0	17.9	8.6	21.3	19.0	12.3	5.6	1.1	.4	Albuquerque, N.M.
100.0	6.7	11.0	11.6	12.0	11.2	19.6	15.6	7.3	3.3	1.3	.4	Phoenix, Ariz.
100.0	3.3	14.6	11.8	13.7	11.6	19.8	12.0	8.5	3.5	1.0	.2	Salt Lake City, Utah
100.0	3.4	6.2	8.1	12.4	8.1	18.5	18.3	16.6	5.9	1.7	.8	Reno, Nev.
100.0	3.0	10.6	13.4	14.2	12.2	19.9	14.5	8.5	2.7	0.8	0.2	4 Pacific cities
100.0	1.8	10.7	14.9	14.3	12.1	19.2	14.4	8.7	2.7	1.0	.2	Seattle, Wash.
100.0	5.1	15.0	15.2	15.4	12.0	17.5	11.6	5.9	1.9	.3	.1	Portland, Ore.
100.0	3.0	6.5	8.9	11.9	9.7	21.3	17.3	15.1	5.2	.9	.2	Sacramento, Calif.
100.0	2.6	6.4	10.2	13.3	14.0	23.4	17.6	8.7	2.8	.8	.2	San Diego, Calif.

TABLE C 7

Owner-occupant and Tenant Families, Average Annual Family Income by 10 Income Groups, 52 Cities by Geographic Division, 1933

	All income groups	$1-249	$250-499	$500-749	$750-999	$1,000-1,499	$1,500-1,999	$2,000-2,999	$3,000-4,499	$4,500-7,499	$7,500 and over
52 cities[1]	1,465	174	378	613	882	1,201	1,707	2,339	3,484	5,430	12,164
4 New England cities	1,712	171	383	608	870	1,202	1,701	2,343	3,523	5,412	13,218
Portland, Me.	1,842	164	392	598	864	1,188	1,686	2,324	3,512	5,234	11,665
Worcester, Mass.	1,907	183	394	613	868	1,238	1,708	2,368	3,503	5,644	11,527
Providence, R.I.	1,606	170	379	606	870	1,194	1,693	2,338	3,522	5,359	13,866
Waterbury, Conn.	2,073	165	385	617	876	1,203	1,760	2,351	3,576	5,512	12,565
4 Mid. Atlantic cities	1,404	164	374	603	919	1,176	1,749	2,297	3,460	5,310	11,888
Binghamton, N.Y.	2,019	136	371	587	910	1,217	1,676	2,326	3,474	5,692	10,922
Syracuse, N.Y.	1,507	171	372	599	954	1,170	1,710	2,281	3,491	5,276	15,165
Trenton, N.J.	1,174	164	373	628	920	1,151	1,683	2,312	3,385	4,970	8,429
Erie, Pa.	1,080	169	379	592	861	1,190	1,938	2,292	3,480	5,500	10,417
6 E. N. Central cities	1,434	172	374	608	885	1,202	1,719	2,344	3,469	5,541	13,220
Cleveland, Ohio	1,391	169	373	604	866	1,196	1,694	2,334	3,479	5,522	14,250
Indianapolis, Ind.	1,821	186	378	622	948	1,236	1,833	2,397	3,456	5,359	11,417
Peoria, Ill.	1,454	164	368	604	865	1,183	1,679	2,330	3,478	5,474	12,086
Lansing, Mich.	1,204	169	377	604	921	1,173	1,696	2,308	3,532	5,073	13,383
Kenosha, Wis.	959	176	380	616	873	1,195	1,704	2,327	3,503	5,317	
Racine, Wis.	918	158	374	606	878	1,209	1,666	2,326	3,276	7,385	7,717
10 W. N. Central cities	1,453	185	376	613	868	1,196	1,700	2,344	3,479	5,410	12,232
Minneapolis, Minn.	1,530	193	386	615	865	1,195	1,695	2,331	3,491	5,450	11,578
St. Paul, Minn.	1,469	178	361	607	876	1,199	1,707	2,355	3,471	5,469	13,382
Des Moines, Iowa	1,455	190	366	607	853	1,174	1,725	2,333	3,459	5,265	13,103
St. Joseph, Mo.	1,473	178	356	613	858	1,195	1,763	2,435	3,404	5,403	10,488
Springfield, Mo.	1,162	155	357	612	876	1,184	1,671	2,344	3,352	5,359	13,600
Fargo, N.D.	1,682	155	479	711	876	1,199	1,707	2,356	3,481	5,000	10,214
Sioux Falls, S.D.	1,545	238	365	601	878	1,193	1,692	2,317	3,421	5,539	11,588
Lincoln, Neb.	1,404	220	388	595	874	1,189	1,672	2,364	3,532	5,467	11,647
Topeka, Kan.	1,373	161	384	628	877	1,206	1,701	2,344	3,534	5,335	12,489
Wichita, Kan.	1,271	162	373	620	862	1,229	1,673	2,317	3,538	5,391	11,817
9 S. Atlantic cities	1,619	173	376	642	873	1,211	1,714	2,352	3,484	5,584	11,540
Hagerstown, Md.	1,315	170	442	621	873	1,187	1,720	2,292	3,471	5,465	9,425
Richmond, Va.	1,999	177	306	636	854	1,188	1,757	2,374	3,496	5,465	11,158
Wheeling, W.Va.	1,073	149	356	597	867	1,198	1,682	2,324	3,423	5,403	12,577
Asheville, N.C.	1,393	159	370	604	881	1,183	1,675	2,284	3,513	5,467	12,629
Greensboro, N.C.	2,000	163	369	589	857	1,167	1,707	2,360	3,541	5,188	12,247
Charleston, S.C.	1,927	225	450	690	853	1,424	1,695	2,373	3,538	5,352	12,872
Columbia, S.C.	1,737	164	369	672	877	1,201	1,756	2,385	3,425	5,591	11,500
Atlanta, Ga.	1,906	193	415	700	891	1,226	1,727	2,375	3,503	5,750	11,843
Jacksonville, Fla.	1,224	153	375	591	867	1,194	1,687	2,336	3,506	5,983	8,475
3 E. S. Central cities	1,257	168	385	623	891	1,225	1,687	2,326	3,452	5,288	11,606
Paducah, Ky.	1,134	145	355	599	871	1,253	1,673	2,410	3,472	5,289	16,100
Birmingham, Ala.	1,211	170	391	630	898	1,223	1,685	2,309	2,445	5,311	11,292
Jackson, Miss.	1,707	171	363	594	850	1,221	1,714	2,384	3,491	5,108	10,250
6 W. S. Central cities	1,630	180	397	607	907	1,204	1,692	2,351	3,458	5,374	12,358
Little Rock, Ark.	1,502	171	425	596	870	1,183	1,691	2,377	3,417	5,300	10,061
Baton Rouge, La.	1,532	168	349	610	930	1,243	1,694	2,524	3,400	5,281	11,450
Oklahoma City, Okla.	1,617	197	361	605	917	1,208	1,696	2,330	3,475	5,316	12,502
Austin, Tex.	1,534	178	382	607	871	1,195	1,646	2,356	3,472	5,454	11,083
Dallas, Tex.	1,712	177	427	615	926	1,212	1,898	2,343	3,400	5,347	13,748
Wichita Falls, Tex.	1,650	151	358	580	861	1,164	1,712	2,312	3,880	5,912	9,993
6 Mountain cities	1,316	161	365	607	877	1,206	1,702	2,347	3,490	5,513	11,189
Butte, Mont.	1,155	154	370	611	901	1,182	1,687	2,331	3,480	5,307	13,245
Boise, Idaho	1,266	186	370	588	870	1,166	1,696	2,318	3,347	5,546	11,167
Casper, Wyo.	1,441	212	368	596	884	1,191	1,682	2,357	3,485	5,279	13,375
Pueblo, Colo.	933	159	368	601	886	1,173	1,652	2,329	3,336	5,600	
Phoenix, Ariz.	1,590	162	373	608	865	1,216	1,692	2,325	3,440	5,854	11,017
Salt Lake City, Utah	1,417	153	360	612	872	1,231	1,730	2,367	3,585	5,472	10,453
4 Pacific cities	1,310	176	380	608	883	1,202	1,690	2,325	3,510	5,297	10,712
Seattle, Wash.	1,278	176	374	609	877	1,207	1,690	2,312	3,536	5,337	10,469
Portland, Ore.	1,218	167	385	595	876	1,190	1,680	2,319	3,465	5,268	10,715
Sacramento, Calif.	1,712	182	389	632	939	1,214	1,703	2,375	3,456	5,264	14,368
San Diego, Calif.	1,371	190	381	620	884	1,207	1,703	2,348	3,547	5,265	9,696

Source: *Financial Survey of Urban Housing*. Based on number of reports as shown in Tables C 5 and 6. Average not shown for fewer than 3 reports.
[1] Geographic division and 52-city averages weighted by number of occupied units, by tenure, in each city (RPI).

TABLE C 7

Owner-occupant and Tenant Families, Average Annual Family Income by 10 Income Groups, 52 Cities by Geographic Division, 1933

←————————————————————— T E N A N T ————————————————————→

All income groups	$1- 249	$250- 499	$500- 749	$750- 999	$1,000- 1,499	$1,500- 1,999	$2,000- 2,999	$3,000- 4,499	$4,500- 7,499	$7,500 and over	
1,082	175	384	611	872	1,192	1,681	2,321	3,409	5,251	10,422	52 cities[1]
1,166	170	412	604	860	1,181	1,676	2,319	3,396	5,278	8,821	4 New England cities
1,290	167	364	598	858	1,182	1,677	2,323	3,403	5,219	10,056	Portland, Me.
1,221	172	379	604	866	1,194	1,683	2,326	3,255	5,750	9,857	Worcester, Mass.
1,124	171	435	603	860	1,178	1,676	2,320	3,433	5,112	8,337	Providence, R.I.
1,223	162	367	619	848	1,176	1,665	2,298	3,438	5,446		Waterbury, Conn.
1,065	160	393	585	865	1,204	1,712	2,300	3,421	5,275	12,250	4 Mid. Atlantic cities
1,408	173	452	576	867	1,299	1,688	2,282	3,221	5,565		Binghamton, N.Y.
1,082	157	398	585	870	1,185	1,706	2,328	3,489	5,300		Syracuse, N.Y.
902	161	368	583	858	1,178	1,716	2,256	3,444	5,025		Trenton, N.J.
924	157	360	593	860	1,196	1,738	2,299	3,413	5,238	12,250	Erie, Pa.
1,151	180	379	637	885	1,184	1,680	2,305	3,415	5,195	10,937	6 E. N. Central cities
1,138	186	372	641	888	1,189	1,688	2,298	3,419	5,165	11,157	Cleveland, Ohio
1,289	171	406	644	881	1,172	1,663	2,325	3,423	5,232	10,343	Indianapolis, Ind.
1,131	164	369	608	864	1,179	1,674	2,322	3,340	5,283	10,950	Peoria, Ill.
966	162	373	599	850	1,168	1,672	2,303	3,465	5,067		Lansing, Mich.
803	158	344	609	870	1,160	1,675	2,231	3,256	6,033		Kenosha, Wis.
837	180	357	601	919	1,207	1,678	2,329	3,415	5,073		Racine, Wis.
1,143	173	393	609	878	1,194	1,685	2,308	3,425	5,194	9,884	10 W. N. Central cities
1,220	175	436	607	883	1,189	1,688	2,314	3,432	5,142	10,000	Minneapolis, Minn.
1,056	159	386	612	874	1,189	1,665	2,293	3,391	4,910		St. Paul, Minn.
1,174	183	371	600	864	1,181	1,690	2,300	3,357	5,180		Des Moines, Iowa
1,176	190	351	616	909	1,218	1,743	2,281	3,587	5,700	10,257	St. Joseph, Mo.
899	168	356	598	869	1,169	1,662	2,343	3,340	5,450		Springfield, Mo.
1,304	159	368	634	878	1,185	1,688	2,363	3,268	5,400		Fargo, N.D.
1,229	161	392	616	874	1,184	1,686	2,348	3,438	5,150	9,466	Sioux Falls, S.D.
1,153	171	357	615	871	1,189	1,672	2,274	3,506	4,888	9,000	Lincoln, Neb.
1,070	160	353	616	863	1,198	1,692	2,307	3,403	5,786		Topeka, Kan.
1,035	181	354	607	876	1,239	1,681	2,328	3,465	5,388		Wichita, Kan.
949	185	371	593	861	1,188	1,677	2,315	3,387	5,280	12,720	9 S. Atlantic cities
920	140	359	603	857	1,165	1,660	2,337	3,439	5,386		Hagerstown, Md.
1,285	242	440	592	875	1,188	1,688	2,318	3,385	5,290	9,730	Richmond, Va.
925	181	366	590	865	1,177	1,652	2,301	3,372	5,600		Wheeling, W.Va.
821	173	356	610	855	1,165	1,655	2,188	3,358	5,020		Asheville, N.C.
1,217	175	351	608	875	1,189	1,683	2,340	3,377	5,193	14,100	Greensboro, N.C.
734	182	345	578	854	1,153	1,648	2,301	3,380	4,958	27,500	Charleston, S.C.
812	157	353	586	929	1,199	1,676	2,359	3,384	5,109		Columbia, S.C.
979	174	358	596	846	1,197	1,684	2,334	3,408	5,468	10,939	Atlanta, Ga.
626	178	356	588	858	1,198	1,693	2,298	3,359	4,813		Jacksonville, Fla.
776	164	358	609	868	1,198	1,679	2,430	3,383	5,175	9,380	3 E. S. Central cities
680	138	363	616	883	1,179	1,664	2,357	3,276			Paducah, Ky.
769	165	359	608	867	1,201	1,680	2,440	3,388	5,184	9,380	Birmingham, Ala.
899	171	348	610	869	1,188	1,685	2,391	3,405	5,100		Jackson, Miss.
1,136	165	366	615	861	1,188	1,672	2,326	3,413	5,366	9,046	6 W. S. Central cities
940	162	372	616	855	1,275	1,662	2,264	3,518	5,271	9,600	Little Rock, Ark.
1,009	164	377	607	855	1,214	1,646	2,372	3,426	5,600		Baton Rouge, La.
1,096	162	351	598	867	1,174	1,666	2,368	3,346	5,528	8,500	Oklahoma City, Okla.
1,168	175	389	595	865	1,183	1,689	2,382	3,411	5,106	9,167	Austin, Tex.
1,233	167	373	632	859	1,175	1,679	2,306	3,417	5,330	9,200	Dallas, Tex.
1,048	158	356	592	862	1,166	1,672	2,298	3,455	5,254		Wichita Falls, Tex.
1,047	181	378	602	865	1,194	1,682	2,330	3,416	5,203	10,080	6 Mountain cities
986	144	392	606	859	1,203	1,686	2,316	3,375	5,133	14,000	Butte, Mont.
1,194	184	358	639	870	1,186	1,670	2,255	3,326	5,558		Boise, Idaho
1,099	156	369	573	857	1,173	1,691	2,244	3,473	5,300		Casper, Wyo.
783	163	351	597	867	1,161	1,662	2,332	3,400			Pueblo, Colo.
1,114	151	357	598	861	1,217	1,672	2,323	3,411	5,300	8,471	Phoenix, Ariz.
1,094	218	395	605	870	1,197	1,692	2,364	3,439	5,117	9,525	Salt Lake City, Utah
1,096	178	395	611	878	1,210	1,682	2,319	3,416	5,322	10,804	4 Pacific cities
1,125	179	438	617	884	1,242	1,681	2,317	3,416	5,353	9,855	Seattle, Wash.
905	169	358	597	876	1,183	1,673	2,309	3,405	5,221	13,200	Portland, Ore.
1,344	192	388	620	874	1,190	1,694	2,303	3,349	5,210	9,980	Sacramento, Calif.
1,192	183	368	614	873	1,195	1,691	2,344	3,459	5,449	9,700	San Diego, Calif.

TABLE C 8

Owner-occupied Dwellings, Average Value and Ratio of Average Value, January 1, 1934, to 1933 Family Income by 11 Income Groups, 52 Cities by Geographic Division

	All income groups	No income	$1-249	$250-499	$500-749	$750-999	$1,000-1,499	$1,500-1,999	$2,000-2,999	$3,000-4,499	$4,500-7,499	$7,500 and over
52 cities[1]	4,588	3,875	3,207	3,466	3,683	3,831	4,193	4,586	5,484	7,000	9,730	15,222
4 New England cities	6,495	5,673	4,909	5,440	5,199	5,498	5,908	6,247	7,175	8,492	11,616	15,959
Portland, Me.	6,095	5,135	4,152	4,792	5,005	4,938	5,244	5,815	6,571	8,193	8,834	13,662
Worcester, Mass.	6,946	7,351	5,639	6,342	5,999	6,174	5,965	6,435	7,045	8,174	10,613	15,189
Providence, R.I.*	6,223	5,230	4,805	5,153	4,844	5,290	5,807	6,094	7,153	8,336	11,960	16,023
Waterbury, Conn.	8,048	6,306	4,875	6,424	6,576	6,235	7,082	7,397	8,051	10,550	12,923	18,650
4 Mid. Atlantic cities	5,351	4,708	4,319	4,369	4,579	4,792	4,970	5,565	6,364	7,406	10,042	13,425
Binghamton, N.Y.	6,290	5,373	4,493	4,745	5,124	5,285	5,271	6,183	7,106	7,658	10,046	10,861
Syracuse, N.Y.	6,188	5,804	5,015	5,150	5,396	5,488	5,651	6,242	7,164	8,135	10,834	14,706
Trenton, N.J.	4,009	3,257	3,316	3,198	3,283	3,725	3,916	4,399	5,103	5,930	8,630	12,814
Erie, Pa.	4,726	3,914	4,062	4,015	4,190	4,400	4,714	5,239	5,841	7,558	10,168	13,426
6 E. N. Central cities	5,741	4,706	4,279	4,497	4,768	4,742	5,272	5,629	6,708	8,510	12,148	21,029
Cleveland, Ohio*	6,305	5,264	4,741	5,001	5,290	5,227	5,806	6,170	7,407	9,335	13,677	25,122
Indianapolis, Ind.	4,936	3,546	3,389	3,319	3,635	3,829	4,241	4,546	5,390	6,919	9,268	15,517
Peoria, Ill.	4,517	3,470	3,039	3,437	3,510	3,439	4,095	4,564	5,755	7,185	9,968	14,543
Lansing, Mich.	3,892	3,575	3,000	3,189	3,427	3,379	4,057	4,098	4,669	6,145	9,627	7,250
Kenosha, Wis.	5,226	5,034	4,379	5,086	5,097	4,943	5,003	5,568	5,886	9,084	11,417	
Racine, Wis.	5,297	4,540	4,639	4,963	5,261	4,982	5,309	5,846	6,582	7,702	9,150	10,717
10 W. N. Central cities	3,791	3,072	2,541	2,738	3,018	3,132	3,415	3,930	4,713	6,016	8,244	12,769
Minneapolis, Minn.	4,391	3,881	3,190	3,302	3,581	3,635	3,944	4,449	5,120	6,419	8,666	13,562
St. Paul, Minn.	3,832	3,151	2,478	2,903	3,042	3,312	3,485	4,131	4,674	5,720	7,447	11,718
Des Moines, Iowa	3,210	2,017	1,851	2,141	2,342	2,594	2,858	3,552	4,191	5,443	7,160	12,325
St. Joseph, Mo.	3,466	2,563	2,077	2,216	2,451	2,669	2,798	3,435	4,354	6,585	12,022	11,506
Springfield, Mo.	2,871	2,002	1,654	1,771	2,294	2,275	2,764	2,848	5,056	5,905	10,291	12,640
Fargo, N.D.	4,972	4,714	3,545	3,691	3,956	3,837	4,492	4,555	5,710	7,591	8,511	9,143
Sioux Falls, S.D.	4,239	2,873	3,119	3,149	3,379	3,282	3,741	4,272	5,158	7,025	9,381	9,838
Lincoln, Neb.	3,697	2,835	2,549	2,460	3,041	2,740	3,228	3,695	4,860	6,263	8,233	17,200
Topeka, Kan.	3,323	2,259	1,988	2,324	2,563	2,907	3,216	3,653	4,338	5,531	7,218	11,072
Wichita, Kan.	2,799	2,482	1,820	1,919	2,371	2,435	2,575	2,888	3,694	5,156	6,977	12,967
9 S. Atlantic cities	4,391	3,640	2,414	2,628	2,980	3,341	3,915	4,339	5,252	7,194	10,025	15,009
Hagerstown, Md.	4,938	2,975	3,518	3,476	4,028	4,230	4,450	5,780	6,786	7,960	10,812	16,875
Richmond, Va.	5,197	5,547	2,501	2,409	2,670	3,117	4,389	4,548	5,617	7,633	10,447	16,458
Wheeling, W.Va.*	3,919	3,120	2,740	3,072	3,282	3,448	3,960	4,606	5,291	7,588	10,587	16,446
Asheville, N.C.	3,870	2,948	2,263	2,267	2,793	3,008	3,427	3,792	5,880	6,379	11,067	16,214
Greensboro, N.C.	5,168	3,400	2,575	2,678	2,835	4,291	4,260	4,713	5,361	7,315	11,303	16,921
Charleston, S.C.	4,844	2,593	1,794	2,415	3,192	3,236	3,956	4,709	5,625	8,078	11,788	11,408
Columbia, S.C.	4,786	5,011	1,959	2,782	3,332	3,951	4,129	5,179	6,569	6,580	8,996	10,689
Atlanta, Ga.*	4,323	3,346	2,252	2,365	2,812	3,070	3,412	3,792	4,738	6,585	9,699	16,445
Jacksonville, Fla.	3,781	3,156	2,113	2,686	2,926	3,574	4,389	4,275	4,793	7,410	7,708	6,500
3 E. S. Central cities	3,255	2,556	1,855	2,191	2,472	3,099	3,299	3,502	4,287	5,884	9,070	11,228
Paducah, Ky.	2,295	1,486	1,214	1,475	1,862	2,037	2,412	2,772	4,045	4,176	5,167	14,833
Birmingham, Ala.*	3,200	2,594	1,849	2,198	2,435	3,055	3,277	3,423	4,286	6,077	9,147	10,583
Jackson, Miss.	4,469	3,156	2,437	2,739	3,265	4,321	4,208	4,706	4,493	5,837	11,738	13,125
6 W. S. Central cities	3,797	3,336	2,425	2,607	2,863	2,993	3,332	3,621	4,609	5,732	8,174	11,339
Little Rock, Ark.	3,280	2,435	1,861	2,008	2,394	2,534	3,012	3,335	3,992	5,337	8,669	9,740
Baton Rouge, La.	3,940	2,404	2,372	2,654	2,588	3,289	3,698	4,512	6,217	7,075	9,213	
Oklahoma City, Okla.	4,125	4,162	2,531	2,903	3,187	3,452	3,568	3,641	4,991	6,085	9,146	12,641
Austin, Tex.	3,901	3,342	1,937	2,293	2,503	2,722	3,407	4,049	5,320	6,687	9,042	13,500
Dallas, Tex.	3,836	3,213	2,859	2,852	3,111	3,090	3,374	3,642	4,292	5,547	7,070	10,655
Wichita Falls, Tex.	2,789	2,840	1,083	1,343	1,492	1,438	2,229	2,592	3,869	4,069	9,297	10,867
6 Mountain cities	3,161	2,365	1,934	2,378	2,665	2,695	2,901	3,210	4,042	5,478	7,772	14,031
Butte, Mont.	2,680	2,076	1,623	2,173	2,249	2,321	2,790	3,016	3,834	5,180	5,840	8,200
Boise, Idaho	3,454	3,114	2,079	2,523	2,945	2,976	2,982	3,873	4,485	6,137	8,588	11,400
Casper, Wyo.	2,891	1,448	1,641	2,139	2,604	1,938	2,462	2,768	3,904	6,722	7,286	10,875
Pueblo, Colo.	1,906	1,563	1,132	1,446	1,909	1,950	2,110	2,353	2,859	3,806	6,300	
Phoenix, Ariz.	4,135	3,912	2,539	3,303	3,152	3,694	3,570	3,621	4,079	6,096	10,223	14,154
Salt Lake City, Utah	3,462	2,316	2,154	2,531	2,873	2,846	3,081	3,396	4,441	5,717	8,079	16,306
4 Pacific cities	3,454	3,175	2,356	2,641	2,883	2,982	3,194	3,548	4,336	5,920	7,776	13,285
Seattle, Wash.*	3,316	3,009	2,133	2,497	2,703	2,919	3,074	3,377	4,336	6,063	8,089	14,500
Portland, Ore.	3,202	2,930	2,187	2,531	2,768	2,755	2,932	3,336	4,072	5,815	7,258	13,024
Sacramento, Calif.	4,234	4,075	3,397	3,102	3,351	3,619	3,953	4,123	4,640	5,401	6,900	11,245
San Diego, Calif.*	3,889	3,615	2,738	2,984	3,319	3,252	3,613	4,082	4,665	5,981	8,305	11,674

Source: *Financial Survey of Urban Housing*. Based on number reporting as shown in Table C 5. Average not shown for fewer than 3 reports.
*Metropolitan district.
[1]Geographic division and 52-city averages weighted by number of owner-occupied units in each city (RPI).

TABLE C 8

Owner-occupied Dwellings, Average Value and Ratio of Average Value, January 1,1934, to 1933 Family Income by 11 Income Groups, 52 Cities by Geographic Division

←——————————— R A T I O   O F   A V E R A G E   V A L U E   T O   I N C O M E ———————————→

All income groups	$1-249	$250-499	$500-749	$750-999	$1,000-1,499	$1,500-1,999	$2,000-2,999	$3,000-4,499	$4,500-7,499	$7,500 and over	
3.1	18.4	9.2	6.0	4.3	3.5	2.7	2.3	2.0	1.8	1.3	52 cities[1]
3.8	28.7	14.2	8.6	6.3	4.9	3.7	3.1	2.4	2.1	1.2	4 New England cities
3.3	25.3	12.2	8.4	5.7	4.4	3.4	2.8	2.3	1.7	1.2	Portland, Me.
3.6	30.3	16.1	9.8	7.1	4.8	3.8	3.0	2.3	1.9	1.3	Worcester, Mass.
3.9	28.3	13.6	8.0	6.1	4.9	3.6	3.1	2.4	2.2	1.2	Providence, R.I.*
3.9	29.5	16.7	10.7	7.1	5.9	4.2	3.4	3.0	2.3	1.5	Waterbury, Conn.
3.8	26.3	11.7	7.6	5.2	4.2	3.2	2.8	2.1	1.9	1.1	4 Mid. Atlantic cities
3.1	33.0	12.8	8.7	5.8	4.3	3.7	3.1	2.2	1.8	1.0	Binghamton, N.Y.
4.1	29.3	13.8	9.0	5.8	4.8	3.7	3.1	2.3	2.1	1.0	Syracuse, N.Y.
3.4	20.2	8.6	5.2	4.0	3.4	2.6	2.2	1.8	1.7	1.5	Trenton, N.J.
4.4	24.0	10.6	7.1	5.1	4.0	2.7	2.5	2.2	1.8	1.3	Erie, Pa.
4.0	24.9	12.0	7.8	5.4	4.4	3.3	2.9	2.5	2.2	1.6	6 E. N. Central cities
4.5	28.0	13.4	8.8	6.0	4.9	3.6	3.2	2.7	2.5	1.8	Cleveland, Ohio*
2.7	18.2	8.8	5.8	4.0	3.4	2.5	2.2	2.0	1.7	1.4	Indianapolis, Ind.
3.1	18.6	9.3	5.8	4.0	3.5	2.7	2.5	2.1	1.8	1.2	Peoria, Ill.
3.2	17.8	8.5	5.7	3.7	3.5	2.4	2.0	1.7	1.9	0.5	Lansing, Mich.
5.4	24.9	13.3	8.3	5.7	4.2	3.3	2.5	2.6	2.1		Kenosha, Wis.
5.8	29.4	13.3	8.7	5.7	4.4	3.5	2.8	2.4	1.2	1.4	Racine, Wis.
2.6	13.7	7.3	4.9	3.6	2.9	2.3	2.0	1.7	1.5	1.0	10 W. N. Central cities
2.9	16.5	8.6	5.8	4.2	3.3	2.6	2.2	1.8	1.6	1.2	Minneapolis, Minn.
2.6	13.9	8.0	5.0	3.8	2.9	2.4	2.0	1.6	1.4	0.9	St. Paul, Minn.
2.2	9.7	5.8	3.9	3.0	2.4	2.1	1.8	1.6	1.4	0.9	Des Moines, Iowa
2.4	11.7	6.2	4.0	3.1	2.3	1.9	1.8	1.9	2.2	1.1	St. Joseph, Mo.
2.5	10.7	5.0	3.7	2.6	2.3	1.7	2.2	1.8	1.9	.9	Springfield, Mo.
3.0	22.9	7.7	5.6	4.4	3.7	2.7	2.4	2.2	1.7	0.9	Fargo, N.D.
2.7	13.1	8.6	5.6	3.7	3.1	2.5	2.2	2.1	1.7	0.8	Sioux Falls, S.D.
2.6	11.6	6.3	5.1	3.1	2.7	2.2	2.1	1.8	1.5	1.5	Lincoln, Neb.
2.4	12.3	6.1	4.1	3.3	2.7	2.1	1.9	1.6	1.4	0.9	Topeka, Kan.
2.2	11.2	5.1	3.8	2.8	2.1	1.7	1.6	1.5	1.3	1.1	Wichita, Kan.
2.7	14.0	7.0	4.6	3.8	3.2	2.5	2.2	2.1	1.8	1.3	9 S. Atlantic cities
3.8	20.7	7.9	6.5	4.8	3.7	3.4	3.0	2.3	2.0	1.8	Hagerstown, Md.
2.6	14.1	7.9	4.2	3.6	3.7	2.6	2.4	2.2	1.9	1.5	Richmond, Va.
3.7	18.4	8.6	5.5	4.0	3.3	2.7	2.3	2.2	2.0	1.3	Wheeling, W.Va.*
2.8	14.2	6.1	4.6	3.4	2.9	2.3	2.6	1.8	2.0	1.3	Asheville, N.C.
2.6	15.8	7.3	4.8	5.0	3.7	2.8	2.3	2.1	2.2	1.4	Greensboro, N.C.
2.5	8.0	5.4	4.6	3.8	2.8	2.8	2.4	2.3	2.2	0.9	Charleston, S.C.
2.8	11.9	7.5	5.0	4.5	3.4	2.9	2.8	1.9	1.6	.9	Columbia, S.C.
2.6	11.7	5.7	4.0	3.4	2.8	2.2	2.0	1.9	1.7	1.4	Atlanta, Ga.*
3.1	13.8	7.2	5.0	4.1	3.7	2.5	2.1	2.1	1.3	0.8	Jacksonville, Fla.
2.6	11.0	5.7	4.0	3.5	2.7	2.1	1.8	1.7	1.7	1.0	3 E. S. Central cities
2.0	8.4	4.2	3.1	2.3	1.9	1.7	1.7	1.2	1.0	0.9	Paducah, Ky.
2.6	10.9	5.6	3.9	3.4	2.7	2.0	1.9	1.8	1.7	0.9	Birmingham, Ala.*
2.6	14.3	7.5	5.5	5.1	3.4	2.7	1.9	1.7	2.3	1.3	Jackson, Miss.
2.3	13.5	6.6	4.7	3.3	2.8	2.1	2.0	1.7	1.5	0.9	6 W. S. Central cities
2.2	10.9	4.7	4.0	2.9	2.5	2.0	1.7	1.6	1.6	1.0	Little Rock, Ark.
2.5	14.1	7.6	4.2	3.5	3.0	2.7	2.5	1.8	1.3	0.8	Baton Rouge, La.
2.6	12.8	8.0	5.3	3.8	3.0	2.1	2.1	1.8	1.7	1.0	Oklahoma City, Okla.
2.5	10.8	6.0	4.1	3.1	2.9	2.4	2.2	1.9	1.6	1.2	Austin, Tex.
2.2	16.2	6.7	5.1	3.3	2.8	2.1	1.8	1.6	1.3	0.8	Dallas, Tex.
1.7	7.2	3.8	2.6	1.7	1.9	1.5	1.7	1.0	1.6	1.1	Wichita Falls, Tex.
2.4	12.0	6.5	4.4	3.1	2.4	1.9	1.7	1.6	1.4	1.3	6 Mountain cities
2.3	10.5	5.9	3.7	2.6	2.4	1.8	1.6	1.5	1.1	0.6	Butte, Mont.
2.7	11.2	6.8	5.0	3.4	2.6	2.3	1.9	1.8	1.5	1.0	Boise, Idaho
2.0	7.7	5.8	4.4	2.2	2.1	1.6	1.7	1.9	1.4	0.8	Casper, Wyo.
3.0	7.1	3.9	3.2	2.2	1.8	1.4	1.2	1.1	1.1		Pueblo, Colo.
2.6	15.7	8.9	5.2	4.3	2.9	2.1	1.8	1.8	1.7	1.3	Phoenix, Ariz.
2.4	14.1	7.0	4.7	3.3	2.5	2.0	1.9	1.6	1.5	1.6	Salt Lake City, Utah
2.6	13.4	7.0	4.7	3.4	2.7	2.1	1.9	1.7	1.5	1.2	4 Pacific cities
2.6	12.1	6.7	4.4	3.3	2.5	2.0	1.9	1.7	1.5	1.4	Seattle, Wash.*
2.6	13.1	6.6	4.7	3.1	2.5	2.0	1.8	1.7	1.4	1.2	Portland, Ore.
2.5	18.7	8.0	5.3	3.9	3.3	2.4	2.0	1.6	1.3	.8	Sacramento, Calif.
2.8	14.4	7.8	5.4	3.7	3.0	2.4	2.0	1.7	1.6	1.2	San Diego, Calif.*

TABLE C 9

Tenant Families, Average Annual Rent per Dwelling Unit and as a Percentage of Average Annual Family Income by 11 Income Groups, 52 Cities by Geographic Division, 1933

	AVERAGE ANNUAL RENT (dollars)										
	All income groups	No income	$1–249	$250–499	$500–749	$750–999	$1,000–1,499	$1,500–1,999	$2,000–2,999	$3,000–4,499	$4,500–7,499	$7,500 and over
52 cities[1]	262	194	156	181	208	235	274	331	407	514	660	941
4 New England cities	294	230	133	212	233	266	293	360	424	529	720	829
Portland, Me.	328	256	228	226	262	287	320	376	440	494	548	679
Worcester, Mass.	304	222	207	226	249	268	296	340	419	508	745	878
Providence, R.I.	287	226	88	205	225	267	289	370	427	544	733	833
Waterbury, Conn.	293	254	191	217	232	239	290	327	404	503	726	
4 Mid. Atlantic cities	289	227	208	218	231	266	299	357	419	528	628	1,380
Binghamton, N.Y.	329	245	208	245	251	273	298	366	414	515	715	
Syracuse, N.Y.	295	241	209	216	224	276	307	369	433	532	554	
Trenton, N.J.	273	204	215	212	233	261	302	346	401	552	777	
Erie, Pa.	264	207	198	206	230	246	283	335	409	505	572	1,380
6 E. N. Central cities	298	210	193	204	234	254	295	351	438	570	745	1,188
Cleveland, Ohio	310	236	209	219	245	266	309	365	453	591	773	1,218
Indianapolis, Ind.	298	159	164	181	223	242	281	344	433	560	720	1,118
Peoria, Ill.	282	229	180	197	228	235	278	335	428	562	724	1,140
Lansing, Mich.	203	130	136	139	163	187	231	257	321	475	610	
Kenosha, Wis.	226	179	182	193	212	212	251	291	354	394	560	
Racine, Wis.	220	161	164	179	195	222	241	289	361	454	674	
10 W. N. Central cities	281	199	177	185	218	242	287	348	424	530	640	908
Minneapolis, Minn.	317	225	205	208	243	268	319	378	455	573	695	975
St. Paul, Minn.	291	190	189	209	241	256	301	373	442	556	612	
Des Moines, Iowa	284	183	178	180	210	237	281	347	434	535	651	
St. Joseph, Mo.	234	136	136	147	176	179	212	264	353	401	658	869
Springfield, Mo.	182	120	104	127	146	203	238	295	368	451	499	
Fargo, N.D.	336	248	233	200	250	275	338	394	466	503	612	
Sioux Falls, S.D.	299	224	198	218	235	245	297	358	421	511	522	380
Lincoln, Neb.	268	189	156	173	206	241	272	329	411	507	568	780
Topeka, Kan.	242	185	127	144	182	210	269	331	398	491	631	
Wichita, Kan.	200	199	124	123	159	179	211	266	334	460	613	
9 S. Atlantic cities	218	157	115	141	169	206	258	323	409	507	648	920
Hagerstown, Md.	232	173	148	178	195	218	257	327	377	407	609	811
Richmond, Va.	285	188	129	147	173	230	302	369	473	582	733	
Wheeling, W.Va.	226	164	147	168	186	221	248	303	381	471	723	
Asheville, N.C.	169	118	88	120	147	185	212	255	326	419	570	1,368
Greensboro, N.C.	198	170	116	132	137	128	162	241	371	459	584	1,333
Charleston, S.C.	176	109	77	120	172	229	274	327	392	501	648	832
Columbia, S.C.	185	128	97	128	139	172	214	228	343	398	489	
Atlanta, Ga.	222	153	110	135	168	195	262	336	424	526	662	
Jacksonville, Fla.	172	161	107	144	172	204	247	292	379	477	516	
3 E. S. Central cities	158	112	86	109	140	171	205	264	338	422	606	800
Paducah, Ky.	146	93	91	109	138	160	198	248	323	415	615	
Birmingham, Ala.	151	111	82	102	134	162	196	258	329	419	453	800
Jackson, Miss.	228	136	121	167	191	258	290	326	427	530		
6 W. S. Central cities	248	176	144	170	196	221	257	306	374	465	555	768
Little Rock, Ark.	191	102	108	133	164	184	238	271	315	433	452	773
Baton Rouge, La.	227	148	121	147	199	217	256	306	407	464	463	
Oklahoma City, Okla.	251	209	145	178	210	232	256	307	371	455	557	840
Austin, Tex.	257	162	113	136	190	236	285	322	397	465	600	863
Dallas, Tex.	276	188	170	194	209	236	272	306	374	465	611	708
Wichita Falls, Tex.	154	130	89	103	118	132	163	202	263	312	375	
6 Mountain cities	243	181	148	169	196	219	255	310	385	489	613	799
Butte, Mont.	247	191	174	189	191	227	271	314	374	504	579	660
Boise, Idaho	287	262	158	187	224	250	290	344	408	460	615	
Casper, Wyo.	220	135	117	121	175	223	221	269	354	447	576	
Pueblo, Colo.	186	130	121	133	169	189	221	281	336	416		
Phoenix, Ariz.	243	182	132	165	205	247	298	374	456	617		874
Salt Lake City, Utah	259	191	161	182	201	227	266	328	414	537	630	809
4 Pacific cities	250	205	160	177	207	228	262	304	368	466	606	824
Seattle, Wash.	255	219	159	176	214	237	266	309	374	483	579	800
Portland, Ore.	204	167	136	151	173	188	236	270	336	402	589	927
Sacramento, Calif.	319	228	198	218	247	274	302	355	418	506	838	1,086
San Diego, Calif.	275	221	177	197	221	245	273	320	377	504	668	618

Source: *Financial Survey of Urban Housing.* Based on number of families reporting as shown in Table C 6. Percentages derived by dividing average annual rent by average annual income as shown in this table and in Table C 7. Geographic division and 52-city percentages thus automatically weighted. Average or percentage not shown for fewer than 3 reports.

[1] Geographic division and 52-city averages weighted by number of rental units in each city (RPI).

TABLE C 9

Tenant Families, Average Annual Rent per Dwelling Unit and as a Percentage of Average Annual Family Income by 11 Income Groups, 52 Cities by Geographic Division, 1933

| | | | | | PERCENTAGE RENT IS OF INCOME | | | | | | |
All income groups	$1-249	$250-499	$500-749	$750-999	$1,000-1,499	$1,500-1,999	$2,000-2,999	$3,000-4,499	$4,500-7,499	$7,500 and over	
24.2	89.1	47.1	34.0	26.9	23.0	19.7	17.5	13.9	12.7	11.6	52 cities[1]
25.2	78.2	51.5	38.6	30.9	24.8	21.5	18.3	15.6	13.6	9.4	4 New England cities
25.4	136.5	62.1	43.8	33.4	27.1	22.4	18.9	14.5	10.5	6.8	Portland, Me.
24.9	120.3	59.6	41.2	30.9	24.8	20.2	18.0	15.6	13.0	8.9	Worcester, Mass.
25.5	51.5	47.1	37.3	31.0	24.5	22.1	18.4	15.8	14.3	10.0	Providence, R.I.
24.0	117.9	59.1	37.5	28.2	24.7	19.6	17.6	14.6	13.3		Waterbury, Conn.
27.1	130.0	55.5	39.5	30.8	24.8	20.9	18.2	15.4	11.9	11.3	4 Mid. Atlantic cities
23.4	120.2	54.2	43.6	31.5	22.9	21.7	18.1	16.0	12.8		Binghamton, N.Y.
27.3	133.1	54.3	38.3	31.7	25.9	21.6	18.6	15.2	10.5		Syracuse, N.Y.
30.3	133.5	57.6	40.0	30.4	25.6	20.2	17.8	16.0	15.5		Trenton, N.J.
28.6	126.1	57.2	38.8	28.6	23.7	19.3	17.8	14.8	10.9	11.3	Erie, Pa.
25.9	107.2	53.8	36.7	28.7	24.9	20.9	19.0	16.7	14.3	10.9	6 E. N. Central cities
27.2	112.4	58.9	38.2	30.0	26.0	21.6	19.7	17.3	15.0	10.9	Cleveland, Ohio
23.1	95.9	44.6	34.6	27.5	24.0	20.7	18.6	16.4	13.8	10.8	Indianapolis, Ind.
24.9	109.8	53.4	37.5	27.2	23.6	17.3	18.4	16.8	13.7	13.2	Peoria, Ill.
21.0	84.0	37.3	27.2	22.0	19.8	15.4	13.9	13.7	12.0		Lansing, Mich.
28.1	115.2	56.1	34.8	24.4	21.6	17.4	15.9	12.1	9.3		Kenosha, Wis.
26.3	91.1	50.1	32.4	24.2	20.0	17.2	15.5	13.3	13.3		Racine, Wis.
24.6	102.3	47.1	35.8	27.6	24.0	20.7	18.4	15.5	12.3	9.2	10 W. N. Central cities
26.0	117.1	47.7	40.0	30.4	26.8	22.4	19.7	16.7	13.5	9.8	Minneapolis, Minn.
27.6	118.9	54.1	39.4	29.3	25.3	22.4	19.3	16.4	12.5		St. Paul, Minn.
24.2	97.3	48.5	35.0	27.4	23.8	20.5	18.9	15.9	12.6		Des Moines, Iowa
19.9	71.6	41.9	28.9	22.3	19.5	16.9	16.1	12.6	11.5	8.5	St. Joseph, Mo.
20.2	61.9	35.7	24.4	20.6	18.1	15.9	15.1	12.0	9.2		Springfield, Mo.
25.8	146.5	54.3	39.4	31.3	28.5	23.3	19.7	15.4	11.3		Fargo, N.D.
24.3	123.0	55.6	38.1	28.0	25.1	21.2	17.9	14.9	10.1	4.0	Sioux Falls, S.D.
23.2	91.2	48.5	33.5	27.7	22.9	19.7	18.1	14.5	11.6	8.7	Lincoln, Neb.
22.6	79.4	40.8	29.5	24.3	22.5	19.6	17.3	14.4	10.9		Topeka, Kan.
19.3	68.5	34.7	26.2	20.4	17.0	15.8	14.3	13.3	11.4		Wichita, Kan.
23.0	62.2	38.0	28.5	23.9	21.7	19.3	17.7	15.0	12.3	7.2	9 S. Atlantic cities
25.2	105.7	49.6	32.3	25.4	22.1	19.7	16.1	11.8	11.3		Hagerstown, Md.
22.2	53.3	33.4	29.2	26.3	25.4	21.9	20.4	17.2	13.9	8.3	Richmond, Va.
24.4	81.2	45.9	31.5	25.5	21.1	18.4	16.6	14.0	12.9		Wheeling, W.Va.
20.6	50.9	33.7	24.1	21.6	18.2	15.4	14.9	12.5	11.4		Asheville, N.C.
16.3	66.3	37.6	22.5	14.6	13.6	14.3	15.9	13.6	11.2	9.7	Greensboro, N.C.
24.0	42.3	34.8	29.8	26.8	23.8	19.8	17.0	14.8	13.1	4.8	Charleston, S.C.
22.8	61.8	36.3	23.7	23.0	19.0	20.5	16.9	14.4	11.4		Columbia, S.C.
22.7	63.2	37.7	28.2	23.0	21.9	20.0	18.2	15.4	12.1	7.6	Atlanta, Ga.
27.5	60.1	40.4	29.3	23.8	20.6	17.2	16.5	14.2	10.7		Jacksonville, Fla.
20.4	52.4	30.4	23.0	19.7	17.1	15.7	13.9	12.5	12.5	8.5	3 E. S. Central cities
21.5	65.2	30.0	22.2	18.1	16.8	15.0	13.7	12.7			Paducah, Ky.
19.6	49.7	28.4	22.0	18.7	16.3	15.4	13.5	12.4	11.9	8.5	Birmingham, Ala.
25.4	70.8	48.0	31.3	29.7	24.4	19.3	17.9	13.3	10.4		Jackson, Miss.
21.8	87.3	46.4	31.9	25.7	21.6	18.3	16.1	13.6	10.3	7.2	6 W. S. Central cities
20.3	66.7	35.8	26.6	21.5	18.7	16.3	13.9	12.3	8.6	8.1	Little Rock, Ark.
22.5	73.8	39.0	32.8	25.4	21.1	18.6	17.2	13.5	8.3		Baton Rouge, La.
22.9	89.5	50.7	35.1	26.8	21.8	18.4	15.7	13.6	10.1	9.9	Oklahoma City, Okla.
22.0	64.6	36.9	31.9	27.3	24.1	20.8	17.4	14.7	11.8	9.4	Austin, Tex.
22.4	101.8	52.0	33.1	27.5	23.1	19.2	17.2	13.6	11.5	7.7	Dallas, Tex.
14.7	56.3	28.9	19.9	15.3	14.0	12.1	11.4	9.0	7.1		Wichita Falls, Tex.
23.2	81.8	44.7	32.6	25.3	21.4	18.4	16.5	14.3	11.8	8.0	6 Mountain cities
25.1	120.8	48.2	31.5	26.4	22.5	18.6	16.1	14.9	11.3	4.7	Butte, Mont.
24.0	85.9	50.8	35.1	28.7	24.5	20.6	18.1	13.8	11.1		Boise, Idaho
20.0	75.0	32.8	30.5	26.0	18.8	15.9	15.8	12.9	10.5		Casper, Wyo.
23.8	74.2	37.9	28.3	21.8	19.0	16.9	14.4	12.2			Pueblo, Colo.
21.8	87.4	46.2	34.3	23.8	20.3	17.8	16.1	13.4	11.6	10.3	Phoenix, Ariz.
23.7	73.9	46.1	33.2	26.1	22.2	19.3	17.5	15.6	12.3	8.5	Salt Lake City, Utah
22.8	89.9	44.8	33.9	26.0	21.7	18.1	15.9	13.6	11.4	7.6	4 Pacific cities
22.7	88.9	40.2	34.7	26.8	21.4	18.4	16.1	14.1	10.8	8.1	Seattle, Wash.
22.5	80.5	42.2	29.0	21.5	20.0	16.1	14.6	11.8	11.3	7.0	Portland, Ore.
23.7	103.1	56.2	39.8	31.4	25.4	21.0	18.2	15.1	12.2	10.9	Sacramento, Calif.
23.1	96.7	53.5	36.0	28.1	22.8	18.9	16.1	14.6	12.3	6.4	San Diego, Calif.

TABLE C 10

Tenant Families, Average Annual Rent per Room (dollars) by 11 Income Groups, 52 Cities by Geographic Division, 1933

	All income groups	No income	$1-249	$250-499	$500-749	$750-999	$1,000-1,499	$1,500-1,999	$2,000-2,999	$3,000-4,499	$4,500-7,499	$7,500 and over
52 cities[1]	57	47	38	43	47	52	58	66	78	91	107	143
4 New England cities	57	49	29	45	48	54	57	66	75	90	110	120
Portland, Me.	63	52	48	47	55	59	62	68	79	84	74	93
Worcester, Mass.	58	47	43	47	50	52	57	62	72	88	116	139
Providence, R.I.*	56	48	20	44	47	54	56	67	76	91	113	117
Waterbury, Conn.	61	54	48	48	49	52	60	65	76	90	107	
4 Mid. Atlantic cities	53	44	39	43	44	49	54	62	69	83	90	189
Binghamton. N.Y.	61	52	39	50	51	52	56	68	71	77	99	
Syracuse, N.Y.	55	46	39	44	43	51	57	65	70	84	81	
Trenton, N.J.	48	37	41	39	42	47	52	57	64	90	120	
Erie, Pa.	47	41	38	38	41	44	49	57	68	77	74	189
6 E. N. Central cities	60	46	42	44	49	52	60	69	82	99	122	159
Cleveland, Ohio*	62	51	46	47	51	54	62	70	84	100	123	152
Indianapolis, Ind.	62	36	36	40	46	50	59	72	85	106	131	183
Peoria, Ill.	61	53	44	48	52	51	58	70	82	104	119	123
Lansing, Mich.	36	24	25	26	29	35	40	44	54	75	84	
Kenosha, Wis.	45	38	39	40	43	42	50	55	60	62	89	
Racine, Wis.	43	32	32	37	38	44	45	55	64	77	112	
10 W. N. Central cities	61	49	44	45	52	55	62	70	82	93	104	148
Minneapolis, Minn.	70	54	50	52	58	64	71	80	91	104	112	152
St. Paul, Minn.	63	49	45	48	56	56	65	73	85	93	100	
Des Moines, Iowa	60	44	40	39	49	52	59	71	83	96	112	
St. Joseph, Mo.	51	36	37	36	41	46	50	57	75	87	103	150
Springfield, Mo.	40	29	27	30	34	39	44	49	67	76	77	
Fargo, N.D.	75	75	67	61	68	62	73	77	85	82	82	
Sioux Falls, S.D.	65	51	55	53	59	58	63	70	78	87	92	103
Lincoln, Neb.	54	41	40	38	45	51	53	62	70	76	93	137
Topeka, Kan.	53	45	33	33	41	46	57	66	80	89	109	
Wichita, Kan.	44	50	32	31	39	40	46	52	63	79	93	
9 S. Atlantic cities	52	45	36	38	42	48	56	66	78	89	103	140
Hagerstown, Md.	43	35	30	33	37	42	45	57	62	68	100	
Richmond, Va.	65	51	38	39	42	51	66	79	93	104	116	119
Wheeling, W. Va.*	51	46	39	41	45	54	54	59	67	78	110	
Asheville, N.C.	32	24	22	26	28	32	37	41	48	59	63	
Greensboro, N.C.	40	37	31	30	30	28	32	45	67	78	78	122
Charleston, S.C.	53	44	41	44	45	53	56	64	71	86	97	133
Columbia, S.C.	49	43	35	38	39	54	50	64	70	75	92	
Atlanta, Ga.*	58	49	39	41	45	50	61	75	87	101	112	154
Jacksonville, Fla.	39	42	27	33	38	42	50	54	70	75	91	
3 E. S. Central cities	38	32	27	29	32	36	42	52	65	76	99	160
Paducah, Ky.	39	30	29	30	35	37	45	55	63	80		
Birmingham, Ala.*	36	32	26	27	30	34	40	50	63	75	101	160
Jackson, Miss.	54	38	36	44	48	55	64	68	82	84	82	
6 W. S. Central cities	57	47	41	45	49	53	57	63	73	82	95	116
Little Rock, Ark.	42	29	30	33	39	40	48	51	58	73	67	110
Baton Rouge, La.	54	44	39	42	51	54	53	60	73	80	77	
Oklahoma City, Okla.	60	58	41	48	54	58	60	67	74	88	103	124
Austin, Tex.	58	43	34	37	46	54	63	69	80	88	95	108
Dallas, Tex.	63	48	49	52	52	56	60	67	78	85	104	114
Wichita Falls, Tex.	33	30	23	25	27	29	35	40	51	55	68	
6 Mountain cities	60	51	40	45	50	53	62	73	86	98	114	155
Butte, Mont.	67	56	50	52	55	60	71	83	91	115	92	125
Boise, Idaho	65	75	43	46	51	54	64	78	89	88	104	
Casper, Wyo.	59	48	38	40	55	57	57	71	75	86	111	
Pueblo, Colo.	43	32	31	32	39	41	48	62	70	82		
Phoenix, Ariz.	59	51	38	46	50	53	59	65	83	93	129	114
Salt Lake City, Utah	63	52	41	47	50	55	65	76	92	105	115	184
4 Pacific cities	60	52	41	46	53	56	61	68	78	90	102	139
Seattle, Wash.*	65	56	43	49	58	62	66	74	87	99	107	136
Portland, Ore.	45	41	31	36	40	42	50	56	65	69	85	175
Sacramento, Calif.	69	56	50	54	59	60	67	76	82	92	106	102
San Diego, Calif.*	65	58	45	52	58	63	65	70	75	99	113	114

Source: *Financial Survey of Urban Housing.* Based on number of reports and average annual rent by income groups as shown in Tables C 8 and 9. Reports on number of rooms per dwelling unit slightly fewer than the number reporting annual rent. The average annual rent per room shown in this table computed for each income group by dividing average annual rent derived from the larger sample by average number of rooms derived from the smaller sample. Average not shown for fewer than 3 reports.

*Metropolitan district.

[1]Geographic division and 52-city averages weighted by number of rental units in each city (RPI).

TABLE C II

Tenant Families, Number reporting, and Percentage of Rent Delinquent by 11 Income Groups, 52 Cities by Geographic Division, 1933

	NUMBER REPORTING	All income groups	No income	$1-249	$250-499	$500-749	$750-999	$1,000-1,499	$1,500-1,999	$2,000-2,999	$3,000-4,499	$4,500-7,499	$7,500 and over
52 cities[1]	157,630	24.8	48.4	52.2	41.3	30.2	21.5	13.0	7.4	5.1	3.3	4.6	6.0
4 New England cities	12,593	24.4	45.4	54.9	46.0	36.2	25.4	14.7	7.1	4.5	4.3	3.0	5.3
Portland, Me.	2,754	21.0	40.2	56.0	41.4	34.1	23.7	14.2	8.8	7.3	5.0	9.7	
Worcester, Mass.	2,815	24.3	48.8	55.1	38.5	34.6	30.4	17.2	9.4	5.4	3.2	5.3	
Providence, R.I.	5,891	24.6	43.6	55.2	48.0	36.6	23.3	13.3	6.1	4.0	4.2	1.4	5.3
Waterbury, Conn.	1,133	26.1	54.2	52.0	51.5	38.8	30.3	19.7	8.0	3.2	6.3		
4 Mid. Atlantic cities	7,307	25.5	39.1	50.2	42.0	30.6	26.9	16.0	8.5	5.4		6.1	
Binghamton, N.Y.	774	15.1	20.0	46.2	38.5	26.3	21.6	13.8	5.8	2.9		8.7	
Syracuse, N.Y.	1,525	16.7	17.9	33.7	30.1	21.0	23.4	10.9	5.1	5.3		11.1	
Trenton, N.J.	2,080	34.2	59.9	62.6	51.9	38.8	25.2	20.0	10.8	6.4	2.6		
Erie, Pa.	2,928	43.4	77.8	75.6	59.9	45.9	39.3	24.4	15.3	6.6	9.3	3.8	
6 E. N. Central cities	36,848	28.0	55.1	56.4	48.5	36.2	26.2	16.4	9.1	6.2	4.0	5.1	4.5
Cleveland, Ohio	27,462	29.7	60.1	58.3	51.7	36.2	27.2	16.7	10.1	7.0	4.6	5.0	3.5
Indianapolis, Ind.	3,183	24.9	53.0	58.2	44.9	37.1	24.2	15.6	7.3	4.3	1.7	1.4	7.1
Peoria, Ill.	2,330	22.9	41.4	54.7	40.3	33.5	21.2	14.6	4.9	5.1	5.6		
Lansing, Mich.	977	23.0	33.0	33.8	36.8	32.0	21.9	15.4	9.4	1.6	3.8		
Kenosha, Wis.	1,002	32.7	29.7	37.0	48.8	40.5	39.8	22.1	10.3	8.9		33.3	
Racine, Wis.	1,894	27.5	31.1	44.3	36.8	34.6	25.5	16.3	7.1	9.2	7.4	18.2	
10 W. N. Central cities	24,890	19.5	43.6	48.5	36.2	26.7	17.8	10.0	6.2	4.0	3.7	3.5	10.0
Minneapolis, Minn.	9,282	19.6	53.6	50.5	37.3	28.4	17.8	10.6	6.7	6.3	3.9	2.3	10.0
St. Paul, Minn.	1,830	18.1	25.8	49.7	30.6	24.4	19.8	7.1	6.1	2.6	3.4		
Des Moines, Iowa	3,117	21.5	44.8	53.7	41.0	30.8	18.5	14.3	6.9	2.5	4.9		
St. Joseph, Mo.	1,282	18.9	46.9	46.1	38.1	28.8	18.1	5.8	5.1	0.9		3.3	
Springfield, Mo.	1,195	24.5	49.1	55.7	38.7	20.2	13.6	11.6	5.6			9.1	
Fargo, N.D.	909	12.9	14.3	29.5	21.4	22.1	9.7	14.9	6.2	2.7		8.2	
Sioux Falls, S.D.	1,525	15.3	33.3	35.8	41.8	21.0	11.5	10.1	7.0	4.4			
Lincoln, Neb.	1,295	21.4	58.1	49.6	38.0	32.0	17.4	11.1	4.6	4.6	2.0		
Topeka, Kan.	2,078	18.8	39.1	39.4	34.9	26.2	16.4	7.9	5.8	1.1	1.7		
Wichita, Kan.	2,377	19.9	36.2	42.5	36.1	20.8	19.2	9.5	6.1	3.0	3.8		
9 S. Atlantic cities	26,687	30.5	54.1	56.6	42.7	32.5	22.8	13.9	7.9	6.8	3.9	3.9	5.0
Hagerstown, Md.	1,275	29.1	54.0	66.0	49.7	31.9	20.1	9.9	7.4	6.7		14.3	5.0
Richmond, Va.	4,171	29.9	56.8	65.6	54.5	39.4	28.7	15.7	9.3	10.1	5.9	8.5	5.0
Wheeling, W.Va.	2,217	38.2	50.6	67.1	54.1	48.1	36.5	23.3	14.6	8.8	6.9		
Asheville, N.C.	1,644	16.4	31.3	33.2	20.6	13.0	16.2	6.3	4.3	3.6	4.2		
Greensboro, N.C.	1,221	13.2	40.0	38.5	26.5	14.7	8.5	7.1	3.8	6.6	8.3		
Charleston, S.C.	2,534	38.2	73.2	60.1	44.0	32.5	22.8	15.4	2.6	4.3	4.0		
Columbia, S.C.	1,583	32.0	60.0	47.5	42.7	31.3	19.6	12.8	8.6	4.8	3.6		
Atlanta, Ga.	9,515	29.6	56.0	56.1	40.5	32.2	20.0	12.8	7.3	5.1	1.6	1.0	
Jacksonville, Fla.	2,527	32.1	49.3	50.5	34.5	23.7	18.5	10.7	6.4	8.7	3.1		
3 E. S. Central cities	9,194	34.5	63.7	57.0	38.6	28.5	21.7	14.0	9.7	5.5	2.3	20.0	
Paducah, Ky.	1,313	39.7	70.0	60.9	46.0	31.6	23.6	14.5	8.6	9.2	5.9		
Birmingham, Ala.	7,173	35.3	65.6	58.1	39.6	28.7	22.1	14.7	9.9	5.2	2.0		
Jackson, Miss.	708	22.9	41.2	44.1	23.2	23.8	16.3	6.7	8.6	5.4		20.0	
6 W. S. Central cities	13,072	20.1	50.5	50.1	37.6	24.8	14.9	10.0	5.4	3.5	1.8	5.4	
Little Rock, Ark.	2,612	34.8	76.0	62.7	53.5	33.4	23.2	14.3	8.0	6.7		7.1	
Baton Rouge, La.	864	32.5	64.0	60.7	48.2	34.7	19.4	9.3	11.2	9.3			
Oklahoma City, Okla.	3,891	17.3	31.3	54.1	30.0	18.7	9.7	10.1	5.1	3.1	1.0		
Austin, Tex.	1,018	19.3	33.3	40.8	36.8	20.9	14.1	12.0	6.2	3.0	1.8		
Dallas, Tex.	3,830	17.1	57.1	47.1	38.1	25.9	15.9	9.0	4.2	2.5	1.9	5.0	
Wichita Falls, Tex.	1,057	16.4	45.5	35.3	28.5	23.5	11.9	7.0	4.5	2.4	4.5		
6 Mountain cities	10,058	24.0	39.3	50.1	38.6	29.5	22.2	10.3	7.1	3.7	3.4	3.4	13.1
Butte, Mont.	2,009	26.1	50.0	48.9	36.8	27.0	25.4	10.0	5.3	7.1	4.2	3.4	
Boise, Idaho	1,114	10.6	17.6	32.9	28.8	12.6	11.2	5.1		2.2			
Casper, Wyo.	698	16.3	27.6	48.0	21.0	22.9	13.6	6.7	5.1	2.7	3.8		
Pueblo, Colo.	917	30.9	52.9	59.4	40.7	31.4	19.2	11.1	3.6				
Phoenix, Ariz.	1,666	13.8	24.1	25.7	23.8	21.6	12.4	7.3	5.0	4.1		4.5	14.3
Salt Lake City, Utah	3,654	29.6	44.5	62.7	50.5	37.6	30.4	13.0	10.2	2.9	3.1	2.9	12.5
4 Pacific cities	16,981	17.7	36.8	42.1	33.3	20.4	14.2	8.8	5.2	4.4	1.2	4.3	
Seattle, Wash.	5,989	18.6	46.4	45.0	33.4	21.8	14.6	9.1	5.6	4.8	0.6	5.2	
Portland, Ore.	4,021	21.2	31.7	46.6	32.6	22.8	13.6	9.2	4.9	4.7	1.3		
Sacramento, Calif.	2,167	13.2	31.3	35.9	29.2	17.1	15.6	10.6	4.5	4.3	2.7		
San Diego, Calif.	4,804	13.3	27.6	33.0	36.1	15.7	13.4	6.8	5.0	3.1	1.5	2.6	

Source: *Financial Survey of Urban Housing.* *Number of reports shown here approximately the same as in Table C 6; for number reporting by income groups see Table C 6.*
Percentage not shown for fewer than 10 reports.
[1]*Geographic division and 52-city percentages weighted by number of rental units in each city (RPI).*

TABLE C 12

Tenant Families, Number reporting, and Percentage of Families Delinquent in Rent by Rent-Income Percentage Groups, 52 Cities by Geographic Division, 1933

◄————————PERCENTAGE DELINQUENT IN RENT————————►
RENT - INCOME PERCENTAGE GROUPS

	NUMBER REPORTING	All groups	1-9	10-14	15-19	20-24	25-29	30-34	35-39	40-49	50-69	70-99	100 and over
52 cities[1]	156,171	25.0	10.6	9.9	12.0	16.4	19.3	24.7	28.8	35.5	40.1	46.9	51.1
4 New England cities	12,519	24.5	8.5	9.5	12.4	14.6	19.1	21.6	28.4	38.9	40.8	47.8	48.7
Portland, Me.	2,730	21.2	5.6	10.7	12.2	15.6	16.4	17.4	22.0	25.4	34.9	41.1	45.9
Worcester, Mass.	2,805	24.4	6.0	10.0	12.7	15.5	19.1	19.3	32.8	37.7	35.6	42.6	49.9
Providence, R.I.	5,855	24.7	10.4	9.4	12.1	14.7	18.3	21.1	26.9	40.0	42.0	51.8	48.0
Waterbury, Conn.	1,129	26.2	4.0	8.3	13.8	11.8	26.0	32.4	34.9	46.0	48.8	38.6	53.6
4 Mid. Atlantic cities	7,258	25.8	11.1	6.6	11.0	14.4	20.7	23.0	31.7	32.5	36.9	45.9	44.3
Binghamton, N.Y.	773	15.1	5.6	4.2	8.5	8.0	15.0	17.4	37.8	14.9	34.4	41.9	25.0
Syracuse, N.Y.	1,513	16.8	7.1	5.5	7.5	10.6	13.7	17.6	20.2	25.4	22.9	34.9	27.2
Trenton, N.J.	2,062	34.6	21.9	8.8	14.0	17.3	26.0	29.5	29.3	42.7	47.4	51.6	60.4
Erie, Pa.	2,910	43.6	13.5	8.8	17.2	24.1	34.3	31.9	52.1	50.7	57.1	65.8	78.2
6 E. N. Central cities	36,459	28.3	13.3	9.6	12.0	16.0	20.3	26.4	29.1	38.5	43.9	48.1	56.8
Cleveland, Ohio	27,185	30.0	10.9	9.6	11.5	15.3	18.9	26.2	28.2	39.3	45.7	52.2	59.8
Indianapolis, Ind.	3,132	25.3	18.8	6.2	12.1	15.4	22.1	26.2	28.3	37.5	42.5	41.0	59.0
Peoria, Ill.	2,306	23.2	7.4	12.1	12.1	12.4	22.1	22.9	37.2	29.9	36.0	47.1	45.9
Lansing, Mich.	968	23.2	15.0	19.3	13.3	23.6	21.8	26.9	30.4	40.4	37.0	33.3	30.2
Kenosha, Wis.	993	33.0	35.7	14.5	20.1	29.9	28.0	40.3	42.0	46.1	42.0	45.8	35.8
Racine, Wis.	1,875	27.7	13.2	16.5	14.8	22.2	26.8	26.9	25.0	35.0	38.2	38.9	39.1
10 W. N. Central cities	24,667	19.7	9.9	7.9	9.3	13.0	14.4	20.1	22.3	28.5	38.7	42.2	46.0
Minneapolis, Minn.	9,224	19.7	9.4	7.3	9.1	11.5	13.1	17.4	18.7	25.1	31.6	39.1	52.2
St. Paul, Minn.	1,814	18.3		7.8	6.0	10.9	11.1	15.8	13.8	29.9	26.1	43.9	36.6
Des Moines, Iowa	3,071	21.8	14.8	10.9	11.0	14.3	17.4	24.1	25.2	23.2	41.7	43.3	51.2
St. Joseph, Mo.	1,271	19.0	7.0	6.7	11.0	12.3	17.0	25.6	37.0	34.7	35.9	47.2	41.4
Springfield, Mo.	1,182	24.8	8.5	9.2	11.9	18.9	20.6	27.6	24.4	42.9	44.9	56.5	56.1
Fargo, N.D.	906	12.9	22.2	2.1	6.1	8.7	7.3	16.3	15.9	15.5	26.5	32.1	23.2
Sioux Falls, S.D.	1,514	15.4	7.7	8.3	7.5	10.9	8.8	15.9	16.2	22.9	24.7	46.7	30.6
Lincoln, Neb.	1,278	21.5	3.1	5.2	9.3	10.9	15.7	25.2	32.1	30.0	41.0	47.9	53.7
Topeka, Kan.	2,053	19.0	8.7	10.3	8.4	16.0	14.0	19.3	24.7	28.6	29.9	44.6	44.9
Wichita, Kan.	2,354	20.0	11.8	9.0	14.2	20.2	20.6	26.1	34.1	37.9	24.2	36.5	38.2
9 S. Atlantic cities	26,512	30.8	13.4	14.0	16.9	22.6	24.9	32.1	36.5	41.5	46.8	55.0	57.1
Hagerstown, Md.	1,263	29.1		13.8	11.2	15.6	20.0	27.7	38.5	46.2	41.8	60.8	59.9
Richmond, Va.	4,145	30.2	13.4	15.0	17.3	22.3	25.4	36.5	37.2	43.9	52.4	51.7	58.8
Wheeling, W.Va.	2,180	38.9	11.8	22.9	24.8	34.7	38.4	42.2	45.2	45.2	53.3	65.8	60.3
Asheville, N.C.	1,632	16.5	8.3	8.9	9.7	13.6	17.3	16.1	26.4	21.1	22.7	46.3	42.0
Greensboro, N.C.	1,208	13.3	1.8	5.1	12.6	14.7	14.3	26.2	20.0	25.0	32.4	30.0	50.0
Charleston, S.C.	2,510	38.7	23.4	21.5	20.4	23.8	24.0	42.6	50.3	54.2	52.7	56.7	69.5
Columbia, S.C.	1,569	32.2	3.1	11.0	19.7	24.4	29.6	29.7	47.3	41.8	41.7	50.7	55.9
Atlanta, Ga.	9,485	29.7	11.1	11.7	15.1	21.9	23.2	27.6	35.9	41.8	49.1	55.9	56.7
Jacksonville, Fla.	2,520	32.1	23.7	12.8	15.4	19.2	21.7	31.7	27.1	38.7	40.0	56.2	53.5
3 E. S. Central cities	9,118	34.6	13.1	17.8	20.4	29.3	27.5	38.5	41.3	49.2	50.2	57.0	64.1
Paducah, Ky.	1,290	40.4	20.9	20.9	16.0	33.3	35.5	33.8	46.6	54.4	56.0	62.1	72.7
Birmingham, Ala.	7,123	35.5	13.0	19.0	21.5	31.0	28.5	41.5	43.9	51.0	52.3	57.6	65.3
Jackson, Miss.	705	23.0	8.3	5.5	13.4	11.5	13.5	15.6	14.3	30.0	27.3	48.2	47.4
6 W. S. Central cities	12,960	20.4	10.4	7.8	9.6	14.4	17.9	21.3	28.7	29.9	36.8	42.2	49.2
Little Rock, Ark.	2,595	35.0	14.3	13.5	19.7	27.7	37.1	38.5	46.6	45.1	52.8	64.5	70.3
Baton Rouge, La.	859	32.7	13.3	15.9	13.6	19.0	25.0	37.5	41.2	39.7	43.4	52.3	68.1
Oklahoma City, Okla.	3,663	17.5	10.1	6.2	7.6	12.0	12.6	14.7	22.1	25.4	33.5	38.8	42.3
Austin, Tex.	1,008	19.4	18.2	8.2	10.4	12.1	18.4	27.8	30.6	27.7	30.2	34.1	38.1
Dallas, Tex.	3,793	17.6	8.1	6.0	6.7	10.9	15.1	16.9	27.9	27.3	35.2	38.1	50.2
Wichita Falls, Tex.	1,042	16.6	8.5	8.9	14.8	23.3	18.0	26.0	16.7	33.3	34.9	45.8	29.5
6 Mountain cities	9,885	24.5	9.9	10.7	11.7	14.9	20.1	24.5	28.2	34.0	41.2	48.5	47.8
Butte, Mont.	1,942	28.9	14.7	10.2	10.2	18.3	19.2	25.6	14.1	28.6	39.6	38.9	53.6
Boise, Idaho	1,092	10.8	3.2	3.3	8.7	2.3	7.3	10.8	20.8	19.5	15.5	26.0	26.0
Casper, Wyo.	674	16.9	8.1	9.0	4.7	16.7	11.9	13.5	21.9	11.4	52.9	63.6	32.9
Pueblo, Colo.	902	31.2	8.6	9.2	18.2	20.2	25.0	23.1	43.2	50.0	53.2	59.6	56.1
Phoenix, Ariz.	1,642	14.0	2.8	6.0	7.4	9.7	12.7	20.4	14.8	21.8	20.7	21.2	29.8
Salt Lake City, Utah	3,633	29.8	13.4	15.0	13.8	15.8	25.5	30.6	36.4	42.7	48.4	60.7	57.5
4 Pacific cities	16,793	17.9	6.8	6.8	7.2	12.3	13.1	18.5	20.8	27.0	33.4	38.5	41.9
Seattle, Wash.	5,935	18.7	7.9	8.5	7.2	12.3	14.2	18.8	19.9	26.2	32.3	39.6	48.4
Portland, Ore.	3,962	21.5	9.3	7.2	8.7	16.6	14.6	21.4	29.2	32.1	41.6	45.3	40.6
Sacramento, Calif.	2,142	13.3	3.8	4.6	4.8	7.4	12.4	14.8	12.2	24.3	25.0	28.1	32.0
San Diego, Calif.	4,754	13.4	2.6	4.2	6.2	8.5	9.3	15.7	15.0	22.8	27.8	31.7	35.5

Source: Financial Survey of Urban Housing.
[1]*Geographic division and 52-city percentages weighted by number of rental units in each city (RPI).*

TABLE C 13

Owner-occupant and Tenant Families, Number reporting, and Percentage of Full Time worked by Principal Wage Earner by 11
Income Groups, 52 Cities by Geographic Division, 1933

	NUMBER REPORTING	All income groups	No income	$1-249	$250-499	$500-749	$750-999	$1,000-1,499	$1,500-1,999	$2,000-2,999	$3,000-4,499	$4,500-7,499	$7,500 and over
52 cities[1]	109,552	62	7	19	31	47	61	74	85	88	89	89	87
4 New England cities	5,367	59	6	16	25	36	50	66	78	83	84	84	79
Portland, Me.	1,155	65	10	17	25	33	50	74	83	85	87	91	85
Worcester, Mass.	1,032	62	11	20	24	32	52	66	78	85	90	82	71
Providence, R.I.	2,731	57	4	16	25	37	50	65	79	82	81	84	78
Waterbury, Conn.	449	61	7	8	30	42	49	64	69	80	91	82	94
4 Mid. Atlantic cities	6,049	60	6	17	31	44	56	70	84	85	86	91	87
Binghamton, N.Y.	482	69	15	15	27	33	48	67	80	85	85	94	100
Syracuse, N.Y.	1,087	62	7	14	29	41	53	70	86	86	90	88	91
Trenton, N.J.	1,981	60	1	24	39	52	61	70	85	84	88	88	85
Erie, Pa.	2,499	50	4	14	29	46	61	71	82	86	79	98	76
6 E. N. Central cities	27,530	58	5	15	26	44	58	72	84	88	91	91	88
Cleveland, Ohio	18,920	56	6	14	25	44	56	71	83	87	91	91	88
Indianapolis, Ind.	2,289	66	4	20	29	46	61	73	86	88	92	92	95
Peoria, Ill.	2,301	63	4	18	29	43	61	75	87	89	91	87	95
Lansing, Mich.	1,005	59	2	12	25	46	60	75	87	94	95	87	81
Kenosha, Wis.	947	51	6	16	28	44	57	69	83	88	91	92	
Racine, Wis.	2,088	48	2	14	27	45	59	74	84	84	86	87	48
10 W. N. Central cities	20,927	67	6	18	28	48	66	79	89	90	91	92	85
Minneapolis, Minn.	6,460	66	6	14	24	41	58	76	89	90	92	90	87
St. Paul, Minn.	1,699	68	4	17	25	45	67	80	91	90	92	94	84
Des Moines, Iowa	2,868	68	5	20	33	52	71	79	90	92	92	96	85
St. Joseph, Mo.	1,079	68	5	24	35	55	70	79	87	93	84	92	90
Springfield, Mo.	1,362	65	5	25	37	60	75	82	90	88	92	85	99
Fargo, N.D.	711	85	7	41	42	62	72	90	91	96	97	99	90
Sioux Falls, S.D.	1,021	70	11	15	32	57	72	82	88	90	89	89	99
Lincoln, Neb.	1,417	64	9	20	29	48	69	81	86	90	90	92	91
Topeka, Kan.	2,127	66	6	21	30	53	66	76	90	91	90	98	76
Wichita, Kan.	2,183	63	6	17	32	56	70	79	88	90	91	85	63
9 S. Atlantic cities	11,017	68	9	28	46	58	70	75	87	89	90	90	92
Hagerstown, Md.	641	77		26	50	65	78	83	91	97	96	91	99
Richmond, Va.	1,916	76	15	30	42	57	69	78	90	93	94	92	87
Wheeling, W.Va.	1,964	55	3	20	33	53	70	75	82	84	88	84	99
Asheville, N.C.	796	68	14	28	49	66	74	74	82	86	88	80	66
Greensboro, N.C.	496	70	13	37	46	63	70	68	77	87	90	91	82
Charleston, S.C.	561	76	12	38	64	63	66	82	85	90	87	88	78
Columbia, S.C.	492	70	3	29	59	60	72	72	85	90	88	93	87
Atlanta, Ga.	3,688	75	12	29	49	61	70	77	90	90	91	92	92
Jacksonville, Fla.	463	63	4	35	56	48	69	67	89	87	91	99	99
3 E. S. Central cities	4,701	63	4	26	43	60	70	80	87	90	94	90	88
Paducah, Ky.	658	62	6	27	44	63	79	85	90	89	90	98	56
Birmingham, Ala.	3,644	62	4	24	43	60	69	78	86	90	94	89	90
Jackson, Miss.	399	74	2	38	38	60	65	84	92	92	96	90	99
6 W. S. Central cities	8,758	70	13	27	39	54	69	80	88	90	92	92	91
Little Rock, Ark.	1,612	67	10	31	40	53	64	76	89	90	91	87	95
Baton Rouge, La.	265	68	3	38	59	72	76	74	90	93	89	97	99
Oklahoma City, Okla.	2,487	69	14	22	37	53	67	81	88	92	94	89	86
Austin, Tex.	910	70	22	32	47	63	73	82	85	85	83	89	99
Dallas, Tex.	2,734	72	12	27	36	50	69	80	87	90	92	96	90
Wichita Falls, Tex.	750	73	19	27	45	62	77	88	92	91	95	93	96
6 Mountain cities	8,716	61	5	17	32	48	65	78	85	90	92	94	93
Butte, Mont.	1,886	51	5	16	29	46	54	68	84	89	91	97	99
Boise, Idaho	1,199	66	10	15	30	46	69	85	89	91	93	93	99
Casper, Wyo.	607	73		28	36	49	70	78	89	94	91	99	95
Pueblo, Colo.	930	50	5	16	33	44	54	73	84	92	91	99	x
Phoenix, Ariz.	885	61	9	17	31	44	67	74	78	89	92	87	90
Salt Lake City, Utah	3,209	65	3	17	33	51	69	82	87	90	92	92	90
4 Pacific cities	16,487	60	8	16	28	44	60	73	86	87	86	84	86
Seattle, Wash.	6,002	60	5	16	28	46	61	75	87	88	89	85	89
Portland, Ore.	4,401	60	9	16	30	48	66	77	87	90	88	89	95
Sacramento, Calif.	2,081	66	18	19	28	42	53	72	85	89	90	89	89
San Diego, Calif.	4,003	55	9	17	22	34	52	64	81	81	72	70	64

Source: Financial Survey of Urban Housing. Percentage not shown for fewer than 3 reports.
[1]*Geographic division and 52-city percentages weighted by number of owner-occupied units in each city (RPI).*
[2]*Geographic division and 52-city percentages weighted by number of tenant-occupied units in each city (RPI).*

TABLE C 13

Owner-occupant and Tenant Families, Number reporting, and Percentage of Full Time worked by Principal Wage Earner by 11 Income Groups, 52 Cities by Geographic Division, 1933

←————————————————— T E N A N T[2] —————————————————→

NUMBER REPORTING	All income groups	No income	$1-249	$250-499	$500-749	$750-999	$1,000-1,499	$1,500-1,999	$2,000-2,999	$3,000-4,499	$4,500-7,499	$7,500 and over	
151,611	66	2	27	43	60	73	84	90	92	93	92	85	52 cities[1]
11,867	65	2	25	39	55	67	79	88	90	90	89	88	4 New England cities
2,629	72	1	23	40	56	74	83	90	94	93	95	99	Portland, Me.
2,545	63	1	21	34	51	63	75	85	89	90	96	84	Worcester, Mass.
5,617	64	x	25	40	56	68	80	88	90	89	86	88	Providence, R.I.
1,076	69	3	36	41	57	67	80	89	90	93	90	x	Waterbury, Conn.
6,940	65	2	25	41	54	70	81	88	91	94	89	74	4 Mid. Atlantic cities
740	76		33	50	58	70	84	92	89	95	99		Binghamton, N.Y.
1,456	65	2	25	42	54	70	81	88	92	98	89		Syracuse, N.Y.
1,964	68		24	36	54	73	81	90	90	95	92		Trenton, N.J.
2,780	54	1	19	37	53	67	79	84	90	83	81	74	Erie, Pa.
35,469	63	3	21	37	55	70	82	89	92	93	93	91	6 E. N. Central cities
26,534	61	2	19	34	54	68	81	89	91	93	93	95	Cleveland, Ohio
3,046	68	6	27	45	58	76	84	89	93	94	93	85	Indianapolis, Ind.
2,243	68	3	24	40	54	72	85	90	92	94	92	74	Peoria, Ill.
938	62		18	34	51	75	83	87	93	96	99		Lansing, Mich.
928	53		20	30	52	68	80	85	89	85	x		Kenosha, Wis.
1,780	52		16	35	52	68	84	92	93	91	96	x	Racine, Wis.
24,023	69	2	23	37	59	77	87	92	93	95	95	97	10 W. N. Central cities
8,983	68	1	18	29	52	74	85	91	92	93	94	96	Minneapolis, Minn.
1,780	67		18	37	61	76	90	94	93	96	98		St. Paul, Minn.
3,012	71	2	24	39	60	77	86	91	95	94	94	x	Des Moines, Iowa
1,232	74		31	48	67	83	88	92	93	95	99	99	St. Joseph, Mo.
1,162	65		27	48	69	81	89	89	96	93	99		Springfield, Mo.
878	77		29	40	67	85	87	93	98	95	95		Fargo, N.D.
1,478	77	7	30	46	70	83	87	94	94	95	99	99	Sioux Falls, S.D.
1,246	70	1	27	35	64	83	89	91	93	99	84	99	Lincoln, Neb.
1,976	70	1	32	48	64	75	87	92	94	99	99	x	Topeka, Kan.
2,276	70	4	29	45	66	81	88	94	95	96	94	x	Wichita, Kan.
25,523	69	1	40	60	71	79	86	91	94	94	94	83	9 S. Atlantic cities
1,214	67		25	53	67	83	87	88	93	98	99		Hagerstown, Md.
4,044	75		38	60	71	78	87	92	94	95	96	90	Richmond, Va.
2,065	62	1	27	45	54	72	80	91	92	90	88	x	Wheeling, W.Va.
1,515	68		36	58	73	80	86	90	92	93	99		Asheville, N.C.
1,161	80	2	47	66	74	87	86	94	93	95	92	79	Greensboro, N.C.
2,453	71	x	56	72	78	84	88	94	95	93	86	33	Charleston, S.C.
1,507	65	1	40	61	75	81	87	92	96	98	89	x	Columbia, S.C.
9,123	70	1	43	62	74	79	85	89	94	95	94	91	Atlanta, Ga.
2,441	62		41	59	74	78	89	95	92	92	98		Jacksonville, Fla.
9,032	59	2	37	57	66	66	84	90	88	88	91	79	3 E. S. Central cities
1,274	58		33	57	70	77	87	90	90	95			Paducah, Ky.
7,071	58	2	36	56	65	63	84	90	87	88	90	79	Birmingham, Ala.
687	68		44	62	73	80	83	90	91	89	99		Jackson, Miss.
12,611	72	3	34	52	67	78	87	92	94	93	94	91	6 W. S. Central cities
2,485	66	1	37	50	69	80	88	91	94	98	99	74	Little Rock, Ark.
803	72		53	67	75	82	91	90	92	91	74	x	Baton Rouge, La.
3,609	71	6	28	47	66	79	86	93	94	95	90	99	Oklahoma City, Okla.
981	69		36	54	65	72	82	87	94	91	91	99	Austin, Tex.
3,711	76	2	35	53	66	77	87	92	93	92	98	89	Dallas, Tex.
1,022	73		34	52	65	87	89	94	96	92	89		Wichita Falls, Tex.
9,786	62	2	20	39	56	71	84	91	92	95	92	91	6 Mountain cities
1,985	55	2	18	38	52	59	79	92	93	97	92	74	Butte, Mont.
1,097	71	6	17	40	62	77	85	94	93	99	99		Boise, Idaho
684	63	3	19	36	58	69	82	91	93	92	99	x	Casper, Wyo.
877	55	1	22	38	55	73	83	92	92	99	x		Pueblo, Colo.
1,620	63	1	24	43	53	70	83	88	88	94	80	88	Phoenix, Ariz.
3,523	65	2	18	38	59	74	86	91	94	92	96	97	Salt Lake City, Utah
16,360	65	3	22	36	59	74	82	90	90	90	91	66	4 Pacific cities
5,775	64	2	21	33	58	70	83	89	90	91	93	71	Seattle, Wash.
3,895	59		18	37	58	75	83	92	92	95	95	66	Portland, Ore.
2,098	73	3	30	42	60	74	82	90	94	95	91	79	Sacramento, Calif.
4,592	70	5	26	37	61	80	81	89	87	81	84	49	San Diego, Calif.

SECTION D

Financing Nonfarm Residential Real Estate

The 48 tables of section D are concerned with the volume, terms, and characteristics of residential mortgage financing. The first 4 tables carry comprehensive data for the country; the others consist principally of sample data.

Table D 1, giving the percentage of properties mortgaged and the percentage debt is of value by three population groups, is derived from the 1920 Census Monograph II. The 1920 data in Table D 2 are also from this source; the 1934 data and the figures in Table D 3 are taken or derived from the Financial Survey.

Table D 4 represents the National Bureau's preliminary estimate of total debt secured by mortgages on nonfarm residential real estate as of January 1, 1934, derived by methods described in Chapter IV, section 3.

Tables D 5–47 are summaries of Financial Survey data. Methods of deriving the weighted geographic division averages are described in Chapter I, section 2.

The term debt as used in section D includes mortgages and deeds of trust of all priorities, land contracts, or sales contracts and all forms of credit secured by nonfarm residential real estate, even though title to the property may still remain in the seller or mortgagee.

The terms property and properties are used in this section as referring to nonfarm residential real estate which is the security on which the credit is based. Whatever the type of property, it is usually considered as a unit for financing purposes; hence this term is generally used throughout this discussion in place of dwellings or dwelling units, as was done in sections A and B which deal with value and rent.

All tables in this section refer to urban nonfarm residential properties, though the nonfarm designation is omitted from table captions. An exception occurs in the New York City areas, where a few properties are used for commercial and industrial purposes.

All data from the Financial Survey are on a sample basis and therefore are not to be taken as having full coverage in any classification for population groups, tenure, priority, or other grouping, or as having the same coverage in different cities. Although the Financial Survey data for individual cities are the number or amount reported in the sample, and not totals for the city, the totals for population groups within geographic divisions and the aggregate usually represent sample figures for several cities weighted by the total number or amount for each constituent city.

TABLE D I

Owner-occupied Dwellings, Percentage Mortgaged and Percentage that Debt is of Value of Total Mortgaged Property, by Population Group, State, and Geographic Division, 1920

	←———PERCENTAGE OF PROPERTIES MORTGAGED———→				←———PERCENTAGE THAT DEBT IS OF VALUE———→			
	All population groups	100,000 or more	25,000-100,000	Under 25,000	All population groups	100,000 or more	25,000-100,000	Under 25,000
United States	39.7	57.6	49.0	29.9	42.6	44.6	42.8	39.9
New England	51.7	68.4	62.7	41.6	43.9	46.2	45.6	40.6
Maine	22.8		33.1	21.1	40.2		42.3	39.1
New Hampshire	30.0		45.7	26.6	39.2		44.6	36.1
Vermont	30.4			30.4	38.2			38.2
Massachusetts	58.7	67.4	65.1	50.2	45.3	47.0	46.6	42.0
Rhode Island	53.4	58.4	63.7	41.5	40.8	42.4	42.0	36.5
Connecticut	64.2	76.8	73.8	55.7	43.0	45.3	44.7	39.9
Mid. Atlantic	51.2	68.5	54.5	39.1	44.8	47.3	43.9	41.2
New York	55.1	72.7	52.6	38.1	44.7	46.5	42.4	39.8
New Jersey	63.5	68.2	71.0	59.0	43.7	46.4	44.9	41.7
Pennsylvania	43.7	63.4	46.5	32.9	45.7	49.4	44.2	41.9
E. N. Central	41.6	59.0	50.4	30.4	41.0	41.9	41.5	39.0
Ohio	42.2	54.9	51.3	31.5	40.9	41.4	41.6	39.6
Indiana	36.7	57.0	50.5	28.7	38.0	41.8	40.2	33.7
Illinois	43.5	63.8	47.1	30.6	41.2	42.3	40.8	39.0
Michigan	43.7	59.5	53.9	29.5	41.4	41.2	42.5	40.4
Wisconsin	38.3	59.5	48.0	30.5	42.1	44.7	42.3	40.1
W. N. Central	32.4	50.9	44.1	25.9	40.4	43.3	40.7	38.2
Minnesota	34.0	50.1	52.2	23.5	38.5	38.9	41.8	37.2
Iowa	28.1	50.5	45.2	22.5	38.8	41.3	41.8	36.7
Missouri	38.1	51.9	41.9	30.2	45.1	48.3	42.5	40.4
N. Dakota	30.7			30.7	39.9			39.9
S. Dakota	27.0		40.7	25.9	38.6		37.5	38.7
Nebraska	32.5	52.9	41.2	25.8	39.4	39.7	37.2	39.6
Kansas	29.7	45.6	40.6	26.8	37.9	42.6	37.9	37.2
S. Atlantic	29.3	48.3	34.6	21.7	41.1	42.9	41.1	39.2
Delaware	47.0	62.8		27.8	41.3	41.5		40.4
Maryland	40.9	46.1	41.9	31.6	40.6	40.2	43.5	41.0
D. C.	55.4	55.4			46.4	46.4		
Virginia	25.8	38.3	36.3	20.9	42.2	44.5	43.7	40.0
W. Virginia	26.4		36.6	23.6	39.4		40.2	38.8
N. Carolina	20.5		33.4	18.6	38.6		39.5	38.3
S. Carolina	22.5		28.7	21.6	40.9		44.1	39.9
Georgia	22.8	48.0	26.3	17.5	41.2	41.1	43.2	40.6
Florida	25.2		38.1	21.4	36.8		38.3	35.7
E. S. Central	22.7	36.2	35.1	18.3	42.0	43.5	43.5	40.7
Kentucky	24.2	34.2	40.5	19.2	40.6	41.7	40.9	39.9
Tennessee	23.4	34.2	34.4	18.1	43.1	44.4	45.9	40.8
Alabama	22.9	42.7	26.1	17.8	43.9	43.8	45.8	43.5
Mississippi	17.8			17.8	39.4			39.4
W. S. Central	26.0	36.4	40.9	21.9	39.2	42.2	40.0	37.4
Arkansas	25.5		40.8	22.9	39.7		40.7	39.1
Louisiana	21.7	30.1	31.5	17.6	40.7	42.7	42.9	37.9
Oklahoma	30.5		51.3	26.5	36.8		38.1	35.9
Texas	25.3	38.9	33.3	20.3	40.1	42.0	42.3	37.9
Mountain	29.5	44.7	36.5	25.8	41.8	42.7	42.1	41.4
Montana	29.0		31.1	28.7	43.6		46.6	43.2
Idaho	35.4		35.4		40.5		40.5	
Wyoming	34.9			34.9	41.4			41.4
Colorado	33.2	42.7	35.8	27.4	41.6	42.2	41.3	41.0
New Mexico	14.5			14.5	39.8			39.8
Arizona	23.4		46.9	20.1	41.5		40.7	41.8
Utah	32.2	48.6	36.6	21.4	42.4	43.6	41.0	40.6
Nevada	12.5			12.5	42.6			42.6
Pacific	38.9	46.1	41.1	32.9	41.4	42.3	42.3	39.6
Washington	39.3	48.8	42.2	31.3	44.0	45.3	46.0	41.0
Oregon	34.8	45.9		26.9	40.4	41.6		38.5
California	39.7	45.1	40.7	35.2	40.8	41.6	41.4	39.4

Source: Census Monograph II, Mortgages on Homes in the United States, 1920; percentage mortgaged 'All population groups' transcribed from Table 26; percentage mortgaged by population group derived from Tables 26, 27, 28, 30, 31, as explained in detail in Part Two, Ch. IV, sec. 1; percentages that debt is of value are transcribed from Table 34. Data as reported by the Census in Monograph II are based on reports from 66.3 per cent of owner-occupied dwellings in the United States (see pp. 17-21).

TABLE D 2

Owner-occupied Dwellings, Percentage Mortgaged, 50 Cities, and Percentage that Debt is of Value of Mortgaged Property, 45 Cities by Geographic Division, 1920 and 1934

	Percentage of properties mortgaged		Percentage that debt is of value			Percentage of properties mortgaged		Percentage that debt is of value	
	1920	1934	1920	1934		1920	1934	1920	1934
50 (45) cities[1] [2]	48.9	55.3	41.5	55.6	8 S. Atlantic cities	37.4	49.8	41.9	56.3
					Hagerstown, Md.	44.7	49.6	44.7	60.9
5 (4) New England cities[2]	65.1	69.8	44.6	54.6	Richmond, Va.	34.2	49.7	43.5	59.4
Portland, Me.	37.3	46.7	42.2	50.5	Wheeling, W.Va.	28.1	35.3*	40.8	49.4*
Nashua, N.H.	38.0	56.8			Asheville, N.C.	22.6	46.9	37.7	66.3
Worcester, Mass.	81.5	83.6	49.8	67.1	Charleston, S.C.	30.2	32.9	45.7	50.3
Providence, R.I.	58.4	63.2*	42.4	49.4*	Columbia, S.C.	25.8	58.4	40.9	57.4
Waterbury, Conn.	79.8	81.1	47.7	60.0	Atlanta, Ga.	48.0	58.3*	41.1	57.3*
					Jacksonville, Fla.	38.3	47.6	43.1	52.2
5 (4) Mid. Atlantic cities[2]	59.5	62.1	41.3	55.9					
Binghamton, N.Y.	51.9	45.3	39.7	45.9	2 (1) E. S. Central cities[2]	40.0	49.6	43.8	61.1
Syracuse, N.Y.	65.8	76.9	40.0	57.0	Knoxville, Tenn.	34.0	43.3		
Trenton, N.J.	73.2	68.8	46.1	58.4	Birmingham, Ala.	42.7	52.4*	43.8	61.1*
Erie, Pa.	49.9	49.7	42.9	57.7					
Williamsport, Pa.	31.9	36.1			6 (5) W. S. Central cities[2]	45.1	53.0	40.2	55.9
					Little Rock, Ark.	39.3	43.8	41.5	62.9
7 (6) E. N. Central cities[2]	56.1	63.7	40.0	56.8	Shreveport, La.	31.5	59.7		
Cleveland, Ohio	59.0	67.0*	38.9	57.2*	Oklahoma City, Okla.	59.3	61.7	40.2	58.2
Indianapolis, Ind.	57.0	63.8	41.8	56.2	Austin, Tex.	27.0	39.2	37.7	46.4
Decatur, Ill.	40.8	50.1			Dallas, Tex.	46.1	53.3	40.3	53.5
Peoria, Ill.	47.5	54.0	41.0	50.4	Wichita Falls, Tex.	41.8	41.4	41.4	66.3
Lansing, Mich.	67.6	57.4	46.3	59.5					
Kenosha, Wis.	62.9	65.3	43.2	53.8	4 Mountain cities	43.8	47.8	43.4	56.7
Racine, Wis.	33.8	67.1	44.5	58.9	Butte, Mont.	31.1	24.2	46.6	41.3
					Pueblo, Colo.	37.0	40.9	44.6	59.2
9 W. N. Central cities	47.3	51.0	39.1	52.1	Phoenix, Ariz.	46.9	55.6	40.7	56.3
Minneapolis, Minn.	54.5	55.9	38.3	52.4	Salt Lake City, Utah	48.6	54.0	43.6	58.0
St. Paul, Minn.	43.6	48.0	40.2	50.0					
Des Moines, Iowa	50.5	49.5	41.3	53.2	4 Pacific cities	45.9	50.5	43.5	55.9
St. Joseph, Mo.	43.8	42.9	42.7	52.5	Seattle, Wash.	50.7	49.2*	46.8	54.7*
Springfield, Mo.	41.0	50.1	39.5	52.9	Portland, Ore.	45.9	51.0	41.6	56.6
Sioux Falls, S.D.	40.7	53.4	37.5	46.5	Sacramento, Calif.	43.6	54.5	47.3	61.8
Lincoln, Neb.	41.2	48.2	37.2	53.6	San Diego, Calif.	36.0	50.6*	37.1	54.4*
Topeka, Kan.	37.7	44.0	37.8	50.4					
Wichita, Kan.	42.9	53.5	37.9	56.8					

Source: 1920, Census Monograph II, Mortgages on Homes in the United States, 1920, Tables 27, 28, 31, and 33; 1934, Financial Survey of Urban Housing
*Metropolitan district.
[1] Geographic division and 50 (45)-city averages weighted by number of owner-occupied dwellings in each city, 1930.
[2] Figures in parentheses are number of cities reporting percentages that debt is of value of mortgaged property.

TABLE D 3

Mortgaged Dwellings, Percentage that Debt is of Value, January 1, 1930, 1933, and 1934, reported by Owners in 1934: Owner-occupied, 52 Cities; Rented, 44 Cities, by Geographic Division

	← O W N E R - O C C U P I E D →			← R E N T E D →		
	1930	1933	1934	1930	1933	1934
52 (44) cities[1] [2]	50.8	55.6	55.6	51.9	60.0	60.4
4 (3) New England cities[2]	50.0	53.9	54.6	55.2	60.5	60.6
Portland, Me.	48.7	50.2	50.5	48.2	52.7	53.4
Worcester, Mass.	59.8	66.1	67.1	59.7	68.8	69.3
Providence, R.I.*	46.4	48.8	49.4	54.6	58.7	58.7
Waterbury, Conn.	51.6	59.7	60.0			
4 (3) Mid. Atlantic cities[2]	46.0	53.7	55.9	51.4	60.3	62.8
Binghamton, N.Y.	43.1	45.7	45.9			
Syracuse, N.Y.	45.1	54.5	57.0	50.8	60.5	62.7
Trenton, N.J.	49.9	55.9	58.4	47.5	57.8	59.7
Erie, Pa.	47.9	54.9	57.7	55.7	60.9	64.5
6 E. N. Central cities	50.2	56.3	56.8	52.2	62.3	64.2
Cleveland, Ohio*	50.1	56.7	57.2	54.6	66.4	67.7
Indianapolis, Ind.	49.7	55.0	56.2	44.8	54.0	57.0
Peoria, Ill.	49.6	51.5	50.4	59.6	60.4	52.5
Lansing, Mich.	55.7	62.4	59.5	45.1	56.5	57.0
Kenosha, Wis.	45.3	52.3	53.8	46.4	35.0	58.4
Racine, Wis.	53.0	58.1	58.9	49.3	56.9	59.8
10 (9) W. N. Central cities[2]	50.1	51.9	52.0	50.4	54.2	55.3
Minneapolis, Minn.	48.9	51.1	52.4	51.8	54.3	56.7
St. Paul, Minn.	47.8	49.7	50.0	46.6	54.8	53.7
Des Moines, Iowa	54.4	55.1	53.2	49.0	51.9	52.2
St. Joseph, Mo.	50.2	51.1	52.5	52.9	56.8	54.5
Springfield, Mo.	55.3	54.8	52.9	46.0	46.5	48.2
Fargo, N.D.	50.4	52.2	50.4			
Sioux Falls, S.D.	46.0	48.2	46.5	49.4	48.4	48.8
Lincoln, Neb.	54.0	55.6	53.6	54.7	59.4	63.3
Topeka, Kan.	52.4	51.5	50.4	60.3	52.7	52.0
Wichita, Kan.	52.4	56.8	56.8	47.5	56.3	57.4
9 (8) S. Atlantic cities[2]	55.3	58.6	56.6	57.7	69.7	65.5
Hagerstown, Md.	51.2	60.7	60.9	68.9	68.0	67.4
Richmond, Va.	60.3	61.4	59.4	67.0	64.6	62.6
Wheeling, W.Va.*	45.5	51.9	49.4	46.3	53.0	51.1
Asheville, N.C.	64.3	66.7	66.3	76.4	88.4	79.7
Greensboro, N.C.	59.5	68.3	61.9	68.2	79.6	61.2
Charleston, S.C.	49.1	50.5	50.3	48.4	50.3	51.9
Columbia, S.C.	54.8	59.5	57.4	58.8	68.5	62.6
Atlanta, Ga.*	56.5	59.2	57.3	54.8	73.4	70.0
Jacksonville, Fla.	52.9	53.4	52.2			
3 (2) E. S. Central cities	54.5	59.4	59.4	41.6	49.9	51.1
Paducah, Ky.	63.9	65.5	58.7	39.8	41.2	48.2
Birmingham, Ala.*	54.3	60.5	61.1	42.1	52.5	52.0
Jackson, Miss.	52.8	51.7	50.4			
6 (5) W. S. Central cities[2]	53.7	58.5	55.4	51.6	57.1	56.7
Little Rock, Ark.	56.6	64.5	62.9	49.6	61.6	62.2
Baton Rouge, La.	49.8	50.1	45.0			
Oklahoma City, Okla.	52.1	60.2	58.2	51.1	57.7	55.5
Austin, Tex.	53.0	51.1	46.4	50.4	49.2	50.9
Dallas, Tex.	54.6	56.7	53.5	52.0	55.7	56.7
Wichita Falls, Tex.	56.9	75.1	66.3	61.9	76.8	72.4
6 (4) Mountain cities[2]	52.0	59.0	55.7	47.7	56.2	57.5
Butte, Mont.	44.2	42.5	41.3	50.9	54.6	52.2
Boise, Idaho	48.7	45.8	43.2			
Casper, Wyo.	65.6	63.4	56.9			
Pueblo, Colo.	58.2	58.9	59.2	46.0	53.4	58.9
Phoenix, Ariz.	47.7	57.8	56.3	44.2	54.3	53.3
Salt Lake City, Utah	52.4	62.4	58.0	49.0	57.4	59.8
4 Pacific cities	52.5	56.8	55.9	50.0	57.1	57.4
Seattle, Wash.*	51.4	55.8	54.7	51.4	59.2	57.2
Portland, Ore.	53.2	57.3	56.6	46.8	49.6	54.9
Sacramento, Calif.	61.4	62.4	61.8	59.6	62.7	64.2
San Diego, Calif.*	49.3	55.6	54.4	45.8	56.4	57.6

Source: *Financial Survey of Urban Housing*
*Metropolitan district.
[1]*Geographic division and 52 (44)-city percentages weighted by total value of mortgaged property in each city, by tenure, 1934 (RPI).*
[2]*Figures in parentheses are number of cities reporting rented mortgaged properties.*

TABLE D 4

Total Mortgage Debt and Percentage Distribution by Geographic Division and Tenure, January 1, 1934 (preliminary)

	AMOUNT (thousands of dollars)[1]			PERCENTAGE DISTRIBUTION BY GEOGRAPHIC DIVISION			PERCENTAGE DISTRIBUTION BY TENURE	
	Total	Owner-occupied	Rented	Total	Owner-occupied	Rented	Owner-occupied	Rented
United States	26,078,684	13,218,660	12,860,024	100.0	100.0	100.0	50.7	49.3
New England	2,580,770	1,522,009	1,058,761	9.9	11.5	8.2	59.0	41.0
Mid. Atlantic	10,236,455	4,716,598	5,519,857	39.2	35.7	42.9	46.1	53.9
E. N. Central	6,783,023	3,496,180	3,286,843	26.0	26.4	25.5	51.5	48.5
W. N. Central	1,461,423	887,931	573,492	5.6	6.7	4.5	60.8	39.2
S. Atlantic	1,586,297	810,454	775,843	6.1	6.1	6.0	51.1	48.9
E. S. Central	384,683	232,640	152,043	1.5	1.8	1.2	60.5	39.5
W. S. Central	824,090	378,487	445,603	3.2	2.9	3.5	45.9	54.1
Mountain	363,886	176,193	187,693	1.4	1.3	1.5	48.4	51.6
Pacific	1,858,057	998,168	859,889	7.1	7.6	6.7	53.7	46.3

[1]*Includes land contracts and debt on vacant properties.*

TABLE D 5

Owner-occupied Dwellings, Number and Percentage Mortgaged by Value Groups, 52 Cities by Geographic Division, January 1, 1934

	All value groups	$1-499	$500-999	$1,000-1,499	$1,500-1,999	$2,000-2,999	$3,000-3,999	$4,000-4,999	$5,000-7,499	$7,500-9,999	$10,000-14,999	$15,000 and over
					NUMBER MORTGAGED							
52 cities[1]	70,197	243	1,333	2,606	4,081	11,128	12,670	10,754	16,135	5,762	3,498	1,987
4 New England cities	4,428	3	8	33	51	262	490	654	1,521	713	509	184
Portland, Me.	676	2	2	7	17	43	91	109	204	105	76	20
Worcester, Mass.	1,190			6	3	44	102	190	448	203	150	44
Providence, R.I.*	2,079	1	6	16	31	154	271	295	707	310	203	85
Waterbury, Conn.	483			4		21	26	60	162	95	80	35
4 Mid. Atlantic cities	4,459		5	67	172	605	865	747	1,270	417	227	84
Binghamton, N.Y.	267					15	32	38	102	48	21	11
Syracuse, N.Y.	1,011		2	5	4	46	126	124	407	178	95	24
Trenton, N.J.	1,627		2	49	125	356	336	271	354	75	39	20
Erie, Pa.	1,554		1	13	43	188	371	314	407	116	72	29
6 E. N. Central cities	21,140	14	95	252	528	1,852	2,984	3,562	6,734	2,678	1,509	932
Cleveland, Ohio*	14,764	8	45	123	232	1,020	1,818	2,342	5,003	2,136	1,243	794
Indianapolis, Ind.	1,773	1	32	48	118	284	329	294	378	142	93	54
Peoria, Ill.	1,479	2	13	49	92	249	290	250	313	110	72	39
Lansing, Mich.	660	3	4	20	46	135	168	121	116	38	6	3
Kenosha, Wis.	748		1	2	13	41	141	168	279	65	27	11
Racine, Wis.	1,716			10	27	123	238	387	645	187	68	31
10 W. N. Central cities	12,611	80	361	674	990	2,356	2,641	2,088	2,361	567	322	171
Minneapolis, Minn.	4,206	3	24	71	163	627	929	896	990	296	136	71
St. Paul, Minn.	911		4	17	37	143	233	215	209	26	20	7
Des Moines, Iowa	1,693	28	81	108	137	349	376	216	305	55	23	15
St. Joseph, Mo.	541	1	26	42	54	134	115	61	68	16	17	7
Springfield, Mo.	799	20	74	123	124	180	98	70	76	14	11	9
Fargo, N.D.	494		1	5	9	43	106	116	154	28	23	9
Sioux Falls, S.D.	654	3	14	18	45	101	131	112	143	50	26	11
Lincoln, Neb.	826	1	26	41	81	195	175	111	127	32	20	17
Topeka, Kan.	1,107	5	36	76	120	222	250	160	181	23	25	9
Wichita, Kan.	1,380	19	75	173	220	362	228	131	108	27	21	16
9 S. Atlantic cities	5,696	18	129	222	381	894	930	736	1,318	489	340	239
Hagerstown, Md.	367	1	7	10	27	62	68	47	78	24	20	23
Richmond, Va.	1,112	2	15	28	51	102	118	141	362	155	95	45
Wheeling, W.Va.*	120			6	2	18	27	13	26	11	11	6
Asheville, N.C.	421	2	26	32	37	79	81	57	59	18	13	17
Greensboro, N.C.	323		4	20	22	32	39	41	86	39	21	19
Charleston, S.C.	213	2	9	6	16	32	33	27	57	14	11	6
Columbia, S.C.	349	3	13	17	18	49	43	42	88	38	30	8
Atlanta, Ga.*	2,493	6	47	96	175	466	477	337	487	169	126	107
Jacksonville, Fla.	298	2	8	9	33	54	44	31	75	21	13	8
3 E. S. Central cities	2,605	20	160	230	236	538	473	335	381	112	79	41
Paducah, Ky.	240	10	30	34	27	54	33	23	18	6	1	4
Birmingham, Ala.*	2,090	9	123	186	196	435	393	259	304	87	67	31
Jackson, Miss.	275	1	7	10	13	49	47	53	59	19	11	6
6 W. S. Central cities	5,403	49	194	325	480	1,192	1,109	632	830	284	198	110
Little Rock, Ark.	874	8	49	67	66	213	178	80	130	46	24	13
Baton Rouge, La.	203	2	15	14	23	32	44	13	32	9	17	2
Oklahoma City, Okla.	1,815	13	54	92	174	381	363	229	275	104	83	47
Austin, Tex.	425	4	31	44	37	79	66	39	67	22	23	13
Dallas, Tex.	1,716	1	11	59	120	396	413	254	295	95	46	26
Wichita Falls, Tex.	370	21	34	49	60	91	45	17	31	8	5	9
6 Mountain cities	4,305	33	197	337	451	1,074	862	551	497	163	85	55
Butte, Mont.	482	6	42	65	68	99	69	46	50	14	14	9
Boise, Idaho	594	3	30	37	66	153	121	77	71	19	9	8
Casper, Wyo.	312	10	26	25	38	79	44	42	22	16	6	4
Pueblo, Colo.	425	10	45	68	60	134	58	20	23	3	3	1
Phoenix, Ariz.	555		8	25	41	116	122	91	87	34	20	11
Salt Lake City, Utah	1,937	4	46	117	178	493	448	275	244	77	33	22
4 Pacific cities	9,550	26	184	466	792	2,355	2,316	1,449	1,223	339	229	171
Seattle, Wash.*	3,297	16	94	213	300	861	769	441	377	97	61	68
Portland, Ore.	2,581	6	55	150	256	682	617	391	272	72	49	31
Sacramento, Calif.	1,276	1	6	34	73	229	302	262	247	66	43	13
San Diego, Calif.*	2,396	3	29	69	163	583	628	355	327	104	76	59

Source: *Financial Survey of Urban Housing.* *Percentage not shown when total number reporting on properties (mortgaged plus free) as shown in Table A 12 is less than 3.*

*Metropolitan district.

[1]*Geographic division and 52-city percentages weighted by number of owner-occupied residential dwellings in each city (RPI).*

[2]*Based upon the number of properties reporting mortgage debt as shown in this table and the total number of properties reporting (mortgaged plus free) as shown in Table A 12.*

TABLE D 5

Owner-occupied Dwellings, Number and Percentage Mortgaged by Value Groups, 52 Cities by Geographic Division, January 1, 1934

← ——————————————————— P E R C E N T A G E   M O R T G A G E D [2] ——————————————————— →

All value groups	$1-499	$500-999	$1,000-1,499	$1,500-1,999	$2,000-2,999	$3,000-3,999	$4,000-4,999	$5,000-7,499	$7,500-9,999	$10,000-14,999	$15,000 and over	
56.1	25.4	33.1	40.4	44.3	51.1	56.0	61.8	63.2	64.9	64.4	60.0	**52 cities[1]**
67.1	21.7	44.1	57.1	54.0	61.3	62.8	68.1	70.3	70.0	69.2	59.8	**4 New England cities**
46.7	40.0	22.2	30.4	44.7	43.4	45.3	52.4	45.4	49.3	50.7	37.7	Portland, Me.
83.6			85.7	60.0	83.0	82.3	88.0	87.3	81.5	82.4	60.3	Worcester, Mass.
63.2	20.0	46.2	47.1	53.4	55.6	58.7	63.4	66.1	67.7	65.3	62.0	Providence, R.I.*
81.1			100.0		77.7	70.3	77.9	89.0	81.8	87.9	58.3	Waterbury, Conn.
64.1		41.2	50.6	44.9	56.4	61.0	59.8	67.7	70.6	71.7	65.4	**4 Mid. Atlantic cities**
45.3					40.5	39.5	44.7	46.7	49.4	44.6	47.8	Binghamton, N.Y.
76.9		66.7	50.0	40.0	67.6	71.6	67.4	80.0	83.6	86.4	77.4	Syracuse, N.Y.
68.8		18.2	57.6	64.4	64.4	70.1	70.0	73.3	78.1	78.0	76.9	Trenton, N.J.
49.7		12.5	46.4	39.4	40.8	49.1	48.4	55.1	55.2	58.1	46.8	Erie, Pa.
65.1	39.4	41.5	45.9	50.9	55.3	59.4	66.8	69.0	71.4	70.0	64.5	**6 E. N. Central cities**
67.0	47.1	39.5	41.7	44.4	53.4	59.3	67.4	71.9	75.9	73.7	67.3	Cleveland, Ohio*
63.8	16.6	56.1	50.5	62.4	62.0	64.1	70.3	66.4	59.2	64.6	59.3	Indianapolis, Ind.
54.0	33.3	34.2	53.3	51.1	51.2	52.2	57.2	53.6	58.8	66.1	60.0	Peoria, Ill.
57.4	37.5	20.0	69.0	67.6	59.5	53.3	56.3	58.8	70.4	54.5	60.0	Lansing, Mich.
65.3			50.0	76.5	50.6	60.8	65.6	70.1	73.9	57.4	52.4	Kenosha, Wis.
67.1			47.6	58.7	56.9	56.7	69.5	71.1	78.2	72.3	66.0	Racine, Wis.
51.1	27.4	29.3	34.9	39.5	46.2	51.4	58.5	60.8	59.9	61.0	53.5	**10 W. N. Central cities**
55.9	33.3	30.4	32.9	39.2	48.9	52.1	61.6	64.5	71.8	65.1	57.3	Minneapolis, Minn.
48.0		18.2	27.9	29.1	37.0	46.3	59.9	59.7	59.1	66.7	50.0	St. Paul, Minn.
49.5	25.7	31.5	35.8	38.8	46.8	56.1	60.0	65.9	66.3	51.1	44.1	Des Moines, Iowa
42.9	6.7	31.3	32.8	37.5	45.3	47.9	47.7	53.5	34.8	44.7	41.2	St. Joseph, Mo.
50.1	46.5	48.1	49.0	49.0	50.4	50.3	56.5	54.3	36.8	45.8	60.0	Springfield, Mo.
58.5			50.0	60.0	57.3	51.4	60.1	63.3	56.0	60.5	64.2	Fargo, N.D.
53.4	23.7	43.7	39.1	49.4	45.9	52.4	56.8	61.9	69.4	50.9	52.3	Sioux Falls, S.D.
48.2	5.9	33.3	37.6	43.1	47.2	52.9	51.6	54.5	50.8	57.1	51.5	Lincoln, Neb.
44.0	18.5	24.7	30.3	41.0	42.9	52.2	46.1	52.9	36.5	65.8	60.0	Topeka, Kan.
53.5	33.3	34.7	50.3	54.2	55.7	55.9	63.3	59.0	55.1	65.6	59.3	Wichita, Kan.
45.8	17.5	22.9	26.8	34.0	41.5	47.5	52.2	56.2	59.1	55.8	55.9	**9 S. Atlantic cities**
49.6	20.0	70.0	29.4	44.3	50.0	56.7	47.5	49.7	43.6	48.8	71.9	Hagerstown, Md.
49.7	8.3	13.8	17.8	30.4	40.3	47.8	58.8	61.3	66.5	62.5	60.0	Richmond, Va.
21.9			15.0	5.9	16.5	24.3	24.1	29.2	42.3	30.6	37.5	Wheeling, W.Va.*
46.9	16.6	33.3	34.7	43.0	46.1	57.0	55.3	52.6	48.6	43.3	48.5	Asheville, N.C.
56.8		13.8	51.3	51.2	46.4	53.4	61.2	67.2	67.2	61.8	67.9	Greensboro, N.C.
32.9	22.2	17.0	16.2	33.3	41.0	36.7	38.0	38.5	31.1	26.8	22.2	Charleston, S.C.
58.4	33.3	35.1	43.6	48.6	64.5	54.4	59.2	66.2	71.7	63.8	47.1	Columbia, S.C.
58.3	19.4	23.5	38.2	44.6	54.0	61.9	68.9	69.1	70.4	69.2	70.9	Atlanta, Ga.*
47.6	18.2	18.6	16.4	49.3	45.0	46.3	51.7	69.4	61.8	72.2	53.3	Jacksonville, Fla.
51.4	13.4	31.4	41.6	43.3	50.9	58.9	65.2	62.0	67.2	63.5	60.3	**3 E. S. Central cities**
30.7	16.1	19.0	27.4	28.4	38.3	40.7	57.5	35.3	33.3	20.0	57.1	Paducah, Ky.
52.4	12.2	32.9	42.4	43.8	50.4	60.2	66.4	63.9	69.0	69.8	62.0	Birmingham, Ala.*
61.5	20.0	30.4	47.6	52.0	65.3	64.4	62.3	70.0	83.0	52.4	50.0	Jackson, Miss.
52.2	15.7	27.9	40.6	48.6	52.1	54.8	57.0	58.2	60.9	60.6	51.2	**6 W. S. Central cities**
43.8	14.3	25.1	33.0	35.9	48.3	49.3	51.3	54.4	51.1	57.1	46.4	Little Rock, Ark.
53.3	16.7	39.5	45.2	62.2	51.6	69.8	37.1	61.5	47.4	65.4	33.3	Baton Rouge, La.
61.7	27.7	42.2	51.7	63.7	60.9	64.7	69.4	61.4	65.4	72.2	59.5	Oklahoma City, Okla.
39.2	16.0	38.2	36.6	36.2	39.6	39.4	37.1	43.5	44.0	44.2	48.1	Austin, Tex.
53.3	5.9	15.1	35.3	44.0	50.8	54.4	61.2	62.4	68.8	61.3	52.0	Dallas, Tex.
41.4	28.0	27.6	43.8	49.2	51.4	40.2	33.3	47.7	47.1	35.7	34.6	Wichita Falls, Tex.
47.3	18.4	26.4	36.3	41.3	50.9	52.6	59.5	55.9	61.9	54.3	56.1	**6 Mountain cities**
24.2	10.2	18.0	19.1	22.7	25.3	27.1	29.3	30.7	38.9	42.4	42.9	Butte, Mont.
45.1	25.0	37.5	39.8	47.8	46.6	44.3	47.0	47.7	52.8	34.6	42.1	Boise, Idaho
44.0	15.3	29.2	34.2	52.8	54.8	44.8	67.7	37.9	64.0	46.1	44.4	Casper, Wyo.
40.9	14.3	20.8	37.2	41.4	55.8	55.2	64.5	62.2	50.0	75.0		Pueblo, Colo.
55.6		26.7	38.5	48.8	55.2	59.5	65.9	56.1	66.7	62.5	42.3	Phoenix, Ariz.
54.0	21.1	28.0	39.4	41.4	54.7	58.6	64.7	63.5	72.0	52.4	66.7	Salt Lake City, Utah
50.4	19.2	27.5	33.7	39.7	47.9	56.2	62.9	59.8	61.5	64.4	66.4	**4 Pacific cities**
49.2	21.9	28.7	34.5	37.7	46.3	56.3	63.0	61.0	62.6	61.0	74.7	Seattle, Wash.*
51.0	18.8	29.1	33.1	40.0	48.2	57.5	65.6	61.8	62.1	75.4	66.0	Portland, Ore.
54.5	20.0	17.1	47.2	50.7	50.1	53.3	60.1	60.2	63.5	53.8	39.4	Sacramento, Calif.
50.6	13.0	26.4	27.2	39.2	50.2	55.1	59.2	53.0	56.8	58.0	58.4	San Diego, Calif.*

TABLE D 6

Rented Dwellings, Number and Percentage Mortgaged by Value Groups, 44 Cities by Geographic Division, **January 1, 1934**

	All value groups	$1-499	$500-999	$1,000-1,499	$1,500-1,999	$2,000-2,999	$3,000-3,999	$4,000-4,999	$5,000-7,499	$7,500-9,999	$10,000-14,999	$15,000 and over
44 cities[1]	14.146	59	357	657	967	2,319	2,391	1,904	2,890	1,137	766	699
3 New England cities	808		2	9	17	47	88	90	279	154	78	44
Portland, Me.	194		2	6	3	13	15	25	53	44	23	10
Worcester, Mass.	208			1	2	7	20	24	74	47	18	15
Providence, R.I.*	406			2	12	27	53	41	152	63	37	19
3 Mid. Atlantic cities	756		10	8	27	96	110	120	223	82	54	26
Syracuse, N.Y.	224			1		4	15	25	93	47	28	11
Trenton, N.J.	248		9	5	25	59	38	29	64	9	6	4
Erie, Pa.	284		1	2	2	33	57	66	66	26	20	11
6 E. N. Central cities	3,904	6	35	90	144	420	502	578	1,083	477	312	257
Cleveland, Ohio*	2,384	2	14	39	45	156	224	346	774	355	240	189
Indianapolis, Ind.	512	4	9	18	49	116	98	56	91	34	18	19
Peoria, Ill.	372		9	18	29	74	70	70	57	15	14	16
Lansing, Mich.	166		1	8	18	38	51	18	25	4	2	1
Kenosha, Wis.	137			2	2	6	25	22	44	11	15	10
Racine, Wis.	333		2	5	1	30	34	66	92	58	23	22
9 W. N. Central cities	2,955	22	105	217	284	560	631	406	415	118	84	113
Minneapolis, Minn.	1,000	2	9	33	44	171	229	162	183	57	45	65
St. Paul, Minn.	227			7	15	33	55	45	45	12	9	6
Des Moines, Iowa	413	6	16	22	50	83	114	44	46	12	9	11
St. Joseph, Mo.	113		8	15	6	22	24	23	9	3	3	
Springfield, Mo.	186	6	11	32	31	50	18	12	17	4	1	4
Sioux Falls, S.D.	188	1	1	10	15	29	35	40	36	10	5	6
Lincoln, Neb.	201		8	17	20	46	49	23	20	7	2	9
Topeka, Kan.	260		18	30	43	48	46	29	32	4	5	5
Wichita, Kan.	367	7	34	51	60	78	61	28	27	9	5	7
8 S. Atlantic cities	1,861	8	58	100	125	323	320	262	393	118	86	68
Hagerstown, Md.	69	1	1	3	5	15	14	9	11	6	3	1
Richmond, Va.	134		4	4	4	15	19	25	38	12	8	5
Wheeling, W.Va.*	830	4	24	45	59	132	159	127	184	44	28	24
Asheville, N.C.	46	1	3	4	7	9	4	9	3	2	3	1
Greensboro, N.C.	76		3	10	3	9	10	10	15	6	6	4
Charleston, S.C.	75		3	6	5	10	13	11	20	5	1	1
Columbia, S.C.	87		5	4	2	9	10	14	24	12	4	3
Atlanta, Ga.*	544	2	15	24	40	124	91	57	98	31	33	29
2 E. S. Central cities	246	5	16	14	29	48	41	28	29	15	10	11
Paducah, Ky.	25	3	3		2	3	4	2	3	1	1	3
Birmingham, Ala.*	221	2	13	14	27	45	37	26	26	14	9	8
5 W. S. Central cities	1,188	14	71	83	107	239	212	117	166	63	53	63
Little Rock, Ark.	184	7	18	24	17	37	24	15	20	7	7	8
Oklahoma City, Okla.	402	2	14	26	43	68	56	38	66	24	25	40
Austin, Tex.	110	4	22	9	7	21	19	9	7	3	4	5
Dallas, Tex.	410		7	15	30	90	97	51	64	29	17	10
Wichita Falls, Tex.	82	1	10	9	10	23	16	4	9			
4 Mountain cities	587	1	27	43	62	126	102	77	79	26	12	32
Butte, Mont.	59		5	8	10	10	7	1	8	2	1	7
Pueblo, Colo.	55		15	9	9	12	3	4	2		1	
Phoenix, Ariz.	166	1	1	5	9	40	30	23	35	11	5	6
Salt Lake City, Utah	307		6	21	34	64	62	49	34	13	5	19
4 Pacific cities	1,841	3	33	93	172	460	385	226	223	84	77	85
Seattle, Wash.*	511		8	26	44	135	113	58	60	12	21	34
Portland, Ore.	445	3	8	35	48	113	96	48	48	19	12	15
Sacramento, Calif.	237		1	8	19	52	46	38	39	18	11	5
San Diego, Calif.*	648		16	24	61	160	130	82	76	35	33	31

Source: *Financial Survey of Urban Housing. Percentage not shown when total number reporting on properties (mortgaged plus free) as shown in Table A 13 is less than 3.*

*Metropolitan district.

[1] *Geographic division and 44-city percentages weighted by total number of rented residential properties in each city (RPI).*

[2] *Individual city percentages are based upon the number of properties reporting mortgage debt as shown in this table and the total number of properties reporting (mortgaged plus free) as shown in Table A 13.*

TABLE D 6

Rented Dwellings, Number and Percentage Mortgaged by Value Groups, 44 Cities by Geographic Division, January 1, 1934

← PERCENTAGE MORTGAGED [2] →

All value groups	$1-499	$500-999	$1,000-1,499	$1,500-1,999	$2,000-2,999	$3,000-3,999	$4,000-4,999	$5,000-7,499	$7,500-9,999	$10,000-14,999	$15,000 and over	
39.8	20.2	14.9	21.7	27.9	34.5	41.6	49.1	54.6	57.6	58.3	68.6	44 cities[1]
52.5		20.0	15.6	36.1	34.2	42.7	42.9	62.4	64.7	72.6	69.8	**3 New England cities**
41.3		20.0	30.0	14.3	23.2	29.4	40.3	43.8	58.7	63.9	55.6	Portland, Me.
69.3		25.0			70.0	55.6	60.0	72.5	81.0	64.3	75.0	Worcester, Mass.
50.2			11.8	38.7	27.6	41.4	39.4	62.4	61.8	75.5	70.4	Providence, R.I.*
51.7		26.7	13.5	16.4	29.6	41.7	50.7	60.3	59.2	68.9	63.6	**3 Mid. Atlantic cities**
67.1					30.8	48.4	55.6	70.5	78.3	80.0	73.3	Syracuse, N.Y.
39.8		37.5	10.4	35.2	32.6	39.2	46.0	67.4	36.0	66.6	50.0	Trenton, N.J.
36.5		20.0	15.4	4.7	25.8	33.5	46.5	40.7	45.6	54.1	57.9	Erie, Pa.
50.7	44.1	21.8	30.8	36.1	40.4	45.6	50.2	58.2	62.6	58.6	71.4	**6 E. N. Central cities**
53.2	25.0	24.1	31.2	33.6	36.3	40.8	52.7	60.4	63.7	64.0	61.6	Cleveland, Ohio*
51.2	80.0	21.4	29.0	44.5	51.3	58.3	47.9	56.9	66.6	48.6	86.3	Indianapolis, Ind.
40.3		16.4	22.5	28.4	38.9	41.7	56.0	46.3	51.7	53.8	80.0	Peoria, Ill.
36.5		5.6	34.8	32.1	33.9	37.5	35.3	59.5	44.4	50.0		Lansing, Mich.
48.2			50.0	50.0	30.0	45.5	37.9	53.7	42.3	78.9	71.4	Kenosha, Wis.
53.5		28.6	33.3	14.3	36.1	35.8	54.5	57.5	78.4	67.6	84.6	Racine, Wis.
37.9	15.4	15.4	23.7	27.2	32.9	44.1	53.7	53.1	55.9	58.0	74.0	**9 W. N. Central cities**
46.3	13.3	14.1	23.1	24.6	38.4	49.2	56.4	58.3	61.3	67.2	75.6	Minneapolis, Minn.
41.4		26.9	31.9	28.7	42.6	51.1	52.9	54.5	69.2	75.0		St. Paul, Minn.
35.4	11.5	13.4	17.2	27.9	31.2	55.1	53.6	56.8	57.1	64.3	64.7	Des Moines, Iowa
24.7	15.1	15.8	13.0	22.9	32.4	65.7	28.1	60.0	37.5			St. Joseph, Mo.
25.4	17.1	8.3	21.1	23.1	36.0	31.0	50.0	47.5	57.1		57.1	Springfield, Mo.
40.8	25.0	7.1	30.0	30.7	36.2	26.0	48.8	48.0	52.6	50.0	50.0	Sioux Falls, S.D.
36.5		16.0	32.7	23.8	34.6	46.2	46.9	52.6	53.8	33.3	90.0	Lincoln, Neb.
26.2		16.4	21.1	27.0	21.5	28.4	37.7	47.1	30.8	55.6	71.4	Topeka, Kan.
38.8	21.9	26.8	29.8	39.2	37.0	48.4	59.6	61.4	56.3	45.5	87.5	Wichita, Kan.
34.3	6.8	11.8	19.1	20.9	33.7	36.9	47.9	56.1	53.6	58.3	60.8	**8 S. Atlantic cities**
26.2	14.3	5.1	9.0	21.4	25.0	37.6	28.4	39.5	43.0	30.0	25.0	Hagerstown, Md.
34.2		12.5	12.9	11.4	27.3	29.2	49.0	55.1	63.2	30.0	35.7	Richmond, Va.
35.3	13.3	18.2	26.5	27.6	31.1	36.1	39.3	47.5	40.0	53.3	51.1	Wheeling, W.Va.*
14.5	6.6	13.6	14.2	22.5	12.6	8.1	23.6	7.8	13.3	62.5		Asheville, N.C.
29.3		8.3	37.0	15.8	47.4	27.0	47.6	44.1	31.6	54.5	57.1	Greensboro, N.C.
23.6		6.3	14.0	15.2	18.2	40.6	50.0	46.5	33.3	7.7	33.3	Charleston, S.C.
33.7		16.1	18.2	13.3	28.1	27.0	53.8	64.9	60.0	50.0	75.0	Columbia, S.C.
40.7	3.8	9.9	18.2	25.2	42.9	48.1	54.8	71.5	68.9	80.5	80.6	Atlanta, Ga.*
21.7	3.0	8.5	13.2	24.8	22.4	27.0	31.2	36.4	43.0	42.1	64.5	**2 E. S. Central cities**
7.1	3.5	2.8		4.9	11.5	20.0	25.0	21.4	33.3	33.3	100.0	Paducah, Ky.
22.9	3.0	9.0	13.2	26.5	23.3	27.6	31.7	37.7	43.8	42.9	61.5	Birmingham, Ala.*
35.9	8.3	15.2	21.7	25.6	36.0	45.3	51.4	55.5	65.8	63.6	74.7	**5 W. S. Central cities**
23.9	5.1	14.6	18.9	18.1	28.7	35.8	62.5	52.6	77.8	58.3	80.0	Little Rock, Ark.
43.1	5.0	16.7	31.0	36.4	39.5	45.9	55.1	55.9	68.6	64.1	78.4	Oklahoma City, Okla.
30.6	25.0	26.2	20.5	22.6	41.2	41.3	40.9	22.6	15.0	50.0	71.4	Austin, Tex.
39.6		12.3	19.2	24.6	36.4	51.3	53.7	60.4	70.7	68.0	71.4	Dallas, Tex.
21.2	5.9	15.1	12.4	14.5	29.8	33.3	20.0	69.2				Wichita Falls, Tex.
35.5	20.0	13.5	18.3	30.0	35.8	38.5	50.9	48.2	70.5	44.3	79.4	**4 Mountain cities**
15.1		8.9	12.5	18.2	14.7	21.2	5.3	23.5	28.6	14.3	50.0	Butte, Mont.
22.5		25.4	22.0	28.1	25.5	23.1	50.0	25.0		25.0		Pueblo, Colo.
43.6	20.0	7.1	17.2	23.6	46.0	40.0	52.3	61.4	64.7	55.6	100.0	Phoenix, Ariz.
42.9		13.3	19.1	38.2	41.0	50.0	64.5	58.6	86.7	55.6	76.0	Salt Lake City, Utah
36.8	16.7	10.3	18.8	25.7	35.4	43.8	54.5	55.4	53.5	57.8	64.6	**4 Pacific cities**
36.4		9.6	15.1	20.4	35.4	48.1	59.2	62.5	41.4	70.0	61.8	Seattle, Wash.*
33.8	16.7	7.5	21.5	27.1	34.2	38.6	46.6	52.7	61.3	50.0	62.5	Portland, Ore.
45.0		6.7	25.8	37.3	37.1	46.9	58.5	57.4	64.3	50.0	71.4	Sacramento, Calif.
38.3		15.8	18.8	28.1	36.3	42.3	55.0	47.2	59.3	50.8	68.9	San Diego, Calif.*

TABLE D 7

Mortgaged Dwellings, Number reporting Value and Average Value by Value Groups: Owner-occupied, 52 Cities; Rented, 51 Cities, by Geographic Division, January 1, 1934

	NUMBER REPORTING	OWNER-OCCUPIED — AVERAGE VALUE (dollars) BY VALUE GROUPS											
		All value groups	$1-499	$500-999	$1,000-1,499	$1,500-1,999	$2,000-2,999	$3,000-3,999	$4,000-4,999	$5,000-7,499	$7,500-9,999	$10,000-14,999	$15,000 and over
52 cities[1]	70,166	5,081	359	782	1,231	1,687	2,456	3,322	4,250	5,780	8,163	11,236	21,327
4 New England cities	4,382	6,635		767	1,182	1,626	2,747	3,365	4,250	5,891	8,340	11,074	19,265
Portland, Me.	660	6,142			1,143	1,659	2,344	3,328	4,242	5,919	8,225	10,810	17,370
Worcester, Mass.	1,187	6,744			1,120	1,600	2,591	3,589	4,295	5,901	8,292	10,933	17,002
Providence, R.I.*	2,074	6,393		767	1,206	1,632	2,881	3,292	4,242	5,889	8,352	11,094	19,255
Waterbury, Conn.	481	8,112			1,175		2,414	3,377	4,217	5,870	8,415	11,344	24,660
4 Mid. Atlantic cities	4,437	5,777			1,237	1,723	2,437	3,330	4,265	5,808	8,199	10,998	20,975
Binghamton, N.Y.	266	6,637					2,727	3,422	4,363	5,857	8,160	10,924	21,727
Syracuse, N.Y.	1,000	6,478			1,220	1,675	2,407	3,329	4,270	5,888	8,319	11,098	22,129
Trenton, N.J.	1,617	4,176			1,304	1,652	2,353	3,302	4,247	5,655	8,085	10,821	19,150
Erie, Pa.	1,554	4,957			1,215	1,928	2,436	3,308	4,211	5,711	8,003	10,942	19,190
6 E. N. Central cities	20,645	6,019	383	797	1,310	1,745	2,496	3,378	4,270	5,859	8,221	11,120	20,691
Cleveland, Ohio*	14,311	6,635	383	762	1,375	1,781	2,540	3,421	4,265	5,864	8,277	11,153	21,633
Indianapolis, Ind.	1,767	4,946		906	1,183	1,682	2,366	3,278	4,270	5,959	8,091	11,060	19,348
Peoria, Ill.	1,467	4,745		792	1,182	1,689	2,366	3,327	4,262	5,693	8,067	11,190	17,884
Lansing, Mich.	647	3,967		850	1,155	1,637	2,446	3,320	4,303	5,648	8,176	10,917	20,467
Kenosha, Wis.	744	5,273				1,729	2,433	3,330	4,272	5,788	8,285	10,867	16,455
Racine, Wis.	1,709	5,529			1,191	1,663	2,650	3,314	4,315	5,802	8,151	11,169	19,041
10 W. N. Central cities	12,536	4,166	325	768	1,197	1,671	2,390	3,299	4,264	5,726	8,123	10,994	22,468
Minneapolis, Minn.	4,186	4,819		795	1,290	1,685	2,431	3,326	4,256	5,712	8,097	11,030	26,559
St. Paul, Minn.	896	4,207		725	1,131	1,665	2,363	3,308	4,229	5,633	8,125	10,820	18,857
Des Moines, Iowa	1,677	3,624	307	735	1,158	1,660	2,363	3,309	4,221	5,730	8,015	10,587	19,820
St. Joseph, Mo.	541	3,756		723	1,138	1,650	2,485	3,220	4,792	6,229	8,188	11,059	19,714
Springfield, Mo.	788	3,004	325	746	1,139	1,626	2,287	3,215	4,239	5,867	8,286	10,909	31,444
Fargo, N.D.	489	5,168			1,060	1,888	2,536	3,319	4,275	5,824	8,452	11,586	19,889
Sioux Falls, S.D.	654	4,538	367	693	1,150	1,682	2,638	3,271	4,242	5,684	8,090	10,808	17,500
Lincoln, Neb.	825	3,860		792	1,175	1,641	2,313	3,276	4,254	5,761	8,222	11,955	16,633
Topeka, Kan.	1,105	3,632	340	903	1,181	1,686	2,353	3,318	4,228	5,631	7,935	11,036	20,700
Wichita, Kan.	1,375	3,002	329	757	1,144	1,639	2,288	3,243	4,218	5,697	8,230	11,462	20,987
9 S. Atlantic cities	6,384	4,964	362	790	1,137	1,665	2,375	3,266	4,221	5,751	8,051	10,983	18,970
Hagerstown, Md.	366	5,275		671	1,110	1,569	2,350	3,241	4,247	5,710	7,729	11,280	19,626
Richmond, Va.	1,112	5,971		769	1,107	1,652	2,316	3,281	4,256	5,862	8,124	11,495	18,182
Wheeling, W. Va.*	828	4,422	275	688	1,156	1,616	2,342	3,235	4,253	5,729	7,818	10,668	18,021
Asheville, N.C.	419	4,132		769	1,150	1,658	2,403	3,219	4,157	5,629	8,271	10,692	18,677
Greensboro, N.C.	321	5,836		750	1,155	1,686	2,381	3,272	4,295	5,791	8,097	10,914	21,833
Charleston, S.C.	212	4,761		700	1,100	1,613	2,250	3,248	4,115	5,832	7,943	10,818	20,500
Columbia, S.C.	346	5,107		769	1,119	1,588	2,709	3,270	4,211	5,714	7,997	10,173	18,750
Atlanta, Ga.*	2,482	4,828	400	911	1,147	1,725	2,401	3,282	4,268	5,761	8,121	11,128	19,316
Jacksonville, Fla.	298	4,513		638	1,133	1,615	2,307	3,281	4,177	5,608	8,095	10,577	18,750
3 E. S. Central cities	2,597	3,737	379	779	1,222	1,630	2,320	3,250	4,179	5,619	8,069	10,376	18,262
Paducah, Ky.	240	2,772	310	874	1,132	1,630	2,300	3,284	4,243	5,811	8,000		15,750
Birmingham, Ala.*	2,083	3,675	383	790	1,239	1,631	2,298	3,240	4,164	5,610	8,030	10,354	18,565
Jackson, Miss.	274	4,538		671	1,150	1,623	2,473	3,300	4,250	5,595	8,353	10,518	17,333
6 W. S. Central cities	5,383	4,130	325	798	1,264	1,664	2,345	3,285	4,219	5,805	8,090	11,168	19,976
Little Rock, Ark.	874	3,682	450	839	1,163	1,655	2,374	3,291	4,213	5,553	7,987	10,487	16,731
Baton Rouge, La.	200	4,292		733	1,146	1,668	2,413	3,243	4,169	5,872	8,111	11,141	
Oklahoma City, Okla.	1,809	4,279	300	710	1,116	1,638	2,347	3,243	4,245	5,771	8,153	11,046	19,423
Austin, Tex.	425	4,199	300	745	1,157	1,711	2,257	3,396	4,146	6,035	7,955	11,085	19,015
Dallas, Tex.	1,716	4,212		882	1,454	1,683	2,348	3,292	4,230	5,867	8,083	11,374	20,896
Wichita Falls, Tex.	359	3,106	271	728	1,149	1,608	2,330	3,300	4,135	5,603	8,143	11,940	24,500
6 Mountain cities	4,288	3,601	361	838	1,164	1,672	2,375	3,299	4,240	5,711	8,139	12,699	26,556
Butte, Mont.	479	3,327	367	922	1,118	1,610	2,247	3,313	4,233	5,600	8,164	10,314	21,489
Boise, Idaho	594	3,515	367	720	1,222	1,695	2,395	3,269	4,230	5,715	8,232	11,222	19,638
Casper, Wyo.	306	3,141	370	892	1,146	1,670	2,363	3,307	4,210	5,718	8,119	10,000	
Pueblo, Colo.	420	2,375	390	729	1,133	1,641	2,346	3,300	4,150	5,587	8,000	12,287	
Phoenix, Ariz.	552	4,249		788	1,132	1,676	2,475	3,272	4,189	5,611	8,212	11,170	18,000
Salt Lake City, Utah	1,937	3,858	350	902	1,179	1,684	2,370	3,307	4,283	5,780	8,143	13,961	30,295
4 Pacific cities	9,514	3,913	345	759	1,232	1,672	2,361	3,276	4,242	5,655	8,062	12,010	24,855
Seattle, Wash.*	3,288	3,907	356	813	1,325	1,676	2,368	3,270	4,259	5,638	8,005	13,169	27,828
Portland, Ore.	2,578	3,812	300	745	1,165	1,657	2,337	3,278	4,241	5,660	8,039	10,820	24,226
Sacramento, Calif.	1,262	4,409		600	1,203	1,692	2,407	3,294	4,250	5,803	8,286	13,033	18,346
San Diego, Calif.*	2,386	4,224	400	732	1,141	1,679	2,364	3,284	4,199	5,618	8,130	10,884	21,993

Source: *Financial Survey of Urban Housing.* *Average not shown for fewer than 3 reports.*

*Metropolitan district.

[1] *Geographic division and 52 (51)-city averages weighted by estimated number of mortgaged properties, by tenure, in each city (RPI). For rented properties, where the number of cities included in the 'All value groups' column is larger than the number for the individual value groups, the weighted geographic division and 52 (51)-city averages in the 'All value groups' column are not strictly comparable to the weighted averages for the individual value groups.*

[2] *Where only average value 'All value groups' is shown, average value by value groups was not obtained by the Financial Survey of Urban Housing either because the number of reports was too small or because of lack of related information for rented properties.*

TABLE D 7

Mortgaged Dwellings, Number reporting Value and Average Value by Value Groups: Owner-occupied, 52 Cities; Rented, 51 Cities, by Geographic Division, January 1, 1934

← RENTED →

AVERAGE VALUE (dollars) BY VALUE GROUPS

NUMBER REPORTING	All[2] value groups	$1-499	$500-999	$1,000-1,499	$1,500-1,999	$2,000-2,999	$3,000-3,999	$4,000-4,999	$5,000-7,499	$7,500-9,999	$10,000-14,999	$15,000 and over	
13,779	6,133	372	761	1,214	1,666	2,418	3,343	4,260	5,846	8,218	11,383	35,583	51 cities[1]
909	7,613			1,083	1,614	2,438	3,328	4,224	6,019	8,417	10,930	26,261	4 New England cities
194	7,474			1,083	1,500	2,392	3,220	4,236	5,979	8,236	10,887	32,240	Portland, Me.
208	7,283					2,529	3,365	4,175	6,146	8,300	10,944	18,887	Worcester, Mass.
397	6,901				1,625	2,415	3,327	4,238	5,984	8,471	10,930	18,887	Providence, R.I.*
110	13,745											27,889	Waterbury, Conn.
828	6,749		656	1,220	1,596	2,390	3,391	4,213	5,794	8,173	10,950	27,104	4 Mid. Atlantic cities
81	8,169												Binghamton, N.Y.
219	7,504					2,375	3,453	4,200	5,850	8,109	10,819	31,722	Syracuse, N.Y.
245	4,020		656	1,220	1,596	2,328	3,213	4,203	5,478	8,344	11,517	16,725	Trenton, N.J.
283	5,704					2,472	3,342	4,255	5,858	8,231	10,920	21,636	Erie, Pa.
3,837	6,690	375	760	1,339	1,696	2,565	3,313	4,263	5,859	8,168	11,184	29,912	6 E. N. Central cities
2,344	8,008		770	1,460	1,702	2,736	3,330	4,269	5,925	8,333	11,352	31,261	Cleveland, Ohio*
512	4,776	375	744	1,178	1,686	2,323	3,288	4,268	5,782	7,937	10,739	26,600	Indianapolis, Ind.
352	5,417		738	1,176	1,604	2,328	3,244	4,169	5,724	7,964	11,843	37,163	Peoria, Ill.
164	3,555			1,171	1,789	2,327	3,349	4,211	5,728	7,775			Lansing, Mich.
133	6,698												Kenosha, Wis.
332	6,875			1,160		2,433	3,303	4,315	5,785	8,186	11,174	24,782	Racine, Wis.
3,015	4,717	317	745	1,147	1,706	2,361	3,315	4,323	5,773	8,252	11,294	29,996	10 W. N. Central cities
998	5,830		786	1,136	1,640	2,367	3,293	4,463	5,696	8,196	11,175	27,795	Minneapolis, Minn.
227	5,186			1,157	1,947	2,397	3,424	4,293	6,011	8,392	11,400	34,267	St. Paul, Minn.
410	4,119	267	688	1,150	1,676	2,353	3,224	4,225	5,800	8,442	11,611	32,309	Des Moines, Iowa
109	3,248												St. Joseph, Mo.
181	3,082	360	722	1,177	1,706	2,256	3,265	4,200	5,706	8,375		25,250	Springfield, Mo.
80	5,146												Fargo, N.D.
188	5,222			1,110	1,753	2,448	3,329	4,163	5,722	7,990	11,100	41,333	Sioux Falls, S.D.
200	4,148		700	1,206	1,645	2,324	3,277	4,204	5,710	7,986		24,389	Lincoln, Neb.
255	3,831		744	1,107	1,660	2,371	3,418	4,261	5,790	8,000	11,100	42,400	Topeka, Kan.
367	3,107	357	724	1,141	1,608	2,326	3,316	4,257	5,681	8,278	11,260	24,471	Wichita, Kan.
1,140	6,260		748	1,157	1,663	2,313	3,485	4,310	5,663	8,213	13,261	48,488	8 S. Atlantic cities
68	4,445												Hagerstown, Md.
133	5,893		825	1,175	1,800	2,187	3,242	4,336	5,929	8,300	10,650	32,800	Richmond, Va.
120	5,791												Wheeling, W. Va.*
39	3,738												Asheville, N.C.
76	6,476												Greensboro, N.C.
75	4,139												Charleston, S.C.
85	5,607												Columbia, S.C.
544	6,990		720	1,150	1,613	2,359	3,573	4,300	5,567	8,181	14,206	54,166	Atlanta, Ga.*
317	5,884		725	1,100	1,619	2,304	3,351	4,188	5,508	7,836	10,838	62,938	3 E. S. Central cities
24	4,458												Paducah, Ky.
218	5,718		725	1,100	1,619	2,304	3,351	4,188	5,508	7,836	10,838	62,938	Birmingham, Ala.*
75	6,919												Jackson, Miss.
1,242	5,141	289	787	1,137	1,640	2,346	3,298	4,247	5,792	8,319	11,104	28,753	6 W. S. Central cities
180	3,883	240	765	1,121	1,625	2,308	3,358	4,180	5,915	7,829	12,333	17,344	Little Rock, Ark.
60	5,327												Baton Rouge, La.
402	6,882		800	1,162	1,621	2,325	3,305	4,258	5,680	8,213	10,720	32,728	Oklahoma City, Okla.
110	3,776	350	686	1,122	1,657	2,352	3,337	4,144	6,086	8,667	11,375	22,600	Austin, Tex.
408	4,749		800	1,127	1,652	2,367	3,276	4,269	5,792	8,428	11,059	29,500	Dallas, Tex.
82	2,522												Wichita Falls, Tex.
664	5,482		833	1,188	1,680	2,402	3,336	4,225	5,807	8,405	10,787	43,991	6 Mountain cities
59	6,334												Butte, Mont.
34	3,894												Boise, Idaho
50	5,068												Casper, Wyo.
55	2,142												Pueblo, Colo.
164	4,858			1,167	1,711	2,405	3,400	4,214	5,824	8,564	10,600	22,900	Phoenix, Ariz.
302	6,892		833	1,200	1,661	2,400	3,298	4,231	5,797	8,308	10,900	56,753	Salt Lake City, Utah
1,827	6,186	467	776	1,181	1,636	2,350	3,360	4,239	6,052	8,185	11,626	46,948	4 Pacific cities
506	8,648		850	1,169	1,562	2,349	3,261	4,247	6,760	8,155	11,286	77,285	Seattle, Wash.*
438	4,509	467	629	1,206	1,673	2,353	3,313	4,248	5,529	8,121	12,292	33,900	Portland, Ore.
235	4,838			1,186	1,721	2,400	3,957	4,274	5,834	8,411	10,818	26,800	Sacramento, Calif.
648	4,867		819	1,171	1,672	2,329	3,318	4,204	5,650	8,206	11,755	24,426	San Diego, Calif.*

TABLE D 8

Mortgaged Dwellings, Number reporting Debt and Average Debt Outstanding (Principal only), All Priorities, by Value Groups:
Owner-occupied, 52 Cities; Rented, 51 Cities, by Geographic Division, January 1, 1934

	NUMBER REPORTING	All value groups	$1-499	$500-999	$1,000-1,499	$1,500-1,999	$2,000-2,999	$3,000-3,999	$4,000-4,999	$5,000-7,499	$7,500-9,999	$10,000-14,999	$15,000 and over
52 cities[1]	68,011	2,823	372	615	916	1,129	1,543	1,934	2,452	3,138	4,230	5,858	10,733
4 New England cities	4,231	3,619		583	664	1,198	1,726	1,905	2,542	3,239	4,455	5,900	9,045
Portland, Me.	643	3,102			-1,057	729	1,351	1,477	1,992	2,955	4,302	5,579	8,526
Worcester, Mass.	1,109	4,522			700	1,133	2,312	2,462	3,161	4,036	5,330	7,232	9,855
Providence, R.I.*	2,009	3,156		583	614	1,252	1,558	1,730	2,359	2,915	4,051	5,406	8,101
Waterbury, Conn.	470	4,868			725		1,750	2,052	2,664	3,748	5,245	6,397	13,420
4 Mid. Atlantic cities	4,325	3,230			1,269	1,304	1,620	1,937	2,565	3,297	4,591	6,021	8,918
Binghamton, N.Y.	261	3,049					1,567	1,641	1,792	2,744	3,993	5,352	7,991
Syracuse, N.Y.	971	3,692			1,425	1,375	1,739	1,996	2,745	3,486	4,712	5,967	8,717
Trenton, N.J.	1,592	2,438			1,166	1,172	1,426	1,906	2,593	3,126	4,577	6,215	10,445
Erie, Pa.	1,501	2,858			940	1,243	1,520	1,975	2,487	3,270	4,617	6,364	8,475
6 E. N. Central cities	19,899	3,419	500	766	1,200	1,281	1,698	2,078	2,546	3,282	4,436	6,060	10,776
Cleveland, Ohio*	13,838	3,794	500	871	1,355	1,375	1,773	2,141	2,635	3,361	4,567	6,002	11,665
Indianapolis, Ind.	1,685	2,781		563	971	1,212	1,563	1,961	2,319	3,187	3,999	6,366	10,108
Peoria, Ill.	1,375	2,393		545	693	815	1,299	1,779	2,218	2,784	4,081	5,172	7,776
Lansing, Mich.	630	2,361		333	950	1,118	1,512	2,112	2,566	3,138	4,692	6,600	8,833
Kenosha, Wis.	725	2,837				1,321	1,844	2,064	2,383	2,984	4,308	6,241	4,300
Racine, Wis.	1,646	3,257			750	884	1,712	1,985	2,680	3,451	4,619	6,020	10,417
10 W. N. Central cities	12,191	2,168	266	500	773	908	1,323	1,747	2,263	2,906	3,798	5,178	11,900
Minneapolis, Minn.	4,084	2,525		585	812	888	1,435	1,804	2,169	2,880	3,822	5,475	16,059
St. Paul, Minn.	879	2,104		375	719	847	1,143	1,640	2,365	2,713	3,275	4,835	9,414
Des Moines, Iowa	1,628	1,928	279	552	769	923	1,352	1,752	2,179	2,954	3,828	5,413	10,700
St. Joseph, Mo.	529	1,973		365	698	876	1,305	1,625	2,833	3,452	4,206	5,224	7,457
Springfield, Mo.	756	1,590	275	485	713	850	1,228	1,776	2,259	2,776	3,426	4,565	9,589
Fargo, N.D.	481	2,605			833	1,044	1,310	1,710	2,278	3,095	3,426	4,565	9,589
Sioux Falls, S.D.	645	2,118	200	442	735	818	1,276	1,701	2,137	2,609	3,224	4,385	7,636
Lincoln, Neb.	795	2,069		452	860	1,006	1,262	1,777	2,227	3,228	4,128	5,600	7,007
Topeka, Kan.	1,069	1,829	320	524	710	900	1,312	1,690	2,183	2,668	4,448	5,048	6,113
Wichita, Kan.	1,325	1,704	233	482	783	1,097	1,358	1,833	2,367	3,160	4,088	4,880	9,780
9 S. Atlantic cities	6,130	2,809	386	515	771	1,037	1,410	1,918	2,497	3,207	4,529	6,087	9,328
Hagerstown, Md.	363	3,215		414	890	777	1,503	1,960	3,032	3,439	5,488	6,358	10,878
Richmond, Va.	1,077	3,544		773	708	935	1,490	2,070	2,688	3,540	4,755	6,826	9,442
Wheeling, W.Va.*	810	2,186	400	483	784	1,049	1,153	1,637	2,019	2,662	3,851	5,478	9,138
Asheville, N.C.	408	2,739		812	866	1,259	1,749	2,435	2,650	3,628	6,665	4,792	10,041
Greensboro, N.C.	293	3,613		600	865	1,084	1,386	1,890	2,583	3,264	5,059	7,367	13,519
Charleston, S.C.	208	2,396		400	633	681	987	1,985	2,300	3,081	3,307	6,482	6,683
Columbia, S.C.	323	2,930		440	562	987	1,602	1,733	2,847	3,365	4,449	5,107	8,600
Atlanta, Ga.*	2,361	2,766	380	448	749	1,099	1,500	1,961	2,557	3,285	4,588	6,533	9,402
Jacksonville, Fla.	287	2,355		338	938	1,045	1,233	1,821	2,363	2,953	4,305	4,392	7,450
3 E. S. Central cities	2,533	2,233	361	642	917	1,148	1,529	2,106	2,521	3,192	4,285	5,291	8,862
Paducah, Ky.	234	1,626	140	460	673	904	1,423	1,959	2,519	3,367	5,067		9,000
Birmingham, Ala.*	2,039	2,264	375	665	974	1,249	1,586	2,135	2,565	3,217	4,384	5,466	8,816
Jackson, Miss.	260	2,285		571	650	591	1,205	1,976	2,233	2,957	3,317	4,155	9,100
6 W. S. Central cities	5,204	2,289	314	601	830	1,006	1,450	1,876	2,440	3,213	4,019	5,891	8,969
Little Rock, Ark.	841	2,317	300	319	766	1,194	1,581	1,958	2,696	3,620	4,818	6,154	8,231
Baton Rouge, La.	186	1,931		400	662	825	1,311	1,707	1,775	2,987	3,078	4,900	
Oklahoma City, Okla.	1,758	2,489	308	477	766	1,055	1,485	1,986	2,458	3,377	4,028	6,345	9,844
Austin, Tex.	416	1,948	367	461	753	857	1,237	1,648	1,900	2,789	3,127	4,114	8,854
Dallas, Tex.	1,676	2,253		773	927	947	1,420	1,799	2,483	3,036	3,960	5,743	8,185
Wichita Falls, Tex.	327	2,060	293	992	857	1,174	1,672	2,146	2,894	3,643	5,057	7,325	11,500
6 Mountain cities	4,203	2,007	259	554	733	1,008	1,498	1,818	2,300	2,992	3,650	6,769	14,678
Butte, Mont.	475	1,373	233	607	681	827	1,180	1,394	1,826	2,136	3,086	2,807	5,588
Boise, Idaho	568	1,518	167	366	632	911	1,141	1,425	1,691	2,415	3,106	3,700	8,100
Casper, Wyo.	300	1,787	240	552	848	1,253	1,308	2,000	2,349	2,695	4,244	4,150	
Pueblo, Colo.	413	1,406	270	498	767	1,163	1,455	1,868	2,255	2,896	2,233	6,400	
Phoenix, Ariz.	537	2,392		775	674	1,015	1,627	1,916	2,234	3,154	4,148	6,520	8,620
Salt Lake City, Utah	1,910	2,236	275	535	747	974	1,585	1,866	2,466	3,187	3,987	8,091	18,190
4 Pacific cities	9,295	2,186	288	580	819	1,109	1,451	1,928	2,365	2,930	4,023	5,926	12,913
Seattle, Wash.*	3,222	2,138	275	437	796	1,003	1,369	1,905	2,297	2,794	4,060	6,643	15,223
Portland, Ore.	2,511	2,044	280	742	819	1,197	1,454	1,900	2,328	2,957	3,963	5,440	12,340
Sacramento, Calif.	1,240	2,724		583	879	1,280	1,671	2,139	2,697	3,525	4,577	6,340	11,923
San Diego, Calif.*	2,322	2,296	333	632	845	1,126	1,535	1,934	2,437	2,927	3,782	4,891	8,926

Source: *Financial Survey of Urban Housing.* *Average not shown for fewer than 3 reports.*

*Metropolitan district.

[1] *Geographic division and 52 (51)-city averages weighted by estimated number of mortgaged properties, by tenure, in each city (RPI). For rented properties where the number of cities included in the 'All value groups' column is larger than the number for the individual value groups, the weighted geographic division and 52 (51)-city averages in the 'All value groups' column are not strictly comparable to the weighted averages for the individual value groups.*

[2] *Where only average value 'All value groups' is shown average debt by value groups was not obtained by Financial Survey of Urban Housing either because the number of reports was too small or because of lack of related information for rented properties.*

Mortgaged Dwellings, Number reporting Debt and Average Debt Outstanding (Principal only), All Priorities, by Value Groups: Owner-occupied, 52 Cities; Rented, 51 Cities, by Geographic Division, January 1, 1934

←——————————————————————— R E N T E D ———————————————————————→

NUMBER REPORTING	All[2] value groups	$1-499	$500-999	$1,000-1,499	$1,500-1,999	$2,000-2,999	$3,000-3,999	$4,000-4,999	$5,000-7,499	$7,500-9,999	$10,000-14,999	$15,000 and over	
						AVERAGE DEBT OUTSTANDING (PRINCIPAL ONLY) BY VALUE GROUPS (dollars)							
13,274	3,719	408	666	1,083	1,130	1,556	2,031	2,575	3,345	4,602	6,503	21,292	51 cities[1]
869	4,872			600	1,225	1,803	1,895	2,605	3,602	5,181	6,786	15,176	4 New England cities
188	3,990			600	900	1,592	1,971	2,412	3,702	4,188	5,757	13,770	Portland, Me.
192	5,047					1,514	2,040	2,832	4,441	5,519	7,169	16,333	Worcester, Mass.
366	4,051				1,258	1,912	1,843	2,556	3,338	5,179	6,773	14,967	Providence, R.I.*
103	11,240												Waterbury, Conn.
803	4,133		522	1,060	1,192	1,429	2,498	2,833	3,551	4,938	6,944	18,077	4 Mid. Atlantic cities
80	4,283												Binghamton, N.Y.
210	4,709					1,225	2,693	2,904	3,593	5,111	6,233	22,586	Syracuse, N.Y.
238	2,398		522	1,060	1,192	1,354	2,020	2,593	2,865	4,113	9,500	10,750	Trenton, N.J.
275	3,659					2,032	2,296	2,803	3,903	5,027	7,137	10,845	Erie, Pa.
3,662	4,294		859	1,616	1,351	1,760	2,071	2,697	3,350	4,574	6,797	20,834	6 E. N. Central cities
2,246	5,425		980	2,163	1,588	2,040	2,171	2,921	3,583	5,242	7,633	23,284	Cleveland, Ohio*
483	2,723		689	839	1,020	1,396	1,983	2,376	3,017	3,200	5,624	16,300	Indianapolis, Ind.
318	2,844		483	833	993	1,098	1,579	2,195	2,829	3,933	4,492	24,585	Peoria, Ill.
157	2,026			760	878	1,428	2,016	2,482	2,929	5,400			Lansing, Mich.
133	3,913												Kenosha, Wis.
325	4,109			1,380		1,617	1,958	2,716	3,611	5,081	6,309	12,986	Racine, Wis.
2,921	2,608	428	494	760	975	1,248	1,817	2,325	2,925	4,468	5,780	17,176	10 W. N. Central cities
966	3,300		471	790	1,124	1,205	1,762	2,446	3,020	4,652	6,614	16,932	Minneapolis, Minn.
223	2,783			757	846	1,313	2,000	2,442	2,895	4,408	4,756	19,883	St. Paul, Minn.
406	2,149	467	519	638	902	1,223	1,616	2,291	2,789	4,417	5,911	17,364	Des Moines, Iowa
107	1,770												St. Joseph, Mo.
174	1,487	500	463	780	983	1,146	1,931	1,767	2,747	4,025		6,200	Springfield, Mo.
77	2,945												Fargo, N.D.
185	2,548			830	764	1,139	1,729	2,053	2,569	2,380	5,740	22,500	Sioux Falls, S.D.
187	2,626		700	960	785	1,228	2,000	2,232	2,853	3,829		19,178	Lincoln, Neb.
247	1,992		361	489	956	1,291	1,730	1,975	2,762	5,675	4,560	23,360	Topeka, Kan.
349	1,782	357	475	772	995	1,369	1,842	2,311	3,119	4,778	5,200	12,614	Wichita, Kan.
1,095	4,097		502	673	971	1,443	2,320	2,709	3,587	5,025	8,153	35,785	8 S. Atlantic cities
59	2,995												Hagerstown, Md.
131	3,689		525	575	900	1,320	2,006	2,268	3,663	5,182	6,700	23,900	Richmond, Va.
119	2,962												Wheeling, W.Va.*
37	2,981												Asheville, N.C.
70	3,964												Greensboro, N.C.
75	2,148												Charleston, S.C.
84	3,510												Columbia, S.C.
520	4,890		493	709	997	1,487	2,434	2,868	3,559	4,968	8,679	40,086	Atlanta, Ga.*
308	2,966		667	1,007	1,224	1,607	2,054	2,620	3,192	4,043	5,850	23,488	3 E. S. Central cities
20	2,150												Paducah, Ky.
215	2,975		667	1,007	1,224	1,607	2,054	2,620	3,192	4,043	5,850	23,488	Birmingham, Ala.*
73	3,026												Jackson, Miss.
1,191	2,924	215	726	969	915	1,446	1,977	2,705	3,231	4,838	6,025	14,232	6 W. S. Central cities
178	2,417	120	541	761	1,163	1,311	2,371	2,600	3,410	4,571	6,667	11,222	Little Rock, Ark.
57	3,165												Baton Rouge, La.
379	3,816		446	672	874	1,437	2,184	2,727	3,411	5,491	5,088	17,058	Oklahoma City, Okla.
105	1,921	333	543	556	957	1,380	1,724	2,389	2,843	3,333	6,450	8,700	Austin, Tex.
393	2,696		971	1,267	885	1,490	1,807	2,763	3,143	4,719	6,424	13,927	Dallas, Tex.
79	1,825												Wichita Falls, Tex.
650	3,095		360	907	1,113	1,475	2,006	2,283	3,906	4,049	5,068	23,783	6 Mountain cities
59	3,307												Butte, Mont.
33	1,758												Boise, Idaho
49	2,453												Casper, Wyo.
53	1,262												Pueblo, Colo.
161	2,589			883	1,656	1,568	1,862	2,123	3,650	3,873	5,800	7,317	Phoenix, Ariz.
295	4,124		360	922	784	1,419	2,093	2,380	4,061	4,155	4,625	33,747	Salt Lake City, Utah
1,775	3,549	467	568	825	1,049	1,513	1,959	2,371	3,396	4,172	6,099	26,286	4 Pacific cities
498	4,944		538	746	889	1,557	1,836	2,132	3,852	4,255	6,276	43,497	Seattle, Wash.*
423	2,475	467	514	797	1,171	1,448	1,916	2,553	3,165	3,717	4,590	18,286	Portland, Ore.
233	3,105			929	1,189	1,650	2,589	2,781	3,437	5,783	6,145	17,260	Sacramento, Calif.
621	2,804		664	926	1,102	1,463	1,936	2,394	2,962	3,891	7,341	13,184	San Diego, Calif.*

TABLE D 9

Percentage of Dwellings Mortgaged by Type: Owner-occupied, 52 Cities; Rented, 44 Cities, by Geographic Division, January 1, 1934

	OWNER-OCCUPIED					RENTED				
	All types [3]	1-family	2-family	Apart-ments	Other dwell-ings	All types [3]	1-family	2-family	Apart-ments	Other dwell-ings
52 (44) cities [1] [2]	56.2	54.8	60.5	69.4	69.1	39.8	36.8	44.1	61.0	49.0
4 (3) New England cities [2]	66.0	61.7	66.5	73.3	80.7	50.0	37.9	48.3	59.0	68.9
Portland, Me.	46.7	44.8	42.4	84.0	63.9	41.3	38.2	38.3	31.0	52.0
Worcester, Mass.	83.6	80.0	84.7	93.9	88.3	69.3	56.7	66.1	61.5	77.9
Providence, R.I.*	63.2	58.0	64.3	65.6	76.6	50.4	34.9	47.2	62.3	67.0
Waterbury, Conn.	81.1	74.4	81.2	82.3	86.6					
4 (3) Mid. Atlantic cities [2]	64.0	62.7	66.8	73.6	65.5	51.4	49.7	54.7	61.1	44.8
Binghamton, N.Y.	45.3	45.6	43.0	64.3	44.4					
Syracuse, N.Y.	76.9	76.0	79.9	80.0	76.3	67.1	64.6	68.5	68.2	55.2
Trenton, N.J.	68.8	64.9	72.8	100.0	68.7	39.8	39.2	46.1	57.1	33.3
Erie, Pa.	49.7	49.0	50.7	54.8	55.3	36.5	33.4	39.9	37.0	38.8
6 E. N. Central cities	64.9	63.7	68.0	77.3	70.6	50.2	46.9	54.5	64.1	54.1
Cleveland, Ohio*	67.0	65.3	71.5	76.9	71.5	53.2	47.4	57.9	63.4	53.0
Indianapolis, Ind.	63.8	64.2	59.2	82.9	67.7	51.2	51.7	48.3	64.5	61.5
Peoria, Ill.	54.0	53.0	61.7	88.2	59.1	40.3	38.5	42.3	70.0	50.0
Lansing, Mich.	57.4	58.0	42.3	82.5	62.1	36.5	35.5	34.1	80.0	53.3
Kenosha, Wis.	65.3	64.5	66.3	88.8	71.4	48.2	45.5	51.9	63.6	42.3
Racine, Wis.	67.1	65.4	54.5	67.9	68.8	53.5	48.1	57.5	62.5	66.2
10 (9) W. N. Central cities [2]	51.2	51.3	47.6	66.5	55.8	38.1	36.8	36.7	61.8	39.4
Minneapolis, Minn.	55.9	57.3	47.6	68.2	56.0	46.2	48.8	38.9	59.6	43.7
St. Paul, Minn.	48.0	47.8	46.6	53.3	58.2	41.4	38.3	38.2	73.3	47.2
Des Moines, Iowa	49.5	49.2	46.8	91.7	65.0	35.4	35.0	34.2	43.8	40.3
St. Joseph, Mo.	42.9	42.6	46.3	83.3	35.4	24.7	27.4	16.1	25.0	20.8
Springfield, Mo.	50.1	49.7	57.9	60.0	52.3	25.4	25.2	48.4	100.0	10.3
Fargo, N.D.	58.5	58.4	54.8	57.1	68.8					
Sioux Falls, S.D.	53.4	52.4	66.7	64.3	57.9	40.8	41.1	32.1	65.0	36.0
Lincoln, Neb.	48.2	47.7	47.2	81.8	54.7	36.5	32.8	41.0	77.8	31.5
Topeka, Kan.	44.0	44.1	38.5	59.5	37.8	26.2	24.9	22.9	54.2	34.9
Wichita, Kan.	53.5	53.5	50.5	70.8	54.0	38.8	37.5	43.2	64.0	38.1
9 (8) S. Atlantic cities [2]	48.7	48.9	46.3	62.5	46.5	37.5	37.7	36.8	58.6	24.5
Hagerstown, Md.	49.6	50.1	45.1	75.0	70.0	25.2	21.8	27.1	41.6	18.2
Richmond, Va.	49.7	50.1	44.5	75.0	49.3	34.2	34.1	36.2	57.1	17.9
Wheeling, W. Va.*	35.3	35.0	34.8	50.0	39.8	21.9	22.0	22.7	18.2	20.5
Asheville, N.C.	46.9	46.7	56.2	50.0	47.1	14.5	15.4	9.9	....	14.3
Greensboro, N.C.	56.8	57.0	53.3	85.7	35.7	29.3	28.9	6.3	25.0	16.7
Charleston, S.C.	32.9	34.3	23.4	40.0	42.9	23.6	16.7	34.1	37.5	26.7
Columbia, S.C.	58.4	60.0	47.5			33.7	30.3	42.8	66.7	31.3
Atlanta, Ga.*	58.3	58.2	59.2	66.7	55.7	40.7	56.7	44.8	71.6	35.5
Jacksonville, Fla.	47.6	45.8	64.2		42.1					
3 (2) E. S. Central cities [2]	51.4	51.3	53.6	67.3	51.5	21.3	20.8	21.9	42.5	18.0
Paducah, Ky.	30.7	29.7	28.6	66.7	52.4	7.1	6.2	10.9		6.3
Birmingham, Ala.*	52.4	52.3	52.1	60.0	55.4	22.9	22.2	22.4	42.4	22.2
Jackson, Miss.	61.5	61.7	67.6	88.9	40.0					
6 (5) W. S. Central cities [2]	52.2	51.7	55.2	64.5	53.2	34.8	32.6	45.5	64.8	27.0
Little Rock, Ark.	43.8	44.0	39.0	18.2	47.1	23.9	22.1	29.6	70.6	13.9
Baton Rouge, La.	53.3	53.5	41.7	33.3	63.6					
Oklahoma City, Okla.	61.7	60.7	69.8	70.0	64.2	43.1	37.3	55.2	67.1	33.8
Austin, Tex.	39.2	39.8	29.3	60.0	31.0	29.2	28.9	24.0	50.0	35.7
Dallas, Tex.	53.3	52.7	55.2	69.8	53.9	39.6	37.2	46.2	63.5	29.6
Wichita Falls, Tex.	41.4	41.6	36.1	18.2	52.2	20.9	20.7	30.0		5.3
6 (4) Mountain cities [2]	47.3	47.3	44.5	52.7	49.3	34.6	33.3	38.6	51.9	34.8
Butte, Mont.	24.2	23.6	23.2	30.0	33.3	15.1	14.7	12.4	18.7	19.0
Boise, Idaho	45.1	44.3	57.8	48.4	51.4					
Casper, Wyo.	44.1	43.1	55.4	45.5	38.2					
Pueblo, Colo.	40.9	40.2	46.0	80.0	48.4	22.5	20.4	34.6	37.5	14.8
Phoenix, Ariz.	55.6	54.9	60.3		67.5	43.6	42.2	40.6	58.3	56.7
Salt Lake City, Utah	54.0	54.4	43.9	62.5	53.8	42.9	40.0	45.6	71.4	39.5
4 Pacific cities	50.4	50.4	43.6	68.5	46.6	36.4	35.2	36.7	62.0	41.4
Seattle, Wash.*	49.2	48.9	44.6	77.6	46.0	36.4	34.6	30.5	72.4	34.6
Portland, Ore.	51.0	51.1	44.9	73.0	45.2	33.8	31.6	39.4	54.9	44.4
Sacramento, Calif.	54.5	55.8	36.0	60.6	44.6	45.0	44.5	40.7	52.6	49.0
San Diego, Calif.*	50.6	50.5	48.9	60.0	51.6	38.3	37.5	38.0	59.1	43.9

Source: *Financial Survey of Urban Housing*. *Percentage not shown for fewer than 3 reports.*

*Metropolitan district.

[1] *Geographic division and 52 (44)-city percentages weighted by total number of residential properties, by tenure, in each city (RPI).*

[2] *Figures in parentheses are number of cities reporting on rented properties.*

[3] *Based on number reporting mortgages on owner-occupied and rented dwellings as shown in Tables D 5 and 6.*

TABLE D 10

Dwellings reporting Distribution of Original Cost to Present Owner, Percentage Distribution of Cost by Form of Consideration, and Percentage of Consideration in the Form of Debt by Period of Acquisition, 1889 or before, to 1934: Owner-occupied, 52 Cities; Rented, 44 Cities, by Geographic Division

	NUMBER REPORTING[2]	FORM OF CONSIDERATION (per cent)			CONSIDERATION IN FORM OF DEBT BY PERIOD OF ACQUISITION (per cent)[3]					
		All forms	Cash	Trade	Debt	1889 or before	1890-99	1900-09	1910-19	1920-29	1930-34
52 cities[1]	81,268	100.0	50.4	3.4	46.2	14.1	22.3	26.7	37.3	48.6	53.1
4 New England cities	2,361	100.0	53.6	0.8	45.6	13.3	22.1	32.5	39.9	48.2	47.6
Portland, Me.	548	100.0	64.9	1.4	33.7	12.2	11.4	22.5	23.9	35.5	47.6
Worcester, Mass.	446	100.0	47.5	1.3	51.2		7.8	36.1	49.5	50.1	49.6
Providence, R.I.*	1,166	100.0	55.0	0.7	44.3	13.4*	27.1	31.9	38.0	47.4	46.4
Waterbury, Conn.	201	100.0	48.6	0.3	51.1			35.9	43.9	56.5	51.7
4 Mid. Atlantic cities	3,128	100.0	47.6	1.9	50.5	26.4	37.1	33.4	45.6	49.0	54.8
Binghamton, N.Y.	250	100.0	60.4	1.7	37.9		44.8	27.1	32.6	39.5	44.9
Syracuse, N.Y.	690	100.0	41.8	1.8	56.4	29.5	35.8	32.8	48.5	58.2	64.5
Trenton, N.J.	675	100.0	50.1	1.3	48.6	9.7	45.7	46.0	46.6	49.2	58.0
Erie, Pa.	1,513	100.0	48.7	2.9	48.4	29.6	28.2	32.2	49.3	35.2	38.6
6 E. N. Central cities	18,473	100.0	49.6	4.3	46.1	16.6	24.9	26.2	38.2	48.1	50.7
Cleveland, Ohio*	12,220	100.0	48.4	4.5	47.1	19.8	77.7	24.7	38.3	49.5	51.0
Indianapolis, Ind.	1,737	100.0	49.7	4.0	46.3	7.9	19.1	22.5	34.8	48.5	54.2
Peoria, Ill.	1,871	100.0	68.2	3.6	28.2	8.3	8.5	13.4	24.3	29.3	36.2
Lansing, Mich.	816	100.0	37.8	7.1	55.1	13.9	32.2	26.0	48.5	58.4	57.7
Kenosha, Wis.	611	100.0	67.2	3.0	29.8	10.6	10.9	26.2	48.8	20.2	31.1
Racine, Wis.	1,218	100.0	43.6	3.0	53.4	13.9	28.2	34.2	51.2	55.3	56.7
10 W. N. Central cities	16,360	100.0	51.2	3.8	45.0	10.9	17.2	26.4	34.5	49.0	55.3
Minneapolis, Minn.	4,494	100.0	48.4	2.3	49.3	2.9	16.6	27.7	38.7	53.3	58.3
St. Paul, Minn.	1,332	100.0	50.1	1.9	48.0	16.4	20.8	41.5	39.4	51.4	60.5
Des Moines, Iowa	2,385	100.0	46.5	5.0	48.5	1.3	8.1	25.2	36.9	53.5	59.9
St. Joseph, Mo.	868	100.0	60.3	2.9	36.8	14.3	35.6	25.4	28.0	41.2	44.3
Springfield, Mo.	1,124	100.0	57.3	8.6	34.1	2.8	20.0	12.7	20.3	39.2	41.0
Fargo, N.D.	632	100.0	56.7	2.3	41.0		19.0	20.0	32.9	42.1	48.5
Sioux Falls, S.D.	873	100.0	48.4	24.8	26.8	65.3	10.2	11.0	22.4	37.4	46.0
Lincoln, Neb.	1,212	100.0	60.9	4.0	35.1	6.0	13.0	13.2	25.2	38.1	44.0
Topeka, Kan.	1,728	100.0	54.7	5.7	39.6	28.6	14.1	14.7	27.5	44.1	46.9
Wichita, Kan.	1,712	100.0	55.9	5.9	38.2	26.0		7.7	21.8	40.2	52.7
9 S. Atlantic cities	8,478	100.0	51.8	2.8	45.4	10.6	22.9	29.9	35.7	46.8	56.7
Hagerstown, Md.	391	100.0	71.8	0.3	27.9	0.7	10.7	26.6	23.7	27.2	42.2
Richmond, Va.	1,483	100.0	47.0	4.3	48.7	20.6	10.8	41.3	31.8	51.0	61.0
Wheeling, W.Va.*	1,425	100.0	64.9	1.7	33.4	12.9	11.6	25.3	29.1	36.9	35.0
Asheville, N.C.	725	100.0	56.4	6.4	37.2		3.3	6.9	30.3	30.6	70.8
Greensboro, N.C.	390	100.0	48.2	6.4	45.4		26.7	22.9	30.1	31.3	72.1
Charleston, S.C.	337	100.0	74.8	0.9	24.3	1.0	11.4	6.7	25.3	27.1	28.2
Columbia, S.C.	393	100.0	55.9	0.2	43.9		28.1	8.1	35.9	46.8	62.5
Atlanta, Ga.*	2,945	100.0	40.2	2.9	56.9	6.1	31.7	36.8	45.4	58.5	66.4
Jacksonville, Fla.	389	100.0	52.8	1.6	45.6	8.6	56.9	26.7	40.1	51.6	64.9
3 E. S. Central cities	4,110	100.0	48.3	3.4	48.3	5.3	20.7	25.4	41.1	50.8	54.8
Paducah, Ky.	508	100.0	65.9	1.5	32.6	4.6	20.3	25.6	34.7	29.9	49.9
Birmingham, Ala.*	3,338	100.0	45.9	3.6	50.5	5.4	24.3	27.6	41.6	53.6	55.8
Jackson, Miss.	264	100.0	53.3	3.4	43.3		1.4	13.4	40.9	44.6	51.7
6 W. S. Central cities	7,475	100.0	47.6	4.5	47.9	8.2	14.5	21.1	35.9	50.4	55.5
Little Rock, Ark.	1,652	100.0	52.2	3.7	44.1	6.9	27.3	26.8	33.7	47.8	53.4
Baton Rouge, La.	207	100.0	46.1	0.5	53.4			5.0	30.2	66.5	62.1
Oklahoma City, Okla.	2,077	100.0	49.7	5.6	44.7		13.1	32.7	45.6	51.4
Austin, Tex.	766	100.0	57.4	2.7	39.9		8.4	14.1	23.9	43.6	55.6
Dallas, Tex.	2,139	100.0	41.3	4.9	53.8	8.5	12.7	30.3	44.2	56.1	60.1
Wichita Falls, Tex.	634	100.0	58.1	4.3	37.6			9.4	22.7	37.4	40.6
6 Mountain cities	7,148	100.0	50.5	4.5	45.0	14.8	21.2	26.5	35.1	48.2	58.9
Butte, Mont.	1,539	100.0	65.9	0.8	33.3		25.4	39.7	48.2	24.3	43.5
Boise, Idaho	1,061	100.0	60.3	5.6	34.1			14.4	22.1	37.3	53.0
Casper, Wyo.	476	100.0	49.7	3.0	47.3			32.7	34.2	42.9	70.3
Pueblo, Colo.	818	100.0	55.1	3.9	41.0	41.0		27.0	27.9	59.4	50.2
Phoenix, Ariz.	737	100.0	55.8	4.0	40.2			6.3	29.7	40.4	55.2
Salt Lake City, Utah	2,517	100.0	43.5	5.4	51.1	9.6	20.4	31.4	38.1	55.3	64.6
4 Pacific cities	13,735	100.0	49.7	4.1	46.2	10.5	14.8	17.5	31.8	49.6	56.2
Seattle, Wash.*	5,153	100.0	46.9	3.9	49.2		19.6	18.6	38.8	53.7	58.0
Portland, Ore.	3,698	100.0	51.6	4.8	43.6	16.0	7.5	17.9	31.0	47.4	54.8
Sacramento, Calif.	1,652	100.0	49.7	2.4	47.9		15.8	22.4	34.7	49.4	58.6
San Diego, Calif.*	3,232	100.0	52.7	4.6	42.7	2.7		12.5	17.2	44.1	53.4

Source: *Financial Survey of Urban Housing.* Percentage not shown for fewer than 3 reports.

*Metropolitan district.

[1]Geographic division and 52 (44)-city percentages weighted by total value of properties, by tenure, in each city (RPI).

[2]Includes only properties purchased for a consideration and excludes those acquired by gift or inheritance.

[3]The percentages shown by period of acquisition do not necessarily indicate that the average of all properties purchased in the earlier years involved less credit than the average of all properties purchased in the later years. The data are based upon reports of 1934 owners and it may be presumed that properties purchased many years prior with large debt assumption were less likely to be owned in 1934 by the early purchasers than properties purchased for a larger consideration in cash.

TABLE D 10

Dwellings reporting Distribution of Original Cost to Present Owner, Percentage Distribution of Cost by Form of Consideration, and Percentage of Consideration in the Form of Debt by Period of Acquisition, 1889 or before, to 1934: Owner-occupied, 52 Cities; Rented, 44 Cities, by Geographic Division

←———————————————————————————— R E N T E D ————————————————————————————→

NUMBER REPORTING[2]	FORM OF CONSIDERATION (per cent)				CONSIDERATION IN FORM OF DEBT BY PERIOD OF ACQUISITION (per cent)[3]						
	All forms	Cash	Trade	Debt	1889 or before	1890-99	1900-09	1910-19	1920-29	1930-34	
10,816	100.0	64.7	4.2	31.1	9.8	12.8	21.5	25.1	34.2	26.1	44 cities[1]
179	100.0	68.8	1.4	29.8			20.2	26.8	32.2	36.7	3 New England cities
53	100.0	76.4	3.2	20.4			34.7	13.7	41.9	54.7	Portland, Me.
28	100.0	66.7		33.3				56.8	22.1	38.8	Worcester, Mass.
98	100.0	68.4	1.5	30.1			18.4	20.4	33.7	33.9	Providence, R.I.*
390	100.0	54.8	4.0	41.2	15.7	2.0	33.9	54.0	32.5	30.7	3 Mid. Atlantic cities
51	100.0	49.6	3.0	47.4			42.9	71.9	29.1	31.3	Syracuse, N.Y.
166	100.0	61.4	1.7	36.9	37.6		17.4	22.8	43.7	37.5	Trenton, N.J.
173	100.0	63.6	7.2	29.2	5.9	2.0	21.1	27.5	35.3	26.3	Erie, Pa.
2,011	100.0	64.0	4.5	31.5	7.0	10.5	19.7	28.1	32.3	17.8	6 E. N. Central cities
1,008	100.0	65.7	3.7	30.6	6.3	10.3	17.7	28.0	40.7	15.9	Cleveland, Ohio*
241	100.0	57.9	5.9	36.2			20.6	24.9	5.7	19.4	Indianapolis, Ind.
345	100.0	65.8	5.3	28.9	14.0		15.2	31.0	34.6	23.3	Peoria, Ill.
165	100.0	54.8	13.0	32.2			53.1	32.8	33.0	28.0	Lansing, Mich.
82	100.0	72.8	1.6	25.6			31.7	26.7	31.4	17.5	Kenosha, Wis.
170	100.0	67.1	6.0	26.9	21.8			43.4	25.5	29.4	Racine, Wis.
2,753	100.0	63.5	5.9	30.6	17.4	19.1	14.6	22.0	35.6	29.5	9 W. N. Central cities
518	100.0	58.7	5.7	35.6	20.0	26.3	20.6	28.6	41.0	31.4	Minneapolis, Minn.
169	100.0	55.4	5.2	39.4		3.3	23.8	21.7	43.4	46.3	St. Paul, Minn.
465	100.0	69.7	5.7	24.6			5.9	26.3	31.1	18.7	Des Moines, Iowa
166	100.0	74.9	4.6	20.5	1.0	12.8	8.7	20.5	24.0	26.3	St. Joseph, Mo.
308	100.0	71.1	10.5	18.4		34.9	5.4	6.3	21.9	15.7	Springfield, Mo.
173	100.0	68.1	5.6	26.3			6.6	12.0	30.7	29.0	Sioux Falls, S.D.
229	100.0	73.6	5.4	21.0			6.5	11.4	27.6	14.8	Lincoln, Neb.
338	100.0	63.3	9.1	27.6			5.7	16.8	33.4	29.6	Topeka, Kan.
387	100.0	74.1	5.8	20.1			2.1	10.8	23.6	21.6	Wichita, Kan.
1,189	100.0	65.9	2.8	31.3		20.8	51.0	13.9	35.5	31.3	8 S. Atlantic cities
46	100.0	88.9	1.6	9.5			7.5		17.4	4.6	Hagerstown, Md.
135	100.0	65.2	1.6	33.2				24.4	28.0	34.3	Richmond, Va.
142	100.0	76.0	1.9	22.1		20.8	9.5	12.8	25.3	23.2	Wheeling, W.Va.*
172	100.0	85.4	2.3	12.3				22.1	29.5	3.9	Asheville, N.C.
98	100.0	71.7	2.3	26.0			6.2	2.8	27.4	36.1	Greensboro, N.C.
93	100.0	90.5	0.2	9.3			5.7	10.4	7.0	17.9	Charleston, S.C.
90	100.0	74.4	3.2	22.4				6.5	25.1	32.8	Columbia, S.C.
413	100.0	53.3	4.2	42.5			82.6	12.0	50.9	38.9	Atlanta, Ga.*
396	100.0	74.8	3.7	21.5			2.6	18.2	26.3	19.9	2 E. S. Central cities
117	100.0	88.3	1.1	10.6					12.2	29.4	Paducah, Ky.
279	100.0	74.3	3.8	21.9			2.6	18.2	26.9	19.5	Birmingham, Ala.*
1,362	100.0	61.8	5.0	33.2			31.9	32.1	38.9	25.8	5 W. S. Central cities
359	100.0	68.8	4.7	26.5			23.7	70.1	33.2	17.7	Little Rock, Ark.
310	100.0	64.5	5.8	29.7				25.8	34.4	25.7	Oklahoma City, Okla.
131	100.0	77.2	4.6	18.2				10.5	12.9	29.2	Austin, Tex.
372	100.0	53.2	4.4	42.4			33.6	35.8	49.5	29.2	Dallas, Tex.
190	100.0	79.0	5.4	15.6				10.2	30.9	6.5	Wichita Falls, Tex.
598	100.0	62.7	4.0	33.3	5.9		18.4	26.4	31.8	43.4	4 Mountain cities
97	100.0	79.2	0.5	20.3			10.9	25.1	25.4	16.8	Butte, Mont.
98	100.0	75.2	3.9	20.9			23.3	11.9	19.5	34.3	Pueblo, Colo.
149	100.0	58.8	5.9	35.3				12.1	37.7	34.8	Phoenix, Ariz.
254	100.0	57.6	4.1	38.3	5.9		19.6	36.8	33.0	56.8	Salt Lake City, Utah
1,938	100.0	64.3	5.4	30.3			11.4	19.8	38.5	23.9	4 Pacific cities
589	100.0	64.5	4.8	30.7			13.3	18.1	42.2	24.5	Seattle, Wash.*
528	100.0	70.0	5.5	24.5			1.8	22.4	32.6	14.1	Portland, Ore.
170	100.0	53.2	3.7	43.1			42.3	36.4	47.5	29.8	Sacramento, Calif.
651	100.0	62.3	7.0	30.7			6.3	14.9	33.9	30.2	San Diego, Calif.*

TABLE D II

Mortgaged Owner-occupied Dwellings, Number and Percentage Distribution by Debt-Value Percentage Groups, 52 Cities by Geographic Division, January 1, 1934

	All percentage groups	1-9	10-19	20-29	30-39	40-49	50-59	60-69	70-84	85-99	100 and over
				NUMBER							
				DEBT - VALUE PERCENTAGE GROUPS							
52 cities[1]	68,385	1,682	3,900	6,057	7,199	8,884	10,144	9,304	10,103	5,263	5,849
4 New England cities	4,239	112	271	342	468	541	591	580	651	343	340
Portland, Me.	643	20	70	72	90	94	83	65	76	35	38
Worcester, Mass.	1,115	14	29	35	70	105	157	178	228	142	157
Providence, R.I.*	2,009	74	157	209	256	286	271	267	265	120	104
Waterbury, Conn.	472	4	15	26	52	56	80	70	82	46	41
4 Mid. Atlantic cities	4,328	67	188	360	423	566	720	668	672	298	366
Binghamton, N.Y.	262	4	23	32	46	42	44	28	26	13	4
Syracuse, N.Y.	973	18	47	60	93	129	160	151	162	76	77
Trenton, N.J.	1,592	18	32	115	154	223	305	265	248	99	133
Erie, Pa.	1,501	27	86	153	130	172	211	224	236	110	152
6 E. N. Central cities	20,180	562	1,186	1,696	2,083	2,617	2,856	2,672	2,896	1,563	2,049
Cleveland, Ohio*	14,115	399	816	1,159	1,438	1,825	1,963	1,879	2,030	1,095	1,511
Indianapolis, Ind.	1,687	29	109	150	167	228	234	233	251	135	151
Peoria, Ill.	1,375	64	106	146	152	194	205	168	162	101	77
Lansing, Mich.	630	17	46	48	57	78	92	62	88	57	85
Kenosha, Wis.	727	15	37	69	90	107	112	87	110	38	62
Racine, Wis.	1,646	38	72	124	179	185	250	243	255	137	163
10 W. N. Central cities	12,240	269	720	1,344	1,566	1,853	1,966	1,574	1,554	700	694
Minneapolis, Minn.	4,097	82	232	445	585	674	690	562	483	193	151
St. Paul, Minn.	893	19	64	109	107	166	157	124	74	42	31
Des Moines, Iowa	1,634	31	85	169	209	232	255	207	226	109	111
St. Joseph, Mo.	529	9	35	65	68	89	76	56	71	30	30
Springfield, Mo.	757	10	54	88	96	98	120	71	92	60	68
Fargo, N.D.	486	8	23	50	54	73	97	76	79	16	10
Sioux Falls, S.D.	645	8	43	83	85	109	128	88	61	21	19
Lincoln, Neb.	796	24	42	90	87	90	123	109	115	61	55
Topeka, Kan.	1,069	40	80	133	127	152	145	122	145	63	62
Wichita, Kan.	1,334	38	62	112	148	170	175	159	208	105	157
9 S. Atlantic cities	6,142	163	364	513	543	763	912	879	983	500	522
Hagerstown, Md.	363	10	15	34	37	34	43	50	65	31	44
Richmond, Va.	1,077	16	40	62	76	127	219	178	192	87	80
Wheeling, W.Va.*	810	42	91	99	89	105	96	98	79	49	62
Asheville, N.C.	408	10	31	41	21	39	42	48	57	52	67
Greensboro, N.C.	293	6	19	23	24	38	40	36	54	27	26
Charleston, S.C.	208	4	20	26	30	28	33	18	22	8	19
Columbia, S.C.	332	14	26	28	31	50	44	41	55	17	26
Atlanta, Ga.*	2,364	53	108	175	203	295	350	364	427	214	175
Jacksonville, Fla.	287	8	14	25	32	47	45	46	32	15	23
3 E. S. Central cities	2,533	83	129	225	230	279	321	283	361	266	356
Paducah, Ky.	234	8	16	29	31	22	27	21	27	17	36
Birmingham, Ala.*	2,039	58	96	166	174	221	258	229	304	226	307
Jackson, Miss.	260	17	17	30	25	36	36	33	30	23	13
6 W. S. Central cities	5,214	141	268	385	532	616	758	764	870	446	434
Little Rock, Ark.	841	12	42	51	74	75	107	132	166	92	90
Baton Rouge, La.	188	10	19	18	24	27	22	22	22	13	11
Oklahoma City, Okla.	1,762	45	75	119	175	183	259	276	343	160	127
Austin, Tex.	416	21	26	52	49	53	74	49	54	25	13
Dallas, Tex.	1,676	46	86	124	195	246	256	243	239	123	118
Wichita Falls, Tex.	331	7	20	21	15	32	40	42	46	33	75
6 Mountain cities	4,209	97	278	410	462	516	614	588	600	362	282
Butte, Mont.	479	18	63	76	59	59	50	53	47	24	30
Boise, Idaho	569	18	49	79	84	116	80	57	61	18	7
Casper, Wyo.	298	10	16	27	31	29	32	37	48	40	28
Pueblo, Colo.	413	5	23	35	41	35	59	57	79	34	45
Phoenix, Ariz.	540	7	15	45	57	62	98	95	84	37	40
Salt Lake City, Utah	1,910	39	112	148	190	215	295	289	281	209	132
4 Pacific cities	9,300	188	496	782	892	1,133	1,406	1,296	1,516	785	806
Seattle, Wash.*	3,225	96	203	331	321	402	490	378	500	239	285
Portland, Ore.	2,512	37	119	185	254	297	381	401	428	192	218
Sacramento, Calif.	1,241	18	46	79	101	121	182	195	220	147	132
San Diego, Calif.*	2,322	37	128	187	216	313	353	322	368	207	191

Source: Financial Survey of Urban Housing

*Metropolitan district.

[1]Geographic division and 52-city percentage distributions weighted by estimated number of owner-occupied mortgaged properties in each city (RPI).

TABLE D II

Mortgaged Owner-occupied Dwellings, Number and Percentage Distribution by Debt-Value Percentage Groups, 52 Cities by Geographic Division, January I, 1934

◄──────────────────── P E R C E N T A G E   D I S T R I B U T I O N ────────────────────►

DEBT - VALUE PERCENTAGE GROUPS

All percentage groups	1-9	10-19	20-29	30-39	40-49	50-59	60-69	70-84	85-99	100 and over	
100.0	2.5	5.8	8.8	10.6	13.2	14.9	13.6	14.7	7.6	8.3	52 cities[1]
100.0	2.9	6.4	8.4	11.2	13.0	13.9	13.9	15.1	7.8	7.4	4 New England cities
100.0	3.1	10.9	11.2	14.0	14.6	12.9	10.1	11.8	5.5	5.9	Portland, Me.
100.0	1.3	2.6	3.1	6.3	9.4	14.1	16.0	20.4	12.7	14.1	Worcester, Mass.
100.0	3.7	7.8	10.4	12.7	14.2	13.5	13.3	13.2	6.0	5.2	Providence, R.I.*
100.0	0.8	3.2	5.5	11.0	11.9	17.0	14.8	17.4	9.7	8.7	Waterbury, Conn.
100.0	1.7	4.9	7.8	10.3	13.4	16.5	15.1	15.5	7.1	7.7	4 Mid. Atlantic cities
100.0	1.5	8.8	12.2	17.6	16.0	16.8	10.7	9.9	5.0	1.5	Binghamton, N.Y.
100.0	1.9	4.8	6.2	9.6	13.3	14.5	15.5	16.6	7.8	7.9	Syracuse, N.Y.
100.0	1.1	2.0	7.2	9.7	14.0	19.2	16.6	15.6	6.2	8.4	Trenton, N.J.
100.0	1.8	5.7	10.2	8.7	11.5	14.1	14.9	15.7	7.3	10.1	Erie, Pa.
100.0	2.7	6.0	8.4	10.3	13.0	14.1	13.2	14.4	7.8	10.1	6 E. N. Central cities
100.0	2.8	5.8	8.2	10.2	12.9	13.9	13.3	14.4	7.8	10.7	Cleveland, Ohio*
100.0	1.7	6.4	8.9	9.9	13.5	13.9	13.8	14.9	8.0	9.0	Indianapolis, Ind.
100.0	4.7	7.7	10.6	11.1	14.1	14.9	12.2	11.8	7.3	5.6	Peoria, Ill.
100.0	2.7	7.3	7.6	9.0	12.4	14.6	9.9	14.0	9.0	13.5	Lansing, Mich.
100.0	2.1	5.1	9.5	12.4	14.7	15.4	12.0	15.1	5.2	8.5	Kenosha, Wis.
100.0	2.3	4.4	7.5	10.9	11.2	15.2	14.8	15.5	8.3	9.9	Racine, Wis.
100.0	2.1	6.0	11.1	12.9	15.7	16.3	13.1	12.0	5.6	5.2	10 W. N. Central cities
100.0	2.0	5.7	10.9	14.3	16.4	16.8	13.7	11.8	4.7	3.7	Minneapolis, Minn.
100.0	2.1	7.2	12.2	12.0	18.6	17.6	13.9	8.3	4.7	3.4	St. Paul, Minn.
100.0	1.9	5.2	10.3	12.8	14.2	15.6	12.7	13.8	6.7	6.8	Des Moines, Iowa
100.0	1.7	6.6	12.3	12.8	16.8	14.4	10.6	13.4	5.7	5.7	St. Joseph, Mo.
100.0	1.3	7.1	11.6	12.7	12.9	15.9	9.4	12.2	7.9	9.0	Springfield, Mo.
100.0	1.6	4.7	10.3	11.1	15.0	20.0	15.6	16.3	3.3	2.1	Fargo, N.D.
100.0	1.2	6.7	12.9	13.2	16.9	19.8	13.6	9.5	3.3	2.9	Sioux Falls, S.D.
100.0	3.0	5.3	11.3	10.9	11.3	15.5	13.7	14.4	7.7	6.9	Lincoln, Neb.
100.0	3.7	7.5	12.4	11.9	14.2	13.6	11.4	13.6	5.9	5.8	Topeka, Kan.
100.0	2.8	4.7	8.4	11.1	12.7	13.1	11.9	15.6	7.9	11.8	Wichita, Kan.
100.0	2.7	6.0	8.4	9.1	12.8	15.0	14.5	15.5	7.8	8.2	9 S. Atlantic cities
100.0	2.8	4.1	9.4	10.2	9.4	11.8	13.8	17.9	8.5	12.1	Hagerstown, Md.
100.0	1.5	3.7	5.8	7.1	11.8	20.3	16.5	17.8	8.1	7.4	Richmond, Va.
100.0	5.2	11.2	12.2	11.0	13.0	11.9	12.1	9.7	6.0	7.7	Wheeling, W.Va.*
100.0	2.5	7.6	10.0	5.1	9.6	10.3	11.8	14.0	12.7	16.4	Asheville, N.C.
100.0	2.0	6.5	7.8	8.2	13.0	13.7	12.3	18.4	9.2	8.9	Greensboro, N.C.
100.0	1.9	9.6	12.5	14.4	13.5	15.9	8.7	10.6	3.8	9.1	Charleston, S.C.
100.0	4.2	7.8	8.4	9.3	15.1	13.3	12.4	16.6	5.1	7.8	Columbia, S.C.
100.0	2.2	4.6	7.4	8.6	12.5	14.8	15.4	18.1	9.0	7.4	Atlanta, Ga.*
100.0	2.8	4.9	8.7	11.2	16.4	15.7	16.0	11.1	5.2	8.0	Jacksonville, Fla.
100.0	3.4	5.0	8.8	8.9	11.1	12.8	11.3	14.3	10.6	13.8	3 E. S. Central cities
100.0	3.4	6.8	12.4	13.3	9.4	11.5	9.0	11.5	7.3	15.4	Paducah, Ky.
100.0	2.9	4.7	8.1	8.5	10.8	12.7	11.2	14.9	11.1	15.1	Birmingham, Ala.*
100.0	6.5	6.5	11.5	9.6	13.9	13.9	12.7	11.5	8.9	5.0	Jackson, Miss.
100.0	2.8	5.2	7.5	10.5	12.3	14.7	14.6	16.3	8.3	7.8	6 W. S. Central cities
100.0	1.4	5.0	6.1	8.8	8.9	12.7	15.7	19.8	10.9	10.7	Little Rock, Ark.
100.0	5.3	10.1	9.6	12.8	14.4	11.7	11.7	11.7	6.9	5.8	Baton Rouge, La.
100.0	2.5	4.3	6.7	9.9	10.4	14.7	15.7	19.5	9.1	7.2	Oklahoma City, Okla.
100.0	5.0	6.3	12.5	11.8	12.7	17.8	11.8	13.0	6.0	3.1	Austin, Tex.
100.0	2.8	5.1	7.4	11.6	14.7	15.3	14.5	14.3	7.3	7.0	Dallas, Tex.
100.0	2.1	6.0	6.3	4.5	9.7	12.1	12.7	13.9	10.0	22.7	Wichita Falls, Tex.
100.0	2.1	6.1	9.0	10.6	11.6	14.9	14.5	14.9	9.1	7.2	6 Mountain cities
100.0	3.8	13.1	15.9	12.3	12.3	10.4	11.1	9.8	5.0	6.3	Butte, Mont.
100.0	3.2	8.6	13.9	14.8	20.4	14.0	10.0	10.7	3.2	1.2	Boise, Idaho
100.0	3.4	5.4	9.1	10.4	9.7	10.7	12.4	16.1	13.4	9.4	Casper, Wyo.
100.0	1.2	5.6	8.5	9.9	8.5	14.3	13.8	19.1	8.2	10.9	Pueblo, Colo.
100.0	1.3	2.8	8.3	10.6	11.5	18.1	17.6	15.6	6.8	7.4	Phoenix, Ariz.
100.0	2.0	5.9	7.8	10.0	11.3	15.4	15.1	14.7	10.9	6.9	Salt Lake City, Utah
100.0	2.2	5.4	8.7	9.7	12.2	15.1	13.8	16.2	8.1	8.6	4 Pacific cities
100.0	3.0	6.3	10.3	9.9	12.5	15.2	11.7	15.5	7.4	8.2	Seattle, Wash.*
100.0	1.5	4.7	7.4	10.1	11.8	15.2	16.0	17.0	7.6	8.7	Portland, Ore.
100.0	1.5	3.7	6.4	8.1	9.8	14.7	15.7	17.7	11.8	10.6	Sacramento, Calif.
100.0	1.6	5.5	8.1	9.3	13.5	15.2	13.9	15.8	8.9	8.2	San Diego, Calif.*

TABLE D 12

Mortgaged Rented Dwellings, Number and Percentage Distribution by Debt-Value Percentage Groups, 44 Cities by Geographic Division, January 1, 1934

	All percentage groups	1-9	10-19	20-29	30-39	40-49	50-59	60-69	70-84	85-99	100 and over
						N U M B E R					
						DEBT - VALUE PERCENTAGE GROUPS					
44 cities[1]	12,829	229	563	913	1,216	1,717	2,095	1,886	2,063	890	1,257
3 New England cities	770	23	49	55	66	72	104	119	132	72	78
Portland, Me.	188	6	9	23	23	23	21	27	23	18	15
Worcester, Mass.	193	4	10	4	13	7	26	32	47	24	26
Providence, R.I.*	389	13	30	28	30	42	57	60	62	30	37
3 Mid. Atlantic cities	724	5	25	34	44	86	150	100	136	55	89
Syracuse, N.Y.	211	1	7	7	14	24	43	35	35	24	21
Trenton, N.J.	238	1	6	10	16	34	71	30	35	10	25
Erie, Pa.	275	3	12	17	14	28	36	35	66	21	43
6 E. N. Central cities	3,667	83	156	276	345	479	536	524	568	291	409
Cleveland, Ohio*	2,251	52	102	159	193	275	310	312	348	195	305
Indianapolis, Ind.	483	4	23	39	51	85	71	74	62	34	40
Peoria, Ill.	318	13	13	40	40	48	59	35	41	9	20
Lansing, Mich.	157	3	5	13	25	21	25	14	24	15	12
Kenosha, Wis.	133	3	4	9	16	20	23	23	18	9	8
Racine, Wis.	325	8	9	16	20	30	48	66	75	29	24
9 W. N. Central cities	2,849	44	122	239	336	469	537	411	404	115	172
Minneapolis, Minn.	966	14	37	79	100	179	173	137	145	43	59
St. Paul, Minn.	225	4	8	11	27	33	61	31	36	10	4
Des Moines, Iowa	407	4	14	40	53	75	76	62	50	12	21
St. Joseph, Mo.	108	1	3	11	7	12	22	25	19	6	2
Springfield, Mo.	175	1	9	17	20	22	37	28	21	5	15
Sioux Falls, S.D.	185	3	12	23	29	34	39	22	15	3	5
Lincoln, Neb.	187	3	8	16	24	22	35	22	33	6	18
Topeka, Kan.	247	9	21	19	35	33	42	38	31	8	11
Wichita, Kan.	349	5	10	23	41	59	52	46	54	22	37
8 S. Atlantic cities	1,098	30	56	65	95	130	156	161	182	97	126
Hagerstown, Md.	59	1	1	4	4	7	10	10	7	6	9
Richmond, Va.	132	1	5	6	15	13	26	21	28	7	10
Wheeling, W. Va.*	120	8	9	10	16	13	16	13	19	7	9
Asheville, N.C.	37	1	2	1	3	4	6	3	4	2	11
Greensboro, N.C.	71		5	10	5	8	11	7	7	9	9
Charleston, S.C.	75	1	7	9	6	12	10	8	11	3	8
Columbia, S.C.	84	3	2	3	12	6	8	13	18	14	5
Atlanta, Ga.*	520	15	25	22	34	67	69	86	88	49	65
2 E. S. Central cities	236	4	7	20	10	29	33	27	41	19	46
Paducah, Ky.	20	1				2	6	1	2	3	5
Birmingham, Ala.*	216	3	7	20	10	27	27	26	39	16	41
5 W. S. Central cities	1,137	24	50	79	93	147	156	162	202	89	135
Little Rock, Ark.	178	11	8	8	7	18	23	28	40	18	19
Oklahoma City, Okla.	379	4	15	35	36	50	51	62	62	24	40
Austin, Tex.	105	2	5	8	10	15	18	10	18	7	12
Dallas, Tex.	395	6	17	22	38	57	54	62	67	32	40
Wichita Falls, Tex.	80	1	5	6	2	7	10	2	15	8	24
4 Mountain cities	569	5	28	34	61	74	121	81	84	23	58
Butte, Mont.	59	3	7	6	9	8	5	4	5	2	10
Pueblo, Colo.	53		2	5	3	4	12	9	8	2	8
Phoenix, Ariz.	162		7	7	17	20	37	25	25	7	17
Salt Lake City, Utah	295	2	12	16	32	42	67	43	46	12	23
4 Pacific cities	1,779	11	70	111	166	231	302	301	314	129	144
Seattle, Wash.*	500	4	22	30	50	79	84	78	81	34	38
Portland, Ore.	424	2	16	33	42	43	81	71	78	26	32
Sacramento, Calif.	233	1	8	12	11	33	24	40	53	23	28
San Diego, Calif.*	622	4	24	36	63	76	113	112	102	46	46

Source: Financial Survey of Urban Housing
*Metropolitan district.
[1]Geographic division and 44-city percentage distributions weighted by estimated number of rented mortgaged properties in each city (RPI).

Mortgaged Rented Dwellings, Number and Percentage Distribution by Debt-Value Percentage Groups, 44 Cities by Geographic Division, January 1, 1934

PERCENTAGE DISTRIBUTION
DEBT - VALUE PERCENTAGE GROUPS

All percentage groups	1–9	10–19	20–29	30–39	40–49	50–59	60–69	70–84	85–99	100 and over	
100.0	1.8	4.5	6.9	9.2	13.2	16.0	14.8	16.2	7.3	10.1	44 cities[1]
100.0	3.1	7.0	6.5	7.8	9.3	14.2	15.6	17.4	8.8	10.3	3 New England cities
100.0	3.2	4.8	12.2	12.2	12.2	11.2	14.4	12.2	9.6	8.0	Portland, Me.
100.0	2.1	5.2	2.1	6.7	3.6	13.5	16.6	24.3	12.4	13.5	Worcester, Mass.
100.0	3.4	7.7	7.2	7.7	10.8	14.7	15.4	15.9	7.7	9.5	Providence, R.I.*
100.0	0.6	3.4	4.1	6.3	11.6	20.2	15.1	18.0	9.4	11.3	3 Mid. Atlantic cities
100.0	0.5	3.3	3.3	6.6	11.4	20.4	16.6	16.6	11.4	9.9	Syracuse, N.Y.
100.0	0.4	2.5	4.2	6.7	14.3	29.9	12.6	14.7	4.2	10.5	Trenton, N.J.
100.0	1.1	4.4	6.2	5.1	10.2	13.1	12.7	24.0	7.6	15.6	Erie, Pa.
100.0	2.0	4.4	7.6	9.7	13.9	14.5	14.3	14.7	7.9	11.0	6 E. N. Central cities
100.0	2.3	4.5	7.1	8.6	12.2	13.8	13.9	15.4	8.7	13.5	Cleveland, Ohio*
100.0	0.8	4.8	8.1	10.6	17.6	14.7	15.3	12.8	7.0	8.3	Indianapolis, Ind.
100.0	4.1	4.1	12.6	12.6	15.1	18.5	11.0	12.9	2.8	6.3	Peoria, Ill.
100.0	1.9	3.2	8.3	15.9	13.4	15.9	8.9	15.3	9.6	7.6	Lansing, Mich.
100.0	2.3	3.0	6.8	12.0	15.0	17.3	17.3	13.5	6.8	6.0	Kenosha, Wis.
100.0	2.5	2.8	4.9	6.1	9.2	14.8	20.3	23.1	8.9	7.4	Racine, Wis.
100.0	1.5	3.9	8.0	11.5	16.3	19.7	14.5	14.7	4.2	5.7	9 W. N. Central cities
100.0	1.4	3.8	8.2	10.4	18.5	17.9	14.2	15.0	4.5	6.1	Minneapolis, Minn.
100.0	1.8	3.5	4.9	12.0	14.7	27.1	13.8	16.0	4.4	1.8	St. Paul, Minn.
100.0	1.0	3.4	9.8	13.0	18.4	18.7	15.2	12.3	3.0	5.2	Des Moines, Iowa
100.0	0.9	2.8	10.2	6.5	11.1	20.4	23.1	17.6	5.6	1.8	St. Joseph, Mo.
100.0	0.6	5.1	9.7	11.4	12.6	21.1	16.0	12.0	2.9	8.6	Springfield, Mo.
100.0	1.6	6.5	12.4	15.7	18.4	21.1	11.9	8.1	1.6	2.7	Sioux Falls, S.D.
100.0	1.6	4.3	8.6	12.8	11.8	18.7	11.8	17.6	3.2	9.6	Lincoln, Neb.
100.0	3.6	8.5	7.7	14.2	13.4	17.0	15.4	12.5	3.2	4.5	Topeka, Kan.
100.0	1.4	2.9	6.6	11.7	16.9	14.9	13.2	15.5	6.3	10.6	Wichita, Kan.
100.0	2.7	5.1	5.7	8.8	11.7	14.5	14.8	17.0	8.6	11.1	8 S. Atlantic cities
100.0	1.7	1.7	6.8	6.8	11.9	16.9	16.9	11.9	10.2	15.2	Hagerstown, Md.
100.0	0.8	3.8	4.5	11.4	9.8	19.7	15.9	21.2	5.3	7.6	Richmond, Va.
100.0	6.7	7.5	8.3	13.4	10.8	13.4	10.8	15.8	5.8	7.5	Wheeling, W. Va.*
100.0	2.7	5.4	2.7	8.1	10.8	16.2	8.1	10.8	5.4	29.8	Asheville, N.C.
100.0		7.0	14.1	7.0	11.2	15.5	9.9	9.9	12.7	12.7	Greensboro, N.C.
100.0	1.3	9.3	12.0	8.0	16.0	13.3	10.7	14.7	4.0	10.7	Charleston, S.C.
100.0	3.6	2.4	3.6	14.3	7.1	9.5	15.5	21.4	16.7	5.9	Columbia, S.C.
100.0	2.9	4.8	4.2	6.5	12.9	13.3	16.6	16.9	9.4	12.5	Atlanta, Ga.*
100.0	1.5	3.1	9.1	4.5	12.4	13.0	11.8	17.9	7.6	19.1	2 E. S. Central cities
100.0	5.0				10.0	30.0	5.0	10.0	15.0	25.0	Paducah, Ky.
100.0	1.4	3.2	9.3	4.6	12.5	12.5	12.0	18.1	7.4	19.0	Birmingham, Ala.*
100.0	1.8	4.4	6.8	8.7	13.3	13.8	14.7	17.4	7.7	11.4	5 W. S. Central cities
100.0	6.2	4.5	4.5	3.9	10.1	12.9	14.6	22.5	10.1	10.7	Little Rock, Ark.
100.0	1.1	4.0	9.2	9.5	13.2	13.5	16.3	18.3	6.3	10.6	Oklahoma City, Okla.
100.0	1.9	4.8	7.6	9.5	14.3	17.1	9.5	17.1	6.7	11.5	Austin, Tex.
100.0	1.5	4.3	5.6	9.6	14.4	13.7	15.7	17.0	8.1	10.1	Dallas, Tex.
100.0	1.2	6.2	7.5	2.5	8.8	12.5	2.5	18.8	10.0	30.0	Wichita Falls, Tex.
100.0	0.6	4.6	5.8	10.3	12.8	22.0	14.7	15.1	4.1	10.0	4 Mountain cities
100.0	5.1	11.9	10.2	15.2	13.5	8.5	6.8	8.5	3.4	16.9	Butte, Mont.
100.0		3.8	9.4	5.7	7.5	22.6	17.0	15.1	3.8	15.1	Pueblo, Colo.
100.0		4.3	4.3	10.5	12.4	22.9	15.4	15.4	4.3	10.5	Phoenix, Ariz.
100.0	0.7	4.1	5.4	10.8	14.2	22.7	14.6	15.6	4.1	7.8	Salt Lake City, Utah
100.0	0.6	4.0	6.3	9.5	13.2	17.1	16.7	17.5	7.1	8.0	4 Pacific cities
100.0	0.8	4.4	6.0	10.0	15.8	16.8	15.6	16.2	6.8	7.6	Seattle, Wash.*
100.0	0.5	3.8	7.8	9.9	10.1	19.1	16.7	18.4	6.1	7.6	Portland, Ore.
100.0	0.4	3.4	5.2	4.7	14.2	10.3	17.2	22.7	9.9	12.0	Sacramento, Calif.
100.0	0.6	3.9	5.8	10.1	12.2	18.2	18.0	16.4	7.4	7.4	San Diego, Calif.*

TABLE D 13

Mortgaged Dwellings, Ratio of Debt to Value by Value Groups: Owner-occupied, 52 Cities; Rented, 51 Cities, by Geographic Division, January 1, 1934

← ———————————— O W N E R - O C C U P I E D ———————————— →

	All value groups	$1-499	$500-999	$1,000-1,499	$1,500-1,999	$2,000-2,999	$3,000-3,999	$4,000-4,999	$5,000-7,499	$7,500-9,999	$10,000-14,999	$15,000 and over
52 cities[1]	55.6	103.6	78.6	74.4	66.9	62.8	58.2	57.7	54.3	51.8	52.1	50.3
4 New England cities	54.5		76.0	56.2	73.7	62.8	56.6	59.8	55.0	53.4	53.3	47.0
Portland, Me.	50.5			92.5	43.9	57.6	44.4	47.0	49.9	52.5	51.6	49.1
Worcester, Mass.	67.1			62.5	70.8	89.2	68.6	73.6	68.4	64.3	66.1	58.0
Providence, R.I.*	49.4		76.0	50.9	76.7	54.1	52.6	55.6	49.5	48.5	48.7	42.1
Waterbury, Conn.	60.0			61.7		72.5	60.8	63.2	63.9	62.3	56.4	54.4
4 Mid. Atlantic cities	55.9			102.6	75.7	66.5	58.2	60.1	56.8	56.0	54.7	42.5
Binghamton, N.Y.	45.9				57.5	48.0	41.1	46.8	48.9	49.0	53.8	36.8
Syracuse, N.Y.	57.0			116.8	82.1	72.2	60.0	64.3	59.2	56.6	57.4	54.5
Trenton, N.J.	58.4			89.4	70.9	60.6	57.7	61.1	55.3	56.6	58.2	44.2
Erie, Pa.	57.7			77.4	64.5	62.4	59.7	59.1	57.3	57.7	58.2	
6 E. N. Central cities	56.8	130.5	96.1	91.6	73.4	68.0	61.5	59.6	56.0	54.0	54.5	52.1
Cleveland, Ohio*	57.2	130.5	114.3	98.5	77.2	69.8	62.6	61.8	57.3	55.2	53.8	53.9
Indianapolis, Ind.	56.2		62.1	82.1	72.1	66.1	59.8	54.3	53.5	49.4	57.6	52.2
Peoria, Ill.	50.4		68.8	58.6	48.3	54.9	53.5	52.0	48.9	50.6	46.2	43.5
Lansing, Mich.	59.5		39.2	82.3	68.3	61.8	63.6	59.6	55.6	57.4	60.5	43.2
Kenosha, Wis.	53.8				76.4	75.8	62.0	55.8	51.6	52.1	57.4	26.1
Racine, Wis.	58.9			63.0	53.2	64.6	59.9	62.1	59.5	56.7	53.9	54.7
10 W. N. Central cities	52.0	81.8	65.1	64.6	54.3	55.4	53.0	53.1	50.8	46.8	47.1	53.0
Minneapolis, Minn.	52.4		73.6	62.9	52.7	59.0	54.2	51.0	50.4	47.2	49.6	60.5
St. Paul, Minn.	50.0		51.7	63.6	50.9	48.4	49.6	55.9	48.2	40.3	45.5	49.9
Des Moines, Iowa	53.2	90.9	75.1	66.4	55.6	57.2	52.9	51.6	51.6	51.4	47.2	54.0
St. Joseph, Mo.	52.5		50.5	61.3	53.1	52.5	50.5	59.1	55.4	51.2	41.4	37.8
Springfield, Mo.	52.9	84.6	65.0	62.6	52.3	53.7	55.2	53.3	47.3	40.5	39.4	54.6
Fargo, N.D.	50.4				78.6	55.3	51.7	51.5	53.3	45.9	40.6	48.2
Sioux Falls, S.D.	46.5	54.5	63.8	63.9	48.6	48.4	52.6	50.8	45.9	50.2	46.8	43.6
Lincoln, Neb.	53.6		57.1	73.2	61.3	54.6	54.2	52.4	56.0	47.4	45.7	42.1
Topeka, Kan.	50.4	94.1	58.0	60.1	53.4	59.4	55.8	50.9	51.6	56.1	42.6	29.5
Wichita, Kan.	56.8	70.8	63.7	68.4	66.9	59.4	56.5	56.1	55.5	49.7		46.6
9 S. Atlantic cities	56.6	106.6	65.2	67.8	62.3	59.4	58.7	59.2	55.8	56.3	55.4	49.2
Hagerstown, Md.	60.9		61.7	80.2	49.5	64.0	60.5	71.4	60.2	71.0	56.4	55.4
Richmond, Va.	59.4		100.5	64.0	56.6	64.3	63.1	63.2	60.4	58.5	59.4	51.9
Wheeling, W.Va.*	49.4	145.5	70.2	67.8	64.9	49.2	50.6	47.5	46.5	46.7	51.3	50.7
Asheville, N.C.	66.3		105.6	75.3	75.9	72.8	75.6	63.7	64.5	80.6	47.9	62.4
Greensboro, N.C.	61.9		80.0	74.9	64.3	58.2	57.8	60.1	55.9	52.8	41.6	59.9
Charleston, S.C.	50.3		57.1	57.5	42.2	43.9	61.1	53.0	67.6	58.9	55.6	50.2
Columbia, S.C.	57.4		57.2	50.2	62.2	59.1	53.0	59.8	60.8	57.0	56.5	45.9
Atlanta, Ga.*	57.3	95.0	49.2	65.3	63.7	62.5	59.8	60.8	57.0	56.5	58.7	48.6
Jacksonville, Fla.	52.2		53.0	82.8	64.7	53.4	55.8	56.6	52.7	53.2	41.5	39.7
3 E. S. Central cities	59.8	95.3	82.4	75.0	70.4	65.9	64.8	60.3	56.8	53.1	51.0	48.5
Paducah, Ky.	58.7	45.2	52.6	59.5	55.5	61.9	59.7	59.4	57.9	63.3		57.1
Birmingham, Ala.*	61.1	97.9	84.2	78.2	77.0	69.0	65.9	61.6	57.3	54.6	52.8	47.5
Jackson, Miss.	50.4		85.1	56.5	36.4	48.7	59.9	52.5	52.9	39.7	39.5	52.5
6 W. S. Central cities	55.4	96.6	75.3	65.7	60.5	61.8	57.1	57.8	55.3	49.7	52.7	44.9
Little Rock, Ark.	62.9	66.7	38.0	65.9	72.1	66.6	59.5	64.0	65.2	60.3	58.8	49.2
Baton Rouge, La.	45.0		54.6	57.8	49.5	54.3	51.9	42.6	50.9	37.9	44.0	
Oklahoma City, Okla.	58.2	102.7	67.2	68.7	64.4	63.3	61.2	57.9	58.5	49.4	57.4	50.7
Austin, Tex.	46.4	122.3	61.9	65.1	50.1	54.8	48.5	45.8	46.2	39.3	50.5	39.2
Dallas, Tex.	53.5		87.6	63.8	56.3	60.5	54.6	58.7	51.7	49.0	62.1	46.6
Wichita Falls, Tex.	66.3	108.1	136.3	74.6	73.0	71.8	65.0	83.7	65.0	62.1	61.3	46.9
6 Mountain cities	55.7	71.7	66.1	63.0	60.3	63.1	55.1	54.2	52.4	44.8	53.3	55.3
Butte, Mont.	41.3	63.5	65.8	60.9	51.4	52.5	42.1	43.1	38.1	37.8	27.2	28.0
Boise, Idaho	43.2	45.5	50.8	51.7	53.7	47.6	43.6	40.0	42.3	37.7	33.0	41.2
Casper, Wyo.	56.9	64.9	79.8	74.0	75.0	55.4	60.5	55.8	47.1	52.3	41.5	
Pueblo, Colo.	59.2	69.2	68.3	67.7	70.9	62.0	56.6	54.3	51.8	27.9	52.2	
Phoenix, Ariz.	56.3		98.4	59.5	60.6	65.7	58.6	53.3	56.2	50.5	58.4	47.9
Salt Lake City, Utah	58.0	78.6	59.3	63.3	57.8	66.9	56.4	57.6	55.1	49.0	58.0	60.0
4 Pacific cities	55.9	83.5	76.4	66.5	66.3	61.5	58.9	55.8	51.8	49.9	49.3	52.0
Seattle, Wash.*	54.7	77.2	53.8	60.1	59.8	57.8	58.3	53.9	49.6	50.7	50.4	54.7
Portland, Ore.	56.6	93.3	99.6	70.3	72.2	62.2	58.0	54.8	52.2	49.3	50.3	50.9
Sacramento, Calif.	61.8		97.2	73.1	75.7	69.4	64.9	63.5	60.7	55.2	48.6	65.0
San Diego, Calif.*	54.4	83.3	86.3	74.1	67.1	64.9	58.9	58.0	52.1	46.5	44.9	40.6

Source: *Financial Survey of Urban Housing.* Based on average debt (principal only) by value groups and average value of mortgaged properties by value groups as shown in Tables D 7 and 8. Percentage not shown for fewer than 3 reports.

*Metropolitan district.

[1] *Geographic division and 52 (51)-city percentages are automatically weighted by use of weighted averages from Tables D 7 and 8. For rented properties where the number of cities included in the 'All value groups' column is larger than the number for the individual value groups, the weighted geographic division and 52 (51)-city percentages in the 'All value groups' column are not strictly comparable to the weighted percentages for the individual value groups.*

TABLE D 13

Mortgaged Dwellings, Ratio of Debt to Value by Value Groups: Owner-occupied, 52 Cities; Rented, 51 Cities, by Geographic Division, January 1, 1934

All value groups	$1–499	$500–999	$1,000–1,499	$1,500–1,999	$2,000–2,999	$3,000–3,999	$4,000–4,999	$5,000–7,499	$7,500–9,999	$10,000–14,999	$15,000 and over	
					RENTED							
60.6	109.7	87.5	89.2	67.8	64.4	60.8	60.4	57.2	56.0	57.1	59.8	51 cities[1]
64.0			55.4	75.9	74.0	56.9	61.7	59.8	61.6	62.1	57.8	4 New England cities
53.4			55.4	60.0	66.6	61.2	56.9	61.9	50.8	52.9	42.7	Portland, Me.
69.3					59.9	60.6	67.8	72.3	66.5	65.5	86.5	Worcester, Mass.
58.7				77.4	79.2	55.4	60.3	55.8	61.1	62.0	53.7	Providence, R.I.*
81.8												Waterbury, Conn.
61.2		79.6	86.9	74.7	59.8	73.7	67.2	61.3	60.4	63.4	66.7	4 Mid. Atlantic cities
52.4												Binghamton, N.Y.
62.7				....	51.6	78.0	69.1	61.4	63.0	57.6	71.2	Syracuse, N.Y.
59.7		79.6	86.9	74.7	58.2	62.9	61.7	52.3	49.3	82.5	64.3	Trenton, N.J.
64.5					82.2	68.7	66.9	66.6	63.3	65.4	50.1	Erie, Pa.
64.2		113.0	120.7	79.7	68.6	62.5	63.3	57.2	56.0	60.8	69.7	6 E. N. Central cities
67.7		127.3	148.1	93.3	74.6	65.2	68.4	60.5	62.9	67.2	74.5	Cleveland, Ohio*
57.0		92.6	71.2	60.5	60.1	60.3	55.7	52.2	40.3	52.4	61.3	Indianapolis, Ind.
52.5		65.4	70.8	61.9	47.2	48.7	52.7	49.4	49.4	37.9	66.2	Peoria, Ill.
57.0			64.9	49.1	61.4	60.2	58.9	51.1	69.4			Lansing, Mich.
58.4												Kenosha, Wis.
59.8			119.0		66.5	59.3	62.9	62.4	62.1	56.5	52.4	Racine, Wis.
55.3	135.0	66.3	66.3	57.2	52.9	54.8	53.8	50.7	54.1	51.2	57.3	10 W. N. Central cities
56.7		59.9	69.5	68.5	50.9	53.5	54.8	53.0	56.7	59.2	61.2	Minneapolis, Minn.
53.7			65.4	43.5	54.8	58.4	56.9	48.2	52.5	41.7	58.0	St. Paul, Minn.
52.2	174.9	75.4	55.5	53.8	52.0	50.1	54.2	48.1	52.3	50.9	53.7	Des Moines, Iowa
54.5												St. Joseph, Mo.
48.2	138.9	64.1	66.3	57.6	50.8	59.1	42.1	48.1	48.1		24.6	Springfield, Mo.
57.2												Fargo, N.D.
48.8			74.8	43.6	46.5	51.9	49.3	44.9	29.8	51.7	54.4	Sioux Falls, S.D.
63.3		100.0	79.6	47.7	52.8	61.0	53.1	50.0	47.9		78.6	Lincoln, Neb.
52.0		48.5	44.2	57.6	54.4	50.6	46.4	47.7	70.9	41.1	55.1	Topeka, Kan.
57.4	100.0	65.6	67.7	61.9	58.9	55.5	54.3	54.9	57.7	46.2	51.5	Wichita, Kan.
65.4		67.1	58.2	58.4	62.4	66.6	62.9	63.3	61.2	61.5	73.8	8 S. Atlantic cities
67.4												Hagerstown, Md.
62.6		63.6	48.9	50.0	60.4	61.9	52.3	61.8	62.4	62.9	72.9	Richmond, Va.
51.1												Wheeling, W.Va.*
79.7												Asheville, N.C.
61.2												Greensboro, N.C.
51.9												Charleston, S.C.
62.6												Columbia, S.C.
70.0		68.5	61.7	61.2	62.9	68.1	66.7	63.9	60.7	61.1	74.0	Atlanta, Ga.*
50.4		92.0	91.5	75.6	69.7	61.3	62.6	58.0	51.6	54.0	37.3	3 E. S. Central cities
48.2												Paducah, Ky.
52.0		92.0	91.5	75.6	69.7	61.3	62.6	58.0	51.6	54.0	37.3	Birmingham, Ala.*
43.7												Jackson, Miss.
56.9	74.4	92.2	85.2	55.8	61.6	59.9	63.7	55.8	58.2	54.3	49.5	6 W. S. Central cities
62.2	50.0	70.8	67.9	71.6	56.8	70.6	62.2	57.7	58.4	54.1	64.7	Little Rock, Ark.
59.4												Baton Rouge, La.
55.5		55.8	57.8	53.9	61.8	66.1	64.0	60.1	66.9	47.5	52.1	Oklahoma City, Okla.
50.9	95.1	79.2	49.6	57.8	58.7	51.7	57.6	46.7	38.5	56.7	38.5	Austin, Tex.
56.7		121.4	112.4	53.6	62.9	55.2	64.7	54.3	56.0	58.1	47.0	Dallas, Tex.
72.4												Wichita Falls, Tex.
56.5		43.2	76.3	66.3	61.4	60.1	54.0	67.3	48.2	47.0	54.1	6 Mountain cities
52.2												Butte, Mont.
45.1												Boise, Idaho
48.4												Casper, Wyo.
58.9												Pueblo, Colo.
53.3			75.7	96.8	65.2	54.8	50.4	62.7	45.2	54.7	32.0	Phoenix, Ariz.
59.8		43.2	76.8	47.2	59.1	63.5	56.3	70.1	50.0	42.4	59.5	Salt Lake City, Utah
57.4	100.0	73.2	69.9	64.1	64.4	58.3	55.9	56.1	51.0	52.5	56.0	4 Pacific cities
57.2		63.3	63.8	56.9	66.3	56.3	50.2	57.0	52.2	55.6	56.3	Seattle, Wash.*
54.9	100.0	81.7	66.1	70.0	61.5	57.8	59.6	57.2	45.8	37.3	53.9	Portland, Ore.
64.2			78.3	69.1	68.8	65.4	65.1	58.9	68.8	56.8	64.4	Sacramento, Calif.
57.6		81.1	79.1	65.9	62.8	58.3	56.9	52.4	47.4	62.5	54.0	San Diego, Calif.*

TABLE D 14

Percentage that Total Debt on Mortgaged Dwellings is of Total Value of All Dwellings, including Dwellings not Mortgaged: Owner-occupied, 61 Cities; Rented, 44 Cities, by Geographic Division, January 1, 1934

	Owner-occupied	Rented		Owner-occupied	Rented
61 (44) cities[1][2]	34.1	32.8	10 (8) S. Atlantic cities[2]	30.6	32.4
			Frederick, Md.	14.0	
			Hagerstown, Md.	32.3	20.0
6 (3) New England cities[2]	36.3	37.0	Richmond, Va.	33.8	29.1
Portland, Me.	23.8	27.6	Wheeling, W.Va.*	19.7	14.8
Nashua, N.H.	23.7		Asheville, N.C.	32.7	13.4
Burlington, Vt.	21.4		Greensboro, N.C.	38.4	30.9
Worcester, Mass.	54.2	49.4	Charleston, S.C.	15.9	15.8
Providence, R.I.*	31.9	34.8	Columbia, S.C.	35.8	32.8
Waterbury, Conn.	47.0		Atlanta, Ga.*	36.5	46.3
			Jacksonville, Fla.	29.8	
5 (3) Mid. Atlantic cities[2]	36.1	36.5	4 (2) E. S. Central cities[2]	33.0	20.5
Binghamton, N.Y.	21.7		Paducah, Ky.	21.6	9.6
Syracuse, N.Y.	45.4	42.3	Knoxville, Tenn.	24.5	
Trenton, N.J.	41.6	27.3	Birmingham, Ala.*	36.6	20.9
Erie, Pa.	29.9	27.4	Jackson, Miss.	31.5	
Williamsport, Pa.	19.0				
			7 (5) W. S. Central cities[2]	31.6	30.3
			Little Rock, Ark.	30.8	26.3
			Baton Rouge, La.	25.8	
7 (6) E. N. Central cities[2]	38.2	37.6	Shreveport, La.	33.8	
Cleveland, Ohio*	39.8	40.4	Oklahoma City, Okla.	37.1	34.8
Indianapolis, Ind.	35.7	33.3	Austin, Tex.	19.7	18.9
Decatur, Ill.	31.1		Dallas, Tex.	31.0	31.0
Peoria, Ill.	28.4	28.4	Wichita Falls, Tex.	29.1	19.1
Lansing, Mich.	35.0	23.2			
Kenosha, Wis.	35.3	32.1	8 (4) Mountain cities[2]	29.9	30.3
Racine, Wis.	41.1	37.7	Butte, Mont.	12.3	11.5
			Boise, Idaho	19.5	
			Casper, Wyo.	27.3	
10 (9) W. N. Central cities[2]	29.1	27.8	Pueblo, Colo.	30.1	15.2
Minneapolis, Minn.	31.8	32.3	Albuquerque, N.M.	33.4	
St. Paul, Minn.	26.3	27.9	Phoenix, Ariz.	32.1	29.2
Des Moines, Iowa	29.6	25.5	Salt Lake City, Utah	34.7	38.9
St. Joseph, Mo.	24.4	16.5	Reno, Nev.	26.5	
Springfield, Mo.	28.1	17.9			
Fargo, N.D.	30.6		4 Pacific cities	31.7	31.4
Sioux Falls, S.D.	26.5	23.9	Seattle, Wash.*	31.4	35.4
Lincoln, Neb.	27.0	30.8	Portland, Ore.	32.5	25.3
Topeka, Kan.	24.3	18.9	Sacramento, Calif.	34.6	34.5
Wichita, Kan.	32.2	27.9	San Diego, Calif.*	29.7	28.3

Source: *Financial Survey of Urban Housing*. Based on number of reports for all properties and mortgaged properties which is approximately the same as shown in Tables A 12 and 13 and D 5 and 6.
*Metropolitan district.
[1] Geographic division and 61 (44)-city percentages weighted by value of all properties, by tenure, in each city (RPI).
[2] Figures in parentheses are number of cities reporting on rented properties.

TABLE D 15

Mortgages, Number and Percentage Distribution by Tenure and Priority, 52 Cities by Geographic Division, January 1, 1934

	←————————————— NUMBER —————————————→						
	OWNER-OCCUPIED				RENTED		
	All priorities	1st mortgages	2ᵈ & 3ᵈ mortgages	Land contracts	All priorities	1st mortgages	2ᵈ & 3ᵈ mortgages	Land contracts
52 cities[1]	73,439	62,864	6,088	4,487	14,259	13,075	881	303
4 New England cities	5,030	4,186	833	11	1,032	887	143	2
Portland, Me.	716	640	74	2	222	195	26	1
Worcester, Mass.	1,410	1,096	312	2	239	208	31	
Providence, R.I.*	2,305	1,983	316	6	440	382	57	1
Waterbury, Conn.	599	467	131	1	131	102	29	
4 Mid. Atlantic cities	4,805	4,247	535	23	878	790	83	5
Binghamton, N.Y.	293	257	32	4	87	80	7	
Syracuse, N.Y.	1,227	964	260	3	261	214	47	1
Trenton, N.J.	1,686	1,559	125	2	248	232	15	
Erie, Pa.	1,599	1,467	118	14	282	264	14	4
6 E. N. Central cities	21,871	18,714	2,223	934	3,930	3,620	257	53
Cleveland, Ohio*	15,592	13,511	1,910	171	2,466	2,243	211	12
Indianapolis, Ind.	1,710	1,518	57	135	497	487	6	4
Peoria, Ill.	1,448	1,262	96	90	332	314	11	7
Lansing, Mich.	634	367	15	252	158	142	2	14
Kenosha, Wis.	760	647	42	71	139	124	8	7
Racine, Wis.	1,727	1,409	103	215	338	310	19	9
10 W. N. Central cities	12,801	10,934	588	1,279	3,001	2,792	100	109
Minneapolis, Minn.	4,348	3,703	157	488	1,020	924	45	51
St. Paul, Minn.	932	805	23	104	229	210	8	11
Des Moines, Iowa	1,639	1,238	42	359	407	385	8	14
St. Joseph, Mo.	552	499	46	7	100	93	5	2
Springfield, Mo.	772	737	31	4	177	169	6	2
Fargo, N.D.	528	460	36	32	79	75	3	1
Sioux Falls, S.D.	660	546	35	79	199	180	8	11
Lincoln, Neb.	841	759	58	24	180	170	4	6
Topeka, Kan.	1,138	967	82	89	251	240	6	5
Wichita, Kan.	1,391	1,220	78	93	359	346	7	6
9 S. Atlantic cities	6,596	5,911	630	55	1,203	1,120	72	11
Hagerstown, Md.	379	352	24	3	67	61	6	
Richmond, Va.	1,227	1,048	173	6	143	128	14	1
Wheeling, W.Va.*	844	770	64	10	125	117	6	2
Asheville, N.C.	423	380	30	13	38	37	1	
Greensboro, N.C.	332	285	47		60	52	5	3
Charleston, S.C.	204	201	3		79	78	1	
Columbia, S.C.	362	329	30	3	89	82	5	2
Atlanta, Ga.*	2,533	2,277	242	14	542	510	32	
Jacksonville, Fla.	292	269	17	6	60	55	2	3
3 E. S. Central cities	2,670	2,422	188	60	337	310	20	7
Paducah, Ky.	239	217	15	7	21	20	1	
Birmingham, Ala.*	2,141	1,947	142	52	228	216	9	3
Jackson, Miss.	290	258	31	1	88	74	10	4
6 W. S. Central cities	5,538	5,049	389	100	1,259	1,187	57	15
Little Rock, Ark.	897	808	63	26	185	182	2	1
Baton Rouge, La.	182	173	6	3	61	56	5	
Oklahoma City, Okla.	1,919	1,720	170	29	400	374	22	4
Austin, Tex.	420	372	19	29	107	97	4	6
Dallas, Tex.	1,779	1,655	114	10	423	398	21	4
Wichita Falls, Tex.	341	321	17	3	83	80	3	
6 Mountain cities	4,289	3,277	145	867	686	617	33	36
Butte, Mont.	472	369	8	95	61	55	3	3
Boise, Idaho	585	489	20	76	37	32	2	3
Casper, Wyo.	302	170	11	121	51	46	2	3
Pueblo, Colo.	421	392	16	13	48	43	2	3
Phoenix, Ariz.	572	477	26	69	183	168	9	6
Salt Lake City, Utah	1,937	1,380	64	493	306	273	15	18
4 Pacific cities	9,839	8,124	557	1,158	1,933	1,752	116	65
Seattle, Wash.*	3,404	2,543	98	763	530	473	25	32
Portland, Ore.	2,624	2,324	140	160	448	413	29	6
Sacramento, Calif.	1,328	1,102	113	113	246	227	13	6
San Diego, Calif.*	2,483	2,155	206	122	709	639	49	21

Source: Federal Home Loan Bank Board tabulation of data from Financial Survey of Urban Housing.
Metropolitan district.
[1]*Geographic division and 52-city percentages weighted by number of loans, by tenure and priority, in each city (RPI).*

TABLE D 15

Mortgages, Number and Percentage Distribution by Tenure and Priority, 52 Cities by Geographic Division, January 1, 1934

← ————— P E R C E N T A G E D I S T R I B U T I O N [1] ————— →								
O W N E R - O C C U P I E D				R E N T E D				
All priorities	1st mortgages	2d & 3d mortgages	Land contracts	All priorities	1st mortgages	2d & 3d mortgages	Land contracts	
100.0	85.3	8.7	6.0	100.0	91.6	6.4	2.0	52 cities[1]
100.0	83.6	16.2	0.2	100.0	86.1	13.7	0.2	4 New England cities
100.0	89.4	10.3	0.3	100.0	87.8	11.7	0.5	Portland, Me.
100.0	77.7	22.1	0.2	100.0	87.0	13.0		Worcester, Mass.
100.0	86.0	13.7	0.3	100.0	86.8	13.0	0.2	Providence, R.I.*
100.0	78.0	21.9	0.1	100.0	77.9	22.1		Waterbury, Conn.
100.0	84.7	14.9	0.4	100.0	87.1	12.6	0.3	4 Mid. Atlantic cities
100.0	87.7	10.9	1.4	100.0	92.0	8.0		Binghamton, N.Y.
100.0	78.6	21.2	0.2	100.0	82.0	18.0		Syracuse, N.Y.
100.0	92.5	7.4	0.1	100.0	93.5	6.1	0.4	Trenton, N.J.
100.0	91.7	7.4	0.9	100.0	93.6	5.0	1.4	Erie, Pa.
100.0	85.6	9.4	5.0	100.0	93.1	5.7	1.2	6 E. N. Central cities
100.0	86.7	12.2	1.1	100.0	91.0	8.5	0.5	Cleveland, Ohio*
100.0	88.8	3.3	7.9	100.0	98.0	1.2	0.8	Indianapolis, Ind.
100.0	87.2	6.6	6.2	100.0	94.6	3.3	2.1	Peoria, Ill.
100.0	57.9	2.4	39.7	100.0	89.9	1.3	8.8	Lansing, Mich.
100.0	85.1	5.5	9.4	100.0	89.2	5.8	5.0	Kenosha, Wis.
100.0	81.6	6.0	12.4	100.0	91.7	5.6	2.7	Racine, Wis.
100.0	85.5	4.2	10.3	100.0	92.9	3.4	3.7	10 W. N. Central cities
100.0	85.2	3.6	11.2	100.0	90.6	4.4	5.0	Minneapolis, Minn.
100.0	86.4	2.5	11.1	100.0	91.7	3.5	4.8	St. Paul, Minn.
100.0	75.5	2.6	21.9	100.0	94.6	2.0	3.4	Des Moines, Iowa
100.0	90.4	8.3	1.3	100.0	93.0	5.0	2.0	St. Joseph, Mo.
100.0	95.5	4.0	0.5	100.0	95.5	3.4	1.1	Springfield, Mo.
100.0	87.1	6.8	6.1	100.0	94.9	3.8	1.3	Fargo, N.D.
100.0	82.7	5.3	12.0	100.0	90.5	4.0	5.5	Sioux Falls, S.D.
100.0	90.2	6.9	2.9	100.0	94.4	2.2	3.4	Lincoln, Neb.
100.0	85.0	7.2	7.8	100.0	95.6	2.4	2.0	Topeka, Kan.
100.0	87.7	5.6	6.7	100.0	96.4	1.9	1.7	Wichita, Kan.
100.0	89.8	9.4	0.8	100.0	92.7	5.7	1.6	9 S. Atlantic cities
100.0	92.9	6.3	0.8	100.0	91.0	9.0		Hagerstown, Md.
100.0	85.4	14.1	0.5	100.0	89.5	9.8	0.7	Richmond, Va.
100.0	91.2	7.6	1.2	100.0	93.6	4.8	1.6	Wheeling, W.Va.*
100.0	89.8	7.1	3.1	100.0	97.4	2.6		Asheville, N.C.
100.0	85.8	14.2		100.0	86.7	8.3	5.0	Greensboro, N.C.
100.0	98.5	1.5		100.0	98.7	1.3		Charleston, S.C.
100.0	90.9	8.3	0.8	100.0	92.1	5.6	2.3	Columbia, S.C.
100.0	89.9	9.6	0.5	100.0	94.1	5.9		Atlanta, Ga.*
100.0	92.1	5.8	2.1	100.0	91.7	3.3	5.0	Jacksonville, Fla.
100.0	90.7	7.1	2.2	100.0	93.0	5.2	1.8	3 E. S. Central cities
100.0	90.8	6.3	2.9	100.0	95.2	4.8		Paducah, Ky.
100.0	91.0	6.6	2.4	100.0	94.7	4.0	1.3	Birmingham, Ala.*
100.0	89.0	10.7	0.3	100.0	84.1	11.4	4.5	Jackson, Miss.
100.0	91.4	6.9	1.7	100.0	94.0	4.9	1.1	6 W. S. Central cities
100.0	90.1	7.0	2.9	100.0	98.4	1.1	0.5	Little Rock, Ark.
100.0	95.1	3.3	1.6	100.0	91.8	8.2		Baton Rouge, La.
100.0	89.6	8.9	1.5	100.0	93.5	5.5	1.0	Oklahoma City, Okla.
100.0	88.6	4.5	6.9	100.0	90.7	3.7	5.6	Austin, Tex.
100.0	93.0	6.4	0.6	100.0	94.1	5.0	0.9	Dallas, Tex.
100.0	94.1	5.0	0.9	100.0	96.4	3.6		Wichita Falls, Tex.
100.0	76.6	3.4	20.0	100.0	89.8	4.8	5.4	6 Mountain cities
100.0	78.2	1.7	20.1	100.0	90.2	4.9	4.9	Butte, Mont.
100.0	83.6	3.4	13.0	100.0	86.5	5.4	8.1	Boise, Idaho
100.0	56.3	3.6	40.1	100.0	90.2	3.9	5.9	Casper, Wyo.
100.0	93.1	3.8	3.1	100.0	89.6	4.2	6.2	Pueblo, Colo.
100.0	83.4	4.5	12.1	100.0	91.8	4.9	3.3	Phoenix, Ariz.
100.0	71.2	3.3	25.5	100.0	89.2	4.9	5.9	Salt Lake City, Utah
100.0	81.9	5.1	13.0	100.0	90.5	5.8	3.7	4 Pacific cities
100.0	74.7	2.9	22.4	100.0	89.2	4.7	6.1	Seattle, Wash.*
100.0	88.6	5.3	6.1	100.0	92.2	6.5	1.3	Portland, Ore.
100.0	83.0	8.5	8.5	100.0	92.3	5.3	2.4	Sacramento, Calif.
100.0	86.8	8.3	4.9	100.0	90.1	6.9	3.0	San Diego, Calif.*

TABLE D 16

Mortgages, Amount and Percentage Distribution by Tenure and Priority, 52 Cities by Geographic Division, January 1, 1934

| | THOUSANDS OF DOLLARS | | | | | | | |
| | OWNER-OCCUPIED | | | | RENTED | | | |
	All priorities	1st mortgages	2^d & 3^d mortgages	Land contracts	All priorities	1st mortgages	2^d & 3^d mortgages	Land contracts
52 cities[1]	183,623.9	166,731.9	7,539.1	9,352.9	48,784.8	46,079.9	1,921.5	783.4
4 New England cities	15,394.0	14,191.8	1,181.8	20.4	4,545.7	4,073.6	467.5	4.6
Portland, Me.	1,973.7	1,837.0	134.6	2.1	773.9	714.9	55.9	3.1
Worcester, Mass.	4,912.2	4,484.9	423.0	4.3	1,086.2	1,020.9	65.3	
Providence, R.I.*	6,258.6	5,872.9	372.1	13.6	1,542.1	1,456.1	84.5	1.5
Waterbury, Conn.	2,249.5	1,997.0	252.1	0.4	1,143.5	881.7	261.8	
4 Mid. Atlantic cities	12,289.8	11,554.5	688.7	46.6	2,967.6	2,850.1	99.9	17.6
Binghamton, N.Y.	783.6	731.0	41.6	11.0	331.1	319.2	11.9	
Syracuse, N.Y.	3,559.5	3,185.5	369.7	4.3	1,049.0	993.1	55.9	
Trenton, N.J.	3,809.3	3,662.3	141.0	6.0	569.8	550.8	17.0	2.0
Erie, Pa.	4,137.4	3,975.7	136.4	25.3	1,017.7	987.0	15.1	15.6
6 E. N. Central cities	68,079.5	61,973.1	3,197.5	2,908.9	16,757.2	15,809.2	727.0	221.0
Cleveland, Ohio*	51,603.5	48,204.0	2,815.5	584.0	12,428.7	11,727.7	652.0	49.0
Indianapolis, Ind.	4,594.3	4,084.1	78.9	431.3	1,325.6	1,308.1	10.8	6.6
Peoria, Ill.	3,246.8	2,921.1	106.2	219.5	904.8	826.7	17.9	60.2
Lansing, Mich.	1,446.5	766.1	8.8	671.6	313.7	275.6	1.9	36.2
Kenosha, Wis.	2,015.4	1,737.2	53.1	225.1	501.8	452.0	11.6	38.2
Racine, Wis.	5,173.0	4,260.6	135.0	777.4	1,282.7	1,219.1	32.8	30.8
10 W. N. Central cities	25,266.7	22,249.4	617.4	2,399.9	7,360.6	6,917.5	175.1	268.0
Minneapolis, Minn.	10,000.7	8,833.4	232.5	934.8	3,163.2	2,882.6	124.1	156.5
St. Paul, Minn.	1,802.5	1,572.6	18.1	211.8	605.7	577.6	6.9	21.2
Des Moines, Iowa	3,051.6	2,311.2	36.7	703.7	859.5	823.2	6.0	30.3
St. Joseph, Mo.	1,002.4	947.6	46.8	8.0	179.8	175.5	1.7	2.6
Springfield, Mo.	1,082.5	1,054.1	22.7	5.7	257.0	243.9	11.4	1.7
Fargo, N.D.	1,237.7	1,131.4	37.5	68.8	214.4	210.1	2.5	1.8
Sioux Falls, S.D.	1,326.8	1,144.2	28.7	153.9	490.1	455.6	4.4	30.1
Lincoln, Neb.	1,613.4	1,514.5	68.6	30.3	467.0	456.3	3.4	7.3
Topeka, Kan.	1,923.6	1,720.4	56.9	146.3	501.2	487.1	7.6	6.5
Wichita, Kan.	2,225.5	2,020.0	68.9	136.6	622.7	605.6	7.1	10.0
9 S. Atlantic cities	17,062.0	16,228.7	729.9	103.4	4,418.7	4,240.8	144.9	33.0
Hagerstown, Md.	1,121.3	1,073.6	37.4	10.3	187.3	179.8	7.5	
Richmond, Va.	3,744.9	3,524.1	209.3	11.5	475.0	451.4	22.9	0.7
Wheeling, W.Va.*	1,696.2	1,591.5	83.2	21.5	345.5	321.2	19.6	4.7
Asheville, N.C.	1,074.2	1,015.9	32.2	26.1	102.7	97.7	5.0	
Greensboro, N.C.	1,059.3	957.6	101.7		241.2	183.1	54.1	4.0
Charleston, S.C.	478.7	471.8	6.9		158.8	156.8	2.0	
Columbia, S.C.	933.9	893.5	31.4	9.0	253.7	237.5	5.7	10.5
Atlanta, Ga.*	6,293.9	6,070.3	206.5	17.1	2,462.3	2,438.0	24.3	
Jacksonville, Fla.	659.6	630.4	21.3	7.9	192.2	175.3	3.8	13.1
3 E. S. Central cities	5,501.4	5,218.6	155.0	127.8	926.6	883.4	25.6	17.6
Paducah, Ky.	369.0	348.8	14.8	5.4	41.6	41.2	0.4	
Birmingham, Ala.*	4,545.2	4,309.7	114.7	120.8	657.7	640.1	12.8	4.8
Jackson, Miss.	587.2	560.1	25.5	1.6	227.3	202.1	12.4	12.8
6 W. S. Central cities	11,784.6	11,398.7	281.9	104.0	3,546.3	3,489.7	46.2	10.4
Little Rock, Ark.	1,917.3	1,838.0	51.5	27.8	448.0	445.4	2.2	0.4
Baton Rouge, La.	347.1	334.8	7.4	4.9	173.1	169.2	3.9	
Oklahoma City, Okla.	4,324.1	4,165.5	128.8	29.8	1,470.3	1,446.4	21.8	2.1
Austin, Tex.	790.9	756.0	12.7	22.2	204.0	195.6	4.6	3.8
Dallas, Tex.	3,747.6	3,660.4	70.1	17.1	1,088.7	1,072.6	12.0	4.1
Wichita Falls, Tex.	657.6	644.0	11.4	2.2	162.2	160.5	1.7	
6 Mountain cities	7,990.5	6,274.7	158.5	1,557.3	2,084.3	1,899.6	84.3	100.4
Butte, Mont.	632.5	512.7	7.1	112.7	189.5	171.1	15.0	3.4
Boise, Idaho	847.7	755.4	19.0	73.3	73.9	67.2	5.4	1.3
Casper, Wyo.	517.9	315.0	11.7	191.2	119.7	100.5	2.5	16.7
Pueblo, Colo.	566.4	542.1	11.1	13.2	58.6	52.2	2.4	4.0
Phoenix, Ariz.	1,246.4	1,126.9	20.4	99.1	464.4	437.0	11.8	15.6
Salt Lake City, Utah	4,179.6	3,022.6	89.2	1,067.8	1,178.2	1,071.6	47.2	59.4
4 Pacific cities	20,255.4	17,642.4	528.4	2,084.6	6,177.8	5,916.0	151.0	110.8
Seattle, Wash.*	6,730.8	5,489.1	102.7	1,139.0	2,484.5	2,400.0	29.5	55.0
Portland, Ore.	5,034.6	4,581.5	118.8	334.3	1,054.4	1,009.1	38.4	6.9
Sacramento, Calif.	3,293.0	2,840.3	97.3	355.4	741.4	694.3	36.5	10.6
San Diego, Calif.*	5,197.0	4,731.5	209.6	255.9	1,897.5	1,812.6	46.6	38.3

Source: Federal Home Loan Bank Board tabulation of data from Financial Survey of Urban Housing. Percentage not shown if less than one-tenth of one per cent.
*Metropolitan district.
[1]*Geographic division and 52-city percentages weighted by amount of debt, by tenure and priority, in each city, 1934.*

TABLE D 16

Mortgages, Amount and Percentage Distribution by Tenure and Priority, 52 Cities by Geographic Division, January 1, 1934

←——————— PERCENTAGE	DISTRIBUTION	———————→						
OWNER-OCCUPIED				RENTED				
All priorities	1st mortgages	2d & 3d mortgages	Land contracts	All priorities	1st mortgages	2d & 3d mortgages	Land contracts	
100.0	90.8	4.4	4.8	100.0	94.9	3.8	1.3	52 cities[1]
100.0	92.4	7.4	0.2	100.0	91.7	8.2	0.1	4 New England cities
100.0	93.1	6.8	0.1	100.0	92.0	7.2	0.8	Portland, Me.
100.0	91.3	8.6	0.1	100.0	94.0	6.0		Worcester, Mass.
100.0	93.8	6.0	0.2	100.0	94.4	5.5	0.1	Providence, R.I.*
100.0	88.8	11.2		100.0	77.1	22.9		Waterbury, Conn.
100.0	91.9	7.7	0.4	100.0	95.5	4.2	0.3	4 Mid. Atlantic cities
100.0	93.3	5.3	1.4	100.0	96.4	3.6		Binghamton, N.Y.
100.0	89.5	10.4	0.1	100.0	94.7	5.3		Syracuse, N.Y.
100.0	96.1	3.7	0.2	100.0	96.7	3.0	0.3	Trenton, N.J.
100.0	96.1	3.3	0.6	100.0	97.0	1.5	1.5	Erie, Pa.
100.0	90.7	4.5	4.8	100.0	94.9	4.0	1.1	6 E. N. Central cities
100.0	93.4	5.5	1.1	100.0	94.4	5.2	0.4	Cleveland, Ohio*
100.0	88.9	1.7	9.4	100.0	98.7	0.8	0.5	Indianapolis, Ind.
100.0	90.0	3.2	6.8	100.0	91.4	2.0	6.6	Peoria, Ill.
100.0	53.0	0.6	46.4	100.0	87.8	0.6	11.6	Lansing, Mich.
100.0	86.2	2.6	11.2	100.0	90.1	2.3	7.6	Kenosha, Wis.
100.0	82.4	2.6	15.0	100.0	95.0	2.6	2.4	Racine, Wis.
100.0	88.0	2.2	9.8	100.0	94.1	2.3	3.6	10 W. N. Central cities
100.0	88.3	2.3	9.4	100.0	91.1	3.9	5.0	Minneapolis, Minn.
100.0	87.2	1.0	11.8	100.0	95.4	1.1	3.5	St. Paul, Minn.
100.0	75.7	1.2	23.1	100.0	95.8	0.7	3.5	Des Moines, Iowa
100.0	94.5	4.7	0.8	100.0	97.6	1.0	1.4	St. Joseph, Mo.
100.0	97.4	2.1	0.5	100.0	94.9	4.4	0.7	Springfield, Mo.
100.0	91.4	3.0	5.6	100.0	98.0	1.2	0.8	Fargo, N.D.
100.0	86.2	2.2	11.6	100.0	93.0	0.9	6.1	Sioux Falls, S.D.
100.0	93.9	4.2	1.9	100.0	97.7	0.7	1.6	Lincoln, Neb.
100.0	89.4	3.0	7.6	100.0	97.2	1.5	1.3	Topeka, Kan.
100.0	90.8	3.1	6.1	100.0	97.3	1.1	1.6	Wichita, Kan.
100.0	95.1	4.3	0.6	100.0	95.7	3.3	1.0	9 S. Atlantic cities
100.0	95.7	3.3	1.0	100.0	96.0	4.0		Hagerstown, Md.
100.0	94.1	5.6	0.3	100.0	95.0	4.8	0.2	Richmond, Va.
100.0	93.8	4.9	1.3	100.0	93.0	5.7	1.3	Wheeling, W. Va.*
100.0	94.6	3.0	2.4	100.0	95.1	4.9		Asheville, N.C.
100.0	90.4	9.6		100.0	75.9	22.4	1.7	Greensboro, N.C.
100.0	98.6	1.4		100.0	98.7	1.3		Charleston, S.C.
100.0	95.7	3.4	0.9	100.0	93.6	2.3	4.1	Columbia, S.C.
100.0	96.4	3.3	0.3	100.0	99.0	1.0		Atlanta, Ga.*
100.0	95.6	3.2	1.2	100.0	91.2	2.0	6.8	Jacksonville, Fla.
100.0	94.9	2.8	2.3	100.0	96.3	2.4	1.3	3 E. S. Central cities
100.0	94.5	4.0	1.5	100.0	99.0	1.0		Paducah, Ky.
100.0	94.8	2.5	2.7	100.0	97.3	2.0	0.7	Birmingham, Ala.*
100.0	95.4	4.3	0.3	100.0	88.9	5.5	5.6	Jackson, Miss.
100.0	96.9	2.3	0.8	100.0	98.4	1.3	0.3	6 W. S. Central cities
100.0	95.9	2.7	1.4	100.0	99.4	0.5	0.1	Little Rock, Ark.
100.0	96.4	2.1	1.5	100.0	97.8	2.2		Baton Rouge, La.
100.0	96.3	3.0	0.7	100.0	98.4	1.5	0.1	Oklahoma City, Okla.
100.0	95.6	1.6	2.8	100.0	95.9	2.2	1.9	Austin, Tex.
100.0	97.7	1.9	0.4	100.0	98.5	1.1	0.4	Dallas, Tex.
100.0	97.9	1.7	0.4	100.0	99.0	1.0		Wichita Falls, Tex.
100.0	78.3	2.0	19.7	100.0	91.2	4.0	4.8	6 Mountain cities
100.0	81.1	1.1	17.8	100.0	90.3	7.9	1.8	Butte, Mont.
100.0	89.1	2.2	8.7	100.0	90.9	7.3	1.8	Boise, Idaho
100.0	60.9	2.2	36.9	100.0	84.0	2.1	13.9	Casper, Wyo.
100.0	95.7	2.0	2.3	100.0	89.1	4.1	6.8	Pueblo, Colo.
100.0	90.4	1.6	8.0	100.0	94.1	2.5	3.4	Phoenix, Ariz.
100.0	72.3	2.2	25.5	100.0	91.0	4.0	5.0	Salt Lake City, Utah
100.0	86.6	2.4	11.0	100.0	96.0	2.2	1.8	4 Pacific cities
100.0	81.6	1.5	16.9	100.0	96.6	1.2	2.2	Seattle, Wash.*
100.0	91.0	2.4	6.6	100.0	95.7	3.6	0.7	Portland, Ore.
100.0	86.2	3.0	10.8	100.0	93.7	4.9	1.4	Sacramento, Calif.
100.0	91.0	4.0	5.0	100.0	95.5	2.5	2.0	San Diego, Calif.*

TABLE D 17

Mortgaged Owner-occupied Dwellings, Number reporting Outstanding Debt by Priority and by Holding Agency, 52 Cities by Geographic Division, January 1, 1934

	All holding agencies	Life ins. co.	Build. & loan asso.	Commer. bank	Savings bank	Mortgage co.	Construct. co.	Title & trust co.	H.O. Loan Corp.	Individual	Other[1]
52 cities	62,864	7,063	11,351	9,413	7,541	5,199	243	1,884	2,158	15,276	2,736
4 New England cities	4,186	72	517	458	1,946	102	5	99	61	741	185
Portland, Me.	640	10	190	45	280	5		2	6	96	6
Worcester, Mass.*	1,096	12	46	54	819	13	1	11	18	46	76
Providence, R.I.*	1,983	43	266	294	641	81	4	64	23	478	89
Waterbury, Conn.	467	7	15	65	206	3		22	14	121	14
4 Mid. Atlantic cities	4,247	108	508	328	815	74	4	47	61	2,150	152
Binghamton, N.Y.	257	6	5	32	67	1		1		139	6
Syracuse, N.Y.	964	43	8	83	674	3	1	10	1	126	15
Trenton, N.J.	1,559	33	197	89	44	49		20	15	1,050	62
Erie, Pa.	1,467	26	298	124	30	21	3	16	45	835	69
6 E. N. Central cities	18,714	1,203	4,003	6,227	2,770	390	63	676	553	2,204	625
Cleveland, Ohio*	13,511	908	1,536	6,023	2,687	143	46	380	389	1,016	383
Indianapolis, Ind.	1,518	145	921	89	31	15	8	101	68	92	48
Peoria, Ill.	1,262	90	870	41	12	9	7	10	16	141	66
Lansing, Mich.	367	45	146	18	17	10	1	7	30	83	10
Kenosha, Wis.	647	3	99	23	7	52	1	147	12	254	49
Racine, Wis.	1,409	12	431	33	16	161		31	38	618	69
10 W. N. Central cities	10,934	1,421	2,416	608	472	1,416	22	366	385	3,339	489
Minneapolis, Minn.	3,703	524	473	239	328	523	5	125	63	1,270	155
St. Paul, Minn.	805	74	76	53	11	90	2	13	33	431	22
Des Moines, Iowa	1,238	239	131	92	47	135	1	11	98	416	68
St. Joseph, Mo.	499	25	112	57	11	95	1	29	5	113	51
Springfield, Mo.	737	53	163	25	6	73	2	10	15	331	59
Fargo, N.D.	460	16	123	36	12	46	2	7	63	129	26
Sioux Falls, S.D.	546	83	13	29	13	179	2	4	29	154	40
Lincoln, Neb.	759	86	316	14	6	39	4	56	12	197	29
Topeka, Kan.	967	82	556	49	37	80	1	18	30	104	10
Wichita, Kan.	1,220	239	453	14	3	156	2	93	37	194	29
9 S. Atlantic cities	5,911	1,293	553	500	270	980	26	181	177	1,591	340
Hagerstown, Md.	352	6	50	25	1	5		1	4	251	9
Richmond, Va.	1,048	172	41	195	22	215	5	75	18	188	117
Wheeling, W.Va.*	770	54	124	178	122	9	9	16	17	168	73
Asheville, N.C.	380	136	48	13	1	73	1	3	14	84	7
Greensboro, N.C.	285	131	54	6	2	26	2	2	4	44	14
Charleston, S.C.	201	8	2	13	3	8	1	4	5	144	13
Columbia, S.C.	329	42	125	8	1	5		3	12	125	8
Atlanta, Ga.*	2,277	682	87	55	118	614	8	75	86	464	88
Jacksonville, Fla.	269	62	22	7		25		2	17	123	11
3 E. S. Central cities	2,422	697	533	103	26	337	8	45	101	475	97
Paducah, Ky.	217	54	33	27	8	3	3	19'	5	59	6
Birmingham, Ala.*	1,947	528	416	69	18	324	5	25	88	383	91
Jackson, Miss.	258	115	84	7		10		1	8	33	
6 W. S. Central cities	5,049	811	1,423	366	106	608	91	61	260	1,160	163
Little Rock, Ark.	808	113	141	229	20	33		11	72	138	21
Baton Rouge, La.	173	3	106	8	1	2		7		34	12
Oklahoma City, Okla.	1,720	306	713	16	14	201	5	17	117	299	32
Austin, Tex.	372	13	35	14	1	53	61	1	3	165	26
Dallas, Tex.	1,655	344	333	93	69	247	12	27	54	408	68
Wichita Falls, Tex.	321	32	95	6	1	42	13	5	7	116	
6 Mountain cities	3,277	336	658	122	179	319	13	190	278	1,070	112
Butte, Mont.	369	2	2	39	4	12	2	12	31	235	30
Boise, Idaho	489	37	185	3	2	14		4	43	185	16
Casper, Wyo.	170	4	72	7	2	2		4	32	43	4
Pueblo, Colo.	392	10	103	4	9	3	4	2	78	161	18
Phoenix, Ariz.	477	54	28	16	43	69	1	12	29	220	5
Salt Lake City, Utah	1,380	229	268	53	119	219	6	156	65	226	39
4 Pacific cities	8,124	1,122	740	701	957	973	11	219	282	2,546	573
Seattle, Wash.*	2,543	364	123	149	626	335	2	107	117	634	86
Portland, Ore.	2,324	425	139	72	90	342	2	83	100	784	287
Sacramento, Calif.	1,102	102	169	119	32	48		4	9	484	135
San Diego, Calif.*	2,155	231	309	361	209	248	7	25	56	644	65

Source: *Federal Home Loan Bank Board tabulation of data from* Financial Survey of Urban Housing

*Metropolitan district.

[1]Includes public bond issues:

First mortgages (Number of reports)		Second and third mortgages (Number of reports)	
Trenton, N. J.	1	Racine, Wis.	1
Kenosha, Wis.	17		
Racine, Wis.	7		
Richmond, Va.	1		
Paducah, Ky.	2		
Seattle, Wash.	1		

TABLE D 17

Mortgaged Owner-occupied Dwellings, Number reporting Outstanding Debt by Priority and by Holding Agency, 52 Cities by Geographic Division, January 1, 1934

◄─────── S E C O N D   A N D   T H I R D   M O R T G A G E S ───────►

All holding agencies	Life ins. co.	Build. & loan asso.	Commer. bank	Savings bank	Mortgage co.	Construct. co.	Title & trust co.	Individual	Other[1]	
6,088	47	181	333	147	359	205	66	4,315	435	**52 cities**
833	2	21	37	41	33	5	8	633	53	**4 New England cities**
74		4	10		3		1	54	2	Portland, Me.
312	2	7	19	20	9		4	230	21	Worcester, Mass.
316		9	6	20	11	5	3	237	25	Providence, R.I.*
131		1	2	1	10			112	5	Waterbury, Conn.
535	2	10	38	13	10	9	3	427	23	**4 Mid. Atlantic cities**
32			1	1				29	1	Binghamton, N.Y.
260	2	1	8	9	7	3	1	219	10	Syracuse, N.Y.
125		4	21	2	2	2	1	90	3	Trenton, N.J.
118		5	8	1	1	4	1	89	9	Erie, Pa.
2,223	11	75	136	58	123	55	17	1,615	133	**6 E. N. Central cities**
1,910	6	42	109	56	107	49	11	1,430	100	Cleveland, Ohio*
57	1	5	13	1	2	2	1	29	3	Indianapolis, Ind.
96	3	14			7			57	15	Peoria, Ill.
15		3	1	1				10		Lansing, Mich.
42		3	2		2	2	3	25	5	Kenosha, Wis.
103	1	8	11		5	2	2	64	10	Racine, Wis.
588	9	29	16	5	20	24	11	417	57	**10 W. N. Central cities**
157	2	2	4		5	1		119	24	Minneapolis, Minn.
23						1		21	1	St. Paul, Minn.
42	1		3		1		2	31	4	Des Moines, Iowa
46		3		1	4	2	1	28	7	St. Joseph, Mo.
31	1	6	4		3			16	1	Springfield, Mo.
36		4		2		3	1	21	5	Fargo, N.D.
35	1	1	1		2			25	5	Sioux Falls, S.D.
58	2	4	1	1	1	3	1	41	4	Lincoln, Neb.
82	2	8	1		2	6	2	58	3	Topeka, Kan.
78		1	2	1	2	8	4	57	3	Wichita, Kan.
630	7	11	61	17	68	39	6	359	62	**9 S. Atlantic cities**
24		2	1		1	2		16	2	Hagerstown, Md.
173	1	1	24	1	21	11		90	24	Richmond, Va.
64	1	4	13	4	1	5	1	26	9	Wheeling, W.Va.*
30			3		3			24		Asheville, N.C.
47	1		6	1	3	12		16	8	Greensboro, N.C.
3								3		Charleston, S.C.
30	1	1	2	1	1			23	1	Columbia, S.C.
242	3	3	12	10	35	9	5	147	18	Atlanta, Ga.*
17					3			14		Jacksonville, Fla.
188	6	7	8	1	28	4	1	119	14	**3 E. S. Central cities**
15		1	2				1	11		Paducah, Ky.
142	3	6	5		27	3		84	14	Birmingham, Ala.*
31	3		1	1	1	1		24		Jackson, Miss.
389	2	8	14	2	30	34	5	251	43	**6 W. S. Central cities**
63	1		13		2	3	2	38	4	Little Rock, Ark.
6				1				1	4	Baton Rouge, La.
170		4			11	11	1	129	14	Oklahoma City, Okla.
19					4			14	1	Austin, Tex.
114	2	3	1	1	12	17	2	57	19	Dallas, Tex.
17					1	3		12	1	Wichita Falls, Tex.
145	3	6	4	3	10	11	7	89	12	**6 Mountain cities**
8					1			6	1	Butte, Mont.
20			3			1		14	2	Boise, Idaho
11	3						1	7		Casper, Wyo.
16		1			1	3		11		Pueblo, Colo.
26					1	2	1	18	4	Phoenix, Ariz.
64		5	1	3	7	5	5	33	5	Salt Lake City, Utah
557	5	14	19	7	37	24	8	405	38	**4 Pacific cities**
98	2	1	7	3	5	1	2	69	8	Seattle, Wash.*
140	2	2	1	1	9	4	3	107	11	Portland, Ore.
113	1	8	5	1	6	2		80	10	Sacramento, Calif.
206		3	6	2	17	17	3	149	9	San Diego, Calif.*

TABLE D 18

Mortgaged Rented Dwellings, Number reporting First Mortgages by Holding Agency, 52 Cities by Geographic Division, January 1, 1934

	All holding agencies	Life ins. co.	Build. & loan asso.	Commer. bank	Savings bank	Mortgage co.	Construct. co.	Title & trust co.	H.O. Loan Corp.	Individual	Other[1]
52 cities	13,075	1,485	2,291	1,690	1,680	1,126	28	450	182	3,555	588
4 New England cities	887	13	83	108	436	18		26	5	153	45
Portland, Me.	195	4	30	28	81			4	2	39	7
Worcester, Mass.	208	2	6	8	155			4	2	14	17
Providence, R.I.*	382	7	47	59	138	16		15		83	17
Waterbury, Conn.	102			13	62	2		3	1	17	4
4 Mid. Atlantic cities	790	20	73	70	187	10	3	15	4	376	32
Binghamton, N.Y.	80	3		13	26		1	2	1	31	3
Syracuse, N.Y.	214	12	1	22	146			4	1	26	2
Trenton, N.J.	232	4	21	6	6	5	1	6	1	167	15
Erie, Pa.	264	1	51	29	9	5	1	3	1	152	12
6 E. N. Central cities	3,620	234	941	906	578	71	5	182	50	495	158
Cleveland, Ohio*	2,243	172	267	844	556	28	1	83	34	170	88
Indianapolis, Ind.	487	23	325	28	9	3	1	48	4	30	16
Peoria, Ill.	314	6	229	8	7	2		6	6	36	14
Lansing, Mich.	142	30	46	11	5	1	1	8	2	34	4
Kenosha, Wis.	124		22	3		9	1	23	3	58	5
Racine, Wis.	310	3	52	12	1	28	1	14	1	167	31
10 W. N. Central cities	2,792	401	550	172	124	361	6	98	28	912	140
Minneapolis, Minn.	924	135	117	62	73	124	1	39	4	318	51
St. Paul, Minn.	210	26	10	15	9	27		6	5	108	4
Des Moines, Iowa	385	81	34	37	21	33	1	2	5	149	22
St. Joseph, Mo.	93	2	19	6	1	19		7		35	4
Springfield, Mo.	169	17	37	9	1	15		2	1	73	14
Fargo, N.D.	75	3	20	7	1	6		2	4	28	4
Sioux Falls, S.D.	180	30	7	10	5	46	1	1	1	67	12
Lincoln, Neb.	170	11	63	2	2	20	2	15	1	50	4
Topeka, Kan.	240	18	122	15	9	26		6	3	31	10
Wichita, Kan.	346	78	121	9	2	45	1	18	4	53	15
9 S. Atlantic cities	1,120	223	71	80	69	194		23	15	373	72
Hagerstown, Md.	61	1	7	5	2	1				43	2
Richmond, Va.	128	12	3	26	4	24		4		42	13
Wheeling, W.Va.*	117	6	7	34	24	5		3	2	24	12
Asheville, N.C.	37	12	2			9			1	9	4
Greensboro, N.C.	52	24	12	1	1	5		1		5	3
Charleston, S.C.	78	4	1	2	1	2			2	56	10
Columbia, S.C.	82	13	26	2					1	40	
Atlanta, Ga.*	510	138	11	6	37	139		15	8	129	27
Jacksonville, Fla.	55	13	2	4		9			1	25	1
3 E. S. Central cities	310	90	47	14	10	42		10	17	64	16
Paducah, Ky.	20	2	4	1	2					6	1
Birmingham, Ala.*	216	49	22	13	6	39		4	15	53	13
Jackson, Miss.	74	39	21		2	3		6	2	5	2
6 W. S. Central cities	1,187	185	271	102	22	175	11	8	25	349	39
Little Rock, Ark.	182	19	28	69	1	17		2	8	30	8
Baton Rouge, La.	56	1	32	2		3		1	1	15	1
Oklahoma City, Okla.	374	83	138	1	1	53	1	2	11	74	10
Austin, Tex.	97		5	1		18	9		1	57	6
Dallas, Tex.	398	76	53	25	19	75	1	3	3	132	11
Wichita Falls, Tex.	80	6	15	4	1	9			1	41	3
6 Mountain cities	617	69	86	24	48	87	2	42	23	219	17
Butte, Mont.	55		1	5	1	6			2	39	1
Boise, Idaho	32	1	10		1			1	1	15	3
Casper, Wyo.	46	3	21	4			1	1	2	12	2
Pueblo, Colo.	43	1	11		2	2			1	24	2
Phoenix, Ariz.	168	13	11	6	22	26	1	2	8	73	6
Salt Lake City, Utah	273	51	32	9	22	53		38	9	56	3
4 Pacific cities	1,752	250	169	214	206	168	1	46	15	614	69
Seattle, Wash.*	473	97	41	19	96	50		22	7	129	12
Portland, Ore.	413	85	16	15	23	50		12	5	169	38
Sacramento, Calif.	227	12	34	28	14	8			1	121	9
San Diego, Calif.*	639	56	78	152	73	60	1	12	2	195	10

Source: Federal Home Loan Bank Board tabulation of data from *Financial Survey of Urban Housing*. For number reporting second and third mortgage loans on rented properties for 'All holding agencies' combined see Table D 15.
* Metropolitan district.

[1] Includes public bond issues:

(Number of Reports)

Worcester, Mass.	1	Minneapolis, Minn.	1	Seattle, Wash.	2	
Kenosha, Wis.	2	Asheville, N.C.	1	San Diego, Calif.	2	
Racine, Wis.	5	Paducah, Ky.	1			

TABLE D 19

Mortgaged Owner-occupied Dwellings, Outstanding Debt by Priority, and Percentage Distribution by Holding Agency, 52 Cities by Geographic Division, January 1, 1934

◄─────────────── ALL PRIORITIES ───────────────►

PERCENTAGE DISTRIBUTION

	DEBT OUTSTANDING ($000)	All holding agencies	Life ins. co.	Build. & loan asso.	Commer. bank	Savings bank	Mortgage co.	Construct. co.	Title & trust co.	H.O. Loan Corp.	Individual	Other[2]
52 cities[1]	183,623.9	100.0	13.7	13.1	15.4	15.9	6.9	0.6	3.1	3.0	23.9	4.4
4 New England cities	15,394.0	100.0	2.9	7.5	13.4	41.8	2.8	0.2	2.8	1.6	22.8	4.2
Portland, Me.	1,973.7	100.0	2.4	25.5	10.0	36.9	0.7		0.6	0.8	22.1	1.0
Worcester, Mass.	4,912.2	100.0	0.9	3.0	5.6	70.8	0.9	0.1	1.0	1.3	10.4	6.0
Providence, R.I.*	6,258.6	100.0	4.0	9.6	16.1	30.7	4.4	0.3	3.3	1.4	26.3	3.9
Waterbury, Conn.	2,249.5	100.0	2.0	2.4	17.3	35.3	0.8		4.9	3.0	31.3	3.0
4 Mid. Atlantic cities	12,289.8	100.0	4.2	4.8	10.0	39.0	1.1	0.2	1.2	0.8	35.7	3.0
Binghamton, N.Y.	783.6	100.0	3.9	0.9	13.4	28.4	0.3		0.1		51.2	1.8
Syracuse, N.Y.	3,559.5	100.0	5.1	0.7	9.6	59.8	0.6	0.2	1.2	0.2	20.2	2.4
Trenton, N.J.	3,809.3	100.0	2.8	11.4	8.5	4.0	3.2	0.1	1.8	1.1	63.0	4.1
Erie, Pa.	4,137.4	100.0	2.5	15.9	10.4	2.4	1.5	0.3	1.6	3.2	57.1	5.1
6 E. N. Central cities	68,079.5	100.0	9.8	20.3	30.3	11.9	2.0	0.7	3.8	3.1	14.5	3.6
Cleveland, Ohio*	51,603.5	100.0	9.7	12.4	40.1	16.2	1.4	0.5	2.3	3.0	11.3	3.1
Indianapolis, Ind.	4,594.3	100.0	13.1	46.4	7.9	1.5	1.3	1.8	9.3	4.0	11.0	3.7
Peoria, Ill.	3,246.8	100.0	10.4	59.5	3.7	0.8	0.9	0.6	1.0	0.9	16.3	5.5
Lansing, Mich.	1,446.5	100.0	14.8	21.4	5.8	3.2	2.2	1.0	1.8	4.8	39.5	5.5
Kenosha, Wis.	2,015.4	100.0	0.4	16.4	3.0	0.6	8.8	0.2	19.9	2.3	39.9	8.5
Racine, Wis.	5,173.0	100.0	0.9	26.9	3.2	1.1	12.2	0.5	2.3	2.3	45.2	5.4
10 W. N. Central cities	25,266.7	100.0	18.2	14.1	4.9	3.5	12.2	0.5	3.2	3.3	36.2	3.9
Minneapolis, Minn.	10,000.7	100.0	22.4	8.5	5.0	6.3	13.3	0.4	3.0	1.7	35.3	4.1
St. Paul, Minn.	1,802.5	100.0	12.1	8.5	4.8	0.9	11.1	0.6	2.1	3.9	53.8	2.2
Des Moines, Iowa	3,051.6	100.0	21.5	6.3	6.7	2.9	9.7	0.5	0.9	6.9	39.9	4.7
St. Joseph, Mo.	1,002.4	100.0	5.6	21.5	9.1	1.6	23.3	0.3	5.9	0.9	22.9	8.9
Springfield, Mo.	1,082.5	100.0	12.6	21.6	6.0	0.5	9.9	0.2	2.1	3.1	37.4	6.6
Fargo, N.D.	1,237.7	100.0	3.7	24.1	6.9	1.7	8.5	0.5	1.3	17.1	30.5	5.7
Sioux Falls, S.D.	1,326.8	100.0	17.2	2.3	6.6	2.4	25.3	0.7	0.3	5.6	32.5	7.1
Lincoln, Neb.	1,613.4	100.0	16.0	36.2	1.8	0.7	6.3	0.5	8.6	1.0	25.9	3.0
Topeka, Kan.	1,923.6	100.0	10.5	51.2	3.5	3.3	8.4	0.5	2.5	4.7	13.8	1.6
Wichita, Kan.	2,225.5	100.0	27.4	27.6	1.3	0.1	10.7	0.9	7.6	2.7	18.9	2.8
9 S. Atlantic cities	17,062.0	100.0	29.8	5.8	9.9	2.9	15.3	0.8	2.7	3.1	24.1	5.6
Hagerstown, Md.	1,121.3	100.0	1.7	8.0	10.2	0.1	0.8	0.2	0.4	1.5	74.4	2.7
Richmond, Va.	3,744.9	100.0	18.7	2.0	19.1	1.9	18.7	1.1	6.5	2.1	20.2	9.7
Wheeling, W.Va.*	1,696.2	100.0	12.8	12.7	26.3	11.1	1.2	1.6	2.2	3.7	20.8	7.6
Asheville, N.C.	1,074.2	100.0	44.8	7.5	8.1	0.7	16.0	0.7	2.1	2.8	15.6	1.7
Greensboro, N.C.	1,059.3	100.0	53.9	12.1	8.4	0.3	7.1	3.0	0.4	1.0	8.5	5.3
Charleston, S.C.	478.7	100.0	7.2	1.6	9.5	0.8	2.2	0.4	2.9	5.0	63.4	7.0
Columbia, S.C.	933.9	100.0	17.4	25.8	2.0	0.2	1.1		1.5	3.9	45.2	2.9
Atlanta, Ga.*	6,293.9	100.0	42.6	2.2	1.9	2.6	25.3	0.4	2.0	3.1	15.9	4.0
Jacksonville, Fla.	659.6	100.0	29.3	5.0	3.1		7.8		1.0	6.1	43.5	4.2
3 E. S. Central cities	5,501.4	100.0	41.6	14.8	4.4	1.0	12.7	0.2	1.7	4.8	15.3	3.5
Paducah, Ky.	369.0	100.0	24.7	10.8	15.7	5.3	1.8	0.3	13.3	1.7	21.0	5.4
Birmingham, Ala.*	4,545.2	100.0	39.6	14.6	3.9	1.0	14.6	0.2	1.3	5.0	15.8	4.0
Jackson, Miss.	587.2	100.0	59.5	17.4	4.0	0.1	3.3	0.3	0.7	4.6	10.1	....
6 W. S. Central cities	11,784.6	100.0	24.2	21.1	6.3	1.8	12.9	1.6	1.4	5.4	22.4	2.9
Little Rock, Ark.	1,917.3	100.0	16.4	10.4	32.3	1.4	8.1	0.2	1.0	9.1	18.5	2.6
Baton Rouge, La.	347.1	100.0	0.7	59.9	9.7	0.4	1.2			5.4	18.3	4.4
Oklahoma City, Okla.	4,324.1	100.0	26.9	31.7	0.9	1.0	12.0	0.4	1.4	7.1	17.2	1.4
Austin, Tex.	790.9	100.0	5.6	9.2	4.0	0.1	15.9	12.9	0.6	0.8	47.8	3.1
Dallas, Tex.	3,747.6	100.0	29.1	13.5	4.9	3.1	15.2	1.1	1.7	4.0	23.1	4.3
Wichita Falls, Tex.	657.6	100.0	23.1	20.4	2.6		14.7	2.6	1.4	1.6	31.8	1.8
6 Mountain cities	7,990.5	100.0	14.6	15.6	4.0	5.4	11.0	1.8	6.9	7.0	30.6	3.1
Butte, Mont.	632.5	100.0	0.3	1.2	14.5	1.4	2.0	0.1	2.7	7.4	60.5	9.9
Boise, Idaho	847.7	100.0	7.0	32.2	1.9	0.2	2.9		1.8	10.1	41.1	2.8
Casper, Wyo.	517.9	100.0	1.6	51.7	5.1	0.8	0.8	0.3	2.7	14.1	22.0	0.9
Pueblo, Colo.	566.4	100.0	3.1	30.6	0.9	1.1	0.8	1.3	0.2	20.2	39.4	2.4
Phoenix, Ariz.	1,246.4	100.0	14.7	4.5	3.9	7.6	12.5	1.1	2.0	8.3	43.5	1.9
Salt Lake City, Utah	4,179.6	100.0	19.1	12.7	3.9	6.6	14.4	2.5	10.4	3.7	23.4	3.3
4 Pacific cities	20,255.4	100.0	17.6	6.8	6.8	10.8	12.4	0.4	3.1	3.5	30.2	8.4
Seattle, Wash.*	6,730.8	100.0	19.2	4.0	4.3	19.0	13.1	0.3	3.9	3.9	28.2	4.1
Portland, Ore.	5,034.6	100.0	22.5	5.6	3.5	3.3	14.9	0.4	4.3	4.8	28.7	12.0
Sacramento, Calif.	3,293.0	100.0	8.2	11.4	9.9	2.8	5.2	0.2	0.3	0.8	40.3	20.9
San Diego, Calif.*	5,197.0	100.0	11.6	12.2	16.0	8.8	10.7	0.7	1.1	2.2	31.6	5.1

Source: Federal Home Loan Bank Board tabulation of data from *Financial Survey of Urban Housing*. *For number reporting loans, see Table D 17. Percentages not shown if less than one-tenth of one per cent.*

*Metropolitan district.

[1] *Geographic division and 52-city percentage distributions weighted by estimated total mortgage debt on owner-occupied properties, by priority, in each city (RPI).*

TABLE D 19

Mortgaged Owner-occupied Dwellings, Outstanding Debt by Priority, and Percentage Distribution by Holding Agency, 52 Cities by Geographic Division, January 1, 1934

					FIRST MORTGAGES							
DEBT OUTSTANDING ($000)					PERCENTAGE DISTRIBUTION							
	All holding agencies	Life Ins. co.	Build. & loan asso.	Com-mer. bank	Sav-ings bank	Mort-gage co.	Con-struct. co.	Title & trust co.	H.O. Loan Corp.	Indi-vidual	Other[2]	
166,731.9	100.0	15.0	13.6	16.5	17.2	7.1	0.3	3.2	3.3	19.7	4.1	52 cities[1]
14,191.8	100.0	3.1	8.0	14.1	44.8	2.9	0.1	3.1	1.7	18.2	4.0	4 New England cities
1,837.0	100.0	2.5	26.9	9.8	39.6	0.5		0.6	0.9	18.2	1.0	Portland, Me.
4,484.9	100.0	1.0	3.2	5.5	76.8	0.9		1.0	1.4	4.4	5.8	Worcester, Mass.
5,872.9	100.0	4.3	10.1	16.9	32.3	4.6	0.2	3.5	1.4	23.0	3.7	Providence, R.I.*
1,997.0	100.0	2.2	2.7	19.2	39.7	0.5		5.6	3.4	23.6	3.1	Waterbury, Conn.
11,554.5	100.0	4.6	5.1	10.4	42.1	1.0	0.1	1.3	0.9	31.5	3.0	4 Mid. Atlantic cities
731.0	100.0	3.8	1.0	13.4	28.4	0.2		0.2		51.2	1.8	Binghamton, N.Y.
3,185.5	100.0	5.7	0.8	10.4	66.6	0.4	0.1	1.3	0.3	12.2	2.2	Syracuse, N.Y.
3,662.3	100.0	2.9	11.7	8.3	4.0	3.2	0.1	1.8	1.2	62.6	4.2	Trenton, N.J.
3,975.7	100.0	2.6	16.3	10.5	2.3	1.6	0.3	1.6	3.4	56.4	5.0	Erie, Pa.
61,973.1	100.0	10.5	21.4	32.7	13.0	1.8	0.4	3.9	3.4	9.6	3.3	6 E. N. Central cities
48,204.0	100.0	10.2	13.1	42.3	17.1	1.2	0.4	2.4	3.2	7.2	2.9	Cleveland, Ohio*
4,084.1	100.0	14.4	49.8	8.0	1.7	0.6	0.8	9.5	4.5	7.2	3.5	Indianapolis, Ind.
2,921.1	100.0	11.2	63.1	4.1	0.9	0.8	0.6	1.1	1.0	11.7	5.5	Peoria, Ill.
766.1	100.0	23.6	27.8	7.4	4.9	2.9	0.1	2.1	9.1	19.7	2.4	Lansing, Mich.
1,737.2	100.0	0.2	17.1	3.1	0.7	8.9	0.1	22.4	2.7	36.4	8.4	Kenosha, Wis.
4,260.6	100.0	1.1	30.4	3.2	1.3	13.2		2.8	2.8	40.1	5.1	Racine, Wis.
22,249.4	100.0	21.3	13.6	5.1	3.7	13.4	0.2	3.6	3.7	31.8	3.6	10 W. N. Central cities
8,833.4	100.0	25.1	8.4	5.4	7.0	14.3	0.2	3.2	2.0	31.0	3.4	Minneapolis, Minn.
1,572.6	100.0	13.9	7.8	5.0	1.0	12.1	0.2	2.1	4.5	51.1	2.3	St. Paul, Minn.
2,311.2	100.0	27.4	7.7	7.7	3.5	12.1	0.1	0.9	9.1	27.2	4.3	Des Moines, Iowa
947.6	100.0	6.0	22.3	9.6	1.5	24.1	0.2	5.7	1.0	20.9	8.7	St. Joseph, Mo.
1,054.1	100.0	12.9	22.0	5.5	0.6	9.9	0.2	2.1	3.2	36.9	6.7	Springfield, Mo.
1,131.4	100.0	4.0	24.7	7.1	1.8	9.2	0.4	1.5	18.7	27.3	5.3	Fargo, N.D.
1,144.2	100.0	19.6	2.5	6.2	2.5	28.8	0.6	0.4	6.5	25.5	7.4	Sioux Falls, S.D.
1,514.5	100.0	16.9	38.0	1.9	0.5	6.5	0.4	9.0	1.1	23.1	2.6	Lincoln, Neb.
1,720.4	100.0	11.6	53.5	3.6	3.4	9.2	0.1	2.7	5.3	9.1	1.5	Topeka, Kan.
2,020.0	100.0	29.8	28.2	1.3	0.1	11.7	0.2	7.9	3.0	15.2	2.6	Wichita, Kan.
16,228.7	100.0	31.2	6.0	9.7	2.9	15.7	0.4	2.8	3.3	22.6	5.4	9 S. Atlantic cities
1,073.6	100.0	1.7	8.2	10.0	0.3	0.7		0.3	1.6	74.7	2.5	Hagerstown, Md.
3,524.1	100.0	19.7	2.1	19.2	2.0	19.3	0.7	6.7	2.3	18.2	9.8	Richmond, Va.
1,591.5	100.0	13.7	13.1	26.6	11.5	1.3	1.4	1.8	3.9	19.7	7.0	Wheeling, W.Va.*
1,015.9	100.0	46.1	7.9	8.0	0.7	16.4	0.7	1.8	3.0	13.7	1.7	Asheville, N.C.
957.6	100.0	59.4	13.3	6.0	0.3	7.7	0.1	0.4	1.1	7.3	4.4	Greensboro, N.C.
471.8	100.0	7.3	1.3	9.6	0.8	2.2	0.7	3.0	5.0	62.9	7.2	Charleston, S.C.
893.5	100.0	17.9	26.9	1.9	0.1	1.1		1.6	4.1	43.9	2.5	Columbia, S.C.
6,070.3	100.0	44.2	2.2	1.7	2.6	25.8	0.2	2.1	3.2	14.1	3.9	Atlanta, Ga.*
630.4	100.0	30.7	5.3	3.3		7.4		1.0	6.4	42.1	3.8	Jacksonville, Fla.
5,218.6	100.0	42.1	15.3	4.6	1.0	12.9	0.1	1.8	5.1	13.7	3.4	3 E. S. Central cities
348.8	100.0	26.2	11.3	16.5	5.2	1.9	0.3	13.8	1.8	17.3	5.7	Paducah, Ky.
4,309.7	100.0	40.1	15.1	4.1	1.0	14.8	0.1	1.4	5.3	14.3	3.8	Birmingham, Ala.*
560.1	100.0	60.8	18.2	4.0		3.3		0.7	4.9	8.1		Jackson, Miss.
11,398.7	100.0	24.9	21.6	6.4	1.8	13.0	1.4	1.4	5.5	21.2	2.8	6 W. S. Central cities
1,838.0	100.0	17.1	10.4	32.9	1.4	8.1		0.9	9.5	17.4	2.3	Little Rock, Ark.
334.8	100.0	0.7	62.1	10.0	0.5	0.9			5.6	16.8	3.4	Baton Rouge, La.
4,165.5	100.0	27.8	32.6	0.9	1.0	12.1	0.2	1.4	7.4	15.4	1.2	Oklahoma City, Okla.
756.0	100.0	5.9	9.7	4.2	0.4	16.0	13.1	0.4	0.8	46.3	3.2	Austin, Tex.
3,660.4	100.0	29.7	13.7	5.0	3.1	15.4	0.8	1.7	4.1	22.3	4.2	Dallas, Tex.
644.0	100.0	23.6	20.8	2.7		15.0	2.4	1.4	1.6	31.0	1.5	Wichita Falls, Tex.
6,274.7	100.0	17.1	15.2	4.0	5.6	11.7	0.7	6.9	9.1	27.2	2.5	6 Mountain cities
512.7	100.0	0.5	0.5	13.0	1.3	2.2	0.5	3.4	9.1	60.9	8.6	Butte, Mont.
755.4	100.0	7.9	35.4	1.5	0.3	3.0		1.8	11.3	35.9	2.9	Boise, Idaho
315.0	100.0	2.6	35.7	6.7	1.0	1.2		3.0	23.1	25.5	1.2	Casper, Wyo.
542.1	100.0	3.2	31.4	0.9	1.2	0.6	1.0	0.2	21.1	38.3	2.1	Pueblo, Colo.
1,126.9	100.0	15.9	5.0	4.4	8.4	12.5	0.2	1.5	9.2	41.5	1.4	Phoenix, Ariz.
3,022.6	100.0	23.9	12.5	3.9	6.9	16.2	0.9	11.4	5.2	16.5	2.6	Salt Lake City, Utah
17,642.4	100.0	19.9	7.0	7.4	11.6	13.3	0.1	3.4	4.1	25.7	7.5	4 Pacific cities
5,489.1	100.0	22.7	4.6	4.3	21.4	14.7		4.4	4.9	19.6	3.4	Seattle, Wash.*
4,581.5	100.0	24.6	4.7	3.7	3.4	15.4	0.2	4.6	5.3	25.5	12.6	Portland, Ore.
2,840.3	100.0	9.5	12.2	11.1	3.1	5.4		0.3	0.9	42.9	14.6	Sacramento, Calif.
4,731.5	100.0	12.6	12.8	17.2	9.5	11.2	0.3	1.1	2.4	29.2	3.7	San Diego, Calif.*

[2]*Includes public bond issues:*

	All priorities	First mortgage (per cent)	Second and third mortgage
Kenosha, Wis.	2.8	3.3	
Racine, Wis.	1.0	1.1	2.4
Richmond, Va.	0.1	0.1	
Paducah, Ky.	3.6	3.8	
Seattle, Wash.	0.3	0.3	

TABLE D 19 (Cont'd)

Mortgaged Owner-occupied Dwellings, Outstanding Debt by Priority, and Percentage Distribution by Holding Agency, 52 Cities by Geographic Division, January 1, 1934

	DEBT OUTSTANDING ($000)	All holding agencies	Life ins. co.	Build. & loan asso.	Commer. bank	Savings bank	Mortgage co.	Construct. co.	Title & trust co.	Individual	Other[2]
52 cities[1]	7,539.1	100.0	0.9	2.2	5.4	2.9	4.3	2.7	1.0	74.4	6.2
4 New England cities	1,181.8	100.0	0.9	3.0	2.4	5.6	2.2	0.5	0.5	79.3	5.6
Portland, Me.	134.6	100.0		5.7	14.0		3.6		0.6	74.9	1.2
Worcester, Mass.	423.0	100.0	0.1	1.4	6.6	8.1	1.3		0.6	74.0	7.9
Providence, R.I.*	372.1	100.0	1.9	4.4		6.8	2.3	1.1	0.6	76.6	6.3
Waterbury, Conn.	252.1	100.0		1.9		0.5	3.0			92.7	1.9
4 Mid. Atlantic cities	688.7	100.0	0.3	0.7	4.0	2.1	2.1	1.0	0.4	85.0	4.4
Binghamton, N.Y.	41.6	100.0			5.5	2.4				86.3	5.8
Syracuse, N.Y.	369.7	100.0	0.3 ✓	0.3 ✓	2.7 ✓	2.1 ✓	2.3 ✓	0.9 ✓	0.3 ✓	86.7 ✓	4.4 ✓
Trenton, N.J.	141.0	100.0			2.0	14.1	2.3	2.1	1.7	0.7	75.7	1.4
Erie, Pa.	136.4	100.0		4.3	8.2	1.6	1.5	2.3	1.5	74.1	6.5
6 E. N. Central cities	3,197.5	100.0	0.9	2.3	7.0	2.3	4.9	2.5	0.6	73.9	5.6
Cleveland, Ohio*	2,815.5	100.0	0.5	1.8	6.0	2.6	4.9	2.3	0.5	76.1	5.3
Indianapolis, Ind.	78.9	100.0	2.2	4.1	23.3	0.2	6.0	4.2	1.5	54.7	3.8
Peoria, Ill.	106.2	100.0	12.1	10.7			4.1			58.4	14.7
Lansing, Mich.	8.8	100.0		10.2	4.6	12.5				72.7	
Kenosha, Wis.	53.1	100.0		2.4	4.0		3.0	6.8	6.2	67.4	10.2
Racine, Wis.	135.0	100.0	0.5	4.7	14.0		3.6	5.9	1.5	62.7	7.1
10 W. N. Central cities	617.4	100.0	1.1	2.2	3.3	0.8	2.7	3.7	1.3	75.7	9.2
Minneapolis, Minn.	232.5	100.0	1.4	1.0	2.6		1.1	0.4		81.6	11.9
St. Paul, Minn.	18.1	100.0						12.7		85.6	1.7
Des Moines, Iowa	36.7	100.0	2.5		5.2		2.4		4.9	68.1	16.9
St. Joseph, Mo.	46.8	100.0		4.7		4.3	11.8	8.1	4.3	53.8	13.0
Springfield, Mo.	22.7	100.0	1.8	6.6	31.7		12.3			45.4	2.2
Fargo, N.D.	37.5	100.0		6.4		2.7		4.8	0.8	77.1	8.2
Sioux Falls, S.D.	28.7	100.0	0.4	3.5	13.9		5.2			67.6	9.4
Lincoln, Neb.	68.6	100.0	2.3	4.5	1.0	2.8	2.9	3.9	1.8	75.5	5.3
Topeka, Kan.	56.9	100.0	1.1	6.0	5.3		5.3	7.0	1.2	67.8	6.3
Wichita, Kan.	68.9	100.0		0.7	2.0	0.1	0.9	9.0	4.1	78.7	4.5
9 S. Atlantic cities	729.9	100.0	1.0	1.4	15.6	1.8	7.3	8.6	1.6	53.0	9.7
Hagerstown, Md.	37.4	100.0		5.1	19.2		1.6	5.6		59.1	9.4
Richmond, Va.	209.3	100.0	0.8	0.2	18.1	0.1	9.1	8.1		52.4	11.2
Wheeling, W.Va.*	83.2	100.0	0.2	4.1	22.6	6.3	0.2	5.4	7.6	36.4	17.2
Asheville, N.C.	32.2	100.0			17.1		4.6			78.3	
Greensboro, N.C.	101.7	100.0	2.1		31.7	0.8	1.4	30.8		19.1	14.1
Charleston, S.C.	6.9	100.0								100.0	
Columbia, S.C.	31.4	100.0	3.5	3.5	7.0	3.5	3.5			77.7	1.3
Atlanta, Ga.*	206.5	100.0	1.3	1.6	6.7	2.3	12.0	4.9	1.6	62.8	6.8
Jacksonville, Fla.	21.3	100.0					13.1			86.9	
3 E. S. Central cities	155.0	100.0	8.3	2.7	2.9	0.4	11.9	2.1	0.3	63.4	8.0
Paducah, Ky.	14.8	100.0		0.7	2.0				5.4	91.9	
Birmingham, Ala.*	114.7	100.0	2.0	3.5	2.6		15.2	2.5		63.5	10.7
Jackson, Miss.	25.5	100.0	34.5		4.3	2.0	2.7	1.2		55.3	
6 W. S. Central cities	281.9	100.0	0.1	3.0	2.9	0.5	8.7	8.8	1.7	64.1	10.2
Little Rock, Ark.	51.5	100.0		2.0	23.3		5.6	6.2	3.1	46.4	13.4
Baton Rouge, La.	7.4	100.0				10.8				33.8	55.4
Oklahoma City, Okla.	128.8	100.0		3.7			9.8	6.7	1.2	72.9	5.7
Austin, Tex.	12.7	100.0					20.5			77.1	2.4
Dallas, Tex.	70.1	100.0	0.4	3.3	0.2	0.7	8.0	14.4	2.4	59.2	11.4
Wichita Falls, Tex.	11.4	100.0					1.7	13.2		63.2	21.9
6 Mountain cities	158.5	100.0	0.7	3.6	2.2	1.1	5.9	8.6	13.3	56.9	7.7
Butte, Mont.	7.1	100.0					2.8			93.0	4.2
Boise, Idaho	19.0	100.0			16.8			1.6		76.9	4.7
Casper, Wyo.	11.7	100.0	13.7						11.1	75.2	
Pueblo, Colo.	11.1	100.0		13.5			12.6	17.1		56.8	
Phoenix, Ariz.	20.4	100.0					7.3	4.9	1.5	71.6	14.7
Salt Lake City, Utah	89.2	100.0		3.7	1.8	1.7	5.8	9.8	19.6	49.2	8.4
4 Pacific cities	528.4	100.0	0.9	1.8	4.4	1.6	7.9	4.9	2.0	70.2	6.3
Seattle, Wash.*	102.7	100.0	2.4	1.3	10.5	2.4	5.2	1.6	3.3	67.3	6.0
Portland, Ore.	118.8	100.0	0.7	0.7	0.3	0.3	11.6	4.4	2.1	72.7	7.2
Sacramento, Calif.	97.3	100.0	0.8	7.6	5.7	0.8	5.5	1.6		72.4	5.6
San Diego, Calif.*	209.6	100.0		0.7	2.6	2.6	7.7	9.5	1.7	69.2	6.0

TABLE D 20

Mortgaged Rented Dwellings, Outstanding Debt reported for All Priorities combined and for First Mortgages, and Percentage Distribution by Holding Agency, 52 Cities by Geographic Division, January 1, 1934

	DEBT OUTSTANDING ($000)	All agencies	Life ins. co.	Build. & loan asso.	Commer. bank	Savings bank	Mortgage co.	Construct. co.	Title & trust co.	H.O. Loan Corp.	Individual	Other[2]
52 cities[1]	48,784.8	100.0	22.2	11.8	12.7	13.3	8.9	0.2	3.3	1.4	20.9	5.3
4 New England cities	*4,545.7	100.0	3.6	5.9	16.4	42.5	3.8		2.7	0.3	19.6	5.2
Portland, Me.	773.9	100.0	4.0	11.4	16.4	42.2			0.4	1.5	19.1	5.0
Worcester, Mass.	1,086.2	100.0	1.7	2.2	4.5	71.3	0.1		2.0	0.5	11.1	6.6
Providence, R.I.*	1,542.1	100.0	5.2	8.1	21.4	32.6	3.8		3.5		22.0	3.4
Waterbury, Conn.	1,143.5	100.0			13.7	40.3	10.6		1.2	0.7	22.5	11.0
4 Mid. Atlantic cities	2,967.6	100.0	8.2	3.9	11.3	37.3	0.9	0.1	2.1	0.7	31.6	3.9
Binghamton, N.Y.	331.1	100.0	12.5		14.5	26.5		0.9	1.4	0.9	41.6	1.7
Syracuse, N.Y.	1,049.0	100.0	10.5	0.2	11.6	53.6	0.1		2.1	0.8	17.3	3.8
Trenton, N.J.	569.8	100.0	2.3	7.5	2.1	3.5	2.2	0.2	6.5	0.4	68.1	7.2
Erie, Pa.	1,017.7	100.0	0.4	17.0	12.6	3.3	3.8		0.6	0.3	58.1	3.9
6 E. N. Central cities	16,757.2	100.0	17.0	22.1	21.6	12.8	3.3	0.3	4.0	1.2	13.5	4.2
Cleveland, Ohio*	12,428.7	100.0	20.7	12.8	27.8	17.4	3.6	0.3	2.2	1.3	10.6	3.3
Indianapolis, Ind.	1,325.5	100.0	9.1	53.8	7.5	1.2	0.5		9.0	0.9	14.6	3.4
Peoria, Ill.	904.8	100.0	2.8	57.0	4.4	3.0	0.2	0.1	1.4	1.4	9.5	20.2
Lansing, Mich.	313.7	100.0	21.5	24.5	7.5	4.1	0.6	2.0	4.7	2.2	26.1	6.8
Kenosha, Wis.	501.8	100.0		21.1	1.9		10.5	0.7	18.1	1.6	42.5	3.6
Racine, Wis.	1,282.7	100.0	2.3	12.9	4.8	0.5	13.7	0.5	6.5	0.4	46.2	12.2
10 W. N. Central cities	7,360.6	100.0	25.3	10.7	5.5	3.6	11.9	0.1	7.0	1.0	30.0	4.9
Minneapolis, Minn.	3,163.2	100.0	28.2	6.2	5.4	4.5	11.6	0.1	8.8	0.3	28.1	6.8
St. Paul, Minn.	605.7	100.0	25.9	3.9	4.5	4.6	11.8		5.2	2.2	40.7	1.2
Des Moines, Iowa	859.5	100.0	32.1	5.2	9.4	4.9	9.4	0.4	0.6	1.4	31.8	4.8
St. Joseph, Mo.	179.8	100.0	3.6	17.4	5.4	1.7	25.3		7.3		33.4	5.9
Springfield, Mo.	257.0	100.0	16.5	20.2	4.2	0.2	12.3		0.5	0.6	35.1	10.4
Fargo, N.D.	214.4	100.0	3.9	22.3	6.8	4.2	3.7		2.1	6.6	42.7	7.7
Sioux Falls, S.D.	490.1	100.0	16.9	1.5	16.8	1.6	17.5	0.3	0.3	0.1	40.6	4.4
Lincoln, Neb.	467.0	100.0	11.0	23.9	0.5	0.6	10.9	0.6	24.4	0.5	26.0	1.6
Topeka, Kan.	501.2	100.0	13.5	42.6	4.1	2.8	15.2	0.2	3.2	1.7	12.1	4.6
Wichita, Kan.	622.7	100.0	38.5	28.7	2.8	0.4	10.9	0.1	2.8	1.3	11.1	3.4
9 S. Atlantic cities	4,418.7	100.0	38.2	3.8	8.6	2.9	19.3	0.1	1.6	1.2	20.6	3.7
Hagerstown, Md.	187.3	100.0	12.0	8.4	7.8	2.7	0.5				64.7	3.9
Richmond, Va.	475.0	100.0	11.1	2.0	16.7	3.8	22.3		2.3		33.4	8.4
Wheeling, W. Va.*	345.5	100.0	6.3	6.9	39.1	21.3	3.4		1.4	1.3	14.7	5.6
Asheville, N.C.	102.7	100.0	38.0	1.1			28.3			4.1	18.7	9.8
Greensboro, N.C.	241.2	100.0	35.4	15.1	26.3	0.1	2.1		0.2	1.1	15.8	3.9
Charleston, S.C.	158.8	100.0	11.8	2.1	3.2	1.2	2.2			5.4	62.7	11.4
Columbia, S.C.	253.7	100.0	21.5	26.4	3.7			0.5		0.8	47.1	
Atlanta, Ga.*	2,462.3	100.0	54.0	0.9	0.6	1.3	26.3	0.2	2.2	1.4	10.7	2.4
Jacksonville, Fla.	192.2	100.0	36.6	2.1	14.5		11.4			0.7	34.4	0.3
3 E. S. Central cities	926.6	100.0	38.7	6.6	6.4	1.2	20.1	0.1	2.2	7.0	14.8	2.9
Paducah, Ky.	41.6	100.0	10.8	8.9	14.4	4.8			29.8		21.9	9.4
Birmingham, Ala.*	657.7	100.0	36.2	5.1	7.2	1.0	22.9	0.1	2.1	7.9	14.7	2.8
Jackson, Miss.	227.3	100.0	58.6	16.7	0.1	1.7	3.7	0.1		1.4	14.6	3.1
6 W. S. Central cities	3,546.3	100.0	27.4	15.8	6.3	1.8	17.7	0.7	0.8	2.2	25.2	2.1
Little Rock, Ark.	448.0	100.0	17.4	8.2	39.6	0.1	12.0		0.5	5.0	12.2	5.0
Baton Rouge, La.	173.1	100.0	14.0	44.1	1.4		5.4		11.6	5.0	17.1	0.9
Oklahoma City, Okla.	1,470.3	100.0	40.2	26.0	0.1	0.2	12.7	0.9	0.2	3.2	15.8	0.7
Austin, Tex.	204.0	100.0		4.0	3.2		23.0	4.3		0.2	60.0	5.3
Dallas, Tex.	1,088.7	100.0	23.3	7.6	6.0	3.8	24.0	0.3	0.7	0.8	31.2	2.3
Wichita Falls, Tex.	162.2	100.0	10.3	11.6	13.6	1.7	12.6	0.1		1.2	44.0	4.9
6 Mountain cities	2,084.3	100.0	20.5	8.5	5.6	8.1	14.8	0.7	6.4	3.9	29.4	2.1
Butte, Mont.	189.5	100.0		0.1	7.1	0.4	2.6			10.1	75.8	3.9
Boise, Idaho	73.9	100.0	3.8	37.5		0.8			12.8	1.6	40.5	3.0
Casper, Wyo.	119.7	100.0	20.5	33.3	7.2			1.3	1.5	5.7	27.4	3.1
Pueblo, Colo.	58.6	100.0	1.4	27.0		3.7	1.5			2.4	56.0	8.0
Phoenix, Ariz.	464.4	100.0	9.8	7.4	4.3	12.4	9.9	1.2	0.9	6.3	45.3	2.5
Salt Lake City, Utah	1,178.2	100.0	29.4	3.4	6.9	8.9	21.3	0.6	9.2	2.6	16.5	1.2
4 Pacific cities	6,177.8	100.0	29.6	8.1	7.5	7.2	5.9	0.1	3.1	0.9	24.1	13.5
Seattle, Wash.*	2,484.5	100.0	38.8	7.8	3.1	7.2	3.6		4.2	0.8	13.2	21.3
Portland, Ore.	1,054.4	100.0	35.7	5.3	2.3	4.8	9.6	0.5	3.6	1.6	29.1	7.5
Sacramento, Calif.	741.4	100.0	7.3	10.5	11.0	5.8	4.3			0.6	53.1	7.4
San Diego, Calif.*	1,897.5	100.0	10.3	10.2	22.1	9.8	9.2	0.1	1.3	0.6	34.8	1.6

Source: Federal Home Loan Bank Board tabulation of data from Financial Survey of Urban Housing. For number reporting outstanding debt on first mortgages, see Table D 18. Percentage not shown if less than one-tenth of one per cent.

*Metropolitan district.

[1] *Geographic division and 52-city percentage distributions weighted by estimated mortgage debt on rented properties, by priority, in each city (RPI).*

[2] Includes public bond issues:

	Per cent All priorities	First mortgages		Per cent All priorities	First mortgages
Worcester, Mass.	1.1	1.2	Asheville, N.C.	3.4	3.6
Kenosha, Wis.	2.0	2.2	Paducah, Ky.	8.4	8.5
Racine, Wis.	2.6	2.5	Seattle, Wash.	3.9	4.0
Minneapolis, Minn.	0.9	1.0	San Diego, Calif.	0.4	0.4

TABLE D 20

Mortgaged Rented Dwellings, Outstanding Debt reported for All Priorities combined and for First Mortgages, and Percentage Distribution by Holding Agency, 52 Cities by Geographic Division, January 1, 1934

DEBT OUTSTANDING ($000)	All agencies	Life ins. co.	Build. & loan asso.	Commer. bank	Savings bank	Mortgage co.	Construct. co.	Title & trust co.	H.O. Loan Corp.	Individual	Other[2]	
46,079.9	100.0	23.2	12.2	13.0	13.8	9.1	0.1	3.4	1.5	18.6	5.1	52 cities[1]
4,073.6	100.0	4.0	6.3	17.0	45.7	3.9		2.9	0.3	15.8	4.1	4 New England cities
714.9	100.0	4.4	11.9	16.7	42.9			0.4	1.6	16.7	5.4	Portland, Me.
1,020.9	100.0	1.8	2.4	4.5	75.9			2.1	0.5	5.9	6.9	Worcester, Mass.
1,456.1	100.0	5.6	8.4	22.6	33.8	3.8		3.7		18.8	3.3	Providence, R.I.*
881.7	100.0			12.0	52.1	13.6		1.6	0.8	18.0	1.9	Waterbury, Conn.
2,850.1	100.0	8.5	4.1	11.7	38.7	0.9	0.2	2.2	0.7	29.0	4.0	4 Mid. Atlantic cities
319.2	100.0	12.9		14.6	27.2		0.9	1.5	0.9	40.2	1.8	Binghamton, N.Y.
993.1	100.0	11.1	0.2	12.3	56.4			2.2	0.8	13.1	3.9	Syracuse, N.Y.
550.8	100.0	2.4	7.8	2.2	3.6	2.2	0.2	6.7	0.4	67.0	7.5	Trenton, N.J.
987.0	100.0	0.3	17.4	12.4	2.7	3.7	0.3	0.6	0.3	58.4	3.9	Erie, Pa.
15,809.2	100.0	17.7	22.9	22.2	13.3	3.1	0.1	4.1	1.3	11.0	4.3	6 E. N. Central cities
11,727.7	100.0	21.7	13.4	28.7	18.2	3.2	0.1	2.3	1.4	7.6	3.4	Cleveland, Ohio*
1,308.1	100.0	9.2	54.5	7.5	1.3	0.4		9.1	0.9	13.7	3.4	Indianapolis, Ind.
826.7	100.0	3.0	57.2	4.2	3.3	0.3		1.5	1.5	7.1	21.9	Peoria, Ill.
275.6	100.0	22.6	25.6	8.6	4.7	0.6	2.3	5.4	2.5	22.9	4.8	Lansing, Mich.
452.0	100.0		21.4	2.1		11.7	0.8	20.1	1.8	38.9	3.2	Kenosha, Wis.
1,219.1	100.0	2.4	13.1	4.7	0.5	14.2	0.5	6.4	0.4	45.9	11.9	Racine, Wis.
6,917.5	100.0	26.9	10.9	5.6	3.8	12.4	0.1	7.0	1.1	27.8	4.4	10 W. N. Central cities
2,882.6	100.0	30.9	6.3	5.8	4.9	12.5	0.1	9.0	0.4	24.2	5.9	Minneapolis, Minn.
577.6	100.0	27.2	4.1	4.6	4.8	11.6		4.9	2.3	39.6	0.9	St. Paul, Minn.
823.2	100.0	33.5	5.4	9.5	4.7	9.8	0.3	0.5	1.5	30.1	4.7	Des Moines, Iowa
175.5	100.0	2.3	16.3	5.7	1.8	25.8		7.6		34.5	6.0	St. Joseph, Mo.
243.9	100.0	17.4	20.7	4.4	0.3	11.4		0.7	0.3	33.8	11.0	Springfield, Mo.
210.1	100.0	3.9	22.7	7.0	4.3	3.8		2.1	6.8	42.6	6.8	Fargo, N.D.
455.6	100.0	18.2	1.6	15.6	1.6	18.7	0.3	0.2	0.1	39.0	4.7	Sioux Falls, S.D.
456.3	100.0	11.3	23.2	0.5	0.6	11.2	0.6	25.0	0.5	25.6	1.5	Lincoln, Neb.
487.1	100.0	13.9	42.3	4.2	2.9	15.4		3.3	1.7	12.2	4.1	Topeka, Kan.
605.6	100.0	39.5	29.3	2.4	0.5	11.2		2.9	1.3	9.4	3.5	Wichita, Kan.
4,240.8	100.0	39.3	3.8	8.4	2.6	20.0		1.7	1.2	19.3	3.7	9 S. Atlantic cities
179.8	100.0	12.5	8.7	8.2	2.8	0.6				63.2	4.0	Hagerstown, Md.
451.4	100.0	11.6	2.1	17.3	3.8	23.1		2.4		30.8	8.9	Richmond, Va.
321.2	100.0	6.8	6.5	41.8	19.0	3.6		1.5	1.4	13.3	6.1	Wheeling, W. Va.*
97.7	100.0	39.9	1.1			29.8			4.3	14.5	10.4	Asheville, N.C.
183.1	100.0	41.4	20.5	21.8	0.3	3.4		0.3		8.0	4.3	Greensboro, N.C.
156.8	100.0	11.9	2.2	3.2	1.2	2.2			5.5	63.5	10.3	Charleston, S.C.
237.5	100.0	21.3	25.4	4.0					0.8	48.5		Columbia, S.C.
2,438.0	100.0	54.6	0.9	0.5	1.2	26.4		2.3	1.4	10.3	2.4	Atlanta, Ga.*
175.3	100.0	35.3	2.3	16.0		11.9			0.7	33.5	0.3	Jacksonville, Fla.
883.4	100.0	38.9	6.6	6.7	1.3	20.7		2.3	7.2	13.2	3.1	3 E. S. Central cities
41.2	100.0	10.9	9.0	14.6	4.8			30.1		22.1	8.5	Paducah, Ky.
640.1	100.0	36.6	5.1	7.4	1.1	23.3		2.2	8.1	13.3	2.9	Birmingham, Ala.*
202.1	100.0	60.0	17.5		2.0	3.7			1.5	10.9	3.5	Jackson, Miss.
3,489.7	100.0	27.9	15.9	6.5	1.8	17.9	0.5	1.0	2.2	24.4	1.9	6 W. S. Central cities
445.4	100.0	17.5	8.2	39.9	0.1	12.1		0.4	5.0	11.8	5.0	Little Rock, Ark.
169.2	100.0	14.3	45.1	0.8		5.5		11.9	5.1	16.7	0.6	Baton Rouge, La.
1,446.4	100.0	40.8	26.4	0.3	0.3	12.7	0.3	0.6	3.3	14.8	0.5	Oklahoma City, Okla.
195.6	100.0		3.0	3.3		24.0	4.5		0.2	60.7	4.3	Austin, Tex.
1,072.6	100.0	23.7	7.6	6.1	3.8	24.3	0.3	0.7	0.8	30.6	2.1	Dallas, Tex.
160.5	100.0	10.4	11.6	13.8	1.7	12.8			1.2	43.6	4.9	Wichita Falls, Tex.
1,899.6	100.0	22.5	8.5	6.1	8.9	16.0	0.2	5.6	4.2	26.5	1.5	6 Mountain cities
171.1	100.0		0.1	7.8	0.5	2.9			11.2	76.7	0.8	Butte, Mont.
67.2	100.0	4.2	40.6		0.9			14.1	1.8	35.1	3.3	Boise, Idaho
100.5	100.0	24.4	31.1	8.5			1.6	1.8	6.8	22.1	3.7	Casper, Wyo.
52.2	100.0	1.6	26.6		4.2	1.7			2.7	56.9	6.3	Pueblo, Colo.
437.0	100.0	10.2	7.8	4.6	13.2	10.4	0.5	0.9	6.7	43.1	2.6	Phoenix, Ariz.
1,071.6	100.0	32.4	3.4	7.5	9.7	23.0		7.7	2.8	13.0	0.5	Salt Lake City, Utah
5,916.0	100.0	30.6	8.3	7.7	7.4	6.0		3.2	1.0	21.9	13.9	4 Pacific cities
2,400.0	100.0	40.2	8.0	3.0	7.3	3.6		4.3	0.9	10.8	21.9	Seattle, Wash.*
1,009.1	100.0	36.3	5.5	2.4	5.1	9.8		3.8	1.6	27.7	7.8	Portland, Ore.
694.3	100.0	7.7	10.7	11.8	6.2	4.6			0.7	50.9	7.4	Sacramento, Calif.
1,812.6	100.0	10.7	10.3	22.8	10.1	9.5	0.1	1.3	0.7	33.2	1.3	San Diego, Calif.*

TABLE D 21

Average Loan Outstanding, All Holding Agencies: First Mortgage by Holding Agency, Owner-occupied and Rented, 52 Cities; Second and Third Mortgages, Owner-occupied and Rented, 52 Cities; Land Contracts, Owner-occupied, 50 Cities; Rented, 41 Cities, by Geographic Division, January 1, 1934

	OWNER-OCCUPIED — FIRST MORTGAGE											2d & 3d MORTG.	LAND CONTRACTS
	All² holding agencies	Life ins. co.	Build. & loan asso.	Commer. bank	Savings bank	Mort-gage co.	Con-struct. co.	Title & trust co.	H.O. Loan Corp.	Indi-vidual	Other		
All cities[1]	$2,672	$4,004	$2,333	$2,852	$2,393	$2,752	$3,162	$2,852	$2,969	$2,482	$2,590	$1,251	$2,087
New England cities	3,306	5,433	2,546	3,881	3,269	3,208	3,075	3,597	3,746	3,248	2,863	1,353	2,267
Portland, Me.	2,870	4,650	2,600	3,980	2,600	1,960			2,733	3,486	3,100	1,819	
Worcester, Mass.	4,092	3,733	3,098	4,569	4,207	3,100		4,145	3,422	4,298	3,399	1,356	
Providence, R.I.*	2,962	5,849	2,225	3,371	2,956	3,322	3,075	3,222	3,748	2,827	2,456	1,178	2,267
Waterbury, Conn.	4,276	6,386	3,587	5,911	3,846	3,267		5,045	4,879	3,891	4,436	1,924	
Mid. Atlantic cities	2,936	4,027	2,579	3,642	3,180	3,465	3,167	3,877	2,899	2,779	3,553	1,360	2,043
Binghamton	2,844	4,700	1,380	3,056	3,104				2,692	2,200		1,300	2,750
Syracuse, N.Y.	3,304	4,230	3,200	3,992	3,149	4,133		4,030		3,094	4,600	1,422	1,433
Trenton, N.J.	2,349	3,203	2,181	3,409	3,370	2,410		3,370	2,847	2,183	2,530	1,128	
Erie, Pa.	2,710	4,012	2,180	3,377	3,103	2,957	3,167	4,031	2,953	2,686	2,865	1,156	1,807
E. N. Central cities	3,240	4,853	3,476	3,406	2,805	3,398	4,110	3,253	3,536	3,214	3,325	1,437	3,046
Cleveland, Ohio*	3,568	5,441	4,101	3,383	3,063	4,071	4,196	3,106	3,985	3,404	3,639	1,474	3,415
Indianapolis, Ind.	2,690	4,052	2,209	3,673	2,187	1,540	4,213	3,858	2,709	3,207	2,952	1,384	3,195
Peoria, Ill.	2,315	3,628	2,119	2,941	2,217	2,689	2,686	3,230	1,831	2,415	2,411	1,106	2,439
Lansing, Mich.	2,087	4,020	1,458	3,128	2,200	2,190		2,300	2,340	1,823	1,850	587	2,665
Kenosha, Wis.	2,685	1,400	3,000	2,304	1,800	2,977		2,648	3,900	2,491	2,756	1,264	3,170
Racine, Wis.	3,024	3,983	3,012	4,091	3,494	3,491		3,852	3,087	2,761	2,737	1,311	3,616
W. N. Central cities	2,053	3,261	1,587	1,863	1,582	2,164	2,656	2,223	2,340	1,858	1,780	1,080	1,905
Minneapolis, Minn.	2,385	4,232	1,568	2,003	1,906	2,416	2,900	2,264	2,754	2,155	1,954	1,481	1,916
St. Paul, Minn.	1,954	2,947	1,608	1,483	1,445	2,120		2,546	2,130	1,866	1,641	787	2,037
Des Moines, Iowa	1,867	2,652	1,360	1,937	1,730	2,063		1,991	2,135	1,511	1,476	874	1,960
St. Joseph, Mo.	1,899	2,268	1,889	1,596	1,255	2,403		1,859	1,880	1,751	1,627	1,017	1,143
Springfield, Mo.	1,430	2,566	1,425	2,320	967	1,432		2,260	2,253	1,175	1,195	732	1,425
Fargo, N.D.	2,460	2,838	2,274	2,239	1,700	2,265		2,329	3,360	2,391	2,312	1,042	2,150
Sioux Falls, S.D.	2,096	2,700	2,177	2,462	2,208	1,841		975	2,576	1,897	2,128	820	1,948
Lincoln, Neb.	1,995	2,974	1,819	2,057	1,300	2,541	1,350	2,434	1,400	1,778	1,359	1,183	1,263
Topeka, Kan.	1,779	2,428	1,655	1,271	1,589	1,978		2,544	3,020	1,512	2,560	694	1,644
Wichita, Kan.	1,656	2,521	1,256	1,871	900	1,519		1,716	1,643	1,579	1,810	883	1,469
S. Atlantic cities	2,681	3,855	1,674	2,985	1,771	2,437	2,577	2,441	3,040	2,221	2,506	1,159	1,771
Hagerstown, Md.	3,050	3,083	1,762	4,284		1,600			4,300	3,195	2,922	1,558	3,433
Richmond, Va.	3,363	4,041	1,783	3,463	3,168	3,165	4,760	3,179	4,472	3,421	2,941	1,210	1,917
Wheeling, W.Va.*	2,067	4,026	1,684	2,374	1,496	2,278	2,456	1,856	3,694	1,867	1,526	1,300	2,150
Asheville, N.C.	2,673	3,446	1,681	6,246		2,289		5,933	2,150	1,655	2,486	1,073	2,008
Greensboro, N.C.	3,360	4,340	2,367	9,550		2,819			2,550	1,595	3,014	2,164	
Charleston, S.C.	2,347	4,313		3,492	1,300	1,313		3,525	4,740	2,061	2,592	2,300	
Columbia, S.C.	2,716	3,807	1,924	2,100		1,900		4,700	3,087	3,138	2,825	1,047	3,000
Atlanta, Ga.*	2,666	3,931	1,549	1,873	1,341	2,551	1,713	1,664	2,250	1,846	2,713	853	1,221
Jacksonville, Fla.	2,343	3,124	1,505	2,929		1,872			2,376	2,160	2,155	1,253	1,317
E. S. Central cities	2,176	3,150	1,499	2,584	2,480	1,969	1,092	2,427	2,630	1,546	1,771	819	2,214
Paducah, Ky.	1,607	1,691	1,197	2,133	2,263	2,200	367	2,537	1,240	1,020	1,675	987	771
Birmingham, Ala.*	2,214	3,276	1,562	2,516	2,494	1,972	1,140	2,420	2,605	1,607	1,777	808	2,323
Jackson, Miss.	2,171	2,960	1,217	3,229		1,850			3,400	1,370		823	
W. S. Central cities	2,249	3,311	1,676	2,285	2,119	2,369	2,019	2,608	2,596	2,056	1,872	712	1,065
Little Rock, Ark.	2,275	2,772	1,357	2,638	1,235	2,376		1,573	2,436	2,312	2,052	817	1,069
Baton Rouge, La.	1,935	767	1,962	4,188					2,700	1,656	933	1,233	1,633
Oklahoma City, Okla.	2,422	3,780	1,906	2,256	3,000	2,511	1,800	3,429	2,635	2,143	1,591	758	1,028
Austin, Tex.	2,032	3,431	2,086	2,243		2,285	1,626		2,133	2,122	931	668	766
Dallas, Tex.	2,212	3,164	1,502	1,954	1,658	2,283	2,358	2,322	2,811	1,997	2,285	615	1,710
Wichita Falls, Tex.	2,006	4,750	1,411	2,883		2,293	1,185	1,840	1,486	1,723	2,325	671	733
Mountain cities	1,960	2,736	1,564	2,298	1,622	1,861	3,791	2,144	2,314	1,909	1,806	1,111	1,899
Butte, Mont.	1,389			1,708	1,650	917		1,433	1,500	1,329	1,473	888	1,186
Boise, Idaho	1,545		1,603	1,448	3,700		1,643		3,475	1,981	1,466	1,356	950	964
Casper, Wyo.	1,853	2,025	1,563	3,014				2,325	2,278	1,867	900	1,064	1,580
Pueblo, Colo.	1,383	1,740	1,651	1,250	733	1,067	1,375		1,465	1,291	622	694	1,015
Phoenix, Ariz.	2,362	3,317	2,029	3,063	2,209	2,046		1,375	3,552	2,128	3,220	785	1,436
Salt Lake City, Utah	2,190	3,159	1,413	2,204	1,751	2,235	4,633	2,218	2,395	2,209	1,979	1,394	2,166
Pacific cities	2,138	2,934	1,871	2,071	1,959	2,306	2,271	2,326	2,342	1,779	2,230	948	1,713
Seattle, Wash.*	2,159	3,421	2,067	1,588	1,877	2,407		2,260	2,279	1,694	2,008	1,048	1,493
Portland, Ore.	1,971	2,649	1,558	2,374	1,750	2,063		2,518	2,437	1,489	2,011	849	2,089
Sacramento, Calif.	2,577	2,645	2,050	2,639	2,759	3,177		2,475	2,856	2,515	3,083	861	3,145
San Diego, Calif.*	2,196	2,586	1,954	2,253	2,143	2,146	2,271	2,048	2,066	2,141	2,694	1,017	2,098

Source: Federal Home Loan Bank Board tabulation of data from *Financial Survey of Urban Housing*. Average not shown for fewer than 3 reports.
*Metropolitan district.
[1]Geographic division and 'All cities' averages weighted by number of loans, by tenure and priority, in each city (RPI).

TABLE D 21

Average Loan Outstanding, All Holding Agencies: First Mortgage by Holding Agency, Owner-occupied and Rented, 52 Cities; Second and Third Mortgages, Owner-occupied and Rented, 52 Cities; Land Contracts, Owner-occupied, 50 Cities; Rented, 41 Cities, by Geographic Division, January 1, 1934

← ——————————————————————— R E N T E D ——————————————————————— →

All[2] holding agencies	Life ins. co.	Build. & loan asso.	Commer. bank	Savings bank	Mortgage co.	Construct. co.	Title & trust co.	H.O. Loan Corp.	Individual	Other	2d & 3d MORTG.	LAND CONTRACTS	
			F I R S T M O R T G A G E										
$3,568	$7,420	$2,881	$3,651	$2,726	$4,653	$978	$3,463	$3,508	$3,180	$5,003	$2,052	$2,497	All cities[1]
4,403	11,202	2,936	5,734	4,173	3,481				3,963	3,284	2,703		**New England cities**
3,666	7,800	2,837	4,257	3,784			775		3,067	5,500	2,150		Portland, Me.
4,908		4,067	5,788	4,998			5,375		4,329	3,619	2,106		Worcester, Mass.
3,812	11,543	2,604	5,576	3,571	3,481		3,560		3,295	2,853	1,482		Providence, R.I.*
8,644			8,131	7,415			4,733		9,318	4,175	9,028		Waterbury, Conn.
4,030	8,786	2,836	4,500	3,513	5,398		4,730		4,212	2,744	1,216	3,900	**Mid. Atlantic cities**
3,990	13,733		3,585	3,335					4,142	1,867	1,700		Binghamton, N.Y.
4,641	9,167		5,555	3,836			5,500		4,985		1,189		Syracuse, N.Y.
2,374	3,225	2,043	2,033	3,333	2,460		6,167		2,208	2,740	1,133		Trenton, N.J.
3,739		3,376	4,221	2,978	7,400		1,933		3,791	3,258	1,079	3,900	Erie, Pa.
4,113	10,577	4,257	3,794	3,145	9,181		2,953	4,011	5,034	4,339	2,882	3,626	**E. N. Central cities**
5,229	14,803	5,868	3,993	3,839	13,504		3,176	4,791	5,258	4,577	3,090	4,083	Cleveland, Ohio*
2,686	5,222	2,194	3,507	1,822	1,900		2,479	3,025	5,967	2,769	1,800	1,650	Indianapolis, Ind.
2,633	4,200	2,065	4,288	3,943			2,117	2,067	1,625	12,943	1,627	8,600	Peoria, Ill.
1,941	2,073	1,537	2,145	2,600			1,850		1,859	3,300		2,586	Lansing, Mich.
3,645		4,391	3,167		5,878		3,957	2,633	3,034	1,533	1,450	5,457	Kenosha, Wis.
3,933	9,867	3,079	4,767		6,168		5,593		3,350	4,415	1,726	3,422	Racine, Wis.
2,531	4,937	1,661	2,284	2,153	2,437		4,902	2,514	1,952	2,072	1,679	2,449	**W. N. Central cities**
3,120	6,607	1,553	2,702	1,949	2,910		6,618	2,550	2,195	2,808	2,758	3,069	Minneapolis, Minn.
2,750	6,046	2,380	1,773	3,078	2,478		4,750	2,660	2,118	1,225	863	1,927	St. Paul, Minn.
2,138	3,406	1,318	2,111	1,852	2,442			2,420	1,664	1,764	750	2,164	Des Moines, Iowa
1,887		1,500	1,667		2,379		1,914		1,731	2,650	340		St. Joseph, Mo.
1,443	2,494	1,368	1,189		1,847				1,129	1,914	1,900		Springfield, Mo.
2,801	2,767	2,380	2,100		1,333			3,550	3,200	3,550	833		Fargo, N.D.
2,531	2,760	1,043	7,120	1,440	1,854				2,649	1,767	550	2,736	Sioux Falls, S.D.
2,684	4,682	1,684			2,545		7,600		2,338	1,700	850	1,217	Lincoln, Neb.
2,030	3,767	1,689	1,367	1,556	2,885		2,650	2,767	1,926	1,980	1,267	1,300	Topeka, Kan.
1,750	3,069	1,469	1,611		1,507		967	1,975	1,070	1,407	1,014	1,667	Wichita, Kan.
3,765	6,418	2,387	3,695	1,805	3,637		3,182	4,250	2,287	2,275	2,085	3,761	**S. Atlantic cities**
2,948		2,243	2,940						2,644		1,250		Hagerstown, Md.
3,527	4,375	3,167	3,004	4,225	4,350		2,675		3,310	3,100	1,636		Richmond, Va.
2,745	3,633	2,986	3,947	2,546	2,320		1,667		1,775	1,625	3,267		Wheeling, W.Va.*
2,641	3,250				3,233				1,578	2,200			Asheville, N.C.
3,521	3,158	3,125			1,260				2,920	2,600	10,820	1,333	Greensboro, N.C.
2,010	4,675								1,779	1,610			Charleston, S.C.
2,896	3,885	2,323							2,880		1,140		Columbia, S.C.
4,780	9,641	1,918	2,267	814	4,629		3,680	4,250	1,950	2,167	759		Atlanta, Ga.*
3,187	4,754		7,000		2,322				2,348			4,367	Jacksonville, Fla.
2,909	4,544	1,505	3,631	1,150	3,631		2,370	3,467	2,007	1,408	1,357	2,245	**E. S. Central cities**
2,060		925					3,100		1,517				Paducah, Ky.
2,963	4,782	1,491	3,631	1,150	3,831		2,350	3,467	1,606	1,408	1,422	1,600	Birmingham, Ala.*
2,731	3,159	1,681			2,467				4,420		1,240	3,200	Jackson, Miss.
2,944	4,620	1,882	2,841	2,142	3,303	978	2,700	3,405	2,427	1,702	765	750	**W. S. Central cities**
2,447	4,105	1,300	2,572		3,159			2,813	1,753	2,775			Little Rock, Ark.
3,021		2,384			3,100				1,880		780		Baton Rouge, La.
3,867	7,117	2,765			3,477			4,291	2,896	790	991	525	Oklahoma City, Okla.
2,016		1,160			2,611	978			2,082	1,400	1,150	633	Austin, Tex.
2,695	3,342	1,545	2,608	2,142	3,473		2,700	2,967	2,489	2,000	571	1,025	Dallas, Tex.
2,006	2,783	1,247	5,525		2,278				1,707	2,633	567		Wichita Falls, Tex.
2,999	5,718	1,867	6,236	3,915	3,373		2,168	3,469	2,313	1,700	2,613	2,674	**Mountain cities**
3,111			2,680		833				3,364		5,000	1,133	Butte, Mont.
2,100		2,730							1,573	733		433	Boise, Idaho
2,185	8,167	1,490	2,150						1,850	1,850		5,567	Casper, Wyo.
1,214		1,264							1,238			1,333	Pueblo, Colo.
2,601	3,438	3,109	3,367	2,623	1,750			3,650	2,581	1,867	1,311	2,600	Phoenix, Ariz.
3,925	6,804	1,153	8,956	4,718	4,657		2,168	3,356	2,477	1,733	3,147	3,300	Salt Lake City, Utah
3,579	6,177	3,515	2,842	2,240	2,328		3,461	3,135	2,287	17,548	1,300	1,692	**Pacific cities**
5,074	9,932	4,688	3,811	1,828	1,736		4,714	2,986	2,004	43,060	1,180	1,719	Seattle, Wash.*
2,443	4,307	3,494	1,593	2,226	1,984		3,167	3,340	1,654	2,068	1,324	1,150	Portland, Ore.
3,059	4,492	2,188	2,921	3,057	3,963				2,923	5,700	2,808	1,767	Sacramento, Calif.
2,837	3,450	2,399	2,722	2,515	2,873		1,992		3,086	2,025	951	1,824	San Diego, Calif.*

[2]Includes public bond issues:

	Owner-occupied	Rented		Owner-occupied	Rented
Worcester, Mass.		**	Richmond, Va.	**	**
Asheville, N.C.		**	Paducah, Ky.		**
Kenosha, Wis.	$3,365	**	Seattle, Wash.	**	**
Racine, Wis.	6,957	$6,040	San Diego, Calif.		**
Minneapolis, Minn.		**			

**Average not shown for fewer than 3 reports.

TABLE D 22

Average Original Loan reported by Owners, January 1, 1934: First Mortgages by Holding Agency, Owner-occupied, 52 Cities, Rented, 30 Cities; and for All Holding Agencies, Owner-occupied and Rented, 52 Cities; Second and Third Mortgages, Owner-occupied, 49 Cities, Rented, 23 Cities; Land Contracts, Owner-occupied, 33 Cities, Rented, 9 Cities, by Geographic Division

	All² holding agencies	Life ins. co.	Build. & loan asso.	Commer. bank	Savings bank	Mortgage co.	Construct. co.	Title & trust co.	H.O. Loan Corp.	Individual	Other	2d & 3d MORTG.	LAND CONTRACTS
All cities¹	$3,318	$4,891	$3,086	$3,532	$3,081	$3,299	$3,711	$3,533	$3,027	$2,985	$3,197	$1,854	$2,995
New England cities	3,970	6,279	3,447	4,785	4,029	3,912	3,675	4,331	3,893	3,628	3,487	1,990	
Portland, Me.	3,757	10,990	3,463	4,861	3,399	2,620			2,983	4,143	4,167	2,156	
Worcester, Mass.	4,316	4,175	3,950	4,740	4,354	3,408		5,218	3,772	4,411	3,976	2,133	
Providence, R.I.*	3,797	6,445	3,047	4,532	3,994	4,166	3,675	3,861	3,839	3,301	3,079	1,740	
Waterbury, Conn.	4,556	7,029	5,147	6,548	3,929	3,833		5,741	4,950	4,026	4,942	2,623	
Mid. Atlantic cities	3,204	4,617	3,255	3,800	3,404	3,297	3,167	4,251	2,973	3,074	3,973	2,180	2,720
Binghamton, N.Y.	3,367	6,217	2,480	3,594	3,481				3,246	2,450	1,833		
Syracuse, N.Y.	3,497	4,623	3,650	4,016	3,300	3,675		4,582		3,448	5,214	2,349	
Trenton, N.J.	2,506	3,529	2,908	3,422	3,618	2,566		3,340	2,987	2,252	2,400	1,680	
Erie, Pa.	3,130	4,815	3,104	3,790	3,390	3,145	3,167	4,394	2,958	2,930	3,482	1,647	2,720
E. N. Central cities	4,195	6,003	4,360	4,483	3,754	4,116	4,836	4,219	3,610	4,044	4,092	2,022	4,097
Cleveland, Ohio*	4,640	6,805	4,995	4,582	4,088	4,918	4,967	4,206	4,074	4,333	4,519	2,122	4,468
Indianapolis, Ind.	3,587	4,986	3,147	4,828	3,293	2,000	4,829	4,915	2,750	4,059	3,527	1,702	4,193
Peoria, Ill.	3,109	4,715	2,951	3,402	2,992	3,378	3,257	3,770	1,919	3,091	3,034	1,296	3,434
Lansing, Mich.	2,612	4,602	2,117	3,517	2,683	3,144		2,363	2,347	2,168	2,990	906	3,797
Kenosha, Wis.	3,017	1,575	3,753	2,800	2,087	3,106		2,903	3,908	2,789	2,913	1,452	4,154
Racine, Wis.	3,381	3,983	3,821	4,584	3,581	3,702		3,987	3,134	2,887	3,011	1,523	4,628
W. N. Central cities	2,479	3,879	2,179	2,169	2,196	2,539	2,798	2,607	2,356	2,195	2,170	1,429	2,880
Minneapolis, Minn.	2,743	4,708	2,133	2,399	2,430	2,702	3,000	2,562	2,767	2,387	2,263	2,114	2,930
St. Paul, Minn.	2,327	3,530	2,112	1,753	2,583	2,478		2,715	2,130	2,199	2,268	897	3,041
Des Moines, Iowa	2,296	3,302	1,885	2,300	1,947	2,616		3,082	2,197	1,880	1,669	1,005	2,983
St. Joseph, Mo.	2,317	2,704	2,537	1,972	1,618	2,844		2,303	1,860	2,081	1,774	1,343	
Springfield, Mo.	1,903	3,476	2,330	2,580	1,083	1,831		2,540	2,253	1,456	1,442	823	
Fargo, N.D.	2,928	3,512	2,997	2,708	2,258	2,568		2,329	3,440	2,891	2,612	1,497	2,947
Sioux Falls, S.D.	2,359	3,220	2,933	2,638	3,092	1,953		1,000	2,579	2,152	2,493	1,129	2,922
Lincoln, Neb.	2,693	4,104	2,563	2,085	1,933	3,029	1,800	2,930	1,433	2,437	1,807	1,353	1,832
Topeka, Kan.	2,335	3,059	2,282	1,767	1,870	2,435		2,884	3,043	1,990	3,310	877	2,297
Wichita, Kan.	2,212	3,304	1,809	1,908	1,667	2,020	2,733	2,311	1,649	2,027	2,197	1,228	2,132
S. Atlantic cities	3,302	4,847	2,352	3,588	2,331	2,992	3,054	3,053	3,058	2,703	2,992	1,893	2,261
Hagerstown, Md.	3,395	4,183	2,538	4,812		1,740			4,300	3,428	3,056	2,280	
Richmond, Va.	3,895	4,822	2,283	3,978	3,486	3,650	4,820	4,093	4,472	3,940	3,161	2,122	
Wheeling, W.Va.*	2,910	5,409	2,260	3,317	2,370	3,033	3,080	2,393	3,706	2,605	2,574	1,673	2,591
Asheville, N.C.	3,807	5,060	2,962	7,569		3,088		8,433	2,229	2,251	4,443	1,597	2,323
Greensboro, N.C.	4,408	5,569	3,262	9,288		3,921			2,625	2,439	3,757	3,020	
Charleston, S.C.	2,797	5,567		4,669	2,850	2,063		3,900	4,800	2,379	2,867		
Columbia, S.C.	3,342	5,007	2,550	3,113		2,120		5,100	3,067	3,693	2,286	1,565	
Atlanta, Ga.*	3,165	4,585	2,222	2,369	1,789	3,075	2,300	2,076	2,267	2,206	3,129	1,706	1,878
Jacksonville, Fla.	2,937	4,489	2,291	3,314		2,217		2,867	2,388	2,505	2,333	1,500	
E. S. Central cities	2,893	4,127	2,198	3,196	2,875	2,736	2,184	3,265	2,706	1,957	2,694	1,460	2,874
Paducah, Ky.	2,373	2,578	1,800	3,296	2,500	3,033	433	3,643	1,320	1,557	2,300	1,227	
Birmingham, Ala.*	2,897	4,239	2,251	3,072	2,900	2,708	2,300	3,240	2,693	1,965	2,720	1,523	2,874
Jackson, Miss.	3,091	4,069	2,019	3,971		2,790			3,400	2,082		1,265	
W. S. Central cities	2,887	4,219	2,348	2,925	2,667	2,988	2,488	3,166	2,627	2,622	2,427	1,152	1,417
Little Rock, Ark.	2,615	3,415	1,861	3,015	1,277	2,503		1,673	2,474	2,574	2,373	1,448	1,434
Baton Rouge, La.	2,897	2,767	3,031	4,950					2,714	2,576	1,018		
Oklahoma City, Okla.	3,098	4,760	2,622	2,619	3,273	3,214	2,220	4,356	2,645	2,698	2,248	1,062	1,245
Austin, Tex.	2,812	5,382	2,856	3,123		3,148	2,356		2,133	2,837	1,844	1,600	1,321
Dallas, Tex.	2,823	3,794	2,138	2,863	2,543	2,887	2,750	2,771	2,868	2,531	2,848	1,110	1,950
Wichita Falls, Tex.	2,733	5,467	1,934	3,125		3,136	2,225	1,871	1,486	2,708	2,317	1,142	
Mountain cities	2,346	3,558	2,134	2,698	2,081	2,053	3,533	2,593	2,337	2,286	2,131	1,311	2,667
Butte, Mont.	1,660			2,321	2,150	1,167		1,800	1,506	1,586	1,603		1,814
Boise, Idaho	1,967	2,707	2,083	3,933		1,879		3,775	1,984	1,660	1,706	1,064	1,500
Casper, Wyo.	2,298	3,300	2,232	3,714				2,550	2,287	2,042	1,350	1,100	2,257
Pueblo, Colo.	1,718	2,820	2,039	1,625	1,267	1,267	1,850		1,556	1,640	939	794	1,662
Phoenix, Ariz.	2,740	4,238	2,893	3,394	2,484	2,333		2,254	3,590	2,375	3,700	1,643	2,441
Salt Lake City, Utah	2,600	3,777	1,938	2,613	2,234	2,381	4,120	2,590	2,397	2,698	2,270	1,421	2,953
Pacific cities	2,683	3,740	2,612	2,651	2,632	2,876	3,225	3,037	2,384	2,102	2,961	1,448	2,552
Seattle, Wash.*	2,703	4,204	2,812	2,173	2,572	2,857		2,939	2,283	1,994	2,844	1,442	2,333
Portland, Ore.	2,539	3,411	2,288	3,035	2,492	2,823		3,238	2,555	1,798	2,681	1,455	3,038
Sacramento, Calif.	3,186	3,635	2,830	3,238	3,800	4,074		3,967	2,856	2,907	3,877	1,419	3,970
San Diego, Calif.*	2,676	3,432	2,689	2,667	2,570	2,471	3,225	2,454	2,070	2,505	3,288	1,460	2,706

Source: *Financial Survey of Urban Housing.* Based on approximately the same number of reports as shown in Tables D 17 and 18. Certain cities omitted from the rented tenure class because detailed tabulations were not prepared for the original amount of the loan by the agency holding the original loan. The average amounts of these loans shown for all agencies. Averages not shown for fewer than 3 reports.
*Metropolitan district.

¹Geographic division and 'All cities' averages weighted by number of loans, by priority and tenure, in each city (RPI). For rented properties where the number of cities included in the 'All holding agencies' column is larger than the number for the individual agencies, the weighted geographic division and 'All cities' averages in the 'All holding agencies' column are not strictly comparable to the weighted averages for the individual agencies.

TABLE D 22

Average Original Loan reported by Owners, January 1, 1934: First Mortgages by Holding Agency, Owner-occupied, 52 Cities, Rented, 30 Cities; and for All Holding Agencies, Owner-occupied and Rented, 52 Cities; Second and Third Mortgages, Owner-occupied, 49 Cities, Rented, 23 Cities; Land Contracts, Owner-occupied, 33 Cities, Rented, 9 Cities, by Geographic Division

◄──────────────────────────── RENTED ────────────────────────────►

All[2] holding agencies	Life ins. co.	Build. & loan asso.	Commer. bank	Savings bank	Mortgage co.	Construct. co.	Title & trust co.	H.O. Loan Corp.	Individual	Other	2d & 3d MORTG.	LAND CONTRACTS	
$4,225	$9,049	$3,618	$4,321	$3,257	$5,172		$4,424	$3,524	$3,496	$6,609	$2,606	$3,580	All cities[1]
5,041	11,140	3,472	6,195	4,717	4,031				4,004	3,597	3,200		New England cities
4,496	9,125	3,803	5,241	4,616			4,339		3,539	6,643	2,022		Portland, Me.
5,154	7,100	4,435	5,356	5,288			5,375		4,307	4,060	2,770		Worcester, Mass.
4,599	12,571	3,147	6,546	4,560	4,031		4,233		3,958	3,150	2,267		Providence, R.I.*
8,870											8,294		Waterbury, Conn.
4,303	8,034	3,627	4,957	3,785	6,420		5,349		4,668	3,471	2,177		Mid. Atlantic cities
4,306											2,300		Binghamton, N.Y.
4,856	9,300		5,910	3,963			6,333		5,596		2,283		Syracuse, N.Y.
2,575	3,620	2,723	2,100	3,900	2,983		5,529		2,351	2,740	1,416		Trenton, N.J.
4,173		4,240	4,641	3,288	8,750		2,900		4,043	3,967	1,661		Erie, Pa.
5,009	12,570	5,092	5,032	3,905	8,749		3,886	4,064	5,200	5,232	3,473	4,435	E. N. Central cities
6,375	17,423	6,767	5,298	4,754	13,200		4,550	4,832	6,055	5,606	3,552	6,115	Cleveland, Ohio*
3,288	6,517	2,925	4,615	2,456	1,933		2,898	3,025	4,807	3,100			Indianapolis, Ind.
3,552	5,783	2,960	5,780	4,000	2,967		3,017	1,975	1,947	15,514	2,595		Peoria, Ill.
2,417	2,334	2,175	3,400	3,125			1,988		2,174	3,700		3,171	Lansing, Mich.
4,052													Kenosha, Wis.
4,176	10,667	4,054	5,308		6,179		5,593		3,414	4,504	2,243		Racine, Wis.
2,988	5,858	2,110	3,246	2,686	2,857		6,339	2,476	2,163	2,640	3,658	3,259	W. N. Central cities
3,639	7,124	2,055	3,465	2,533	3,352		7,825	2,550	2,418	4,061	3,658	3,410	Minneapolis, Minn.
3,252	7,830	2,920	1,980	3,778	2,789		6,833	2,660	2,288	1,600		2,855	St. Paul, Minn.
2,525	4,200	1,809	2,524	2,090	2,890			2,420	1,888	1,918		3,057	Des Moines, Iowa
1,927													St. Joseph, Mo.
1,752	3,206	1,827	1,222		2,513				1,267	2,015			Springfield, Mo.
3,185													Fargo, N.D.
3,368		2,887	1,225	20,220	2,200	1,913			2,769	1,818		4,173	Sioux Falls, S.D.
3,192	5,627	2,049			3,111		8,393		2,866	2,380			Lincoln, Neb.
2,507	4,439	2,264	1,920	1,763	3,071		3,950	2,767	2,253	1,990			Topeka, Kan.
2,155	3,883	1,744	1,813		1,720		1,269	1,975	1,347	1,875			Wichita, Kan.
4,251	10,676	2,269	2,467	1,161	5,067		4,277	4,250	2,165	2,536	1,975		S. Atlantic cities
3,463													Hagerstown, Md.
3,590											3,165		Richmond, Va.
3,766													Wheeling, W.Va.*
3,239													Asheville, N.C.
4,157													Greensboro, N.C.
2,392													Charleston, S.C.
3,408													Columbia, S.C.
5,298	10,676	2,269	2,467	1,161	5,067		4,277	4,250	2,165	2,536	1,259		Atlanta, Ga.*
3,637													Jacksonville, Fla.
3,994	5,516	2,514	4,677	1,800	3,850		2,733	3,467	1,842	1,708	1,492		E. S. Central cities
4,295													Paducah, Ky.
3,415	5,516	2,514	4,677	1,800	3,850		2,733	3,467	1,842	1,708			Birmingham, Ala.*
7,318											1,492		Jackson, Miss.
3,604	5,583	2,866	3,453	2,767	4,125		4,067	3,404	3,057	1,822	1,066		W. S. Central cities
2,896	4,620	2,215	2,854		3,788			2,813	2,143	3,100			Little Rock, Ark.
3,802													Baton Rouge, La.
4,758	8,539	3,598			4,311			4,291	3,580	800	1,329		Oklahoma City, Okla.
2,348													Austin, Tex.
3,307	3,916	2,540	3,579	2,767	4,079		4,067	2,967	2,918	2,200	882		Dallas, Tex.
2,461													Wichita Falls, Tex.
3,383	6,222	3,241	7,155	4,243	4,135		2,183	3,509	2,574	1,799	3,048	5,113	Mountain cities
3,618													Butte, Mont.
2,548													Boise, Idaho
3,268													Casper, Wyo.
1,410													Pueblo, Colo.
2,888	4,217	4,070	4,120	2,743	2,074			3,650	2,763	1,917	3,020		Phoenix, Ariz.
4,297	7,478	1,721	9,056	5,183	5,427		2,183	3,420	2,456	1,725	3,065	5,113	Salt Lake City, Utah
4,261	7,745	3,986	3,147	2,815	2,780		4,632	3,135	2,523	22,791	1,475	3,254	Pacific cities
6,135	12,486	4,197	3,970	2,303	2,196		6,171	2,986	2,226	56,933	1,447	3,448	Seattle, Wash.*
2,916	4,857	4,763	2,114	2,971	2,388		4,822	3,340	1,889	2,610	1,527		Portland, Ore.
3,681	6,200	3,035	3,454	4,329	4,850				3,329	6,033	1,738		Sacramento, Calif.
3,220	4,622	3,287	2,923	2,779	3,187		2,264		3,272	1,900	1,377	2,692	San Diego, Calif.*

Includes public bond issues:

	Owner-occupied	Rented
Kenosha, Wis.	$3365	
Racine, Wis.	7029	$6040
San Diego, Calif.		4367

TABLE D 23

Average Term of Loan, Average Years of Term Expired, and Average Years to run after 1933, by Priority: Owner-occupied, First Mortgages, 52 Cities; Second and Third Mortgages, 26 Cities; Land Contracts, 19 Cities; Rented, First Mortgages, 27 Cities, by Geographic Division, January 1, 1934

	OWNER-OCCUPIED									RENTED [2]		
	1st MORTGAGES			2d & 3d MORTGAGES			LAND CONTRACTS			1st MORTGAGES		
	Term of loan	Years expired	Years to run after 1933	Term of loan	Years expired	Years to run after 1933	Term of loan	Years expired	Years to run after 1933	Term of loan	Years expired	Years to run after 1933
						(YEARS)						
All cities [1]	10.2	4.3	5.9	8.0	3.8	4.2	11.0	4.4	6.6	9.1	3.7	5.4
New England cities	14.3	6.1	8.2	9.6	4.9	4.7				13.5	5.3	8.2
Portland, Me.	12.8	5.1	7.7									
Worcester, Mass.	12.6	4.1	8.5	9.5	5.1	4.4				12.6	3.9	8.7
Providence, R.I.*	15.2	7.2	8.0	9.7	4.8	4.9				13.8	5.8	8.0
Waterbury, Conn.	12.5	3.2	9.3	9.5	4.7	4.8						
Mid. Atlantic cities	11.8	6.4	5.4	9.5	5.3	4.2				9.2	4.0	5.2
Binghamton, N.Y.	9.8	6.0	3.8									
Syracuse, N.Y.	12.8	7.6	5.2	9.7	5.6	4.1						
Trenton, N.J.	13.3	6.2	7.1	10.4	4.6	5.8				11.6	5.0	6.6
Erie, Pa.	9.2	4.2	5.0	7.0	3.9	3.1				7.5	3.3	4.2
E. N. Central cities	11.0	4.6	6.4	7.8	3.5	4.3	12.7	5.5	7.2	11.0	4.8	6.2
Cleveland, Ohio*	11.2	4.8	6.4	7.8	3.6	4.2	11.2	4.0	7.2	11.4	5.1	6.3
Indianapolis, Ind.	11.4	4.6	6.8	8.1	2.7	5.4	12.3	5.3	7.0	10.5	4.5	6.0
Peoria, Ill.	11.3	4.8	6.5	8.2	2.5	5.7	12.3	4.0	8.3	11.0	4.4	6.6
Lansing, Mich.	9.8	3.0	6.8				12.9	5.6	7.3			
Kenosha, Wis.	7.1	3.3	3.8				12.7	7.0	5.7			
Racine, Wis.	9.2	3.7	5.5	6.5	2.5	4.0	15.2	7.6	7.6	7.7	3.4	4.3
W. N. Central cities	7.7	2.8	4.9	6.4	2.9	3.5	10.4	4.2	6.2	7.2	2.9	4.3
Minneapolis, Minn.	7.1	2.5	4.6	5.7	2.5	3.2	9.5	4.0	5.5	6.9	2.7	4.2
St. Paul, Minn.	7.0	2.6	4.4				10.4	4.2	6.2	6.8	3.1	3.7
Des Moines, Iowa	9.2	3.1	6.1	6.0	2.6	3.4	11.9	4.9	7.0	6.8	2.8	4.0
St. Joseph, Mo.	7.4	3.4	4.0									
Springfield, Mo.	7.4	2.6	4.8							7.1	2.4	4.7
Fargo, N.D.	8.6	2.3	6.3									
Sioux Falls, S.D.	7.1	2.6	4.5				10.0	3.9	6.1	6.3	2.5	3.8
Lincoln, Neb.	8.8	3.5	5.3							7.7	3.1	4.6
Topeka, Kan.	9.5	3.5	6.0	8.5	3.7	4.8	10.4	3.6	6.8	8.7	3.4	5.3
Wichita, Kan.	8.9	3.4	5.5	7.1	3.5	3.6	10.2	3.7	6.5	8.6	3.5	5.1
S. Atlantic cities	8.3	3.2	5.1	6.0	2.6	3.4				6.1	2.3	3.8
Hagerstown, Md.	6.3	2.5	3.8									
Richmond, Va.	6.5	2.9	3.6	5.5	2.7	2.8						
Wheeling, W.Va.*	10.9	4.6	6.3	8.7	2.7	6.0						
Asheville, N.C.	12.0	6.1	5.9									
Greensboro, N.C.	10.1	4.1	6.0									
Charleston, S.C.	7.4	3.0	4.4									
Columbia, S.C.	9.3	3.3	6.0									
Atlanta, Ga.*	7.5	2.6	4.9	5.3	2.4	2.9				6.1	2.3	3.8
Jacksonville, Fla.	8.3	2.9	5.4									
E. S. Central cities	9.5	4.9	4.6	5.5	2.2	3.3				8.3	2.9	5.4
Paducah, Ky.	9.0	3.6	5.4									
Birmingham, Ala.*	9.3	5.1	4.2	5.5	2.2	3.3				8.3	2.9	5.4
Jackson, Miss.	11.1	3.8	7.3									
W. S. Central cities	9.0	3.2	5.8	6.2	2.4	3.8				7.7	2.6	5.1
Little Rock, Ark.	8.1	2.4	5.7	4.9	2.2	2.7				6.1	2.0	4.1
Baton Rouge, La.	12.4	5.6	6.8									
Oklahoma City, Okla.	10.2	3.4	6.8	6.1	2.3	3.8				9.2	2.6	6.6
Austin, Tex.	8.3	3.5	4.8									
Dallas, Tex.	8.2	3.0	5.2	6.7	2.6	4.1				7.2	2.8	4.4
Wichita Falls, Tex.	8.1	3.2	4.9									
Mountain cities	8.6	2.8	5.8	7.3	2.5	4.8	10.8	3.8	7.0	6.8	2.2	4.6
Butte, Mont.	6.0	1.8	4.2									
Boise, Idaho	8.5	2.9	5.6				7.5	2.7	4.8			
Casper, Wyo.	9.5	2.2	7.3				9.0	2.1	6.9			
Pueblo, Colo.	9.7	2.4	7.3									
Phoenix, Ariz.	6.9	2.5	4.4							6.0	2.0	4.0
Salt Lake City, Utah	9.1	3.2	5.9	7.3	2.5	4.8	11.4	4.2	7.2	7.3	2.4	4.9
Pacific cities	9.8	4.1	5.7	6.4	2.7	3.7	10.4	4.1	6.3	8.0	3.5	4.5
Seattle, Wash.*	9.0	3.4	5.6	5.5	2.2	3.3	9.6	3.8	5.8	7.7	3.1	4.6
Portland, Ore.	12.0	5.6	6.4	7.3	3.4	3.9	11.6	4.7	6.9	10.2	5.3	4.9
Sacramento, Calif.	9.5	4.1	5.4	6.1	2.5	3.6	15.8	6.1	9.7	7.9	3.1	4.8
San Diego, Calif.*	7.6	2.7	4.9	6.4	2.4	4.0	11.6	4.1	7.5	6.3	2.5	3.8

Source: *Financial Survey of Urban Housing.* The number of reports from which these data were derived, except land contracts, may be found distributed according to term of loan in Tables D 24 and 25.

The number of owner-occupied land contract reports are:

Cleveland, Ohio	112	Minneapolis, Minn.	418	Boise, Idaho	72
Indianapolis, Ind.	109	St. Paul, Minn.	91	Casper, Wyo.	123
Peoria, Ill.	76	Des Moines, Iowa	307	Salt Lake City, Utah	477
Lansing, Mich.	223	Sioux Falls, S.D.	67	Seattle, Wash.	648
Kenosha, Wis.	46	Topeka, Kan.	81	Portland, Ore.	121
Racine, Wis.	164	Wichita, Kan.	78	Sacramento, Calif.	101
				San Diego, Calif.	106

*Metropolitan district.

[1] Geographic division and 52 (27)-city averages weighted by number of loans, by tenure and priority, in each city (RPI).

[2] Sample data inadequate to show average terms on second and third mortgages and land contracts.

TABLE D 24

First Mortgages, Number by Term in Years: Owner-occupied, 52 Cities; Rented, 47 Cities, by Geographic Division, January 1, 1934

	All terms of loan	1 year or less	2 years	3 years	4 years	5 years	6 or 7 years	8 or 9 years	10 years	11 or 12 years	13 or 14 years	15 years or more
52 cities	43,579	2,565	799	4,469	1,246	6,458	2,654	2,632	5,581	5,639	2,792	8,744
4 New England cities	1,335	26	5	20	10	24	21	51	103	397	140	538
Portland, Me.	309	9	1	7	4	5	5	15	49	112	19	83
Worcester, Mass.	164	2		5	1	7	4	5	9	55	13	63
Providence, R.I.*	811	14	2	6	4	9	9	29	43	220	106	369
Waterbury, Conn.	51	1	2	2	1	3	3	2	2	10	2	23
4 Mid. Atlantic cities	1,473	61	17	82	34	354	63	57	127	232	83	363
Binghamton, N.Y.	89	2	1	9	3	27	3	7	8	6	6	17
Syracuse, N.Y.	99	1		10	4	13	4	6	15	9	6	31
Trenton, N.J.	299	3	1	3	2	7	4	9	21	79	31	139
Erie, Pa.	986	55	15	60	25	307	52	35	83	138	40	176
6 E. N. Central cities	11,033	1,572	75	478	118	561	297	406	925	2,222	1,301	3,078
Cleveland, Ohio*	7,151	1,481	43	125	56	285	138	221	437	989	961	2,415
Indianapolis, Ind.	1,300	23	6	8	7	109	34	48	211	384	207	263
Peoria, Ill.	1,121	8	11	23	11	54	24	33	128	584	61	184
Lansing, Mich.	287	2	3	16	7	44	31	52	43	12	14	63
Kenosha, Wis.	336	43	5	78	16	21	29	23	27	57	5	32
Racine, Wis.	838	15	7	228	21	48	41	29	79	196	53	121
10 W. N. Central cities	9,342	155	161	1,433	313	2,390	589	559	1,325	931	301	1,185
Minneapolis, Minn.	3,144	35	42	805	107	829	179	147	348	242	104	306
St. Paul, Minn.	707	4	12	133	33	258	37	47	60	40	8	75
Des Moines, Iowa	1,108	20	24	73	33	339	69	53	102	65	40	290
St. Joseph, Mo.	396	16	12	104	18	52	23	47	35	25	24	40
Springfield, Mo.	597	26	20	134	30	67	40	33	134	37	20	56
Fargo, N.D.	369	15	6	23	10	113	32	30	30	20	4	86
Sioux Falls, S.D.	476	10	15	50	19	202	32	21	42	18	10	57
Lincoln, Neb.	620	11	4	43	18	136	37	55	158	61	29	68
Topeka, Kan.	880	7	12	40	18	146	39	37	184	300	20	77
Wichita, Kan.	1,045	11	14	28	27	248	101	89	232	123	42	130
9 S. Atlantic cities	4,737	284	124	513	171	1,172	344	261	601	401	175	691
Hagerstown, Md.	162	76	4	5	1	4	5	2	2	41	3	19
Richmond, Va.	886	87	47	280	47	72	49	58	62	46	25	113
Wheeling, W.Va.*	347	11	7	9	5	18	29	33	79	45	18	93
Asheville, N.C.	369	19	9	12	9	36	37	29	75	53	17	73
Greensboro, N.C.	252	13	4	5	6	17	30	13	62	40	8	54
Charleston, S.C.	103	20	5	8	5	12	8	9	12	4	3	17
Columbia, S.C.	215	3	8	24	9	8	21	10	72	24	5	31
Atlanta, Ga.*	2,176	32	31	134	79	983	151	95	216	131	82	242
Jacksonville, Fla.	227	23	9	36	10	22	14	12	21	17	14	49
3 E. S. Central cities	2,151	97	48	175	62	278	175	192	307	221	120	476
Paducah, Ky.	180	8	6	12	3	19	23	14	39	16	8	32
Birmingham, Ala.*	1,760	79	38	158	56	242	134	162	231	181	101	378
Jackson, Miss.	211	10	4	5	3	17	18	16	37	24	11	66
6 W. S. Central cities	4,281	133	85	289	141	720	396	387	778	481	229	642
Little Rock, Ark.	629	74	25	115	24	34	53	34	55	51	27	137
Baton Rouge, La.	146	4	5	2	1	7	6	4	17	27	34	39
Oklahoma City, Okla.	1,560	18	13	44	30	223	91	105	409	248	92	287
Austin, Tex.	294	5	6	16	16	35	61	44	43	30	16	22
Dallas, Tex.	1,404	22	31	100	57	380	147	174	200	99	52	142
Wichita Falls, Tex.	248	10	5	12	13	41	38	26	54	26	8	15
6 Mountain cities	2,705	68	114	467	111	242	236	242	389	250	116	470
Butte, Mont.	217	24	42	31	10	25	27	13	6	2	4	33
Boise, Idaho	442	13	13	48	15	47	75	49	70	33	17	62
Casper, Wyo.	147	7	1	11	6	11	18	16	23	12	3	39
Pueblo, Colo.	335	5	14	45	8	19	18	51	33	35	13	94
Phoenix, Ariz.	382	4	18	127	17	49	23	28	50	11	9	46
Salt Lake City, Utah	1,182	15	26	205	55	91	75	85	207	157	70	196
4 Pacific cities	6,522	169	170	1,012	286	717	533	477	1,026	504	327	1,301
Seattle, Wash.*	2,097	37	42	296	85	243	206	182	314	198	110	384
Portland, Ore.	1,861	41	25	244	61	191	107	116	306	131	90	549
Sacramento, Calif.	841	15	46	63	58	85	77	56	178	54	43	166
San Diego, Calif.*	1,723	76	57	409	82	198	143	123	228	121	84	202

Source: *Financial Survey of Urban Housing*
Metropolitan district.

TABLE D 24

First Mortgages, Number by Term in Years: Owner-occupied, 52 Cities; Rented, 47 Cities, by Geographic Division, January 1, 1934

All terms of loan	1 year or less	2 years	3 years	4 years	5 years	6 or 7 years	8 or 9 years	10 years	11 or 12 years	13 or 14 years	15 years or more	RENTED
7,474	326	229	1,071	261	1,476	475	417	858	916	432	1,013	47 cities
140	9	3	4	1	4	3	5	6	31	14	60	3 New England cities
21		1	1		1			1	6	2	9	Worcester, Mass.
113	9	2	1	1	3	3	5	5	25	12	47	Providence, R.I.*
6			2								4	Waterbury, Conn.
178	5	5	16	6	61	9	6	15	24	13	18	3 Mid. Atlantic cities
21		2	5		9		1	2		1	1	Binghamton, N.Y.
31	2	2	1			1		2	7	7	9	Trenton, N.J.
126	3	1	10	6	52	8	5	11	17	5	8	Erie, Pa.
1,798	154	29	88	22	152	57	65	177	439	221	394	5 E. N. Central cities
988	148	19	20	9	68	23	36	60	153	138	314	Cleveland, Ohio*
385	2	4	7	4	49	12	10	72	139	52	34	Indianapolis, Ind.
236	1	1	9	2	13	8	9	32	114	15	32	Peoria, Ill.
57	1	1	15	1	7	2	5	5	12	3	5	Kenosha, Wis.
132	2	4	37	6	15	12	5	8	21	13	9	Racine, Wis.
1,992	41	51	322	78	569	141	121	275	179	58	157	10 W. N. Central cities
611	14	14	157	20	140	36	39	76	49	23	43	Minneapolis, Minn.
159	1	6	28	9	59	9	7	9	10	7	14	St. Paul, Minn.
278	10	6	23	14	123	23	16	21	9	7	26	Des Moines, Iowa
74	4	5	28	2	6	6	10	6	6		1	St. Joseph, Mo.
110	5	6	30	4	10	9	5	20	6	3	12	Springfield, Mo.
54	1	2	8	2	26	1		4	2	1	7	Fargo, N.D.
121	1	2	10	8	65	9	3	12	3	2	6	Sioux Falls, S.D.
124	1	3	10	9	36	16	5	17	14	1	12	Lincoln, Neb.
206	3	4	14	1	35	12	14	60	55	2	6	Topeka, Kan.
255	1	3	14	9	69	20	22	50	25	12	30	Wichita, Kan.
729	30	29	102	37	283	53	26	68	40	20	61	8 S. Atlantic cities
16	5		2				1		4		4	Hagerstown, Md.
89	11	8	44	5	4	5	5	2	3		2	Richmond, Va.
39	2		1		2	2	5	11	5	2	9	Wheeling, W.Va.*
27			4	1	5	6		3	2		6	Asheville, N.C.
48	1	1	1	2	2	8	2	10	8	3	10	Greensboro, N.C.
43	2	4	8	1	5	2	2	13	2	1	3	Columbia, S.C.
432	6	16	36	27	239	26	9	27	13	11	22	Atlanta, Ga.*
35	3		6	1	6	4	2	2	3	3	5	Jacksonville, Fla.
210	11	10	18	5	44	14	11	20	22	6	49	3 E. S. Central cities
13			1		3	3	1	2	1	1	1	Paducah, Ky.
140	9	10	16	3	33	6	6	6	14	3	34	Birmingham, Ala.*
57	2		1	2	8	5	4	12	7	2	14	Jackson, Miss.
868	31	29	84	40	198	82	77	124	74	38	91	6 W. S. Central cities
124	15	11	26	11	11	15	7	5	7	2	14	Little Rock, Ark.
34			1	1	2		1	5	6	6	12	Baton Rouge, La.
279	5	3	10	6	61	22	21	57	38	16	40	Oklahoma City, Okla.
75	1	3	8	8	13	16	11	9	2	2	2	Austin, Tex.
312	7	9	36	12	106	26	32	37	16	10	21	Dallas, Tex.
44	3	3	3	2	5	3	5	11	5	2	2	Wichita Falls, Tex.
406	6	28	142	16	47	32	27	29	16	13	50	5 Mountain cities
22	2	7		1	3	3	1	1	2		2	Butte, Mont.
26		1	8	1	1	6	2	2	4		1	Boise, Idaho
33	1	2	8		4	5	6	3		2	2	Pueblo, Colo.
124	1	9	46	6	18	12	7	9	2	3	11	Phoenix, Ariz.
201	2	9	80	8	21	6	11	14	8	8	34	Salt Lake City, Utah
1,153	39	45	295	56	138	84	79	144	91	49	133	4 Pacific cities
329	7	13	67	13	56	29	18	40	30	23	33	Seattle, Wash.*
268	6	3	75	9	22	17	13	33	22	6	62	Portland, Ore.
137	2	12	17	11	16	16	12	17	12	7	15	Sacramento, Calif.
419	24	17	136	23	44	22	36	54	27	13	23	San Diego, Calif.*

TABLE D 25

Second and Third Mortgages on Owner-occupied Dwellings, Number by Term in Years, 46 Cities by Geographic Division, January 1, 1934

	All terms of loan	1 year or less	2 years	3 years	4 years	5 years	6 or 7 years	8 or 9 years	10 years	11 or 12 years	13 or 14 years	15 years or more
46 cities	3,620	349	143	417	241	646	443	291	305	358	173	254
3 New England cities	271	5	3	19	11	34	35	27	38	41	14	44
Worcester, Mass.	108	1	–	5	3	17	12	13	16	19	6	16
Providence, R.I.*	108	2	2	9	7	13	16	10	11	13	6	19
Waterbury, Conn.	55	2	1	5	1	4	7	4	11	9	2	9
4 Mid. Atlantic cities	264	5	6	10	17	82	37	21	23	17	12	34
Binghamton, N.Y.	16	1	1	2		8	3	1				
Syracuse, N.Y.	121		1	2	4	39	20	12	10	8	7	18
Trenton, N.J.	37	1	1		3	1	4	2	9	5	3	8
Erie, Pa.	90	3	3	6	10	34	10	6	4	4	2	8
6 E. N. Central cities	1,238	191	34	123	49	133	110	86	88	207	116	101
Cleveland, Ohio*	1,050	183	29	85	41	106	95	77	69	162	108	95
Indianapolis, Ind.	44	3		3	2	8	6	2	6	8	4	2
Peoria, Ill.	63	1	1	8	4	13	1		5	28		2
Lansing, Mich.	10		2	2		1	2	1	2			
Kenosha, Wis.	23	2		6	1	2	3	3	2	2	2	
Racine, Wis.	48	2	2	19	1	3	3	3	4	7	2	2
10 W. N. Central cities	425	28	21	58	27	112	42	27	50	36	9	17
Minneapolis, Minn.	90	4	6	18	7	25	10	6	7	2	1	4
St. Paul, Minn.	20	1	3	3	2	8		2			1	
Des Moines, Iowa	36	4		7	2	8	2	7	3	2		1
St. Joseph, Mo.	35	3	3	4	1	8	8	4	1	1	1	1
Springfield, Mo.	27	1	1	6	1	5	5	1	6	1		
Fargo, N.D.	23	1	2	1	2	9	4		1	1	1	
Sioux Falls, S.D.	25	4	1	6	2	5	2	1	2	1		1
Lincoln, Neb.	41	4	1	6	4	14	1	1	3		2	5
Topeka, Kan.	72	4	1	4	1	19	3	2	14	24	1	2
Wichita, Kan.	56	3	3	3	5	11	7	3	13	4	2	2
8 S. Atlantic cities	484	42	27	63	43	128	82	39	26	18	3	13
Hagerstown, Md.	18	6		2	1	2	3		1	2		1
Richmond, Va.	139	8	11	25	9	23	32	18	5	6	1	1
Wheeling, W. Va.*	17	1	1		3		3	2	1	3		3
Asheville, N.C.	17	7	1		1	2	2	2	2			
Greensboro, N.C.	38	4		1	5	8	7	2	6			5
Columbia, S.C.	14	1	1	5	2	4	1					
Atlanta, Ga.*	226	14	11	28	21	87	32	14	10	6	2	3
Jacksonville, Fla.	15	1	2	4	1	2	2	1	1	1		
2 E. S. Central cities	145	21	7	16	19	25	20	17	9	3		8
Birmingham, Ala.*	129	21	6	14	18	21	19	13	8	2		7
Jackson, Miss.	16		1	2	1	4	1	4	1	1		1
5 W. S. Central cities	297	31	17	36	29	50	50	28	25	15	7	9
Little Rock, Ark.	52	7	6	10	5	7	6	6	2	2		1
Oklahoma City, Okla.	132	18	9	12	13	19	19	9	16	9	5	3
Austin, Tex.	17	1	1	4	2	2	5	1	1			
Dallas, Tex.	86	4	1	9	8	20	17	11	6	4	2	4
Wichita Falls, Tex.	10	1		1	1	2	3	1				1
4 Mountain cities	97	6	6	22	10	8	16	6	8	5	3	7
Boise, Idaho	16	3		3	2		2	1	4			1
Pueblo, Colo.	12		1	2		2	3	3		1		
Phoenix, Ariz.	20	1	3	7	3	2	3					1
Salt Lake City, Utah	49	2	2	10	5	4	8	2	4	4	3	5
4 Pacific cities	399	22	22	70	36	74	51	40	38	16	9	21
Seattle, Wash.*	61	5	3	11	7	12	9	5	5	1	2	1
Portland, Ore.	101	6	4	20	11	14	8	9	9	8	4	8
Sacramento, Calif.	81		8	10	9	22	10	8	10		1	3
San Diego, Calif.*	156	11	7	29	9	26	24	18	14	7	2	9

Source: Financial Survey of Urban Housing. Similar data for rented properties are available for 17 cities, but the samples were so small that it seemed inadvisable to present them here. This information may be had from the files of the National Bureau of Economic Research.
*Metropolitan district.

TABLE D 26

Number of Reports, Unweighted Average Contract, and Effective Interest Rates (per cent) by Priority for Identical Properties: First Mortgages, Owner-occupied and Rented, 52 Cities; Second and Third Mortgages, Owner-occupied, 49 Cities; Rented,
20 Cities; Land Contracts, Owner-occupied, 33 Cities; Rented, 9 Cities, by Geographic Division, January 1, 1934

| | FIRST MORTGAGES | | | | | | SECOND AND THIRD MORTGAGES | | |
| | OWNER-OCCUPIED | | | RENTED | | | OWNER-OCCUPIED | | |
	Number reporting	Contract rate	Effective rate	Number reporting	Contract rate	Effective rate	Number reporting	Contract rate	Effective rate
All cities[1]	25,263	6.29	6.73	3,351	6.39	6.93	1,400	6.54	7.06
New England cities	1,032	5.99	6.18	117	6.00	6.13	116	6.92	7.60
Portland, Me.	215	6.05	6.22	35	6.13	6.29	15	7.40	7.57
Worcester, Mass.	127	5.68	5.75	18	5.78	5.80	30	6.60	7.01
Providence, R.I.*	597	6.15	6.43	52	6.07	6.25	43	7.47	8.47
Waterbury, Conn.	93	5.84	5.89	12	6.00	6.06	28	6.14	6.59
Mid. Atlantic cities	993	5.69	5.98	125	5.74	6.08	95	5.89	6.47
Binghamton, N.Y.	68	5.95	6.27	14	5.87	6.50	9	5.94	6.88
Syracuse, N.Y.	109	5.50	5.73	19	5.63	5.82	44	5.89	6.45
Trenton, N.J.	225	5.91	6.16	25	5.92	6.62	16	5.88	5.98
Erie, Pa.	591	5.95	6.48	67	5.97	6.47	26	5.87	6.73
E. N. Central cities	6,326	6.23	6.53	834	6.23	6.57	607	6.34	6.72
Cleveland, Ohio*	4,203	6.18	6.49	511	6.15	6.46	522	6.35	6.76
Indianapolis, Ind.	460	6.41	6.70	135	6.43	6.88	6	6.50	6.53
Peoria, Ill.	612	6.69	7.08	73	6.71	6.95	32	6.42	6.60
Lansing, Mich.	207	6.37	6.57	27	6.59	6.74	6	6.62	6.92
Kenosha, Wis.	273	6.09	6.42	22	6.39	6.76	13	5.62	5.84
Racine, Wis.	571	5.97	6.30	66	6.04	6.46	28	5.94	6.21
W. N. Central cities	5,231	6.18	6.82	825	6.16	6.83	122	6.19	6.85
Minneapolis, Minn.	2,152	5.97	6.65	264	5.99	6.69	43	6.26	7.30
St. Paul, Minn.	485	5.94	6.57	87	5.93	6.58	6	6.00	6.42
Des Moines, Iowa	401	6.17	6.83	129	6.32	6.97	6	6.17	6.48
St. Joseph, Mo.	211	6.32	6.94	36	6.03	6.56	7	5.14	5.19
Springfield, Mo.	330	7.27	8.12	44	7.39	8.18	8	7.03	7.24
Fargo, N.D.	169	6.52	6.61	22	6.61	6.83	5	6.80	6.80
Sioux Falls, S.D.	207	6.33	6.96	48	6.05	6.90	7	6.14	6.26
Lincoln, Neb.	262	6.27	6.67	55	6.30	6.78	11	5.95	6.23
Topeka, Kan.	532	7.24	7.69	53	6.84	7.40	22	7.06	7.06
Wichita, Kan.	482	6.61	7.40	87	6.50	7.43	7	6.29	7.49
S. Atlantic cities	2,729	6.42	7.26	334	6.58	7.53	123	6.50	7.02
Hagerstown, Md.	132	5.91	6.29	18	5.81	6.09	9	5.33	5.46
Richmond, Va.	489	6.04	7.02	48	6.00	6.88	27	6.26	6.86
Wheeling, W.Va.*	200	6.18	6.48	28	6.00	6.29	11	6.09	6.41
Asheville, N.C.	223	5.95	6.47	5	5.90	6.58	5	6.00	6.88
Greensboro, N.C.	123	5.98	6.26	21	6.00	7.05	5	6.00	6.32
Charleston, S.C.	89	6.89	7.60	14	6.57	7.04			
Columbia, S.C.	118	7.19	7.94	19	6.61	7.15	1		
Atlanta, Ga.*	1,249	6.66	7.73	165	6.85	7.95	61	7.11	7.90
Jacksonville, Fla.	106	6.80	7.92	16	6.78	7.88	4	7.50	7.50
E. S. Central cities	1,564	6.89	7.46	98	6.74	7.44	102	7.20	7.35
Paducah, Ky.	78	6.03	7.10	4	6.00	6.80	2		
Birmingham, Ala.*	1,416	6.96	7.52	64	6.75	7.47	93	7.29	7.47
Jackson, Miss.	70	6.66	7.20	30	6.78	7.32	7	6.86	6.89
W. S. Central cities	1,952	7.17	7.80	352	7.07	7.85	68	7.74	8.00
Little Rock, Ark.	228	6.43	7.30	50	6.58	7.65	7	7.14	8.40
Baton Rouge, La.	38	7.31	7.62	9	7.11	8.47			
Oklahoma City, Okla.	632	7.09	7.77	95	6.69	7.41	35	8.04	8.14
Austin, Tex.	193	7.58	7.83	35	7.61	8.21	7	7.43	7.43
Dallas, Tex.	716	7.34	7.96	140	7.43	8.17	14	7.57	7.74
Wichita Falls, Tex.	145	7.25	7.77	23	7.20	8.08	5	8.00	8.14
Mountain cities	1,568	7.23	7.65	157	7.34	7.94	32	7.85	8.15
Butte, Mont.	233	7.93	8.36	9	8.22	9.82			
Boise, Idaho	222	7.46	8.20	14	7.64	8.65	2		
Casper, Wyo.	43	6.86	7.49	11	7.09	7.33	1		
Pueblo, Colo.	184	6.72	7.24	14	6.79	7.74	2		
Phoenix, Ariz.	228	7.57	8.04	44	7.63	8.30	10	8.00	8.17
Salt Lake City, Utah	658	7.17	7.50	65	7.18	7.62	17	7.82	8.14
Pacific cities	3,868	6.60	7.22	509	6.65	7.37	135	6.86	7.32
Seattle, Wash.*	1,527	6.68	7.27	122	6.59	7.19	38	6.96	7.30
Portland, Ore.	888	6.30	6.78	129	6.24	7.33	29	6.61	7.25
Sacramento, Calif.	444	6.70	7.38	50	6.98	7.68	17	6.88	7.12
San Diego, Calif.*	1,009	6.86	7.73	208	6.91	7.74	51	7.00	7.48

Source: *Financial Survey of Urban Housing*. *Percentage not shown for fewer than 3 reports.*
Metropolitan district.
[1]*Geographic division and 'All cities' percentages weighted by estimated total debt, by tenure and priority, in each city (RPI).*

Number of Reports, Unweighted Average Contract, and Effective Interest Rates (per cent) by Priority for Identical Properties: First Mortgages, Owner-occupied and Rented, 52 Cities; Second and Third Mortgages, Owner-occupied, 49 Cities; Rented,
20 Cities; Land Contracts, Owner-occupied, 33 Cities; Rented, 9 Cities, by Geographic Division, January I, 1934

SECOND AND THIRD MORTGAGES RENTED			LAND CONTRACTS OWNER-OCCUPIED			RENTED			
Number reporting	Contract rate	Effective rate	Number reporting	Contract rate	Effective rate	Number reporting	Contract rate	Effective rate	
89	6.53	7.43	2,124	6.47	6.68	38	6.39	6.52	All cities[1]
12	7.04	8.46							New England cities
2									Portland, Me.
1									Worcester, Mass.
4	8.00	8.88							Providence, R.I.*
5	6.10	8.04							Waterbury, Conn.
13	5.54	5.69	3	5.67	5.97				Mid. Atlantic cities
2									Binghamton, N.Y.
5	5.60	5.66							Syracuse, N.Y.
1									Trenton, N.J.
5	4.80	6.00	3	5.67	5.97				Erie, Pa.
34	6.34	7.28	407	6.33	6.46	7	6.08	6.08	E. N. Central cities
26	6.35	7.30	56	6.25	6.36	4	5.88	5.88	Cleveland, Ohio*
			26	6.87	7.06				Indianapolis, Ind.
2			42	6.33	6.44				Peoria, Ill.
			166	6.05	6.14	3	6.33	6.33	Lansing, Mich.
			29	5.98	6.23				Kenosha, Wis.
6	6.00	6.28	88	5.97	6.07				Racine, Wis.
3	6.00	6.20	511	6.20	6.46	15	6.24	6.38	W. N. Central cities
3	6.00	6.20	239	6.10	6.48	8	6.31	6.44	Minneapolis, Minn.
			48	5.89	6.07	3	6.00	6.17	St. Paul, Minn.
			91	6.35	6.57	2			Des Moines, Iowa
									St. Joseph, Mo.
									Springfield, Mo.
			7	7.14	7.30				Fargo, N.D.
			34	6.54	6.66	2			Sioux Falls, S.D.
			7	5.71	5.76				Lincoln, Neb.
			47	7.24	7.31				Topeka, Kan.
			38	6.93	6.99				Wichita, Kan.
6	6.57	6.88	18	6.49	6.72				S. Atlantic cities
									Hagerstown, Md.
3	6.00	6.17							Richmond, Va.
			4	6.50	6.63				Wheeling, W.Va.*
			9	5.88	5.91				Asheville, N.C.
									Greensboro, N.C.
									Charleston, S.C.
									Columbia, S.C.
3	7.33	7.83	5	7.00	7.54				Atlanta, Ga.*
									Jacksonville, Fla.
2			39	7.17	7.65				E. S. Central cities
									Paducah, Ky.
			39	7.17	7.65				Birmingham, Ala.*
2									Jackson, Miss.
7	8.00	10.15	40	7.15	7.48				W. S. Central cities
			3	6.00	6.10				Little Rock, Ark.
									Baton Rouge, La.
1			9	6.94	7.56				Oklahoma City, Okla.
			23	8.00	8.17				Austin, Tex.
6	8.00	10.15	5	7.50	7.80				Dallas, Tex.
									Wichita Falls, Tex.
			517	7.26	7.40	1			Mountain cities
			55	7.32	7.41				Butte, Mont.
			37	6.81	7.09				Boise, Idaho
			48	8.26	8.43				Casper, Wyo.
			3	6.67	6.67				Pueblo, Colo.
			26	7.79	7.99				Phoenix, Ariz.
			348	7.13	7.25	1			Salt Lake City, Utah
12	6.89	7.20	589	6.54	6.81	15	6.82	7.04	Pacific cities
5	6.80	6.98	433	6.80	7.10	6	6.83	6.97	Seattle, Wash.*
2			53	6.33	6.39				Portland, Ore.
			53	5.28	5.76				Sacramento, Calif.
5	7.00	7.46	50	6.60	6.75	9	6.80	7.23	San Diego, Calif.*

TABLE D 27

Contract and Effective Interest Rates (per cent), Simple and Weighted Averages by Priority: First Mortgages, Owner-occupied and Rented, 52 Cities; Second and Third Mortgages, Owner-occupied, 49 Cities; Rented, 23 Cities; Land Contracts, Owner-occupied, 33 Cities; Rented, 9 Cities, by Geographic Division, January 1, 1934

	FIRST MORTGAGES								SECOND AND THIRD MORTGAGES OWNER-OCCUPIED			
	OWNER-OCCUPIED				RENTED							
	Contract Interest Rate		Effective Interest Rate		Contract Interest Rate		Effective Interest Rate		Contract Interest Rate		Effective Interest Rate	
	Simple average	Weighted[2] average	Simple average	Weighted[2] average	Simple average	Weighted[2] average	Simple average	Weighted[2] average	Simple average	Weighted[2] average	Simple average	Weighted[2] average
All cities[1]	6.26	6.18	6.73	6.54	6.40	6.25	6.93	6.76	6.51	6.44	7.06	7.02
New England cities	5.94	5.93	6.18	6.17	5.96	5.88	6.13	6.20	6.83	6.76	7.60	7.85
Portland, Me.	6.01	6.00	6.22	6.10	6.07	6.04	6.29	6.11	7.02	6.24	7.57	11.63
Worcester, Mass.	5.65	5.64	5.75	5.71	5.70	5.47	5.80	5.76	6.82	6.70	7.01	9.03
Providence, R.I.*	6.06	6.06	6.43	6.45	6.06	6.00	6.25	6.40	7.20	7.17	8.47	7.42
Waterbury, Conn.	5.92	5.90	5.89	5.84	5.90	5.93	6.06	6.06	6.04	6.05	6.59	6.53
Mid. Atlantic cities	5.63	5.65	5.98	5.91	5.62	5.72	6.08	6.03	5.85	5.87	6.47	6.41
Binghamton, N.Y.	5.82	5.80	6.27	6.18	5.78	6.35	6.50	6.18	5.63	5.67	6.88	7.45
Syracuse, N.Y.	5.43	5.46	5.73	5.69	5.46	5.54	5.82	5.83	5.86	5.87	6.45	6.34
Trenton, N.J.	5.89	5.92	6.16	6.03	5.87	5.77	6.62	6.29	5.88	5.92	5.98	5.85
Erie, Pa.	5.94	5.94	6.48	6.36	5.94	5.95	6.47	6.48	5.96	5.98	6.73	6.69
E. N. Central cities	6.19	6.18	6.53	6.45	6.22	6.15	6.57	6.46	6.32	6.19	6.72	6.54
Cleveland, Ohio*	6.14	6.14	6.49	6.42	6.14	6.09	6.46	6.35	6.32	6.18	6.76	6.58
Indianapolis, Ind.	6.41	6.34	6.70	6.52	6.46	6.34	6.88	6.76	6.61	6.53	6.53	6.38
Peoria, Ill.	6.58	6.56	7.08	6.88	6.64	6.39	6.95	6.76	6.30	6.26	6.60	6.40
Lansing, Mich.	6.30	6.20	6.57	6.41	6.49	6.35	6.74	6.75	6.55	6.53	6.92	6.82
Kenosha, Wis.	6.08	6.09	6.42	6.38	6.24	6.24	6.76	6.69	5.94	5.84	5.84	5.47
Racine, Wis.	5.96	5.95	6.30	6.34	5.98	5.96	6.46	6.47	5.83	5.85	6.21	6.36
W. N. Central cities	6.19	6.09	6.82	6.54	6.22	6.08	6.83	6.72	6.37	6.29	6.85	6.55
Minneapolis, Minn.	5.98	5.92	6.65	6.31	6.02	5.91	6.69	6.68	6.12	6.08	7.30	6.62
St. Paul, Minn.	5.93	5.93	6.57	6.46	5.96	5.94	6.58	6.50	6.21	6.07	6.42	6.29
Des Moines, Iowa	6.21	5.91	6.83	6.48	6.36	6.18	6.97	6.64	6.53	6.60	6.48	6.10
St. Joseph, Mo.	6.30	6.21	6.94	6.80	6.25	6.12	6.56	6.69	6.02	5.97	5.19	6.01
Springfield, Mo.	7.31	7.04	8.12	7.51	7.26	7.00	8.18	7.58	7.14	7.06	7.24	7.01
Fargo, N.D.	6.55	6.38	6.61	6.40	6.62	6.64	6.83	6.92	6.62	6.58	6.80	6.97
Sioux Falls, S.D.	6.25	6.12	6.96	6.57	6.19	6.01	6.90	6.71	6.97	6.72	6.26	6.80
Lincoln, Neb.	6.32	6.22	6.67	6.52	6.32	6.14	6.78	6.66	6.38	6.32	6.23	6.67
Topeka, Kan.	7.19	7.03	7.69	7.51	7.16	6.86	7.40	6.99	7.16	6.93	7.06	6.85
Wichita, Kan.	6.67	6.48	7.40	7.11	6.69	6.34	7.43	7.23	6.96	6.67	7.49	6.44
S. Atlantic cities	6.41	6.25	7.26	6.91	6.63	6.32	7.53	7.25	6.48	6.47	7.02	7.03
Hagerstown, Md.	5.88	5.87	6.29	6.12	5.92	5.73	6.09	5.64	5.79	5.98	5.46	6.03
Richmond, Va.	5.98	5.97	7.02	6.72	6.00	6.00	6.88	6.83	6.04	6.12	6.86	6.86
Wheeling, W.Va.*	6.16	5.93	6.48	6.39	6.05	6.05	6.29	6.15	6.05	6.03	6.41	5.93
Asheville, N.C.	5.96	5.95	6.47	6.39	5.94	5.83	6.58	6.35	6.00	6.00	6.88	7.28
Greensboro, N.C.	5.96	5.97	6.26	6.35	5.98	5.98	7.05	7.75	6.04	6.10	6.32	7.28
Charleston, S.C.	6.84	6.71	7.60	7.12	6.65	6.42	7.04	6.87				
Columbia, S.C.	7.11	6.87	7.94	7.39	6.99	6.94	7.15	6.72	7.53	7.27		
Atlanta, Ga.	6.66	6.40	7.73	7.25	6.83	6.35	7.95	7.60	7.08	6.90	7.90	7.55
Jacksonville, Fla.	6.94	6.78	7.92	7.35	7.25	6.80	7.88	7.14	7.55	7.77	7.50	7.86
E. S. Central cities	6.87	6.59	7.46	7.09	6.72	6.39	7.44	7.17	7.08	7.04	7.35	7.23
Paducah, Ky.	6.16	5.93	7.10	7.29	6.24	6.16	6.80	6.70	6.15	6.73		
Birmingham, Ala.*	6.93	6.63	7.52	7.10	6.72	6.37	7.47	7.19	7.31	7.13	7.47	7.25
Jackson, Miss.	6.71	6.52	7.20	6.93	6.81	6.60	7.32	7.11	6.49	6.79	6.89	7.14
W. S. Central cities	7.21	6.99	7.80	7.45	7.15	7.07	7.85	7.50	7.62	7.51	8.00	7.93
Little Rock, Ark.	6.50	6.26	7.30	6.88	6.61	6.32	7.65	7.34	6.88	6.23	8.40	6.86
Baton Rouge, La.	7.27	7.17	7.62	7.55	7.31	6.78	8.47	7.61				
Oklahoma City, Okla.	7.12	6.82	7.77	7.38	6.91	7.02	7.41	6.98	7.84	7.76	8.14	8.42
Austin, Tex.	7.61	7.41	7.83	7.52	7.61	7.59	8.21	9.16	7.78	7.61	7.43	7.14
Dallas, Tex.	7.36	7.22	7.96	7.63	7.37	7.21	8.17	7.76	7.52	7.58	7.74	7.76
Wichita Falls, Tex.	7.50	7.22	7.77	7.48	7.53	7.12	8.08	8.02	8.00	7.87	8.14	8.14
Mountain cities	7.21	7.02	7.65	6.60	7.32	7.06	7.94	7.36	7.37	7.37	8.15	7.68
Butte, Mont.	7.95	7.82	8.36	8.32	8.10	7.45	9.82	8.71				
Boise, Idaho	7.43	6.95	8.20	7.91	7.75	7.64	8.65	8.17	7.38	6.75		
Casper, Wyo.	7.03	6.93	7.49	7.31	6.94	6.85	7.33	7.05	6.98	7.30		
Pueblo, Colo.	6.67	6.62	7.24	7.08	7.36	7.04	7.74	7.16	7.36	7.53		
Phoenix, Ariz.	7.57	7.31	8.04	7.60	7.53	7.39	8.30	7.94	7.65	7.79	8.17	8.21
Salt Lake City, Utah	7.14	6.97	7.50	5.83	7.16	6.86	7.62	6.97	7.35	7.32	8.14	7.58
Pacific cities	6.57	6.34	7.22	6.92	6.70	6.42	7.37	7.06	6.86	6.85	7.32	7.09
Seattle, Wash.*	6.67	6.25	7.27	6.95	6.69	6.26	7.19	6.79	6.93	6.87	7.30	7.06
Portland, Ore.	6.21	6.09	6.78	6.45	6.36	6.20	7.33	7.10	6.58	6.69	7.25	6.99
Sacramento, Calif.	6.70	6.58	7.38	7.14	6.89	6.82	7.68	7.23	7.03	6.83	7.12	6.83
San Diego, Calif.*	6.86	6.79	7.73	7.48	6.93	6.88	7.74	7.66	7.00	7.00	7.48	7.31

Source: Financial Survey of Urban Housing. Contract interest rates based on total number reporting interest rate. This number of reports is shown in Table D 28 for first mortgages; for other priorities the number of reports is approximately the same as shown in Table D 15. Effective interest rate based on number reporting both contract and effective interest rates. This number of reports is shown in Table D 26. Percentage not shown for fewer than 3 reports.

*Metropolitan district.

[1] Geographic division 'All cities' percentages weighted by estimated debt, by tenure and priority, in each city (RPI).

[2] Individual interest rates in each city weighted by amount of principal outstanding for specified priority.

TABLE D 27

Contract and Effective Interest Rates (per cent), Simple and Weighted Averages by Priority: First Mortgages, Owner-occupied and Rented, 52 Cities; Second and Third Mortgages, Owner-occupied, 49 Cities; Rented, 23 Cities; Land Contracts, Owner-occupied, 33 Cities; Rented, 9 Cities, by Geographic Division, January 1, 1934

SECOND AND THIRD MORTGAGES RENTED				LAND CONTRACTS OWNER-OCCUPIED				LAND CONTRACTS RENTED				
Contract Interest Rate		Effective Interest Rate		Contract Interest Rate		Effective Interest Rate		Contract Interest Rate		Effective Interest Rate		
Simple average	Weighted[2] average	Simple average	Weighted[2] average	Simple average	Weighted[2] average	Simple average	Weighted[2] average	Simple average	Weighted[2] average	Simple average	Weighted[2] average	
6.55	6.40	7.43	7.16	6.46	6.42	6.68	6.54	6.40	6.33	6.52	6.40	**All cities[1]**
6.69	6.54	8.46	8.38									**New England cities**
6.59	6.58											Portland, Me.
7.04	6.64											Worcester, Mass.
7.33	7.10	8.88	9.83									Providence, R.I.*
5.95	5.96	8.04	6.97									Waterbury, Conn.
5.83	5.82	5.69	5.71	5.46	5.84	5.97	6.18					**Mid. Atlantic cities**
5.75	5.65											Binghamton, N.Y.
5.83	5.83	5.66	5.57									Syracuse, N.Y.
6.00	5.92											Trenton, N.J.
5.81	5.79	6.00	7.38	5.46	5.84	5.97	6.18					Erie, Pa.
6.35	6.24	7.28	6.78	6.28	6.24	6.46	6.45	6.15	6.04	6.08	5.89	**E. N. Central cities**
6.36	6.25	7.30	6.78	6.19	6.27	6.36	6.44	6.11	5.86	5.88	5.60	Cleveland, Ohio*
6.36	6.03			6.72	6.58	7.06	7.02					Indianapolis, Ind.
				6.32	6.38	6.44	6.50					Peoria, Ill.
				6.08	6.04	6.14	6.12	6.20	6.25	6.33	6.24	Lansing, Mich.
				6.03	6.01	6.23	6.17					Kenosha, Wis.
5.98	5.99	6.28	6.57	5.94	5.93	6.07	6.02					Racine, Wis.
6.02	5.19	6.20	6.19	6.22	6.22	6.46	6.38	6.16	6.12	6.38	6.26	**W. N. Central cities**
6.02	5.19	6.20	6.19	6.05	6.05	6.48	6.39	6.09	6.09	6.44	6.27	Minneapolis, Minn.
				6.04	6.02	6.07	6.01	6.20	6.09	6.17	6.23	St. Paul, Minn.
				6.38	6.38	6.57	6.45	6.29	6.14			Des Moines, Iowa
												St. Joseph, Mo.
				6.86	6.86	7.30	6.94					Springfield, Mo.
				6.37	6.22	6.66	6.65	6.55	6.46			Fargo, N.D.
				6.06	6.23	5.76	5.93					Sioux Falls, S.D.
				7.20	7.35	7.31	7.35					Lincoln, Neb.
				7.01	6.96	6.99	6.91					Topeka, Kan.
												Wichita, Kan.
6.55	6.56	6.88	6.84	6.18	6.95	6.72	6.55					**S. Atlantic cities**
												Hagerstown, Md.
6.05	6.06	6.17	6.16									Richmond, Va.
												Wheeling, W.Va.*
				5.82	7.57	6.63	6.45					Asheville, N.C.
				5.92	5.96	5.91	5.98					Greensboro, N.C.
												Charleston, S.C.
												Columbia, S.C.
7.22	7.24	7.83	7.75	6.93	6.86	7.54	7.17					Atlanta, Ga.
												Jacksonville, Fla.
6.33	6.02			7.13	6.75	7.65	6.90					**E. S. Central cities**
												Paducah, Ky.
				7.13	6.75	7.65	6.90					Birmingham, Ala.*
6.33	6.02											Jackson, Miss.
7.53	7.74	10.15	11.71	6.66	7.35	7.48	7.50					**W. S. Central cities**
				6.50	6.35	6.10	6.00					Little Rock, Ark.
												Baton Rouge, La.
7.72	7.93			5.07	7.23	7.56	7.71					Oklahoma City, Okla.
				8.00	8.00	8.17	8.20					Austin, Tex.
7.30	7.50	10.15	11.71	7.68	7.66	7.80	7.73					Dallas, Tex.
												Wichita Falls, Tex.
7.78	7.76			7.18	7.22	7.40	7.36	6.89	6.74			**Mountain cities**
				7.54	7.55	7.41	7.69					Butte, Mont.
				6.62	6.92	7.09	7.10					Boise, Idaho
				8.17	8.12	8.43	8.77					Casper, Wyo.
				6.67	6.35	6.67	6.43					Pueblo, Colo.
7.70	7.84			7.80	7.82	7.99	7.88					Phoenix, Ariz.
7.80	7.74			7.03	7.08	7.25	7.16	6.89	6.74			Salt Lake City, Utah
7.13	6.91	7.20	7.36	6.60	6.48	6.81	6.44	6.79	6.71	7.04	6.95	**Pacific cities**
6.97	6.95	6.98	7.39	6.78	6.66	7.10	6.57	6.79	6.73	6.97	6.93	Seattle, Wash.*
6.90	6.73			6.39	6.34	6.39	6.38					Portland, Ore.
7.16	7.05			5.82	5.58	5.76	5.73					Sacramento, Calif.
7.60	6.95	7.46	7.32	6.65	6.48	6.75	6.44	6.79	6.66	7.23	7.02	San Diego, Calif.*

TABLE D 28

Mortgaged Dwellings, Number reporting Contract Interest Rates on First Mortgages by Tenure and by Interest Rate Groups, 52 Cities by Geographic Division, January 1, 1934

	All contract interest rates	4.0 or less	4.1-4.9	5.0	5.1-5.9	6.0	6.1-6.9	7.0	7.1-7.9	8.0	8.1-8.9	9.0	9.1-9.9	10.0	11.0	12.0
						OWNER-OCCUPIED										
52 cities	62,628	563	59	4,182	1,895	32,500	2,535	12,331	1,128	6,534	256	197	24	402	4	18
4 New England cities	4,195	13	6	224	717	3,003	44	78	11	97		2				
Portland, Me.	633	4		30	6	543	19	19	9	3						
Worcester, Mass.	1,110	3	3	71	673	324	19	11		6						
Providence, R.I.*	1,981	6	3	94	17	1,715	6	48	2	88		2				
Waterbury, Conn.	471			29	21	421										
4 Mid. Atlantic cities	4,247	21	3	761	163	3,274	8	4	5	5		1	2			
Binghamton, N.Y.	257	2		17	52	185			1							
Syracuse, N.Y.	975	1	1	527	67	376	1		1	1		1				
Trenton, N.J.	1,572	6	1	146	35	1,377	1	2	1	2		1				
Erie, Pa.	1,443	12	1	71	9	1,336	6	2	2	2			2			
6 E. N. Central cities	18,756	114	22	967	104	12,873	940	3,228	210	282	3	10		3		
Cleveland, Ohio*	13,602	84	11	669	50	10,155	336	1,999	64	225	3	6				
Indianapolis, Ind.	1,506	5		87	13	463	503	387	11	36				1		
Peoria, Ill.	1,226	7	5	34	18	418	26	603	93	19		3				
Lansing, Mich.	359			40	4	143	50	121	1							
Kenosha, Wis.	654	5	2	26	3	521	10	71	16							
Racine, Wis.	1,409	13	4	111	16	1,173	15	47	25	2		1		2		
10 W. N. Central cities	10,854	62	7	678	536	6,119	342	1,628	288	961	123	64	10	35		1
Minneapolis, Minn.	3,707	25	2	194	323	2,853	73	177	4	50	1	1	1	3		
St. Paul, Minn.	803	6	1	60	49	656	1	15	2	13						
Des Moines, Iowa	1,242	9		139	28	628	103	281	7	45	1			1		
St. Joseph, Mo.	497	7		14	13	328	9	60	7	59						
Springfield, Mo.	732	2		21	9	107	3	219	26	319	4	20		2		
Fargo, N.D.	456	2		71	3	98	24	197	15	42		3	1			
Sioux Falls, S.D.	540	4		34	21	342	26	71	1	30		1	1	9		
Lincoln, Neb.	747	1	3	36	41	441	23	105	42	38		8		9		
Topeka, Kan.	910	2		47	24	200	19	141	139	204	115	5	2	11		1
Wichita, Kan.	1,220	4	1	62	25	466	61	362	45	161	2	26	5			
9 S. Atlantic cities	5,899	28	4	275	128	3,414	166	1,116	24	728	1	3	1	8		3
Hagerstown, Md.	350	2	2	30	12	303						1				
Richmond, Va.	1,048	2		23	9	1,005	4	1	1	1				1		1
Wheeling, W. Va.*	762	9	2	35	1	567	10	94	12	29		1	1	1		
Asheville, N.C.	380			16	5	356		1	1	1						
Greensboro, N.C.	296	1		6	3	283		3								
Charleston, S.C.	201			9		41	4	120	1	25				1		
Columbia, S.C.	332	2		14		81	7	88	1	138				1		
Atlanta, Ga.*	2,269	10		122	97	702	132	773	8	418	1	1		4		1
Jacksonville, Fla.	261	2		20	1	76	9	36		116						1
3 E. S. Central cities	2,361	12	2	154	38	767	201	325	31	814	2	2		11		2
Paducah, Ky.	209	3		6	2	179	2	3		7		1		5		1
Birmingham, Ala.*	1,897	8	2	135	35	466	181	311	29	721	2			6		1
Jackson, Miss.	255	1		13	1	122	18	11	2	86		1				
6 W. S. Central cities	4,956	14	1	314	110	990	149	1,004	278	1,778	58	77	7	167	3	6
Little Rock, Ark.	795	2		84	14	365	19	181		103	4	7	1	15		
Baton Rouge, La.	170	2		7	1	13		65	8	73				1		
Oklahoma City, Okla.	1,697	6		142	83	341	46	259	227	415	17	46	4	102	3	6
Austin, Tex.	358	2		3		18	6	79	19	230				1		
Dallas, Tex.	1,627	1	1	65	12	207	69	374	21	812	5	21	2	37		
Wichita Falls, Tex.	309	1		13		46	9	46	3	145	32	3		11		
6 Mountain cities	3,287	32	1	316	4	318	63	842	89	1,385	29	28	3	153	1	3
Butte, Mont.	366	11		36		25		6	1	179		8		100		
Boise, Idaho	502	1		43		47	4	66	2	331		3		5		
Casper, Wyo.	160	4		34		18		6	4	78	9	2		4	1	
Pueblo, Colo.	385	12		95	1	43		103	39	78	1	2	3	6		2
Phoenix, Ariz.	483	1		34		48	10	47	2	310	1	2		28		
Salt Lake City, Utah	1,371	3	1	74	3	137	49	614	41	409	18	11		10		1
4 Pacific cities	8,093	267	13	493	95	1,742	622	4,106	192	484	40	10	1	25		3
Seattle, Wash.*	2,523	23	6	159	44	446	352	1,259	32	183	3	5		9		2
Portland, Ore.	2,341	230	6	134	25	892	215	671	25	132	1	1		9		
Sacramento, Calif.	1,101	5	1	98	6	169	8	724	39	35	13	1		1		1
San Diego, Calif.*	2,128	9		102	20	235	47	1,452	96	134	23	3	1	6		

Source: Financial Survey of Urban Housing
*Metropolitan district.

Mortgaged Dwellings, Number reporting Contract Interest Rates on First Mortgages by Tenure and by Interest Rate Groups, 52 Cities by Geographic Division, January 1, 1934

								RENTED								
All contract interest rates	4.0 or less	4.1-4.9	5.0	5.1-5.9	6.0	6.1-6.9	7.0	7.1-7.9	8.0	8.1-8.9	9.0	9.1-9.9	10.0	11.0	12.0	
12,979	87	6	530	411	6,630	689	2,986	207	1,233	58	48	3	79	7	5	52 cities
896	6	2	43	133	659	16	16		17				3	1		4 New England cities
195	3		9	1	162	12	8									Portland, Me.
214	3		11	123	68	2	3		1				3			Worcester, Mass.
382		2	16	3	337	2	5		16					1		Providence, R.I.*
105			7	6	92											Waterbury, Conn.
779	4		141	54	576	1	1	2								4 Mid. Atlantic cities
73			5	23	44	1										Binghamton, N.Y.
214	2		103	20	88			1								Syracuse, N.Y.
233			27	11	193		1	1								Trenton, N.J.
259	2		6		251											Erie, Pa.
3,621	21	1	103	27	2,398	289	688	41	51	1	1					6 E. N. Central cities
2,239	14	1	67	17	1,748	47	301	7	37							Cleveland, Ohio*
482	3		6	1	139	211	114	1	7							Indianapolis, Ind.
323	1		13	6	82	6	183	27	4	1						Peoria, Ill.
147			2	1	67	16	60		1							Lansing, Mich.
125			3		88	5	25	4								Kenosha, Wis.
305	3		12	2	274	4	5	2	2		1					Racine, Wis.
2,750	12		86	131	1,639	115	464	52	182	28	21	2	14	3	1	10 W. N. Central cities
925	4		25	84	714	30	56	2	8				2			Minneapolis, Minn.
206	1		13	7	177	1	4		3							St. Paul, Minn.
382			9	5	214	44	97	4	7				2			Des Moines, Iowa
105	2		2		71		20	1	9							St. Joseph, Mo.
168			2	2	35	2	53	5	54	1	14					Springfield, Mo.
73			7		18	4	37	2	5							Fargo, N.D.
178	1		3	5	132	8	21	1	7							Sioux Falls, S.D.
149	1		4	8	88	7	22	13	4	1		1				Lincoln, Neb.
225			8	9	61	4	42	17	50	24	5		5			Topeka, Kan.
339	3		13	11	129	15	112	7	35	2	2	1	5	3	1	Wichita, Kan.
1,131	1	1	25	15	593	34	298	6	153	1	3		1			9 S. Atlantic cities
68	1		2	1	64											Hagerstown, Md.
131					131											Richmond, Va.
120			3		111		4		1	1						Wheeling, W. Va.*
33		1	2	1	28				1							Asheville, N.C.
68			1	1	66											Greensboro, N.C.
79			4		23		49		3							Charleston, S.C.
83			1		19	4	37		22							Columbia, S.C.
490			11	12	138	28	194	6	98		3					Atlanta, Ga.*
59			1		13	2	14		28				1			Jacksonville, Fla.
302	3		20	5	101	31	54	1	87							3 E. S. Central cities
17					15				2							Paducah, Ky.
209	2		18	5	58	20	46	1	59							Birmingham, Ala.*
76	1		2		28	11	8		26							Jackson, Miss.
1,141	3		46	26	259	41	257	52	394	12	19		29	1	2	6 W. S. Central cities
172			9	6	77	7	44	1	21	1	1		5			Little Rock, Ark.
58			1		8		22	4	22				1			Baton Rouge, La.
344			27	15	104	5	65	37	63	5	10		11		2	Oklahoma City, Okla.
94			1		3	3	24	3	58	1			1			Austin, Tex.
392	2		6	5	49	25	94	5	190	1	7		7	1		Dallas, Tex.
81	1		2		18	1	8	2	40	4	1		4			Wichita Falls, Tex.
609	3		34	2	57	22	181	13	255	7	3	1	27	2	2	6 Mountain cities
53			3		6		1		28	1	1		13			Butte, Mont.
32			1		1		6		23				..	1		Boise, Idaho
41	2		3		15		1	1	13	1	1		4			Casper, Wyo.
49			3		4		23	3	13				1	1	1	Pueblo, Colo.
164	1		13	1	11	2	18	3	108				7			Phoenix, Ariz.
270			11	1	20	20	132	6	70	5	1	1	2		1	Salt Lake City, Utah
1,750	34	2	32	18	348	140	1,027	40	94	9	1		5			4 Pacific cities
471	1		14	12	95	77	239	4	26	1	1		1			Seattle, Wash.*
421	31	2	10	2	151	39	156	3	25				2			Portland, Ore.
226			3	1	33	4	164	10	9	1			1			Sacramento, Calif.
632	2		5	3	69	20	468	23	34	7			1			San Diego, Calif.*

TABLE D 29

Mortgaged Owner-occupied Dwellings, First Mortgage Contract Interest Rates, Simple and Weighted Averages by Holding Agency, 52 Cities by Geographic Division, January 1, 1934

	All[3] holding agencies	Life ins. co.	Build. & loan asso.	Commer. bank	Savings bank	Mortgage co.	Construct. co.	Title & trust co.	H.O. Loan Corp.	Individual	Other
52 cities[1]	6.26	6.09	6.72	6.34	6.32	6.44	6.57	6.24	5.00	6.26	6.14
4 New England cities	5.94	5.93	6.21	5.94	5.92	6.04	6.75	5.85		5.96	5.92
Portland, Me.	6.01	5.67	6.23	5.94	5.96	5.90			5.00	5.95	4.83
Worcester, Mass.	5.65	5.77	5.85	5.84	5.59	5.89		5.73	5.00	5.85	6.01
Providence, R.I.*	6.06	6.02	6.39	5.99	6.04	6.21	6.75	5.87	5.00	6.02	5.95
Waterbury, Conn.	5.92	5.93	5.93	5.92	5.98	5.67		6.00	5.00	5.90	5.93
4 Mid. Atlantic cities	5.63	5.91	6.05	5.92	5.49	5.83	6.00	5.94	5.00	5.85	5.89
Binghamton, N.Y.	5.82	5.83	5.90	6.05	5.59					5.88	5.83
Syracuse, N.Y.	5.43	5.93	6.09	5.87	5.24	5.75		5.91		5.82	5.92
Trenton, N.J.	5.89	5.87	6.04	5.92	5.78	6.00		5.93	5.00	5.87	5.80
Erie, Pa.	5.94	5.92	6.02	6.02	6.00	5.95	6.00	6.03	5.00	5.94	5.91
6 E. N. Central cities	6.19	6.11	6.72	6.14	6.20	6.50	6.27	6.09	5.00	5.96	6.02
Cleveland, Ohio*	6.14	6.01	6.78	6.10	6.18	6.42	6.22	6.05	5.00	5.86	6.05
Indianapolis, Ind.	6.41	6.18	6.60	6.35	6.34	7.06	6.44	6.28	5.00	6.36	5.86
Peoria, Ill.	6.58	6.27	6.79	6.11	6.15	6.58	6.50	6.00	5.00	6.04	6.24
Lansing, Mich.	6.30	6.06	6.51	6.59	6.46	6.62		6.50	5.00	6.45	6.05
Kenosha, Wis.	6.08	6.25	6.45	6.00	6.17	6.07		6.00	5.00	6.06	5.92
Racine, Wis.	5.96	6.02	6.17	6.05	5.94	5.95		6.02	5.00	5.88	5.83
10 W. N. Central cities	6.19	5.98	6.57	6.22	6.26	6.17	5.89	6.12	5.00	6.14	6.19
Minneapolis, Minn.	5.98	5.90	6.34	5.94	5.95	6.02	5.80	5.90	5.00	5.93	5.94
St. Paul, Minn.	5.93	5.85	6.25	6.05	5.83	6.02		6.11	5.00	5.92	6.00
Des Moines, Iowa	6.21	6.14	6.31	6.30	6.36	6.33		6.60	5.00	6.39	6.30
St. Joseph, Mo.	6.30	6.09	6.75	6.10	6.45	6.36		6.28	5.00	6.16	6.00
Springfield, Mo.	7.31	6.25	7.81	7.08	6.83	7.22		6.85	5.00	7.39	7.30
Fargo, N.D.	6.55	6.47	7.01	6.90	6.92	7.13		6.36	5.00	6.55	6.55
Sioux Falls, S.D.	6.25	6.02	6.99	6.38	7.75	6.18		6.50	5.00	6.46	6.28
Lincoln, Neb.	6.32	5.96	6.69	6.71	6.53	6.11	6.00	5.93	5.00	6.12	6.22
Topeka, Kan.	7.19	6.09	7.82	6.89	6.96	6.29		6.24	5.00	6.54	7.61
Wichita, Kan.	6.67	6.19	7.25	6.71	7.33	6.32	6.33	6.32	5.00	6.56	6.63
9 S. Atlantic cities	6.41	6.08	6.74	6.54	6.69	6.59	6.71	6.47	5.00	6.58	6.39
Hagerstown, Md.	5.88	5.75	6.00	6.00		6.00			5.00	5.85	6.33
Richmond, Va.	5.98	5.98	6.12	6.00	6.00	6.00	6.00	6.02	5.00	5.98	5.98
Wheeling, W. Va.*	6.16	5.95	6.85	6.05	6.28	6.67	6.11	6.07	5.00	6.10	6.00
Asheville, N.C.	5.96	5.97	6.06	6.00		6.00		6.00	5.00	6.00	5.67
Greensboro, N.C.	5.96	5.98	6.00	6.14		6.00			5.00	6.00	
Charleston, S.C.	6.84	6.00		6.96	6.88	7.00		6.63	5.00	6.95	6.77
Columbia, S.C.	7.11	6.33	7.72	7.13		7.60		6.33	5.00	7.00	7.00
Atlanta, Ga.*	6.66	6.17	6.97	6.97	7.21	6.91	7.31	6.92	5.00	7.07	6.69
Jacksonville, Fla.	6.94	6.25	7.62	7.08		6.81			5.00	7.48	6.90
3 E. S. Central cities	6.87	6.26	7.55	7.04	7.20	7.05	7.75	6.76	5.00	7.28	6.47
Paducah, Ky.	6.16	6.04	6.30	6.04	6.00	6.00	6.67	6.10	5.00	6.42	
Birmingham, Ala.*	6.93	6.27	7.59	7.05	7.26	7.12	7.80	6.79	5.00	7.50	6.47
Jackson, Miss.	6.71	6.29	7.69	7.29		6.94			5.00	6.10	
6 W. S. Central cities	7.21	6.52	7.81	7.33	7.50	7.22	7.92	7.00	5.00	7.35	7.22
Little Rock, Ark.	6.50	6.12	7.55	6.40	6.91	6.74		6.95	5.00	6.43	6.86
Baton Rouge, La.	7.27		7.34	7.56					5.00	7.65	6.75
Oklahoma City, Okla.	7.12	6.06	7.91	7.35	7.39	6.98	8.20	6.34	5.00	7.29	7.11
Austin, Tex.	7.61	7.42	7.45	7.62		7.46	7.89		5.00	7.68	7.33
Dallas, Tex.	7.36	6.82	7.87	7.47	7.74	7.50	7.67	7.54	5.00	7.56	7.39
Wichita Falls, Tex.	7.50	6.91	8.10	7.57		7.22	8.00	7.57	5.00	7.39	7.60
6 Mountain cities	7.21	6.55	7.93	7.42	7.28	7.58	6.95	7.49	5.00	7.19	7.39
Butte, Mont.	7.95			8.08	8.50	9.00		8.83	5.00	8.10	8.90
Boise, Idaho	7.43	6.67	7.98	7.67		7.82		7.50	5.00	7.53	7.63
Casper, Wyo.	7.03	6.00	8.03	8.00		8.13		7.70	5.00	6.79	7.33
Pueblo, Colo.	6.67	6.10	7.75	7.50	6.00	7.00	6.75		5.00	6.84	6.99
Phoenix, Ariz.	7.57	6.48	8.55	7.88	8.00	7.95		7.43	5.00	7.83	7.80
Salt Lake City, Utah	7.14	6.70	7.74	7.13	7.23	7.41	7.00	7.40	5.00	6.97	7.21
4 Pacific cities	6.57	6.23	7.16	6.86	6.86	6.69	7.29	6.71	5.00	6.78	5.88
Seattle, Wash.*	6.67	6.27	7.28	6.97	6.90	6.67		6.77	5.00	6.80	6.70
Portland, Ore.	6.21	6.18	6.99	6.61	6.73	6.47		6.50	5.00	6.62	4.63
Sacramento, Calif.	6.70	6.19	7.17	6.97	6.84	6.80		6.50	5.00	6.87	5.73
San Diego, Calif.*	6.86	6.25	7.19	6.99	7.00	7.04	7.29	7.02	5.00	6.93	6.29

Source: Financial Survey of Urban Housing. The number of reports on which these interest rates are based is shown for 'All holding agencies' in the owner-occupied section of Table D 28. The distribution of the number reporting by agency holding the loan is approximately the same as shown in Table D 17. Rates not shown for fewer than 3 reports.

*Metropolitan district.

[1] *Geographic division and 52-city percentages weighted by estimated debt on first mortgage loans in each city (RPI).*

[2] *Individual interest rates for each agency and city weighted by amount of principal outstanding on first mortgage loans by agency holding the loan.*

[3] *Includes public bond issues:*

	Per Cent	
	Simple average	Weighted average
Kenosha, Wis.	6.00	6.00
Racine, Wis.	5.64	5.21

TABLE D 29

Mortgaged Owner-occupied Dwellings, First Mortgage Contract Interest Rates, Simple and Weighted Averages by Holding Agency, 52 Cities by Geographic Division, January 1, 1934

All[3] holding agencies	Life ins. co.	Build. & loan asso.	Commer. bank	Savings bank	Mortgage co.	Construct. co.	Title & trust co.	H.O. Loan Corp.	Individual	Other	
			W E I G H T E D A V E R A G E S [2]								
6.18	5.98	6.73	6.26	6.26	6.39	6.55	6.18	5.00	6.18	6.09	52 cities[1]
5.93	5.92	6.28	5.93	5.92	6.06	6.95	5.85	5.00	5.91	5.86	4 New England cities
6.00	5.61	6.26	5.96	5.99	5.92			5.00	5.93	3.66	Portland, Me.
5.64	5.74	5.89	5.79	5.59	5.83		5.76	5.00	5.76	6.01	Worcester, Mass.
6.06	6.01	6.54	6.00	6.04	6.23	6.95	5.85	5.00	6.00	5.91	Providence, R.I.*
5.90	5.95	5.95	5.90	5.98	5.82		6.00	5.00	5.83	6.00	Waterbury, Conn.
5.65	5.91	6.06	5.93	5.48	5.98	6.00	5.94	5.00	5.86	5.90	4 Mid. Atlantic cities
5.80	5.84	5.91	6.03	5.57					5.87	5.85	Binghamton, N.Y.
5.46	5.94	6.11	5.91	5.24	6.00		5.91		5.82	5.90	Syracuse, N.Y.
5.92	5.90	6.00	5.83	5.75	6.00		5.95	5.00	5.91	5.88	Trenton, N.J.
5.94	5.87	6.02	6.00	6.00	5.92	6.00	6.01	5.00	5.96	5.92	Erie, Pa.
6.18	5.99	6.75	6.11	6.18	6.41	6.26	6.06	5.00	5.91	6.02	6 E. N. Central cities
6.14	5.96	6.81	6.09	6.20	6.35	6.21	6.04	5.00	5.83	6.05	Cleveland, Ohio*
6.34	6.12	6.62	6.22	6.33	6.85	6.47	6.17	5.00	6.21	5.90	Indianapolis, Ind.
6.56	6.28	6.83	6.00	5.43	6.53	6.43	5.91	5.00	6.09	6.18	Peoria, Ill.
6.20	6.00	6.50	6.68	6.37	6.59		6.54	5.00	6.33	6.04	Lansing, Mich.
6.09	6.10	6.54	6.00	6.21	6.06		6.00	5.00	6.06	5.99	Kenosha, Wis.
5.95	5.79	6.18	6.03	5.87	5.94		6.09	5.00	5.87	5.76	Racine, Wis.
6.09	5.92	6.62	6.13	6.24	6.10	5.88	6.05	5.00	6.02	6.14	10 W. N. Central cities
5.92	5.82	6.38	5.91	5.87	5.98	5.84	5.88	5.00	5.91	6.00	Minneapolis, Minn.
5.93	5.86	6.33	6.12	5.95	6.00		5.98	5.00	5.93	5.98	St. Paul, Minn.
5.91	6.04	6.29	6.18	6.13	6.18		6.42	5.00	5.70	6.13	Des Moines, Iowa
6.21	6.02	7.06	5.98	6.61	6.18		6.24	5.00	6.04	6.07	St. Joseph, Mo.
7.04	6.09	7.88	6.78	6.71	6.91		6.38	5.00	7.18	7.14	Springfield, Mo.
6.38	6.50	7.06	6.91	8.05	7.03		6.38	5.00	6.42	6.33	Fargo, N.D.
6.12	6.01	7.30	6.32	7.63	6.12		6.67	5.00	6.17	6.11	Sioux Falls, S.D.
6.22	5.92	6.66	6.22	6.23	6.01	6.00	5.91	5.00	6.01	6.17	Lincoln, Neb.
7.03	6.03	7.85	6.56	6.71	6.17		6.29	5.00	6.30	6.67	Topeka, Kan.
6.48	6.13	7.27	6.58	7.56	6.26	6.00	6.19	5.00	6.35	6.61	Wichita, Kan.
6.25	6.02	6.66	6.44	6.46	6.46	6.41	6.28	5.00	6.43	6.32	9 S. Atlantic cities
5.87	5.97	6.00	6.00		6.00			5.00	5.84	6.11	Hagerstown, Md.
5.97	5.97	6.09	5.99	6.00	6.02	6.00	6.01	5.00	5.96	5.98	Richmond, Va.
5.93	5.85	6.84	6.01	6.01	6.17	4.92	5.41	5.00	5.51	5.91	Wheeling, W. Va.*
5.95	5.94	6.01	6.00		6.00		6.00	5.00	6.01	6.00	Asheville, N.C.
5.97	5.96	6.00	6.02		5.98			5.00	6.00	6.12	Greensboro, N.C.
6.71	5.87		7.01	6.82	7.00		6.79	5.00	6.91	6.67	Charleston, S.C.
6.87	6.26	7.76	7.41		7.01		6.30	5.00	6.77	6.84	Columbia, S.C.
6.40	6.04	6.81	6.69	6.86	6.80	7.16	6.43	5.00	6.91	6.51	Atlanta, Ga.*
6.78	6.26	7.57	7.13		6.80			5.00	7.30	6.95	Jacksonville, Fla.
6.59	6.20	7.52	6.98	6.88	6.88	7.82	6.58	5.00	6.98	6.20	3 E. S. Central cities
5.93	6.04	6.36	6.04	6.00	6.00	7.45	6.19	5.00	6.29		Paducah, Ky.
6.63	6.19	7.54	6.93	6.92	6.99	7.84	6.60	5.00	7.20	6.20	Birmingham, Ala.*
6.52	6.31	7.76	7.58		6.42			5.00	5.71		Jackson, Miss.
6.99	6.40	7.75	6.96	7.14	7.33	7.70	6.80	5.00	7.20	7.23	6 W. S. Central cities
6.26	6.04	7.60	6.26	6.62	6.57		6.78	5.00	6.16	6.69	Little Rock, Ark.
7.17		7.33	7.07					5.00	7.36	7.20	Baton Rouge, La.
6.82	6.01	7.80	6.73	7.05	6.91	7.47	6.15	5.00	7.12	7.25	Oklahoma City, Okla.
7.41	7.30	7.25	7.39		7.24	7.90		5.00	7.44	7.34	Austin, Tex.
7.22	6.67	7.82	7.20	7.35	7.92	7.83	7.26	5.00	7.48	7.28	Dallas, Tex.
7.22	6.59	8.09	7.54		7.03	8.03	8.00	5.00	7.27	7.74	Wichita Falls, Tex.
7.02	6.58	7.91	7.25	7.30	7.40	6.86	7.23	5.00	7.13	7.27	6 Mountain cities
7.82			8.02	8.24	8.52		8.42	5.00	8.14	7.87	Butte, Mont.
6.95	6.49	7.97	7.62		7.71		7.22	5.00	7.44	7.81	Boise, Idaho
6.93	6.55	7.96	8.00		8.25		7.77	5.00	7.01	7.93	Casper, Wyo.
6.62	6.14	7.77	7.12	6.61	7.00	6.84		5.00	6.67	6.73	Pueblo, Colo.
7.31	6.36	8.63	7.67	8.00	7.75		7.08	5.00	7.70	7.86	Phoenix, Ariz.
6.97	6.77	7.69	6.99	7.15	7.19	6.87	7.16	5.00	6.93	7.04	Salt Lake City, Utah
6.34	5.71	7.07	6.76	6.76	6.57	7.22	6.68	5.00	6.72	5.67	4 Pacific cities
6.25	5.00	7.12	6.87	6.78	6.51		6.68	5.00	6.76	6.40	Seattle, Wash.*
6.09	6.13	6.91	6.42	6.62	6.38		6.45	5.00	6.54	4.57	Portland, Ore.
6.58	6.15	7.05	6.94	6.64	6.58		6.72	5.00	6.84	5.53	Sacramento, Calif.
6.79	6.22	7.22	6.96	6.99	6.97	7.22	7.00	5.00	6.87	6.02	San Diego, Calif.*

TABLE D 30

Mortgaged Rented Dwellings, First Mortgage Contract Interest Rates, Simple and Weighted Averages by Holding Agency, 30 Cities by Geographic Division, January 1, 1934

	SIMPLE AVERAGES										
	All[3,4] holding agencies	Life ins. co.	Build. & loan asso.	Commer. bank	Savings bank	Mortgage co.	Construct. co.	Title & trust co.	H.O. Loan Corp.	Individual	Other
30 cities[1]	6.39	6.11	6.95	6.47	6.42	6.57	6.00	6.27	5.00	6.45	6.35
3 New England cities	5.97	5.88	6.21	5.96	5.91	5.93		6.05		6.06	6.18
Portland, Me.	6.07	6.00	6.67	5.94	6.00			6.00		5.86	6.29
Worcester, Mass.	5.70	5.50	5.80	5.88	5.63			6.00		6.18	5.93
Providence, R.I.*	6.06	6.00	6.32	5.99	6.00	5.93		6.07		6.04	6.26
3 Mid. Atlantic cities	5.60	5.98	5.91	5.97	5.45	6.06		5.97		5.86	5.96
Syracuse, N.Y.	5.46	6.00		5.95	5.25			6.00		5.83	
Trenton, N.J.	5.87	5.80	6.08	6.00	5.64	6.20		5.64		5.86	5.88
Erie, Pa.	5.94		5.84	6.00	6.00	6.00		6.00		5.96	6.00
5 E. N. Central cities	6.22	6.07	6.75	6.09	6.21	6.45	6.00	6.04	5.00	6.02	6.09
Cleveland, Ohio*	6.14	6.02	6.81	6.04	6.13	6.34		6.02	5.00	6.04	6.08
Indianapolis, Ind.	6.46	6.24	6.61	6.23	6.50	7.00		6.07	5.00	5.98	6.10
Peoria, Ill.	6.64	6.08	6.90	6.02	6.00	6.33		6.00	5.00	5.80	6.11
Lansing, Mich.	6.49	6.47	6.60	6.73	6.40	6.00	6.00	6.50	5.00	6.40	6.65
Racine, Wis.	5.98	6.00	6.29	6.00		5.96		6.00		5.91	5.88
8 W. N. Central cities	6.20	5.97	6.62	6.21	6.05	6.16		5.90	5.00	6.15	6.10
Minneapolis, Minn.	6.02	5.88	6.40	6.02	5.92	6.06		5.99	5.00	5.98	6.00
St. Paul, Minn.	5.96	5.92	6.39	6.19	6.00	5.98		5.58	5.00	5.95	6.00
Des Moines, Iowa	6.36	6.11	6.50	6.31	6.36	6.48			5.00	6.52	6.16
Springfield, Mo.	7.26	6.35	8.04	7.11		7.00				7.23	6.88
Sioux Falls, S.D.	6.19	6.03	6.33	6.35	6.60	6.04				6.28	6.38
Lincoln, Neb.	6.32	6.05	6.94			5.94		6.07		6.10	5.00
Topeka, Kan.	7.16	6.00	7.92	7.23	6.33	6.42		5.90	5.00	6.44	6.22
Wichita, Kan.	6.69	6.18	7.30	6.38		6.55		6.06	5.00	6.53	7.35
1 S. Atlantic city	6.83	6.17	7.60	7.67	7.14	7.01		6.54	5.00	7.27	6.92
Atlanta, Ga.*	6.83	6.17	7.60	7.67	7.14	7.01		6.54	5.00	7.27	6.92
1 E. S. Central city	6.72	6.16	7.16	7.08	6.92	7.03		6.92	5.00	7.15	7.17
Birmingham, Ala.*	6.72	6.16	7.16	7.08	6.92	7.03		6.92	5.00	7.15	7.17
3 W. S. Central cities	7.11	6.35	7.87	7.17	7.60	7.01		7.00	5.00	7.38	6.68
Little Rock, Ark.	6.61	5.95	7.78	6.56		6.81			5.00	6.64	6.50
Oklahoma City, Okla.	6.91	6.01	7.76			6.73			5.00	7.34	5.55
Dallas, Tex.	7.37	6.72	7.98	7.28	7.60	7.29		7.00	5.00	7.55	7.72
2 Mountain cities	7.27	6.70	7.96	7.36	7.35	7.56		7.36	5.00	7.25	7.00
Phoenix, Ariz.	7.53	6.54	8.27	8.00	8.00	7.74			5.00	7.65	7.00
Salt Lake City, Utah	7.16	6.77	7.83	7.11	7.09	7.49		7.36	5.00	7.09	7.00
4 Pacific cities	6.70	6.22	7.23	6.80	6.83	6.74		6.64	5.00	6.84	6.44
Seattle, Wash.*	6.69	6.17	7.16	6.76	6.86	6.80		6.67	5.00	6.83	6.83
Portland, Ore.	6.36	6.23	7.28	6.70	6.56	6.64		6.23	5.00	6.72	4.53
Sacramento, Calif.	6.89	6.36	7.20	6.90	6.86	6.25				6.90	7.00
San Diego, Calif.*	6.93	6.26	7.37	6.97	6.99	6.89		6.92	5.00	6.95	6.86

Source: Financial Survey of Urban Housing. The number of reports on which these interest rates are based is shown for all agencies in the rented section of Table D 28. The distribution of the number reporting by agency holding the loan is approximately the same as shown in Table D 18. Rates not shown for fewer than 3 reports.

*Metropolitan district.

[1] *Geographic division and 30-city percentages weighted by estimated debt on first mortgage loans in each city (RPI).*

[2] *Individual interest rates for each agency and city weighted by amount of principal outstanding on first mortgage loans by agency holding the loan.*

[3] *Includes public bond issues:*

	Per cent: Simple average	Per cent: Weighted average
Racine, Wis.	6.00	6.00
San Diego, Calif.	5.83	6.40

[4] *The data do not allow the presentation of contract interest rates by agency holding the loan for all 52 cities. Contract interest rates for all agencies combined for the 52 cities are shown in the first mortgage rented section of Table D 27.*

TABLE D 30

Mortgaged Rented Dwellings, First Mortgage Contract Interest Rates, Simple and Weighted Averages by Holding Agency, 30 Cities by Geographic Division, January 1, 1934

— W E I G H T E D   A V E R A G E S [2] —

All[3,4] holding agencies	Life ins. co.	Build. & loan asso.	Commer. bank	Savings bank	Mort-gage co.	Con-struct. co.	Title & trust co.	H.O. Loan Corp.	Indi-vidual	Other	
6.24	5.99	6.98	6.37	6.35	6.49	6.00	6.19	5.00	6.30	6.20	30 cities[1]
5.87	5.83	6.33	5.84	5.87	5.94		5.93		5.81	6.11	3 New England cities
6.04	6.07	6.58	5.92	6.00			6.00		5.89	6.18	Portland, Me.
5.47	5.28	5.80	5.76	5.53			5.90		5.38	5.93	Worcester, Mass.
6.00	6.00	6.50	5.86	5.98	5.94		5.93		5.96	6.17	Providence, R.I.*
5.65	5.98	5.96	5.98	5.45	6.03		5.99		5.89	5.94	3 Mid. Atlantic cities
5.54	6.00		5.97	5.27			6.00		5.88		Syracuse, N.Y.
5.77	5.81	5.91	6.00	5.57	6.11		5.94		5.74	5.79	Trenton, N.J.
5.95		5.98	6.00	6.00	6.00		6.00		5.97	6.00	Erie, Pa.
6.15	5.94	6.73	6.07	6.19	6.43	6.00	6.03	5.00	5.87	6.03	5 E. N. Central cities
6.09	5.86	6.79	6.03	6.13	6.51		6.01	5.00	5.83	6.01	Cleveland, Ohio*
6.34	6.16	6.58	6.16	6.40	6.32		6.05	5.00	5.96	6.14	Indianapolis, Ind.
6.39	6.08	6.82	6.01	6.00	6.00		6.00	5.00	5.96	5.73	Peoria, Ill.
6.35	6.26	6.41	6.75	6.42	6.00	6.00	6.44	5.00	6.31	6.68	Lansing, Mich.
5.96	6.00	6.37	6.00		5.97		6.00		5.92	5.60	Racine, Wis.
6.06	5.88	6.74	6.11	5.97	6.06		5.81	5.00	6.05	5.85	8 W. N. Central cities
5.91	5.78	6.52	5.87	5.83	6.01		5.95	5.00	5.96	5.66	Minneapolis, Minn.
5.94	5.95	6.87	6.07	6.00	5.97		5.58	5.00	5.92	6.00	St. Paul, Minn.
6.18	5.97	6.44	6.17	6.13	6.19			5.00	6.43	6.10	Des Moines, Iowa
7.00	6.18	8.17	6.80		6.65				6.99	6.66	Springfield, Mo.
6.01	5.94	6.18	6.81	6.38	6.12				5.63	6.20	Sioux Falls, S.D.
6.14	5.97	6.95			5.96		5.99		6.06	4.45	Lincoln, Neb.
6.86	5.76	7.95	7.26	6.61	6.13		5.96	5.00	6.09	6.31	Topeka, Kan.
6.34	5.97	7.14	6.33		6.24		5.42	5.00	6.12	6.79	Wichita, Kan.
6.35	5.96	7.25	7.30	7.16	6.88		6.27	5.00	7.03	6.65	1 S. Atlantic city
6.35	5.96	7.25	7.30	7.16	6.88		6.27	5.00	7.03	6.65	Atlanta, Ga.*
6.37	5.94	7.23	7.32	6.99	6.50		6.79	5.00	7.17	7.08	1 E. S. Central city
6.37	5.94	7.22	7.32	6.99	6.50		6.79	5.00	7.17	7.08	Birmingham, Ala.*
7.05	6.32	8.54	7.14	6.96	6.97		7.00	5.00	7.07	6.77	3 W. S. Central cities
6.32	5.93	8.08	6.31		6.48			5.00	6.59	6.19	Little Rock, Ark.
7.02	5.97	9.77			6.45			5.00	6.90	6.06	Oklahoma City, Okla.
7.21	6.71	7.53	7.29	6.96	7.53		7.00		7.31	7.50	Dallas, Tex.
7.01	6.71	8.03	7.29	6.93	7.26		7.34	5.00	7.03	7.15	2 Mountain cities
7.39	6.63	7.90	8.00	8.00	7.76			5.00	7.50	7.32	Phoenix, Ariz.
6.86	6.74	8.08	7.01	6.50	7.06		7.34		6.84	7.08	Salt Lake City, Utah
6.42	6.07	7.09	6.55	6.73	6.69		6.55	5.00	6.78	5.95	4 Pacific cities
6.26	5.91	7.05	6.38	6.78	6.79		6.55	5.00	6.76	6.02	Seattle, Wash.*
6.20	6.12	6.77	6.46	6.41	6.53		6.08	5.00	6.59	4.44	Portland, Ore.
6.82	6.60	7.10	6.82	6.51	6.24				6.91	6.83	Sacramento, Calif.
6.88	6.19	7.47	6.96	6.96	6.75		6.97	5.00	6.93	6.71	San Diego, Calif.*

TABLE D 31

Mortgaged Dwellings, Number reporting Effective Interest Rates on First Mortgages by Tenure and Holding Agency, 52 Cities by Geographic Division, January 1, 1934

	OWNER-OCCUPIED										
	All holding agencies	Life ins. co.	Build. & loan asso.	Commer. bank	Savings bank	Mortgage co.	Construct. co.	Title & trust co.	H.O. Loan Corp.	Individual	Other[1]
52 cities	25,263	3,482	4,937	3,151	2,128	2,676	115	749	850	6,205	970
4 New England cities	1,032	24	245	116	362	31		20	16	178	40
Portland, Me.	215	4	91	8	71					39	2
Worcester, Mass.	127	2	13	4	82	3		1	1	8	13
Providence, R.I.*	597	17	134	97	181	27		15	10	93	23
Waterbury, Conn.	93	1	7	7	28	1		4	5	38	2
4 Mid. Atlantic cities	993	30	203	81	96	6	2	10	14	512	39
Binghamton, N.Y.	68	2	1	10	16			1		36	2
Syracuse, N.Y.	109	13		4	64	1		1		23	3
Trenton, N.J.	225	7	66	13	6				2	118	13
Erie, Pa.	591	8	136	54	10	5	2	8	12	335	21
6 E. N. Central cities	6,326	508	1,645	1,850	701	156	28	226	187	843	182
Cleveland, Ohio*	4,203	356	648	1,751	673	58	20	104	128	358	107
Indianapolis, Ind.	460	66	235	42	7	3	1	44	21	26	15
Peoria, Ill.	612	57	428	22	8	2	5	7	2	61	20
Lansing, Mich.	207	25	88	13	8	4	1	5	17	42	4
Kenosha, Wis.	273	3	41	8	2	24	1	55	6	119	14
Racine, Wis.	571	1	205	14	3	65		11	13	237	22
10 W. N. Central cities	5,231	718	1,109	339	235	755	8	182	146	1,574	165
Minneapolis, Minn.	2,152	311	256	165	183	332	3	71	32	727	72
St. Paul, Minn.	485	42	52	32	4	59	1	7	14	267	7
Des Moines, Iowa	401	81	49	40	13	54		4	31	110	19
St. Joseph, Mo.	211	16	46	28	6	50		8	2	40	15
Springfield, Mo.	330	34	72	12	5	40		4	4	139	20
Fargo, N.D.	169	7	41	12	2	18		1	26	55	7
Sioux Falls, S.D.	207	28	7	10	4	81	2	2	8	56	9
Lincoln, Neb.	262	39	99	7	3	16	1	26	2	67	2
Topeka, Kan.	532	52	310	30	15	49		10	12	50	4
Wichita, Kan.	482	108	177	3		56	1	49	15	63	10
9 S. Atlantic cities	2,729	707	239	169	91	535	10	86	75	673	144
Hagerstown, Md.	~132	1	23	9		1		1	1	91	5
Richmond, Va.	489	79	19	90	9	107	1	33	6	87	58
Wheeling, W.Va.*	200	28	43	27	21	4	2	8	6	43	18
Asheville, N.C.	223	87	26	4		49	1	2	11	38	5
Greensboro, N.C.	123	63	22	3	1	9	2	1	2	16	4
Charleston, S.C.	89	2		6	1	4			4	69	3
Columbia, S.C.	118	15	54	2		3		2	6	35	1
Atlanta, Ga.*	1,249	405	43	27	59	345	4	38	33	249	46
Jacksonville, Fla.	106	27	9	1		13		1	6	45	4
3 E. S. Central cities	1,564	445	343	58	13	246	5	24	59	308	63
Paducah, Ky.	78	28	12	10	1	2	1	5	1	16	2
Birmingham, Ala.*	1,416	384	308	46	12	241	4	19	58	283	61
Jackson, Miss.	70	33	23	2		3				9	
6 W. S. Central cities	1,952	336	493	128	38	270	48	25	92	448	74
Little Rock, Ark.	228	35	32	69	3	26			16	36	8
Baton Rouge, La.	38		30	2		1			1	2	2
Oklahoma City, Okla.	632	122	237	5	9	81	1	5	51	109	12
Austin, Tex.	193	5	18	10		27	37		2	87	7
Dallas, Tex.	716	159	128	38	26	116	5	12	17	171	44
Wichita Falls, Tex.	145	15	48	4		19	5	5	5	43	1
6 Mountain cities	1,568	156	307	63	81	180	7	92	126	507	49
Butte, Mont.	233		1	28	1	6	1	8	14	156	18
Boise, Idaho	222	14	96	1	2	7		4	20	70	8
Casper, Wyo.	43		17	1					12	13	
Pueblo, Colo.	184	3	48	2		1	3		38	85	4
Phoenix, Ariz.	228	27	17	7	26	33		7	14	95	2
Salt Lake City, Utah	658	112	128	24	52	133	3	73	28	88	17
4 Pacific cities	3,868	558	353	347	511	497	7	84	135	1,162	214
Seattle, Wash.*	1,527	235	66	100	398	228	2	47	69	339	43
Portland, Ore.	888	160	68	31	32	139		24	44	295	95
Sacramento, Calif.	444	45	66	56	6	15		1	2	207	46
San Diego, Calif.*	1,009	118	153	160	75	115	5	12	20	321	30

Source: *Financial Survey of Urban Housing*

*Metropolitan district.

[1] Includes public bond issues:

Owner-occupied		Rented	
(number of reports)			
Kenosha, Wis.	5	Racine, Wis.	1
Racine, Wis.	2	Seattle, Wash.	2
Richmond, Va.	1	San Diego, Calif.	1
Paducah, Ky.	1		
Seattle, Wash.	1		

[2] Where only number 'All holding agencies' is shown, number by agency holding the loan was not obtained by *Financial Survey of Urban Housing* either because the number of reports was too small or because of lack of related information for rented properties.

TABLE D 31

Mortgaged Dwellings, Number reporting Effective Interest Rates on First Mortgages by Tenure and Holding Agency, 52 Cities by Geographic Division, January 1, 1934

← R E N T E D →											
All[2] holding agencies	Life ins. co.	Build. & loan asso.	Commer. bank	Savings bank	Mortgage co.	Construct. co.	Title & trust co.	H.O. Loan Corp.	Individual	Other[1]	
3,351	436	494	373	288	337	4	113	33	738	111	52 cities
117	2	17	12	42	1		5	2	20	4	4 New England cities
35		7	4	14			2	2	6		Portland, Me.
18		1	1	11					2	3	Worcester, Mass.
52	2	9	7	17	1		3		12	1	Providence, R.I.*
12											Waterbury, Conn.
125	5	18	7	6	10	1	2	1	53	8	4 Mid. Atlantic cities
14											Binghamton, N.Y.
19	4		1		9		1	1	3		Syracuse, N.Y.
25	1	7		3					10	4	Trenton, N.J.
67		11	6	3	1	1	1		40	4	Erie, Pa.
834	68	239	199	124	11		39	9	94	29	6 E. N. Central cities
511	52	70	180	121	3		15	6	52	12	Cleveland, Ohio*
135	9	85	12	3	2		14	2	2	6	Indianapolis, Ind.
73	4	60	2				3		2	2	Peoria, Ill.
27	3	12	2				1		8	1	Lansing, Mich.
22											Kenosha, Wis.
66		12	3		6		6	1	30	8	Racine, Wis.
825	131	117	56	34	122	2	28	6	244	27	10 W. N. Central cities
264	45	29	19	19	44		14	2	81	11	Minneapolis, Minn.
87	12	3	5	3	11		4	3	45	1	St. Paul, Minn.
129	25	12	16	6	16				47	7	Des Moines, Iowa
36											St. Joseph, Mo.
44	6		13	3			6		15	1.	Springfield, Mo.
22											Fargo, N.D.
48	7	2	3	1	17	1			14	3	Sioux Falls, S.D.
55	7	19	1		5	1	5		16	1	Lincoln, Neb.
53	10	17	5	3	9		1	1	6	1	Topeka, Kan.
87	19	22	4	2	14		4		20	2	Wichita, Kan.
334	48	3	2	7	45		5	1	44	10	9 S. Atlantic cities
18											Hagerstown, Md.
48											Richmond, Va.
28											Wheeling, W.Va.*
5											Asheville, N.C.
21											Greensboro, N.C.
14											Charleston, S.C.
19											Columbia, S.C.
165	48	3	2	7	45		5	1	44	10	Atlanta, Ga.*
16											Jacksonville, Fla.
98	17	3	4	2	14		4	2	16	2	3 E. S. Central cities
4											Paducah, Ky.
64	17	3	4	2	14		4	2	16	2	Birmingham, Ala.*
30											Jackson, Miss.
352	58	44	30	4	57		3	4	78	7	6 W. S. Central cities
50	8	5	21	1	7			2	5	1	Little Rock, Ark.
9											Baton Rouge, La.
95	26	20	1		20		2	1	22	3	Oklahoma City, Okla.
35											Austin, Tex.
140	24	19	8	3	30		1	1	51	3	Dallas, Tex.
23											Wichita Falls, Tex.
157	15	10	4	14	22		15	3	25	1	6 Mountain cities
9											Butte, Mont.
14											Boise, Idaho
11											Casper, Wyo.
14											Pueblo, Colo.
44	3	3	1	10	9		1	1	.15	1	Phoenix, Ariz.
65	12	7	3	4	13		14	2	10		Salt Lake City, Utah
509	92	43	59	55	55	1	12	5	164	23	4 Pacific cities
122	32	7	6	23	13		6	1	31	3	Seattle, Wash.*
129	32	6	1	8	19		1	3	46	13	Portland, Ore.
50	5	10	5	3					25	2	Sacramento, Calif.
208	23	20	47	21	23	1	5	1	62	5	San Diego, Calif.*

TABLE D 32

Mortgaged Owner-occupied Dwellings, First Mortgage Effective Interest Rates (per cent), Simple and Weighted Averages by Holding Agency, 52 Cities by Geographic Division, January I, 1934

	All[3] holding agencies	Life ins. co.	Build. & loan asso.	Commer. bank	Savings bank	Mortgage co.	Construct. co.	Title & trust co.	H.O. Loan Corp.	Individual	Other
52 cities[1]	6.73	6.56	7.31	6.73	6.85	7.30	7.10	6.83	5.25	6.60	6.62
4 New England cities	6.18	6.37	6.47	6.25	6.06	6.40		6.15	5.22	6.11	6.16
Portland, Me.	6.22	5.78	6.40	6.03	6.19					6.03	
Worcester, Mass.	5.75		5.79	6.00	5.64	5.73				5.94	6.25
Providence, R.I.*	6.43	6.41	6.84	6.50	6.27	6.70		6.18	5.25	6.24	6.12
Waterbury, Conn.	5.89		6.20	5.71	5.94			6.00	5.12	5.89	
4 Mid. Atlantic cities	5.98	6.36	6.51	5.98	5.82	6.52		6.41	5.24	6.28	6.27
Binghamton, N.Y.	6.27			6.47	6.51					6.13	
Syracuse, N.Y.	5.73	6.54		5.78	5.30					6.31	6.10
Trenton, N.J.	6.16	6.04	6.47	5.83	5.90					6.05	6.19
Erie, Pa.	6.48	6.05	6.54	6.45	7.04	6.52		6.41	5.24	6.48	6.90
6 E. N. Central cities	6.53	6.39	7.08	6.46	6.66	7.46	6.70	6.42	5.18	6.23	6.42
Cleveland, Ohio*	6.49	6.35	7.15	6.41	6.54	6.95	6.69	6.36	5.18	6.15	6.49
Indianapolis, Ind.	6.70	6.51	6.90	6.66	7.21	10.47		6.63	5.21	6.53	5.96
Peoria, Ill.	7.08	6.59	7.28	6.71	7.28		6.80	6.61		6.49	6.78
Lansing, Mich.	6.57	6.27	6.80	6.72	7.01	7.00		6.60	5.29	6.66	6.28
Kenosha, Wis.	6.42	6.50	7.09	6.26		6.60		6.23	5.08	6.33	6.23
Racine, Wis.	6.30		6.46	6.48	6.10	6.39		6.68	5.12	6.13	6.69
10 W. N. Central cities	6.82	6.63	7.20	6.80	6.86	6.95	7.50	7.15	5.25	6.73	6.85
Minneapolis, Minn.	6.65	6.65	6.91	6.74	6.53	6.82	7.50	6.84	5.20	6.54	6.72
St. Paul, Minn.	6.57	6.54	7.29	6.56	6.68	6.67		7.89	5.14	6.46	6.56
Des Moines, Iowa	6.83	6.61	6.99	6.78	7.14	7.21		7.03	5.37	7.13	6.84
St. Joseph, Mo.	6.94	6.16	7.33	6.72	7.00	7.08		7.25		6.87	6.80
Springfield, Mo.	8.12	6.91	8.38	8.12	7.82	8.20		8.00	5.38	8.19	9.22
Fargo, N.D.	6.61	6.37	7.12	7.08		7.31			5.04	6.66	6.34
Sioux Falls, S.D.	6.96	6.61	7.41	7.01	8.58	6.86			5.56	7.38	6.44
Lincoln, Neb.	6.67	6.59	7.00	6.67	7.70	6.68		6.57		6.23	
Topeka, Kan.	7.69	6.73	8.26	7.11	7.19	7.20		6.78	5.23	6.95	6.80
Wichita, Kan.	7.40	6.93	7.79	6.97		7.50		7.42	5.60	7.41	7.67
9 S. Atlantic cities	7.26	6.70	7.88	7.25	8.03	7.83	8.10	8.02	5.36	7.39	7.15
Hagerstown, Md.	6.29		6.09	6.08						6.30	7.46
Richmond, Va.	7.02	6.48	7.71	6.99	7.00	7.65		7.05	5.47	6.69	7.03
Wheeling, W. Va.*	6.48	6.25	7.28	6.29	6.60	7.98		6.69	5.27	6.05	5.99
Asheville, N.C.	6.47	6.32	6.68	6.53		6.73			5.32	6.67	6.12
Greensboro, N.C.	6.26	6.28	6.22	6.50		6.51				6.16	6.15
Charleston, S.C.	7.60			7.20		7.53			5.08	7.85	7.43
Columbia, S.C.	7.94	6.67	8.33			8.90			5.12	8.43	
Atlanta, Ga.*	7.73	7.05	8.70	8.03	9.10	7.92	8.10	9.03	5.28	8.18	7.59
Jacksonville, Fla.	7.92	6.87	7.84			8.51			5.77	8.61	8.15
3 E. S. Central cities	7.46	6.79	8.15	7.63	7.53	7.71	7.75	6.98	5.35	7.84	6.78
Paducah, Ky.	7.10	6.79	7.43	7.92				6.36		7.29	
Birmingham, Ala.*	7.52	6.78	8.16	7.62	7.53	7.85	7.75	7.01	5.35	8.17	6.78
Jackson, Miss.	7.20	6.85	8.32			6.80				5.79	
6 W. S. Central cities	7.80	7.23	8.44	7.78	8.58	7.94	7.92	7.63	5.40	7.88	7.66
Little Rock, Ark.	7.30	7.07	8.46	7.21	8.57	7.76		7.17	5.38	7.13	7.15
Baton Rouge, La.	7.62		7.62								
Oklahoma City, Okla.	7.77	7.02	8.49	7.74	8.26	8.01		7.44	5.52	7.88	7.53
Austin, Tex.	7.83	7.22	7.79	7.76		7.81	8.13		5.20	7.82	7.76
Dallas, Tex.	7.96	7.47	8.52	7.86	8.85	7.98	7.80	7.93	5.33	8.07	8.29
Wichita Falls, Tex.	7.77	6.95	8.98	8.75		7.57	8.78	7.40	5.40	7.86	
6 Mountain cities	7.65	6.90	8.28	7.57	7.82	8.35	6.61	7.91	5.29	7.62	8.00
Butte, Mont.	8.36			8.29		11.80		9.61	5.19	8.38	9.07
Boise, Idaho	8.20	6.82	8.85			8.99		7.90	5.74	8.23	8.03
Casper, Wyo.	7.49		8.22						5.39	7.89	
Pueblo, Colo.	7.24	6.87	8.32				6.33		5.44	7.43	7.88
Phoenix, Ariz.	8.04	6.90	8.86	8.10	8.57	8.56		8.00	5.12	8.32	
Salt Lake City, Utah	7.50	6.92	8.01	7.33	7.56	7.95	6.67	7.76	5.26	7.28	7.94
4 Pacific cities	7.22	6.70	8.07	7.46	7.58	7.40	7.68	7.20	5.27	6.68	6.47
Seattle, Wash.*	7.27	6.55	8.12	7.66	7.44	7.27		7.36	5.30	7.48	7.45
Portland, Ore.	6.78	6.55	8.01	6.80	7.33	7.09		6.48	5.28	7.24	5.02
Sacramento, Calif.	7.38	6.55	7.73	7.78	7.98	7.30				7.64	6.12
San Diego, Calif.*	7.73	6.88	8.23	7.93	8.02	8.22	7.68	8.01	5.21	7.69	7.00

Source: Financial Survey of Urban Housing. For number of reports upon which these interest rates are based see the owner-occupied section of Table D 31. Rates not shown for fewer than 3 reports.

*Metropolitan district.

[1]Geographic division and 52-city percentages weighted by estimated debt on first mortgage loans in each city (RPI).

[2]Individual interest rates for each agency and city weighted by amount of principal outstanding on first mortgage loans by agency holding the loan.

[3]Includes public bond issue:

	Per cent	
	Simple average	Weighted average
Kenosha, Wis.	6.74	6.86

TABLE D 32

Mortgaged Owner-occupied Dwellings, First Mortgage Effective Interest Rates (per cent), Simple and Weighted Averages by Holding Agency, 52 Cities by Geographic Division, January 1, 1934

← — — — — — — — — — — W E I G H T E D   A V E R A G E S [2] — — — — — — — — — — →

All[3] holding agencies	Life ins. co.	Build. & loan asso.	Commer. bank	Savings bank	Mortgage co.	Construct. co.	Title & trust co.	H.O. Loan Corp	Individual	Other	
6.57	6.37	7.22	6.63	6.66	7.00	7.06	6.64	5.22	6.49	6.44	52 cities[1]
6.17	6.41	6.60	6.36	6.06	6.43		6.10	5.11	6.08	6.09	4 New England cities
6.10	5.77	6.38	6.01	6.11					5.99		Portland, Me.
5.71		5.96	6.31	5.62	5.57				5.90	6.19	Worcester, Mass.
6.45	6.45	7.00	6.52	6.29	6.80		6.13	5.12	6.22	6.04	Providence, R.I.*
5.84		6.18	5.85	5.92			6.00	5.09	5.85		Waterbury, Conn.
5.91	6.30	6.39	5.87	5.74	6.36		6.25	5.18	6.12	6.12	4 Mid. Atlantic cities
6.18			6.20	6.44					6.06		Binghamton, N.Y.
5.69	6.48		5.83	5.27					6.09	6.12	Syracuse, N.Y.
6.03	6.02	6.40	4.85	5.92					6.01	5.99	Trenton, N.J.
6.36	5.97	6.39	6.67	6.70	6.36		6.25	5.18	6.37	6.22	Erie, Pa.
6.45	6.29	7.07	6.36	6.54	7.03	6.63	6.36	5.19	6.06	6.29	6 E. N. Central cities
6.42	6.25	7.17	6.32	6.51	6.90	6.63	6.35	5.16	5.96	6.32	Cleveland, Ohio*
6.52	6.45	6.79	6.54	6.81	7.92		6.35	5.17	6.38	6.01	Indianapolis, Ind.
6.88	6.51	7.17	6.19	6.63		6.69	6.20		6.22	6.73	Peoria, Ill.
6.41	6.22	6.81	6.74	6.95	7.01		6.62		6.52	6.22	Lansing, Mich.
6.38	6.14	6.88	6.18		6.67		6.20	5.08	6.27	6.31	Kenosha, Wis.
6.34		6.44	6.45	5.74	6.36		6.64	5.81	6.13	6.43	Racine, Wis.
6.54	6.14	7.11	6.68	6.72	6.76	7.35	6.90	5.19	6.51	6.76	10 W. N. Central cities
6.31	5.64	6.88	6.56	6.45	6.72	7.35	6.80	5.17	6.43	6.66	Minneapolis, Minn.
6.46	6.47	7.14	6.64	6.96	6.51		6.82	5.11	6.37	6.57	St. Paul, Minn.
6.48	6.42	6.67	6.56	6.77	6.86		7.10	5.24	6.69	6.40	Des Moines, Iowa
6.80	6.19	7.25	6.84	7.16	6.77		7.46		6.39	7.24	St. Joseph, Mo.
7.51	6.56	8.31	7.06	7.72	7.62		7.63	5.22	7.59	8.32	Springfield, Mo.
6.40	6.39	7.17	7.79		7.21			5.03	6.59	5.81	Fargo, N.D.
6.57	6.42	7.07	6.80	8.07	6.71			5.23	6.49	6.33	Sioux Falls, S.D.
6.52	6.47	6.97	6.60	6.06	6.53		6.63		5.96		Lincoln, Neb.
7.51	6.82	8.19	6.94	7.19	7.07		6.96	5.25	6.68	6.90	Topeka, Kan.
7.11	6.78	7.72	7.05		6.97		6.98	5.50	7.07	7.71	Wichita, Kan.
6.91	6.63	7.36	7.07	7.11	7.47	8.19	7.09	5.38	7.02	6.90	9 S. Atlantic cities
6.12		6.10	6.10						6.10	6.91	Hagerstown, Md.
6.72	6.47	6.68	6.79	7.17	6.94		6.84	5.55	6.59	6.87	Richmond, Va.
6.39	6.19	7.27	6.23	6.35	7.37		6.72	5.32	5.93	6.01	Wheeling, W.Va.*
6.39	6.41	6.25	6.18		6.76				6.28	6.09	Asheville, N.C.
6.35	6.30	6.20	6.89		6.57				6.13	6.10	Greensboro, N.C.
7.12			7.34		7.47			5.06	7.43	7.54	Charleston, S.C.
7.39	6.60	8.13			8.39			5.10	7.54		Columbia, S.C.
7.25	6.86	8.04	7.72	7.34	7.79	8.19	7.35	5.29	7.68	7.27	Atlanta, Ga.*
7.35	6.99	7.59			7.90			5.63	7.80	7.44	Jacksonville, Fla.
7.09	6.66	8.05	7.36	7.23	7.47	7.81	6.77	5.28	7.22	6.40	3 E. S. Central cities
7.29	6.51	7.61	9.75				6.33		6.24		Paducah, Ky.
7.10	6.64	8.04	7.25	7.23	7.56	7.81	6.79	5.28	7.61	6.40	Birmingham, Ala.*
6.93	6.86	8.24			6.87				4.91		Jackson, Miss.
7.45	6.98	8.28	7.64	8.21	7.63	8.06	7.30	5.30	7.58	7.79	6 W. S. Central cities
6.88	6.84	7.79	6.90	7.49	7.44		6.86	5.26	6.70	6.84	Little Rock, Ark.
7.55		7.54									Baton Rouge, La.
7.38	6.85	8.32	8.00	7.83	7.60		7.29	5.34	7.51	7.80	Oklahoma City, Okla.
7.52	7.34	7.33	7.44		7.34	8.11		5.25	7.51	7.55	Austin, Tex.
7.63	7.09	8.57	7.54	8.71	7.78	7.99	7.36	5.28	7.84	8.05	Dallas, Tex.
7.48	6.68	8.50	7.70		7.31	8.68	8.00	5.45	8.02		Wichita Falls, Tex.
6.60	4.78	8.14	7.24	7.60	7.97	6.61	7.60	5.50	7.53	7.74	6 Mountain cities
8.32			8.14		11.07		9.02	5.22	8.76	7.63	Butte, Mont.
7.91	6.62	8.54			8.71		7.90	5.44	8.03	8.35	Boise, Idaho
7.31		8.16						5.34	8.04		Casper, Wyo.
7.08	7.09	8.20				6.58		5.28	7.13	8.47	Pueblo, Colo.
7.60	6.72	8.94	7.66	8.41	8.21		7.60	5.11	8.03		Phoenix, Ariz.
5.83	3.39	7.81	7.03	7.32	7.58	6.62	7.46	5.72	7.26	7.52	Salt Lake City, Utah
6.92	6.60	7.90	7.29	7.29	7.03	7.49	7.06	5.22	7.23	5.95	4 Pacific cities
6.95	6.63	7.94	7.45	7.23	6.91		7.18	5.22	7.30	6.51	Seattle, Wash.*
6.45	6.45	7.87	6.71	6.97	6.69		6.48	5.24	6.94	4.89	Portland, Ore.
7.14	6.50	7.61	7.50	7.52	6.73				7.49	5.91	Sacramento, Calif.
7.48	6.82	8.02	7.76	7.78	7.96	7.49	7.71	5.21	7.43	6.52	San Diego, Calif.*

TABLE D 33

Mortgaged Rented Dwellings, First Mortgage Effective Interest Rates (per cent), Simple and Weighted Averages by Holding Agency, 30 Cities by Geographic Division, January 1, 1934

	All [3] holding agencies	Life ins. co.	Build. & loan asso.	Commer. bank	Savings bank	Mortgage co.	Construct. co.	Title & trust co.	H.O. Loan Corp.	Individual	Other
30 cities[1]	6.93	6.73	7.52	6.75	6.79	7.51		6.85	5.45	7.06	6.94
3 New England cities	6.14		6.46	6.10	6.17			5.73		6.07	6.10
Portland, Me.	6.29		7.14	6.05	6.19					6.12	
Worcester, Mass.	5.80				5.68						6.10
Providence, R.I.*	6.25		6.39	6.11	6.34			5.73		6.06	
3 Mid. Atlantic cities	6.03	6.75	6.63	6.62	5.73					6.26	6.33
Syracuse, N.Y.	5.82	6.75			5.33					6.17	
Trenton, N.J.	6.62		7.07		6.07					6.44	6.85
Erie, Pa.	6.47		6.44	6.62	6.87					6.47	6.10
5 E. N. Central cities	6.56	6.37	7.11	6.35	6.49	6.66		6.33	5.43	6.53	6.77
Cleveland, Ohio*	6.46	6.35	7.20	6.29	6.34	6.67		6.25	5.43	6.54	6.88
Indianapolis, Ind.	6.88	6.42	6.88	6.58	7.03			6.60			6.45
Peoria, Ill.	6.95	6.43	7.01					6.13			
Lansing, Mich.	6.74	6.47	6.83							6.66	
Racine, Wis.	6.46		6.84	6.20		6.55		6.77		6.29	6.37
8 W. N. Central cities	6.84	6.67	7.54	6.89	6.46	7.11		6.73	5.63	6.60	6.60
Minneapolis, Minn.	6.69	6.65	7.07	6.74	6.47	6.86		6.83		6.54	6.59
St. Paul, Minn.	6.58	6.43	8.10	7.12	6.30	7.09		5.85	5.63	6.32	
Des Moines, Iowa	6.97	6.82	7.32	6.64	6.50	7.89				6.88	6.57
Springfield, Mo.	8.18	6.80	9.03	7.40		8.00				8.29	
Sioux Falls, S.D.	6.90	6.84		7.87		6.75				6.34	6.90
Lincoln, Neb.	6.78	6.59	6.98			7.02		7.00		6.44	
Topeka, Kan.	7.40	6.84	8.63	7.24	7.07	6.51				6.95	
Wichita, Kan.	7.43	7.04	8.51	6.75		7.60		8.08		6.74	
1 S. Atlantic city	7.95	7.28	8.83		7.79	8.17		8.48		8.40	7.80
Atlanta, Ga.*	7.95	7.28	8.83		7.79	8.17		8.48		8.40	7.80
1 E. S. Central city	7.47	6.82	7.37	7.08		7.72		7.68		8.09	
Birmingham, Ala.*	7.47	6.82	7.37	7.08		7.72		7.68		8.09	
3 W. S. Central cities	7.80	6.92	8.38	8.05	8.10	8.15				7.99	7.46
Little Rock, Ark.	7.65	6.45	8.58	7.81		8.56				7.26	
Oklahoma City, Okla.	7.41	6.65	7.98			7.85				7.74	6.00
Dallas, Tex.	8.17	7.25	8.69	8.10	8.10	8.34				8.34	8.76
2 Mountain cities	7.81	7.36	7.96	8.27	8.03	8.26		7.59		7.85	
Phoenix, Ariz.	8.30	7.50	9.20		8.62	8.48				8.22	
Salt Lake City, Utah	7.62	7.31	7.47	8.27	7.80	8.17		7.59		7.70	
4 Pacific cities	7.37	6.94	7.81	7.27	7.32	8.32		7.44	5.43	7.47	6.84
Seattle, Wash.*	7.19	6.78	7.60	7.07	7.20	8.08		7.32		7.20	
Portland, Ore.	7.33	6.85	8.00		7.53	9.14			5.43	7.84	4.05
Sacramento, Calif.	7.68	7.56	7.98	7.58	6.93					7.76	
San Diego, Calif.*	7.74	7.16	8.11	7.67	7.62	8.22		7.76		7.73	9.30

Source: _Financial Survey of Urban Housing_. For number of reports upon which these interest rates are based see the rented section of Table D 31. Rates not shown for fewer than 3 reports.

*Metropolitan district.

[1]Geographic division and 30-city percentages weighted by estimated debt on first mortgage loans in each city (RPI).

[2]Individual interest rates for each agency and city weighted by amount of principal outstanding on first mortgage loans by agency holding the loan.

[3]The data do not allow the presentation of effective interest rates by agency holding the loan for all 52 cities. Effective interest rates for all agencies combined for 52 cities are shown in the first mortgage rented section of Table D 27.

Mortgaged Rented Dwellings, First Mortgage Effective Interest Rates (per cent), Simple and Weighted Averages by Holding Agency, 30 Cities by Geographic Division, January 1, 1934

| ← WEIGHTED AVERAGES [2] → | | | | | | | | | | | |
All [3] holding agencies	Life ins. co.	Build. & loan asso.	Com- mer. bank	Sav- ings bank	Mort- gage co.	Con- struct. co.	Title & trust co.	H.O. Loan Corp.	Indi- vidual	Other	
6.74	6.54	7.42	6.77	6.70	7.21		6.70	5.41	6.88	6.87	**30 cities**[1]
6.22		6.73	7.66	6.19			5.69		6.06	6.08	**3 New England cities**
6.11		6.99	6.05	6.11					6.02		Portland, Me.
5.76				5.63						6.08	Worcester, Mass.
6.40		6.71	7.82	6.40			5.69		6.06		Providence, R.I.*
6.01	6.55	6.55	6.65	5.71					6.19	6.11	**3 Mid. Atlantic cities**
5.83	6.55			5.41					6.09		Syracuse, N.Y.
6.29		6.74		6.08					6.23	6.21	Trenton, N.J.
6.48		6.47	6.65	6.51					6.49	6.06	Erie, Pa.
6.45	6.26	7.03	6.26	6.44	6.29		6.27	5.39	6.39	6.67	**5 E. N. Central cities**
6.35	6.25	7.12	6.20	6.29	6.28		6.19	5.39	6.39	6.63	Cleveland, Ohio*
6.76	6.27	6.71	6.49	7.01			6.50			6.87	Indianapolis, Ind.
6.76	6.34	7.00					6.17				Peoria, Ill.
6.75	6.44	6.88							6.61		Lansing, Mich.
6.47		7.07	6.34		6.41		6.76		6.26	6.45	Racine, Wis.
6.72	6.67	7.43	6.82	6.30	6.81		6.79	5.62	6.50	6.19	**8 W. N. Central cities**
6.68	6.76	7.09	6.72	6.38	6.59		6.84		6.46	6.02	Minneapolis, Minn.
6.50	6.42	7.99	7.00	6.05	7.16		6.11	5.62	6.30		St. Paul, Minn.
6.64	6.65	6.76	6.51	6.17	7.11				6.59	6.55	Des Moines, Iowa
7.58	6.70	9.14	7.15		6.79				7.91		Springfield, Mo.
6.71	6.52		7.36		6.74				6.39	7.03	Sioux Falls, S.D.
6.66	6.49	6.91			6.61		6.87		6.40		Lincoln, Neb.
6.99	6.57	8.57	7.51	7.16	6.45				6.45		Topeka, Kan.
7.23	7.06	8.23	6.77		7.09		8.11		6.75		Wichita, Kan.
7.60	7.04	8.50		7.89	7.89		7.65		8.24	7.63	**1 S. Atlantic city**
7.60	7.04	8.50		7.89	7.89		7.65		8.24	7.63	Atlanta, Ga.*
7.19	6.72	7.45	7.02		7.42		7.55		8.02		**1 E. S. Central city**
7.19	6.72	7.45	7.02		7.42		7.55		8.02		Birmingham, Ala.*
7.33	6.74	8.31	7.77	8.19	7.67				7.33	7.93	**3 W. S. Central cities**
7.34	6.38	8.96	7.40		7.79				7.06		Little Rock, Ark.
6.98	6.53	7.96			7.68				6.94	7.18	Oklahoma City, Okla.
7.76	7.10	8.64	7.96	8.19	7.75				7.85	8.73	Dallas, Tex.
7.25	6.87	8.01	8.02	7.41	8.13		7.47		7.76		**2 Mountain cities**
7.94	7.41	9.31		8.49	8.57				7.72		Phoenix, Ariz.
6.97	6.65	7.49	8.02	6.98	7.95		7.47		7.77		Salt Lake City, Utah
7.06	6.54	7.52	6.76	7.02	8.23		7.36	5.44	7.23	6.91	**4 Pacific cities**
6.79	6.28	7.13	6.40	6.96	7.66		7.29		7.03		Seattle, Wash.*
7.10	6.66	7.89		6.86	10.00			5.44	7.22	4.31	Portland, Ore.
7.23	6.85	7.89	6.82	6.58					7.46		Sacramento, Calif.
7.66	6.97	8.06	7.66	7.50	8.13		7.54		7.67	9.20	San Diego, Calif.*

TABLE D 34

Mortgaged Owner-occupied Dwellings, Number reporting Contract Interest Rates on Second and Third Mortgages, by Holding Agency, 38 Cities by Geographic Division, January 1, 1934

	All[1] holding agencies	Life ins. co.	Build. & loan asso.	Commer. bank	Savings bank	Mortgage co.	Construct. co.	Title & trust co.	Individual	Other[2]
38 cities	5,797	44	165	321	143	340	195	77	4,110	402
4 New England cities	827	1	21	38	40	31	6	9	634	47
Portland, Me.	74		4	9		3		2	55	1
Worcester, Mass.	311	1	8	19	20	7		4	231	21
Providence, R.I.*	309		8	8	19	11	6	3	234	20
Waterbury, Conn.	133		1	2	1	10			114	5
4 Mid. Atlantic cities	537	2	8	37	12	12	9	6	430	21
Binghamton, N.Y.	32					1		2	29	
Syracuse, N.Y.	264	2		8	9	8	3	2	221	11
Trenton, N.J.	124		3	21	2	2	2	1	90	3
Erie, Pa.	117		5	8	1	1	4	1	90	7
5 E. N. Central cities	2,191	12	72	133	60	124	55	23	1,578	134
Cleveland, Ohio*	1,902	6	41	107	59	109	50	16	1,411	103
Indianapolis, Ind.	57	1	5	14	1	1	1	2	29	3
Peoria, Ill.	88	3	13			7			52	13
Kenosha, Wis.	44	1	4	2		2	2	3	25	5
Racine, Wis.	100	1	9	10		5	2	2	61	10
9 W. N. Central cities	553	9	24	16	4	20	23	12	393	52
Minneapolis, Minn.	153	1	2	4		5	1		116	24
Des Moines, Iowa	38	1		3		1		2	29	2
St. Joseph, Mo.	45		3		1	4	2	1	28	6
Springfield, Mo.	33	1	5	4		3			19	1
Fargo, N.D.	34		2		2		3		21	5
Sioux Falls, S.D.	34	1	1	1		2		1	25	4
Lincoln, Neb.	60	2	3	1		1	3	1	45	4
Topeka, Kan.	77	3	7	1		2	6	2	53	3
Wichita, Kan.	79		1	2	1	2	8	5	57	3
6 S. Atlantic cities	574	7	9	59	15	63	40	9	316	56
Richmond, Va.	174	1		22	1	21	13	1	90	25
Wheeling, W.Va.*	63	1	5	13	4	1	5	1	24	9
Asheville, N.C.	27			3		4			20	
Greensboro, N.C.	50	1		7	1	4	12		18	7
Columbia, S.C.	30	1	1	2	1		2		22	1
Atlanta, Ga.*	230	3	3	12	8	33	8	7	142	14
2 E. S. Central cities	171	6	8	5	1	27	5		106	13
Birmingham, Ala.*	137	3	7	4		25	4		81	13
Jackson, Miss.	34	3	1	1	1	2	1		25	
3 W. S. Central cities	331	2	6	13	1	19	30	4	220	36
Little Rock, Ark.	57		1	13		3		2	33	5
Oklahoma City, Okla.	167		3			10	11		130	13
Dallas, Tex.	107	2	2		1	9	16	2	57	18
1 Mountain city	65		5	1	3	6	4	6	34	6
Salt Lake City, Utah	65		5	1	3	6	4	6	34	6
4 Pacific cities	548	5	12	19	7	38	23	8	399	37
Seattle, Wash.*	97	2	1	7	3	5		1	69	9
Portland, Ore.	133	2	2	1	1	9	4	3	103	8
Sacramento, Calif.	111	1	7	5	1	6	2		79	10
San Diego, Calif.*	207		2	6	2	18	17	4	148	10

Source: *Financial Survey of Urban Housing*
*Metropolitan District.
[1]Data for 'All holding agencies' only are available for 11 cities:
(number of reports)

Lansing, Mich.	14	Wichita Falls, Tex.	17
St. Paul, Minn.	28	Boise, Idaho	24
Hagerstown, Md.	36	Casper, Wyo.	12
Jacksonville, Fla.	20	Pueblo, Colo.	14
Paducah, Ky.	13	Phoenix, Ariz.	31
Austin, Tex.	18		

[2]Includes public bond issue: Racine, Wis. 1 report

TABLE D 35

Mortgaged Owner-occupied Dwellings, Second and Third Mortgage Contract Interest Rates (per cent), Simple and Weighted Averages by Holding Agency, 38 Cities by Geographic Division, January 1, 1934

	All [3] holding agencies	Life ins. co.	Build. & loan asso.	Commer. bank	Savings bank	Mortgage co.	Construct. co.	Title & trust co.	Individual	Other
	←				SIMPLE AVERAGES					→
38 cities[1]	6.50	6.13	6.71	6.51	6.46	6.75	6.71	6.75	6.48	6.37
4 New England cities	6.83		6.69	7.01	6.69	7.11	7.92	7.80	6.88	6.27
Portland, Me.	7.02		6.50	6.11		8.67			7.17	
Worcester, Mass.	6.82		6.81	7.14	6.78	7.14		7.50	6.81	6.43
Providence, R.I.*	7.20		6.63	7.00	6.63	7.45	7.92	8.00	7.30	6.30
Waterbury, Conn.	6.04					6.10			6.04	6.00
4 Mid. Atlantic cities	5.85		5.65	5.78	5.56	5.75	5.70		5.87	5.85
Binghamton, N.Y.	5.63								5.60	
Syracuse, N.Y.	5.86			5.75	5.56	5.75	5.67		5.88	5.82
Trenton, N.J.	5.88		6.00	5.88					5.87	6.00
Erie, Pa.	5.96		5.30	6.00			6.00		5.99	6.00
5 E. N. Central cities	6.32	5.94	6.65	6.38	6.54	6.73	6.47	5.94	6.25	6.33
Cleveland, Ohio*	6.32	5.92	6.67	6.36	6.54	6.75	6.47	5.94	6.26	6.32
Indianapolis, Ind.	6.61		6.70	6.86					6.55	6.67
Peoria, Ill.	6.30	6.50	6.88			6.50			6.06	6.54
Kenosha, Wis.	5.94		6.50					6.00	5.74	6.00
Racine, Wis.	5.83		5.89	6.12		6.20			5.81	5.78
9 W. N. Central cities	6.39	7.00	6.91	6.53		6.13	7.39	7.00	6.31	6.50
Minneapolis, Minn.	6.12			6.50		6.00			6.10	6.21
Des Moines, Iowa	6.53			6.50					6.55	
St. Joseph, Mo.	6.02		6.67			6.63			5.77	6.50
Springfield, Mo.	7.14		8.56	7.00		6.67			6.83	
Fargo, N.D.	6.62						7.33		6.41	6.60
Sioux Falls, S.D.	6.97								6.88	7.25
Lincoln, Neb.	6.38		6.17				7.00		6.34	6.25
Topeka, Kan.	7.16	7.00	7.86				7.83		7.02	8.00
Wichita, Kan.	6.96						7.63	7.00	6.84	7.00
6 S. Atlantic cities	6.43	7.17	6.95	6.52	6.91	6.55	6.34	7.29	6.36	6.40
Richmond, Va.	6.04			6.32		6.10	6.00		5.98	6.00
Wheeling, W.Va.*	6.05		6.86	6.15	6.00		6.00		5.96	5.78
Asheville, N.C.	6.00			6.00		6.00			6.00	
Greensboro, N.C.	6.04			6.00		6.00	6.00		6.11	6.00
Columbia, S.C.	7.53								7.36	
Atlanta, Ga.*	7.08	7.17	7.00	7.21	7.38	7.29	7.00	7.29	6.98	7.29
2 E. S. Central cities	7.14	7.79	7.54	6.50		7.64	7.50		6.96	7.53
Birmingham, Ala.*	7.31	8.00	7.54	6.50		7.64	7.50		7.16	7.53
Jackson, Miss.	6.49	7.00							6.22	
3 W. S. Central cities	7.59		6.83	6.73		8.05	7.86		7.57	7.71
Little Rock, Ark.	6.88			6.73			7.67		6.73	7.00
Oklahoma City, Okla.	7.84		6.83			8.40	8.00		7.80	7.92
Dallas, Tex.	7.52					7.56	7.75		7.56	7.67
1 Mountain city	7.35		8.60		7.33	6.92	7.25	7.50	7.50	5.92
Salt Lake City, Utah	7.35		8.60		7.33	6.92	7.25	7.50	7.50	5.92
4 Pacific cities	6.86		6.71	7.05	6.67	6.92	6.97	6.64	6.81	7.15
Seattle, Wash.*	6.93			7.00	6.67	7.00			6.88	7.33
Portland, Ore.	6.58					6.61	7.00	6.00	6.55	6.75
Sacramento, Calif.	7.03		6.71	7.00		7.17			6.97	7.60
San Diego, Calif.*	7.00			7.12		7.03	6.94	7.25	6.92	7.20

Source: *Financial Survey of Urban Housing.* For number of reports upon which these contract interest rates are based see Table D 34. Rates not shown for fewer than 3 reports.

*Metropolitan district.

[1] Geographic division and 38-city percentages weighted by estimated debt on second and third mortgage loans in each city (RPI).

[2] Individual interest rates for each agency and city weighted by amount of principal outstanding on second and third mortgage loans by agency holding the loan.

[3] The data do not allow the presentation of contract interest rates by agency holding the loan for more than 38 cities. Contract interest rates for all agencies combined are shown for 49 cities in second and third mortgage, owner-occupied section of Table D 27. The data do not allow the presentation of effective interest rates for owner-occupied properties by agency holding the loan. Effective interest rates for all agencies combined for these properties are shown in the second and third mortgage, owner-occupied section of Table D 27.

TABLE D 35

Mortgaged Owner-occupied Dwellings, Second and Third Mortgage Contract Interest Rates (per cent), Simple and Weighted Averages by Holding Agency, 38 Cities by Geographic Division, January 1, 1934

←————————————————— W E I G H T E D   A V E R A G E S [2] —————————————————→

All [3] holding agencies	Life ins. co.	Build. & loan asso.	Commer. bank	Savings bank	Mortgage co.	Construct. co.	Title & trust co.	Individual	Other	
6.42	6.17	6.76	6.55	6.30	6.71	6.69	6.51	6.40	6.28	**38 cities**[1]
6.76		6.73	7.26	6.55	6.95	7.85	7.51	6.84	6.07	**4 New England cities**
6.24		6.18	6.00		9.17			7.08		Portland, Me.
6.70		7.16	6.80	6.46	6.02		6.75	6.78	6.08	Worcester, Mass.
7.17		6.49	7.65	6.61	7.71	7.85	8.00	7.24	6.09	Providence, R.I.*
6.05					6.23			6.05	6.00	Waterbury, Conn.
5.87		5.87	5.80	5.36	5.67	5.79		5.88	5.87	**4 Mid. Atlantic cities**
5.67								5.64		Binghamton, N.Y.
5.87			5.77	5.36	5.67	5.77		5.89	5.85	Syracuse, N.Y.
5.92		6.00	5.91					5.91	6.00	Trenton, N.J.
5.98		5.75	6.00			6.00		5.99	6.00	Erie, Pa.
6.19	6.01	6.74	6.32	6.37	6.68	6.38	5.67	6.12	6.21	**5 E. N. Central cities**
6.18	6.00	6.76	6.27	6.37	6.69	6.38	5.66	6.12	6.19	Cleveland, Ohio*
6.53		6.83	7.08					6.35	6.70	Indianapolis, Ind.
6.26	6.20	6.85			6.78			6.06	6.46	Peoria, Ill.
5.84		6.69					6.00	5.65	6.22	Kenosha, Wis.
5.85		5.75	6.27		6.14			5.86	5.67	Racine, Wis.
6.31	6.33	7.02	6.52		6.07	7.36	6.50	6.26	6.25	**9 W. N. Central cities**
6.08			6.53		6.00			6.08	5.99	Minneapolis, Minn.
6.60		6.34						6.56		Des Moines, Iowa
5.97		6.86			6.28			5.67	6.60	St. Joseph, Mo.
7.06		8.51	6.71		6.57			7.24		Springfield, Mo.
6.58						7.06		6.50	6.68	Fargo, N.D.
6.72								6.63	6.07	Sioux Falls, S.D.
6.32		6.43				7.00		6.26	6.06	Lincoln, Neb.
6.93	6.33	7.66				7.80		6.81	8.00	Topeka, Kan.
6.67						7.66	6.50	6.59	6.26	Wichita, Kan.
6.39	6.92	6.75	6.60	6.90	6.51	6.34	6.94	6.34	6.43	**6 S. Atlantic cities**
6.12			6.71		6.05	6.00		5.99	6.00	Richmond, Va.
6.03		6.99	6.04	6.01	6.00	6.00		5.90	6.06	Wheeling, W.Va.*
6.00			6.00		6.00			6.00		Asheville, N.C.
6.10			6.00		6.00	6.00		6.52	6.00	Greensboro, N.C.
7.27								7.08		Columbia, S.C.
6.90	6.92	6.62	7.11	7.37	7.26	7.00	6.94	6.76	7.26	Atlanta, Ga.*
7.06	7.79	7.48	6.48		7.65	7.62		6.80	7.70	**2 E. S. Central cities**
7.13	8.00	7.48	6.48		7.65	7.62		6.87	7.70	Birmingham, Ala.*
6.79	6.99							6.53		Jackson, Miss.
7.49		6.64	6.58		8.58	7.83		7.46	7.56	**3 W. S. Central cities**
6.23			6.58			7.41		6.69	6.14	Little Rock, Ark.
7.76		6.64			9.19	8.12		7.57	7.86	Oklahoma City, Okla.
7.58					7.73	7.59		7.58	7.67	Dallas, Tex.
7.32		9.33		7.67	6.83	7.02	7.93	7.16	6.40	**1 Mountain City**
7.32		9.33		7.67	6.83	7.02	7.93	7.16	6.40	Salt Lake City, Utah
6.85		6.32	6.95	6.20	7.35	7.09	6.82	6.72	7.32	**4 Pacific cities**
6.87			6.86	6.20	7.00			6.83	7.35	Seattle, Wash.*
6.69					8.08	7.19	6.00	6.39	7.26	Portland, Ore.
6.83		6.32	7.00		7.15			6.73	8.00	Sacramento, Calif.
7.00			7.00		7.02	7.00	7.59	6.93	7.07	San Diego, Calif.*

270

TABLE D 36

Mortgaged Dwellings, All Priorities, Number reporting Payments and Average Annual Payment (dollars) required for Interest and Principal, by Value Groups: Owner-occupied, 52 Cities; Rented, 51 Cities, by Geographic Division, January 1, 1934

O W N E R - O C C U P I E D

AVERAGE ANNUAL PAYMENT REQUIRED (INTEREST AND PRINCIPAL)

	NUMBER REPORTING	All value groups	$1-499	$500-999	$1,000-1,499	$1,500-1,999	$2,000-2,999	$3,000-3,999	$4,000-4,999	$5,000-7,499	$7,500-9,999	$10,000-14,999	$15,000 and over
52 cities[1]	68,067	351	124	137	165	181	224	270	319	384	497	660	1,128
4 New England cities	4,206	329		80	104	127	166	188	240	304	412	537	732
Portland, Me.	625	354			102	151	189	208	255	350	476	571	885
Worcester, Mass.	1,116	336			114	110	202	236	240	306	391	488	690
Providence, R.I.*	1,991	323		80	99	131	155	179	249	307	417	561	710
Waterbury, Conn.	474	345			113		148	140	183	258	394	476	880
4 Mid. Atlantic cities	4,296	254			122	102	151	153	205	259	350	455	659
Binghamton, N.Y.	252	241					145	156	155	209	338	392	499
Syracuse, N.Y.	966	281			143	95	163	140	210	270	351	438	681
Trenton, N.J.	1,596	182			75	94	110	144	192	231	315	512	745
Erie, Pa.	1,482	257			110	129	162	198	233	287	391	482	607
6 E. N. Central cities	20,037	441	142	154	205	204	251	302	354	431	555	721	1,209
Cleveland, Ohio*	13,889	482	142	172	228	220	259	309	365	438	570	719	1,279
Indianapolis, Ind.	1,717	405		102	173	195	259	319	363	454	566	791	1,323
Peoria, Ill.	1,417	365		122	142	165	209	285	348	451	547	693	1,093
Lansing, Mich.	625	330			157	183	228	322	358	403	587	720	547
Kenosha, Wis.	732	261				132	210	189	225	273	359	547	495
Racine, Wis.	1,657	313			136	115	190	201	249	333	412	618	973
10 W. N. Central cities	12,190	285	78	112	141	147	199	244	299	357	460	602	1,254
Minneapolis, Minn.	4,065	318		136	151	140	194	242	274	353	463	610	1,936
St. Paul, Minn.	877	256		50	93	103	163	210	280	308	395	696	854
Des Moines, Iowa	1,625	271	83	123	157	171	217	248	299	390	520	547	864
St. Joseph, Mo.	532	250		93	120	138	210	207	419	353	315	408	887
Springfield, Mo.	777	199	98	89	115	146	187	232	271	343	396	586	583
Fargo, N.D.	475	316			188	150	250	255	282	333	356	582	898
Sioux Falls, S.D.	636	243	83	130	142	124	196	199	249	255	276	570	884
Lincoln, Neb.	801	300		125	161	181	218	285	321	399	530	617	979
Topeka, Kan.	1,064	302	58	136	164	178	233	305	354	403	600	680	677
Wichita, Kan.	1,338	279	71	139	177	221	237	299	376	438	580	482	1,091
9 S. Atlantic cities	6,146	371	134	114	170	196	227	298	341	420	548	703	912
Hagerstown, Md.	359	241		46	81	87	127	186	251	264	363	432	666
Richmond, Va.	1,068	411		120	130	164	210	284	340	420	525	683	910
Wheeling, W.Va.*	787	314	38	105	155	207	206	259	289	378	458	706	973
Asheville, N.C.	408	413		152	224	240	309	409	432	535	927	551	956
Greensboro, N.C.	303	516		123	189	241	273	349	438	474	759	1,003	1,331
Charleston, S.C.	204	246		34	108	97	124	257	260	280	262	590	637
Columbia, S.C.	327	357		99	102	165	211	258	349	433	435	691	660
Atlanta, Ga.*	2,407	393	176	141	205	217	261	322	369	455	588	773	947
Jacksonville, Fla.	283	308		52	178	191	176	291	286	365	522	511	736
3 E. S. Central cities	2,525	354	207	175	222	240	289	347	374	460	535	671	1,005
Paducah, Ky.	225	288	66	125	189	228	258	278	397	504	926		1,355
Birmingham, Ala.*	2,040	354	216	180	227	252	287	352	377	459	525	683	958
Jackson, Miss.	260	381		161	204	165	318	343	348	445	438	590	1,167
6 W. S. Central cities	5,193	368	87	198	186	228	272	338	396	468	522	779	1,161
Little Rock, Ark.	840	306	89	106	151	230	237	269	346	436	495	745	932
Baton Rouge, La.	185	315		133	177	166	269	314	310	454	408	598	
Oklahoma City, Okla.	1,765	394	78	145	163	201	268	345	403	511	546	860	1,416
Austin, Tex.	411	367	90	149	181	260	269	345	413	492	572	698	897
Dallas, Tex.	1,653	369		279	206	242	276	342	403	431	492	749	1,070
Wichita Falls, Tex.	339	371	143	214	269	289	352	417	447	540	698	850	1,136
6 Mountain cities	4,195	301	104	133	153	189	249	285	348	404	463	832	1,434
Butte, Mont.	471	239	68	224	182	174	233	254	257	306	362	426	490
Boise, Idaho	580	273	107	115	152	191	248	262	303	365	445	536	951
Casper, Wyo.	295	318	150	145	187	240	297	357	430	399	531	363	
Pueblo, Colo.	413	216	75	98	158	222	238	230	334	320	250	797	
Phoenix, Ariz.	538	314		130	137	166	246	278	286	411	441	637	1,035
Salt Lake City, Utah	1,898	329	110	134	152	182	249	301	376	442	532	1,028	1,711
4 Pacific cities	9,279	318	110	126	172	208	242	297	332	381	533	694	1,490
Seattle, Wash.*	3,204	339	109	124	195	223	257	319	346	391	511	751	1,941
Portland, Ore.	2,519	282	64	117	142	183	205	272	312	368	572	715	1,405
Sacramento, Calif.	1,239	348		120	199	218	261	306	347	417	520	670	781
San Diego, Calif.*	2,317	320	193	152	157	210	264	287	326	361	522	535	907

Source: Financial Survey of Urban Housing. Average not shown for fewer than 3 reports.

*Metropolitan district.

[1] Geographic division and 52 (51)-city averages weighted by estimated number of mortgaged properties, by tenure, in each city (RPI). For rented properties where the number of cities included in the 'All value groups' column is larger than the number for the individual value groups, the weighted geographic division and 52 (51)-city averages in the 'All value groups' column are not strictly comparable to the weighted averages for the individual value groups.

[2] Where only average annual payment 'All value groups' is shown, average annual payment by value groups was not obtained by Financial Survey of Urban Housing either because the number of reports was too small or because related information was lacking for rented properties.

Mortgaged Dwellings, All Priorities, Number reporting Payments and Average Annual Payment (dollars) required for Interest and Principal, by Value Groups: Owner-occupied, 52 Cities; Rented, 51 Cities, by Geographic Division, January 1, 1934

← ——————————————————————————— R E N T E D ——————————————————————————— →

NUMBER REPORTING	All[2] value groups	$1- 499	$500- 999	$1,000- 1,499	$1,500- 1,999	$2,000- 2,999	$3,000- 3,999	$4,000- 4,999	$5,000- 7,499	$7,500- 9,999	$10,000- 14,999	$15,000 and over	
						AVERAGE ANNUAL PAYMENT REQUIRED (INTEREST AND PRINCIPAL)							
12,968	440	57	158	167	182	210	262	310	399	525	705	2,456	51 cities[1]
844	420			60	101	188	182	233	330	482	626	1,353	4 New England cities
179	378			60	133	161	288	288	308	447	470	1,326	Portland, Me.
195	338					184	144	197	302	364	451	962	Worcester, Mass.
367	404				98	192	183	239	341	521	694	1,474	Providence, R.I.*
103	755												Waterbury, Conn.
778	316		37	62	73	112	233	187	255	368	502	1,465	4 Mid. Atlantic cities
74	370												Binghamton, N.Y.
206	346					93	269	163	254	369	463	1,797	Syracuse, N.Y.
237	164		37	62	73	99	143	195	180	272	635	775	Trenton, N.J.
261	305					172	197	245	309	430	517	1,035	Erie, Pa.
3,622	523	73	241	210	219	253	284	353	428	574	765	2,425	6 E. N. Central cities
2,205	646		236	256	253	286	292	360	456	626	864	2,639	Cleveland, Ohio*
490	385	73	276	159	165	221	293	364	417	503	634	2,149	Indianapolis, Ind.
327	375		98	117	157	181	218	331	399	571	604	2,662	Peoria, Ill.
156	251			127	202	203	254	305	308	528			Lansing, Mich.
127	373												Kenosha, Wis.
317	311			120		140	213	244	257	381	461	848	Racine, Wis.
2,855	319	47	131	117	152	173	221	268	339	486	639	2,342	10 W. N. Central cities
945	395		163	136	164	160	211	277	332	483	763	2,078	Minneapolis, Minn.
218	323			67	141	172	175	226	300	468	453	3,610	St. Paul, Minn.
396	262	35	94	122	134	150	231	253	315	468	648	1,820	Des Moines, Iowa
106	169												St. Joseph, Mo.
174	196	40	81	87	145	164	268	258	266	358		1,163	Springfield, Mo.
76	288												Fargo, N.D.
182	360			122	131	128	132	160	280	218	750	5,442	Sioux Falls, S.D.
178	359		178	119	129	195	266	277	360	408		2,676	Lincoln, Neb.
242	289		62	103	182	205	256	299	334	810	682	2,858	Topeka, Kan.
338	252	63	99	148	167	228	273	340	475	591	496	935	Wichita, Kan.
1,066	481		79	151	151	181	318	335	421	568	867	4,137	8 S. Atlantic cities
62	267												Hagerstown, Md.
130	421		33	100	108	137	211	258	318	640	541	3,772	Richmond, Va.
116	330												Wheeling, W.Va.*
35	406												Asheville, N.C.
70	628												Greensboro, N.C.
72	175												Charleston, S.C.
77	401												Columbia, S.C.
504	571		95	169	166	197	357	363	458	542	985	4,269	Atlanta, Ga.*
293	497		139	164	253	225	301	365	558	388	659	2,270	3 E. S. Central cities
15	322												Paducah, Ky.
205	398		139	164	253	225	301	365	558	388	659	2,270	Birmingham, Ala.*
73	1,027												Jackson, Miss.
1,142	425	58	87	178	194	254	296	372	432	725	848	1,872	6 W. S. Central cities
172	288	58	153	106	141	187	237	269	357	733	675	1,237	Little Rock, Ark.
57	384												Baton Rouge, La.
363	568		88	176	204	262	339	384	513	704	634	2,594	Oklahoma City, Okla.
92	386		122	173	174	284	339	374	568		1,113	1,893	Austin, Tex.
380	388		68	194	202	258	274	384	373	736	977	1,536	Dallas, Tex.
78	300												Wichita Falls, Tex.
630	401		142	203	172	184	234	301	476	437	621	2,881	6 Mountain cities
52	480												Butte, Mont.
33	269												Boise, Idaho
47	451												Casper, Wyo.
55	162												Pueblo, Colo.
157	283			318	289	165	195	242	397	324	638	690	Phoenix, Ariz.
286	538		142	134	102	196	257	337	523	505	610	4,207	Salt Lake City, Utah
1,738	445	37	145	147	186	211	264	301	407	479	631	3,079	4 Pacific cities
476	667		187	165	228	217	258	292	494	493	633	5,720	Seattle, Wash.*
418	289	37	75	133	155	176	251	278	334	389	561	1,864	Portland, Ore.
230	315			147	170	208	310	370	444	722	544	1,296	Sacramento, Calif.
614	336		154	135	165	238	269	309	341	454	733	1,208	San Diego, Calif.*

TABLE D 37

Mortgaged Dwellings, All Priorities, Average Annual Payment required for Interest and Principal as a Percentage of Value of Property, by Value Groups: Owner-occupied, 52 Cities; Rented, 51 Cities, by Geographic Division, January 1, 1934

	OWNER-OCCUPIED											
	All value groups	$1-499	$500-999	$1,000-1,499	$1,500-1,999	$2,000-2,999	$3,000-3,999	$4,000-4,999	$5,000-7,499	$7,500-9,999	$10,000-14,999	$15,000 and over
52 cities[1]	6.9	34.5	17.5	13.4	10.7	9.1	8.1	7.5	6.6	6.1	5.9	5.3
4 New England cities	5.0		10.4	8.8	7.3	6.0	5.6	5.6	5.2	4.9	4.8	3.8
Portland, Me.	5.8			8.9	9.1	8.1	6.2	6.0	5.9	5.8	5.3	5.1
Worcester, Mass.	5.0			10.2	6.9	7.8	6.6	5.6	5.2	4.7	4.5	4.1
Providence, R.I.*	5.1		10.4	8.2	8.0	5.4	5.4	5.9	5.2	5.0	5.1	3.7
Waterbury, Conn.	4.3			9.6		6.1	4.1	4.3	4.4	4.7	4.2	3.6
4 Mid. Atlantic cities	4.4			9.9	5.9	6.2	4.6	4.8	4.5	4.3	4.1	3.1
Binghamton, N.Y.	3.6					5.3	4.6	3.6	3.6	4.1	3.6	2.3
Syracuse, N.Y.	4.3			11.7	5.7	6.8	4.2	4.9	4.6	4.2	3.9	3.1
Trenton, N.J.	4.4			5.8	5.7	4.7	4.4	4.5	4.1	3.9	4.7	3.9
Erie, Pa.	5.2			9.1	6.7	6.7	6.0	5.5	5.0	4.9	4.4	3.2
6 E. N. Central cities	7.3	37.1	19.3	15.6	11.7	10.1	8.9	8.3	7.4	6.8	6.5	5.8
Cleveland, Ohio*	7.3	37.1	22.6	16.6	12.4	10.2	9.0	8.6	7.5	6.9	6.4	5.9
Indianapolis, Ind.	8.2		11.3	14.6	11.6	10.9	9.7	8.5	7.6	7.0	7.2	6.8
Peoria, Ill.	7.7		15.4	12.0	9.3	8.8	8.6	8.2	7.9	6.8	6.2	6.1
Lansing, Mich.	8.3			13.6	11.2	9.3	9.7	8.3	7.1	7.2	6.6	2.7
Kenosha, Wis.	4.9				7.6	8.6	5.7	5.3	4.7	4.3	5.0	3.0
Racine, Wis.	5.7			11.4	6.9	7.2	6.1	5.8	5.7	5.1	5.5	5.1
10 W. N. Central cities	6.8	24.0	14.6	11.8	8.8	8.3	7.4	7.0	6.2	5.7	5.5	5.6
Minneapolis, Minn.	6.6		17.1	11.7	8.3	8.0	7.3	6.4	6.2	5.7	5.5	7.3
St. Paul, Minn.	6.1		6.9	8.2	6.2	6.9	6.3	6.6	5.5	4.9	6.6	4.5
Des Moines, Iowa	7.5	27.0	16.7	13.6	10.3	9.2	7.5	7.1	6.8	6.5	5.2	4.4
St. Joseph, Mo.	6.7		12.9	10.5	8.4	8.5	6.4	8.7	5.7	3.8	3.7	4.5
Springfield, Mo.	6.6	30.2	11.9	10.1	9.0	8.2	7.2	6.4	5.8	4.8	5.4	1.9
Fargo, N.D.	6.1			17.7	7.9	9.9	9.7	6.6	5.7	4.2	5.0	4.5
Sioux Falls, S.D.	5.4	22.6	18.8	12.3	7.4	7.4	6.1	5.9	4.5	3.4	5.3	5.1
Lincoln, Neb.	7.8		15.8	13.7	11.0	9.4	8.7	7.5	6.9	6.4	5.2	5.9
Topeka, Kan.	8.3	17.1	15.1	13.9	10.6	9.9	9.2	8.4	7.2	7.6	6.2	3.3
Wichita, Kan.	9.3	21.6	18.4	15.5	13.5	10.4	9.2	8.9	7.7	7.0	4.2	5.2
9 S. Atlantic cities	7.5	37.0	14.4	15.0	11.8	9.6	9.1	8.1	7.3	6.8	6.4	4.8
Hagerstown, Md.	4.6		6.9	7.3	5.5	5.4	5.7	5.9	4.6	4.6	3.8	3.4
Richmond, Va.	6.9		15.6	11.7	9.9	9.1	8.7	8.0	7.2	6.5	5.9	5.0
Wheeling, W.Va.*	7.1	13.8	15.3	13.4	12.8	8.8	8.0	6.8	6.6	5.9	6.6	5.4
Asheville, N.C.	10.0		19.8	19.5	14.5	12.9	12.7	10.4	9.5	11.2	5.2	5.1
Greensboro, N.C.	8.8		16.4	16.4	14.3	11.5	10.7	10.2	8.2	9.4	9.2	6.1
Charleston, S. C.	5.2		4.9	9.8	6.0	5.5	7.9	6.3	4.8	3.3	5.5	3.1
Columbia, S.C.	7.0		12.9	9.1	10.4	7.8	7.9	8.3	7.6	5.4	6.8	3.5
Atlanta, Ga.*	8.1	44.0	15.5	17.9	12.6	10.9	9.8	8.8	7.9	7.2	6.9	4.9
Jacksonville, Fla.	6.8		8.2	15.7	11.8	7.6	8.9	6.8	6.5	6.4	4.8	3.9
3 E. S. Central cities	9.5	54.6	22.5	18.2	14.7	12.5	10.7	8.9	8.2	6.6	6.5	5.5
Paducah, Ky.	10.4	21.3	14.3	16.7	14.0	11.2	8.5	9.4	8.7	11.6		8.6
Birmingham, Ala.*	9.6	56.4	22.8	18.3	15.5	12.5	10.9	9.1	8.2	6.5	6.6	5.2
Jackson, Miss.	8.4		24.0	17.7	10.2	12.9	10.4	8.2	8.0	5.2	5.6	6.7
6 W. S. Central cities	8.9	26.8	24.8	14.7	13.7	11.6	10.3	9.4	8.1	6.5	7.0	5.8
Little Rock, Ark.	8.3	19.8	12.6	13.0	13.9	10.0	8.2	8.2	7.9	6.2	7.1	5.6
Baton Rouge, La.	7.3		18.1	15.4	10.0	11.1	9.5	7.4	7.7	5.0	5.4	
Oklahoma City, Okla.	9.2	26.0	20.4	14.6	12.3	11.4	10.6	9.5	8.9	6.7	7.8	7.3
Austin, Tex.	8.7	30.0	20.0	15.6	15.2	11.9	10.2	10.0	8.2	7.2	6.3	4.7
Dallas, Tex.	8.8		31.6	14.2	14.4	11.8	10.4	9.5	7.3	6.1	6.6	5.1
Wichita Falls, Tex.	11.9	52.8	29.4	23.4	18.0	15.1	12.6	10.8	9.6	8.6	7.1	4.6
6 Mountain cities	8.4	28.8	15.9	13.1	11.3	10.5	8.6	8.2	7.1	5.7	6.6	5.4
Butte, Mont.	7.2	18.5	24.3	14.5	10.8	10.4	7.7	6.1	5.5	4.4	4.1	2.3
Boise, Idaho	7.8	29.2	16.0	12.4	11.3	10.4	8.0	7.2	6.4	5.4	4.8	4.8
Casper, Wyo.	10.1	40.5	21.0	16.3	14.4	12.6	10.8	10.2	7.0	6.5	3.6	
Pueblo, Colo.	9.1	19.2	13.4	13.9	13.5	10.1	7.0	8.0	5.7	3.1	6.5	
Phoenix, Ariz.	7.4		16.5	12.1	9.9	9.9	8.5	6.8	7.3	5.4	5.7	5.8
Salt Lake City, Utah	8.5	31.4	14.9	12.9	10.8	10.5	9.1	8.8	7.6	6.5	7.4	5.6
4 Pacific cities	8.1	31.9	16.6	14.0	12.4	10.2	9.1	7.8	6.7	6.6	5.8	6.0
Seattle, Wash.*	8.7	30.6	15.3	14.7	13.3	10.9	9.8	8.1	6.9	6.4	5.7	7.0
Portland, Ore.	7.8	21.3	15.7	12.2	11.0	8.8	8.3	7.4	6.5	7.1	6.6	5.8
Sacramento, Calif.	7.9		20.0	16.5	12.9	10.8	9.3	8.2	7.2	6.3	5.1	4.3
San Diego, Calif.*	7.6	48.3	20.8	13.8	12.5	11.2	8.7	7.8	6.4	6.4	4.9	4.1

Source: *Financial Survey of Urban Housing.* Percentages in this table are based upon average values of mortgaged properties as shown in Table D 7 and average annual payment required for interest and principal as shown in Table D 36. Percentage not shown for fewer than 3 reports.

*Metropolitan district.

[1]Geographic division and 52 (51)-city percentages automatically weighted by the use of weighted averages from Tables D 7 and 36. For rented properties where the number of cities included in the 'All value groups' column is larger than the number for the individual value groups the weighted geographic division and 52 (51)-city percentages in the 'All value groups' column are not strictly comparable to the weighted percentages for the individual value groups.

TABLE D 37

Mortgaged Dwellings, All Priorities, Average Annual Payment required for Interest and Principal as a Percentage of Value of Property, by Value Groups: Owner-occupied, 52 Cities; Rented, 51 Cities, by Geographic Division, January 1, 1934

← ——————————————————————— R E N T E D ——————————————————————— →

All value groups	$1-499	$500-999	$1,000-1,499	$1,500-1,999	$2,000-2,999	$3,000-3,999	$4,000-4,999	$5,000-7,499	$7,500-9,999	$10,000-14,999	$15,000 and over	
7.2	15.3	20.7	13.8	10.9	8.7	7.8	7.3	6.8	6.4	6.2	6.9	51 cities[1]
5.5												4 New England cities
5.1			5.5	6.3	7.7	5.5	5.5	5.5	5.7	5.7	5.2	Portland, Me.
4.6			5.5	8.9	6.7	8.9	6.8	5.2	5.4	4.3	4.1	Worcester, Mass.
5.8				6.0	7.3	4.3	4.7	4.9	4.4	4.1	5.1	Providence, R.I.*
5.5					8.0	5.5	5.6	5.7	6.2	6.3	5.3	Waterbury, Conn.
4.7		5.6	5.1	4.6	4.7	6.9	4.4	4.4	4.5	4.6	5.4	4 Mid. Atlantic cities
4.5												Binghamton, N.Y.
4.6					3.9	7.8	3.9	4.3	4.6	4.3	5.7	Syracuse, N.Y.
4.1		5.6	5.1	4.6	4.3	4.5	4.6	3.3	3.3	5.5	4.6	Trenton, N.J.
5.3					7.0	5.9	5.8	5.3	5.2	4.7	4.8	Erie, Pa.
7.8	19.5	31.7	15.7	12.9	9.9	8.6	8.3	7.3	7.0	6.8	8.1	6 E. N. Central cities
8.1		30.6	17.5	14.9	10.5	8.8	8.4	7.7	7.5	7.6	8.4	Cleveland, Ohio*
8.1	19.5	37.1	13.5	9.8	9.5	8.9	8.5	7.2	6.3	5.9	8.1	Indianapolis, Ind.
6.9		13.3	9.9	9.8	7.8	6.7	7.9	7.0	7.2	5.1	7.2	Peoria, Ill.
7.1			10.8	11.3	8.7	7.6	7.2	5.4	6.8			Lansing, Mich.
5.6												Kenosha, Wis.
4.5			10.3		5.8	6.4	5.7	4.4	4.7	4.1	3.4	Racine, Wis.
6.8	14.8	17.6	10.2	8.9	7.3	6.7	6.2	5.9	5.9	5.7	7.8	10 W. N. Central cities
6.8		20.7	12.0	10.0	6.8	6.4	6.2	5.8	5.9	6.8	7.5	Minneapolis, Minn.
6.2			5.8	7.2	7.2	5.1	5.3	5.0	5.6	4.0	10.5	St. Paul, Minn.
6.4	13.1	13.7	10.6	8.0	6.4	7.2	6.0	5.4	5.5	5.6	5.6	Des Moines, Iowa
5.2												St. Joseph, Mo.
6.4	11.1	11.2	7.4	8.5	7.3	8.2	6.1	4.7	4.3		4.6	Springfield, Mo.
5.6												Fargo, N.D.
6.9			11.0	7.5	5.2	4.0	3.8	4.9	2.7	6.8	13.2	Sioux Falls, S.D.
8.7		25.4	9.9	7.8	8.4	8.1	6.6	6.3	5.1		11.0	Lincoln, Neb.
7.5		8.3	9.3	11.0	8.6	7.5	7.0	5.8	10.1	6.1	6.7	Topeka, Kan.
8.1	17.6	13.7	13.0	10.4	9.8	8.2	8.0	8.4	7.1	4.4	3.8	Wichita, Kan.
7.7		10.6	13.1	9.1	7.8	9.1	7.8	7.4	6.9	6.5	8.5	8 S. Atlantic cities
6.0												Hagerstown, Md.
7.1		4.0	8.5	6.0	6.3	6.5	6.0	5.4	7.7	5.1	11.5	Richmond, Va.
5.7												Wheeling, W.Va.*
10.9												Asheville, N.C.
9.7												Greensboro, N.C.
4.2												Charleston, S.C.
7.2												Columbia, S.C.
8.2		13.2	14.7	10.3	8.4	10.0	8.4	8.2	6.6	6.9	7.9	Atlanta, Ga.*
8.4		19.2	14.9	15.6	9.8	9.0	8.7	10.1	5.0	6.1	3.6	3 E. S. Central cities
7.2												Paducah. Ky.
7.0		19.2	14.9	15.6	9.8	9.0	8.7	10.1	5.0	6.1	3.6	Birmingham, Ala.*
14.8												Jackson, Miss.
8.3	20.1	11.1	15.7	11.8	10.8	9.0	8.8	7.5	8.7	7.6	6.5	6 W. S. Central cities
7.4	24.2	20.0	9.5	8.7	8.1	7.1	6.4	6.0	9.4	5.5	7.1	Little Rock, Ark.
7.2												Baton Rouge, La.
8.3		11.0	15.1	12.6	11.3	10.3	9.0	9.0	8.6	5.9	7.9	Oklahoma City, Okla.
10.2		17.8	15.4	10.5	12.1	10.2	9.0	9.3		9.8	8.4	Austin, Tex.
8.2		8.5	17.2	12.2	10.9	8.4	9.0	8.4	8.7	8.8	5.2	Dallas, Tex.
11.9												Wichita Falls, Tex.
7.3		17.0	17.1	10.2	7.7	7.0	7.1	8.2	5.2	5.8	6.5	6 Mountain cities
7.6												Butte, Mont.
6.9												Boise, Idaho
8.9												Casper, Wyo.
7.6												Pueblo, Colo.
5.8			27.2	16.9	6.9	5.7	5.7	6.8	3.8	6.0	3.0	Phoenix, Ariz.
7.8		17.0	11.2	6.1	8.2	7.8	8.0	9.0	6.1	5.6	7.4	Salt Lake City, Utah
7.2	7.9	18.7	12.4	11.4	9.0	7.9	7.1	6.7	5.9	5.4	6.6	4 Pacific cities
7.7		22.0	14.1	14.8	9.2	7.9	6.9	7.3	6.0	5.6	7.4	Seattle, Wash.*
6.4	7.9	11.9	11.0	9.3	7.5	7.6	6.5	6.0	4.8	4.6	5.5	Portland, Ore.
7.5			12.4	9.9	8.7	7.8	8.7	7.6	8.6	5.0	4.8	Sacramento, Calif.
6.9		18.8	11.5	9.9	10.2	8.1	7.4	6.0	5.5	6.2	4.9	San Diego, Calif.*

TABLE D 38

Mortgaged Owner-occupied Dwellings, Average Annual Payment required and Average Annual Payment as Percentage of Average Original Loan: First Mortgages by Holding Agency, 52 Cities; Second and Third Mortgages, All Holding Agencies, 49 Cities; Land Contracts, All Holding Agencies, 33 Cities, by Geographic Division, January 1, 1934

$\longleftarrow$ AVERAGE ANNUAL PAYMENT REQUIRED (DOLLARS) [1] $\longrightarrow$

	FIRST MORTGAGE											2d & 3d MORTG. [5]	LAND CONTRACTS [5]
	All [3] holding agencies	Life ins. co.	Build. & loan asso.	Commer. bank	Savings bank	Mortgage co.	Construct. co.	Title & trust co.	H.O. Loan Corp.	Individual	Other		
All cities[1]	320	490	366	327	298	342	414	330	204	267	305	233	373
New England cities	290	470	353	339	297	399	350	284	252	225	283	195	
Portland, Me.	329	527	418	366	275	318			268	283	265	215	
Worcester, Mass.	276	289	388	325	250	608		305	327	300	358	208	
Providence, R.I.*	294	523	315	338	321	355	350	273	226	198	260	176	
Waterbury, Conn.	273	444	511	364	238	320		312	275	233	302	236	
Mid. Atlantic cities	207	392	283	254	191	250	180	243	187	205	290	241	242
Binghamton, N.Y.	215	375	290	236	206					210	128	212	
Syracuse, N.Y.	208	422	256	265	175	288		238		239	406	263	
Trenton, N.J.	169	271	298	229	199	149		196	169	133	179	168	
Erie, Pa.	237	456	326	263	211	262	180	304	206	195	217	169	242
E. N. Central cities	410	605	495	402	351	420	563	380	239	382	387	235	445
Cleveland, Ohio*	445	669	560	433	383	506	592	371	269	388	436	243	494
Indianapolis, Ind.	387	548	363	392	342	245	524	502	179	482	330	272	477
Peoria, Ill.	356	534	350	300	261	318	350	383	162	341	326	151	384
Lansing, Mich.	270	469	284	363	272	359		170	160	169	198	152	393
Kenosha, Wis.	228	153	481	183	123	195		176	251	169	217	144	439
Racine, Wis.	272	379	434	277	235	229		239	198	176	208	126	490
W. N. Central cities	252	417	276	226	259	249	266	278	165	195	214	208	380
Minneapolis, Minn.	271	483	269	256	260	267	242	266	193	200	234	318	405
St. Paul, Minn.	216	376	268	163	336	234		302	130	183	212	178	404
Des Moines, Iowa	240	360	243	255	222	258		368	173	186	169	140	357
St. Joseph, Mo.	235	366	295	208	105	267		213	150	193	148	169	
Springfield, Mo.	193	430	256	203	140	177		137	163	141	126	122	
Fargo, N.D.	280	425	380	181	220	210		254	235	249	256	229	467
Sioux Falls, S.D.	211	331	356	236	396	164		133	182	175	205	162	378
Lincoln, Neb.	289	407	326	251	250	303	343	289	121	201	189	157	243
Topeka, Kan.	292	382	307	216	266	256		365	211	211	359	119	297
Wichita, Kan.	265	373	258	231	237	222	310	270	118	220	207	167	290
S. Atlantic cities	336	514	321	325	265	350	322	339	209	258	306	315	326
Hagerstown, Md.	222	542	307	292		96			268	190	272	209	
Richmond, Va.	346	461	348	339	288	316	308	388	292	319	278		369
Wheeling, W.Va.*	292	667	303	266	225	429	342	264	236	220	306	193	349
Asheville, N.C.	401	479	379	508		393		817	149	286	420	230	322
Greensboro, N.C.	458	562	414	614		466			180	242	367	433	
Charleston, S.C.	250	479		518	240	413		553	388	192	211		
Columbia, S.C.	339	489	344	540		296		297	234	293	262	163	
Atlanta, Ga.*	354	481	289	271	274	356	320	289	158	262	325	346	304
Jacksonville, Fla.	301	472	359	257		270			181	235	267	204	
E. S. Central cities	338	461	306	339	286	328	286	434	188	229	294	248	369
Paducah, Ky.	285	322	243	402	160	260	143	348	118	222	270	177	
Birmingham, Ala.*	339	473	312	330	294	330	296	440	192	229	296	267	369
Jackson, Miss.	357	446	293	371		343			191	233		190	
W. S. Central cities	352	487	330	369	330	372	325	380	179	302	342	228	208
Little Rock, Ark.	286	382	288	299	172	277		225	189	256	328	273	223
Baton Rouge, La.	318	427	321	500					236	300	234		
Oklahoma City, Okla.	372	550	359	356	397	373	320	449	188	299	276	213	206
Austin, Tex.	372	511	393	534		397	372		177	351	279	398	173
Dallas, Tex.	352	444	315	356	318	388	320	370	179	300	418	213	273
Wichita Falls, Tex.	362	672	273	324		394	334	343	41	364	355	169	
Mountain cities	275	437	315	276	282	249	571	287	175	251	256	260	352
Butte, Mont.	208			285	460	174		171	134	205	181		338
Boise, Idaho	261	402	330	350		274		525	156	176	270	180	262
Casper, Wyo.	298	340	339	398		307		403	187	258	313	188	336
Pueblo, Colo.	212	355	307	193	216	183	258		123	191	157	140	218
Phoenix, Ariz.	277	554	450	271	280	231		232	234	211	335	271	396
Salt Lake City, Utah	305	443	273	284	283	278	680	267	182	303	268	314	361
Pacific cities	290	433	350	318	308	302	321	330	167	208	281	246	335
Seattle, Wash.*	309	469	334	306	321	324		333	156	210	333	246	327
Portland, Ore.	259	390	346	353	301	296		354	166	169	190	236	367
Sacramento, Calif.	324	471	372	314	324	361		373	253	271	339	236	370
San Diego, Calif.*	293	420	381	282	288	241	321	259	150	245	311	263	316

Source: Financial Survey of Urban Housing. The number reporting average annual payment required is approximately the same as that shown in Tables D 17 and 15. Average or percentage not shown for fewer than 3 reports.

*Metropolitan district.

[1] Geographic division and 52-city average annual payment weighted by number of loans, by priority, in each city (RPI).

[2] Percentages derived by dividing the average annual payment in this table by the average original amount of loan as shown in Table D 22. Geographic division and 52-city percentages automatically weighted by the use of weighted averages in this table and in Table D 22.

TABLE D 38

Mortgaged Owner-occupied Dwellings, Average Annual Payment required and Average Annual Payment as Percentage of Average Original Loan: First Mortgages by Holding Agency, 52 Cities; Second and Third Mortgages, All Holding Agencies, 49 Cities; Land Contracts, All Holding Agencies, 33 Cities, by Geographic Division, January 1, 1934

←——— AVERAGE ANNUAL PAYMENT AS PERCENTAGE OF AVERAGE ORIGINAL AMOUNT OF LOAN[2] ———→

All [4] holding agencies	Life ins. co.	Build. & loan asso.	Commer. bank	Savings bank	Mortgage co.	Construct. co.	Title & trust co.	H.O. Loan Corp.	Individual	Other	2d & 3d MORTG. [5]	LAND CONTRACTS [5]	
					FIRST MORTGAGE								
9.6	10.0	11.9	9.3	9.7	10.4	11.2	9.3	6.7	8.9	9.5	12.6	12.5	All cities[1]
7.3	7.5	10.2	7.1	7.4	10.2	9.5	6.6	6.5	6.2	8.1	9.8		New England cities
8.8	4.8	12.1	7.5	8.1	12.1			9.0	6.8	6.4	10.0		Portland, Me.
6.4	6.9	9.8	6.9	5.7	17.8		5.8	8.7	6.8	9.0	9.8		Worcester, Mass.
7.7	8.1	10.3	7.5	8.0	8.5	9.5	7.1	5.9	6.0	8.4	10.1		Providence, R.I.*
6.0	6.3	9.9	5.6	6.1	8.3		5.4	5.6	5.8	6.1	9.0		Waterbury, Conn.
6.5	8.5	8.7	6.7	5.6	7.6	5.7	5.7	6.3	6.7	7.3	11.1	8.9	Mid. Atlantic cities
6.3	6.0	11.7	8.5	5.9					6.4	5.2	11.6		Binghamton, N.Y.
5.9	9.1	7.0	6.6	5.3	7.8		5.2		6.9	7.8	11.2		Syracuse, N.Y.
6.7	7.7	10.2	6.7	5.5	5.8		5.9	5.5	5.9	7.5	10.0		Trenton, N.J.
7.6	9.5	10.5	6.9	6.2	8.3	5.7	6.9	7.0	6.7	6.2	10.3	8.9	Erie, Pa.
9.8	10.1	11.4	9.0	9.4	10.2	11.6	9.0	6.6	9.4	9.5	11.6	10.9	E. N. Central cities
9.6	9.8	11.2	9.5	9.4	10.3	11.9	8.8	6.6	9.0	9.6	11.5	11.1	Cleveland, Ohio*
10.8	11.0	11.5	8.1	10.4	12.3	10.9	10.2	6.5	11.9	9.4	16.0	10.7	Indianapolis, Ind.
11.5	11.3	11.9	8.8	8.7	10.6	9.3	10.2	8.4	11.0	10.8	11.7	11.2	Peoria, Ill.
10.3	10.2	13.4	10.3	10.1	11.4		7.2	6.6	7.8	6.6	16.7	10.4	Lansing, Mich.
7.6	9.7	12.8	6.5	6.0	6.3		6.1	6.4	6.1	7.4	9.9	10.6	Kenosha, Wis.
8.0	9.5	11.4	6.0	6.6	6.2		6.0	6.3	6.1	6.9	8.3	10.6	Racine, Wis.
10.2	10.8	12.7	10.4	11.8	9.8	9.5	10.7	7.0	8.9	9.9	14.6	13.2	W. N. Central cities
9.9	10.3	12.6	10.7	10.7	9.9	8.1	10.4	7.0	8.4	10.3	15.0	13.8	Minneapolis, Minn.
9.3	10.7	12.7	9.3	13.0	9.4		11.1	6.1	11.8	9.3	19.8	13.3	St. Paul, Minn.
10.5	10.9	12.9	11.9	11.4	9.9		11.9	7.9	9.9	10.1	13.9	12.0	Des Moines, Iowa
10.1	13.5	11.6	10.5	6.5	9.4		9.2	8.1	9.3	8.3	12.6		St. Joseph, Mo.
10.1	12.4	11.0	7.9	12.9	9.7		5.4	7.2	9.7	8.7	14.9		Springfield, Mo.
9.6	12.1	12.7	6.7	9.7	8.2		10.9	6.8	8.6	9.8	15.3	15.8	Fargo, N.D.
8.9	10.3	12.1	8.9	12.8	8.4		13.3	7.1	8.1	8.2	14.3	12.9	Sioux Falls, S.D.
10.7	9.9	12.7	12.0	12.9	10.0	19.1	9.9	8.4	8.2	10.5	11.6	13.3	Lincoln, Neb.
12.5	12.5	13.5	12.2	14.2	10.5		12.7	6.9	10.6	10.8	13.6	12.9	Topeka, Kan.
12.0	11.3	14.3	12.1	14.2	11.0	11.3	11.7	7.2	10.9	9.4	13.6	13.6	Wichita, Kan.
10.2	10.6	13.6	9.1	11.4	11.7	10.5	11.1	6.8	9.5	10.2	16.6	14.4	S. Atlantic cities
6.5	13.0	12.1	6.1		5.5			6.2	5.5	8.9	9.2		Hagerstown, Md.
8.9	9.6	15.2	8.5	8.3	8.7	6.4	9.5	6.5	8.1	8.8	17.4		Richmond, Va.
10.0	12.3	13.4	8.0	9.5	14.1	11.1	11.0	6.4	8.4	11.9	11.5	13.5	Wheeling, W.Va.*
10.5	9.5	12.8	6.7		12.7		9.7	6.7	12.7	9.5	14.4	13.9	Asheville, N.C.
10.4	10.1	12.7	6.6		11.9			6.9	9.9	9.8	14.3		Greensboro, N.C.
8.9	8.6		11.1	8.4	20.0		14.2	8.1	8.1	7.4			Charleston, S.C.
10.1	9.8	13.5	17.3		13.9		5.8	7.6	7.9	11.0	10.4		Columbia, S.C.
11.2	10.5	13.0	11.4	15.3	11.6	13.9	13.9	7.0	11.9	10.4	20.3	16.2	Atlanta, Ga.*
10.2	10.5	15.7	7.7		12.2			7.6	9.4	11.4	13.6		Jacksonville, Fla.
11.7	11.2	13.9	10.6	9.9	12.0	13.1	13.3	6.9	11.7	10.9	17.0	12.8	E. S. Central cities
12.0	12.5	13.5	12.2	6.4	8.6	33.0	9.6	8.9	14.3	11.7	14.4		Paducah, Ky.
11.7	11.2	13.9	10.7	10.1	12.2	12.9	13.6	7.1	11.7	10.9	17.5	12.8	Birmingham, Ala.*
11.5	11.0	14.5	9.3		12.3			5.6	11.2		15.0		Jackson, Miss.
12.2	11.5	14.1	12.6	12.4	12.4	13.1	12.0	6.8	11.5	14.1	19.8	14.7	W. S. Central cities
10.9	11.2	15.5	9.9	13.5	11.1		13.4	7.6	9.9	13.8	18.9	15.6	Little Rock, Ark.
11.0	15.4	10.6	10.1					8.7	11.6	23.0			Baton Rouge, La.
12.0	11.6	13.7	13.6	12.1	11.6	14.4	10.3	7.1	11.1	12.3	20.1	16.5	Oklahoma City, Okla.
13.2	9.5	13.8	17.1		12.6	15.8		8.3	12.4	15.1	24.8	13.1	Austin, Tex.
12.5	11.7	14.7	12.4	12.5	13.4	11.6	13.4	6.2	11.9	14.7	19.2	14.0	Dallas, Tex.
13.2	12.3	14.1	10.4		12.6	15.0	18.3	2.8	13.4	15.3	14.8		Wichita Falls, Tex.
11.7	12.3	14.8	10.2	13.6	12.1	16.2	11.1	7.5	11.0	12.0	19.8	13.2	Mountain cities
12.5			12.3	21.4	14.9		9.5	8.9	12.9	11.3		18.6	Butte, Mont.
13.3	14.8	15.8	8.9		14.6		13.9	7.9	10.6	15.8	16.9	17.5	Boise, Idaho
13.0	10.3	15.2	10.7		10.8		15.8	8.2	12.6	23.2	17.2	14.9	Casper, Wyo.
12.3	12.6	15.1	11.9	17.0	14.4	13.9		7.9	11.6	16.7	17.6	13.1	Pueblo, Colo.
10.1	13.1	15.6	8.0	11.3	9.9		10.3	6.5	8.9	9.1	16.5	16.2	Phoenix, Ariz.
11.7	11.7	14.1	10.9	12.7	11.7	16.5	10.3	7.6	11.2	11.8	22.1	12.2	Salt Lake City, Utah
10.8	11.6	13.4	12.0	11.7	10.5	10.0	10.9	7.0	9.9	9.5	17.0	13.1	Pacific cities
11.4	11.2	11.9	14.1	12.5	11.3		11.3	6.8	10.5	11.7	17.1	14.0	Seattle, Wash.*
10.2	11.4	15.1	11.6	12.1	10.5		10.9	6.5	9.4	7.1	16.2	12.1	Portland, Ore.
10.2	13.0	13.1	9.7	9.0	9.9		9.4	8.8	9.3	9.7	16.6	9.3	Sacramento, Calif.
10.9	12.2	14.2	10.6	11.2	9.8	10.0	10.6	7.2	9.8	9.5	18.0	11.7	San Diego, Calif.*

[3] Includes public bond issue: Kenosha, Wis., $212; Racine, Wis., $373.
[4] Includes public bond issue: Kenosha, Wis., 6.3 per cent; Racine, Wis., 5.3 per cent.
[5] Summary of all agencies reporting.

TABLE D 39

Mortgaged Rented Dwellings, Average Annual Payment required and Average Annual Payment as Percentage of Average Original Loan: First Mortgages by Holding Agency, 52 Cities; Second and Third Mortgages, All Holding Agencies, 23 Cities; Land Contracts, All Holding Agencies, 9 Cities, by Geographic Division, January 1, 1934

| | ← A V E R A G E   A N N U A L   P A Y M E N T   R E Q U I R E D [1]   (DOLLARS) → | | | | | | | | | | 2d & 3d MORTG. | LAND CONTRACTS |
| | F I R S T   M O R T G A G E S | | | | | | | | | | | |
	All[3] holding agencies	Life ins. co.	Build. & loan asso.	Commer. bank	Savings bank	Mortgage co.	Construct. co.	Title & trust co.	H.O. Loan Corp.	Individual	Other	[6]	[6]
All cities[1]	409	940	429	414	338	495		429	226	322	609	335	434
New England cities	362	1,141	357	433	372	290		281		243	243	342	
Portland, Me.	346	737	417	446	348			280		201	263	236	
Worcester, Mass.	306		432	345	302			290		235	307	245	
Providence, R.I.*[5]	361	1,182	328	458	396	290		279		250	221	295	
Waterbury, Conn.[5]	528											718	
Mid. Atlantic cities	277	628	366	253	222	353		329		336	244	252	
Binghamton, N.Y.[5]	337											206	
Syracuse, N.Y.	283	732		269	209			330		422		276	
Trenton, N.J.	160	266	280	123	203	226		327		130	199	116	
Erie, Pa.	309		424	303	266	440				274	275	174	
E. N. Central cities	495	1,304	556	466	398	974		367	269	559	461	376	401
Cleveland, Ohio*	608	1,767	728	508	434	1,049		410	295	510	460	387	483
Indianapolis, Ind.	383		708	338	419	372		316	233	808	344		
Peoria, Ill.	355	702	320	635	266	400		425	210	137	1,383	316	
Lansing, Mich.	233	260	252	154	270			119		192	315		340
Kenosha, Wis.[5]	323												
Racine, Wis.	313		448	286		624		336		212	296	157	
W. N. Central cities	299	653	271	305	293	293		643	157	176	211	464	453
Minneapolis, Minn.	362	784	269	384	289	337		706	143	197	279	464	463
St. Paul, Minn.	311	963	343	148	374	276		685	158	176	110		434
Des Moines, Iowa	252	444	227	226	194	320			160	168	188		409
St. Joseph, Mo.[5]	160												
Springfield, Mo.[5]	188	474	258	82		197				95	206		
Fargo, N.D.[5]	270												
Sioux Falls, S.D.	257	226	150	1,591	278	158				173	145		555
Lincoln, Neb.	365	596	252			341		1,269		219	237		
Topeka, Kan.	291	473	310	146	318	255		380	247	189	193		
Wichita, Kan.	247	369	254	188		229		148	158	126	203		
S. Atlantic cities	410	1,055	355	310	210	494		498	215	205	278	422	
Hagerstown, Md.[5]	256												
Richmond, Va.[5]	339											612	
Wheeling, W.Va.*[5]	316												
Asheville, N.C.[5]	378												
Greensboro, N.C.[5]	526												
Charleston, S.C.[5]	164												
Columbia, S.C.	334												
Atlanta, Ga.*	534	1,055	355	310	210	494		498	215	205	278	307	
Jacksonville, Fla.	310												
E. S. Central cities	478	643	290	825	388	434		278	207	202	162	208	
Paducah, Ky.[5]	333												
Birmingham, Ala.*[5]	395	643	290	825	388	434		278	207	202	162	208	
Jackson, Miss.[5]	982												
W. S. Central cities	408	628	384	421	362	478		510	226	278	194	238	
Little Rock, Ark.	283	549	289	258		396			151	148	270		
Baton Rouge, La.[5]	368												
Oklahoma City, Okla.	520	929	442			520			287	284	87	291	
Austin, Tex.[5]	395												
Dallas, Tex.	382	454	368	455	362	468		510	203	301	245	200	
Wichita Falls, Tex.[5]	304												
Mountain cities	365	782	347	565	429	417		280	217	206	172	667	752
Butte, Mont.[5]	457												
Boise, Idaho[5]	311												
Casper, Wyo.[5]	428												
Pueblo, Colo.[5]	169												
Phoenix, Ariz.	266	458	570	315	275	194			215	218	137	286	
Salt Lake City, Utah	465	983	209	720	525	556		280	218	199	193	895	752
Pacific cities	435	823	533	346	299	279		508	222	210	2,201	243	356
Seattle, Wash.*	661	1,345	591	390	293	224		700	219	205	5,562	378	366
Portland, Ore.	279	527	616	335	305	218		549	192	143	174	180	
Sacramento, Calif.	348	657	411	326	422	560				273	492	218	
San Diego, Calif.*	308	455	412	302	254	308		196	257	260	200	275	328

Source: Financial Survey of Urban Housing. The number reporting average annual payment required is approximately the same as that shown on Tables D 15, 18, and 34. Average or percentage not shown for fewer than 3 reports.

*Metropolitan district.

[1] Geographic division and 'All cities' average annual payment required weighted by number of loans, by priority, in each city (RPI). Where the number of cities included in the 'All holding agencies' column is larger than the number for the individual agencies, the weighted geographic division and 'All cities' averages and/or percentages in the 'All holding agencies' column are not strictly comparable to the weighted averages and/or percentages for the individual agencies.

Mortgaged Rented Dwellings, Average Annual Payment required and Average Annual Payment as Percentage of Average Original Loan: First Mortgages by Holding Agency, 52 Cities; Second and Third Mortgages, All Holding Agencies, 23 Cities; Land Contracts, All Holding Agencies, 9 Cities, by Geographic Division, January 1, 1934

←————————AVERAGE ANNUAL PAYMENT REQUIRED AS PERCENTAGE OF AVERAGE ORIGINAL AMOUNT OF LOAN[2]————————→

FIRST MORTGAGES

All[4] holding agencies	Life ins. co.	Build. & Loan asso.	Commer. bank	Savings bank	Mortgage co.	Construct. co.	Title & trust co.	H.O. Loan Corp.	Individual	Other	2d & 3d MORTG. [6]	LAND CONTRACTS [6]	
9.7	10.4	11.9	9.6	10.4	9.6		9.7	6.4	9.2	9.2	12.9	12.1	All cities[1]
7.2	10.2	10.3	7.0	7.9	7.2		6.5		6.1	6.8	10.7		New England cities
7.7	8.1	11.0	8.5	7.5			12.4		5.7	4.0	11.7		Portland, Me.
5.9		9.7	6.4	5.7			5.4		5.5	7.6	8.8		Worcester, Mass.
7.8	9.4	10.4	7.0	8.7	7.2		6.6		6.3	7.0	13.0		Providence, R.I.*
6.0											8.7		Waterbury, Conn.[5]
6.4	7.8	10.1	5.1	5.9	5.5		6.2		7.2	7.0	11.6		Mid. Atlantic cities
7.8											9.0		Binghamton, N.Y.[5]
5.8	7.9		4.6	5.3			5.2		7.5		12.1		Syracuse, N.Y.
6.2	7.3	10.3	5.8	5.2	7.6		5.9		5.5	7.3	8.2		Trenton, N.J.
7.4		10.0	6.5	8.1	5.0				6.8	6.9	10.5		Erie, Pa.
9.9	10.4	10.9	9.3	10.2	11.1		9.4	6.6	10.8	8.8	10.8	9.0	E. N. Central cities
9.5	9.8	9.3	9.6	9.1	7.9		9.0	6.1	8.4	8.2	10.9	7.9	Cleveland, Ohio*
11.6	10.9	11.6	9.1	6.7			10.9	7.7	16.8	11.1			Indianapolis, Ind.
10.0	12.1	10.8	11.0	6.7	13.5		14.1	10.6	7.0	8.9	12.2		Peoria, Ill.
9.6	11.1	11.6	4.5	8.6			6.0		8.8	8.5		10.7	Lansing, Mich.[5]
8.0													Kenosha, Wis.[5]
7.5		11.1	5.4		10.1		6.0		6.2	6.6	7.0		Racine, Wis.
10.0	11.1	12.8	9.4	10.9	10.3		10.1	6.3	8.1	8.0	12.7	13.9	W. N. Central cities
9.9	11.0	13.1	11.1	11.4	10.1		9.0	5.6	8.1	6.9	12.7	13.6	Minneapolis, Minn.
9.6	12.3	11.7	7.5	9.9	9.9		10.0	5.9	7.8	6.9		15.2	St. Paul, Minn.
10.0	10.6	12.5	9.0	9.3	11.1			6.6	8.9	9.8		13.4	Des Moines, Iowa[5]
8.3													St.Joseph, Mo.
10.7	14.8	14.1	6.7		7.8				7.5	10.2			Springfield, Mo.[5]
8.5													Fargo, N.D.[5]
7.6	7.9	12.2	7.9	12.6	8.3				6.2	8.0	13.3		Sioux Falls, S.D.
11.4	10.6	12.3			11.0		15.1		7.6	10.0			Lincoln, Neb.
11.6	10.7	13.7	7.6	18.0	8.3		9.6	8.9	8.4	9.7			Topeka, Kan.
11.5	9.5	14.6	10.4		13.3		11.7	8.0	9.4	10.8			Wichita, Kan.
9.6	9.9	15.6	12.6	18.1	9.7		11.6	5.1	9.5	11.0	21.4		S. Atlantic cities
7.4													Hagerstown, Md.[5]
9.4											19.3		Richmond, Va.[5]
8.4													Wheeling, W.Va.*[5]
11.7													Asheville, N.C.[5]
12.7													Greensboro, N.C.[5]
6.9													Charleston, S.C.[5]
9.8													Columbia, S.C.[5]
10.1	9.9	15.6	12.6	18.1	9.7		11.6	5.1	9.5	11.0	24.4		Atlanta, Ga.*
8.5													Jacksonville, Fla.
12.0	11.7	11.5	17.6	21.6	11.3		10.2	6.0	11.0	9.5	13.9		E. S. Central cities
7.8													Paducah, Ky.[5]
11.6	11.7	11.5	17.6	21.6	11.3		10.2	6.0	11.0	9.5			Birmingham, Ala.*
13.4											13.9		Jackson, Miss.[5]
11.3	11.2	13.4	12.2	13.1	11.6		12.5	6.6	9.1	10.6	22.3		W. S. Central cities
9.8	11.9	13.0	9.0		10.5			5.4	6.9	8.7			Little Rock, Ark.[5]
9.7													Baton Rouge, La.[5]
10.9	10.9	12.3			12.1			6.7	7.9	10.9	21.9		Oklahoma City, Okla.[5]
16.8													Austin, Tex.[5]
11.6	11.6	14.5	12.7	13.1	11.5		12.5	6.8	10.3	11.1	22.7		Dallas, Tex.
12.4													Wichita Falls, Tex.[5]
10.8	12.6	10.7	7.9	10.1	10.1		12.8	6.2	8.0	9.6	21.9	14.7	Mountain cities
12.6													Butte, Mont.[5]
12.2													Boise, Idaho[5]
13.1													Casper, Wyo.[5]
12.0													Pueblo, Colo.[5]
9.2	10.9	14.0	7.6	10.0	9.4			5.9	7.9	7.1	9.5		Phoenix, Ariz.
10.8	13.1	12.1	8.0	10.1	10.2		12.8	6.4	8.1	11.2	29.2	14.7	Salt Lake City, Utah
10.2	10.6	13.4	11.0	10.6	10.0		11.0	7.1	8.3	9.7	16.5	10.9	Pacific cities
10.8	10.8	14.1	9.8	12.7	10.2		11.3	7.3	9.2	9.8	19.2	10.6	Seattle, Wash.*
9.6	10.9	12.9	15.8	10.3	9.1		11.4	5.7	7.6	6.7	11.8		Portland, Ore.
9.5	10.6	13.5	9.4	9.7	11.4				8.2	8.2	12.5		Sacramento, Calif.
9.6	9.8	12.6	10.3	9.1	9.7		8.7		7.9	10.5	20.0	12.2	San Diego, Calif.*

[2] Percentages derived by dividing the average annual payment required in this table by the average original amount of loan as shown in Table D 22. Geographic division and 'All cities' percentages automatically weighted by the use of weighted averages in this table and in Table D 22.

[3] Includes public bond issue: Racine, Wis., $368; San Diego, Calif., $337.

[4] Includes public bond issue: Racine, Wis., 6.1 per cent; San Diego, Calif., 7.3 per cent.

[5] Sample inadequate to obtain averages or percentages by individual agencies.

[6] Summary of all agencies reporting.

TABLE D 40

Mortgaged Dwellings, Number reporting Method of Paying Principal and Percentage Distribution by Method: First Mortgages, Owner-occupied and Rented, 52 Cities; Second and Third Mortgages, Owner-occupied, 52 Cities; Rented, 23 Cities, by Geographic Division, January 1, 1934

| | ←————————————————O W N E R - O C C U P I E D————————————————→ | | | | | | | | | |
| | FIRST MORTGAGES PERCENTAGE DISTRIBUTION | | | | SECOND AND THIRD MORTGAGES PERCENTAGE DISTRIBUTION | | | | |
	NUMBER REPORTING	All methods	Straight[2] term loans	Amortized loans[3]	Other loans	NUMBER REPORTING	All methods	Straight[2] term loans	Amortized loans[3]	Other loans
All cities[1]	63,839	100.0	38.2	39.3	22.5	6,190	100.0	39.9	36.4	23.7
New England cities	4,237	100.0	59.0	24.2	16.8	844	100.0	53.5	21.8	24.7
Portland, Me.	645	100.0	34.9	38.0	27.1	77	100.0	48.0	26.0	26.0
Worcester, Mass.	1,103	100.0	82.4	13.2	4.4	315	100.0	47.3	21.3	31.4
Providence, R.I.*	2,020	100.0	49.0	29.1	21.9	318	100.0	56.9	22.0	21.1
Waterbury, Conn.	469	100.0	91.5	6.2	2.3	134	100.0	54.5	20.9	24.6
Mid. Atlantic cities	4,265	100.0	82.8	10.6	6.6	542	100.0	40.2	22.6	37.2
Binghamton, N.Y.	253	100.0	81.4	5.9	12.7	31	100.0	41.9	19.4	38.7
Syracuse, N.Y.	970	100.0	90.0	2.9	7.1	264	100.0	36.3	22.0	41.7
Trenton, N.J.	1,554	100.0	83.9	14.6	1.5	126	100.0	55.6	20.6	23.8
Erie, Pa.	1,488	100.0	65.3	27.3	7.4	121	100.0	53.7	32.2	14.1
E. N. Central cities	19,088	100.0	22.3	46.0	31.7	2,260	100.0	36.1	42.1	21.8
Cleveland, Ohio*	13,769	100.0	20.0	35.4	44.6	1,942	100.0	33.7	42.1	24.2
Indianapolis, Ind.	1,559	100.0	13.0	77.8	9.2	60	100.0	30.0	58.3	11.7
Peoria, Ill.	1,319	100.0	10.9	83.6	5.5	95	100.0	47.4	44.2	8.4
Lansing, Mich.	371	100.0	34.2	52.6	13.2	16	100.0	50.0	37.5	12.5
Kenosha, Wis.	648	100.0	77.8	18.7	3.5	44	100.0	75.0	25.0	
Racine, Wis.	1,422	100.0	66.3	32.1	1.6	103	100.0	76.7	13.6	9.7
W. N. Central cities	11,090	100.0	42.4	36.5	21.1	600	100.0	46.6	39.5	13.9
Minneapolis, Minn.	3,749	100.0	43.9	28.4	27.7	153	100.0	46.4	40.5	13.1
St. Paul, Minn.	812	100.0	53.5	26.7	19.8	29	100.0	37.9	44.8	17.3
Des Moines, Iowa	1,262	100.0	35.8	38.0	26.2	40	100.0	42.5	37.5	20.0
St. Joseph, Mo.	508	100.0	50.8	35.8	13.4	46	100.0	45.6	37.0	17.4
Springfield, Mo.	757	100.0	50.6	39.4	10.0	34	100.0	55.9	32.3	11.8
Fargo, N.D.	462	100.0	58.0	33.6	8.4	36	100.0	50.0	44.4	5.6
Sioux Falls, S.D.	548	100.0	66.8	20.8	12.4	37	100.0	51.4	32.4	16.2
Lincoln, Neb.	767	100.0	30.8	56.1	13.1	61	100.0	63.9	24.6	11.5
Topeka, Kan.	977	100.0	17.5	70.3	12.2	84	100.0	46.4	46.4	7.2
Wichita, Kan.	1,248	100.0	20.3	61.7	18.0	80	100.0	37.5	46.3	16.2
S. Atlantic cities	6,017	100.0	38.6	35.0	26.4	660	100.0	29.9	46.3	23.8
Hagerstown, Md.	352	100.0	81.8	15.9	2.3	35	100.0	68.6	28.6	2.8
Richmond, Va.	1,056	100.0	54.2	16.8	29.0	182	100.0	25.8	50.6	23.6
Wheeling, W.Va.*	770	100.0	40.1	43.7	16.2	64	100.0	56.3	32.8	10.9
Asheville, N.C.	382	100.0	14.6	60.5	24.9	28	100.0	53.6	35.7	10.7
Greensboro, N.C.	300	100.0	18.0	49.3	32.7	50	100.0	32.0	44.0	24.0
Charleston, S.C.	203	100.0	73.4	17.7	8.9					
Columbia, S.C.	340	100.0	38.8	51.8	9.4	32	100.0	53.1	37.5	9.4
Atlanta, Ga.*	2,341	100.0	28.3	35.6	36.1	248	100.0	13.7	52.8	33.5
Jacksonville, Fla.	273	100.0	45.0	34.1	20.9	21	100.0	47.6	38.1	14.3
E. S. Central cities	2,448	100.0	23.6	49.7	26.7	189	100.0	31.8	30.8	37.4
Paducah, Ky.	217	100.0	22.1	54.4	23.5	15	100.0	46.6	26.7	26.7
Birmingham, Ala.*	1,968	100.0	25.7	45.9	28.4	142	100.0	31.0	31.0	38.0
Jackson, Miss.	263	100.0	10.3	73.0	16.7	32	100.0	31.2	31.3	37.5
W. S. Central cities	5,128	100.0	21.1	58.0	20.9	386	100.0	26.8	52.0	21.2
Little Rock, Ark.	824	100.0	40.9	41.5	17.6	61	100.0	27.9	42.6	29.5
Baton Rouge, La.	176	100.0	11.3	77.3	11.4					
Oklahoma City, Okla.	1,744	100.0	16.5	67.2	16.3	176	100.0	34.7	47.1	18.2
Austin, Tex.	374	100.0	18.4	61.0	20.6	21	100.0	19.0	61.9	19.1
Dallas, Tex.	1,678	100.0	22.6	50.8	26.6	110	100.0	19.1	56.4	24.5
Wichita Falls, Tex.	332	100.0	10.2	70.8	19.0	18	100.0	22.2	77.8	
Mountain cities	3,316	100.0	39.0	49.2	11.8	146	100.0	33.6	50.9	15.5
Butte, Mont.	366	100.0	65.0	23.8	11.2					
Boise, Idaho	507	100.0	33.9	62.5	3.6	23	100.0	34.8	56.5	8.7
Casper, Wyo.	174	100.0	22.4	71.8	5.8	11	100.0	9.1	54.5	36.4
Pueblo, Colo.	398	100.0	37.2	54.8	8.0	16	100.0	43.7	43.8	12.5
Phoenix, Ariz.	483	100.0	61.9	25.9	12.2	32	100.0	34.4	46.9	18.7
Salt Lake City, Utah	1,388	100.0	31.6	53.4	15.0	64	100.0	32.8	53.1	14.1
Pacific cities	8,250	100.0	35.1	46.1	18.8	563	100.0	30.4	53.8	15.8
Seattle, Wash.*	2,571	100.0	32.3	47.7	20.0	98	100.0	44.9	46.9	8.2
Portland, Ore.	2,367	100.0	33.4	45.2	21.4	142	100.0	30.3	53.5	16.2
Sacramento, Calif.	1,118	100.0	39.5	47.3	13.2	113	100.0	19.5	49.5	31.0
San Diego, Calif.*	2,194	100.0	42.0	44.0	14.0	210	100.0	23.8	61.9	14.3

Source: *Financial Survey of Urban Housing*

*Metropolitan district.

[1]Geographic division and 'All cities' percentages weighted by number of loans, by tenure and priority, in each city (RPI).

[2]Principal payable at end of term.

[3]Regular installments.

Mortgaged Dwellings, Number reporting Method of Paying Principal and Percentage Distribution by Method: First Mortgages,
Owner-occupied and Rented, 52 Cities; Second and Third Mortgages, Owner-occupied, 52 Cities; Rented, 23 Cities, by Geographic
Division, January 1, 1934

←					R E N T E D					→
FIRST MORTGAGES					SECOND AND THIRD MORTGAGES					
PERCENTAGE DISTRIBUTION					PERCENTAGE DISTRIBUTION					
NUMBER REPORTING	All methods	Straight[2] term loans	Amortized loans[3]	Other loans	NUMBER REPORTING	All methods	Straight[2] term loans	Amortized loans[3]	Other loans	
13,274	100.0	43.4	32.7	23.9	841	100.0	41.5	31.6	26.9	All cities[1]
899	100.0	60.9	16.6	22.5	155	100.0	52.3	22.9	24.8	New England cities
195	100.0	46.7	23.1	30.2	31	100.0	71.0	9.7	19.3	Portland, Me.
211	100.0	86.3	6.6	7.1	33	100.0	54.6	21.2	24.2	Worcester, Mass.
387	100.0	50.9	20.4	28.7	56	100.0	48.2	23.2	28.6	Providence, R.I.*
106	100.0	91.5	4.7	3.8	35	100.0	60.0	28.6	11.4	Waterbury, Conn.
787	100.0	85.5	6.9	7.6	107	100.0	33.9	16.0	50.1	Mid. Atlantic cities
80	100.0	82.5	1.3	16.2	12	100.0	66.6	16.7	16.7	Binghamton, N.Y.
210	100.0	90.5	1.9	7.6	48	100.0	25.0	14.6	60.4	Syracuse, N.Y.
235	100.0	88.1	9.8	2.1	25	100.0	76.0	12.0	12.0	Trenton, N.J.
262	100.0	73.7	20.2	6.1	22	100.0	54.6	31.8	13.6	Erie, Pa.
3,693	100.0	24.0	50.1	25.9	255	100.0	43.6	36.9	19.5	E. N. Central cities
2,273	100.0	23.7	36.3	40.0	215	100.0	41.9	38.1	20.0	Cleveland, Ohio *
496	100.0	14.1	76.0	9.9						Indianapolis, Ind.
338	100.0	14.8	78.4	6.8	17	100.0	53.0	29.4	17.6	Peoria, Ill.
144	100.0	41.7	48.6	9.7						Lansing, Mich.
127	100.0	76.4	19.7	3.9						Kenosha, Wis.
315	100.0	77.2	20.3	2.5	23	100.0	78.3	13.0	8.7	Racine, Wis.
2,833	100.0	45.6	28.1	26.3	45	100.0	51.1	26.7	22.2	W. N. Central cities
944	100.0	41.6	25.6	32.8	45	100.0	51.1	26.7	22.2	Minneapolis, Minn.
210	100.0	58.1	15.7	26.2						St. Paul, Minn.
383	100.0	43.9	19.8	36.3						Des Moines, Iowa
105	100.0	65.7	21.9	12.4						St. Joseph, Mo.
168	100.0	58.9	31.6	9.5						Springfield, Mo.
77	100.0	72.7	14.3	13.0						Fargo, N.D.
180	100.0	76.1	11.1	12.8						Sioux Falls, S.D.
175	100.0	34.9	46.3	18.8						Lincoln, Neb.
243	100.0	27.2	58.8	14.0						Topeka, Kan.
348	100.0	25.3	48.8	25.9						Wichita, Kan.
1,156	100.0	54.2	20.8	25.0	51	100.0	27.6	42.0	30.4	S. Atlantic cities
70	100.0	81.4	12.9	5.7						Hagerstown, Md.
131	100.0	67.2	8.4	24.4	18	100.0	33.3	11.1	55.6	Richmond, Va.
120	100.0	54.1	31.7	14.2						Wheeling, W. Va.*
37	100.0	37.9	29.7	32.4						Asheville, N.C.
69	100.0	17.4	46.4	36.2						Greensboro, N.C.
79	100.0	78.5	15.2	6.3						Charleston, S.C.
86	100.0	47.7	40.7	11.6						Columbia, S.C.
506	100.0	45.2	20.8	34.0	33	100.0	24.2	60.6	15.2	Atlanta, Ga.*
58	100.0	69.0	13.8	17.2						Jacksonville, Fla.
312	100.0	38.6	36.4	25.0	13	100.0	38.5	53.8	7.7	E. S. Central cities
21	100.0	28.6	47.6	23.8						Paducah, Ky.
215	100.0	43.7	29.3	27.0						Birmingham, Ala.*
76	100.0	10.5	76.3	13.2	13	100.0	38.5	53.8	7.7	Jackson, Miss.
1,203	100.0	33.4	39.9	26.7	53	100.0	36.6	30.2	33.2	W. S. Central cities
184	100.0	55.5	26.6	17.9						Little Rock, Ark.
59	100.0	30.5	55.9	13.6						Baton Rouge, La.
380	100.0	22.1	54.2	23.7	30	100.0	26.7	30.0	43.3	Oklahoma City, Okla.
100	100.0	31.0	31.0	38.0						Austin, Tex.
398	100.0	36.7	31.7	31.6	23	100.0	43.5	30.4	26.1	Dallas, Tex.
82	100.0	32.9	47.6	19.5						Wichita Falls, Tex.
623	100.0	52.1	30.3	17.6	30	100.0	30.0	30.0	40.0	Mountain cities
54	100.0	55.6	25.9	18.5						Butte, Mont.
32	100.0	46.9	43.7	9.4						Boise, Idaho
47	100.0	25.5	68.1	6.4						Casper, Wyo.
49	100.0	51.0	42.9	6.1						Pueblo, Colo.
168	100.0	69.6	17.3	13.1	10	100.0	30.0	30.0	40.0	Phoenix, Ariz.
273	100.0	45.4	28.6	26.0	20	100.0	30.0	30.0	40.0	Salt Lake City, Utah
1,768	100.0	44.2	32.9	22.9	132	100.0	38.0	43.8	18.2	Pacific cities
470	100.0	35.1	35.8	29.1	31	100.0	35.5	58.1	6.4	Seattle, Wash.*
422	100.0	45.7	30.8	23.5	29	100.0	44.8	24.1	31.1	Portland, Ore.
228	100.0	53.9	30.3	15.8	21	100.0	33.3	28.6	38.1	Sacramento, Calif.
648	100.0	51.7	31.8	16.5	51	100.0	35.3	52.9	11.8	San Diego, Calif.*

TABLE D 41

Mortgaged Dwellings, Number reporting Frequency of Payment (Interest and Principal) and Percentage Distribution by Frequency: First Mortgages, Owner-occupied and Rented, 52 Cities; Second and Third Mortgages, Owner-occupied, 52 Cities; Rented, 23 Cities, by Geographic Division, January 1, 1934

| | ←————————————————————— OWNER-OCCUPIED —————————————————————→ | | | | | | | | | | |
| | FIRST MORTGAGES PERCENTAGE DISTRIBUTION | | | | | SECOND AND THIRD MORTGAGES PERCENTAGE DISTRIBUTION | | | | | |
	NUMBER REPORTING	All frequencies	Monthly	Quarterly	Semi-annually	Annually	NUMBER REPORTING	All frequencies	Monthly	Quarterly	Semi-annually	Annually
All cities[1]	62,455	100.0	43.7	14.1	31.2	11.0	5,926	100.0	46.7	11.7	28.0	13.6
New England cities	4,123	100.0	21.4	6.3	62.2	10.1	789	100.0	21.1	8.5	57.4	13.0
Portland, Me.	616	100.0	37.8	7.8	42.2	12.2	65	100.0	38.5	16.9	24.6	20.0
Worcester, Mass.	1,098	100.0	16.1	21.5	55.9	6.5	308	100.0	13.0	16.6	59.7	10.7
Providence, R.I.*	1,963	100.0	23.5	1.4	64.0	11.1	290	100.0	26.9	4.1	55.5	13.5
Waterbury, Conn.	446	100.0	10.1	8.3	72.0	9.6	126	100.0	11.9	7.1	66.7	14.3
Mid. Atlantic cities	4,227	100.0	12.1	1.7	70.6	15.6	525	100.0	11.4	15.7	59.7	13.2
Binghamton, N.Y.	253	100.0	6.3	1.2	69.6	22.9	30	100.0	26.7	6.7	46.6	20.0
Syracuse, N.Y.	945	100.0	2.3	1.4	81.6	14.7	255	100.0	5.1	16.1	65.9	12.9
Trenton, N.J.	1,552	100.0	17.7	3.2	69.4	9.7	123	100.0	17.9	32.5	39.8	9.8
Erie, Pa.	1,477	100.0	32.9	1.4	46.2	19.5	117	100.0	41.9	3.4	41.9	12.8
E. N. Central cities	18,894	100.0	48.2	35.0	11.2	5.6	2,178	100.0	56.9	21.4	9.8	11.9
Cleveland, Ohio*	13,631	100.0	35.9	53.3	6.8	4.0	1,883	100.0	57.1	25.0	7.8	10.1
Indianapolis, Ind.	1,552	100.0	82.2	0.4	10.1	7.3	57	100.0	73.7	1.8	7.0	17.5
Peoria, Ill.	1,306	100.0	87.0	0.3	8.0	4.7	89	100.0	61.8		19.1	19.1
Lansing, Mich.	366	100.0	66.7	1.9	19.7	11.7	15	100.0	53.3	6.7		40.0
Kenosha, Wis.	640	100.0	23.0	0.4	58.3	18.3	40	100.0	25.0		52.5	22.5
Racine, Wis.	1,399	100.0	39.7	0.3	48.6	11.4	94	100.0	27.7	6.4	40.4	25.5
W. N. Central cities	10,776	100.0	41.3	1.4	39.9	17.4	573	100.0	56.0	2.2	19.0	22.8
Minneapolis, Minn.	3,654	100.0	32.1	2.1	49.7	16.1	145	100.0	55.2	2.1	20.7	22.0
St. Paul, Minn.	805	100.0	30.2	1.0	47.4	21.4	29	100.0	58.6		24.1	17.3
Des Moines, Iowa	1,229	100.0	42.7	1.1	30.7	25.5	37	100.0	51.4	2.7	13.5	32.4
St. Joseph, Mo.	490	100.0	40.6	1.0	40.2	18.2	44	100.0	61.4	2.3	13.6	22.7
Springfield, Mo.	747	100.0	43.6	1.6	38.6	16.2	35	100.0	48.6	5.7	25.7	20.0
Fargo, N.D.	431	100.0	48.3	0.7	30.4	20.6	32	100.0	59.4		15.6	25.0
Sioux Falls, S.D.	522	100.0	29.1	0.8	45.4	24.7	38	100.0	44.7		23.7	31.6
Lincoln, Neb.	741	100.0	62.2	0.4	21.2	16.2	57	100.0	38.6	5.3	22.8	33.3
Topeka, Kan.	968	100.0	76.5	0.7	14.9	7.9	83	100.0	63.8	2.4	19.3	14.5
Wichita, Kan.	1,189	100.0	68.6	1.0	22.1	8.3	73	100.0	69.8	1.4	9.6	19.2
S. Atlantic cities	5,851	100.0	43.9	11.9	29.3	14.9	624	100.0	70.9	6.7	10.5	11.9
Hagerstown, Md.	343	100.0	21.3	4.7	51.0	23.0	30	100.0	43.3		30.0	26.7
Richmond, Va.	1,025	100.0	20.2	24.2	38.5	17.1	176	100.0	76.1	6.3	8.5	9.1
Wheeling, W.Va.*	694	100.0	63.1	15.1	9.8	12.0	48	100.0	50.0	16.7	10.4	22.9
Asheville, N.C.	385	100.0	64.4	1.3	19.0	15.3	29	100.0	51.7	10.3	6.9	31.1
Greensboro, N.C.	296	100.0	47.6	2.4	40.5	9.5	50	100.0	62.0	8.0	10.0	20.0
Charleston, S.C.	197	100.0	21.8	40.1	13.2	24.9						
Columbia, S.C.	328	100.0	57.9	16.2	11.9	14.0	28	100.0	53.6	3.6	21.4	21.4
Atlanta, Ga.*	2,316	100.0	43.8	2.3	39.4	14.5	244	100.0	84.4	1.2	9.9	4.5
Jacksonville, Fla.	287	100.0	46.8	24.0	14.6	14.6	19	100.0	52.6	21.1	10.5	15.8
E. S. Central cities	2,434	100.0	60.9	2.1	27.6	9.4	187	100.0	68.4	2.1	11.2	18.3
Paducah, Ky.	211	100.0	58.8	2.8	16.1	22.3	13	100.0	23.1		15.4	61.5
Birmingham, Ala.*	1,963	100.0	57.7	2.1	30.9	9.3	142	100.0	71.1	2.8	10.6	15.5
Jackson, Miss.	260	100.0	82.7	1.5	10.8	5.0	32	100.0	68.7		12.5	18.8
W. S. Central cities	5,044	100.0	62.3	0.7	22.6	14.4	371	100.0	70.5	1.4	11.4	16.7
Little Rock, Ark.	791	100.0	51.8	0.5	24.5	23.2	58	100.0	67.2	5.2	3.5	24.1
Baton Rouge, La.	178	100.0	88.8	0.6	2.2	8.4						
Oklahoma City, Okla.	1,721	100.0	70.1	0.7	19.6	9.6	166	100.0	70.5	1.2	10.2	18.1
Austin, Tex.	373	100.0	59.5	0.8	17.2	22.5	19	100.0	78.9		5.3	15.8
Dallas, Tex.	1,643	100.0	55.1	0.8	28.9	15.2	107	100.0	70.1	0.9	16.8	12.2
Wichita Falls, Tex.	338	100.0	75.2	1.2	11.5	12.1	21	100.0	71.4			28.6
Mountain cities	3,237	100.0	61.5	8.1	20.4	10.0	140	100.0	71.4	3.7	10.8	14.1
Butte, Mont.	340	100.0	50.3	26.2	4.7	18.8						
Boise, Idaho	507	100.0	64.5	1.2	23.9	10.4	23	100.0	65.2	4.4	17.4	13.0
Casper, Wyo.	174	100.0	83.9		4.0	12.1	11	100.0	63.6	18.2		18.2
Pueblo, Colo.	378	100.0	73.3	1.6	18.0	7.1	15	100.0	80.0		20.0	
Phoenix, Ariz.	478	100.0	34.7	5.7	48.5	11.1	29	100.0	65.5	3.5	20.7	10.3
Salt Lake City, Utah	1,360	100.0	64.6	10.7	15.3	9.4	62	100.0	72.6	3.2	4.8	19.4
Pacific cities	7,869	100.0	55.1	15.6	20.6	8.7	539	100.0	72.3	7.3	9.5	10.9
Seattle, Wash.*	2,497	100.0	56.5	4.6	29.6	9.3	94	100.0	54.3	5.3	22.3	18.1
Portland, Ore.	2,179	100.0	43.3	22.7	23.5	10.5	130	100.0	72.3	5.4	9.2	13.1
Sacramento, Calif.	1,093	100.0	90.6	1.6	1.9	5.9	112	100.0	90.2	0.9	1.8	7.1
San Diego, Calif.*	2,100	100.0	57.5	31.4	5.5	5.6	203	100.0	78.3	14.3	3.0	4.4

Source: *Financial Survey of Urban Housing*
*Metropolitan district.
[1] Geographic division and 'All cities' percentages weighted by number of loans, by tenure and priority, in each city (RPI).

TABLE D 41

Mortgaged Dwellings, Number reporting Frequency of Payment (Interest and Principal) and Percentage Distribution by Frequency: First Mortgages, Owner-occupied and Rented, 52 Cities; Second and Third Mortgages, Owner-occupied, 52 Cities; Rented, 23 Cities, by Geographic Division, January I, 1934

	FIRST MORTGAGES PERCENTAGE DISTRIBUTION					SECOND AND THIRD MORTGAGES PERCENTAGE DISTRIBUTION						
NUMBER REPORTING	All frequencies	Monthly	Quarterly	Semi-annually	Annually	NUMBER REPORTING	All frequencies	Monthly	Quarterly	Semi-annually	Annually	
12,589	100.0	36.3	14.7	34.1	14.9	798	100.0	44.0	13.5	30.3	12.2	All cities[1]
877	100.0	16.4	7.2	63.9	12.5	149	100.0	24.8	6.4	54.5	14.3	New England cities
187	100.0	20.3	11.8	44.9	23.0	32	100.0	6.2	9.4	34.4	50.0	Portland, Me.
212	100.0	14.6	21.7	58.0	5.7	35	100.0	14.3	8.6	65.7	11.4	Worcester, Mass.
378	100.0	17.5	1.8	66.7	14.0	52	100.0	30.8	3.8	53.9	11.5	Providence, R.I.*
100	100.0	9.0	12.0	71.0	8.0	30	100.0	20.0	13.3	50.0	16.7	Waterbury, Conn.
715	100.0	10.9	2.2	69.4	17.5	100	100.0	7.3	23.8	55.6	13.3	Mid. Atlantic cities
66	100.0	7.6	1.5	80.3	10.6	11	100.0	9.1	9.1	72.7	9.1	Binghamton, N.Y.
215	100.0	3.3	2.8	70.2	23.7	48	100.0	2.1	29.2	56.2	12.5	Syracuse, N.Y.
212	100.0	14.6	1.9	78.3	5.2	19	100.0	26.3	5.3	52.6	15.8	Trenton, N.J.
222	100.0	28.4	1.3	55.0	15.3	22	100.0	40.9		36.4	22.7	Erie, Pa.
3,597	100.0	46.8	31.4	13.4	8.4	251	100.0	43.6	25.5	15.3	15.6	E. N. Central cities
2,222	100.0	28.8	56.8	9.0	5.4	206	100.0	44.2	27.2	13.1	15.5	Cleveland, Ohio*
491	100.0	77.6	0.4	11.6	10.4							Indianapolis, Ind.
330	100.0	78.5	0.3	8.5	12.7	23	100.0	60.9		13.0	26.1	Peoria, Ill.
142	100.0	52.1		32.4	15.5							Lansing, Mich.
119	100.0	26.1	0.8	53.8	19.3							Kenosha, Wis.
293	100.0	21.9	1.0	60.4	16.7	22	100.0	13.6	4.6	72.7	9.1	Racine, Wis.
2,656	100.0	31.0	2.4	44.5	22.1	43	100.0	41.8	11.6	23.3	23.3	W. N. Central cities
900	100.0	27.1	2.3	46.8	23.8	43	100.0	41.8	11.6	23.3	23.3	Minneapolis, Minn.
208	100.0	17.3	4.3	49.5	28.9							St. Paul, Minn.
342	100.0	24.8	1.5	53.8	19.9							Des Moines, Iowa
87	100.0	28.7	1.2	59.8	10.3							St. Joseph, Mo.
163	100.0	32.5	1.2	39.9	26.4							Springfield, Mo.
77	100.0	22.1	2.6	44.1	31.2							Fargo, N.D.
157	100.0	13.4	3.2	43.9	39.5							Sioux Falls, S.D.
168	100.0	50.0	1.2	30.3	18.5							Lincoln, Neb.
233	100.0	62.7	2.6	24.0	10.7							Topeka, Kan.
321	100.0	52.3	2.5	32.1	13.1							Wichita, Kan.
1,087	100.0	27.7	16.2	36.8	19.3	44	100.0	76.2	4.7	7.5	11.6	S. Atlantic cities
71	100.0	19.7	1.4	45.1	33.8							Hagerstown, Md.
126	100.0	10.3	27.8	37.3	24.6	14	100.0	64.3	7.1	14.3	14.3	Richmond, Va.
116	100.0	45.7	11.2	6.0	37.1							Wheeling, W.Va.*
34	100.0	44.1		32.4	23.5							Asheville, N.C.
66	100.0	39.4	3.0	47.0	10.6							Greensboro, N.C.
65	100.0	16.9	46.2	29.2	7.7							Charleston, S.C.
72	100.0	43.0	25.0	15.3	16.7							Columbia, S.C.
490	100.0	28.0	2.0	54.3	15.7	30	100.0	83.4	3.3	3.3	10.0	Atlanta, Ga.*
47	100.0	25.6	36.2	19.1	19.1							Jacksonville, Fla.
289	100.0	46.6	4.4	35.5	13.5	12	100.0	100.0				E. S. Central cities
22	100.0	45.5	4.5	22.7	27.3							Paducah, Ky.
193	100.0	41.4	5.2	38.9	14.5							Birmingham, Ala.*
74	100.0	77.0		17.6	5.4	12	100.0	100.0				Jackson, Miss.
1,143	100.0	43.1	1.8	31.5	23.6	56	100.0	56.0	5.9	29.1	9.0	W. S. Central cities
165	100.0	35.7	1.2	37.6	25.5							Little Rock, Ark.
57	100.0	57.9		5.3	36.8							Baton Rouge, La.
367	100.0	59.9	1.1	27.8	11.2	30	100.0	70.0	3.3	26.7		Oklahoma City, Okla.
85	100.0	40.0	3.5	25.9	30.6							Austin, Tex.
388	100.0	31.4	2.3	39.2	27.1	26	100.0	46.1	7.7	30.8	15.4	Dallas, Tex.
81	100.0	50.6	2.5	16.0	30.9							Wichita Falls, Tex.
552	100.0	44.5	15.1	32.1	8.3	26	100.0	80.2	8.2	11.6		Mountain cities
42	100.0	45.2	35.7	2.4	16.7							Butte, Mont.
31	100.0	64.5	3.2	25.8	6.5							Boise, Idaho
38	100.0	81.6		10.5	7.9							Casper, Wyo.
49	100.0	59.2		18.4	22.4							Pueblo, Colo.
147	100.0	29.9	8.2	56.5	5.4	8	100.0	75.0	12.5	12.5		Phoenix, Ariz.
245	100.0	41.6	24.9	27.4	6.1	18	100.0	83.3	5.6	11.1		Salt Lake City, Utah
1,673	100.0	44.1	18.5	26.5	10.9	117	100.0	70.2	9.6	15.9	4.3	Pacific cities
437	100.0	44.4	4.4	41.4	9.8	29	100.0	62.1	10.4	24.1	3.4	Seattle, Wash.*
389	100.0	29.3	26.5	32.9	11.3	20	100.0	70.0	5.0	25.0		Portland, Ore.
223	100.0	73.5	1.8	3.6	21.1	18	100.0	77.8		22.2		Sacramento, Calif.
624	100.0	47.1	36.7	8.0	8.2	50	100.0	76.0	16.0	4.0	4.0	San Diego, Calif.*

TABLE D 42

Mortgaged Dwellings, Percentage Reduction from Original Loan and per Annum: First Mortgages, Owner-occupied, 52 Cities; Rented, 27 Cities; Second and Third Mortgages, Owner-occupied, 26 Cities; Land Contracts, Owner-occupied, 19 Cities, by Geographic Division, January 1, 1934

| | OWNER-OCCUPIED | | | | | | RENTED [2] | |
| | FIRST MORTGAGES | | SECOND AND THIRD MORTGAGES Percentage Reduction | | LAND CONTRACTS | | FIRST MORTGAGES Percentage Reduction | |
	From original amount	Per annum	From original amount	Per annum	From original amount	Per annum	From original amount	Per annum
All cities [1]	19.0	4.6	32.6	8.8	29.9	6.9	15.5	4.3
New England cities	16.0	2.6	31.4	6.5			13.4	2.4
Portland, Me.	23.4	4.6						
Worcester, Mass.	5.7	1.4	35.6	7.0			3.6	0.9
Providence, R.I.*	22.4	3.1	31.2	6.5			16.9	2.9
Waterbury, Conn.	5.7	1.8	26.1	5.6				
Mid. Atlantic cities	9.7	1.8	37.0	6.9			9.4	2.7
Binghamton, N.Y.	15.5	2.6						
Syracuse, N.Y.	4.9	0.6	38.4	6.9				
Trenton, N.J.	6.2	1.0	31.4	6.8			6.1	1.2
Erie, Pa.	24.9	5.9	26.9	6.9			10.8	3.3
E. N. Central cities	22.6	4.9	30.2	8.6	26.0	4.9	18.5	3.7
Cleveland, Ohio*	23.0	4.8	31.8	8.8	24.3	6.1	19.1	3.7
Indianapolis, Ind.	25.6	5.6	22.6	8.4	25.7	4.8	17.8	4.0
Peoria, Ill.	25.6	5.3	13.4	5.4	28.6	7.2	25.2	5.7
Lansing, Mich.	20.3	6.8			29.2	5.2		
Kenosha, Wis.	10.8	3.3			25.2	3.6		
Racine, Wis.	10.3	2.8	9.4	3.8	21.5	2.8	4.8	1.4
W. N. Central cities	16.6	5.9	26.4	9.9	29.4	7.2	15.8	5.5
Minneapolis, Minn.	12.6	5.0	27.7	11.1	34.9	8.7	13.7	5.1
St. Paul, Minn.	15.9	6.1			34.0	8.1	15.0	4.8
Des Moines, Iowa	18.4	5.9	23.4	9.0	14.5	3.0	14.8	5.3
St. Joseph, Mo.	17.2	5.1						
Springfield, Mo.	25.6	9.8					18.8	7.8
Fargo, N.D.	15.5	6.7						
Sioux Falls, S.D.	11.6	4.5			32.4	8.3	29.0	11.6
Lincoln, Neb.	25.3	7.2					17.3	5.6
Topeka, Kan.	23.6	6.7	17.8	4.8	29.8	8.3	17.8	5.2
Wichita, Kan.	25.3	7.4	27.5	7.9	31.8	8.6	20.8	5.9
S. Atlantic cities	18.3	5.8	40.0	14.0			9.2	4.0
Hagerstown, Md.	10.5	4.2						
Richmond, Va.	13.4	4.6	43.8	16.2				
Wheeling, W.Va.*	28.4	6.2	17.4	6.4				
Asheville, N.C.	29.6	4.9						
Greensboro, N.C.	24.0	5.9						
Charleston, S.C.	17.0	5.7						
Columbia, S.C.	19.7	6.0						
Atlanta, Ga.*	16.0	6.2	48.2	15.9			9.2	4.0
Jacksonville, Fla.	19.6	6.8						
E. S. Central cities	25.4	5.4	46.8	21.3			8.0	2.8
Paducah, Ky.	32.6	9.1						
Birmingham, Ala.*	24.4	4.8	46.8	21.3			8.0	2.8
Jackson, Miss.	30.1	7.9						
W. S. Central cities	21.7	6.8	38.4	15.9			17.8	6.8
Little Rock, Ark.	13.7	5.7	39.4	17.9			14.3	7.2
Baton Rouge, La.	32.6	5.8						
Oklahoma City, Okla.	21.7	6.4	33.2	14.4			18.5	7.1
Austin, Tex.	27.5	7.9						
Dallas, Tex.	21.6	7.2	45.1	17.3			17.8	6.4
Wichita Falls, Tex.	24.9	7.8						
Mountain cities	17.2	6.2	22.8	9.1	27.1	7.2	8.6	3.9
Butte, Mont.	16.2	9.0						
Boise, Idaho	22.1	7.6			35.3	13.1		
Casper, Wyo.	19.5	8.9			29.1	13.9		
Pueblo, Colo.	19.6	8.2						
Phoenix, Ariz.	13.4	5.4					11.0	5.5
Salt Lake City, Utah	17.3	5.4	22.8	9.1	26.6	6.3	7.7	3.2
Pacific cities	20.3	5.3	34.2	12.9	35.9	8.9	17.4	5.3
Seattle, Wash.*	20.0	5.9	27.5	12.5	41.6	10.9	18.0	5.8
Portland, Ore.	22.7	4.1	43.1	12.7	30.2	6.4	20.2	3.8
Sacramento, Calif.	18.8	4.6	37.1	14.8	20.8	3.4	16.5	5.3
San Diego, Calif.*	17.7	6.6	30.0	12.5	23.1	5.6	13.6	5.4

Source: Financial Survey of Urban Housing. Percentage reduction from original amount of loan based upon the average amount of the original loans and the average amount of the loans outstanding for properties reporting year loan was contracted. The percentages shown may be approximated very closely by using the average amount of the original loans and the average amount of the loans outstanding, by agency holding the loan, as shown in Tables D 22 and 21, respectively. The percentage reduction per annum is obtained by dividing the total percentage reduction by the average years expired as shown in Table D 23.

*Metropolitan district.

[1] Geographic division and 'All cities' percentages weighted by estimated total debt, by tenure and priority, in each city (RPI).
[2] Sample data inadequate to show percentage reduction for second and third mortgages and land contracts.

TABLE D 43

Mortgaged Dwellings, Years required to pay off Existing Debt at Average Rate of Retirement: Owner-occupied, First Mortgages, 52 Cities; Second and Third Mortgages, 26 Cities; Land Contracts, 19 Cities; Rented, First Mortgages, 27 Cities, by Geographic Division, January 1, 1934

| | OWNER-OCCUPIED | | | RENTED[2] |
	1st mortgages	2d & 3d mortgages	Land contracts	1st mortgages
All cities[1]	21.7	11.4	14.5	23.3
New England cities	38.5	15.4		41.7
Portland, Me.	21.7			
Worcester, Mass.	71.4	14.3		111.1
Providence, R.I.*	32.3	15.4		34.5
Waterbury, Conn.	55.6	17.9		
Mid. Atlantic cities	55.6	14.5		37.0
Binghamton, N.Y.	38.5			
Syracuse, N.Y.	166.7	14.5		83.3
Trenton, N.J.	100.0	14.7		30.3
Erie, Pa.	16.9	14.5		
E. N. Central cities	20.4	11.6	20.4	27.0
Cleveland, Ohio*	20.8	11.4	16.4	27.0
Indianapolis, Ind.	17.9	11.9	20.8	25.0
Peoria, Ill.	18.9	18.5	13.9	17.5
Lansing, Mich.	14.7		19.2	
Kenosha, Wis.	30.3		27.8	
Racine, Wis.	35.7	26.3	35.7	71.4
W. N. Central cities	16.9	10.1	13.9	18.2
Minneapolis, Minn.	20.0	9.0	11.5	19.6
St. Paul, Minn.	16.4		12.3	20.8
Des Moines, Iowa	16.9	11.1	33.3	18.9
St. Joseph, Mo.	19.6			
Springfield, Mo.	10.2			12.8
Fargo, N.D.	14.9			
Sioux Falls, S.D.	22.2		12.0	8.6
Lincoln, Neb.	13.9			17.9
Topeka, Kan.	14.9	20.8	12.0	19.2
Wichita, Kan.	13.5	12.7	11.6	16.9
S. Atlantic cities	17.2	7.1		25.0
Hagerstown, Md.	23.8			
Richmond, Va.	21.7	6.2		
Wheeling, W. Va.*	16.1	15.6		
Asheville, N.C.	20.4			
Greensboro, N.C.	16.9			
Charleston, S.C.	17.5			
Columbia, S.C.	16.7			
Atlanta, Ga.*	16.1	6.3		25.0
Jacksonville, Fla.	14.7			
E. S. Central cities	18.5	4.7		35.7
Paducah, Ky.	11.0			
Birmingham, Ala.*	20.8	4.7		35.7
Jackson, Miss.	12.7			
W. S. Central cities	14.7	6.3		14.7
Little Rock, Ark.	17.5	5.6		13.9
Baton Rouge, La.	17.2			
Oklahoma City, Okla.	15.6	6.9		14.1
Austin, Tex.	12.7			
Dallas, Tex.	13.9	5.8		15.6
Wichita Falls, Tex.	12.8			
Mountain cities	16.1	11.0	13.9	25.6
Butte, Mont.	11.1			
Boise, Idaho	13.2		7.6	
Casper, Wyo.	11.2		7.2	
Pueblo, Colo.	12.2			
Phoenix, Ariz.	18.5			18.2
Salt Lake City, Utah	18.5	11.0	15.9	31.3
Pacific cities	18.9	7.8	11.2	18.9
Seattle, Wash.*	16.9	8.0	9.2	17.2
Portland, Ore.	24.4	7.9	15.6	26.3
Sacramento, Calif.	21.7	6.8	29.4	18.9
San Diego, Calif.*	15.2	8.0	17.9	18.5

Source: *Financial Survey of Urban Housing*. The years required to pay off existing debt are obtained by dividing the average annual percentage reduction, as shown in Table D 42, into 100.0 per cent.

*Metropolitan district.

[1] Geographic division and 'All cities' averages automatically weighted by the use of weighted averages from Table D 42.

[2] Sample data inadequate to show average years required for second and third mortgages and land contracts.

TABLE D 44

Mortgaged Dwellings, Percentage with Payments in Arrears, All Priorities by Value Groups: Owner-occupied, 52 Cities; Rented, 44 Cities, by Geographic Division, January 1, 1934

← ——————————————————————————— O W N E R - O C C U P I E D ——————————————————————————— →

	All value groups[2]	$1-499	$500-999	$1,000-1,499	$1,500-1,999	$2,000-2,999	$3,000-3,999	$4,000-4,999	$5,000-7,499	$7,500-9,999	$10,000-14,999	$15,000 and over
52 cities[1]	41.9	58.0	55.1	51.1	48.8	45.6	41.9	40.3	39.5	39.7	39.4	41.8
4 New England cities	27.4			43.8	29.0	38.6	29.2	30.2	26.6	27.7	23.3	15.7
Portland, Me.	28.1				28.6	41.9	34.9	27.4	24.0	26.5	26.8	26.3
Worcester, Mass.*	24.3					40.9	32.0	29.2	23.0	21.0	15.9	26.2
Providence, R.I.*	29.3			43.8	29.0	38.5	27.4	31.2	28.9	31.3	25.9	12.3
Waterbury, Conn.	22.0					33.3	32.0	27.6	20.6	19.6	20.5	11.4
4 Mid. Atlantic cities	28.7			49.8	47.8	34.7	29.6	25.9	28.5	27.8	26.1	25.0
Binghamton, N.Y.	26.2					42.9	32.3	28.6	20.4	28.3	33.3	9.1
Syracuse, N.Y.	22.9					28.3	21.0	19.8	24.2	22.4	19.4	29.2
Trenton, N.J.	26.3			27.0	26.7	24.7	28.7	22.8	25.9	34.2	28.2	26.3
Erie, Pa.	48.4			72.7	69.0	57.6	52.5	44.4	47.9	36.0	38.2	21.4
6 E. N. Central cities	58.3		67.9	62.5	64.2	60.2	60.4	57.2	57.2	56.0	53.9	54.4
Cleveland, Ohio*	61.9		68.4	64.0	65.1	61.3	62.9	62.4	62.6	61.5	59.3	57.8
Indianapolis, Ind.	53.3		76.7	58.7	67.2	61.8	59.4	47.8	47.7	45.6	36.3	42.6
Peoria, Ill.	38.7		30.8	34.7	38.2	46.3	42.2	35.6	36.1	33.3	36.3	
Lansing, Mich.	50.1			60.0	48.7	55.0	54.6	48.7	37.7	47.4		42.1
Kenosha, Wis.	52.8				78.6	50.0	51.1	55.1	52.6	47.7	57.7	54.5
Racine, Wis.	62.4			90.9	73.1	64.7	60.6	55.9	63.8	59.7	70.2	68.8
10 W. N. Central cities	35.2	54.9	43.5	46.5	40.3	40.6	34.7	32.9	29.9	28.8	35.3	46.7
Minneapolis, Minn.	37.4		36.1	52.2	48.4	42.9	38.6	35.8	33.1	28.7	40.0	45.1
St. Paul, Minn.	25.3		37.5	22.2	37.2	23.6	22.2	21.5	25.0	25.0		
Des Moines, Iowa	33.2	46.4	46.2	37.4	38.2	34.9	30.6	25.7	31.9	27.3	30.4	46.7
St. Joseph, Mo.	31.3		50.0	35.7	34.6	37.1	26.1	31.1	21.2	18.8	25.0	
Springfield, Mo.	29.5	40.0	29.0	27.2	32.2	29.5	33.3	29.0	20.8	21.4	38.4	
Fargo, N.D.	25.1											
Sioux Falls, S.D.	27.6		28.6	61.1	27.3	27.1	31.3	24.8	22.1	34.7	11.5	36.4
Lincoln, Neb.	43.7		60.0	57.5	46.8	47.3	41.5	43.6	32.8	30.0	47.4	53.3
Topeka, Kan.	45.2		50.0	56.8	53.0	49.3	49.8	40.1	29.8	36.4	36.0	55.6
Wichita, Kan.	49.9	75.0	56.8	52.3	50.9	49.7	45.8	51.1	44.9	44.4	50.0	46.7
9 S. Atlantic cities	37.2		56.7	47.2	46.5	41.8	36.4	33.8	32.3	34.5	33.1	36.2
Hagerstown, Md.	16.4				17.4	27.9	13.4	13.0	16.0	12.5	10.0	8.6
Richmond, Va.	21.3		37.5	22.2	23.5	28.1	23.7	14.3	21.9	22.3	16.1	13.3
Wheeling, W.Va.*	48.7		60.9	48.8	63.8	57.0	55.8	40.5	39.4	36.4	50.0	45.8
Asheville, N.C.	48.8		50.0	60.0	58.3	48.1	45.0	38.9	42.4	70.6	46.2	62.5
Greensboro, N.C.	44.8			44.4	71.4	45.2	35.1	30.8	41.5	50.0	55.0	50.0
Charleston, S.C.	21.8				25.0	34.5	20.0	23.1	18.2	7.7	9.1	
Columbia, S.C.	51.3		53.8	75.0	50.0	55.6	60.5	51.2	45.9	38.9	53.3	
Atlanta, Ga.*	38.1		64.4	53.1	46.4	41.7	35.9	36.1	32.4	32.9	33.1	40.0
Jacksonville, Fla.	37.6				53.1	35.8	26.2	46.7	32.0	47.6	23.1	
3 E. S. Central cities	57.3		76.1	71.3	65.1	56.7	53.8	53.0	51.8	47.5	48.1	58.1
Paducah, Ky.	46.3		58.6	53.3	48.1	40.4	38.7	47.8	44.4			
Birmingham, Ala.*	59.0		77.2	72.7	65.6	57.8	56.2	55.5	52.0	48.8	46.3	58.1
Jackson, Miss.	50.9			70.0	69.2	56.3	44.7	39.2	53.4	38.9	60.0	
6 W. S. Central cities	41.2	49.7	53.0	48.7	44.9	40.1	38.7	40.7	38.1	41.5	40.2	39.7
Little Rock, Ark.	47.9		71.7	47.7	47.7	48.6	40.6	52.5	45.7	52.3	40.2	46.2
Baton Rouge, La.	45.5		73.3	76.9	68.2	40.0	37.2	23.1	28.1		47.1	
Oklahoma City, Okla.	43.0	50.0	48.0	43.3	47.6	40.4	40.3	44.4	42.1	46.1	48.8	43.2
Austin, Tex.	46.7		70.0	47.6	50.0	39.7	48.5	51.3	46.0	36.4	43.5	23.1
Dallas, Tex.	35.6		46.2	50.0	37.1	36.3	34.1	35.2	33.0	36.2	34.0	38.5
Wichita Falls, Tex.	49.6	47.6	58.6	53.3	57.9	52.2	47.7	35.3	34.5			
6 Mountain cities	44.4	64.5	48.4	46.4	48.1	45.0	44.1	41.0	40.4	48.1	55.8	40.1
Butte, Mont.	44.7		52.4	50.8	45.6	38.5	49.3	37.0	40.0	50.0	35.7	
Boise, Idaho	28.8		39.3	27.3	21.7	29.1	28.3	20.0	35.7	52.6		
Casper, Wyo.	33.6	50.0	26.9	33.3	27.8	34.6	27.9	35.0	35.0	50.0		
Pueblo, Colo.	46.8	70.0	42.2	43.3	51.8	48.9	43.9	45.0	50.0			
Phoenix, Ariz.	43.2			58.3	51.3	35.1	44.6	41.8	35.3	46.9	57.9	54.5
Salt Lake City, Utah	47.4		53.1	47.8	52.5	50.5	47.4	43.8	40.4	47.4	57.6	36.4
4 Pacific cities	37.1	62.5	40.9	39.8	41.7	38.2	34.6	33.9	36.3	37.5	38.0	47.3
Seattle, Wash.*	43.7	62.5	47.3	48.1	51.4	44.4	41.7	39.4	40.1	37.1	40.0	59.4
Portland, Ore.	36.0		35.8	35.4	37.8	38.6	30.9	34.1	39.0	42.9	45.8	32.3
Sacramento, Calif.	24.4			33.3	31.4	24.7	26.5	19.9	21.1	30.6	19.5	46.2
San Diego, Calif.*	29.4		34.6	30.9	30.4	29.0	28.4	27.4	29.8	32.0	28.0	45.6

Source: *Financial Survey of Urban Housing.* The number of reports upon which the percentage with payments in arrears is based is approximately the same as those shown in Tables D 5 and 6. Percentage not shown for fewer than 3 reports.

*Metropolitan district.

[1] Geographic division and 52 (44)-city percentages weighted by number of mortgaged properties, by tenure, in each city (RPI). For rented properties where the number of cities included in the 'All value groups' column is larger than the number for the individual value groups the weighted geographic division and 52 (44)-city percentages in the 'All value groups' column are not strictly comparable with the weighted percentages for the individual value groups.

[2] Where only percentage with payments in arrears 'All value groups' is shown, percentage with payments in arrears by value groups was not obtained by the Financial Survey of Urban Housing either because the number of reports was too small or because related information was lacking for rented properties.

Mortgaged Dwellings, Percentage with Payments in Arrears, all Priorities by Value Groups: Owner-occupied, 52 Cities; Rented, 44 Cities; by Geographic Division, January 1, 1934

All value groups[2]	$1–499	$500–999	$1,000–1,499	$1,500–1,999	$2,000–2,999	$3,000–3,999	$4,000–4,999	$5,000–7,499	$7,500–9,999	$10,000–14,999	$15,000 and over	
						RENTED						
45.7		67.9	53.7	47.2	48.9	45.0	45.2	44.9	47.7	47.4	51.7	44 cities[1]
30.9				16.7	43.5	20.2	31.1	29.1	35.5	40.9	27.7	3 New England cities
31.7					16.7	20.0	54.2	27.5	25.6	43.5	50.0	Portland, Me.
27.3						15.8	21.7	29.0	26.1	23.5	57.1	Worcester, Mass.
31.9				16.7	46.2	21.6	31.7	29.3	39.3	45.9	16.6	Providence, R.I.*
28.5				44.0	45.4	37.1	23.3	24.2	33.1	29.7	27.3	3 Mid. Atlantic cities
23.3						40.0	13.0	19.7	28.3	25.9		Syracuse, N.Y.
21.9				44.0	25.0	13.5	25.0	8.0				Trenton, N.J.
47.1					59.4	45.5	50.0	47.7	46.2	40.0	27.3	Erie, Pa.
66.1		90.0	60.4	61.0	66.3	65.1	65.8	63.3	67.9	65.4	65.0	6 E. N. Central cities
68.0		90.0	57.1	57.5	65.4	61.1	69.6	66.1	71.8	73.0	72.7	Cleveland, Ohio*
69.1			72.2	66.7	75.0	78.4	66.0	65.2	57.6	44.4	50.0	Indianapolis, Ind.
40.1			29.4	50.0	27.9	32.8	35.3	36.4	85.7	100.0	62.5	Peoria, Ill.
61.5				82.4	68.9	66.6	52.9	41.7				Lansing, Mich.
50.0												Kenosha, Wis.
65.2					60.0	65.6	62.5	68.2	65.5	65.2	68.2	Racine, Wis.
36.0		38.3	50.6	39.0	36.2	35.6	34.3	33.4	37.8	40.9	42.1	9 W. N. Central cities
40.0			48.4	48.8	38.2	33.6	40.0	36.0	52.7	40.9	54.9	Minneapolis, Minn.
24.1				26.7	31.3	26.4	18.6	20.5	25.0			St. Paul, Minn.
34.9		33.3	68.2	26.0	24.4	41.7	39.5	38.6	25.0		9.1	Des Moines, Iowa
26.2												St. Joseph, Mo.
23.6			19.4	26.7	28.0	17.6	25.0	11.8				Springfield, Mo.
32.2			50.0	26.7	35.7	21.9	27.5	45.7	20.0			Sioux Falls, S.D.
38.5			35.3	35.0	37.0	39.6	30.4	30.0				Lincoln, Neb.
46.8		50.0	71.4	51.2	37.0	51.1	35.7	26.7•				Topeka, Kan.
47.5		39.4	50.0	49.2	53.3	50.8	42.9	48.1	33.3			Wichita, Kan.
36.2		53.3	52.2	32.5	36.6	32.0	38.3	31.7	35.6	42.4	51.7	8 S. Atlantic cities
19.4												Hagerstown, Md.
25.5					28.7	26.3	16.0	15.8	18.2			Richmond, Va.
41.4												Wheeling, W. Va.*
54.1												Asheville, N.C.
35.5												Greensboro, N.C.
21.9												Charleston, S.C.
34.5												Columbia, S.C.
40.3		53.3	52.2	32.5	40.2	34.1	46.4	37.5	41.9	42.4	51.7	Atlanta, Ga.*
57.4		64.9	83.4	98.6	70.7	79.3	46.7	84.9	59.9			2 E. S. Central cities
34.8												Paducah, Ky.
58.0		50.0	64.3	76.0	54.5	61.1	36.0	65.4	46.2			Birmingham, Ala.*
40.5		55.9	42.2	36.3	38.1	38.0	41.2	32.3	44.4	33.5	55.2	5 W. S. Central cities
42.1		62.5	47.6	33.3	37.8	41.7	46.7	17.6				Little Rock, Ark.
43.9		46.2	44.0	38.1	40.3	46.4	33.3	44.6	54.5	40.0	56.4	Oklahoma City, Okla.
45.8		86.4			55.0	26.3						Austin, Tex.
36.2			40.0	35.7	34.1	33.7	45.1	27.4	37.9	29.4	54.5	Dallas, Tex.
48.8												Wichita Falls, Tex.
48.7			55.6	48.5	45.1	38.4	55.7	48.4	55.5		52.6	4 Mountain cities
59.6												Butte, Mont.
55.6												Pueblo, Colo.
37.3					41.0	28.6	23.8	53.1	45.5			Phoenix, Ariz.
52.7			55.6	48.5	47.6	44.3	75.0	45.5	61.5		52.6	Salt Lake City, Utah
41.0		56.3	41.7	42.1	41.1	39.5	39.6	42.7	36.5	37.5	48.9	4 Pacific cities
47.4			50.0	46.7	43.3	47.3	42.1	55.2	54.5	42.9	64.7	Seattle, Wash.*
46.4			58.1	48.9	50.0	43.8	43.2	42.6	36.8	36.4	33.3	Portland, Ore.
26.5				42.1	30.0	29.5	26.3	18.4	11.8	36.4		Sacramento, Calif.
32.0		56.3	13.6	28.8	33.5	27.9	37.5	34.2	20.0	31.3	41.9	San Diego, Calif.*

TABLE D 45

Mortgaged Dwellings, Number reporting and Average Payment in Arrears, All Priorities by Tenure, 52 Cities by Geographic Division, January 1, 1934

	OWNER—OCCUPIED		RENTED	
	Number reporting	Average amount (dollars)	Number reporting	Average amount (dollars)
52 cities[1]	30,243	467	6,119	582
4 New England cities	1,161	369	264	516
Portland, Me.	183	397	60	490
Worcester, Mass.	276	344	54	342
Providence, R.I.*	598	365	122	439
Waterbury, Conn.	104	498	28	1,602
4 Mid. Atlantic cities	1,445	393	249	507
Binghamton, N.Y.	67	387	15	1,066
Syracuse, N.Y.	225	447	50	573
Trenton, N.J.	420	229	53	215
Erie, Pa.	733	415	131	374
6 E. N. Central cities	11,989	593	2,416	691
Cleveland, Ohio*	8,747	653	1,555	818
Indianapolis, Ind.	925	487	347	533
Peoria, Ill.	563	329	141	457
Lansing, Mich.	320	377	96	332
Kenosha, Wis.	382	536	65	784
Racine, Wis.	1,052	499	212	504
10 W. N. Central cities	4,520	365	1,096	409
Minneapolis, Minn.	1,540	403	394	456
St. Paul, Minn.	224	370	53	564
Des Moines, Iowa	547	332	140	312
St. Joseph, Mo.	167	281	28	293
Springfield, Mo.	226	279	42	194
Fargo, N.D.	121	755	15	258
Sioux Falls, S.D.	175	423	59	328
Lincoln, Neb.	350	379	77	712
Topeka, Kan.	492	275	118	268
Wichita, Kan.	678	302	170	260
9 S. Atlantic cities	2,282	418	397	617
Hagerstown, Md.	58	247	13	531
Richmond, Va.	231	328	27	386
Wheeling, W. Va.*	389	581	48	626
Asheville, N.C.	210	528	20	222
Greensboro, N.C.	138	641	27	635
Charleston, S.C.	44	241	16	994
Columbia, S.C.	172	417	29	389
Atlanta, Ga.*	931	334	217	706
Jacksonville, Fla.	109	346		[2]
3 E. S. Central cities	1,463	484	173	506
Paducah, Ky.	106	311	8	110
Birmingham, Ala.*	1,220	519	123	450
Jackson, Miss.	137	291	42	834
6 W. S. Central cities	2,242	431	511	463
Little Rock, Ark.	414	446	72	350
Baton Rouge, La.	90	235	32	218
Oklahoma City, Okla.	764	504	172	756
Austin, Tex.	194	395	49	331
Dallas, Tex.	605	397	146	338
Wichita Falls, Tex.	175	390	40	524
6 Mountain cities	1,822	372	311	387
Butte, Mont.	213	399	34	132
Boise, Idaho	165	273	10	513
Casper, Wyo.	101	378	21	256
Pueblo, Colo.	195	392	30	340
Phoenix, Ariz.	235	321	59	465
Salt Lake City, Utah	913	385	157	399
4 Pacific cities	3,319	373	702	634
Seattle, Wash.*	1,413	425	240	993
Portland, Ore.	913	336	199	356
Sacramento, Calif.	304	264	61	373
San Diego, Calif.*	689	316	202	362

Source: Financial Survey of Urban Housing

*Metropolitan district.

[1] Geographic division and 52-city averages weighted by number of mortgaged properties with payments in arrears, by tenure, in each city (RPI).

[2] Data not available.

TABLE D 46

Mortgaged Dwellings, Number reporting Payments in Arrears on First Mortgages and Percentage Distribution by Holding Agency: Owner-occupied, 52 Cities; Rented, 30 Cities; and Number reporting Payments in Arrears on Second and Third Mortgages: Owner-occupied, 49 Cities; Rented, 23 Cities, by Geographic Division, January 1, 1934

			←————————————— O W N E R - O C C U P I E D ————————————→										
			F I R S T M O R T G A G E S										
	NUMBER REPORTING	All holding agencies	Percentage Distribution by Holding Agency										2d & 3d mortg.
			Life ins. co.	Build. & loan asso.	Commer. bank	Savings bank	Mortgage co.	Construct. co.	Title & trust co.	H.O. Loan Corp.	Individual	Other[2]	
All cities[1]	26,717	100.0	11.4	21.8	13.4	14.4	7.9	0.4	2.6	0.7	22.6	4.8	3,383
New England cities	986	100.0	2.7	12.0	11.6	43.2	2.3	0.2	2.7	0.4	17.8	7.1	362
Portland, Me.	175	100.0	1.7	32.6	8.0	48.0					9.7		33
Worcester, Mass.	183	100.0	0.5	4.9	5.5	67.8	3.8		0.5		4.4	12.6	156
Providence, R.I.*	556	100.0	3.6	13.7	14.2	33.1	2.3	0.3	3.6	0.4	22.3	6.5	119
Waterbury, Conn.	72	100.0	1.4	4.2	8.3	59.7			2.8	1.4	18.0	4.2	54
Mid. Atlantic cities	1,283	100.0	5.4	10.5	9.9	24.6	1.3	.0	0.8	0.1	42.8	4.6	271
Binghamton, N.Y.	60	100.0	1.6	3.3	16.7	16.7			1.7		58.3	1.7	13
Syracuse, N.Y.	139	100.0	8.7	.7	12.2	45.3	0.7		0.7		26.6	5.1	127
Trenton, N.J.	393	100.0	3.3	23.9	4.1	2.5	2.8		0.2	0.3	58.8	4.1	51
Erie, Pa.	691	100.0	1.6	24.0	6.7	2.3	2.0	0.1	1.2	0.3	56.3	5.5	80
E. N. Central cities	11,053	100.0	6.4	31.2	30.4	13.9	1.8	0.3	3.2	0.8	8.8	3.2	1,397
Cleveland, Ohio*	8,405	100.0	6.7	14.4	44.7	20.2	1.1	0.3	2.8	0.8	6.1	2.9	1,230
Indianapolis, Ind.	811	100.0	6.9	73.4	4.4	2.1	1.1	0.6	3.7	1.1	4.5	2.2	28
Peoria, Ill.	505	100.0	5.1	74.3	2.0	0.6	0.4	0.6	0.4		10.5	6.1	40
Lansing, Mich.	168	100.0	14.9	46.4	5.3	6.0	4.8		1.8		19.0	1.8	10
Kenosha, Wis.	314	100.0	0.3	22.9	2.3	0.6	9.2	0.3	16.6		37.6	10.2	24
Racine, Wis.	850	100.0	0.8	38.9	1.9	1.1	10.2		2.2	0.8	39.1	5.0	65
W. N. Central cities	3,802	100.0	13.6	24.9	5.0	3.4	11.6	0.2	2.7	0.6	33.2	4.8	286
Minneapolis, Minn.	1,273	100.0	16.7	18.5	4.7	6.8	13.0		2.5	0.5	32.6	4.7	74
St. Paul, Minn.	186	100.0	9.1	14.5	5.4	1.1	10.8	0.5	1.6	0.5	51.1	5.4	15
Des Moines, Iowa	383	100.0	23.2	8.4	9.7	4.2	10.7		1.0	0.3	39.4	3.1	19
St. Joseph, Mo.	152	100.0	2.6	32.9	11.2	...	17.8		3.3		21.7	10.5	13
Springfield, Mo.	213	100.0	5.2	40.4	2.3	0.5	7.5		1.4	0.5	36.6	5.6	15
Fargo, N.D.	106	100.0	4.7	37.7	6.6	1.0	10.4	0.9	1.0	2.8	25.5	9.4	16
Sioux Falls, S.D.	132	100.0	10.6	3.8	6.8	0.8	27.3		1.5	1.5	37.9	9.8	14
Lincoln, Neb.	330	100.0	9.4	48.8	1.8	0.9	5.2	1.2	7.3	0.6	20.9	3.9	26
Topeka, Kan.	428	100.0	6.1	70.3	3.7	2.8	7.0		2.1	0.5	6.6	0.9	47
Wichita, Kan.	599	100.0	21.0	40.2	1.2	0.2	11.7	0.3	6.0	1.3	15.9	2.2	47
S. Atlantic cities	2,055	100.0	21.6	12.7	7.4	6.9	15.5	0.4	3.1	0.3	26.7	5.4	344
Hagerstown, Md.	50	100.0	2.0	26.0	6.0		4.0				60.0	2.0	11
Richmond, Va.	179	100.0	14.5	11.7	14.5	2.2	21.8		5.6	0.6	20.7	8.4	73
Wheeling, W. Va.*	364	100.0	5.0	22.8	19.8	17.0	1.1	1.1	2.2	0.8	21.7	8.5	34
Asheville, N.C.	191	100.0	35.1	16.8	4.2	0.5	15.7	0.5	0.5	0.5	23.6	2.6	24
Greensboro, N.C.	127	100.0	51.2	11.0	3.2	0.8	13.4	1.5	0.8		11.8	6.3	24
Charleston, S.C.	42	100.0			14.3	4.8	7.1		2.4		69.0	2.4	
Columbia, S.C.	168	100.0	13.1	48.8	1.8	0.6	1.8		1.2		29.1	3.6	17
Atlanta, Ga.*	835	100.0	29.2	2.3	2.3	9.4	25.4	0.3	4.2	0.1	22.8	4.0	151
Jacksonville, Fla.	99	100.0	28.3	18.2	....		6.1		1.0		42.4	4.0	10
E. S. Central cities	1,382	100.0	26.3	29.1	3.2	1.0	14.3	0.4	1.3	1.0	18.7	4.7	122
Paducah, Ky.	98	100.0	18.4	22.5	11.2	4.1	1.0	3.1	10.2	1.0	24.5	4.0	11
Birmingham, Ala.*	1,152	100.0	25.0	27.8	2.6	0.9	16.7	0.3	0.9	1.0	19.4	5.4	93
Jackson, Miss.	132	100.0	38.6	40.1	3.8		4.5		0.8	0.8	11.4		18
W. S. Central cities	2,086	100.0	16.1	33.3	5.0	2.4	14.0	2.2	1.1	0.8	21.6	3.5	239
Little Rock, Ark.	384	100.0	19.0	25.3	23.4	2.9	8.3		1.6	2.1	15.6	1.8	43
Baton Rouge, La.	77	100.0	2.6	51.9	5.2	1.3	1.3			1.3	23.4	13.0	
Oklahoma City, Okla.	723	100.0	15.4	49.1	1.1	1.0	13.1	0.1	1.3	0.7	16.3	1.9	110
Austin, Tex.	170	100.0	2.4	9.4	3.5	0.6	17.6	18.2			41.8	6.5	10
Dallas, Tex.	573	100.0	21.0	25.5	4.2	4.2	16.8	1.2	1.0	0.7	21.6	3.8	61
Wichita Falls, Tex.	159	100.0	6.9	32.7	1.3		12.6	5.0	2.5	0.6	35.9	2.5	15
Mountain cities	1,342	100.0	10.8	28.9	3.0	6.5	10.4	0.7	4.9	1.8	29.7	3.3	76
Butte, Mont.	158	100.0		0.7		9.5	.5.7	0.6	3.8		70.2	7.6	
Boise, Idaho	136	100.0	7.3	47.1	0.7		3.7		0.7	2.2	34.6	3.7	13
Casper, Wyo.	57	100.0	5.2	57.9	5.3		3.5				28.1		6
Pueblo, Colo.	183	100.0	1.6	44.3	1.1	2.2	0.5	1.1	1.1	3.3	39.3	5.5	10
Phoenix, Ariz.	201	100.0	9.9	9.0	3.0	10.4	15.9	0.5	2.5	1.0	46.3	1.5	17
Salt Lake City, Utah	607	100.0	16.6	27.7	3.1	8.9	14.5	0.8	8.2	1.8	15.7	2.7	30
Pacific cities	2,728	100.0	16.3	11.2	7.1	13.4	12.8	0.2	2.8	1.0	28.1	7.1	286
Seattle, Wash.*	1,049	100.0	15.5	7.5	5.4	24.5	13.7	0.2	4.5	1.3	22.8	4.4	58
Portland, Ore.	822	100.0	22.6	8.4	2.1	5.0	15.9		2.7	0.7	30.9	11.7	79
Sacramento, Calif.	256	100.0	8.2	22.6	14.1	3.1	3.5		0.8		39.5	8.2	43
San Diego, Calif.*	601	100.0	10.3	19.0	16.3	10.5	9.5	0.3	0.6	1.2	29.0	3.3	106

Source: Financial Survey of Urban Housing

*Metropolitan district.

[1]*Geographic division and 'All cities' percentage distributions weighted by number of first mortgage loans, by tenure, in each city (RPI).*

[2]*Includes public bond issues:*

Owner-occupied	(per cent)	Rented	
Kenosha, Wis.	3.5	Racine, Wis.	2.0
Racine, Wis.	0.5	Seattle, Wash.	0.9
Paducah, Ky.	2.0	San Diego, Calif.	1.0

TABLE D 46

Mortgaged Dwellings, Number reporting Payments in Arrears on First Mortgages and Percentage Distribution by Holding Agency: Owner-occupied, 52 Cities; Rented, 30 Cities; and Number reporting Payments in Arrears on Second and Third Mortgages: Owner-occupied, 49 Cities; Rented, 23 Cities, by Geographic Division, January 1, 1934

←——————————————————— R E N T E D ———————————————————→

F I R S T   M O R T G A G E S
Percentage Distribution by Holding Agency

NUMBER[3] REPORTING	All holding agencies	Life ins. co.	Build. & loan asso.	Commer. bank	Savings bank	Mortgage co.	Construct. co.	Title & trust co.	H.O. Loan Corp.	Individual	Other[2]	2d & 3d MORTG. NO. REP.	
	100.0	13.8	22.2	12.3	12.8	10.8	0.1	2.6	0.4	20.8	4.2	515	**All cities**[1]
	100.0	2.9	7.7	17.5	48.8	2.4		2.4		13.7	4.6	78	**New England cities**
64	100.0	1.6	6.2	14.1	60.9			1.6		12.5	3.1	13	Portland, Me.
45	100.0	4.5	4.4	6.7	66.7	2.2		2.2		4.4	8.9	18	Worcester, Mass.
114	100.0	2.6	8.8	21.1	42.1	2.6		2.6		16.7	3.5	28	Providence, R.I.*
20												19	Waterbury, Conn.
	100.0	4.1	8.7	9.8	1.1	36.7		2.2		33.2	4.2	47	**Mid. Atlantic cities**
14												1	Binghamton, N.Y.
35	100.0	5.7		11.4		60.0		2.9		17.1	2.9	30	Syracuse, N.Y.
56	100.0	3.6	17.8	3.6	1.8	7.1		1.8		55.4	8.9	6	Trenton, N.J.
126	100.0	0.8	23.0	10.3	3.2	1.6		.8		56.3	4.0	10	Erie, Pa.
	100.0	6.7	39.3	22.8	14.8	1.5	0.2	4.0	0.4	7.2	3.1	203	**E. N. Central cities**
1,542	100.0	7.7	14.5	37.5	24.6	1.5	0.1	3.8	0.6	5.6	4.1	169	Cleveland, Ohio*
340	100.0	3.2	78.8	4.4	1.8	0.9		4.7	0.3	5.0	0.9		Indianapolis, Ind.
126	100.0	2.4	84.9	0.8	2.4	0.8		0.8		5.5	2.4	15	Peoria, Ill.
82	100.0	28.1	37.8	4.9	6.1	1.2	1.2	6.1		12.2	2.4		Lansing, Mich.
62													Kenosha, Wis.
205	100.0	1.0	20.0	3.4	1.2	7.8	1.2	4.9	1.1	50.2	9.2	19	Racine, Wis.
	100.0	19.3	24.5	5.3	3.5	11.5		2.1	0.1	29.8	3.9	27	**W. N. Central cities**
365	100.0	18.6	16.1	4.9	4.7	14.8		3.8		32.1	5.0	27	Minneapolis, Minn.
45	100.0	24.5	13.3	11.1	2.2	6.7				42.2			St. Paul, Minn.
132	100.0	25.0	9.9	7.6	6.1	12.1				34.8	4.5		Des Moines, Iowa
27													St. Joseph, Mo.
38	100.0	5.3	44.7	2.7	2.6					42.1	2.6		Springfield, Mo.
15													Fargo, N.D.
49	100.0	14.3	6.1	2.1	2.0	30.6				32.7	12.2		Sioux Falls, S.D.
69	100.0	8.7	50.7	1.4	1.5	2.9		5.8		21.7	7.3		Lincoln, Neb.
115	100.0	7.8	68.7		2.6	7.8		0.9	0.9	7.8	3.5		Topeka, Kan.
163	100.0	24.5	45.4	1.2	1.2	14.1		2.5		8.0	3.1		Wichita, Kan.
	100.0	26.7	2.0	1.0	10.4	27.7		2.5	0.5	23.8	5.4	29	**S. Atlantic cities**
16													Hagerstown, Md.
23												9	Richmond, Va.
47													Wheeling, W. Va.*
20													Asheville, N.C.
27													Greensboro, N.C.
17													Charleston, S.C.
31													Columbia, S.C.
202	100.0	26.7	2.0	1.0	10.4	27.7		2.5	0.5	23.8	5.4	20	Atlanta, Ga.*
23													Jacksonville, Fla.
	100.0	21.1	13.0	8.1	3.3	15.5		1.6	1.6	26.8	9.0	8	**E. S. Central cities**
9													Paducah, Ky.
123	100.0	21.1	13.0	8.1	3.3	15.5		1.6	1.6	26.8	9.0		Birmingham, Ala.*
40												8	Jackson, Miss.
	100.0	20.0	26.1	6.2	3.4	18.3	0.3		0.5	21.7	3.5	36	**W. S. Central cities**
73	100.0	16.4	15.1	41.1	1.4	5.5			2.7	16.4	1.4		Little Rock, Ark.
32													Baton Rouge, La.
167	100.0	26.9	43.1			0.6	15.0		0.6	8.4	5.4	20	Oklahoma City, Okla.
50													Austin, Tex.
147	100.0	16.3	17.7	2.7	5.5	23.1	0.7			31.3	2.7	16	Dallas, Tex.
37													Wichita Falls, Tex.
	100.0	18.1	13.3	4.4	9.9	17.5		5.7	2.2	26.7	2.2	21	**Mountain cities**
34													Butte, Mont.
12													Boise, Idaho
21													Casper, Wyo.
24													Pueblo, Colo.
59	100.0	11.8	8.5	6.8	11.9	16.9			3.4	37.3	3.4	5	Phoenix, Ariz.
140	100.0	22.1	16.4	2.9	8.6	17.9		9.3	1.4	20.0	1.4	16	Salt Lake City, Utah
	100.0	19.0	13.1	9.3	10.1	8.4		2.2	0.1	32.1	5.7	66	**Pacific cities**
226	100.0	26.6	11.9	2.2	17.3	10.2		3.5		26.1	2.2	15	Seattle, Wash.*
187	100.0	25.7	4.8	4.3	2.7	6.5		2.1	0.5	40.6	12.8	16	Portland, Ore.
58	100.0		22.4	8.6	6.9	3.5				51.7	6.9	10	Sacramento, Calif.
204	100.0	8.8	19.6	24.5	8.8	9.8		1.5		24.0	3.0	25	San Diego, Calif.*

[3]*Where only number reporting is shown, number and percentage distribution by agencies was not obtained by Financial Survey of Urban Housing either because the number of reports was too small or because related information was lacking for rented properties.*

TABLE D 47

Mortgaged Dwellings, Percentage with Payments in Arrears, All Holding Agencies: First Mortgages, by Holding Agency, Owner-occupied and Rented, 52 Cities; Second and Third Mortgages, Owner-occupied, 52 Cities; Rented, 23 Cities, by Geographic Division, January 1, 1934

| | OWNER-OCCUPIED | | | | | | | | | | 2d & 3d MORTG. |
| | FIRST MORTGAGES | | | | | | | | | | |
	All holding agencies	Life ins. co.	Build. & loan asso.	Commer. bank	Savings bank	Mortgage co.	Construct. co.	Title & trust co.	H.O. Loan Corp.	Individual	Other	3/
All cities[1]	39.9	41.2	52.3	36.6	40.2	42.2	58.3	36.2	11.2	36.5	43.3	51.2
New England cities	24.3	34.7	25.8	23.1	25.5	23.2		24.5	8.5	22.3	35.1	40.6
Portland, Me.	27.3	30.0	30.2	31.1	29.6					17.9		42.9
Worcester, Mass.	16.5	9.1	20.0	17.9	15.0	50.0		9.1		17.8	28.4	47.7
Providence, R.I.*	27.7	42.6	28.0	26.1	28.9	15.3		31.3	8.7	25.6	39.1	36.6
Waterbury, Conn.	15.5		20.0	9.0	21.2			9.1	7.1	10.9	21.4	40.9
Mid. Atlantic cities	24.1	32.9	49.6	24.5	21.3	42.8		16.7	5.6	31.0	43.2	48.7
Binghamton, N.Y.	23.6			31.2	15.1					25.5		41.9
Syracuse, N.Y.	14.3	27.3		20.5	9.3			9.1		29.4	46.7	48.3
Trenton, N.J.	25.1	38.2	45.0	18.0	24.4	22.4		4.8	6.7	22.1	26.2	40.8
Erie, Pa.	46.8	40.7	54.2	36.8	50.0	63.6		47.1	4.4	47.2	52.1	65.6
E. N. Central cities	57.2	54.2	71.3	53.7	56.5	61.6	58.7	50.8	17.4	46.4	54.7	60.4
Cleveland, Ohio*	61.1	60.2	77.1	61.6	61.1	64.2	58.7	59.3	18.5	49.9	61.3	62.4
Indianapolis, Ind.	52.0	38.9	62.5	40.0	50.0	52.9		30.3	13.2	36.7	35.3	46.7
Peoria, Ill.	38.1	28.3	40.6	25.0	25.0			20.0		36.3	44.3	40.0
Lansing, Mich.	45.0	54.3	52.7	50.0	52.6	80.0				38.6	30.0	62.5
Kenosha, Wis.	49.3		69.9	30.4		56.9		37.1		48.0	67.7	52.2
Racine, Wis.	59.3	63.6	73.6	48.5	56.3	53.0		61.3	18.9	53.3	62.3	61.9
W. N. Central cities	32.8	33.5	43.0	29.3	24.0	30.8		28.8	9.1	31.1	36.7	45.8
Minneapolis, Minn.	34.0	39.6	48.7	24.8	26.6	31.6		25.8	11.1	32.5	37.3	45.9
St. Paul, Minn.	23.0	23.0	34.2	18.9	16.7	22.0		21.4	3.0	22.1	45.5	50.0
Des Moines, Iowa	30.5	35.7	24.2	40.7	33.3	30.1		33.3	1.0	35.6	18.2	45.2
St. Joseph, Mo.	30.2	16.0	42.4	30.9		29.0		17.2		28.7	31.4	28.3
Springfield, Mo.	28.8	20.4	49.1	20.8		22.2			6.7	24.1	20.3	41.7
Fargo, N.D.	22.8	29.4	32.0	18.9	7.6	28.9			4.7	21.2	38.4	43.2
Sioux Falls, S.D.	24.7	17.3	35.7	31.0	7.7	20.8			6.9	33.6	32.5	37.8
Lincoln, Neb.	43.0	36.5	48.9	46.2		44.7		43.6	18.2	34.8	44.8	42.6
Topeka, Kan.	43.7	31.7	53.0	33.3	31.6	37.0		47.4	6.9	26.7	.	53.4
Wichita, Kan.	48.2	51.6	52.1	50.0		44.3		37.5	21.6	48.7	41.9	56.0
S. Atlantic cities	35.3	34.2	44.1	32.0	50.0	30.6		39.8	6.1	36.8	33.0	51.5
Hagerstown, Md.	14.5		27.1	11.5						12.3		30.6
Richmond, Va.	17.1	14.9	48.8	13.5	18.2	17.9		13.5	5.6	20.1	12.7	39.5
Wheeling, W.Va.*	48.0	32.7	65.4	42.4	50.4			53.3	17.8	50.0	40.8	52.3
Asheville, N.C.	50.0	48.9	62.7	66.7		41.1			7.1	54.2		75.0
Greensboro, N.C.	42.8	48.9	25.0			56.7				33.3	53.3	47.1
Charleston, S.C.	21.4			46.1						20.8	7.6	
Columbia, S.C.	50.6	51.2	62.6							40.2		58.6
Atlanta, Ga.*	35.7	34.7	21.8	32.2	63.2	33.5		44.9	1.2	40.4	37.5	59.4
Jacksonville, Fla.	36.1	44.4	81.8			24.0				33.6	33.3	45.5
E. S. Central cities	56.7	51.4	73.5	44.6	52.6	58.7		44.1	13.5	55.0	68.9	59.3
Paducah, Ky.	46.0	33.3	66.7	42.3				45.6		42.9		18.6
Birmingham, Ala.*	58.5	53.9	75.5	44.8	52.6	58.5		44.0	13.5	57.5	68.9	64.1
Jackson, Miss.	49.6	43.2	60.9			60.0				44.1		50.0
W. S. Central cities	39.8	38.0	47.5	37.6	41.2	44.3	56.1	36.9	6.7	37.2	39.1	59.3
Little Rock, Ark.	46.7	62.9	65.1	40.0	50.0	50.8		50.0	11.1	42.3	33.3	69.4
Baton Rouge, La.	42.5		36.0							51.4	76.9	
Oklahoma City, Okla.	41.8	36.6	49.4	50.0	46.7	46.8		52.9	4.3	39.1	43.7	63.2
Austin, Tex.	45.8	33.3	44.4	42.9		58.8	50.0			43.0	42.3	41.7
Dallas, Tex.	34.3	34.3	42.9	26.4	34.8	37.6	58.3	21.4	7.4	30.8	32.4	53.5
Wichita Falls, Tex.	47.3	34.4	53.6			47.6	47.1			47.5		71.4
Mountain cities	42.0	38.1	61.5	36.3	45.1	43.9		34.2	12.5	41.4	41.2	47.8
Butte, Mont.	42.8			37.5		75.0		50.0		47.4	40.0	
Boise, Idaho	27.3	23.8	34.4			35.7			6.9	24.8	31.2	50.0
Casper, Wyo.	33.1		44.6							36.4		50.0
Pueblo, Colo.	46.1	30.0	75.0						7.6	45.0	55.6	55.6
Phoenix, Ariz.	41.8	36.4	64.3	37.5	46.7	48.5		35.7	6.9	41.9		51.5
Salt Lake City, Utah	43.8	43.9	62.0	35.8	44.6	40.2		31.8	16.9	42.6	38.1	43.5
Pacific cities	35.0	38.6	51.5	30.7	39.0	34.9		31.6	9.8	32.7	38.8	51.3
Seattle, Wash.*	41.2	44.9	63.9	38.5	40.5	42.5		43.9	11.9	38.1	55.2	58.0
Portland, Ore.	35.0	43.0	50.4	23.9	45.6	37.2		26.8	6.0	32.8	31.4	54.1
Sacramento, Calif.	23.0	19.8	34.1	29.5	25.0	18.4				20.7	15.4	37.4
San Diego, Calif.*	27.7	26.5	36.2	27.4	30.3	22.8		15.4	12.5	27.0	29.0	49.5

Source: Financial Survey of Urban Housing. For number reporting 'All holding agencies' combined see Table D 46. Percentage not shown for fewer than 10 reports.

*Metropolitan District.

[1]*Geographic division and 'All cities' percentages weighted by number of loans, by tenure and priority, in each city (RPI). For rented properties where the number of cities included in the 'All holding agencies' column is larger than the number for the individual agencies, the weighted geographic division and 'All cities' percentages in the 'All holding agencies' column are not strictly comparable with the weighted percentages for the individual agencies.*

TABLE D 47

Mortgaged Dwellings, Percentage with Payments in Arrears, All Holding Agencies: First Mortgages, by Holding Agency, Owner-occupied and Rented, 52 Cities; Second and Third Mortgages, Owner-occupied, 52 Cities; Rented, 23 Cities, by Geographic Division, January 1, 1934

← ————————————————————————— R E N T E D ——————————————————————————— →

F I R S T   M O R T G A G E S

All[2] holding agencies	Life ins. co.	Build. & loan asso.	Commer. bank	Savings bank	Mortgage co.	Construct. co.	Title & trust co.	H.O. Loan Corp.	Individual	Other	2d & 3d MORTG. 3/	
44.1	50.7	57.2	45.1	43.4	44.3		40.4	23.2	38.8	45.6	57.7	All cities[1]
27.3		21.4	40.6	31.3	18.8		20.0		20.3	26.3	48.9	New England cities
32.8		13.3	32.1	47.6					21.1		38.2	Portland, Me.
21.3				19.1					14.3	25.0	46.2	Worcester, Mass.
29.5		22.2	41.4	33.3	18.8		20.0		22.1	26.7	49.1	Providence, R.I.*
19.4											55.9	Waterbury, Conn.
24.2	18.2	50.3	27.9		14.0				28.6	38.3	52.9	Mid. Atlantic cities
17.7											8.3	Binghamton, N.Y.
16.3	18.2		20.0		14.0				24.0		61.2	Syracuse, N.Y.
23.5		45.4							18.2	33.3	22.2	Trenton, N.J.
47.2		53.7	46.4						46.4	41.7	40.0	Erie, Pa.
65.4	63.3	76.5	59.3	67.1	78.3		56.4	29.4	51.2	51.3	74.8	E. N. Central cities
67.7	71.7	79.6	67.4	67.1	79.3		67.4	29.4	52.1	70.0	75.1	Cleveland, Ohio*
68.0	45.8	78.4	55.6				34.8		56.7	20.0		Indianapolis, Ind
37.3		42.5	10.0						19.4	23.1	65.2	Peoria, Ill.
57.7	79.3	64.6	40.0						29.4			Lansing, Mich.
49.2												Kenosha, Wis.
66.3		75.9	58.3		61.5		71.4		62.4	70.4	76.0	Racine, Wis.
34.4	43.4	51.4	29.6	28.2	34.4		30.9		29.2	32.4	58.7	W. N. Central cities
38.7	46.6	49.2	30.0	23.9	40.9		35.0		36.9	33.3	58.7	Minneapolis, Minn.
22.1	40.7	60.0	31.3		11.5				18.4			St. Paul, Minn.
34.7	40.7	39.4	26.3	38.1	48.5				31.9	27.3		Des Moines, Iowa
25.5												St. Joseph, Mo.
22.2	11.8	43.6							21.9	7.1		Springfield, Mo.
19.7												Fargo, N.D.
27.5	23.3				31.9				24.2	54.5		Sioux Falls, S.D.
37.7	54.5	47.3			10.0		26.7		29.4			Lincoln, Neb.
47.1	50.0	62.7		30.0	33.3				30.0	40.0		Topeka, Kan.
46.4	50.0	59.2			48.9		22.2		24.5	35.7		Wichita, Kan.
35.2	38.6	33.3		55.3	38.1		33.3		37.2	42.3	55.6	S. Atlantic cities
21.9												Hagerstown, Md.
17.4											47.4	Richmond, Va.
40.2												Wheeling, W.Va.*
54.1												Asheville, N.C.
37.0												Greensboro, N.C.
22.0												Charleston, S.C.
34.8												Columbia, S.C.
38.8	38.6	33.3		55.3	38.1		33.3		37.2	42.3	60.6	Atlanta, Ga.*
39.0												Jacksonville, Fla.
56.5	54.2	72.7	76.9		51.4			13.3	62.3	84.6	57.1	E. S. Central cities
36.0												Paducah, Ky.
57.7	54.2	72.7	76.9		51.4			13.3	62.3	84.6		Birmingham, Ala.*
52.6											57.1	Jackson, Miss.
41.3	42.9	48.1	21.7	44.4	42.3			9.1	30.0	54.0	56.3	W. S. Central cities
41.5	68.4	42.3	45.5		23.5				43.3			Little Rock, Ark.
52.5												Baton Rouge, La.
43.7	52.3	51.4			45.5			9.1	18.9	81.8	60.6	Oklahoma City, Okla.
47.2												Austin, Tex.
36.6	31.6	47.3	16.7	44.4	44.2				34.3	36.4	53.3	Dallas, Tex.
45.1												Wichita Falls, Tex.
45.6	59.8	60.4		43.0	44.4		33.3	20.0	42.2		64.7	Mountain cities
59.6												Butte, Mont.
37.5												Boise, Idaho
48.8												Casper, Wyo.
49.0												Pueblo, Colo.
36.0	58.3	45.5		31.8	38.5				31.0		45.5	Phoenix, Ariz.
50.2	60.8	69.7		50.0	48.1		33.3	20.0	49.1		76.2	Salt Lake City, Utah
40.2	50.4	55.7	35.4	28.9	34.5		30.9		38.4	40.3	49.2	Pacific cities
46.6	60.6	64.3	26.3	39.0	43.4		33.3		45.7	30.0	45.5	Seattle, Wash.*
45.4	54.5	56.2	57.1	20.0	24.0		33.3		45.8	54.5	51.6	Portland, Ore.
25.9		38.2	18.5	28.6					25.2		47.6	Sacramento, Calif.
31.6	31.6	50.0	32.7	23.7	32.8		25.0		25.5		51.0	San Diego, Calif.*

[2] Where only percentage with payments in arrears 'All holding agencies' is shown, percentage with payments in arrears by individual agencies was not obtained by Financial Survey of Urban Housing either because the number of reports was too small or because related information was lacking for rented properties.

[3] All agencies reporting.

TABLE D 48

Mortgaged Dwellings, Two New York City Areas, Number of Loans and Aggregate Amount by Priority and Holding Agency; Percentage Distribution of Aggregate Loans, each Priority by Holding Agency; Average Amount, Average Interest Rate, Average Term, and Average Reduction of Original Loan by Priority and Holding Agency, 1934

| | ←——LOWER EAST SIDE, 87 BLOCKS——→ | | | | ←——HARLEM, 40 BLOCKS——→ | | | |
| | PRIORITY | | | | PRIORITY | | | |
	First mortgage	Second mortgage	Third mortgage	Fourth mortgage	First mortgage	Second mortgage	Third mortgage	Fourth mortgage
a. Number								
All agencies	1,303	366	65	1	1,198	426	75	5
Life Insurance Company	20				37			
Building & Loan Assoc.	1				10	2		
Commercial Bank	46	3			92	8	1	
Savings Bank	598				415	5		
Mortgage Company	30	4	3		55	2	1	
Title & Trust Company	19				31	1		
Home Owner's Loan Corp.					7			
Construction Company	1					1		
Realty Company	17	17	2		12	25	4	
Institution	48	2			25	3		
Individual	403	307	53	1	409	346	67	4
Estate	84	12			60	8	1	
Other	36	21	7		45	25	1	1
b. Aggregate Loans (dollars)								
All agencies	23,643,506	2,779,849	372,907	3,000	22,589,180	3,681,867	474,930	27,800
Life Insurance Company	674,250				1,889,840			
Building & Loan Assoc.	70,000				49,527	2,840		
Commercial Bank	797,305	9,000			1,851,000	336,900	5,500	
Savings Bank	10,826,245				8,272,364	36,100		
Mortgage Company	1,166,650	32,600	4,000		1,079,325	12,350	5,575	
Title & Trust Company	579,140				314,350	9,500		
Home Owner's Loan Corp.					54,006			
Construction Company	21,000					5,150		
Realty Company	219,725	118,072	34,210		275,580	220,660	19,300	
Institution	869,541	13,000			456,100	28,700		
Individual	6,054,425	2,331,777	276,708	3,000	6,007,569	2,702,943	437,055	23,450
Estate	1,331,290	99,075			1,147,209	52,330	6,500	
Other	1,033,935	176,325	57,989		1,192,310	274,394	1,000	4,350
c. Percentage Distribution of Aggregate Loans								
All agencies	100.0	100.0	100.0	100.0	100.0	100.0	100.0	100.0
Life Insurance Company	2.9				8.4			
Building & Loan Assoc.	0.3				0.2	0.1		
Commercial Bank	3.4	0.3			8.2	9.2	1.1	
Savings Bank	45.8				36.6	1.0		
Mortgage Company	4.9	1.2	1.1		4.8	0.3	1.2	
Title & Trust Company	2.4				1.4	0.2		
Home Owner's Loan Corp.					0.2			
Construction Company	0.1					0.1		
Realty Company	0.9	4.2	9.2		1.2	6.0	4.1	
Institution	3.7	0.5			2.0	0.8		
Individual	25.6	83.9	74.2	100.0	26.6	73.4	92.0	84.4
Estate	5.6	3.6			5.1	1.4	1.4	
Other	4.4	6.3	15.5		5.3	7.5	0.2	15.6
d. Average Amount (dollars)								
All agencies	18,145	7,595	5,737	3,000	18,856	8,643	6,332	5,560
Life Insurance Company	33,712				51,077			
Building & Loan Assoc.	70,000				4,953	1,420		
Commercial Bank	17,333	3,000			20,120	42,113	5,500	
Savings Bank	18,104				19,933	7,220		
Mortgage Company	38,888	8,150	1,333		19,624	6,175	5,575	
Title & Trust Company	30,481				10,140	9,500		
Home Owner's Loan Corp.					7,715			
Construction Company	21,000					5,150		
Realty Company	12,925	6,945	17,105		22,965	8,826	4,825	
Institution	18,115	6,500			18,244	9,567		
Individual	15,023	7,595	5,221	3,000	14,688	7,812	6,523	5,863
Estate	15,849	8,256			19,120	6,541	6,500	
Other	28,720	8,396	8,284		26,496	10,976	1,000	4,350

Source: See Part Two, Ch. IV, sec. 4
[1] *Interest rate weighted by amount of loans.*

Mortgaged Dwellings, Two New York City Areas, Number of Loans and Aggregate Amount by Priority and Holding Agency; Percentage Distribution of Aggregate Loans, each Priority by Holding Agency; Average Amount, Average Interest Rate, Average Term, and Average Reduction of Original Loan by Priority and Holding Agency, 1934

e. Average Interest Rate (per cent) [1]

Holding Agency	LOWER EAST SIDE, 87 BLOCKS — PRIORITY				HARLEM, 40 BLOCKS — PRIORITY			
	First mortgage	Second mortgage	Third mortgage	Fourth mortgage	First mortgage	Second mortgage	Third mortgage	Fourth mortgage
All agencies	5.39	5.85	5.88	6.00	5.61	5.96	5.96	6.00
Life Insurance Company	5.42				5.67			
Building & Loan Assoc.	6.00				5.93	6.00		
Commercial Bank	5.35	6.00			5.68	5.94	6.00	
Savings Bank	5.25				5.51	6.00		
Mortgage Company	5.81	5.69	6.00		5.76	6.00	6.00	
Title & Trust Company	5.49				5.79	6.00		
Home Owner's Loan Corp.					5.41			
Construction Company	6.00					6.00		
Realty Company	5.71	6.00	6.00		5.84	6.00	6.00	
Institution	5.24	6.00			5.65	6.00		
Individual	5.50	5.84	5.84	6.00	5.65	5.95	5.96	6.00
Estate	5.33	6.00			5.52	5.95	6.00	
Other	5.76	5.82	6.00		5.75	6.00	6.00	6.00

f. Average Term (years and months)

Holding Agency	LOWER EAST SIDE — PRIORITY				HARLEM — PRIORITY			
	First (yrs mos)	Second (yrs mos)	Third (yrs mos)	Fourth (yrs mos)	First (yrs mos)	Second (yrs mos)	Third (yrs mos)	Fourth (yrs mos)
All agencies	10 6	5 11	3 7		7 6	5 7	6	
Life Insurance Company	20 4				7 1			
Building & Loan Assoc.	10 3				11			
Commercial Bank	13 7	4 7			5 10	1		
Savings Bank	11 8				7 10			
Mortgage Company	13 4	4 8	4		6 9	10		
Title & Trust Company	14 1				5 10	11		
Home Owner's Loan Corp.					14 5			
Construction Company	6				5 4	4	3 4	
Realty Company	7 1	6 2	8		5	5		
Institution	9 5	21 4			7 6	5 9	6 1	
Individual	8 6	5 9	3 6	open	8 7	3		
Estate	10 10	6 4	2 5		8 11	4 2	11 6	
Other	7 4	6 8	2 5					

g. Average Reduction of Original Loan (per cent)

Holding Agency	LOWER EAST SIDE — PRIORITY				HARLEM — PRIORITY			
	First mortgage	Second mortgage	Third mortgage	Fourth mortgage	First mortgage	Second mortgage	Third mortgage	Fourth mortgage
All agencies	18.7	25.2	19.0	00.0	7.3	14.7	3.6	7.9
Life Insurance Company	21.6				5.0			
Building & Loan Assoc.	44.0				18.0	55.2		
Commercial Bank	24.0	47.1			3.5	0.5	00.0	
Savings Bank	19.6				9.2	0.8		
Mortgage Company	12.6	00.0	00.0		3.4	30.4	00.0	
Title & Trust Company	13.6				13.0	00.0		
Home Owner's Loan Corp.					00.0			
Construction Company	41.7					14.2		
Realty Company	18.2	38.4	39.9		10.9	13.9	5.2	
Institution	17.5	00.0			7.1	9.5		
Individual	17.9	24.1	18.8	00.0	7.4	15.8	3.6	9.3
Estate	20.7	37.3			9.5	7.4	00.0	
Other	11.2	23.5	0.9		1.8	20.3	00.0	00.0

SECTION E

Nonfarm Residential Construction

Tables E 1–6 summarize National Bureau estimates, prepared by methods described in Chapter V. Detailed descriptions of the processes, together with discussions concerning the nature and limitations of the data and the methods of handling, are in the text and footnotes of Part Two that describe methods of estimating construction, referred to above. Table E 7 was derived from Bureau of Labor Statistics building permit data, as part of the process of estimating value of residential construction (see Ch. V).

TABLE E 1

Dwelling Units Built by Type, Class of City, and Geographic Division, 1920-1936 (thousands of units)

	1920	1921	1922	1923	1924	1925	1926	1927	1928	1929	1930	1931	1932	1933	1934	1935	1936
Total	247	449	716	871	893	938	849	810	753	509	286	212	74	54	55	144	282
A Type of Dwelling																	
1-family	202	316	437	513	534	573	491	454	436	316	185	147	60*	39	42	111*	211*
2-family	24	70	146	175	173	157	117	99	78	51	28	21	7*	4	3	7*	12*
Apartments	21	63	133	183	186	208	241	257	239	142	73	44	7	11	10	26*	59*
Total	247	449	716	871	893	938	849	810	753	509	286	212	74	54	55	144	282
B Class of City[1]																	
1 120 central cities	95	192	319	393	404	431	396	355	313	203	113	83	24	17	19	51	104
2 Environs: 2,500 and over	36	71	120	152	156	166	156	157	143	90	52	38	12	9	8	20	40
3 Environs: under 2,500	18	35	60	75	77	82	77	78	71	45	26	20	6	5	5	12	27
4 Total environs (2 + 3)	54	106	180	227	233	249	234	235	214	135	77	58	18	13	13	32	68
5 96 met. dist. (1 + 4)	150	299	499	620	637	680	629	590	528	338	190	140	42	31	33	83	172
6 Other urban	64	96	135	153	156	155	129	131	138	107	59	43	20	14	13	35	61
7 Total urban (5 + 6)	214	395	633	773	793	835	759	721	665	445	249	184	62	45	46	118	232
8 Rural nonfarm[2]	33	55	82	97	100	103	90	89	88	64	36	28	12	9	9	26	50
9 Total nonfarm (7 + 8)	247	449	716	871	893	938	849	810	753	509	286	212	74	54	55	144	282
C Geographic Division																	
New England	11	20	37	45	53	60	45	44	45	28	15	14	5	4	3	4	10
Mid. Atlantic	44	101	187	233	249	255	255	257	218	128	84	67	19	14	19	35	67
E. N. Central	50	74	134	181	191	192	186	178	160	110	37	19	5	3	4	17	37
W. N. Central	20	35	52	63	53	60	45	35	36	30	16	15	6	4	4	9	13
S. Atlantic	37	57	83	91	106	118	101	85	81	49	29	29	13	9	9	36	58
E. S. Central	8	19	29	37	42	46	39	37	39	24	12	6	3	2	2	6	20
W. S. Central	33	56	66	66	59	64	56	63	68	59	37	24	8	7	6	16	32
Mountain	6	13	17	15	17	20	14	14	14	14	8	6	2	1	1	3	6
Pacific	38	74	111	140	123	123	108	97	92	67	48	32	13	10	7	18	39

* *Revision of data published in Bulletin 65, Table 3.*
[1] *Addition of some individual items differs from subtotals owing to rounding; see Table EM 10 for details.*
[2] *Excludes rural towns and villages (under 2,500) and unincorporated areas in environs of metropolitan districts considered as urban.*

TABLE E 2

Aggregate Value of Residential Construction by Class of City, 1920-1936 (millions of dollars)

	1920	1921	1922	1923	1924	1925	1926	1927	1928	1929	1930	1931	1932	1933	1934	1935	1936
Total New Residential[1]	1,122	1,841	3,115	3,980	4,244	4,754	4,314	4,064	3,813	2,623	1,456	1,005	282	204	214	585	1,202
Housekeeping Units by Class of City																	
1 120 central cities	475	910	1,524	1,924	2,086	2,263	2,043	1,851	1,612	1,102	585	412	106	71	77	225	499
2 Environs: 2,500 and over	213	356	589	821	911	1,036	989	978	899	569	345	254	68	57	58	139	261
3 Environs: under 2,500	92	128	235	301	316	356	351	368	348	219	132	102	25	21	21	53	120
4 Total environs (2 + 3)	305	484	824	1,122	1,228	1,392	1,340	1,347	1,248	787	477	356	93	78	80	192	381
5 96 met. dist. (1 + 4)	780	1,394	2,348	3,046	3,314	3,655	3,383	3,198	2,859	1,889	1,063	768	199	149	157	417	881
6 Other urban	214	274	434	513	528	570	499	492	530	404	218	153	57	38	36	109	200
7 Total urban (5 + 6)	994	1,668	2,782	3,559	3,842	4,225	3,882	3,689	3,389	2,293	1,280	921	256	187	193	526	1,081
8 Rural nonfarm[2]	74	104	175	216	223	250	230	221	223	160	89	66	23	16	17	54	109
9 Total nonfarm (7 + 8)	1,068	1,771	2,956	3,775	4,065	4,475	4,112	3,910	3,613	2,453	1,369	987	279	203	210	580	1,191
Nonhousekeeping Units	54	70	157	206	179	279	202	154	200	171	86	17	3	2	3	5	11

[1] *Addition of some individual items differs from subtotals owing to rounding; see Table EM 11 for details.*
[2] *Excludes rural towns and villages (under 2,500) and unincorporated areas in environs of metropolitan districts considered as urban.*

TABLE E 3

Dwelling Units Built, Number and Percentage Distribution by Type and Period, 1920-1936

	THOUSANDS OF UNITS				PERCENTAGE DISTRIBUTION			
Type of Dwelling	1920-24	1925-29	1930-36	1920-36	1920-24	1925-29	1930-36	1920-36
Total	3,176	3,859	1,107	8,142	100.0	100.0	100.0	100.0
1-family	2,002	2,270	795	5,067	63.0	58.8	71.8	62.2
2-family	588	502	82	1,172	18.5	13.0	7.4	14.4
Apartments	586	1,087	230	1,903	18.5	28.2	20.8	23.4

TABLE E 4

Dwelling Units Built, Number, Aggregate Value, and Percentage Distribution, by Class of City and Period, 1920-1936

	120 Central cities	Environs	Other urban	Rural nonfarm[1]	Total nonfarm
1920-29					
Number of units (thousands)	3,102	1,867	1,264	802	7,035
Percentage distribution	44.1	26.5	18.0	11.4	100.0
Aggregate value (millions of dollars)	15,789	10,077	4,457	1,876	32,199[2]
Percentage distribution	49.0	31.3	13.9	5.8	100.0[2]
1930-36					
Number of units (thousands)	411	279	245	172	1,107
Percentage distribution	37.1	25.2	22.1	15.6	100.0
Aggregate value (millions of dollars)	1,975	1,657	812	375	4,819[2]
Percentage distribution	41.0	34.4	16.8	7.8	100.0[2]
1920-36					
Number of units (thousands)	3,513	2,146	1,509	974	8,142
Percentage distribution	43.1	26.4	18.5	12.0	100.0
Aggregate value (millions of dollars)	17,764	11,734	5,269	2,251	37,018[2]
Percentage distribution	48.0	31.7	14.2	6.1	100.0[2]

[1]*Excludes rural towns and villages (under 2,500) and unincorporated areas in environs of metropolitan districts considered as urban.*

[2]*Housekeeping units only.*

TABLE E 5

Dwelling Units Built, Number and Percentage Distribution by Geographic Division and Period, 1920-1936

	NUMBER (thousands of units)			PERCENTAGE DISTRIBUTION		
	1920-29	1930-36	1920-36	1920-29	1930-36	1920-36
United States	7,035	1,107	8,142	100.0	100.0	100.0
New England	388	55	443	5.5	5.0	5.4
Mid. Atlantic	1,927	305	2,232	27.4	27.6	27.4
E. N. Central	1,456	122	1,578	20.7	11.0	19.4
W. N. Central	429	67	496	6.1	6.1	6.1
S. Atlantic	808	183	991	11.5	16.5	12.2
E. S. Central	320	51	371	4.6	4.6	4.6
W. S. Central	590	130	720	8.4	11.7	8.8
Mountain	144	27	171	2.0	2.4	2.1
Pacific	973	167	1,140	13.8	15.1	14.0

TABLE E 6

Increase in Number of Families and Dwelling Units Built by Decades, 1890-1929 (thousands)

	1890-99	1900-09	1910-19	1920-29
Increase in number of nonfarm families	2,262	3,445	4,109	5,541
Number of new nonfarm dwelling units built	2,417	3,952	3,890	7,035

TABLE E 7

1-Family Dwellings for which Building Permits were issued, Average Cost (dollars), 257 Cities by Geographic Division and Class of City, 1920-1936[1]

(Figures in parentheses represent the number of cities for which data were reported in the designated year.)

Class of City / Geographic Division	1920	1921	1922	1923	1924	1925	1926	1927	1928	1929	1930	1931	1932	1933	1934	1935	1936
113 Central cities[2]	(108) 4,301	(113) 3,755	4,082	4,110	4,326	4,624	4,714	4,809	4,896	4,915	4,936	4,757	3,950	3,755	4,037	4,218	4,439
13 New England	(13) 4,612	3,980	5,313	5,616	5,949	6,009	6,096	6,122	6,398	6,350	6,170	5,615	4,677	4,515	5,098	4,780	4,676
27 Mid. Atlantic	(26) 5,788	5,373	5,308	5,527	5,561	5,642	5,751	5,661	5,566	5,656	5,802	5,572	4,532	4,252	4,140	5,969	6,147
21 E. N. Central	(21) 4,396	4,322	4,199	4,312	4,763	4,861	5,054	5,141	5,461	5,453	5,591	5,409	4,868	4,574	4,720	5,752	6,050
11 W. N. Central	(11) 3,707	3,397	3,708	3,542	3,634	3,782	4,036	4,105	4,257	4,206	4,290	4,168	3,736	3,574	3,456	4,141	4,269
14 S. Atlantic	(12) 4,865	4,597	4,762	4,660	4,652	4,908	4,541	4,502	4,975	5,241	5,295	5,210	4,737	4,226	4,966	4,921	4,954
6 E. S. Central	(6) 4,210	4,210	3,585	2,691	2,742	3,770	3,493	3,754	3,638	3,649	3,629	3,320	2,597	2,593	2,188	3,198	3,099
9 W. S. Central	(8) 3,791	2,851	3,156	3,029	3,024	3,274	3,638	3,814	3,802	3,701	4,063	3,943	2,393	2,200	2,866	3,117	3,283
2 Mountain	(2) 3,004	3,004	3,576	3,204	3,821	3,936	4,354	4,699	4,873	4,830	5,035	4,183	4,732	4,257	4,510	4,962	4,589
10 Pacific	(9) 3,161	2,568	2,880	2,909	3,145	3,400	3,690	3,886	3,924	4,087	3,881	3,747	3,191	3,216	3,243	3,696	3,930
64 Satellite cities	(35) 6,773	(64) 4,771	5,183	5,273	5,399	5,695	5,972	6,239	6,471	6,429	6,779	6,784	5,312	5,625	5,840	5,754	5,785
24 New England	(18) 5,982	4,676	5,823	5,972	6,079	6,406	6,374	6,485	6,958	7,187	7,085	6,283	5,388	6,004	6,238	6,214	6,599
18 Mid. Atlantic	(12) 8,936	6,475	6,562	6,672	7,017	6,660	7,065	7,543	8,665	9,076	9,401	8,990	6,712	6,997	6,722	6,891	6,991
12 E. N. Central	(4) 5,349	4,970	5,214	5,235	4,921	5,587	5,657	5,897	5,360	4,892	5,810	6,036	5,165	4,460	6,117	5,300	5,844
4 W. N. Central	.....	.....	.....	.....	.....	.....	.....	.....	.....	.....	.....	.....	.....	.....	.....	.....	.....
S. Atlantic	.....	.....	.....	.....	.....	.....	.....	.....	.....	.....	.....	.....	.....	.....	.....	.....	.....
1 E. S. Central	(1) 2,308	3,007	3,110	3,500	4,500	4,000	3,100	3,091	3,395	3,195	3,760	3,732	4,130	1,500	3,000	3,000	3,455
W. S. Central	.....	.....	.....	.....	.....	.....	.....	.....	.....	.....	.....	.....	.....	.....	.....	.....	.....
Mountain	.....	.....	.....	.....	.....	.....	.....	.....	.....	.....	.....	.....	.....	.....	.....	.....	.....
4 Pacific	.....	3,511	3,307	3,592	3,881	3,777	4,499	4,449	4,426	4,488	4,386	4,649	3,636	3,493	3,771	4,380	4,219
80 Other urban	(44) 3,456	(79) 3,088	(80) 3,323	3,454	3,484	3,794	3,973	3,864	3,969	3,901	3,820	3,669	3,004	2,804	2,816	3,224	3,410
6 New England	(4) 3,088	3,139	3,751	4,475	4,384	4,826	5,372	5,258	5,107	5,497	4,841	4,335	3,829	3,471	3,284	2,711	3,413
7 Mid. Atlantic	(3) 4,644	4,877	5,013	4,728	4,912	5,768	6,463	5,907	5,842	6,842	7,468	6,289	4,881	4,567	4,720	4,256	4,840
33 E. N. Central	(17) 3,418	3,060	3,704	3,579	3,597	3,902	3,952	3,980	4,080	4,162	4,089	4,020	3,482	2,860	3,001	3,944	3,644
8 W. N. Central	(6) 4,240	3,305	3,585	3,157	3,642	3,907	3,977	3,996	4,002	3,889	3,865	3,561	2,889	2,539	2,600	3,175	3,063
13 S. Atlantic	(6) 3,187	2,988	2,942	3,332	3,383	3,593	3,942	3,783	4,002	3,481	3,606	3,337	2,745	2,966	2,851	3,103	3,530
4 E. S. Central	(3) 2,535	2,157	2,961	2,578	2,532	2,976	3,730	2,960	2,276	2,540	2,143	2,226	1,297	1,810	1,907	2,184	2,342
3 W. S. Central	(3) 3,616	(3) 2,724	3,156	2,759	2,501	2,625	3,087	2,851	3,077	3,004	2,780	2,438	1,778	1,316	1,945	2,635	3,215
5 Mountain	(2) 1,818	2,055	1,518	3,943	2,467	2,867	3,068	3,431	3,011	3,116	2,832	3,098	2,810	2,864	1,851	2,987	3,296
1 Pacific	(1) 3,264	1,964	4,033	3,943	3,836	4,374	3,933	3,747	3,627	4,127	4,368	4,438	3,526	2,457	2,851	3,448	4,102
257 cities[3]	(187) 4,316	(256) 4,161	(257) 4,088	4,132	4,328	4,591	4,752	4,835	4,936	4,934	4,993	4,834	3,943	3,856	4,062	4,227	4,432
43 New England	(35) 4,918	4,161	5,343	5,658	5,829	6,102	6,174	6,246	6,609	6,714	6,462	5,797	4,859	5,064	5,423	5,379	5,534
55 Mid. Atlantic	(41) 5,994	5,465	5,405	5,606	5,667	5,732	5,876	5,838	5,868	6,061	6,206	5,951	4,775	4,592	4,374	4,201	5,687
68 E. N. Central	(42) 4,296	4,144	4,210	4,274	4,586	4,784	4,938	5,000	5,263	5,179	5,331	5,199	3,581	4,638	5,388	5,456	4,014
19 W. N. Central	(17) 3,781	3,383	3,691	3,552	3,636	3,799	4,028	4,087	4,226	4,149	4,210	4,052	3,561	3,392	3,262	3,926	3,926
27 S. Atlantic	(18) 4,586	4,233	4,376	4,365	4,446	4,727	4,437	4,343	4,716	4,857	4,981	4,976	5,431	3,982	4,642	4,579	4,661
11 E. S. Central	(10) 3,910	3,112	3,517	2,742	2,788	3,725	3,489	3,624	3,745	3,381	3,299	3,011	2,273	2,417	2,136	2,991	2,946
12 W. S. Central	(10) 3,787	2,837	2,920	2,969	2,962	3,218	3,603	3,786	3,745	3,646	4,004	3,841	2,316	2,085	2,774	3,079	3,277
7 Mountain	(4) 4,014	2,678	2,876	3,104	3,504	3,662	3,937	4,038	4,114	4,126	4,028	3,883	4,279	4,013	3,934	4,506	4,231
15 Pacific	(10) 3,163	2,662	2,931	2,987	3,228	3,444	2,874	3,933	3,977	4,144	3,948	3,830	3,253	3,238	3,284	3,758	3,959

Source of basic data: Bureau of Labor Statistics

[1] Figures in parentheses represent number of cities for which building permit data were reported in designated year.

[2] Except for 1920-21 as noted.

[3] Since these averages incorporate several revisions of basic data, they agree with data previously published for 257 cities in 1930-32 and 1935-36 alone; see *Statistics of Building Construction* (Bureau of Labor Statistics Bulletin 650, 1938), p. 8.

Index

Annexations, 45

Banks
  number reporting by population groups, 13–4, 65
Building activity, 11
  rate, 43
Building permits, 41–3, 51–3, 66–7

Census, Bureau of the, 15, 42, 45
Census of Population, 15, 18
CHAWNER, L. J., 59–61
Construction
  method of estimating, 41–61
  nonfarm residential, 10–1
  stages of estimates, 41
Contracts awarded
  F. W. Dodge Corporation, 53, 55–61, 66–7
Coverage, 15–6
Credit, 7–10

Debt, see mortgage debt
Definitions
  dwelling unit (dwellings), 1, 19, 56
  rent, 18–9
  residential, 1
  tenure, 18
  value, 18
Delinquencies, 5–7
Dodge, F. W. Corporation
  contracts awarded, 53, 55–61, 66–7
Dwelling units (dwellings)
  defined, 1, 19, 56
  number built, value, 11, 47–50
  occupied, vacant, 23
  ratio of units built to increase in families, 44, 46–7

Estimates
  construction, 41–61
  limitations, 56
  value
    details, 20–8, 28–32
    major steps necessary, 19, 28

Families
  quasi, 45
  farm, nonfarm, total, 1–2, 54–5
  use in estimating construction, 43–5
Farm and Village Housing, 53
Financial Survey of Urban Housing, 15
Financing, 39–41
  interest rates, 10

lending agencies, 9
nonfarm residential, 7–10
term of loan, 10

Geological Survey, U. S.
  building permits, 46, 67

HALLAUER, F. J., 43, 45
HOLDEN, ARTHUR, 41
Housing costs
  contrast by regions, 3–5

Income, 37–9
  comparison by years, 6–7
  in relation to rent and value, 5–7
  limitation of data, 38
  method of enumeration, 38
Interest rates, 10

Labor Statistics, Bureau of
  building permits, 41, 43, 45
Lending agencies, 9

Mayor's Planning Committee, 41
Methods
  estimate of
    aggregate value, 1930 and 1934, 11–4
    construction, 41–61
  presentation, 15–6
Metropolitan districts
  overlapping, 44
Mid-point
  use, displacement, correction, 30–1, 33–4
Mortgage debt, 8
  by tenure, lending agency, 9
Mortgaged properties
  by tenure by debt-value ratios, 8–9

National wealth, 1
New York Building Congress, 41
New York City Tenement House Department, 46, 67

Permits, see Building permits
Philadelphia Housing Association, 55

Ratios
  dwelling units built to increase in number of families, 47
  mid-point correction factor, 30–1, 34
  nonfarm families to total families, 27
  vacancy factor, 23–4

LIST OF PUBLICATIONS

LIST OF PUBLICATIONS

* *Out of print.*

17 PLANNING AND CONTROL OF PUBLIC WORKS (1930)
   Leo Wolman   260 pp., $2.50
*19 THE SMOOTHING OF TIME SERIES (1931)
   Frederick R. Macaulay   172 pp.
20 THE PURCHASE OF MEDICAL CARE THROUGH FIXED PERIODIC PAYMENT
   (1932)
   Pierce Williams   308 pp., $3.00
*21 ECONOMIC TENDENCIES IN THE UNITED STATES (1932)
   Frederick C. Mills   639 pp.
22 SEASONAL VARIATIONS IN INDUSTRY AND TRADE (1933)
   Simon Kuznets   455 pp., $4.00
23 PRODUCTION TRENDS IN THE UNITED STATES SINCE 1870 (1934)
   A. F. Burns   363 pp., $3.50
24 STRATEGIC FACTORS IN BUSINESS CYCLES (1934)
   J. Maurice Clark   238 pp., $1.50
25 GERMAN BUSINESS CYCLES, 1924–1933 (1934)
   C. T. Schmidt   288 pp., $2.50
26 INDUSTRIAL PROFITS IN THE UNITED STATES (1934)
   R. C. Epstein   678 pp., $5.00
27 MECHANIZATION IN INDUSTRY (1934)
   Harry Jerome   484 pp., $3.50
28 CORPORATE PROFITS AS SHOWN BY AUDIT REPORTS (1935)
   W. A. Paton   151 pp., $1.25
29 PUBLIC WORKS IN PROSPERITY AND DEPRESSION (1935)
   A. D. Gayer   460 pp., $3.00
30 EBB AND FLOW IN TRADE UNIONISM (1936)
   Leo Wolman   251 pp., $2.50
31 PRICES IN RECESSION AND RECOVERY (1936)
   Frederick C. Mills   561 pp., $4.00
32 NATIONAL INCOME AND CAPITAL FORMATION, 1919–1935 (1937)
   Simon Kuznets   100 pp., 8¼ x 11¾, $1.50
33 SOME THEORETICAL PROBLEMS SUGGESTED BY THE MOVEMENTS OF
   INTEREST RATES, BOND YIELDS AND STOCK PRICES IN THE UNITED
   STATES SINCE 1856 (1938)
   F. R. Macaulay   586 pp., $5.00
   The Social Sciences and the Unknown Future, a reprint of the in-
   troductory chapter to Dr. Macaulay's volume: 35 cents; in orders
   of 10 or more, 25 cents.
34 COMMODITY FLOW AND CAPITAL FORMATION, Volume I (1938)
   Simon Kuznets   500 pp., 8¼ x 11¾, $5.00
35 CAPITAL CONSUMPTION AND ADJUSTMENT (1938)
   Solomon Fabricant   271 pp., $2.75
36 THE STRUCTURE OF MANUFACTURING PRODUCTION, A CROSS-SECTION
   VIEW (1939) *C. A. Bliss*   234 pp., $2.50
37 THE INTERNATIONAL GOLD STANDARD REINTERPRETED, 1914–34 (1940)
   William Adams Brown, Jr.   1420 pp., $12
   * Out of print.

38 RESIDENTIAL REAL ESTATE, ITS ECONOMIC POSITION AS SHOWN BY
   VALUES, RENTS, FAMILY INCOMES, FINANCING, AND CONSTRUCTION,
   TOGETHER WITH ESTIMATES FOR ALL REAL ESTATE (1940)
   D. L. Wickens   320 pp., 8¼ x 11¾, $3.50
39 THE OUTPUT OF MANUFACTURING INDUSTRIES, 1899–1937 (1940)
   Solomon Fabricant   685 pp., $4.50

FINANCIAL RESEARCH PROGRAM

I *A Program of Financial Research*
1 REPORT OF THE EXPLORATORY COMMITTEE ON FINANCIAL RESEARCH
   (1937)   91 pp., $1.00
2 INVENTORY OF CURRENT RESEARCH ON FINANCIAL PROBLEMS (1937)
                                                 253 pp., $1.50

II *Studies in Consumer Instalment Financing*
1 PERSONAL FINANCE COMPANIES AND THEIR CREDIT PRACTICES (1940)
   Ralph A. Young and *Associates*   170 pp., $2.00
2 SALES FINANCE COMPANIES AND THEIR CREDIT PRACTICES (1940)
   Wilbur C. Plummer and *Ralph A. Young*   298 pp., $3.00
3 COMMERCIAL BANKS AND CONSUMER INSTALMENT CREDIT (1940)
   John M. Chapman and *Associates*   318 pp., $3.00
4 INDUSTRIAL BANKING COMPANIES AND THEIR CREDIT PRACTICES (1940)
   R. J. Saulnier   192 pp., $2.00
5 GOVERNMENT AGENCIES OF CONSUMER INSTALMENT CREDIT (1940)
   J. D. Coppock   216 pp., $2.50
6 THE PATTERN OF CONSUMER DEBT, 1935–36 (1940)
   Blanche Bernstein   238 pp., $2.50
7 THE VOLUME OF CONSUMER INSTALMENT CREDIT, 1929–38 (1940)
   Duncan McC. Holthausen in collaboration with
   Malcolm L. Merriam and *Rofl Nugent*   137 pp., $1.50

CONFERENCE ON RESEARCH IN NATIONAL INCOME AND WEALTH

STUDIES IN INCOME AND WEALTH   (Volumes I–III together, $7.50)
Volume I (1937), 368 pp., $2.50; Volume II (1938), 342 pp., $3.00;
Volume III (1939), 500 pp., $3.50.

CONFERENCE ON PRICE RESEARCH

1 REPORT OF THE COMMITTEE ON PRICES IN THE BITUMINOUS COAL
   INDUSTRY (1938)   144 pp., $1.25
2 TEXTILE MARKETS—THEIR STRUCTURE IN RELATION TO PRICE
   RESEARCH (1939)   304 pp., $3.00
3 PRICE RESEARCH IN THE STEEL AND PETROLEUM INDUSTRIES (1939)
                                                224 pp., $2.00

NATIONAL BUREAU OF ECONOMIC RESEARCH
                              1819 Broadway, New York, N. Y.
     European Agent: Macmillan & Co., Ltd.
                              St. Martin's Street, London, W.C.2